AUGUSTINE THE BISHOP

---

hARPER ⚡ TORChBOOKS

*A reference-list of Harper Torchbooks, classified
by subjects, is printed at the end of this volume.*

"God has humbled himself —
and still man is proud!"

Sermo CLXII, 6.

F. VAN DER MEER

AUGUSTINE THE BISHOP
Religion And Society
At The Dawn Of The Middle Ages

Translated by
Brian Battershaw
and
G. R. Lamb

HARPER TORCHBOOKS ♦ The Cathedral Library
Harper & Row, Publishers
New York and Evanston

TO
BERNARD HALLWARD

AUGUSTINE THE BISHOP

Copyright © Sheed & Ward Ltd., 1961

First published 1961 by Sheed & Ward Ltd., 33 Maiden Lane, London W.C. 2, and 64 University Place, New York 3, N.Y., and reprinted by arrangement.

First HARPER TORCHBOOK edition published 1965 by Harper & Row, Publishers, Incorporated, 49 East 33rd Street, New York, N.Y. 10016.

This book is a translation of *Augustinus de Zielzorger*, published by Uitgeverij het Spectrum, Utrecht and Brussels.

CONTENTS

	page
INTRODUCTION	x

PART 1
THE CHURCH OF HIPPO REGIUS

1. A Prisoner in the Lord	3
THE UNEXPECTED CALLING OF AUGUSTINE	3
AFRICA, CARTHAGE AND THE HARBOUR TOWN OF HIPPO	10
SARCINA EPISCOPATUS	14
2. The Town and the Country	16
THE TOWN OF HIPPO REGIUS	16
THE BASILICA MAJOR	20
THE PROVINCE	25
3. The Pagans	29
A DWINDLING MINORITY	29
POLEMICS	31
THE ENDING OF PAGANISM	37
4. The Legacy of Paganism	46
POMPA DIABOLI: WILD BEAST FIGHTS, RACES AND THE THEATRE	47
SUPERSTITION	56
AUGUSTINE'S STRUGGLE AGAINST ASTROLOGY	60
AUGUSTINE'S VIEWS ON THE POWER AND IMPOTENCE OF THE DEMONS	67
5. The Jews	76
6. The *Pars Donati* and the Heretics	79
THE DONATIST SCHISM AND THE QUESTION OF REUNION BY FORCE	79
THE DONATISTS IN HIPPO	102
MANICHEANS, ARIANS AND PELAGIANS	117
QUI POSUIT FINES TUOS PACEM	125
7. Day-to-Day Pastoral Work	129
AUGUSTINE'S OWN COMMUNITY	129
THE ELEMENT OF SIMPLICITY: *IDIOTAE* AND MEN OF CULTURE, RICH AND POOR	132
VOLATILITY: THE PINIANUS EPISODE	140
THE INDIFFERENT	148
A CASE OF SCRUPLES: AUGUSTINE THE PROBABILIST	153

	page
THE MURMURERS OF THE YEAR 410	157
PRAYER: THE LETTER TO PROBA	164
CHURCH ATTENDANCE	169
FASTING	177
SEXUAL MORALITY	180
THE NEW PEOPLE	190
8. THE CLERGY AND THE ASCETICS	**199**
THE *EPISCOPIUM* AS MONASTIC COMMUNITY	199
THE MONASTIC IDEAL	206
THE VIRGINS	217
THE CLERGY	225
9. THE BISHOP	**235**
AUGUSTINE IN CLOSE-UP: APPEARANCE, HEALTH AND DOMESTIC LIFE	235
THE CIRCLE OF FRIENDS	241
THE LETTERS	247
THE CADI	255
THE ELECTION OF ERACLIUS	270
THE DEATH OF AUGUSTINE	273

PART 2
THE CULTUS

10. THE THEORETICAL ASPECT	**277**
THE LETTERS TO JANUARIUS	277
WORD AND SACRAMENT	279
SACRAMENT AND COMMUNITY	282
ESSENTIALS AND INESSENTIALS	285
SACRAMENTS AS SACRED SYMBOLS	298
THE POWER AND LIMITATIONS OF SYMBOLS	301
SYMBOLISM AND REALISM	306
11. AUGUSTINE'S LITURGICAL PRACTICE	**317**
THE PURITANICAL TRAIT	317
THE SINGING OF THE PEOPLE	325
THE EMPHASIS ON UNDERSTANDING	337
THE BIBLE AND THE LITURGY	342
12. BECOMING A CHRISTIAN	**347**
INITIATIO CHRISTIANA	347
EMERGENCY BAPTISM AND INFANT BAPTISM	349
THE CATECHUMENATE	353
THE *COMPETENTES*	357

		page
	EASTER EVE	361
	THE OCTAVE OF EASTER	379
	PENANCE AFTER BAPTISM	382
13.	A SUNDAY IN HIPPO	388
	THE INSTRUCTIONAL SERVICE	389
	THE SACRIFICE OF THE FAITHFUL	397

PART 3
PREACHING

14.	THE HANDBOOK FOR PREACHERS	405
	THE FOURTH BOOK OF *CHRISTIAN KNOWLEDGE*	405
	THE BIBLE AND RHETORIC	406
	THE NECESSITY OF INTERPRETATION	406
	THE THREE AIMS: EXPLANATION, EDIFICATION, CONVERSION	409
	THE NEED FOR LIVING EXAMPLE	411
15.	THE SERVANT OF THE WORD	412
	AUGUSTINE AS PREACHER	412
	THE TRADITIONAL MATERIAL	414
	THE POPULAR FORM	417
	THE DEPTH OF AUGUSTINE'S THOUGHT	432
	THREE CASTS OF THOUGHT	438
	RESULTS	449
16.	*INSTRUCTION FOR BEGINNERS*	453
	THE GUIDE FOR DEOGRATIAS AND ITS PLAN	453
	THE TYPES OF CATECHUMEN	454
	THE CATECHIST	455
	THE STORY OF REDEMPTION AS THE ESSENCE OF INSTRUCTION	458
	EXHORTATION	461
	EXAMPLE OF A TWO-HOUR CATECHISM	461
	EXAMPLE OF A HALF-HOUR CATECHISM	466

PART 4
POPULAR PIETY

17.	THE CULT OF THE MARTYRS	471
	AUGUSTINE AND THE CULT OF THE MARTYRS	471
	GENERAL AND LOCAL DEVOTION TO THE SAINTS	475
	THE MOTHER OF OUR LORD	484
	AUGUSTINE'S CRITICISM OF ERRONEOUS VIEWS	487
	BURIAL *AD SANCTOS*	492

		page
18.	THE FEASTS OF THE DEAD	498
	THE FAMILY FEAST	498
	THE COMMEMORATIVE CELEBRATIONS OF THE CHURCH	506
	THE *REFRIGERIA* AFTER THE MASS CONVERSIONS	510
	THE FIRST PROTESTS	515
	THE PROHIBITION IN HIPPO	520
	THE ACCEPTANCE OF THE FAMILY FEASTS	525
19.	BELIEF IN MIRACLES	527
	PRIMITIVE POPULAR BELIEFS	527
	VISIONS	531
	MIRACLES	539
	THE MIRACLE RECORD	544
	THE TALE OF THE TEN ACCURSED CHILDREN OF CAPPADOCIA	549
	AUGUSTINE'S CRITICAL SENSE AND HIS CREDULITY	553

EPILOGUE

20.	AUGUSTINE AND OUR OWN DAY	561
	THE STAMP OF THE AGE	561
	AUGUSTINE'S ORIGINALITY	566
	HIS MODEL: AMBROSE	570
	WAS AUGUSTINE A RIGORIST?	572
	EXIT ANTIQUITAS	581
	AUGUSTINE THE MAN OF THE EARLY CHURCH: AUGUSTINE THE GENIUS: AUGUSTINE THE UNCONDITIONAL CHRISTIAN	585

NOTES	591
LIST OF ABBREVIATIONS	658
INDEX	661

LIST OF ILLUSTRATIONS

		facing page
1.	The Church Centre at Cuicul (Djemila)	8
2.	The complex of buildings at Cuicul	9
3.	Fourth-century basilica at Cuicul	24
4.	Reconstruction of an African town church	25
5.	Apse (Tebessa)	104
6.	Mosaic from Tabraca	105
7.	Book-cupboard (Mausoleum of Galla Placidia, Ravenna, 450)	120
8.	Altar (Baptistery at Ravenna, 458)	121
9.	"Ecclesia Mater" (Santa Sabina, Rome, 422–32)	200
10.	Ambrose (S. Vittore in Ciel d'Oro, Milan, 470)	201
11.	Augustine (fresco in the Lateran Library, *circa* 600)	216
12.	"Dominus legem dat" (Baptistery, Naples, 470)	217
13.	Jonah (fragment of a sarcophagus, Louvre, early fourth century)	296
14.	*Lipsanotheca* from Brescia (?370)	297
15.	Baptistery at Cuicul	312
16.	Font at Cuicul	313
17.	Ambulatory of the Baptistery at Cuicul	392
18.	Font at Timgad	393
19.	Floor mosaic in the Basilica of Cresconius (Cuicul)	408
20.	Reliquary from Aïn Zirara (Vatican)	409
21.	Grave mosaic from Tabraca (Musée du Bardo, Tunis)	488
22.	The Four Seasons, on a country estate (Musée du Bardo, Tunis)	489
23.	Mosaic of Theodoulos (Museum of Sousse)	504
24.	Market-place, Timgad	505

SOURCES OF THE ILLUSTRATIONS

15 and 18, Service des antiquités d'Alger; 6, 21, 22, 23, Service des antiquités de Tunisie; 1, 2, 3, 19, Ofalac, Algiers; 16, 17, Eichacker, Algiers; 20, Museo Cristiano, Vatican; 12, 14, Alinari; 5, 24, Lévy-Neurdein; 7, 8, 9, 10, 11, Wilpert, *Mosaiken und Malereien*; 13, Gerke, *Vorkonstantinische Sarkophage*

INTRODUCTION

HISTORIANS keep telling us that we have a more intimate knowledge of St. Augustine than of any other individual in the whole world of Antiquity. But who really knows him, and what exactly is it that we know? Before Bertrand's book came along, Augustine was a name. He is now a novel; an edifying novel, if you like (since the author's source of material was the *Confessions*), and also a fascinating one. No-one can ever forget the description of Carthage, "where the cauldron of filthy loves boiled over all about me",[1] or the singing community of Ambrose in the Basilica of Milan; nor will anyone, I fear, banish wholly from his mind that nameless woman companion who returns to Africa without her child, to devote the remainder of her life to God.[2]

Thus today Augustine the sinner is known to all. So is Augustine the convert. But what do men know of Augustine the saint?

It would almost seem as though the figure of Augustine could hold men's interest up to the point of his conversion. After that, the tendency is for people to forget both the man and the saint, and merely to remember the genius. Yet even the genius is somehow forbidding, for Augustine the genius is hidden away in eleven great folios of strangely scintillating Latin, a fitting subject for the scholar and especially for those industrious human bees, the philologists.

Besides these eleven great tomes, there has grown up a whole library of books intended almost exclusively for the initiated. True enough, men here and there still read the *Confessions* (or at any rate the first nine or ten books of them), and among such readers there are always those who put the book down deeply moved and ask in a bewildered way for something more. Into the hands of such a one may perhaps come a translation of some other work of Augustine's, but his awe before those eleven forbidding folios remains.

It is in a way natural enough that the ordinary worldly person should see a sort of "happy ending" in a conversion and feel no particular concern in what happens afterwards. That "afterwards" stretches before his mental eye as a sort of monochrome plain, dull after what he conceives to be the manner of all virtue. So it may well be that thousands of readers have been profoundly moved by this or that passage in the *Confessions*, without ever giving a thought to what happened in the period concerning which the *Confessions* are silent; and yet most of such readers would concede that the most important part of this man's life only begins after the old man has been put off and the new put on.

That certainly has been the Church's view. What has chiefly remained in the mind of the Church is not the Augustine who went astray and so dramatically turned back from his errors and his sins, nor the Augustine whom a declining world of Antiquity endowed with such exquisite sensibility. Rather was it the man, who, having found his treasure after seeking it for thirty years, had forty-three years left to turn it to account. The man whom the Church saw fit to canonize was the Bishop of Hippo Regius.

He was never an ordinary bishop, he was not even an ordinary bishop of genius. Most ordinary men, even most gifted ordinary men, who had happened to stand thus in the foreground of events and in the full glare of African Church history, would still have remained as impersonal in their orthodoxy as the Church itself. Had Augustine been such a man, he might well have been of moment to the historian; to the great multitude he would have made little appeal. But Augustine was not such a man; the pious men who studied these folios in every age have known better.

Nor was he baptized on the deathbed of his sensibility. He remained the incomparable one—even in the grey habit which was indistinguishable from that of those who shared his habitation and who for forty years saw him go about in such attire.[3] In his writings he remained till the day of his death one of the world's greatest artists in thought—and he was nearly seventy-six when he died. He was also one of the most intuitive of poetical minds, for whatever one may say of him and in whatever mood we encounter him, the mark of the artist is palpable and unfailing.

But the magic and attraction of the man did not lie in his writings alone. The story of his early years reveals something of the compelling power of his personality, and to the end, though living in strangely humble circumstances, he continued to draw men to himself.

The great man lived in a small world. He was hardly more than a sort of episcopal dean, and a great deal of his work was that of an ordinary priest; he was the kind of bishop whom the more casual officials cheerfully kept waiting in their anterooms.[4] There was, in fact, beneath the genius, a very humdrum Augustine who lived in what was really a large but very ordinary presbytery and who could be approached by anybody about pretty well any business that his caller fancied.

Viewing him through the perspective of history, we gain the impression that the saint's real home was Carthage and that this was the city from which he dominated Church history in his day. Undoubtedly there were years in which nearly half of his time was spent in the capital, but the truth is that Carthage was still essentially the exception and Hippo the rule. True, Augustine belonged to the Church as a whole; nevertheless his desire was to belong in an especial manner to the Church in Hippo, and it was in the daily cure of souls in that locality that he conceived his first duty to lie.

He was to an exemplary degree a resident bishop, and that in a bishopric considerably the worse for wear. Augustine in Hippo was a figure very like that of Bossuet, but not the Bossuet of the Court who now and then spent a little time in Meaux (and that by preference in the little garden house behind the hornbeams). Rather was he a Bossuet working in Boulogne or Toulon and daily surrounded by beggars and petitioners. Never again did he cross the sea to Italy. Alypius attended to that sort of thing for him; or, if the message he had to send was of minor importance, a simple acolyte or subdeacon performed the service. Nobody at the Court of Ravenna knew what he looked like, and Rome, after thirty years, remained equally ignorant; for the "second founder of the ancient Faith"[5] worked upon the spirits of others by means of his own spirit and not by measures of ecclesiastical policy.

His was no key position in the Church, yet as he wrote at his desk or spoke from the *cathedra* in the third-rate place which was his home wave upon wave went out over the world. What many readers of Augustine's writings do not realize is that his simple *cathedra* was more important to him than his pen. It was the needs and cares of ordinary Christian folk that supplied both the matter and manner of his loftiest writings, so that the main function of his genius was to serve the pastor of souls. It is not altogether wrong to say that we owe Augustine the saint to the strange and surprising fact that Augustine the genius was little more than a parish priest.

Even that humble task he took on against his will. Indeed, he was literally forced into it, and ultimately, before the end of his life, he handed over this all-too-restricted sphere of his work to a younger man, for the councils of his country now laid greater tasks upon his shoulders. Yet in between these two events there are thirty-five years of humble labour in one of the Lord's less prepossessing vineyards, in that same Hippo where his priestly work began.

From 391 till 426, he was every inch a pastor of souls, and this despite the monastic life which he lived together with his clergy, despite the care for the churches of all Africa which his metropolitan put upon him, and despite his growing literary fame. What ultimately compelled him to travel was the concrete demands which were made upon him by the necessities of the Church. It was the fear of seeing truth clouded over and violence done to the purity of the Church's doctrine, for what was in question was freedom and grace and the unity and holiness of the Church—those very matters which most deeply touched his mind. Of his greater works, one only owes its existence to pure interest in speculation—that on the Trinity. The others all came into being to meet the particular needs of the time.

The monastery which he conducted became a pastoral training school. Possidius, his biographer, tells us that no fewer than ten bishops came forth from it, most of them men who definitely set their mark on the African Church.[6] Augustine therefore led the strange life of the founder of an order, who was both a bishop and the rector of a seminary and at the same time the pastor of a large urban church—a life not unlike that of M. Olier at Saint-Sulpice, though with Augustine there was less devotion to the doctrine of *ama nesciri* and less concern with the niceties of personal style.

In this book the reader will find a compilation of such knowledge as we possess concerning the external activities of this man. For the most part we are concerned with very simple facts, with the saint's ordinary doings and preoccupations, with his judgements upon conditions and men, with speculations, sometimes of quite a subtle kind, on matters so essentially practical as the catechism and so unpretentious as the liturgy of that day. There is little more here than a number of pleasing or pointed sayings and some fascinating anecdotes concerning the ancient world, together with some stories of a somewhat conventional kind about priests and the priestly life. And perhaps there is a certain danger in drawing the portrait of so great a man with such a multiplicity of small strokes. Indeed, the reader who is already equipped with a certain amount of knowledge and who will therefore find little, if anything, that is new, may be tempted to ask whether it is wise to relegate the gigantic fact of Augustine's genius to an almost secondary place and to discard the advantages of that factor of distance which in this case undoubtedly helps to give stature to the saint. Like so many gifted men, Augustine was a complex character, a strange compendium of tenderness and inflexibility, and the charm which draws us to him is great indeed. Is the technique of the "close-up" best suited to reveal him?

There is only one excuse for my boldness in employing it. It is that his friend, housemate and only true biographer, Possidius, both saw and desired to see him after this fashion. The only real and original piece of hagiography we possess about this saint is this small *Vita* by Possidius, which in form tends rather to suggest one of the biographies of Suetonius;[7] but true saints suffer little by being thus portrayed by one of their housemates, even by so pedestrian and unimaginative and honest a biographer as Possidius, a man whom Harnack designates as "wholly unreceptive to genius".

Perhaps it would have been simpler to translate this little book of Possidius', which is contained in the Maurist edition of Augustine's works and there runs to less than twenty columns, and to leave it at that. Alternatively, one could take a portion of that wonderful work of elaboration and completion performed by Le Nain de Tillemont in the pages (there are nearly a thousand of them) of his incomparable *Vie de saint Augustin*.[8] But the readers of

Possidius were probably more thorough than we are, and would certainly, after finishing his little book, have taken up the manuscripts containing Augustine's other works, and Tillemont, despite his merits, has his defects. These great gentlemen of Port-Royal do tend to be a little on the grand and long-winded side.

It seems indicated, therefore, that we should keep in a general way to Possidius' portrait but provide it with a background. This is not too difficult, for Augustine's thousand sermons and some two hundred of his letters throw a sufficiently direct light on Augustine the shepherd of souls. By making a selection from both of these sources and supplementing it by occasional reference to the greater works and adding a few as yet little known facts from African archaeology, it is possible to add the quality of life to the beauty which the portrait already displays, and above all to furnish that portrait with an adequately broad frame.

It cannot be expected of a simple fisherman that he should catch all the fish in this particular sea. Even Tillemont confessed as much when he said, "I cannot possibly tell everything, but it is equally impossible to tell what should be left out." In these circumstances the best course for the writer is to confine himself to a restricted number of themes that all have a sort of connection with one another.

In the pages which follow only three of these themes are treated in any considerable detail: Augustine's practice in liturgical affairs, in preaching and in the matter of popular devotion. It is, of course, natural enough that something should be said concerning the general theory out of which that practice sprang. However, the reader who seeks an adequate synthetic presentation of Augustine's whole moral and ascetic philosophy must be referred to more competent authorities.

To prevent the discussion of these three themes from remaining too much in isolation, and to give them a common background of cultural history, the three chapters dealing with liturgy, preaching and popular devotion are prefaced by yet a further chapter which deals with the special features of the Church of Hippo Regius. In this the attempt is made to draw a reasonably clear picture of the environment, long since vanished, in which Augustine wrote his letters and preached his sermons, and in which, in so humble and yet in so inspired a manner, he carried on his daily work for souls. This environment and the Church which it contains, though palpably things of the world of Antiquity, are nevertheless so thoroughly human and at the same time so completely Christian that they have a most powerful fascination for the Christian of today. Indeed, whether the reader be priest or layman, Catholic or Protestant, the account of these things may well induce certain reflections in him, for placed as they are in the lovely landscape of what was—

despite the Donatists—an undivided Christendom, they remind us that Augustine and his Church belong to us all.

I have three misgivings concerning this book. First, that it is not the work of a classical scholar; secondly, that it is rather like a collection of anecdotes dealing with cultural history; and finally, that instead of achieving a certain intimacy with the saint, it may merely succeed in applying to him a very limited perspective. The first of these misgivings has to some extent been removed through the kind collaboration of a specialist. As to the other two, I can only say that I have taken them into account and have still made no attempt at anything in the nature of a synthesis. Yet perhaps in some cases the very best kind of synthesis is provided by nothing more than a readable presentation of the facts, and it may well be that this multiplicity of little stones does, after all, make up a good fifth-century mosaic.

This may sound like presumption, but, if the reader will forgive me, I share with St. Augustine a certain belief in the "daimonic"—especially in the magical and compelling power of that kind of historical writing which claims to do nothing else than give an exhaustive and faithful rendering of a multitude of small details.

Some people will fear that to show a Father of the Church in his ordinary commonplace surroundings will make a commonplace thing of the man himself; they may consider it unpardonable to disregard his immortal writings in favour of a few perhaps quite secondary happenings, the report of which mere chance has preserved. To such I would reply that those who have read a presentation of Augustine's mind compiled entirely on the basis of his writings may find it somehow refreshing to glance at the writer himself and see how he passed his time from one day to another. That is a less ambitious form of study, though it is certainly an easier one; but great saints are in certain respects like the pillars in French cathedrals—they can be looked at from close at hand because they are fashioned according to a human measure and never in any circumstances seem either too great or too small for a healthy human eye. In St. Peter's in Rome, the giant columns seem normally proportioned as one enters the church, but as one comes closer that feeling of proportion disappears. As against this, one can go quite close to a Gothic pillar without experiencing any such result. Every part appears to be of the right size, wherever one sees it from, and the plinth is never so high that you can't lean on it. Whatever service it performs, every part is instinct with the style of the whole, and the upward thrust begins at the very foot of the pillar.

Augustine had this Gothic character in his nature. He was always great, not great merely on this occasion or that; yet he was at all times too preoccupied with the important things to play the great man. In his ordinary workaday relations he was easygoing, though there was never absent in him a certain magic and brilliance, for he was fundamentally an artist; he was, moreover, essentially an artist in sympathy, and that is why he never failed in charm.

So far as one can tell from his letters and his sermons, he preferred to associate either with humble folk or with the nobility, and it is these two classes that he is in the habit of describing from the pulpit. With the bourgeoisie, however, whom he either passes over in silence or treats with a certain irony, he seems to have had little in common. But there was in his outward bearing nothing of a Bossuet—nothing at least of that Bossuet who was everlastingly climbing aboard the king's coach, who was so adept at treating *de haut en bas* those of a different mind from his own, and who so loved to be painted by a draper's showman like Rigaud. Nor was there anything in him of the somewhat sanctimonious and interminably professorial gentlemen of Port-Royal. Though he had likes and dislikes, he was a man everlastingly hungry for human intercourse. Rather does he suggest a St. Francis of Sales, but without the latter's humanistic honey (and without St. Jane Frances de Chantal) or possibly a St. Bernard who has made his peace with Cluny and quietly shakes his head over La Trappe. He admired St. Anthony and his anchorites, but he himself loved to gather his friends around him and was concerned to ensure that he should always be surrounded by people of a like mind to his own, and also that once he had left his study he should never for a moment be alone.

He was no mystic in the strict sense of the word; indeed, the mystical state was unknown to him, even if now and then he could gain a foretaste of the inexpressible joy of that sight of God which his merits were ultimately to ensure.[9] We have the Church's assurance for the statement that the virtue he displayed in his life was of the heroic order, but there is so little that is demonstrative in his sanctity, and that sanctity is so free not merely from the extravagant but even from the extraordinary, that only few saints are fitted in equal degree to bring comfort to us poor ordinary sinners. There was so much that was human in that glowing heart, and yet that same heart knew only too well that the warmth within it betokened nothing more than the happy gift of sensibility. It was not in itself necessarily a sign of that love of God which the Holy Ghost pours into the soul.

Yet we need not spend much time in searching out the virtue which Augustine practised to such a heroic degree. It was humility. It was his gift of sympathy and his ability to suggest to others that he shared their feelings that made that naturally proud spirit into a man of charm; but it was his humility that made him into a saint. Has he not told us himself that he abandoned neo-Platonism because Christianity taught him that the Infinite Majesty came to us in humility?[10] In the Word made flesh the supreme Truth became kindly and indeed irresistible, so much so that fishermen and other working folk could receive it. It was this which moved him, and this realization was among the greatest gifts of grace which he received. Until his death he was to preach that the essential mystery of the Faith is the Incarnation and that the first lesson of the Incarnation is humility. After that all seemed vanity to him, save only the humble man's love. "God humbled himself," he once cried from the pulpit, "and yet man stays proud."[11]

Augustine's biographer, Possidius, thought it sufficient that he should immortalize the works of humility and that in his short account of Augustine's life he should concentrate on the pastor of souls. Though he gives us elsewhere an exact account of the different works in which Augustine's genius found expression, the little stories of daily life answered Possidius' purpose, for in a certain sense it is the humbler works described in these little tales that are the truly decisive things in Augustine's life.

This was well known to his pious biographer. To his visible embarrassment he could record no miracles,[12] for Augustine had worked none and his merit lay simply in this: that he most humbly followed the precepts he enjoined on others. Many centuries before Thérèse of Lisieux, he trod the Little Way. That is why Possidius concludes the description of Augustine's life with the words of the Gospel: "He that shall do and teach" the Commandments "shall be called great in the Kingdom of Heaven."[13]

In general the Latin text of quotations has deliberately not been given. Otherwise the notes would have been as voluminous as the text itself. Passages in inverted commas have, however, been literally translated. The other quotations are short but faithful condensations of the original. The documentation is at the end of the book. The edition of Augustine's works which has been used is the Maurist edition in eleven volumes. Where necessary, as in the case of letters, use was made of the relevant volumes of the *Corpus Scriptorum Ecclesiasticorum Latinorum*, and further of the "Sermones Post Maurinos Reperti" of Dom Morin.[14]

I am very far from having read all that has been published on this subject. That would be like drinking up the sea.[15] A number of works published just before or during the War remained unavailable to me. A number of works to which I have currently referred and also some monographs on special questions are named in my notes.

I am deeply grateful to Dr. Christine Mohrmann, who has been good enough to check quotations for philological mistakes and has made a number of corrections. I have also received valuable information from Professors Brom and Sassen. I also wish to express my indebtedness to the directors and staff of the University, Franciscan and Augustinian libraries in Nijmegen, who, despite difficult circumstances, placed their shelves at my disposal and were always ready to help.

I owe especial thanks to Professor Leschi in Algiers, Superintendent of Antiquities in Tunis, and to Mlle Allais, director of the Djemila excavations, for information supplied and other help.

PART 1
THE CHURCH OF HIPPO REGIUS

1

A PRISONER IN THE LORD

THE UNEXPECTED CALLING OF AUGUSTINE

IN the spring of the year 391[1] Augustine journeyed from Tagaste to the harbour town of Hippo Regius. The object of that journey was to bring help in his spiritual difficulties to a certain Godfearing man, a member of the Imperial Corps of Couriers.[2] Perhaps Augustine hoped to lead him to a way of life similar to his own, for Augustine had been a monk for three years now and was living with great simplicity deep in the heart of the country. The house which sheltered him there had belonged to his parents, and in it he shared his life with a number of pious literary friends, the proceeds of an inherited estate, which they had acquired in common, providing for the community's support. Such was the manner of life of that sometime Professor of Rhetoric who for thirteen years had been lecturing on this subject—mostly at the Imperial residence of Milan—but was now hidden by the cowl of the monk. The beauty of words mattered to him no longer. He had seen the worthlessness of that art, and he had abjured it, though he could never wholly relinquish it.

He was a lonely man—a son who four years previously had lost a mother whom he could never forget, and who had but lately lost a friend most dear to him; and he was also a father who had lost his only child. In his little country monastery he had listened to that child reading the Scriptures, and had been moved and delighted by that precocious young mind. He had marvelled at the answers made to him by this boy of sixteen and written them down, so that they can still be read in the dialogue known as *The Teacher*. Young Adeodatus was taken away from him when the lad was eighteen years of age and we can but believe that he was found fit to see God, as though he were too good and too perfect for this world.[3] Or again, it may be that his death was intended as a punishment for Augustine, even as Bathsheba was punished in the death of her son. Augustine never spoke or wrote of that death. Only in the *Confessions*, in which he could not be silent, does he say that he is wholly without fear and full of joy when he thinks of him; for Augustine never doubted that he was among the blessed,[4] so blameless had been his days since baptism. But indeed we know little of Augustine's inner life in those days.

In the middle of the barren acre of his speculations, Providence seized Augustine, like another Habbakuk, by the hair. On that Sunday, when he was present at the Eucharist with the rest of the people in the great church at Hippo, the aged Bishop Valerius happened to mention his intention of having a new priest chosen. Augustine, who had been recognized that day in the town, was, to his complete surprise, firmly seized and led to the *exedra*, where Valerius sat, while those who thus did violence to him called out that this was the man who should be chosen. They knew how he had lived; they knew of his eloquence and of his ascetic life. And they were determined not to let him go. Valerius, an old man, a Greek by descent, who spoke Latin imperfectly, had long expressed a desire for a priest who was both learned and a master of the spoken word. He was later to say that a prayer which he had made for years was answered on this day and that the inmost wish of his heart was fulfilled.

It was vain for Augustine to resist or even to refuse outright; it was vain even for him to shed tears. The dignitaries who surrounded him believed that the mere honour of priestly status was too slight for him, and assured him that they would later make him a bishop, and though it was not this consideration which caused him to yield, yet yield for some reason at last he did, and Valerius laid his hands upon him.[5]

Thus Augustine, like many another at this time, was literally dragged to the priest's bench. He knew that all over Africa men desired him for their bishop, and for that reason on his infrequent journeys he had been at pains to avoid any place where he knew a bishopric was vacant, but in Hippo he had felt himself particularly secure. True, the bishop of that place was old, but his health was sound, and that had dispelled any hesitation Augustine might have felt in going there. And now that very thing had happened to him which, though on a greater scale, had happened in Milan to that distinguished man, Ambrose, whom Augustine so much admired.

It had not been his fate to achieve intimacy with that eminently practical aristocrat; now the very practical problems with which he was suddenly made familiar had little about them to suggest the atmosphere of aristocracy; Augustine the man of delicate speculative mind was suddenly plunged into the turmoil of a great harbour town, and, to make things worse, it was a town in which the schismatics set the tone in all religious matters. For the schismatics had the biggest church, the biggest numbers, the fattest livings and leaders who yielded nothing in obstinacy and determination to the Arnauld family of Port-Royal, though they possessed little of the latter's virtue or breeding. As against this, the Catholic bishop, though he understood men well enough, had not the art of holding them.

Augustine could indeed transfer something of the cloistered atmosphere of his old life to Hippo, for Valerius gave him a house and garden near the cathedral;[6] but the life of contemplation was over. He had become a prisoner of the Lord,[7] though in a contrary sense to that which applied to the Apostle. He was now far removed from the schools of philosophy and the eternal Ideas, for what he saw before him now were the actualities of ordinary life. On the other hand, his very body and senses were now made familiar with the mysteries of the Faith, for these became concrete realities in the daily services and bound him more closely to his people, divided though they were by a senseless schism and all too often deprived of all knowledge of the truth.

Divine truth he had himself struggled for many years to attain, and yet now he was among men who could be talked away in hordes by any glib heretic, or whose grandparents had happened to be rebaptized. His people were sheep who followed the shepherd nearest at hand, not souls who possessed the truth because they had had, even for a short time, to fight their way towards it.

Here he was then, by nature a thinker and a recluse, but now compelled to drive his pitiful flock together with the aid of the customary crook and a couple of very unpretentious sheepdogs. What use was it here to speak of the schooling of the will, or to refer to the *lex aeterna*, or to rouse that desire for the spiritual perception of God achieved, as it were, with the delicate edge of the soul?

It was only a few months since he had proved to his friend Nebridius, who was now dead, that true wisdom, which concerns itself with death, can only thrive when an absence of worldly cares ensures tranquillity. Perhaps—so he had said at that time—a few "leaders of the Church" receive, as a grace granted to their office, the power to remain calm and wise in the midst of the whirl of business. He himself would never have that ability.[8] Now it was precisely this grace for which he had to pray.

Gradually his eye focused on new realities. He saw the Christian folk with their seemingly petty needs and cares and the mysterious solidarity of all the redeemed. The author of the *Soliloquies* and of *On the Quantity of the Soul*, the man who, in order to strike a weapon from the Manicheans' hands, had expended so much vain labour in expounding the allegorical interpretation of the first two chapters of Genesis, the man who had never ceased to peer into himself and had looked up towards eternal truth as the sole fountain of the life of bliss, the man who so confidently believed that even in this life the sight of God was possible—this same man now took the first step on that long road that led from introspection and the neo-Platonic doctrine of contemplation to those tangible realities among which his mother had moved in so natural and uninhibited a fashion. He discovered prayer, the Church, the

Communion of the Saints, the sacraments, the Word of God and Jesus Christ, our Lord. Now it was no longer his own religious experiences that formed the subject of his thoughts but the Scriptures, the Church and the true God.

Soon he was to explain in that beautiful little piece of writing, *The Uses of the Faith*, that the Faith enables us to understand why things are what they are, yet before explaining the uses of the Faith it was necessary to drive that Faith into the heads of the fisherfolk, old soldiers and business men who made up his congregation. Thus his ordination as a priest was the second great turning-point of his life. At his baptism he had received the life of grace; on that Sunday morning there came to him, with some measure of violence, his vocation.

He was soon to discover that in heavenly things there are no great and learned men, but that all human beings, with their weaknesses, are much of the same measure as, like little birds, they snatch after the spiritual food which is brought to them by their mother, the Church. The redeemed was not the wise man, but he whom Christ had purchased and made his own. He looked about him. Who was it that in this world he had now entered was held in respect? The answer was, "The Martyrs." Who was it whose hands and cheeks were kissed in deference? The *continentes*. The sweetest and purest of sounds was the voice of the humble—the speech of ordinary people made articulate in the ancient vernacular rendering of the Psalms. Was he himself indeed a teacher at all? Had he not, like any other, first to learn? It was so that we might learn from him that the Word had been made flesh and dwelt among us. God himself descended to our own lowliness and remained patient in the midst of fools, sinners and men of little faith, sometimes even calling the children to himself, for he was not the God of the learned and the philosophers. Augustine, servant of the servants of Christ (as he was wont to style himself in his letters), began to be a part of his own folk—as indeed it was fitting that he should.

One of the first things we hear concerning his new activity has to our minds little of the extraordinary about it. Augustine is commanded by Valerius to preach in the great church in his bishop's presence. Actually, Augustine was the first man to preach in Africa as a mere priest, for it was the custom there to leave preaching entirely to the bishop—a bad custom, says St. Jerome,[9] who, being a priest himself, had a rather special interest in the matter. Here the West differed from the East. In Jerusalem, for instance, any priest present at the divine service could speak, if he felt moved to do so, the bishop speaking last; not that there were not criticisms of this arrangement, such as those of the nun Aetheria, who thought that it took up too much time.[10]

Valerius, however, who himself came from the East, seems to have thought differently; and since he was wholly without jealousy,[11] the presence of the famous young orator caused him immediately to break the prevailing rule. Some of Augustine's fellow-priests took exception to this[12] and it was shortly afterwards that Pope Celestine forbade the bishops of Italy to permit their priests to preach. But Valerius' example was imitated—a development which may have been due to the quality of the young preacher in question.

Augustine, on this occasion, asked for a short leave of absence to enable him to work his way into Holy Scripture, for the man who shortly before had completed that glowing masterpiece, *The True Faith*, perhaps the most beautiful essay of his time on the essence of Christianity, looked upon himself as a mere layman when it was a matter of serving God by means of the spoken word. His bishop was actually living a few doors away from him in the same complex of buildings, but Augustine addressed a long letter to him on this occasion, a letter which we still possess.

It is an edifying composition and one clearly intended not for the bishop alone but for a wider circle of readers. It is a triumph of style and an excellent example of a certain noble pathos that sometimes marks Augustine's writing. It is also the first anxious cry in which is expressed that sense of responsibility which the care of souls inspired. He writes:

> There is nothing easier and nothing more pleasant, or more respected of men, than the office of a bishop, a priest or a deacon, as long as one carries it out without overmuch solicitude and in a manner calculated to please the people [*si perfunctorie atque adulatorie res agatur*]. Yet nothing is more wretched, more pitiful and more deserving of the condemnation of God. As against this, nothing is more difficult and more dangerous, and yet at the same time nothing is more blessed in the eyes of God than to fulfil one's priestly duties in the manner which our Captain commands. I am very far from having been trained since childhood for this service, and now that I am called upon to make my fellow creatures think upon their sins and to heal their sinful nature, I feel like a man who is ignorant of the very nature of an oar but is suddenly called upon to act as mate on a vessel. That was why at my consecration I wept in secret. Spiritually I am still a weakling and need the physic of the Holy Writ [*Scripturarum ejus medicamenta*]. This I must study at all costs, though hitherto I have lacked the time. Today I know at first hand what a man who serves the Sacrament and the Word of God really needs. May I not strive to obtain what I as yet do not possess? Do you want my labours to be in vain, Father Valerius? Where is your charity? Surely you love me, and your Church? I am sure you do—love your Church, and me too. But you think I am a fit and proper person, whereas I have come to know myself better than that, even though it has been through sorrow and shame. Perhaps Your Holiness will say, "What are

the gaps in your knowledge, then?" But I find it much easier to say what I possess, than to say what I should like to possess. Through my colleagues I asked you for a short leave of absence until Easter; now I should like to ask you personally, in writing.

What answer should I be able to give the Lord on the Day of Judgement? That I could not ask because I had been far too occupied with the administration of the Church's goods? Suppose he then said to me: "You wicked servant, if anyone had made a false claim to any of the Church's lands, then you would naturally have embarked upon a court case and if necessary entered an appeal overseas and remained away a whole year without making any complaint. And all for the sake of a bit of land which the poor needed to still their hunger—as though they cannot appease it far better in my living orchards, as long as these are diligently cultivated. How comes it then that you lacked the time to learn to cultivate my orchard?" How should I answer him? Tell me that. Would you have me say: "Father Valerius held me to be well instructed. The more he loved me, the less desirous was he to give me the occasion for learning these things"? Think well upon this, Father Valerius, I conjure you by the goodness and strictness of Christ.[13]

So at last he was granted leave of absence and could spend some months preparing himself. When the season of fasting came, he began, a recruit among recruits, his first catechizing of the *competentes* enrolled for that year, and it is typical of the man that even in that pedestrian activity he never failed to emphasize his unworthiness and inexperience.[14] Then at length he began to preach, and since he carefully committed his first sermons to paper, they are still in our possession, in two collections: those on the Sermon on the Mount (which in his old age he was still thoroughly to work over, and which there are several quotations from in our breviaries) and those on Genesis. His fame grew; he began disputing publicly with heretical leaders, and soon he became the Lacordaire of Africa. He preached both from the steps of the apse immediately in front of Valerius' *cathedra*, and at private gatherings; he gave impromptu conferences, and formal lectures with text in hand. When he dealt with topical questions—and in the year 400 religious problems were as topical as they were to be in 1520—both Catholics and dissidents came to hear him and, in the discussion which followed his address, would make notes of his sayings on the spot, like people at a political press conference. After the lecture many would ask for permission to copy the manuscript.[15]

Then at the Plenary Council of Africa which was held in the *domus ecclesiae* at Hippo in 393 (the presiding bishop of which, Aurelius, Bishop of Carthage, was his intimate friend) it was the young priest Augustine who was

1 The Church Centre at Cuicul (Djemila)

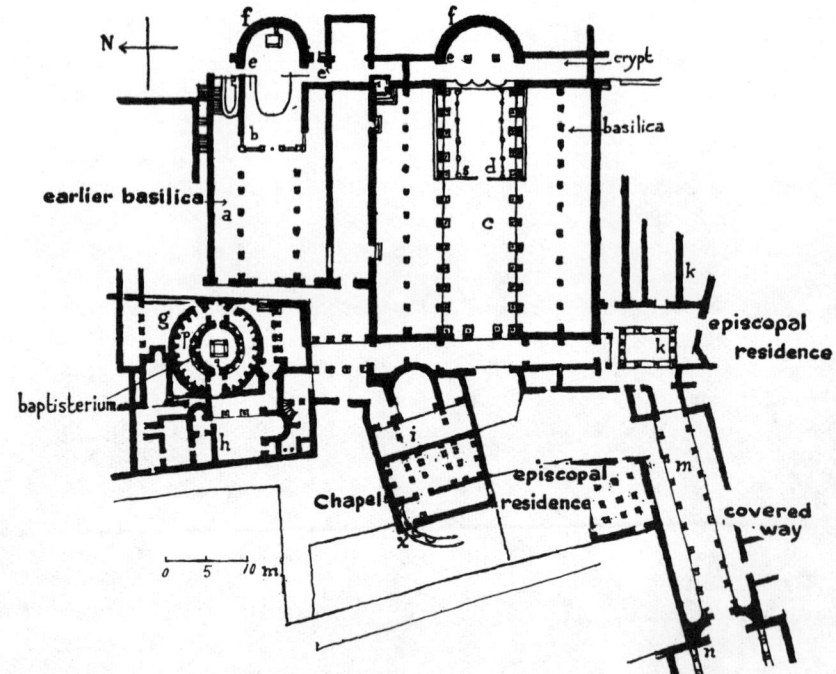

2 The complex of buildings at Cuicul, after A. Ballu (ground-plan)

Cuicul was a small town at the western extremity of Numidia, a settlement of discharged soldiers with only a few thousand inhabitants. Apparently it was a place of pilgrimage. The complex of buildings is on rising ground in the south-western part of the suburbs.

KEY: (a) Fourth-century basilica, 102 ft. by 45 ft., with mosaic floor and inscriptions containing Donatist names; (b) *Cancelli* with altar area, raised 19 in. above floor level; (c) The great basilica, 114 ft. by 78 ft. with five naves and pillars in front of the central piers. Mosaic floor with hunting scenes and other motifs, e.g., a cockfight. Built under Bishop Cresconius at the beginning of the fifth century; (d) *Cancelli*; under the floor (of later date) an inscription alluding to the return of the Donatists—"... decurrit ... in unam congeriem" (i.e., with the community) and with a reference to the reconciliation of heretics—"... sacramento dei medicinam sumere [s]chismae"; (e) Opening connecting with the three crypts (apparently containing graves of local saints); (f) Apses of two crypts (no trace of the upper apses); (g) *Baptisterium* with associated buildings, including hot and cold baths; the inner rotunda, with its cupola, has a diameter of 14 ft. 3 in. and a height of 10 ft. 6 in. There is an *oculus* in the cupola; (p) Barrel-vaulted ambulatory with dressing accommodation. Mosaic floor; (q) *Piscina* with mosaic depicting fish, and inscription including the words [t]empus erit omnes in font[e] [renasci]; covered by a stone baldachin on four short pillars (see pl. 16), with an *oculus* in the baldachin and a lamp below it, of which the iron ring was found; (h) *Consignatorium* (?); (i) Chapel; (kk) Episcopal residence; (m) Covered way, with pillars; (n) Approach to the town; (x) Traces of an older baptistery.

permitted to give the great dogmatic address on the Faith and the confession of faith.[16]

Neither Valerius nor Hippo would now let him go. Some years after the council, the old bishop, fearing—and that not without reason—that other communities might forestall him, wrote to Bishop Aurelius that he wished to keep Augustine for Hippo and to have him raised to the episcopacy beside himself, with right to succeed to the bishopric. When thereafter his neighbour, Megalius of Calama, the senior bishop and Primate of Numidia, made a visitation, Valerius took the occasion of acquainting him with his plan. He also made it known to the accompanying bishops and to his own clergy and people, and the great church reverberated to the echoes of their acclamation.

Augustine himself was concerned at the unexpected honour, all the more so since the consecration of a new bishop while the holder of the bishopric in question was still alive went contrary to custom. He would only agree after they had satisfied him that such a thing frequently occurred not only overseas but in Africa itself. Actually the practice was forbidden under the eighth canon of Nicaea, though neither Augustine nor Valerius was aware of this.[17]

But something happened to upset Megalius, an irascible old gentleman, and he roundly refused to consecrate Augustine, on the ground that imputations had been made against the character of the latter's life. It was said that, with her husband's knowledge, Augustine had given a woman a love potion and had thus seduced her, and in the end Megalius wrote the synod an angry letter, of which Augustine's enemies were at a later date to make copies only too gladly. However, thanks to the efforts of the synodal commission, it was disclosed that the love potion was merely a harmless *eulogion* (a blessed keepsake similar to the *prosphora* in the East) and that the whole story was based upon slander.

To his credit, the aged pastor humbly asked pardon and, despite his years, came personally to Hippo to attend the celebration.[18] The thing seems to have made a deep impression on Augustine. He was both touched and angry, and when Megalius died he could not help alluding, in a letter to a close friend, to the mingled feeling aroused in him by the memory of the man, and take the occasion to reflect on the danger of losing one's temper.[19]

Thus when the good "Father Valerius" died, in 396, Augustine, then aged forty-two, ascended the *cathedra* of the Church of Hippo. He was now deprived of any opportunity for a merely egotistical display of genius; from that point onwards he regarded "the service of the ministry of the mysteries of God" as his highest duty. He kept back nothing of his gifts for himself, and he could say with a good conscience, "I speak of that by which alone I live. I distribute that by which I am sustained."[20] As he put it on another occasion, "What are we ourselves if you should be lost? Is it true that we are one thing for ourselves and another for you? For ourselves, we are Christians; for you we are bishops and priests. It was not to the clergy, it was not to the bishops and priests that the Apostle spoke when he said: 'Ye are the members of Christ.' He said it to the people, to the believers, to the Christians."[21]

AFRICA, CARTHAGE AND THE HARBOUR TOWN OF HIPPO

It was not long before the African Church, thanks to its synods and their presiding bishop, Aurelius of Carthage, was taking up a great deal of his time. And she was by no means the least among the Churches of the ancient world.

Africa was no place of exile that lay far from the world of men, nor merely the granary of Rome, the best field of investment for large landowners, or the home of good orators and good jurists. It was the cradle of Christian Latinity. While everywhere else Christianity was being preached in Greek, it was in Africa that it assumed a Latin dress (with a highly individual character of its own), and it was here that the Holy Scriptures were translated into popular Latin of a remarkable kind. Ever since Tertullian's era, it was the African Church which had, more than any other, concerned itself with the practical problems of the day: Church discipline, Church unity and the validity of the sacraments were discussed, fought over and finally settled, and they were dealt with with all the serious-mindedness, the breadth of vision and the subtlety (sometimes also the fanaticism) of the national character. If the East was the Sorbonne for Christianity as a whole, Africa was the intellectual battlefield of Latin Christianity—rather like nineteenth-century France. But a certain gloomy seriousness in all matters that concerned the Faith, a courage that sometimes tended to degenerate into cruelty, and a certain peculiar conservatism recall—in another direction—certain features later displayed by the Church in Spain; Augustine himself clung with his whole heart to the existing order.

The coastal strip of Africa, and in particular the region of Africa Proconsularis, was in those days a wealthy and thickly-populated country. It was without villages, but covered with innumerable small towns, and had much of the character of Andalusia or Apulia today. Each of these typically Roman *municipia* and *coloniae* had its bishop; in most towns there were two of them, a Catholic bishop and a schismatic. Catholics and Donatists emulated one another in increasing the number of their bishops and playing them off against each other. As in modern Greece or in the Patriarchate of Constantinople, every place of any importance had a bishop of its own. When, fifteen years after Augustine's death, Africa was conquered by Gaiseric, and Pope Leo the Great took over the two Mauretanias, which had been cut off but still remained free, he was indignant about the bishops residing in hamlets or on simple country estates. He forbade such degradation of this high office and ordered that bishops should not be appointed in places which could be adequately served by an ordinary priest.[22] With its five to seven hundred episcopal sees, the African Church of the year 400 was like a mosaic of autonomous communities, far too numerous and far too small, held together only by the synods which took place regularly after 391, and by the bond, external and yet vague, with Rome and other Churches overseas.

Carthage was a natural centre, but there was nothing in the nature of a metropolis in any of the different provinces. The bishop of an ancient and respected bishopric was simply entitled "Bishop of the First Seat"[23] while the senior bishop of the province was called the Primate. Thus the last-named dignity was wholly independent of the size of the town concerned and was usually held by very old men. Yet from now on Aurelius was to take over the general leadership, thus carrying out the plan of a single man, Augustine.

Augustine forged this plan predominantly in Hippo, although its execution frequently took him to Carthage, for the Bishop of Hippo was genuinely anxious to live in his own town; he would indeed have preferred to absent himself hardly at all from that harbour town of his, and though the complete fulfilment of his wish was denied him, he was never again to leave Africa, nor did he ever again set foot upon a vessel. Not once did he go to that Court, "rich in fame", at Ravenna—to which he could, after all, easily have had access, for its anterooms were filled not by fellow-bishops alone but by many a humble priest who came there with letters of introduction from Rome.[24]

Actually such men rarely came to Ravenna for any constructive purpose. Some came to intrigue, some because they were in want, others again came seeking promotion or to lodge an appeal. All came for some personal reason. Bishop Gratus of Carthage had complained as far back as 343 of this discreditable state of affairs, and in Augustine's day it moved Pope Innocent to anger.[25]

Once, in 419, with a view to healing a schism which confused elections had brought into being, Honorius had summoned a council,[26] and Augustine was invited to lead an African delegation. But though at this time he enjoyed in Italy an incomparable fame, it never entered his mind to cross the sea. It was Alypius who went to Rome and also brought greetings from him to Jerome in Palestine. And it was again Alypius who, in 420, was called upon to hand over in Rome Augustine's paper, *Against the Two Letters of the Pelagians*, which Augustine had dedicated to Pope Boniface.[27] Augustine himself remained at home.

Certainly, in the beautiful opening words of the work just referred to, he recalls the friendship shown him by the Bishop of Rome, who "although he should really stand so much higher" than the ordinary pastors, was yet willing to be their friend. This was his thanks for the confidence that had been placed in him.[28] And elsewhere we encounter recollections of Roman acquaintances of thirty years ago. But nowhere is there a word to suggest anything like homesickness for the beloved city that had undergone such heavy trials.

It may be that a certain conscious restraint was at work in this, for Augustine, who had so brilliantly formulated the prerogatives of the See of Peter,[29] who had skilfully utilized the prestige and the verdict of Rome against the Pelagians, had nevertheless in various matters to take a certain stand. There was, for instance, the question of certain forms in which appeals to Rome had to be made, and there were also cases of Roman interference. We do not know whether he held quite as firmly to native tradition as did some of his brother bishops whose ideal came near to that of an African Church existing *sui juris*—at least, as far as Church discipline and administration were concerned. Perhaps he was not sufficiently juridically-minded to come to grips with this issue, but however that may be his ultramontanism, or rather ultramarinism, was mystical rather than political.[30] For both the courts in question his tendency was to let others *navigare ad comitatum*.

Seafaring was in itself distasteful to him. What prevented him from making even the smallest journey by sea, let alone from voyaging to Italy, what prevented him from "sharing the travails of the sea and of lands beyond the sea" with his brother bishops, was, he once wrote to his clergy and his people, not lack of devotion but physical inability.[31] He always immediately suffered from seasickness and was too weak to travel far. Incidentally, he had hated travel since youth. The journey from Hippo to Carthage had even then seemed a long one,[32] and when he was a bishop well on in years he was never oblivious of the trouble to which others had put themselves when they came to Hippo to see him. There were, of course, the Roman roads paved with their firm blocks of stone, but the Circumcellions, and later the barbarians, prevented these even from being safe.[33] Till the end of his life, however, he continued to move around in Africa; there was no synod that he did not feel compelled to attend, no ecclesiastical committee on which he neglected to be present, no heresiarch whom he did not feel called upon publicly to controvert, and of course time and again he would be asked to go out and preach somewhere on a feast day.

For to preach he was compelled whenever he was passing through a place and the bishop could catch him for a moment.[34] And though his neighbours would gladly come and visit him, they were unwilling to preach in his church, even when he was an old man. They much preferred to listen. During a short sermon to his own people he once jestingly said in reference to the parable of the talents: "My brothers and fellow-bishops honour me and cause my heart to rejoice by their presence and their visits, but they refuse to help me when I am tired. This, then, I say to you, brethren, while they are present themselves, that you, our audience, may come to our rescue when I beg them to say a word. They too should lend at interest what they have received, and work instead of excusing themselves."[35] In his old age he wrote in the preface to the *Retractations*: "If there was a need for preaching to the people, and I happened to be present, I was hardly ever allowed to keep silent and listen to others, and thus to be quick to listen and slow to speech, as James the Apostle enjoins."[36]

For the most part he remained in Numidia and the thickly-populated neighbouring province of Africa Proconsularis. Once, at the bidding of Pope Zosimus, he went as far as Caesarea in Mauretania, though we do not know why.[37]

Nevertheless, Carthage became his second home, and by necessity. The great metropolis with its dozens of basilicas and its marble fora and its theatres (of such evil repute), its imposing walls,[38] colourful harbour district and all the fascinating coming and going of its half-million inhabitants, was no longer the stronghold of patriotic heroes described in *Salammbô*, but it was a swarming trade-centre, full of greed and lust, and yet also a garden of sacred *memoriae*.* Carthage was dear to Augustine because of its associations with his student days; now it became the chief scene of his synodal activities, the place of his most memorable encounters and the place where his most noteworthy sermons were preached. At least sixty of the sermons that have come down to us were preached in Carthage, thirty-four of these being on the Psalms.[39] During the final crisis of Donatism he spent as much time in Carthage as he did in Hippo, and then his pulpit in Carthage makes one think of that of Lacordaire and Didon in Notre-Dame. We find him preaching there on St. Cyprian's day,[40] or round about that time, and a few times on the great feast days which normally would have been spent in Hippo.[41] There he appeared on all councils, where his formulations were often incorporated word for word in the final resolutions. The Church has made these declarations her own and has reverently quoted them down the centuries.

And yet he hated being away from home, for once away from there, hardly any kind of business failed to draw him in. This happened despite the fact that during these absences his wish—so he writes even as a young priest— was to conform strictly to Church rule and to engage in no kind of activity save with the permission of the local bishop or one of his assistant priests.[42] When once, some days before the feast of St. Cyprian, he had concluded a sermon on Gal. vi.1 and the people called out to him to remain in the town till the day of the feast itself, he promised on this occasion to do so, but only because "the holy old man", Aurelius, had so commanded him. He declared that he would fast with the rest during the days which followed (from 11 to

---

* See p. 19.

13 September)—which was another way of preparing his sermon—but he would do so, he declared, with a heavy heart because he "could not endure the cries of longing from his people" even when they reached his ears by letter,[43] for the Christians of Hippo wanted him back at home. While still a priest he wrote to Aurelius that his people were liable to get restless while he was away.[44]

When, after he had become a bishop, overwork compelled him to make a long stay in the country—this was in the summer and autumn of 410—he begged his flock not to mourn over his long absence or the poor health which had occasioned it, for these things were quite as painful to himself as to anybody else.[45] There was a certain Pinianus whose wife, Melania, and mother-in-law, Albina, had founded two large monasteries in his paternal home town of Tagaste and had richly endowed the local basilica with golden vessels and with land.[46] They were Roman millionaires who did this because of their liking for its bishop, Alypius, and from a desire to do him honour. When Augustine returned from the country, these people expected a visit from him, but Augustine wrote to Pinianus that absence from Hippo might hurt and even cause scandal[47] to his people, who were already agitated in their minds because of the approach of the Goths and the fall of Rome (Calabria had already gone up in flames) and the disturbances created by the Donatists. This was not a mere excuse (although, still convalescent as he was from his illness, he may well have been frightened by the cold journey into the mountains during the rainy season).[48] It was truly the voice of his conscience.

Sarcina Episcopatus

Yet up to the end of his life he never lost the sense of the burden of his calling. The office of bishop is for many a coveted honour; for others, pious though they remain, it gives an undoubted opportunity for display. For some, again, it is merely an administrative task, while yet others look upon it as a step in a successful career and, from the religious point of view, a sinecure. Augustine, the greatest bishop of his time, felt his office to be, before all else, a burden. *Sarcina episcopatus*—this phrase kept slipping from his lips, even on the anniversary of his consecration, as though it represented a self-evident truth.[49] When he warned monks against idleness, he was by no means enacting the part of a man who imposes a burden on others while not lifting a finger himself. He confessed that he would much prefer to do manual work at certain fixed times after the manner of men living in a regular monastery and to spend the remainder of his time in reading or prayer. That would be much pleasanter than having to concern himself from day to day with the affairs of other people.[50] Instead of preaching, how much rather would he have meditated on the word of God;[51] time and again one finds him saying in letters to his friends that he is too busy and cannot get away for a moment. "It is exceptional if a few drops of time are allowed to fall for me."[52]

Rarely was it that he could feel undisturbed, and how else could he have fared in the midst of what was all too often unspiritual business? Leo the Great wrote some years later from his great quiet palace of the Lateran: "It is in the nature of the human spirit to deny something to the substance subject to it, so that it may dwell in the halls of the spirit, free from bodily desires, and find time for heavenly wisdom."[53] Here in Hippo it is true that personal desires were silent—that was not the trouble, and Augustine certainly denied himself enough; yet how could he keep his mind quiet among all the people who daily overwhelmed him in his *secretarium* with all the confusion that the three lusts of this world can create? Yet even while he felt this pressure, he knew and believed that Christ's yoke must be easy, whatever might appear to the contrary, and so went courageously on his way. And although he never had time to spare, and was sometimes compelled to dictate at night, his writings alone furnish the proof of an industry and endurance that excelled even that of Luther or Origen. Perhaps that same thought was in his mind that was ever with his fellow-bishop, Martin of Tours, the thought that was uttered by him as he lay dying, a year after old Valerius, in Candes on the Loire in distant Gaul: "Lord, if thy people needeth me, I will not refuse my labours."[54]

2

THE TOWN AND THE COUNTRY

THE TOWN OF HIPPO REGIUS

HIPPO REGIUS had originally been founded by the Phoenicians, and in Augustine's time was a typical provincial town, sometimes referred to as a *colonia*[1] and sometimes as a *municipium*. Until quite recently it seemed to have disappeared almost completely. We do not know when it was that Hippo declined and Bône arose—Bona-la-Hadida, which lies one-and-a-half miles further to the north, on the site of the Seybousse, and has inherited the harbour. From Possidius and others we learn that the town where Augustine, worn out with cares, died on 28 August 430, was besieged by the Vandals, but relieved over a year later; and that shortly afterwards, however, it was abandoned by a large part of its population, and occupied and plundered by the Vandals, into whose hands it had fallen as the result of a treaty. We also learn that Providence preserved the library of the diocese, including the best manuscripts of Augustine's works, and that there was still a bishop there at the time of the Byzantine restoration.[2] But later on this glorious name and all its memories are lost under the overpowering and oppressive inundation of Islam.

Hippo, then, faded away, and as shortly afterwards as the Middle Ages there was nothing left to be seen of it; both Leo Africanus and the learned Arab al Bakri say as much, explicitly. Even twenty years ago anyone visiting the famous scene from Bône saw only three things. There was, of course, the beautiful curve of the lovely coastline, rich in vegetation and nestling close to the Djebel Edough, with the Cap de Garde to the left in the distance and the sea at one's feet. There was the new basilica of St. Augustine next to the hospice of the Little Sisters of the Poor, high on the top of a wooded hill above the site of the city.[3] And there was a small museum containing some damaged specimens of Roman sculpture and a few very fine mosaic floors from the Roman villas. And that was all. A section of Punic wall; some cisterns of Hadrian's day and the ruins of waterworks older still; some pedestals of statues, bearing the names of the citizens in honour of whom they had been erected;[4] a torso from the baths; a head of Vespasian; some Corinthian capitals, and finally, the inevitable fragments of mosaic pavements with their Nereids, fishermen, hunting-scenes, cupids, peacocks, bunches of grapes and geometrical motifs—that was all that was left, the principal items being in the museum. The Christian remains consisted of a mere handful of inscriptions, partly of the Byzantine period,[5] some Vandal *fibulae*, a piece of a comb, on which is depicted Habbakuk flying into Daniel's den with his breakfast, and three *ampullae* once brought as souvenirs from the grave of St. Menas, which was Egypt's most popular place of pilgrimage at the time.[6]

However, in 1924 excavations were begun. Erwam Marec stirred up active concern about the "great scandal of Hippo Regius",[7] and during the next twenty years the Department of Archaeology, in co-operation with the local academy and scholars like Gsell, Albertini and Leschi, managed to acquire the most important parts of the town area. As a result about seventy-five of its hundred and fifty acres have been uncovered. The forum, the baths of Septimus Severus, some smaller baths on the south side, the theatre and a small residential quarter—all these have been excavated. What is more, between the forum and the baths there has been found a block of ecclesiastical buildings which are so strikingly in agreement with what Augustine casually mentions about his surroundings that in interpreting their discoveries the excavators automatically went on the hypothesis that its various parts were in fact those of the town's episcopal centre.[8]

As regards the town itself, the excavations have not revealed any complete buildings. What they have revealed is an area of ruins—still only partially cleared—between the St. Augustine's hill and the Seybousse (the ancient *flumen Ubus*). It is a site full of foundation blocks and blocks of marble, fallen columns (some of them re-erected), lower courses of walls, and pieces of pavement. There is a plundered forum full of pedestals, which has, incidentally, proved to be the largest of all African provincial fora. Much of what is missing can be reconstructed, and not by pure conjecture alone.

A typical unhealthy[9] harbour town of the Mediterranean had much the same appearance then as it has now: piled blocks of dirty white houses rising steeply from the sea, dusty and blazing in the glare of the sun. Since, moreover, as excavations have shown, there was little difference in size between one provincial town in Africa and another, and since in their general layout and their public buildings they were as much alike as peas in a pod, we need have no hesitation in supplementing the remnants of the monuments of Hippo with those of Timgad, Dougga, Djemila or Sbeitla, those astonishingly well-preserved towns of the Numidian and Proconsular interior.[10] Admittedly, the ruins of Hippo have their distinctive features, such as the lowness of the walls above ground and the thoroughgoing destruction of the sculptural decoration. And another more important difference lies in the fact that Hippo Regius was not a creation of the Roman military occupation but a very ancient town and port as well.

None the less, the picture soon becomes a familiar one. Hippo too had its wide, scorching forum, with on one side the *curia* and the principal temples of the old cult on their high *stylobata* and with the remnants of a temple court. On the other side was the echoing market basilica with its *exedrae* and side-aisles; around it the porticoes for shopping and the evening constitutional —a queer mixture of the present-day Italian *galleria* and the Arabian *suk*, for long stretches of its walls were honeycombed into rows of box-like little shops, each shut off by a stone counter under which the shopkeeper had to crawl in the morning in order to get in. The forum also had its speaker's rostra and what would be from our point of view a presumptuous superfluity of statues—emperors, generals, magistrates and deserving citizens (and one, curiously enough, of the historian Suetonius). Right across the enormous square ran the dedicatory inscription, in fine capitals, of C. Paccius Africanus, a proconsul of Nero's day well known to us from Tacitus. You would also have seen somewhere a sundial let into the pavement, and in one corner there would have been a row of public latrines with running water emptying into a drain. Round this ancient core of the town were the houses, hidden behind whitewashed walls on which, by the sides of the unpretentious street doors, one could see the name-plates—*tituli*—of the owners.[11] Mules jogged down the unevenly paved streets between very narrow footways, and there was the occasional carriage. In summer Hippo is oppressively hot, but in the winter it is delightful; so that it is not surprising that on the sea-front an elegant residential quarter has been discovered, with some of the finest among the mosaic pavements.[12]

There was plenty of entertainment. Hippo possessed an amphitheatre (still undiscovered); many years previously a *flamen Augusti* and *duumvir* had provided a gladiatorial show which lasted for three consecutive days, for which he was offered a statue by each *curia*;[13] but those days were over. The remains of a theatre have been found, and quite a sumptuous one too; and there was probably a stadium as well, for the bishop is constantly inveighing in one breath against zither-players, pantomimists, revue artists, charioteers and fighters of wild animals.[14] The baths of the period (two of them have been brought to light) were public establishments, serving also as assembly rooms where people met one another, gave parties and delivered lectures; in one of them, the Baths of Sossius, the bishop held his public dispute with the Manichee Fortunatus[15]—the kind of affair which today would be arranged in a private room at a hotel.

There is not much beauty in the African ruins of the later imperial period; banal capitals, soundly constructed but shoddily finished buildings and an endless series of statues showing all the characteristics of soulless mass-production. The only thing which delights us again and again (Hippo is no exception) is the new-born luxury art of the mosaic, known to us mostly from the pavements and later from the tombs, with its profusion of decorative discoveries, and its colour-schemes which retain something of the old tastes while at the same time giving us a glimpse of what was to come. Small wonder that not one of the ancient authors has described the monuments of Africa, or even as much as mentioned them.

Hippo, which was called Regius because, so it was said, the old Numidian kings liked to live there, was by no means the least among the Numidian towns.[16] Everything goes to show that after the metropolis of Carthage it certainly ranked second in Africa Romana; and it is an open question whether Cirta, the capital of Numidia (present-day Constantine) was a larger town. Even after the excavations we do not know how big it was; it has been estimated to have had between thirty and forty thousand inhabitants.[17] The grain of the *annona*[18] was exported from its harbour, and this meant that there was a regular shipping service to Rome and that Augustine had a postal service directly at his door. Greek ships called here too—you could always hear men swearing in Greek in this place, he once said in a sermon[19]—so that Hippo was connected with both East and West.

The town was a good place for the bishops to meet one another as they travelled around, for it lay half-way between the two capitals of Cirta and Carthage. In October 393 a synod was held in the *secretarium* of the great church, a meeting which Augustine called a "plenary council of the whole Church".[20] Further, the town was fortified. It had a coastal guard under a tribune[21] and strong walls as well, and it was to Hippo in 430 that numerous bishops fled (as did also Boniface, the imperial commander), and there endured a siege of fourteen months.[22] Yet in spite of all this, Hippo remained a provincial town, and no-one will compare the *cathedra* of Augustine with the pulpit of Notre-Dame or with Newman's pulpit in St. Mary's, Oxford.

In the outer districts of the town, there were a number of Christian basilicas. We hear of the Leontiana, a church in which the bishop celebrated the anniversary of his consecration and which had been built by a certain Leontius,[23] one of Augustine's predecessors. We also hear of a number of churches or chapels dedicated to local martyrs, of whom we know nothing beyond the bare fact of their martyrdom—a certain Bishop of Hippo named Theogenes, who lived in Cyprian's time, is a case in point. Alternatively, we find them vaguely named after unidentified groups, such as "The Twenty Martyrs", "The Eight Martyrs",[24] and so on. Then there were churches built on the cemeteries outside the cities and known as *memoriae* or *martyria*. Hippo could also, at the time of Augustine's death, point to a number of communities of *continentes* which Augustine himself had founded, it could point to the monastery containing the cathedral clergy, a large convent and a monastery for lay monks. The costs of one of these institutions had been borne by the wealthy priest Leporius, who had, at Augustine's instigation, built the "Basilica of the Eight" and also a pilgrims' hostel or *xenodochium*.[25] Outside the centre of the town but still within the walls, and probably not so far away from the centre as it was in the unwalled city of Timgad or Tigzirt,[26] there was the new core, the heart of the *Ecclesia Hipponensis*, the complex of buildings surrounding the *basilica major*.

THE BASILICA MAJOR

It is little enough that we know from the texts about this subject; in fact we are wholly dependent on the occasional brief but illuminating references by Augustine himself. Yet it is clear that we have to deal with an extensive complex of buildings probably very similar to the recently excavated remains of the ecclesiastical centre in the neighbouring Cuicul (plates 1, 2, 3) which, both as regards their extensiveness and the excellence of their preservation, are inferior only to the buildings of Salona in Dalmatia, and contain the best preserved baptistery in Africa.

In Hippo this complex contained the "Basilica of Peace" or "Great Church" —*basilica pacis sive major*[27]—with its baptistery[28] and the adjoining devotional chapel for the relics of St. Stephen.[29] It further contained a *secretarium*, which served as the depository of the archives and as a meeting and reception room. In Nola the main purpose of such a building was inscribed in verses over the door:

> This in truth is the place where the sacred vessels are guarded;
> Hence the procession departs bound for the worship of God.

There also belonged to the complex the *episcopium* or bishop's palace, where Augustine lived in community with his monks, and which therefore constituted a bishop's palace and canonry in one. There was, in addition, a *xenodochium*, and finally a number of secondary buildings, including those rooms with gardens where Augustine had lived as a priest in community with a few like-minded men, and which now housed a community of lay monks. This little monastery lay *intra ecclesiam*, that is to say, within the enclosing wall of the complex.[30] Close to the bishop's residence lay the convent, where the bishop's sister acted as superior till about 420. In the same quarter of the town there was also situated the large basilica of the Donatists.[31]

The conjectures suggested by the texts have in fact been confirmed by the excavations. The large block of ecclesiastical buildings between the Baths of

Severus and the forum has been unanimously recognized as being the town's episcopal centre, and as an organic whole which, despite the traces left by the Vandals and the Byzantine restoration, goes back in the main to the time of Augustine.

The buildings are not situated on the outskirts of the town, as is the case in other places; furthermore, the main church lies above some non-ecclesiastical buildings (a house, and a kind of factory for making "purple"), so that it seems likely that the Christian community had taken over what was already a building site. Three streets, paved in the familiar manner with large stones, and with a gutter down the middle, surround the main block, which thus takes up a complete *insula*. To the east of it is a very old-fashioned basilica with pillars and a fairly sumptuous mosaic pavement; this lies so very near to the main church on the west that it reminds one at once of the letter in which Augustine says that the people could hear the noise the Donatists made in their church, so short a distance was there between the two. It might indeed well be that of the Donatists.

In the main block the *basilica major* stands out. And if it is indeed the *basilica pacis*, then we know the exact spot where Augustine used to preach: in the middle of the bench for the presbyters on the dais of the apse the open space for the *cathedra* is clearly visible. The church fronts right onto the street and there is practically no narthex; opposite the main door an enclosure wall rises abruptly under the slope. To the right of the basilica there is a very modest *baptisterium*; the piscina is not more than six feet by nine, and there would only just be room for the bishop, one person to be baptized, and one deacon or deaconess. Baptism was obviously administered privately and one at a time—for reasons of decency, apart from anything else, since all *infantes* were baptized naked. The space surrounding the baptistery is much larger and has splendid mosaic pavements, which gives us sure grounds for surmising that it is the location of the *consignatorium*, where the bishop performed the post-baptismal rites and, in particular, administered the anointing with chrism (as part of what we now term the sacrament of confirmation) to the newly-baptized. The font itself was covered with a baldachin, the four columns of which have been re-erected; it is not now possible to determine whether the baptismal water had to be brought in in vessels or came flowing down through spouts. To the left of the main church there is a trefoil-shaped building, which is also decorated with a sumptuous mosaic pavement and connected with a spacious portico adjoining a very large hall. This hall is supposed to have been used as the council-chamber of 393; and the trefoil-shaped building may well have been the votive chapel or *martyrium* of St. Stephen at the side of the cathedral. To the west of this *cella trichora* there are a number of very simple cells, all alike: these are thought to have formed the domestic monastery which Augustine set up in his residence. The rooms on the north-east side of the block of buildings, which are rather office-like, are thought to have been used by the deacons for the distribution of charity; remains found in them seem to indicate that grain and other provisions were stored there.

Will all these identifications prove to be definitive? The area as yet unexcavated may always produce surprises; but it would be certainly remarkable if in this town, which is not very large, a second block of buildings were found which tallied as perfectly with what we know from the texts. The situation of the *martyrium* of St. Stephen presents a difficulty, admittedly. From a passage in the *City of God* it would appear that it not only could be reached directly from the cathedral, but was so near to it that in the apse of the cathedral the cries before the chancel of the chapel could be heard. Those who identify the chapel with the *cella trichora* must be counting on very loud voices.

For the rest, the *basilica major* which has been discovered does not differ in any way from the usual African town churches of the pre-Byzantine period. It is neither a very large nor a very striking building. Its measurements—60 by 126 (or, including the apse, 147) feet are those of the average fairly large main church in this area; only one or two Carthaginian churches, like the enormous and eccentric Damous-el-Karità, are larger. Augustine himself says somewhere of this standard type that it has an oblong ground-plan and that the front is considerably narrower than the side-walls.[32]

Only the foundations of the church are left. But we know enough of dozens of other cathedrals in Numidia and African Proconsularia to assume that Augustine's cathedral must have been a sober and modest building. It contained no seats, not even along the walls, for the congregation remained standing, after the manner still to be seen in the Orthodox East. Augustine tells us[33] that here and there, in certain places overseas, people used to sit, but that this was most unusual. In the Syrian hinterlands the custom of squatting on mats seems to have grown up at a fairly early date.

Men and women stood separately.[34] It also appears—or at any rate we are told this of Italy by an unknown contemporary of Ambrose—that virgins had a special place of their own shut off by a balustrade, and certainly there is in the Louvre a crudely chiselled *tabula ansata* with the inscription:

```
        VIRG
    B  INUM  B
        CANC
```

which seems to mean, "Choir of Virgins. All Good Things to the Good" (*Virginum Cancellus B[onis] B[ene]*).[35] In the nave there was not much more than a square wooden altar (plates 4 and 8)[36] behind which there was a rectangular space, shut in by balustrades, for the officiating clergy, the choir and, in Easter week, for the newly baptized.[37] We do not know the position of the reader's *pulpitum*, but it was not in a place of honour, for the readers were only well-drilled boys "whose voices had not yet broken". We know that some reading took place from the apse,[38] but there is never any talk of an ambo.

The bishop himself always spoke from the apse, which was raised a few steps higher than the nave and was thus called *absida gradata*[39] or *locus superior*, and so had in Africa retained its purpose of an *exedra*[40] or sitting-place, and tribune (*tribuna*), thus following the pattern of the ordinary profane market basilica. At the back of the apse and backed ultimately by the semi-circular walls ran the stone sigma-seats for the priesthood, these seats being ranged one behind the other in two tiers on the pattern of an amphitheatre. Up against the wall and at its centre, and raised upon a couple of additional steps, stood the bishop's *cathedra*, covered by a precious rug,[41] the symbol of the "overseer's" high office, "for the marble chair remains, only the person seated upon it changes".[42] It was from this high seat that Augustine was in the habit of speaking, and in doing so he was truly an *epi-skopos*, which he himself has translated *superintentor* or "one who looks down from above".[43] Sometimes when the church was very full, he stood upright upon the top step.[44] The paucity of furniture inside the church made it possible for larger numbers to be packed into it (on such occasions as Masses for martyrs[45]) than its actual size would lead one to assume. As many as two thousand may sometimes have been gathered there.

There is no reason to suppose that the interior of the church was particularly impressive. We hear of costly hangings in the houses of the well-to-do. The higher a man's social rating, the bishop says, the more *vela* will be hanging in his house,[46] so a *velum* may often well have hung between the pillars of the church. Some kind of decorative curtain, either of worked leather or of heavy wool, might well have hung behind the door, which usually opened inward, as one can see on the famous Sarcophagus 176 in the Lateran, with its two representations of church buildings,[47] and as one can also see it in mosques and in the churches of the South. Such a curtain would, among other things, serve to keep out the flies, and would be especially useful if the door was left open, as it well might be. The only other decorative things would be the sacred vessels, the chalices, basins, ewers and so on, which were of gold and silver.[48] We hear nothing of a gold-covered *confessio*, or of massive golden dedicatory offerings of so many hundred pounds, of the kind mentioned in the *Liber Pontificalis* for the churches of Rome. In all probability the limits of decorative effect were represented by a marble covering of the walls going up to the height of a man and possibly embellished with intarsia, some mosaic work in the cupola of the apse, a number of candelabra or lamp holders[49] and an elaborate mosaic floor.

This last was never absent (plates 4 and 19). If anyone wanted to do something for the church, he presented a piece of mosaic: "Such and such a one has covered [*tesselavit*] so and so many feet of mosaic" is what the inscriptions say in such a case. The only really ancient representation that we possess of the interior of a church of this date is the mosaic over a grave in a small cemetery basilica in Tabraca. It shows a representation, which seems vaguely Egyptian in character, of what was presumably a pretty average basilica, the picture being intended as a symbol of Mother Church—a conception with which Augustine was familiar.[50] All that this picture shows in the way of equipment is three wax candles which burn upon a cube-shaped altar, the latter being railed off by a *transenna*. Further one can see an *oculus* or round opening in the dome of the apse, a triumphal arch with three arcades of pillars with gilded capitals and, in the midst of them, the steps of the apse; see also the pillars and barred windows of the nave, the tiled roof, a pointed gable, a curtain over a doorway, and finally between the pillars of the left-hand colonnade (which must be imagined as being rather further away from the beholder) the birds and flowers of the mosaic floor.[51] Most of the floors delight us by their delicate colouring, in which slate blue and rust brown predominate, usually against a greyish-yellow background. Moreover, there is continual fascination for the eye in the intertwined bands and other geometric motifs, sometimes no more than a quite simple playing around with little wedges and squares.

In contrast to the mosaics, the actual architectural remains are often mediocre or worse (and the same applies to the graphic quality of the inscriptions), while virtually nothing remains in the way of sculpture. Often the capitals of pillars have been taken from temples and are entirely out of place in their new positions; as to Christian motifs, we sometimes find a small cross in relief upon a wall or a *chrismon* carved on a coping stone, and here again the inscriptions are full of mistakes.

From the character of hundreds of other ruins found elsewhere we may infer with confidence that, like the rest, the churches of Hippo were simple, quickly erected and somewhat impermanent structures which manifested no marked characteristics, architecturally or otherwise, that might be called specifically African. They varied occasionally in their general ground plan, but otherwise one of these African churches was pretty much like another. The element of variation and surprise does not enter in Africa till we come to the Byzantine period some hundred years later. Till then there is no sign of a vaulted nave, or of any attempt at achieving a really ambitious decoration of the apse. All that we find is that in a few towns there is a

3 Fourth-century basilica at Cuicul

4 Reconstruction of an African town church

remarkable tendency to multiply naves, with seven or even nine naves sometimes running alongside of one another. Usually, however, the dimensions are less ambitious and conformity to type is the rule.

Thus when thinking of Augustine's church we must in no wise visualize anything suggesting the great period of Roman architecture, nor yet such magnificent Christian edifices as Santa Sabina or San Paolo Fuori le Mura. The vision of an Augustine picturesque with heavy locks casting his spell over thousands as he moves in sweeping vestments and fluttering *omophorion* against the background of an edifice which in its turn is a sort of Ulpian Basilica[52] magnified by the imagination, is the stylized product of a fancy which piety has driven to overstatement.

The truth was somewhat different. Augustine bore neither cross nor ring, his figure was slight, his features somewhat sharp, his head shaven; he was usually wrapped in a cloak or *birrus* (probably dark in colour) open in front; it was thus attired that he generally occupied the *cathedra*. From here he looked down on the faithful thronging before the steps beneath him and into a very simple church with three naves, a building which, except for the light cast by the high-placed windows, resembled more than anything else one of those domeless mosques that were the successor of the Christian basilica in Syria and North Africa. The beauty, such as it was, of this daughter of a king lay within. Victor Vitensis describes the interior of such a church with a single sentence. "At the time of the Vandal persecutions someone in a vision saw the church of Faustus in Carthage in its accustomed splendour, blazing with the lights of its candles, and shimmering with its curtains."[53]

On the outside Augustine's church was no doubt much built around, and the effect must have been massive, though in the absence of towers there can have been no feeling of height. It sat broadly on the ground, but there was nothing to tempt the eye upwards. Probably in some ways the whole effect was similar to that produced by a mosque with its *madrasa* in Tlemcen or Cairo—a somewhat neglected complex of cool pillared buildings, narrow passages with courtyards full of a kind of heavy heat, and small windows in walls of blinding white. Somewhere there must also have been a few dusty shrubs near a covered fountain, the murmur of which could just be heard. All this must have been very like what we can see today, save only that, gleaming in the tremulous blue of the air, there rose over all the sign of the Cross.

The Province

The town lay on the edge of a wide hinterland, the Regio Hipponensium Regiorum,[54] which, as is indicated by the boundary stones that have come to light, stretched out about fifteen miles toward the north-west, something over twenty miles in the direction of Tabraca and a similar distance in that of Calama.[55] The diocese or *parochia*[56] of Hippo was apparently somewhat larger than this, for we hear of someone coming up to Hippo for baptism from the Municipium Tulliense[57] which was even further away. We also hear of a spot called Fussala (where Augustine was one day to make a bishop of a reader) and this Fussala was stated to be on the outskirts of the territory adjoining the town, though it was actually over thirty miles away.[58]

Towards the interior the land was covered with large estates. On these, small tenant farms surrounded the house of the lord of the estate and its park. Poor *coloni* toiled wearily, as did hordes of slaves who still spoke the Punic tongue and worked under the whip of the overseer, while the stewards wrangled with the tax officials. It was the countryside that we know so well from the mosaics of the middle period of the Empire (Plate 22). There we can see walled-in ploughlands, huge villas, occasional quarries of marble,[59] and lonely herds upon the hills beside the main road. There also are shown thieves and rogues, while up in the mountains is the hunter's country where the great gentlemen have their sport, "caring naught for heat or cold, for ravines or rushing brooks, for bites or broken limbs, content with the coarsest fare and the dirtiest water—and all this to bring down a boar or a stag, the death of which brings even more delight to their hunters' hearts than is ever vouchsafed their palates when these same beasts come roasted on to the table."[60]

These estates were sometimes part of the imperial domain or *saltus*, while in other cases they were the property of Roman senators[61] or of other wealthy folk, whose homes might be in Campania or Sicily or possibly close by in Africa itself; in yet other cases the estates belonged to the Church.[62] They were administered by stewards[63] or agents who also acted as tax collectors,[64] or by a manager, who would then be accounted as the head of the whole *familia rusticana*. The owners, who usually lived far away, were rarely seen but were for all that the objects of envy. If anyone saw a large country house, then he would ask one of the workmen, "Whose is this magnificent estate?"— for, after all, the average person could not read the *tituli* on the walls—and when the answer came—"It belongs to this senator or that"—he would sigh, "Lucky man!" or, "Those people can really live."[65]

The *coloni*[66] were small tenant farmers, who were for all practical purposes serfs and probably in many cases paid their rent in kind.[67] They were simple, rough people who treated a slave very much like one of themselves. They cursed heaven when there was a thunderstorm, and bought charms against hail; some among them would invoke demons to bring about a bad harvest, so that they could sell supplies at exorbitant prices.[68]

As far as religion went, such men were quite helpless in the hands of their lords. We hear that they occasionally became Christian in swarms (and even remained so)[69] along with their lord or his steward. On other occasions they would go over to the *pars Donati* in exactly the same fashion and were duly rebaptized[70]—and possibly, having done so, repeated this performance and returned to the Catholic Church.

The whole interior spoke the Punic tongue which it had used for centuries— we hear practically nothing of Berber's being used—a circumstance which proved an almost insuperable obstacle to preachers of the Gospel.[71] For even the interior was nominally Christian, and almost every large estate, and indeed almost every little settlement of farmers, had its own house of God.[72] The landlords were in the habit of putting up a basilica on their land for themselves and their people, and would then look around for a permanent priest. We hear of house-chapels and oratories and of *memoriae* in honour of the martyrs. Not far from Hippo there was found a memorial stone, on which are shown two doves drinking from a single vessel. The founding of a chapel by a newly-baptized couple is commemorated thereon in the following words:

> What the first fruits of our virtue were may be read and seen here, for the new building which you behold was begun and completed by reason of our care.[73]

It was not always the lords who did the building. An inscription on the ruins of a church north of Aures tells that the inhabitants of the village of Venusianum had begun the structure, while those of Mucrion had contributed five pillars and those of Cusalete six, and that all of them together had paid for the mosaic on the floor of the apse. The inhabitants of Cusalete had in addition provided for all further equipment. The priest Rogatus and a certain Aemilianus are recorded as having directed the building operations.[74]

Mass was only said occasionally in the smaller house-chapels. In the bishopric of Hippo we hear of a priest who had to serve four hamlets, though it is true that he had a reader to help him.[75] Everywhere in Africa there have been found remains of those lonely little rural churches, which for the most part repeat the three-nave pattern, though it so happens that in the diocese of Hippo we have only found a solitary one, that of Verdier, some six miles south of Hippo itself. This lies among a multitude of gravestones, one carrying an inscription in memory of the *custos*, a simple subdeacon.[76] Few recognizable traces remain of the little house-churches.

Descriptions have just been given of the character of some of the great estates, and it was estates of this kind, vast in extent and worked by hundreds of slaves, that were sold by the younger Melania and her husband during their stay in Africa. Men did not have to be actual saints to be alive to the monstrous character of such forms of property, nor need we wonder that the countryfolk of Africa grew embittered, for embittered they became, and the fanaticism of the Donatist Circumcellions gave expression to an urge to revolt which was in part at least social in its origins—the revolt which ultimately took shape in a naïve and short-lived attempt at dictatorship.

Over that same countryside Augustine was often to ride, surveying as he went the rich treeless cornfields[77] of Numidia—"naked Getulia". As he rode, he would ever reflect upon the miracle that most men had long ceased to regard, the miracle by which God daily brings forth vast harvests from a single grain of wheat.[78] A hundred little manifestations of nature, or of man in contact with nature, would suggest to his mind, as it did to the Psalmist, some simile of a spiritual truth. His sermons abound in this kind of thing. He sees the ploughman at work, and tells his flock that they must cultivate good works in the winter which is this life, and do so for the sake of the future which is to come, even as the sower and the ploughman must continue with their work under a dark sky and in unceasing rain and cold, for they that sow in tears shall reap in joy.[79] Or again, a piece of straw caught on a thorn hedge brings to his mind the chaff of the Church, blown over to the Donatists;[80] the olive, containing as it does pulp and oil in one, suggests the press that will separate one from the other and so the Last Judgement.[81] Similarly the leaves trodden underfoot,[82] the flight of birds of passage and their strange foreknowledge of the onset of winter,[83] smoke going up from a heap of dung,[84] the blossom and fruit of the lemon tree, the little flowers[85]—all are raw materials for this great artist. Nothing seems to be missed. He sees an olive grower grafting a shoot,[86] he sees a goat standing on its hind legs to nibble the olive leaves, and can no more resist applying these themes than could the sculptors of the Roman sarcophagi. Yet it was not these diminutive idylls that filled his spirit. When he rode along the military highway, saw from afar the ordinary folk sweating beside their cattle,[87] and greeted the labourers by the roadside with the customary "The blessing of the Lord be upon you",[88] then he thought of the helplessness of these poor people. He knew only too well what manner of creatures lived in this seemingly friendly countryside—men with strong hearts, hirelings and labouring slaves. He knew only too well the distance that separated these people from the civilized Roman city and from the Church which belonged to that city (even though it was in the country that it had its estates), the Church which spoke the tongue of the governing class. He knew the gulf between such Roman civilized things and this rightless, unstable and all-too-inflammable Berber folk who still used the ancient Punic speech—and yet, praise God, upon those fields he often heard them sing.[89]

3

THE PAGANS

A Dwindling Minority

THE urban population was predominantly Christian, and the bishop could say, of his congregation of fishermen, sailors, weavers, market gardeners, merchants, business men, soldiers, officials, literary men and ascetics, that there was no house without a Christian, and hardly a house where the Christians did not outnumber the pagans.[1] Even so, there were still many pagans who occupied high positions, and that not only in the cities, where their influence was often not inconsiderable and where they put many difficulties in the Catholics' way. This happened in Calama, for instance, the centre of Possidius' diocese, and in Madaura, the home of Apuleius.

The fact is that the influence of the local magnate was all-embracing. Even in the country surrounding Hippo one could hear folk ask who would still remain a pagan, if such and such a great lord turned Christian.[2] This probably meant that a whole hamlet really belonged to such a man; the inhabitants might well have wished to become Christians themselves, but they watched what was done by their lord and did not dare to act on their own.

The senators in the capital still remained true to their ancient gods, but we do not know whether in Africa their example was followed by the *curiales* and *duumviri* of the smaller towns. Possibly this would have been the case less frequently than it actually was, had the Christian not shown a distinct tendency to keep out of public affairs. We know that round about the year 400 Christians found it impossible to avoid civic office with all the burdens that it entailed, but, if we are to accept pagan testimony of this point, it was the Christian rich who wriggled out of the magistracy more than anyone else. It is even said that many a man became a cleric because he feared for his family estates and wanted to avoid office in order to save his money. There was yet another explanation for the paucity of Christians in high office, for we learn from Augustine's letters that high officials tended to postpone their baptism, believing all too often that as soldiers or in a Government office it was impossible for them to lead a life that was pleasing to God.[3]

Elsewhere the failings of Christians took a different form. We hear of Christians in Andalusia at the time of Constantine who sought to obtain priestly posts in that province for the sake of the honour and income attached to them, a practice which aroused great indignation among the clergy.[4]

In contrast to its Roman counterpart, the aristocracy was Christian almost to a man.[5] In a few towns you would have had to use a lantern to find a pagan, and no-one there mocked at the new faith.[6] The verses of the proud Spaniard Prudentius might well have applied to Africa, when he wrote:

> Rare indeed are the fools that cling to the creed of the pagan,
> Giving a rickety faith grudging observance of rite,
> Striving, now that the darkness has fled, to recapture the darkness,
> Standing blind to the light after the dawn of the day.[7]

A powerful bait was the Christian care for the poor, which resulted in many sham conversions, though even the pagan would, in a crisis, come running to the deacon and even, on occasion, make use of the bishop's court. And so, as Augustine pointed out in a sermon, the word of the Psalmist was fulfilled: "He hath made the nations subject to us and laid the heathen at our feet."[8]

It began to be advantageous to join what was now the religion of the Court, of the Imperial Government—and also of the majority. And though a bishop as yet carried no crozier, it was not a bad thing to be within reach of one— a fact which the poor and socially helpless knew all too well.

There were also, of course, conversions that resulted from some personal crisis; thus we hear of a doctor who vowed by the sickbed of his small and only daughter that he would become a Christian if her life could be spared, a vow which he ultimately fulfilled, though somewhat belatedly.[9] Naturally enough, there were admirable people among the pagans, people who, as Augustine pointed out, fed the hungry and clothed the naked as lovingly as any Christian. Such people had to be handled with great tact,[10] he declared, for they would be won over to the truth by gentleness rather than by argument. In one respect they resembled their own gods of stone, and yet God could awaken these cold stones into life, making them true children of Abraham.[11]

Though the majority's way of life was not always markedly Christian, public opinion was nevertheless informed by a somewhat dour pro-Christian bias. That at least can be inferred by the way people reacted in the harbour and the market-place to the least sign of pagan presumption, and this spirit came out even more strongly when Christians were gathered together in their church. Once Augustine had to present an elderly, highly-placed but somewhat evil-living convert to his congregation. It was the banker Faustinus, and it was suspected that it was his ambition to attain the magistracy which had caused him to change horses. The basilica rang with the cry "No pagan for mayor, no pagan at our head!" which caused the bishop to hurry along with such apt scriptural references as that concerning the labourers who arrived at the eleventh hour, and the hundredth sheep. He knew, he said, what they thought of this man. For years the refrain had been "Who is it that has undertaken this or that against the Christians?" and the answer was, "Faustinus"—always "Faustinus". But now one might well ask, "Who is it that fears Christ?" and to this the answer would indeed be "Faustinus", and that answer would be true. Augustine therefore begged his hearers now to show a love for the man which would exceed their previous hatred of his errors. He also assured them that the unhappy victim of their uncharity had declared that he did not covet office at all, but merely desired to be a Christian.[12]

Yet whatever the motives behind the conversions, the numbers of those who mocked at the Christians was steadily declining.[13] Augustine states that they were growing less from year to year, and that in some places not one of them remained. If Christians were to stay away from the theatre, the mere handful of pagans would of necessity become ashamed of their small numbers, and would run from the empty seats.[14] Since every diminution brought their numbers nearer to zero, pagans must be reconciled either to their own disappearance or to an acceptance of the Faith.[15]

POLEMICS

Influential pagans were to be found first and foremost in the ranks of the old freethinkers, who just could not go along with the religious excitement that almost universally prevailed. They were men who, for the most part, were indifferent in matters of religion. There were still men in all walks of life who held on to traditional practices through laziness and sheer dullness of mind; there were others who clung to them from sentiment or even from obstinacy which prevented their admitting their errors to themselves;[16] yet others did so because they desired no curb upon their sexual licence, or even from sheer frivolity.

One group was annoyed by what they considered the banality of the so-called new Christian customs,[17] another (and this was a not wholly unjustifiable ground of objection) by the everlasting doctrinal quarrels.[18] There was some mocking at what was to outsiders the inexplicable ease and speed with which sins were forgiven at baptism, for this seemed like a charter to continue the indulgence of desires to the very last moment, when after a long licentious life[19] a deathbed baptism would settle all accounts. Others were more understanding, and indeed many a good heart lurked under this Voltairian ridicule—many a heart of which grace might at any time take instant possession.[20]

Yet the learned and intellectual opposition to Christianity had not by any means died out—this at any rate was the case in Africa. There were still literary amateurs who felt that the prestige of the ancient culture weighed too heavily in the scale. Such a man was the orator Maximus, from that very conservative place, Madaura. To Maximus it was incomprehensible that anyone should visit the graves of a few murdered plebeians in preference to the dignified temples of the gods, or that anyone could neglect the ancient immortals in order to honour men with such barbarous and disgustingly Punic names as Miggin, Sanam, Lucitas or the "arch-martyr" Namphamo (a catalogue that probably referred to the otherwise now nameless martyrs of Madaura).

It was in this sense that Maximus wrote to the monk Augustine when the latter had just exchanged rhetoric for asceticism,[21] and his short letter contains this pertinent question: "The old gods could be publicly worshipped, as is fitting, whereas your god is kept behind lock and key, and no-one knows exactly who he is. What is one to make of that?—and just who is this god?" Maximus concluded his letter with the words, "Give me a straight answer without the customary tricks of eloquence or any of those dialectical games which can at a pinch make all things seem equally credible."

The author of that admirable little work *The True Worship of God* was better equipped than anybody else to satisfy such curiosity and he did so forthwith. Augustine's skirmishes with Maximus are a sort of light counterpart to the debate over the Altar of Victory in the Roman senate chamber which Ambrose, the man Augustine so greatly honoured, carried on in the grand manner with Symmachus. The tone on either side was equally courteous. Maximus retained copies of the correspondence, which were always available for inspection.[22]

Augustine, in replying to his questioner,[23] was naturally the more detailed of the two, though there is an easy spontaneity about his writing and a certain delicate irony. Its substance was a short version of the arguments which he was at the end of his life to develop in so comprehensive and unforgettable a manner in the *City of God*. To be visible was beneath the dignity of God, but his works were glorious enough to hold all those captive who could take pleasure in them. The martyrs are not gods but brave and simple men who are all the more to be honoured for their simplicity, whereas the pagan gods were either demons, or ordinary men who had wrongly had divinity attributed to them,[24] for they were men who had all too often done shameful things and now were made objects of worship at the games, which themselves were all too often a place of instruction in the ways of shame. As to the alleged worship of the dead, no Catholic Christian ever dreams of engaging in that.

Augustine then asked Maximus whether he did not think that he himself was making pagan religion ridiculous. His line of argument would certainly make one suppose that. As to these comic Punic names, Namphamo simply meant "Good Foot"—as they both, being Africans, knew very well, and this was not so absurd as "the Dirt God", "the Sewer Goddess", "Bald Venus", "the Anaemia God"[25] and other names of pagan deities. Before jesting so lightly about God, however, let him take care lest he fall into the sin of blasphemy. All this was a question which must be most seriously treated, and he himself was not disposed to make sport of it. Since that was the attitude he had always deliberately taken, his friend could hardly expect him to change it.

Maximus admitted that there could only be one supreme "father god without a son", a being who had had no beginning. Only a madman would deny this. That gods lived on Olympus was of course a Greek fable. Nevertheless, he found satisfaction in seeing numbers of gods in the market place of his town, for God's limitless powers were distributed over the whole universe and we might surely adore these under various names and under the guise of visible images, and thus in the various cults worship God "piece by piece and as it were in his members". In the matter of names, he preferred the beautiful ancient ones over those that were new and plebeian. The honouring of angels and martyrs was really the same thing as honouring heroes and gods.[26] One feels in all this an essentially modern note, save only that one misses the technical terms of modern religious studies. We might well have before us an exchange of letters between Lucius and Delehaye.

There is even more charm in the short letters which Augustine, when already a bishop, wrote to a Platonizing *littérateur* named Longinianus, whom he referred to as a righteous man. Longinianus had put some questions to him concerning, among other things, the value of the old purification rites, which Longinianus held to be indispensable for a man seeking to rise to the contemplation of God; for it was, he held, the duty of man ever to seek to rise upwards towards the one true God, the Creator of all things, and he did this through purity of life, through seeking converse with the gods (or as Christians would say, with the angels) and through the use of purification rites, as the ancients had always taught.[27]

For his part the bishop had asked his correspondent what he thought of Christ, "for I know that your estimation of him is not small".[28] Longinianus replied that he recognized his greatness but did not accept him as the Son of God; he admitted, however, that he did not quite know what to make of him or of that "ghost god" of the Christians.

Augustine respected this point of view, but asked his correspondent, in the next letter, to establish as far as he could the true value, whatever it might be, of the purification rites, and, if possible, to prove it. Was purification the consequence of a good life, or was it its cause; or was it perhaps a part of a good life? It was only when this point had been cleared up that a really searching discussion could take place of the other matters.[29] It is unfortunate that the rest of the correspondence has been lost. Longinianus had a soft spot in his heart for "the most excellent of Romans", who had met him in this friendly fashion. Never, so he wrote, had he met a man with so burning a desire to know God, nor had he encountered the like in book or story from the past.[30]

It is also worth our while to note the bishop's answer to the dignitaries of Madaura. These had remained pagan despite the closing of the temples in 399. When after his dispute with Maximus these men had occasion to send Augustine a letter (through the mediation of a certain Florentius), they wished "our father Augustine everlasting salvation in the Lord" and then begged him to use his authority and good offices on behalf of the bearer, who had important business in Hippo. They closed their letter with the following words: "We desire, sir, that God and his Christ may preserve you for a long and happy life in the midst of your clergy."[31]

Augustine was at first delighted, for he thought that the people of the town were about to turn Christian, but when his messenger had assured him that they did not contemplate anything of the kind "and had their idols firmly locked in their hearts as in their temples" he expressed astonishment in his reply at these Christian-sounding words, for, he said, he refused to believe that they had been used in irony. Further, he adjured his brothers and fathers in Madaura (in which he had been to school as a youth) to have serious fear of the judgement of God, and to recognize this judgement in the terrifying examples provided by the fate of the Jews, by the decay of paganism, and by the closing of the temples, and not to throw his own most well-intentioned warnings to the wind and so bring down a judgement upon themselves even more dreadful than these. Let them read the signs of the times, for the name of Christ was in every man's mouth and one saw emperors throw off their diadems and prostrate themselves at a fisherman's grave.[32] It was in a similar sense that he was later to write to a pagan citizen of Calama, urging him to reflect that times had changed. Paganism had outlived its usefulness and was perishing of its own rottenness.[33]

He was always courteous. It is true that in a confidential letter he spoke of the miracle-workers Apollonius of Tyana and Apuleius as sorcerers (the pagans still compared these men with Christ) and claimed that their miracles vanished to nothing when compared with those of the Prophets, not to speak of the miracles of Christ himself and of that greatest miracle of all, the fulfilment of the prophecies. In the same letter, however, he admitted that he found Apollonius a more respectable person than "Jupiter with his incests and his rapes". As to Apuleius, who was so anxious to have a statue erected to himself, he declared that he was a gifted artist in life and said nothing worse of him than that he was an excellent business man.[34] In a piece of writing that was intended for the public as a whole, he even praised Apuleius as a noble

Platonist and mentioned him in the same breath as Plotinus, Iamblichus and Porphyry.[35]

Apart from the *arcana* of the sacraments, most pagans were fairly well instructed concerning Christian doctrine, which, after all, they could study in the biblical writings.[36] Thus, a certain Carthaginian intellectual once put six very precisely formulated questions to the priest Deogratias. They dealt with points concerning which, as a man of the world, the Carthaginian experienced difficulties. These points were the resurrection of the body, the universal effectiveness of Christ's redemption (which seemed to be made impossible by the fact that the world had been going on for many centuries before him), the correspondence between the sacrificial practices of the Old Testament and those of the pagans, the incongruity of eternal punishment for a sin committed in time, the sonship of God and the miracle of Jonah—all questions which Deogratias preferred to pass on to the learned Bishop of Hippo.[37]

We find that the young sceptic Volusianus had similar difficulties. Volusianus, however, was genuinely anxious to have them resolved, for at that time not all sceptics were indifferent. (Probably this man was the son of that Pontifex Maximus Albinus, who had secretly remained a pagan, and whom Jerome once describes as dandling his grandson on his knees while the latter very solemnly sang him alleluias.[38] If this is correct, he was on his mother's side a relative of Melania.)

Volusianus had, while quite a young man, occupied a very important post, and was at this time living in Carthage. He cultivated the society of Catholics of his own rank, and discussed religion with them. This was, of course, just then the fashionable thing to do, and Volusianus on these occasions used all the finesse by which this kind of discussion tended to be marked. A couple of letters which happen to have been preserved enable us to get an excellent picture of the kind of mixed literary salon which he no doubt frequented. Upon the urging of Volusianus' pious mother, Augustine had briefly written to him somewhat as follows. He should read the Scriptures; they are, he says, honest and worthy documents. They do not creep into your soul with the aid of prettily painted words. They strike into the heart of any man who is less concerned with words than with their content. Above all, he should read the letters of the Apostles. Augustine would not fail to help him over any difficulties he might encounter.[39]

Volusianus felt flattered. He showed the bishop's letter round his club and said, "If they were not too numerous for a single letter, I would gladly put all questions before him that are in my heart." Then the conversation, which till that moment had been on oratorical composition and its importance, naturally began to turn on religion and passed on to a discussion of the Christian mysteries. Thus came the unavoidable question. How was it possible for the incomparable One to conceal himself for nine months in the womb of a virgin? Did not this suspend the laws which rule the world? Also, the miracles which he wrought as a grown man were surely not unique. The company resolved that a letter should be written to the bishop and that his reply should be requested. Volusianus wrote to him briefly but with elegance and apprised him of the questions in point, closing with the words: "Your reputation is at stake. When dealing with other members of the priesthood, we do not become greatly concerned if they prove ignorant on some matter, but when it is a case of Bishop Augustine, then we can only say, 'What that man does not know is not part of Christian law.' "[40]

Being unwilling to make his letter overlong, Volusianus communicated certain questions which he did not touch upon in writing to his fellow club member, the *tribunus et notarius* Marcellinus, who was Augustine's intimate friend. The questions touched, among other things, on the unmilitary attitude of Christians and their lack of loyalty to the Empire. Marcellinus wrote a pressing letter to his friend, begging him to reply but also to use great care in doing so, since his letter would undoubtedly go from hand to hand, and to give particularly thorough treatment to the question of alleged Christian disinclination to serve the State in arms or otherwise. There had been, so Marcellinus declared at the end of his letter, a large landowner in the club who had spoken words of praise about Augustine, though he may possibly have meant these ironically, and who had declared himself dissatisfied with the answers of the Christian club members. This man had, however, gone further and said that even Augustine would not be able to give him a satisfactory reply on the points at issue.[41]

Augustine replied with a complete tract in letter form, a piece of writing particularly meticulous and also couched in terms very flattering to the person he was addressing, for even among his friends Augustine spoke of Marcellinus as of a beloved son, the bond being further strengthened by the Christian ardour of Marcellinus' mother, with which the bishop was well acquainted.[42]

Augustine's letter, which dealt with the Incarnation and the Church, became in due course a classical document for theologians, a document which was quoted by such men as Leo the Great, Theodore and Cassian, and twice referred to at a general council.[43] Marcellinus received yet a second letter which dealt with the remainder of the questions raised and this,[44] like the first, was also duly read out in the club.

It is true that this dignified tone only prevailed in such places as the select club here referred to, and possibly in an earnest man's study. Converts had much to endure from their families.[45] And on the street, religious controversy rarely rose above the level of mutual insult and ridicule. Worshippers of a crucified scoundrel and of an unreasoning baby, simpletons, ne'er-do-wells, despisers of life, traitors—these were samples of the kind of thing the Christians had to put up with.[46] Or they were asked: "What has Christ achieved?", the answer to which was that he had caused idiots to squander their substance on idlers, and that the world, which once had been so rich, so jolly and full of roaring good times, had become a place of boredom.[47] Nevertheless, the tide had turned, and that irreversably. The new and rising faith was not to be withstood. Around 400 its advance was as irresistible as was to be that of unbelief in the second half of the eighteenth century.

The Ending of Paganism

The old cult was coming to an end anyway. Under Valentinian II and Theodosius both public and private sacrifices had been forbidden. This prohibition applied not merely to divination from entrails of slaughtered beasts, but to all the ancient cults, even to the offering of wine and incense to the gods of the hearth, and to the garlanding of household gods. The temples, which had still been open as recently as 382, "because of the masterpieces which were to be seen there", were now closed. At least, a law was passed to this effect,[48] and this law was actually enforced (and drastically so) wherever the arm of the State could reach and Christians could assist it—which means over the whole of the East and in a few towns of the West. In those regions not a single altar sent up its smoke, not a single sacred tree had any garland to show, the statues stood desolate upon the market place, and all the herms and Priapuses had been removed. In Africa progress was not quite so fast. There it was not till the Draconian measures of Honorius that the whole cult completely disappeared, and before this could be achieved a number of edicts, namely those of the years 399, 407, 408 and 415, had to order idols and other objectionable objects to be removed from the temples, and the temples themselves to be closed. Temples for the most part were not actually pulled down— it was fortunate that zeal did not run to such excess—but the altars were destroyed, the appropriations for the upkeep of these institutions and for the actual games were cancelled, the personnel were sent back to their homes and temple property was confiscated and put to more worthy uses.[49]

In his youth Augustine had himself seen the depraved eunuchs of the Mother of the Gods go through the streets of Carthage "with damp hair, white powdered faces, swinging hips and feminine gait", in order to beg for their own support. He had observed the Goddess of Heaven (the old Phoenician Tanit) being carried around in solemn procession and seen a crowd of thousands witness the washing of the Mother of the Gods in April. The rites which accompanied this ceremony had, it is true, the sanction of Antiquity, but were so vulgar that the matrons who unblushingly witnessed them may well have learned things which otherwise would never have entered their minds.[50]

All that was now over. The first turning-point, as far as Africa was concerned, was the year 399. In that year the *comites* Gaudentius and Jovius had the temples of Carthage closed, the closing of the provincial temples following gradually.[51] Some few years back Augustine in a sermon had pointed out that the prophets in the Old Testament had told the story of the fall of ancient gods, and that his own time was witnessing a similar thing. Now, he declared, they were seeing prophecies of long ago being fulfilled;[52] the gods were being hidden in far-away places, while, for fear of the Christians, sacrifices had to take place in secret,[53] and those who had so long been faithful could now see the temples standing empty; the basilicas, which were often equipped with the pillars and capitals of temples that had been pulled down, were every Sunday full of people.

Augustine declared himself well content with this process of liquidation by law.[54] He likened the orthodox Emperor, who seriously attacked the hydra of polytheism, to that Persian king who had thrown the avengers of the dragon into the lions' den, while Daniel, whose balls of pitch had caused the dragon to burst, had been restored by him to honour. His thoughts also went back to Nebuchadnezzar, who, after his conversion by the three young men, had caused the idol of Bel to be torn down and strictly forbidden all blasphemy against the true God.[55] Probably this analogy often occurred to artists of that time, for we find these two themes frequently occurring in the carvings on Roman sarcophagi.

The fact that in this process of liquidation many statues and other monuments were lost and that cultured connoisseurs tended to make the most fearful outcry about this, left the Christians cold. They felt exactly as their brother Christians of Antioch had felt some decades previously when Julian the Apostate expelled Babylas, the patron saint of their city, from the neighbourhood of Apollo's temple in Daphne. On that occasion the Christians carried the saint's relics in procession to safety and most provocatively sang as they went the verse from the psalm, "May they become even as the graven images of their hand, yea and all who trust therein."[56]

It would have been an easy matter for Augustine to have all statues of gods destroyed by merely speaking the word. For never did the sixteenth-century Reformers of Holland destroy the sculptures in their churches with greater fury and satisfaction than the Christian mob wrecked the marble statues, beautiful and unsightly, clothed and naked alike. This was especially the case after the Government appeared, by the law of 399, to have given approval to such practices and even to have enjoined them. Indeed, it might be said that Augustine himself on occasion came very near to touching the iconoclastic nerve. One Sunday of June 401, he was preaching in Carthage, where, though the temples had been closed two years previously, paganism was still offering stubborn resistance. Augustine on this occasion seized on a verse of the psalm which had just been sung—"Lord, who is like unto thee?" —and congratulated his congregation on their zeal against idols. He also assured his hearers that both the bishop and he himself entirely shared their views, and when, immediately thereafter, he reminded the people in that closely packed church that even in Rome the temples had been closed and the idols destroyed, the words resounded through the church, apparently spoken by the congregation in unison, "In Carthage, as in Rome." Later still, he asked, "If the Roman gods have disappeared from Rome, why do they remain here?" and added, "If they could walk, they would answer that they had fled to this place. Think well, dear brethren, think well! I have said what I have said. It is for you to draw the conclusions." At this point wild applause broke out, for the shorthand-writers record a threefold uttering of the cry "Dii romani!"[57]

Moreover, there is obvious satisfaction expressed in his description of the devastation of temples in Carthage in 399—"... in part completely fallen into ruin, in part pulled down, in part closed or used for some purpose other than their original one, the statues broken into pieces, burnt, carried off or utterly destroyed."[58]

The sacred groves were uprooted, the chapels in them carried away, the altars thrown down, and sacrifices in them forbidden on pain of death.[59] That many people held these things dear was no ground for allowing them to continue, for they only served the purposes of lust or the deceptive arts of demons. Augustine admired the success of Constantine, who had founded a city without temples on the Bosphorus, and also that act of the strict Theodosius, who, when removing the statues of Jupiter which his counter-Emperor Eugenius had erected in the Alps, laughingly gave the golden lightning-flashes to his soldiers, who declared that they wanted to be struck by them.[60] He likened the government that abolished these abuses to a tutor who cries to boys playing in the dirt, "Stop it, wash your hands", and then gives them a book and a better way of employing their energy.[61]

If need arose Augustine did not scruple to seek out overbold pagans in their own dens and expose them; for having got the worst of the struggle, the pagan party was still eager to strike back whenever it could. When in some obscure place the pagan mob saw the chance of getting its own back on a Christian minority (a thing that was liable to happen in any spot which was still predominantly pagan, and in which the *curiales* were willing to close an eye), the temptation all too often proved irresistible. When in Colonia Sufetana in Byzacena the statue of Hercules was overturned—this was probably in the year 399—sixty Christians were killed by the pagans and the town council coolly demanded that the damage be made good. The council, admittedly, was basing its demand on the ordinary rights of property, which applied to community property as much as to any other. We still possess the letter which Augustine sent on this occasion. "Your monstrous and infamous crime," he wrote, "your incredible cruelty, causes the earth to tremble and reverberates to heaven. Blood gleams in your temples and public places. You have buried the laws of Rome and he who has murdered the largest number sits covered with praise presiding at your town council. But now to the main point. You speak of your Hercules. He was yours. You shall have him back. There is assuredly a quarry nearby here, and no lack of stone or even of different kinds of marble. There are also plenty of sculptors to choose from—and your god is being carefully chiselled, smoothed and made beautiful. Moreover, we will throw in a little red lead so that you may have him a bright crimson and thus add a really riotous note to your festivities. For if you say, 'This was our Hercules', we must needs put our pennies together and buy you back your god from any sculptor whom you fancy. But then you too must return to us the lives of those sixty."[62]

Nine years later, after the murder of Stilicho in the year 408, the pagans again began to stir in the different towns. There was an outbreak in Calama, where Possidius was bishop, and this caused Augustine again to declare his attitude. At the Calends of June the pagans surprised everybody by organizing one of the processions "which a little time previously had been forbidden by law".[63] They danced and junketed provocatively in front of the church door, and when some of the priests bade them remember the law, they greeted them with stones. A week later, when the thing seemed to be dying down, the bishop reminded the council of the law and the penalties it imposed. The reply was another rain of stones upon the church. Then, however, it was as though heaven was minded to give its own answer, for on the same day a hailstorm visited the town, and hailstones coming down on top of cobblestones did make a momentary impression.

Yet hardly had the shock this caused passed away, hardly was the sky clear, before what till now had been a minor brawl had grown into a riot which lasted from midday till far into the night. The mob, no longer content with throwing stones, sought to set the basilica on fire. After that it moved to the houses of the priests and soon everything was out of hand. The diaconal storehouse was plundered, and its contents distributed to the accompaniment of uproar (and here even Christians did not scruple to get hold of a bit of the loot), while the monastery was emptied of all that could be taken from it. A monk who dared to go out into the street was killed. Possidius, who had escaped in the nick of time, heard from his hiding-place the shouting of the raging horde. "Where is the bishop? If we haven't the bishop, we might as well not have come." Meanwhile the *curiales* did not stir a finger, although it would not have been too difficult to avert further disaster, for a wealthy foreigner succeeded in rescuing a few of the ascetics from the crowd and thus saved them from certain death—and all this, says Augustine, for the sake of wretched idols made of silver. No doubt, he says, it was by the manufacture of these that many of the townsfolk made their living.[64]

The people of Calama, when they came to their senses, were not too happy about what had occurred. The thing had clearly gone too far, and when shortly after this the great bishop visited Possidius and his flock and comforted them, some of the notables of the place sought an audience from him and asked him to plead the town's cause. One of these, a certain Nectarius, who had taken no part in the disturbances, wrote him a letter in which he admitted that the town had incurred a heavy guilt. He nevertheless asked Augustine to use his influence so that possible proceedings and questionings under torture might be prevented. The town council promised to make good any damage that had been done, and were anxious that the innocent (which meant the notables) should not suffer along with the guilty (which meant the common people).[65] Augustine in reply coolly remarked that he could well appreciate the council's love for their home (in this connection he did not fail to refer to an even better home) but that he himself wanted to see exemplary justice done (though he had no wish to have anyone executed or tortured) so that other towns might not be tempted to follow Calama's example. In any case, it was not for him but for the Government to decide.[66]

In the meantime Possidius travelled to the Court in order to get satisfaction. He passed through Nola on his way, and in that city visited Paulinus, thus combining business with pleasure. He was not the only bishop to cross the sea at this time, for Fortunatus of Sicca was also travelling to Court on behalf of the synod, and in the following year an official delegation took ship for Italy, there being by that time complete anarchy all over Africa.

Pagans and Donatists were now making common cause, numerous priests had been murdered and bishops were having their hair torn out. So when Severus of Milevis journeyed through Hippo, Augustine gave him a letter to Olympiodorus, the *magister officiorum* who was the *homo novus* at the Court. In this he asked for the Government to intervene, and, having no appetite for tolerance where the cult of demons was concerned,[67] pressed for strict enforcement of the old laws.

The result was that Honorius revived the laws and imposed heavy penalties, though not the death penalty, and threatened to get the garrison to intervene if there was any recurrence of the trouble.[68] Hereupon Nectarius, who had reckoned with the Government's pigeonholing the whole affair and so had simply lain low for eight months, hastened to write a further letter to Hippo. He complained that the penalties were much too severe, and proposed a general pardon because "as the Stoics were in the habit of saying, all sins were equally great",[69] implying by this that we are all equally imperfect. The bishop rejoined in a cool and dignified manner, saying that none of those who were to be punished was to be deprived of his livelihood, and then passed on to other matters.[70] We do not know exactly how the affair ended.

Further, we do not know quite what is meant by Augustine's remark about silver idols, and it may be that the cause of the trouble was not so much the destruction of statues but a threat to a trade in objects of pagan devotion. The fanatical fury against idols, which was quite in the manner of the Old Testament, was really a serious pastoral problem, for the bishops were as little in sympathy with the destruction of monuments by irregular methods as the high State officials themselves. The question was, of course, connected with two others, namely with that of toleration and that of property rights. Augustine was very sensible of this. He would himself from time to time ridicule the wooden, stone, bronze, marble and even gold and silver gods who "even when they are furnished with golden eyes see just as little as the cheaper ones",[71] and, as we have seen, he sometimes preached against the statues, but we can assume that his only intention was that his hearers should banish them from their imagination. He once declared it to be untrue that Christians were everywhere snuffling about after images and that they promptly destroyed them when they found them, and the proof of this was that statues could still abundantly be seen in the gardens of private villas. Christians knew this well enough, he said, but nevertheless left them untouched since God had not yet delivered them into their hands.[72] The people who really destroyed the statues were the Donatist gangs who, while the temples were still open, were in the habit of thus deliberately provoking crowds of young pagans on festival days, not because they set great store by the destruction of statues but in order to ensure their own death and thus to win a cheap and easy martyrdom; and later they used the same tactics even on private ground which they had no right to enter.[73]

The truth is that the liquidation of the equipment of the old religion was looked upon by Augustine as a concern of the State, and anybody who interfered at his own risk and on his own authority was in his opinion justly liable to punishment. If the Circumcellions did this kind of thing with the deliberate purpose of courting death, they certainly did not deserve the name of martyrs. Only those who lose their lives when acting with proper police authority or because they happen accidentally to be present at a confiscation "may be said to earn a shadow of martyrdom".[74] Actually, Augustine was glad that his Christians were not in the habit of destroying idols, altars and mascots on other people's ground, though they gladly did this when such a piece of ground had been acquired for the Church, or by a Christian purchaser, and especially when, as sometimes happened, an absentee owner had asked the congregation to perform such cleansing and was thankful to them for undertaking it. Then they could do what the Israelites did in Canaan, "for we are no guardians of idols".[75] Yet nobody was permitted to steal from a temple or to appropriate temple property simply because the true owners were no longer there; otherwise it might appear as though Christians were not acting from zeal but rather from avarice. Christians, said Augustine, had no wish to rob. They desired only to destroy error.[76] There seems to have been no objection, however, to putting to Christian use materials that once served a heathen purpose. Both Catholics and Donatists were ready enough to use materials from disused temples for their basilicas, nor did the bishop frown upon this. Indeed, whenever he preached at the consecration of a sometime temple, he did not fail to make appropriate references to the fact.[77]

Naturally, the pagans sometimes took their revenge on a Christian basilica for the dismantling of one of their temples, but feeling seems to have died down pretty quickly and the defeated party soon enjoyed the toleration which tends naturally to be extended to the innocuous. The wine of the ancient culture was thus duly bottled, and its fruits put into preserve. Its educational schemes, textbooks, schools, style, language, its poetry and allegories—all the human legacy of Antiquity, in fact—remained undisturbed, and as long as there is such a thing as humanist education that legacy, with its glory and its limitations, is likely to endure.

Meanwhile, the horizon darkened. The complaint that the world had since Christ's day changed for the worse was now taken up by the Christians themselves—even the proverb "God sends no rain. The Christians are to blame" contrived to live on. The bishop advised men to think nothing of this; men must go through the press if the best is to be got out of them just as the olive must be crushed to produce the oil.[78]

When Rome fell in 410, all the old reproaches were revived, as though that event had not resulted from a decline spreading over centuries.[79] It was also in these days that Augustine began, in the first books of the *City of God*, his thorough and decisive refutation of the ancient faith. This was again done at the instigation of Count Marcellinus; this time, however, it was not for the benefit of a small select circle, but for the world and for all time.

The pastor of souls who corresponded with pagans in so cautious and courteous a manner now stood forth as judge and accuser settling his final account with the pagan world. He showed the gaping void which its vast façade concealed. He pointed scornfully to the old frivolous fables of the Greeks, nor did he spare the old-established gods of Latium. He showed neither understanding nor sympathy for the often surprising origins of this nature-religion which only the later humanizing poets had turned into a stupid and indecent novel; but then no one at that time was in a position to show such understanding and sympathy. Neither Augustine nor his adversaries realized that the whole of the ancient cult was nothing but a vast growth upon what had for centuries been a stagnant pool. They judged the quality of the dead flame from its ash. Augustine, however, did succeed in exposing the true nature of the new splendour by which for the last time the old myths were illuminated. He did join issue with the theosophical neo-Platonists, these Modernists of the fourth and fifth centuries who vainly sought to turn the whole mythological apparatus into a vast allegory of the cosmic struggle towards light. This man who, because the Bible contains truth, was able to find hidden meanings in almost every word of it, refused to admit the possibility that these profane traditions, which, as he held, were founded on falsehood, could have any concealed but valid meaning. He would not admit that Saturn, who devoured his own children, might be a serviceable symbol of time. No truth could be gathered from fables[80]—and that, precisely, was the point. The new faith was not a product of the poetic imagination. It was founded on historical fact, on a true story turning upon the axis of Christ, a story which really dated back far longer than all others and gave a prospect of eternity. He also set his face against what was the most intellectually pleasing of all the pagan countermovements of that day, that almost lyrical adoration of ancient Rome, which was partly a religious and partly a political manifestation and much in evidence at the select clubs.

In this book, *The City of God*, Augustine sought to try conclusions with all that ancient culture of lies, and he did so with a much wider sweep of the visionary eye than had previously been the case, for in the second half of the book the argument between the old culture and the new becomes part of the everlasting battle between good and evil. Now it is no longer a case of myth against history, but of truth against lies, of God against Satan, while in the background there rises the house built by self-seeking set over against the house of the heavenly Father, which is itself as great as any *civitas* and will stand for ever.

All around him paganism was dying. Either it was dying in the baptismal pool or it was just dying.[81] A rumour had for a time gone around that Peter had been able to put a spell on the world for 365 years. After that the Christian religion would disappear and the whole company of gods would again stand on their pedestals and all would be as it was before. Yet as the years passed, and particularly when the year 400 was reached, the last gods were tumbled down, and many men's eyes were opened.[82] Paganism—which till recently had been strong by reason of so many atavistic survivals—disappeared from the politics of the provinces and then from those of the whole Empire. The last images of gods were still to be found for a few years in a number of the out-of-the-way haunts of the harbour towns, or in a few corners of distant *latifundia*, but even the inhabitants of *pagi* were no longer pagans.[83] Paganism, as a religion, was confined to tramps and to the captives of the wars and to the barbarous Berber tribes beyond the Empire,[84] beyond the lowering mountains of Jebel Aures.

4

THE LEGACY OF PAGANISM

IT was easier for people to drive idols out of their sacred buildings than to drive them out of their minds and imaginations.[1] Nobody knew better than Augustine how much paganism was still hovering about in ghostly fashion inside many baptized heads, and how true it was that even anointed eyes, that had had the sign of the cross made over them, could often not be drawn away by any power on earth from the unseemly spectacles in which they took delight. The cults could be destroyed, but the public jollifications which from time immemorial had been connected with them remained, as did the traffickers in various kinds of superstition. The first of these stood under the protection of State law, for though the State might well fail to provide security or bread, it never failed to supply circuses. As to the second, it was kept alive by that very powerful human instinct which causes men always to seek some secret means of getting the better of their irrational fears.

The Christianizing of people in masses had commenced less than a hundred years before and had certainly been over-hurried. There is, the bishop once said, not a man among us who has not one or more pagans among his grandparents.[2] Hundreds of thousands were crowding into the mother-house of the saints, yet the bishop could not refrain from the thought that the fish within the great fish-net[3] which had been nearly rent asunder, had as yet been most imperfectly sorted; his mind kept running on the words of the psalm, "They have increased beyond all numbering",[4] and that other verse from Isaiah, "Thou hast multiplied the nation but not increased the joy."[5]

Augustine's Christians were lively southerners and were still bogged up to the neck in the customs of pagan society. They felt at ease in that environment, much as they felt at ease in the lukewarm water of their pagan *thermae*. The Church had now become a public thing and a part of ordinary men's lives, and precisely because she had now entered that field, her attractive power was threatened by the pagan legacy, by the things with which the ordinary man chiefly associated the pagan cults. There was thus more chaff than wheat upon the threshing floor of the Church, a circumstance that occasioned Augustine many a sigh, and though that is the way of most threshing floors, the thing was particularly true of a great port like fifth-century

Carthage, with its five or six hundred thousand inhabitants and the loose morals that are inseparable from such a place.

Anybody here could call himself a Christian—the drunkard, the miser, the cheat, the gambler, the adulterer and the evil liver, and the theatre-maniac; so also could people that put charms around their necks, sorcerers, astrologers and every kind of fortune-teller; "persons who, though they take the name of Christian, have nevertheless a passion for such things, give their time to them, approve them, and let themselves be talked into yet further affection for them". It is "masses, coarsened and corrupted after this fashion, who bring at any rate their bodies into the church".[6]

"To hunt, to bathe, to gamble, to laugh, that is to live."[7] Thus runs the celebrated inscription from the middle period of the Empire, found in the last century in the forum of Timgad, and even in Augustine's day it still might have been taken as an expression of the outlook of the typical Carthaginian, Christian or otherwise. One of the first things that would have disedified a new convert in Carthage was the fact that the same people who filled the churches on feast days also filled the theatres on days of heathen festival, both places being occupied to capacity on these occasions.[8] The same kind of thing was, of course, true of other places than Carthage, though perhaps to a lesser extent. The temples were closed, but the old gods still ruled on the stage, in the schools, in the secret drug shops and at all festivals.

Pompa Diaboli: Wild Beast Fights, Races and the Theatre

When, in the night of the Pasch, the bishop solemnly asked those he was to baptize, "Do you renounce the devil and all his pomps?" those addressed had an unclear idea of what was meant by worldly temptations and were probably clearly conscious only, for a moment, that they would not find their eternal salvation in the theatre. This represented something of a change. In Tertullian's day, two hundred years before, those undergoing baptism had had something very concrete in their minds. The *pompa* which they were renouncing were the whole apparatus of cult and pleasure, and the pleasure was generally quite as harmful as the cult. The resolve had in such cases been quite definite to avoid both.[9]

Yet in the Christian society of the year 400, the stage throve more than it had ever done before. This was the vulnerable spot of which every pastor was conscious, and the cross of every bishop who still thought in traditional Christian terms, for "wherever the towering mass of the theatre is erected, there the foundations of [Christian] virtue are undermined, and while in that department an insane expenditure gives [to the sponsors] a glorious report, men mock at the works of mercy".[10]

Generally speaking, Augustine was not one of those preachers who thundered in the grand manner against the theatre. His inclinations did not lie in that direction, and he disliked giving descriptions of anything that might be described as *risqué*. But when he feels in censorious mood, it is the theatre against which he inveighs in nine cases out of ten. He knew it well, having been an ardent enthusiast in his youth.[11] His sermons on this subject do not always make it clear whether he is attacking Hippo or some other town. Many of his most violent utterances probably refer to Carthage,[12] nor do we know the nature of public entertainments in Hippo, or how often they took place; but his remarks no doubt were applicable anywhere.

Public games were of three kinds. First, there were those in the amphitheatre, "the den of bloodlust".[13] The strongest attraction was the animal baitings; these were always part of the actual *munera* which were free to all, the cost being borne by the high officials. These games were in all respects modelled on those in the capital, and their essential feature was the netting of baited and starved beasts which would then be fought by hunters or goaded against one another. Leopards, panthers, lions, tigers and bears—the more outlandish the beasts the better—all were used, preferably in whole packs. Brightly uniformed hunters spread the nets on one side while the goading was done by others. "Two fellows against nine bears", says Quodvultdeus; it is as though the Holy Writ had never said, "Give not to the beasts the lives of those that acknowledge thee."[14] Sometimes prisoners and convicts also fought. It was a spectacle of racing dogs and of big game leaping into the air, of torn bodies and streaming blood—a sight compared with which the best bullfight was child's play. It was an expensive kind of amusement. We read in the letters of that time[15] how high officials, even when they were Christians, concerned themselves with the purchase of bears[16] and giraffes, and of their various complaints in that connection; the mishaps in transport, those unfortunate occurrences when the most superb specimens quite inexplicably showed themselves too bored to fight, and, by no means least, the blasé public, which refused ever to be satisfied. Yet despite these setbacks—so the bishop tells us—the same men continued to empty their strong-boxes or sold a villa to cover the insensate costs involved. They spend ten thousand sesterces, we are told, in order to dress up their hunters as brightly as possible,[17] and do not stop for a moment to reflect that these men too have souls and that their Lord Jesus Christ "has hunters as much as any other kind of men among his quarry".[18] We hear of a friend of Augustine's early years, the wealthy Romanianus, himself a Christian, bringing bears even to little Tagaste to be part of the *munera* there, and of how these *munera* were to surpass anything the town could remember.[19] All concerned went home the poorer, the *editor* with an empty purse, the stupid public with an empty soul—and yet, God save the mark, this kind of thing was called a *munus*, or gift.[20]

The worst horror, the gladiatorial games, a form of entertainment on which even the phlegmatic Alypius had once gone completely mad,[21] had for some time been forbidden (the prohibition in Rome came in 410), but the bishop refers once or twice to the rabble of sword-fighters and their criminal ways,[22] and even in Augustine's time there were still sea-fights or *naumachiae*, during which the arena was filled with water and galley-slaves in small boats were set to fight each other. Augustine makes a contemptuous reference to them in a sermon preached at the *memoria* of Cyprian.[23]

A day of *munera* was a high festival, the culminating point of a whole period of festivities, sometimes of several periods, and on such days the church often remained practically empty.[24] On such an occasion the bishop said, "Once we were so foolish as to sit there ourselves, and do you not think that many future Christians are sitting there now, yes—who knows?—perhaps many future bishops."[25] Then all the faithful were praised from the pulpit, especially those who at first had wavered between church and theatre, but had eventually come to church after all because they would not give way to "the most evil hunter in all the world, the devil". Augustine also pointed to the miracle that Christians were to be found even among the professional hunters of the arena, and that the Lord himself was a hunter who not only made those who witnessed animal-baiting displays his quarry, but the very men who fought with the beasts; and that he had done this before innumerable spectators, so that the words of Scripture applied, "They have looked upon me and have regarded me." For he had allowed his martyrs to "fight" in public, to be gored and torn to pieces and to become a spectacle for angels and men.[26] He then added with a happy inspiration, it is not for nothing that the broad way leads to the amphitheatre, for it is the road to death.[27]

It was on one of these occasions when the games were on and church attendance poor in consequence, that he expounded the verse from the Psalms, "They have multiplied beyond number": "There is a certain number, and there are men and women over and above that number. The number is the number of the heavenly Jerusalem. For the Lord knows his own. He knows them all, the God-fearing Christians, the faithful Christians, the Christians that keep the Commandments, walk in God's ways, refrain from sin or confess their sin if they have fallen. All these belong to the number. Yet they are not the only ones, for there are also those who are over and above that number. There are only few present here today in comparison with the multitudes that are present on feast days. How full are then the churches! Then they push and thrust and crowd against the walls and almost suffocate in the crowd. Yet these are the same people who, on a festival, run to the theatre. These are the people that are beyond and above the number, but we say this with the intention of making them part of the number. They do not hear us now, because they are not here. They should, however, hear it from yourselves when church is over."[28]

Another form taken by the games was chariot-racing, which took place in the circus, a long narrow race-track with rounded corners. No stadium ever attracted such vast numbers as did this old dusty track on which small two-wheeled cars, each with four horses, raced around the *spina*, the "backbone", which was the part running down the middle of the course.[29] On these occasions also, the church remained half empty, not so much from any deliberately misdirected will as from custom. Many, says the bishop, are influenced by the arrangements they happen to have made with their friends. Some, as a result of this, go to church, others to the circus. "How many of the baptized prefer to fill the circus rather than the basilica, and set up their stalls or complain if they are denied the opportunity to do so"[30]—for even in those days there was a sort of fair connected with the races, which was held on the anniversary of the city's foundation.[31]

Wherever they were held, whether in the capital or some provincial city, such races were accompanied, in greater or less degree, by the kind of folly of which we read in the accounts that have come down to us of the Hippodrome at Byzantium. There was always the same insensate roaring of the crowd, the same wild gambling, the same passionate partisanship for one of the four colours, the same fury of disappointment on the part of those whose colour had lost, the same everlasting quarrels when partisans shouted up the colour they favoured,[32] the same adoration of a popular charioteer, which almost approached modern film-star worship, the same kind of mass magnetism that a champion of sport[33] always seems to command; there was the same never-ending chatter about favourites and fancies.[34] We can to some extent recapture the atmosphere of these events in the right kind of *plaza de toros*.

Incidentally, the amphitheatres of Africa still astonish us by their size. That of Thysdrus, one of the out-of-the-way towns of Byzacena, is only slightly smaller than the Colosseum and is, one might add, just as well preserved. None of the Fathers of the Church ever succeeded in preaching them empty. "Is it then not madness to yell your head off just to encourage a charioteer? No, do not say so. Nothing is more delightful."[35]

Cheaper, in every sense of the word, than the type of entertainment already described, was a third kind, the theatre proper. Augustine always speaks with a certain revulsion of the great games, which devoured so much money, but it needs the thought of the theatre and all its vulgarity to make him really angry. When he speaks of the three forms of concupiscence, or of vice in general, it is to the theatre that his finger invariably points. Nor did the theatre deserve much better; one could scarcely witness the performances, let alone tell of them, without blushing.[36]

The personnel consisted largely of prostitutes (*scorta*) and procurers, and the repertoire was made up of little more than miming to the music of flutes and zithers, and was in effect the lowest kind of cabaret; for the subjects were the amours of the old gods, and every kind of tainted story from fable or brothel, all represented with that complete lack of inhibition that was characteristic of the ancient world. The *ludi scenici* in honour of Flora were particularly bad. They knew no limits whatever. The demon of the theatre, said Augustine, was not satisfied with ordinary sacrifices of birds or even of human blood, but "wanted to see the immolation of all human modesty".[37]

In past times there used to be a *compère*, the bishop tells us. But he had now disappeared, so that a stranger could not really understand the plots and intrigues behind it all.[38] Sometimes the scanty survivals of ancient tragedy were put on the stage ("parricide and incest", says Tertullian); also dramatized incidents from the epics, such as the Trojan Horse, the shade of Creusa, the wanderings of Aeneas and the despair of Dido—scenes which at one time had brought tears to young Augustine's eyes, which had caused him positively to weep with delight when he read them,[39] and even more so when he saw them enacted. As a student he had been mad on the theatre, and once, when a rising author, he had won the first prize in a contest for a dramatic fragment in verse.[40] On that occasion he had been crowned by the proconsul in the capitol at Carthage.

Sometimes the performance was turned into a sort of revue, with a dancer or even a ballet,[41] and thus became a costly affair, involving the expenditure of entire fortunes, for it made a good impression to have first-class performers. Yet this expenditure, so the bishop complained, with all the contraptions for the *deus ex machina*, could show us nothing but things like the cruelties of Jupiter, his idle chatter and his wearisome adulteries.[42] Often, of course, the whole business sank to a very ordinary fair-show with tight-rope walkers, sword-swallowers and jugglers, the kind of thing you could see any day on the street.[43]

The average African must often have failed to understand why the Church should have had such things so much on her mind. He was used to the free and easy ways of the public baths, and for the most part lacked any kind of inhibition in all that pertained to the physical, while in conversation he thought nothing of calling a spade a spade, a habit which—at least, to our way of thinking—was not conspicuous even in sermons by its absence. That being so, this same average African could see no connection between a millstone that was allegedly being hung around his neck and the quick patter of jokes, parodies on licentious gods, or any other feature of these usually flute-accompanied representations. They set the whole house roaring and, even if they made him no wiser, seemed no worse than a waste of his time; nor could he understand how the baptism which had given him his Christian name could be said to enter into the affair.

Yet the old bishop, usually so mild and gentle, refused to take things calmly. He was well aware how excellently these cinemas of Antiquity were attended. His flock knew their mythology, but most of them knew it not from Virgil but from the boards.[44] The fact is that he looked upon the theatre as a school of vice, a disgrace to a Christian town and, thanks to those who plied their trade there, a proximate occasion of impurity.[45] He knew that the basic theatrical fare turned on matters which the Christian should not even name, and yet he knew from first-hand knowledge that the great majority of his "Easter lambs" were among the theatre's regular patrons. Small wonder that he most emphatically and without qualification forbade all visits to it, or that he should have used words such as those he used in Carthage at Cyprian's grave: "Why do you not contemplate Cyprian and seek to be like him? You may, if you wish, vent your anger against me, or curse me and say, 'Become like him yourself!' Yet you have no just cause for anger when I give you such counsel. But I will spare you and will merely ask that you join me and that you simply make a change in the customary objects of your interest. For those men upon whom you so often have gazed are men without honour, and if that is so, can those who look upon them claim to deserve good repute? Those who pay such people should surely set bounds to their hunger for pleasure. If they did so, there would suddenly be a dearth of dirt upon the market. Why then do you encourage what you must needs disapprove? For there must surely be something very wrong with things if the lack of honesty in those whom you glorify leaves you untainted. Do I dare to forbid you the theatre? Indeed I do dare it. This place gives me the courage to do so, as does he who has set me here. The ancient Roman strictness, which held all manner of actors to be devoid either of honour or right, would have enjoined me to do precisely this, and very excellent that would have been."[46]

It was useless, and he knew it. Also he knew exactly what the population of the town thought of the matter. When streams of people came out of the amphitheatre, or the Odeon when "that cave began to spew forth the depraved multitude", and it so happened that, while their minds were still full of the delights they had experienced, they recognized a passing priest, they would say, "Poor things! They must give up a lot",[47] and that was about as far as the matter went. A bishop, they said, had naturally to preach against the theatre—that was only right and proper. He was used to seeing things that way and it was his job to exaggerate a bit; moreover, it was quite entertaining to listen to him—particularly his clever play with words. Thus on one occasion he developed over a great part of one of his sermons the theme of the ten-stringed psaltery from the ninth psalm. "Use but the lyre of the Lord and you may be both a zither player and a slayer of wild beasts. Strike the first string, which is that of religion, and the beast Superstition falls down dead. When you strike the second, which is the commandment not to take God's name in vain, the beast Heresy falls dead—and so you kill all the principal sins with the Ten Commandments."[48]

Nowhere was this question such a burning one as in the theatre city of Carthage,[49] and it was rarely that Augustine preached there without inveighing against the theatrical spectacles which everybody was attending. When Nineveh did penance after three days, the prophecy of Jonah was fulfilled, so Augustine claimed, for such a conversion was equivalent to a devastation, and if such a thing were to happen in Carthage—if all the theatre-maniacs were suddenly converted—that too would suggest something like a devastation, so that people would ask, "What has happened to this Carthage of ours?"[50]

In Hippo itself it would seem that there were fewer things inviting prohibition than elsewhere. It appears from an inscription[51] that there was probably an amphitheatre there, besides which there was a circus and an ordinary theatre too. The last, to judge from Augustine's sermons, was very well patronized, though it is doubtful whether there were regular performances in the other two places. It is somewhat surprising to learn that there were neither actors nor prostitutes actually resident in Hippo; for when the bishop was passing through the town of Bulla Regia in Africa Proconsularis, where they appear to have abounded, and was invited to preach, he cried angrily from the pulpit:

> Oh, brothers of Bulla—such folk are not to be found anywhere else, and perhaps it is their presence here that causes people to come to your city. Then you say to them, "What have you come for? Theatrical folk? Women of easy virtue? You can find them all in Bulla." Are you not ashamed that yours should be the only city in which such disgraceful merchandise can be bought? In our good Hippo we have scarcely any of this. When there is a demand for such people, they are sent for from Bulla. "Granted," you say, "but we are no worse than Carthage." But Carthage is a town full of Jews and pagans, while you yourselves are Christians. We know exactly how large your city is. You can do nothing here without your bishop knowing it. So be careful, for theatrical performances are at this moment being arranged. Do not attend them. Then indeed shall we see how
>
> > Men at empty benches stare
> > And blush that they themselves be there.[52]

Then, after conjuring his hearers either to mend their ways or move to some other place, he said:

> I see a mere handful of you sitting there. And yet the day of the sufferings of Christ will soon be coming; soon Easter will be here. Then these walls

will scarcely hold all that will come. Then the church will be full—full of the same people who now fill the theatres. Compare the two places and then beat your breasts.

Perhaps you will say to me, "Naturally, as a priest and bishop, you don't go in for that kind of thing, but we are only layfolk." But what manner of life do you layfolk lead? It is you that maintain the prostitutes and make them what they are—as though prostitutes had not souls as much as you yourselves, and as though it had not been written, "The harlots and the publicans shall enter the Kingdom of Heaven before you." Or you say, "I am only a catechumen." A catechumen! Have you one forehead to receive the sign of Christ, and another to take to the theatre? If go to the theatre you must, then change your foreheads before you go. Rather follow the example of your neighbour town of Simittu. There recently an imperial official organized one of these dirty affairs and none of the dignitaries of the town—no, not a workman or a Jew—went to see it. It was God's will that I should chance to pass here. My colleague forced me to preach. [*Applause.*] No, do not applaud, for even for that applause I must render an account and it is thus more of a burden than an honour. Yet I cannot be silent about these things. See to it that later on I have a good report of you."[53]

The public games and performances constituted one of the most important legacies of the old religion. Every temple had once had its own legend and its own festival. Now the temples were closed, the sacrifices fallen into disuse and the legends forgotten, but the festivals remained, and nobody wanted to miss them. The laws promulgated by the emperors in the fourth century for the closing of the temples expressly declare that there was no intention of abolishing the festivals, especially in the provinces.[54] In Africa Honorius, who was a strict Christian, had in 407 forbidden the old processions, then at a later date permitted them, and once more, still later, forbidden them again, but he had never touched the public entertainments. So it was that, thanks to these entertainments, paganism retained its roots among ordinary people, and needless to say, people of all religions took part in them, much as today they take part in a harvest festival or tread the lees in the South, or as, even in some Protestant countries, children still carry lighted candles through the streets at Martinmas.

At the Calends of January, though the old custom of putting on stag-antlers (*cervulum facere*) was tending to fall into disuse, people still gave each other *strena* or New Year's gifts of copper coins. But the bishop made a day of penance out of this somewhat disorderly New Year celebration. He ordered Psalm cv to be read, which has the verse, "Save us, O Lord our God, and gather us together from among the heathen", and he told his flock in his sermon: "If you cannot fast, then make a light breakfast. You say, 'I know that if I give *strena* to my friends, I shall get them back', but if you give money to the poor, do you receive nothing in return? In this matter take the Jews as your example, for they certainly do not engage in these practices." Actually, Augustine had on this occasion little ground for complaint, for the church was exceptionally full.[55]

Whatever reminded him of the orgiastic licence of the old festivals filled him with horror. Once he gave a warning as early as New Year's Day against the practice of self-baptism on the Feast of St. John in June, a pagan custom in which some people had indulged in good faith in the previous year. Certain people had been forbidden the sacraments because of this, and there had been some murmuring in consequence. This was why the bishop issued his prohibition six months in advance.[56] Augustine was not the sort of man whose heart clings to ancient usage.

Actually the practice of *cervulum facere* continued to persist, though Bishop Pacianus of Barcelona wrote an entire book against it under the title *Cervulus*, and long after Christian Africa had disappeared it continued to flourish in Merovingian Gaul.

Also at the end of March, about the time of the vernal equinox, which of course was in the middle of the fasting season, there was still the "Blood Day" which had originally been celebrated in honour of Attis and Cybele. This was described by the bishop as "the feast of some woman or other whose golden earrings, when torn from her ear-lobes, were miraculously increased in weight by reason of the blood which attached to them"—and because of this many women and girls stayed away from church, "as though the blood of the Lamb did not weigh far more heavily than the blood from the ears of this woman, with which the demons aped in advance the sacrament of the blood of Christ" This last was a frequent sentiment of Augustine's, for since the world had become Christian the demons, he said, were playing their part as the apes of God, and now that they could no longer openly seduce Christians they did so under the semblance of Christian rites. "You can see it plainly," Augustine once heard a priest of Attis triumphantly tell a group of Christians, "Attis, the man under the headdress, is also Christ."[57]

In the year 418, when the last day of this five-day festival happened to fall on a Sunday, he deliberately kept the faithful breathless with a two-hour sermon on the Gospel of St. John, so that the festivities were over when they left the church.[58]

The Church continued to oppose these depraved old festivals and eventually succeeded in invoking the strong arm of the law and getting them stopped. Meanwhile, however, she found a powerful counter-measure in the new feasts which had become customary in a few churches in commemoration of the martyrs. The Church provisionally recognized these feasts and so kept them under her control. They provided an indispensable counter-attraction, or—to use the even stronger expression employed by other bishops—a visible triumph of the saints over the demons.

SUPERSTITION

There was yet another link in being with the pagan past. It was less conspicuous than the festivals, yet it was quite as tough and much more dangerous. That link was provided by the old practices of superstition. Nor were these practices among Christians always so very old, though the old ones seemed to thrive and assert themselves more vigorously than the new.

Many a Christian sailor would not put out to sea "without forgetting the haven of Christ for the sirens of superstition" and secretly calling on Father Neptune. Many an expectant Christian mother still sought refuge with Mother Juno or with the Goddess of Heaven.[59] Augustine declared that Saturn and the Goddess of Heaven had nothing more to say to men in Carthage. Yet a hundred years later Salvianus was to write that the Goddess of Heaven was still reigning, particularly among the upper classes. Bishop Aurelius had had her great temple cleaned up (for it was already overgrown with weeds from the temple gardens that had run to seed) and had solemnly celebrated Easter there, but the old memories were so powerful that he abandoned the building and had it pulled down.[60]

The great mass of people still preferred to make doubly sure. Their spirits may have thirsted after God, but not their flesh and not their hearts, and when they were troubled about their money, their cattle, or about water or wine, then they forgot God and fled to Jupiter, to Mercury, to the Goddess of Heaven, or to "who knows what demons or princes of this world".[61]

Christ does not provide for our temporal needs, they said; let us therefore live on a sound footing with the ancient gods. So we honour the ancient gods and the powers of darkness for our temporal purposes, and Christ for the sake of eternity. We honour the demons along with God, though reluctantly and in a far lesser degree.[62] People had no hesitation in talking like this, even to Christians who strictly lived up to their beliefs. Even when the bishop asked them why they still consulted astrologers and astronomical almanacs, he was told that it was not Christ's affair to help them in their business or pick propitious days for their ventures—"as though Christ had not said, 'No man can serve two masters', and yet soon they will be telling me that we must serve God for our everlasting life and the devil for our temporal one".[63] Others would tell him that this business about everlasting life was never a certainty. Of course, they were good Christians, that went without saying, but just how much did they really know about the next world? Had anybody ever come back from there to tell us what things were like? As to the Resurrection, did you ever hear your father talk to you from the grave since you buried him? The mockers would say at a burial, "There he lies in his grave; let him make us hear his voice if he can. One day we shall be lying there just like that and if one day our family brings an offering for the dead, they will simply eat it themselves and we shan't be a penny the better." Such were the "Catholic brothers who turned up their noses" when there was a sermon on the resurrection of the body.[64]

So it was that many still attended the old pleasant festivals, where these were still maintained, from motives in which ancient piety was mixed up with a good measure of indifference. In the temple of the city of Carthage they even lay alongside the sacrificial genius tables, giving the excuse that the *genius* was not really a god at all,[65] and as of old, they used the old gods to swear by, and did not scruple to drink to them. They also crept away, cautiously and privately, to fortune-tellers, baptized and otherwise, and to the sorcerers and the quacks.[66] For in cases of sickness or misfortune, and particularly in the matter of averting the evil eye and pacifying the ever-present demons, it was surely prudent to apply the principle of making doubly sure.

And after all, why should one not continue to try out the little ways of the past? The devils, the gods and the stars were still powerful things and full of wisdom. They had not wholly disappeared. It is true that men no longer served them with their whole heart, but they feared them none the less. Were the heavens not filled with evil demons, those evil spirits of the air, of which the lector read in church? What if they were one's enemies? People were actuated not by fear quite as much as by a habit, and this was why women in love wore a little ribbon on some hidden part of their bodies, or in pregnancy called on Juno and the Dea Coelestis; why country folk hesitated to move a statue from its accustomed place.[67] "If all is well, they remain to outward appearance Christian, but if anything goes wrong, off they go to the soothsayers."[68] Those are your Christians, people say. It is so simple, says Augustine, to praise the Lord in the daytime when all is well—say, after a good delivery or an unhoped-for recovery from sickness—but to raise up one's hands and praise the Lord in the night of the soul when all goes amiss, what man does that?[69] It is all "fear, fear". Such a man was helped by the old tricks; why should your own case be different? "You are a Christian and seek counsel of the astrologers! 'What of it?' comes the retort. 'The man got this or that for me, and without him I certainly should not have obtained it.' 'And the name of Christ, does that mean nothing to you?'—and the answer is a wrinkling of the nose."[70] And so it was that many people went off to those last remaining branches of the old business, the little houses where the charms and magic could still be bought. There it was whispered to them how long they had to live, whether or no they would be lucky in love or win a lawsuit or back the winner at the races. There were sold the amulets which the bearer had, in the prescribed manner, to wear next to his skin, or the charm which he had to tie round his head (*ligaturae*) as a cure for headache.[71] There, when prayer had failed, the infallible prescriptions were made up. All manner of things were to be had in those places; strips of paper with certain letters upon them, which had always to be carried about with one (*characteres*),[72] diagrams enabling one to do one's own prophesying, specifics, called *remedia*, or in the case of the professedly more respectable ones, *physica*—"as though the real doctors, the *physici*, were not utterly opposed to the whole business". There one could get medallions with mysterious signs upon them, little earrings and the small ostrich bones which had to be worn on the little finger.[73] "There lies one of the faithful on his sickbed, writhing in pain. He prays, and is not heard, or rather he is heard, put to the proof and chastized for his own good, as a child is chastized before it may once more enter the room. Then comes temptation. An old woman comes to his bedside, or a man (in so far as such a creature deserves the name of man), and tells him to tie something about himself, or try this bit of magic or that, and then, it is said, he will recover. 'Such and such a man tried it and was helped by it. You can ask him yourself.' Yet the patient remains obdurate and does not give way. He does not allow himself to be talked over. He puts up a fight and if necessary becomes a martyr in his own bed."[74] "For he says 'I would rather die than resort to such means as these. Let God chastize me if he will, let him summon me if he will, or save my life if he will. Why should I purchase a few days of life if the price is the damnation of my soul?' He looks very ill indeed, he lies there and struggles for breath, he can barely move his limbs or his tongue, and yet this exhausted man wins his victory over the devil." So much power has such a man in his heart. The martyrs won their crowns in the amphitheatre, this man in his bed, and yet the triumph of such a man remains as hidden as his heroic struggle.[75]

Yet they all did it—even the well-to-do. Like the woman with an issue of blood in the Gospel, who represents the Church in a pagan world, many rich people gave their whole fortunes to quacks, to the interpreters of signs and omens, to fortune-tellers, to men and women professing to have second sight, and to temple prophets.[76] Our prayers are not heard, they would say, when the bishop set his face against these things, however hard we pray, and we have ourselves heard the sorcerer call upon the names of God and his angels[77] —for all who were compelled to make their living out of what remained of paganism made a point of courting the Christians. The vendors of amulets wrote on their magic papers the names of Christ, Michael and Gabriel, or the words, Κ Ε Β Ο Η Θ Ι, κύριε βοήθι, "Lord help us", "a coating of honey on a bitter poison".[78] Is it not clear as day, they would then be told from the pulpit, the demons are the apes of God, proper *mangones*, pedlars who sell glittering rubbish? God is a good Father who does not spare the rod, the devil a dangerous counsellor who in a twinkling has you in his bag. Have a care which of these takes you along, and whither—to the Kingdom of Heaven, or into the sack of hell.[79]

Catechumens would actually come to instruction wearing amulets. In his little handbook *Instruction for Beginners*, Augustine charges the deacon Deogratias of Carthage, for whom this piece of writing was intended, to examine his pupils on this point and enlighten them.[80] A brother bishop once asked him whether a baptized child could be harmed by magical devices used upon it by parents who happened to know no better—a question to which Augustine, of course, replied in the negative.[81] In the same letter he recalled the miracle told by Cyprian of a child to whom an ignorant nurse had given a piece of pagan sacrificial bread. When after this the child was taken to church and the deacon, despite the child's resistance, gave it a little consecrated wine, it threw the wine up "out of its desecrated entrails". Possidius once asked him what he was to do about men who came to Communion in his church in Calama wearing in their ears small rings which they refused to take off. Augustine replied that if things were so bad that a positive prohibition was of no effect, then Possidius should see to it that they did not actually justify their superstition.[82]

In the second book of his *Christian Knowledge* Augustine mentions some of the more harmless practices connected with the fear of certain omens and influences, practices which in many cases still live on today in southern Europe and are found equally among the Christians of Naples and Cadiz and the Muslims of Tunis. Today, the humbler kind of Italian dislikes meeting anyone whom he suspects of having the Evil Eye, and should he do so he immediately touches himself or puts his hand on iron. If by any chance he meets a priest on a lonely platform in the early hours of the morning, he will forthwith go and touch the rails. The Africans of Augustine's day were much the same. If you had any encounter which you felt somehow to be ominous, there were certain fixed rules that had to be followed. If anybody had the hiccups, his friend would tell him to hold his left thumb with his right hand.[83] If you were walking side by side with anybody, and a boy or a dog or a stone came between you, then there was a threat to your friendship with the person who was walking beside you. You must tread on the stone, smack the boy's face and give the dog a kick. But the dog, says the bishop, has a habit of avenging the boys who are thus assaulted, and ends by sending to a real doctor the superstitious fool who has profited nothing from his magic. Whoever passes his own house should put his foot on the doorstep, whoever sneezes while putting on his shoes should get back into bed, whoever knocks himself against anything in the street should go back to his own house. If anybody discovered that mice had been gnawing his clothes he was much more concerned over the omen than over the damage. It would have been better, said Augustine, if such people had remembered Cato's joke. When once a trembling friend told him that the mice had eaten his shoes, Cato replied that it would have been a much more serious portent [*monstrum*] if the shoes had eaten the mice.[84]

AUGUSTINE'S STRUGGLE AGAINST ASTROLOGY

But never is Augustine more emphatic than when attacking the astrologers, the pseudo-scientific cheats of his day. Nearly all his Christians believed astrology to be an exact and genuine science (this despite the fact that it had been forbidden by Theodosius) and accepted its practitioners as true, though somewhat expensive, men of learning. In earlier times they had been called birthday specialists, *genethliaci*. Now people called them *mathematici*.[85] In reality they were anything but serious students of Hipparchus or Eratosthenes; common swindlers working a territory which was made profitable by the element of learning and mystery which appeared to surround it.

In his youth, Augustine had himself been enslaved by their books, and though his old friend, Vindicianus the physician, warned him that the whole thing was nonsense, and his young comrade Nebridius laughed at him about it, he could not leave it alone.[86] Eventually, however, he came to realize the worthlessness of horoscopes.[87] The disappointment caused him by that Manichean oracle Faustus contributed to this. Then there was the continued contrast between what may often have been the correct calculations of genuine astronomers and the theorizing of the astrological prophets. Finally, there was the case where two persons born at the same hour of the same day had a wholly different course of life, one being born wealthy, with everything the heart could desire at his command, the other a poor devil of a slave. Even in those days, Augustine had already been struck by the fact that soothsayers may prophesy a certain number of happenings correctly, doing this not by reason of their art but by pure chance.[88] He saw that these successful prophecies would be remembered and discussed, while the faulty predictions were forgotten. And after all, sometimes prophets do happen to be right, just as a person opening a book at random may well light on a passage which most aptly fits a subsequent situation.[89]

It is doubtful whether Augustine ever really did understand the principles of the horoscope, or knew his way about "those different parts of the circle of beasts" in relation to which the significance of the hour of birth was determined, for a very complicated calculation was involved, depending not only on the star under the sign of which the birth took place, and the quarter of the heavens in which the sun at that moment happened to be, but on dozens of other factors such as the constellations which formed squares and triangles with the dominant constellation. Then there were the four *cardines*, the houses of the planets, the twelve divisions of the heavens—none of these could be left out of account. Take it for all in all, the ultimate product was something like a mathematical masterpiece, the refinements of which had been thoroughly developed by the astrologers in order to impress the customer with their own importance, but which nevertheless left plenty of loopholes if the calculations should prove to be misleading. Whether a particular prediction was correct or not, however, it was the bishop's practice to let the science more or less rest on its own assumptions and merely to question the philosophical principles which underlay it. He showed how contradictory they were. Without mincing his words, he declared the whole thing to be pretence. There were of course those among them, he admitted, who really calculated how the stars stood in relation to one another when a particular birth took place,[90] yet all their wisdom either existed solely in their own imagination or was plain deceit, for a man's destiny does not depend on the hour of his birth. If that were so— this was his most devastating argument, though he had partly borrowed it from Cicero and Diogenes—if that were so, the destiny of twins would always be identical[91]—and yet what says the Holy Writ of Jacob and Esau, who incidentally were, as St. Paul tells us, conceived *ex uno concubitu*,[92] and were born as a sort of twin birth with the heel of the one in the hand of the other? And if people say that in this case there were two distinct births, one following upon the other, then surely in the moment between the two births the constellation might have undergone a fundamental change—for one should always think how "vast is the change that is wrought by a small, nay, a trumpery shifting"[93] —he asked how an astrologer could possibly establish such a slight deviation from the first stellar pattern, a mere fraction of the angle of a minute in the trajectory of the sun; and if he could not do so, what use were all his tables?[94] And if, taking their cue from Nigidius Figulus in this matter, people said that even a very small angle at the calculator's end corresponded to a very large space in the actual dome of heaven (the dome that revolves with such incredible rapidity), then this must necessarily be a reflection on the accuracy of any observation and render any calculation problematical.[95] And what of cases where there is complete synchronization of conceptions? Should this factor have no influence on the destinies concerned, even if there is some separation in the actual moments of birth? Indeed, may we not assume that influences are already at work at the moment of conception, by which the hour of birth itself is influenced? Why, then, do people jabber about an unalterable destiny, if that destiny can be changed between conception and birth?

Why should destiny be unalterable and incapable of being influenced by the will? And what exactly happens in the case of twins of different sex? One of these may be a commander, always on his travels, while the other remains a spinster, tied down to a country estate. There are people who do their sowing under the guidance of astrologers. Yet in such cases, though the sowing takes place on the same day, one crop will be harvested, while the other is destroyed by a fire. Or are crops and cattle not subject to the stars, but only human beings, though it is precisely the latter who have free will?[96]

Augustine does not trouble to disprove that the will itself can be influenced by the stars, for those who are philosophically trained know well enough that the material cannot determine the spiritual, nor can the higher be determined by the lower; though he does not go so far as Cicero, who held the will to be so fully sovereign that he denied any possibility of predicting human action, and even of God's foreknowledge of it.[97] And what remains of divine power, if all is decided by the destiny imposed by the stars? If, as against this, the stars exert their influence under the direction of God, so that it is God who compels us to do evil, we do injustice to the shining heavenly senate in regarding them as evil's originators. Yet, if that argument is admitted, how can God judge us, being himself a partner in our guilt?[98]

So it is all madness. If you live subject to this madness and take it seriously, then, says Augustine, you are the author of your own deception. And yet if through astrology you are really in contact with the demons, then the Apostle's warning must be held to apply to you—"I would not that you should be made partakers with devils."[99] And who will deny that astrologers are indeed the accomplices of the Evil One? "There they sit and calculate. They reckon out the distance and course of the stars and the speed with which they complete their orbits, together with all their positions and their various movements. They observe, they describe, they guess. They appear great and learned, but all their learning is nothing more than a condoning of sin—*excusare excusationes in peccatis*.[100] For they say, 'You will become an adulterer, for you stand in the sign of Venus—you will become a hero of the knife, for you belong to Mars.' To another they say that he will become a miser, for he stands under Saturn, and to yet another that he will become a skilful trickster, since he is bound to Mercury. This means that Mars is the murderer, and not the man who used the knife, and that it is Venus who deceives his friend. Have a care lest you yourself be not damned for these things, rather than Mars or Venus."[101]

Bad as were the astrologers, their clients were no better, for these were just as ready as the astrologers themselves to blame their *fatum* instead of blaming Satan. "And when you ask what manner of thing this *fatum* may be, then they say it is the bad stars, and if you ask further and say, 'But who made the stars?', they are compelled to answer, 'God.' In this way they are ultimately forced into the position where either by implication, or putting their argument through a long tube [*canna*] or quite directly, they must blame their misdeeds on God."[102] Thanks to this way of thinking, many never think of the sacrament of penance.

Augustine then set his face against the kind of fatalism that "sets the ordinary man perpetually thinking of the position and power of the stars under which he has been born or conceived".[103] He considered such ideas a sort of moral plague, because they deny the freedom of the will and make all moral responsibility impossible. Is it not outrageous, he asks, to suppose that a dog is free to choose between doing a thing and leaving it undone, but that a man is not—simply because the man has been born under a particular star? "These cheats seek to blame the stars for the moral ruin which they spread (and which causes them to be shunned by decent people) by trying to persuade you that it is from the stars that evil comes."[104]

Yet the evil into which men were led by this kind of thing was a fact, and Augustine is outspoken enough on the subject. What, he asks, do we hear daily from the counterparts of the sinful woman in the Gospel, her counterparts in shame though not by any means in the penitent confession of sins? "These harlots, these adulteresses, these immoral women deny their sins if they do not come to light, but if they are caught or commit their sin openly, then they defend themselves. Oh, how convenient is their excuse, and how readily it comes to hand, and yet how impudent, though we hear it every day —aye, and how blasphemous! If God had not wanted that, they say, 'I would not have done it! God has so willed it. It is my *fortuna*, my destiny.' "[105] Nobody in the world dares to say that adultery is good or that murder is permissible, or that a man may steal. Yet everywhere the cry is, "If God had not willed it, I should not have done it. Tell me what I can do against my fate!"[106]

While these stupid geese deceived themselves after this fashion, said Augustine, it was evident that the real professional astrologers did not really believe their own words, for their practice gave the lie to their contentions, and of course in ordinary life the theories they held were quite unworkable. Had an astrologer wished to be consistent, "then he must not beat his slaves when they have made some blunder till he has told the shining gods of the firmament exactly what he thinks of them".[107] If he looks up for a moment at home from his ivory tablets and sees his wife flirting with a friend, or leaning too far out of the window, then he gives her a thrashing, and if she cries out, "Don't beat me, beat Venus if you can", he says, "You idiot, that kind of thing may be good enough for the customers, but it isn't good enough for the boss!"[108] No, the astrologers themselves did not act on these principles. They sold the people the death of their souls and got their money by that; nor did they catch their prey in the woods, but rather did so at their leisure on the market place. There people positively ran to them, and used their money to buy themselves a master, and then went away as the slaves of Jupiter, Saturn or Mercury.[109] The astrologers did not point this out, of course, but merely laughed up their sleeves.

But they never gave up their trade for as long as they lived. It was too profitable to them for that. Once Augustine presented a converted astrologer to his congregation, a man that had brought his books along to be burned. On this occasion Augustine said (the incident is a good illustration of the pastoral methods of the time): "Though he had been baptized, this man was tempted by the devil and for a time practised as a *mathematicus*. Himself seduced, he seduced others. Himself deceived, he deceived others, betraying them and speaking many lies against God, who gave men the power to do good and avoid evil. This man here declared that it was not their own will that caused them to be unfaithful in marriage, but Venus, that it was not their own will which committed murder, but Mars, that it was not God that wrought justice, but Jupiter; and he made many other blasphemous statements." Yet now, Augustine declared, the man shuddered at these lies. He was converted, and it seemed as though this had happened by reason of the great fear that was in his heart. Had he been a pagan, one might have supposed that the purpose of his conversion was to obtain some clerical office, but he came to them as a penitent simply seeking mercy. Augustine, therefore, was compelled to recommend him both to their hearts and to their eyes, and he enjoined his people carefully to observe the man's way of life, to put him in touch with the brethren who were not present and to see that the seducer did not win back his heart. Like his brother Christian at Ephesus in the story of the Apostles, "he has brought his books with him for burning, those books in place of which he might himself have had to burn. Now the books are going into the fire, so that his own soul may in due course be refreshed". "But you will say, How many Christians has this man relieved of their pennies? To how many has he sold his lies? Why, to those same people to whom we have so often said, 'Dear people, how long will your hearts remain dull and why do you love vanity and seek after lies?' "[110]

For countless minds were still held captive by fear of evil stars. Business men made careful note of unpropitious or so-called "Egyptian" days.[111] Everywhere Augustine heard men saying, "This year I shall plant no vines, for it is a leap year; this month I shall not go travelling with my merchandise, for the month stands under such and such a star; I am not going out, for it is an unlucky day; this venture will surely be lucky, for the moon is in such and such a position; I shall get that girl, for my stars are favourable; I shall close that bargain, for the day is right; today I will have my mare served—or again, I shall do nothing today, for fate is against me."[112]

Believing Christians said openly to his face, "On the day after the Calends, I never travel." People even came to him at the bishop's palace, people "who, as the saying is, did not know where they belonged", to warn him in confidence not to go out on this day or that. Men were so little inclined to make fun of the stars that even the bishop usually refrained from touching on the subject except in a very lighthearted way and with a smile upon his lips.[113] Later he declared in his little handbook that it was only St. Paul's concern over this matter that decided him to treat this kind of sin as grave. It was the general practice of the time, and for this reason he did not expel a layman from the Church on account of it, or degrade a priest.[114] Nevertheless, he did not keep his own opinion of this "accursed plague" to himself, and preached that even daily almsgiving could not obtain forgiveness, if the habit was persisted in.[115] For after all, the intention was to obtain certain information from demons, and he called that an adultery of the soul, committed in a house that was hostile to Christ.[116] His practice in regard to astrological books was to have them burnt out of hand.[117]

Meanwhile, he never failed to refute any objections to his views. Thus his opponents pointed out that the date of Easter was allowed to depend on the course of the stars. Even an earnest Christian like Januarius, who sent him a long list of liturgical questions, once came out with this point without realizing that he was riding a Manichean hobby-horse.[118] Then there was the passage in Genesis, "... that they shall be to you as signs and times and days and years", and also those passages from the Gospel according to St. John, "Mine hour is not yet come", and "His hour was not yet come", and again, "The hour is come."[119] There were some people who, when they heard these passages read, would say, "You see, even Christ was under a *fatum*."[120] Then the bishop would cry out, "If your heart were not so dull, you would not look upon this as a trump card of destiny. *Fatum* means 'word', it comes from *fari*; how can the Word of God, which contained everything before anything was created, itself have a *fatum*?"[121]—and he pointed to that other phrase, "I have the power to lay down my life and to take it up", and proved that the Evangelist only meant the hour in which a certain prophecy was to be fulfilled.[122] Then they came up with such things as the "acceptable time" in the Second Epistle to the Corinthians,[123] and, naturally enough, with the Star in the East which had led the Wise Men to Bethlehem. In regard to this latter difficulty, Augustine was anything but at a loss for a reply. Even if all men were subject to the stars, the Son of God would not be subject on that account. Moreover, this star did not stay upon its course but pointed the way to the Child. Christ did not therefore appear in obedience to the stars, but was their Master. It was not the star that gave Christ's life its miraculous pattern, but it was Christ that caused the star's miraculous appearance.[124] Further, the star was a phenomenon that only occurred once, and that for a definite end: "It did not rule over him with decrees, but did service to him as a witness. It did not subject him to its dominion, but served him by being a sign of his coming", and it appeared as a new star to accompany the new birth. If men must talk of a *fatum*, then the star was not the *fatum* of Christ, but Christ the *fatum* of the star.[125] And what was this star but a glorious tongue in the sky which proclaimed the glory of God and the Epiphany of the Lord here on earth?[126] They are the same thoughts that Gregory the Great was later to compress into the simple sentence, "The Child did not go to the star, but the star to the Child."[127]

The belief in the stars was so strong that Augustine was ready to take arms against it on the slightest provocation. When, as a young priest, it fell to him to expound the text from Galatians, "Ye hold to days and months", the passage did not suggest the Jewish practices of the Galatians, but rather the "astrologers and Chaldeans among the people in our Church". "There are enough that run to them", he declared, "before they dare undertake anything or start any kind of building, and in this way they literally become the slaves of weak elements that are in themselves in need of help."[128] "As in Juvenal's day, there are people who will not even have intercourse with their wives without consulting one of these living almanacs beforehand, and will even have a horoscope cast when one of their beasts is to be paired or is to have young."[129] The evil was so widely spread that he could always safely assume its existence. Thus he could say, "If your boy fell ill, perhaps you called in the *mathematicus*"[130] or, "A man has stolen. That is a sin, but to avoid detection he goes to the *mathematicus*. Had you but been content with stealing—why did you commit a second sin? For here are two sins. When you are told that this is unlawful, you spurn your bishop—and that is a third sin; and when you hear men say, 'Expel him from the Church', you go over to the Donatists, and that is a fourth sin."[131]

Again and again, whenever there was mention in the Psalms of sun, moon or stars, he thought it necessary to remind his superstitious hearers that Holy Scripture uses the heavenly bodies for purposes of metaphor, but that these metaphors are metaphors and nothing more. Thus Scripture applies the term "Sun of Righteousness" to Christ and also to the wise. The Church, that true witness in heaven, is symbolized by the moon. But the moon also symbolized that low-lying Jericho of our mortality (for the translation of the Hebrew word "Jericho" is "moon"). That is why it is written of eternity, "Until the moon is taken away". Yes, he says, our flesh, which must first be resurrected and then made imperishable for ever, is also called the moon.[132]

The Apostle compares the true Christians who undeviatingly pursue their way with stars in the heavens following the courses appointed for them by the

Creator.[133] But must we on that account worship the stars? We do not pray to lions because it is written that the Lion of Judah has conquered, nor do we worship mountains because we sing, "The mountains skip like lambs and the hills like young sheep."[134] To Januarius he wrote, "If comparisons of that kind mean that the Holy Writ is concerned with astrology, then it is also concerned with the mixing of poisons when it says, 'Be ye wise as serpents', and with the bird omens of the augurs when it adds, 'and guileless as doves'."[135] He frowns on the very word *fatum*, even when this is not used as referring to the stars but to the will of God, though he sought no quarrel with men of good will because of this word.[136]

Strange to say, however, he looked upon the result of a throw of dice or the drawing of a lot as an expression of God's will. God himself had spoken by means of a lot in the choice of Matthew. Such a thing might therefore well be an indication of the will of God. If the clergy wish to fly from a particular town, he says, then the lot should decide who should go and who should remain behind to minister to the people.[137]

It was, however, the cruder kind of superstition which was the real legacy of paganism, and it was quite ineradicable. It was a dark power ever-present, and no kind of exorcism could drive it out. It was both a result of unbelief and a substitute for faith. It was a survival from a degeneration of primitive life, but also a symptom of genuine power on the part of devils. It was a thing with which it was impossible truly to come to grips. The bishops could drive it underground, but they could get no hold on it. It eluded them, and they tended to see in it something more than folly. They regarded it as a demonic reality.

Augustine's Views on the Power and Impotence of the Demons

Augustine himself was firmly convinced that the pomps of the theatre, fortune-telling, astrology and the other black arts, in short the whole legacy of paganism, were parts of a single apparatus. He held that this apparatus was definitely in the service of the demons, and this explained the wonderful, nay, the astonishing perfection with which it worked and why it could have become so effective an instrument of seduction.

Naturally enough, he identified the "vile beings in the air which are called demons"[138] with the fallen angels of Holy Scripture and with the evil spirits in the air of which the Apostle speaks.[139] These beings were usually conceived of at this time as being partly spiritual, though possessing bodies of a kind of volatile substance. They were immortal but subject to evil passions and were invisible as they haunted the world.[140] In this view Augustine was at one with the best minds of the Church in his day, and like them he held that evil spirits had succeeded, over a period of centuries, in getting themselves or their creatures worshipped as gods, for men were convinced that the old gods really existed, whether they were human beings to whom the demons caused worship to be paid (and it was thus that some people still regarded them) or demons in the proper sense of the term. Did one not sing in the ninety-fifth psalm, "All the gods of the Gentiles are devils"?[141]

To find out what Augustine thought of their true nature and their power, it is well to read his little book, *The Demons' Art of Prophecy*.[142] He wrote it in the year 409, being moved to do so by certain discussions he had with layfolk on this subject. In these he had fought to elucidate how it was that the demons had so exactly foretold the carrying-off of Serapion in Alexandria, a wholly unanticipated event which occurred in the patriarchate of Theophilus in 391.[143] One can examine the views expressed in this little book in conjunction with those to be found somewhat later in *The City of God*.[144] Demons—so he tells us—are in certain respects powerful, for they possess three dangerous advantages. They have a subtle, ethereal and all-penetrating power of perception, speed of movement, and, above all, a very long experience. This does not put them on a higher level than men, for even dogs have certain senses, such as the sense of smell, better developed than we. Similarly, bees are able to detect honey in a way that men cannot. Vultures and eagles are speedier than man, elephants are stronger, snakes are more long-lived and even have the power to renew their youth. A malignant old man, moreover, tends to be more sly than a decently-minded youth, and in his own field the narrow specialist is always more experienced than the man of wisdom. Nobody should therefore be impressed by the demonic arts. The effect they create is the same as that produced by jugglers and tightrope walkers. They are simply spiritual *épateurs*. Their senses are sharper, but not their intelligence. Now, one day, "our own bodies will also be immortal, but that immortality will not be designed for eternal torture but will be of a nature consonant with the purity of our souls". Though, however, the demons live in higher regions, "their despair is shamed by our holy hope, nor does it behove us to strive to ascend to God by means of a piled-up hierarchy of physical heights; rather should we mount on a ladder of spiritual analogies".[145] That they can prophesy in certain cases merely means that they announce their own tricks in advance,[146] and also that they notice many things which escape human observation. Augustine, however, later abandoned a belief which he held in earlier days, namely that because of the peculiarly airy texture of their own bodies they could penetrate into the body of a man and could merge themselves into his thoughts by presenting lively pictures to his imagination,[147] and at the same time thus become aware of his secret thoughts and motives. That the idols would one day fall was something which had long been known to them from the words of the

Prophets. For a long while they had been silent on this matter and it was not surprising, now that the end of their reign was approaching, that they should begin to speak of it.

Demons are often in error, he says, even though they sometimes contrive to hide their ignorance.[148] Yet they have only one object in mind, which is to harm mankind, and this they can do so far as God permits it.[149] They fill the earthly air with seeds of disease and the hearts with evil thoughts and lascivious images. It is obvious that they must still be united by secret bonds to the places where once they were worshipped. Moreover, they lord it here on earth and on all the lower side of the lower planetary sphere, the nethermost part of heaven, and consequently they can tell better than human beings what goes on up above, and God may even permit them to gain some knowledge of the intentions of the good spirits; and it may well be that the latter guide the stars, in so far as every visible creature is guided by an invisible one, a creature which in this case must be angelic. It is possible that the demons communicate the knowledge they thus piece together to the *mathematici*, by means of secret signs, signs which may be prearranged or of which they infuse an intuitive understanding. Thus by reason of men's fear of the stars they keep them enmeshed in a demoralizing superstition.[150]

In the second book of his *Christian Knowledge*, Augustine enters into a theoretical examination of superstition, and here too returns to the mysterious part played by the demons. Under "superstition" he includes everything that has been devised by men regarding the alleged origin of the gods and also regarding their worship. The term "superstition" then involves two different kinds of activity: the substitution of the worship of creatures for the worship of God, and the practice of seeking and following the advice of demons which is communicated by means of prearranged signs. The first of these activities comprises the whole of the ancient cults, the second the whole business of the augurs and *auspices* together with the whole business of *ligaturae, remedia*, magic formulae, necromancy and the rest.[151]

The element of wrong in all this lay in the freely made decision to make bargains with demons, and in the heeding or interpreting of the signs by which they made themselves understood. It is worth noting that these are almost exactly the grounds on which the Church of today condemns spiritualism, which it does not by any means invariably regard as founded on fiction but treats as though it were quite possibly just such a converse with evil spirits as the men of Augustine's day had in mind. Men, Augustine tells us, resort to such practices "from curiosity, from torturing anxiety, or from a kind of slavish habit of self-abasement, but it brings nothing but plagues and death". Naturally, the signs which people receive, or suppose themselves to receive, from demons, mean nothing in themselves. The respect some people show them does not derive from any genuine magic power they possess, but purely from the attention which others pay them and the significance which they read into them.[152] We Christians have also our signs which have a hidden meaning, but these were given to us as a result of divine love and out of regard for men's love of God; those other signs were discovered by grasping and conscienceless men, and in accordance with a divine decision the men who traffic in these things, who indeed strive after nothing but evil, are exposed to the wiles of the bad angels "to whom this nethermost part of the universe is made subject by divine Providence in accordance with a well-ordered scheme"—and who have an interest in sowing in men's hearts the seeds of this immoral faith in the stars and confirming it by correctness of prophecy.[153]

That, and not the fact that horoscopes are cast, is the reason why their prophecies are occasionally fulfilled, though of course chance sometimes has a part in it. Holy Scripture is not silent on this last and warns against it, telling us not to believe the words of certain prophets even if what they speak comes true; the reference here being to demons. We must rather despise such people, and must act as St. Paul acted in the case of the woman with the pythonical spirit who brought to her masters much gain by divining.[154] Elsewhere, too, he says clearly that if the astrologers sometimes predict the future "with astonishing accuracy", then they speak from a secret inspiration, which they receive without knowing it, this inspiration being in itself a form of deceit and the work of seducers.[155]

Thus Augustine saw in the demonic apparatus a kind of counterpart to the sacraments of the Church.[156] On the one side were the simple but effective signs of grace, on the other the complicated diagrams of a disreputable pseudoscience, which based itself on the whisperings of demons. Here the divine impulse towards purity and contemplation, there the devilish tempting of men to base things and the trapping of them in the net of self-seeking. Here the love which edifies, there loveless knowledge which puffs men up and seduces them.[157] This line of thought makes his way of looking at the sacraments all the clearer because of his very act of contrasting them with their opposites. In it we can also hear from time to time the dominant theme of the second part of the *City of God*, namely, the struggle which never ceases here on earth between self-seeking which forgets God and the divine selflessness which forgets itself.

It would, however, be wrong to suppose that his consciousness of the existence of demons darkened his outlook on the world. This world has been redeemed, and that not by tribute paid to Satan. In the matter of man's redemption he sees Satan rather as the secret accuser of the Book of Job, as the tormentor who is allowed for a time to torture his victim, but never as an adversary with whom God deals on terms of equality. The devil is the Unrighteous One who must inevitably, because of his unrighteousness, be worsted by the righteousness of Christ. He is conquered not by God's power but by his justice.[158] Augustine frequently expresses himself in very forthright terms. Thus he is bold enough to say in a sermon that Christ on the Cross was a bait for Satan, but the Cross proved a mousetrap. There the Lion of Judah, who went like a lamb to the slaughter, trapped the roaring lion who goeth about seeking whom he may devour.[159] Elsewhere he follows a related train of thought. The drama of our reconciliation is played out upon the Cross, but it is played out between Father and Son. The devil has no part in it.[160] Moreover, although Augustine sees the space between the moon and the earth as a field in which, despite the world's redemption, God permits the devil a certain power, his power remains nothing more than a source of temporary resistance, a mystery of unrighteousness but no obstacle to the full glory of the Redemption.

Moreover, the prince of this world has already been kicked out of it. There is no need to flirt with the demons in order to be happy and even powerful in this world. Let people think of the government of Constantine, that government that was "happy beyond all that was ever desired". Constantine dared to break with the demons for good,[161] and today at the graves of the martyrs the demons everywhere depart, fleeing before the piety of the exorcists.[162]

Augustine thought in the terms of the world of late Antiquity; that explains why his belief in demons was to him a belief in a very real thing. Like nearly all his contemporaries, he visualized the whole of creation, from the flaming ether of the Empyrean to the innermost kernel of this little earth, as being filled with life, even though he could find no proofs of this in Holy Scripture. Matter could not create its own motion; it must therefore be moved by something else, which must necessarily be something higher than itself—a spirit. The universe was therefore moved and kept going by forces that were partly or wholly spiritual; in other words, it was filled with life, and of what else could that life consist save of good and evil angels?—"for every visible thing in this world stands under the direction of an angelic power".[163]

According to the science of his day, the universe consisted of a series of heavenly spheres enclosed one inside the other. Inside the firmament of the stars were the seven planetary spheres, and outside it was the Empyrean. These heavenly spheres revolved at vast distances around their centre, which was the earth. The size of the planetary spheres was so great that their relation to the diminutive earth was that of a ball to a dot.[164] In the lowest part of the heavens, beneath the moon's sphere, the demons hovered, and for this reason the devil was called the power in the air.[165] The spirits which had not fallen, on the other hand, had their habitation far above them, namely from the firmament of stars right up to the Empyrean, though Augustine did not venture to say exactly where this habitation was and what was its nature. In the year 415 he seems to have thought that the Thrones, Dominations, Principalities and Powers spoken of in Holy Writ were something more than angels pure and simple; he believed that they were to be found in the sphere of heaven and "are different, one from the other", though he did not know what precisely were the differences between them, and "it is really hardly our concern, whether they are possessed of reason and have a spirit". As far as the moon and the stars are concerned, he says, "they are too remote from the instruments of our senses and our spirit for us to discover whether spirits live there or no".[166] Six years later he declares that he will not venture to decide the question whether sun, moon and stars belong to the above-named angel-like powers or whether they are simply light-diffusing bodies, moved from without and without any living spirits upon them.[167]

It is obvious that such a conception of the universe, which pictures it almost as a vast living thing animated by thousands upon thousands of spirits and, as it were, breathing power at every point, could easily absorb the biblical devils. This also explains why the Christians were not disposed to treat demonic influences lightly. The Church herself, who from the moment of receiving anyone as a catechumen seeks with the sign of the cross and with words of conjuration to guard him against all demons, was wholly conscious that she was battling with very concrete embodiments of evil. The demons were in retreat, but they were not departing willingly.

It is perhaps a pity that Augustine, instead of seeing the stars only as the lamps set before God's throne, should so largely have connected them with swindling astrologers. Yet in his rhetorical and allegorical way, Augustine did not fail to praise the marvels of the shining heavenly mechanism. The stars, "a most noble senate in a glittering *curia*",[168] "whose ways are in the heavens and who both by day and night proceed on their appointed paths and are undisturbed by the insults inflicted when men give them the names of heathen gods, put us and our distractions to shame".[169] They are given to us as times and seasons. They form the heavenly clock by which we can tell the days, the seasons of the year and the years themselves, and they are, moreover, a guide to sailors.[170] He is still ready to accept the almanac, but that is as far as he will go. Genuine astronomical knowledge may perhaps be pursued in certain cases without making the student a slave to the superstitions "of those who decipher the *fatua fata*", but such men stand in dangerous proximity to the demonic sphere of influence and only here and there enable us to calculate phenomena with any exactitude.[171] Also, such knowledge is quite useless to the interpreters of Holy Writ, save only perhaps that it may be a starting-point, so that we can proceed from a contemplation of the beauty of the heavenly bodies to the higher beauties of the soul, and so discover the great Artificer who is at work within our own breast.[172] Once he had attained that point of view, Augustine managed to forget the demons, and he hears the heavens singing the praises of God as clearly as the Psalmist. Then he too can say: "Thou lookest upward to the heavens and beholdest" ("le silence éternel des espaces infinis..."). "Look thou up to the innumerable host of the stars, look about thyself and see what swims in the water or creeps upon the ground or flies through the air or circles in the sky."[173] "I look up to the heavens, to the beauty of the stars, I marvel at the rays of the sun, which suffices for sowing by day, and the moon, which comforts us in the darkness of the night. Glorious is all this, and to be praised and marvelled at, and I marvel at it and praise it, yet I thirst after him that hath made these things."[174] And another time: "Ask the beauty of the earth, the beauty of the sea, the beauty of the wide firmament and the beauty of the sky, ask the stars in their well-governed courses, the sun which illuminates the day with its rays, the moon which dispels the darkness when the night comes, the creatures that multiply in the waters or live upon the land or fly in the air, the hidden souls and the visible bodies, the visible things that are guided from without and the invisible powers that guide them, and they will reply, 'Yes, we are beautiful', and their beauty is their hymn of praise."[175] Also, speaking in a manner very reminiscent of the Book of Wisdom ("If they were able to make judgement of the world, how did they not more easily find out the Lord thereof?"), he censures the astrologers, who have become learned by reason of their studies and are thus able to divine the date of a solar or a lunar eclipse, yet forget the Creator and stop short at his creatures.[176] It need hardly be said that in all the passages which mention sun, moon and stars he indulges in his game of allegory. Christ on these occasions is the sun, and the sun illumines the moon, which is the Church. The moon of the Church, however, is partly light and partly dark, because its brightness is often concealed by the fleshliness of its bad members. It wanes in order to grow again, and thus is a symbol of the resurrection of the body.[177] The heavens, which show forth God's glory, are the Apostles.[178]

A man who can speak in this fashion is not one whose world has been radically corrupted by demons. Rather has that world been symbolically transfigured. And the manner in which he deals with superstition's unhappy victims gives no indication of his having demons on the brain. It is gratifying to see that on these occasions he is quite capable of completely forgetting his devils, and instead of dwelling upon the subject of the world's demon-infested background, he will suddenly, in his sermons, say something about the poor-spirited conduct of his flock in this connection, though he will bring this in incidentally, as though it were hardly a subject worthy of his pulpit. More than once, perhaps, he convinced the more foolish among his hearers that they were being frightened by a turnip ghost, and even if he did not achieve anything remarkable in this connection, at least his hearers were left in no doubt about the fact that their dubious practices "were not permitted by the bishop or the Church".

Not that he was not fully in earnest in his views of the devilish nature of the ancient cult. All that had been touched by the belief in the ancient gods has in his eyes to some extent been defiled, and this comprised places, festivals, the names of months and days, buildings, works of art, yes, even those verses of the classical poets which once heard are never forgotten. He did not feel that demons really still lurked behind these things, but there still clove to them the irrepressible memory of a poisoned past. He would gladly have seen a change in the names of the days of the week, so that all Christians, instead of speaking of *dies lunae, Martis, Mercurii, Jovis, Veneris,* would have called them *feria secunda, quarta, quinta, sexta,* or *secunda, tertia, sexta, Sabbati,* according to what he described as "the ritual language of the Church". The first day of the week had already been Christianized. The *dies dominicus* had already irrevocably displaced the *dies solis,* and so it has remained in all Romance languages up to this day. Also the designation *sabbato* had largely become customary among Christians.[179]

As to the meaning of planets, Augustine would point out that these had been there much longer than the gods and that men had only given them the names of deified heroes through lack of understanding,[180] for the supposed gods were merely human beings. "Let us see whether the science of history will not succeed in showing us the graves of these pseudo-gods here on earth, so that the idle talk of poets does not fasten their stars onto the heavens, but confines itself to the proper business of poetry." And—he continues in the same mocking vein—"has chastity become of so little account that Venus has her star, but not Minerva?"[181]

Yet the once-so-powerful demons were withdrawing everywhere. The instrument of their power, the heathen cults, seemed to Augustine like a primeval forest which had once covered the world with an impenetrable mass of superstition, and which was now slowly but surely being uprooted by Christ. Hence the words of the Psalmist, "Invenimus eum in campis silvae"—we found him in the country of an uprooted forest, in that country where the Church had found room for ploughland and houses.[182]

The whole organization of the ancient worship of the gods seemed to him a glittering net for souls, that was once spread by the demons over the whole earth but had now been torn in pieces by the Redeemer and his Bride, the Church. Christians need no longer fear the meshes of this net, but they could still be entangled in it if they did not walk circumspectly on their way. It was still their task to heal the world of its infection, and that not so much by making the sign of the cross but by the blameless character of their lives.

Once men honoured the statues of the gods, nor was it really remarkable that they should thus have herded swine; but that was over now, and the prodigal son had returned from the wilderness.[183] At some places demons were still on the watch, but they were no more than chained dogs which could still bark savagely enough but could only bite those who went too near them.

Nothing justifies us in assuming that he regarded statues, fountains, withered garlands, turf altars and the remnants of secret meals as a kind of demonic germ-carriers. He did not fear contacts with stone and marble. The thing of which he had a much more real fear was the spiritual contact involved in reading the beloved authors of Antiquity, whom in his old age he used to quote without giving their names. "As those lines of somebody or other go", he would write on these occasions, as though he did not know his Vergil as well as Dante was later to know him. Indeed, the works of the great classical writers were in his library—well preserved in their leather containers. In Augustine's day people were no longer at pains to turn their heads away from an idol that happened to be left standing, nor did one blow upon a statue, if one happened to come upon it in some grove, in order to make it impotent for evil, though this had been the practice in the days of Minucius Felix and Tertullian. Still less did anyone bother about the closed temples. The world belonged to Christ, the Lord of the Earth and all contained therein, although there was still room in the air for the powers of evil. For a thinker like Augustine, demonic influence had its domain in the realm of the spirit, and that was why it could only reach men via their own wills. It is only through the free consent of a man's will that he can become a partner in their desecrating guilt. A pure mind, however, soon brings their wicked designs to naught. It was along these lines that Augustine made answer to those who asked his advice concerning such matters as intercourse with pagans and dealings with desecrated goods,[184] for not all Christians could always find the right line in these matters[185] and only a few could form an objective judgement of them.

Augustine was the last man to underrate the power of evil. The whole of the ancient cult had been in the service of evil. Paganism had left behind a demonic legacy, but Augustine was not afraid of dealing with it or of liquidating it in its theoretical aspects. He knew what purpose God had wanted it to serve. Once the impressive façade of the old religion had deceived the entire world; now, after the divine campaign, there was nothing left but a heap of ruins; yet those very ruins helped to testify to God's victory. The prophecy of Daniel was fulfilled. "And behold...one like the Son of Man came...and there were given to him power and glory and a kingdom and all peoples...shall serve him."[186] The seer of the *City of God* would certainly have subscribed to what Baudelaire wrote in his intimate journals, namely that paganism and Christianity mutually demonstrate each other.

5

THE JEWS

INCONSPICUOUS among the multitude and yet occasionally forcing men's attention upon themselves, mysterious and omnipresent, there were always the Jews. The bishop could not help being aware of them, for there were many of them in Hippo,[1] while in Carthage the numbers were very large indeed.

Augustine knew their customs. He would speak of their festivals at Easter and Whitsun, of the lighting of lamps on the eve of the Sabbath and of their *cena pura* on Good Friday.[2] He knew that there were many good Jews, and that many Jews sought to govern their lives by God's commandments, and though they were sometimes the occasion of violent outbursts on his part, he could also speak of them with great tenderness. He could be angry, however, about their excessive attention to business and their occasional brazenness. They were regular patrons of the theatre[3] and made more noise there than anybody else. They keep the Sabbath, he said, so that they can idle and eat titbits, and their rest upon this day is only a fleshly one. It would be better if they spent their Sabbath doing useful work upon the land, instead of creating an uproar in the theatre, and it would be better if their women spent the Sabbath at the spinning wheel, even though that occupation was forbidden, "instead of dancing shamelessly on their roofs" to the rhythm of the tambourine.[4] They were, he also complained, a querulous lot. If they incurred some well-deserved punishment, they would sulk (or pretend to do so) as though they were being blamed for everything that went wrong.[5]

Augustine wrote a treatise on the claims of the Jews and made numerous references to this subject elsewhere. Thus he asks, of what use to them is it to be called Israel, for the name wanders around and their crime remains.[6] He finds hard words for their blindness, and is continually reinterpreting the Psalms to call attention to this characteristic. They are, he claims, worse than the demons, who have at least recognized the Son of God. And yet they are more to be excused than the heretics, for they allowed the inscription over the Crucified One to remain, and if they have found a stumbling-block in the smaller stone which is Christ in the lowliness of his earthly life, the heretics bay against the mountain Christ which is the Church.[7] He shows us the rabbis asking the everlasting and angry question, "What are you doing with our books?" He shows their acrimony in all discussions. Never, he says, do they fail to hand gall and vinegar to Jesus as he battles with death.[8] He knows that they still boast that they have conquered the cozener Christ,[9] and he observes that, after being despised for centuries, they are suddenly admired by all the enemies of Christianity because of their hatred of the Church. Celsus and Julian admire their faithfulness to their old tradition, while Porphyry praises them for their killing of Christ. Yes, the latter, referring to the oracle of Apollo, goes so far as to declare that they possess the true wisdom.[10]

Without ceasing, Augustine adjures his catechumens to concern themselves seriously with the objections of the Jews and with their erroneous interpretation of the Old Testament. For these ancient books are no longer truly theirs at all. "They are as blind men when they read them and as the deaf when they sing from them."[11] He compares them to the slaves who, when they have carried their young master's books to school, sit in front of the door while the lesson is going on. They are the *ci-devant* librarians of the Church and can now and then elucidate some doubtful passage in a text. They are the older ones who can serve those younger than themselves, as Esau served Jacob. Yet far from having a part in the heavenly Jerusalem foretold by their prophets, they may not, thanks to the Emperor's order, even set foot in the earthly Jerusalem[12]—the Jerusalem which today is a city full of basilicas, crowding around the cross and the empty grave. Yet never does he forget their older rights, for as he says with St. Paul, the grafted branches must not boast against those that have been broken off.[13]

In an incomparably beautiful sermon on the parable of the prodigal son, he compares the Jews to the elder son who, when the younger one returns, is vexed by the killing of the fatted calf. The Jews are vexed because those worthless people, the pagans, have been granted a short cut and can now sit down to partake of the mystical meal, and Augustine draws a picture of the godfearing Jew who has begun to think about the riddle of the Church, and must stand by and watch as the human race marches on under the banner of Christ. He is like that same son who comes home out of the fields and stands before the house. In just this manner such a Jew's mind runs on this Church and he asks himself just what manner of thing she may be. He sees the Law in his own home, says Augustine, and sees that we also have the Law. The Prophets are in his home too, yet we also have the Prophets, but he also sees that we have sacrifice daily, though in his home the sacrifice is no longer. He sees that though he was upon the field of his father, yet he may not partake of the fatted calf. And then he hears the *symphonia*, the harmony of our unity. This *symphonia* moves him as do the voices, the choir and the solemnities and the eucharistic feast, and he stands by the Church and listens, and is stirred as he recognizes his own psalms, and surely the Father will sooner or later say to him, "My son, has your place not always been in my house?"[14]

Few have had so moving and yet so true a vision of Israel, and that is not surprising, for Augustine saw all things, including, of course, the Jews, through the light of Holy Scripture. I am of course not now speaking of the commercial Jews, says Augustine, but of the thoughtful and reflective type. But oh, how rare it is for the elder son to come back home again![15] They have become like the rich man and his brethren, those unhappy men who had Moses and the Prophets. Nay, they are worse than these, for they do not believe, though One has risen from the dead.[16]

6

THE *PARS DONATI* AND THE HERETICS

WAS the symphony of unity always so very impressive? It was fortunate that Augustine's Jew did his listening so close to the Basilica Pacis; had he listened somewhat further off, sounds from a very different symphony might have reached his ears. For within the same block, church music might have been sounding from yet another and larger church—one which belonged to a bitterly hostile community, the *pars Donati*. The bishop could hear that music during his own worship.[1]

A much greater trial than that created by the dying influence of paganism was the hydra of schism among the Christians themselves, a monster that was continually growing new heads. Eighty-eight heresies were numbered by Augustine in his book on this subject—all, he says, born from the one mother-monster, pride,[2] and begotten, we might add, of the obtuseness of the self-centred. Not all heresies flourished in Africa, but the more obstinate among them were thoroughly at home there. In Hippo itself there was little sign of an early Christian idyll. When Augustine arrived there, the town was wholly in the hands of the *pars Donati*, and this counter-Church was to be the great cross of his life.

The Donatist Schism and the Question of Reunion by Force

The schism, a result of personal animosities, had started some hundred years before. When in the year 305 a certain Caecilianus was consecrated Bishop of Carthage, a group of Numidian bishops refused to acknowledge him. They did so on the ground that his consecrator, Felix of Aptunga, had been one of those who, during the persecution of Diocletian, had delivered up the sacred books, and had thus, they said, made his own orders invalid. This event stirred to action a certain Carthaginian camarilla at the head of which was a highly-placed lady named Lucilla (of whom, incidentally, Optatus tell us that before receiving Communion she would always kiss a small bone, said to be a martyr's, but of doubtful authenticity). Now, Lucilla had already had occasion to censure Caecilianus, and when he was made a bishop, her camarilla took the law into its own hands and made a friend and protégé of hers, named Majorinus, bishop in his place; when, after losing a lawsuit, they had carried the matter to the episcopate of Africa Proconsularis and then to Rome, Arles and to the Emperor himself, one after the other, they finally went into definite opposition. After that the party developed into a regular African counter-Church. Looking back at it over the centuries, this new party appears to us like a gigantic weed, a symptom of the disease which the excessive demands made on men by the recent age of persecution had brought into being. It was the strangest mixture of African and Numidian particularism, early Christian idealism and personal resentment, but the Church which it created rose up in every town and locality as a rival to the Church Catholic, altar being set against altar in every neighbourhood where a Catholic church was to be found. Everywhere at the edges of the ancient towns two great basilicas towered over the houses, one Catholic, one non-Catholic. Though the churches differed in no way from one another in appearance, their congregations sometimes treated each other to rude remarks (and sometimes to worse); but in the main they simply ignored each other, though they continued to suspect each other of all kinds of infamies. The membership of the protesting or (if that expression is preferred) conservative Churches was often larger than that of the Catholic ones. Even in 411, the Donatists were in the majority in the province of Numidia, both in town and country, while in Africa Proconsularis they were a troublesome minority that caused the Catholics no little anxiety.[3]

As always, from the very start the schismatics also became heretics. They were the Anabaptists and Rigorists of the fourth and fifth centuries. They held that the true Church could only consist of the pure—the Catharism typical of so many heretics, which in this case makes the term "heretic" particularly applicable—and for this reason they held that the validity of the sacraments depended on the purity of the ministrant. Naturally, only they themselves were pure and they avoided as unclean the hierarchy which their founders had condemned and looked upon them as being hand in glove with the *traditores*, the cowards who had handed over the Sacred Books in Diocletian's day. For this reason also they baptized afresh all those who had undergone baptism by the existing hierarchy, and consecrated an unspotted hierarchy of their own. They paid no heed to their isolated position among the Churches both of the East and the West, and maintained that the *pars Donati* was the one true Church. "Only Africa smells fresh. Apart from Africa, the whole world stinks"—that was the attitude, St. Paul's words that we all have the sweet savour of Christ being apparently spoken in vain, and "the price of Christ's blood [was] so small that it only sufficed to redeem Africa. Alternatively, perhaps the Africans weighed so heavily in the scale that they alone could be redeemed".[4]

There were men both among their leaders and their members who had to be taken seriously. The great Donatus is a case in point, as is also the exegete Tyconius. Such men vaguely recall the outstanding qualities of the early Jansenists. Yet in contrast to the Port-Royal movement, Donatism was from its inception a popular movement, poor in original ideas, but nevertheless full of people who were easily inflamed and drawing from these its principal strength. Indeed, once the leaders had got the Punic-speaking masses on to their side, no power on earth could heal the schism.

The Donatists had the Puritans' power of obstinate endurance, and in due course could count more than three hundred bishops in Africa, which Catholics considered excessive in relation to the actual numbers of their following; also, despite their strictness they tolerated the presence in their midst of the most disreputable elements; they did this simply because these elements happened on occasion to be useful to them and because their presence was preferable to a submission to the Catholics. Under Julian the Apostate, who took a malicious delight in showing favour to anything that made for Christian disunity, they were firm supporters of the Government, while under Constantius and Honorius, who pursued a very different policy, they complained bitterly that their deputations were not received, and when the Government began to deal drastically with their excesses and even with the movement as such, they suddenly turned round and asked what the bishops had to do with the Court, or the Emperor with the Church.[5] From this time onwards they began to conspire against the State, supporting such rebels as Firmus, Gildo and Heraclian. One of their chief ornaments, Bishop Optatus of Thamugadi, came to be known chiefly as "the Gildonian".[6]

The Donatists behaved like embittered integralists. They claimed to be the exclusive possessors of the only pure tradition and held that duty called them to that tradition's lone and bitter defence. Despite the fact that externally and in matters of ritual they were wholly indistinguishable from the Catholics, we are told that they avoided the latter like the plague, cursing their sacraments as arts of the devil and declaring the Catholic Canon of the Eucharist (which they referred to as *carmen* instead of by the more customary *prex*[7]) to be a sorcerer's formula. More and more they developed an idiom of their own. For instance, instead of the "Deo gratias" that Cyprian had hallowed for ever upon his deathbed, they deliberately affected "Deo laudes", and this became a sort of party slogan which in their churches they chiselled on the capitals of the columns and on the keystones and inscribed on the graves of their martyrs, so that one can always tell when excavating a ruined church whether it is Donatist or not.[8]

They did not speak of their leaders as bishops of the Catholic Church, but as bishops of the Catholic Truth and True Christianity, or as bishops of the Holy

Gospel.⁹ They were indeed very fond of playing off the Gospels against the Church, which they also reproached with relying on the secular sovereign and which allegedly "throve by bloody bites and grew fat upon the flesh and blood of the saints".¹⁰ With unvarying emphasis they voiced their misgivings concerning an institutional priesthood. How, they asked, could an unholy man make others holy? How can the dead call others to life, how can one who is not possessed of the Spirit impart the Spirit to others by the laying-on of hands? How can the blind open other men's eyes? How can a Church be content to see unsanctified men in its high places? The Universal Church is not the Church that spans the earth, but the Church which keeps the Commandments and the sacraments. For the world beyond Africa, and particularly for "the innumerable Eastern Churches",¹¹ they cared very little. Alone in Rome, the city which, we are told by Optatus of Milevis, had forty basilicas, they possessed a "haunt" between the hills outside the walls, a circumstance which earned them the nickname of "mountaineers".¹²

This Optatus was the first author to attack them, and he led a campaign against their second great leader, Parmenianus, whom he refuted in his book *The Schism of the Donatists*. In that work he describes the sect in telling words, words which in a most lively manner conjure up the strange atmosphere of that time. Outwardly, he said, there is very little difference between the Donatists and ourselves, the general Church routine is the same as ours, they have the same lessons, the same faith, the same sacraments, the same mysteries.¹³ They too say that a true Church must have certain things that immediately distinguish it for what it is, namely, it must have a *cathedra*, an angel who touches the baptismal pool (the bishop),¹⁴ the living water of the Spirit, and in addition, the unbroken seal of the *symbolum* (the sealed fountain of the Song of Songs), an altar and a priesthood. Yet the Donatists "have been cut out from the root of the Mother-Church by the sickle of envy and now lie scattered around as rebels",¹⁵ for while even in a geographical sense the Catholic Church spans the world and is at unity with the authentic *cathedra* in Rome, this unity being confirmed by letters sent from that place to churches all over the world, the Donatists stand wholly isolated.¹⁶

Nor did they desire it otherwise. The new chosen people had no wish to waste even a word on the Catholic Samaritans. It is said that they even wiped the pavement on which a Catholic had been standing. What was even worse, they made use of strong-arm squads of embittered proletarians—men who might perhaps have had dreams of an earthly Kingdom of Heaven—who were continually falling upon the *cellae*, the lonely farms, country houses and churches of the Catholics—hence their name of Circumcellions.¹⁷ In every place which was not strong enough to defend itself against them, these bands would come and plunder supplies, carrying off food and spilling away the drink. They would set the basilicas on fire, books and all, and manhandle the clergy. In the final stages of their career, when the cause of Donatism was already failing, they made a practice of throwing lime and vinegar into Catholics' eyes and so blinding them, "a thing unknown even among barbarians".[18] There was nothing from which they shrank; they forced men under threats to hand over the notes of their debtors, to destroy contracts, to set free the most depraved of their slaves, and they would set recalcitrant masters to the treadmill.[19] In this fashion they defied the police for more than a century. Indeed, this Jacquerie infested the whole land of Numidia, to the great annoyance ultimately of the Donatists themselves.

When the opportunity occurred, they even seized churches. This occurred in the case of the principal church of Cirta, which had been built by Constantine. They took possession of this place by force, nor could any threats induce them to relinquish it, so that the Emperor, who was averse to violence, was compelled to have a new basilica built for the Catholics at the State's charge, without collecting any compensation from the robbers.[20] The Catholics did not regain all their property even under Constantius. Julian the Apostate had handed all their own churches back to the Donatists, together with those they had taken by force, and after his death the Catholics were unable to put sufficient pressure on the police to regain their property; consequently they were compelled to acquiesce in the theft and build emergency basilicas.

Although the rabble of the Circumcellions had really little in common with the *pars Donati*, the regrettable fact remained that the hotheads among the latter definitely took them into the service of their cause. They used them as shock troops, called them "soldiers of Christ" and "wrestlers" (*agonisticos*[21]), and even clerics and bishops did not scruple to lead their raids. Optatus of Timgad earned the name of "Destroyer of Africa", and even the moderate Bishop Macrobius was drawn into the business.[22] These "Clubs of Israel"[23] inspired such terror that whole hamlets were rebaptized on the occasion of an attack, for these Donatist bands were as free with blood as they were with holy water.[24] "Their feet are swift unto the shedding of blood"—Augustine had only to quote that verse from the Psalms and everyone would know what he had in mind. The police knew it as well as he, and would occasionally take strong measures.[25] Yet it was difficult to put one's hands on the real culprits. Moreover, when the police finally got on their trail the Donatists concerned would frequently take their lives. With the cry "Deo laudes" on their lips, they would on such occasions hurl themselves into an abyss or drown themselves— practices which were later to be followed by the Old Believers in the day of Archpriest Avvakum. Augustine says that men of good will feared the cry of "Deo laudes" as they feared the roaring of lions,[26] and that it had gained so evil a notoriety that everyone who heard it ran away in terror, so as not to see

God offended by that terrible leap[27] (for in this way the deed was usually done). The men leapt into those deep rocky clefts that are so frequent in the Aures mountains, which were in a sense the Donatist's paradise. The devil had only to call out to one of them, "Throw yourself down", to awaken the belief that martyrdom was in his grasp—as though Christ had not said, "Get thee behind me Satan, thou shalt not tempt the Lord thy God." These hysterical suicides once caused Augustine to abandon his customary delicacy and to ask during a sermon at Cyprian's grave why those who were so obsessed with the desire for a martyr's death never employed the rope, which offered a much more comfortable method of taking one's life. He observed that the Donatists showed a quite singular unanimity in avoiding its use. It seemed, he said, that they preferred to follow the devil himself rather than his disciple, Judas.[28]

These Donatist fanatics usually went about "under the guise of professional wandering ascetics",[29] and seemed to vie with one another in their search for martyrdom, to ensure which they made bargains with both pagans and Catholics. Even today excavation is bringing graves to light the inscriptions on which refer to the alleged murder of these would-be saints by the *traditores*. In Ala Miliaria such an inscription was discovered relating to a certain Robba, an elderly virgin and a sister of a bishop, who in the year 414 "was murdered by the *traditores*".[30] Though such accusation should be treated with caution it should not be thought, however, that Catholics, where they were in the majority, were invariably mild in their demeanour. In the year 411, for instance, the Bishop of Abora in Africa Proconsularis announced that any persons proclaiming themselves Donatists would be stoned.[31]

At the moment when Augustine was received into the hierarchy, the schism had reached a temporary stalemate. The persecution had died down. Only older men could still remember the dragonnades of such officials as Paulus and Macarius. The period of Macarius had been particularly noteworthy in so far as, after 347 and Constantius' decree of compulsory unification, the Donatists lost all their churches, numbers of their people being killed, while refractory priests were banished. In those days, so Optatus tells us, "there was peace everywhere, the devils in the temples and those who were far away, exiled in strange lands, being the only ones that mourned".[32] Fourteen years later, Julian the Apostate, foreseeing that the Christian sheep would tear each other to pieces without any further prompting, had recalled all the exiles and ordered his provincial governors to remain neutral. Thus, immediately after their reunion, the Donatists had relapsed into schism. Under the leadership of the returning exiles they had stormed the churches and had washed them with salt water, for the ordinary water had been made unclean by the allegedly bogus baptisms for which the *"traditores"* had used it. They had planed off the surface of the wood from the altars and scratched away the limestone from the walls, relegated the reputedly sham sacraments of their oppressors to the dustheap, poured the oil from the lamps out of the window, burnt the books, thrown the Eucharist to the dogs, imposed the great penance on all who had partaken of the "sham sacraments", declared all baptism and all consecrations of priests and virgins to be null and void and reconsecrated the persons concerned.[33]

For thirty years conditions remained virtually unchanged. The Donatists enjoyed a somewhat precarious religious freedom. In order to make their propaganda more forceful Gratian and Valentinian had made the act of rebaptizing a punishable offence, but spirits had grown calmer, and it seems probable that the Vicarius Africae, Flavianus, to whom it would have fallen to enforce the law, was himself secretly a Donatist.[34] Most certainly he failed to interfere, and so the law became obsolete.

Thus the schism went on from year to year and acquired the persistence of an inveterate habit, and soon nobody believed that it was possible to solve the problem—until three new personalities appeared on the scene in 391, namely Aurelius and Primianus, who took over the Catholic and Donatist bishoprics respectively at Carthage, while Augustine became a priest in Hippo.

One year later the strictly orthodox Theodosius issued a general edict, imposing on all heretics a fine of ten pounds of gold for secret consecrations and for professing irregular use of the title of bishop. Any building in which such a consecration had taken place was ordered to be confiscated. Moreover, though the Donatists were not actually named in this connection, all schismatic clergy were declared incapable of inheriting or making testamentary dispositions, and actually a certain nobleman, who was disputing with a Donatist community an inheritance which the latter had obtained under his sister's will, succeeded in recovering the property after the Donatists had already taken possession.[35]

The Catholics now suddenly became alive to the fact that they had the right type of man among their number and could make themselves masters. The bishops, however, had no intention of contesting at one stroke all the legacies by which the Donatists had benefited, nor of denying to their Donatist colleagues the right to call themselves bishops. "There were laws," Augustine was to write, "but we allowed them to sleep in our hands, as though they had never been made at all"[36]—even so they were conscious of the strength of their position "and the Catholic Church began once more to raise its head".[37]

As to the Donatists, Primianus had hardly been installed before he became gravely compromised, and that in two ways. In the first place, his congregation espoused the cause of the Gildonian rebellion, and the Court did not remain in ignorance of this. Secondly, one of his deacons, a certain Maximianus, started a schism within the schism.[38] The circumstances recalled those of the Caecilianus affair in 312. Again there was an intriguing woman mixed up in the business, and again there was a personal quarrel (though of course Maximianus professed to have a genuine grievance) and the Catholics looked on with a certain malicious pleasure while the pattern was further repeated. Primianus caused a great synod duly to condemn, remove and excommunicate the twelve bishops who had consecrated the schismatic, and was finally driven to call in against the Maximianists that very secular authority concerning whose interference he had on other occasions so bitterly complained. Small wonder that Augustine lost no opportunity to use the *argumentum ad hominem* against him. "Usually they crawl like serpents, but give them the opportunity and they will roar like lions, aye, and use all the violence of lions."[39] He also pointed out their dogmatic inconsistencies. Maximianus had condemned Primianus with the help of a hundred bishops from Africa Proconsularis and Byzacena. Primianus, who had contrived to muster three hundred and ten, mostly from Numidia, condemned Maximianus and the twelve bishops who had consecrated him, and threatened the rest with excommunication if they did not return. When they really got down to it, however, Primianus and his party were ready to catch on the rebound those who had gone over to the other camp, without any rebaptism or reconsecration.[40] Other small schisms had occurred before this and yet others were still to follow, but "The Gildonian" and his Numidian henchmen raged like wild beasts against Maximianus' party and invoked the laws of the Empire against dissidents, laws which had in point of face been framed against themselves. Here and there they got the upper hand sufficiently to expel the new schismatics from their churches and actually began to act as though they were followers of the Catholic bishops and almost to speak in their name.[41] They caused one of the consecrators of Maximianus, a certain Salvius of Membressa, to be dragged out of his house by the mob of a neighbouring town. These hung dead dogs round his neck and danced about him like madmen.[42] The other splinter Churches did not dare to assert themselves against such people. One of these splinter groups, that of the Rogatists, the mildest of all the sects, had, according to Augustine, only a handful of followers. We have a letter of Augustine to Vincentius, the leader of the Rogatists, in which he dwells upon this fact: "And while it is written, 'In all places from the rising of the sun unto the going down thereof... the Lord saith' (note that 'the Lord saith' well. It is not 'Donatus saith' or 'Rogatus saith' or 'Vincentius saith', but 'the Lord saith') and 'the whole world is full of his glory, *fiat, fiat*', you sit in Cartennae with your ten remaining Rogatists and say, 'non fiat, non fiat'."[43]

Yet despite these difficulties all the sects, both great and small, continued in being, and indeed it soon became difficult to tell one lot of the demonstrative aspirers to sanctity from another. Meanwhile, Aurelius and his party were working in a number of synods (including that of Hippo in 393) for the reform of their own Church, a work which they felt required their attention before they could give serious thought to the problem of reunion. Augustine, however, during this time left no attack unanswered but repeated both the old arguments of Optatus and the new ones which bore on the Maximianist affair, with a patience that seemed inexhaustible and with a mildness of spirit that nothing was able to disturb. The whole sharpness of his mind and all the resources of his old art of dialectics were employed, as he expounded the true character of the Church and insisted on the objective reality of the sacraments. He and his friends did not desire the compulsory abolition of the party of their opponents. What they desired was reconciliation—and so they decided to seek counsel from Rome and Milan on the question whether, in view of the great shortage of priests in Africa, a dispensation could be granted to such Donatist priests as came back to the fold, so that those who had not engaged in rebaptism and had come over in a body with their congregation could retain their priestly office. They also asked whether the laying-on of hands which was customary in the case of baptized minors who returned to the Church—the rite was a kind of confirmation of their penance—should be considered as disposing of all further impediments.

Nor was Augustine discouraged by Pope Anastasius' warning not to trust the opposing party too readily. In the end, however, the decision was made to leave the whole matter to the local bishop.[44] In this way the doors were opened to the schismatic clergy. Unfortunately this liberal spirit proved useless. Deputies from the synods, who were sent to every place where the Maximianists had a church, received no reply.

From the year 403 onward the idea of an honest exchange of views between the two parties gained strength among the Catholics. Since the Donatists refused all personal contact with their opponents, various town governments were brought into the affair. The invitations, together with the reasons for them, were entered in the register of every town. The other party could then enter their reply without incurring the risk of a personal meeting. Thus it might happen that the Catholic bishop would appear at the town hall, and present the documents attesting his authority, together with his invitation; he would have them both recorded and withdraw. Then his schismatic opposite number would arrive and cause the documents to be read to him, and appears sometimes to have composed his reply on the spot.

Primianus' own reply in the records of Carthage was as follows. "It would be shameful for the sons of the martyrs to meet with the race of *traditores*. They come up against us with the letters of many emperors, though we ourselves have nothing but the Gospel. The True Church is that which suffers persecution, not that which persecutes."[45] The Numidian bishops were personally not inimical to the notion of a meeting, but for the most part replied that they must first consult their brothers in office—this happened, for instance, in Hippo and Calama. However, on a hint passed by Carthage they ultimately refused in a body and usually in insulting terms. Thus in the town hall of Calama, Crispinus had the following answer to Possidius recorded. " 'Fear not the word of a sinful man.' Secondly, 'Beware that thou sayest naught into the ear of one bereft of good sense, so that he mock not thy prudent word, when he has heard it.' Finally, I summarize this my reply in the words of the patriarch [Job]: 'All the godless fly before me and I desire not to know their ways.' " The reply was typical of the sect, but it merely proved that the "most learned old age" of Crispinus had nothing to teach Possidius, "the young recruit of yesterday", and Crispinus was the joke of the town.[46]

But the mob rose to a man and made common cause with the Circumcellions, who now appeared everywhere on the scene, and as soft words gave place to acrimony, ruffians began to lurk on the highways whenever Augustine was to preach anywhere. Once he escaped certain death by the fortunate accident of losing his way.[47] A priest of the neighbourhood, however, was set upon under the walls of Calama, while a few days after the scene in the town hall Bishop Possidius was discovered in the attic of a farmhouse by a gang which was led by a priest. The gang surrounded the house and attacked it with fire and stones and despite the protests of the villagers, who feared reprisals upon themselves and who succeeded in putting out the fire, contrived to break the door in. They wounded the cattle which were within, and beat the bishop till he fell senseless, though the leader of this assault was careful not to risk actual murder.[48] The Bishop of Bagai (the town was an active breeding-ground of schism) was caught in his church, which had just been recovered by legal process, and beaten with sticks and even with one of the feet of the wooden altar under which he had hidden when the church doors were broken open. Thereupon he was dragged outside and left lying on the ground, covered with blood. When the small number of his faithful carried him away that evening, singing psalms as they went, the other party suddenly appeared, recaptured his person and, since he still breathed, threw him down from a tower. He landed on a dunghill, where a poor man discovered him, while *ventrem exonerans*. The man called his wife, who was waiting close at hand with a light. Then the pair roused the faithful, and so the bishop's life was saved.[49]

Thus the policy of reconciliation came to nothing. The synod of the year 404 sent deputies to the Court to ask not for the actual abolition of the sect but for the application of the existing laws against breaches of the peace. This was a most moderate demand. A certain number of bishops had expressed the opinion that unity could only be achieved by force and they cited the case of Tagaste. At the time of Macarius this whole town had come over to the Catholics and remained faithful; Augustine, however, would have none of this. In his view the normal protection by the State against those who disturbed public order was quite sufficient. The law of 392 against heretics covered this point.[50]

But meanwhile the Bishop of Bagai had displayed his scars to the Court overseas and other victims were sitting in the antechambers.[51] Honorius took drastic action and forbad the schism. The churches were handed over to the orthodox, and the recalcitrant clergy fled across the border. Laymen who secretly came together for purposes of rebaptism received heavy penances and were even subject to confiscation of their goods. A rebaptized person lost his legal status. If he was a slave and had acted under duress, he could seek asylum in the Church and so gain his freedom. The Donatists thenceforth ranked as ordinary heretics, and the act of rebaptism as sacrilege. There was, however, never any question of a death penalty for these offences.[52]

The reunion decree was strictly carried out with regard to the basilicas. The heretical clergy went underground, or retired. We hear nowhere of any exiles. Many Donatist congregations came over. The first contacts with the Catholic clergy were wholly satisfactory, and people began to feel what a senseless thing the schism had been. The Donatist Bishop of Bulla kept only a single member of his flock, that of Gratianopolis not a solitary one (later he was angrily to declare that the members of his congregation would have had their houses pulled down had they failed to conform). The bishops of Sufazar and Bazaritana settled their problems by resigning.[53]

The idea of a serious exchange of views now once more began to influence people and we find that certain Donatist bishops who happened to be at the Ravenna Court in the year 406 asked the Praefectus Praetorii to arrange a discussion with a Catholic bishop who chanced to be visiting there. The bishop, however, very properly did not respond to the suggestion, since, as an isolated individual, he felt he had no authority to act.[54]

For all this, however, hatred burned all the more fiercely in Numidia, the true focal point of the trouble, and a fresh wave of excesses forced the bishops to renew their accusations. The basilica of Bagai was consigned to the flames, all its books being burned, in Constantine the heretics pulled down all the altars, while in Sitifi the church was seized, together with money, corn and vehicles, and one of the priests was subjected to torture. A Donatist bishop went so far as to boast that he had reduced four churches to ashes with his own hands, and numerous priests were blinded or subjected to other kinds of maltreatment.[55]

The climax was reached when Stilicho was murdered, an event which caused the rebels to think that, as far as they were concerned, the storm was over. A provincial toleration edict made the situation more confused than ever, and in 408 Augustine was constrained to send an urgent request for help to Olympiodorus, the *homo novus* at Ravenna.[56]

It was not till 411 that the situation began to be clarified. In that year, at the request of the Synod of Carthage and by order of the Emperor Honorius, a great religious discussion took place in the hall of the Baths of Gargilius, to which all bishops of both parties were invited and which large numbers actually attended.[57] This was really the beginning of the end for the Donatists as a sect, and they understood well enough that they no longer had a future. The Catholic bishops, on the other hand, felt so strong that they declared themselves ready to lay down their office if the debate went to their disadvantage, but they knew in advance how it would end, though they also knew that whatever the result there would continue to be two bishops in every town. That is why they made the very magnanimous proposal that should the Donatists be the losers they would not be required to divest themselves of their title of bishop. If, on the contrary, the Catholics were defeated, they would place themselves at the Donatists' disposal and follow their counsel. If in any city the people refused to tolerate the existence of two bishops, both bishops should retire, and the newly-elected bishop should be consecrated by the bishop of some community which happened to have a single bishop, for as Catholics they could only abhor the human errors of their opponents,[58] not their orders, which were from God. Probably they all felt that their spectacular public proceedings were a little dubious in character, but they acquiesced in them not as defendants who had to establish their innocence—*causa finita erat* since 312—but because they wished to bring clearly before their adversaries' eyes the judgement that had already been entered against them.[59]

With Alypius and especially with Augustine among their advocates, the Catholic cause was in good hands. Count Marcellinus had arrived by the Emperor's order to act in the capacity of *cognitor*, and his duty was to call the conference together, to preside over it and at the end of the debate to give judgement. He was ready to make considerable concessions though he had already, "from personal goodwill", provisionally restored their churches to the Donatists.[60] Meanwhile, Augustine, on his side, was preaching most effectively in the Catholic churches of the capital on the follies of the rebaptizing sect, asking with the Apostle whether Christ was divided or whether his hearers had been baptized in the name of Paul, "and if not in Paul's name, then still less in that of Caecilianus or Donatus. And yet you say, 'I will not relinquish Donatus, I will not relinquish Garus, Lucius, Parmenianus' and God knows who else. A thousand names, a thousand schisms! You run after one man and so dissipate the patrimony of which you know that it stretches from sea to sea, unto the uttermost parts of the earth. Why do you not hold on to this? Because you are holding on to a man. But what is a man? A rational being made out of earth. And you are against us because you lick earth." He spoke of the coming conference and read Psalm cxviii. 96: "I have seen the end of all perfection. Thy commandment is exceeding broad", and asked, "What then is the end we pursue? The broad commandment. The end of the commandment is—what you are already saying with me—'Love from a pure heart' "[61]— for the people had recognized the text and spoke the last words in unison, and while he spoke of the coming peace within the Church, he exposed the folly of those who wanted anything rather than peace, "who hate peace as a man with inflamed eyes hates the light". His words have a truly magnificent ring:

> And now it is announced to those people that the Christians are to make peace with one another, and hearing this they say to one another, "Woe unto us—why is this? Concord is at hand." Now what is the significance of those words, "Woe unto us! Concord is at hand"? Have you been told that a wild beast is at hand, or that a fire is about to break out? No, concord will come, light will come, and therefore, dearly beloved, I enjoin your love that you show these people your Christian and Catholic mildness. Those with whom you have to deal are sick men. Their eyes are inflamed and need long and gentle treatment. Let no man now seek to chaffer as over a bargain, let him not even enter into discussion on religious matters, for that might cause a spark to fly. Perhaps you will have insults hurled at you. If so, bear with them, and pretend not to hear them. Take the words I say to you literally. To nurse the sick means to nurse the sick. It does not mean two people starting an argument. Be patient, I adjure you, my brethren. "But I cannot bear it", you will say, "when a man speaks contemptuously of the Church." Yet in such a moment this is just what the Church demands of you—namely, that you should bear it with meekness when she is despised. "But", you will say, "he is attacking my bishop. Shall I remain silent while he speaks evil of my bishop?" Let him do it. Do you do this for your bishop —refrain for his sake from getting into an argument. Take counsel with yourself so that you understand the real need of the moment and pray for him.[62]

Take particular care, dear brethren, that nobody who is not expected there enters the conference room, yes, avoid even passing the place, if you can. You have read the proclamation of His Excellency on this subject, even if this was put up for the benefit of others than yourselves, for you fear God and are at pains to respect the warnings of your bishop. Let us avoid being the occasion of any kind of disturbance and let us give no excuse for any crowd to gather. Perhaps you will say, "We should like to know what we *can* do?" Well, we will make a suggestion, and it is a very pious one. We are debating for *you*, do *you* pray for *us*. Strengthen your prayers by fasting and almsgiving, give them wings that they may fly to God. If you will do your share in this manner, you may be more useful to us than we are to you.[63]

In this fashion Augustine did more than ten brigades of police could have done to maintain order in the town.

Although the Donatists had good speakers at their command, they made a somewhat pitiful impression, and this though they turned up in full strength and even made a sort of triumphal entry, while the Catholics arrived without any particular ceremony or fuss. Nor did the reason for the Donatist failure on this occasion lie solely in the fact that they felt themselves to be the weaker party, and so tended to look upon the whole conference as a rather cruel farce —which it most certainly was not. The trouble was that they deliberately acted like men under an unfair handicap, and began systematically to sabotage the whole proceedings. In order to avoid disturbances, it had been decided to limit the delegates to eighteen a side, of whom seven were to be speakers, seven advisers and four supervisory officials. The Catholics appeared with eighteen delegates, the Donatists with considerable numbers, but the Donatists refused to declare which of these were actual delegates and which were not. Two whole days were wasted by their obstructive tactics on points of procedure. They completely upset the order of business, against which they raised continual protests. They insisted on verification of credentials and lists of the names of those taking part. They also insisted on confronting every Catholic with his opposite number from the same town, were silent when they should have spoken and spoke on all matters concerning which they should have kept silent. They forced the meeting to record all the minutes in longhand because they could not read the shorthand record, and even "refused to sit down together with sinners". In consequence of this last everybody had on the first day to stand for eleven hours (although it was a hot June day) including the courteous and patient official who was presiding and who did his utmost to be genuinely impartial. The confrontation of the various pairs of local opposite numbers tended sooner or later to result in the hurling of abuse. The following dialogue provides a fair sample.

> PETILIANUS OF CIRTA: Yes, that is the man, the persecutor of the Church in the town where I am bishop.
>
> FORTUNATUS: Yes, indeed, I am from that town where all the altars have been broken.
>
> PETILIANUS: Let it be recorded in the minutes that you are a persecutor. In due time you will hear what you deserve to hear.

Or:

"Do you know him?"
"I should say I do—from all the difficulties he has put in my way."

Or:

SEVERIANUS: There are no Donatists with us.
ADEODATUS: What! Why, this man sits among my people, though it is true he has hounded my clergy away.
SEVERIANUS: He lies. God is my witness.
MARCELLINUS: Will Your Holiness tell us plainly whether there is or is not a bishop in this village?
ADEODATUS: He sits among my people. The village is as good as mine.[64]

No wonder that Marcellinus had constantly to intervene, first to make an end of these battles of words and then to stop downright sabotage.

During the third meeting, which was held after a five-day interval, Augustine, who till now had been silent, intervened suddenly in the debate. The Catholics had handed in to Marcellinus a short declaration of principles. Shortly afterwards the latter received a very violent rejoinder from the Donatists, or rather "from the bishops of Catholic truth, which suffers persecution but does not persecute".[65] Emeritus, one of the seven Donatist speakers, was rash enough to submit this rejoinder for debate, and with it, of course, the whole subject with which it professed to deal. Hereupon Augustine attacked him and fairly let fly. He dealt with the two main questions, that of Caecilianus and that of the true Church, and in this way built up an excellent exposition of his case.[66] On that same evening Marcellinus gave his decision, and he gave it in favour of the Catholics and declared that their opponents had been led away into heresy and schism.

Soon thereafter the edict was promulgated which abolished the sect, forbade them to meet together and handed over all their property to the Catholic Church. It also declared estates on which the Circumcellions had been in the habit of mustering as confiscated, but it left the persons of the bishops alone. When the Donatists appealed against the edict, a new edict provided heavy penalties for all priests and laymen who would not join the Catholic Church. Slaves who refused to follow their masters were to be whipped into concurrence. Anyone offering resistance to the handing over of Donatist property was to be banished.[67] Imperial commissioners were to travel from town to town chiefly for the purpose of supervising the liquidation of Donatist assets, and it appears that these commissioners really did play a determining part in this whole affair. Certain resolutions of the council of 418 are evidence of this. According to these resolutions Catholic bishops who showed too little zeal in reconciling Donatists were to be brought by their colleagues before the provincial governor. They had to make good their arrears in this duty under threat of excommunication. If, however, no commissioner had appeared in a locality to arrange for the transfer of the property the absence of mass conversion was not to be made a reproach to the bishop concerned. Bishops were also forbidden to produce fictitious lists of reconciliations.[68]

All this was, to put the matter bluntly, a forcing of consciences, but it was also for Donatists the beginning of the end. "Huge masses, whole armies in fact", went over "to Catholic peace"—priests, bishops and people often going over in a body,[69] and with the Church property there also returned the poor.[70] Even the Circumcellions, says Augustine, hid their wolfishness under the sheep's clothing of the official Church.[71]

In the country, however, it frequently happened that protagonists of reunion had a rough reception. We hear of the burning of books, of farmhouses burnt to the ground, of a bishop having his tongue cut out and a hand hacked off, of a priest who lost a finger and an eye, and of yet another priest who lost his life.[72]

But if many a man "did not feel at home in the new surroundings" it was shown that Catholics and ex-Donatists could live with one another, and could do so permanently. Many confessed that they had long been Catholic in thought, but had been deterred from showing their hand by fear of violence. Those whose reconciliation was mere pretence were at least compelled to listen to the truth. Only a small minority remained obdurate.[73] The Donatist bishops could move about freely, and they retained their title of bishop, but in cases where they refused to co-operate they were deprived of jurisdiction. Of the latter kind, those who simply refrained from celebrating Mass were left in peace, but the majority fled or went underground.[74]

As to the bishops who returned to the fold, Augustine, both in his sermons and in a letter to Marcellinus, proposed a certain course of action. He saw well enough that "people no longer wanted two bishops", and now suggested that both should function in a single basilica, one on the *cathedra*, the other in a more subordinate position. They should conduct worship in turn until one of them died.[75] It is impossible to say to what extent this suggestion was acted on, but we do know that those who did not return were not hounded down. They disappeared into a dignified leisure or went into the mountains. In the year 418 some thirty of them had a secret meeting (there had been two hundred and seventy-nine in 411) and resolved that those who had not preached in the churches of the *traditores* and had not offered the Sacrifice there should be allowed to keep their rank and be received back into the pure Church.[76]

Augustine could not help seeing the finger of God in these sudden mass reunions. He greeted the draconian decrees of Honorius which promoted them with the same enthusiasm with which Bossuet received the news of the revocation of the Edict of Nantes. For years he had opposed the suppression of heresy by force.[77] He knew from personal experience the price that had to be paid for the finding of truth.[78] Was it not he who once, in somewhat different circumstances, uttered that profound saying that only wicked men make war upon the wicked?[79] His tone towards the schismatics was always definite and firm but also always courteous. Even in matters of litigation he was always the bishop. In the year 401, the counter-bishop of Calama, Crispinus, who had not even suspended the organizer of the assault on Possidius, was held responsible for this disgraceful business. He was accused, summoned before the Proconsul, and after a public debate with Possidius formally convicted of heresy. On the strength of Theodosius' law, which now for once was carried into effect, he had a fine of ten pounds in gold imposed on him. Hereupon Possidius, Augustine and his colleagues asked the Proconsul to reduce this sum, to which the Proconsul agreed, and though Crispinus forfeited this relief by appealing his case to the Emperor, his opponents had nevertheless given proof that even when dealing with a schismatic and before a judge they could be true bishops.[80]

Augustine desired persuasion; he did not wish for force. In his writings over a long period he defended two principles, first that error as such could not claim toleration, but, second, that no man must be forced into the Faith against his will. Service to demons must be extirpated and forbidden, but laws against heresy and schism should be no more than warnings. It was only the excesses of the Circumcellions and the palpably malicious intentions of the Donatist leaders that induced this essentially mild man to become a supporter of the laws in question, to demand their application (though this was to be tempered by moderation), and finally, when he could actually point to a number of excellent results, to approve the compulsory imposition of the Faith as the lesser evil.

As early as 411 the laws of Honorius occasioned the remark that "the Lord has broken the teeth of the lion",[81] and that now there would be an end to the lion's boldness. After that date Augustine becomes capable of speaking in glowing terms of the Emperor's right in this matter. And who was it, he began to ask, who had first demanded the application of the law against schismatics? It was the Donatists, who at the Council of Bagai had invoked the laws against the Maximianists. So what had they to complain of? They had suffered the fate of Daniel's accusers. The lions which they had set on others had turned on them.[82]

So it is not the radical Optatus of Milevis, but Augustine, who must be regarded as the true father of the Inquisition, the great reputation which for centuries Augustine enjoyed contributing no doubt to his influence in this respect. As to the soundness of his principles one may form one's own opinion;

but the manner in which he applied them, indeed his whole point of view, was thoroughly dangerous.[83]

Yet to the very end he never incited officials towards severity; rather, he urged moderation. Never did he join with Optatus of Milevis in falling back on the zealots of the Old Testament and defending the death penalty in matters of religion. That went too far. He was horrified by the idea of a Church that shed blood. Rather should bishops, in case of capital offences, always make use of the right of intervention. This he did himself even on behalf of the men who had murdered Restitutus, one of his own priests, because, so he wrote to the Proconsul Apringius, one must always leave the enemies of the Church time for repentance.[84] Killing heretics was a horrible thing. Their blood would dishonour the martyrdom of the true servants of God.[85] No death penalty, he wrote to the Proconsul Donatus, and begged him for the sake of Christ not to neglect mildness or fail to recognize what the Church's attitude was in this matter, otherwise churchmen could never accuse anybody before him, though no-one but these had the right to bring such accusations.[86] In a letter to Count Boniface, in which he develops in its complete form his theory concerning the suppression of erroneous doctrines, he defends this point of view with great force.[87] On another occasion he wrote to his friend Marcellinus that he, personally, wished to see no other instruments used during a judicial examination than those used by schoolmasters and parents—in other words, the rod and the whip but not the rack, pincers ("ploughing nails") or fire, and he praised him because when hearing a case concerning the murder of a priest, he had confined himself to rods. He wrote in a similar sense to Marcellinus' brother, the Proconsul.[88]

Yet Augustine did not live in the eighteenth century. He did not smile when the truth was at stake. Also, he did not believe that mankind could be educated without punishments, and so he came to take a more positive view of force in the service of morality. The forcible reunion proved to be a success when it was completed. To everybody's surprise it turned out that there were thousands of Donatists who were Donatists merely from habit and who felt it as a relief when they no longer had to maintain the rigid and unyielding attitudes of their sect. What did they know of the great quarrel? Their grandparents had been rebaptized, they knew nothing of any other religion and saw no point in arguing about such things. They sang the same alleluias, heard the same Gospel, celebrated the same Easter, believed in the same Christ, and despite this, one man went to one church and one to another. Nobody saw any way out. Their ancestors were to blame for it all.[89] That was what many thought—and their thinking never got any further. They were like snakes biting their own tails. And so Augustine began to meditate on the *compelle intrare* of the Gospel.[90] How could one deal with this ossified attitude except by seizing hold of the people? We must not worry, he had preached in the past, if we are inconvenient. Ice must not be melted, it must be broken, and boys often cry when they have to go to school. People will say, "The Apostles forced nobody." That was true; they were fishermen. They threw their nets out upon the high seas and were content with what they caught. But after he sent the fishermen God sent the hunters, as the prophet Jeremiah prophesied, and "these hunters are ourselves, our duty being to beat up souls from the undergrowth of those great heretical mountains named Arius and Photinus and Donatus".[91]

Going in and taking hold of them was the only way of dealing with the bands of fanatics. They were men sick of a fever, who attacked their physicians in their delirium. Half of them were apparently dead, sick with a sleeping sickness, the other half were madmen. These last were wild and difficult to handle. The others were merely lazy and would not wake up properly. They said, "So it is, Lord, so it is, and there is nothing to be done about it. My father died in such a place in the Donatist faith and my mother, another Donatist, is buried in such another." "Then I say to that man, 'But you aren't dead and buried yet. You're alive. Your parents were Christians of the Donatist persuasion. Their parents were perhaps Christians too, but their grandparents and great-grandparents were most certainly pagans—why then are you not a pagan?' "[92]

The overwhelming majority were now having their eyes opened, he declares, and only a small remainder are still obstinate. That justifies people in using force. Banishment was the usual punishment. Then they could see the extensiveness of that Catholic Church which at home they preferred to combat rather than try to get to know it.[93] As to the confiscations, everybody looked on the right of property, where immovables like basilicas and Church lands were concerned, as standing under the protection of the laws of the Empire, which bound men in conscience, provided, of course, it did not command them to do wrong. The State's function was to ensure law and order, and the Emperor was lord in the temporal sphere. They should thank God that the Emperor supported the Church in its difficult task, for he was the only one capable of doing so effectively, and though the bishops might say nothing of the matter, he showed that he understood his duties very well when he listened attentively to readings in church from the holy books and heard how Hezekiah and Josiah had the high places removed, how Darius had the idols destroyed and the King of Nineveh decreed a penance.[94]

That, roughly, was Augustine's line of thought. He also said that tolerance was the normal principle on which a bishop should act, but that sometimes force became unavoidable, for though the best kind of men were drawn by love, yet the majority needed fear to move them.[95]

It was not his fault if, in addition to his preaching, legal sanctions proved to be necessary, for nobody ever brought greater selflessness or greater gentleness to the task of reunion than did he. He refused to speak of honest folk who happened to have been born Donatists as "heretics".[96] He resolutely defended the view that priests who had not been rebaptized could continue under certain conditions to exercise their office and even conduct special worship for their own congregations when these had returned in a body to the fold.[97] He pressed the converted lawyer, Castorius, a particularly gifted man, to take over the office of his brother, a Donatist bishop, who had considerately retired in order to avoid personal rivalries.[98] (Incidentally, the speech of thanks which a former Donatist priest made in one of his churches seems, to judge by the style, to have been dictated by himself.[99]) He valued those who returned no less highly than those who had always remained faithful, and was only too ready to recognize that many had come over to him at great cost to themselves. He himself composed the epitaph for the deacon Nabor, who after his return to the Church was murdered by his sometime fellow-sectarians. This epitaph is full of allusions to the contrast between true martyrdom and the sham martyrdom of so many Donatists. In the Latin it is an acrostic, with the first letter of each line spelling out the word *Diaconus*.

> Here lie at rest the remains of one whom piety praises.
> Nabor the name of the man, whom Donatists cruelly murdered.
> Long did he live with them. Then to the one true Church of the Founder
> Turned he, seeking oneness of mind and oneness of doctrine.
> Now he is wrapped in the purple of blood. Most faithfully served he,
> Seeker of holy things. No death here born out of madness,
> This was no murder of self. True martyrdom here thou beholdest.
> Read each line's first letter to learn of the office he served in.[100]

The sheep that were secure in their pens in Hippo he left behind, and despite his grey hairs went searching for those that were lost. He was not afraid and refused an escort of soldiers. Friendly to all and fearful of none, he rode through Numidia, as once St. Francis of Sales was to ride through Savoy, and on one occasion through the astonished city of Geneva. He preached in numerous cities, both great and small. After the popular religious exercises which he instituted in Cirta and Carthage, he could quite truthfully speak of mass conversions. They wrote to him from Cirta, the capital of Numidia, that only his mild bearing and patient exposition of the truth had produced these results—much as the drunkard Polemo had given up drinking when, during a drunken fit, he had heard Xenocrates expound the virtue of moderation.[101] He found among such people much ignorance of the true nature of the Church, but little actual hatred, and he also found that in so far as they could be said to have made an actual act of choice, this was influenced by human rather than by theological considerations. Certainly Augustine's personal and deep devotion to the Church proved at least as infectious as did the fear of the Emperor's *executores*.

True, that Augustine on occasion did not mince his words. Those who still continued to make outcry about the interference by the secular power were mercilessly reminded that they themselves had invoked that power against the Maximianists, which only shows that this mildest of men could be brutally frank when occasion demanded. When the Donatists began to spread a story around that Marcellinus had been bribed, or at any rate that, being a Catholic himself, he had been biased, and also that they had not had full freedom of speech and that the whole conference had been a put-up job, the synod sent a stinging letter to the Donatist leaders, in which the statements were completely refuted. Augustine was the author of that letter.[102]

Incidentally, in the "zealous churches" of Carthage, Tagaste, Constantine and Hippo, the bishops ordered the complete minutes of the conference to be read out at Mass during Lent.[103] Since, however, these were much too long and since far too much of their space was taken up by the records of the obstructive manoeuvres of the Donatists, Augustine composed a short but extremely effective summary, the so-called *Breviculus Collationis*, which made excellent reading from the pulpit. He followed this up with a very bold pamphlet, *To the Donatists after the Conference*, which was far from flattering to its addressees. "Away then, with *pars Donati*", he says in this latter work, "away with the sect that has so often been condemned, which has spread so many slanders and such outrageous lies, which has been so often refuted and which has proved its inability to defend its arguments and has in so many respects been utterly put to shame. Let them by all means seek to attract attention and make themselves important with their stories of bribed judges—as though a defeated party ever failed to come out with a yarn of that kind!"

As to the crowds whom the Donatists had led astray, he would ask them why they still listened to men who had been so plainly defeated. Let them mark the lies of their leaders, when these said that the conference only ended at dead of night, that they dared not leave the hall and had been threatened with death. How often had they themselves said that if only both parties could meet and discuss things, truth would come to light. Well, that was precisely what had happened.[104]

Yet he spoke more of the Church than he did of the schism, and showed that he thought love a better theme than hatred. Certainly his mind moved along very similar lines to that of another great reconciler, St. Francis of Sales. He who speaks of love is by that very act speaking against heresy, even though he may never name that subject. Surely it was with a clear conscience that he read in the Psalms, "With them that hated peace I was peaceable, when I spoke to them they fought against me without cause."[105]

Yet he could not win everybody. Many of his old enemies remained embittered against him. When in the year 420 the energetic commissioner Dulcitius came to Numidia to liquidate the last vestiges of schism in what had been its principal breeding-ground, and threatened those who refused to hand over their churches with exile and even with death, Bishop Gaudentius of Thamugadi, Optatus's successor and one of the speakers at the conference, shut himself up in his basilica with the remainder of his faithful and wrote to him that if the church was seized he would set fire to it and perish in the flames with all his flock.[106] Dulcitius was alarmed and gave way. He wrote back saying that none wished the bishop's death, and asked as a personal favour that he should flee. He then sent Gaudentius' letters to Augustine. The latter replied, "Your Excellency has no right of life and death, and you should not have threatened this man with death. I congratulate you, however, on the moderation you displayed, which is good for the prestige of the Church. And though we are very busy and have refuted such idle chatter in previous writings and made innumerable concessions, pointing out that it is not the fact of being killed but the cause which makes the martyr, I will myself deal with the letters of Gaudentius if you think this is in the interests of the people of Thamugadi"[107]—for Gaudentius had himself in the meantime written to Augustine in a rather desultory fashion.

Gaudentius' letters to Dulcitius, however, were excellently conceived and contained sharp attacks, saying that the Church was only man-made and that peace with blood was not peace at all, that Christ had sent forth prophets and not kings,[108] apostles, but not soldiers. In reply Augustine reminded him of what the Donatists had themselves done against the Maximianists and asked him whether he himself had given heed to the Prophets and the Apostles.[108] Augustine's reply takes up a whole book, in which the accusations made by Gaudentius are patiently refuted point for point. It must, however, be admitted that Gaudentius carried on the controversy with equal calmness, and that his letters do not in any way suggest a man who proposed to burn down a church with himself inside it. It does appear, however, from certain of Augustine's allusions, that some of the Donatist bishops had actually preferred death by fire to the peace of the Catholic Church, and had not waited for Gaudentius to set them an example.[109]

It chanced that in the year 419 in distant Caesarea in Mauretania, Augustine encountered the sometime Donatist bishop, Emeritus. He greeted him, started a conversation with him and by his ingratiating manner persuaded him to enter the church, where a number of Augustine's fellow-bishops were waiting for him among a large number of Christians of both persuasions, including many Donatists who had returned to the Church. The upshot of the affair was somewhat of a disappointment for him, for after Augustine had held forth on the question of the day, he asked Emeritus to speak and say freely what was in his mind. Emeritus concurred, but barely spoke ten words, and when the speaker of the moment suddenly asked him in the middle of his discourse and right there in that crowded church, whether, having been a witness to the event, he would now declare who had won the victory in Carthage, he merely replied that the minutes showed whether he had gained the victory or been defeated, and whether he had declared himself conquered by the truth or had yielded to force. Augustine: "Why did you come here?" Emeritus: "To do what you wanted me to do." Augustine: "I asked you why you came here. If you had not come here I should not have had occasion to put such a question." Hereupon Emeritus said to the shorthand writer, "Put that down." Augustine: "You did not come here without a reason, but if you keep silence under the pressure of truth, then your motive in coming here was to make a false pretence to those present." Long silence, whereafter Emeritus continued to listen to the sermon "like one dumb" and thereafter to the reading by Alypius of certain official documents. Finally came words from Augustine himself. "Let us pray for him. How can we know the intentions of God? For it is written, 'There are many thoughts in the heart of a man, but the will of the Lord shall stand firm.'" However, Emeritus did not again open his lips.[110]

Twenty years after the end had come, when the Vandals were falling upon the triumphant Church and, like wild beasts, were tearing it to pieces, it was made manifest that there were in Africa many men who had thus kept silence, but who now were enabled once more to rear their Donatist heads and proclaim the old catchwords; for we hear of Donatists right down into post-Byzantine times. Even so, the sect was virtually reduced to impotence in 411. Augustine had helped truth to victory, and the State compelled men to recognize that truth. Thirty-five years later Quodvultdeus was to write from Carthage, "The adder is trodden underfoot. The brazen serpent on the cross has eaten the serpent of heresy, even as Moses' staff consumed the serpents of the sorcerers."[111]

Today we can no longer form a true picture of the fanaticism of this struggle. There was very little humour in it. When a thousand years later the deadly earnest of Port-Royal produced within the Church a new secret *pars Donati*, and one marked with all the peculiar distinction that marks old French Catholicism, its younger members would gleefully drown little Jesuit dolls in the pond of the monastery garden, while adults could find pleasure in the biting satire of the *Lettres provinciales*. The records of Donatism, however, can show us nothing but solemn and sanguinary stupidity over which shines, like a solitary sun, the luminous intelligence of Augustine and his glowing heart, that heart whose warmth was so vainly shed upon these men.

The Donatists in Hippo

We have had a general overall view of the development of Donatism, and there can be no doubt of the leading part that Augustine played in this affair. All that, however, belongs to the history of Augustine the Father of the Church. What we are interested in is the work in the little town of Hippo of Augustine the pastor of souls.

When he came there, the diocese was predominantly Donatist. In the town itself the schismatics were in the majority, and a very oppressive and tyrannous majority they were, nor was the heresy by any means confined to the lower orders. In the country things were as bad as in the towns. In Siniti there was a Donatist bishop, and the life of the Catholics was about as pleasant as it has been for them within recent times in Ulster. The little locality of Fussala had not a single Catholic, nor had the village of Thiava, and several of the richest landowners belonged to the sect.[112] Relations with Catholics had long been bad. Intercourse with pagans could be pleasant enough, but any kind of religious contact with the Donatists was quite impossible. Simple folk could enjoy the festivals together, could chat with those of a different persuasion from their own and even marry them, but it never occurred to them to discuss matters of religion with them.

Shortly before the reign of Julian the Apostate, Faustinus, the schismatic Bishop of Hippo, had strictly forbidden his people to bake bread for Catholics. We know of the case of a baker who was lodging with a Catholic deacon and refused to put his landlord's bread in the oven.[113] The silent hatred was so great that the faithful merely smiled when two deacons who had come over from the Donatists lapsed after a time back into heresy.[114] Many came over to the Church when they thought there was something to be gained by it, and then, when their expectations were disappointed, promptly returned to the Donatists "just as chaff which whirls up from the threshing floor is sometimes caught on a thorn bush and is then blown back again by the next puff of wind". Yet these, so said Augustine, suffer the same fate as the chaff; they will be thrown into the everlasting fire.[115]

As they nearly always do, the Catholics boasted of their converts and abused all those who lapsed, and lapses undoubtedly occurred. Short-tempered people who had been rebuked by a priest believed they could get their revenge by changing their religion. A young coxcomb who beat his mother and threatened her with death received a warning from Augustine and immediately went over to the schismatics, and, "still lusting after the blood of his mother", could be seen standing in his white garments within the *cancelli* for all to see.[116] A subdeacon from the country who had been shut out of a nunnery joined the Circumcellions, together with two nuns, who, like himself, were *coloni* on an estate, and doubtless all gave themselves over to the drunkenness and promiscuity which were characteristic of that body.[117] Though a certain amount of mutual spying went on, neither of the two parties knew much about the other. Watchmen were posted at all the doors of the Donatist churches, who asked unknown visitors whether they were Catholic, and if they said they were, forbade their entry. As against this, the Catholics were only too pleased if those of a different persuasion came to listen to their services, even if they came with the intention of denouncing them afterwards or made fun of the sermon after leaving the church.[118]

Even so, it is rare for us to hear of actual clashes. On one occasion the bishop complains that a Catholic lady living on a country estate was insulted by a Donatist priest and called a traitor and a persecutor of the Church, but this seems to have been an isolated case. Moreover, the priest was angry because a hysterical country girl (*corruptae mentis*) who had wanted to take the veil with the schismatics, despite the fact that she was a Catholic catechumen, had in consequence received a thrashing from her father. Augustine not only put an end to the beating but also was able, like David of old, to prevent the faithful from dealing summarily with this new Shimei.[119]

There was, further, the problem of mixed marriages. Augustine spoke sometimes of the unnatural division in those families "where husband and wife are one when they rise from their bed, but are no longer one when they approach the altar", who "make a union of their bodies and swear faith to one another by Christ and yet tear Christ's body asunder by the difference of their religious professions", who "live in one house and eat together but who cannot sit together at the Lord's table". He spoke of children born of a single couple who went to different churches.[120]

Later, after the compulsory reunion, Augustine was to be horrified by the questions which were put to him by large numbers of the more simple-minded among the faithful. Was it lawful to give out that you were a Donatist so that you could spy among them? Was it lawful for a wife to commit adultery with a Donatist in order to get from him the names of other heretics? For the most part, however, Catholics and Donatists managed to live peaceably side by side.

When Augustine first preached at Hippo as a young priest in 391, his schismatic colleagues looked askance at him because heretics came to hear him preach quite as frequently as did his own parishioners, so that there was always a mixed congregation in the great church.[121] It was vain for the clergy just down the road in the Church of the Saints to issue warnings and say, "What business have such people here? What do they want with us? Let them stay with the Catholics, since they are so fond of them—but nobody should speak to them, nobody should visit them and nobody should listen to what they say."

"Yes", said Augustine in his sermon, "that is what they say. They are like the deaf adders of the psalm, they stop their ears so that they may not hear the voice of the sorcerer."[122] The sometime professional orator spoke with so much distinction that after he had been in Hippo some eighteen months adherents of both parties made a joint request that he should attack the theosophist who was conducting the Manichean community, a task which he undertook with considerable success.[123]

Yet Augustine did not rest till he could carry his attack right into the ranks of the heavily entrenched Donatist clergy. In the following year, 392, he wrote in the name of the absent Valerius a long letter to his "dearly beloved master and honoured brother Maximinus", the Donatist Bishop of Siniti, which was just within the diocese of Hippo, for he had heard that the latter had re-baptized the Catholic deacon of the village of Mutugenna, "as though he were a heathen", and received him into his clergy. "I was disappointed," he wrote, "for I had been told that you would never do such a thing, and I could not believe that you were behind it. Yet now I have visited the village, and find that the young man has disappeared, and have heard from his heartbroken parents that he has 'gone over to the others'. Has he indeed been rebaptized? I beg of you to let me know forthwith what has happened to him. I will have your answer read out in my church. I prefer to write to you about this personally rather than that you should learn of my feelings from common friends. If you respect Catholic baptisms, we could have a talk together and no doubt there would soon be peace between us. Could we not have a conference in the presence of the faithful and really speak our minds—I would gladly wait till the soldiers have left the town? We could then talk things over in a cool, detached and sensible manner, and basing our arguments on Holy Scripture, have a proper exchange of ideas."[124] That, unfortunately, is the last we know of this particular affair. Perhaps Maximinus was called to order by his colleagues. Fifteen years later he became a Catholic.[125]

Augustine did not neglect to protect his people from the insidious effect of Donatist catchwords, and sometimes did so to the detriment of good artistic taste. It was probably as early as 393 that he composed an alphabetical psalm against the *pars Donati* for the more unlettered among his followers. This tells in very simple verses the story of the origin and development of the schism, its malice and the only possible cure for it. As an introduction he used the metaphor, drawn from the Gospel, of the torn net, which represents the Church, from which the fish only too gladly slip away.[126] It is a sort of ballad, of very slender literary merit, an interminable didactic poem of 293 verses arranged in twenty strophes of twelve lines each, and the first word of every strophe begins with a different letter of the alphabet, the letters going from A to U. The poem starts with a *prooemium* and ends with a *prosopopoiea* of

5 Apse (Tebessa)

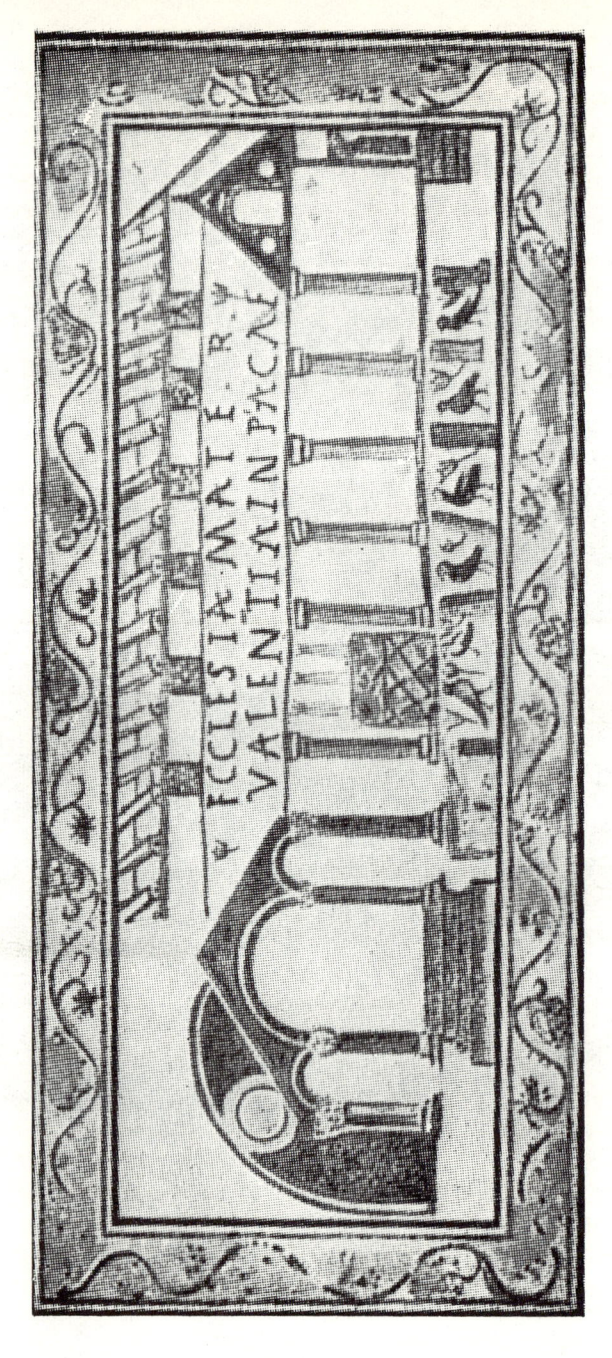

6 Mosaic from Tabraca

the Catholic Church. The verses, which all end either with a short *e* or with an *-ae*, probably for melodic reasons, are marked by a certain amount of alliteration, and consist of two trochaic tetrameters separated by a caesura. This was a type of verse form with which ordinary folk at this time were well acquainted—particularly since it was common in the *cantica* of the theatre and the cabaret. In Augustine's verses the *ictus* or stress has taken the place of the quantities which had once governed classical versification. Thus, apart from the quasi-poetry of Commodianus, these verses are the oldest example we have of rhythmic Latin folk poetry.

More important, however, than any question of literary form is the insight which we can gain here into Augustine's pastoral and didactic methods. His practice was to have the strophe sung by a soloist, at the end of which the congregation would chime in with the refrain or *hypopsalma*, which was written in the same metre as the rest. Augustine has himself revealed his intentions to us. He wanted the nature of the Donatist issue brought to the knowledge of the simplest person and thus to stamp it into the memory even of the most uneducated. He tells us that he deliberately kept away from the classic forms of prosody because observance of the rules of quantity would have compelled him to employ words which ordinary people were not accustomed to use.[127] The idea was not entirely his own, however. His didactic poem was also meant to refute the fiery hymns of Parmenianus, the schismatic Primate of Carthage, hymns which had become the popular battle-songs of the Donatists. Rightly or wrongly, it has been alleged that Augustine not only took his trochaic metre from the theatre, but also used the melody of a profane popular song.[128] So it came about that the delicate-minded author of the *Soliloquies* did not scruple to descend to the doggerel of a music-hall ditty. It is perhaps unfortunate that he stuck to Latin, for many Punic-speaking peasants thus remained outside effective range.

A few verses from the song may be quoted here to show the kind of thing it was.

Refrain

Unity's triumphant children   test the soundness of your doctrine.

Prooemium

Hateful 'tis to judge the evil   if regard you have for creatures,
Yet the wicked ne'er, 'tis certain,   can possess the heavenly Kingdom.
If you tear another's garments   none will bear this unprotesting,
Much the greater guilt your portion   if Christ's seamless robe you sunder.
Who then did the thing so sinful?   Let us closely mark the story.

Unity's triumphant children   prove the soundness of your doctrine.

First Strophe

Oh, the surfeit of the wicked   greatly doth confirm the brethren.
'Tis for this, most sure, the Master   stoutly sought to gird and arm us.
He compared the realm of heaven   to a net cast on the ocean,
Gathering fishes in abundance   fish of every kind and colour.
When the fishermen have landed   then the motley catch is sorted,
Into barrels—that's the good ones   back the bad go in the ocean.
Whoso truly knows the Gospel   let him learn (and let him tremble)
By the net the Church is shown him   'Tis the world that is the ocean,
And the mingling of the fishes?   Mingled thus are good and evil.
And the strand? That is the Judgement   when will come the dreadful sifting.
Those who wickedly the net tore   loved this "ocean" all too greatly.
Never will they see the barrels   these denote the blessed mansions.

Unity's triumphant children   test the soundness of your doctrine.

Second Strophe

You that listen well may ask us   who it was that tore the net thus.
Proud they are, as proud as Satan   and they tell us they are holy.
These the men that did the rending   setting altar against altar
Fighting for the "great tradition"   trading thus their souls to Satan,
And the crimes that they committed   they would put on others' shoulders,
For 'twas they that sold the Scriptures   though they name ourselves as
   guilty.[129]

Few people will look upon this strange composition as a masterpiece, for it may safely be said that the original is quite as bad a piece of doggerel as the translation. But one must judge the thing on its own level, and taken in this way it is at least a clear indication that Augustine had left his ivory tower for ever. It is, further, the only genuine "penny-plain-tuppence-coloured" picture of Donatism. We have here the contemporary slogans in all their crudity, for despite its admirably logical design, the song only abandons at its very end the naïve tone with which it opens. It tells us first of the origin of the evil, of the election of Majorinus, of the failure of the judges overseas to get their judgement implemented (the words *causa finita est*, which were later to become so celebrated, turn up here for the first time), it tells us also how, more or less as an act of revenge for their lost lawsuit, the Donatists began the business of rebaptizing. Then follow the strophes about the inevitable presence of sinners in the Church. Was not Judas one of the Apostles? Did not the Lord compare his Church to a net full of different kinds of fish? Then comes the question of the validity of the sacraments. If the unworthiness of a priest invalidates baptism, why do the Donatists not have members of their own sect rebaptized?—for these may have been baptized by one who had offended while already in their own ranks. These then, the song continues, are the essential points of our quarrel. Do not, therefore, come to us with your old reproach about the *tempora Macariana* and the acts of retribution by Macarius and Paulus.

> Nay, but if such men were cruel   we ourselves would disavow them.
> Yet if slanders be your stories   God himself will judge the matter.[130]

We admit, says the song, that even with us there is much chaff among the wheat. Has not John the Baptist said that the Lord will cleanse his threshing floor? And has not the Lord himself said that the Church is a field full of tares? And must we remind you of the Circumcellions?[131] Is then the chaff amongst us a reason for cutting yourselves away from the field which is the Catholic Church?

Augustine goes on to say, as Optatus of Milevis had said before him, that the Catholic Church is a vine. Woe betide him who cuts himself away from its root! Even if the severed branch looks fair, its life is only an illusion, a seeming life.

> What avails the seeming beauty   if the branch from root be severed?
> Welcome, brothers, if your wish be   with the vine to be united,
> For the sight of you before us   lying severed, moves our pity.[132]

And again like his predecessor Optatus, he points to the unity with the chair of Peter as the essential characteristic of the living Church. There is the rock, made visible in the succession of Roman bishops, which links the present bishop with Linus and Peter, and so with the Lord.

> Count the bishops in succession   sitting on the chair of Peter
> In the sequence of the Fathers   one doth follow on another.
> Here the Rock is and hell's portals   never shall prevail against it.[133]

Augustine does not fail to show to what impossible positions the insistence on purity must lead. When you meet somebody, he says, filled with the faith of those old Roman bishops, he will say to you, "Brother, why do you wish to baptize me afresh? I am a believing Christian; what may have happened in the past is forgotten, nor do I know what it is that may possibly render me defiled, nor can I tell by looking at you whether you are yourself defiled or no. I do not know what goes on in your heart, but if that which I do not know of myself may defile me, then you might very well defile me yourself. Even if I look upon you as undefiled, I have only to look on those with whom you associate and ask whether all these are not defiled by secret sins. Indeed, are you yourself really free of them? And if you say that what I do not know will not harm me, then I am not going to worry about what has been done by myself in the past." And yet he says, you would have the effrontery to rebaptize even such a man as this![134] Woe to you who fight with such dishonest weapons for the cause of your *cathedrae,* you who make such an uproar about being the only true holy ones even though your hearts must speak quite differently, for you know well enough what worthless fellows there are among you. Moreover, you cannot say, as we can, that good and bad are mixed up in the net. Indeed, you yourselves have torn that net in twain. Nor can you say that one must put up with the chaff among the wheat, for then we would reply that you might have thought of that in years gone by, for your Catholic brethren were certainly no worse than Judas, with whom the Apostles shared their evening meal, though they knew what he was guilty of. These men were not defiled by the foulness in other men's hearts, and yet you have the effrontery to baptize your Christian brethren afresh.[135]

After this unsparing onslaught, he suddenly lets Mother Church put in an appearance.

Yet when Mother Church attempts to   speak to you of peace and concord,
Cries to you "My sons, what have you   what, my sons, against your Mother?
Say, why fled you from my keeping   why forsook me? Grant me answer.
Crimes you charge against your brothers   'Tis by that I'm cleft asunder.
When the pagan heel was on me   great was then your Mother's anguish.
Many a child of mine deserted   left me, but 'twas fear that drove them,
Fear'd you aught? Nay, none oppressed you   nor constrained you to rebellion.
Still you're mine, you say, yet know you   that's a word that has no substance,
For *Catholica* my name is   Yours, it seems, is *pars Donati.*
'Twas the Apostle that enjoined me   e'er to pray for this world's princes.
Prayer was answered, yet you rage that   faith in Christ, profess the princes.
Strange indeed a child should rage so   when a Mother's prayer is answered.
When the princes brought me gifts then   you would nought of them, you spurned them,
And in this forgot the Prophets   who foretold it, aye, and clearly,
That the princes of the peoples   would to Mother Church their gifts bring.
By rejecting them you showed men   that the Church was not among you.
Thus coerced, Macarius acted   more in sorrow than in anger.
Tell me when I harmed you, where in   all the world you suffered by me,
Where't may be I thrust the sinner   out from me, and where't may not be.
Suffer him until he's healed of   evil or is brought to judgement.

> Tell me, tell me, why you left me   in your own death crucified me?
> If your hatred such for sinners   why then suffer them amongst you?
> Yet if sinners you can suffer   be at one with us, so suff'ring,
> For we know no second baptism   nor set altar against altar.
> Now ye suffer many sinners   and your suffering's rewardless.
> What you owe to Christ, you pay it   not to Christ but to Donatus."

The poem closes with the lines:

> Oh, if you had ears to hear us   unity's the theme we sing you.
> Soon or late One comes to judge us   take we heed of his demanding.[136]

As soon as Augustine had been made a bishop, and so could claim equal status with the schismatic hierarchy, he made haste to get in touch with his opposite number among the Hippo Donatists. The latter, who was named Proculeianus, had already told a layman who was a friend of both bishops that he was not averse to a conference with Augustine, if this could be held in the presence of some reputable citizens. Augustine wrote a most friendly and, indeed, moving letter "to his honourable and beloved master Proculeianus". In this he offered to let the latter select his own witnesses, but if he preferred it, he was, Augustine said, prepared to start the debate by correspondence or as a purely private conversation.[137] Proculeianus answered that he preferred a conference, on the understanding that the whole discussion should turn on Holy Scripture. Also he suggested that the conference might take place in connection with a synod of his Church at Milevis, where Proculeianus hoped to find more eloquent partners. Augustine, in reply, suggested that he himself should be represented by Bishop Samsucius of Turris, a speaker whom Proculeianus had no cause to fear, since Samsucius had never learned the art of impromptu speaking. In the same letter he reproached him with the rebaptism of that degraded son who had sworn to his mother that he would join the Donatists and that he would afterwards drink her blood. If they approved of that kind of thing, the man's "sanctifiers" might as well get him to carry out the second part of his vow within the octave.[138] Proculeianus made no further reply, and let it be known that he wished to receive no more letters. Shortly afterwards, when one of Proculeianus' priests took part in a rebaptism —which technically constituted a criminal act of sacrilege—Augustine formally reported the matter and had the report filed at the town hall. He further sent Proculeianus a letter through a Government official who was a common friend, in which he requested Proculeianus to put an end to these practices and, if he was unwilling to do so, to make no complaint if an official report was filed. He refrained, however, from more drastic action, as he did not wish official pressure to be brought to bear in such a case.[139]

A few years later Augustine established friendly relations with a small group of earnest Donatists in the little town of Thubursicum. In due course these people came to speak of the proceedings of the synod of 322, the synod which had deposed Caecilianus because he had been consecrated by the "traitor" Felix of Aptunga. Augustine gave them the full facts about the Catholic synod which had refuted the dissidents and removed them from their office. Next day he made a two-day journey to another town in order to be able to show them a complete record of the proceedings. Later he summarized his arguments in a letter the leading idea of which—a very inspiring one—was that the Catholics' true documents were not a lot of old records, but the Church of God, which was spread over the whole world, a document which none can ever destroy.[140] It was probably under pressure from this small circle of friends that the aged Donatist bishop Fortunius agreed to a public discussion, which took place in his own house, Augustine being willing to make the journey thither out of respect for Fortunius' grey hairs. Unfortunately, the faithful anticipated that the thing would be a thoroughly sensational affair. They streamed to the bishop's house—so Augustine was later to tell—as though it had been a theatre— and nothing could make them keep quiet. Although it was quite impossible for them to follow the discussion, there was no end to their interruptions. Also the shorthand-writers suddenly refused to go on, and in the general uproar the Catholics, who declared themselves ready to take the shorthand-writers' places, completely failed to get any proper record down. Indeed, the little we know of this discussion comes from a letter which Augustine wrote from Hippo to these same friends at a somewhat later date. From this it appears that Fortunius, a very simple-minded old man, simply did not know what the whole thing was about. Thanks to a letter from the Arian Fathers of Sardica, he seems to have been under the impression that he was in communion with the Churches of the whole world. As against this, he was compelled to admit that a strict interpretation of his own professed views made it impossible for him to recognize even Ambrose as a true Christian. At last, lamenting the persecution to which his own Church was subject, he declared that he would be ready at some later date to join with nine other colleagues and meet an equal number of Catholic bishops in debate—a promise which in all probability was never kept.[141] Such was the fate of Augustine's generous offers. When the force of his argument began to tell upon his opponents they had a disconcerting habit of quietly withdrawing from the field. There was, for instance, the case of a certain Bishop Honoratus, who had proposed an exchange of views by letter. Augustine opened the debate in a positive tone by demonstrating that the Catholic Church alone could be held to fulfil the prophecies of universality.[142] Honoratus failed to reply. Again, it had long been reported that Crispinus, from neighbouring Calama, had been eager to cross swords with Augustine. The treatment meted out to the Maximianists provided Augustine with the occasion for writing to Crispinus and again applying the *argumentum ad hominem*[143]—but Crispinus, too, was silent. Shortly after this, Crispinus bought up the imperial estate of Mappalia, and some eighty wretched *coloni* were "plunged muttering and sighing into the depths"—were rebaptized, that is to say, against their will. Augustine wrote that he had no intention of causing a fine of ten pounds in gold to be imposed upon him, though such a fine was provided for by the law, for "we do not seek to inspire fear by any human agency, we leave that to Christ". He did, however, propose that they should each present his views to the peasants concerned through the mouth of a Punic interpreter and let them choose for themselves. A similar procedure might, Augustine said, be adopted where Crispinus' opponents had been guilty of coercion.[144] Again there was no reply.

And yet Augustine was not discouraged. He sent letters in every direction to acquaintances who, from mere force of habit, were living in schism or were in danger of being influenced by shallow talk, his own nephew[145] being among those so addressed. There was, for instance, the case of a certain Generosus. This man had been approached by a Donatist cleric from Cirta, who maintained that he had a commission from an angel to convert him. Augustine took the somewhat obvious course of referring to Gal. i.8: "But though we or an angel from heaven preach a gospel to you besides that which we have preached, let him be anathema." He also pointed to that very palpable proof of the identity of the true Church and of the Apostolic Succession, namely the list of the occupants of Peter's chair, the unbroken line going from Linus to Anastasius, thirty-six names in all.[146]

In this same period he wrote, in a quite different genre, the lengthy works attacking the internal contradictions of the Donatist's poorly thought out idea of the Church; the books in question are *Against the Letter of Parmenianus, Against the pars Donati, Baptism, Against the Letters of Petilianus, Against Cresconius, The Unity of the Church and the Donatists*.

What gives this strangely monotonous drone of controversy interest and life is the fact that through it all we are so vividly aware of a personality that is both witty and patient—the personality of Augustine, shepherd of souls. Who can remain unmoved as he reads in the book on baptism (Augustine's chief theoretical work), that passage in which he speaks of Cyprian; Cyprian, whose views were at variance with his own, Cyprian who was most certainly wrong, but who, despite all this, would not sever himself from the Church? Or that famous passage in which he says that the learned tend rather more frequently than others to be wrong in their doctrinal conclusions, so that ecclesiastical decisions very often violate their instincts? (This is all too true, and circumstances often arise in which only a humble love for the Church can prevent such men from treading the path of a Luther or a Döllinger.[147]) Surely, too, there is something out of the ordinary in that cheerful persistence with which Augustine, having given a certain answer three times to the ruffianly Petilianus of Cirta, was ready yet a fourth time to defend exactly the same truth against the schoolmaster Cresconius.

Petilianus, a sometime lawyer and now Bishop of Cirta, had referred to those baptized into the Catholic Church as "souls defiled by a bath of guilt, depraved souls more defiled than any filth". He spoke of their *cathedra* as a seat of plague, called their leaders forgers and simulators of the holy mysteries. He spoke of their eucharistic celebrations as a sacrifice to the gallows and of their faithful as heathen.[148] As to Augustine, Petilianus did not scruple to attack his personal character, a relatively easy thing to do, since the *Confessions* were there for the whole world to read. Petilianus threw Augustine's past in his face, called him a priest of the Manichees and a smuggler of magic charms, and asserted that his consecrator had suspected him of immorality and that he was, in point of fact, an adulterer and—worst infamy of all—a master of the insidious arts of rhetoric and dialectics.[149] Augustine replied that even if he were personally utterly put to shame, and that by one who because he has been an advocate calls himself a paraclete, his cause would still triumph, for Catholics do not draw their strength from frail human creatures but from the Church, from the sacraments, which come from God, and not from their ministers. He was used to slander, he claimed, he had even been accused of burning the Sacred Books—and in this manner Augustine very quietly catalogued from his *cathedra* the various charges made against himself, without even troubling to rebut them.[150]

In Carthage his bearing was much the same. There on one occasion, citing actual records, Augustine showed that an inner necessity compelled schism ever to breed further schism.[151] The sermon was widely discussed and roused the fury of his enemies. Again his past was thrown in his face, but this merely produced the comment in his next sermon that his enemies were compelled to attack his person because they could do nothing against his cause. "They speak of many things of which they do not know, and of many others of which they know only too well, yet these last are things that belong to my past and which I have dealt with much more drastically than my critics have ever dealt with their own errors, for I have put them behind me and utterly broken with them." He then advised his hearers that, if the subject of his personal character came up again, they should say quite simply, "Augustine is a bishop of the Catholic Church. He carries his own burden and will one day have to render to God an account of it. I know that he clings to the company of the good. If he is himself evil, he will know it; yet even if he is good, it is not to him that I cling, for in the Catholic Church I have learned, above all things, never to make man the foundation of my trust."[152]

When in Hippo, or elsewhere, the invitation to a debate which had again been duly recorded at the town hall was greeted with contemptuous silence, Augustine directed a final appeal, but not in his own name but in that of the Catholic Church, to certain reputable laymen who had shown themselves rather more approachable than their clerical fellow-sectarians. "To you, Donatists," his appeal began without any further introduction, "speaks the Catholic Church, saying, 'My friends, how long will your heart be a morass? Why do you pursue vanity and why do you seek after lies? Why do you remain cut off from the whole world?' "—and he closes his letter with the question "When the wolves refused to submit to cross-examination by the shepherds, why did the sheep not there and then decide to stop visiting the wolves in their lairs?"[153]—but it was all in vain.

In Hippo, too, the compulsory reunion brought a number of fresh problems in its train—as we can see even from Augustine's more casual references. He speaks, for instance, of "the newly-converted whom I must in no wise desert",[154] and warns against the slanderous tongues that were wagging on the subject of the transfers of Donatist Church property. "What such-and-such a man long ago bequeathed to Faustinus is being snapped up by Augustine"—that was the kind of whispered malice that was going the rounds—to which Augustine would reply that, as people knew well enough, these goods belonged neither to Augustine nor to Faustinus. They belonged to the Dove (the Church), and that both by divine right and by the law of the land—or was there some third kind of justice which could dispose differently of the matter?[155] In Hippo itself, the great basilica of the Donatists had, of course, been handed over to the Catholics, and Augustine had a little collection of documents affixed to the wall from which the justice of the transfer was apparent. These documents related to a number of civil and ecclesiastical suits but also contained selected Bible texts and a commentary by Augustine on the whole affair. Augustine had originally made it known to the Donatist congregation that he would be prepared to let them inspect all the documents concerned, and it was only when an anonymous pamphlet was circulated which attacked this whole plan that he had them exhibited in the manner described. "In this way", he tells us, "this work was published."[156]

Peace and concord were certainly not the universal fruits of this compulsory reunion, and indeed in the countryside that reunion was for a long time not even effective, for the rabble maintained the upper hand. When Maximinus (that Bishop of Siniti of whom mention has already been made) was reconciled to the Church while overseas, the Donatist bandits sent a crier into his village to proclaim that any persons who held to him would have their houses set on fire. A priest whom, shortly before Maximinus' return, Augustine had sent to Siniti to visit the few Catholics who lived there, was mishandled and chased away from the place, while the returning travellers, when they actually arrived, were welcomed with the greeting "Hands off our people, or you're done for!"

All manner of renegade scum found sanctuary with the "saints", but woe to the priests who returned to the Mother Church. They would be found upon the roads senseless and often even nigh to death. The priest Restitutus of the Villa Victoriana, who had already become a Catholic of his own free will, was dragged from his house, beaten, thrown into a marsh and then exhibited in a shirt of reeds, his release not being brought about till after some twelve hours, when Proculeianus intervened from fear of legal proceedings. Yet another village priest, Marcus, a convert, escaped with his bare life.[157]

In the year 406, Bishop Proculeianus died and was succeeded by Macrobius. Now, while Macrobius, himself a pleasant enough fellow, was making his entry into Hippo surrounded by a swarm of fanatical country priests, there suddenly appeared upon the scene, to the horror of the citizens, none other than the Circumcellions. These created so much disturbance that at Mass next day Macrobius, who at least believed in order, addressed them through a Punic interpreter and told them exactly what he thought of them. Furious at such ingratitude (had they not been the ones who had helped the party to gain its churches?[158]) the Circumcellions immediately left the basilica.

So this strange performance ended in a retreat, and so indeed the whole Donatist cause was soon to end, for however much Catholics might have been cowed during the anarchy that followed Stilicho's death, they could still fall back on public opinion and the law. However, a number of acts of revenge by the defeated faction somewhat marred the joy with which Catholics were filled in 411 through reunion with their separated brethren. Thus, acting under the leadership of one Donatus, a renegade deacon, some rump elements of the sect succeeded in waylaying a number of converts. In this way Restitutus, who has been already referred to, was finally trapped and killed on a remote estate. Another priest, Innocentius, lost a finger and an eye. The guilty persons were arrested, and it actually fell to Augustine to plead for their lives.[159]

Fear of the law now caused the large landowners round Hippo to close their little schismatic churches. Macrobius, however, was part incited and part compelled by his henchmen to try one last desperate throw. "Surrounded by a rabble of both sexes" (among whom were the murderers of Restitutus), he went in person from hamlet to hamlet, reopening one church after another. On the estate of one of the wealthiest owners he took advantage of the absence of the steward, a strict Catholic, to reorganize the churches and say Mass there.[160]

Despite these setbacks, Augustine unceasingly urged his faithful from the *cathedra* in no wise to abandon the work of reunion but to live in peace and amity with their difficult neighbours—and he himself carried this policy to the uttermost extremes. "There is news", he said on one occasion shortly after the conference. "One of our priests has had his tongue cut out by them. They are madmen. Yet we must love even such men as these."[161] Not that he could not strike a different note. When in the last days of 411 the murderers of Restitutus and the torturers of Innocentius (both priests and laymen) were condemned, he had the report of the proceedings read out in all the churches of his diocese. He felt it was most desirable that the ruffians in the villages should be informed about these things.[162]

Between the years 405 and 411, there had been hardly any respite from the disturbances which visited his diocese. He suffered cruelly under this. In 409 the barbarian atrocities in Spain moved him to write some comforting words to the Spanish priest, Victorianus. In this letter he remarks in passing, "We too have nothing but misery here, for instead of the barbarians we have the Circumcellions, and it is an open question which is the worse of the two. They murder and burn everywhere, throw lime and vinegar into the eyes of our priests; only yesterday I heard of forty-eight helpless persons who were compelled to submit to rebaptism in this place."[163]

The year 411, however, was the final turning-point, and a few years later peace reigned over the whole province. Now Augustine began the systematic reform of the country churches. Not that he had previously forgotten his poor Punic folk. When the famous senator Pammachius had succeeded, by means of his letters and the weight carried by his name, in getting the serfs on his estate to break in a body with Donatism, Augustine could not congratulate him too warmly. He was genuinely happy that even in distant Rome the great man could still give a thought to the poor wretches who were at the very heart of schism, and pressed him to move other landowners in the metropolis to do likewise.[164] He further urged the ex-proconsul Donatus, who had large estates in Africa, to follow Pammachius' example and apply it to his own estates in Hippo and Siniti,[165] while Festus, another great landowner, who had given his serfs written instructions to join the Catholic Church, was urged to take yet more effective action.[166]

The case of the millionaire Donatist, Celer, called for special treatment. He was the largest landowner in the diocese, and it was to him that the little churches which had been the object of Macrobius' intentions belonged. Also, Augustine had once lent him a book on the question of schism. Augustine now sent him his personal invitation to enter the unity of the Catholic Church.[167] We still possess the long, subtly eloquent letter which he wrote to yet another Donatus, the Donatist priest of the village of Mutugenna. This man had violently resisted the enthusiasts who had sought to drag him by force to the Catholic Church. When he was fetched he threw himself down from his mule and finally hurled himself into a river from which, fortunately, he was rescued by some clerics. What could Augustine do save raise this spiritually fallen man gently up and remind him of the words "...and if I give my body to be burned and have not charity...?"[168] In Thiava and Fussala—the latter till then had been entirely Donatist—he was at pains to nominate special Punic-speaking bishops, a small matter but nevertheless an index of his zeal for souls, and neither the unsatisfactory conduct of the young Bishop of Fussala nor a certain lack of prudence on Augustine's part can detract from the purity of Augustine's intentions. In the letter which he wrote to Pope Celestine, begging him not to send his recently converted Numidians, who had had so much to scandalize them, from the frying pan into the fire, we can detect a tenderness for souls that is quite unmistakable.[169]

No, this business of reunion was no easy matter, and the year 411 was on the whole a particularly bitter one for Augustine. To his friends in Tagaste he wrote that even those who appeared to love him were angry with him, that he was no longer equal to his task and was tired of life. He felt the "lust of death" in his heart, where "the savour of death can already be smelt before reason foresees it".[170] Some called him too venturesome, some too cautious and considerate. In either case men failed to see the holiness of his intentions. Even in his beloved Hippo men did not understand him, though Hippo now had a new face and Donatism had melted there like snow under the sun. Only a fraction of his faithful could really help him, for the faithful were far less tolerant than their large-minded bishop. When the stream of returning converts began to flow, "they were met by their brothers with mistrust and above all was this true of those *perfidi* whose falling-away Catholics had witnessed with their own eyes". In a sermon of this fateful year 411, Augustine bitterly reproached such men with working against the cause of reconciliation. Only a few days before that sermon was preached they had howled a rebaptized Donatist out of the Church, after he had publicly confessed his sins. "We must tell you, beloved," Augustine said in reference to this, "that our entrails are wrung by this. We must confess that zeal of this kind is displeasing to us. I know that you did what you did out of zeal for God. I know it and I do not doubt it. Yet you must also pay heed to the words of the Apostle when he complains of those 'who have a zeal of God but not according to knowledge'.[171] Think well of what you have done. Today this man is not admitted amongst you, tomorrow he may die. From whose hands will his soul be demanded? You say, 'He was a hypocrite.' I reply, 'But he asks to be received among you. I can prove that he asks to be received. Do you prove that he is a hypocrite!' My Christian friends, you must tell me very clearly how you know that he is a hypocrite. You say he is anxious about his employment—yes, truly we know that many are concerned about their business and in the past became Catholics for that reason. Then, when the pressure relaxed, many such men returned to the schismatics. Yet there were others who did not return. These last who did not return had also been anxious about their business, yes, up till the very day they came over to us, but after they had thus come over they learned something—and they remained. How do you know that this man is one of those who will one day be unmasked as a dissimulator? In particular, how can you be sure of it now, when the truth is shining out with all the clarity of the sun (for it did so at the Carthage conference) and error has been exposed in a manner utterly disastrous to itself? Have we toiled and expended ourselves for such folly as this? ... The Lord has helped us and now we are beginning to surmount many of our difficulties. It may well be that this man, whom we had at least brought to the point where he was ready to be one of us, did indeed have some less creditable motive than appears. But who are you to judge the heart? My Christian friends, be satisfied with what your eye beholds and concede that it does behold it, and leave what it cannot behold to God."[172]

Yet now, he continues, the thing had happened, and he was compelled to listen to foolish people saying that when the Donatists came over to the Church they were not received. That is why he wanted to put this matter right, clearly and publicly. He further pointed out that the man who had asked to be reconciled had certainly not acted under pressure, for all that was necessary in order to make a formal breach with the schismatics was for a man to inscribe his name with the Catholics as a penitent. Once he had done this he no longer had to fear the law; the actual penance could be postponed for as long as such a man pleased. It is interesting to note that on this occasion Augustine added a warning against the impression being created that penance could be dispensed with on the grounds that penance had already been done once on the occasion of a previous lapse into Donatism, and that to do it now would mean doing it twice over.[173] One can see from this how childishly this little people thought, how blind it was and how blind its leaders.

In his last years Augustine ceases altogether to mention Donatism, and when he died, nineteen years after the great conference, unhappy, beleaguered Hippo was at least united in the Faith.

Manicheans, Arians and Pelagians

There were still a number of wolves that required the shepherd of Hippo's attention. When as a young priest he first began to preach, he immediately came up against the Manicheans, a sect which over a period of nine years he had learned to know—and learned to fear. Manicheism, with its pseudo-scientific air, its puritanism, its somewhat nebulous cosmic dualism and its perverse denial of value to creation, had really very little in common with Christianity at all. There was a Manichean community in the town, at the head of which stood the renegade priest, Fortunatus, a pleasant enough person in himself, and certainly a busy one. About a year after Augustine's arrival in Hippo, the latter's fellow-priests had urged him to challenge this man to a debate, as did also certain Donatist laymen. Augustine met him at the Baths of Sossius and made things so impossible for him that he was forthwith compelled to leave the town.[174] Twelve years later, in 404, when he was already a bishop, Augustine was granted an even more satisfying experience, when he disputed publicly in the church with the *electus* Felix, a man who, compared with Fortunatus, was possibly "of inferior literary culture, but otherwise far better equipped". At the end of that disputation Augustine watched as Felix signed a declaration anathematizing Mani, and then received him into the Church.[175]

Till his last days Augustine did not desist from dealing most thoroughly with this strange heresy which damned flesh and blood and so treated Christ's human nature as accursed, which preached an esoteric doctrine of self-redemption out of darkness and really resolved itself into an abstruse gnosis, a terror of sex, and the practice of abstinence. There are a whole number of Augustine's books that deal with the subject.[176]

The bishop drew his faithful into this controversy along with himself. Thus when a disciple of Mani named Addas Adimantus had, in certain writings, raised the question of alleged contradictions in the Old Testament, Augustine dealt with the matter publicly from his *cathedra* before publishing his arguments in book form.[177] In the year 420 some zealous Carthaginian Christians brought him an anonymous codex which had been offered for sale on the quays of the harbour after public readings had been given from it which excited great interest. Augustine exposed the book as a disguised Marcionite attack on the story of creation, the Jewish laws, and indeed against the whole of the Old Testament, and refuted it in an essay of his own.[178] He dealt similarly with an Arian sermon reproduced in pamphlet form, which somebody had sent him.[179] Sometimes he had occasion to issue warnings concerning apocryphal writings which here and there made their appearance, such as an apocalypse of the Apostle Paul, dealing with his transports in the third heaven. Another book, entitled *The Secrets of Moses*, also fell into this category. There was also some idle talk among certain pagans about some letters of Christ addressed to Paul, which no-one had ever seen and which were supposed to contain magic formulae.

A letter written by Augustine to Bishop Ceretius describes a hymn which our Lord is supposed to have sung before ascending the Mount of Olives; the Bible which was for "fleshly" eyes did not contain this song, but the knowledge of it was widespread among the Priscillianists, where it was called "the King's Secret". Augustine proved that the expressions in the text were somewhat muddled paraphrases of biblical texts. This fabrication, he said, was widely known. He claimed that there were certain other matters, however, which this sect kept secret under oath.[180]

Within the province of Hippo he found the strange community of the Abelites, which condemned human propagation, honoured the virginal Abel and maintained the continuity of their sect by adopting children. Every male member lived together with a woman, but the pair practised continence. They took a boy and a girl into their house, and thanks to the poverty in the land and the great number of large families, children were not difficult to come by. When the adoptive parents died, the children continued this process.

After a great deal of effort Augustine succeeded in making the last stronghold of this sect see reason, a not inconsiderable task, for it was nothing less than an entire village.[181] It was Augustine's doing also that a curious remnant of an earlier time, the Tertullianist community in Carthage, handed over their last remaining basilica to Bishop Aurelius.[182]

Everyone who reads the sermons is struck by the frequency and emphasis of his preaching on the unity of substance between the Father and the Son.[183] There were, however, few Arians or Eunomians in Africa, and there seems reason to believe that even the African bishops did not know overmuch about the great battles of the councils in the fourth century. In 343 about thirty African bishops appeared at Sardica, and in 359 at least a few of them were present at Rimini, for it would seem as though certain semi-Arian elements were trying to strike up a partnership with the Donatists.[184] However, no single African plays any noteworthy or indeed noticeable part in this controversy. And yet none of the orthodox bishops failed to grasp the nature of the issues at stake or their unique importance. Augustine knew very well what he was about when he applied his best talents and a very great portion of his time to his work on the Trinity.

Augustine's personal contacts with Arians were infrequent but, when they occurred, remarkable. The first was occasioned by a piece of Arian writing which he received from a certain Elpidius, a person till then unknown to him, who had conceived a fixed determination to convert him. Augustine replied in great detail and in a tone that was not unfriendly.[185] The second Arian he encountered was a doctor, who had abjured his errors after chancing to hear one of Augustine's sermons, but was subsequently at little pains to make his family follow him. Augustine wrote to him, giving him a brief reminder of his duties and a long exposition of the doctrine of the one-ness of substance of the Father and the Son, and of the *latria* due to Christ. At the same time he wrote a short letter to his bishop, in which he requested the latter to beg the doctor not to take offence at the cheap paper and poor handwriting of his letter and to say that his letters even to his bishop were no better in this respect; further, the doctor was requested to reply as soon as possible and say what impression Augustine's letter had made on him—a typical example of his anxious care for souls.[186] We hear of two other encounters, both of which took the form of public discussions.

The first of these was with the *comes domesticorum* Pascentius, an elderly and somewhat moody gentleman, who had incurred the hatred of his taxpayers by reason of his obduracy, and who was feared by the episcopacy because of a certain habit of ridicule. The debate was arranged in Carthage at Pascentius' own suggestion, for Pascentius believed that his position would carry great weight and also had a weakness for public speaking, but it proved a comic and even slightly painful affair. The account of it illustrates in an admirable way the usefulness of the technical terms of theology[187] and the importance, in a debate of this kind, of understanding of their meaning. Augustine, as was his practice, insisted that everything said be accurately recorded by the official reporters. Pascentius objected to this, giving as his excuse that he did not wish to go on record with utterances that were technically illegal, but he agreed to the presence of witnesses, among them Alypius and several bishops. At a very early stage of the proceedings he lost his good humour, though on the morning of the debate he had received Augustine with every courtesy and congratulated him upon his fame, Augustine replying with the customary polite cliché—that *fama* had cheated Pascentius in this particular—Pascentius opened the debate and it soon became apparent that he was completely ignorant of theology and was not an opponent whom Augustine need take seriously at all. He began by praising Ambrose's opponent, Bishop Auxentius of Durosturum, as a paragon of orthodoxy. Hereupon Alypius asked whether this Auxentius had been an Arian or a Eunomian. What, answered the Count, I condemn both Arius and Eunomius, and it would be a good thing if people were to condemn Homoousios too. When the bishops explained to him that *homoousion* was not a person but a theological term, Pascentius asked them to show him this word in Holy Scripture, saying that if they could do so he would immediately become one of them. But although it was explained to him that the word was Greek and that for this reason the word was not found in a Latin Bible, and that he would do better to enquire whether the thing it meant was or was not to be found in the Bible, Pascentius remained obdurate and continued with his argument.[188]

At length he declared that he believed in God the almighty Father, the invisible and incomprehensible, and in Jesus Christ, his Son, God, Lord, born before all time, through whom all things were made, and in the Holy Ghost. Augustine declared that this was entirely sound, and that he could himself

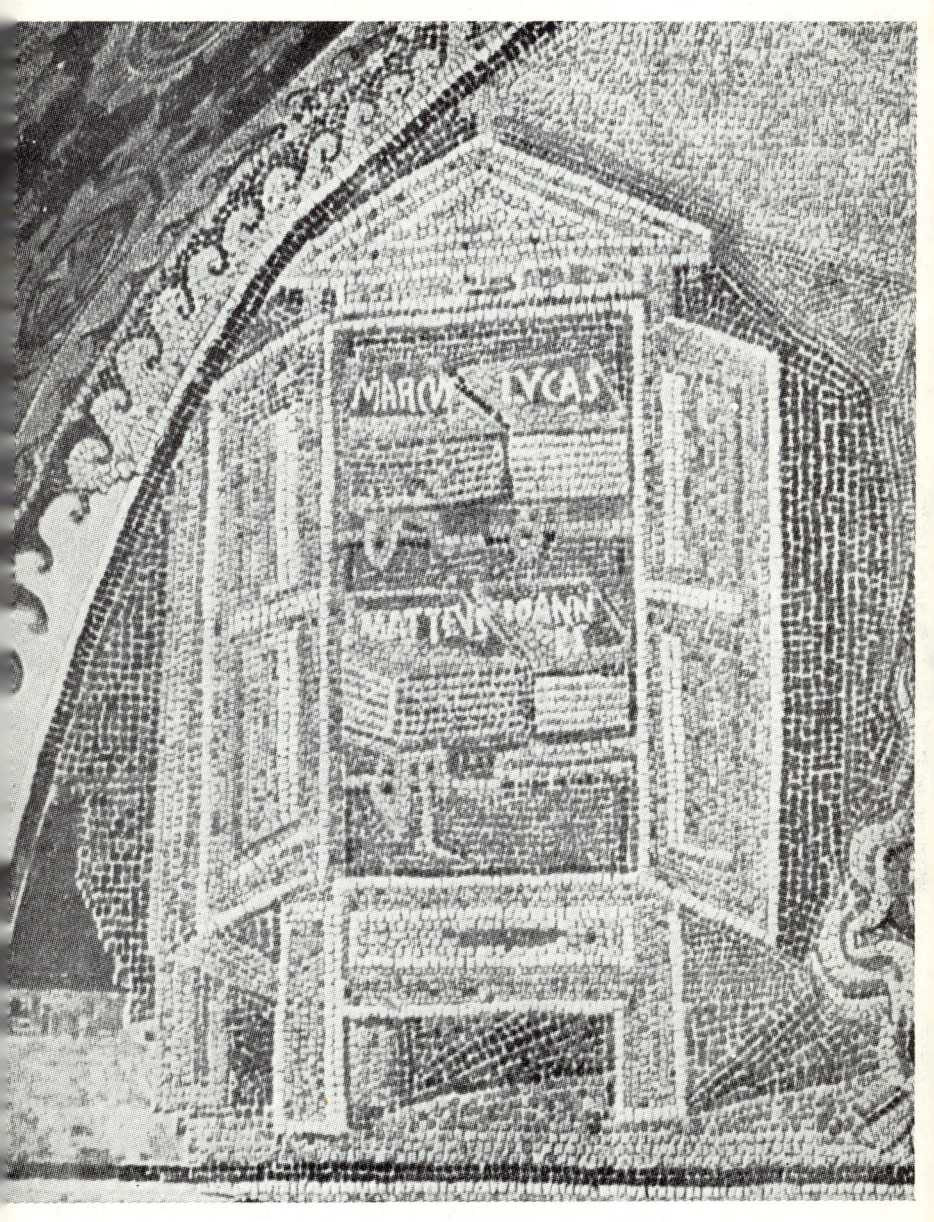

7 Book-cupboard (Mausoleum of Galla Placidia, Ravenna, 450)

8 Altar (Baptistery at Ravenna, 458)

sign such a profession if he had it before him. Pascentius then took a sheet of paper, wrote the sentence down and gave it to the bishop to read. The latter, however, pointed out that he had written "unbegotten" instead of "incomprehensible". He then asked whether the Father is referred to as "unborn" in the Bible. "Yes", said Pascentius.

"Where is that?" said Augustine.

Here a friend of Pascentius joined in.

"Do you assert", he said, "that the Father was ever begotten?"

"No."

"Well, if he was never begotten, he is unbegotten."

"True", said Augustine, "and that only shows that a word may not be in the Bible and still mean something that is very much in the Bible, and that is exactly what we say of *homoousion*."

After a short silence Pascentius remarked: " 'Unbegotten' could hardly be in the Scriptures. It would be insulting to the Father."

"Did you insult him then when you wrote it with your own hand?"

"Yes, it would be better if I had not done so."

"Then you must cross it out again."

"No, I stick to my statement that the Father is unbegotten."

"Which only shows again that an expression which is correct even in a profession of faith may not be contained in Holy Scripture at all."

At this Pascentius took the paper from him and tore it to shreds.[189]

After dinner the talk was continued, shorthand-writers being present, for Pascentius had at length agreed to this. However, he talked much too rapidly for the shorthand-writers to follow him, and when Augustine asked him to keep his promise and to write down a profession of his faith as he had undertaken to do, Pascentius suddenly cried out, "You are trying to trap me so that you can have something against me in black and white" (with reference, of course, to the law against Arianism).

The bishop, while remaining calm, could not entirely conceal his irritation at this remark, and although Pascentius insulted him immediately thereafter Augustine nevertheless regretted such observations as he did let fall, and felt that in view of the count's exalted station he owed an apology, which he later gave in writing.[190]

Needless to say, the discussion yielded no further results, for the atmosphere was by now completely spoiled. At length the count's utterances showed that he did not regard the Son as God after all. Augustine pointed out that in the morning he had accepted the Godhead of the Son, and that this showed how desirable it was to have the talk recorded. Hereat Pascentius grew very angry, saying that it would have been better if he had contented himself with knowing Augustine only by reputation, since on closer acquaintance he proved to be a very different person, whereupon Augustine remarked that he had himself said as much at their first meeting.

"And you were right", was Pascentius' retort.

And that was the end of it—at least, as far as that conversation was concerned.[191] Even so, Pascentius boasted everywhere that he had got the better of the famous Augustine, and had made his own profession of faith right in the bishop's face, which others had lacked the courage to do. This caused Augustine to send him a written account of the proceedings which he duly had confirmed by the witnesses, and to appeal seriously to his conscience. He included in his memorandum a lengthy explanation of his own position.[192] He signed his own name to the letter but out of respect for Pascentius' rank omitted explicitly to name him as the addressee. This piece of writing contains the famous words, "Nobody has much difficulty in getting the better of Augustine; the great question is 'How?'—with the help of truth or by noisy talk? It is really very simple. If people notice that you have a burning interest in a certain matter, they will be pleased to make the opportunity of ingratiating themselves with so powerful a man by prudent applause. It is not to a man's advantage to triumph over another but very much to his advantage to triumph over himself."[193] Pascentius did not even read this letter, though he did send a reply to a second much shorter letter,[194] and did this with a simulated courtesy that was really a fresh affront. In the latter missive he expresses his surprise that his beloved brother still persists in his former error. Augustine, he said, was like a thirsty man who on a very hot day had drunk marsh water, and to whom it is therefore useless to offer a drink of fresh water, since he has stuffed himself up inside. Which of the Three, he asked, was really the one God? Was there perhaps a threefold person who bore that name? There was really very little point in writing much. It would be better for Augustine, if he were so certain of his ground, to come and confer with him in a spirit of peace, along with the other bishops of his party.[195] The weakness which Pascentius was covering up was made very clear by a casual remark of Augustine's in yet another letter: If, he says, I had changed my mind between morning and evening as you did, you would not say that I had drunk marsh water—but what was even worse, namely that I was double-tongued.[196]

Another debate held some twenty years later, this time with a man who did know some theology, was equally unsatisfactory. In the year 428, when the old bishop, having more or less drawn clear of the Donatist affair, needed all his strength to combat the Pelagians, he observed to his dismay the entry into the town of a well-known Arian bishop, Maximinus. Maximinus had come to Hippo at the instigation of the Vandal Count Sigisvult, whom the Empress Placidia, now desperate and misled by erroneous information, had called to her aid against the rebel commander Boniface. Maximinus had no success and was loud in his complaints that Augustine was ruining his business—probably among the soldiers of the garrison—and that he had attacked him in one of his sermons as a blasphemer. The sermon in question was on the words "Whoso believeth on me believeth not on me but on him that sent me", and attacked Maximinus as a blasphemer because he was reported to have said that one could also speak of God and the Apostles being one.[197] This may seem a relatively mild essay in the field of heresy, but we must remember that it took place in a town where the Catholics were in the majority and that majority had the law behind it.

After the priest Eraclius had tried unsuccessfully to bring the two men together for a talk, Augustine himself eventually succeeded in bringing about a public discussion. Maximinus was a formidable opponent. He was an excellent speaker and scriptural texts dropped one after another from his lips. The beginning of the affair was certainly interesting. Maximinus insisted on certain conditions, one of which was that terms not found in Holy Scripture were not to be used, this on the ground that Scripture itself declares that "They serve not who teach the commandments of men." When Maximinus said this Augustine interrupted him with the words, "I will not agree to that but would rather come to the point immediately. Tell me forthwith what you believe with reference to Father, Son and Spirit", and when his opponent answered by referring to the formula of Rimini, Augustine said, "I merely repeat what I asked just now, when you failed to answer me; tell me what you really believe." But Maximinus evaded the question and made further discussion impossible by indulging in a long monologue which lasted till evening. In this he completely lost himself in a mass of quite secondary matters, and dealt at enormous length with points which were not controversial at all. On the next day he went off to Carthage on the pretext of pressing business, and there boasted of a great triumph.

The indefatigable Augustine, however, did not let the matter rest, but proceeded to refute Maximinus in two exhaustive essays. The first attacked his methods of controversial sabotage, the second his doctrine. The friend of the Goths replied not a single word, although he had given a written promise to do so.[198] He revenged himself twelve years later, however, when the butcher Gaiseric had overrun Sicily.[199] Twelve bishops of that island had refused Maximinus Communion and they were duly reported to the conqueror. As regards these disputations and the verbal sparring and shadow-boxing which they so often involved, one does not know which to wonder at most—the popularity of the performances themselves (due no doubt to the respect in which were held the whole art of public speaking and the not inconsiderable intellectual training which it involved), or the earnestness and persistence of Augustine's opponents, with their strange mixture of cunning and good faith.

And yet once more it was Augustine who in his old age was called by God to do battle with Pelagius and his followers, "those strong and swift spirits",[200] who overestimated the purely human part in the work of redemption. They were surrounded by the lustre with which their strict asceticism endowed them, and many of the best minds read their writings, even if it was only for "the rich style, sharp as a hair".[201]

Augustine would not rest till he had made an end of this process of subtle poisoning and neutralized it. And who was better qualified than Augustine to silence these eulogizers of the natural goodness of man? Just how uncorrupted is this human nature of ours he knew from his own unhappy experience, and he held with all the passion of which he was capable to the truth to which he had thus attained. And here were men who were prepared to build a whole system of Christian asceticism on this monstrous ineptitude! What remained of Christ if the whole work of redemption amounted to nothing more than following certain moral precepts and a divine example? Augustine's innermost being was outraged by such an idea, and he threw himself body and soul into the business of doing battle with it and, perhaps because a certain element of the personal was involved, his struggle carried him to heights of excellence which he had never attained before. He became the very essence of himself, and in this controversy steps into the foreground and stands unique among the Fathers of the Church. Ambrose looked back to some extent to the Stoa, but Augustine became *par excellence* the teacher of the doctrine of divine grace and the great interpreter of the Epistle to the Romans. Augustine was supremely the propagator of the idea of an elect, the man who brought to the bar of truth the reality of our fallen human nature, the spiritual father of both Calvin and St. Thomas. No theologian who deals with this question can afford to pass him by. But Augustine's appearance on the scene as the champion against Pelagianism belongs to the general history of the Church, the fight being carried on largely outside Africa. It has only an indirect bearing on the story of the pastor of souls.

On innumerable occasions during these last years he preached, and that with quite unusual fervour, on God's absolute sovereignty in the dispensing of grace, on our helplessness and the power of grace. He returned to the subject again and again; indeed, he did it so often that he felt constrained to apologize since his Carthaginian hearers began to be bored by it,[202] for these addresses were given more frequently in Carthage than anywhere else. Even in Carthage, however, Pelagianism never attained to the dimensions of a popular movement. Despite the importance of the whole question it never did more than become the occasion of a crisis in theological circles and among ascetics. It was the learned caste and not the common people which took exception to the words "Give what thou commandest and command what thou wilt."[203]

The extent to which this dangerous and subtle heresy caused disquiet in Hippo we do not know. It may to some extent have done so in the monasteries. We do know, however, that the ascetics of Hadrumetum, a community which was a daughter foundation of Hippo, took the liveliest interest in the fight and that some of them drew erroneous conclusions from Augustine's very positive formulations. The result was that their abbot, Valentinus, wrote a letter on the subject of grace in which he issued a warning against going to the opposite extreme and thus wholly denying the freedom of the will.[204] Indeed, somebody had actually got up and said that Augustine's interpretation made all admonitions by a superior entirely senseless.

So it came about that the bishop sent to Hadrumetum his books *Grace and Free Will* and *Admonition and Grace*, as well as a number of letters in which he begged the abbot to send him for further instruction two of his monks, for these two monks had taken exception to certain expressions used by Augustine in a letter to the Roman archdeacon Sixtus.[205] The books and letters of "the truly holy Father Augustine whom we esteem above all things and whom we honour with pious joy" were received—so wrote the abbot—as the passing glory of God was received by Elijah in his cave.[206] Is there a more telling proof of the passionate earnestness with which the initiated followed this battle about grace than the fact that a year before the barbarians landed simple monks had no hesitation in travelling to and fro from the coast of Byzacena to Uzalis and Hippo to hear something which truly satisfied them concerning such matters as the value of ascetic effort, the direction of prayer and the sureness of their salvation? This desire for enlightenment is as moving as Augustine's own conscientiousness, which drove him to write the two books *The Predestination of the Saints* and *The Gift of Steadfastness* for the benefit of two laymen, Prosper and Hilarius, in distant Southern Gaul. They were unknown to him, but they had written to him that they were the only ones in that country who defended his views and that all others took exception to them—which seems to show that even then Provence was marked by that contentious character which has made it famous in history.[207]

Qui Posuit Fines Tuos Pacem

Augustine could rightly claim that in bringing back the separated brethren he had indeed most fully expended himself. He was in a position to say that, after truth itself, it was he who was the true conqueror of Donatism. More than any Government edict, it was the luminous quality of Augustine's logic that won the victory. Yet his arguments were few and always much the same. Schism, he says, is a worse sin than handing over the books, and you persist in your schism. You wish men to call you saints. How can you suffer an Optatus or the Circumcellions in your midst, which you do for fear of further divisions? Did Christ die only for Africa? And if you give your bodies to be burned, what profit have you if you have not charity? And you have no charity while you remain in schism. And yet he never forgot the more popular argument. Thus the heretics made great play with quoting from Habb. iii.3—"God will come out of Africa, and the holy one from the shadowy mountain." "Imagine trying to apply that text to treeless Numidia! There is hardly a twig to be found there to whisk away the flies with, and the people live in caves!"[208] Generally, however, he was in more serious vein.

He taught his Christians not to be too greatly scandalized by these spawning sects. They played a necessary part in that they caused good men to come forward to give battle for the Faith and stimulated them to search more earnestly in the Scriptures. Also, they schooled men in patience. The petty squabbles of small-minded people within the Church are nothing worse, he said, than the stirring of a child within its mother's womb.[209] Watchful overseer that he was, he unmasked the false leaders as children of the devil and antichrists, and, despite their sacraments and their piety, called their communities severed limbs of the Church, empty of the Spirit, and because of their severance dead and given over to corruption.[210]

Donatism must be seen as one of the many revolts of alleged purists who find that the visible Church falls short of some private formula of perfection conceived by themselves. It may also perhaps be viewed as a reaction, largely conditioned by local circumstances, of proletarian elements against the partnership of Church and State. Whatever it was, Donatism was so pitifully poor in ideas that one can only look upon its very origin as a sort of insensate misunderstanding, for even if a minor ideological content is conceded to it, what could those emotional masses understand of the points of ecclesiastical theory on which the arguments of their leaders so often turned? Such people, indeed, were generally not concerned with religious beliefs at all, but were chiefly interested in the various tales of infamy which abounded concerning their opponents. Thus Donatists were only too ready to believe that what Catholics sacrificed upon their altars was something essentially different from what they themselves sacrificed—and they certainly believed that it was something devilish.[211] They did not engage with their opponents in learned arguments about the Church. Their debates were rather more in the nature of recriminations concerning alleged beatings-up, raids by the police, legal coercions and the like. To read a certain meaning into the whole affair, one must try to visualize its effect on Augustine and the deeper insight these controversies awakened in him. It was in Augustine's person that the Church, till then a thing rooted in the world of hard facts, with its theories still imperfectly formulated, grew conscious of the real nature of its unity, of the reasons which necessitated that unity and of all the finer shades of meaning which an attempt to define it must take into account. Hard experience of the facts before him taught Augustine that the rending apart of the body of the Church was a worse thing than any handing over of books or any breakdown of clerical discipline, that honest conviction cannot always claim the rights that are the privilege of the truth, that the sacraments are still valid even when passed into wrongful hands outside the Church, that the worthiness of the office continues despite the unworthiness of the office-holder, that the visible element in the Church also represents an objective reality, that there is no spiritual health for a Christian whose spiritual life is in separation from that of his fellows (for such a life is the fruit of a man's being a law unto himself and all too easily leads to unbelief).

They were right when once they cheered him as he announced as a text the Psalmist's words, "he who set thy path toward peace". For that text was spoken by him out of the very depths of his heart. "What is it that makes you cheer?" he cried. "Dear brethren, see that you do indeed love peace. It delights our heart when from your own hearts comes the echo of this love. Do you too take delight in that sound. Surely you do, for your applause came before I had uttered a word, before I had even made a beginning of speaking."[212] To restore peace and safeguard it when it was restored—that was his aim, and it is a matter that those people should especially reflect on who compare Augustine with Luther, that almost alarmingly gifted and strangely irritable man who held himself to be too great and too ample a recipient of grace to suffer the tragic Church of Leo X. Less impetuous but not less irritable, and certainly a man of much more subtle mind, Augustine is in some ways actually closer to the frivolous Renaissance pope than to the great man of prayer, for he was less concerned with saving his own soul than with saving the Church. Buried deep under the faith by which he lived, was it not in the last resort his sound commonsense, his natural modesty, his sense of proportion, his respect for existing institutions, his fear of any kind of fanaticism—was it not, in a word, all things in him that went to make up the type of the Christian humanist (a type we can never afford to lose), that caused him to be filled with horror by the action of those would-be great ones who thought that because they were themselves scandalized by little men, they were entitled in their turn to scandalize those same little men by leaving the Church?

It is his refutation of Donatism that causes Augustine to stand out as the great human hammer for the undoing of heresy, and that more than anything else entitles him to be called a pillar of the Catholic Church. No man has more movingly described the misery of those people who leave the Church for any one of the innumerable reasons that make men do this—some scandalous happening, some *idée fixe*, some personal antipathy or whatever the thing may be.

Nobody has ever made us feel more intensely that here alone lie the means of salvation from which no man may turn away, that here is the ark amid the flood of subjective religious experience. "Oh", he once cried in the crowded basilica at Caesarea to a congregation containing quite a number of heretics, among them a schismatic bishop whom Augustine himself had induced to come there—"Oh, it is true enough that this man can get everything he wants outside the Church—he can enjoy the dignity of office, he can receive the Sacrament, he can sing 'Alleluia' and answer 'Amen', he can hold to the Gospel. He may in the name of the Father and the Son and the Holy Ghost both have and preach the Faith, but he will not find salvation outside the Catholic Church!"[213]

Augustine has taught the Church for all time, as he taught the Church in Africa, that "no man may look on God as a merciful Father unless he is prepared to hold in honour his Mother the Church".[214] Yet that does not by any means set the measure of his achievement. In dealing with heresy he did more than merely cut and stab; he also healed. He did more than merely chase away the wolves from the flock; he brought together again the sheep that had been scattered. He was St. Robert Bellarmine, St. Francis of Sales and St. Charles Borromeo in one, and his touching solicitude for the actual human members of the *pars Donati* outweighs the fact that in the matter of forcing consciences he played, at least in theory, the role of a Bossuet. He was, perhaps, a poor politician and a great theologian. What he has chiefly taught posterity as a pastor of souls is to see those who hold heretical beliefs as strayed sheep rather than as the carriers of loathsome infection, the strayed sheep for which, as a bishop of the true Church, he bore as much responsibility as he did for the herd that was guarded secure in its fold, the herd that knew its home full well and was comfortable in that knowledge.

7

DAY-TO-DAY PASTORAL WORK

Augustine's Own Community

IT is extremely difficult, almost impossible, to reconstruct a picture of such a congregation as that of Hippo from the quick periodic glimpses which the great man's utterances afford, or from his fortuitous *obiter dicta*. As we read his letters and his sermons it is always borne in upon us that the shadier sides of life are the ones that tend most frequently to draw attention to themselves. Letters in which men and things are shown in their true proportion or even in their true nobility hardly ever get published, while the more picturesque kind tend either to distort or to be satirically tinged. Madame de Sévigné was certainly never guilty of deliberate slander, but no-one who reads her letters will take her or her acquaintances for particularly good Christians, although nearly all of them were just that. Madame de Sévigné herself was indeed a granddaughter of St. Jane Frances de Chantal, of whom she honestly tried not to be too unworthy. Augustine's letters, moreover, lack the catharsis of a really sincere friendship, such as that which reconciles us to the tirades of Jerome. As with the letters of so many pastors of the kind that can be approached by pretty well anybody, we gain in Augustine's case the impression that such a man's duties are concerned with both people and things that are exceptionally difficult, and that clerical life is a continual preoccupation with the unpleasant.

As to the sermons, of course, it is natural enough that a preacher should in the main refrain from actually flattering his hearers. He will mix the good with the bad; he will tend to exaggerate the contrasts, though he will pass over the spicier subjects in silence. In the fifth century, which had few pietistic leanings, it was not usual to engage in religious idylls. Apart from expounding the Scriptures, preachers confined themselves largely to the maxim *insta, obsecra, increpa*, and that not always in *omni patientia et doctrina*. Nearly all Church Fathers are accounted pessimists. A man like the majestic Leo, who never loses his self-control and who never uses a commonplace expression (he was in Augustine's day still a simple acolyte[1]) is a white raven among a flock of black ones, ravens that usually do a good deal of unpleasant croaking on the subject of morals. In reading these old preachers our feelings are very much like those of the hero in *Le Diable boiteux*; the roofs are suddenly torn off the houses, and what we then see is hardly calculated to delight us.

Now, Augustine was not a man who loved the sensational. Even in the pulpit he remains the thinker who never loses his sense of proportion. He is also the true lyricist who allows his glowing heart to speak. It is only to achieve the utmost clarity of meaning that he sometimes steps down among the prosaic facts of everyday life and makes use, more or less incidentally, of those shrewdly-observed illustrations from the life that was about him, illustrations which sometimes make us feel as though we were looking through a chink in a wall. Even these are humdrum enough. Human life as we see it reflected in the *sermones* is sometimes moving and sometimes repulsive, but usually a pretty ordinary affair. Parish life in one age is remarkably like parish life in another. The differences are mostly differences of local colour; in this case, the background of Africa in late Antiquity.

Hippo seems to have been a pretty dirty place. We know that on the night before the Feast of St. John the street boys could gather whole heaps of refuse of which they would make little bonfires to greet the summer solstice; the smell would permeate the entire town and the bishop would be unable to see the sky for smoke.[2] And there is no doubt that if it was dirty physically, Hippo was not much cleaner morally. Indeed, it was far from being the unblemished kind of place that enthusiasts for early Christianity might perhaps have imagined. Augustine was not a man who readily became indignant, and even in the pulpit his quick and flexible mind is playful rather than critical. Even so, he tends, with one or two exceptions, to speak of good men rather in the abstract, yet not to hesitate to be most specific about the bad ones; and so it is that those parishioners of Hippo to whom our attention is especially drawn are scarcely the most edifying specimens.

All Africans are scoundrels, the bilge-water of the Roman Empire—so wrote Salvianus of Marseilles many years after Augustine's death.[3] He must, of course, be accounted a prejudiced writer, since his object was to prove the degeneracy of all Romans and so to demonstrate that the collapse of the Empire, and its supersession by the barbarians with their new potentialities, was a just dispensation of fate. The failings which the bishop's utterances suggest as the besetting sins of this people were more or less confined to anger, coarseness and weakness. These provide ample material to keep the preacher going but produce a rather wearisome effect upon the reader. To the above-mentioned we might add swearing, stealing, cheating, quarrelling, extravagance, the sins of sensuality and excessive love of pleasure, and to complete the list we should also name the two national characteristics mentioned by Arnobius as early as the third century: namely, prying and practical joking, both habits that have their roots in a certain venial malice common to hot-blooded people.[4]

The great mass of people took no part whatever in public life. All that happened was blindly accepted as the decree of fate. Small wonder that apart from religion their interests turned wholly on the satisfaction of their elementary desire to sustain life and enjoy themselves. The mild climate, a surfeit of leisure, the slenderness of their needs and their ineradicable optimism all contributed toward that end.

Unfortunately they were dishonest, suspicious and quarrelsome. All transactions were governed by contract, and rich men often did not know at any given time how many lawsuits they had running. One need hardly make further mention of their delight in festivals and no doubt, though, like all southerners, they were temperate in the matter of drink, they would occasionally overdo it. "It is a great disgrace when a man whom no mere iron can subdue is overcome by wine"—so the bishop once ventured to write to the commander of the imperial troops,[5] while to the leader of the Rogatists, that rigidly puritanical offshoot of the Donatists of which mention has already been made, he wrote: "Who is so blind that he does not know how many men there are everywhere who have abandoned themselves to drink? Take any ten names of your own sect and see if you do not find at least one in any such ten is a drunkard."[6] Not a few clerics caused scandal by drunkenness. Indeed, Augustine was at some pains to put an end, at least within the confines of church property, to the carousals that took place from time to time on the graves of the martyrs.[7] Even on Easter morning he had to adjure the newly-baptized *infantes* not to come to the afternoon worship in too merry a condition,[8] and on Sundays one would everywhere hear songs in praise of wine.[9]

From the workships sounded light-hearted little tunes and the more *risqué* these were the more popular they were and the more lasting their popularity, many holding their place for years in the people's affection. Unfortunately both words and music came from the theatre.[10] The songs sung at weddings were as vulgar in their content as in their accent—that rasping Punic accent by which one immediately recognized the Libyan, and with which St. Jerome has his fun.[11]

These were the faults of the people among whom Augustine worked, and they were no more grave than those of any other men living in an equally seductive climate and at an equally low level of existence. They were all faults derived from the national character and from the pagan past. Perhaps Ambrose's remark about women in general and Eve in particular might aptly be applied to this little African people—namely that they sinned rather from the instability of their spirit than from malice.[12]

The Element of Simplicity: *Idiotae* and Men of Culture, Rich and Poor

Every reader of the sermons will be moved by the simple manner in which the truths of the Faith are presented therein. What the fullness of Augustine's spirit here put into words was clearly intended for quite uneducated people. The impression we gain concerning Augustine's parishioners is that they must have been very simple people, for he explains everything to them in the most elementary manner and with a multitude of repetitions. Many came to hear, and often bishops were sitting in the apse; when he preached in Carthage, high officials and literary connoisseurs stood on the steps of the sanctuary. But the majority of his audience were unlettered men. He himself distinguished between a minority that had a good knowledge of Scripture, and the great majority who had scarcely any knowledge of it whatever. When after the manumission of a slave or an ecclesiastical election the official record for the *gesta episcopalia* had to be signed by some of those present, it was presumably always found that one or the other could not write his name, for Augustine said that the signing should be left to those capable of it.[13] When we reflect on what the excavations have brought to light in regard to the level of literacy among stonemasons, we are driven to the conclusion that the number of illiterates must have been very large indeed. This makes it all the more surprising that Augustine's congregation could understand him, that it grasped the point of his play on words and that its applause was by no means confined to the less genuinely witty of Augustine's remarks, for there is no indication of the existence of any little group of devout church mice building up Augustine's reputation as a preacher. On the contrary, it was not the quietly devout who cheered him. Rather was his a broad-based popularity. At the same time it rested on the enthusiasm of people who really got pleasure from his apt inspirations and who rather prided themselves on their discernment for so doing.

There was a good deal of reading in Hippo—on the part of the few. Possidius speaks almost with tenderness of the magnificent episcopal library, and apparently Augustine could command the services of so many copyists that on one occasion he was able and willing immediately to make a gift of his *Confessions* to a highly-placed literary enthusiast who was a complete stranger to him.[14] As against this, however, instances occur where Augustine has to be less accommodating. Where the applicants are strangers, or even when the applicant is, like Evodius of Uzalis, a friend, but asks for more than one book, Augustine sometimes asks the enquirer to send his own copyist to Hippo.[15] By ordinary standards he was most generous in making gifts of his books, but it must be remembered that in those days an author was his own publisher, and readers were limited to a comparatively small circle.

Augustine also tended to make more promises than he could always remember to fulfil. His correspondence seems to indicate that a new book was distributed quickly and easily and that, at any rate among the educated, both clerical and lay, there was a positive mania for reading and writing. Even the nuns had their library.[16] Whether there were in the *secretarium* of the cathedral at Hippo any arrangements similar to those obtaining at Nola, we do not know. In the latter place codices of the Bible were available for all to read, and Paulinus had the following verses inscribed over the door:

> Whoso is moved by the holy desire to reflect on the Scriptures
> Here at peace can he sit and engage in the pious perusal.[17]

Most certainly even the laymen who corresponded with Augustine had very extensive scriptural knowledge—as, for that matter, did the ordinary folk who listened to his sermons. It is difficult to believe that this was entirely acquired by listening to the readings in church. "Everywhere in the world", Augustine says in one of his sermons, "Holy Scripture is not only recited and sung, but is also publicly offered for sale." Whether when bought it was always read is of course open to doubt. Africa in this respect would scarcely have attained the level of cultured Constantinople, and even here, though Chrysostom once gave wealthy laymen the advice to read on Saturday evening, in the codices written in gold letters on purple, the pericope for the following day, he knew well enough that nobody would do anything of the kind. The books were kept as showpieces in the bookcases, and that was as far as the thing went.[18] We also hear of simple folk who, when they had a headache, would get somebody to put a codex of the Gospels on their heads. The custom, when faced by some decision, of opening the Gospels at random and seeking guidance from what one saw, was at this time also already in force.[19] We cannot deduce from the existence of such practices that those who engaged in them could necessarily read, but they seem to show that codices of the Bible were by no means rareties, and even that priests and deacons were not indisposed to lend them out for purposes which were, strictly speaking, very far from liturgical.

There were elementary schools under the direction of *ludi magistri*, where there was a great deal more thrashing than instruction. The first little prayer which the bishop could remember from his boyhood ran, "O God, please don't let me get a thrashing at school today!"[20] Whoever could come anywhere near affording it sent his children to a *grammaticus*, as the principal would be called in those rather curious private schools where the poets were read, explained and learned by heart. After that the further schooling for those with any pretence to education was pretty standardized, and even a pious middle-class woman like Monica thought that her clever boy, as soon as he had finished his schooling in Madaura, must go to the school of rhetoric in distant Carthage, nor could the evil reputation of the Carthage students deter her from this.[21] It was twenty years before her son ever had doubts about the value of this kind of training. A knowledge of reading was indispensable before a man could make any claim whatever to have lifted himself above the herd. Technical ability in some craft rated for very little.[22] So much was this last the case that even a distinguished architect would pride himself less on his plans and designs than on his knowledge of Vitruvius. It was an age in which men boasted of the extent of their reading, an age of interminable versified epitaphs and dedications, and even the walls of the basilicas (and in Africa, the floors) were liberally sprinkled with these things. In the last resort the ancient culture had remained above all a literary culture. Now it was approaching its end, and the old forms, which had been stereotyped by the schools, were threatening to burst asunder under the pressure of the new Christian ideas—a thing that was happening also to the old words under the stress of new meanings. The fact is that the old culture was peeling away like an old skin leaving the new skin beneath. Yet at this very time any Roman or even any barbarian who could summon up the slenderest justification for so doing, seemed more ready than ever to boast of such conventional literary culture as he was able to display. People of standing made a point of seeing that their codices were well annotated. It made a good impression to quote poetry at table, and perhaps after the meal to bring the discussion round to the question of unusual, especially scriptural, turns of phrase.[23] It was even better if one could trot out some agonized concoction of an epigram or some little set speech, and it was worth a fortune if a man could transform some dull letter into a sort of torrent of polished compliments. There were people who, to the very end of their lives, expended their whole energy on these stylistic exercises.

Yet if we take the population as a whole, the truly lettered only formed a small caste in the towns and a tiny fraction in the villas and on the land, and we know that Tagaste and probably also Hippo did not possess a high school, for we know that on one occasion not a single codex of Cicero was to be found in the latter place. "I should have to send for it from Carthage", the bishop wrote to a young literary snob, "and might as well have a professional teacher of rhetoric come along with it, considering that the science has fallen asleep even in schools."[24] Above all, the countryside was mentally backward, as we can see from the weird sects that sprang up all over the place, partly on the fringes of Donatism. There were men who sought death in the flames, and men who dreamed of a pure Church, and men who, like the Abelites, rejected human propagation and ensured continuity for their sect by adopting children,[25] childishly radical sects like those which were later to grow up in Russia on the edges of the Raskolniki, the Skoptsi and the Khlysti—and the extremists among the Old Believers.

The people were poor. The bishop knew well enough what manner of folk were before him in the basilica. The rich men were few and the poor were many.[26] In the town he could see the huts packed closely together behind the wide-walled palaces, and he knew that inside they were black with smoke. "Smoky" is his standard epithet for the houses of the poor.[27] True that the poor in spirit sometimes lived in marble halls; yet how many of the rich did not count among the poor when it came to proclaiming the Gospel and a knowledge of the Scriptures! And the materially poor constituted the overwhelming majority.

Then there was slavery, the foundation of the whole culture of Antiquity, on which no man as yet dared lay a finger. Like St. Paul and all Fathers of the Church,[28] St. Augustine was more concerned to ennoble the existing relation between master and slave than to reconstruct the social order or to preach the sharing of labour, an idea which at that time had occurred to nobody and would have been technically quite impracticable. That those who were distinguished by superior understanding should keep the wilder elements in subjection, that those who as fathers of families, heads of households, kings and princes, made peace secure both in their home and in the Empire, should enjoy a higher measure of authority, appeared to Augustine part of the natural order of things. To ensure "peace and order" God had arranged for the distribution among kings and emperors of certain rights over mankind,[29] though this subordination of one rational order to another was a consequence and a punishment of sin and did not derive naturally from man's uncorrupted nature.[30]

The number of slaves was still unbelievably large.[31] There were, literally, slaves in every house. A wealthy household often numbered hundreds of them, but even a poor deacon would have a few. Thus it was that when the clergy of Hippo one day formally renounced all worldly possessions they were compelled to liberate a number of slaves who, in point of fact, were already living in a monastery.[32]

Nobody thought much about cursing slaves as a man might curse his cattle, and in this there was little to choose between pagans, Jews and Christians; such expressions as "wretch", "fool", "Satan", "devil", were the mildest the slaves had to endure.[33]

The old punishments were still legal[34] and Augustine knew only too well what it meant to see a slave receive a whipping from the overseer, to watch him look up like a beseeching dog, until his master should say the short releasing word, *Parce*.[35] It sometimes fell within his duties to speak the *manumissio*, a short and rather charming little ceremony which is described in one of his sermons. The slave is led into the church by his master. Silence is requested and the document attesting his freedom is read out or possibly composed on the spot. Then the slave's master says, "I give this man out of my hands. He has faithfully served me in all things." And with these words he tears in two the contract of sale[36]—on the whole, a more sensible reward for services stretching over a period of many years than the testimonials of the modern world, with their stereotyped phraseology. The liberation of one's slaves was generally recognized as constituting a good work. The aristocratic ascetics set a good example in this respect. It is told of Melania that she once gave their freedom to more than a thousand slaves on a single day. The freedman was, of course, faced with the problem of finding a livelihood, so that many preferred to remain as slaves in their warm nest, and indeed many a slave wanted for nothing and many a freedman had to beg his bread.[37] It was a frequent practice to call freedmen to "the nobility of the cloister", and many such men came in this manner to the *cuculla* and so obtained a roof over their heads. In the cloister they lived on a footing of equality with the free-born, for the Church knew no respect of persons. It was, however, expected that freedmen would pitch into their work with somewhat greater energy, since they had been used to work all their lives, and could not plead the effects of an over-delicate upbringing as an excuse for indifferent performance.[38]

Yet there is no sign of anything in the nature of a propaganda for wholesale liberation of slaves. Indeed, the world was uncomfortably full of freedmen, while the effect of Christianity made slavery itself more bearable; for Christian sermons influenced both master and man. The Stoics had condemned needless cruelties to slaves and urged their masters to show benevolence in their treatment of them.[39] But what had been no more than the pious admonition of the Stoics was prescribed as a stern duty by the new religion, for which the equality of all men before God was anything but an empty phrase. Now one began to see mistresses nursing their sick slaves; highborn ladies would take all their servants along with them when they entered the cloister and there treat them as their equals,[40] nor was it considered remarkable that a lady of great estate should exchange the kiss of peace with one of her farm-servants at the eucharistic feast. Augustine never dared to ask slave-owners to beg a slave's pardon after inflicting an unjust punishment or losing their tempers with him, but he advised them quietly to humble themselves before God; and to show the man concerned, by means of a friendly word, that the injustice of which he had been made a victim was at least recognized.[41] He did not hesitate to say in his sermons that a slave must not be handled in the lighthearted manner in which a man might deal with his own money or his own horse, and that this was no less true when a slave's market value happened to be lower than that of a horse.[42] Last but by no means least, a slave whose master flew into a rage against him could always seek sanctuary in the ever-open church, and in the cool air of that holy place could wait till the storm had blown over. He could also ask his master to sell him if the two failed completely to get along together.[43]

The South has always been a country of contrasts and on the whole the relations between men of sharply contrasting condition were often more human than might be supposed. As in old Spain, a nobleman and a beggar might well talk and deal with one another with less constraint than that which today exists between men of the lower and upper middle-class. Even a miser tended to have more affection for a faithful slave than he had for his money. "He is worth more to me than anything else in the world", says one of these. "He is not for sale. And why do you think I say that? Because he is a good dancer and a good cook? No. Because he is true as gold."[44]

Life was not always hard. Then, as now, poor people in that favoured South were easily satisfied, though they might completely lose their composure over a trifle. Had Augustine himself not been deeply moved many years before in Milan, by the happy expression on the face of a poor devil who had drunk somewhat too deeply, while he himself was running around in utter misery, because a panegyric which he was composing upon the Emperor was not taking proper shape?[45] Such people have a natural friendliness. After an evening's drinking, or even after a single glass of wine, they would never fail to cry "Thank you" to the landlord. Above all, the children had a glorious life. Most of them did not have to go to school, and they were rarely punished and always spoiled. Sometimes the slaves would sing a merry song upon the fields, sometimes a hymn.[46] And even the rich were sometimes friendly. When the psalm was sung in church, "Blessed is the man who regardeth the needs of the poor", Augustine would think of the many rich men who never ceased giving alms to his poor and his church and his monasteries, and then he would praise them: "They are the cedars of Lebanon. See how many sparrows—how many, that is to say, of the little ones of this world, who have given up their little bit of goods and gear and family life to make a new home upon these heights of the spirit—see how many of these have built their nests in these cedars!"[47] Even thieves were liberal. "Yes", they would say to Augustine, "I got my fortune by stealing, but I support the poor... *agapes facio*."[48]

There were poor people, too, who were also at home in Lebanon. For instance, there was the porter of a schoolmaster in Milan, whose story Augustine was later to tell from the pulpit. One day this man found a purse with two hundred *solidi*, and had a notice announcing the find put up. The owner duly appeared and begged him to accept ten per cent as a reward and when the man refused this, to accept at least ten or even five *solidi*; but he only gave way when the other lost his temper, and even then he went straight off and gave the money to the poor. "This Christian at the church door", said Augustine, "had a higher place than the pagan in the *cathedra*."[49] Needless to say, others, when they found a purse, cheerfully cried out: "Ha! Here is a present from God!" and let it rest at that.[50]

There is great warmth of heart, though spiced with a certain irony, in the aphorisms and anecdotes about riches and poverty of which the sermons are full. Whatever the Church Fathers may have thought of property, they certainly never keep off the subject. And one wonders what they would have thought of the later Puritans, who managed to connect the riches they amassed in commerce and by thrift with the message of the Gospels. But, though he was no respecter of wealth, it never occurred to Augustine to flatter the poor. All too often, he claims, they have the rich man's desires. They cannot pass a country house without asking the owner's name and sighing: "These lucky people! They can really live!"[51] They sing from the Fifty-first Psalm, "Behold the man that made not God his helper, but trusted in the abundance of his riches and prevailed in his vanity." But while they sing, they think of their own shabby clothes and look enviously at the dress of their neighbour in church, and then say to themselves, "That refers to him."[52]

There are beggars, he says, who fall asleep from the cold, but dream of luxury and fall into a rage when, on waking up, they see the rags of their parents. Poor people, as well as rich, must suffer a punishment without respect of birth, when they do wrong. For with poor and rich alike, God does not look to the contents of your strong-box or the size of your house, but to the thoughts in your minds.[53] Nevertheless, it is with the eyes of one baptized that Augustine looks upon the state of the poor. Nor does he ever, when doing so, forget the Sermon on the Mount. Poverty is a fact—a normal fact, if you will—but it is no disgrace. Rather, it is a means of freedom, and that is why the ascetics imitate the poor. The poor are our porters who carry our luggage of good deeds into heaven.

When we help them it is as though we gave a sailing ticket to somebody who for the time being happens to be in Africa, but is a citizen of a city far away, to which we ourselves desire to go—for they are also citizens of the City of God, which is their heavenly kingdom.[54] And our Lord Jesus Christ is their surety.[55] Augustine has always got a good word to say for tramps. A beggar, he says, who asks you for a penny, generally sings God's commandments before your door.[56] One day he closed his sermon with the following words: "I will not conceal from you why I have asked for alms. When I came here, I was stopped by some poor men who asked that I should say a good word for them, for they have not recently received overmuch from you. They no doubt expect something from us clergy, and we do what we can; but our means are limited. This means that we are more or less your emissaries." And hereupon there was loud applause. "You hear what I say and you cheer me. Thank God for that."[57]

Augustine's sermons are innocent of anything that might be called a satire on riches as such, but there are numerous allusions which show clearly enough what he thought of the reputed joys of property and of the claim to greatness that rests on the magnitude of a man's possessions. He knew the rich, their bad taste, their triviality, the self-indulgence which ultimately made them its slaves, and their meanness, which often far exceeded that of poorer men. He knew what their houses looked like from the inside, with their golden ceilings, marble statues, couches of ivory with soft cushions upon them, their innumerable hangings and their curtains of silk, and the crowd of musicians that would be gathered before their doors on any occasion that offered a pretext—a birthday, a banquet or a wedding.[58] He had seen those pretentious monuments beside the road[59]—those tall mausoleums which caused Jerome to ask whether corpses really needed silk and marble before they could lie down and rot in comfort.[60] And he asks his hearers whether they could tell a rich man's bones from those of a poor one if they could see them under the ground. Where, then, is rank? Augustine tells men that they should reflect on the state in which they were born; it is one of nakedness, and the nakedness of the rich is the same as the nakedness of the poor.[61]

He mentions people who try to bribe some poor devil or to force him under threats, if he is a slave, to spread slanders about a rival or an enemy. If that should happen the man so tempted or coerced should answer with Holy Scripture, that the man who lies "brings death unto his soul".[62] He indulges his irony over the pride of the rich and their eagerness to make others keep their distance. They are people, he says, who judge men by the fineness of their clothes and never think of the skin beneath, which is much the same in one man as in another.[63] In heaven there will be no tunics to appraise. There the poor look like angels because of the splendour of their righteousness.[64] And are not the poor much happier? Can they not get much more from looking at the starry heavens than the rich can get from looking at their gilded ceilings?[65]

There are people, he says, who can get enough to live on from some well-administered piece of property and so are under no necessity to work, but even these cannot free themselves from their anxieties. They are approached on all sides for money, and common decency compels them to help finance the public games for the mob. What an honourable task, he then adds in mockery—to spend as much as possible on these desperadoes of animal-baiters, and on buying up whole menageries of animals, most of which will die on the journey![66] It must, however, be admitted that others among the rich are as avaricious of money as any of the poor. A poor man may steal out of need but "with the rich their iniquity hath come forth, as it were, from fatness",[67] as the Psalmist says. Moreover, all who are not rich dream continually of becoming so, and are willing to hazard all for the chance. Indeed, the energy with which the children of darkness serve Mammon is one of his favourite themes. True, they are ridden by yet another demon—their love of ease.

While one of these demons says "Up with you and be doing", the other says, "Sleep on. Why stir abroad on such a cold morning?" But then the first says, "Out with you, and bother the weather."[68] What pains men take for the sake of a bit of money!

One day the sight of the harbour inspired him to give his heart free rein on the following Sunday. "What is it that sends all these people out onto the sea, aye, right to India? Hunger for money—avarice. They do not know a word of the Indian tongue but the word 'avarice' seems to be understood everywhere. When a storm breaks out they call on God for help, but God answers 'Why? Did I send you out to sea?' "[69] Ever and again one sees the corpse of a shipwrecked sailor lying upon the shore amid the wreckage of his ship and one says "Poor devil," (as one wipes away a tear) "he lost his life from love of gold"[70]—and yet the very man who says this may well plunder the corpse and sail away and so continue till his own life is forfeit.

Augustine really sums up all he has to say on the subject of riches and poverty by declaring that all lust for possessions is vanity. The wise man is he who has schooled himself to forgo these things, and the poor of Hippo knew that their great bishop in his well-endowed church lived more truly poor than any of them.

Volatility: The Pinianus Episode

When we consider the humble kind of folk Augustine was dealing with and the social contrasts in his congregation we cannot help being impressed by the extent to which people were completely carried away by his sermons. Preacher and congregation vie with each other in their excitement. The joint proceedings —for one must really call them that—are nearly always *staccato*, sometimes *scherzo* or *furioso*, but invariably *vivace*. This unusual liveliness, presumably a heritage of Berber blood, was fortunately displayed as much in spiritual matters as in the people's outward bearing. The people of Hippo remind us of Neapolitans. They were probably quick-witted, as southerners have remained to this day, but they lacked depth, and that is why we must picture them as volatile and unstable, despite their generous impulses, and also, despite their wit, as thoroughly superstitious.

For their bishop they had a tenderness which could on occasion be definitely embarrassing. That is evident enough from their disquiet during his absences[71] and from their ready response whenever he made a request; nor is this surprising, for the bishop was learned, pious, famous and kind. Who would not be proud of him and show him devotion? Had he not freed Africa of the bigmouthed Donatists? For the most part they accepted blindly whatever he said, and never dreamed of bringing an independent judgement to bear—

provided always that nothing was involved that interfered with their convenience. The sheep followed behind the shepherd, nor did it ever enter their minds to question his guidance. Indeed the bishop himself sometimes wished that they were more critically-minded and less naïvely obedient. He would have preferred a keener sense of personal responsibility. For Augustine's people were as uncritically behind him as the Donatists were behind their own bishop. A little more criticism, Augustine said openly from the *cathedra*, would have been an excellent thing.[72]

They easily lost their composure. In the restless days of the winter of 410-11, just before the reunion with the Donatists, Augustine wrote to the Valerii in Tagaste, "The people of Hippo, whose servant the Lord has made me, is in many respects, one might almost say in every respect, so weak that the slightest setback is liable to make it positively ill. Now it is undergoing a trial of such a magnitude that it would scarce have been able to surmount it had it been much stronger than it is. When I returned from my holiday in the country my absence had produced a dangerously irritable condition."[73] That was why he did not go out to meet his exalted guests.

Such volatility of character generally goes hand in hand with a propensity to violent rages, and the people of Hippo certainly were a violent lot. Augustine knew them well; he knew the hotheads who broke pencils when some task proved difficult, or let fly at animals, or hurled their tools away, and who would have their knives out on the slightest provocation.[74] He knew well enough that there were thoroughly vicious elements among them—ruffians who would plunder shipwrecked sailors in cold blood; children who beat their own mothers; so-called respectable men of the middle classes who maltreated their wives, as did the Russian merchant classes in the time of the Czars.[75] But there is no need to give further examples. Some of the facts related earlier about the Circumcellions are eloquent enough. Augustine often preached on the subject of "Rage" and of the desire for revenge—the besetting sins of the South. "Rage is the mote, hatred the beam, but if you feed your rage it will sooner or later became a beam too. For a mote which you nourish is bound to turn into a beam in the end. Take care, therefore, that your motes do not turn into beams, and let not the sun go down upon your wrath. Do you yourself feel that you are turned white with hatred when you rebuke another for losing his temper? Put by your hatred, then, and your rebuke will truly be justified. If you do not do this the beam will be in your own eye and the mote in that of your neighbour. And why will you have a beam in your own eye? Because you disregarded it when it was a mote. You went to sleep with it. You got up with it. You cosseted it. You watered it with false suspicions and you nourished it by giving credence to flatterers, who have spoken evil to you about your friends. In this way you have made a beam of what before was a mote. Take, therefore, the beam out of your own eye and do not hate your brother. Are you frightened now or are you not frightened? I say to you, do not hate, and yet you feel secure and answer me, 'Well, what is hatred?' 'What harm is there in hating your enemy?' Yet if you think hatred a matter of small account, then let me tell you something that will surprise you. Whosoever hates his brother is a murderer. He who hates is a murderer. Can you say to me, 'It's all one to me whether I am a murderer or not?'" "He who hates is truly a murderer. No, you have mixed no poisons, you have not sallied forth with a sword; you have made no bargains with accomplices; arranged no meeting-place; you have not appointed a time; and, finally, you have not committed a crime. All you have done is to hate, and therefore, although you have not killed another you have brought about your own death." A little later, after a magnificent passage, on the words "Forgive us our debts as we forgive our debtors", he says, "But your soul will not forgive, and it mourns because you say to it, 'Do not hate.' Say then to your soul, 'How canst thou mourn, O my soul? How canst thou torture me with grief? Why dost thou mourn? Get rid of thy hatred and do not destroy me utterly. Why dost thou vex me with thy misery? Trust in God. Thou art sick. Thou dost battle for breath. Thou knowest that thou art sick with malice, because thou canst not put away thy hatred. Trust in God. He is a physician. For thee he hung upon the cross and to this day he has not been revenged. Why wilt thou be avenged? The reason for thy hatred is that it is a means of revenge. See thy Lord hanging there. See him hanging. And giving thee his commands from the cross as though it were his seat of office. See him hanging there, preparing a physic from his blood for one like thyself, preparing it for thee, for thou art sick. See him hanging there, thou that wouldst be revenged. Hear his prayer, 'Father, forgive them, for they know not what they do.' "[76]

But the vendetta had been a flourishing institution long before Augustine spoke these words. Once a disturbance arose the people would listen to no-one. "Then no man dare go out in the street to try and stop them. Even we ourselves dare not do that." So the bishop declared from the pulpit one St. Laurence's Day, when the crowd had lynched an officer whom, it must be admitted, they had some reason for disliking, and had mutilated his body. "And then people are so ready to say, 'We must take no notice of what is done by the people, for what is done by the people cannot be punished.' Indeed? Can God not punish it?"[77]

This sermon on the lynching is a masterpiece of improvisation, and a superb illustration of Augustine's skill of making a synthesis of ideas which are really far removed from one another. It also shows that he could develop a rough and brutal style when dealing with rough and brutal things. After making a few brief references to the martyrs and their powers of self-control, he let the theme of St. Laurence rest and used the last half-hour fairly to let fly. He heaped the bitterest reproaches on the guilty, while at the same time adjuring them in the most affecting manner to mend their ways. He did not conceal his anger, but vented it freely. Nor did he refrain from uttering what was really a personal complaint. "Now that you have killed this man," he said, "I have only to say a word on this matter, and immediately you retort, 'How sad that the bishop did not pray more earnestly for him.'" Immediately after this he appealed in the most moving fashion to their honour, and explained what irresistible power would be theirs if they were to practise meekness, and how it would then be possible for the peaceful man to fetter the hands of the transgressor; how the father could then control his son, the master his servant, and the priest his layfolk. A moment later he made quite clear his conviction that their victim was lost for ever. "Do not curse him in his grave," he said, "for an evil man is dead. He is doubly to be mourned—because he is dead and he is evil. He is doubly to be mourned because he has died a double death. He has died both the temporal and the eternal death. I fear the worst. Do not rage any further against him, for only the wicked rage against the wicked. Others deal mildly with them."[78] Is it so very remarkable that the church should sometimes have resounded with weeping?

They showed the same passion in the causes of God. They not merely shouted an unwelcome convert out of the church, but shouted strangers whom they happened to like on to their bench of priests. That had been Augustine's own experience, as it had been the experience of Paulinus in Barcelona, and of Ambrose in Milan. Twenty years after his own enforced consecration under Valerius, that church saw an equally astonishing scene which Augustine describes in a letter to Melania's mother, Albina,[79] in great detail. It is a scene which makes us realize, as no detailed description could do, what an embarrassing and inconvenient thing the herd of Hipponesians could at times become. Melania, the younger, and her husband Pinianus, were of the House of the Valerii. They were enormously rich and after their flight from Rome they lived for a time in Tagaste. Since the early death of their children they had lived as *continentes* and were busying themselves with the liquidation of Melania's inheritance. Together with Alypius, the Bishop of Tagaste, they visited Augustine in the spring of 411, after the latter had been unable to go to them in the previous winter.[80] While they were praying among the faithful in the great church the crowd, at the end of the Introit, began to shout that they wanted Pinianus as a priest and that he was to remain in Hippo and that they would in no wise let him go. Augustine came into the body of the church and declared that he would certainly not consecrate the man against his will. He declared that he had given him a promise to that effect, and that if the people insisted on keeping him as a priest in violation of that promise, they would not have Augustine as a bishop for very much longer.[81] Then he went back to his seat in the apse. By this answer the people were "moved for a moment, as a flame is beaten down by the wind only to blaze out again more fiercely than before". They called out that if Augustine would not consecrate another was to do it. Hereupon Augustine told the notables who, in the meantime, had come into the apse, that he would not dream of allowing anything of this kind to happen in his own church, and that Pinianus, if he were to be consecrated against his will, would only leave Hippo the more quickly. But the little group of men, which in any case could hardly hear Augustine through the shouting, did not believe that he meant what he said.

Meanwhile the crowd, which was standing packed together by the railings of the apse, began to give vent to its resentment against Bishop Alypius, for the latter had acted as host to the wealthy Romans. They continued to shout so wildly and so persistently as they stood on the steps of the apse, that both bishops began to fear a disaster, though it later became plain that the people who were making all the noise had no serious hostile intentions.

Augustine said nothing. He was determined not to utter a word, since he was afraid that otherwise he could not keep his promise, and was seriously considering leaving the church, so as to forestall its possible desecration. But, on reflection, he did not do so, since he was afraid to leave Alypius alone, and equally afraid to make a path for himself and Alypius through the crowd. At this moment the horrified Pinianus succeeded in getting a priest named Barnabas to make his way to the apse with a message to Augustine. Pinianus said that he would declare on oath that if consecrated against his will, he would leave Africa.

The bishop was careful to avoid thus pouring oil upon the flames. He stepped down from the apse and the people made room for him. Immediately hereafter a second messenger from Pinianus, a certain Timasius, contrived to reach him, and let him know that if no actual force was used, Pinianus might consent to stay in Hippo. Augustine made no reply, but turned round, rapidly mounted the steps again, and whispered to Alypius what Pinianus had let him know. Alypius angrily answered that he wanted to be left out of it. Whereupon Augustine, not knowing what to do, turned to the crowd, and amid a sudden silence, let them know what Pinianus had said. There was a certain amount of whispering, and then a few men in front began to call out, "He is to swear that if later he becomes a priest he will only be a priest in Hippo." Augustine told him this and Pinianus declared that he agreed. There was thunderous applause when Pinianus's answer was read out. But immediately, there was a demand that he should take the promised oath there and then. Pinianus, however, delayed, on the grounds that such an oath would need some formulating, and also because he was disinclined to bind himself to remain in the town.

What would he do in an emergency? A raid by the barbarians, for example? At this stage Melania interrupted him, pointing out how bad the climate was, whereupon her husband told her to be quiet.

The bishop found these objections natural enough, though actually he did not think that Pinianus would be faced with the difficulty he anticipated, since, in the event of a barbarian attack, the whole town would be evacuated. But he thought it better not to go into the matter publicly, since the people would become suspicious and would look upon the phrase "Except in the case of extreme need" as a trick for evading the obligation undertaken. And in point of fact, he proved to be right. When the deacon started to read the declaration it was well received but hardly had he spoken the words "Except in the case of extreme need", than the shouting broke out again. Hereupon Pinianus had the offending phrases struck out and the declaration read a second time after this correction had been made. Although Augustine was deadly tired, Pinianus did not wish to appear before the congregation alone, so they appeared together. The newly-elected priest told them that all they had heard from the deacon had indeed been written by himself and was looked upon as having the binding force of an oath. And he repeated yet again, word for word, what he had dictated. "Deo gratias!" was now the cry. But it was followed by demands that the document should be signed immediately. The bishop sent the catechumens away, for they were not voting Church members, and the rule which forbade them to be present at the Sacrifice most probably forbade their presence at the laying-on of hands. Hereupon Pinianus signed. The suspicious notables, however, also insisted upon the signature of both bishops. And Augustine had already half-written his name when the outraged Melania intervened (*contradixit*), and seems actually to have torn the document from his hands, for Augustine himself says, "I obeyed her", and nothing came of the signing.[82]

This impossible scene not only was the occasion of considerable annoyance and of a very bad fright for Augustine himself, but it estranged his highly-placed friends. Alypius was upset because the mob had shouted such outrageous insults at him and the bishop, and he also wrote a letter to his friend in which he expressed astonishment that another bishop should allow anybody to take an oath in his presence with such far-reaching consequences. But there was more to come, for old Albina, Melania's mother, wrote a very stiff letter from Tagaste in which she reproached Augustine with his passive attitude and expressed her disgust at the shameless avarice of his congregation, for she correctly assumed that they were not so much concerned with the ascetic achievements of Pinianus as with the charitable donations and foundations which they might expect to get out of him. Augustine defended his parishioners against this accusation with considerable wit, but unfortunately to little purpose. To his friend Alypius he wrote: "It was really a very unpleasant business. The fact is that while you have been suspected of avarice by the ignorant multitude I have incurred the identical suspicion but from the lights of the Church. I cannot leave such stings in the hearts of my dear friends. There is the ugly suspicion against my people. Albina almost shouted it in my face [*pene clamavit*], and so did her children on that day in the apse. I don't say that there weren't a certain number of my people who had unworthy motives, but the intentions of most of them were quite honest. None of my monks joined in the clamour, and there was only one monk, who came from Carthage, who was not a member of my community, and even he did not shout at you. I made enquiries about that. Of course, Pinianus must keep his promise and that without reservations, for the oath must be held to bind in the sense in which the other party interprets it. Even the heathens did not dare to say that an oath taken under duress is invalid. Think of Regulus; and after all, my people did not force him to commit perjury or demand anything evil of him. Nor can it possibly be said that they did not correctly understand the oath, or drew unjustifiable inferences from it, for they said nothing when, by pure chance, Pinianus was compelled to leave town the next day. So they know exactly what was sworn and what was not sworn, and Pinianus most certainly did not promise to refrain from going wherever he wanted to, he merely promised to return to Hippo."[83]

To Albina he wrote much more fully.

I must comfort you, and I will try to show you, if I can, that your suspicions have no foundation. Why do you accuse my people of the meanest kind of avarice? They called out for something that was good. They wanted a good priest. Is that avarice? Why should you think my people are so very interested in donations made to the Church? I was invited here as a priest when I possessed nothing whatever and had just got rid of the little bit of land that I had inherited from my father. So that, if you take the monies of my Church into account (which, as everybody knows, I have to administer), I am twenty times richer now than I was when I came here. As against this, Pinianus would be a comparatively poor man, if you take his accustomed way of life into account; so you cannot say that my people were clamouring for him because he was rich, but rather because he despised riches; and even if there were some beggars among those who created the uproar and these beggars hoped that a bit of money would drop their way, well, begging by a poor man is not a sign of avarice. Or is the reproach made indirectly against my clergy, which would mean that it is made against me? That at least would not be entirely unreasonable, for here the assumption is that we are sustained by church property, and that we only spend our money within the bishopric and the monastery. Very little of this money goes to the poor and nobody could prove what becomes of it, so that your reproach if reasonably interpreted could only be held to refer to ourselves.

So what am I to do now? How can I establish my innocence? This is a matter of conscience, of which only God can judge. Now you force me to confirm something with an oath, and that is worse than to order somebody to take an oath or to incite him to do so; and this last is exactly what you accuse me of in your letter, though your accusation is quite untrue. I am not angry with you because of this, despite the fact that your own anger is directed against me and my people, but because the wound in your heart, as also my own good name, force me to do so, I call God as my witness and declare to you that I only carry on with the administration of Church property against my will and look upon it as a hideous burden. If I could get rid of this task, I would do so; and Alypius feels in this matter just as I do. No, I am not angry with you; rather do I feel grateful to you for respecting my office and not saying what you think to my face, but rather letting me know by discreet and honourable though rather indirect means, what your feelings in this matter really are.

He ended by demolishing, with a clever play on words, the suggestion that an oath given under duress was not binding. How can that be said? he asks. A man who is consecrated as a priest must not, on that account, go into exile and he will surely not prefer becoming guilty of perjury to undertaking this exile—I mean this service in the priesthood—and should I rather have brought my Church into confusion than accept what so excellent a man as your son was offering me?[84] And so this very significant event ends with two witty letters of defence which teach us more than anything else could have done about the circumstances prevailing in the Hippo congregation and of the violence of the Hippo people.

Long ago Tillemont voiced the suspicion that these two letters were not the end of the story. Probably what happened was that, thanks to the eloquence of Augustine, Pinianus was released from his promise,[85] for he remained for seven years in Tagaste and then went to the East and later back again to Italy, where he died as an abbot keenly interested in agriculture, and with a community of some thirty monks around him.[86] Neither Pinianus nor Melania could long remain angry with Augustine, if indeed they were ever angry at all. They wrote to him from Jerusalem in 418 about an encounter with Pelagius, and he replied by sending them his works *The Grace of Christ* and *Original Sin*, which he dedicated collectively to his three friends.[87] And in the next year they sent cordial greetings from Bethlehem [88] via Jerome. It was not unusual for the ascetic practices of the Valerii to make them figures of some interest. One day they were proceeding with the older Melania on a journey to visit St. Felix of Nola and his servant Paulinus, who was a man of their own rank and a distant relative. They had fetched the old woman from Naples with a number of luxurious coaches and magnificently caparisoned horses, but as they were passing through Campagna the senators and lawyers suddenly began to vie with one another in throwing their silk togas and gold-embroidered *stolae* and their costly fur mantles at the elder Melania's feet, and covered themselves with the edges of her worn widow's mantle, and sought everywhere to touch her greasy hempen habit, as though they wished to rid themselves of the infection of their wealth by drawing towards themselves the very filth of poverty.[89]

When a people honours a thing it wants to possess it and will use force in order to do so if the opportunity occurs. Whatever may have been the true feelings of the people at Hippo, they were quite prepared to compel these saintly rich men to restrict the circle of their friends to their own neighbourhood and to force the Mammon of their unrighteousness, such as it was, to exercise its influence in their immediate vicinity. Hippo still belonged to the old realistic world of Antiquity. In the Middle Ages, people stole saints after their death in order to attract alms. In Hippo they stole them while they were still alive and their alms along with them.

The Indifferent

As in the sphere of morals, so also in that which pertains to the formal practice of religion, it is the weaker brethren that we hear about most. There are, for instance, the permanent catechumens who are ready enough to listen to a fine sermon, who make the sign of the cross and call themselves Christians, but who, when Lent comes round, refuse to be inscribed as *competentes* and put off their baptism till they happen to be gravely ill or have got into a panic in some emergency. If there was an earthquake or a pestilence, if the barbarian showed himself in the neighbourhood threatening fire and sword, then they came rushing to the priests for baptism. That was quite the usual thing, and it was one of the reasons why the clergy were not allowed to leave if a town was threatened with siege.[90] There was an earthquake in Sitifi, the capital of the neighbouring province of Mauretania, which was later to be separated from Augustine's own, and the inhabitants were forced to spend five days in the fields. On that occasion two thousand were baptized.[91] It was the same in other parts of the Empire. When Alaric was nearing Rome in 410, there was a panic and crowds besieged the baptisteries, which went on baptizing uninterruptedly. When there were severe earth-tremors in Jerusalem, resulting in considerable damage to buildings at the Holy Places, more was wrought in an instant by terror than had been achieved by a whole century of preaching. Everybody rushed to be baptized, catechumens, heathens, Jews—the latter wearing the cross upon their clothes—and the baptisms ultimately numbered seven thousand. Augustine said in one of his sermons that he frequently heard of such things from brothers who were entirely trustworthy. "Everywhere God seeks to fill our hearts with terror so that he need condemn no man."[92] In Constantinople, he said, he had heard stories of a vision of fire from heaven which was shortly to destroy the town. A highly-placed officer had seen this in a dream and had told his bishop about it. The bishop had apparently made the matter public and the whole town had done penance much as Nineveh had done it long ago. After that a fiery cloud actually did appear over the town—some said later that they had smelled sulphur—and everyone fled to church "and forced anyone who was competent to do so to baptize them". People were baptized in the street, in the public squares and in ordinary houses, and in any of these places absolution was given and prayers sent up for mercy. Perhaps, said Augustine, some of those who were at that moment listening to him had witnessed the scene. Suddenly the rumour spread that the whole town would be consumed on the following Saturday, whereupon the inhabitants, led by the Emperor and the patriarchs, fled the place and went many miles away. After that people watched from a village church. They saw smoke appear for a short space of time over the town, and there were screams of panic.

The spell was quickly broken, however, when messengers arrived who reported that in the fateful hour nothing whatever had happened. Everyone went home again and found his doors still standing open. There had not even been any thefts. God had sought to make them better men by giving them all a salutary fright. That was how Augustine concluded his tale, which has all the appearances of being true.[93]

Augustine never sought to make easy excuses for those who kept putting off baptism. Some did this from indifference and through the lack of any serious element in their dispositions, some from that peculiar laziness which Augustine had himself had occasion to observe in his own father Patricius, for Patricius, after being a catechumen for many years, was only baptized in 371, when he was actually on his death-bed and Augustine himself was already seventeen years of age.[94] There were others who pointed to some baptized blockhead, who was a scoundrel into the bargain, and haughtily demanded whether they were not better men than he. Augustine's comment on these occasions was that Christ himself had been baptized "for the sake of the proud men who were still to come". "It often happens that a catechumen knows more of his religion and leads a better life than many others who have been baptized. He sees how badly instructed a baptized person can often be and that his way of life is often much less recollected and much less chaste than his own. He himself never thinks of women, yet he sees Christians, who, while remaining innocent of actual adultery, practise little self-control toward their wives. Even so, no man has a right to puff himself up and say, 'Why should I be baptized? Why should I desire to partake of something that happens to be possessed by another who is my inferior both in the matter of conduct and knowledge?' The Lord will answer him, 'How much is he thy inferior? As much as thou art mine? Or is perhaps the servant greater than the master?' "[95]

In most cases the motive for avoiding baptism lay in the desire of such men not to be bound. They wanted to be free to sin and then get rid of their sins cheaply and all at once when the appropriate moment came. Augustine did not mince matters in this connection. They think, he said, that as catechumens they can make light of their adulteries, and then have the effrontery to compare themselves with the woman in the Temple who "also was not condemned".[96]

This whole evil was one with which Augustine never wearied in doing battle. Even the anniversary of his consecration found him in fighting mood. I care naught, he cried out on this occasion, that today of all days you expect to hear something pleasant from me. I must warn you in the words of Holy Scripture: "Defer it not from day to day, for his wrath shall come on a sudden." God knows that I tremble in my *cathedra* myself when I hear those words. I must not, I cannot, be silent. I am compelled to preach to you on this matter and "to make you fearful, being myself full of fear".[97] How dangerous, he says, is every delay! How many rascals are saved by being baptized on their death-beds? And how many earnest catechumens die unbaptized?—which, for Augustine, is equivalent to saying that they are lost for ever.[98] He compares the carefree condition of mind that such people often display with the dread sleeping-sickness of an old man, who keeps on saying "Let me sleep", although the doctor keeps warning those around him that sleep is the one thing he must not do. And do not make it a reproach to me, he continues, that I disturb your peace of mind. How can I comfort you when the threat comes from God himself? For I am but the steward, not the father of the house.[99] "You say, 'I will do it later, I will do it tomorrow. Why do you frighten us? Have we not been promised forgiveness?' Yes, forgiveness is promised you, but it has not been promised to you that you shall see tomorrow."

Each year as the Lenten season approached and the time came for candidates for baptism to inscribe their names, Augustine's zeal grew in intensity. He was like the man in the parable who constrains the guests to come in. Then he would say, "See, it is Easter. Enter your names for baptism. If the feast itself does not inspire you to do this, let at least your curiosity impel you to find out what is really meant by the words 'Whoso eateth my flesh and drinketh my blood remaineth in me and I in him', and to share with myself the understanding of 'Knock and it shall be opened to you', for I too stand here and knock. Open to me! It is in your ear that I am calling and it is against your heart that I am knocking.... And do you faithful also admonish these men by the purity of your lives."[100]

Nor did he feel any constraint in broaching this subject even to exalted personalities. Sometimes he did this by letter, as is shown by the last part of his long missive to his friend Count Caecilianus of Carthage. Caecilianus had complained of Augustine's long silence and Augustine now assured him of his unalterable affection, but he did not fail to let his correspondent feel that he, Caecilianus, had, through his negligence, become guilty, in part at least, of the death of his intimate friend the tribune Marcellinus, who had been most unjustly executed. There had even been rumours of Caecilianus's complicity in the affair, but Augustine refused to give them credence.

Having once made his reference to these rather embarrassing matters and being thus already in process of pouring out his heart, he continued in this outspoken vein: "And if you are willing to listen to the truth, here is another matter which greatly disturbs me. It is that despite your advanced age and the exemplary character of your life you still elect to remain a catechumen. Cannot believing Christians serve the public weal all the better by being good and devout men themselves? For what is the object of all your planning and worrying save to serve men well? If that were not so it would be better to spend your nights and your days in sleep instead of sitting and waking over official business which never yet brought anybody much profit; but I do not doubt that your excellent ——"[101] Here the text breaks off just before the end of the letter, which is a great pity, for we should have very much liked to see how Augustine concluded it; but we can see from it, as we can from innumerable other examples, that eminent men considered a public career incompatible with the status of a baptized person.[102]

To Marcianus, another old friend, who had at long last become a catechumen, he wrote a glowing letter of congratulation which he concluded with a gentle reminder to the man to present himself for baptism as soon as possible. This letter is a masterpiece of reserve and of pastoral diplomacy and is built up on the theme that he did not fully and truly "possess" his friend until he possessed him in Christ. Complete accord over heavenly things is the noblest foundation of friendship—even Cicero had known that.[103]

His attitude was very similar towards the *excommunicati*—the people, that is to say, who had been given a public penance or had even asked for it on their own account. Such men seem often to have been quite undisturbed by having to remain cut off from the rest of the congregation from one year to another. Indeed, they seemed to regard the special part of the church to which they were confined as a particularly fashionable place, for they did not stir a finger to bring about their *reconciliatio*, and looked on quite contentedly while others went to Communion. Were these indeed penitents? "No," says the bishop, "that name is a mask, for your wickedness remains. I seem to see *poenitentes* here in large numbers, but if I look more closely I see they are *malviventes*. What should be a place for humility has become a place for flirting with evil. This I say to you, that you call yourselves penitents but are in reality nothing of the kind. What shall I say to you? Shall I praise you? But I do not praise you in this. What can I do except sing my hackneyed old song? Turn about and be converted, this I beg of you. No man knows when his end is coming and each of you is walking around with his own trap ... I beseech you, brethren, if you have no care for yourselves at least have compassion on *me*." *"Poenitentes, poenitentes"*—so once he began a sermon—"if indeed you are in truth *poenitentes* and not *irridentes*, change your lives, be reconciled to God."

General absolution with laying-on of hands seems to have been a pretty frequent occurrence, but it must sometimes have been a very sorry affair. An endless stream would come up to have hands laid upon them, so the bishop tells us, and not one of them was truly prepared to lead a better life.[104]

Despite his glowing heart, Augustine could be very harsh in his judgements on the indifferent. His mind probably moved on much the same lines as Dostoievsky's Bishop Tikhon, who held that the indifferent man really had no faith at all but only fear—and even that comparatively rarely, if he happened to be a sensual man.[105] He could always mercilessly expose the merely cynical man of pleasure, for he knew him well enough. "Such a man may well grow old, but his lust will not grow old along with him and he may well say to himself, 'We are told that "the countenance of the Lord is against them that do evil things: to cut off the remembrance of them from the earth", but see how old I have grown, and yet from my earliest youth to the present day I have indulged my desires. Many a chaste youth have I helped to bury and it is I, the evil-liver, who have survived those of blameless life.' "[106]

Yet he can also turn to those superficial people, whose frivolity has little in it of malice but yet has dangers of its own. For instance he speaks of the shallow remarks that can be heard in cases of sudden death. "When a dead man is carried to his grave, people think of death. Then men say 'Oh, poor man, he was such a vigorous fellow; only yesterday he was out walking', or, 'I saw him in the street only a week ago and he said this and that to me. Really, a man is nothing at all!' That is how they whisper, and that is how they talk when making their visits of condolence, when they see the man on his bier, when they watch the funeral ceremonies, when they see the corpse carried out and watch the burial. But when the dead man is buried, such thoughts are buried too and the fear of death disappears. As they go home from the funeral they will even have forgotten who it was they had carried out for burial and they return to their swindles, their thieving, perjury and drunkenness and to all the other lusts of the flesh, to the pleasures that disappear, I will not say, when they have been indulged in up to the limit of a man's desire, but in the very moment in which they are being enjoyed. What is even more disastrous, is that the fact that they have just buried a man becomes a reason for doing what they call 'using their common sense'. 'Let us eat and drink', they say, 'for tomorrow we die.' "[107]

The final argument which he applied to the indifferent was that from the pains of hell, and he applied it with both clarity and force. Many a man at that time would say to himself, "I am baptized. A baptized person cannot be lost for ever. My life has, of course, been evil and I shall certainly have to be cleansed by purgatory, but I give alms and that covers a multitude of sins." But the bishop swept these evasions aside. All the Apostles, he said, thought very differently in this matter.[108] Once Christ had descended into hell and had freed all those whom he wished to free,[109] but since then hell had become a prison which would never again be opened. And even if he did not wish to exclude the possibilities of certain temporal reliefs,[110] the punishment was eternal.

Once when a thoroughly bad character was murdered, he did not fear to tell a crowded church not to rage against the man who was quite badly enough off as it was.[111] We cannot help being struck by the fact that he never thought it necessary to refute in the pulpit the arguments against the eternal character of the pains of hell. Probably he never encountered anyone who denied that character or said, as Baudelaire said in reference to George Sand, that a true Christian could not possibly believe in hell—because he himself had most pressing grounds for wishing to see it abolished.

A CASE OF SCRUPLES: AUGUSTINE THE PROBABILIST

That layfolk could go to the other extreme is shown by the letter of a certain Senator Valerius Publicola. Publicola was the only son of the elder Melania, and was the husband of Albina and the father of the younger Melania. He was the owner of some estates at the southern edge of the Empire, and naturally enough his tenants tended to be very much concerned with the problem of the barbarians, in this case the tribe of the Arzuges.[112] The long list of questions which he put to Augustine showed him clearly to be the victim of scruples and to be almost pathologically concerned with the question of defilement. Almost half the questions which he puts are actuated by a fear of demonic influence. Is it lawful, he asks, for travellers or officials on the borders of the

Empire to allow a barbarian, when undertaking to look after their luggage, to swear that he will do so by the local gods, who, after all, are demons, and is it in such circumstances lawful to give him a monetary reward? Publicola asks for an unequivocal answer which will leave no loopholes, otherwise he will be more tortured by doubts than ever.

Is it lawful, he goes on, to draw a profit from crops which have been delivered with an oath of this kind? Further, if the information that such an oath has been sworn comes from the owner's steward and the steward only has that information from hearsay, from witnesses, that is to say, of whom one alleges that the oath was sworn while the other is in some doubt so that the swearing of the oath is not a certainty, does the rule stated in the First Epistle to the Corinthians concerning the partaking of the meat of sacrifice apply? If so, what should be done with the crops or the proceeds thereof? Must they remain untouched until clear proof has been forthcoming that no such oath was actually sworn? Does such an oath only defile a Christian who has permitted it to be sworn, or does it also defile the goods in question? And what is the position when a pagan tribune allows a barbarian to swear such an oath? And if I send a messenger to the Arzuges does the oath defile the messenger?[113]

Is it lawful for a Christian knowingly to eat anything taken from a threshing-floor or a wine-cellar, if sacrifices have been made to the gods in such places? Is it lawful for him to gather wood in a sacred grove? If he brings meat from market and is in doubt whether it is sacrificial meat or no, and finally comes to the conclusion that it is not, that being the correct conclusion, and acts accordingly, does he commit a sin? If somebody first says that the meat is sacrificial meat and then denies it, saying that he told lies on the first occasion, is it lawful for the Christian to eat it or sell it?[114] If a Christian loses his way and is in danger of dying of hunger and in extreme necessity finds food in a deserted temple, is it lawful for him, assuming that the district in question is entirely uninhabited, to eat some of this food or must he die?[115] If a barbarian or a Roman tries to kill him, is it lawful for him to kill his assailant in self-defence, or must he merely seek to restrain him without killing him? And how do the words "Resist not evil" apply in this case? Does he become guilty of murder if he puts a wall round his property and enemies are killed at this place?[116] Is it lawful to drink from a fountain at which wine has been sacrificed? Is it lawful to drink from the fountain in a deserted temple, if an idol is still standing there, though nothing else occurs in that place? May a Christian take a bath either in a private house or in a public establishment if sacrifice is still offered there? If pagans bathe there on a festival day may he bathe there together with them or must he bathe alone? If pagans, returning on such a festival from the worship of their idols, go straight into the pool and there commit some idolatrous act (he probably means some ritual ablution or a kissing of hands or other greeting to a statue in the corner) and the Christian knows of this, may he still enter the pool after them? If at a dinner a Christian has refused to eat sacrificial meat, but is later offered that meat either at his business or at another meal, and fails to recognize it, does he commit a sin? May he buy fruit or vegetables or eat them if they come from a garden which belongs to an idol or to one of the idol's priests?[117] Publicola ends his list by quoting a few texts from the Pentateuch, from the Book of Joshua and from the Book of Judges, which he applies to his own problems with undeniable skill, for instance, the verse "Neither shalt thou bring anything of the idol into thy house lest thou become an anathema like it."[118] He then asks for enlightenment, and ends hastily with the words "God protect you. I greet you; pray for me."

Is it not a strange thing that a Roman living in a marble palace on the Coelian Hills should bring to light the formula of probabilism for the benefit of his petty tenants on the edges of the Empire? Publicola's questionnaire is a pitiful performance, as also is his style, and both express a purely formalistic type of Christianity. As one reads his letter it is difficult not to conclude that casuistry goes even further back than to the time shortly before Escobar and the *Lettres provinciales*, and was not invented by professional moralists at all but by layfolk. The casuist who, in this case, was under the necessity of answering him, wrote him a letter which is of interest not only for the light it sheds on the whole question of lay piety, but because it is an important document in the history of moral theology, and this despite the fact that Augustine had enough sense to ignore the great majority of the questions altogether.[119]

The first sentences contain a touch of irony. Augustine says that Publicola's letter had made him almost as warm as the writer—not that he himself was particularly perturbed by these questions, but because he burns to bring his questioner peace of mind. You ask me for a final and definitive answer, he continues, but I cannot promise to give you that, for though I may be convinced of the correctness of some answer myself, you may remain unconvinced (clearly Augustine was no stranger to the obstinacy of scrupulous people). Nevertheless, I have thought the thing over and think that I should answer you as far as I can.

Now, he says, in this matter of a promise confirmed by an oath to heathen gods, I do not think you have any need to worry, for although Holy Scripture forbids us to swear an oath, it does not forbid us to accept an oath from another. And indeed, out in that part of the world we may have no choice but to do this, if we want to be certain that engagements are kept and the peace of the Empire preserved. Further, a Christian, in so far as he is able, should try and prevent a part of any crop from being sacrificed, but if this should happen, the remainder is not necessarily defiled any more than is the pool in a bathing establishment. After all, we still have to breathe the air even when the smoke of sacrifice has ascended through it, and we continue to drink at the fountain even when water for sacrifice has been fetched from it. All that you must guard against is creating the impression that you honour the gods—in other words, you must avoid giving scandal.[120]

When you officially confiscate a temple you must take nothing from it for your own use; that would create the impression that your zeal was merely a cloak for avarice. Compare this with the text from Deuteronomy. It is, however, quite lawful for you to devote the confiscated temple to some other purpose—that merely means converting as human beings are converted.

As regards eating, he goes on, there is no need for you to be more strict than Paul, who only forbade men to eat deliberately from the table of sacrifice, "for the earth is the Lord's and all that there is therein", and further, "Every creature of God is good."[121] If it were not lawful to eat what had been grown in a temple garden, how could Paul have eaten in Athens, since the whole city was dedicated to Minerva? Do we not all enjoy the light of the sun, to which sacrifices are unceasingly offered? And what of the wind, which so to speak takes up and consumes the smoke of sacrifice and to whom sacrifices are also actually made? Not resisting evil means to refrain from taking delight in revenge, it does not mean failing to observe the courtesies of public intercourse, nor does it mean the waiving of the right of self-defence. And as regards that wall which might perhaps come to mark the spot where men were killed, is it unlawful to shoe a horse because it might one day kick somebody? Did not Paul accept an armed escort? Are we forbidden to have trees in our garden because somebody might hang himself on one of them? Or a window because somebody might jump out of it?

As regards the question about the starving person, the answer is that he may eat even when he has ground to fear that it may possibly be sacrificial meat. Only in the event of his having absolute certainty on that point would it be better for him to display Christian fortitude and leave it alone.[122] Apart from the last of these answers, which is dictated by a reverence for St. Paul and which may well strike us as extreme, Augustine argues very much along the lines of the old Jesuits, and—*n'en deplaise* Pascal and his Augustinianizing friends—unmistakably belongs to the probabilists. Also, he has no belief in the power of demons to infect food. All this is quite important, as is also the proof here supplied that eminent people round the year 400 knew their Bibles remarkably well, that their Latin was execrable and that they were not always blessed with that perfect love which casteth out fear.

The Murmurers of the Year 410

Then there was a group of people who resembled the Jews in the wilderness. These were the murmurers; they were something different from the ordinary grumblers who every year complained that the winter had never been so cold nor the summer so hot. There will always be men like this, said Augustine; one generation will always praise the times that have gone before, and the previous generation will praise those even further back and they will take a fancy to those times because they have not lived in them themselves, for "It is the present that bites most sharply."[123] But these murmurers were men who would not accept the dispensations of God, for the old biblical sin of murmuring had reappeared in this declining world of pleasure-lovers and slaves, a world which the prestige of the Roman name still carried along and which was soon to be smashed into pieces under the hammer blows of the barbarians. One heard both Christians and pagans complain of "these wretched Christian times", one heard them say how well things had gone before, how the amphitheatres were falling into ruin and nothing was kept in repair.[124]

This was a theme which Augustine was to treat in the twenty-two books of his *City of God*, and one which was to fill the whole world after the fall of Rome in the year 410, and was, as the sermons clearly show, to find its echo even in Hippo. Quite suddenly the shadow of the great "decline and fall" had fallen, even over secure Africa. The horror of August 410 was even greater than that of June 1940. One saw refugees—among them aristocrats with some of the greatest Roman names—coming off the ships wild-eyed and shabby; one heard them tell of the horrors that had befallen Rome—of palaces burnt, of the Gardens of Sallust smoking and in ruins, of rich men being hunted down, of blood on the marble fora, of the barbarians' carts full to overflowing with stolen and damaged treasures.

Entire families had been annihilated, senators murdered. Virgins dedicated to God had been raped. The aged Marcella had been beaten nearly to death, because she could produce no hidden gold, and insisted on begging for only one favour—that the honour of her young companion Principia should not be violated.[125] Men became terrified as they heard of these things, and the story spread while the refugees themselves hastened to leave the little harbour town behind and make for Carthage, where they immediately secured their regular seats at the theatre and where, since Roman refugees were added to the rest, life became wilder than ever. For "the Bourbons never learn anything and never forget anything", whatever the age in which they happen to live. Twenty years later Carthage was to fall without a blow. While it was being taken games were in progress, so that, if Salvianus is to be believed, the shouts in the amphitheatre drowned the trumpets of the Vandals, and it was none other than Genseric himself who chased the weaklings out of the town.[126]

The effect which the fall of Rome had on men's minds was decisive; it had been shown that the Eternal City was not eternal at all, it was as though the world itself had been decapitated. "How are the towers fallen", the ascetics read in Jeremiah, but they thought of the towers of the Aurelian Wall. "How forsaken is the town that once was full of people", thought the pious when they heard the terrible stories of the sack, stories of dogs barking in the empty palaces, of starved survivors coming out of the basilicas after five days and standing wringing their hands over the corpses in the streets while the carts with the gold and silver and the captured youths and maidens rolled triumphantly southwards along the Via Appia.

Augustine himself was shattered by the news.[127] He had the fate of the Empire very much at heart. It was too closely bound up with the fate of the Church for him to feel otherwise. Two years previously he had read in a letter of the priest Victorianus how the Vandals had overrun the unhappy country of Spain, how they had burnt the basilicas and killed without exception all the priests on whom they could lay their hands, how they had in fact behaved precisely as the Communists behaved in 1936. He had been deeply moved, and indeed felt that suffering almost as though it were his own.[128] In that same year of 409, when other barbarians threatened the Eternal City for the first time, he felt called upon to rebuke a woman named Italica for having written to him four times without saying a word about conditions prevailing in Rome. Surely you will understand, he wrote, that we should wish to have certainty about things that are reported to us as rumours, rumours which seem too monstrous to be believed, for as we would rejoice with the joyful, so we would shed tears with those that weep. What are we to make of this omission of yours? he continued. Perhaps there is a proud reserve at the bottom of it?[129]

He was on the country estate where he passed a whole summer by doctor's orders when he heard how the city had fallen quite suddenly, almost without a struggle. His first act was to write to Hippo and appeal both to clergy and people not to waste their time in lamentations, but to lend a hand and give hospitality to the refugees that were streaming in, and to clothe them, and to make a better showing in this than they had done hitherto.[130]

The event had yet other effects; pagans said quite openly what they thought —Rome had fallen because it had forsaken its gods,[131] and even the Christians began to sing the same tune though with slightly different words. "Where now are the *memoriae* of the Apostles", the bishop could hear the people say, "What has Rome gained for possessing Peter and Paul? Once Rome stood upright, now it is fallen."[132] There were Christians who murmured in this fashion. Augustine could not point out to the Christians, as he could to the pagans, that a pagan like Rhadagasus had sacrificed every day to the gods and had been quite as much conquered as anybody else, and that the conqueror

Alaric was himself a Christian.[133] (He could hardly make that point to Christians, for after all, was not Alaric an Arian?) And how could he explain why the Eternal City should have fallen now, of all times, when it was surrounded by a circle of famous martyrs' graves? Had there not been fifty just men in Rome, or even thirty, or even ten as in Sodom?[134]

Augustine admitted in a sermon that this last question had been very emphatically raised in connection with the eighteenth chapter of Genesis, and it must be admitted that his answers are not wholly satisfactory. Rome, he said, had not been destroyed like Sodom; it had only been chastised, and fortunately the facts were not so bad as the first reports led one to believe. So many people, he said, got away in time and have now returned home again; others were living in safety in Africa, and could be seen in their midst; prisoners were being ransomed, while Alaric's respect for the graves of the Apostles and for the first see of the Church helped in a marked manner to mitigate the disaster. Indeed, it had been instrumental in saving thousands of lives. All who had sought sanctuary in the great basilicas had been safe, and the report was going around that the gold vessels from St. Peter's had, by pure chance, been discovered hidden in the house of a widow, and that Alaric had returned them to the church under guard. This again showed that Christianity and Christianity alone had been able to teach the barbarians the elements of humanity.

God had indeed used Alaric to chastise Rome, but he had also used him to spare and protect it. Nor did Rome have to suffer what Job had to suffer. It did not have to witness its own decay, and however much Rome had had to bear, the pains of hell were very much worse. Let men think of the wealthy glutton and his thirst. Most certainly there were many just men in Rome—many more, indeed, than fifty—but if those just men were truly wise they would recognize that they were sinners and so deserved punishment; also, how many saints had gone to their eternal refreshment? The true city consists not of walls but of its citizens. No, the thing had been sent as a trial, but not as a condemnation.[135]

For the Christians the bishop had ready a specifically Christian formula, though of a very radical kind; it was a line of thought which is to be traced through, indeed which may be said to govern, the various sermons of the years 410 and 411.[136] The catastrophe of Rome had been an act of divine intervention; God was a physician who cut away the diseased flesh from out of the body of our culture. The world was a furnace in which the straw was consumed, while the gold came out ennobled and purified. It was the press which separated the oil from the pulp; the pulp was black and must flow away to the place for which it was fitted, which was the drain; the waste matter was made worse by the process, the oil improved. He who murmured was of the residue; he who looked into his own soul and amended his life was the good oil.[137] On the feast day of the Prince of the Apostles in 411, ten months after the sack, it seemed quite natural for him to revert to the fate of Rome in his sermon, and to that complaint which it seemed impossible to silence—"Where are now the *memoriae* of the Apostles?" Augustine replied to this (and it was a superb example of his ready wit in the pulpit) by referring to St. Paul's words on the relative character of all earthly suffering. It is written "that the sufferings of this time are not to be compared to the glory that is to come which will be revealed in us." If that was how St. Paul felt, let no man today think in terms of the flesh; there was no time for that, the world was being shaken so that all things within it were being changed; the old man was being put off, the flesh was being pressed in the press. Let free reign be given, therefore, to the spirit. " 'There is St. Peter's body in Rome', say the people, 'there is the body of Paul and the body of Lawrence, and the bodies of other holy martyrs lie in Rome; and Rome is misery, Rome is a ruin, Rome is in mourning, trodden under foot and burned out. So many people have perished there through hunger, through pestilence and the sword. Where now are the *memoriae* of the Apostles?' What say you there? True, true, I have said it myself, I have spoken of the misery of Rome, and I am asked where now are the *memoriae* of the Apostles. True, they are there in Rome, yes, they are there, but you do not have them within yourself. Oh, if only they were within you, those *memoriae* of the Apostles, whoever you may be, you who speak so foolishly, and judge so foolishly, you who, having been called by the Spirit, yet judge by the flesh; O that they were within you! If you would only 'memorize' the Apostles, then you would see whether it is earthly or heavenly happiness that is promised you, for if the *memoria* of the Apostle is indeed alive within you, then give ear to him when he says, 'For that which is at present momentary and light of our tribulation worketh for us above measure exceedingly an eternal weight of glory . . . for the things which are seen are temporal, but the things which are not seen are eternal.'[138] In Peter himself the flesh was temporal, and yet you will not accept that the stones of Rome are temporal too. The Apostle Peter is reigning with the Lord, the body of the Apostle Peter lies buried somewhere and is a reminder to us which has for its purpose the awakening of our love for the eternal, so that you may not cleave to the earth with your thoughts, but with the Apostle direct them towards heaven. Mark well the direction in which the Apostle is seeking to drive you. 'When ye are risen with Christ then look up to what is above and not to what is of this world'—you hear it in this one word 'Sursum'. Lift up, lift up your hearts. And if you are able to hear this, are you still sad, do you shed tears because wood and stone have fallen down, and because mortal men have died?" "Can the Goth take away anything that is watched over by Christ? Was it the purpose of the Apostles' *memoriae* to safeguard your idiotic theatres? Did Peter die and was his body buried in Rome, so that not a stone of your theatres should be displaced?"[139]

No, God is just. He snatches their unwholesome sweets out of the hands of naughty children. Ah, my brothers, says Augustine, let us make an end both of our sins and our murmuring. Surely it behoves not Christians to complain because Rome happens to burn in the Christian era? Rome has burnt three times, under the Gauls, under Nero, and now under Alaric. What use is there in eating your heart out about that? Why do you turn and gnash your teeth against God? Because something is burning which has burned quite often before. Romulus' Rome is burning—there is nothing remarkable about that. One day the whole world that God has created will burn. You remark that the Christian sacrifices should have saved the town, but why should they have done this any more than the heathen sacrifices should have saved your mother city of Troy?[140] Rome burned because it was necessary to make the world pause and reflect—and, he adds, I may say this: that the world today is far more guilty than the old world of Troy, for it has had the Gospel preached to it.[141]

Augustine was not afraid to go still further and to say that the world which was collapsing under his eyes was not worth sorrowing for, and he pointed to the martyrs of the time of Constantine, whose contempt fell on a world that was not in decay, but still full of happiness; they despised a world that was still in bloom while his hearers could not turn away from one that was decaying and full of thorns; rather, let them take a lesson from the collapse of their house. What is it worth, he continues, O you people who have such wonderful knowledge of the value of things, you who know how to haggle, and to chaffer away a bit off the price in every bargain that is offered you? Be certain of this, that your faith is worth more than heaven and earth put together.[142]

Not that these people were always pleased to hear such words. If the heavenly wisdom "was like the hen of the Gospel that kept the egg of Christian hope under her wings then there were always scorpions which would attack the egg, and if the hen, in her turn, rounded upon them, they would sting another", and he himself was that other. Yes, he cried, vent your anger against me if you will; however deeply we may be moved we shall not curse you back, and if we are slandered by you we shall only pray for you the more. For it is true, he said, that they cover me with slander. "Let him keep off the subject of Rome", that is what they say of me, "let him say nothing of Rome." Yet I do not accuse Rome; Rome is merely for me a spur to send my supplications up to God, and I use it as an example wherewith to warn you. For did we ourselves have no brothers there, and are not our brothers there still? Does not a great part of Jerusalem, that city of pilgrims, have its habitation there?"[143]

The emphatic quality of his defence shows us how serious was the complaint against him. It is true that preachers who use their pens will often express ideas which have filled their minds when they were at their desks. And the fact that Augustine was treating a similar subject in his study (where he was working on the first five books of the *City of God*) may in part explain his choice of that subject for the pulpit. But few people will say that it completely explains it. As against this, however, it has already been pointed out how deeply the fall of Rome affected him, and that though he did not look upon the Empire as eternal, he was nevertheless quite unable to conceive of a world in which that Empire would no longer exist. The end of the one was the end of the other. He could not see the Middle Ages looming up behind the ages of barbarism. His conviction was that "the Empire has been subjected to trial, it has not been transformed", and because this had happened before, he felt that the possibility still existed that it would rise again. What had happened gave no grounds for despair, for who knew the mind of God?[144] Even the ancients could accept the ruin of a city with resignation and allow the sight of it to set them dreaming, and in point of fact one of his fellow-Christians, Ausonius, a somewhat worldly man, gave expression to that same classic calm in some verses which he wrote about this time:

> What's so dire in the death of a man or the end of a building?
> Whether it's stones or fame, death is the end of it all.[145]

Augustine was a loyal Roman. *Romanitas* and *humanitas* were in his eyes inseparable from one another. Although he saw in the Roman State a certain demonic element (though this was hidden and its existence was difficult to prove), he preached obedience to the powers of this world in all things not forbidden by conscience. He held up as an example those Christian soldiers under Julian the Apostate who rejected the Pontifex and his futile sacrifices, but for all that scrupulously obeyed the Emperor's commands.[146] It does not matter, he was later to write, under what kind of a government we live, so long as it does not actually compel us to do evil. If the worst comes to the worst we must endure a government that is thoroughly bad and so earn for ourselves in the midst of the earthly State a place in the heavenly one.[147] This is very definitely a negative attitude, and nothing could be further removed from a mere deification of the State. For all that, he lays it down as a matter of duty time and time again (and he does this with great emphasis) that the laws and authority and customs of the country must be respected.[148]

He was capable of reminding higher officials of their duties and of using great warmth when he did so,[149] and was by no means disinclined to defend the interference of secular authority, particularly when that interference served the cause of ecclesiastical unity;[150] while in the pulpit he could thunder against those who sought to achieve a special righteousness by circumventing the law.[151] He could also speak with enthusiasm of the potentialities latent in the office of a Christian emperor, potentialities which were realized in the person of his hero Theodosius.[152] The same man who had once declared that if the factor of justice is eliminated the great empires are nothing but bands of robbers, declared both in his writings and in his sermons that the Roman Empire owed its ascendancy to the superior morality of its citizens, a morality which could often serve as an example to Christians. Despite the fact that many of its wars had been waged to satisfy avarice and the lust for power, he held that it had nevertheless brought many peoples peace, and guaranteed an undisturbed order.[153] Although theoretically the Roman Empire clove to this world, in so far as it had been corrupted by original sin and had been fettered by the chains of demons, he nevertheless more than once spoke of it as one of the aids by which the City of God was to be called into being, and even as one of its aspects.

Never did he criticize the weaker emperors; even when Marcellinus was judicially murdered, he complained of the military bully in Africa who had so ruthlessly carried out the sentence, but not of the men in Ravenna by whom that sentence had been imposed.[154] While in his celebrated letter to Count Boniface he alludes quite plainly to the undeservedly ungracious treatment which Boniface had received, but says not a word about the Empress;[155] and yet how bluntly and bitterly that same Boniface is reproached by him with having, in 427, handed over Africa to his mutinous troops to work their will with in any way they pleased, and all this because of a purely personal grievance.[156] Even where they are more discreet, there is no question of what Augustine's words are intended to convey. It is that even a man whose worth has not been recognized, and who has in consequence suffered some injustice, must never become a traitor to the dynasty and the Empire. What must he have thought when shortly afterwards, in 429, the embittered man summoned the Vandals from Baetica to Africa, so that it was a Roman general who drew back the bolt at the Pillars of Hercules, and who thus unwittingly gave the sign for the downfall of Christendom in Africa?

There seems some justification for the opinion that it was Augustine who, at the eleventh hour, when the barbarian had already begun to ravage Mauritania, brought about a reconciliation between the Emperor and his commander-in-chief. His fellow-bishops shared his attitude; they remained unswervingly loyal, and one cannot help noticing that neither Gildo nor Heraclian obtained the slightest support from the Catholics, although they enjoyed very active support from the Donatists.

Augustine, however, was more concerned with the immortal souls of men than with the blows of temporal misfortune. All the warnings he uttered to that world to which he undoubtedly belonged, and which, when all is said and done, had done something more than merely build theatres, were inspired by that consideration. They were not only directed against the venerable ruin of dying Rome, but against those grumblers and men of little faith who in the desert of fifth-century Christianity, mourned for the comfortable establishment that had provided for their material needs, and for the fleshpots of paganism in general.

Prayer: The Letter to Proba

Probably it was those same dissatisfied people who also complained, "God does not hear us, what use is it to pray?" The little old secret ways accomplished much more; why not try them again? After all, they were *remedia*. "True", the bishop answered, "they are *remedia*, but they come from the bad angels, and both those that ask for them and those that offer them will burn together."[157] "Somebody says, 'All these years, I have been baptized; then something happened to me. I got ill, ran to church every day, and yet things remained as they were; then I tried the secret remedy, and now I am well again—and don't forget this, for I heard it myself: the magician calls upon the names of God and of the angels.' True enough, but those are angels of whom the Apostle says that we shall ourselves judge them."[158] And then he referred to the wonderful story of the Apostle Paul. Paul prayed earnestly but in vain, most desperately did he pray to God to compel the angel of Satan who struck him with his fists in the face (i.e., gave him severe headaches) to depart. He begged for this a second and a third time, and lo and behold, it was not Paul but the demon who was heard. Are you, then, he says, better than Paul? Have you spent a day and a night in the deep? Have you been beaten three times with rods, or stoned? The example of Paul robs you of any excuse. It is better to be cleansed with Paul by pain, "for power cometh to its fullness in weakness". What is it that the fullers do with linen? They beat it. Or the goldsmiths, with gold that is not purified? They make it hot. We too must be in a position to say, "Only when I am weak am I strong."[159] God is not always willing to hear everyone; many miracles occur in our St. Stephen's Chapel, but many men go away without being heard. In such cases it is God's desire to heal the soul rather than the body.[160] No, not even our prayer that evil shall be removed is always heard immediately; we must suffer the chaff upon the threshing floor. The just can indeed attain to justice, but they cannot always get the benefit of the final judgement. It is written in the Psalms, "The Lord will not cast off his people", but it is also written, "Until justice is turned into judgement".[161]

So also did he speak to the half-hearted who were vexed because they saw sinners living at peace with the world, and regretted their own virtuous lives. "Do we not every day hear such blasphemous talk from the mouths of the faithful, mouths through which there enters the body of Christ? If anybody sees some worthless fellow who has occasioned him particular annoyance living in comfort, he immediately starts to sigh and to say 'Oh dear, what is the good of behaving decently?' Am I not speaking the truth? Do people not speak after this fashion? And if I ask such a man, 'Are you a Christian?' then he says, 'Yes, I am a Christian, but Christ is of little use to me.' Yet how can you say that, my friend? Did Christ, whom you follow, luxuriate in the banquets of this world? Think what has been suffered on your behalf, and by whom! Think how great is that suffering, and by whom and for whom it has been endured! And now you murmur and say, 'He was God, and so he could endure everything, but I am only a man.' Holy Apostle Paul, make us truly learn what you have said, and you who complain, listen carefully and do not close your ears! 'Christ suffered for us, leaving you an example that you should follow in his steps.'"[162]

Others again complain, "Such-and-such a man lives an evil life, and yet he is happy." You are in error, Augustine says. He is not happy, he is like a sick man laughing in his delirium. Soon the illusion of his seeming pleasures will fall away and he will be in very real pain. "Oh dear," these men of little faith begin to cry, "is it just that the wicked should flourish while the good should have to suffer?" But God answers, "Is this your faith? Is that the kind of thing I promised you? Did you become Christians to have a comfortable time in this world? Does it worry you that the wicked should prosper for a time, when those very wicked will soon be worried by the devil?"[163] Yet Augustine was prepared to admit "that no sea is as deep as the riddle why God permits the good to suffer, while the wicked flourish".[164]

It was hardly to be expected that Augustine would be particularly enthusiastic about those Christians who had been baptized with the thought in their minds, "Now my luck will turn, now I shall prosper." Such people, he said, are like the woman who marries a rich man only for his money. "If you ask of your wife that she should love you for yourself alone, should you love God for some reason other than himself? Do you not, as a Christian, sing the psalm 'I will freely sacrifice to thee'?"[165] Nevertheless, Augustine did not deny that it was quite lawful, when praying, to ask for temporal benefits, for it is God who turns all evil things into good, and from whom all good things come, and who heals not only a man but his horse, his sheep and even his chickens, as indeed it is written in the psalm, "Men and beasts thou wilt preserve, O Lord."[166]

On the difficult question, what things above all we should pray for, we have Augustine's moving letter to Faltonia Proba.[167] She was a noble lady of the

Gens Anicia and a widow of the "Perpetual Prefect" Probas, and the mother of not less than three consuls, which meant, in those days, a particularly expensive form of parenthood. Probas, by the way, was a typical eleventh-hour Christian, for he was laid in that precious and very pronouncedly Christian sarcophagus (which we can still see in the Museo Petriano)[168] while still in his baptismal robe and still dripping with the water of baptism. One day Faltonia had met Augustine and, referring to the passage in the eighth chapter of Romans, "We know not what we should pray for", had asked his advice on that very point. In his reply, Augustine tells her to pray for a happy life. But what is a happy life? To do whatever we want? Certainly not; even Cicero knew better than that. Is it the will to be decent in one's dealings? No, it is not that either. Is it not even the care for the wellbeing of one's family? Or for the temporal wellbeing of any other creature? No, care remains care, and is not pure happiness. Is it the high office that you wish for your children (assuming, of course, that you wish them this so that they do good to others)? No, it is not that either. Certainly it is lawful to pray for good health or friendship or for the wellbeing of your families, but true happiness depends on none of these things. Why, he says, do you not pray in the manner that is shown in the Scriptures? "One thing I have asked of the Lord, this will I seek after, that I may dwell in the house of the Lord."[169] That is happiness. Refer everything back to that one prayer, ask for everything that is necessary to enable you to dwell in God's house. You will then pray for the thing that is most salutary to yourself. In asking for the happy life you are then asking for the highest good.[170]

That is why you need not burden yourself with many words, he goes on, for God knows without this what it is that you are trying to say. Yet despite this knowledge on the part of God, it is written that we must always pray and never cease, and must be as persistent as the widow before the unjust judge. For the Apostle says that if she "is a widow indeed and desolate, let her continue in prayers night and day".[171] And although in the eyes of the world Faltonia is anything but *desolata* (which means incapable of being comforted), yet as a Christian she is that very thing, for her *solatium* will only come in the future life.[172] What is one to make of this paradox? Surely this: God does not wish to know our will, he knows that already, but he does wish to deepen our knowledge, and so to purify our desire, so that by means of prayer and contemplation we are made ready to accept whatever it is he sends. That is a very great thing, though we are often too small to match up to it; that is why it is written, "Be ye also enlarged and bear not the yoke with unbelievers."[173]

From time to time we should also pray in actual words, so that by clear definition we may call to mind what we are praying about, and grow conscious of the extent to which our longing has grown; and thus intensify that longing, "for the more glowing the feeling which gave rise to it the more effective our prayers will be".[174]

To pray unceasingly means to be everlastingly longing for the happy life in God. This longing must not be allowed to grow cold through the preoccupations of everyday life, and it must be stirred up at certain fixed times so that it may be brought to glow. It is written, "May your earnest prayers be known before God."[175] This means that they should be made known to our own minds, and that before God who lets us pray; not that we should boast of our prayers before men. Perhaps it also means that these prayers should be made known before the angels who are with God and who bear our prayers to him, who advise us, and who are able to convey to our minds, either clearly and explicitly, or in such a manner that the mind becomes unconsciously aware of it, the nature of the divine will.[176]

Long prayers made during such times as our necessary preoccupations permit are neither wrong nor purposeless, but even this does not mean making many words, as some men think. "For a multitude of words does not necessarily indicate an enduring good disposition. It is written of our Lord that he spent the night in prayer, and that, wrestling with death, he prayed the longer. What else did he do on that occasion than give us an example? At that time, this being the appropriate moment, he was himself a petitioner; now he has become, along with the Father, a hearer of prayers." In Egypt, Augustine continued, the brothers use a large number of quick short prayers which they ejaculate together, so that their devotion may not die away or become blunted. As long as their devotion lasts they are enjoined not to cease from uttering these prayers, though it is sometimes easier for them to express themselves with simple sighs and tears.[177]

There follows at this point an admirable exposition of the seven petitions in the *Our Father*, which Augustine interprets one after another, as being all directed to the blessed life in the heavenly kingdom. Further, he shows that all other prayers, including those in the Psalms and the sapiental books, which so many Christians daily repeat, all ultimately go back to these seven petitions, and he finds that everyone who prays for something that cannot be referred back to one of these seven petitions is uttering a "fleshly" prayer. He also gives us an example of how *not* to pray.[178]

Fasting and almsgiving fortify prayer; they seek to touch God as it were with hands, though God cannot be touched. They fulfil what is written in the psalm, "In the day of my trouble I sought God with my hands."[179] The passage from Romans means that just those things are salutary for us that do not appear to be so—that is to say, our trials. Paul himself experienced this with the sting that might not be taken away. That is why we must patiently pray for deliverance from our trials. If our prayers are heard—particularly our prayers concerning temporal matters—this should not lead us to boast, for even the legion of devils which went into the swine were heard. If we are not heard then we must say, "Not my will but God's will be done."[180] Thus we pray in a sort of learned ignorance and that is why Holy Scripture says that the Spirit prays for us with unspeakable sighs—in other words, that it is he who lets us pray, by inspiring us with a longing for something that we do not yet know.[181] He ends this long letter to Proba with a reference to those two biblical widows who shared her fate—Anna the mother of Samuel and Anna the daughter of Phanuel—and to their incessant prayer. And he adds at the end the words, "Pray for me."[182]

The letter to Proba belongs to the general literature of edification, and contains no details concerning the life of prayer for the guidance of ordinary people, nor do we learn much elsewhere about what prayer should be used in "the chamber", on rising, on retiring or in the family circle.[183] But we also hear few complaints concerning negligence in prayer. Reading the passages in the sermons about prayer, and comparing them with each other, we gain the impression that under the pressure of circumstance there was really a very great deal of praying. Simple people, of course, often prayed very selfishly; they begged for riches,[184] they wailed upon their sick beds and trembled at the thought of death, and in this scorching country, they prayed again and again with tears and clamour, for rain.[185] Here, too, one sees that necessity teaches men to pray, and no doubt prayers for temporal benefits will continue till the last day.

There was perhaps little meditation in our sense of the word, and even in the monasteries there may not have been very much of it. Also, there was little communal prayer in church. Communal prayer in church seems to have been limited to short acclamations by the people. There was, however, a great deal of singing in church, and men loved to pray in private and prayed often, such prayer being spontaneous, after the manner of Southerners. Many, says the bishop, do not even wait till cock-crow, but get up in the middle of the night to pray; so strong is their urge to pray that they will not wait for the customary hour for prayer. They are like the man in the psalm: "In the hour of the night I was there and cried."[186]

On several occasions Augustine had something to say about the actual outward conduct of his faithful when praying. Men uttered their prayers out loud much more often than they do today; they prayed straight from the heart and accompanied their prayer with lively gestures. We hear of some ill-mannered boys who listened to some poor fellow praying in church and then bawled his prayers after him in the street.[187] Many prayed with sighs and tears.[188] Many suffered from swollen knees;[189] others could show bumps on their heads, due to their beating their heads against the ground. A man did not feel any sense of embarrassment when he stepped before the altar of a *memoria* in torn clothes and with dishevelled hair, and broke into loud sobs about his troubles.[190] When the words "Forgive us our trespasses", or "I confess", or even the one word "wicked", sounded through the church, then "fists fairly flew at men's breasts" with a resounding impact. "There is no respite from the thunder of the people beating their breasts, and very properly so, for the cloud in which God dwells is always full of thunder."[191] Many passed the night vigils in church with endless kneeling down and rising again, and it was customary, when making the general confession, or when making some specially earnest prayer, for men to prostrate themselves completely on the ground and to touch the ground with their foreheads.[192]

Whether men were always as inwardly moved as their outward posture suggested, is of course an open question. Augustine himself is always quite satisfied if people strike their breasts in penitence. He looks upon this as a sign of a contrite heart.[193] But when people beat their breasts every time the word "wicked" occurs and yet still continue in their wickedness, he refers to this as putting a plaster over one's sins for the sake of appearances,[194] and also compares it with the ceaseless hammering of the mosaic workers when busy on the floor of a church. Moreover, the demonstrative gestures of prayer were liable to become a mere habit. "You throw your bodies to the ground, you bend your necks, confess your sins and pray to God; I see where your body lies but I ask myself where your spirit is; I see your limbs stretched out, but show me whether your attention is standing upright or whether it has not been washed away by the flood of your thoughts." Profane and evil thoughts "are liable to come to the surface while you are on your knees", yet how can men permit that to happen? Would I, asks Augustine, who am your equal, not feel insulted if, in the middle of a conversation with me, you were to turn aside and give orders to a slave and leave me standing? And yet you treat God like that every day.[195] But if troubles came to a man, then his distractions disappeared like so much dust, and the frightened soul found its way to the sanctuary with the ever-open doors. Which brings us to the subject of visits to the church.

Church Attendance

Although they gladly showed their Catholic teeth to heretics and were fond of listening to a sermon with plenty of plays upon words in it, most Hipponesians were, in Augustine's eyes, very far from being Church folk. On feast days they fairly crowded into the great church, for then the "mass of the theatre public" came along, not so much driven by piety, as attracted by the air of general festivity,[196] and also to see all the people in their fine clothes, which they had put on for a recognized holiday. The bishop was by no means edified to see the nave packed full, for the back of the church was never quiet and his weak voice could in any case never be heard there properly. It was only "when there was a great quiet" that people could follow him.[197] When they could not do so he would cut his sermons short and let people know why he was doing this. Thus, he cut short an address on the wedding at Cana when he came to the question of the real mystery of these happenings—the significance of the six vessels, and of the Master of the Feast, of Mary's conduct, and so on. Not unkindly, he said: "I would rather deal with this tomorrow if your holiness agrees. I would rather not make things too difficult for my infirmity or your own, for it is possible that many people have come here today not to listen to a sermon, but to help us to celebrate the feast. So, I invite those people who want to listen to the rest of what I have to say to come tomorrow. In this way I shall avoid giving short measure to the zealous and at the same time I shall not weary the indifferent."[198] The result was that the subject which he had treated in a somewhat brief and superficial manner on the day of the feast was, on the following day, handled at his leisure for the benefit of his regular patrons,[199] and there were enough of these, even in Carthage.

In 412, a good year after the conference with the Donatists, he was preaching in Carthage on the eve of St. Cyprian's Day and was giving an exposition of the Seventy-second Psalm.[200] After he had been speaking for two hours (the sermon covers more than fourteen folio columns), he suddenly broke off with the words "I've forgotten for how long I have been speaking, but I have come to the end of the psalm, and to judge from the smell [that is to say, the smell of sweat] I gather that I have been giving a very long sermon. But I am helpless in the face of your enthusiasm. Your very violence disarms me, and I hope that this very violence will help you to conquer the Kingdom of Heaven."[201] We must not forget, of course, that in the years following August 411 Augustine was not only the most famous man in Carthage, but the most famous man in the whole Latin half of the Empire; and even so, the honour that was paid him in his native town was somewhat less than that which he received in the capital, where, on his own admission, he spoke with more polish and preparation.

Nevertheless, on certain days—such, for instance, as the Feast of the Ascension—the churches were largely full of people "who were much more anxious to get out than to come in". In particular, the fashionable people found that the whole business was much too long-drawn-out. They could find time for a breakfast that lasted far into the evening, but not for a festival sermon.[202] Of course they came to church; that was only right and proper. Christianity was the religion of the State and of the Court; it was only a matter of good form for them to take part. They did not actually attend Mass merely for the sake of their lackeys, as was the case in France in the eighteenth century, but they contented themselves with an absolute minimum of passive standing around, for which they could just find the time. These African *viri clarissimi* in Carthage are very like the titled men of pleasure in the pages of Tolstoy, or for that matter, like Napoleon, who could just spare twenty minutes on Sunday to put in an appearance in a room at the Tuileries. On Easter Sunday, when a true joy reigns everywhere and the packed multitude sings "Alleluia"[203] at the top of its voice, there are still many whose thoughts are with the party that they will be having that evening, and above all, with the long Easter drink they will be taking after a fortnight's abstinence.[204] Feast days are drinking days.[205] Even the *infantes*, who had been baptized that very day, are warned on that Easter morning not to be drunk when they appear at Vespers in the afternoon. But, they would ask, did you not yourself preach to us that we should rejoice and indulge ourselves a little?[206] Even on the feasts of the martyrs men would toast each other by the graves and, for the ordinary man, this was the culminating point of the feast. True, they came into the church on these feast days. "I go there", they said, "and put on my best clothes"—and they called this celebrating the feast.[207]

Augustine would cast his eye over this seething festive crowd, which seemed much more suited to a theatre than to a church, and observed it with feelings of mingled pity, revulsion and love. In his heart he yearned for his faithful. But he makes honest efforts on behalf of these rare birds of passage, and he speaks to them in simple yet forceful terms. On days like these, he says, my church is like a field full of tares, and like that net which gathers good and bad. Now I see those multitudes before me who, in the critical hours when heresies threaten us, will cause the net, which is the Church, to split. For today it is just the people who make so much noise in the elections, the theatre-maniacs and agitators, who come to church. And he compares his own church with the true Church as a whole, and wonders whether the Mother Church as a whole was not filled up too suddenly. "Let us look at it more closely. Has not so great a multitude been gathered together in the Church that the chaff at the moment entirely hides the wheat? How many thieves, drunkards, blasphemers and theatre-maniacs are now not members of it? And are those who crowd into the churches not the same identical ones who crowd into the theatres, and who seek, by means of their noisy conduct, to achieve the same results as they succeed in achieving in the theatre? When some spiritual advice is given, or some spiritual duty is laid down, they oppose it and resist. They follow their flesh and withstand the Holy Spirit. They do the very same thing of which Stephen accused the Jews. In this very town, my brethren, have we not cause to know—and your holiness will surely recollect the matter as well as I do—in this very church, have we not cause to know how great was the danger in the midst of which God put an end to the drinking parties in the basilica? Did not the ship of our Church nearly founder on that occasion, as a result of the uproar created by worldly men? And how did that result? Surely from the excessive number of fish that had been provisionally caught in the net?"[208]

Naturally, "fish" of that kind were not of the silent sort. They ran in and out, chattering everlastingly. They concluded bargains, discussed the news of the town, greeted their friends and acquaintances and made appointments with their lady friends (Augustine had himself done the latter many years before when a student in Carthage).[209] They also indulged in exhaustive gossip about their neighbours. If a newcomer made an appearance you could always hear a couple of the supposedly pious start whispering, "Is not that that lunatic from the circus? Is he not the man who went crazy about this or that gladiator, or about this or that variety artiste?"[210] It was exactly the same as in Milan, where the buzz of voices during the reading of the lessons never ceased, and no reader ever succeeded in silencing it.[211]

On Sundays and on ordinary fast days the church was well attended, but rather less well on Saturdays.[212] The octave of Easter counted as part of the feast and also coincided with the regular holidays of the citizens.[213] Augustine made a point of preaching every day within the octave, and often did so both morning and afternoon.[214] The full morning worship would then consist of the Eucharist preceded by readings, of the psalm of the day, and of a sermon or *tractatio*.[215] The evening worship would consist of readings from the Scriptures, with or without a *tractatio*, and of the singing of psalms and hymns. Because this evening act of worship took place at the time when the lamps were ordinarily lit, it was called the *lucernarium* or *vespertinum*.[216]

We find no trace in Augustine's writings of a corresponding early-morning worship "at cockcrow", which was customary in other places and was something quite apart from the ordinary vigils.[217] Eucharist and Vespers were expressly referred to as the "daily acts of worship".[218] During the week these acts of worship, which were almost of a private character, seem to have been attended, not only by the monks, the virgins, the cathedral clergy and occasionally by the bishop, but also by many other pious men "who hungered for an edifying word, and, in the country, by those quiet and secluded *continentes*, the widows, old people and children. Thus, we hear of a chapel on an estate where the head of the establishment sang Vespers in the evening with the nuns.[219] In the town the church rarely remained empty, and Augustine would be at pains on these occasions to make his sermon suitably pointed and forceful. He would, for instance, intentionally say a word against those who looked upon their faithful visiting of the church as a kind of draft entitling them ultimately to cash in on the possession of heaven. "Such people interpret the words of the Psalmist, when he tells us to bring offerings of praise to God, as though he referred to the imposition of a tax, and they calculate the thing to themselves after this fashion: 'Now, I shall get up early every day, go to church, join in the singing of one morning hymn, and of a Vesper hymn in the evening, and I shall sing one or two hymns at home. Then the account will be even.' "[220] But he could on occasion also praise them, these regular patrons of his. "Consider now this ant of God. Every day it gets up early, runs into church, hears the lesson read and joins in the singing of the hymns and chews over on what it has heard. It goes in and out of church like a little ant upon its path, an ant which is making provision for the winter."[221] Men who possibly went to church conspicuously often, had occasionally to pocket an insult from their friends, a fact of which Augustine was well aware. "What do they say to you then, these carpers and critics?" he cried. "Do they twit you with being a great apostle? Do they say 'You have certainly been up to heaven like Elijah?' Do they say, 'You have your legs hanging out of the sky?' and, 'Where are you coming from now?' And then you do not venture to say, 'I come from church', because then you would be told, 'Aren't you ashamed to confess that—you, a man? That's the place where widows and old women go.' An evil tongue thus makes you ashamed of doing good. Pride is thus broken by the judgement of ordinary men, and good men blush under the jibes of worthless mockers."[222]

The trouble was that people made fun not only of sentimental old women who could not keep their pious instincts to themselves, but of the whole Christian interpretation of life, and of Christian earnestness. If there was somebody who did not drink or who did not run around with women or who did not go to the circus, and if such a person, on top of everything else, was a conspicuously frequent churchgoer, then his whole circle of friends would start twitting him: "Old boy, you're a grand fellow—a Peter, an Elias, a super-Apostle."[223] And those that mocked him this way were not heathens but Christians, and like the snarer of birds in the Psalms they first puzzled him by their seductive calls, and then, with their false jollity and their cutting words, got him trapped in the gin.[224] They meant no harm, but their frivolity often degenerated into malice, for the more frivolous their own lives the more critical their attitude was towards true piety. "The less these depraved individuals care about their own sins, the greater is their malignant curiosity in respect of others. For they do not seek to make men better, but only for something upon which they can fasten their teeth."[225] Generally they preferred to tease the earnest Christian when there were several of them against one, so that their victim was embarrassed and at a disadvantage. Then that victim might well sigh and say with the Psalmist, "Who shall rise up for me against the evil-doers?"[226]

Yet when the bishop looked over his flock he found there were more mockers than actual free-thinkers and when he said, "I hope you will come tomorrow in great numbers, for I have something important to tell you", then he would see the church full next morning.[227] Few came on the days dedicated to such saints as were not natives of Africa. Even on the feast of the Princes of the Apostles the church would be half empty, and the bishop would ask his congregation, "Do you not love Peter and Paul? Actually, I am putting that question to those who are not present today, for to those who have at least put in an appearance here I wish to express my thanks."[228]

Church attendance was worse if a performance had been announced at the theatre, and then Augustine knew very well that only the old faithful ones would turn up, nor did he fail to show that he was aware of it.[229] One day, for instance, when a performance took place on the same day as the feast of St. Laurence and it was stiflingly hot into the bargain, he began his sermon with the words "The martyrdom of St. Laurence is famous—at least it is famous in Rome, though it does not seem to be so here, for I see that only a few of you have come, and yet we here are no more capable of taking away the victor's crown of St. Laurence than are the people of Rome. Why that crown has not made its appearance in this city, I do not know. However, let this little gathering listen to the little we have to tell, for we ourselves have not much strength, tired as we are, and this heat does not make things easier." Actually, this short sermon only lasted a quarter of an hour.[230] In Carthage once on the same festival, he began his sermon with the remark that it was hardly worth while preaching when there was so little interest, but that he would preach all the same in honour of the martyr. It so happens that on that day he preached exceedingly well.[231]

When all the circumstances are taken into account, church attendance was really not so bad, for the services were very long and tiring. On ordinary Sundays the Fore-Mass alone consisted of three excerpts from Holy Scripture, a reading from the Apostle, or, as we should say, the Epistles, a psalm, which was sung antiphonally (our own Gradual is all that remains of this), and then the Gospel. Hereupon followed the sermon. As he was about to begin his sermon the bishop might quite possibly say, "We have listened and sung, and harkened with great attention to the Gospel."[232] The length of the sermon seems to have varied from half an hour to an hour and a half or even two hours, except on days where the worship was lengthier, and on these the bishop would content himself with an address lasting perhaps ten minutes, though he always apologized on these occasions.

During all this time the people would stand packed closely together before the *cancelli* and the steps of the apse. They had to stand like this for hours. When the memory of a particularly popular martyr was being honoured, an account of that martyr's passion made the service even longer.[233] Augustine himself knew well how tiring this was. "We have had a long account read to us", he once said on the feast of St. Vincent of Saragossa, "and the day is short. We must not now impose upon your patience with a lengthy sermon; we know that you have stood there and listened with a great patience, indeed you have done so for so long that you have to some extent suffered with the martyr. May God who hears you love you and crown you for it."[234] And though the faithful had always to stand, he himself remained quietly seated while he spoke.

He regretted the whole arrangement very much, for standing caused people to tire and to be easily distracted.[235] When he noticed this he would cut his sermon short with a word of sympathy. "I should not like to detain you for long, especially since you must be tired of standing while I sit here and talk."[236] Yet he found plenty of opportunities for praising their faithfulness in appearing in church, their endurance and what was sometimes their overwhelming interest —and indeed the real enthusiasts could never have enough.[237] Sometimes they found a long sermon all too short and wanted to have some more.[238] One day when he was a guest preacher he closed his sermon, which had lasted at least three full hours (it takes up twenty-five folio columns), with the words, "Perhaps I have spoken for much too long, but thanks to the tenseness with which you have listened to me, I did not notice it. If I have offended in this way please forgive me; first of all because I have acted at the request of others, secondly because you have hung on my words with such avidity, though we ourselves confess that we have been equally dependent on your good will."[239] At the close of a long sermon he could pay the following delicate compliment to his audience: "I never become aware of the fact that you are growing tired, and yet God knows that I fear that I sometimes ask too much of you, or at least ask too much of a certain number of the brethren; yet I see the interest which so many of you display, who ask of me this labour and this care, and I am glad that your interest is greater than that of the fools in the amphitheatre. If those people in the theatre had to stand for all this length of time they would really soon stop looking at the spectacle."[240]

The applause which he continually earned was something more than a proof of their readiness with their voices and their hands. It proved a genuine receptivity for the seed which Augustine scattered with so much zest. With Augustine "the daily rain of admonitions"[241] only rarely degenerated into the melancholy drip of the modern homily. When he gave his subtle lectures on the Gospel according to St. John, lectures which went on for hours, people came streaming in for months in the rawest and coldest of weathers,[242] and this despite the fact that they could hear him preach almost daily—on one occasion indeed they could have heard him on seven days in succession.[243] Even outside the season of Lent and Easter he sometimes spoke four times a week, and invariably on the Saturday and the Sunday.[244] Most probably he also spoke on Saturday evenings during the ancient evening worship, that relic of the older Sunday vigil which has been retained up to this day in the parish churches of the Orthodox East.[245] This age of interminable speeches seems to have been blessed with a gift for interminable listening.

We do not know how many people were usually present at Mass on weekdays. Augustine speaks of the "daily physic of the body of the Lord".[246] And there is no doubt that wherever Mass was daily celebrated it was possible for anybody to go daily to church without exciting attention, and there to receive the Sacrament, for nobody, except penitents, attended Mass without doing this. How many came in this fashion we do not know. We do not even know exactly in what neighbourhoods Mass was daily celebrated. In his letter to Januarius, the bishop refers to great local differences in eucharistic practice, and he says that in the East the Eucharist is not the daily Bread of the overwhelming majority, but that it is so in the churches of the West.[247] Here and there he speaks of the daily celebration, and in one place he says that Christ has designed this sacrament as "the daily sacrifice of the Church".[248] But even that would not exclude the possibility that in Africa, just as in Rome, the sacrifice was sometimes omitted. He never complains, however, that the faithful remain away when the body of Christ is distributed. His complaints only refer to the penitents who neglected to set their affairs in order, and who for that reason might not receive Communion. But even secret sinners, or at any rate those who had not been publicly forbidden to receive the sacrament, did not always dare to show themselves, for Augustine was not afraid to "send away at the *cancelli*" shameless people whom he knew to be adulterers.[249] Still, we may safely assume that all the others present in the church came forward without exception when the sacrament was distributed, extending their hands to receive the holy bread and drinking a drop of the wine, and saying "Amen" when they had done both these things. For the pious this was their daily bread, while the least pious partook of it at least once a week.

People communicated fasting, for even in those days it was demanded "by the dignity of so great a sacrament that the body of the Lord should enter the mouth of the Christian before any other food".[250] We do not know whether, in the year 400, the old house Communions were still in practice; there are certain references to them in Tertullian and Cyprian,[251] which means that the practice was in force at the beginning and in the middle of the third century. In that ancient time of persecution Communion was received early in the morning in the bedroom, "before any meal had been partaken of"; husband and wife took the sacred elements from a small container (*arca*) in which they brought home a part of the sacred gift of the altar. Probably this house Communion was originally intended for the sick and for those who for other reasons could not leave their homes. The practice was also possibly resorted to on weekdays, since Mass was not a daily occurrence. Some think that the special circumstances created by the persecution had something to do with it.[252] If that is so, the habit fell into disuse when the persecution ceased, and when, even in Africa, daily Mass become customary. We can, however, see from certain observations by Basil and Jerome that house Communion was still practised in Augustine's time in Alexandria and Rome, though we do not know to what extent.[253] Certainly it was not unusual for the faithful to preserve a piece of the blessed bread and to keep it at home or carry it about with them on their journeys as a means of warding off evil.[254] From this we can conclude that people were not forbidden to leave a part of the bread unconsumed. Moreover, from Augustine's letter to Januarius it is clear that there were certain differences of opinion, probably among married layfolk, over the question whether daily Communion was desirable. This was not because the sacrament was not valued, but because such people, in their ordinary lives, and particularly after marital intercourse, considered themselves unworthy to receive it.[255]

Fasting

We are rather better informed on the subject of fasting. These passionate people observed their fasts in a manner that makes us ashamed. They fasted like the Russian peasant of old. Their practice, as far as it is known to us, seems to bear the mark of an Oriental strictness, but actually it was in accord with the general early Christian rule. During the period of fasting, people refrained for forty days from visiting the baths—a heavy sacrifice, despite the fact that the spring in that part of the world was usually cold and rainy. They abstained from meat, from certain kinds of fruit, and drank no wine, and they took no food at all until sunset. In other words, the *prandium* was taken at the time of the *coena*, which means that they did not breakfast till the evening. Even then the repast was very simple. The man of the people contents himself with vegetables, with a little piece of "smoky" bacon (and two or three little cups of the wine of the country).[256] People suffering from stomach troubles, and invalids in general, were allowed to choose both their food and the time of their meals, and in certain cases to drink a little wine mixed with water—an indulgence which St. Paul, it will be remembered, recommended to Timothy.[257] Married people were gently but emphatically counselled by the bishop to refrain from marital intercourse, and that in accordance with the spirit of St. Paul, not with a view to lessening each other's rights, but in order to strengthen the life of prayer. "Let your body, which has been made soft by fleshy tenderness, now be thrown upon the ground to be wholly governed by prayer. Let your hands, which till now have been interlocked in embraces, be spread apart in the gesture of prayer."[258] Here we have a moving picture of the ancient piety. We see husband and wife praying together in their bedroom with their hands lifted up and outspread, while the little oil lamp burns, the initials of Christ being turned towards the east. We do not know of course, whether these general directives given by the bishop were binding under sin, but it seems clear that those who observed them were not considered pious beyond the ordinary.[259]

There were several days of fasting before all the great feasts and before certain saints' days,[260] and some of the wildest and noisiest of the old pagan festivals were turned into days of penance, a practice which recalls the forty hours of prayer during carnival time.[261] Good Friday and Easter Saturday continued to be, as of old, in an especial manner days of heavy fasting, for they were naturally days to which a peculiar sanctity attached.[262] This had been the rule in Africa since the time of Tertullian, and we may well believe that these were days which no man dared desecrate, though the tendency to make up for lost time at Easter was often very palpable. Many people regularly observed a more or less strict fast on Wednesdays and Fridays; Wednesday being accounted a fast day because it was the day on which the Sanhedrin determined to put our Lord to death, and Friday because it was the day on which Christ actually died.[263] However, they avoided fasting on Thursdays, because that was the fast day of the Jews. There was a certain amount of controversy[264] on the subject of the Saturday fast. In Rome and in a number of Churches in the West and in Africa, there was fasting in memory of our Lord's humiliation through his burial. Augustine tells us that this practice obtained in the Churches in his immediate vicinity. In other Churches, and these included the Churches in Carthage and Hippo, and indeed the great majority of the Churches of Africa, fasting was not observed on this day, because it was the day of Christ's rest in the grave after his passion. Many zealous laymen quite ardently emulated the ascetics, who usually fasted five days a week and always abstained from meat and wine; many of the *continentes* contrived to go wholly without food for three days or more. In his early work *The Customs of the Church and the Customs of the Manichees*, Augustine referred the preachers of theory of abstinence to these miracles of self-control.[265]

Even if we make allowances for climate and the relative complexity of our life, the average level of achievement in this matter of fasting puts us to shame. The supersession of the banqueting chambers of Trimalchio and Lucullus by the refectories of Tabennisi and Hippo was indeed a revolution in manners. Yet in the sermons of Augustine on the subject of fasting[266] there are no special eulogies on the high level of observance—indeed there is hardly a mention of it; all we can find is an occasional remark addressed to the over-scrupulous who would not even make use of a pot during fast time if meat had once been cooked in it.[267] Of a heretic or a Jew who fasts, he says, on one occasion, that he is like a rider who has tamed a horse and then allows it to bolt with him.

Naturally enough he brings up all the classical themes in this connection. The precedent for our forty days' fast has been set by Moses, Elias and Christ, representing the Law, the Prophets and the Gospel.[268] Fasting sets us half-way between the angels and carnal men.[269] It is a very necessary aid in our battle with our appetites. In regard to marital continence, he speaks of it as the school of self-control, and states that it is well within the bounds of the possible and weakens any inclination to adultery. Let men think of widows, widowers and the many *continentes*. Fasting chastens the flesh but brings pure gain to the spirit. He who cannot fast should give alms, and he who cannot give alms should forgive his enemies. For there can be no excuse for not doing that. What the Christian saves through fasting should find its way to Christ, who is hungry in his poor.[270]

Yet we also hear of people who fast in the morning so that they may indulge themselves all the more in the evening; who spend more money on fish and choice vegetables than they usually spend on meat. So much so, indeed, that although their diet remains technically *maigre*, they are often in danger of dissipating within a comparatively short time the whole of their patrimony on this extravagance. Such men would in no circumstances miss the self-indulgence for which fast times give them the occasion; instead of wine they drink the most costly cider; the long period over which they deny themselves food only serves them as a means to increase their appetite and when the time comes "they hurl themselves at their loaded tables like cattle rushing to the trough, they pour a veritable avalanche of dishes into their stomachs and make their bellies swell, by feeding them a greater volume of food than they can possibly digest during the time of their fasting". Men who practise such fasts as these are "deliciosi potius quam religiosi". Their fasting is a service to their belly and not to God; so far from battling against the commands of their appetites, it is a loyal servant to them.[271]

This drastic representation shows a suspicious similarity to what he had previously written about Manichean abstinence, in which he spoke of the Manichees as refusing all manner of legitimate foods "because of the seal of their mouths", but belching twice daily behind mountains of highly-seasoned vegetarian dishes.[272] No doubt the parallelism occurred to Augustine himself, for he warns his people against having a mania for ritual purity;[273] perhaps the great orator wanted to make a little joke for the benefit of his good parishioners.

Sexual Morality

The subject of *continence* in marriage opens up the whole question of conjugal morality. It was the pride of the Church in those days to show the world, and in particular to show such misguided deniers of life as the Manichees, what manner of thing Christian marriage could be.[274] But it was a source of great grief to her to stand by and see in how childish a fashion people sought to reconcile the old conceptions with the new. The new conceptions, so people said, were excellent for women, but the old ones were necessary for men, and they still tended to overlook, in the case of a man, conduct which would bring a woman into ill repute.

Augustine was in the main most sparing in rebuke, but he makes frequent references to the sin of adultery. "All Africa is lit with torches of obscenity. It is not a land for human beings to live in but a burning Aetna of unchastity." "There is not an African who is not a slave to lewdness", is what Salvianus was later to write, though admittedly he was addicted to exaggeration. Even the just Augustine says that almost the whole human race is marked with this blemish and that this is the sin which it has to battle against more than any other.[275] Augustine felt compelled to say something on this matter and felt he could do so without offence to decency. He said what he had to say in a fashion that was brief, discreet but very definite; he spoke objectively about the strength and irrationality of the sexual instincts, though he refrained from digressing into needless detail, nor did he adduce any other examples when praising chastity than that of Joseph in the house of Potiphar and that of the constant Susannah.[276] But his listeners found the subject definitely wearisome, and said that it was his hobby horse. Once, when he was explaining the "ten-stringed psalter" (the Ten Commandments) and had come to the fifth (which is our sixth), he said, "And now, take no heed of what I tell you myself, but listen only to the word of God. Control your wrath. I have now come to the fifth string. Can I pass it over? Far from it. I shall never cease to strike it."[277] The ill humour of Augustine's hearers is rather painfully like the annoyance expressed by the courtiers of Versailles concerning Bourdaloue "tonnant à tort et à travers contre l'adultère", and is all too clear an indication of the character of his critics. Incidentally, Augustine tells us quite clearly who the latter were. "Those men who do not want to be faithful to their wives (and there are a good many of them) cannot bear to hear me talk like this, but talk like this I will whether they like it or not. I know that there is many a man who rages against me inwardly when his wife reproaches him with his unfaithfulness, and who then thinks, 'Of course that man's been here again', or 'My wife's been in church again.' Perhaps he even breaks into a rage, but then his wife can surely answer him and say, 'Why do you curse a man whom you have just been cheering in church?'"[278]

Nobody bothered much about young bachelors or young widowers who visited prostitutes "for their dog's-weddings".[279] But the bishop would bring them back to reality, if necessary by means of the very outspoken kind of letter which he wrote to a literary friend of his.[280] The subject broached was the sin rich men so often committed with their female slaves. In such a case the husband was in an advantageous position. If the wife had been caught with a slave she would have been brought to the forum, but nothing would happen if it was the husband who had been guilty of the offence. Public feeling in this matter was so strong that many a wife sincerely believed that it was quite lawful for her husband to do something that was forbidden to herself.[281] "Oh, come," the men would say, "God cares nothing for the sins of the flesh."[282] Many were furious that the bishop dared say openly that keeping a concubine is quite as bad as resorting to a prostitute. They even dared to challenge him on this point and to make complaints. "The woman I have got is no prostitute, she is my concubine. Holy bishop, you have called my concubine a prostitute. Surely you don't imagine that I would resort to a prostitute? I neither do this nor do I touch a woman who belongs to another. The woman whom I keep is my own serving maid. May I no longer do what I please in my own house?" He had his reply ready to hand: "I tell you, it must not be. All those that do this will go to hell and will burn in everlasting fire. If you remain deaf to me, God will still hear me warning you. If you pay no heed to these things the angels will still heed them full well. And as for your concubine, is it I who speak in this fashion? Far from it; it is the Apostle who has proclaimed this. You are reproaching me, but it is the Apostle who merits your reproach. I do but desire to see you restored to your senses and spiritual health. Why do you rage like a madman against me on this account? Are you a married man who talk like this? You know that you are. Very well, whether you like it or not, any woman who sleeps with you other than your wife is a prostitute. This is what I have said. And now you can go and tell her if you like that the bishop has insulted her."[283]

Unfortunately, those who spoke in this fashion had the law on their side. And Augustine had no hesitation in pointing out the conflict between Paul and Papinian, between "the law of heaven" and "the law of the forum".[284] The law permitted both divorce and the keeping of concubines. Holy Scripture and the Church strictly forbade both. In the pulpit he said he knew very well why people would not have their names inscribed for baptism. The chief reason was that the persons concerned had not the remotest intention of amending their lives in this particular.[285] And in his book on *Faith and Works* he refers to the ecclesiastical rule which enjoined that public women, actors and other publicly-known sinners should be refused baptism, if they would not abandon their way of life. He further insisted on strictly examining the married life of all *competentes*. Unfortunately, this intention was not always carried out. Moreover, many candidates for baptism, who were guilty of persistent irregularities of one kind or another—who might for instance be living with a divorced woman—continued in their sinful habits up to the day of their baptism and in some cases never even thought that their conduct was other than permissible.[286] After baptism, it is true, this kind of thing was rare, and even divorce was something of an exception. Even the mighty ones of the earth were held back from the last, whether it was through fear of hell or out of respect for Christian opinion, or because they did not wish to risk suddenly hearing the *non licet tibi* from some exceptionally bold bishop.[287] Augustine adjured those who had been baptized not to go to perdition along this slippery way. "You are encompassing your ruin, my children. Will you not believe me? O you faithful who hear me, if you have committed a sin of this kind, do not persist in it, but beg God for forgiveness. I will say this again so that nobody can say that he has not understood me. If you have defiled yourselves by some illicit union, then consummate your penance as the Church has laid it down and let the Church pray for you. Do not say, 'I will do it quietly by myself. I will confess to God.' Have the words 'what you have loosed upon earth', no meaning? And must a man from the people feel ashamed where the Emperor Theodosius knew no shame at all?"[288]

He urged the women to defend their honour and to stand firmly upon their Christian rights, and he did this in words that left nothing to be desired in the matter of clarity. "Let the women listen to me. Let them show jealousy towards their husbands. I will not urge husbands to show jealousy towards their wives, because I know well enough that they will do that without prompting from myself. I do not want the Christian wife to be over-patient, on the contrary I want her to be a jealous wife. I say this with all emphasis. I order it. I command it. Your bishop commands it. And Christ commands it through me. Yes, I say this and I command it to you. Do not suffer it if your husbands make themselves guilty of unchastity. Appeal against them to the Church. In all other things be subject to your husbands, but where this matter is concerned defend your cause."[289] It is true that here and there he would find fault with women who made the infidelities of their husbands known to him, but did so out of jealousy rather than from a zeal for souls, and then showed themselves dissatisfied when they heard nothing further of the matter, as though there was anything else that Augustine could do than talk privately to the guilty parties.[290] But his patience was even less with those women who were actually proud of their reputation of being experienced married women who were clever enough not to see what they were not meant to see; although even these he found preferable to women whose main characteristic was an entirely loveless piety.

The husband was the head of the house. What, then, was the position when the head was no longer to be depended on? "When the master of the house lives a worse life than his wife, does not then the house stand on its head?"[291] As to those who mock at chastity, he points out, they do not hesitate to demand it of their wives. In fact, they insist on it in them, and certainly in their daughters, though while doing so they are ready to threaten the chastity of other women.[292] Moreover, while the wife remains chaste because a strict watch is kept upon her, the husband can only preserve his chastity through manly discipline.[293] Augustine was prepared, when speaking privately to men, or when writing to them, to make even more forceful utterances. A highly-placed friend of his youth had lost his wife and had begun to lead a very irregular life. When this man asked Augustine to write him some words of comfort, the latter told him exactly what he thought. How dared his correspondent, who was now the slave of a daily increasing number of mistresses, make an appeal to his old friendship and make such a request to a bishop! If he ever wished to see his virtuous wife again, that wife who had loved him despite the viciousness of his life, he must begin to lead a chaste life himself.[294]

On the subject of women's love of adornment his observations are moderate and restrained. He was anything but sharp-tongued. Even in his letters one seeks in vain for those satirical remarks about make-up, jewellery, provocative perfume or provocative gait, which Tertullian, Cyprian and, among Augustine's contemporaries, Jerome, and even the dignified Ambrose, were so fond of regaling their contemporaries with. It is not from Augustine but from others that we learn that the walking feminine fashion-plates of the time strutted around "with complete islands and woods on their slender little necks", exactly as they had done in the third century, that they dyed their hair gold and wore towering coiffures, that a real tear still made a deep furrow in the coating of powder on their soft cheeks.[295] Augustine is brief and to the point. For a woman to rouge and paint her face is a form of deceit. It belongs to the same category of wrongdoing as infidelity. And it does not even really please the husband. Incidentally, it is quite lawful for a married woman to make herself beautiful for her husband. That, he says to Possidius, you cannot, as her bishop, forbid her to do; but she should not wear her hair uncovered.[296] It would be quite wrong to imagine that Augustine went about with his eyes shut; he merely used a certain discretion and was careful to seize the right occasion. Commenting on the text from the Psalms, "Their daughters decked out after the similitude of a temple", he spoke as follows: Let us be brief. Let us on this occasion seek not to offend any woman's sense of delicacy. Let them rather enquire themselves what they are putting on and what we are ashamed to mention.[297] On another occasion he was rather more cutting, but then he spoke not of the woman's folly but of the man's; if she says, "I don't like to see you in your heavy cloak", then he will take off the cloak; if she says to him in the middle of winter, "I prefer to see you in your spring cloak", then the love-sick dolt will take off his heavy woollen mantle, for he would rather "freeze than displease"—and for whom? For a shameless woman. And why? Because she will condemn him? Or bring him into prison? Or have him tortured? No, he only trembles that he may hear the words, "You will never see me again." If a shameless woman says this to you and frightens you by saying it, he asks, why are you not frightened when God says it to you?[298] Sometimes he takes a shot at the young fop: " 'Your hair isn't cut properly', says the serious old gentleman to his young sprig. 'It creates a bad impression if you run about with a mane like that.' But the young man knows well enough that a certain young person likes to see him wear his hair that way." Generally speaking, Augustine confines his dealings with this subject to a few telling but indirect allusions. "You will never go about in worn and shabby clothes, but you don't seem to mind going about with a shabby soul."[299]

Augustine's views of the rights and duties of married people seem by our standards to be severe, but in general they are in accord with the conceptions of his time. He was, on the whole, against early marriages. Heed me, young people, he says, marriage is an iron fetter; other fetters can be loosed by us here in the church, but not this one. I say this lest you think that you can seek asylum here with us and have your marriage dissolved. We, your bishop, rivet this fetter with double rivets, but you are not compelled to put your foot into it. What says the Apostle? "If thou art tied to a wife seek not thy freedom, but if thou art free seek not a wife."[300] As against this, he looked upon the young married state as unsuitable for men of uncontrolled character.[301]

Conjugal intercourse was, in Augustine's opinion, only permissible if there was an express purpose of producing children. He was fond of quoting the words written on the little tablets of the marriage contract—"liberorum procreandorum causa"—and he asked those who believed that everything was permitted whether they looked upon themselves as pagans, and on their mothers and fathers-in-law as procurers.[302] And if through weakness people demanded greater latitude and went beyond the bonds of the contract, then they should at least respect the marriage bed. They might then, as a concession to their weakness, and so that Satan should not lead them into temptation, demand the *debitum* and should not refuse it to one another, except by mutual agreement and for a limited time. It is in any case a venial sin, for it is written, "Dico secundum veniam".[303] He imagined that the saintly men of patriarchal times had only approached their wives for the purpose of begetting progeny, and had looked upon the work of the flesh as a humiliating duty, and for this reason alone had been permitted to have more than one wife.[304]

This last was the argument he applied against those who cited the example of the Patriarchs, not only to justify the keeping of concubines, but also to attack the ideal of virginity, as Jovinian had done in Rome. Jovinian had cried out to the nuns, "Do you think that you are better than Sarah or Mother Anna?" and his sermons had caused even elderly virgins "to plunge into matrimony".[305] Augustine looked upon the concupiscence which is inherent in the work of the flesh, as a punishment for original sin and the root of spiritual death. He meant by this that the sexual instinct no longer obeys the will, but comes into play independently of it and with disproportionate frequency. This was what he said in the pulpit: "Love your wives but love them chastely. Insist on the work of the flesh only in such measure as is necessary for the procreation of children. Since you cannot beget children in any other way, you must descend to it against your will, for it is the punishment of Adam, our original parent. Let us not be proud of our punishment. It is the punishment of man, who has deserved to procreate mortality because sin has made him mortal; and God has not taken this punishment away. Men should call to mind from what distant place he has been recalled and what is the nature of his ultimate call. He should yearn for that embrace in which there can be no more corruption."[306] He even dared to write (and the passage probably reveals his true thoughts) that marriage is only a relative good, and that it would be better if all men were to refrain from it—assuming always that this was done with a pure heart, a "good conscience and an unfeigned faith", for then the number of the elect would be completed sooner, the City of God perfected earlier and the end of the world would be upon us at an earlier date. Does not the Apostle say that he would that all men were as himself?[307]

It is for the psychoanalyst to decide whether in such radical utterances we are not being confronted with an unmastered fear complex with regard to women. Augustine can, however, strike another note, and it sometimes happens that the cry of his own heart is suppressed and that he talks very sound sense. Chaste married folk can attain blessedness, together with the virgin. They will shine together like stars, "differing in the quality of their brightness but all in the same heaven".[308] He knows that true continence is not necessarily given with the external control of the body, but represents above all a virtue of the soul, and what may be lacking in external conduct may well suddenly find expression in a spiritual attitude. For this reason he is prepared to treat the Patriarchs as being on an equality, in this particular, with the Fathers of the Desert, and to rate a married woman who is truly devoted to God more highly than a proud virgin.[309] Chastity can, moreover, appear to him not as a form of fear, but as an expression of the rightly directed will; not as a lack of love but as a better and more honest kind of love.[310]

In regard to the realities of married life, he says quite clearly that lust as a rule tends to respect no limits in its fury, but he is compelled to admit that among married people there is as much goodwill to be found as there is human weakness. The widespread tendency to infidelity brought many a bitter word from the pulpit: "Does it mean that I have baptized in vain for all these years, since there is nobody who truly fulfils his duty? I cannot believe it. If that were true I would rather not be a bishop. But I hope that there are people who are faithful to their duties, and I believe that there are such people, for it is one of the sorriest parts of my office that I am generally compelled to know all too well who are the adulterers and yet not to know who are the chaste."[311]

He preferred, however, to speak less of marriages that had suffered damage, and more of the ideal marriage. He emphasizes that the man was the head of the woman and the woman his servant. She must call him her lord. When government is in the hands of a woman then you have a *pax perversa*. But in the matter of conjugal rights husband and wife are equal.[312] Much more frequent than mere rebukes are those utterances in which he urges married people to cultivate harmony with one another and show their love in practical ways. In particular, he urges the husband to show delicacy of feeling and respect towards the mother of his children, for the woman's lot is not an easy one. We may remember that he praised Monica because she could handle her ill-tempered husband despite his intermittent fits of rage, and because he had never seen her, as he had seen so many others, with bruises on her face.[313] Yet he could censure on occasion, and he was particularly severe on those married women who enforced continence on their husbands and so violated the obligations of love under the pretext that they were aiming at Christian perfection. There was, for instance, the case of the pious Ecdicia, who had prematurely put on widow's weeds and had given her fortune away to a number of wandering monks, and thus by her conduct driven her husband to an immoral way of life. Augustine wrote to her in very strong terms to remind her of her duties towards her husband and her son, and to make it plain to her that she had driven her husband into adultery. He ordered her for the sake of the child to try and restore a happier relation with her husband, to pray for him and to write to him immediately in a humble tone, promising to be subject to him in all things if he would return.[314]

Yet it is not only his championship of the institution in such cases as these, where false piety had virtually produced a divorce, that entitled Augustine to be reckoned amongst the great eulogists of Christian marriage, for such he was despite his professed contempt for the physical, which in its turn is probably mixed up with his neo-Platonist aversion to the lower manifestations of love, and perhaps even more with his conception of the nature of original sin. His own unhappy experiences in youth may also have some bearing on the matter. Although he wrote a little book on *The Excellence of Widowhood*, he refused to condemn a second marriage in principle and in this he differed from certain Greek Fathers of the Church. The condemnation of a second marriage seemed to him to smell too much of the heresy of Novatian and Tertullian.[315] So we look in vain among Augustine's utterances for such bad jokes as Jerome's story, who told how he had seen a man who had buried twenty wives and a woman who had buried twenty husbands enter on Christian marriage together.[316] At the end of the fourth century Jovinian the despiser of virginity had condemned the Catholics' low estimation of sex life as a Manichean infection. He insisted that it was impossible to praise continence without lowering the status of marriage, and to prove his point he made a great showing with a number of Jerome's letters, which were admittedly somewhat cynical, and in which Jerome spoke contemptuously of sex—the same Jerome who was always surrounded by a circle of pious feminine intellectual aristocrats to whose conversation he attached the greatest value. In order to strike the weapons from Jovinian's hands[317] Augustine first wrote a little book entitled *The Good in Marriage*, and somewhat later a second one on *Holy Virginity*, though both these books were written some years after Jovinian had made his first appearance. In the first of these he praised the three great goods of marriage—children, faithfulness and sacramental union. In the second he praised the state of virginity as the more perfect of the two because in it we begin the life of angels even before our bodies are resurrected. At the same time he saw in the virginal state one only suitable to those who had been especially called to it, a state which can only possess true value among the humble, and one which is liable to be defiled by pride. It is better to be holy as a virgin than chaste in marriage, but infinitely better to be a humble married woman than a proud virgin.[318] In a lecture to some *continentes* he was bold enough to say that virgins usually have so excellent an opinion of themselves that they think themselves better than their own parents because the latter have been married. What ingratitude, he comments, and where do they imagine they would have been without their parents? If such people are puffed up, then certainly they are not better than their parents; and if by chance they are better then they will certainly be more humble.[319]

He knows full well how many people are happy in marriage and that happiness is possible even in a mixed marriage.[320] And when he speaks of those who practise continence by mutual consent he has higher praise for the living harmony between than he has for their continence.[321] He knows how many married Christian folk practise all the virtues for which their station calls. In his sermons on married love the same note of tenderness can be detected as in the heartfelt words in so many epitaphs of this time in which a husband or wife seeks to honour the memory of a lost mate:

To my dear, chaste wife.

To my most excellent companion who lived so-and-so many years with me wholly without quarrels.

To my sweet, unforgettable wife.

To my good, chaste and most exceptional wife who was always of one mind with me throughout her life.

But no doubt equally affectionate thoughts were often concealed in the standing formula: "NN. conjugi benemerenti"—"To my most deserving wife."

We may assume that in the main the bond of the family was very strong, as it is in the South to this day, for there among the ordinary people *il babbo e la nonna* do not have to rot in almshouses or homes for the aged, but as a rule spend their declining years contentedly in some little back room of the house surrounded by the love of their children and grandchildren. We hardly ever hear, says the bishop, of a child that does not honour its parents, although that does happen here and there. Particularly among the poor, it seems to be the general rule, for a young fellow to work his fingers to the bone for his old father wholly without hope of reward.[322] Many a woman stood faithfully by her husband even when the latter had become poor, and was proud to help carry his burden.[323] Children in those days were happy little creatures who missed nothing and were usually made much of. There was only one thing that they were afraid of, and that was school.

Strangely enough, education is a theme which Augustine rarely broaches. He gives no more than a general warning against the spoiling of children, and urges parents, when the children have grown older, not to let their various affairs pass unnoticed. The last sentiment was inspired, no doubt, by a memory of the unhappy licence which he had been accorded in his own youth.[324] For the circumstances prevailing in his own home had been far from perfect. The unforgettable picture which he has drawn for us of his mother as a wife did not by any means represent his ideal; a simple instinctive mutual understanding was in his view a more desirable thing than a miracle of tact.

Only rarely and quite incidentally does he speak of what was the curse of dying Rome, namely *orbitas*, childlessness. There were no children in the houses of the great, and it was the rich rather than the poor who excused themselves for only having two or three children by saying that they did not want the other children that they might have had to live a life of poverty. Many parents (so says the bishop) with two or three children are afraid to have more, lest the others should have to beg their bread.[325] On another occasion he makes a remark in passing about people who are so niggardly that they even look upon fruitfulness as a burden, though the truth is that no increment in worldly goods brings so much happiness as the steady augmenting of a man's wealth in children. This fear of poverty sometimes drives them to the worst kind of *impietas*, for it is these avaricious people who, together with the unmarried mothers, expose their children to die, and forget the duties of parenthood.[326] Yet it is a matter for some astonishment that Augustine never expressly and publicly throws the light of his eloquence upon this evil; apparently it was not a theme for the pulpit. Whether he deliberately evaded it, and, if so, for what reason, we have no means of knowing. This silence concerning the subject of race suicide is one of the riddles of the pastoral life of this time. Perhaps the thing is in some way connected with that reverence for continence which then prevailed everywhere. In his book on *Marriage and Desire* which, as an old man, he sent to his friend Valerius in Ravenna, he says quite openly that now, after Christ, it was no longer a time in which to marry and propagate; rather was it a time to sanctify the souls which were already in existence, and he quotes Eccles. iii.5, "A time to embrace and a time to be far from embraces." But what was little more than an incidental remark on the part of the old Jewish sceptic in his litany of resignation and weariness of life was for Augustine something very different. It was a conscious and reasoned indifference towards anything that would needlessly prolong an age which was already in decay and which had already, to some extent, been overrun by the forces which were to supersede it. For all that he remains the great defender of marriage, and that not only so that he may wash the institution clean from the accusations of Julian of Eclanum. He does not venture to designate as an evil a good which at worst is inferior only to greater goods, and in the married relationship he can say exactly where the good ceases and the evil begins.

Somewhat later in the same treatise—it is worth noting that these remarks *are* confined to a treatise and that they do not occur in a sermon—he uses language of great violence about those whose lack of conscience permits them to lay hands on the fruit of the womb before birth: "Sometimes their sadistic licentiousness goes so far that they procure poison to produce infertility, and when this is of no avail they find one means or another to destroy the unborn and tear it from its mother's womb. For they desire to see their offspring perish before it is alive" (he implies by this that the soul is not infused until some time after conception), "or, if it has already been granted life, they seek to kill it within the mother's body before it is born. If both parties engage in these practices then they are no married pair at all, and if they have done these things from the beginning then they have not entered into the married state together but merely into that of immorality. In cases where only one of the parties is guilty, then I venture to state that either the woman is the harlot of the man or the man commits adultery with his own wife."[327] Augustine also touched on the question of calculated periodic abstinence from intercourse (there is nothing new under the sun), and in an early work of his made what is today a quite untranslatable remark, to the effect that the contemptible Manichees were endeavouring to spread the practice among Catholics.[328]

THE NEW PEOPLE

Such, broadly speaking, are the things that we know of the people of Hippo and Carthage, the people that heard these sermons, which certainly do not owe their fame to the quality of the audience who listened to them. Yet, if they formed but a shabby background to the bishop's own figure, and if he singularly failed to turn them into people of true Christian stature, who as Christians could stand on their own feet, and who could, in those threatening times, give a reasoned defence of their faith—if, in short, these people were really sheep and had no mind of their own—it is nevertheless true that the overwhelming majority of them sincerely wanted to be something more than nominal Christians. Yet even the existence of nominal Christians was a consideration, and the very fact that there were large numbers of these did not leave the bishop unmoved. Superior in their numbers and in the power of their faith, he said, could they not meet any evil face to face if they so desired, even the evils which followed from the aberrations of their own passions? In the sermon that followed upon the disturbance in which the hated officer was lynched, Augustine declared, "One thing I know, and it is known to all. There are houses in our town in which there is not a single pagan to be found, and there is not a single house in which there are no Christians. And if we examine the thing carefully we shall find that there is not a single house in which there are not more Christians than pagans. That is certain, and you confirm it [No doubt at this point there were cries of "True, true!"]. It is therefore obvious that nothing evil could happen if the Christians did not want it to happen. You can make no objection to that. Hidden evil can of course occur, but evil cannot occur openly if the Christians seek to prevent it, for every man can keep his slave or his son under control; a strict father or uncle or teacher, or a good neighbour, or in fact anybody older than he can administer suitable reproof to the wilder kind of youth and can help tame him. If that were done we should all have far fewer occasions for displeasure."[329] Yet the name of Christ does not live only upon their lips. The all-too-human element which he describes is of less importance than the divine element about which, for the moment, he is silent. True, he states repeatedly, the good only constitute a handful in the midst of a multitude of evil ones. Everywhere there is more chaff than wheat, even among the clergy. "Do you perhaps believe that weeds do not come creeping right up to the apse?"[330] Yet now and then he contradicts himself on this point with as much force as that with which he had made the original assertion, for he says the smallness of the numbers of the good is only relative. The number is made to appear small by the greatness of the numbers of the evil. There are a great many good, but it is only the good who know that.[331] Gradually the Christian leaven was causing the dough to rise. There was a good deal of biblical wisdom in proverbs:

> What the people's mouth declares
> Many a wholesome lesson bears

was a rhyming couplet which Augustine introduced into one of his sermons. Do not think too much evil of yourselves, he continued, even if you are not all just you are all faithful, and the just man lives by faith. Reflect in whose image you are created, and through whose blood you have been redeemed. Calculate your own worth according to the price that has been paid for you. Consider what you eat and what you drink, and what it is to which your "Amen" subscribes. Truly you need not fear to sing, "Rejoice in the Lord, O ye just. Praise becometh the upright."[332]

During Lent he saw the faithful Christians standing at his feet and next to them the *continentes* of the great monasteries. Among the latter were people of every degree. Some had been schooled in the liberal arts. For these he spoke too slowly. For the others, the uneducated, he spoke too fast and passed too quickly from one thing to another, so that he often felt constrained to repeat in simpler words some scintillating thought to which he had already given expression. He had encountered such pious circles in Rome and Milan. Now he saw them before himself in Africa and in his own town. They were quiet people and they lived secluded lives together under the direction of an overseer who was sometimes a layman but more often a priest. They made provision for their own support, practised strict fasting and silence, but remained faithful to the rule that nobody was to be forced to do what was over-difficult.[333] These were the men and women who heard the word and kept it, who knew Scripture and gladly helped both each other and strangers.[334] Sometimes there were special lectures for them in the church. Hundreds of people followed this life of self-denial. Already, in his youth, he had been able to challenge the Manichees with the words "You have hardly a single one who could be counted among the elect. We have thousands of blameless ones."[335]

But in the press of the world, in the cities, in Hippo and Carthage and Rome and Milan, Augustine learnt to know many whose dealings with the goods of this world might aptly be described by the words "utebantur tamquam non utentes". We learn of the celebrated physician Gennadius who, even as a young man, had given away all his property, although in those days he still doubted the existence of a life after death. His good deeds were rewarded by a vision of the heavenly choirs which was vouchsafed to him in a dream, while philosophy familiarized him with the conception of life on a superphysical plane. To the day of his death he remained poor, for he gave away all the money that he came by and treated his patients for nothing, as did later in distant Persia those ἰατροὶ ἀνάργυροι, Cosmas and Damian.[336] We have another little sketch of a doctor at a sick bed. All hope has been abandoned and people are standing around with tears in their eyes and look to him in anxious expectation. "After a short hesitation the doctor says modestly in language which seems almost like our own, 'Pray for him. The good God can do everything.'"[337]

We hear also of remarkable Christians. We hear, for instance, of that Court functionary Pontitianus, a man of the world with long experience of men and affairs, who threw himself on to the ground in the church in long and repeated prayers.[338] There were also convinced Christians among those who were bearers of the *dignitates*: the proconsuls Donatus and Apringius, Macedonius the *vicarius*, the tribune Dulcitius and Count Valerius, were all devout Catholics who accounted it an honour that they might look upon Augustine as their spiritual adviser. Then there was Marcellinus, who was *tribunus et notarius*, which means "secretary to the Imperial Cabinet". He was a man of most cultivated mind, most learned in the Scriptures and the father of an exemplary family. He was also, despite his *chlamys* and his spurs, a saint. Augustine had got to know him at the conference of the year 411, over which Marcellinus had presided as Imperial Commissioner. His fame had preceded him to Africa and since the occasion of the conference he had been one of the bishop's dearest friends. He paid for his zeal for the *pars catholica* with his life, for when in 413 Count Marinus, an irresponsible adventurer, had contrived to suppress a soldiers' rising under a certain Heraclian, he had Marcellinus and his brother Apringius taken prisoner and executed quite suddenly in a public place in Carthage.[339] It was said that he acted in this way "out of jealousy or because he was corrupted". The truth was, however, that he acted under pressure from the Donatists. One day before his execution Apringius, who had led a worldly life, said to his brother, "I can understand that I should have to undergo this fate as a just punishment for my sins, but you who, as we all know, have lived the life of a conscientious and zealous Christian, to what evil deed can you ascribe this misfortune?" Marcellinus answered, "Even if all you say about my life were true would it be a small benefit for God to confer on me, to have my sins punished now, instead of having them saved up for the Last Judgement? To let me suffer now is an act of mercy, even though it means the shedding of my blood." Augustine had scoured the town, desperate and miserable, and had visited people all over the place, to try and prevent the execution from being carried out. Caecilianus, however, who was secretly Marcellinus' enemy, had deluded Augustine with false hopes that his efforts would be successful because a mission had arrived at Court, with Marinus' knowledge and approval, with a request for mercy. Now he heard of this conversation, and with that zeal for souls which was peculiar to him he returned to this subject when seeing Marcellinus privately in prison. Having in mind the possibility of some secret impropriety he asked Marcellinus directly whether there was yet anything for which he ought to undergo the great ecclesiastical penance. Hereupon this man, who was usually so reserved, took the bishop's right hand in both his own, and said with rather a nervous smile: "I declare by the sacraments which have been administered by these hands that I have never known any other woman than my wife, either before marriage or afterwards." It is the bishop himself who has given us an account of this little scene, which he described in that brave and moving letter to the weakling who could not bring himself to prevent the execution, although he had the power to do so.[340] Augustine not only lamented the death of his friend, but vindicated his honour and has perpetuated his memory. The words which he wrote on this occasion have played their part in bringing it about that the Church should now honour this great man of the world as a saint. "How excellent was his conduct in all occasions! How true a friend he was! How eagerly he sought knowledge of the Faith, how sincere he was in his piety, how honourable in his marriage, how just and moderate as a judge, how patient towards his enemies, how kind to his friends, how humble before the saints and how loving towards all! How quick he was to render a service to another when there was any question of that, how modest when he asked such a service for himself! How pleased he was over a good deed, and how grieved over a shortcoming! How gloriously honest he was, how full of glowing kindness and considerate solicitude, how merciful in helping others, how generous in forgiving them, how confident in his prayers! How great was his contempt for worldly goods, how great his hope for the everlasting ones! Gladly would he have abandoned all worldly business and put on the girdle of the *militia Christi*, but this was forbidden him by the marriage bond by which he was already fettered when he began to desire even better bonds than those. When that desire came those lesser bonds could no longer be loosed."[341]

It is a moving thing to watch how even the most respected among the lay folk wavered between self-denial and indulgence and how the passionate quality of the faith of those days would gradually draw them on. We are dealing with people here whom we must not seek in the confined setting of Hippo. Augustine used to meet them in Carthage or on a journey, or make the encounter through a chance exchange of letters. There is, for instance, the figure of the tribune Boniface who was one day to become commander-in-chief in Africa (*comes domesticorum Africae*), the best general of the Empire, who had preserved Africa for the Regent and Valentinian III. Whilst he was still fighting against the Berbers as a tribune he had asked Augustine what he could do to become a good soldier. Augustine had replied in a long letter in which he had gently admonished him to drink a little less. After the death of his wife Boniface had seriously thought of becoming a monk, and, in a conversation in Tubunae, he had confided his resolve to Augustine and Alypius. These, however, had dissuaded him from this course, since his services against the barbarians were indispensable. Shortly after this he was called to Court, and before departing for Italy came to Hippo to say goodbye; but it so happened that Augustine was so tired that he could not have a proper talk with him at all.

After a time the rumour began to circulate that he had married an Arian woman, later, that he had had a daughter baptized as an Arian and had taken concubines, and also that he had allowed the troops whom he had left behind to engage in unrestrained plunder. His friends were horrified and it was only when a deacon in whom Augustine reposed particular confidence was travelling to Italy that Augustine summoned up the courage to send a long letter in which he made plain to him how deeply he had fallen. He was ready, he said, to believe that the rumours were exaggerated, but he adjured him to turn forthwith from his present ways. The question of his fall from the Empress's favour was one with which he could not very well concern himself, but this did not deter him from his duty of urging Boniface to do penance, or, if his second wife objected to that course, to be most strict in the fulfilment of his duties.[342] We do not know what the general replied. In the two years that followed, namely 428 and 429, he was again fighting in Africa, alternately against the weak Empress's barbarian auxiliaries and on their side. Whatever he may have thought about poor Galla Placidia, his love for Augustine remained unchanged. He seems, therefore, after all, to have been the kind of man that Augustine in his stern letter expected him to be, "a man of whom it might be said 'Rebuke a wise man and he will love thee'".[343] When the bishop was dying it was Boniface who was defending beleaguered Hippo against Genseric.

Everywhere one saw the miracle of Christian family life, with the woman spiritually strong, a Christian who, though she remained humble, yet knew her own worth. We have a marvellous portrait of just such a woman in the figure of Mother Nonna, as Gregory of Nazianzus has unforgettably depicted her for us. "The woman who night and day stands upright like a pillar as she sings her psalms, who never speaks in church, never turns her back to the altar, never spits on the holy floor, who never gives her hand or a kiss to pagan women and does not even offer them salt and bread when she greets them; who never raises her eyes when she passes a defiled house, who wishes to hear no song nor any novelty from the theatre and will not suffer herself to be told of any of these things. Who never makes a complaint before receiving the Eucharist and never wears a mourning dress at Communion, who no longer has tears in her eyes when she has sealed them with the holy figures and whose tears cease to flow when she has made the sign of the cross."[344] And who can help thinking of that woman whom no false hopes any longer beguiled, who could count no earthly happiness her own, but who had nevertheless grown old in virtue and who, since she walked in the security of the Faith, had never yet lost heart—who can help thinking of that Mother Monica, who followed her son over land and sea although he had run away from her, who at last, after that conversation in Ostia, obtained in some mysterious way the certainty that he would never be lost again, and who fell sick far from her home and suddenly declared at the age of fifty-six, "What further business have I here?"[345] When Augustine said of his mother that her spiritual pangs of childbirth had been far greater than her physical ones,[346] he undoubtedly saw behind the figure of Monica the figure of that other mother, the Church. Whoever sees the mosaic of the two elderly women above the inner door of Santa Sabina in Rome (Plate 9), the two figures which represent the Church from the time of circumcision and from the time of paganism, will instinctively recall that undying association of ideas in Augustine's mind which caused him always to see the Church in the form of an aged mother. This impression will be made all the stronger by the fact that the two figures in Santa Sabina are definitely elderly figures and so stand in strong contrast to the royal virgins of Rheims and Strasbourg. Even if we do not see Monica in quite so sharp a focus as we do Nonna, she is nevertheless a much more attractive personality, and certainly not less admirable than her Cappadocian contemporary.

And so there are all manner of bright stars glittering in the deep, dark sky of that time, and it would hardly be reasonable to forget the stars and only have eyes for the darkness. When Augustine spoke to the newly baptized he adjured them not to neglect to see the good among the mediocre and the downright evil: "And if you can't find a good man, then woe betide me. My God, what am I saying there? If you cannot find a good man—that would mean that we have been baptizing all these years for nothing, for it would mean that nobody keeps the vows which he made on that occasion. That I cannot believe, I am confident that there are good men among them, I firmly believe that there are such people."[347]

And there certainly were, although it was often God alone who knew their names. Every year between Easter and Whitsun he saw that strange group of *infantes* standing by the altar, people who in the middle of their lives had declared themselves ready to turn their backs completely on the past. He himself ventured to say what was in his mind on these occasions: "Speaking generally, people are full of praise for the Church of God. *Magni christiani*, they say—'They're tremendous fellows, these Christians, there is nobody like them, and the Catholic Church is a tremendous thing. All these people love one another and serve one another in any way they can. All over the world people fast and pray and sing hymns; in peaceful accord with one another men sing the praises of God.' "[348] True, people might also say, and in fact they did say it, that there were grasping and vicious men among them, and men that couldn't keep away from the theatre; that even in the monasteries everything was not gold that glittered. "Even so, all the evil in this world cannot wash out the good." Time and again he would point to the spectacle of this new nation of fasting and praying men and women who were full of goodwill to one another. He was anxious neither to criticize too sharply nor to be too reckless in his praise, but he could not help seeing that mankind had undergone a change, and that the old vices were losing ground. And even though in his old age he would speak in the pulpit of the little flock of the elect as a mere handful which grace and divine predestination would separate and save out of the avalanche of the *massa damnata*, he refused to regard anyone as lost, as long as there was still time for him to be saved. As he looked about him he saw how frequently the hot African temper could swing over from the extremes of vice to the extremes of heroic virtue. No evil man lived in this world in vain. The wicked were granted their power in order to steel the good, and every one of the wicked could change himself and become good. Men who had been stealing the property of others would quite suddenly begin giving their own property away to the poor.[349] Every day he could see how one man would fall while another would raise himself up; but to fall was human, while the raising up was a work of God. He knew the power of the example set by the few. He had once described it, that slow raising of the dough by means of a small piece of yeast. Was it not an incomparable blessing for mankind that nobody any longer worshipped either any earthly or even any heavenly creature, but only the one God whose nature could only be apprehended by the heart and the mind? And that this was no longer a matter of learned controversy, but the simple faith accepted and proclaimed by the ordinary man and woman in the street. Then there was the example of those who fasted and were truly masters of themselves, who lived lives of perfect chastity, who despised death, who spent themselves and denied themselves and were ready to renounce great fortunes. Even if those who practised these virtues were scattered and few, while those who practised them rationally were fewer. the great mass of men heard of them and saw them and was inspired. It could value such things and secretly begin to be ashamed of its own unworthiness. Ordinary men experienced their inability to rise to these heights as a weakness and a reproach, and even that was a step in the right direction and, as it were, a small spark of virtue.[350] And in all the works of love the Christian had a monopoly.[351]

No, baptism was not a last desperate leap undertaken to avoid the perils of eternity. Those who stepped out of the baptismal pool did indeed constitute a new nation. "A true renovation occurs in this holy bath and a new man is made, and having been thus made new, he becomes steadily better from day to day, though with some progress is quicker than with others. For one sees, if one watches carefully and without prejudice, that many really do make progress in this new life. As the Apostle says, 'Though our outward man is corrupted yet the inward man is renewed day by day.' "[352]

Nor did he fail to see this miracle, though it was usually a very unobtrusive one, in his own town. There, as elsewhere, he could see souls that were made anew through the grace of the Church. There was no need for him to make any *retractatio* in regard to that solemn apostrophe to the Church which he had uttered as a young man:

> Thou, O Mother Church, instructest us children in childish fashion. Thou teachest youths with power and the aged in quietude, and thou teachest every one of these not only in accordance with the ripeness of his years but in accordance with the ripeness of his understanding. Thou dost subject the wife to her husband in chaste obedience, not for the satisfaction of lust, but for the propagation of children and that the bond of the family may be preserved. Thou makest the husband the head of the wife, not that the weaker sex may thereby come short, but because this is the law of honest love. Thou subjectest the children to the parents that they may freely serve them, and givest to the parents a loving dominion over their children. Thou unitest brother with brother in the bonds of faith which are stronger than those of blood and bring men more truly close to one another. All the ties of blood and marriage thou makest more close through mutual love, while preserving in this all the workings of nature and of the will. Thou teachest the slave to be devoted to his master, not through the compulsion of his status but from the joy which his service affords him. And by directing their thoughts to the most high God the common Lord of mankind, thou renderest the master gentle to the slave, and makest him eager to guide rather than to punish. Thou makest one citizen to be at unity with another and nation to be at unity with nation, and thou causest the memory of our first parents to bind all men together not merely into a society but into brotherhood. Thou teachest kings to care for their peoples and remindest the

peoples that they must bow before their kings. Thou teachest without ceasing to whom honour is due or affection or respect. Thou showest who must be feared, who comforted, who admonished, who warned, who disciplined, who rebuked and who should suffer in his body, and thou showest that not all things are due to all men, but only that love is due to all and injustice to none.[353]

8

THE CLERGY AND THE ASCETICS

The *Episcopium* as Monastic Community

AUGUSTINE had not read in vain St. Paul's injunction that a bishop should first rule his own household. When he first took over the bishopric and became the leader of its clergy he immediately carried through an unobtrusive reform. He proposed that he should lead, together with them all, that life in community which up till then he had led as a priest in company with a few like-minded men. He turned the bishop's palace into a monastery, that is to say, into a community of priests, deacons and subdeacons living under direction of their bishop without lay brothers or novices, all undertaking the obligation to live according to a common rule. The first bishop in the West who, to use the expression of Ambrose, united the spheres of monastic discipline and pastoral activity (which till then had been separate), the first bishop, that is to say, who sought to live in community with his cathedral clergy, was Eusebius of Vercelli, who made a beginning of the *vita communis* after a journey to Egypt round about the year 340. There followed Paulinus of Nola, the sometime soldier Victricius of Rouen, then finally came Augustine between the years 391 and 396, and shortly thereafter that other famous soldier Martin of Tours.[1] Whether Augustine knew of these first attempts we cannot be certain. Probably he was in this instance carrying out a plan which he had long formulated as a wish. It is certainly a plan that carries the stamp of his own mind, though its essential idea may have already been realised in Nola and Vercelli without his being aware of it. He was, however, certainly the first to introduce the idea of clergy living in community into Africa. It was impossible for him, as a bishop, to live behind closed doors in the bishop's palace, as he had lived, while still a priest, in the monastery within the cathedral grounds. A bishop who was inaccessible to visitors would appear inhuman, and indeed he says as much himself—and those who, despite everything, insist on seeing him *par excellence* as the great humanist, will find their views confirmed in that utterance.[2] And so Augustine was driven to find his own solution of this problem. He did so by leaving his own door open while the doors of the priests who remained scattered around were kept closed, and social intercourse, which he had twice sought to limit strictly to those who were like-minded with himself, was now extended to people who were performing some part in the general business of worship. Life in community according to a common rule had long been the ideal of nearly all ascetics in the Christian world of that time. In Augustine's view this kind of life was even more suited to the clergy than to anybody else. It was in any case natural for a priest to live continently, even if he were married,[3] and it was quite customary for his wife to withdraw herself as a *continens*, after which all that could be required would be the voluntary surrender of his house and property. It was a practical ideal, for life in community provided opportunities for mutual education and it also opened the possibility of that which is the desire of all generous and sympathetic minds, namely, a place where ideas can be hammered out and where ready mental intercourse can always be obtained. Augustine recognized that he could render no greater service to the Church in his part of the world than by creating a new elite, educated under his supervision, in his own house and largely by his own efforts, for there was quite obviously a shortage of priests with adequate intellectual training.[4] That end could hardly be achieved with the kind of cleric of the great towns whom Jerome has drawn for us, for these seem to have been rather vain men who lived and went about very much as they pleased, and were interested in almost everything except the counsels of the Gospel. Not that the urban clergy was in any danger of degenerating into a mere bureaucracy; that danger only affected archdeacons and a few other administrative ecclesiastical officials, but even the best of these men had often to care for their families, practise a trade of some kind in some small place, or, what was even worse, they would have to be on the watch to see that their children did not run to the theatre, contract mixed marriages so that they might legally come of age sooner, or possibly contribute to the cost of public games as holders of public office and so cause scandal.[5] That is why he began to try and isolate from the town the clergy whom he found at Hippo, and to gather them together in the neighbourhood of that little monastery and garden which he himself gave up, but later used as a kind of seminary for the priests who were to come. He asked them straight out whether they were prepared to renounce their property for the benefit either of the Church in Hippo or some other Church, or if necessary for the benefit of their families, and to share with him his house, his table and the sacraments in a life of complete poverty and continence. "He who is ready to live with me", he was bold enough to say, "will possess God."[6] They all declared themselves prepared.

Although he himself was the mildest person in the world he would refuse to allow anybody, whoever he might be, to evade even the smallest part of his promise. He says himself that for years it had never occurred to him to try and find out whether his brother monks had disposed of their fortunes or

9 "Ecclesia Mater" (Santa Sabina, Rome, 422–32)

10 Ambrose (S. Vittore in Ciel d'Oro, Milan, 470)

how they had done so; he was neither a business man nor an inquisitor. When, however, towards the end of his life, it appeared that one of his priests was administering a fortune for himself and had even made a will, he took energetic action. Since the matter had become publicly known and his own community had thus become the subject of talk, he did not hesitate publicly to expose the priest who had been the occasion of this scandal. Among other reasons for his action was the fact that the congregation had a right to make their wishes known in the choice of his college of priests and Augustine always met the wishes of his congregation, as far as he was able, and as far as this was in accord with customary practice.[7]

To remove this stigma from his house he discussed the whole matter from the pulpit and we know exactly how he did it, from the shorthand writer's record. He carried out his purpose in two addresses,[8] and the records throw so strong a light on the circumstances within the diocese and on Augustine's own honesty and openness that it is worth reproducing them in detail.

One day the bishop asked his listeners to come in rather greater numbers to the church next morning because he had an important communication to make to them. When next day he had a large number before him (he was then already in his seventies) he began to speak to them as follows: "We live for you and not for ourselves, so that I am emboldened to say with the Apostle, 'Be my successors, for I am the successor of Christ.' That is why I will not permit even one of us to have the opportunity of leading an evil life. Placed here as I am, I must have a care not only for my own conscience but for my reputation. You know that we all live here in the manner described in the Acts of the Apostles. We have all things in common and nobody is permitted any possessions."[9]

He spoke of the circumstances in which he had entered the bishop's palace, and of the introduction of communal life there, and then pointed out that the priest Januarius had offended against the rules of that life. The congregation knew him well, he said, and knew how he had come to the place. Yet although he had given the impression that he was renouncing all rights and his property, he was secretly administering money for a daughter who was a minor and who was living in a convent close by. Now, seeing death close before him, he had made a will in favour of the Church at Hippo and had disinherited both his daughter and a son who was a monk in that Church. Augustine said that he had known nothing of this, that he did not concern himself with such matters or pay particular regard to them, and when he had heard about the affair, he could not believe it. Since, however, there could now be no doubt about the facts, he had decided to refuse the legacy. There was also a quarrel now between the two children, who were both religious. He did not doubt that he could settle that quarrel with the aid of a committee from the congregation, and would be able to determine the exact legal position. But as to the money, he would administer that until the two people were of age, but not thereafter.[10]

Naturally, he knew that many people would say, "Bishop Augustine is such a kindly person that he gives everything away and that is why nobody will make any gifts to the Church in Hippo." Such people, said Augustine, invariably bit when they spoke praise, and put their teeth into people's flesh while they caressed it with their lips. Others, he continued, would say "The Church gets everything!" He said that his own position recalled the words of the Gospel, "We have piped to you and you have not danced. We have mourned for you and you have not wept", for whatever he did was wrong. Well, then, if they wished to hear him say it, he would admit that he accepted gifts. He had accepted a legacy from Julianus, who was childless. But he would not accept one from a shipowner like Boniface, because if there were to be a shipwreck the odium of that would fall on the Church. Also, they had no money to pay damages. They had no strong-box (*entheca*), since their money was paid out to the poor as soon as it came in. If they asked him whether it was lawful for the Church to inherit, he would say, "Christ may receive a portion which may be given to him as a matter of duty. If there are three children then he may be the fourth, if there are ten then he may be the eleventh; but he must not be the only one, if others are thereby disinherited." If a man wished to disinherit his children for the benefit of the Church, he should go elsewhere and not to Augustine, and even then he would hope that God would see to it that he would find no-one to accept his money. And here he cited the example of the Primate of Carthage. A childless man had made over the whole of his property to the Church, retaining only the usufruct. When, unexpectedly, children were born to this man, Aurelius freely returned to him all he had given.[11]

Augustine then declared that he had called all his clergy together and asked them whether they were prepared to abide by their previous decision. "Brothers," he had said, "if you still have any possessions, give them away; you have the Church which cares for you." He had given them up to Epiphany to decide. Turning then to the congregation, he reminded them that it was he himself who had made the decision to consecrate no-one as a priest who would not join his community; the understanding had been that anybody who left the community would lose their clerical status. Now he declared before the face of God that he proposed to change his decision. If any of his clergy wished to keep their property they could live where they pleased and, if they so desired, leave his Church; they would not lose their clerical status on that account, though that status, once they had received it with the tonsure, might rather be called a burden than an honour. But he wanted no hypocrites; it was far worse to have hypocrisy than to change a decision that one had made.

As to those who decided to retain their property, he would not judge them, but would leave the judgement to God. But while now everyone was free to do as he pleased, they should reflect that if they left this Church, they would already, to some extent, have fallen. He knew that such men would find their defenders both in his own Church and with the other bishops. There would be people who would say, "What wrong has this man done? Why should he be degraded because he lives outside the diocese?" He would, he repeated, compel no-one to live in community, and he knew very well how anxious they were to retain their status. He would leave them that save only in his own house. As to what he would do after Epiphany, he would announce that later, and he would also let them know how the quarrel between the brother and the sister had been resolved. He concluded by asking indulgence for the talkativeness of old age and also for his weakness and hesitancy, for they saw that his years were heavy upon him and that his powers were failing. He asked their prayers so that he might serve them for as long as a soul was in his body.[12] No doubt his parishioners thought that the hesitancy of this charming old man gave no ground for serious concern.

When after Epiphany he again stepped into the pulpit his first words were, "We are indeed a spectacle for men and angels." He claimed some praise, but was also prepared for criticism; but, he said, "We must seek, with God's help, to preserve both our life and our good name, so that those who would praise us are not made ashamed by those who would censure us." He then asked for their very special attention and asked Lazarus the deacon to read verses 32 and 35 from the fourth chapter of the Acts of the Apostles: "And the multitude of believers had but one heart and soul, neither did any one say that aught of the things he possessed was his own: but all things were common unto them ... and distribution was made to everyone according as he had need." When Lazarus handed over the codex to his bishop (no doubt so that he might bless it, as is still customary today), Augustine said, "I myself will read it over to you, for I would rather read you this passage than defend my cause with my own words", and he read it a second time with great emphasis and signs of deep emotion, concluding with the words, "You have now heard what is our desire, pray that we may be able to achieve it."[13]

Hereupon he explained the whole matter again and gave his reasons for discussing it publicly, after which he told them what had happened, saying that he had good news for them, since all were agreed, priests, deacons, sub-deacons and also his nephew Patricius.[14] Apparently he had had the legal and financial position of everyone concerned most carefully examined, for there followed in each man's case a detailed account of the residual possessions remaining with him, and of the steps that had been taken to prevent any man even giving the impression of possessing anything. A great deal had to be done in this connection, for in the press of business many legal points had been overlooked, which now had to receive belated attention. He began with the deacons, who had always been the administrators of Church property.

Valens, who owned some property jointly with his brother, the latter being a subdeacon under Bishop Severus of Milevis, was to liberate his slaves after the estate had been distributed, and to hand over his lands to the Church.

The mother of Patricius had died during that year. Patricius was to share the estate with his sisters.

Faustinus, a sometime soldier, who had been baptized in Hippo, possessed immovable property only. He had parted with this, to use the legal term, *corpore non jure*, and had thereafter bestowed no further attention on it. He now handed over half to his brothers, the other half to the poor Church of his native town.

Severus, whom God had afflicted with blindness, had bought a little house for his mother and sister, using for this purpose the money of some pious laymen who were known to Augustine. Augustine declared that he would himself supervise this matter in accordance with the laws of piety. The few lands which Severus possessed at home would be handed over to the local Church, which was in want.

They knew, he said, that the Deacon of Hippo was poor, but the few slaves that he possessed would forthwith be freed before the episcopal court in the presence of himself and the congregation.

Eraclius, Augustine then went on to say, was sufficiently well known to them. They could see with their own eyes what his benefactions had done for the Church. St. Stephen's Chapel had been built with the money which he had handed over. He had also used his credit to buy an estate with borrowed money and was still paying off the debt, so that for the moment the Church had no benefit from it. Augustine himself had persuaded him to do this since he feared the reproaches of his mother, who might well consider that Eraclius was too young to give away the property, which he had inherited from his father. For this reason Augustine had also given him the following counsel: insofar as he desired to use his patrimony to make some benefaction he was to invest it in a villa, the ownership of which could be restored to him at any time. The house next to the chapel opposite the cathedral had recently been given away by him—immediately after it had been completed, in fact. His mother was to receive it. His slaves, who were already living in a monastery, were that day to receive their freedom.

All Augustine's subdeacons were poor and lived according to rule with the rest.

That left only the priests. These had brought nothing to the Church but their love. Since, however, rumours were in circulation about their alleged riches, it was necessary for him to make a statement. Leporius, who came from a very noble house, had come to him poor. He had given all his property away elsewhere. On the property that had once belonged to him he was now administering the monastery which he had built for his relatives. At Augustine's request he had built their house of pilgrimage and with the help of the money which the members of his congregation had themselves subscribed, the Basilica of the Eight Martyrs. The house which he had purchased with the intention of breaking it up and using the tiles for the guest house was now being let for the benefit of the Church, since the necessity of carrying out his original purpose had not arisen. They should therefore no longer say "by or in front of or behind the priest's house", for it no longer belonged to him.[15]

They were saying that their priest Barnabas had bought the villa of Eleusinus. That was untrue. He had made a gift of it to the monastery. Augustine himself could certify that, since there seemed to be a certain amount of incredulity in the matter. Happy Barnabas! He had done so good a work that nobody would believe the story. Also, there was a rumour that Barnabas was in debt and had asked Augustine to give him for ten years the proceeds of the Villa Victoriana. That was untrue, but perhaps the rumour had arisen because Barnabas was the administrator of the monastery and consequently had debts to liquidate. Moreover, since they could only find a single tenant for the farm and that tenant was unwilling to pay more than forty *solidi*, Barnabas was working the farm himself, which was a much more profitable arrangement. The proceeds of that farm were now being devoted exclusively to the reduction of debts. Actually, Augustine said, he would be only too pleased to be rid of the thing and he wished that somebody would come forward, preferably one of those who had been circulating these stories, and work it for the benefit of the monastery; then Barnabas could be relieved of it forthwith. He asked most pressingly for this, for if no layman came forward he would in any case sooner or later have to put somebody else in charge of it. In regard to the land on which Eleusinus had founded his monastery, Barnabas had been the nominal owner in the title deeds, but it had been transferred to the monastery.

In regard to the quarrel between brother and sister, it had come to an end of its own accord, as was only right and proper between religious.[16] It was certain, Augustine said, that after his sermon there would again be a lot of gossip, and since some of it would certainly reach his own ears he would, if necessary, return to it without naming names, but giving all the details.

If they wished to make a gift let them give it to the treasury and not to an individual priest. If his congregation were God's acre, then the treasury was their crib. Let them make no gift, even of a *birrus*, or of a linen tunic, otherwise than for the common good of all—and he begged them not to present him personally with some *birrus* of exceptionally rich workmanship. Ordinarily that would be fitting enough in the case of a bishop, but not in that of Augustine, who had been born of poor parents. No, let them rather give him one which he could give away to some poor man or to a deacon or a subdeacon; otherwise he would merely sell it. Splendid clothes would merely embarrass him; they were unsuited to his office and out of keeping with the counsels which he himself had given, nor did they suit his figure or his grey hair. In conclusion, he said, let nobody tear the servants of God to pieces. If they should be slandered, it was true that the reward of those servants would be greater; but so would be the punishment of the slanderers.[17]

Then suddenly the old man became the bishop again; humble in his own person, he reminded them of the authority of his office. In concluding his sermon he declared that if he ever again caught anyone in possession of property or drawing up a will, then he would strike him from the list of his clergy. Such a man might summon a thousand councils against him, he might travel where he would to carry out his purpose (Augustine had in mind the Court and the Curia overseas), he might live where he pleased, but so help him God and as he was a bishop, he would not recognize such a man as a member of his own clergy. They had heard what he had said and so had those of whom he had spoken. They had heard him gladly. He prayed that they would faithfully follow his rule.[18]

It was rare for Augustine to intervene with such energy as this, but here the priesthood, the very pith of the tree of the Church, was at stake. Augustine's own institutions (the cathedral chapter and the orders and congregations within his Church) had vitality insofar as they were inspired by his own uncompromising attitude, and insofar as they fell short of this, that vitality diminished. Many a zealous bishop who came later may well have envied Augustine his clergy and may have thought that it was very much easier to found the first cathedral chapter community than to reform it at a later stage. Fortunate indeed was Augustine, who needed but to give a couple of days' thought to this matter in order to do all he needed. One cannot help in this connection calling to mind the unfortunate Bishop Fauchet of Pamiers,[19] who needed nine years to carry out his reforms and was compelled to let the holders of his choir stalls die off one by one before he could achieve what he wanted.

The Monastic Ideal

Augustine's ideal was undoubtedly a strictly monastic one. It was not the life in community, but sexual continence and the renunciation of all personal property, that in his view made the truly spiritual man. The question has been raised, whether it was the philosopher and artist or the Christian that this ideal reflected. Certainly there was no other Christian ideal at that time. All the energy that today goes into missionary activity or spiritual exercises or Catholic Action and the youth movements, was concentrated in those days in that ascetic life which now suddenly began to appear everywhere in much the same form. The time of the martyrs was over, the springtime of the monastery had come.

Augustine had early seen the great potentialities that lay in free renunciation. Even before his conversion he had seen in this a way of freeing himself from the tyranny of physical appetites, and a means of creating the right kind of atmosphere for study, for serious conversation, and for the higher forms of male association. He had been the life and soul of that plan, according to which ten people were to form a Platonic study circle on the country estate of the wealthy Romanianus. But when it was a question of turning one's back on the world, his womenfolk would have nothing to do with it, and the whole plan burst like a soap-bubble.[20] When he was thirty-two years of age, he had quite suddenly, and apparently by mere chance, got to know of the ideals of Christian asceticism. One day when he and Alypius were entertaining Pontitianus, who came from the same part of the country as they themselves, and held a high position at Court, their guest saw a codex of St. Paul lying on one of the side tables and so the conversation came round to the Faith. Pontitianus broached the subject of the Egyptian hermits and when he realized that his host had never heard of these he began talking about their founder Anthony. At length, when he saw how intently they listened to him, he began to tell of an experience which he and another dashing young staff officer had had in Germany. One day while they were in Trèves and were roaming about the vine-clad hills by the Moselle while the Emperor was at the amphitheatre, they chanced to hear in a hermit's hut of the wonderful life of St. Anthony. They heard how that man, on entering a church, had caught the words, "If thou wilt indeed be perfect, sell all thou hast, and give it to the poor, and follow me", and had then and there begun to follow this counsel and had continued following it all his life. Hereupon both officers severed all connection with their lady friends, sold all they had, and lived exactly after the fashion of the hero of that tale which they had heard in Trèves. Augustine called Alypius aside and said to him, "What kind of fellows are we? Blockheads get up and conquer heaven! What are *we* doing, we and our precious system? Just wallowing about in flesh and flood."[21] After that he never forgot the life of St. Anthony. On that same day in that same garden and by that same codex of St. Paul the hour of the *tolle, lege* sounded. From that moment onward he was filled with the desire to see these new saints, who were the successors of the martyrs, with his own eyes. He discovered that there were ascetics in the suburbs of Milan, in a house founded by Ambrose. Later he visited others in Rome. He was immensely edified by these people and by their strict but kindly overseers. They kept themselves by handicrafts and performed the most incredible fasts; the women, widows and virgins, spun and wove and lived in community under the supervision of experienced superiors.[22] Shortly after this in his book *The Customs of the Catholic Church*, he glorified the anchorites of the East, though he had not seen them, and only knew of them by repute. One of his motives here was to hold up to the Manichees the marvellous powers of self-denial which these men displayed, for the Manichees were immensely proud of their own practice of these virtues. Augustine alleged that though these ascetics might, in some people's opinion, go too far in their neglect of human affairs, yet only shortsighted people could overlook the enormous advantages that flow to us all from their prayer and example, and this despite the fact that we may be quite unaware of them. He praised their state as the very summit of holiness, the very highest that man could hope to attain, and one that spread glory over the whole Christian movement.[23] But his greatest admiration he reserved for the cenobites. In that same work of Augustine's youth there is a passage which we find reproduced both in Anatole France and Flaubert. In this Augustine describes that crowd of thousands of people which, at the end of the day's work, streamed out from all directions into the deserts of Syria and Egypt to listen to one or other of the venerable Fathers. They came soberly and in silence and listened reverently but intently; they would take in his words with sighs and with tears in their eyes, but also with feelings of suppressed joy. And only after they had heard him would they partake of a meal, at which they would eat no meat and drink no wine. At least three thousand desert ascetics came together, all people who lived by the work of their hands. Every group would be subject to a dean, who would sell their baskets and other plaited work, while any proceeds over and above their needs would be given to the poor; whole shiploads of grain would sometimes be dispatched to some hungry country from this source. This latter circumstance was widely known.[24]

After his seven months in Cassiciacum, his baptism and a year in Rome, Augustine founded in 388 his first small monastery in the house of his parents in Tagaste; he was joined there by his son Adeodatus, Alypius, Severus, Evodius and a few others. It was a congregation that was founded on certain principles, but was not bound under vows. Although they followed the Italian example, they nevertheless laid an emphasis on studies which was peculiar to themselves. They had discovered the highly realistic rule for their life in the celebrated verses of the fourth chapter of the Acts of the Apostles, concerning the community of possessions.[25] A great deal of work, no doubt, was done, but it was brain-work, and though these men owned no personal property and lived very simply, they lived undisturbed, and relatively carefree, and exclusively in the company of laymen. To be free from business and so be made more like unto God—that was the thing for which they now had time, Augustine wrote quite simply to his intimate friend Nebridius, without ever guessing how selfish and presumptuous were those words.[26] So he lived for three years and wrote his books *On Music, The Teacher, The Customs of the Catholic Church and the Customs of the Manichees, On The True Religion, A Commentary on Genesis Written Against the Manichees* and a book containing answers to approximately eighty questions. In addition to this he carried on correspondence both with his Christian friends and his pagan acquaintances.

Thus Tagaste was anything but a Grande Chartreuse, but still less was it a convalescent home for anticlerical intellectuals. However, it pleased God to tear him away suddenly and for ever from this secure nest, in which almost all his dreams had been fulfilled. We do not know whether the little community dissolved itself, but the founder disappeared into the ordinary routine of Hippo, taking his philosophy, but hardly his idyll, along with him. Part of the community went along with Augustine from Tagaste to the garden of Valerius, and vocations—*boni propositi fratres*[27]—were soon forthcoming. The brotherhood in Tagaste, where Alypius was later to become a bishop, also began to multiply and to supply foundations to the Churches in the neighbourhood. Augustine carried his monastic life along with him into the bishop's palace, and up to the hour of his death he remained inflexibly a monk. And what is even more important, he loved to remind both his friends and less intimate acquaintances that though he was a bishop and man of letters he was first and foremost a cenobite monk, a preacher of self-denial, and a servant of the new servants of Christ.

A monk in those days was still essentially a white blackbird, whose peculiar plumage did not by any means always make him an object of esteem. People were far less impressed by actual asceticism than they were in the East. They were ready to take some note of ascetical *tours de force* if they were dished up and publicized as exotic *mirabilia*. They were less interested if they occurred quietly in the house next door. Above all, Rome, which was the seat of a paganism that still clung obstinately to its traditions, and was all too ready to mock at anything new, looked askance at the new phenomenon, while even the venerable Church herself, according to Duchesne, "had some difficulty in abandoning the idea that Christian perfection was the duty of all, and not the speciality of a certain elite". Jerome himself was to encounter that attitude, and his ascetical salon on the Aventine Hill fell suddenly into disrepute through the death of Blesilla, who had collapsed, according to the reports that began to circulate, under the mortifications which Jerome had imposed.[28] We also hear in Carthage that "the black ones did not enjoy a high estimation in public opinion".[29] When Bishop Aurelius wanted to subject them to the laying-on of hands, and thus admit them to the clergy proper, the ordinary secular priests protested, which caused the Emperor Honorius officially to lay it down that the consecration of monks, as a measure of necessity, was entirely in order.[30] As against this Pope Innocent, to whom the secular clergy carried their complaint, decided in the opposite sense, and in Rome no monk was ordained as a priest. In this matter of ordination it was Augustine's own wish that the monks should not in any way prove a disturbing element. And when one day Aurelius, acting in good faith, accepted into his own clergy two monks who had run away from Augustine's own monastery, one being a priest and one a laybrother, Augustine intervened with a letter which contains among others the remark that this was an insult to the whole clerical order, and that he himself confined his consecrations to the very best. Even a good monk, he said, only rarely makes a good showing as a priest. Things might go to a point where people would say, "A bad monk—good enough for holy orders—...as they now say, 'A poor flute-player—good enough to conduct an orchestra.'"[31] Shortly after this, in September 401, Carthaginian bishops were forbidden by the Synod, under pain of excommunication, to accept into their clergy monks who had left their monasteries or who had quarrelled with their abbots. It also forbade them to make such men overseers in monasteries.[32] Even the Donatists started taking shots at these "blackbirds"; one of their leaders, Petilianus of Cirta, vented his venom against the whole institution of monasticism, which he described as a senseless innovation, made all the more suspect by the fact that a rhetorician of such doubtful repute as Augustine had imported it into Africa. Augustine retorted that Petilianus was badly instructed, or at any rate that he pretended to be so, for monks were known to the whole world.[33] Yet the seedlings which Augustine had planted continued to grow quietly to maturity, and to have most happy relations with their respective congregations. Monks as yet claimed no special privileges or exemptions, nor was there as yet any friction between the monastic orders and the episcopacy, for normally only lay brothers lived in the monasteries. Contrasts, so far as these existed, were at best to be found between the Augustinians, who lived in community, and the clergy of the towns, who had always lived scattered about, each man on his own. The phenomenon of the monastic clergy was a purely Catholic thing and such monastic clergy were indisputably recognized as an elite.

Augustine had a sharp eye and even sharper words for the failings of monasticism. He detested the wandering monk quite as much as St. Benedict was later to do. So long as monks lived in the desert or in large well-regulated houses, they were a burden only to themselves, and a source of edification to others; but for a long time now wandering monks had established a foothold in nearly all the suburbs of the East, and swarmed like hostile locusts on temples, councils, on an insufficiently orthodox bishop or on anything else of which they did not happen to approve. Usually they spent their time making pilgrimages, visiting each other and hanging around and begging. Augustine knew all too well that the worst examples of shipwrecked lives are to be found in the monasteries.[34] He mocks at these rather dubious people, "who are always journeying though nobody has ever sent them, who belong nowhere in particular and never either really stand or sit". They are always hunting for a customer to buy sham relics of the spiritual masters, are always under the alleged necessity of visiting relatives in distant places, and never, in any circumstances whatever, refrain from begging.[35] He also makes fun of the long-haired eccentrics who have at least this resemblance to the fowls of the air, in that they do not like to be plucked, and who "certainly fear that shorn sanctity will prove less remunerative than its hairier manifestations"; who defend their shabby locks by appealing to the Nazarenes, who, like themselves, never permitted the shears to touch their heads, and who seek to deprive of its force the Pauline injunction against men who cultivate their hair by saying that they are not men at all but eunuchs. Madness, says Augustine. How do they get such ideas? Is it necessary for them to be so completely idle that they cannot afford a haircut? And yet, insofar as these people appeal to Samuel and Samson, Augustine thought it proper to defend the men of Old Testament times, for the long hair of such men was a symbol of the veil of the Law, which, among others, hid the face of Moses, and which, according to St. Paul, was a symbol of the blindness of the Jews, and therefore should properly be abolished under the new dispensation. Not all these long-haired men—*criniti*—were men of bad will. He loved them all, and was on the whole more merciful than Jerome, who draws us a detailed picture of these hirsute people with their chains, manes, goatee beards, bare feet and black habits, and exposes them as hypocrites. All that Augustine asked was that they should cover their heads with a hood instead of with the hairy veil of the Law, and that the better ones among them should, in God's name, get their hair cut.[36] People who seek sanctity in the neglect of their persons are, according to Augustine, just dirty fellows. He seems to share the view of the wicked Rutilius Numatianus, that ragged clothing is often a deceit, for it often covers a vain coxcomb or a hypocrite, and serves the wolf as sheep's clothing.[37]

Round about the year 400 Augustine wrote a small treatise, at the request of Bishop Aurelius, in which he defends the assertion that monks should not live from gifts but by the work of their hands. The book has the title *On the Work of Monks*, and is not directed against the cathedral clergy, which was fully occupied with the cure of souls, and so was fully entitled to use church property for its support, but against certain lay brothers in the monasteries who thought they had done sufficient if they simply lived lives of self-denial, and who justified themselves by the words of the Gospel: "Consider the fowls of the air and the lilies of the field, which toil not neither do they spin..."[38] There were monks in Carthage who not only said this out loud but practised what they preached, for hardly a hundred years had passed after the deaths of St. Paul and St. Anthony before these contemners of the world turned up who,

> ... brillants de santé
> S'engrassaient d'une longue et sainte oisiveté.

They must have formed a strange contrast with those pale emaciated faces who, so Libanius tells us, were always to the fore when a temple was to be desecrated. Augustine thought that they might quite profitably just disappear. Monks should not spend their spare time just sitting still but devote it to ascetical exercises and works of mercy. They must only accept alms for those among them who are sick or who are engaged in the cure of souls. He drew attention to St. Paul's work as a tentmaker, and when people asked him whether he really knew exactly how St. Paul had spent his time he would retort sharply that St. Paul was at least no clown and that he was neither an adulterer nor an idler.[39] And when, again, they asked him who would attend to the singing of psalms, he would tell them to sing psalms at their work, as though they were a divine rowing song.[40] When, yet again, they asked him whether they had not deliberately renounced all work, he would retort, "Then renounce your meals too!" What, he asked, was the good of reading the Scriptures if you did not carry out what you read into practice? Very often plebeians enter the monastic life in order to take things easy, or slaves do so, who obtain their freedom from their masters for this purpose, and who find it grand fun to look on while *delicati* do the rough work and they themselves can live together on an equal footing with men who till then would not even have looked at them. Even so, these *delicati* had no reason for having too good an opinion of themselves. They had not been better educated, but merely more softly educated; but that did not mean that the well-to-do were to be debased so that the poor should get false ideas about themselves. It did not mean that senators were to enter the monastic life to be industrious while working men entered it to be idle.[41] And what did all these idlers do but chatter and criticize monasteries that were more strict than their own? For chatterboxes were not only to be found in nunneries.[42] He also did not forbear to make fun of the excuses used by the workshy. If they wanted to live according to the Gospel, then they must not gather their grain into barns—*colligere in apothecas* (to quote the African translation of the Bible)—for what are *apothecae* but depositories where things are deposited for a rest—but these people have nothing to rest from. They imitate the fowls of the air chiefly by picking up things wherever they can. Everybody is expected to give them free access to his fields and orchards. How unfortunate that there are still watchmen! It would be even better if they had wings. Then they would scatter like chaff immediately the alarm was given.

They appeal, he says, to the gathering of ears by the Apostles; but why, then, do they go into the country to the farmers at a time when nothing eatable can be gathered? And if, indeed, they only ask for sustenance for a single day, and truly profess to live from hand to mouth, why do they have barns and permit all kinds of things to be brought into their houses? The birds of the air cheerfully gather the little they need from the fields rather than allow themselves to be locked into a cage.[43] The man who had written so many wonderful passages concerning true freedom from bodily needs, and concerning the life that has been made independent of all extraneous support,[44] could permit himself a joke or two, on this subject, in the slightly Rabelaisian vein.

It was in much the same spirit that he wrote to monastic communities outside Africa; for instance, to Eudoxius, the abbot of the island of Capraria.[45] He also found individual monks being given money and other valuables haphazardly. He pointed out to the younger Melania how quickly the proceeds of an estate that had been sold could be used up, and how much better it was to make an endowment of real property—that is to say, a piece of land, or a house, and in particular a house that was unencumbered by debt and produced a regular income.[46] He wrote to that Ecdicia of whom mention has already been made, that she must stop handing over great estates to unknown monks without her husband's knowledge and to the detriment of the fortune of her little son. Those who sought sanctity by the wrong door were redirected by Augustine to the right one. The letter to Ecdicia shows us in a particularly striking way how carefully he proceeded when he recommended asceticism. Probably the woman here in question belonged to that class of wealthy but frustrated females who find that in the religious life they can give reign to their desire to attract attention, and who see in that life their last chance of making themselves important. Augustine had no hesitation in telling her that it was silly to wear widow's weeds and assume airs of superiority towards her husband (who was still alive). She should not try and repel her husband by wearing sombre clothes, but use sincerity towards him. She had no right to force him into a promise to renounce his conjugal rights, and the best thing she could do was to take off her widow's veil and to dress in accordance with her station.[47] There was never any question about his views in this matter. The ascetic life was for those who had an aptitude for it. They were the only ones who should attempt it. True, he felt that in the case of widows—and this applied even to those who were highly placed—their very widowhood practically constituted a call to the ascetic life, and indeed, that the state of widowhood is for this very reason a great good. He wrote a whole book on this subject which he dedicated to the noble widow Juliana, a daughter-in-law of Proba. Actually, the well-known letter to Proba on the subject of prayer is also, though less expressly so, an exposition of the potentialities of the state of widowhood, in addition to being a masterpiece of tactful admonition. He points out to the first lady in Rome that among so many people she too, as a Christian, is a lonely soul. In the eyes of this world she is a lady of the highest rank, rich and the mother of a highly respected family. She thus appears to be anything but forlorn, yet she is anxious about her prayers— though that alone is a sign of God's grace, for God has permitted even the rich to enter the Kingdom of Heaven; yet that anxiety is a sign that despite all her external good fortune she feels herself forsaken, a widow—as the Apostle says, "Vere vidua et desolata." He reminds her of that unceasing loneliness of the Christian soul, that cross which no man, Christian or other, may escape: "In all our human relationships nothing will appear friendly to us unless we have some other being who is truly our friend; but how rarely in this life do we find such a being, a being on whose character and conduct we can truly rely, and, indeed, who knows even himself so well that he can be certain how he will act on the morrow?"[48] Thus it is that in this life the Christian is ever forlorn; he is a soul that lives in a state of longing, and is for that reason ever drawn towards solitary prayer—and with infinite tenderness Augustine now touches on the evangelical counsel of detachment. Even if Proba is bound by the duties of piety not to renounce her great fortune, she must reflect that she will one day have to give an account of her stewardship. Let her then not seek to get more from her vast wealth than is necessary for her full bodily wellbeing (for that is a thing that is by no means to be despised, and one that is in this life most necessary, until such time as our mortality has put on immortality). So let her take care of her health. Therefore, " 'If riches abound, set not your heart on them', for the widow 'who liveth in pleasure is dead while she is living'."[49]

Augustine's delicacy, which he so effectively used when it was a question of directing the great on to the road of self-denial, was matched by his energy when he was called to the aid of lesser people who had found this road but were forbidden to tread it. For people who, without loss of their composure, could watch their parents, or widows and old men, disappearing into the monastic life, were usually most unwilling to let their children enter it. In a sermon about the obedience of Abraham and his sacrifice of Isaac the bishop said: "I say this not without sorrow and shame. When it is not their money-bags but their children through whom parents are tried—in a word, when they are tried in the manner in which Abraham was tried, and their daughters and sons dare to come out openly with what is in their minds, when these say to them, 'Let me go, I want to be a virgin, I want to be a servant of God', then they are told *Nec salva sis,* 'Even if it costs your salvation, by God, you shall not do what you want to do but what *I* want!' What would you do if somebody were to say to you, 'Murder your son', or 'Murder your daughter'? You have been promised everlasting life, and it lies before you and you take up arms against it, you doubt and resist—and you call yourselves Christians. 'But what do you mean, Sir?', you will reply. 'Because I am a Christian, may I have no grandchildren?' You ask me whether you may have grandchildren. Shall I tell you just why you are failing, though you may have spent all yesterday fasting? If you are not, then sing with me what that other man sang: 'O Lord make me know my end and what is the number of my days, that I may know what is wanting to me.' "[50] He thought that a girl who truly dreamt of him who was beautiful above the sons of men might, if need be, even enter a convent against the wishes of her parents.[51] Life is short and the world full of vanity, and only he is wise who can read the signs of the times; he who, in a world which is crumbling away on all sides, seeks that lofty way, narrow but secure, that leads out of it. That was the thought that never forsook Augustine; the perpetual motive in his spiritual guidance.

It is true that as he grew older even his ascetic ideal underwent a change. His presumptuous "to be free from business and so be made more like unto God",[52] gave way to a humble listening to God's word, and to a grateful receiving of God's mercy. At the end of his letter to the nuns of Hippo, the letter which contains his rule, he could charmingly describe his dedicated virgins as "lovers of spiritual beauty smelling sweetly of the savour of Christ".[53] At the same time he never ceased to stress that all this amounted to nothing more than simple conformity with the love and humility of Christ. Perhaps the fact that he continually stresses humility as the touchstone of perfection explains why he says comparatively little about external obedience. In the matter of chastity everyone knows that once he had obtained his release from the flesh, this man, who reacted so quickly to stimulus, showed himself unwilling to make the least compromise where the physical was concerned. "Nothing is so powerful in drawing the spirit of a man downwards [the actual words are 'to hurl him from his Acropolis'] as the caresses of a woman and that physical intercourse which is part of marriage." These fierce words from his *Soliloquies*[54] were written before his baptism. They came from the depths of his soul and he most strictly held to them. He went even further. No woman might set a foot over the threshold of his house. No woman might speak to him except in the presence of some other person and outside his reception room. He did not even make an exception for his own elder sister and his nieces, all three of them nuns, not even when it was a matter of some problem of conscience.[55] He was neither a prude in his speech nor excessively hard on the weak, but he was convinced that if a man would serve God and his intention to do this was serious, then sexual continence was the minimum with which he must begin. The holy fountain of life, he said, remained defiled by the blemish of lust, even in the ordered garden of marriage. It was better to leave it untouched. The *continens* had chosen the better part. Fortunately, however, he never repeated the angry words from the *Soliloquies*, and instead of providing modern psychoanalysts with symptoms from which to diagnose fears and resistances, he confined himself to singing in simple and beautiful terms the praises of virginity.

That spiritual life was incompatible with any kind of luxury, he knew from Holy Scripture, from his own experience, and from that of all other wise men. He was fond of referring, when the opportunity occurred, to the ancient Roman simplicity, and of speaking of consuls behind the plough, such as Cincinnatus and Valerius, who toiled like peasants.[56] Yet he also knew that poverty must not be a source of worry and that the poverty which is pleasing to God did not mean a painful want, but that external simplicity which is the outward witness of self-denial. More than once he said that a servant of God was fully entitled to use whatever was necessary for his health, and that was a principle that did not apply only to a pampered lady like Proba.[57] Thus we can trace no sign of fanaticism in his conception of poverty, and it is only rarely that his conscience pricks him because of those few pleasant things with which he could not help being surrounded and which he could not do without—his books, his friends, the convenience of having a staff of copyists, his library and a place where he could work. He often speaks of fasting, but never of anything in the nature of methodical mortification; we never hear him praise the extreme penitential practices of the Desert Fathers. He is not at home with the flickering light of the *Apophthegmata*, but belongs rather in the eminently sensible circle of Cassiodorus, of the Massilians and St. Benedict. As a monk he is no Berber but a good Latin, nor did he preach that most extreme of all mortifications, complete solitude—and indeed, who would have found it harder at that time to deny himself friends?[58] A man who lives alone is evil and weak, he said; that is why Holy Scripture says "Woe to the solitary man." The same Scripture also contains the psalm, "Look, how good and pleasant it is when brothers dwell together." "This is the psalm which has brought the world its monasteries; at the sound of it those brothers leapt up who desired to live together. This verse was a trumpet call for the assembly, and sounded over the whole world; and those who were living in separation from one another came together."[59] It is true that the word *monachos* came from *monos*, but that must not necessarily mean "alone", it can also mean "one", and can refer to that one heart and soul which are a necessity if people are to live together in one house.[60] He knew the misery of an enforced living together with persons who are not sympathetic to one, but what applies in a

11 Augustine (fresco in the Lateran Library, *circa* 600)

12 "Dominus legem dat" (Baptistery, Naples, 470)

safe harbour applies also in a monastery: it is better to live crowded together but protected, than to be driven hither and thither without hope of safety upon the high seas. And then the novices! Every newcomer is at one and the same time a new chance and a new risk. It is true that many of them are mere children (though in most cases children who have been well brought up), but must not every harbour have an entry? Is it not written, "Prove all things and hold on to that which is good"? Let men endeavour to keep evil thoughts from their hearts if they can.[61]

Most certainly he had little ground for complaints about his monasteries, or, for that matter, about the general practice of asceticism in Africa, though, as he himself wrote, hypocrisy is to be found in every walk of life.[62] In that same passage there is also the very positive statement that in the City of God it is the mass that finds the hire, while the *continentes* are the battling army.[63] His own monks never begged. His housemates were busy with the cure of souls; those who were not plaited baskets or did other honest work. The sisters copied books; they spun and wove; and elsewhere they directed a home for foundlings.[64] And all employed the time when they were not at work in praising God in prayer and quiet spiritual reading.[65] So they lived in that quiet atmosphere which, since their day has attracted innumerable souls and created some of the most beautiful habitations in the world. It was a province wholly unknown to Antiquity and one full of savour of piety and of that rare elixir of self-denial which gives peace of heart, and which one cannot help feeling in the silence of the cloister.

THE VIRGINS

For Sister Martina of the Mother of God of the convent of Discalced Carmelites at Drahtem in Friesland.

The women threw themselves into the new ideal less conspicuously, perhaps, but, if anything, more ardently. Among the ascetics of the Latin West they were in the overwhelming majority. Their communities were as a rule more numerous than those of the men, and many houses, including those of Tagaste and Hippo, counted more than one hundred sisters. In that world of Antiquity women were not permitted a profession; their sphere was confined to the interior of the house and to the housework connected with it. For the mistresses this meant receiving visitors and giving orders, for the slave women fetching water, clearing up and cooking. It was the male slave who did the shopping. In such circumstances the convents threatened to degenerate into homes for old maids, though they were also often homes for women of very independent minds. Widows and spinsters were always mingling among the virgins in the cloister and perhaps were often a useful counter-balancing element to those young freed slave girls who were often received in groups into a single house. All, without exception and without regard to their past, were spoken of as "dedicated to God" and as *sanctimoniales*, they were accounted brides of him "who grazes his flock among lilies surrounded by virgins". Their state was honourable in a double sense. In church they stood together in a particular place quite close to the altar—so at least it was in Rome and Milan; they were also greeted by the girls and matrons with special confidence and respect and received the kiss of peace before all others.[66] At special celebrations they had a place of honour—pews full of the hoods of nuns during a canonization in St. Peter's are nothing new—and needless to say, that place of honour never remained empty. They missed nothing; no ecclesiastical function failed to be of interest to them, nor did any of the great personages of the Church. Even in those days a visiting bishop was met by "flocks of singing *sanctimoniales*".[67] Whenever His Excellency had occasion to appear with any ceremony the "black doves" came fluttering out of their dovecotes. The picture drawn for us by the poet of *The Virgin's Hymn* (which was composed about this time), when he describes the heavenly procession surrounding the Lamb, may well have been suggested to him by the actual ceremonial entry of a real bishop:

> Where'er thou go'st they follow thee
> The virgins and their praise of God
> Thou canst not 'scape their hymns of joy
> And sweet, most sweet, the sound of them.[68]

If the ideal of self-denial drew women towards the cloister, that of virginity was even more powerful, for in those days it represented an escape from the brutal sphere of the *epithalamos*. Let us remember in this connection the kind of thing Ausonius would recite in the intimacy of his family circle. In virginity, too, they were realizing the evangelical counsel and their own choice was here made glorious by the Apostle's words. The holiest longings of such girls have been well expressed by the poet of the *Virgin's Hymn*:

> To have no knowledge of the wounds
> Corruption makes upon the soul.[69]

So many were attracted by the idea of purity that it often happened that shortly before her marriage a shadow seemed, to a young bride, to fall over her future way of life, and she would suddenly abandon both her jewellery and her love. And there was occasionally some excitement when a daughter of one of the great houses thus suddenly fled from the fire-red *flammeum* of Hymen in her eagerness for the virgin's veil. Nevertheless, the world was in those days already Christian, so that when this happened there were no audible lamentations and one only heard the rejoicings of the pious, who tended to look on this heroic decision as a personal victory for Christ their Lord. In one such instance the young noblewoman, Demetrias, who came from the house of the Anicii Probi and was a daughter of Juliana and a granddaughter of Proba, was passing a few days in Tripoli and suddenly abandoned her plans of marriage (both Augustine and Alypius had a hand in this matter) and appeared in the habit of a nun before her mother and grandmother. These were not immediately prepared to give their approval. When, however, at last she had obtained their consent and, in the year 414, received the veil from Aurelius's hand, the wildest delight spread among all the ascetics. It should, however, be noted that the family made certain that everybody was told about the affair, nor did Demetrias forget to send Augustine a memento from the feast[70] (*apophoretum*); and Jerome, too, had to be notified.[71] Even the Irishman Pelagius, who in those days still had the reputation of a strict monk, was duly apprised. He wrote the exalted postulant a long letter which gave Augustine the occasion to sound a warning, for that letter already contained a few drops of Pelagian poison.[72] It must all have been a strange experience for her grandmother Proba. Proba had installed three sons as consuls one after another and on these occasions had paid the cost of the appallingly expensive public games "without experiencing any difficulty whatever". Now, instead of the troops of lions and tigers which had been exhibited before her when her sons attained the summits of their careers, she had displayed before her eyes swarms of virgins, for Demetrias took a whole crowd of slave girls along with her on her new way of life. Jerome wrote that there was not a village in Africa where the news was not known. Italy had ceased to mourn. Every city on the ocean's fringe was speaking of it: "Only a single province knew her as an affianced bride. The whole world knows her now as a virgin of Christ."[73] The whole thing was taken most seriously. Both in the highest circles and throughout the masses there was a murmur of admiration, if one of these fashionable ladies gave up her swarms of eunuchs and servants, her delicate table and her gardens. In the Middle Ages nobody bothered much about this kind of thing—there were too many princesses to be found among the abbesses—while in the eighteenth century people shrugged their shoulders in a gesture of commiseration. When Louis XV's daughter Louise took the veil in a Carmel Paris hardly mentioned the matter—though the age of Louis XIV may have approximated rather more closely to the year 400 in this respect, and indeed when the Duchesse de Luynes and the Duchesse de Noneville could cause the world of Paris to gather before the grille of the Grandes Carmélites, we must admit that a *prise de voile* was a very important event. But in Augustine's time the admiration for such a thing was more intense, for the sacrifice was more radical. Here Louise de la Vallière could hardly have competed.

Incidentally, asceticism penetrated right up to the Court. Ravenna still cherishes the memory of that tragic and politically ambitious daughter of Theodosius, Augustine's Empress Galla Placidia, who spent whole nights in prayer in the lonely Basilica of St. John (which she had herself erected) bewailing her endless banishment. The very name of that curiously large-eyed woman seems to breathe an air of solemn peace and suggests a combination of detachment and melancholy splendour. Something of all this is suggested by her grave, that glorious mosaic structure which is hidden away in a little cruciform brick building covered with simple tiles. She was a woman who made a better ruler than the men she was compelled to marry and who longed to the end of her days for the oratory and the veil. In Constantinople lived Galla Placidia's niece, the saintly Empress Aelia Pulcheria. Entangled in a web of intrigue and watched over by a crowd of orthodox eunuchs, this woman, together with her two veiled sisters, sang psalms day after day in the palace of Theodosius II. For the sake of the Empire she later became the virginal bride of the upstart Emperor Marcianus. Her successor Eudoxia, a woman of great literary culture, was a convert coming from the Athenian Guild of Poets. When she became Empress she loved to hear from connoisseurs the praises of her panegyrics, but she also had a beginning made on the codification of Roman law. She ended her days, strict and pious, in almost utter poverty in that paradise of all *continentes*, Jerusalem.

It is obvious that the excitement which a woman like Demetrias could occasion was due to her great name and her wealth. The ordinary *velatio* was unnoticed. It was one of the most intimate ceremonies of the ancient Church, and one least likely to have any connection with the turbulence of public life. Untouched by personal ambition or political intrigue—for the thing had no official significance—it left no traces save a suggestion of oases of untouched womanhood in a world that was essentially masculine to the point of animalism.

A full century and a half before the idyll of Subiaco the Church Fathers had often had their own sisters as superiors of convents. They were not always as intimately linked with these as were the twins Benedict and Scholastica, who could be separated neither in the womb nor in the grave, but only by the rule of the cloister, and on whose honoured grave on the height of Monte Cassino there could, until 1944, be read the lines

> Whom their mother brought to the world in one birth
> Mother earth received into a single grave.

But in the Communion of the Saints it was rare for sisters to let their brothers tread the way of perfection alone. On the contrary, they had usually gone on ahead, nor is anything more calculated to arouse our respect in this melancholy age of late Antiquity, which held women in such low esteem, than the veiled mothers, sisters and nieces of the Church Fathers. These holy women, the forerunners of the abbesses and ecstatics of the Middle Ages, are the first of that long line of mighty women at the head of whom stands Lydia the seller of purple and the grandmother of Timothy, while Genevieve and Hroswitha, Gertrude and Catherine are followed by Angélique Arnauld, Teresa of Avila and Louise de Marillac, Sophie Barat and Cécile de Bruyère, and all the mothers of the abbeys, the congregations, the schools and the hospitals. But those early ones remained in the background of Church history, that being in accordance with the spirit of the age of the *gynaeceum*. Nevertheless, in the lives of their celebrated sons, brothers, uncles and cousins they played a modest but nevertheless indispensable part, of which the world outside knew very little, or which it quickly forgot even when its attention was drawn to it.

Even so, the Cappadocians gave due honour to their saintly grandmothers, aunts and sisters by means of letters and eulogies. Jerome owes part of his fame and also the inspiration for some of his best prose to a group of *moniales* who had been schooled in letters. Ambrose dedicated his book *On the Virgins* in unforgettable fashion to his sister Marcellina on the occasion of her receiving the veil at Christmas from the hand of Pope Liberius; the book contains a reproduction of the papal address.[74] Augustine, however, who glorified his mother as no-one had ever done before, is silent about her daughter, his elder sister. She was a widow and lived only a house away as the superior of a great convent in Hippo, where also lived other nieces and relatives of his, including possibly the daughters of his brother Navigius.[75] Never did he set foot in her house except on the most urgent occasions; we do not even know her name.

Apparently this woman ruled the house without any statutes and also without any difficulty, for it was only round about the year 420 that there seems to have been any trouble. When it did arise, it was due to a rebuke which the new superior, Felicitas, had administered, and which produced a minor revolt. The rector Rusticus was helpless (what else can you expect from a man with a name like that?). He had only just been appointed and it appears that the dissatisfied party was relying on him, or possibly on his popularity, in order to bring about the superior's removal, though the latter had held her office for some years. Rusticus declared that he would rather leave the place than be the cause of her resignation.[76] Augustine had no wish to carry out a visitation. Not that he was without feeling for his sisters. He had himself founded their community and brought it to maturity. But he believed at first that he would succeed by mildness, and so he wrote to the superior, and, quite secondarily, to the rector; and also, to the sisters, a letter couched in very amicable terms, in which he admonished them all to keep their love for one another and to let no quarrels develop because of a well-meant rebuke. Such a rebuke, he says, "is either engendered by love or is sent to test our love."[77] When that proved of no avail he wrote a second letter which was rather more explicit and considerably more energetic, and in this he gave free rein to his indignation and called a spade a spade. His decision was to keep both the rector and the superior and he used the occasion to publish and impose a very carefully worked-out house rule.[78] It will be observed that he was careful to do it all in writing. Apparently he knew already from experience the truth that he was later to express in words which had no malice but are marked nevertheless by a touch of irony—"Fly from the bars of a nunnery. Otherwise you will only lose time and get nothing for your pains but a lot of talk."

Naturally he was careful not to write in this sense. If I do not come in person, he said, it is only out of my consideration for you. It is because, as the Apostle said to the Corinthians, I do not want my presence to increase your disorder or my own sorrow, and I say this although you have requested me to come. I have become used to thinking of you as an oasis of goodness in this wicked world. "You did run well. Who hath hindered you? Know you not that a little leaven..." but I prefer not to continue the quotation.[79] How is such a thing possible, he goes on; a schism in a convent and against a mother who has been looking after most of you for years and has cared for you and instructed you and given many of you the veil? It isn't as if you wanted to get rid of the rector; the person of whom you are seeking to get rid is your own superior, who long served here under the direction of my revered sister.[80] The house rule, which takes up four-fifths of the letter,[81] begins simply and tellingly with the remark that they are come together "that you should dwell in your house, and before God above, being of one heart and one soul and having nothing that you can call your own"—again, the ideal of the fourth chapter of the Acts. Then follow short pregnant directives concerning the duties and the customary failings in a community of women. This famous letter, No. 211, is pure gold for him who has the patience to listen to the deep wisdom which it contains, hidden in these apparently simple little pointers. It is also valuable because of the charming and most human picture which it provides of life in the convent of that time.

There was to be no question of any respect for persons. Both the superior and the rector were allowed to remain in their respective offices and indeed were expressly confirmed in them by Augustine's action, though the rector was only concerned with such tasks as were beyond the capacity of the superior. The bishop reserved the right to intervene if necessary.[82]

In the community of the convent there were the usual small jobs. One, or possibly two, sisters were charged with the care of clothing. Where necessary more might be called upon—for instance, when it was necessary to beat the clothes in order to get out the moths. One sister was in charge of the larder, another of the infirmary, another of the library, for there really was a library. And believe it or not, the lending desk was open every day at certain hours. In those days one did not forget in the convents of women, any more than in the monasteries of men, what was written about "growing in the knowledge of God".[83] Evagrius incorporated in his rule the words, "Let the rising sun, O virgin, find thee with a book in thy hand."

The wardrobe was made up of the clothing which each of the sisters had brought along with her, and of what she had woven herself, but the mistress of clothing was under no obligation to hand out the old clothing to its former owner. Every sister had to be content with whatever was given. The only provision made was that the wardrobe was always to be accessible. The superior decided how often the clothing had to be washed, and whether that work was to be done by the fullers. It was her task to see that the sisters were not to grow accustomed to the pleasant sensation of always having a clean dress.[84] The storekeeper was under no obligation to give all the same food. The more tastily-prepared dishes were given to the sisters of the better families, the poorer ones only received them when they were ill and were told to account themselves fortunate insofar as they were strong enough for a coarser diet to agree with them. Strictly speaking, therefore, the robust poor should have been the object of envy to the delicate rich. Although they were of most diverse origins all wore the same clothes,[85] a dark *tunica* with a mantle, a girdle, shoes and veil. The hairnet was not to be visible through the veil, nor was the hair to appear, either as the result of untidiness or of deliberate arrangement.[86] It would seem, therefore, that the sisters of Hippo did not by any means make themselves hideous by means of sackcloth or sinister-looking hoods, in the fashion followed by certain nuns described by Jerome who, according to him, looked like night owls.[87] The rule only lays down that they are not to wear conspicuous clothing and that it is not the clothes which make a person pious. We also hear that the more highly placed were instructed to look upon it as an honour if they were allowed to associate with the poorer ones, and that they were not to let the fact that they had brought a large dowry to the house become the occasion of secret pride. As against this, the poor were not to think themselves superior to those "who had enjoyed a certain respect in the world", for then the convent would only be of service to the rich who deliberately suffered humiliation there, and ruinous for the poor, in that they became puffed up.[88] There was a chapel, but Mass was not said there and it was only used for prayers at certain hours of the day. Some of the rules are concerned with this modest office. "Never cease to pray at certain fixed hours and times. Let no-one use the oratory for any other purpose than that for which it was built and which has given it its name, and if there are some who wish to pray there otherwise than at the fixed hours, insofar as they have the time, let no-one disturb them who is engaged in some other occupation in that place, that is to say, in cleaning or talking. When you pray to God in your psalms and songs of praise, then let that which sounds in your voice be alive in your heart and only sing that which is directed to be sung; that which is not directed to be sung you are not to sing."[89] At table somebody should read aloud, "for not only must your mouth take food, but your ears must receive God's word".[90] Fortunately it is not laid down here, as in the case in the letter of Caesarius of Arles, that the superior is not to choose a reader "with a sweet-sounding voice". His rule further shows us that Caesarius would have nothing to do with any kind of painting, coloured curtains or silks in the chapel. He forbids any ingenious needlework, only simple black or white crosses being allowed, and these must be sewn, and not woven in. Embroidery was only permitted on the *mappulae*, the handkerchiefs which were held in the hand for show, and in the sweat cloths.[91] But Augustine is silent on these matters.

The sisters passed their time in prayer, reading and in handiwork, such as spinning and weaving. Probably they also copied books.[92] They never went out alone or in smaller numbers than three at a time. Once a month, also three at a time, they bathed in the municipal baths, though the sick were allowed to go more often. There was also a doctor connected with the house.[93]

There are the usual darker patches in the picture, for this rule, too, has its negative side. It is obvious from it that sulkiness over a motherly rebuke, talebearing and jealousy, were factors which had to be reckoned with. The bishop expressly and most emphatically refers to the duty of taking back an angry word after a quarrel. The superior is the only one in such a case who, by reason of her position, can look upon herself as released from the duty of apologizing, but she must allow people to perceive that she recognizes that she has been in the wrong, and make good the painful impression by means of some little kindly act; and to the Lord of her conscience she must confess her guilt.[94] The worst things which the lawgiver sought to prevent—take note, to prevent—were an unconciliatory spirit after any kind of difference, any kind of forwardness or flirtatiousness, a thing that was, of course, forbidden to the Christian woman in the world also, whether single or married. Forbidden, too, is the secret acceptance of little notes or presents from male acquaintances.[95] There is express warning against ogling; and to look about one in the street is unworthy of a virgin. To exchange glances with men is equivalent to a first yielding to lust, and "staring is an abomination to the Lord".[96]

At the end comes the direction that the reading of the rule is to be heard once a week and that on this occasion everyone must search her own conscience as though regarding herself in a mirror.[97] There was no *clausura*, but in accordance with the decision of the Third Council of Carthage, which applied everywhere, no cleric or monk was permitted to set foot within the convent except with the express permission of the rector or the bishop, and even then only if accompanied by people of known probity.[98] The bishop himself gave the example here by only speaking to the superior when this was absolutely necessary, and always in the presence of two witnesses. The grille, that symbolic rampart of virginity (which has nothing in it of the spirit of the harem or the *gynaeceum*, or of the macabre poetry of the *sépolte vive*, but everything to do with that secret garden of the Song of Solomon and with the ancient *salvator ponetur in ea murus et antemurale*)[99]—that grille did not yet exist. Such a hedge only grew up when the garden of contemplation had reached its highest point of refinement. Hippo's gardens of virgins were still young and tender, and Africa was not France. It was not capable of producing a Saint Jane Frances de Chantal. Unlike M. de Genève, Augustine never knew the delightful companionship of a holy and witty woman.

Everyone knows how wonderful was the tree that grew from the seedling which was the celebrated Letter 211, a letter which Possidius overlooked in the list of Augustine's works. All cathedral and college chapters, a whole order with all its branchings, and innumerable congregations, can be traced back to this document and so owe their origin to this minor disturbance in the *episcopium*. It is not impossible that amongst others Benedict knew at least of the spirit of this rule and that through Gaudiosus of Abithinae, an African bishop who had fled to Naples.[100] As is so often the case, the simple solution of a question of spiritual discipline, which was originally intended to apply to a limited circle, became the rule of life for whole generations.

The Clergy

Despite frequent complaints about the shortage of priests, the clergy in Africa were numerous. In Carthage a bishop was consecrated on almost every Sunday of the year, and when the Vandals broke in there were about five hundred clerics, if we include the lectors, who were mostly boys.[101] To every urban Church there belonged, besides the bishop, a number of presbyters, deacons, acolytes and lectors. Thus, in 424, Augustine had in his Church at least six deacons and three priests, while in 427 he had seven priests, of whom two had been deacons in 424 and had since been ordained. Also in that same year of 427 two of those who had been priests in 424 were still with him.[102] As we have seen, the lectors were mostly boys, who were given this office because of their clear voices but could not, of course, rise any higher during boyhood.[103]

Jerome has pointed out the disadvantages that are inherent in the elective system of appointing priests, for, says he, the best qualified men are not ambitious and so do not come to the fore, while the bishops who preside at elections often seek to please their wealthier parishioners or even their own relations.[104] The recruitment of clergy, however, was greatly simplified through the rise of monasteries and through the spread of the Augustinian system of having bishops and clergy living together under rule. This last was imitated everywhere and provided an excellent atmosphere for training candidates for the priesthood. As regards the general quality of the clergy, it seems likely enough that the mere existence of the Donatist counter-Church caused men to be particularly careful of their manner of life, and most certainly the Catholic clergy whom we encounter in Donatist documents do not disgrace their office.[105]

There is a letter of Augustine's which he wrote, shortly after his election to the priesthood, to his friend Aurelius, who had lately become Bishop of Carthage. In this he airs a number of matters that happen to be burdening his heart, and, among other things, has some bitter remarks to make on the clergy, their jealousy, their greed and their self-seeking.[106] Yet shortly before writing that letter, he had written to Valerius, and it is plain from this last communication that the esteem in which the clerical office was held was very great indeed.[107] In his later writings we hear now and then of some incident that causes scandal, of some precipitate act and of the usual disputes concerning jurisdiction, but we hear much oftener of honest zeal and of wholehearted devotion to the cause of God.

It is true that it is often made obvious that the clergy were in the main very simple folk, so much so that Augustine often felt called upon to reprimand certain half-educated snobs who found a source of amusement in the barbarisms, solecisms and faulty pronunciation of which both bishops and priests were occasionally guilty; he would urge such men rather to lift up their hearts to God during the public prayers than to take note of such things. He admitted that the clergy sometimes did mispronounce their prayers and on occasion did not even know the meaning of the words they were uttering. He did not condone this, for the people should surely know what it was that their "Amen" confirmed. Nevertheless, as a matter of piety, the better instructed should bear with the ignorance of others.[108] Easter Eve, when baptisms took place, was an occasion when these words were particularly relevant, for many people of standing who did not come to Church at any other time would then be present; also, there might well be a number of persons who had rank and a name among the candidates for baptism. It is this circumstance that Augustine has specially in mind when he makes one of his references to the faulty rendering of prayers by the clergy when people of education are present, though he insists that this does not affect the validity of baptism, which is all that matters.[109] The Council of Milevis of the year 401 laid it down that all priests should use the prescribed formulae, with particular emphasis on the *preces* (the prayers of intercession before the *praefatio*), the *orationes* (said "when the sacrificial gifts on the altar are consecrated and divided") the *missae* (the prayers of dismissal, also called *interpellationes*), the *praefationes*, the *commendationes*, the laying-on of hands. Further, it was decreed that new prayers originating from other places, which neighbouring priests wanted to take over or copy, must be first examined and approved by competent members of the synod—a sort of inter-synodal *imprimatur*. This last provision was also made in Carthage as early as in 397, together with the order that at the altar the priest was to address himself to the Father and not to the Son, and that in the *preces* no-one was to address the Son in place of the Father, or the other way round.[110] Quodvultdeus wrote to Augustine in a somewhat similar sense from Carthage, saying that in that great town some of the clergy had little education, and adding with true modesty, "I have only to think of myself."[111]

Outside the cities, we may well suppose that the clergy had for the most part no education at all, while the majority of the bishops were, no doubt, like Augustine's friend Samsucius from the village of Turris near Hippo, who had not been trained in the liberal arts but had nevertheless an excellent understanding of the truths of the Faith.[112]

The country priests, together with their subordinate clergy, formed a caste apart. They had often grown up in serflike status as *coloni* on the estate where the little basilica happened to be situated. They had been ordained for the service of the church of a particular property or a particular village and had for the most part been elected by the local folk.[113] Serfs they continued to remain, and were under compulsion to provide for their rent either personally or through others; they had no business elsewhere. Only with the express permission of the Bishop of Carthage could they be called to another place,[114] and even then they remained under the obligation to compensate their lord. Further, they were forbidden to alienate the property of their church or to give it away to other churches without the bishop's permission,[115] and indeed in course of time these country churches and their congregations acquired a definite legal status with certain specific rights. Thus, in 427, we find the synod laying it down that the bishop must not allow the cathedral church to benefit from any gifts on the part of the diocesan churches, though the administration of the latter was entirely and exclusively in his own hands.[116]

Despite their dependent position, the country clergy were something of a disturbing element. They liked to be the kings of their own castles. The type of the opinionated village priest, with somewhat limited horizons, who is a law unto himself, is as old as the Church. Thus we find the priest of Badesile reading out of apocryphal books because he happened to consider them attractive, and allowing his village to become a gathering place for Manichees and other heretics.[117] Another typical case is that of the priest of Subsana who consecrated his reader Timotheus in connivance with his landlord but without the knowledge of his bishop (in this case Augustine himself), as subdeacon of his own little church. Unfortunately Timotheus had already promised his services under oath to Bishop Severus of Milevis, and Augustine had some difficulty in convincing his friend that he had kept faith with him and had been innocent of any underhand dealings. Timotheus had ultimately to stay in Subsana. The priest was severely rebuked, but there was, however, nothing to be done. Timotheus had carried out the duties of reader in one of the churches of the bishopric of Hippo and the Synod of Milevis ruled in the year 402 that "anyone who has carried out the office of reader, be it only a single time in one church, may not be held bound to perform any spiritual office in another".[118]

Sometimes it would happen that a village priest pulled so many strings and for so long that his congregation would send a deputation to the Primate in Carthage with the request that their good shepherd be made a bishop so that their own church would achieve independence. That this was possible is shown by a canon of the synod dated 397,[119] though the Fathers were careful to make it a condition that the permission of the existing bishop should be obtained, for "there are people who seek to create a post for themselves, and having done so will have nothing to do with their brethren. Moreover, the more worthless the man, the more he desires to be his own master and to be like a tyrant in his fortress. Many of these puffed-up and contumacious priests dare even to defy their bishops; yea, and by hospitalities and all manner of unlawful means, they cause their congregations to show them unmerited favours and to request that they be made bishops over them."[120] As always—one need only think of the most flourishing period of the Holy Synod in Russia—the Hierarchy was unanimous against the emancipation of country clergy.

It was in the country, where the town folk could not bear to live, that these "barbarous and uneducated clergy"[121] felt themselves to be in their element. They spoke Punic like the neighbouring farmers. They were in fact pastors who stood very near to their own people, and perhaps because of this they were at times insufficiently careful of the dignity or even the obligations of their office. Certainly this was true of the deacons. We have already noted the case of the subdeacon who went over to the Donatists with two fellow serfs, both of them dedicated virgins.[122] There was also the case of the sub-deacon Rusticianus, who preferred to sit around in the drinking shops of Hippo rather than in his village inn. On one such occasion his bishop asked him what he was doing away from his village and why he deserted his post. "You are tied to a wife", the bishop said. "Do not seek a divorce."

Rusticianus, however, complained that there was no-one in his village with whom he could associate. He entertained on quite a scale and was entertained in return, borrowed money, got into debt and, in fact, led such a riotous life that his village priest excommunicated him. Rusticianus then went over to the Donatists, was rebaptized, and shortly afterwards seized and killed during a nocturnal hold-up.[123] We hear also of a certain Abundantius, another member of the village clergy, who, late on Christmas Eve, said goodbye to his friends in Gippi with the declared purpose of going home, and thereupon had a meal and passed the night with a woman of ill repute. Augustine reported him to his bishop. He was removed from his office and sent back to Bulla, whence he came, with a very moderately phrased letter to his village priest. He could, he was told, appeal to a commission of six bishops if he wished. Augustine would have nothing more to do with him.[124]

Augustine was certainly not the man to protect those who had offended either in morals or doctrine. Reference was made above to the priest of Badesile who was suspended by Aurelius of Carthage. This man came to Augustine asking for his intervention, but Augustine, who thoroughly distrusted him, refused to receive him or to do more than advise him to abstain in future from the reading of uncanonical books.[125] In another case, however—that of his own priest Leporius—he acted very differently. Leporius, while in the South of France, had expressed certain erroneous views concerning the Incarnation, but had withdrawn them on receipt of a reproof from the local bishop. When he returned to Africa Augustine received him in a most friendly fashion simply because Leporius had acknowledged his error.[126]

Even in his own house people sometimes took the wrong road. Once when he was in Carthage news came to him that the priest Boniface and the monk Spes were accusing each other of a very grave offence. Augustine wrote to his clergy and notables that they were to send both men to the grave of St. Felix, where the judgement of God was to be asked for. In the meantime he ordered the priest's name to be struck from the diptychs, and gave instructions that no letter of recommendation should be given him. Although he inclined to believe the priest rather than the monk and was certainly unwilling to lay hands on the latter, though Spes had on several occasions begged most pressingly for ordination, Augustine was determined not to adjudicate the matter lightheartedly, but to do everything in his power to attain certitude. There is nothing worse, he said, than corruption among the elite and he quoted the Apocalypse: "He who is holy, let him become holier, and he who is defiled let his defilement increase." He knew, he said, his own fallibility. He was only a man living among men, nor did he have the presumption to believe that his house was better than Noah's Ark, in which at least one worthless man was found, or than the house of Abraham, from which also one man had to be expelled.[127] Some of those whom he had reared were to prove a bitter disappointment to him. There was, for instance, the case of Paulus. This man became Bishop of Cataqua, a wretchedly poor little place in Byzacena, and at first brought many schismatics back into the Church; but he lived beyond his means and far beyond what his station required. Paulus' major interest began to centre on money. He speculated, got head over ears in debt and was compelled to witness the sale of all his property and effects. He contrived, however, to retain a certain amount of money; with this he acquired a heavily-mortgaged imperial estate. He bought this property in the name of the Church, however, and so evaded taxes. He further applied Church funds to his personal use and committed so many other irregularities that Augustine broke off all connection with him, and after his death had to clear his heavily compromised successor at Court.[128]

A very young monk, a mere lad, who suffered considerably at the onset of puberty and became the victim of neurotic attacks, used after these to tell strange tales of what he had seen in heaven and hell, whither he had journeyed in the company of an old man and a boy. Augustine allowed him to remain in his house, and in due course the boy's heavenly acquaintances prophesied to him that during the forty-day fast he would not suffer at all, and somewhat later gave him the advice to wade up to his waist in sea water. As a matter of fact, the attacks really did cease during the forty-day period, while the sea water, supplemented by medical aid, proved beneficial to his other trouble. In the end, however, when the lad grew up, he ran away from the monastery.[129]

What literally turned Augustine's hair grey in his old age was the young lector Antonius, who had been brought up from childhood in Augustine's own house. When, after endless trouble, the hamlet of Fussala had been won back from Donatism, Augustine had contrived to arrange for a Catholic bishop to be installed there. The Primate of Numidia had come over for the consecration, and then at the last moment the candidate concerned refused, quite suddenly, to accept the office. To save the situation, and incidentally to save his own face before the Primate, who had made a long journey to be present, he was reckless enough, as he himself ruefully confesses, to put forward the name of the young lector Antonius, who had at least the ability to speak Punic to recommend him. Antonius was duly consecrated; unfortunately he proved nothing less than a tyrant who engaged in wholesale plundering and roused the whole population against himself. He also lived in adultery, and —so at least the story went outside the village—was guilty of even graver sins than that; there was in fact talk about rape. A synod which was called together in Augustine's house called him to order and deprived him of jurisdiction. In view of his youth, however, he was not deprived of his office nor banished from his bishopric. Hereupon the scoundrel secretly appealed to Pope Boniface, having first pulled wool over the eyes of the old Primate of Numidia and induced the latter to give him a letter recommending his cause. The Pope, who thus judged the matter on completely misleading evidence, sent a legate to Africa with instructions that this bishop, who had neither been removed nor excommunicated, should be reinstated, and that his rebellious congregation should be brought to obedience, if necessary with the aid of the civil power. We still possess a letter on this matter which Augustine (who was profoundly moved) wrote to Pope Celestine, the successor of Boniface. In this he adjures Celestine not to subject the unfortunate people of Fussala to an authority which would be a hundred times worse than that of the old schismatical leaders. Indeed, so bitterly did Augustine's conscience reproach him on account of what he considered an unpardonable error that he offered to lay down his episcopal office.[130] We do not know how the matter ended, but everything points to the fact that Augustine's exposition opened Celestine's eyes.

The case of Antonius was not the only one of its kind. There was also that of a priest, Apiarius, from the diocese of Sicca. Like Antonius, Apiarius succeeded in winning over the Curia, and here, too, the result was papal intervention and the sending of a legate. These regrettable incidents moved the synod of 426 to request the Bishop of Rome "not to make it too easy for people from this part of the world to obtain an audience and not to receive into your own community those who had come under the ban of the African Church"; such intervention in the territory of other bishops was equivalent to the introduction into the Church of "the pride of the world". The Fathers further forbade not only all clerics and priests, but even the bishops, of the African Church, to make any further appeals to Rome.[131]

About the African clergy as a whole Augustine has only good things to say. He most unequivocally withdrew the bitter things he had said about them in his youth. Even in regard to Carthage we find no trace in his writings of those rather colourful scandals about whose existence in Rome and elsewhere Jerome finds it impossible to be silent. Here are no clerics reading love songs and saucy stories, running after young serving girls, visiting the baths, and spending hours in the care of their skins. Here are none of the clerics who are more often to be found as hangers-on at some rich man's table than comforting some poor family whom God is proving by suffering. Here we hear nothing of the practice of appointing a gastronomic leader for every province, nor of clerics systematically ingratiating themselves with old men who are near to death and even "catching their spittle in their hands when they cough", nor yet do we hear of long morning visits paid to wealthy widows who like to hear the town gossip from a sharp tongue.[132]

There were, of course, always people like Felicia, the converted Donatist sister, who had their doubts about the clergy. We know of Felicia from a letter which Augustine wrote to comfort her. Probably her doubts derived in part from the happenings in Fussala, though they may also have been due to a native prudery. Augustine wrote to her that to the end of time there would always be two kinds of shepherds in the bishops' seats, the true guardians of the flock and those who sought the office for the sake of gain, for there are both sheep and goats among the shepherds, even as there are among their flocks.[133] It is illuminating to compare the way of life of clergy of Augustine's time with the kind of thing that went on under Cyprian, in what was still the heroic age of the martyrs, for clerics, under that same Cyprian, were living together with virgins who bore the innocent-sounding title of "Syneisacts", but had nevertheless, when the bishop took steps to end this practice, all to be examined by midwives.[134] If we then look at the character of Augustine's cathedral clergy, as it is revealed to us in the two sermons on the above-mentioned Januarius, we immediately realize how intolerable and unthinkable in Augustine's day would have been the crude improprieties of Cyprian's times, and how much more sharply defined, despite the great status enjoyed by the priesthood in the world, had become the quality of clerical life in those two hundred intervening years.

Naturally enough the clergy was criticized, and the more highly-placed people tended to take exception to their decisions. Indeed the complainants were many,[135] both in Africa and elsewhere. There is perhaps something to be learned concerning people's attitudes towards the latter from a certain law of the Empire which denied the clergy a simple right enjoyed by any pagan prostitute or charioteer. This was the right to inherit under a will, and though it was continually evaded by means of trusts,[136] its existence is significant. We also encounter the worldling's malicious pleasure, when he catches a member of the clergy committing an offence which he would be quite ready to overlook were it committed by another. This is a type of reaction which is as old as the world itself. It is the revenge which men take on those who claim in one way or another to be professional practitioners of virtue. Augustine once quoted the Psalmist's words, "They that sat in the gate spoke against me: and they that drank wine made me their song." If a priest or a virgin did something wrong, people immediately said, "Aha! that's what they're all like! Only we can't find them out"—although such people, when they came across an ordinary case of adultery, would never dream of thinking any the worse of their mothers and wives on that account.[137]

Incidentally, Augustine had certain very definite rules for dealing with gossip about the clergy. Where it was a case of heretics seeking to besmirch somebody's good name, the thing was to be ignored, but where the talebearers belonged to the faithful, the matter must be further investigated.[138] As to those "foolish, pitiful and misguided men", who if they really came upon a vicious cleric, preferred to imitate the bad sides of his character rather than follow the good precepts which he preached, he likened them to "travellers who think they need go no further because the milestones which spell out their destination do not go along with them".[139]

Although this was the way many people felt, and although the priestly order was extremely powerful, there was in Africa no real anticlericalism, nor did anything Augustine said or wrote provide any basis for such a thing, for never in Augustine is there any trace of the biting satire of Jerome, with his society priests and his nuns that seem to have escaped from the pages of the Decameron.[140] If Augustine knew these types at all, he probably did so only from hearsay; for his correspondence shows that though he had from time to time to concern himself with matters that were distinctly disedifying, yet that same correspondence shows to how great an extent other bishops and priests were at one with him in all spiritual matters and how closely they cooperated with him in their pastoral work. Certainly he knew that there were things to be reformed, but a clergy that seeks reforms is by that very token a good clergy, and it is not irrelevant to this general consideration that wherever Augustine opened a monastery, it was filled. He himself was surrounded by like-minded men to whom the words of his early work *On the Customs of the Church* might well apply, namely that they should so live that men would marvel at the worthiness of their lives, this being especially necessary in the time in which they lived; for they lived amid the troubles of the world and consorted with all manner of men. They were guides to the sick and not to the whole, and they must themselves stand firm against pestilence before they could arrest its course in others—and how difficult it was to tread this road of the golden mean, and to preserve a recollected spirit while doing so.[141]

There were, of course, exceptions to the general rule, and few will think the worse of Augustine because he was sometimes mistaken in his man, all the more so since he confesses this himself and with a heart full of sorrow humbles himself before the Pope. It is true enough that his protégés sometimes ended badly. Paulus and Antonius are cases in point. Yet could St. Vincent de Paul prevent De Retz from taking the wrong road, or that good Father de la Porrée prevent the aberrations of Voltaire, who was the apple of his eye?

The clerical office was greatly respected. "I know", he says in a sermon, "that men strain after this honour",[142] and he adds that whoever chooses the priestly profession can always, if he so desires, make things easy for himself, since nothing is more pleasant than to perform this office in a manner calculated to ingratiate oneself with men, and make an outward show, and nothing more burdensome than to exercise it in the way that God intended.[143] The nature of Augustine's choice is evident in all he did. When he died his biographer could give him especial praise for leaving behind him so numerous a clergy and so many cloisters both for men and women, all peopled by exemplary *continentes* and under the direction of worthy superiors.[144] The saint left behind him a seedbed of sanctity and what was really the first seminary for priests. It was an imperfect thing, but its essential features were to be repeated through the ages. Augustine could not know what Genseric and Huneric had in store for the African clergy, but though their churches were destroyed their spirit survived and has continued to be effective to this day.

9

THE BISHOP

AUGUSTINE IN CLOSE-UP: APPEARANCE, HEALTH AND DOMESTIC LIFE

POSSIDIUS has devoted a great part of his *Life* to a description of Augustine's life within the house, and what he tells us about that is more precious than many panegyrics. The author does not scorn to recount a number of quite minor details and to retail anecdotes and chance sayings. At the end he even says a few words about the external appearance of his hero, and though these are unfortunately somewhat vague, they still enable us to infer that even in his last years Augustine was very far from being an invalid and that the sharpness of his understanding remained with him to the end.

With his shaven head always uncovered and wrapped in his dark *birrus*, Augustine must have looked like some gaunt Benedictine abbot who happens to have put ring and pectoral aside. We do not know whether this monastic *birrus* was always *cucullatus*, that is to say, whether it was equipped with a hood. From the meagre representations that are available to us it would seem that around the year 400 it was more like a short choir mantle with a strap. The *cuculla* proper, with its fixed hood, into which the *birrus* developed and which became the customary monastic dress, seems at this time not yet to have established itself. In the mosaic of the little chapel of San Vittore in Ciel d'Oro there is an undoubtedly authentic portrait of Ambrose which dates to the time shortly after his death (Plate 10).[1] In it the saint wears white stockings and black shoes which just cover his toes and heels, and a white *tunica dalmatica* with thin stripes, which reaches to his ankles and has wide sleeves with borders on them. Over this he wears a dark reddish-brown *paenula* or *casula*, a long bell-shaped garment with an opening for the head. This garment was folded back so as to leave the right arm uncovered up to the elbow, the left arm and hand being left covered. This *casula* is the garment worn by priests and bishops in the sixth-century mosaics in Ravenna and Rome, and it is from this that our own chasuble and the Greek *phelonion* (the Russian *risa*) are derived. Although this *casula* appears also, in Africa, to have been among the normal articles of clothing in the fifth century—that is at least the inference to be drawn from the sepulchral mosaics at Tabraca (Plate 21)—

and seems, according to one passage in the *City of God*, to have been worn even by artificers, we hear of nothing in Augustine's house save tunics and *birri*, of undergarments, that is to say, and mantles.[2] Once we hear of a gift consisting of a number of goat's-hair mantles. These *cilicia* formed part of the normal equipment of a monk. In the East people seem to have been familiar with waterproof cloaks which could be made to stand upright like Bedouins' tents; there were several sorts of these, however, one being made of soft Cilician Angora wool.[3] In the matter of personal appearance, Ambrose wore his hair short, but he cultivated a small narrow beard and a drooping moustache, and in general there seems to have been little in the way of a hard-and-fast rule, either tonsorial or sartorial. We do not know what was worn at the altar, but there is nowhere any mention of a special dress for that occasion.

The oldest representation we have of Augustine is a damaged and mediocre fresco in what was formerly the Lateran Palace—the room was once the library of Gregory the Great—and it shows us a rather delicate-looking old man wearing the distinguished dress of the fourth century and sitting occupied with his books in a great armchair. His hair is cut short, and his face clean-shaven. He wears a white tunic with red shoulderstraps, and on top of this a white pallium covering one shoulder. Despite the conventional character of the clothing and the fact that the picture was painted some hundred and seventy years after his death, the portrait may nevertheless be based on actual memories that were handed down (Plate 11).[4]

It seems—and this is particularly true of the period following his forty-fifth year—that, like St. Paul, he had a delicate constitution and was tortured by recurrent attacks of debility, a thing not uncommon with people of nervous but determined character.[5] He hated travel, and as far back as 389 his friend Nebridius noticed that a journey from Tagaste to Carthage had perceptible effects on his health.[6] Like Erasmus, he could bear neither the sea nor the winter cold,[7] yet time and again, if he felt he really had to make a journey, he would set out on it. In his later years his letters are full of references to his weakness "which is known to everybody".[8] Yet despite this, in 418, when he was sixty-five years old, we find him journeying to distant Caesarea in Mauretania under instructions from Pope Zosimus, and in the following year undertaking the journey to Carthage, though, as a matter of fact, that was the last time he made it.[9] It so happens that we know that in his youth he tended continually to be in an overexcited state and was once seriously ill. When he resigned his professorship in Milan, he pleaded ill-health, alleging on one occasion shortness of breath and constriction of the chest, on another stomach pains.[10] Later we hear of his suffering from haemorrhoids, which keep him in bed. In 410 he has an attack of fever which endangers his life, after which we hear of his taking a rest cure on a country estate near Hippo. (It was, incidentally, an infectious disease that brought about his death.)[11]

Augustine only knew the great blessing of perfect health from distant memory, but he knew the nature of it and its value and could bring the topic effectively into his sermons. "What strange things are our insides," he once said, "and in what strange ways we get to know about them! When we are well, we are not conscious of them at all, and if we are not conscious of them, that is a sign that we are well. You tell a man, 'Watch your stomach', and he replies, 'What's this thing you call a stomach?' Oh happy ignorance! He does not even know where his stomach is, because he is always well."[12] Augustine did not share that enviable ignorance, yet there is no indication that he gave the impression of being in failing health. Like so many vital and sensitive people the effect he had on people was no doubt that of an intensely lively person who was perhaps occasionally worn down by the intensity of his work; for that work of his devoured him. When the administrator interrupted him he would dispose of him with a hurried "Yes" or "No", and then dive back into that atmosphere which was truly his own, the atmosphere of the study, in which he would immerse himself "after accomplishing the necessary temporal things", which were to him "a burden and a pain". Then he would once more "meditate upon heavenly things", or dictate the ideas that had come to him, or correct the manuscript of what had been dictated on a previous occasion; and this he did day and night, never ceasing from work from one day to another, and often carrying his work far into the night and forfeiting his repose.[13]

Like so many artists, Augustine had many almost feminine traits. He was emotional and intuitive and guided largely by impulse. He could show a sudden wild enthusiasm for a thing and with equal speed let it disappear from his mind. Yet it is easy to lay too much stress on that side of his character and equally easy to draw false inferences from his style. Certainly, his works are full of appeals, lamentations and sighs, but that was the convention of the time and part of its fashion of literary pathos. It by no means denoted an inability to discipline his feelings. Words and sentiment in abundance were what was expected of the writer in this period, and brevity was accounted a sign of mental indigence, a laconic style only being permissible in the epigram.

Yet despite the lustre of his style and its smooth perfection Augustine remains the writer who actually had far more to say than any of his contemporaries, and the author of innumerable seminal ideas, for he was a man who could always set a limit to that mere artistry in words in which he delighted, and could harness his wittiest inspirations to the chariot of his theological theme. Finally, there is the sheer volume of his output. His great works were never left incomplete, and we can but marvel at the way his delicate sensibility was made the handmaid of a most virile capacity for sheer hard work.

He liked to dictate till far into the night—a practice in which Ambrose never indulged, for Ambrose would never be a burden to anybody. Augustine, on the other hand, forgot everything and everybody when any piece of work really gripped him. When, being then over seventy years old, he was at one and the same time engaged on the *Retractations* concerning his three hundred and thirty works, and on the refutation of Julian of Eclanum, he devoted the day to the one task and the night to the other.[14] To sum up, this man who, whenever he says anything, seems to be saying it for the first time, but also to be saying it in its final and unalterable form, may on occasion have fallen into rhetorical exaggeration or into a somewhat emotional torrent of words. Yet for all that he never ceases to be the servant of order in the truest sense, and never relaxes his efforts to realize that order. When we read his works, we hear a man engaged in the clear and forceful exposition of his cause.

He lived poorly. He once declared that the income of his bishopric was more than twenty times the amount of the little legacy which he had given away in Tagaste, but all went into the hands of others and ultimately found its way to the deacons for distribution.[15] He resembled that Roman priest from Illyricum who was a contemporary of his and who was

> Rich for the poor, yet poor for himself, and in that he fled from
> All the goods of this world, might hope for celestial reward.[16]

He called the poor his fellow-poor,[17] and on the anniversary of his consecration called poor men to his table; the others were asked to content themselves with partaking of the word of God, which had the quality of not becoming smaller when many shared it.[18]

As to his clothes, he wore whatever anybody gave him, sometimes, no doubt, with the deliberate intention of giving pleasure to the donor. Thus the good sister Sapida begged him to wear a tunic which she had originally woven for her brother who had since died. She told Augustine that it would be a source of comfort to her if he would wear the garment, and Augustine replied, in a quite charming little letter, that he was already doing so.[19] In general, he wore the same sort of clothes as those who shared his house. Reference has already been made to the gift of a consignment of goatskin mantles. These were sent him by his friend Palatinus, who in making this gift was not concerned to benefit one individual but, as was right and proper, the community.[20] For the rest, Augustine avoided both carelessness and elegance in his attire. Even his bedclothes were always plain, though they were invariably clean.

The diet consisted mostly of vegetables and cereals, and there was also wine.

Meat was served to the sick and when guests were present. On the latter occasions the reader would be given the signal to stop somewhat earlier, so as to provide opportunity for conversation.[21] Nobody absented himself from meals, and the taking of meals in the town was forbidden. Ladies who wished to leave something for the sick were permitted to do so, and anyone requiring special nourishment was allowed to take a trifle before breakfast, but again was forbidden to partake of any food outside.[22] Only the spoons were of silver, the vessels being of earthenware, wood and marble. Whoever at table uttered an oath such as "By God", or $\nu\grave{\eta}\ \tau\grave{o}\nu\ \theta\epsilon\grave{o}\nu$, as one could hear the Greeks say in the harbour, or "By my eyes", or "God knows it", or "God is my witness: I appeal to God upon my soul that I speak the truth", or anything of that kind, lost one drink (for nobody was permitted more than a certain number of draughts from his cup).[23]

He had put up a little distich in the refectory which read: "Whoso loves to detract from the good name of those that are absent, let him know that there is no place for him at this table." Once when some friendly fellow-bishops made it apparent that they did not take this too seriously, Augustine remarked with some heat, "Either those verses must be removed or I shall immediately retire to my room."[24] Possidius does not tell us whether he actually carried out this threat. Augustine's table was always laid for any guest, as the door of his room was always open for any visitor, for, as he argued, it was better to be ready to receive a scoundrel than to turn away an honest man in error.[25]

He had no heed for administrative problems, and little aptitude for business details. Possidius never saw him with a key in his hand or a signet ring on his finger; and indeed he left the management of all temporal matters entirely to others, and when the yearly statement of income and expenditure was read over, he scarcely troubled to listen and it was obvious that he took no interest in it whatever.[26] To the mother of one of the wealthiest heirs in Rome he wrote that the care of Church property was something that he endured but did not desire,[27] and he would much rather have entrusted laymen with the task. But no laymen were willing to undertake it, so that he was compelled to hand everything over to an administrator.

From the incident with Januarius which has already been related we can see how anxious he was that the Church should accept no gifts which put her under indeterminate obligations or which might leave the claimant to an inheritance under a sense of grievance. It was for this reason that Augustine preferred to be a legatee rather than an heir.[28]

Augustine's pontificate coincides with a period of vigorous building activity on the part both of Catholics and Donatists, and many more churches were built than was actually necessary. Yet it is strange how rarely the Church Fathers speak of this matter. Augustine is said to have founded several churches and a number of *martyria*, yet in all his three hundred works he hardly alludes to the subject at all. He disliked undertaking new building, Possidius tells us, because of the distractions this necessarily entailed. He left such things largely to others and we do not find that on any occasion he really concerned himself with them; at most he took care to see that the building was not laid out on too ambitious a scale.[29]

There is a chance record of something Augustine said on the subject of building when he was a guest preacher in the Basilica Margarita in Hippo Diarrhytus, the modern Bizerta. The bishop of that church was planning to pull it down and replace it by a larger one, for despite the existence of two much larger churches in the town, it was apparently much too small for local needs. The bishop had to endure some criticism on this account, and Augustine came to his aid by observing that God in his cosmos was always pulling down the old in order to put something better in its place.[30] On another occasion, in a sermon which he gave at the *mensa* of Cyprian in Carthage, he preached in support of the collections for a graveyard basilica.[31] If his hearers on such an occasion were not too liberal, he could use sharp words such as these: "Yes, hard stones! Unwatered ground, or rather, ground watered in vain! You keep all you have for yourselves, and then you say, 'I did not know. I did not know it was needed. No man spoke to me of it.' What? Nobody spoke to you of it? Christ and the Prophets say to you without ceasing, 'Blessed is the man that regardeth the needy and the poor.' Do you not see that your bishop's treasury is empty? Yet you see how the building is growing, the building which you will soon be entering to pray. Do you perhaps imagine that your bishops are able to put by money? Pray God that I have not spoken in vain! The Jews with their stony hearts gave their tenths, but you ... Yes, you sigh, but your sighs do not help us much; yet if you sigh, does that not mean that you are suffering pangs? And if you are suffering pangs you must surely bring forth something. What avail these groans if nothing results from them? Your bowels are twisting themselves, does that mean that there is something in them that had better come out?" We must admit that even Augustine had the makings of a money-raiser.[32]

He himself never had money for building. The foundations which went under his name were always paid for by others. Thus the cost of building the famous Chapel of St. Stephen was born by his priest Eraclius. Certainly Augustine did not seek to dissuade others from making efforts of this kind, for he looked upon it as a good work and one pleasing to God. There was, he maintained, no better way of making friends with the Mammon of unrighteousness. When the time came for consecration, he would speak with both wit and enthusiasm. Apart from that he would keep aloof from the whole affair, and so it was on most other occasions where the problem of ways and means was concerned. It is true that he once went so far as to follow another of Ambrose's precedents and have the sacred vessels melted down (a course to which some of his clergy took grave exception), but the need was urgent, for there were prisoners to be rescued from the Berbers. For the rest, he would now and then remark that his poor box was empty or let the faithful know that their contributions to the funds of the church and *secretarium* fell somewhat short of requirements. Even Ambrose said things like that, so he felt that it was quite permissible.[33]

The Circle of Friends

Although Augustine's mind was wholly directed to the things of the spirit, nobody would have called him either a recluse or unapproachable. His house was always open, and he was not a man who could live without friends. The urge was irresistible to discuss with his housemates whatever filled his mind in his study, and Possidius gives us an idea of what it meant for those housemates to have such a man in their midst. Augustine ruled not only over their house but over their spirits and over their hearts. Thus it was that the oneness of mind which the words from the Acts had caused them to seek after developed in many cases into that spiritual friendship which is the distinguishing mark of a good monastery. This oneness of mind rested on two things: first, on the fact that they were all continually occupied with the one thing necessary; secondly, on their conviction that their father and director would, on the Day of Judgement, have to render his account in respect of every one of them. It was God's service that had brought them together, not personal sympathy or the accident of election, and it was this common service of God that was by far the strongest bond. When one of his oldest personal friends had at last become a catechumen and Augustine had "torn myself free from a mass of work, one might almost say...wrestled myself free and stolen away from it" in order to congratulate him, he reminded him of Cicero's beautiful definition of friendship as "rerum humanarum et divinarum cum benevolentia et caritate consensio", and at the same time declared that it was oneness of mind in regard to heavenly things that carried oneness of mind in human things along with it. The most important element in their friendship had hitherto been lacking, for he had not possessed his friend in Christ, but now he possessed him wholly.[34]

Augustine's circle of friends was by no means confined to those who either shared his house or lived as distant memories in his mind. He was an eager and frequent visitor and one who did not shirk wearisome journeys. If there were certain human things for which he had imperfect understanding, these certainly did not include that clerical sociability which had from time immemorial been customary. Incidentally, he was lucky in his neighbours; some had been his housemates before they themselves became bishops. Alypius sat in Tagaste, some forty miles away, though fortunately the road was good. Profuturus was in somewhat distant Cirta, Severus in Milevis and Evodius in Uzalis. His nearest neighbour was Possidius of Calama. They were all important personalities who played the leading parts at the synods. Yet he was quite as intimate with men who were far less in the public eye. There was, for instance, that old ill-educated farmer-bishop who had grown up on one of the great estates, whom Augustine visited during his last illness. When the old man indicated by a gesture that it would soon be over with him, Augustine said to him in a kindly tone, "You will live for a long time yet, brother, the Church has need of you", but the other answered, "If I need never die, well and good, but if die I must, why not now?" Augustine was much impressed by that answer and often alluded to it.[35]

Alypius, that rough, dry man, so sparing of words, remained Augustine's friend to the end, and, shrewd man of the world that he was, may well have assisted him on more than one occasion with practical advice. It was Alypius who undertook journeys for him, who arranged contacts, knocked at the doors of Government officials; and who, when in his sixties, crossed the sea to Italy no less than three times on business relating to the Pelagian affair. One of the best anecdotes in all early Church history affords us an excellent picture of him, for it concerns one of the few remarks that are on record from those uncommunicative lips. On the occasion of the great debate of 411, the Donatists had, for reasons of their own, entered on their lists the name of an entirely fictitious bishop, who, they said, had died on the way. The whole story was extremely suspicious, and was in fact quite manifestly a fabrication. Nevertheless, the Donatists brazened the thing out, and when one of them blandly asked, "Is it not man's lot to die?" Alypius retorted, "To die, yes, but not to cheat!"[36]

Through the synods Augustine became acquainted with innumerable bishops, and in the case of his friend Aurelius, the Primate of Carthage, he was always in and out of his door. A saying was current at the time and has been handed down to us, that in these days Augustine was the heart of the African Church and Aurelius its brains. It would be truer to say that Augustine was the brain and Aurelius the hand.

With his fellow-bishops he exchanged the courtesies that were customary among the clergy, including sometimes the little piece of consecrated bread which was elsewhere called *eulogion* or *eulogia*, and which was on one occasion sent him by Paulinus of Nola as "a token of unanimity".[37] How gracefully he could fashion a little letter excusing himself from attending the consecration of a church on the ground that he preferred not to travel in winter, and how intimate are those short notes in which he jokes with his sometime housemate

Severus, whom he calls his *alter ego* and who lived, alas, so far away![38] He wrote courteously even to the schismatic bishop Proculeianus, reminding him of the respect in which his office was held by others even if not by himself.[39]

Sometimes there were quarrels even with his best friends, such as Severus, and occasionally Augustine put himself in the wrong. In such cases, however, he was glad to be the loser[40] and would afterwards most humbly apologize. For all that, in a matter of Church discipline he would stand firm even against a brother-bishop, and now and then would not hesitate to admonish him in a manner that was both brotherly and forceful. When his warnings to his protégé Paulus, the Bishop of Cataqua, proved vain, he broke off all connection with him, and did not hesitate, when Paulus' successor had to straighten matters out, to send all the documents relating to the former's misconduct to the *magister officiorum* in Ravenna. His respect for the Empire's law was stronger than any sentiment he may have had about a sometime pupil.[41]

Another bishop had improperly assumed the title of primate of a province (an honour which, according to Numidian custom, went by seniority, and not necessarily to a bishop of one of the larger towns), and had irregularly issued invitations to a synod. In addition he had, in issuing these, made a number of errors in the matter of precedence. Augustine saw to it that he was duly reproved. He also wrote him personally a short, cool letter in which he urged him to come to an understanding with the particular bishop who could, as a matter of right, claim to be regarded as the senior in the province, or at any rate to come to an agreement with the other bishops as to who had the most years of service.[42]

We find a number of personalities cropping up in his immediate entourage whose exact place within the bishopric is difficult to determine, but who definitely belonged to the clergy and stood very close to Augustine. We hear, for instance, of a certain deacon Lucillus, whom he loved "with fondest affection", and with whom he would in no circumstances consent to part, not even to Bishop Novatus of Sitifi, who was Lucillus' own brother, one of the reasons being that Lucillus spoke such excellent Latin, which was the exception in Hippo, though it was common enough in Sitifi, which was the provincial capital.[43] We hear of people who attended to the despatch of his letters—for instance, of a certain priest Firmus who was friendly with Count Valerius, and also of a deacon, Paulus, who rated high with Count Boniface. He also seems to have had special goodwill towards two Roman acolytes, Albinus and Leo.[44]

A great number of his works were written at the request of his brother-bishops. Thus he answers a long questionnaire from his old adviser Simplicianus, who in the meantime had succeeded Ambrose in Milan, but he did the same for men of lesser rank too. Quodvultdeus, the Carthaginian deacon, asks him for a comprehensive work on all the heresies, if such a thing be possible, and states that local information on this subject is imperfect. What he wants is a short summary of each particular heresy and a brief condensation of the standard Catholic refutation.[45] Augustine replies with a provisional discussion of eighty-eight heresies, which he deals with one after the other though without actually refuting them. (Augustine, by the way, seems largely to have based this book on previous compilations.) Another Carthaginian deacon, who was later to be the priest Deogratias, received on request the priceless little first catechism for candidates for baptism. On the whole, however, the burden of official work that the synod placed on his shoulders, and the little daily cares for his own church, prevented him giving much time to such friendly offices.

Although as a controversialist Augustine was the personification of courtesy, he was not wholly immune from the malady of *furor theologicus*, and his thirty-year battle for doctrinal purity ended by making him a number of enemies. Naturally enough, a number of Donatists used the *Confessions* to attack his personal life. The fanaticism of religious disputes being what it is, that was only to be expected.[46] Towards the end of his life, however, there was one man—and he had, so it happened, an excellent pen—who in his books began systematically to defame him. That man was Julian of Eclanum, the son of one of his old friends. In Julian's writings Augustine is variously referred to as "the Manichee", "the Traducianist" (the man, that is to say, who believes that the soul is begotten at the same time as the body—this was a dig at Augustine's conception of original sin), "the detestable Punic quarrel-seeker", "the Punic Aristotle"; he was also spoken of as the agitator who sought to raise the whole of Italy against a couple of ascetics and who had sought to bribe the Court of Ravenna with eighty pounds of gold, and as the man who, "if I as much as mention the senate of the old philosophers, seeks to rouse all the workmen against me". Even Alypius did not escape unscathed but was referred to as "the servant of the Punic babbler's shame".

Augustine was further referred to as a slanderer, who himself empties the Church treasuries to cover the cost of his witch-hunts after heretics, who feeds up horses with the money that belongs to the poor, in order to use them for bribing high officials. Even Monica was attacked. Had she not, in her youth, been wholly given over to drink? Did not Augustine say as much in his *Confessions*?

This last caused Augustine to strike back: "What has my mother done to you, you foul-mouthed fellow? Yet small wonder that you cannot bear her, since you cannot bear the grace of God, that grace of God which enabled her to free herself from the weakness of her youth. I knew your parents as honourable Catholics. I call them fortunate in having died before they could see you as a heretic."[47] What else could one expect of a heresy which was now only kept alive by a few cranks, the arguments on both sides having long been exhausted? When things got to that stage, it was hardly surprising that obstinate and ill-conditioned persons lost their tempers, and started to accuse their opponents of being mere babblers.

As to the laymen, Augustine had not waited till he had become a leading personality of the Church before cultivating relations with the great world. The pleasant memories of all those people whom he had thus encountered formed the legacy which he took with him into his cell. Later that cell was transferred to his bishop's palace, and here, as we have already noted, his door was open for every man, and the world came to him of its own accord, though it did so mostly by letter. Yet there were visitors in plenty, and many a meeting when he was in Carthage. After 410 there was a stream of refugees, and in his old age travellers came to see him from all over the world. Thus in his long life Augustine visited and received many of the greatest in the Empire. There were the fugitives of rank like Faltonia Proba, Juliana and Demetrias from the house of the Anicii Probi, Pinianus and Melania, with their mother Albina, of the house of the Valerii Maximi and of that of the Ceionii. Those who could not visit him often wrote from abroad. Then there were the high officials and high-ranking military officers in Carthage with whom he corresponded officially on Church affairs, and there was the Court of Ravenna, which contained men who were not only persons of cultured mind but well instructed and exceedingly communicative Christians. There were thus plenty of lay people with whom he could discuss, either by letter or directly, the great religious issues of the day, and no doubt a circle would frequently form about him which was ostensibly for the discussion of episcopal business but which in fact soon became a literary and philosophical discussion group. His was the last of the great Christian-Platonic academies before Pico della Mirandola and Marsilio Ficino.

The representatives of the Carthaginian Government were very great personages—*illustres, spectabiles* and even *clarissimi*, that is to say, people of senatorial rank who wore the purple edging on the *chlamys* and were usually all aglitter with golden spurs, signet rings and shoulder-buckles. They must have contrasted strangely with the black-clothed bishop in their midst. Of the Court folk Augustine probably only knew Count Valerius, and Olympiodorus, the *magister officiorum* at Ravenna, indirectly and from their letters. The first of these was an exemplary family man;[48] of the second we only know that he was an enemy of Stilicho, and his successor. He seems to have been a rather shadowy and, according to Sozomen, rather a dubious figure, though Augustine, who needed him as an intermediary, writes to him as to a man whom he held in high esteem.[49]

The great men of Africa were for the most part known to him personally— the proconsuls Apringius and Donatus, the latter a great gentleman and a sincere Christian who brought his father into the Church;[50] then there was Macedonius the *vicarius Africae*, a most upright man who travelled the straight road and did not hesitate to put questions on any matter he had at heart.[51] There were further the *tribuni et notarii* Dulcitius and Marcellinus, the brother of Apringius—Dulcitius, who showed such great energy as imperial commissioner for reunion until he recoiled in horror before the holocausts of Gaudentius.[52] And of course there was Boniface[53] the *tribunus* and later *comes domesticorum*—Boniface, so temperamental and hungry for life and yet fundamentally so kindly a man. There was Caecilianus,[54] Marcellinus' successor; and many others.

Among all these men Marcellinus, who ultimately died a martyr, was dearest to him.[55] Thanks to the glowing words with which Augustine honoured him after his death, the lovely, tragic figure of Marcellinus seems to shine out against the background of his time. He was in that world of bishops and monks a lone layman, and one of the few saints who did not turn his back upon the world, but in the midst of the burdens of high political office gave a true example of Christian life.[56]

Augustine, then, was undoubtedly a man who cultivated his connections with the world and was alive both to the value of the influence of his highly-placed acquaintances, and to their spiritual and intellectual interests. Many of them he made famous for ever by a couple of letters or by a word of praise or a highly personal dedication. We owe a whole series of works, among them some of Augustine's greatest, to the initiative, the persuasion, sometimes to the simple request, of some of these distinguished personalities. While he was still a priest he dedicated his dialogue *On the Happy Life* to the consul Manlius Theodorus, to whom he was bound by an affection which later he condemned as too worldly.[57] *On the Uses of the Faith* was written for Honoratus, who asked the Manichean question, why faith should be a better foundation than knowledge. *On the Excellence of Widowhood* was written for matron Juliana; *The Contemplation of God*, really a letter, but longer than many a book, for Paulina;[58] *On Marriage and Desire* for Valerius in distant Ravenna.[59] To Dulcitius, who put eight questions to him, he sent extracts from books in which these matters had been previously dealt with.[60] For Dulcitius' brother Laurentius, who lived in Rome and who asked for this, he wrote his celebrated handbook, also known as *Faith, Hope and Love*, the oldest theological textbook for laymen. His first writings against the camarilla of Pelagius, on sin, forgiveness and infant baptism, as also *On the Letter and the Spirit*, he dedicated to Marcellinus. To the latter is also dedicated the *City of God*, and it is to his initiative that the origin of this work is to be attributed. Marcellinus did not live to witness its completion, though it was due to the tragic memory of this man that this completion was achieved.[61]

The origin of many of Augustine's works can be traced to an exchange of letters, and many of Augustine's replies to enquiries grew occasionally into small dissertations, some of which are reckoned by Possidius among Augustine's actual books. And this brings us to the subject of Augustine's letters.

The Letters

Not least among the sources from which we know Augustine and his pastoral work are his letters. Some two hundred of these have come down to us, though he wrote far more than that. An active interchange of letters was in the fifth century as inevitable among the pious as it was among the literate, and sometimes the nearest colleague lived so far away that letters were the only means of keeping in touch with him. It was accounted a matter of good form to impart at least as much finish to any letter as would prevent either the writer or the recipient from feeling qualms about seeing it published. Letter-writing was in fact a form of literary activity that was very much in fashion and widely practised, and whatever Augustine the bishop may have thought privately about this rather frivolous pursuit, it would have been morally and socially impossible for him to write like a clerk in an office. The Bishop of Hippo had a reputation to sustain, and he knew very well that his letters were widely circulating—so much so that Jerome, when he was about to receive a letter, would hear of copies circulating before he received the original. Deacon Sinnius once saw a copy of such a letter on a small island in the Adriatic.[62]

No bishop in all the Christendom of that day—Jerome was only a priest, a fact of which he would often give Augustine an ironic reminder[63]—received so many letters, from so far afield. Occasionally one of them would be lost; the long and rather unpleasant argument with the dour old man in Bethlehem can only be attributed to the fact that the first letters wandered all over the place for years, Augustine having entrusted them to an individual who was less conscientious than might have been desired. Thanks to an indiscretion, they became public property, though they were intended to be confidential communications containing advice and information for Jerome alone. The latter, however, heard of their contents through third parties, and was led to believe that they were an underhand attack on himself.[64]

There are plenty of other examples to show that the world was an unreliable place as far as the letter-writer was concerned. Paulinus of Nola once waited four years for a reply which had, in point of fact, already been sent to him. Augustine, when Paulinus' reiterated questions made plain what had occurred, wrote a fresh letter and sent a copy of the first of the missing ones along with it. There was no copy of the second available.[65] When he sent to Jerome in Bethlehem a copy of his book on the origin of the soul, five years went by without his receiving an acknowledgement, though he had sent the book "not in a spirit of presumption" but simply for comment and criticism.[66] Once he had to wait so long for a reply from Valerius, though the latter was in the capital, that he grew anxious, till three letters suddenly turned up together.[67]

Moreover, unless the letter-writer could employ his own courier (which was a fairly common practice), it was not only problematical whether the letter would arrive at all; there was also little guarantee of its contents not being divulged, and considerable danger of forged substitutes. It was this last consideration that caused Augustine to take special precautions when writing an official letter to Bishop Victorinus, who in 404 had irregularly sent him an invitation to the provincial synod of Numidia. On this occasion he sent him his own seal, a man's head, probably a portrait of himself.[68] Yet despite all these difficulties he received letters from all over the Christian world, from bishops Paulinus and Simplicianus in Italy and from matrons like Fabiola and Italica. Letters came from Gaul from the isle of Lérins, and from Prosper, who did not know him personally at all but had nevertheless an immeasurable and almost wearisome admiration for him; they came from Rome, from officials at the Curia and from such future popes as Deacon Celestine and the priest Sixtus, who for a time inclined to Pelagianism but returned to orthodoxy;[69] they came from Spain, from Victorianus and later from Orosius, and from Jerusalem and Bethlehem.

In some ways Augustine's letters remind us of that other letter-writer, Cicero. They certainly have a liveliness that is unique and proclaim a quite remarkable ability on the writer's part to convey the impressions in his mind. The themes are nearly always arresting, for the letters seem to deal with most of the burning issues of the day, though they frequently descend to the trivial and the humdrum, and this to a degree that evoked an irritated remonstrance from Erasmus.[70] Unlike Cicero, however, Augustine finds no place in his letters either for friendship or for the discussion of his own affairs. When Augustine became a priest he had already written all the letters of friendship to Nebridius. There were no others of this kind.

After that phase he can still write warmly but he never writes intimately—not even to Severus or to Paulinus or Marcellinus. If a resurrected Boissier were ever to present us with a book on *Augustin et ses amis* he would have to use other material than the letters. Augustine himself steps into the background. His voice in his letters is quite unmistakable, as is the fire of his personality, but he thinks of everybody and everything except himself. Nowhere does he pour his heart out. He betrays neither his preferences nor his antipathies. At most he complains gently of an excess of work which makes it impossible for him to send prompt answers, or he expresses the wish that he could devote himself more fully and with less interruption to his studies, for "there is hardly even a little drop of time for any but the regular tasks".[71] Nowhere do his humility and his self-control become more apparent than in his letters. The intellect is always paramount. If feeling enters into his writing, it is feeling about objective realities outside himself, even though they may be expressed with the pathos which was peculiar to the time.

Here and there a quiet irony is discernible between the lines, and then we suddenly see, says De Labriolle, how witty he could have been, if he had wanted to. But Augustine did not want to be witty. What he wanted to be was a teacher of truth, and when it was truth that he was expounding, a letter might well grow into a dissertation. Even here, though he expounds his thought with that warmth that was peculiarly his own, the reader still searches in vain for a clear subjective reaction. After the publication of his *Confessions*, in which he reinterpreted into a song of praise that former life of his which was the occasion of many a reproach, it is as though he felt that his own heart was the concern of nobody, not even of himself. He is a servant now of the Church and of the truth and nothing more. It was this feeling and not any purely literary consideration that caused him, shortly before his death, to revise not only his greater and smaller works but also such copies of letters as had been retained.[72]

His style fluctuates, depending to a very considerable degree on the identity of the person he is addressing, but it always remains something distinct from the formal polished epistolary manner that was in fashion at the time, and always there is in it at least a faint echo of the superb pathos of his earlier works. It is true that the letters he wrote as a young priest still bear the marks of a certain artifice, and when he began his correspondence with Paulinus of Nola a certain amount of time passed before he showed signs of forgetting that he was dealing with a sometime patrician. His first letter is profoundly respectful, and those which immediately follow it, although marked by increasing warmth (which was reciprocated), remain exceedingly polite; they also show a most careful eye for form and are almost unctuously religious.[73] As to his first letter to Jerome, he polished this as though it were a work submitted for an examination, though this was in some ways not unnatural. Alypius had brought Jerome Augustine's greetings, but Augustine had never seen the man; he had immense respect for his scholarship, but had nevertheless ventured to criticize some of his translations from the Hebrew, and had even politely protested against his rendering of one of the passages in Galatians. As has already been related, this first letter was lost, the contents becoming public knowledge. There were similar misadventures with the second, but at this stage the old lion began to roar.

Augustine did everything in his power to put matters right,[74] but even so he would not give way in the matter of Paul's conduct in withstanding Peter to his face. Augustine quite rightly thought that Peter was not guilty of hypocrisy but simply of error, and that his humility when a bold subordinate spoke his mind and corrected him was something far more rare and even more holy than Paul's "ability to put himself in the right", useful as that was to men, and grounded on the freedom of love.[75] So Augustine held his ground, though he did permit his colleague Praesidius to look at the later letters to see if they were too sharp in tone.[76]

It all ended well. Augustine yielded to the superior philological attainments of Jerome, while in the matter of Peter the great man gave way before the pleas of Augustine's generous heart, and did so in words which even today can still move and edify.

Faltonia Proba, whom he met after 410, wrote him a short note which said little more than "How is Your Holiness?"[77] Augustine replied in terms of profound respect, and in the long and explicit letter which he wrote to her at her express request on the right method of prayer he obviously never forgets for a moment that he is addressing one of the first ladies in the Empire.[78] He did not become less formal till Faltonia sent him a memento on the occasion of her granddaughter's admission to the cloister. Even then he went no further than a somewhat precious encomium of the ancient race of the Anicii Probi and an elaborate conceit about the "mystical birth not from a pregnant body, but from a growing spirit in which a glowing heart takes the place of nursing breasts, a birth that comes from no bodily womb, but one that is heavenly and comes forth from prayers", "... this young creature preferred, rather, to endow her great family with heavenly treasure than to marry and multiply its numbers; she preferred, rather, while still in the flesh herself, to imitate the life of the angels than out of that flesh to increase the number of those who must take on mortality." Despite all this the letter was not longer than the obligatory half-page.[79]

He wrote with especial warmth to those married folk who resolved in the middle of their lives to practise continence. In most of these cases this resolution proved to be less sensational than in that of Paulinus and Theresia, the luminaries of Nola.[80]

The better the style of the letter he received, the more care he took over the reply. The poor man of Hippo knew well enough how to write for the worldling's ear, though he lamented having to perform the task. A number of notes, by no means all of them short, are solely concerned with the making of acquaintances, with visits and the sending of greetings, or with the sending, copying or dedication of books, the latter usually involving fulsome compliments on both sides. Yet behind Augustine's polished periods there always glows that ripe and inimitable wisdom which is the secret of the Christian humanists.

Many of these letters have a truly vintage sparkle. In the year 429 the young Count Darius came to Africa as the confidential emissary of the Court. His mission was to reconcile with the Empress that rebel Boniface, who had enticed the Vandals to Africa and was now shuddering at the possible consequences of his own act. Darius was the offspring of an ancient Christian house. Augustine, of whom men said that it was he who had brought the rebel to reason, was only known to him from his books, though these books had played a not unimportant part in his life. He had had in his youth a certain romantic weakness for the ancient cults, and it was from this that the reading of Augustine had delivered him. When colleagues informed Augustine of the young man's "excellence and learning", he immediately wished him luck in his peace mission, and wrote that though age and infirmity made it impossible for him to come and visit him he would be glad of a word from him, and sent his greetings both to Darius himself and to his little son.[81] Darius hastened to reply in a most elegant letter in which he expresses his longing to see Augustine's "starlike face" and to hear the "voice that had so often sung of heavenly things". "We cannot yet make an end to the war by means of the word," he writes, "yet I may confess to Your Holiness that though we have not wholly extinguished it we have at least postponed its recurrence." He had, he claimed, dammed up the evil while it was at its height. Then he asks Augustine to plead daily for him with Christ "the heavenly Prince and Lord of all", who, he says, while he was still walking Judaea, had by a letter to a certain king (Abgar of Edessa) healed the latter's body and given safety to his great town. So might he now show mercy to the Roman commonwealth and to Darius himself. In the same letter he asks for a copy of the *Confessions*, sends greetings from his little son Verimodus, and states that he is giving his courier something for the bishop's library and also some medicine made up from the prescription of his personal physician.[82] Augustine, who must have smiled at the mention of his "singing voice" (for he suffered from hoarseness), replied with a witty observation about praise in general but with particular reference to the way in which bishops should listen to their own praises. He praises the exquisite style, but confesses that this was not the only thing that gave him pleasure in reading the letter, for, says he, he is "far from being made of horn" —"neque mihi cornea fibra est". He does not forget the answer of Themistocles, who once complained of the music that was being played him, and, when asked what he wanted to hear, replied, "My own praises." "I read that somewhere or other", he adds, as though he did not know that he was quoting Persius and Plutarch. Together with the *Confessions* he sends Darius his essays on "Faith in Things Unseen", "Patience", "Continence" and "Providence", and his little book *Faith, Hope and Love,* and requests Darius to let him know what he thinks of them, or possibly to enter into a correspondence with him about them. If Darius cannot find time to write, he is asked to let Aurelius of Carthage know what his reactions were.[83]

The appearance of a major work by Augustine seems to have been eagerly awaited. We find Macedonius, the *vicarius Africae*, impatient for the appearance of the *City of God*, of which he had been promised a copy. When the first three books appeared and Macedonius received no copy, he reminds the author of his promise. Augustine replies with a long letter, couched in terms that vary between deference and intimacy, and sends the books. Macedonius reads them from start to finish and is delighted. "I am spellbound by your wisdom as by a miracle", he writes. "Everything in the book is at once clear, learned and sublime, so much so that I can say that I have never read the like of it. I have already read the whole thing through, for there was neither a dull moment in it nor a passage that was sufficiently dry to tempt me to lay it aside and attend to other matters. You have laid your hand upon me and so withdrawn my own hand from all other business, and you have so entranced me, that I do not know what to admire most, the essentially priestly character of the book, its philosophic exactitude, your mastery of ancient history or the beauty of the style, the charm of which is such that ordinary layfolk will be unable to put the work down till they have finished it, and when they have finished it will begin it all over again."[84] Augustine reciprocates by writing Macedonius a brilliant letter on the theme that true happiness is only to be found in God.[85]

Then there was the problem of his sincere but sceptical admirer Volusianus. When it fell to Augustine to answer his somewhat hackneyed but not unskilfully formulated objections, he knew full well that his reply would be read out in a fashionable club with a high level of literary taste and quite a few pagans in the audience. Augustine rose to the occasion, however, and in that reply surpassed himself. But then Augustine really never fell below his own level. In the letter which he subsequently wrote to Marcellinus, for instance, it is quite clear that, despite the easy style and the conversational tone, Augustine never forgets who he is—or, for that matter, whom he is speaking to.[86] The spice of some verbal conceit is rarely absent. Even in a touching letter of condolence to the virgin Sapida, he cannot forbear to write, "Sapida, remember your name and 'quae sursum sunt sape'", and in regard to the woven *tunica*, which she wanted him to wear, he writes: "Your brother has no longer need of clothing that is corruptible, for he is clothed in raiment that is incorruptible."[87] A little letter which he wrote to Valerius, whom he sincerely admired, at Ravenna, is a marvel of tact. In it he says how glad he is to dedicate a book to him, namely that *On Marriage and Desire* which accompanies the letter. The reason he has dedicated this book to Valerius, he says, he will learn in the preface; he had really written it especially for him and "it was as though I was speaking to you personally all the time, for I know who you are and of your practice of chastity in marriage. I do not know you personally, it is true, but I have heard so much of you that I feel I can see into your mind."[88] Could this man have guessed that after fifteen hundred years we should still be reading his praises?

The famous man was pestered with the most incredible questions. A young Greek, Dioscuros, had taken a couple of courses in the West, and now thought himself entitled to claim in his home town the position of an expert on Latin literature and philosophy. Shortly before his departure for the East this young sprig had the impertinence to send Augustine a list of questions on philosophical problems, with the request for an immediate reply, as his ship, a grain ship for Rome, was lying in the harbour ready to sail.[89] For a moment the bishop was perplexed. Did the young fellow really believe that a bishop had nothing better to do than to break his nails in the disentangling of philosophical knots, or to act as the obedient servant of a conceited young careerist? Did he believe that he was suddenly to become deaf to the clamour of his duties so that he might answer unimportant school questions on Cicero's dialogues, and pretty unintelligent questions at that? It was with some difficulty that Augustine kept his patience, but in the end, far from fobbing him off with a few empty words, he wrote him a long and detailed letter, in which an impulse to sarcasm did not go beyond a fatherly "Oh, my Dioscuros", and in which he sought to direct him with a few friendly words to the true fountain of wisdom. As to philosophy, so the letter runs, this subject has fallen somewhat into neglect. The books are not even available in Hippo, and he does not doubt that it is the same where the young man has come from. Personally, he continues, I should look upon this kind of enquiry as the following of a wrong trail, and it is hardly part of my office to concern myself with Cicero's *Rhetoric*. Do not let the storms raised by little Greeks unduly disturb you. You can spend your time to better purpose by absorbing yourself in the doctrines of the Faith.[90]

Even those of his lay friends who in general deserved to be taken more seriously could at times put some remarkably silly questions, though at that time they may not have sounded quite as silly as they do now; for it was a time when people frankly accepted the miraculous and when science consisted chiefly in gaining knowledge of curious and inexplicable happenings and correlating them with one another (this was called "explaining" them, but then, is the setting up of a working hypothesis correlating the results of measurements something so very different?) What power of knowing God is possessed by an embryo? That question, for example, was raised in regard to St. John leaping for joy in Elizabeth's womb.[91] What happened to the sun at the time of our Lord's death? Whence comes the human soul? Is it begotten or created? And if the latter, when? At the moment of conception or later? Then, of course, there were everlasting questions about the Virgin Birth. Dulcitius the tribune sent him a list of eight questions, which contained the following: Do sinners who have been baptized never get out of hell? Do the dead derive any benefit from the food ritually placed on their graves? Must those who are carried off to God on clouds still suffer death? Was Samuel truly conjured up by the witch of Endor? How did Sarah escape from Pharaoh and Abimelech without being raped? Was the spirit upon the waters the Holy Ghost?[92] Even the excellent Marcellinus came along with the question, how the Egyptian sorcerers had been able to display their art when all the waters had been turned to blood. Augustine imperturbably answered that this was done by means of sea-water or with water from the country of the Jews.[93] The character of most of these questions is not difficult to discern; they do not originate from any real thirst for knowledge, but from the boredom of fashionable society. In place of bridge people in those days passed their evenings in riddles and jokes. With all this, however, Augustine became a kind of oracle among the eminent in regard to all biblical questions. The pagan Volusianus in Carthage wrote directly to Augustine that other priests would always have this or that gap in their knowledge, but that with Augustine this was impossible.[94] "O oracle of the Spirit!" a young man wrote to him in a wearisomely elaborated letter containing one or two pitiful conceits and five halting hexameters. Augustine sent a friendly reply but permitted himself one small thrust at the end by saying that he had almost become that which his correspondent had called him, namely *loquax*, which the unhappy lad had written instead of *eloquens*. Further, the fifth of his hexameters had six feet. That is a mistake, said Augustine—or perhaps you wanted to see whether I should notice it?[95] No doubt Augustine set a higher value on the intentions of the questioners than on the actual questions themselves. Many of these correspondents were probably just trying to look important, while others were just trying to get a short letter in Augustine's own hand; Augustine may well have been aware of this, but the fact remained that these people did display an interest in Holy Scripture and were concerning themselves with the things of God, and so in answering them he played his part as a servant of the servants of Christ. Naturally, he preferred answering the enquiries of fellow-priests and theologians and his most important letters are undoubtedly addressed to priests. Many concern themselves with the great problems of the day and are short summaries of lengthier documents which he was preparing for synod or Curia, or of passages in learned polemical works. Others are dissertations on some special subject, like the beautiful letter to Evodius on the preaching of Christ to the spirits in prison referred to in the First Epistle of Peter, or the letter to Paulina on the contemplation of God, or that on the

Trinity and the transfiguration of the body to Consentius.[96] The letters to Paulinus and Jerome are of a similar character, dealing, as they do, with a number of exegetical questions and questions of textual criticism.

It is refreshing to observe how he never loses his charm or his nimbleness of style. Never does he fail to strike an individual note, even when writing quite official political letters to the great men of Africa, and never, when there is any occasion for that, does he lose his warmth of heart. Read that letter of comfort to Victorianus, written during the persecution in Spain (for there have always been burning churches in that dry, poor, courageous land) and you will learn how one priest can comfort another.[97] Read the correspondence between Augustine and Paulinus if you want to hear how two servants of God can delight in a common ideal. If you would learn who was the greater in the kingdom of humility, Jerome or Augustine, you will find a complete collection of material for that enquiry in the sixteen letters which they exchanged with one another. But if you want to learn what was at the bottom of Augustine's heart, first, last and all the time, read the best things in any letter that you have picked at random. You will immediately recognize the man who said, "Give me souls. Then you may take all else."

The Cadi

A bishop in those days was a very great man. Even if he lived with his clerics in a monastic community, he did not in any way resemble a metropolitan in old Czarist Russia; he did not, like the latter, live withdrawn from the world in his monastic residence in some provincial town, nor was he, again like the latter, on certain specified occasions received politely but with unmistakable coolness by the governor, who invariably kept up a running conversation right through the liturgy. Nor must we think of a French bishop of the time following on the separation of Church and State, when a bishop might be honoured if he possessed some special personal quality, but was normally completely ignored. It would be truer to say that Augustine was the secret or, rather, the openly revered spiritual governor of the town. He could have had an easy life, if he had wanted it, and even a pleasant one. Wherever he appeared men asked his blessing. He alone in the church spoke the solemn, usually wholly biblical, formulae of benediction.[98] When, after a long absence, he returned to Hippo, he was escorted when he went abroad again, and surrounded by crowds of flatterers. It's a fine thing, he once wrote to a Donatist bishop, to have a raised *apsis* with steps leading up to it, a carpet over the *cathedra*, crowds of singing nuns to fetch you, but what will these things avail a man before the judgement throne of Christ?[99] Oh, he once cried from the pulpit, now I stand up here above you, but only a short while ago I stood below among you all, and who knows how many future bishops are below me now?[100] Or again: "I can see you come in and go out from here, but I do not see what goes on in your hearts or what you do in your homes, and yet I am your watchman"—he goes on, but, if the Lord doth not watch over us and keep our house, he watcheth in vain that keepeth it. "In order that you may hear our voice better, we are raised somewhat above you, but higher still there is Another who judges us; yet it is through you that the judgement of us will be determined. To be a teacher is a perilous vocation, much more dangerous than being taught. The hearer of the word has much less to fear than the speaker thereof."[101]

At the consecration of a bishop, the sermon was usually a panegyric, not necessarily on the person of the new bishop, but on his office, and Augustine kept to this custom; but whether he was speaking on the anniversary of his own consecration or was a guest preacher at the consecration of somebody else, his theme was always the heavy responsibility that a bishop must bear.[102] One of these addresses, delivered at a consecration shortly before the year 411, began with the following moving words:

> Today, through God's generous mercy, a bishop is being consecrated, and for this reason we are called upon to say something. We must do this so that we may ourselves thereby be reminded of the significance of this occasion, that we may instruct the man who is now taking on this office, and finally, that we may give some instruction on the matter to you who listen to us. Well, then, a man who is the overseer of such a congregation as this must know above all else that he is a servant. I say that he should not consider it beneath his dignity to be the servant of many, for the Lord of Lords did not consider it beneath his dignity to be a servant to ourselves. Once the fleshly substance of those followers of our Lord Jesus Christ who became our Apostles let it come to pass that a lust for honour and regard crept in among them and the smoke of self-esteem crept into their eyes, for we read that a dispute broke out among them as to who should be the greatest; but immediately our Lord, like a physician, pressed out this abscess, and, calling little children to himself he said, "Unless ye become like children ye shall not enter the Kingdom of Heaven."[103]

In that same sermon, and in words of great simplicity and clarity, he explains how worthless it is to be a bishop only in name:

> What use is it to an unfortunate man to be called Felix? If you see some poor devil of a beggar called Felix you can say to him, "Come, Felix", or, "Go away, Felix", or, "Sit down, Felix", or, "Stand up, Felix", but for all your calling him Felix, he still remains *infelix*. Yet a man who is called bishop, but is really no bishop at all, may well be compared with such a

man as that. What does he gain from the honour of his title? Only an increase in his guilt. For the people draw no distinction between the true bishop and the false; they still say, "Have you seen the bishop?", "Have you been to the bishop?", "Where are you coming from?"—"From the bishop", "Where are you going?"—"To the bishop." Yet if he would indeed be what his name proclaims him to be, then let him not hearken to my words but sit beside me and hearken to another. Let us be school-fellows in the school of the Master Jesus Christ and let us learn from him, whose *cathedra* is now in heaven, because here on earth it was once a cross. What he has taught us is the way of humility.[104]

Humble he came amongst us, he, our Creator, coming as a creature, he who created us became for us a man in time, though he was God before all time, and this he did that we might be released from the things of time.

Then, turning to the exposition of the Epistle of the day (which was from Timothy and contained the passage giving the picture of the ideal bishop), he dwells upon the passage "If a man desireth the office of a bishop he desireth a good work", and then says, "Seek not the name, but the task. 'I should like to be a bishop', says somebody: 'Oh, if only I were a bishop.' Let us assume you could become one; but is it the name or the task you seek? If it is the task, then it is indeed true that you seek a good work, but if it is the name, you can enjoy that though your works be very bad indeed; but the punishment in such a case is severe indeed. You say, 'He must be a bishop, for he sits upon the *cathedra*.' True—and a scarecrow might also be called a watchman in a vineyard." He does not omit to advise the faithful of what their attitude should be when a bishop's seat has been unworthily occupied, for here the teaching of the Church and her practice are quite unambiguous. The dignity of the office does not, as the Donatists taught, depend upon the worthiness of the holder. Bread remains bread even upon an earthenware platter. Do not, he says, regard the crudeness of the vessel, but think only of the store-cupboard from whence the bread has come. No bishop, even though he is himself a thief, will say to you from this *cathedra*, "Steal", but only "Thou shalt not steal", for he has received that from God's store-cupboard. "The Lord and Bishop of Bishops has seen to it that your hopes shall not stand or fall with a single man. See, in the name of the Lord I tell you as your bishop, that I myself do not know what manner of man I am, and you know it far less than I. True that I have some notion of what I am at this particular moment; but of what I shall be later—how can I have any knowledge of that whatever? Peter dared to say 'Faithful to thee till death', but the Physician who saw into the very veins of his heart said, 'Unto death? Verily, I say unto thee, before the cock crow, thou shalt deny me thrice.' "[105]

This was the manner in which Augustine did not hesitate to speak of the first office in the Church, of the temptations which it carries with it, and of the fallibility of man, once he is placed upon the rock of dignity. Not being himself the inhabitant of a glass house, he could afford to speak freely.

Augustine was a servant of servants, if ever man was. Even as an author he was ready to descend to the level of the uneducated. For them he did something that surely no other man of his literary stature has ever done; he completely denied his own style. As a priest he composed the doggerel psalm against the Donatists, probably the first example of Latin folk poetry. A year later he wrote *The Christian's Battle*, a book on the battle with the devil, and so a distant predecessor of Scupoli's *Combattimento Spirituale*. It was written in very simple language, and so suited to those who usually spoke Punic and would have difficulty with literary Latin but could get along well enough with the ordinary conversational Latin of the day.[106] In his old age he put together a number of texts which had the character of moral maxims. He called this work *The Mirror*, and it was conceived as an anthology for very simple people, both layfolk and priests.[107] Further, as everyone knows, in the pulpit he never used language that was above his hearers' heads, but always chose his words in such a fashion that everyone would understand him.

Many of those who heard him were known to him personally. Nietzsche found him plebeian, because he lacked the peculiar pride of cool reasoning, because of his addiction to hyperbole and even to what might be considered sentimentality, but above all because of his somewhat extravagant manner of laying himself bare before God and of abasing himself before him.[108] By this he only confirms for us Christians that Augustine did not suffer from *hubris*, for we happen not to believe that a broken and a contrite heart necessarily brings us down to the level of dogs, and have unfortunately no place for the Superman in our scheme of things. Yet there really is something in what Nietzsche says. All great Christians tend naturally to be vulgar, for they feel with and for the great mass of men. The great spiritual aristocrat of Hippo really did vulgarize his Platonism. In the last analysis he neither stood outside the crowd, nor did he even seek to tower over it from within, for he always remained a small man before God.

Augustine knew full well that truth which Ambrose had once expressed in a letter to Vigilius, the Bishop of Trent: "The first thing is to know the congregation which has been entrusted to you by God."[109] Never did he hesitate to visit the sick, to pray with them and to lay his hands upon them, and he was equally solicitous for the widow and the orphan;[110] that, in those days, was as far as visits by priests to parishioners usually went. For the tide flowed the other way. It was the laity that went to the priest, and that not only to receive his blessing. Almost unnoticed, the bishop had become a city judge, and the powers which his predecessors had exercised during the persecution by virtue of Church law and apostolic tradition now had behind them the weight of a vastly increased authority, for the bishop's decisions were now binding under the civil law. As the *cadi* was soon to do from the pages of the Koran, so since the fourth century the Christian bishop declared the law on the principles of the Holy Writ. Perhaps this was the most burdensome part of his office. What must Augustine have thought when he saw in the Gospel the passage "And one of the multitude said to him: Master, speak to my brother, that he divide the inheritance with me. But he said to him: Man, who hath appointed me judge or divider over you?"[111] The Lord had turned away, but Augustine had to carry out the task which Christ had refused, of dividing inheritances. Nevertheless Augustine did seek at least to do this work in the spirit of Christ, though that was not always easy, for whether it was in an audience, before the tribunal or during a visit, most people allowed business considerations completely to overshadow any thought of Christian values.

Possidius tells how, despite an ineradicable aversion to what he considered to be useless and timewasting activities, Augustine would nevertheless perform all such duties with the utmost punctiliousness. Every morning and every noon, he could be found seated in his *secretarium*, surrounded by his *notarii* and their notebooks for the *gesta episcopalia*, and accessible to everyone who required his services as an arbitrator.[112] The care of the poor was largely dealt with by the deacons, but all judicial matters fell on his shoulders alone, and as far as these were concerned, there was not a moment's respite. Anybody that was in any sort of a difficulty ran pale and distraught to the bishop's palace, often after his official hours; people pushed their way into his study and threw themselves on their knees. When he asked them what was the matter, they would cry "Libera me!" and when Augustine asked them "What from?" there would be a long rigmarole of complaints, apprehensions real and imaginary, complaints of slander, persecution, threatened imprisonments and the rest, all always ending with the same appeals for mercy and protection.[113] Or it would be, "My slave has run away!", "My brother has accused me unjustly!", "My brother-in-law wants to swindle me out of an inheritance!", "My son has run away!", "My wife has run off with another man!" They came with their despairs, their quarrels, their family difficulties. They came with all manner of problems never foreseen by the law. They came to be comforted, sometimes only to complain or to pour out their hearts or vent their rage, and the bishop used the opportunity to shame the arrogant, to appeal to the conscience of those that had gone astray, to make an end to innumerable feuds, to cause restitution to be made, to give effect (when he was able) to the counsels of the Sermon on the Mount, "and", says Possidius, "publicly to expose the sinners, so as to inspire a salutary fear in others".[114] Many asked for an interview outside official hours and would then confess their secret sins. Augustine confessed that he often did not know whether there were grounds for imposing the semi-public ecclesiastical penance, and the fact that he felt that he could not ask advice from others was a source to him of serious disquiet; we have here beginnings of private auricular confession and of the secrecy of the confessional.[115] Thus it was that pastoral work, Church discipline and episcopal jurisprudence all merged into one another, and thus everlastingly the muddied waters of human weakness merged with the river of Augustine's life.

These legal preoccupations, with their picturesque and patriarchal air, with their concern often limited to questions of cattle and land, were among the most important social phenomena of this time—profoundly irritating as they were to Augustine. They meant that the legal procedure of the time, with its sanctions and its appeal to force, had been replaced by a procedure in which persuasion and good counsel played a determining part. A great part of the smaller folk had developed the habit of resorting to the bishop's arbitration tribunal instead of going to law. Judicial authority was beginning to pass from the strict representative of the laws of the Empire to the mild man who judged issues by a purely religious yardstick. The ordinary judge was armed with the law and with penal powers; the bishop's only weapons were the respect in which he was held and his ability to utter the liberating words, though we do learn that on occasion he seems to have claimed what may be called the power of the rod, for a slave was once condemned by a sentence of Augustine to receive from his master the thrashing which he had no doubt deserved.[116] Augustine in the public hall of the bishop's palace was a precursor of the later *defensor civitatis* and of the medieval princes of the Church.

No wonder that the holy *cadi* put all the lay officials in the shade. Christians and pagans, heretics and schismatics, all came to him.[117] It is simply terrible, he writes to Marcellinus, all come to me, and I can, unfortunately, neither run away nor ignore them.[118] Even a bishop could not please everybody, however. Before judgement is given, Augustine said in one of his sermons, both parties say that they will accept the verdict. Protest against it or ignore it? They would not dream of such a thing. "Whatever you decide," they say, "may we be anathema if we do not loyally accept it." Yet when the doors of the *secretarium* are opened (the *secretarium* where the secret deliberations are held, and which derives its name from that circumstance)—when what is written on the tablets is read out and the judgement made known, then one of the two parties is sure to start blindly cursing the judges. Yet, Augustine asked, what was he to do? The decision must necessarily be against one of the parties and in favour of the other, and the judgement must obviously be irrevocable. Still, however the judgement reads, it is sure to get him into trouble in one way or the other. If he decides in favour of the richer of the two, the other will say, "He has certainly been bribed", if in favour of the poorer then it will be, "He does that only so as not to make it appear that he is against the poor."[119] For there were people who did not even credit him with common honesty. Indeed, there were those who actually sought to make the bishop a party to their swindles and underhand tricks—who coveted, say, another man's country estate and actually sought his counsel as to how they might steal it from him. "We have actually experienced such a thing, though it seems incredible even to ourselves."[120]

In these and certain others delicate matters, Augustine, as he himself tells us, kept to certain rules, which were roughly the same as those followed by Ambrose. So at least those in the latter's confidence are reputed to have declared, and these, no doubt, included Simplicianus. Some of these rules were: Never ask a woman in marriage for somebody else. If a man wishes to join the army, do not go out of your way to encourage him. Never accept an invitation to a meal in your own town. In a quarrel between husband and wife, never attempt to judge between them, except at the request of both parties. As against this, always endeavour to be present at the signing of a marriage contract, either to add your signature to the document or to give your blessing. In general, be no respecter of persons. Better to accept no legacies at all than to compromise yourself by so doing. Seek rather to resolve quarrels by gentleness than by the exercise of your authority, and, as St. Paul says, learn to treasure it if the faithful prefer to go to the bishop rather than to the civil authorities, and so avoid much litigation.[121]

He took particular care over the appeals for mercy against sentences which had been passed, for in those days such appeals were within the bishop's recognized province. He frequently intervened in this fashion, but always with so much tact, with such reasonable suggestions and in so winning a form, that Macedonius, the *vicarius Africae*, when thanking him for the first three books of the *City of God*, congratulated him on the moderation he had shown in the exercise of his powers. Macedonius added that such conduct contrasted most agreeably with the intransigence displayed by certain other bishops.[122]

In a previous communication Macedonius asked whether Augustine regarded such interventions, which had the sanction of custom, as a legal right, and if so, on what grounds he proposed to claim it, "since he himself was very doubtful whether it could be derived from religion".[123] Augustine answered him at some length, saying that the Church had no intention of deliberately interfering with the normal course of law, but sought to confine herself to the rescuing from the executioner of those guilty of capital offences, and to the safeguarding of their souls from an unshriven death. When she had accomplished this she imposed suitable penances on the culprit. Her endeavour thus was to rescue both the latter's body and his soul. All this was surely legitimate enough, for members of the civil court frequently intervened, on their part, before the bishop's tribunal. Indeed Macedonius himself had recently done this in Carthage on behalf of a priest who had been quite properly censured.[124] Moreover, a bishop had free access to all prisons, which seemed to imply that he had a natural concern in such matters.[125]

If occasion arose he did not hesitate to appeal to the conscience of a judge,[126] and could make hell hot for the pitiless and unfeeling imperial official. He never forgot that it could sometimes be part of a bishop's function to chastise, and he was not the man to be a respecter of the great. A certain Romulus, whom he himself had baptized, was threatened by him in a letter with "wrath that is piling up before the judgement seat of God", because he was squeezing double the taxes due from some wretched *coloni*. Augustine opened proceedings with a full salvo: "Truth is sometimes sweet and sometimes bitter, but even when it is bitter, it has a healing quality, and I must warn you." It may seem to you a small matter, he continued, but the evil is so great that if you realized it and could put a curb on your greed for a moment and could hold this truth before your mind, you would implore God with tears for forgiveness. And do not say to me, "It is all my agent's doing." You yourself pocket the money. Last Saturday I sent you a message, asking you not to leave the town without coming to see me. You said you would do this. Yet you got up on Sunday; you were, as I hear, in church; you prayed there and went home again. You did not wish to talk to me. May God forgive you! There is nothing else for me to say, and he knows that I mean it. Am I so far removed from the bowels of Christ that I can remain indifferent when one whom I have begotten through the Gospel behaves as you do?

Augustine then gives a number of details, the significance of which is no longer quite apparent to the modern reader, to prove that the guilty individual is hedging and prevaricating, and then writes: "But what use is it to say more? Perhaps it would only make you angry and then you would take it out of the poor devils who are at your mercy, but this I swear to you upon my soul, that I fear more for you than I do for these. If you believe me, *Deo gratias*. If not, I must comfort myself with what is written: 'Speak first peace, and if thou art a son of peace, then peace will rest upon him: and if not it will return to thee.' The mercy of God protect you, dear sir and dearly beloved son."[127]

Augustine looked upon such fatherly warnings and reproofs as being in an especial manner a part of his task, nor did he hesitate to enter a rich man's house and say, like John the Baptist, "This is unlawful." He knew well enough that in the eyes of the great a bishop who dared open his mouth was a bad bishop and one that kept silent a good one.[128] Yet he felt himself under a duty of being a conscience *ab extra*, and a conscience that could not be bought. Must not a shepherd on occasion call more loudly than other men? Sometimes even in anger? (For he believed that there was such a thing as religious anger.) It was a good thing sometimes to be angry, for such anger was not the product of hatred, but of anxious and sorrowing love. People are sometimes angry with their children, yet who hates his children? What does any man do who sees a child running towards a rushing stream? He cries out loudly and angrily—and if he does not, it is his fault if the child drowns.[129]

He could lash out, if there was occasion for it and love commanded him to do so, even in his own circle. In the pulpit he can give a drastic description of how a rebellious soul sometimes frantically withstands such admonition: " 'If I am evil and am content to bring about my own ruin, what business is that of yours? Evil is what I want to be and ruin is what I desire.' If a man says that, then my desire to help him is all the greater, and help him I will, even at the risk of annoying him. Heaven preserve us from saying to you, 'Live as you please. Don't worry, God condemns no-one. Only hang on to your Christian faith. And if you want to amuse yourselves in the theatre, don't hesitate to go there. What's the harm? God's mercy is great, and after all, he forgives everything.' If we were to say that, how few people we should offend and how surely we should get the multitude of men on our side!"[130] If his duty demanded that he be unsparing, he would spare no-one: "We sigh over the sins of our brothers. We cannot get over them. We worry about them and sometimes we reprove the individuals concerned. Indeed, we are continually occupied with reproof. All who listen to our sermons will bear witness how often brethren who have done wrong are reproved by us and, by God, not too gently."[131]

He protested, naturally enough, when the police violated the asylum of his church and thus literally intervened in the ecclesiastical sphere.[132] This right of asylum played quite an important part in the life of that time, and it was quite a usual thing for a desperate man, who had the police on his heels, to rush into the church and a moment later to seat himself, gasping for breath, under the altar, with the fringe of the crumpled altar cloth about his shoulders. From there he would look triumphantly toward the door, while the police either quietly made off or stood impotently venting their rage. The feet of the altar and the knobs of the *cancelli* in those days protected many a life, and also saved many insolvent debtors from prison. The cool basilicas were priceless refuges in this hot land of hot-blooded men; in them, one lived literally under the protection of the Almighty. Even under the terror of Count Marinus people were, in Carthage, secure in a church, and when that maniac himself realized that his conduct was frowned on in Ravenna, and his fall was obviously imminent, he too followed the example of his brothers and fled onto ecclesiastical ground—the ground of that Church which "he had caused so terribly to mourn", but which could not, on that ground, deny him her protection.[133]

From this right of asylum arose the strangest situations. After the lynching incident on St. Laurence's day, to which several references have been made already, such large numbers of the very worst elements sought refuge within the church walls that Augustine, after his sermon, begged the faithful not to stay away from church. He could see to it, he said, that the unruly mob did no-one any harm. The church was adequately protected by the laws of the Empire and even the people who had sought asylum on this occasion would not dare to raise a hand against their Mother. Indeed, the best way of preventing any excesses was for the faithful to continue their normal church-going. The church, he continued, is not a refuge just for a handful of people. It is a refuge for all, and he who at the moment has no ground for seeking this refuge should have a care lest he should have such grounds on some future occasion. Mark, beloved, that there are three kinds of people who flee into the church: the good who flee from the evil, the evil who flee from the good, and the evil who flee from the evil. But we must make no distinction between any of these. If we let the guilty be carried off, where are the innocent to hide? Therefore, it is best to have an asylum for both. Bear this in mind. If you do you will appear in large numbers and give these lawless folk ground to think twice before doing any further wrong.[134]

Augustine spared no pains to be an effective advocate for his somewhat demanding flock even where, as was sometimes the case, the matter was one of some delicacy. This kind of thing added much work to that which his official duties entailed. How far his kindness of heart would go in this respect is shown by the strange case of a certain Fascius. This man was unable to pay arrears of taxes amounting to seventeen *solidi*, and so fled to the church. The tax collectors demanded that he should be handed over or that, alternatively, the Church should pay the debt. Augustine saw how ashamed the man was of his predicament, and so instead of going to diaconal funds, he personally borrowed the money from a certain Macedonius and paid the debt. Unfortunately Fascius, having thus for a time been freed from his obligations, disappeared and, despite his promises of repayment, continued to remain in hiding. Thus, when the loan from Macedonius became due for repayment, Augustine had to ask his congregation for a special collection. He did this in writing, having, in the press of the Whitsun services, forgotten to mention the matter from the pulpit, and being at the time on his travels. He obviously did not expect very substantial relief, for he writes to his clergy that the deficit is to be made good from Church funds.[135]

As against this Augustine was, when the circumstances warranted it, quite ready to defend the rights of layfolk in cases of asylum, when these were victimized by a hotheaded priest. There was, for instance, the case of Count Classicianus, whom Bishop Auxilius of Nurco had put under a ban, because the former had allegedly seized, with the help of an armed escort, fugitives who had sought asylum. What had really happened was that Classicianus, accompanied by the escort proper to his rank, had requested Auxilius to deny asylum to certain peasants who had failed to keep promises to which they had sworn on the Gospel (and actually the latter had shortly afterwards had qualms of conscience and left the church of their own accord). Fortunately, Augustine succeeded in putting an end to the whole nonsensical business by means of a tactful letter couched in moderate terms. To Classicianus he wrote that he thought it absolutely necessary for certain limits to be put on the right of asylum and that it was his intention to get a decision on this at the next synod, and, if necessary, to refer the matter to Rome.[136]

In general, however, Augustine worked consistently for leniency and for the humanizing of the judicial and penal machinery. When one of his priests was murdered, he wrote to Marcellinus, begging him not to put witnesses to the torture; beating, he said, was quite sufficient.[137] Three letters of his are extant in which he pleads for that rather curious legal dispensation, whereby any prisoner could be permitted to enjoy, in the town in which he had been arrested, a period of conditioned liberty for thirty days, so that he might put his affairs in order before actually entering on his confinement. The case in point was that of Faventius, a tenant farmer, who had fled into the church at Hippo for fear of his rich and powerful lord. He had remained in hiding there for a time, but had at last grown careless and ventured abroad. One evening, when returning home from supper, he had been seized by a body of armed men under an officer, and arrested. After that he had disappeared, and the fear was that he had been taken off to the provincial court at Cirta, his wealthy landlord having brought this about by means of his money. Augustine immediately had enquiries made through the commander of the coastal guard as to Faventius' whereabouts; in due course it was found that Faventius was in Cirta, as supposed. When the priest who had been sent to see him was denied access, Augustine wrote three short but effective letters and also a protest against the violation of the right of asylum. The letters were to the president of the Cirta court, to his friend the *consularis* Generosus, and to the Bishop of Cirta.

Augustine greatly disliked this never-ending business of intervention, which was all too often without result.[138] In the case of Marcellinus, for instance, both Augustine and Aurelius of Carthage were told by Marinus that a messenger had already been sent to Ravenna with an appeal for mercy, and that for the time being nothing was to happen—this though the execution had already been ordered. Caecilianus, who was a secret enemy of Marcellinus, though we do not quite know why, had visited Augustine on the day before the execution, and pointing to the altar, had sworn by the sacred Mysteries that all was going well.[139]

Unceasingly they criticized him. Once, when preaching on the sin of self-glorification, he felt called upon to defend his frequent intercourse with the great of this world, an intercourse into which, he declared, he was forced by necessity. On another occasion someone would say, "Why did he not reprove such a one more earnestly? Had he done so, the man would not have behaved as he did." "Should I have reproved him publicly, then, along with you all?" Augustine asked. "And how do you know that I did not reprove him? But you shall know the truth. I did reprove him, and he would not listen. I reproved him privately where you could not hear me." Then there were other voices. "What business has the bishop to spend his time with officials and all such manner of folk?" Here too Augustine had his reply: "It is often said of us, 'He's been to one of those Government offices again', and yet you know that it is the needs of you all that drive us to go to such places, from which we would much rather keep away. It is your own needs that compel us to observe certain hours and certain forms, to stand before doors and watch others go in (worthy and unworthy alike), until our turn comes at last to be announced, and often we are not admitted at all. It is your needs that compel us to suffer humiliation, to make abject petitions, to rejoice if ever so rarely we achieve something and to be sad when on other occasions we fail. Who would bear this if he were not compelled to bear it? By all means set us free from these tasks, if you do not approve of them. Spare us these interventions, give us a respite from these duties, for we would be only too delighted to have nothing more to do with Government offices."[140]

Yet to the end of his life he did not cease to busy himself in such matters and to write letters. The respect in which he was held increased with the years, and so it was that in the end there was nobody who was so successful in getting things done. Leisure he never enjoyed. He understood neither the art of keeping out of things nor yet the much more difficult art of keeping his distance, though this last was something which, as a young professor of rhetoric, he had so greatly admired in the dignified Ambrose. Ambrose had exchanged the *sella* for the *cathedra* and his Papinian for the Bible, yet despite the more exalted norms of the divine law-book, he still remained the Roman official, though working in a different sphere. Though crowds of people were trying to get to Ambrose at all times of the day, and though he was an essentially approachable man, and saw people without appointment, he had a curious aptitude which enabled him only to bestow his time where he wished to do so, and he somehow managed to do his reading undisturbed without having actually to bolt his door; for reading was Ambrose's unceasing occupation, and for the most part he followed it without the services of a reader, and without anything in the nature of a discussion-group. He avoided both of these things possibly because without them he could read faster, or possibly (at any rate in the case of the discussion group) because he tended to suffer from hoarseness and wished to spare his voice. Augustine himself could not divine the reason, but confirms that he always read alone and never aloud.

The young man from Tagaste hardly knew Ambrose, but felt an irresistible longing to put his intellectual difficulties before him, and he would much have preferred to speak to him alone outside of his official hour of audience; but when he saw him in his room, bent over a book, never raising his eyes but only moving his lips, and had waited for some time with all manners of questions pulsing through his mind, he would ultimately turn and creep away on tip-toe. He simply did not dare to disturb him.[141] How often, in later years, when the press of callers was upon him, he must have thought of that silent man in the bishop's palace at Milan.

He possessed himself, as a bishop, nothing of this *gravitas Romana*. He was a child of people of rank; yet he did not know that kindliness that is mixed with a shade of condescension, which draws the man in the street and yet keeps him at a distance. He was much too lively a person, much too much of a charmer and, for that reason alone, a man who was easily accessible. He had grown accustomed to regarding himself as the humble servant of all and just because of that became, despite his learned works, the ideal parish priest, who was welcome everywhere.

Nothing was too slight to make claims on his time. We have no less than four letters concerning the engagement of a young girl who was a minor and as whose guardian he acted in the name of the Church, and whom he was most anxious not to see betrothed to a pagan.[142] With his own hand he wrote a long letter of spiritual counsel to a young girl, Florentina, who was, as her mother wrote, at first too embarrassed to answer him.[143] It was this kind of thing that caused Erasmus to say that his letters were often rather trivial. Often he makes his excuses to the person to whom he is writing, saying that he would like to dictate a long letter, but that he has not the time.[144] The truth is that when it came to dictating, his whole inclination lay elsewhere. Dictating meant, for him, working on a book. That was his only relaxation, and as an old man he indulged in it until far into the night,[145] but dictating pointless letters was a thing that he resented having to do, and he did it unwillingly.

It was the same with the popular tribunal, which he felt was a waste of his time and with which he sometimes actually showed impatience. It was one of the things that caused his great plans to lie fallow for years, and one of the reasons why his *City of God* remained for so long a torso. I'm sick of it all, he once said to Marcellinus when the latter kept on urging him to finish the book, but I can't help myself. "If I were to give you an account of how the hours of my days and nights are spent, and let you see how many of them I have to spend over unnecessary things, it would make you quite sad; you would also be astonished at the number of things which I cannot put off and which pluck me by the sleeve and prevent me from doing what you are questioning and begging me about—the things which I would so gladly do myself, but which, to my unspeakable regret, I am not in a position to do."[146] No doubt this was but one of many complaints of distraction through other people's business, "tumultuosissimas perplexitates causarum alienarum".[147]

Among other things, his life of prayer suffered. In a letter to Abbot Eudoxius and his monks, who lived on Capraria, the Isle of Goats in the Tyrrhenian Sea, he confessed that he often envied him his cloisterlike quiet, for one could live more quietly in the midst of the waves of the sea than in his audience chamber. "Remember us in your prayers, for you say them, as I believe, more attentively and more soberly than we." Our own prayers, he says, are weakened by the dark confusion of mundane business, and are, as it were, wounded thereby, for although we have no business of our own, yet those who compel us to go a mile with them and with whom we then go twain, bring so much of it into our house that we can scarcely breathe, but we find comfort in the help of him of whom it is written, "Let the sighing of the prisoners go up before thee."[148]

Once on the anniversary of his consecration, he enumerated all the things that were demanded of him: "To rebuke those who stir up strife, to comfort those of little courage, to take the part of the weak, to refute opponents, to be on guard against traps, to teach the ignorant, to shake the indolent awake, to discourage those who want to buy and sell, to put the presumptuous in their place, to mollify the quarrelsome, to help the poor, to liberate the oppressed, to encourage the good, to suffer the evil, and to love all men."[149] "To be ever preaching, disputing, reproving, edifying, to be on hand for every man—that is a great burden and one which lies heavily on man." "No-one can long more than I to be free from troubles and cares, for nothing is better, nothing is more sweet, than to browse among the heavenly treasures, away from all distraction and noise." "Yet it is the Gospel itself that makes me fear that way of life. I might well say, 'What do I get by boring people, by reproving the evil, by telling them, Don't do this. Stop doing that? Why should I feel myself responsible for others?' It is there that the Gospel holds me back."[150]

To build on the foundation of humility, that was the beginning of all things. When at the end of his life the Vandals flooded over Africa, and Hippo was cut off by land, Honoratus of Thiava asked him what he should do in the event of the barbarians' besieging him. Augustine replied that the bishop and his clergy must in no circumstances flee. For it was a worse thing that the living stones should go to ruin in their absence than that they should witness the falling down of the stones that were lifeless. Also, at such a time people invariably rush into the church. Everyone wants something; one man wants to be baptized, another to be reconciled, a third to do penance, all need comfort and the Holy Sacrifice. How can even one man be weak and "the bishop not burn"? What if any man should die in the ban of the Church, or die without having been born again? Surely, also, no man should be allowed to go out of this world without the viaticum of the Body of Christ? When we are no longer there, he says, men do nothing but run around and curse.[151]

Augustine knew well enough that these petty worries were a primary duty. Mundane preoccupations often brought with them the opportunity to give good advice or to rebuke a sinner; they brought with them the possibility of quiet influence and of setting a good example, a chance to bring about the enlivening of consciences and give spiritual direction. Administration was the least among the thieves of his time. That vile blood-sucking creature that tends to grow so fat in a modern presbytery was left by Augustine to his accountant, but for the rest there was hardly anything on which he would turn his back, for Augustine knew that many an opportunity of serving a soul begins with a chance encounter. If this man had lived in the rather cramped surroundings of an average modern presbytery, how meticulously he would have exploited all the potentialities of parish visiting! How he would have thrown himself into the business of religious exercises and mission weeks! And he would surely have admired the serious manner in which parish visiting is carried on in certain Protestant circles, and the concern shown there for the devout.

Augustine must often have recalled what the Psalmist says about the dumb beast before the face of God—"Ut jumentum factus sum apud te"—but also the words which follow it—"Et ego semper tecum."[152] Yet even the beasts of burden are saved—"Homines et jumenta salvabis"[153]—and efficiency experts in the presbyteries may not be so fortunate. The wise exegete Tyconius, that beacon among the *Pars Donati*, once pointed out that a churchman could always make a good career if he simply showed zeal in administration and correctness in celebrating the Mass. Then, he says, simple folk think him pious, while the eminent, towards whom he should close an eye, think him intelligent and efficient. Yet even these are "one with the beasts"; they are the Pharisees who sit on the seat of Moses; one must, of course, do what they say, but one should not follow their example.[154] Augustine could have got ahead quickly enough, but he wanted no career. His wish was only to proclaim the Word and to be a conscience for all. Harnack once said that Augustine and Ambrose took upon themselves the duties of watchmen for the integrity of God's word, counsellors and judges, and that at a time when the true nature of these duties seemed likely to be forgotten.[155] One may doubt whether the average bishop of that time was, in fact, beginning to be nothing more than either a liturgical expert or an administrator. Yet we cannot get away from the essential uniqueness of the figure of Augustine, who created order in so many homes and so many souls and patiently examined the wounds of all. One certainly cannot call the fifth century to mind without immediately thinking of him, and indeed the picture of this man is still an inspiration to every hard-working parish priest.

THE ELECTION OF ERACLIUS

Postpone it as he might, the hour had to come when he was compelled to choose between his work in Hippo and achieving something for the Church as a whole. He was too old to devote himself effectively to both. He therefore decided to provide for the needs of Hippo by having a coadjutor elected, hoping thus to be enabled, during the few years which remained to him, to serve the Catholic cause in that field in which he was irreplaceable. Six days before the Calends of October in that year in which Theodosius was consul for the twelfth time and Valentinian for the second—on 26 September 426, that is to say—he called his people together to hear an announcement. Probably the best tailpiece that can be found to the story of Augustine and his people is the record of the scene which followed,[156] in which the *notarii* even noted down the number of acclamations—the record which Augustine himself revised, giving it its final shape.

He sat upon his *exedra* with two brother bishops. Seven priests were grouped around him, the whole of his clergy being present and also a great crowd of people. After a few introductory remarks he spoke as follows:

Here below we are all subject to death, and every man's end is certain. Yet as little children we hope to become boys, as boys, to become youths, as youths, to see maturity, and when that comes, we confidently anticipate middle age and hope to experience old age at the end. [One sees here the six periods which Augustine professed to see both in the life of the individual and in the story of man.] No man knows whether he will reach old age or no, but he generally hopes to reach it. Even so, however, he does not know how long it will last; he is only certain of one thing, that there is nothing to follow it. God willed that I should come to this town as a young man, but now my youth is past and I am an old one. I know only too well that when a bishop dies his Church is liable to be disturbed by the scheming of quarrelsome and self-seeking men, and I must have a care that things which I myself have to my sorrow been compelled to witness shall, in so far as I can prevent it, not become the portion of this town. As you know, beloved, I have just come from the Church of Milevis. The brethren there, and in particular the servants of God, had asked me to come because after the death of my brother and fellow-bishop Severus, of holy memory, they feared dissension.

I went there and in his mercy the Lord helped us according to his will, for they peacefully accepted him whom Severus had chosen while he yet lived. For there had been a slight difficulty. Brother Severus had thought that it would suffice if he named his successor in the presence of his clergy. He never discussed the matter with his people, and so there was among some of these a feeling of disappointment. Yet it has pleased God to let that feeling disappear and give place to one of pleasure, and they have now consecrated the candidate whom their late bishop had named. So now, in order to forestall any possible complaint, I desire to make known my own wishes to you all, for these wishes are, as I honestly believe, in accordance with the will of God. I wish the priest Eraclius to be my successor.

Twenty-three times the people (who had been taken completely by surprise) called out, "Deo Gratias! Praised be Christ!", then sixteen times, "Christ, hear us! Long live Augustine!", and then eight times, "Father, Bishop!" When all was quiet again Augustine continued:

It is not necessary that I should say anything in praise of Eraclius. I admire his wisdom, but will spare his modesty. It is enough that you all know him, and I will only say that I know my desire is the same as your own, and that if I did not know this I could now put it to the test. However that may be, my wish is now made plain, and this is the thing that, despite my frosty old age, I ask of God with glowing prayers in which I request and direct you to join. May God melt all your minds together into the unity of the peace of Christ, and then confirm them in the conviction which he has created in our own. He has sent us this man. May he protect him and keep him without blemish or reproach, so that he who in my life has been my joy may exercise my office after my death. You see that the *notarii* are taking note of all we say, and that they also note what you say yourselves, so that neither my words nor yours "fall to the ground"; and in order to make it all more plain we will immediately have this matter entered in the Church records, for I should like to see this matter settled, as far as it is possible to settle finally any human thing.

Hereupon the congregation called out thirty-six times, "Deo Gratias! Christ be praised! Christ, hear us! Long live Augustine!", the last being again repeated thirteen times, Then, eight times, "Father, Bishop!", then twenty times, "Worthy is he and righteous", then five times, "Well deserved! Most worthy!", then six times, again, "Worthy is he and righteous!" ("Dignus et justus est", a curious borrowing from the language of the liturgy and an echo of the Greek *axios*.) When all was quiet again, Augustine asked for a prayer and again they began to shout—sixteen times, "Thanks for your decision!", twelve times, *"Fiat, Fiat!"*, and six times, "Father, Bishop Eraclius!"

Then Augustine recalled to the older ones in the congregation the circumstances of his own consecration, which had already taken place in the lifetime of Valerius, a thing that was contrary to the canons of Nicaea, though neither he nor Valerius had known this at the time. For this reason, he declared, Eraclius would remain an ordinary priest for the present and would only become bishop when God willed it. He went on:

> Nevertheless, I will now do something which I have as yet neglected to do. You know what it was that I was anxious to do some years ago, though at that time you would not let me do it. We had agreed with one another that in view of the scriptural studies which my fathers and fellow-bishops of the two provincial synods of Carthage and Numidia had enjoined me to undertake, nobody was to disturb me for five days in the week. This was entered in the record and approved by acclamation, and I will have the record, with the note of your acclamations, read out. For a short while you kept to your bargain, but you have ever since most outrageously failed to keep it, for you leave me no time to do what I want to do. Both morning and afternoon, you take all my time. I beseech you most earnestly, for Christ's sake, that you will agree to my handing over all my more time-consuming tasks to this young man whom I have this day in Christ's name designated as my successor, namely the priest Eraclius.

"Thanks for the decision!", the people cried out thirty-six times. Then Augustine thanked them and also thanked God for their ready concurrence, and begged them to bring all matters to Eraclius which hitherto they had brought to himself. In special cases Eraclius would come to him for advice. Thus they themselves would lack nothing, while he would at last be enabled, "if God still grants me a little time, to devote this remainder of my life not to idleness and indolence, but to Holy Scripture. Let no man therefore envy me my *otium*, for my *otium* will contain a great deal of *negotium*." He concluded:

> I see that I have now agreed with you in all things concerning which it was my duty to agree with you in the matter which caused me to call you here. So, to conclude, I ask all of you who are able to do so to sign this document, and now I need your final confirmatory answer. Please let me hear it in an acclamation which will signify your consent.

"*Fiat, fiat!*" they called out: "Worthy is he and righteous!", together with many other customary acclamations in honour of the newly-elected bishop-to-be: "Long-deserving, Long-worthy! Christ, hear us! Protect Eraclius!" Hereupon Augustine closed with the beautiful words: "Now the time has come for us to concern ourselves with the things of God at the altar. During the common prayer, beloved, I shall take you all to my heart, and that most earnestly, having in mind all your cares and needs, and I shall pray to the Lord for this our Church and for myself and for the priest Eraclius."[157]

Such were the dispositions which the old man made for his Church in the matter of the apostolic succession, while in his thoughts he was already taking leave of his episcopal office.

The Death of Augustine

How he took leave of his clergy is known to us.[158] Great was the number of those he left behind; he had indeed provided to the very best of his powers for the service of the Church. He had become old and feeble, the bishop of a beleaguered city, and none was more tortured than he by the thought of the collapse of the Empire, the sufferings of the Church and all the decay of that indescribably tragic time. Now they heard him praying to God that he might regard them and free their city, or, if he willed otherwise, that he might strengthen his servants, so that they might bear the trials he had sent and that he might in the end call him to himself.

In the third month of the siege he became gravely ill. Already aflame with his fever, he greeted them all again and requested them to leave him alone and not to enter his room save when the physicians came or to bring him necessary refreshment. Often had he recalled with admiration the words with which the dying Ambrose had comforted his clergy some thirty years before, when these had besought him not to leave the Church and themselves: "My life has not been such that I would need to be ashamed to go on living amongst you. Nevertheless, I do not fear to die. We have a good Father." These words, he said, were quite inimitable and most carefully weighed. What might, perhaps, appear presumptuous in the first part of the utterance was entirely offset by the words at the end. For the first words related to what men might know about a man, and Ambrose had been entitled to utter them, since he had led a life that was entirely pure, while the final ones were spoken by him as a man who is approaching the judgement of God and knows that all is mercy there.[159] Yet Augustine himself did not dare to repeat these words. He was more humble than Ambrose, and had a greater conviction of sin. He had said in intimate conversation with those about him that even good Christians and priests should not leave this life without undertaking a penance. Penance was in those days not a matter of a few pious devotions but a weighty word for a very serious business; it meant exclusion from the table of the Lord. Such penance he now undertook in solitude, and after he had put all else out of his mind, he remained alone with those simple feelings of faith, hope and love, in which we men often see the signs of a divine virtue. Yet over all this there hung for him now the dark veil of remorse. He thought not so much of his five talents, or of the scandals he might have caused, his responsibilities and his innumerable writings. It was something different from all this, for Augustine did not belong to those who go hence, like little children, content and confident.

Ten days he lay alone, his eyes unceasingly fixed on the parchment with the penitential psalms, which he had nailed to the walls, and he wept continually as he repeated the words to himself. Thus he died. To his Church he bequeathed two things: the memory of his humble and indescribably lovable personality, and his great library, the archive of his spirit. In the matter of miracles, Possidius recalls two; one was a simple cure, following a dream in which a sick man had been told to go to Bishop Augustine and to get him to lay his hands on him, the other was a rather ordinary case of exorcism.[160] This, in the fifth century, was nothing very remarkable. There was no will. The poor man of God had nothing to dispose of.

PART 2
THE CULTUS

10

THE THEORETICAL ASPECT

The Letters to Januarius

ON several occasions Augustine expressed his views on what we call "the cultus", though he only did so incidentally. The most remarkable of these utterances are in two letters to a certain Januarius, of whom we know nothing, save that he was a layman who, in the year 400, put a number of liturgical questions to him. Some of these were of a purely practical nature. Thus, Januarius asked what rule he should follow in fasting and communicating, since practice varied from one place to another. Other questions were more theoretical. How does it come about, he asked for instance, that the date of Easter depends on the Sabbath and on the moon?

Augustine dealt with the first set of questions immediately, in a short letter. He waited some time before replying to the rest, and then did so in an epistle which is really almost a book. To judge from the concluding sentences, he wanted to see both letters in the hands of many others readers, "for I am confident that yours is not a jealous love". Moreover, he himself did not forget these letters, for he came to speak of them in the *Retractations*. For our purposes they are probably his most important liturgical document.[1]

The question whether the cultus is in itself important is not raised in these two treatises—for that is what they really are, despite the unsystematic character of their construction, which, such being the nature of the letter, rather suggests an informal chat. But then, the importance of the liturgy was in those days not something which it would have occurred to anybody to question. As to its theological aspects, Augustine was equally under no necessity of expressing any purely personal opinion, for he was on what was really common ground. His conception comes out very clearly in a well-known passage in the *City of God*, in which he shows that he looks upon his ideas as self-evidently clear. Unlike the Greeks, he says there, we have no single unequivocal word to denote "the service due to God", for the Greeks use the word λατρεία, which covers a much narrower ground than our *servitus* or *cultus*, for it is used exclusively for the worship of God, and not for the honouring of any other being. In the same manner, instead of our *religio*, with its different shades of meaning, they use the precise θρησκεία, and instead of the equivocal *pietas*, they say θεοσέβεια, which has a purely religious connotation.[2] Somewhat later he says, "The service which the Greeks call λατρεία is owed by us to him [i.e., to the one true God] both in the sacraments and in ourselves, for we are in our totality a temple, just as each one of us is a temple in himself, for he has laid it upon himself both to dwell amongst us all when we are gathered together in unity of spirit, and also to make his habitation in each of us individually, and when he dwells amongst us all he is not greater than when he dwells in a single one of us, for he can no more become greater by being extended than he can become smaller by being divided up."[3]

Thus Augustine distinguishes between the personal and inward worship of God and the sacramental and external worship, between the subjective and the objective forms of prayer, between piety and the cultus. In the same breath, however, he says that the two forms interpenetrate, since God's presence permeates the individual in the same manner in which it permeates a congregation. In all this one cannot help noticing that he identifies public and sacramental worship as a matter of course. What we call "liturgy" he obviously regards as a λατρεία, which is performed by means of the sacraments instituted by Christ and the Church.

Now, in the two letters to Januarius he writes in exactly the same way, though here he gives us an actual definition of λατρεία; and we find this whole idea further amplified in the twentieth book against Faustus the Manichean, for here he says that the offering of sacrifice is very specially part of a latreutic cult, for it constitutes a *latreia* reserved exclusively to God. Hence, when such a sacrifice is offered to idols we speak of *idol-latria*.[4]

To return, however, to the letters to Januarius. In the first of these we find the following basic ideas expressed, the passage being obviously a reaction to Januarius' excessive preoccupation with matters of secondary importance:

> The first thing I should like you to do is to fix your mind firmly on what is the real starting-point of this whole question. It is that our Lord Jesus Christ has, as he himself says in his Gospel, imposed on us a yoke that is sweet and a light burden. In order to give effect to this intention he has welded together the community of his new people, through the bond of the sacraments, which are few in number, easy to administer and receive, and yet of supreme importance. There is, for instance, baptism, made holy by the name of the blessed Trinity, there is, further, the partaking of the Lord's body and blood, and there are all the other forms mentioned in the canonical writings, excepting always the ceremonies of bygone times, which we read of in the five books of Moses, and which today have been abolished. As to those sacraments which we preserve, not because they are mentioned in Scripture, but because they have been handed down by tradition and are

observed all over the world, it is clear that they were recommended and instituted either by the Apostles themselves or by Plenary Councils. I refer, for instance, to our celebrating every year the sufferings of the Lord, his resurrection, his ascent into heaven, and also the coming down of the Holy Ghost; and there are many similar usages, which are observed by the whole Church, wherever it has been spread.[5]

These few words contain a complete theory of the nature and function of the traditional cultus. We can summarize them as containing the following points: The cultus is simple and is carried out by means of a few simple sacraments. These last stamp the Christian community with its peculiar character. The cultus owes its origin to the Apostles and the Church. The criterion for its form is oecumenical practice.

Word and Sacrament

The thing that Augustine stresses most about the liturgy is its simplicity. He says this on more than one occasion. The typical Christian *colere* and *adorare* are simple, restrained and transparently intelligible. This remark, of course, presupposes some scriptural knowledge, and a sense of the contrast of Christian practice with the manifold and shadowy ceremonies of the old dispensation. There are much fewer sacraments now than in the Old Testament, and this is a consequence of the freedom which Christ has purchased for us. "For the old sacraments," he writes elsewhere, "which were kept and celebrated by virtue of the Law, had no other function than to proclaim the coming of Christ. When Christ had fulfilled them by his coming, they were abolished, and they were abolished because they had been fulfilled, for he came not to destroy the Law but to fulfil it, and since then sacraments have been instituted of greater effect and greater usefulness, easier to celebrate, and fewer in number, as was fitting since the righteousness of the Faith was revealed and the servile yoke, which was suited to a hardened and fleshly people, was removed from the sons of God, who are now called to freedom."[6] One wonders whether, when he wrote that, Augustine was also thinking of the complicated formalism and endless repetitions of the rites of the old Roman State religion, or of the noisy and ostentatious celebrations of the various mystery sects and of other unofficial cults such as that of the Dea Coelestis. It is impossible to say exactly, but he had certainly seen something of the Dea Coelestis as a student in Carthage and had been anything but edified. It was not so much the cult of the emperors, but those more or less Romanized local cults with which he reproached the pagans, calling these cults "a regular *officium* of shamelessness".[7] We may well assume that he saw in the simplicity and purity of the Christian rites the divine corrective of the poisonous seductions of the ancient demons. The Jewish *sacramenta* were useful and transitory. The Greek ones, when not actually obscene, lacked any useful purpose, for however subtly one interpreted them, Greek mythology could only lead to pantheism, leading men to cosmic allegories and "whoring them away from God". Now, Christ had abolished the signs that were useless and shown men the meaning of the useful ones, and these last might, in a certain sense, be allowed to remain, but only as a spiritual exercise for those who grasped their spiritual significance.[8]

Thus it was that Augustine found the liturgy not so much rich as simple, not intoxicating but illuminating. The Christian mysteries are sober, and there are but few of them: "The Lord and likewise the commands of the Apostles have, instead of handing over many, handed over only a few—the sacrament of baptism, the feast of the body and blood of the Lord; they are easy to make use of, most wonderful for those that understand them, and they are administered with great decency [*observatione castissima*]"[9]—one is tempted to translate "without orgiastic or aesthetic excess". This is no platitude, about "serving God in spirit and in truth". Augustine means his words to be taken in a perfectly concrete sense and that is how he experiences the matter. "The worship of God—such is the intention of God in his mercy—shall be a thing of freedom. This means that there shall be as few sacraments as possible, and these shall be intelligible to every one." Materially only little is needed for administering them—in fact, only corn, water, wine and oil; and on another occasion he remarks in passing that the Christian sacrifice is "so pure and so easy".[10]

So there are only few sacraments. Now, every reader will notice that Augustine calls all kinds of things *sacramenta*. It is true that when he is called upon to give examples he chooses, more or less as a matter of course, baptism, the Eucharist and extreme unction, and he obviously sees these as something separate from the other sacraments. But it is clear that for him the word *sacramentum* is still something very imprecise. This comes out very strongly in the letter to Januarius. Here he uses the word *sacramentum* for the constituent element of the externally visible cultus, and its meaning is obviously much wider than it is with ourselves. Almost in one breath he refers to baptism and the Eucharist as sacraments, and applies the same word to the annual celebrations of Christ's resurrection, which we refer to as feasts. Elsewhere he speaks of the following as *sacramenta*: the sign of the cross, salt, exorcisms, contemplation, the penitential garment; the bowing of the head, the transmission of the *symbolum*, the taking off of shoes, and the other rites of the catechumenate, and of the entry on the period of being *competentes*; the octave of Easter, penance, the laying-on of hands, reconciliation, the great fasts, spiritual songs, the Lord's Prayer; and many other things. Their common characteristic is that they are all of some spiritual importance and are externally visible.[11]

The great majority of *sacraments*, however, are not done but spoken, not performed but read, not seen but heard and understood, not used for and in worship by way of symbolic action but in sermons for purposes of preaching the Christian message.

These "spoken" sacraments are literally without number, but all play the same part; they are indirect symbols or signs. They are the mysterious but always suggestive signs of our salvation. They can be historical facts or spoken similes, but they are all symbols of a reality that is higher than that denoted by the literal interpretation of the words employed, or the bare facts that they relate. The book in which they are almost all contained is Holy Scripture. For all things there in addition to the truths of the Faith and the commandments and counsels are "hidden sacramental mysteries".[12] No happening recorded therein, no person mentioned, however unimportant, no fact, however strange or repellent (Jacob's lie, for example), but has some significance within the general framework of Revelation. It is no longer a simple fact or a simple lie, but a *mysterium* or a *sacramentum*, in other words, a picture in word or action of a higher truth. What all sacraments have in common is this holy showing-forth. A disguising yet revealing symbol is always their mark.

But the world of symbols is no burden and no yoke. Even if there is no end to the number of symbols, they do not make the practice of the Faith difficult, for they are not in the nature of laws. They serve only to make the truths of the Faith better known, and only a few of them enter into the actual cultus. Thus, the majority of them are things heard and only a few are things seen. "The symbols which serve to proclaim divine truth are treated by us with great reverence, even when they make use of all manner of common things such as the winds, the sea, birds, fishes, trees, cattle, flowers and human beings. In our sermons we often make use of all manner of such symbols, but when it comes to celebrating the sacraments of Christian freedom, then we are most sparing, confining ourselves to water, wine, corn and oil." As to the rites of the cultus of the Old Testament, these "have only been handed down to us so that we may understand them as signs".[13]

The innumerable sacraments, therefore, that are made use of in a sermon, are contrasted with those few by means of which, in the cultus, we bring λατρεία to God, and by means of which we enjoy our Christian freedom under the New Testament. Augustine does not explain why the divine dispensation has separated off these few sacraments from the many sacraments of the word. He merely shows that this is the case. One idea is foreign to him, though it might well fit into the general scheme of his thought. It is that those sacraments which are sacraments in our sense of the word are instruments of divine mercy capable of being effective in those spiritual depths where words cannot perform this function, and the spirit can no longer, with bare words, make itself understood by the soul.

Augustine does not see in the sacraments of the cultus something that is of a contrary nature to the word, or something subordinate to it. Rather does he see them as something that is joined to it. They have the true mark of a sacrament, which is that it is a sign (a sign which obviously has some spiritual effect), and they are only distinguishable from the word by the clarity with which they convey their meaning and by the pregnancy of their symbolism. Both kinds of sacrament were instituted by Christ, the Apostles or the Oecumenical Church. For all that, Augustine continually stresses in his other writings that it is the few sacraments, i.e., the sacraments in our sense of the word, and not the many sacraments of the word, on which the Church is built up.

Sacrament and Community

It is, after all, those sacraments that are few and simple that make the Christian community a visible thing. This thought comes out very clearly indeed in the first lines of the letter to Januarius, and we also find it elsewhere in Augustine's writings. In the work against Faustus the Manichee he relates this idea to the general principle which was also applied and affirmed by Thomas Aquinas. "It is impossible for men in any religious denomination, be it true or false, to create an ordered and united community, if they are not bound to one another through some common dependence on a sign or a sacrament. The effect of these sacraments is indescribably great and to treat them contemptuously is to be guilty of sacrilege. For to despise what is indispensible for complete union with God is to become godless."[14]

According to this line of thought, the sacraments not only give her visible character to the Church and in a sense build her up externally; they also give her her internal unity, since they are indispensible for eternal salvation and are not to be found outside the Church herself. There is in the Church nothing more concrete than the diffusion of grace through the appointed means of salvation. Thus it is that the unity of the Church is based on the unity of baptism and the Eucharist. This was an argument against the Donatist anabaptists; whosoever duplicates the sacrament of baptism which the Catholic Church has built up, does violence to the Church's unity. This duplicates the Church by schism, for the sacraments exist only in the Church and nowhere else. Whosoever despises the sacraments prepares his own ruin; but also, he who seeks them outside the Church finds no salvation. A sacrament may, it is true, be validly administered outside the Church, and an evildoer can receive it; Simon Magus was baptized and Saul was truly a prophet, so that Donatist baptisms are valid. For all that, sacraments received outside the Church do not bring salvation, for they cannot give to the recipient "the love of God which is poured out in our hearts". Thus, although water is poured out, the spirit of love is missing. Here that applied which was mystically written in the Psalms, namely, that "the Lord covers the higher places" (that is to say, the "more excellent way" of St. Paul) "with water".[15] For the Spirit only acts within the true Church. He animates the Church alone, and nothing outside it. That is why, outside the Church, the sacraments are valid but dead. They are dead signs for members that are soul-less, because they have been cut off. That is why a person being reconciled after lapsing into heresy or schism is not rebaptized, though hands are laid upon him; and for that reason it is only within the unity of the Church that sins can be forgiven. Thus it is that the partaking of the sacraments in common, the *societas sacramentorum*, is a necessary condition of sanctity, and thus is it that Augustine comes to look upon the Mother Church as the sole true servant of the dispensing of grace. Augustine sees her as a virgin mother, made fruitful by the Holy Ghost, who, within herself and in the compass of her three dimensions (in the actual Churches in different places of the world, that is to say), brings forth children from the womb of her baptismal pools, even when her individual earthly servants are heretical or unworthy. It is only this "one chaste and perfect dove" that baptizes, even when hawks pour out the water.[16] It is this one bride who, from the womb of her slave-women and herself, by reason of the sacraments, as it were, bears children from her husband's seed.[17] Yet it is the "sacrament of the body of the Lord" that is in an especial manner the bond of ecclesiastical unity. This is the essential sacrament of the faithful, which the uninitiated do not know and must not taste. "The faithful, however, know the body of Christ for as long as they do not fail to be the body of Christ themselves. They must themselves become Christ's body if they desire to live by Christ's spirit." "Dost thou desire to live from the spirit of Christ? Then be in Christ's body. It is my spirit which gives my body life, and it is by thy spirit that thine own body lives. The body of Christ can only live from the spirit of Christ. For this reason the Apostle Paul, when he speaks of the Bread [John vi.50], says that we, 'being many, are one bread, one body'. O mystery of piety, O symbol of unity, O bond of love!" In the same sermon he calls the Eucharist quite simply "the sacrament of unity of the body and blood of Christ".[18] When he speaks of the Eucharist elsewhere he rarely omits to point out that the faithful, by partaking of the body of the Lord, become one with another, and part of the Church-body of the Lord.

This thought also inspires him when he is called upon for the first time to explain this the greatest of all sacraments to the newly baptized on Easter Sunday, the occasion being the second celebration which they were permitted to attend. It is to be noted that he does not speak of a real presence, though the whole Church of that time expressly believed in it, even if it did not give expression to this belief in its liturgical life; nor does he speak of participation in the crucified, resurrected and glorified humanity of the Lord, though his brother bishops in the East were alive to that. He only speaks of what he himself experiences in this mystery, namely, of men becoming one with one another and with Christ, and thus becoming of one body and one blood. It is this that is the general tenor of his explanation of the Eucharist. To the candidates for baptism he has nothing else to say in his explanation of the mystery. And what precisely is the effect of this sacrament? Augustine gives the answer to that question in a sermon on the Lord's Prayer to the *competentes*: "The Eucharist is our daily bread and our power for good, which is shown forth therein, is unity, that is to say, that we are made into his own body, and having been made into his body, we ourselves become what we receive."[19]

The "Amen" which the faithful pronounce when they receive the sacred elements into their hands and into their mouths, he looks upon as a confirmation of their devotion to the indivisible Church, an act of *social* loyalty. The deacon says, "Body of Christ", and when thereupon they answer "Amen", they are to say to themselves, Yes, we are all the one Church-body of Christ. "If you are then indeed the body of Christ," he says in one of his addresses to those who are making their first Communion, "then the secret of this mystery lies here upon the table, and you yourselves receive your own secret. Your 'Amen' is your declaration of what you have become. It is, so to speak, your signature, for you hear the words said, 'Body of Christ', and you reply 'Amen', and if this your answer is to be true, you must yourselves be members of Christ's body." "Christ the Lord has in this sign made an image of ourselves, for he desired that we should all belong to him in common, and in his own meal he has sanctified our peace and our unity."[20] This sacrament is "your bond, the bond of unity through which you are bound to one another as his body"—and for this reason, he continues, you must have a care that there are no divisions among you. Also, in that which is offered up he recognizes the totality of the one Church. "This is the sacrifice of Christians," he writes again, introducing the passage from St. Paul on many being one body in Christ, "and in the sacrament of the altar with which the faithful, being initiated, are acquainted, the Church continually experiences this; for in that which is offered she is herself most plainly shown forth, and is sacrificed herself."[21] Then he refers back to the very ancient simile from the *Didache*, the symbol of the grains of corn which, though once scattered over many hills, have now come together into a single piece of bread, and of the cup of wine, pressed from many grapes which have ripened in vineyards widely separated from one another.[22] From time to time he is almost overwhelmed by the thought of all the altars upon which the bread is laid and the fact that there is only a single meal among them all—the love-pledge of that one Church which, though spread abroad in innumerable places, yet gathers herself into a single unity, and which, though scattered over the whole world, is not divided. "How many portions of bread will today lie on the altars of Christ over the whole world?" he once cried upon an Easter Sunday before his congregation and the newly baptized. "And yet it is but a single bread and we all, despite our numbers, are but one body!"[23] Thus in the two sacraments of baptism and the Last Supper he saw the Christian community made visible and built up. Concerning the psychological (or, if you prefer, phenomenological) aspects of the process by means of which men are bound to another in the liturgy, Augustine said nothing. The experience of becoming one with many he certainly had, and most fully; and on the subject of the people joining in song he expressed himself in some sentences that are unforgettable. But he never attempted a theoretical analysis of the thing. Paul Valéry, writing of the pseudo-liturgy of our concerts, said something that has a considerable bearing on this matter: "It is the liturgical function which is brought into play when a whole audience melts into one, so that each part of this totality is the victim of the enchantment. And it is this gathering together of a thousand people, who all shut their eyes for the same reason, who experience the same raptures, who feel at unity with themselves and at the same time with so many of their neighbours who have now so completely become like themselves—it is this phenomenon which is the religious foundation for any living unity that exists in multiplicity, and is at the bottom of its unity of feeling." But Augustine, who so often felt his heart pounding in Church and his eyes filling with tears, distrusted that feeling and prayed only for better understanding. Even in the worship of God Augustine distrusted emotion and, as always, asked only for wisdom, intellectually apprehended.[24]

Essentials and Inessentials

As regards the actual scope of the cultus—or, which is for him the same thing, the actual number of the proven and authentic sacraments—Augustine only takes into account what can be referred back to the plenary councils and to Holy Scripture.[25] Not that it ever occurred to Augustine to set Holy Scripture up against tradition. He had had too much experience for that, for practice at that time, as indeed it is now, was based wholly on tradition. Even where institutions of supreme importance, like baptism and the Eucharist, could be proved from Scripture to have a divine foundation, there were many secondary features and local variations. Here there was only one criterion, the closeness of the approximation to the practice of the Universal Church, and in particular to that of certain famous metropolitan sees like those of Rome and Jerusalem, since these took pride of place as apostolic foundations and by reason of their revered traditional orthodoxy.[26] "When the whole world judges its judgement must be sound"—this applied to liturgical practice as much as to anything else. No individual teacher, no Father of the Church, however great he might be and however beloved, carried any weight against the universal consensus of the Church. The truth of this last lesson had been driven home by bitter experience, for during his struggle with the Donatists the latter had always justified their practice of rebaptism by Cyprian, who had held that converted heretics should be baptized afresh.

In his work on baptism Augustine has no hesitation in setting up the authority of the Church against his own spiritual father and countryman, and he formulates the essential antithesis between error and loyalty to the Church: "Have done with Cyprian's authority in the matter of second baptisms, but be edified along with me by Cyprian's example when he safeguards the unity of the Church." This question of baptism had at that time not yet been treated *ex professo*, and yet the Church was already following the salutary principle of "correcting in heretics and schismatics what was worthy of correction while not stressing that on which she was in agreement with them; of healing the wound, but not that which was whole." Augustine continues: "I assume that this habit derived from the tradition of the Apostles. Thus, there are many things which are not actually written down in their writings, nor in those of the councils of their successors, and were nevertheless looked upon as deriving from themselves, since they were things which the whole Church observed."[27]

In the early Church, in which doctrine and tradition, action and speech, sacrament and dogma so completely merged with one another, a bishop might not arbitrarily change a general practice, he might not assess lightly the value of any particular rite when this rite was authentic, nor might he over-value the rite when it was purely local. The most he was permitted was to introduce quite minor variations of customary practice, but its essential meaning had to be that which was determined by the universal Church, "for it is entirely just that the whole should have precedence over the part".[28]

In this letter to Januarius Augustine seeks to prove that apart from the sacraments of baptism and the Eucharist, the character of which no-one is likely to question, the celebration of the Lord's Day in place of the Sabbath and the introduction of the great feasts of Easter, the Ascension and Pentecost, are all founded on the mysteries of the life of Christ, and so based directly on

Holy Scripture.[29] Nevertheless, he looks upon the keeping of Sunday and the observance of the festivals of the ecclesiastical year as things duly ordained by the Apostles and the councils. Although he fills page after page in seeking to prove to Januarius, who has put a question to him on the matter, that the calculation of the date of Easter rests on a combination of sacred numbers which all refer to the symbol of the moon (which stood for the Church), and although he similarly explains the transition from Sabbath to Sunday by the significance of the numbers seven and eight, nevertheless here as elsewhere his observations on the holy seasons are essentially simple.

And indeed it was less difficult then than it is today to regard the cultus as essentially simple and illuminating. Word and meaning had not yet become divorced from one another. Symbols and commemorative celebrations had not yet become too far removed from what they referred to. The formalism of later times was still in the future; there were fewer accretions, and what there were were rudimentary. The liturgy of the ancient Christian basilica was like the basilica itself. It was like a roomy, solemn hall of festival, with lamps and curtains, but without statues or other decorations. It was not in the least like a late Gothic cathedral, filled to its uppermost corner with works of art and covered with the dust of many centuries, half-hidden in the dim light. Augustine belongs to the cool and roomy atmosphere of Sta. Sabina, not to the twilight of a fairy palace like the Cathedral at Milan. As to the commemorative festivals, the great Christian feasts, these were confined to the Christian week and the annual Easter cycle.

The week which had been taken over from the synagogue still reflected the six-day work (*hexameron*) of creation, with God's day of rest at the end of it. As such it was sung in the hymns of the Hours of Ambrose, and it contained, besides the Lord's Day, also the two ancient fast days, Wednesday and Friday. Saturday was not a day of fasting in Milan, nor was it such in most of the bishoprics of Africa, but it was treated as a fast day in Rome and elsewhere.[30] The Lord's Day was essentially the day of his resurrection.[31] Certain things which Augustine says in this connection go back to an extremely ancient tradition, which regarded the Lord's Day not as the first but as the eighth day of the week. Augustine's spirited observations on this point, which are duplicated in Ambrose and originally come from Origen, were in due course reverently copied down by his successors, but Januarius and the laymen of his day would only have heard of such views from the sermon of some initiated preacher, and though Augustine was fond of dilating on this subject from the *cathedra*, this teaching was not a recognized part of his people's liturgical possessions.

Sunday, so Augustine held, was not only the first day of the week, but also the eighth. The eighth day does not signify the transitory rest of the Sabbath, but the eternal rest of the life to come, of which the flesh itself will be a partaker after the Resurrection. Here he is playing with the gnostic and neo-Platonist idea of the *ogdoas*, a word which denotes not only the upper sphere of the heavens but also the τέλειος αἰών or νοητὸς κόσμος. After six times a thousand years of the present era there was to come a seventh thousand, the millennium of the Chiliasts. After this, again, there was to be a short empire of the demons, and then there would begin the new creation which is the era of eternity.[32] Then, he says, God will no longer rest in himself from his present creation, but from the new creation which he will bring about in ourselves, for it is he who is already working now through grace in his saints, and will only cease doing this when these have gone to their eternal rest. That was why the older Sabbath signified rest in this our mortal life; but Sunday signifies rest in eternity. For this reason the Jews ate their paschal lamb in the hour of Christ's death and before the Sabbath, while we eat our paschal lamb, Christ, on Easter Sunday, that is to say after the Sabbath, on this very "eighth day" in fact, the day after the great Easter Sabbath.

This sacrament of the number eight was also known to the Prophets. Examples are furnished by the practice of circumcizing on the eighth day and by the mysterious superscription over many psalms, *Pro octava*.[33] Augustine might have added that this was the reason why so many baptisteries were built in the form of an octagon, around an octagonal *piscina* surrounded by eight pillars; such buildings take their shape from the shape of perfection itself, and are a source of eternal life marked by the number of eternity. A poet—perhaps it was Ambrose himself—has made this thought the subject of a poem which can be seen on the baptistery of Thecla in Milan:

> Eight are the choirs in number that in this church were erected,
>   Eight are the sides of the pool, fitting the gift that it brings.
> Seemly it was in the builder to use this numeral holy
>   For the baptismal hall. Here may a people be saved.[34]

The ecclesiastical year contained in those days only a very limited Proper, actually only the Easter cycle, which still had a closed unitary character. As at the end of the second century and at the beginning of the third, so around the year 400 Christians were in the habit of thinking of one central annual feast in which the whole mystery of Christ was commemorated in one. This was Easter, and all that preceded or followed it was included in it. Nevertheless, about this time the commemorations of the different mysteries began to be differentiated from one another.

Augustine regards the matter as follows. The essential centre of the Christian year is the Pasch. Its time is mysteriously determined by the holy numbers, which in their turn connect it, by means of ideas deriving both from the Old Testament and the New, with the courses of the sun and moon. The term *sacramentum paschale* referred to three holy days, the Friday of the Lord's death, the Saturday on which he rested in the grave, and the Sunday of his resurrection—"sacratissimum triduum crucifixi, sepulti, suscitati".[35] This three-day Pasch is the climax and the dramatic turning-point of the sacred story, and in every year this very heart of the process by which our salvation is effected is treated as a sacramental thing and celebrated *in sacramento*. Then we come once again, as St. Paul says, to be crucified and buried with Christ and to be resurrected with him.

The word "pasch" does not come from πάσχειν, but from a Hebrew word that means *transitus*, or a passing through. It signifies a "phase"—"the passing through amongst us of our Lord". It is the passing through of all of us from death to life, from battle to victory, from expectation to fulfilment, from hope to rest—as St. John says, "We have passed over from death to life." This renewal of life occurs in us only through faith, for although we are only given the hope of things to come, nevertheless the new life has already begun within us, and from that moment onward the inner man "is renewed within us day by day".[36]

In theory Augustine still adheres to the sublime and movingly simple conception of Easter held by Irenaeus, the Alexandrians and Hippolytus of Rome and the majority of his Greek contemporaries, who saw the redemption of the world as one single great mystery, as a single great drama of the God-Man and also of the whole of humanity, a drama of which the resurrection to immortality formed the divine *catharsis*. Today the Churches of the East still hold this conception, for they too, in their view of the work of redemption, stress the fact that the process whereby we partake of the divine nature has already in principle begun, and it is this belief which finds expression in their overwhelming Easter celebrations. With us in the West, on the other hand, the celebration of the Christian mystery, the mystery of the Redemption, centres in the Cross, and thus, in the opinion of some, has become fragmentary and one-sided (though others again hold that it has been wonderfully individualized, purged of neo-Platonic phantasies, purified so as to accord with the Scriptures, and humanized). It is a little as if there were no end to the damaged condition of creation, and our expectation of a future harmony might never allow us to look beyond that condition; as though St. Paul had not seen creation, the whole cosmos, swept up in the resurrection of the Lord.

The fact is that, thanks to medieval theories of the nature of the Redemption, the most drastic of which can find justification in a number of passages from Augustine's own writings,[37] and thanks still more to the element of pathos that entered into our celebrations of the Passion, as these developed in the honouring of the relic of the Cross at Jerusalem, and later in the monasteries of the high Middle Ages, the Cross has gradually come to overshadow the shining grave of our Lord, and seems sometimes to obscure his glory. As against this, however, we can still discover in our present *triduum sacrum*, slightly distorted though it has become, all the essentials of the ancient pattern. We still worship in a shining basilica, though it may have been somewhat rebuilt on medieval lines and be filled with Baroque decoration; and in the sorrowful Matins of Easter Saturday there are still allusions to the mystical rest within the grave, allusions full of the savour of our eternal resting place, "where all tears will be wiped away from our eyes".

What is to be celebrated on each of these days, Augustine writes, is shown clearly enough in the Gospels—an interesting observation, as an example of the essentially historical approach; for indeed, the Christian story is a piece of verifiable history and not a mere timeless myth. It is, however, the Fathers of the Councils, he continues, who have determined how Easter must be celebrated, on which days and in which month of the year.[38] In answer to an anxious question of Januarius, whether the connection between the date of Easter and the course and changing shape of the moon might not compromise a Christian feast, Augustine comes out, as might be expected, with a flood of mystical figures. He apologizes for his pedantry. It all looks very complicated, he says, but there is really nothing in it; he simply happens to have studied the matter in his youth.

Actually, his exposition[39] is bizarre rather than interesting, and amounts, roughly speaking, to little more than the following. The moon may once indeed have been an object of worship (and indeed what African, seeing the sickle of the moon, could help thinking for a moment of the Dea Coelestis, the ancient Tanit, who in her turn was another version of the Phoenician Astarte, the symbol of all that somewhat ambivalent fecundity that beckons to men in the light of the moon?). But neither the fact that the moon has once been worshipped nor that it is recognized as a symbol, need compromise the Church. For all creatures can serve as symbols, both those of heaven and those of earth. Further, the moon is the symbol of the Church, for the Church, like the moon, is that true witness in the heavens of which the Psalmist speaks, and, like the moon, her face is sometimes darkened. This happens when, in the wicked children of Adam (of whom it is written that the fool is as changeable as the moon), she removes herself from the sun of righteousness—or, if this is preferred, when she holds back her light (Augustine, on this occasion, does not enter into the question whether, from the physicist's standpoint, it is more correct to say that the moon is lit up by the sun, or that it absorbs and gives out light).[40] Further, Easter falls into the first month of the lunar year—*mensis novorum*—because of the renewal of life through Christ. That the sun at that time stands in the Sign of the Ram is of no consequence, since the

Ram, though more suitable to that purpose than any other creature, does not appear as a *sacramentum* in Holy Scripture. Easter has its place in the third week because of the trinitarian figure three, which also determines the length of the three-day feast. The figure three also reminds us in which period we live, namely, the third; the first being that before the Law and the second that under the Law.[41] Finally, Easter falls between the fourteenth and the twenty-first day of the first month, and is thus related to two figures which are both determined by the figure seven.

The figure seven brings Augustine to that of seventeen, which, after fifty, is the great number of perfection, since both seven and seventeen are made up of one and seven, which together, once again, make eight.[42] The forty days of fasting relate back to Moses, Elijah and our Lord himself, that is to say, to the Law, the Prophets and the Gospels. They are the symbol of this life of toil, which is the *denarius* with which, under the four quarters of heaven and throughout the four seasons and in a world made up of four elements, we purchase our heavenly reward. Now, four tens are forty, and if we add the figure ten, we come to the heavenly perfection of Pentecost.[43] The season of Easter lasts fifty days, and this figure of fifty, in itself the symbol of plenitude (for it is seven times seven plus one), denotes our spiritual Easter, that is to say, the joys of heaven; for that is the final reward, the *denarius*, paid to us after the forty days' fasting, which is this life.

Being once on the subject, Augustine cannot refrain from explaining to Januarius the mystery of the 153 fishes in the Good Friday Gospel, for 153 is three times fifty plus three and signifies perfection in the name of the Trinity.[44] Finally, Augustine discourses in great detail about that sign "without which no sacrament can be ritually administered", the only iconographic symbol that had a really conspicuous place in the churches of that time: the bare cross without any figure upon it. He adds these expositions to those of the mystery of the *triduum*. The rest in the grave and the Resurrection refer to the life to come, in respect of which we can only have faith and hope; but the Cross refers to our life here below and we experience it in ourselves through selfless love. Each of its four arms has its own significance; the cross-piece with the outstretched hands denotes our happiness in our work, the upper part, our expectation of reward, the upright, our long-suffering patience, the part that is buried in the earth, the hidden Christian mystery, for it is written, "being rooted and founded in charity, you may be able to comprehend with all the saints what is the breadth and length and height and depth". Thus Augustine looks upon the extension of the Cross as a symbol of our moral life, and—how can it be otherwise?—of ourselves, who are nailed on the Cross with the nails of the fear of God, for it is written in the Psalms, "Pierce thou my flesh with thy fear", and again, ". . . having a desire to be dissolved and be with

Christ".[45] In this manner Augustine puts aside for the moment his objective tone in order to delight himself and his readers with a kind of edifying game.

At Easter, the day of the rebirth of all things, the neophytes also are reborn. For this reason the forty-day fast coincides with the last stages of the catechumenate, so that the octave of Easter is marked by the white garments of the *infantes*. In his letter to Januarius Augustine only makes quite casual mention of the octave of the newly baptized, but in his sermons during the Easter octave he never forgets to remind both his congregation and "the band of newcomers" within the *cancelli*, of the correspondence of their own status with both the transitory and the eternal Easter. This period of rejoicing lasts fifty days. The old name of Pentecost for the whole period was apparently no longer in use, but the seven weeks were still regarded as a single whole, despite the fact that the official holiday ended on Low Sunday, and that on this day the newly baptized put off their baptismal robe and their clean shoes along with it.[46]

With Easter was closely associated the memory of the Ascension,[47] and the season was not regarded as coming to an end till the beginning of the eighth octave, when there fell that "day of plenitude" which is called Pentecost today. In traditional fashion, Augustine sets the handing down of the Law on Sinai over against the outpouring of the Holy Ghost in that upper chamber in Jerusalem; in the first case God's finger wrote the Old Law upon tables, in the second that same finger of God, the finger of God's right hand, wrote the New Law with fire upon men's hearts.[48] Both Easter and Pentecost are founded upon Holy Scripture as firmly as upon a rock; the great fast, on the other hand, and the Easter octave of the baptisms, upon the practice of the Church; the singing of "Alleluia" during the fifty days of joy is found everywhere, though there are places where it is sung at other seasons than this. Augustine cannot say whether it is the universal practice to pray standing up during Easter and on ordinary Sundays, but it is clear that the Church does not favour kneeling at these times.[49] The fifty days of Easter, together with the forty days of preparation, form the actual Proper.

Other feasts than these have an altogether different significance. Christmas is of comparatively recent origin. It does not, strictly speaking, commemorate a mystery, but a particularly unique *natale*, a birthday, and one falling on a specially suggestive day. Augustine knows that it replaces the birthday of *Sol Invictus*, although this pagan festival was only celebrated at a few places and was originally a peculiarity of the Roman city calendar. This fact, however, seems to have been widely known in Africa, since Augustine says in a Christmas sermon, "Let us celebrate this day as a feast not for the sake of this sun, which is beheld by unbelievers as much as by ourselves, but for the sake of him who created the sun."[50] He also believes, however, that there is a reliable tradition which gives 25 December as the actual date of the birth of our Lord. According to this same tradition the birth of John the Baptist took place six months before the eighth day before the calends of January, that is, on the eighth day before the calends of July—which means, unfortunately, that it fell on the 24th, and not on the 25th, of June.

Broadly speaking, however, the feast of St. John coincides with the summer solstice and Christmas with the winter solstice. This fact does not particularly disturb the good bishop. He merely points out that at Christmas the days begin to grow longer and on the feast of St. John to grow shorter, a symbol to show that the one had of necessity to become greater, while the other had to grow less. He goes on, incidentally, to say some angry words about the fires made by gutter urchins to celebrate the solstice.[51]

Epiphany, the manifestation of the Lord, was in Augustine's view little more than a kind of counterpart to Christmas. In reality it was much more a feast of abstract ideas. "This star rose for us in the East", says Augustine, but "we celebrate it nevertheless for the sake of the unity of all Churches", a remark which is not only noteworthy because of the clever use of a double meaning in the Latin word for "star", but also because of the allusion to what was firm criterion for the acceptance of any particular custom, namely the consensus of all the Churches. It is because they do not accept this truth but believe that the true Church does not extend beyond Africa that the Donatists, those underminers of the unity of the Church, refuse to keep this feast.[52] Incidentally, the Epiphany is another feast which belongs to those *natalia* which are not celebrated as "sacraments" by means of a mystical dramatization, but as ordinary commemorative anniversaries.[53] The steadily growing number of these feasts includes also the innumerable anniversaries of the deaths of martyrs. Augustine's letter to Januarius shows that he paid but scant attention to these. They are, for him, secondary matters which have only local significance.

So the cycle of the year turns in the rhythm of the sacred numbers upon the axis which is the vigil of Easter, when life conquers death and new men are raised up out of the pools of life. This being the nature of the Proper, it must be admitted that it must have seemed appropriate enough to speak of the mysteries which Easter called to mind, and of the whole manner in which they were commemorated, as simple, and to point out in this connection how small was their number, for not even Augustine's manipulation of texts and numbers could alter the fact that the liturgy of those days still preserved much of its ancient and original character.

Augustine looks upon anything that cannot be referred back to Holy Scripture, to the councils or to oecumenical practice, as of minor importance. The content and reason for any particular practice interests him less than that it should proceed in a dignified and orderly fashion.[54] It is in this sense that he replies to certain questions of Januarius on this matter, and it is astonishing to see the number of things that he regards as secondary. For instance, there is the question of fasting. Some people fast on Saturdays, others do not. My mother Monica, says Augustine, discovered that people fasted in Rome on Saturdays, but not in Milan. When I told Ambrose of this, he gave me the advice to conform to the local custom, whatever it might be, and this I have done, for I entirely agree with him.[55] We have a very detailed letter on this subject which Augustine addressed to the young priest Casulanus in 397, in which he explains by means of a complicated mystical analysis why we fast on Wednesdays and Fridays, but not on Sunday.[56]

As to daily Communion, he says, some find this good; others do not. Those that hold the latter opinion say one should only communicate when one is well prepared, only on those days, that is, when one's life has been entirely pure and continent. Others say that it should only be done on Sunday, others again that we may do it on Saturday too. In all this, of course, the number of times Mass is celebrated in a particular place plays an important part. The grounds for the different opinions are equally varied. Some say that one should only approach so sublime a sacrament when one is worthy to receive it; others declare that if the pestilence of our sins is so great that we feel we should refrain from seeking this means to our salvation, we must submit to the authority of the bishop concerned and ask him to impose a penance; this may, it is true, mean that we are for a time forbidden to approach the altar. What we must not do is to act according to our own judgement and the mood of the moment. One can see that there was a regular debate going on, and one that vaguely recalls *De la fréquente communion*, though mercifully the arguments seem to have been marked by greater brevity.

Augustine's view is as follows. Personally, he says, I am for daily Communion. If anyone has not actually merited the Church's ban, there is no reason why he should deprive himself of the daily physic of the body of Christ. I do not, however, wish to force my views on anybody, and, to put an end to this dispute, the best thing seems to me to be to enjoin both parties to remain with one another in the peace of Christ, and to let every man do what seems best to his own conscience. Zacchaeus joyfully brought the Lord into his house, but the centurion said, "Lord, I am not worthy that thou shouldst enter under my roof." These two men did not quarrel about their respective opinions; they both were in emulation with each other in honouring the Lord; and, he says, I can understand the attitude of either.[57]

Bathing on Maundy Thursday—why, he is asked, is this the universal practice in Africa? It means that on this day there is no fasting, for bathing and fasting cannot be combined. Elsewhere the practice does not obtain. Is it obligatory? Well, says the bishop, my own opinion is that this bathing is a survival from the period following on 313, when there was a perfect flood of converts. In that period there were so many candidates for baptism who had all not bathed for forty days, and who wanted to have a good wash before the baptismal rites on Easter eve; and the result is that since then everybody washes on that Thursday and puts on clean linen.

In that case should Mass be celebrated once on that day or twice, and should the second celebration take place in the morning or the evening? For the evening Mass has been specially arranged for those that have fasted. Now, the practice in this matter varies from place to place but the determining factor seems to be whether people bathe and dine or whether they don't. Admittedly, there are some people who say that at least one Mass should be celebrated after the *coena*, because it is written, "Simili modo postquam coenatum est." Augustine says, however, that this last argument is nonsense. As regards the twofold celebration, he claims that the one in the morning is for those who do not intend to fast and who wish to take a bath, while the other is for those who have kept up their fasting till late. These people do not bathe, but they have their *coena* late and then go to church afterwards. As to this last, he says, the practice of celebrating the Holy Sacrifice in the evening and of communicating after partaking of food is founded on the memory of the Last Supper, which was celebrated after the meal. Naturally, however, we force nobody to eat before partaking of the evening Eucharist.[58]

Another question arose. Why did certain bishops undertake the washing of the feet of the newly-baptized not within the octave of Easter but on Maundy Thursday? Augustine answers that this was no doubt because these bishops did not wish the faithful to look on this ceremony as a completion of baptism, and had changed the time for this reason. In his opinion this was a most excellent idea.[59] On another occasion, to explain the washing of the feet, he brings in an allusion to the words of Jesus that he who has taken a bath must still wash his feet, if he would be completely clean. This washing, he says, is a symbol of our readiness to do penance, which, even after baptism, must continue to wipe away the dust of life's highway from the feet of the Christian pilgrim.[60]

In both letters he expressly says that he cares very little about the fact that such secondary ceremonies should vary from place to place. Let people observe the local practice, whatever it is, for the matters concerned here are never important. He says in this connection, "In regard to all such matters where there are variations of practice, such questions as whether we do or do not fast on a Saturday, whether we should communicate daily, or miss a day, or communicate only on Saturday and Sunday, or on Sunday only, we are completely free to make our own choice. The best rule of conduct for the earnest and intelligent Christian is to follow the practice of the local community, wherever he happens to be. For whatever does not offend against faith or morals should be regarded as indifferent, and local practice should be followed out of regard for the community concerned." Similarly he says in the letter to Casulanus, "Where Holy Scripture lays down nothing definite, the usage of God's people and the decisions of our predecessors should be treated as law."[61]

In this connection he comes to speak of the value of ecclesiastical tradition, where secondary matters are concerned. "As to your enquiry concerning the solemnities of Maundy Thursday," he says, "my reply is that when something is prescribed by the authority of divine writings, we must never hesitate to do what we read therein, nor should we enter into arguments about the exact manner in which these instructions are to be carried out, but, rather, seek to understand the mystery that is hidden here as best we can. Our attitude should be similar when the Church follows a certain observance the whole world over. Then, too, it would be presumption, nay, it would be madness to spend time discussing whether one should conform to it or not. However, neither of these two conditions applies to the question raised by you, for we are here dealing with practices which vary from one place to another, and here everyone should follow the custom of the local Church, whatever it may be; for none of these things offends against the Faith and they are all equally morally indifferent, whereas our duty of introducing innovations or improvements only arises when faith or morals are at stake; for the altering of a tradition, even when in itself salutary and useful, is liable, because of the very element of novelty, to cause confusion. All the more harmful, then, is the disturbing effect of a change that serves no good purpose."[62]

An example of a practice which is both oecumenical and useful is fasting before Communion. In this Augustine sees the breath of the Spirit and he will not allow this custom, which is universal in the Church, to be called in question by an appeal to Holy Scripture. "It has pleased the Holy Ghost that in honour of so sublime a sacrament the body of the Lord should enter the mouth of a Christian before any other food. Even though the Lord himself partook of it after a meal, this does not mean that the brethren are not to meet together for this sacrament until they have partaken of their midday or evening meal. Even less should it follow immediately after a meal, after the practice of the people of Corinth, whom the Apostle rebukes and corrects. The Saviour partook of it when he did because he wanted it to be the last act that he performed before setting out upon the way of his passion, so that he might thereby stress the greatness of this mystery and cause it to be imprinted all the more deeply on the hearts and memories of the Apostles. Nor did he give to these any precise directions as to the manner and time of partaking of the

13 Jonah (fragment of a sarcophagus, Louvre, early fourth century)

14 *Lipsanotheca* from Brescia (?370)

sacrament, preferring, as he did, to leave the regulating of all these matters to those same Apostles whose task it was to be to establish order in the Churches. If he had enjoined them always to take the sacrament after eating other food I cannot believe that anybody would have dared to change this custom." It was on the strength of the authority thus vested in him, he says, that St. Paul could write concerning this part of our worship, "The rest I will set in order when I come."[63]

But ecclesiastical and apostolic tradition does not concern itself with things of secondary importance. On that point Augustine leaves no room for doubt whatever, though in applying this principle he shows a certain caution. "I cannot approve", he says, "the introduction of what might be called pseudo-sacraments over and above the customary ones, even though out of regard for certain holy but rather difficult people I refrain from criticizing such things too sharply. Yet I cannot help deploring the fact that people so often pay little regard to those things which are prescribed for us in Holy Writ for our salvation, and are nevertheless so full of preconceived ideas about trifles that they are more prone to be shocked by a man who, during his octave as a neophyte, touches the floor with his bare feet, than by one who buries his reason in drunkenness. My own opinion, therefore, is that all such things which are not covered by the authority of Holy Scripture, nor determined by episcopal councils nor confirmed by the usage of the universal Church, but are practised in the most diverse ways according to the custom of diverse places, so that one can never really tell the reason why some particular custom has been introduced—my opinion is that these things should be abolished, wherever this can be done, with as little delay as possible. For although one may be unable to find anything in such practices that is contrary to the Faith, they nevertheless weigh down religion with a servile ballast, whereas God's mercy desired that it should be free. Otherwise the state of the Jews would be more bearable than our own, for although these have not purchased their freedom, yet at least it is the weight of the Law that bows them down, and not the pretensions of man. Nevertheless, the Church of God, being filled with much chaff, and having many weeds growing round about it, is ready to tolerate much, even though she will not suffer what is contrary to faith or morals, nor accept it nor pass it over in silence."[64]

These powerful words, which must have been devoured at Port-Royal and which would certainly have delighted Calvin, if only that last sentence, with its most catholic "Ecclesia multum tolerat", had been struck out, provide a most unmistakable expression of Augustine's personal attitude. He was not the man to have much regard for what might be termed pseudo-liturgical practices, or who would have looked on with pleasure as the severe simplicity of the old Christian liturgy blossomed out into a scented medieval pleasure-garden. Here he is for a moment the father, if not actually of the Puritans, then most certainly of the Cistercians and Trappists—and, let us frankly admit it, of the best of the Jansenists. That his African Church was concerned for the purity of the *lex supplicandi* is shown by the number of conciliar resolutions that seek to preserve the healthy and traditional liturgical style.[65] There can be no doubt that Augustine was the moving spirit behind more than one of these proceedings, and it is Augustine's spirit that speaks through many a dry ordinance and many a simple prohibition of some popular custom.

And yet that process which compels a living organism to grow and form a multiplicity of branches was certainly not viewed by him with hostility. He yearned for no bureaucratic uniformity. When, in that long letter to Casulanus, which he wrote before he became a bishop, he touched on the subject of Saturday fasting, he showed plainly enough that he could see a good side to the variation of practice between one place and another. What is the point, he wrote, of getting all wrought up about the question whether it is better to fast on Saturdays like the Romans or to abstain from fasting like the Orientals? What is the point of getting excited about the question whether Rome alone has preserved the apostolic usage of Peter, from which the other Churches have departed, or has denied the tradition of Peter, while Jerusalem and Ephesus have preserved the usage of James and John? We shall never get to the bottom of the matter, so why not make an end of this fruitless dispute? Then the Faith will be one under the different observances, all of which leave its truths untouched; for "all the glory of the king's daughter is within", and it is this very diversity of usage to which the Psalmist refers, when he sings of the garment of the royal maiden who is the Church, and who is "clothed around with varieties".[66]

Sacraments as Sacred Symbols

What does Augustine understand by a sacrament? First and foremost, a sacred sign. This ancient word *sacramentum*, once used in reference to the military oath, had in Africa long had a wider and specifically Christian significance, that of a ritual symbolic sign. The term, in other words, suggested not only a rite but also a sign which both veiled the truth and revealed it. In every case it suggested some holy reality which the symbol held fast, and since Tertullian's day this somewhat elastic word, which once had had so many shades of meaning, had more and more become a synonym for a μυστήριον.

Augustine is primarily concerned with the sacrament's function of being a sign. Every holy sign—every sign, that is to say, which the words either of Scripture or of the Church refer to things divine—he calls a "sacrament".

"It would take us too far", he writes to the pagan Volusianus, in reference to the sacrifices of the Old Testament (which God did not require for himself but merely intended to serve as helpful signs to men), "it would take us too far to give here a comprehensive exposition of all the diversity of the different signs, but if they relate to things divine, they are called 'sacraments'."[67] There are thus two things with which he is concerned when formulating his conception of what constitutes a sacrament: the holy reality to which it refers, and the fact that it is a sign of that reality. The word "sign" here is used in the sense of a symbol. A sacrament is something which has a meaning beyond itself, a "visible word". "The word comes to the element and it becomes a sacrament."[68] In a sacrament God writes the words of his revelation, like a schoolmaster writing upon a blackboard, and so makes them plain and unmistakable.

Now, all things can serve as signs. Indeed, according to Augustine's neo-Platonic philosophy, every word was a sign, the meaning of which became apparent to our minds either through the memory of some impression which our senses had received in the past, or by pure reason. Its characteristic was that it awakened our spirit to some higher reality; and the higher that reality, the better known it is to us, he says, in the realm of the spirit. For we apprehend the deepest realities like "old acquaintances"; otherwise we could never love a person or a thing at first sight, for love is the flaming up of memory.[69] In symbols we speak of symbols of other symbols, which are ultimately all related to one another in the imperishable highest reality which is God. The cosmos, which is ordered according to number and measure, is a world of progressive approximations to originals, so that the relations between things are not determined by direct causality alone, but by the extent to which they partake of the nature of the originals which they copy. If we reflect that this was the typical mental background of the age, it becomes easy to understand that it should come quite naturally to Augustine to write, "Many creatures serve us in the nature of likenesses, so that the divine mysteries may thereby be represented. Christ is called a Lamb, a young Bull, the Lion of Judah, and a Rock, and the Church the Mount of Sion. Not only from among earthly things but from the heavenly bodies, such as the sun and moon, the images showing forth the mysteries are chosen, their function being to signify to us a mystical truth ["ad informationes mysticas"]."[70] The symbols which are thus given a sacred meaning are called "sacraments".

The part which these simple images, and the even simpler elements, play in their capacity of signs, is that of indicating and revealing. "The signs of things divine are visible, but we honour in them realities that are invisible."[71] They are therefore true symbols, visible signs of things that not only are invisible, but cannot be made visible. In this way, in the Gospel, the wine jug, bread and water represent refreshment, food and cleansing that is purely spiritual. They are the visible clothing of mystical truths. In much the same way the literal sense of inspired texts of Scripture covers the true but hidden meaning with a simple but significant veil. Like the wise Donatist Tyconius, Augustine regards Holy Scripture as "an immeasurable forest of prophecy".[72] This forest is nowhere bare; everywhere there is the same dense foliage of inspiration, and from all the tree-tops of it there rustles the one word, "Christ".

The miracles in the Gospels also play this part of signs. They are the first dramatizations of the secrets of salvation which were later revealed. "A man was sent to the pool of Siloam. Could Christ not have opened his eyes without spittle? He certainly could have done this, but the actual circumstances of the miracle are, so to speak, the words of the sacrament."[73] Actually, this beautiful thought, which Augustine expresses when discussing the symbolic actions of Christ with the blind man, is attributable to Origen, but thanks largely to Ambrose, this general conception had, by the year 400, for some time been common property. We find it unmistakably present in certain rites that have grown customary in baptism and at the Eucharist, for instance in the *ephpheta*, in the touching of mouth and ears with fingers and spittle, in the breaking of bread and in the blessing of the chalice. This idea also dominates the iconography of the third and fourth century in Italy, Southern Gaul and the neighbouring lands. It governed the choice of subject among the artists of the oldest catacombs and among the carvers of sarcophagi in Rome, Arles and Africa. There we continually find the man who was blind from birth and the man who took up his bed as the classical symbols for baptism for the forgiveness of sins; the miracle of the loaves, with their baskets full of pieces, and the miracle of Cana, symbolize the Eucharist, while the healing of the woman with an issue of blood, as well as the adoration of the Magi, show forth the calling of the pagan world.

Those who cannot see beyond the external and visible quality of the sign and who cannot progress beyond the literal meaning of the words of the Bible are to be pitied, for in both instances it is right to say that while the spirit enlivens, the letter kills. As against this, the least of symbols, if understood, can greatly uplift the spirit, for it was for this purpose that the things of this world were created.

The fact is that Augustine the sometime Platonist is already wandering in a wholly symbolic medieval world. When he looks upon the heavenly bodies and thereby reflects upon the words ". . . and let them be for times and seasons, and for days and years", then his thoughts do not turn so much to their time-determining functions in the natural order; rather does he see in their ordered course a symbol of Christ's government of his Church, and hears with the ears of the spirit the harmony of the Apostles' choir, or again, the regulated progress of those stars becomes the emblem of the Christian's undiverted path.[74] On another occasion the stars will call to his mind those mystical numbers by which also the way of our salvation is shown forth, and by which the courses of the stars are themselves determined. Even the most humble objects here below can serve to make our spirit rise upward. "Not only the heavens and the stars, but even the lesser creatures, provide visual symbols for the communication of the mysteries. There is a kind of eloquence in the truths of salvation which enables it to lead those who seek truths from the visible to the invisible, from the fleshly to the spiritual, from the temporal to the eternal."[75]

The Power and Limitations of Symbols

It is in the nature of a symbol to uplift the spirit. The very fact that it has more meanings than one gives it a mystical elevating power. Symbols and allegories are the natural means of directing men to the divine; they are, indeed, the natural signposts. The symbolic representation of the mysteries of the Faith has the effect of a burning torch which is thrown into the inflammable substance of our spirit.

In a discussion in which Augustine dilates on our duty to put the temporal behind us and to desire the rest not of the earthly but of the everlasting Sabbath, he uses these words:

> To nourish and, so to speak, to breathe upon, this fire of love so that we are drawn into it and lifted up by it towards our everlasting rest, this—
> —mark it well—is the sole purpose of any kind of symbolism. For that which is borne in upon our minds by means of symbols moves us more strongly and tends more to awaken our love than what is presented to us as a bald fact and not in the language of mystical signs. It is difficult to say why this should be so. Yet it is true that everything that is made known to us by way of allegory affects us more strongly, moves us more deeply and tends more to excite our reverence. My own opinion is that our sensibility is not inflamed to the point of real fervour while it is still enmeshed in the concrete. Once, however, it has been lifted up by means of symbols out of the realm of the material and carried into the sphere of that spiritual truth to which these symbols refer, then this very transition causes it to be caught up and set on fire as though by a torch, so that with a more violent, yea, more burning, passion than ever before, our soul hurries towards that state of rest which is only to be found in the ultimate contemplation of eternal things.[76]

There are other passages where he speaks of the importance and effectiveness of this indirect method of communicating truth. How many passages in Holy Scripture, he remarks on one occasion, seem to possess this quality of holding a hidden secret! That is just why we call them mysteries, but it is just this expedient of talking in riddles that "sharpens our love for the truth and causes us to shake off our indolent refusal thereof". How true this is we can teach ourselves by seeking to disentangle some truth from an allegory,[77] and then observing that this same truth, if it were directly and simply presented to us, might not have impressed us to anything like the same extent. It is the habit of Holy Scripture "not only to feed our souls openly with truth but also to teach us by means of a hidden truth; for the same things are often presented therein both in a form in which we are able directly to apprehend them, and also in the form of hidden allusions. In this way, so that we may not grow weary of what has been directly revealed, a truth that has been plainly set forth is shortly thereafter covered over again and is thus endowed with a fresh attraction for our minds, so that we learn the lesson with increased pleasure. In this salutary fashion the troublesome are corrected and small spirits are nourished, while great ones are provided with a source of delight."[78]

Nowhere does he describe so clearly the why and wherefore of this psychological fact as in the passage already referred to in the second letter to Januarius. The essential feature in a symbol is not its charm but its ability to uplift, for this causes our spirit to be turned away from the material towards the immaterial. What the symbol really brings about is a transition or leap. It is the leap from the superficial to the deeper meaning, the sudden lifting up of one's mind from a lower to a higher order of truth. This *transitus* we may aptly translate by the word "transport"; it is the emotional quality that is the essential characteristic of the kind of intuition which the symbol brings about, for man is naturally moved by the contemplation of truth.

Here Augustine touches the essential structure of religious experience as such, for the two factors which combine to determine this are, first, sensitivity to symbol—to the symbolic power of a word, that is, behind which there looms a higher truth; and, second, the desire for oneness with the First Cause of all things. It is noteworthy, however, that Augustine seems to take the view that blindness to symbols in matters of faith does not result from a certain natural endowment, or lack of it, neither is it simply the characteristic of a certain type of mind; he is quite certain that it must be ascribed to a man's selfish and uninhibited surrender of himself to his lowest instincts. Those who cannot look upward and whose gaze cannot penetrate beyond the material are those who delight in fixing their minds on the chaos of their lusts. Eyes which are clear can see. Those that have been wilfully dimmed can see no longer, "and if your eye is no longer clear can you have aught save darkness within you?"

Myriads of creatures whose material nature is uncomely nevertheless, because they are signs, participate in God's perfection, and have a part in the plan within his mind. For this reason they are good, beautiful and true, while even the doings and interrelations of fallible and imperfect creatures here below are a reflection of the relations of things imperishable. Admittedly, our powers of perception can take in nothing of the former, and are confined within their own world of immediately recognizable objects (for a light falls on the soul from above and not from below, and that which can be immediately apprehended, we recognize from the light given by our inner teacher).[79] And being thus limited to the apprehension of the material world, we only bring our minds to bear on a world of shadows, and lose ourselves, as it were, in the different shades of a mist. Yet for all that, these frail, fleeting and so typically changeable things that are in themselves of so little account, are creatures of God. As such, they are both good and real, though their reality is of an impermanent kind and is like the notes of a chord that sound for a moment in harmony and then pass away. Thus it is that these shadows have value and meaning, for they are the last, nethermost and outermost reflections of the everlasting reason which is at the kernel of creation the outermost vapour around the shining cosmos. The reason why things exist, therefore, is to show forth the divine nature under a circumscribed form, and in this sense to be a sign and a likeness—*similitudo*—of a divine mystery; to be, each in its appointed place, an indication or symbol of a divine intention, or, to put the matter in more concrete form and in the terms of revelation, an indication of an element in the economy of salvation.

We find this idea not only among the neo-Platonists, but among all true poets, from the Pseudo-Dionysius (in whose writings the good Richard Hooker found an excellent weapon against the oversimplifications and degradations of Puritanism) right up to the Symbolists of last century. "Holy things which can be perceived by the senses", says Dionysius, "are images of that which can only be spiritually perceived and are to these last both the signposts and the way." "In certain almost supernatural states of the soul," says Baudelaire, "the whole limitless depths of life are revealed in the drama which is before our eyes, even when that drama is itself quite commonplace, for it becomes the symbol of something more profound."[80]

It cannot be otherwise. The picture which we behold is gradually filled with a religious content. Much as all problems of the philosopher sooner or later lead him round to theology, so the poets discover the existence of a divine mystery behind the symbols of ordinary experience. Sometimes it happens that from mere intuition they pass on to the full light of the Faith, and from poetry to prayer. It is also noteworthy, as Chesterton somewhere points out, that the language of religious symbolism is never precious or artificial, but is, on the contrary, the one really simple thing that poets use, for though religious symbols have more to say than profane ones, they are nevertheless very simple themselves.

The same author points out that the true Christian symbols deal entirely with the relations between God and man, and always assume a personal God. The Way, the Truth, the Light, the Word—these things are not abstractions, but refer in a most concrete manner to the person of Christ himself. He also has this to say: "Wherever men begin to talk much and with great solemnity about the forces outside man, the note of it is barbaric."[81] This last remark is especially true of Augustine, who so significantly exchanged the lofty imprecisions of neo-Platonic theosophy for that direct relationship between God and man which centres in and about Christ. Despite the fact that his whole language of symbols is based on the phenomena of nature, Augustine never speaks of Nature, but only of men and the three divine persons. His universe is moral and spiritual. Nature, which the inherited treasury of his language so often induces him to bring into the picture, is nevertheless, so to speak, not spelt by him with a capital N. Nature is for him merely something that ancient usage has made to serve by way of an allegory.

Augustine's theory of the uplifting power of the symbol appears to us today to be an insufficient explanation of the true nature of a sacrament. Indeed, it does not even approximate to it, for it takes regard of only one of the aspects of a sacrament, its function of serving as a sign; and one gains the impression that he completely overlooks the true character of its efficacy, for he never mentions this at all. Also, in the δρώμενα the emphasis is all on the symbol and not on the rite, though in Africa the meaning of the word *sacramentum* had for two hundred years embraced both elements, and had, indeed, firmly combined them. Like so many of his theories, however, this one was closely connected with his conception of the progressive ascent of the soul to the contemplation of God—a legacy, this, of his neo-Platonist youth, and one which, though it was purified by the study of the Scriptures, remained with him to the end of his life. It is a highly personal and somewhat visionary point of view, and it makes him see the cultus, even though he regards this as an essentially simple thing, as a vast allegory that continues in the style of Revelation—a Holy Writ way of looking at things that fits in admirably with the typological interpretation of Scripture and with the general neo-Platonic conception of the universe, but which the reality behind the means of grace in the New Testament can easily transcend. The actual sacraments, as we use the term, appear, in Augustine's writings, as a number of particularly holy and effective allegories of the process of salvation, but they do so in the company of a thousand others that are not sacraments at all, but mere signs and indications. All boundaries become blurred and the whole of creation is transformed into a mystical ladder into heaven which is erected within the narrow scene of a man's own soul.

Above all, it is a theory which argues a profound poetical experience and an emotional attitude that is highly personal. This does not surprise us in a man who said, "If I could know thee, I would know myself." His whole thinking and his whole piety had long been moving between these two poles, God and the soul; indeed, in the period immediately following his conversion this was the essential pattern of his thought: "God and the soul!—I would know them both. Nothing besides? Nothing besides!"

His personal contact with God he experienced first and foremost in himself, and he experienced the existence of God chiefly in the contemplation of his own soul. There was the picture that most resembled the Creator. To know God one must descend into oneself and know oneself. Like Plotinus, he thought that with the help of the reflection in one's own soul one could rise upward towards that which it reflects, yet in distinction from that most religious philosopher, he knew as a Christian that this ascent must begin with a sense of the vast gulf between the original and its image, and with a realization of one's own misery; in other words, with humble self-knowledge. Not even in honest introspection, but only in a sense of one's own helplessness and dependence, lay the beginnings of true wisdom.

Now, it must be observed that however much this theory of Christian perfection is permeated by the wisdom of Holy Scripture, its starting-point still remains self-knowledge. For this reason, despite a certain objective terminology, it never progresses beyond a kind of subjectivism, any more than does his theory of illumination through Christ the inward Teacher.

It is no mere chance that Augustine, this man who continually pours his heart out and praises God out of his innermost soul, should be the creator of the language of Western piety. Till Bernard of Clairvaux, he was the fieriest heart in the Church; with him begins the true "histoire littéraire du sentiment religieux". His piety was essentially an inner piety—particularly in the first half of his episcopate—and he thus often creates the impression that he attaches less importance to the outer rite than to the inward realities which these produce in him, or of which the rites are a reflection. And this seems true whether we regard those inward realities as the workings of divine grace, or as purely human feelings that correspond to them. Sometimes the rite seems a gift of God to which the soul responds; at other times it appears to be regarded mainly as a means of expressing religious feeling. Sometimes it appears as a device for coming to the aid of man's passionate striving for happiness, a purpose which it achieves by awakening faith, hope and charity within him; then, again, it is one of the steps by which men of restless heart ascend towards their ultimate rest in God. Finally, however, every prayer, every effect of grace through word or sacrament, begins and ends in the sanctuary of the heart, to which God alone has access. The fact is that he is entirely governed by the ideal of the "happy life", and that he never gave up this eudaemonist notion of complete self-development; and this turned all his discernment into a kind of inner eye, and caused him to turn that inner eye unceasingly upon the mirror of his own consciousness.

Some of his most beautiful utterances attract us precisely because of their heartfelt tone, that *tour dévot* which was rare in that period of eternal arguments and subtleties. It is this tone that makes him appear so like the great religious geniuses of the sixteenth and seventeenth centuries, and makes it plain why he was so popular in those times. When he speaks of the true *latria*, his words sound as though this was carried out entirely in our hearts. "Because what is upward belongs to him, therefore our heart is his altar. [*Sursum cor*] We are reconciled with him through his only Son, our Priest. We bring him bloody sacrifices when we fight unto blood for the truth. We waft sweet incense to him when we burn with pious and holy love before his face. To him do we give back his own gifts that are within and to him do we make a gift of our own selves as well. To him, when we celebrate the great feasts and keep the appointed days of remembrance, we dedicate the memory of the good things he has done to us so that at no time an ungrateful forgetfulness may creep in. To him do we offer the Host of our humility and praise upon the altar of our heart in the fire of glowing love. So that we may see him as he should be seen and may cleave to him, we are cleansed from all foulness of sin and of all evil desire, and are consecrated to his name, for he is the fountain of our salvation and the goal of our striving; and the good, that ultimate goal concerning which the philosophers dispute so ardently, is nothing else than the act of cleaving to him."[82]

This is the unchanging theme of his piety. "My happiness is to cleave to God." The cultus is a *pietas*, a θεοσέβεια, an act of shy and hesitant love, for "God is honoured by those that love him".[83]

Augustine was of a theocentric nature. He certainly did not overestimate the value of the external cultus. There has surely never been a man who was further removed from formalism.

Symbolism and Realism

Augustine was, it is true, a man whose gaze was continually fixed, as by a spell, upon his own abundant inner life, and one full of unceasing anxiety for his own salvation; yet the very business of the cure of souls made him a defender of the external and objective and turned the symbolist into a realist. Ever dissatisfied with himself and finding no rest within his own being, his soul was unceasingly being driven towards the divine centre of things, and yet in every crisis it turns outward to the objective. Then he accepted God's ordering, to which the creature must submit. When a crisis arose he showed himself to be a man of order and authority; indeed, he showed himself something of an authoritarian. It was no mere chance that from the time of his baptism in the middle of his life he began suddenly to speak with a quite peculiar clarity and force of the objective character of the effects of the sacraments. It was the necessity imposed by his war with the Donatists, with their perversion of the whole sacramental doctrine, that caused him to make his own views about the sacraments precise. The issue at the parish level was not only what the disposition of men's souls should be when they received a sacrament, but also, and even primarily, the validity or otherwise of baptism, the question whether this rite had any real sense or meaning at all; for if the effectiveness of a sacrament depended on the moral condition of the person administering or receiving it, why had the Church, despite the fame of her martyr Cyprian, so persistently avoided second baptisms and set her face against that heretical practice?

It was ever his concern to reconcile within the great reality of the Church those two apparently contradictory things, holiness and visibility; the effectiveness of what was divine and the insufficiency of its human administration. He saw that insufficiency less, of course, in the actual visible objective means employed by Christians than in the subjective state of the visible administrators. Yet it was impossible to call in question the very instruments of salvation, for the whole visible Catholic Church stood or fell by their objective validity. How could a man believe that this validity depended upon the sanctity of whatever person chanced to be administering them? Did such a person own the sacraments? Were they his property? Of course not. Nobody had any rights over them except the Church, and the Church vouched for them on the strength of a divine command. For the Holy Ghost works only through the true Church.

This is his solution: the sacraments can be valid even outside the Church and in evil members, but what they give depends on whether the recipient has the love of the Holy Ghost. "What then is the sacramental gift in baptism, the Eucharist and the other sacraments? This gift was even received by Simon Magus." Saul too was a prophet, and the means of grace can be received externally by the wicked; but those whose dispositions are not good receive them in vain. They do not receive the spirit, for they have not in common with us "the love that is poured out by the Holy Ghost into our hearts". Therefore they will hear, when the time comes, the words "I know you not."[84]

Men are fallible, not the sacraments. Men are unworthy, but the sacraments are not therefore invalid. For the holy signs are not there merely to teach us; they are not only indicators of a mystery outside themselves. They place that mystery before us and actualize it. This is true of a "sacramental commemoration" like Easter, which is not merely a recalling of the Resurrection that followed after the Passion, but "signifies" also our own transition from death to life, although that is a thing that here below we can only apprehend through faith and hope, and one that will only truly become real on the last day.[85]

All this is particularly true of the two most important sacraments, baptism and the Eucharist, since these, according to Augustine, are filled by a much greater spiritual reality. They are something more than signs or symbols that hold a Christian community together, and something more than mere memories of the baptism and the last supper of our Lord, for they cause one of the facts in the process of our salvation to be re-enacted in the faithful. They continually place before us and actualize that fact. Nor are they simply "mystical signs that proclaim the sufferings and resurrection of Our Lord which now belong to the past".[86] What they do is this: they cause a historic event in this process of salvation to be actually present as a means of the individual salvation of every one of us, and so "insinuate the spiritual gift" which "the divine power makes effective by means of them".[87] Translated into modern parlance, they are channels of the grace they signify. The sacraments of baptism and of the laying-on of hands at consecration constitute an initiation which is not repeated, for in them something is handed over once and for all; they imprint a mark upon the soul that is imperishable, like the branded mark upon a soldier.[88]

The signs which the *sacramenta* provide resemble the realities they represent; that is why they take the names of those realities, and one may often speak of the sign as of the reality, for the sign which acts as a symbol for something becomes an actual channel of that which it signifies. It is worth noting how strongly Augustine underlines this last. In his letter to Bishop Boniface in which he deals with the well-known difficulty about infant baptism —how can children who cannot even speak become members of the body of the faithful when they have as yet no faith?—he adduces impressive proofs of his beliefs. Indeed, he does this at some length, quoting his dead friend Nebridius, "who detested settling important problems with a hurried word". That being so, it seems only right to quote him in entirety.

> When Easter is before our door, we often use such an expression as "The passion of the Lord tomorrow" or, "The passion of our Lord in two days' time", although in point of fact this passion took place many years ago and only happened once. Similarly, on the Lord's Day we say, "Today is the day of our Lord's resurrection", although in actual fact many years have passed since he rose from the dead. Why is nobody so foolish as to give us the lie on this account? Obviously because they know that we give this name to this day because of its similarity to the actual day on which these

events took place.... The day takes its name because it corresponds in the year's cycle to the actual day of these happenings, and because the *sacramentum* of the feast causes us to speak as though a particular thing was happening on this day when in point of fact it really happened a long time ago. Christ himself was only offered up once. Yet is not Christ offered up for the people, not only at Easter but daily in the *sacramentum*? And surely, if a man were to be asked whether he was truly being offered up and were to say that this was so, he would not be lying. For if the *sacramenta* had not a certain resemblance to the things whose *sacramenta* they are, they would not be *sacramenta*. It is because of their similarity to the things they represent that they usually take their name from those same things. As, then, the sacrament of the body of Christ is truly his body, and as that of his blood is truly his blood, so the sacrament of the Faith [by which he means baptism] is the Faith itself. Faith is, after all, nothing but the possession of faith. And if one who is standing godfather to a little child answers, in reply to the question put at baptism, that the child believes, although that child can as yet have no consciousness of the Faith, then in giving that answer he means that it has the Faith through the sacrament of faith. In similar fashion he answers [probably when giving the responses concerning the renouncing of the devil] that it is converted to God, and he means by that answer, which he must give for the completion of the sacrament, that this takes place through the sacrament of conversion. For the Apostle himself says that "we are buried together with him by baptism into death".[89] He does not say, "We have made a representation of his burial." He did not wish the sacrament of so great a matter to be known by any other name than that of the matter itself.

Thus it is that the sacrament of faith makes this little child one of the faithful, even if this does not happen after the same fashion as it does with men who have desired the Faith of their own accord. In the child's case the answer of the godfather that it believes makes it one of the faithful, though it does not assent to the matter with its reason. It suffices that it has received the matter's sacrament. When it reaches the age of reason, it need not repeat the sacrament, but it must seek to grasp its meaning and endeavour by means of its will to adapt itself to the truth thereof. For so long as it is incapable of doing this, it remains protected by the sacrament against the powers of evil. The sacrament is also effective in another manner, for should the child leave this life before it has attained the use of its reason, it is nevertheless, thanks to the power of the sacrament, and through the recommendation of the Church's love, saved from that damnation which came into the world through the failing of man.[90]

Rarely has the objective effectiveness of the sacraments been more clearly explained or proved by more original arguments than in this passage, the importance of which did not escape the medieval theologians. True, the full and complete formulation of the Church's doctrine is not yet present, yet nobody could mistake Augustine's meaning; the signs represent the gifts that they themselves bestow and bestow what they signify. As commemorative rites, the sacraments cause to be present among us one of the mysteries by means of which our salvation is effected. In baptism they sacramentally re-enact the death of sin and the arising of the life of grace, and also cause these things truly to take place. In the sacrament of the altar they cause the sacrificial death of Christ to be truly present, while on the great feasts the mysteries once more become realities.

If the recipient of a sacrament should have grown weak in his faith, the Church is there to vouch for the sacrament's validity through her own words of faith. Now, this word of faith is an essential element. There is a passage in Augustine in which he writes in regard to baptism, "Whence does the water obtain its peculiar power? Through the word, but not because that word has been spoken, but because it has been believed." He also says in this connection while commenting on the words "Ye are pure already, because of the word I have spoken unto you", "Even in the water the word purifies. Take away the word and what is the water but water? But the word comes to the element and it becomes a sacrament and so in itself a word made visible."[91] He also speaks in a similar sense elsewhere about the word and the element of bread.[92] In all this the fact that the element is made truly holy is due to the Spirit which works through the medium of the Church, and will only work through the true Church. Outside the true Church the sacrament may indeed be found, and it may be in all respects a true sacrament, yet despite its validity it cannot there bear any fruit of holiness. That is why Augustine can also say in reference to the bad Christians within her own community and the heretics outside it, that the Church has indeed borne them but has brought them into the world in vain, and that it would have been better for them if they had not been born at all.[93]

Just how this process of sanctification takes place through and within the Church Augustine does not know, and in his great work on baptism he makes it especially clear in regard to infant baptism that he cannot grasp how in the circumstances the sacrament becomes effective, though it has never occurred to him to doubt the usefulness of a practice that has been in existence for centuries, and one that Origen, even in his day, had already declared to be of apostolic origin.[94] His defence of baptism as such, however, convinced him that the sacrament worked a true sanctification and left an indelible mark, and that this was true even when little children received it—despite the fact that these, not having yet attained the age of reason, could not yet live by a faith made effective in love. Indeed, so far from "believing with their hearts and confessing with their mouths", a thing of which even the penitent thief was still capable, they often greeted the mystical words with howls and screams at the very moment when the mystery was being completed.[95] During his battle with the Pelagians, who denied original sin, and who therefore necessarily looked upon infant baptism as senseless and were consequently the continual objects of Augustine's criticism, he wrote some words the meaning of which is quite unmistakable. The Lord, he said, pours the grace of his spirit in secret even into the hearts of little children and makes them part of his body. It is the Church that brings them to birth from the baptismal pool. She is the Lord's bride, and she does this through the potency of his spiritual seed. "Mother Church does this as a whole. As a totality she brings them to birth both individually and collectively."[96]

What distinguishes Augustine's thought from that of the Middle Ages is that the functional and symbolic characters of the sacramental symbol are not yet separated. In this particular matter Augustine would have got along much better with the modern psychologist, who would see the symbolic aspect of the sacrament not as one among a number of characteristics but as the vital element in the whole rite.[97] As against this the psychologist would say that Augustine looked upon the symbolism of the sacrament too much and too exclusively as something designed to act upon the understanding. Another and rather more superficial difference between Augustine and later theorists lies in the fact that the word *sacramentum*, as used by him, was not yet confined to the seven actual sacraments, but was used for many other things of the most diverse character. Thus it is used, as in the letter to Boniface quoted above, for the annual commemoration (we might even say "representation") of the Redemption, for the daily actualization of the sacrificial death of our Lord and for the putting on of our dead, buried and resurrected Lord in baptism, a thing that is done once and not repeated.

There were no real differences of opinion concerning the Eucharist, but because the Donatists had torn the body of Christ (which is the Church) in twain, Augustine felt impelled continually to remind the faithful of the true nature of this sacrament, which he represented as the sacrosanct bond of love, peace and unity, to which no man may do violence. Its presence upon all altars amounted to a continuing silent but divine protest against schism. How could men who partook of this same body in order to become themselves parts of this one body, tear this body of the Church apart?

Augustine's conflict with the Donatists thus explains his extremely strong emphasis on the social function of the Eucharist. And this in turn affords an explanation of the surprise and disappointment experienced by many when they come to read his most heartfelt outpourings concerning the sacrament of the body of Christ. The line of Augustine's thought is wholly in a direction which they do not expect and which they cannot, perhaps, accustom themselves to grasping, even with their best efforts. He wrote at an epoch when the worship[98] of the body and blood of Christ consisted simply in reverent reception, handling and consumption; at such a time men had not yet adverted to the idea of looking for the factual presence, which can be continually worshipped, behind the signs which they grasped and the means of grace of which they availed themselves. And in consequence the words *figura* and *signum corporis Christi* sounded otherwise in their ears than they do now.[99] Thus in his debate with Adimas the Manichean, in which he had occasion to prove that the biblical injunction to refrain from eating the blood of a beast ("for the blood is for the soul") is to be taken symbolically, he writes, "Even the Lord did not hesitate to say, 'This is my body', although he only gave us a sign for his body."[100] Yet when on one occasion he speaks of the symbol or sign of the body and blood of Christ and on another of the actual body and blood themselves, then these are the expressions of two convictions simultaneously entertained, which in no way exclude one another. It is not a case of ideas vacillating between two extremes, that of an inspiring and spiritualizing symbolism and a traditional realism. It is merely that a consistent body of ideas finds varying expression. There is absolutely no reason to suppose that Augustine, who speaks of this mystery in such a matter-of-fact way, conceived of it otherwise than, say, the author (almost certainly Ambrose) of those mystical catechisms contained in the two little books, *The Mysteries* and *The Sacraments*, when he compares the transformation of the elements with the transformation of the water into wine at the marriage in Cana with that of Moses' staff into a serpent, and with other marvellous transformations in the material world. Augustine does not do this but he does, on one occasion, draw the attention of some of the newly baptized to the transformation of the bread and the wine, and compares it to the equally invisible and yet equally real transformation which has taken place within themselves.[101] For Augustine, as much as for anybody, this sacrament is the very secret of the Church's heart, the hidden secret of the living community. "It is the sacrifice of the New Testament," he writes to the catechumen Honoratus, "and it is only after your baptism that you will learn how, when and where it is offered." Even the newly-baptized *infantes*, who see the secret thing lying upon the altar and partake of it together after the celebration, do not know the true origin or manner of it.[102] It is surrounded by a wall of silence and the whole matter takes place behind closed doors. Everyone knows that it is our daily physic against human weakness—and indeed some take it as a corrective against bodily ills—but only the initiated know the real inwardness of it.[103]

15 Baptistery at Cuicul

16 Font at Cuicul

Naturally Augustine employed the terminology of his age, and it should be remembered in this connection that the expressions "sacrificial meal" and "sacrificial repast" are of relatively recent coinage, and not wholly in keeping with the spirit of the early Church. Concerning the identity of the sacrifices on the altar and the cross, Augustine is acquainted with no other theory than that expressed in the simple words that the Lord is "sacramentally offered up every day", and that his death "is made sacramentally present among us", but we must remember that he grew up familiar with the ideas of sacrifice and altar and that in the main he uses the same words as we do ourselves. Though there may have been a shade of difference between the way he experienced sacrifice and communion and the way we feel today, he lived them, nevertheless, just as we do. As far as the Real Presence is concerned, it nowhere appears that he experienced this affectively, that he meditated on it or had devotion to it; such an attitude was foreign to that age, at least in the West.

He is not a medieval man; in connection with the sacrament of the altar he does not yet think of identity with the glorified risen Lord; he does not yet know a "Eucharistic Christ". It does not occur to him to approach immediately the human form of the Lord behind the appearances, to throw himself directly, tenderly, at His feet, and in the deep human emotion of this encounter, to forget the sacramental veil, even to misunderstand it and thus change it into an instrument of new and limitless self-abasement. And yet he was taught the same things that we learn ourselves. He knows that there is no greater mystery, and that man, in receiving it, is like Zacchaeus, who was afraid to take the Lord in, or like the centurion, who held that his roof was too unworthy for the Lord to enter under it.[104] The Eucharist is the "flesh which no-one eats before adoring it", "the same flesh that walked here upon the earth and was taken from the flesh of Mary and is therefore earth of this earth. That is why the Psalmist can say, 'Adore the footstool of his feet', for this footstool is the earth" (these words are taken from a celebrated passage which he has almost literally transcribed from his teacher Ambrose).[105] When he reads in his Bible how David acted like a madman before the gates of Gath, that "his face was changed", and—to use the expression in Augustine's ancient text—he "carried himself in his hands", and when he then asks himself what the spiritual significance of this passage can be, he thinks immediately of David's antitype, Christ, at the Last Supper; for when Christ spoke the words "This is my body", he was in a certain sense carrying his own body in his hands, and Christ too changed his face in his humility, and in that humility gave us his body and his blood, for had he not been humble he would not have suffered himself to be eaten and drunk.

As a mother turns the food for her children to milk within her own body, so the Son of God, by becoming man, has turned, for us men, the Word, the food of the angels, into the milk of the Eucharist.[106] And the rich who receive Christ "in the body of his humility but do not follow him" are like those "rich of the earth" in the psalm, who "have eaten and adored"—for no man can refrain from adoration—whereas "the poor shall eat and be filled".[107]

In another passage he speaks with more restraint. In his book against Faustus, who had ventured to compare the Manichean celebration with bread and chalice to the Catholic sacrament, he says: "Our bread and our chalice are not just the first ones we happen to get hold of, nor do they come into being in the order of nature; they do so mystically by reason of a permanent consecration, and whatever does not come into being in this mystical fashion, even when it is bread and a chalice of wine, is ordinary food which is consumed, but is no sacrament of religion. First it must be blessed, and God must be thanked for all his gifts, both spiritual and temporal."[108]

Augustine often contrasts the visible sign with the invisible reality it represents, and the sacramental with the historic reality: " 'It is spiritually that you must understand that which I have spoken to you'—so said the Lord to the Apostles, 'who were troubled'; it is not this body which you behold that you must eat, nor is it the blood thereof (which is shed by those who crucify me) that you must drink. I have entrusted a sacrament to you that will give you life if you understand it spiritually. For although it is celebrated in a visible form, it should nevertheless be thought of as invisible."[109] The command to eat is "a symbolic expression. It enjoins us to remain partakers in the sufferings of our Lord and so to do honour to the sweet and salutary memory of the flesh that was crucified and wounded for our sake"[110]—all of which is a most felicitous reference to the apostolic injunction to remain partakers of the sufferings of Christ and also to that other command, "Do this in remembrance of me." The act of eating is itself symbolic and spiritual, though the body is real, and we do this eating not with our teeth but with our hearts: "Why do you trouble about your teeth? See that your soul is in good condition."[111]

There are other passages in Augustine in which he resorts to an even greater realism. In expounding the meaning of the blood of Abel, the blood that cries to heaven, his thoughts turn to the blood of Christ that cries louder than that of Abel, and accuses the Jews of fratricidal murder, both in Holy Scripture and in the Eucharist. He continues: "The blood of Christ has a mighty voice here on earth, for when they have partaken of it, all the peoples cry: 'Amen.' That is the unmistakable voice of the blood. The blood of its own accord cries out from the mouth of the faithful whom it has redeemed."[112] That blood is upon every altar whence the holy Victim is distributed, "blotting out the handwriting of the decree that was against us".[113] "Christians celebrate that sacrifice that was completed by Christ for the fulfilment of all the other sacrifices which had prophetically shown it forth, and they do this by means of the holy presence among them of the body and blood of Christ, and by partaking thereof."[114] He also sees the body and blood of the Lord in the fatted calf of the parable, which is offered up to the Father and provides a feast for the whole house of the Church.[115] The Father had desired no sacrifice, yet he had prepared a body for his Son, and it is this body which is now offered up, and is distributed to all who assist at the sacrifice, even if they are unworthy.[116] And with a certain splendid simplicity he says, in the twentieth book against Faustus, in which he speaks of the relation between the shadowy sacrifices of the Old Testament and the sacrifices of the Cross and the Eucharist: "Full often do we offer up sacrifice to God in the memorial churches of the martyrs according to that rite which, by the revelation of the New Testament, he has placed us under the duty of observing. This rite belongs to the cultus that is called *latria* and which is due to God alone. The flesh and the blood of this sacrifice was anticipated symbolically, before the coming of Christ, by the slaughtering of beasts. In the sufferings of Christ the true sacrifice at last took place. After his ascension into heaven we celebrate it in this commemorative sacrament. Thus the difference between the sacrifices of the Jews and that of the pagans is that between an anticipation which resembles the reality and one which does not."[117]

These occasional flashes are, however, really secondary to the idea which time and again illumines his mind—namely, that through the eating of Christ's body and the drinking of his blood we become one with him and with each other. This sacrament is the bond of unity, peace and love; "it is our own mystery that lies on the table of the Lord".

For Augustine the cultus was essentially built up on the *sacramenta*. He was convinced that it had always been so and did not feel the need to say much about it. The cultus, as such, had not yet become a problem. It was not till the circumstances of a heated controversy compelled him to make them so that his formulations became more precise, his whole attitude more carefully considered, his expressions more concrete. This occurred not only in his public disputations but in his utterances from the *cathedra* and during catechism, where in any case learned abstractions are of little use and things have to be called by their proper names. Here, indeed, he was concerned less with the Eucharist and more with the sacraments of baptism, extreme unction and the laying-on of hands; for the Eucharist was uninterruptedly repeated, whereas baptism, extreme unction and holy orders were sacraments that were only administered once, and the worst offence of the schismatics was precisely that they repeated these sacraments. Small wonder that Augustine used time and time again to paint in glaring colours the confusion that these errors brought about, and did this even for the benefit of quite simple souls. Again and again he reminds them that the validity of a sacrament has nothing to do with the worthiness of the recipient, and explains to them that such a sacrament, though unworthily received, could still regain its effectiveness; nor did he hesitate to use the most drastic examples to drive home his theory of the indelible mark. When arguing with Julian of Eclanum, who made light of the supernatural reality in the sacrament, he praised the realistic language of the Punic peasants, who when they wanted to speak of baptism or the Eucharist, simply used the words "salvation" and "life".[118]

Yet when he was not seriously concerned with any question of actual error, he gave full freedom to the playful side of his mind. Then, particularly when dealing with the symbolic side both of the genuine sacraments and of those other things which he included under the term, he delighted in those harmonies of number, word and idea with which he was so often preoccupied and which so frequently seem strange to us. If we desire a correct picture, we must remember this, and we must also keep in mind the fact that his most lively imagination seizes on illustrations as it goes along, combines allegories and cheerfully employs the first analogy (invariably a brilliant one) that comes to hand to prove his point. Further, we must call to mind that everything that he says or writes springs from the intuition of the moment rather than from any firm theological theory. If we take all this into account, we shall soon get used to those apparent contradictions which alarm the more prosaic type of reader but which, for the more poetically inclined, are a never-ending source of astonishment and delight.

11

AUGUSTINE'S LITURGICAL PRACTICE

ADMIRERS of Augustine's theoretical brilliance cannot but be struck, when they turn their eye to the humble realities among which he worked, by the sobriety of his liturgical practice. The verbal luxuriance of his symbolic interpretations is here offset by an almost puritanical simplicity. A description of the Augustinian liturgy leaves one feeling miles removed from a world that cultivates *la religion de la pompe attendrissante*. Indeed if one were to seek a word that expressed the atmosphere of that time better than any other one would probably choose the opening words of Compline, "Fratres, sobrii estote et vigilate"—"Brothers, be sober and vigilant."

THE PURITANICAL TRAIT

Augustine has not a word to say about the splendours of the basilicas. It is most rarely that he even mentions the heavy draperies, vessels of silver and gold, the bowls and vases, sieves and chalices, the lamps and candelabra, which, according to the schedule of a confiscation order respecting the church at Cirta, had been part of the customary furniture of any urban church for at least a hundred years.[1] We hear, it is true, that on one occasion Augustine did what Cyprian had done (and somewhat later Ambrose), namely, that he had the precious vessels melted down to provide ransom for a number of prisoners.[2] He had little taste for the splendid attire that might have been held to suit his high office, and usually told those who presented him with it that he would certainly sell it;[3] whether this disdain extended to liturgical vestments we cannot say. Even this last is probable enough, however, for in those days even the higher clergy wore their ordinary clothes at worship, or at best a white festival garment. Without making any distinctions between one another Augustine and his housemates would, when occasion arose, take a cloak from the communal rack, and all wore the same uniform tunic made of ordinary wool.[4]

He cared little about the decorations in his church. Every historian of art knows the fun he made of the stupid fellows who actually thought that Christ had written letters to Peter and Paul, because they were represented in so many places with letters in their hand. That, he said, was the kind of thing that happened when people sought Christ "not in the holy codices but on painted walls". The allusion here is clearly to those representations, which we know so well from Italy, of the theme "Dominus legem dat", representations in which the Lord is shown handing to the two Apostles a partially unrolled scroll[5] (Plate 12). On another occasion he says, "The fleshly appearance of our Lord is most diversely imagined and represented and yet it only took a single form, whatever that was. We do not know what it was like, and we know as little of how the Virgin Mary looked. Moreover, as regards the Faith which we have from our Lord Jesus Christ, the salutary thing is not that our imagination should form a picture of him, for such a picture may well be far from the reality, but that our understanding should make it clear to us that he was a man." We do not know, he says, what he or his mother looked like but we know that he was a man and born of a virgin.[6]

He dislikes pictorial representations of things that are divine. On the words "Sit on the right hand of the Father" he comments as follows: "He who interprets this right hand in a human sense is in danger of becoming guilty of the blasphemy of those who, as St. Paul says, 'confuse the glory of God who perisheth not with the picture of man that perisheth'. Such a misleading picture of God must not be set up in a Christian temple, still less in the heart, which is God's true temple."[7] That the plastic arts could be gravely abused in this connection is proved by the case of Marcellina, an adherent of the gnostic sect of the Carpocratians, who burned incense in her house before the ikons of Jesus, Paul, Homer and Pythagoras. This anecdote, by the way, bears a suspicious resemblance to that other one about the *lararium* of Alexander Severus, where, next to the statues of the divine emperors, of Apollonius of Tyana, of Abraham and Orpheus, there was also a statue of Christ.[8]

In his old age he writes angrily to his opponent Julian of Eclanum, "You make fun of me because I am supposed to have learned from paintings that Adam and Eve had shown feelings of modesty. For my part, I did not learn this from painters of vain pictures, but from the Writer of divine writings." Because Julian, who maintained that our feelings of modesty came from nature and were not the result of the Fall, explained the view objected to by referring to the lines of Horace

> ... as of right, from now on at all times,
> Poets and painters dared to touch whatsoever might please them

Augustine added that even a poet or a painter could not have talked him into such a piece of impertinence. Even those people, he says, who, as it is so charmingly put, may dare anything they please, would be ashamed to think of anything so ludicrous and fantastic (despite the fact that it apparently expresses your own opinion), and no painter would dare to treat lust and innocence as though they were in the same category.[9] Rather exceptionally, his anger at this attack does not express itself in any unfriendliness toward artists, who invariably depicted Adam and Eve with one hand modestly upon their fig-leaves, a convention which can be seen in many remains.

That the honour done to a picture was really intended for the person it represents is in Augustine's view (to the considerable satisfaction of Calvin) a typically heathen argument, and he sets his face against it with a determination that, in a neo-Platonist, seems astonishing; but in this matter the philosopher was subordinating himself to the somewhat prejudiced Bible student. Actually, he is less concerned here with Christian art (which as yet had not produced much and confined itself to portraits, historic scenes and relatively unpretentious symbols), and is really thinking of the pagan pantheists, who declared that behind the idols and most certainly behind such mighty manifestations as the sun, the stars, the sea and the earth, they merely worshipped the *numina* that govern these things, of which the things themselves are symbols. But, says Augustine, however seductively such people may talk, it is still a lie to give a picture, which is a work of human artifice, the name of one of God's creatures, and even if it were not so, the adoration of a picture is equivalent to paying divine honours to a creature. In actual fact, however, one can see from the practices of such people that their cult is directed to the picture of gold and silver rather than to what is behind it, for they pray with their face toward the statue of the sun and their back to the sun itself, and with their eyes upon Neptune and their back to the sea. We Christians, who also use golden vessels, call them holy, but we only regard them as having become so through the use to which they have been put in celebrating the mysteries; we know that they have no hands or ears or eyes and we do not adore them; we merely use them in adoring God.[10]

A puritanical, one might almost say a dour and resentful, note towards the fine arts marks a number of utterances of his later years. In his *Retractations* he refers to his early writings defending the deeper significance of the Plotinian myth (and also to his glorification of aesthetics) as mistakes, and calls the myth itself "a stupid, tasteless fable". The love of beauty referred to there had only to do with aesthetic trifles and was therefore by no means the twin sister of philosophy.[11] Where literature was concerned, however, his own nature was stronger than his theories; he spoke of wanting to know no more of these "glittering vanities", but his words are contradicted, and that in a very pleasing manner, by the fact that from sheer force of habit he continually quotes his favourite authors.

Painting and the plastic arts, however, have their business settled by him in one short phrase. He says that their achievements may on occasion be considerable, but that they are entirely superfluous.[12] The pagan artists merely helped to keep lewd stories in circulation,[13] while the Christian ones (so no doubt he thought) did no more than divert men's minds to no purpose. The fact is that he obviously cared as little for the plastic arts as for painting. However it must be admitted that the last was at that time purely decorative, and in Italy and Asia Minor largely served the purposes of historical documentation. Nevertheless, we can well understand that Calvin was only too pleased to play up Augustine's somewhat ill-tempered remarks and use them to contradict the saying of Gregory the Great that pictures were the books of the uneducated.[14]

As a pupil of the old Platonists he was acquainted with at least one theory of aesthetics, but the whole point of this was that it sought to transmute aesthetic experience and express it in terms of a purely rational process. Naturally, therefore, it damned any notion of art for art's sake, and looked upon any consciousness of beauty that could not be expressed in terms of something other than itself as mere animal enjoyment. In his early work on music he seeks to give a scientific interpretation of music by a theory of rhythm and intervals; this provided a kind of key to principles of harmony, which could be mathematically deduced and which, in their turn, were a reflection of the cosmic harmony of the spheres. None of this, however, had the least connection with singing or playing or with instruments or composition.

As to the fine arts' function of creative imitation, Augustine regarded this at best as a form of decent technical proficiency, a mere artisan's kind of excellence. He rejects all delight in beauty of form as such, "for thieves get their pleasure in just the same way". It is true that sculptors express something that divine wisdom expresses in a beautiful body, but all this does not amount to much and should not be overrated.[15]

Beauty is essentially transcendent. What we experience of it in the sensible world is nothing but a weak reflection, a *vestigium* (though that *vestigium* is nowhere absent, even in what we call the ugly and the formless); and it is that footprint that the artist invariably uses all his skill to mark and stress. Some of this sounds rather like a theory of expressionism, and shows us that Augustine was conscious of the relative and complementary character of beauty and ugliness, light and darkness, and of the intervening territory between formlessness and form (an attitude which, based as it was on the optical perceptions of shades of colour, was, according to Alois Riegl, typical of late Antiquity).

But all this is only to be found in the works of his youth, and even there it only occurs as a sort of reminder of the general principle that all created beauty is a thing reflected and derived.[16] For the "footprint" of beauty is, strictly speaking, nothing else than that mysterious form[17] by which unity is given to all individuals which bear its mark, and which dwells in a creature, such as a tree, and also in a work of art, such as an architecturally successful building. In the last-named case it does this because of the inherent rhythm of its construction and the felicitous ordering of its parts, factors which in their turn reflect the mathematical ordering of the world; while in living creatures the unity of form is the expression of the soul, which gives it unity and life. The essential element of beauty is therefore unity; and the key to a work of art, the secret of its beauty, by getting on the track of which we get at its real inwardness and are able to explain it, is its rhythm; by means of this rhythm we become sensible of its unity. In its wanderings through earth and sky the reason feels that nothing can satisfy it except beauty, which means beauty expressing itself through the individual forms, the forms giving expression to it by their proportions, the proportions, through their *numerus* or rhythm. Let it be noted, however, that the wanderer is not sensibility but reason; and the result of this wandering is that Augustine elevates the essentially inferior order of natural phenomena to the superior level of geometrical forms and thereupon reorders the latter into mathematical and geometrical systems.[18]

It would almost appear that sculpture alone was excluded from the dignity with which all pictures and symbols are endowed. If Augustine, in his early works, found himself under the necessity of illustrating his theories by reference to one of the arts, he tended to turn to architecture. His prejudice here does not derive from prudery, for a distaste for the nude was alien to him—he took the free and easy ways of the baths as a matter of course. Rather did it rest on a philosophical conception, namely his distrust of mere splendid appearances. It was a characteristic that made him dislike anything in the nature of ostentation. Even the spikenard of Lazarus' sister only has value for him because of its mystical and prophetic significance.[19] His prejudice against artists as a class, and above all against the musicians who were engaged for banquets and for the cabarets, was also due quite as much to his Platonic heritage as to the low social status of this kind of person.

Thus Augustine's religious experience was never a matter of feelings or impressions, and the external forms of the cultus are never valued aesthetically by him. The remarks that come naturally to our tongues when we leave a Benedictine abbey after Vespers, or after hearing a Mass by Palestrina, would have been alien both to the nature of his work and to his time. Never once does it occur to him to say that it had been a beautiful service, or that the singing had been particularly good, or the worship particularly impressive. Round about the year 400 the Church for the first time possessed in Prudentius a poet who could sound the echoes of the newly revealed divine harmonies on the traditional instrument of Pindar. She has, however (at any rate in the West), not yet found the time to take delight in the laying out of her pleasure-gardens. Paulinus and Prudentius sing of what is in their hearts, or biblical happenings, of the fame of the martyrs and the folly of the heathen, they sing of the piety of the people and perhaps of the brand-new buildings over the martyrs' graves, but never in any sense do they really lend their poetic gifts to the cultus, nor are their verses ever a reflection of Christian art.

To judge from the utterances of the Greek Fathers, one would not think that there was such a thing as primitive Christian art at all. Atticists like the Cappadocians and Asterius of Amaseia draw the usual comparisons between the expressionism of contemporary Christian painters and the dramatic power of a Polygnotus, a Zeuxis, a Euphranor or any other of the ancient Hellenic celebrities, whom, because of their more sober use of colour, people would praise as the very antipodes of such Greek impressionists as Callimachus and Kalais. (Nobody, of course, was actually acquainted with the works of these "Old Masters"; nevertheless, their works belonged to the accepted classical heritage.) It was not realized that the new themes synchronized with an actual rebirth of art.[20]

Undeniably Augustine the artist sometimes gives himself away. He is continuously using the word "beautiful" and even when he is dealing with something that he wants to treat as a purely intellectual problem, he conceives of the matter in bodily terms. Why does a man have such strange, superfluous things as a beard and nipples? Because they make for beauty. God gave them to the body not because they were necessary or useful but as ornaments. "Take away the nipples from the male breast and you will see how much that is beautiful you have removed and how much ugliness you have brought into being."[21] In the *Confessions* he says that in those moments when his love of God is most intense, it is as if he were conscious of a shining light, a melody, a taste, a perfume, an inward embrace.[22] The poor bodily covering trembles and is illuminated when God condescends to touch our spirit. Is this not exactly what he experienced in Milan when he burst into tears at the sound of the singing?

> Alors de toutes parts un dieu se fait entendre;
> Il se cache au savant, se révèle au coeur tendre:
> Il doit moins se prouver qu'il ne doit se sentir.[23]

In his professed and stubborn resistance against any mere carrying away of the reason by beauty there may well be a protective instinct at work, for it is impossible not to feel that in the liturgy he did not "feel God in his heart". And on the eve of Easter, which was observed with the same intensity of devotion and with the same splendour as in old Russia, this man who was always an artist at heart completely betrays himself, for he is full of delight at the fantastic illumination of his church, which, with its hundreds of hanging lamps and packed masses of people, must have provided a picture not unlike that to be seen in the mosque of Sidi Okba (which was to be built soon after this is not far from Hippo in Kairouan) when the new moon marked the end of Ramadan. Then he shows all his accustomed skill in weaving those lamps and flames into his metaphors, his sermon being sometimes one long play with the idea of light. He builds a hundred delicate bridges between light and virtue, illumination and knowledge, the arising of the light and divine renewal, spiritual progress and clear sight. Then he speaks of the Father as the Source of light, and of the Son, the Reflector of his glory; then baptism is simply spoken of as illumination, for its symbol is the opening to the true light of the eyes of those who have been born blind, the opening of the eyes to that light which can illuminate every man that comes into this world.[24] The very light that falls on them seems to determine Augustine in the choice of his texts: "Night shall be as day. For you were heretofore in darkness, but now, light in the Lord . . . Arise, be enlightened, O Jerusalem, for the glory of the Lord is risen upon thee . . . For God, who commanded the light to shine out of the darkness, hath shined in our hearts . . . Night shall be my light in my pleasures . . . Enlighten my eyes, that I never sleep in death . . . Covered in glory, thou didst come down from the summit of the everlasting mountain."[25] Doubtless it was necessary that Christ should be resurrected in the night, since by his resurrection he has lightened our darkness, for not without cause it was sung of him so many years ago, "Thou, O Lord, wilt cause my light to shine. Thou, my God, wilt lighten my darkness."[26]

No doubt the fact that he actually heard these texts being sung may have been an added inducement to quote them, yet it is no mere chance that almost in the same breath he describes the gleam of the lights in the church, a spectacle which obviously moves him considerably. Even the indifferent, he declares, must feel uncomfortable and disquieted on this night; the very heathen are ashamed, and seekers after truth cannot sleep through tension. Indeed, he says, all men must needs watch with us through this night, because even if they take to their beds they cannot close an eye.[27] Then joy and triumph quite overpower him and he cries out, "What large and manifold multitude has this feast not called together in every place! The sun has gone but not the day, for a shining earth has taken the place of the shining sky. God, to whom we cry, 'Thou wilt lighten my darkness', that God is now lighting up our hearts. With delighted eyes we behold the gleam of these lamps, and thus, with an illuminated spirit, we can understand the meaning of this shining night."[28]

On at least one occasion he succumbs to the temptation to allude to a picture (which seems to have been in the chapel of St. Stephen built by

Eraclius) of the stoning of Stephen while Saul holds the garments as "a very pretty piece of painting", and he uses it in his sermon—which may well have been given when the chapel was consecrated. In this sermon, after pointing the contrast between the lamb Stephen and Saul, "the tearing wolf Benjamin", he turns to the end of the chapel and addresses the two painted or possibly mosaic figures "who look down upon [us] all and have themselves heard all my words" and, in a moment where he has once again become the rhetorician, asks them for their intercession.[29] Augustine also knows how many are the places where the moving picture of Abraham's sacrifice is to be seen, with Isaac on the altar while Abraham is startled out of his terror by the heavenly voice. This picture once moved Gregory of Nyssa to tears, and he has described it with such exactitude that we can recognize it feature by feature on the monuments. "Isaac is cowering on one knee upon the altar with his hands tied behind his back, while Abraham stands close behind him and with his left hand draws up the boy's hair. He bends over forward and looks into this face that in so pitiful a fashion looks up into his; the right hand, holding the sword, is raised, ready to deal the deadly thrust. Already the sword's point touches the body and it is only at that moment that the call reaches him in the name of God, the call that prevents the deed." Augustine knew these representations: "These sublime happenings have been sung by so many lips and depicted in so many places that nobody can be ignorant of them, even those who act as though they had never noticed these things." To judge from this, Augustine himself can hardly have been greatly moved by what he saw.[30]

And what has Augustine to tell us of the world of the basilicas? The answer is, "Nothing." It is by the purest chance that he makes any remark at all about the basilica in which he happens to be preaching. On one occasion, for instance, he was preaching in the huge basilica at Carthage. The words of Psalm ciii, "Thou stretchest out the heavens like a pavilion", which he was expounding, seem to have made a particular impression on him, for he looked about him and said, "Consider this huge building. Every individual workman was only responsible for a part of this vast roof, and yet every such workman has expended enormous trouble and pains on his task"—but God has stretched out the whole of the heavens like a skin—and even that is only a figure of speech, for God does this entirely without effort.[31] Apart from such incidents as these, however, Augustine has no eye for churches. Thus, when he is preaching at the consecration of a new basilica he hastens from the dead stones to the living congregation; then, after a few perfunctory words of praise, he leaves the subject of the earthly building and hurries on his way to the Jerusalem of the world to come.

The Singing of the People

There was, however, one thing, though it was hardly an essential matter, in which Augustine could take genuine delight; it was the singing of the people. In his letter to Januarius he writes: "When they are not being read to or when there is no exposition of the Scripture going on, when the bishop is not praying and the deacon is not reciting the common prayer of the litany before the offering of the sacrifice, what better thing can the people do than sing? I know of nothing better than that."[32]

For few things, he says, are more calculated to fill the soul with pious thoughts or to loose the passion of divine love. It is certainly our duty sometimes to omit a good thing that may displease our weaker brethren, so that we may thus prevent a greater evil; but in the case of singing this should be introduced forthwith whenever it is clear that the gain of the zealous will outweigh the harm suffered by the over-critical. Can it not be amply defended by Holy Scripture? The Lord himself and his Apostles have shown the way and have commanded it. Here in Africa, he admits, the thing hardly thrives as yet. "Most church members are indifferent [*pigriora sunt*]." The Donatists make a better job of it, though naturally they sing in an unseemly manner. "They fortify their inebriation by psalms which ordinary men have composed," (the fifth-century equivalent of *Ancient and Modern*!) "whereas we in the true Church sing the divine songs of the Prophets." The Donatists do not confine themselves to their church, however, but sing their songs in the streets and proudly tell their Catholic rivals, "Your church is so dull."[33] In other words, Moody-and-Sankey has always proved successful, and community hymn-singing was, even in the fifth century, not a monopoly of the true Church. Even Augustine, with his jingle against the *pars Donati*, had sought to provide an antidote to the popular fighting songs of Parmenianus.

Singing had always been the practice of Christian communities, but the larger the congregation the less people joined in the singing—which seems to be an invariable law. We do not know just in what manner the people either in the East or the West joined in with their songs at the end of the fourth century. Through the very circumstance that since the settlement of 313 the numbers of the faithful had so enormously increased, and the basilicas had become larger and the ritual richer and more disciplined, popular participation in worship seems actually to have decreased. It seems by Augustine's day to have dwindled to the calling out, or possibly the singing, of the old short ejaculations, which were, admittedly, most suitable for large numbers of people. In Africa we hear of many such acclamations, as they seem to have been called. They are cries of concurrence or approval after a prayer, the answer to a greeting, the responses in the dialogue before the Preface, expressions of thanks and praise and the refrains of the litanies:

> Amen!
> And with thy spirit!
> We have, to the Lord!
> Worthy and just!
> *Fiat! Fiat!*
> *Deo gratias!*
> *Christo laudes!*
> *Exaudi Christe!*[34]

There was also of course the Psalter, the essential, and for long the Church's only, book of song. The singing of psalms had been taken over from the Hellenistic synagogues in the *diaspora*: for this reason both words and melody sounded strange to the true Greek ear. According to ancient custom the whole psalm was sung through by a soloist in an ornate, somewhat shrill melody with many melismas, while a number of other singers, or possibly the whole congregation, repeated one particular verse after each different verse sung by the soloist.[35] For some time, however, it had been the custom (which seems to have been an imitation of that of the Aramaic communities of Mesopotamia and Persia and then to have taken root in Syria) to divide the whole congregation into two choirs and have the psalm sung antiphonally verse by verse. This Syrian practice, which was so much livelier and also took less time, and which seemed to exercise a peculiar fascination on people, had been introduced in Milan by Ambrose, who knew the East. There in the marble Portian Basilica the holy Psalms of David, with all their many unforgettable associations with the time of the martyrs, were sung for the first time verse by verse in their venerable Latin translation, the singing being done by two massed choirs. Ambrose tells us that the success of this experiment was very great, for the congregation, which nothing could induce to keep quiet during the readings, immediately stopped making any further disturbance once the psalm had started and joined in the singing with enthusiasm. How impressive the thing was we can learn from the *Confessions*, for Augustine himself, though he had not yet been baptized, was in the congregation, and he could not restrain his tears.[36] A number of passages give grounds for the belief that when he was bishop, Augustine introduced this antiphonal method of psalm-singing in Hippo; but with what measure of success we do not know.[37] There is a casual mention of the fact that the Psalms were sung in Hippo "consona voce, ore consono, dulci concentu",[38] but this probably only means that the people joined in the singing. As against this there are continual references to a soloist mistaking the number of the psalm he has to sing.[39] All we do know is that verses of the Psalms were sung in unison, for when Augustine quotes a verse from the Psalms he often adds, "As you [or "as we"] have just sung", though this may of course only refer to the verse that was used as a refrain.[40]

It seems to be clear, however, that communal singing was unknown in Africa before 393 when the *vir tribunitius* Hilarus, "one of the usual anti-clerical grumblers", protested vehemently against the singing of psalms during the eucharistic prayers and the distribution of the holy gifts, this singing being a practice that had just been introduced in Carthage. Augustine thought it worth the trouble to answer him, though the little essay which he wrote on this occasion has unfortunately been lost;[41] but Church folk have been pretty much the same throughout the ages. Active co-operation has always proved difficult to attain, and if it is ever displayed, it rarely lasts. No doubt the first fine enthusiasm disappeared not long after 393 or 396. Round about the year 500 the bishop Caesarius tells of the Church in Arles that however loudly the deacon might cry *flectamus genua*, his parishioners remained "standing upright as stiff as pillars". They did not even bow their heads, let alone bend their knees,[42] and we may well doubt whether the law of liturgical inertia was in the year 400 miraculously suspended for the benefit of the African Church. Quite probably many of the songs of the Church were popular. We hear that numbers of people preferred to sing psalms at their work rather than the latest hits from the theatre. And, after all, there are plenty of examples of this kind of thing today. In Friesland in the laundries and behind the hedges and board fences you hear little else but "Know Ye Not the Name", sung to the tune of "Home, Sweet Home", and among the Catholics hymns from the evening devotions, like "Heart of Jesus, Thou art Weeping." English missionaries used to tell how the people of Chungking, who once could not sing at all, used to sing the hymns from the Chinese hymn-book in the street.

A particular favourite in Africa was Psalm cxxxii, "Ecce quam bonum et quam jocundum". "This melody is so sweet", Augustine once said from the pulpit, "that even those who do not know the Psalter sing at least a verse of the psalm. It is as sweet as that love which enables brothers to live together and it is the loving singing and understanding of this sweet melody that has called the monasteries into being."[43] Men dreamed of the Psalms, they sang them casually on the decks of ships, in the garden, in the kitchen and in the fields. Here in the country—so write Paula and Eustochium from Bethlehem to Marcella—only the Psalms break the stillness. One hears them everywhere, behind the plough, at the gathering of the grapes; the shepherds pipe them and they are the love-songs of the neighbourhood. Augustine gave monks the advice to sing psalms while at work, "like a divine rowing song", it being of course assumed that they knew them by heart.[44] These strange oriental songs with the alien-sounding words of a clumsily translated Jewish text, with their running parallelisms of sentences and ideas and their bizarre melismas upon a single word, had, despite all these difficulties, conquered the reluctant hearts of men and won over ears that had been attuned to the formal metres of Antiquity. They had done this even in the Latin West, with all its traditions of literary discipline and purity. Time and again it has been proved that "the sighing of the dove of the spirit in the cleft of the rock" is a timeless thing. They can no longer be called the property of Israel, for today the Church has been singing them for a longer time than they were ever sung in the synagogues before Christ.

Even educated people could not banish the Psalms from the background of their minds once they had heard them, and Monica once had occasion to punish young Licentius in Cassiciacum, because late one evening he sang in a somewhat unsuitable place *laete et garrule* a verse from Psalm lxxix:

> O Lord of Hosts, turn our lot
> Show us thy face and we shall be saved.

He found the melody so strange that he could not get it out of his head and although he jokingly replied, "Do you think that God would not have heard me if an enemy had locked me into that place?", he came to Augustine's bedside next day and whispered to him that he could not get this verse out of his head, because his spiritual crisis was not yet past, and that he had been right to speak these words in the midst of uncleanness, for that place was itself a kind of picture of his own soul.[45]

But the great experience of Augustine's youth was not the familiar traditional singing of psalms (though the joining in of the congregation had produced a wholly new effect), but the first hymn, which all the people joined in singing. Never could he forget the effect of the singing of this song of praise, which his own father in Christ, Ambrose, had composed, and which he heard for the first time in the latter's cathedral church. That was in April 387 when, together with Alypius and his son Adeodatus, he had just been baptized. He himself has told us the story: "How I wept on that occasion at your hymns and your songs of praise, being so deeply moved by the voices of your sweet-sounding Church. These voices penetrated into my ears and your truth drop by drop entered my heart and from that same heart a warm piety rose up so that my tears flowed, and as they flowed I was happy."[46]

These people sang in their basilica with real fervour. They knew that their famous congregation was the starting-point from which their new method of communal singing and the new hymns of their bishop were to conquer the whole Latin world, so much so that within a comparatively short space of time those same hymns were being quoted against the heresy of Nestorius by Pope Celestine at a synod in Rome.[47] The real origin of this new method of singing, though not of Ambrose's hymns, is to be found in some strange and dramatic events that had occurred about a year before. Ambrose was being persecuted by the Dowager-Empress Justina, an Arian, and the congregation was unwilling to leave its bishop unguarded at night. So bishop and congregation remained that night in the church, surrounded by a crowd of heretics. It was now Ambrose's concern to see that his friends did not have time hanging too heavily on their hands. If they were read to, they would only start chattering and become restless; so the bishop hit on the idea of dividing them into two large choruses which sang first the Psalms and then their own hymns for the hours of the day and night, hymns which were already probably known to a small circle of ascetics and other personal intimates. The result was so overwhelming that the Arians spread the story round the town that Ambrose had bewitched the people by his songs. Monica was present on this occasion and her son, who was still "cold to the spirit of God", could judge both from his mother's account and from the excitement in the town how moving the experience must have been. Afterwards he went to the church and heard for himself, and neither he nor his mother could ever forget what they witnessed on that occasion.[48] He seems to have been particularly impressed by the hymns, which struck him as unique. They were, compared with the Psalms, so essentially Latin. They also had nothing in common with the fiery, brilliant and almost dithyrambic songs of praise which the Christian Greeks had sung since the time of the odes of Solomon and the days of Ephrem. The songs of Ambrose had a distinct resemblance to their author, that friendly patrician who tended to be rather sparing of his words, whose stern sense of duty made him a little stiff, and who, for all that, was never unkind. Ambrose was the scion of a noble house who could afford the luxury of being simple, and here too his hymns bear the imprint of his personality. There is in them not a superfluous word, yet they show exactly what is in his mind. They have been compared to the altar described in Exodus and Deuteronomy, that altar that was made of unhewn stone, because the work of the chisel was too small a thing for God.[49]

The metre used was simple and one that flowed easily. It was the iambic dimeter, a metre to which the popular ear was well attuned. The melody used was also a simple one, almost wholly without melismas, so that every word had a note to itself and the force of the words was thus not weakened—an excellent old Greek custom. Despite its clarity, the verse tended at times to be somewhat clumsy, but the meaning was as clear as the words of any popular song; and the hymns were just the right length, eight strophes, four for every chorus. Till then no Christian poet had ventured to stray outside the vocabulary of Virgil and Lucretius, and Christian poets had substituted profane synonyms for the familiar Christian terms. Ambrose had the courage to take the whole Christian treasury of words and to use that deep, strong and resounding speech which men were accustomed to hear from the altar, from the pulpit, in the Psalms and in readings from Holy Scripture.[50] The songs of praise for the different times of the day all started by proclaiming the hour of day and at the same time invoked the Creator. Each then treated of one of the six days of the *hexameron*, then mounted upward by almost imperceptible stages from the transitoriness and symbolism of the first creation to a vision of the second creation, which would appear with Christ and would be imperishable, and which has in a certain sense already begun. Then we have pictures of the different hours of the day, each with its peculiar atmosphere: cockcrow at dawn, which frightens away the demons and dispels our sleep, and is a warning to us of the fall of Peter; the glow of morning, with the rising sun, which is a reflection of the glory of the Father; the burning sting from the "flaming wheel" of the sun at midday, which causes us to think of the agonies of dissension and of passion; the dying-away of the light on the horizon when the lamps are lit and we would fain call out to the Light of the world, "Abide with us, for the shades of night are falling." At length we come to a prayer for help in the struggle between light and darkness which now takes place, not in the firmament but in the unstable heart of man.[51] Some of the hymns deal with the mysteries of Christ, while others sing of the patience and the crowns of the martyrs and virgins.[52] All are illuminated by certitude, realism, faith and the peace of true knowledge. There was nothing soft in any of these hymns, scarcely even anything tender, and as strophe after strophe was sung alternately by one half of the congregation and then by the other, they transformed the basilica of Ambrose, which had once been beleaguered by the Arian mob, into the impregnable fortress of the true faith. For the hymns were solemn confessions of doctrine, "verses which spoke the truth".[53]

Monica knew them all by heart. In the rather abstruse debate on the happy life in which the young philosophers at Cassiciacum allowed her to take part, there was mention of an analogy to the Trinity. Monica very subtly intervened with a verse from the evening hymn of Ambrose, saying that Ambrose had already said all there was to be said, for the words ran

> Hear our prayer, O Trinity!

Then she drew attention to the three divine virtues and so wound up the discussion in exemplary fashion.[54] But the songs were to play as important a part in Augustine's life as in that of his mother. When he returned from her funeral in Ostia, which even in those days was an indescribably melancholy place, he found that his tears would not come. In his wretchedness he went to the baths, yet came out of the steam bath unrelieved and with the same bitterness in his heart. Then he went to sleep and woke up feeling less troubled and almost at peace, and while he lay alone upon his bed and alone in the world the hymn came into his mind that his mother had quoted that evening in Cassiciacum, the song of praise for the hour when the lamps were lit:

> God, Creator of all things,
> Thou turn'st the heaven's axis,
> And clothest the day with limpid light,
> And night with loveliness of sleep.
>
> Thus rest can heal the worker's limbs
> And send him to his task restored
> Thus is the weary soul refreshed
> And anxious sorrow banished.[55]

Small wonder that when he became a bishop, he was at pains to see that his congregation was made acquainted with this hymn, and although in the whole of his works only four of Ambrose's hymns are quoted,[56] we know that they were sung in Hippo. Once, when preaching at Christmas on the Virgin Birth, he reminded his hearers of the hymn "which you have just sung":

> Shepherd of Israel, heed, O heed,
> Enthroned above the Cherubim,
> Ephrem, appear, awake the power
> Within thyself and haste to come.
>
> Saviour of all the peoples, come,
> Show what was born of the virgin's womb;
> Let the whole world gaze in wonder,
> For such a birth befits God alone.
>
> Forth from his chamber let him go,
> The royal hall of pure virtue.
> Now shall the dual-natured giant
> Go quickly on his way.
>
> Proceeding from one Father,
> He doth return to that same Father.
> His sally forth doth reach to hell
> Yet he returns to God's throne.

It was the Christmas carol of Milan.[57]

We do not know whether Augustine composed any hymns himself. Certainly he is not the author of the *Exultet*, though his Easter sermons show him to be well acquainted with it. We know that strange ballad against the Donatists which he composed in the early years of his office, but that is a thing apart. When Hilary of Poitiers, who, after Ambrose, was the first composer of hymns in the Latin West, complained that the obstinate people of Poitiers would not join in the singing of his beautiful hymn to Christ, "Christ, Thou Wast Before All Ages",[58] he does not seem to have realized that the complicated metre (alternating Glyconics and Asclepiads) was altogether too much for them. Whether Augustine with his ballad went rather too far in the opposite direction is a matter that everyone who cares to plough through twenty strophes must decide for himself.

It is perhaps worth mentioning, however, that this rather forced composition, stuffed full though it is with biblical and typically Christian turns of phrase, is nevertheless grammatically flawless throughout. But it has another important aspect, too, for it is a reminder of a truth all too often forgotten, namely that we owe the origin of rhythmic poetry to the Christian Church; for it was she who broke the somewhat pedantic fetters of the ancient prosody and so liberated popular song and allowed it to take its rightful place. Indeed, one may say that folk song of the more serious kind was born and grew up in this, the oldest home of ordinary people.

This piece of doggerel also proves that saints are all really very much alike, for Augustine obviously thought very much along the lines of St. Martin of Tours, and might equally well have said, "Lord, if thy people hath need of me, I will not refuse the work." Like St. Martin of Tours he also tore his cloak—his literary cloak—for the sake of the nakedness of the *idiotae*, the unlettered, and the fragments of that cloak have, like those of that other, become venerated relics.

Yet Augustine did not always come out as an advocate for singing in church, at least not in theory. No doubt he was acquainted with Porphyry's remark about "wordless prayers in chaste silence", and of his condemnation of music in worship, and it is part of his neo-Platonist heritage if he speaks of the joy of the angels in heaven being a wordless relishing of God in holy silence.[59] He knew out of his own experience something of "the lust of the ear". In a passage in the *Confessions* which every reader of that work will remember, he speaks of the weakening and distracting effect of any singing that made an excessive appeal to the emotions. He tells there how he had often thought that hymns should be done away with and that the Psalms should be sung in the manner which Athanasius had enjoined on his readers in Alexandria, namely with such slight modulations of the voice that it almost amounted to a recitative. Later he was to see the uses of singing in general and of the singing of the people in particular, and he was to say so in his writing; for he saw that a text will more readily strike root in a soul if it is sung to a moving melody, and that even the prophet David struck his harp for other reasons than those of mere sensuous pleasure.[60] How often, he points out, there is talk of singing and of playing in Holy Scripture! In the old Temple the voices and the instruments must have made an overwhelming noise, and was it not St. Paul himself who commanded us to edify one another by the singing of psalms and spiritual songs?

Yet despite all this the author of the *Confessions* had, even as late as 415, not yet made up his mind. He knew his sensitive heart all too well and found that what might be good for others all too often disagreed with himself. We find him writing this:

> The lust of the ear had caught me in its mesh and made a slave of me, but thou didst loose my bonds and make me free. Even now, I confess that I do not fear to surrender myself to the delights of sound if they are uttered by a pleasant and well-trained voice, so long as thy word gives life to them, and yet I do not suffer myself wholly to be made prisoner by them, but free myself when the time comes that I desire to do this. Yet if not only the melody but the very words themselves demand entrance into my mind, then they are entitled to a worthy place in my heart, and I find it hard to know which one I should prepare for them. For sometimes it seems to me that I do them more honour than they deserve. I sometimes feel that the holy words inflame my heart to greater inward piety and more glowing devotion when they are sung than when they are not, and that all the affections of the heart have their corresponding modes in voice and song, and that these last excite them because of the mysterious relationship which they possess with them. Yet for all that my sensual pleasure, to which the spirit must never be sacrificed, lest that spirit lose its power, all too often deceives and seduces me. Then the senses do not hold themselves patiently back, as they should, and give precedence to reason. Rather do they take control, though it was reason that permitted their entry. Thus I sin unconsciously in this matter, though I become aware of it afterwards. On the other hand, there are occasions when I am over-cautious in respect of this deceit, and err on the side of excessive severity. Indeed, there are times when I wish that all the pleasant melodies to which the Psalms of David are sung could be kept far removed both from my own ears and those of the Church. The thing that I have heard of Athanasius, the Bishop of Alexandria, seems to me to point to a far safer course, for he enjoined that the Psalms should be sung with as little modulation of the voice as possible, so that the delivery was rather that of a recitation than of a song.

Yet when I think of the tears I have shed when listening to the singing in thy Church in the period immediately after my return to the Faith, and when I reflect further that it is less the melody of the song which touches me than the content of the text that is sung (for touch me it does, so long as the tune is suitable and the singer's voice is clear), then I see how useful a thing this singing is. Thus I am swayed to and fro between the lust of my senses and my recognition of the salutary character of this institution, which I can attest from my own experience. On the whole I incline to say that the customary singing in church is a good thing, though I do not wish to dogmatize on the matter. I recognize that even in weaker spirits the charming of the ear may lead to an increase in devotion. Should, however, the song make a greater impression on me than the words that are sung, then I know that I am committing sin worthy of punishment. That then is how matters stand with me.[61]

"Oh this rhetorician! How I laughed!" wrote Nietzsche to Overbeck concerning such confessions as these—and on this occasion many will concede that he was justified. What is more questionable than such refinements of scruple, and what more unsatisfactory than a writer thus putting himself before a mirror, even when he is a saint and the mirror that of his own conscience? Yet what caused Augustine to fear for himself caused him no fear where others were concerned.

It is often obvious that he remained consistently receptive to music. When he expounds the Psalms word for word, he likes to linger over the names of musical instruments. He speaks of Psalm xliv as an epithalamium, and expends some pains in explaining this expression.[62] When dealing with the "zither and the ten-stringed psaltery", he points out that the sounding-box of the psaltery is above, while that of the zither is below, and instead of parading his Pythagorean erudition, as he does in his somewhat abstruse work on music, he now indulges in a pious allegory. In this he speaks of playing upon the ten strings of the ten commandments which come from above, while our difficulties come from below. In another place he speaks of Christ playing on the psalter in his miracles, but on the zither in relation to his human needs. The sound from above and the sound from below—this signified the spirit and the flesh, heavenly and earthly things.[63]

He also speaks of the different functions of precentor and choir,[64] and of the singing of "Amen" after a solemn prayer, which is, so to speak, an underlining of it and a confirmation by the whole congregation. It means "Verily, verily"; and when the Lord himself wants to emphasize something he too says, "Amen, Amen, dico vobis"—"Verily, verily, I say unto you"; and this word is deliberately left untranslated, so that by reason of this very veil of mystery it may attain to greater honour.[65]

Often he speaks of the moving quality of the long-drawn alleluias, especially at Easter. They are "the new song of the new man". When we hear it our spirit is in a sense transformed. We then have already a kind of foretaste of the City of God beyond. We only hear it at Easter and on Sundays because otherwise even so glorious a sound as this would become wearisome, yet in heaven we shall hear it everlastingly, for that is where the song belongs. Yet "when it returns at a certain season, with what joy do we greet it and with what poignant feeling of homesickness do we not bid it farewell!"[66]

Nor is he ignorant of the incomparable power of spontaneous song. When it falls to him, in expounding the Psalms, to explain the word *jubilatio*,[67] he finds a correspondence between that rejoicing which can find no articulate words and can only express itself in an inarticulate cry, and God, who is inexpressible and cannot be comprehended in words. When, in praising God, we become conscious of the insufficiency of mere words, then we must needs do something like singing without words. We can then but utter a sound of gladness: "Make a sound of rejoicing, for to sing well for God means to do that very thing. For what does that imply? It means that try as we may, we cannot find words to express the song that is in our hearts." Thereupon he reminds us, in a charming passage, of those sounds of joy in our ordinary lives, of that wordless carolling in which men sometimes feel most compelled to indulge on a fine morning in the fields and by which even slaves express their cheerfulness at the harvesting of the grapes. "When at harvest time or in the vineyard or at any other work that they do with zest, men feel the desire to sing and their pleasure in the words of the song is too intense to be expressed in words, then they do not bother to pronounce them at all but just begin to utter joyful sounds. And towards whom are such joyful noises more in place than to the unutterable God? For unutterable is he indeed whom no man can express in words, and since you cannot so express him and yet must not keep silent concerning him, what else can you do but utter joyful sounds and let your heart thus express its rejoicing without words, for thus the infinite depth of your joy can break through the limitations which words must needs impose."[68]

Augustine knew well enough all the occasions when men naturally turn to song. He had surely listened to children singing their gay, friendly little ditties.[69] He knew that travellers sing while on the way, especially at night, if only to dispel their fear of loneliness and robbers—for then there is a rustling all about them which fills them with shuddering fear, or, what is if anything worse, silence; and the more silent the night the more uncanny. Augustine advised his monks to sing on their journeys whether they rode or walked, exactly as he enjoined them to sing at their work at home.[70] Yet there is another side to the picture, for rarely has a preacher drawn a more telling sketch of the psalm-singing churchgoer or shown greater insight in pointing out his weakness than does Augustine in that sermon on the text "Deliver me, O Lord, out of the hand of the sinner, and out of the hand of the transgressor of the law and the unjust." Everyone who sings this thinks of some personal experience, says Augustine. As soon as he hears these words from the reader or in the refrain—we are here apparently concerned with the more old-fashioned manner of singing the Psalms—he thinks of the little incidents of his personal life. He thinks of some enemy, some person that has traduced him or has sought to have him put in prison, or of some other who has published some libellous piece of writing against him. Then "you will see him singing with intense emotion, with the expression on his face adapting itself to the spirit of the psalm and with tears often coursing down his cheeks. He sighs between the words that he sings, and whoever has no special skill in reading men's thoughts will be wholly taken in by the outward appearance and will say: 'How deeply this man is stirred, as he listens to this psalm! See how he sighs, how deeply he sighs!'—and then the man, in his turn, begins again to sing and puts into the song all the power that is in him. Yes, he sings with the very marrow of his bones, with voice, face and profound sighs all showing how deeply he is stirred, 'Deliver me, O Lord, from the hand of the sinner and out of the hand of the transgressor of the law and of the unjust' —and yet all the time he is merely thinking of his personal enemy."[71]

The above roughly summarizes what we know of the nature of Augustine's concern for singing in Church, though the fact is that we do not know very much. It does seem clear, however, that in the worship of that time there was very little said in a low voice, but a great deal of reading aloud and singing, and that the congregation now and then took part in the latter, and that when they did so they did it with a will. And Augustine, who was the greatest artist of his day and who for that very reason often tended to be something of a purist and a Puritan, let his people sing; and he did this because that singing, profoundly moving and edifying as it was, was, after its own kind, a lovely thing and a source of joy to all, so much so that he could not suppress a feeling of triumph at having beaten the theatre at its own game.[72]

Whatever one may think of his somewhat over-subtle theories, Augustine had an exquisitely sensitive ear and an enormous capacity for enjoyment. It was also an extremely discriminating one. In the last book of the *City of God*, which he wrote in his old age, he has a remark that the theatre could achieve wonders for the eye, but that what it inflicted on the ear was intolerable.[73] Perhaps it was because music was, in a rather special way, an echo of an ultimate perfection, that its debasement especially offended him. In his last letter to Jerome he compared the ordering of the universe by measure and number to a musical composition which was so beautiful "that if we could hear it we should feel ourselves gently touched by a quite inexpressible joy". In that same passage he speaks of the art of modulating the voice as "a gift of divine generosity and an indication of a much greater thing than itself".[74] Once when he was speaking on the text from the Psalms, "I shall go over into the place of the wonderful tabernacle, even into the house of God, with the voice of joy and praise, the noise of one feasting", the words started a significant and typical train of thought. The tabernacles were, of course, for him those holy men who are God's tabernacles on earth, and the noise of feasting was that of the endless feasting in God's house that centres around the holiest thing of all. "In this hall of the perpetual feast there goes forth a sweet sound most soothing and delightful to the inward ear, and whosoever goes about in the temporal tabernacle is irresistably drawn into this inner place of sanctity. A kind of seductive loveliness draws him on, and it is as though in this house of God someone were softly playing upon an instrument."[75] Augustine was one of those great and happy men who sometimes catch the sound of the distant heavenly music.

The Emphasis on Understanding

That Augustine should have been intolerant of any luxury in his house and that he should have permitted singing in church only by doing a certain violence to his nature—all this reflects the same essential trait in his character as that which made him, in worship, insist above all things on a clear understanding of what was going forward. When a congregation no longer understands its cultus the highest traditions degenerate into mere soulless routine. With all his tolerance for local custom and practice, he was sternly critical of the mere inertia of habit. The enthusiast for symbolism wanted the symbols really to speak. Whoever presented himself as a candidate for baptism had to be carefully instructed in the meaning of every detail, from the moment of the bread of exorcism (a part of the "sacrament of salt") throughout all succeeding stages;[76] and it was an essential part of his way of looking at the sacraments as symbols that he should insist on their being celebrated in such a way that there could never be any doubt as to their meaning.

The poor devil who recited his verses from the psalm as a sort of prayer for revenge had at least recited them with some vague though distorted sense of their meaning, but there were men, he said, who were mere singing automata and who sang "like trained finches, parrots, ravens and magpies"; and these the bishop besought to remember that they were rational beings and so had the duty of noting the meaning of the texts they sang.

People who sing frivolous songs, says Augustine, know very well what they mean, and the more daring they are the better they know it. Must not we "who, in the Church, have learned to sing the divine words" from time to time reflect on what is written in the psalm: "Fortunate is the people that understands its cries of joy"?[77] He wanted his Christians to know what they were doing and do it properly. It is not long tradition that begets routine and automatism, but faulty sensibility deriving from insufficient knowledge. That was why, throughout his life, Augustine never ceased explaining to his people even the commonest of the words and gestures of the liturgy. In this respect he was very much a liturgical priest.

In his exposition of texts there is literally nothing that he passes over. First, of course, come the many foreign words and technical expressions that would have struck people when the text was being read: the weights, measures, names, seasons, domestic details, also the musical instruments, customs, clothes, the superscriptions and the meanings of such words as *evangelium* and *Christus*. All this came within the scope of his expositions, which dealt with each text word by word and were very much like those that had become customary in the schools in the study of the profane poets. Occasionally this biblical erudition has a certain admixture of worldly learning, as when in dealing with the expression *quarta sabbatorum* he names both the Christian and the profane days of the week and compares them with one another.[78]

Actions as well as words have to be expounded; even the pious gestures that have almost begun to partake of the character of reflexes, such as the attitude in prayer. He preaches about the bowing of the head and the bending of the knee, about sighing and about raising one's eyes to heaven. He speaks of "knees that have got callouses on them from praying",[79] of beating one's breast, of throwing oneself down and touching the floor with one's forehead,[80] these last being the ancient gestures of humility, of supplication and of penitence, which the Greeks call *metanoeae* and which to this day continue to play their part in the liturgy of Good Friday in certain strict religious orders, while among the simple Orthodox of Eastern Europe they enter into the normal daily life of prayer. In an early sermon he remarked that Christians prayed standing, and when they speak the words "who art in heaven", "turn towards the East from where the revolving sky starts to turn"—not because God lives in the sky and not elsewhere, or as though he were less real elsewhere, but because the sky is more exalted than the earth, and this gesture therefore signifies the upward striving of the soul towards him who is more exalted than herself;[81] an explanation that seems rather bald compared with the customary notion that Christ ascended into heaven in the direction of the rising sun and will return from that part of the heavens at the appointed time, and that this will be the place of the heavenly paradise to come. People also looked upon the East as the symbol of the heavenly kingdom of light—of everything good and positive, in fact; of the true light and of the sun of righteousness.[82] Cockcrow at early morning is the signal for the first prayer,[83] he says, for it is the hour when the demons flee and so the time to arise from our beds, our salvation being again a stage nearer.

When we see a man at prayer we recognize in his outstretched arms the Cross. In this attitude of prayer, which we can see in the praying figures on African graves, and which was customary in the whole world, Augustine too sees the shape of the cross, just as Justin and Tertullian had done before him, and with it an inward adaptation to the Crucified. Moreover, it is the Holy Spirit which has prescribed it, for it is written, "Lift up your hands to the Lord", and, "In thy name will I lift up my hands, and I will praise thee all my days."[84] Kneeling or stretching out one's hands, however, is not by any means essential. One can make a good prayer without these things, for one can pray sitting or lying down, and for every prayer the principle applies that the more spontaneous it is, the better.[85] But at least he who prays must understand what he says, and that is why Augustine is so anxious always to explain the acclamations of the liturgy. The Hebrew "amen" is a freely given confirmation and, as it were, an underlining of the prayer by the soul. The "alleluia" means "Praise the Lord." In accordance with ancient custom, it is sung for the fifty days after Easter.[86] He also explains the greeting given from the apse, "The Lord be with you", and also the dialogue which dates back to the very first days of the Church and which no Church ever omits before the prayers at the Sacrifice, and especially the words "Lift up your hearts." His expositions of these things are endless, nor does he ever weary of telling us that the only true home for the human heart is above and that here below all is subject to corruption.[87]

Augustine's congregation were in the habit of reacting to whatever was read or preached with all the liveliness of their temperament. They shouted comments, sighed, laughed, like children at the cinema. When a few stereotyped expressions occurred such as "Have mercy on us", or at the word *Confiteor* or at "Forgive us our trespasses" in the Our Father, they made a practice of very audibly beating their breasts.[88] When the speaker made some telling remark they loudly acclaimed him, and protested as loudly when there was anything in his utterances of which they disapproved, but Augustine insisted that even these spontaneous outbursts should be in accordance with good sense.

Once on a saint's day when the epistle was read in which St. Paul enumerates all those who will in no wise enter the Kingdom of Heaven, Augustine, in his sermon, said somewhat unexpectedly, "When mention was made of murderers, you were not particularly perturbed, but when mention was made of loose livers, then, as I could well hear, you beat your breasts. I heard it plainly enough, heard it and saw it. What I was prevented from seeing in your bedchambers, that I saw plainly enough by reason of the sound I heard when you beat your breasts. Throw the sin away from you, my brethren, for to beat your breast and then to continue sinning is merely to plaster over your sins. My brethren, my children, be chaste!"[89] He has a very direct explanation for the effect of this act of beating the breast. It achieves its end very well indeed, for through it the swelling in our breast bursts open into confession.[90] On another occasion the reader read out the passage from Matthew, "I confess to thee, Father of heaven and earth, because thou hast hidden these things from the wise", and at the words "I confess" the basilica resounded with the sound of the multitude beating their breasts. What point was there in that? asked Augustine. "Hardly has the word *confiteor* left the reader's lips, before there is this thunder of breasts being beaten"—but, he says, think for a moment. Here it does not mean "I confess", in the sense of confessing a sin, but "I glorify."[91] Apparently this was not an isolated instance, for he keeps emphasizing this point in the sermons that have come down to us.[92] And how many Christians misused the sign of the cross? "How many of our brethren— we must confess it to our sorrow—run off today after those vanities, that swindle and nonsense, and forget the place for which they have been chosen, and when they get a fright in the circus, they immediately make the sign of the cross, and thus with the very mark of the cross upon them they stand in a place which they would leave at once if they truly had the sign of the cross upon their hearts. What use is it to make the sign of the cross in such circumstances as these? God does not want men who make pictures of his signs, but those who act upon them."[93]

But he was not the man to try and force through all improvements at once. The desire for a "sensible form of worship" and one that closely followed Holy Scripture, meant, if it was to be realized, that all the different parts of something that had grown up organically as a living tradition would have to be minutely scrutinized in order to reform them by what was after all often a purely personal criterion. A man who is concerned to understand and order matters that are essential, and to cause that to be held in honour which truly deserves it, does not waste his time on trifles. Augustine was not the man to be perpetually finding fault with the traditional liturgy. The advice he gave to Januarius on the justification of local tradition, the necessity for treating the common tradition of the Church as the foundation of everything else, and the dangers of *admiratio populi*, was scrupulously followed by himself. In the last chapter the reader will see how mercilessly he rooted out the pious irregularities that had crept into the cultus of the martyrs even in his own parish. As against this, when it was a matter of secondary importance he was ready to forgo his own wishes. At any rate, he was willing to do this when those wishes conflicted with a tradition that had at least some kind of grounds for it, even when the case for it was argued with a certain arbitrariness and obstinacy. For the case of Hippo under Augustine was not very different from that of Russia under Nikon, of London under Laud, of Oxford under Pusey; the people wanted no changes in the order of worship. It would sometimes suffer something new to be introduced, but never suffer anything to which it was accustomed to be left out. Above all, nothing must be altered. When the singing of songs of praise from the Book of Psalms was introduced in Carthage to fill in the time while the Sacrifice was being offered and the Host distributed, a certain Hilarus, a distinguished gentleman (he was *vir tribunitius*), protested loudly, and behaved "as laymen all too often do towards the servants of God".[94]

Augustine tells in one of his letters to Jerome of something that occurred to the Bishop of Oea, the present Tripoli, who had acquired one of the new codices of the Bible after Jerome had revised the text. He was reading the story of Jonah out of it, and in naming the marvellous shrub that grew over the sleeping prophet in a single night, he referred to it as ivy instead of the traditional gourd. Immediately there was a shout of "Wrong!" Above all it was the Greeks who would have nothing to do with this translation from the Hebrew, because they had an uneasy feeling that it did not correspond with their own. The good bishop was therefore compelled to desert his Hebrew authorities and he did so "because he did not wish to lose his flock nor they their gourd".[95] We know well what was really behind this. For nearly two hundred years Christians in the west had seen a certain picture on graves, sarcophagi, church walls and innumerable other places. It was the little slender figure of the prophet stretched out naked and fast asleep under the *cucurbita* with the hanging gourds: one arm was nearly always over his head and his legs were crossed, and the whole manner of presentation suggested an Endymion who has somehow wandered off into the Bible. (Plates 13 and 14.)[96] What were they to make of this ivy that had somehow appeared from nowhere in the hallowed and familiar picture?

In Hippo things were much the same. Once on Good Friday Augustine, instead of following custom and reading the account of the Passion in St. Matthew, read it from all four Gospels. His people found it strange and there was some unrest. In the following year Augustine did not repeat the experiment, though in a subsequent sermon he alluded to the incident and used the occasion to make a somewhat caustic remark: "The people in this case heard something they were not accustomed to and were upset by it, but he who truly loves Holy Scripture and does not want to remain an *idiota* all his life will take notice of everything and examine it all most carefully."[97] But it did little good. Had he not himself written that local tradition should be respected and that if everything were regulated down to the smallest detail, we should have a yoke to bear that would be worse than that of the Jews? And even the Law of the Jews at least came from God, and did not come, like so many liturgical innovations, from some overzealous liturgical enthusiast, who, regardless of the state of his learning (or lack of it), is determined to experiment.

The Bible and the Liturgy

Many elements in the worship of that time reached deep into men's daily lives, for in those days the whole of Christian life turned on the sacraments. Although they were in their essentials hundreds of years old, they spoke an exceedingly simple language, and though here and there one person or another might have missed their meaning, there was for the vast mass very little ambiguity. There was as yet no dead language obtruding itself between the liturgical act and men's understanding of it, and, at any rate in the towns, every word that was spoken in the church was understood by all. It was not an esoteric language that disguised meanings; only the symbol to some extent did that. For this very reason, it was that much easier for Augustine to prevent worship from degenerating into mere routine; language and the spirit of the time were all on his side.

The manner in which he deals with the most important rites, though these have themselves by now become distinctly hieratic, gives one the impression that he is deliberately seeking, as far as possible, to underline their dramatic moments, to explain them and to make their speech come alive. He remained the old skilful rhetorician who could turn every situation to the best advantage. If ever there was a systematic instructor on the field of liturgy, Augustine was that man. It is not true that he added many new customs to the various very ancient initiation rites. For instance, the sermon which was given at the imparting of the Creed, the provisional recitation of the latter by way of test, the solemn imparting of the *Our Father* (again with an exposition), the teaching and explanation of the Ten Commandments, even the idea of a coherent catechism course—none of these things originated with Augustine.[98] Yet he does seem to have reconstituted certain details in a more meaningful form and to have, so to speak, made all rites more luminous through his brilliant interpretation of them.

As against this we cannot help noticing that he is only rarely satisfied with explaining a rite in terms of its original significance, and seems to give little thought to its actual historical origin, though it is precisely this that often reveals its meaning better than anything else. Time and again he permits his imagination to play with the innumerable *sacramenta* which serve the purpose of proclaiming the Gospel and which, he quite humbly believes, are all taken from Holy Scripture (although in seeking to derive them from that source he often has to make some quite secondary aspect of a word or an event the basis of his argument, and even then often rests that argument on very dubious etymology). Yet the strange thing is that among all the tempting byways of his world of symbols, he never strays very far, but in the end is content to stick to a small number of themes which he continually repeats in varying form. So excellently are these chosen, however, and so great are their potentialities that we always end by hearing the divine harmonies again, and his words induce in us the right attitude for hearing the word of God.

And that was the essential thing, for behind Augustine's rejection of luxury on the one hand and his detestation of thoughtless and unintelligent routine on the other (as also behind his zeal for a correct understanding of rites and symbols) there lay, governing everything else, a deep reverence for that word of God which has been revealed to us. The first thought that comes to him when his mind turns to the subject of worship in church is not the ritual and sacramental side of the cultus but the eternal dialogue between God and man. The *Confessions* put the thing with classical brevity: "My mother went to church twice a day, she went in the morning and the evening without ever allowing anything to keep her away, and she went not to hear idle tales and the gossip of old women, but so that she might hear thee in thy words, and so that thou mightest hear her in her prayers."[99] In church "God speaks in the lessons while we speak in our prayers"; the church is the place where the feast of the Holy Scriptures "is always ready".[100] That is why his emphasis is always on the speaking God, for God has his word, and when we pray we do this by means of rites and expressions which are taken from God's word; yes, we even pray in the very Person of the Word made flesh, as we are gathered around his altar and into his body, which is the Church.

The whole work of Augustine owes its very flesh, its very bones and marrow, to the word of God. His whole vocabulary is permeated by the rich and somewhat crude speech of the old translations of the Bible; both the old African translation and the Italian played their part in this, though it was the latter of these two that Augustine preferred, "because it holds more closely to the sense of the original words, and renders their meaning with greater clarity". A number of scholars think that Augustine revised a certain number of the books himself.[101] Whatever be the truth of this, it would be difficult to point to a man who was more completely filled by Holy Scripture than was Augustine. Origen is the learned visionary, Jerome the "three-tongued" scholar, but Augustine is, above all, the believing Bible student. From the days of Cassiciacum till the time of his death he literally lived in Holy Scripture, and had in it so simple a faith that despite his strong critical instinct, he could never wholeheartedly accept the version which Jerome had revised from the original texts; for Augustine never wavered in his conviction as to the providential promulgation and verbal inspiration of the Septuagint, nor did he ever doubt the legend that it had originated in seventy separate cells.[102] These merely human corrections—the very idea, in fact, that "the Hebrew books could contain anything that had escaped so many most expert translators"—was a surprise "more painful than [he] could describe", nor did he hesitate to express himself in this sense to his fellow Bible student, an older man and undoubtedly his superior in philological erudition. It was only after a long correspondence about a number of specific texts that he surrendered, and that not without reservations.[103]

About the zenith of his life he started the systematic planning of his work on Christian knowledge which he only completed shortly before his death. It is quite obvious that he intended this to be a handbook designed to bring about a deeper understanding of Scripture. The sky darkened as he grew older, but as he said in an unforgettable simile, "as little as the night can extinguish the stars in the heavens, so little can the injustice of man extinguish the spirits that are set in the firmament of Holy Scripture".[104]

No greater mistake could, however, be made than to suppose that this man of the Bible meant his veneration of the Bible to be regarded as a belittling of the sacramental cultus, or that any remark of his has that implication. If anything, the opposite was true. Almost unconsciously he proceeded from the assumption that the traditional sacraments, which had been guaranteed by the oecumenical Church, all served to give expression to the real meaning of Scripture, and that their animating spirit lay in the biblical mysteries. He is also anxious that the Bible should be read in the traditional sequence, which in the year 400 already corresponded to the ecclesiastical year, and included some arrangement, of which we know very little, for a *lectio continua* of the most important books.[105] The manner in which he picked out his pericopes, and thus to some extent put his own emphasis on the texts, was in complete accord with the custom of the time, which permitted considerable freedom in the choice of the readings. In this matter of Bible readings, as in so many others, Augustine strictly observed traditional usage. In Easter week he interrupted his continuous commentary on the Gospel according to St. John and preached on the gospel of the day, which dealt with appearances of the risen Christ.[106] At Easter time he read, as we still do today, the Acts of the Apostles, "which, according to a fixed custom, we begin to read on Easter Sunday".[107] In much the same way, on the commemorative days of the martyrs he adhered to the customary readings, but on these days he himself chose the pericope on which to preach, and had this read out before the sermon. There was hardly anyone who in his preaching clung more closely than Augustine to the liturgical texts. There is hardly a sermon that does not refer to the epistle, the psalm (or antiphon) of the day—he always knew exactly what they were— or to the gospel of the day, which by that time was already fixed. "As we have just heard", he would then say, "As you have just heard from the precentor", or "As you yourselves sang a few moments ago." "Today we celebrate the feast of the holy martyr Laurence; the readings which you heard just now were most fitting for this holy feast." "We have heard and sung and have reverently followed the reading of the Gospel." In this way he once began a sermon, naming all three types of reading in one sentence.[108] On another occasion he says, "We have heard the story; let us now seek the meaning of the mystery."[109]

One can safely say that both at the celebration of the Eucharist and at the evening worship Augustine invariably expounded the Scriptures, either choosing a text of his own, or one from one of the prescribed passages for the day. In this he was following an ancient rule, for the sermon was still essentially a commentary on what had been read. Even when he was dealing with some live question of the moment or was making an appeal for a special collection, or preaching in connection with a consecration, he never failed to refer back to the sacred texts on which he built up his discourse and which were the foundation of his arguments. As to the Christian mysteries and the sacraments, it will be seen in the chapters that follow that he allowed no solemn initiation to pass by without explaining the rites in question with all the biblical stops out. This man, who once wrote that God can sometimes sanctify a person "without the mediation of man" and without visible sacraments (though never a man who is a despiser of those visible sacraments),[110] this man who also said that the communal character of the sacraments was the essential condition of holiness, cannot be said ever to have underrated the external apparatus of sanctification. In words of high praise he tells an opponent (and ourselves) that the Punic peasants, who could not speak the Latin of the towns, referred to baptism simply as "salvation" and to the Eucharist as "life".[111] Yet for all that, the value he attached to the sacraments was never disproportionate. They belonged to the world of signs, which, together with faith and hope, would one day disappear; whereas love, and that which was shown forth in the signs, would remain for ever. If sanctification is brought about first in one way, then in another, then the purpose of that is to keep us humble and to remind us that holiness "is not achieved by human pride but by means of heavenly grace". Thus, the Samaritans received the Holy Ghost after baptism through the laying-on of hands, while the hundred and twenty converted of the first Pentecost received it while they were praying and without the laying-on of hands; Cornelius, again, and those of his house, received it when they heard the word of God, and before they were baptized.[112]

Nor did he fall into the error of identifying reverence for the word of God with a predilection for a particular type of preaching. Thus he once wrote in respect of a piece of exposition, "External instruction is only a means to an end, a reminder. The one who truly teaches our hearts has his *cathedra* in heaven."[113] He knew that the voice of this heavenly teacher could express itself equally well through word and sacrament, and could achieve the same results both as to the objective infusion of grace and the power of its impression on the minds of those who truly believed. He knew that we can hear this voice equally well at the altar and when we sit at the feet of a preacher or are bent over our texts. He also quite sincerely believed that the all-embracing word of God, which manifests to us the reality of the fullness of Christ, is presented to us both in the sacraments and in the Scripture under the same moving and uplifting disguise, namely that of the symbol. For Augustine word, sign and interpretation formed an indissoluble unity, for he interpreted Holy Scripture as he both read it and saw it shown forth in the signs of the sacraments. He interpreted it, that is to say, as an all-embracing allegory. This is the element that unites his celebration of the mysteries with his preaching, and it provides the real explanation of both. In the next chapter, which deals with the important rites of the *initiatio Christiana*, the reader will see how closely word and sacrament interpenetrated.

12

BECOMING A CHRISTIAN

Initiatio Christiana

THE emphasis placed on the explanation of gestures and signs is easy enough to understand if one reflects how in those days the whole of Christianity was in the eyes of simple folk a kind of mysterious entity consisting essentially of just such holy signs. Even the educated man outside the Faith looked upon it as something like that. Certainly Christianity could be studied from the sacred books, but to become a Christian meant being initiated stage by stage into the mysteries or *sacramenta*.[1] The true Christians, of course, knew that becoming a Christian began with having faith, and that this faith was a gift of grace. They knew the words of Jesus, "No man cometh to the Son unless the Father draw him." No man in the early Church was more concerned to keep alive the idea of the supernatural origin of grace than was the preacher of Hippo. Above everything else the Christians knew that the essence of Christianity was nothing less than a completely new life in the Lord Jesus Christ, a complete moral turn-about, a true conversion, for the new life in Christ killed the old life of our corrupted nature, the old darkness could no longer assert itself against the new, all-penetrating light.

It was precisely in this that the Christian religion differed from the various mystery religions that surrounded it. Faith was a gift but it also demanded complete conversion. It demanded not merely a certain vague assent of the intellect, but the whole man.[2] Yet for all that this distinction was often imprecise to the mind of the fourth and fifth centuries and on the men of that time the impression conveyed by Christianity was still that of a closed temple, full of divine secrets. It opened itself to the initiated—that is to say, to those who believed and were baptized.

The door of this temple was the sacrament of rebirth, before which were arrayed a whole row of introductory sacraments, forming a sort of antechamber to the temple. In those days the words "mystery" and "sacrament" sounded familiar to everybody. No-one doubted the fundamental interconnection of all things, their symbolic potency, or the divine effectiveness of certain symbols. Nobody was surprised or antagonized by the fact that Christ should have instituted mysteries of his own. Augustine loved to show how simple they were, how small was their number, and how different they were from the external mysteries of the demonic cults and from the fleshly ceremonies of the Law of the Old Testament.[3] Yet for all that they remained for ordinary people just mysteries in the ancient sense of the term.

Whoever was born of Christian parents lived and moved in these mysteries and felt at home therein; they became a matter of habit and instinct. The outsider, however, looked upon them with a certain nervous hesitancy, all the more so since there was no way of being initiated into them at one stroke. That initiation had necessarily to take place, in part at least, step by step and had to take place in the presence of the whole community, usually once a year.

It was this latter circumstance that was the occasion of Augustine's expounding even the most elementary of the holy mysteries at least once a year to a number of new candidates. At such times he also took the opportunity offered by their presence of refreshing the memories of those who had grown up in the Faith, but in whom familiarity had all too often begotten forgetfulness of the meaning of their own practices. Year in, year out, people came to him with the more or less vague intention of becoming Christians; some presented themselves as would-be catechumens and got no further. Yet every year a certain number would have their names inscribed as *competentes* and these were then baptized together on Easter Eve. We do not know exactly how large was the average number in a town like Hippo, but certainly there were some hundreds—enough, at any rate, for the individual to disappear in the crowd.[4] All these, including the catechumens, were called Christians. The various stages of the initiation, which could, if the person concerned so desired, be extended over an entire lifetime, formed a single coherent entity, and one full of meaning, in which the great sacrament that came at the end could not be divorced from the various lesser ones that preceded it; so that Augustine could say to candidates who had finally completed their initiation: "In this life you possess Christ through faith, through the sign of the cross, through baptism and through the food and drink of the altar."[5] That was the customary and most impressive progression, and this had now become the manner in which, over a period of centuries, the "putting-on of the Lord Jesus Christ" had come to be carried out in all Churches. Thus the normal process of initiation was not what it often is today, a somewhat belated declaration of faith, or the repetition of the baptismal vow originally made by a godfather, and the following of this by a solemn First Communion, which is in reality no first Communion at all, and which is followed in its turn by an entirely separate and usually hurried confirmation. The sacraments of baptism, confirmation and the Eucharist themselves constituted the initiatory process, and acted on the mind with all the force of a single vital perception of reality; for normally the person concerned underwent this experience with all his faculties fully developed, and often long after he had attained the age of reason. Moreover, the thing was done in the presence of the whole congregation.

The solemnities which accompanied the different stages of the initiation were in themselves so impressive that they naturally stirred a preacher to memorable utterance, and so enabled him effectively to combine word and sacrament. Strange though it may sound, it seems to be established that Augustine left behind no systematic catechetical courses (such as those of Cyril of Jerusalem, of Theodore of Mopsuestia and Ambrose) which carried the candidate right through the process of initiation. Further, this man, who wrote no less than seven books on the objective character of baptism, apparently left no description of the actual ceremony, though Tertullian had done this in a somewhat sketchy form some two hundred years previously, while during Augustine's own lifetime both Theodore of Mopsuestia and Ambrose composed detailed works on the subject. Even in his account of his own baptism in the *Confessions* he only mentions the actual rite in a single sentence, after which he immediately passes on to tell of the way the fear occasioned by the thought of his past life suddenly fell like a stone from his heart, and of the tears he shed when he heard the singing of the congregation in Milan. Perhaps the discipline of secrecy, to which particular importance was attached around the year 400 and on which Augustine was always insisting to the faithful, had something to do with this. For the *Confessions* were intended for circulation outside the Church, and for this reason and quite apart from the question of secrecy (concerning which Ambrose had given definite instructions), it is likely enough that the author would have written more guardedly than was his custom.[6] Whatever be the truth of that, however, Augustine's allusions to the rite of baptism would have been intelligible enough to the initiated, though they would have meant little for others, for they give nothing in the nature of a description of what actually took place, but merely refer to the proceedings by their customary name and give no further explanation. Nor do we really find that explanation in any of the addresses to the newly baptized which have come down to us. These merely afford us a few hurried and imperfect glances beyond a curtain that has only been slightly drawn aside.

Emergency Baptism and Infant Baptism

Normally initiation took place publicly and with great solemnity. It usually occurred once a year, on Easter Eve. As a rule only adults were present. If children were there they would be at least of an age when they already had the faculty of speech. There were, of course, still many in the towns who were never baptized at all. Not that these were actual pagans; there were at that time hardly any real pagans left. But people were often rather afraid of actually going through with baptism, and in many cases postponed it as long as they possibly could. Innumerable Christians remained catechumens all their lives and continued in that state even after marriage. Even among the truly believing, parents who had themselves undergone baptism preferred not to have their children baptized. Only sickly children, and those who were born underweight or subsequently appeared to be likely soon to die, were taken by their mothers to the priest, who then immediately baptized them, gave them the Eucharist under both forms, as is customary still today in the East, and, if this was still possible, went through all the other ceremonies.[7] We also learn that women in monasteries had any foundling they took in immediately baptized.[8] Often children died on the way to the church, because, even where the child was on the point of death, parents hesitated to baptize it themselves in their home.[9]

Further, Augustine had often to rebuke people because they hoped that baptism, extreme unction and the sacrament of the altar would bring health back to some little sick body and so expected a temporal reward for their faith.[10] Even this first and greatest of the sacraments was in danger of being treated by the people as a sort of anti-demonic medicine, to the use of which no-one, it was held, could object, since "it came from the Church"—and was there not a wicked demon behind every illness? Where healthy children were concerned, however, people preferred not to take them to the baptismal pool. Augustine himself, when as a little boy he was suffering from spasms of the stomach and was in danger of death, had asked his mother for baptism. He was at that time a catechumen, and Monica had prepared everything for an emergency baptism. When, however, she saw that the crisis was past, she had put it off again,[11] thinking it better to wait till he had reached the years of discretion.

Augustine did not share this pusillanimity; he even saw a kind of crime in such calculation, for it meant that parents were blind to the danger to which they were exposing their children, since these might always die quite suddenly, and the high infant mortality rate of those days increased that probability. Moreover, such an attitude was bound to produce the impression among the young that they were perfectly free to sin up to the time of their baptism, which could after all take place at an advanced age. Augustine, who had so stressed the effectiveness of baptism against the "Anabaptists" of that day, could not say enough concerning the absolute necessity of this sacrament for salvation. He insistently adjured his hearers not to defer baptism as far as they themselves were concerned and not to keep their children from it, or to withhold it from anyone in danger. As to the baptism of minors, he looked upon this, like Origen, as an apostolic tradition: "This tender age can bear a significant and weighty witness, for was it not the children who were first permitted to shed their blood for Christ?"[12]—the *mystère des saints Innocents* —in the sense of Péguy and so many other fallen soldiers. He also appeals to the practice of Cyprian and to the fact that so many mothers do hasten to the baptismal pool, that Mother Church is ready to receive them all, and that even the little child makes its condition known, in so far as it is able to do so, for at baptism it does not begin to laugh but to weep.[13] Moreover, these little ones, though they are as yet incapable of any evil act, are nevertheless already dead at the root through original sin; therefore he adjures the adults to take their fate to heart, to speak for those that have as yet no speech, and to beg for those that weep.[14] Further, it is not only the faith of the parents that stands surety for that of the children, but the Church itself, which as a community of the saints continually proclaims that faith through the former's mouth; and all this goes forward by virtue of the power of the sacrament which has been given to the Church and of the hope which is based on that.[15]

He has similar ideas on the baptism of the dying and the unconscious. He expressly emphasizes the effectiveness of such emergency baptism, which can be validly carried out by a layman or even by a pagan; nor is its validity impaired when it is carried out as a joke or by way of mockery, so long as the person committing this act of sacrilege observes the correct forms and performs the act in the name of the Blessed Trinity, and the one being baptized is "free of any hypocrisy and receives it with a certain faith and the words of the Gospel"—that is to say, so long as he has the necessary intention. He admitted, however, that he preferred not to give a final decision on this question but rather to wait until a Church synod could consider it.[16]

An emergency baptism when there was danger of death was admittedly as sober an affair as it is today. Often there was very little solemnity about it, and that was true not only in the case of newly-born children but in the case of unconscious adults. Augustine tells us that a young friend whom he himself had been instrumental in leading astray into the Manichean heresy had been baptized with the sweat of death upon him. The people thought, he had mockingly remarked, that they could thus prolong his life—as though that which Augustine had given him was not far more valuable. When the young man began to recover and seemed a little livelier, Augustine could find nothing better to do than to make fun of the whole business. To Augustine's own astonishment, however, the young man, being filled with the power of grace of the reborn, was indignant over this, despite his weakness, and protested against such a thing's being made fun of. When, shortly afterwards, he died, Augustine could never forgive himself for his tactlessness.[17] Such incidents must often have occurred. Every unbaptized person who lay dying was baptized in the same hurried manner, partly from faith, partly from fear and often from motives less worthy than that. Fundamentally, for all that, the thing was a matter of faith.

Even in doubtful cases Augustine always advised baptism. If anyone is seriously ill and is not capable of learning the *symbolum* (creed) by heart, he is to be questioned article by article and can then simply answer, "Yes." If there is occasion for haste, he need not even be asked whether he still bears anybody hatred or have any similar question put to him.[18] But is it not a disgraceful thing that a man should receive baptism in this fashion through his own fault and have to answer the questions, so to speak, at the gallop?[19] And how many die before they can be baptized, sometimes after a lifelong catechumenate? "Yes, beloved, when people get ill, they send somebody round to the church or have themselves carried there in person; then they are baptized and renewed and it will be for their good."[20] Better late than never. If one comes to a catechumen and finds him already unconscious he should be baptized, although, so Augustine tells, most people are afraid of doing this because it is written, "Throw not that which is holy before the dogs." Although one does not know in such a case whether the person in question truly consents, it is nevertheless better to baptize a person against his will than to deny baptism to a person who desires it, and this is all the more true in cases where there is no absolute certainty but the degree of probability that baptism is actually desired is high—a curious example of Augustine's practical probabilism. He would quite readily baptize a man who was *in extremis*, though he had been living with a divorced woman and had refused, while he had his health, to mend his ways. If such a person recovered, however, he had to abide by the general rules laid down for those baptized, and was made to put his matrimonial affairs in order.[21] His great anxiety was to let no-one die unbaptized. We should remember that he was quite unable to conceive of a pious catechumen's being saved if he died a sudden death and was not baptized at the time.

If ever there was a man who held that the solemn paraphernalia of the actual rite was of little importance, but that the sacrament of baptism by water was indispensible for salvation, that man was Augustine. For that reason, as time went by, he showed himself increasingly inclined not to confine even the solemn and formal ceremony of baptism to Easter Eve. Though shortly after this Leo the Great was to threaten the bishops of Campania, Picenum and Samnium with deposition if they should continue to baptize at any other time than the vigils of Easter and Pentecost,[22] Augustine seems never to have had any serious concern in the matter, and might well have followed this course even if the dangers of delay had not influenced him as powerfully as they did. Concerning the practice of fixing Easter Eve as the date for baptisms he says, "Grace does not flow more freely on that occasion than on any other, but the joy we feel upon this feast is a kind of invitation to choose this day for baptisms."[23] Here once more the pastor of souls gets the better of the mystic.

THE CATECHUMENATE

Whoever wished to become a Christian went to the bishop's palace and introduced himself to one of the priests, or else was introduced by some Christian friend who would then vouch for him. After this there would be a lengthy sitting in the reception room. It would literally be a "sitting", for Augustine considered it "dangerous" to talk to a single person or a small group for long without offering them a seat; only a large group could be allowed to stand.[23a] The applicant or applicants would occasionally be accompanied by a number of acquaintances who had already been baptized and wished to improve their knowledge; the bishop or the priest or deacon who received them noted down the names and enquired after the reasons for the conversion. These last were of the most varied kind. People sought to be received from motives of pure timeserving, some came because they wished to please their master or their protector, others from fear of their landlords, others, again, in order not to lose the custom of Church folk. Yet others appeared because they wished to marry a Christian girl. Finally, there were those who had already studied the Scriptures and had come to think for themselves.[24] Yet even in the hearts of the mere simulators who came from motives of temporal gain or slavish fear, there was never wholly lacking some little spark of the fear of God and fear of the Judgement and of the pains of hell, of that imperfect penitence, in a word, that often, through the mere hearing of the word of God, can change over into love—for even the smallest of such sparks is already breathed on by grace.[25] This first visit to the presbytery was a delicate moment, which Augustine has often described, for such a man would have seen many good and bad men both inside and outside the Church. Now at last, he would have made up his mind to become a Catholic.[26]

Then the catechist would begin an address which might last anything from half an hour to two hours. In it he would give a short description of the secret of the Faith and of the duties of a Christian, but he did so without actually bringing in the actual text of the *symbolum* or the mysteries of initiation. We know the atmosphere and the themes of these introductory courses very well from the wonderful little work, *Instruction for Beginners*, which is described in a later chapter.

Apparently the cleric started by asking whether the applicant accepted what he had heard and was prepared to live in accordance with it, and no doubt the answer will have been, as it is today, the scarcely audible "Yes" that was expected.[27] This instruction was in due course brought to a conclusion by a little solemnity consisting of four rites. The candidate received the sign of Christ, namely the cross, upon his forehead. Hands were then laid upon him and a kind of exorcism was performed, during which evil was "breathed out of him",[28] for it was believed that the devil literally possessed the unbaptized, as though they were his property, just as the Holy Ghost took possession of the baptized. Finally he received for the first time the "sacrament of salt", probably together with a piece of the exorcism bread, the blessed bread that was given to non-communicants.[29] These four *sacramenta* were looked upon as shadows of the actual sacraments of initiation; they were a sort of conception within the womb of the Church which preceded the actual birth therefrom.[30] The signing with the cross was a shadow of baptism, the laying-on of hands a shadow of confirmation, while the handing over of bread and salt was a shadow of the Eucharist that was to come.

From this point onwards, however, the candidate belonged to the "great house".[31] He was a catechumen and a Christian. He could come to church and hear the sermon, as could any pagan or any Jew (for to these, too, the doors stood open, and preachers were particularly careful to avoid any subject the mention of which would violate the discipline of secrecy). There were not many such subjects. "What things do we treat as secret?" Augustine once asked from the pulpit. "Only the sacraments of baptism and the Eucharist."[32] When he came to speak of these or other delicate subjects such as the relationship of the three Persons of the Trinity,[33] then he never forgot that he was speaking to a mixed audience. When he was speaking, for instance, of the priesthood of Melchisedech, he was able to say, "I say this for the faithful. If the catechumens do not take my meaning, let them shake off their indolence and come speedily to an understanding of these things."[34] After the sermon, and before the offerings for the sacrifice were brought out, all such persons were sent away by means of the short formula which in those days was called *missa*.[35] The congregation of the faithful, however, remained assembled in the church behind closed doors, and it was the duty of the porter at the door to ask everyone who sought to enter and who was not known to him personally whether he was baptized; this was to prevent any catechumen "forcing his way into the presence of the mysteries".[36]

Of the four *sacramenta* here in question, that of the cross was certainly the most impressive. It was this that marked a man as a Christian. Hundreds who pressed around the steps of the apse possessed as yet nothing that could be called Christian except a vague good will and the signing upon them of the cross, and sometimes that was all they had till the day of their death. Augustine frequently had occasion to make a special appeal to the sense of honour of these unhappy cross-bearers. Certainly the cross was the thing that terrified the devil, it was the sign of our victorious conquest over evil. As once the blood of the lamb had done when smeared on the doorposts, so today this sign, which men often tattoed their foreheads with, scared away the angel of destruction. Augustine, however, could not approve of his sheep simply looking upon it as a powerful "apotropaeic" sign, a means of warding things off, for it was a great deal more than that.[37] "It is", he says, "first and foremost the distinguishing mark, the *character* of the soldiers of Christ,[38] a sort of rough and hurried monogram of Christ, and as such an ever-present reminder of the fact that you who sign yourselves with it are Christians." Although it has now "moved from the place of execution to the foreheads of emperors",[39] it still reminds us of the self-abasement of God. We must never forget that it is not the star of the Wise Men that has become the sign of Christ but the thing of disgrace, the cross.[40] Further, it is the daily reminder of suffering, and this reminder should never vanish from our altar, our lips or our forehead, for in all the sacraments the cross is indispensable; at baptism, at the Eucharist, at extreme unction, everywhere.[41] It is drawn with our thumb and forefinger on our foreheads, because the forehead is the seat of shame and we must never be ashamed because of the cross of the Son of Man.[42] In the Latin idiom we say of a shameless person, "This man has no forehead", but our forehead is signed with the cross of Christ.[43] That being so, it was natural that Augustine should have sharp words for those who were incapable of tearing themselves away from the theatre, for instance, and it is to be feared that this was just what the majority could not do. "And this is what men permit themselves, who, though they may not have been baptized, are nevertheless already Christians. Perhaps a catechumen thinks he can allow himself this. He says, 'I am only a catechumen.' Indeed—only a catechumen? Have you then one forehead to bear the cross of Christ and another wherewith to go to the theatre? Are you determined to go to that place? If so, first change your forehead." How, he says, can we claim that we are carrying the cross on our foreheads when we have lost it from our hearts? And this many of us have done, for if indeed we carried the cross in our hearts we should not be in such a place.[44]

There are occasional allusions to the "sacrament of salt" but nowhere is there a full explanation of it. Salt usually suggests to him the "apostolic salt which drives away the stink and foulness of sin". He also regards it as a symbol of the gift of discernment by which we distinguish between heavenly and earthly goods.[45] Yet sometimes, again, he understands it in a different sense and one which is tied up with some rather complicated allusions to various scriptural texts that mention salt, the salt of the earth, the salt of the sea, of this world;[46] even the pillar of salt into which Lot's wife was turned is not forgotten. Lot's wife was turned into the salt of that prudence which she lacked, and so she warns us never after baptism to turn around and gaze at the Sodom of our sinful past; otherwise we may ourselves be turned into the salt that destroys corruption—in other words, a dreadful warning to others. All of which is surely something of an exegetic masterpiece.[47] In the little handbook which he wrote for Deogratias he told him to explain that "this thing which has now been consecrated by a blessing has here an altogether different significance from that attaching to it in its ordinary daily use". Explain to them further, he goes on, what was the function of the sermon which they have just heard, how it must add savour to their spirit; and that this consecrated matter is a symbol of that savouring. In this general connection you must remind them that Holy Scripture has a spiritual meaning, even though the sense seems fleshly.[48]

None of this seems very precise, and one cannot help thinking that this particular rite had, by Augustine's day, become little more than a ceremony; nobody any longer had any really clear idea of what it meant. No doubt the majority of catechumens will have thought of some kind of safeguard against spiritual corruption—a kind of antidemonic specific. It was likely enough that they did so, for the salt was always handed around in small quantities, and this procedure was coupled with a laying-on of hands which seems to have had an exorcistic intention. Perhaps here and there some rather pedantic person will have thought of the salt for the newly-born which was customary among the Romans on the *dies lustricus*. The catechumens appear to have received their "sacrament of salt" with much the same regularity that the faithful received the Eucharist and the Greeks and Russians of today receive the *prosphora* bread when they refrain from communicating. Two consecutive councils enjoined that the catechumens were, even on the solemn days of Easter, to receive nothing but "the customary salt".[49]

By the year 400 the majority of the catechumens had begun to come from Christian families, so that there could no longer be any question of violent curiosity or excited anticipation in respect of the holy secrets.[50] The institution of the catechumenate as such, in the days of the martyrs a time of rigorous testing, had most pitifully degenerated. Of what had originally often been a two-year period of probation and study, nothing remained but the four signs, the solitary address and the weekly hearing of the preliminary stages of the Mass. Indeed, for those large numbers of people who remained catechumens and never dreamed of enrolling as *competentes*, and only underwent baptism on their deathbeds, their first catechism remained their last. There was no further instruction; from then onward they were dependent on what they could learn from ordinary sermons—sermons, that is to say, which were directed not exclusively to them, but to pagans, heretics and Jews, all of whom could come and listen, if they so desired.[51] No doubt they listened, but they did not understand; they were *audientes*, not *intelligentes*.

The catechumenate was the customary status of the nominal Christian, the man who lacked the courage for baptism but was ashamed to be called a heathen. Their name denotes "hearers", Augustine said, but they do not understand and remain dumb.[52] They trust in Jesus, but Jesus does not yet trust himself to *them*. When we ask a catechumen whether he believes in Christ, he says, "Yes, I believe", and crosses himself. He already carries the cross of Christ on his forehead and is not ashamed of the cross of his Lord. Thus he already believes in his name, but if you ask him, "Do you eat the body and drink the blood of the Son of Man?" then he has no notion what all that is about.[53] Though he might continually cross himself like some moujik of the old days (and in those days many did just that, though they may have done it less clumsily and unfortunately, like the Old Believers, with two fingers instead of three) a catechumen who did not go forward was a Christian who sinned through presumption and remained both deaf and blind. Augustine compared the half-healed state of the catechumen, who was really neither one thing nor the other, with the man born blind, whom Jesus had touched with his spittle, but who had not yet entered the Pool of Siloam.

> Ask a man if he is a Christian. If he is a pagan or a Jew he will immediately answer "No", but if he says, "Yes", then ask him further whether he is a catechumen or one of the faithful. If he says that he is a catechumen, then he has been anointed. Why was that? Ask him and he will answer you. You need really only ask him in whom he believes. Just because he is a catechumen, he says, "In Christ" (the anointed one). Mark that I now speak equally for the benefit of catechumens and of the faithful. What is it that I have said concerning the spittle and the slime? That the Word has been made flesh (the Word, spittle from the head of the Father, has been mingled with the slime of our flesh). The catechumen has therefore been anointed by the Anointed One and he has this ointment upon his blind eyes. The catechumens themselves hear me speak these things, but all that is not sufficient for that for which they have been anointed. They must hurry to enter the bath if they will have sight in their eyes.[54]

The *Competentes*

If, however, towards the time of fasting a catechumen enrolled as a *competens*—that is to say as a "seeker along with others"[55]—then things became serious, for the old strict period of probation had shrunk down to the seven weeks before baptism. The candidate for baptism was, however, accounted as a recruit of Christ and underwent a thorough training.[56] If he was married he had to practice continence. He was forbidden to bathe and had to fast till evening. Above all, he had to have true repentance for his previous life, for he was no longer a little child but was free to use his will.[57] Unbathed and with their clothing neglected, the *competentes* stood apart in a special portion of the church where the whole congregation could see them, and no doubt their long fasts added to their feeling of discomfort. The special solemnities that surrounded them at this stage may also well have helped to produce a desire for self-renewal not less sincere and not less pathetic than that engendered at the popular missions of the last century. During all this time they were "chastised with instructions and catechetical advice", nor did it ever occur to Augustine to confine himself to the dogmatic explanation of the mere skeleton of the Faith. He used the opportunity to hit out as hard as he could against pagan amusements and sought with all his might to inculcate a certain amount of moral responsibility into those under his care. He again emphasized that actors, stage-managers, pimps, prostitutes and gladiators would in no circumstances be received. He repeated St. Paul's catalogue of vices and left no doubt in the minds of his hearers that those who did these things would in no wise enter the Kingdom of Heaven, even though they were formally baptized.[58] Who it was that then carried on with the chastisement,[59] and where this occurred, and whether the candidates were treated to special addresses in an adjoining room or listened with the rest in the church where the sermon no doubt would have contained some passage specially directed towards them—these are matters which we have no means of deciding.[60] We do learn that "in the night" they were on several occasions questioned one after another before the entire congregation about their conduct and their resolutions, and that quite possibly on at least the first of these occasions they underwent some kind of bodily examination to check whether they suffered from possession, leprosy or ritual uncleanliness. This procedure was known as the *scrutinium*, and during it it was the candidate's duty to search his conscience and awaken true repentance within himself for his past sins. This *scrutinium* was combined with a "blowing-out" and exorcism of the Evil One, because the candidates were looked upon as his slaves in the sense of genuinely being his property.[61] Even in the case of little children these exorcisms were never omitted. It was a very ancient custom, the existence of which Augustine would frequently use as an argument against the Pelagians and their denial of original sin. For if they did not believe the Evil One to be present what were they blowing at save the image of God? And that was an insult to God's majesty. Augustine used the same argument against the Donatist "Anabaptists", because these dared to use a similar exorcism in the case of one filled by the Holy Ghost, that is to say, a baptized person.[62] Contemptuously and almost hissing,[63] the exorcist blew at the unseen enemy and blew him out of the body of the man concerned. Then, using the form of one of those very ancient prayers which call down the power of the Supreme God against the arch-enemy, he would cry, "Come out of him, Accursed One!" And just as men believed that the devil possessed the unbaptized person as his property, so also they believed that, once he had been driven out of him, he would flee into the wilderness, as in the time of Christ.[64] While "the Evil One, the blower-in of unfaithfulness", was "roundly abused in the terror-inspiring name of the almighty Trinity",[65] the *competentes* stood barefooted upon a rough rag or upon a *tunica* made of animal skin. "They did not actually put on a penitential garment, but in mystical fashion stood upon it", so that they might learn "to tread into the earth the goatskins of their vices and to tear to rags the goats that stood upon the left",[66] for a tunic of animal hide was something more than the penitential shirt or *cilicium*. It was intended to recall to our minds the clothing, after the Fall, of our first parents. It was also an excellent symbol of our fallen nature, which Christ, the new Adam, had put on in order to raise it up and transform it into a new kind of raiment.[67] It symbolized in the baptismal candidates their own past sins and whole manner of life, which, because they now considered it bestial, they trod underfoot and utterly repudiated. Meanwhile, they sought to fathom their own hearts and sought to assist in the driving-out of the Evil One by cultivating a sincere hatred for their sins and seeking to repent of them. This wretched business of standing barefoot in the cold of a spring night had not been exactly an enjoyable experience for Augustine himself at the time of his own conversion. He always suffered from cold, and it was the first thing he thought of when Alypius presented himself as a *competens*, but, according to Augustine, Alypius did not worry about that, not even in chilly Italy.[68]

On a certain day towards the end of the fasting period, probably on the Saturday before what is our First Sunday of the Passion,[69] the *competentes* had the *symbolum* recited to them word for word: the term means "handshake" or "bargain", an expression taken, so says Augustine, from the vocabulary of business, but meaning in this instance the confession of faith; it was identical, except for a very few words, with our twelve articles of faith.[70] The various secrets were already known to the *competentes*, but the lapidary formula which was accounted apostolic and which they were supposed to learn by heart at the beginning of the Easter Vigil had never been heard by them before. It was a formula that was nowhere set down in writing but had been orally handed down.[71] It came under the discipline of secrecy, though it was not to this that Augustine referred when discussing the absence of any written record, but to the passage in Jeremiah in which it is foretold that God, in the new covenant, will not write his law upon tables, but in the hearts of men.[72]

This handing-over of the confession of faith was accompanied by a short celebration during which the bishop usually gave a fairly detailed summary of the different articles. Four such special sermons on "The *Symbolum* for Catechumens" have been preserved.[73] The first was obviously delivered before, and the others after, the handing-over of the *symbolum*. In all of them there are the usual allusions to the Arian heresy concerning the Trinity and also to the Donatist errors concerning the visibility, nature and holiness of the Church. They are sternly dogmatic summaries of Christian doctrine but by no means dull, and marked occasionally by undeniable grandeur in their conceptions. The candidates were enjoined by the bishop to repeat most diligently what they had heard, preferably to their spiritual parents, the godfather and godmother who would lift them out of the baptismal pool. He further admonished them to recite it, by way of test, to him personally and to do this at cockcrow one week from the day on which he was speaking after a solemn night of vigil. When the time for this test before him came, they were not to be anxious. "Be calm," he says, "we are your father and have neither rod nor whip. We are not like the schoolmaster in your school. A man can easily stumble over a word. All that matters is that he should not stumble over the Faith."[74] And whoever had not yet mastered the matter still had a whole week—up to Easter Saturday, in fact. For all that, Augustine did insist on a test. "You cannot hear it, like the *Our Father,* every day in the church. You must therefore say it to yourselves daily at rising and retiring. Give your *symbolum* back again and again, give it back to the Lord. Memorize it, do not be too idle to be continually repeating it, for saying it over to yourselves time and again is the very best way of preventing yourselves from forgetting what it says. Don't say, 'I said it over yesterday, or even today and I have said it daily. I know it perfectly.' Do you not dress yourselves when you get up? Then dress your soul by recalling the *symbolum* to your memory."[75] One of these sermons contains some very practical directions for the conduct of this ceremony, so much so, indeed, that we find it hard to resist the conclusion that it was Augustine himself who devised its actual form.

After the test recitation by the candidate of the *symbolum* or Creed, which probably took place on the Saturday before Palm Sunday,[76] there followed the solemn recitation and exposition of a second holy text, the *Our Father*—first the *symbolum* or Creed, then the prayer, for, so says Augustine in the words of St. Paul, "How will they call upon him if they do not believe on him?"[77]

This occasion was also graced by sermons, and again four of these are preserved.[78] In them Augustine gives a moving analysis of the *Our Father,* which may in some respects be compared to that other given in his letter to Faltonia Proba. His real inspiration here is Cyprian's famous book on the Lord's Prayer, that pearl of African literature, which was still used for the catechumenate in the Church at Carthage.[79] He first explains *how* and then *what* we should pray, and the connection of these two things with one another. Under the term "daily bread" he understands both our physical bread and the word of God and the Eucharist. The prayer for forgiveness is part of the normal way to secure the remission of sins committed after baptism, it is a sort of daily baptism which we all most painfully need.[80] If anyone is unable to remember the Lord's Prayer from one reading, that is not too terrible, for he hears it daily from the altar,[81] and incidentally it is contained in every codex of the Gospels.

Easter Eve

At last came the days in which the novices, as Ambrose called them, "were initiated into the more complete mysteries".[82] On Maundy Thursday they were permitted to break their fast and to take a bath in the *thermae* of the town, because "the bodies would otherwise have an unpleasant smell when they entered the baptismal pool".[83] In the afternoon, in some Churches, including possibly that of Hippo, the bishop washed their feet in memory of the example and the command which the Lord himself gave on this day.[84] They did not attend the celebration of the Lord's Supper which was held at the exact hour of this event. Only the initiated were admitted to that, and these had fasted all day (or at least postponed their meal till darkness had fallen) in order to follow the Lord even in this particular and only to receive the mystery "after they had partaken of the meal".[85] Many fasted during the forty-day fast, but all Christians did so on Good Friday and Easter Saturday and that very strictly, and naturally enough this practice was followed by those about to be baptized.[86]

On Good Friday the basilica resounded with the psalm which our Lord had prayed upon the cross, the twenty-first psalm, and all listened, deeply moved, to the story of the Passion according to St. Matthew, and also to a sermon on that subject, which sometimes took the form of an exposition of the psalm of the cross.[87] On Saturday evening, however, when darkness fell and the lamps were lit, the holy pasch began.[88] Lamps, innumerable lamps, flamed up in the basilicas and the houses; it was the greatest *lucernarium* of the entire year—and thus the night of suffering turned suddenly into the day of the Resurrection.

Easter Eve had begun, the most joyful vigil of Christendom, not a vigil for a handful of people, but the feast of a multitude that could not be numbered. We can scarcely imagine the festive excitement and the joy, the real delight which this occasion kindled in Christian hearts. It was something even more intense and exalted than our modern Christmas midnight Mass and, though there was in it much less sensibility and human tenderness, it had a mystical comprehensiveness that outdid even our holiest feasts and a boldness in its joy which we no longer seem to know, but of which the nocturnal Easter liturgy of the Russians might perhaps give us some conception. We of today carry the delicate human sensibility of the Middle Ages in our blood, and the Christian mysteries have become for us the objects of a gentle piety, but for the Church folk of those times they were the celebration of a mighty victory, and Easter, the nocturnal feast of light, represented triumph over the demons, triumph over sin and triumph over death.

We can picture it. As long as the stars still stand in the heavens, the barred windows of the great church continue to give out a deep glow. The gold and silver lampholders have been lighted and gleam in the reddish light of the oil lamps. The crowd streams on—there is a perpetual coming and going. The curtains at the doors and the *vela* between the pillars have been gathered up. The light falls right into the courtyard with its barren-looking shrubs. It falls onto the people that keep pressing in through the open doors. One can hear a low murmur of voices and yet over all there is quiet, for the vesper bell is as yet unknown in the Christian world.

All through the night in the interior of the church there sounds a continuous whispering and scraping, that humming, as of a beehive, which you may still hear on the eve of any great feast in Rome, Jerusalem or Seville. The crowds move around and the tied-up curtains flutter against them, now showing only the crosses, doves and peacocks woven into their upper portions, the lower parts being tied together—only around the apse those curtains still hang down with all their splendour fully extended, behind the great candelabra, each as tall as a man, reminding us of the seven lamps of the Apocalypse.

Over and above the shuffling and the buzz of voices one can hear the readers read one lesson after the other, the readings alternating with the shrill melodies of psalms and hymns. The first chapters of Genesis, the story of the passage of the Red Sea from Exodus and that of the Easter lamb, the song of triumph of Mary, the sister of Moses, with her timbrel, the story of Jonah and the hymn of the three young men in the fiery furnace, sound out across the often indifferently attentive crowd in the nave. The lessons are so long, says Augustine, that "we can give no proper exposition of them, and even if we were to do so, you would soon lose the thread and your attention would wander."[89]

Nevertheless the bishop, though he is tired almost to death, must give an address. He does not speak for long, though he is full of joy and wholly carried away by the occasion. Some of these sermons of the night and the early morning are preserved to us. They are a few dozen in all,[90] and they all expound the same theme—the light in the darkness.

While thousands of eyes shine upon him and the festive garments add colour to the scene, while the jewellery of the women, the metal hanging lampholders, the gilt on the rafters, the marble of the pillars and the golden vessels all gleam in the soft light, Augustine begins to speak. He gathers together into a single whole everything that bears on this theme of light that dispels the darkness, using all the references that have occurred in the various readings that have just been given, or any other relevant text from Holy Scripture, and so he gives his Easter sermon. He recalls the verse that has just been heard from the story of creation—"And God said, let there be light, and there was light"—he speaks of the parting between light and darkness, the darkness of sin which has brought us since the days of our first parent into the darkness and the shadow of death. He speaks of the true light which suddenly shone in the darkness and which the darkness could not comprehend. He reminds his hearers of the words of the Apostle, "Ye also were once in darkness, but now ye are in the light of the Lord."[91] Then the thought takes hold of his mind that they are all watching together as men watched in the days of the Apostles and he cries out certain words in which we can still feel that lingering but eager expectation of a Second Coming, that Second Coming which stretches out ever more distantly beyond the horizons of time. "Be watchful," he cries, "and continue in your watchfulness, for it is this humble and lowly attitude of expectation which turns our night into a shining day. In this house of prayer we have lit all the lights. May God, who once caused light to shine in the darkness by his word, cause light to blaze forth in our hearts, so that we may be inwardly illumined."[92]

Such are Augustine's words to his flock. They are directed both to the tried and proven Christian, as also to those who eagerly await their baptism. These last had already heard an address in which the bishop, basing his remarks on Romans vi.4, had spoken of the "sacrament of the pool" as "being buried together with Christ and arising with him again" to a new life.[93] They had also a not altogether pleasant ceremony behind them, for before the lessons of the vigil had begun, they had had to stand on a raised platform and each one of them had had to "give back" the *symbolum* of the creed to the bishop before all the people.[94] Even children of seven, "who at that age could already both lie and speak the truth", took part in this.[95]

This was the indispensable profession of faith, which was a vital stage in the business of becoming one of the faithful. There is a story of a certain Dioscoros, a physician, who secretly got out of this public profession and was shortly thereafter almost completely paralysed. Dioscoros thereupon made a written declaration, stating that a dream had revealed to him that his affliction was a punishment for his most wrongful act. This same man had, shortly before this, been afflicted with blindness, because, so it was said, he had delayed in the keeping of a vow in which he had promised to be baptized if his little daughter recovered from an illness.[96]

We have no certain knowledge whether Africa followed the custom of Rome, but we may assume that the "giving-back" of the *symbolum* was the occasion of celebration, and that the people crowded in to take part in it, and that for this very reason persons of rank and standing who were preparing for baptism disliked the whole business. One man at least, however, put any such feeling behind him. This was the celebrated rhetorician and neo-Platonist Marius Victorinus. Marius Victorinus had, all his life, defended paganism "with a tongue that drowned the voice of the whole world". When in old age he was baptized, the suggestion was made to him, as it was often made to sensitive people, that he should perform his "giving-back" privately and thus avoid a publicity which might be embarrassing to him; but the man was worthier than his counsellors, and replied that he had so long defended lies in public that he would gladly for once publicly confess the truth.[97]

Let us return to our picture. At the end of the vigil, which was probably at cockcrow, the hour of rebirth is considered to have arrived. Once again the bishop speaks to the candidates. In a few brief words he repeats his explanation of the significance of the sacrament which they are now soon about to receive and which will be the most decisive thing in their whole lives. He recalls those famous words which once determined the course of his own life, there in the garden of the house in Milan: "The night is passed and the day is at hand. Let us therefore cast off the works of darkness and put on the armour of light. Let us walk honestly, as in the day, not in rioting and drunkenness, not in chambering and impurities, not in contention and envy. But put ye on the Lord Jesus Christ."[98] And as he speaks the cry sounds in their hearts as it did in the old *passio* of Cecilia: *"Eja, milites Christi!"*— "Come now, soldiers of Christ!"

Now it is the turn of those present in that church themselves to choose between light and darkness, and they do so by turning towards the west, the region of the sun's departure and of darkness and the demons; and there comes the question, "Doest thou forswear the devil? And his angels? And his pomp?" The meaning of this word *pompa*, originally used in a specific sense for the temples, theatres and the whole imposing apparatus of paganism, had by now become somewhat shadowy and only conveyed a somewhat vague suggestion of the temptations of this world, but the old ritual question was still put and ritually answered, and with faces turned westwards, the candidates now renounced the Evil One.[99] This done, they turn about to the east, the direction of the arising light and the symbol of him who once "triumphed over the sunset". They dedicate themselves to their true Lord and turn finally to God.[100] Then they go in procession to the baptismal chapel, which lies outside the great church itself, but is part of the same complex of buildings (Plates 2, 15), and they sing as they go the forty-first psalm, "which is rightly considered the voice of the catechumens hurrying to the holy bath": "As the hart panteth after the fountains of water, so my soul panteth after thee, O God."[101]

The baptistery too is blazing with lamps and the curtains are withdrawn between the pillars that carry the roof of the holy pool (Plate 18; cf. 16).[102] This pool itself is, as we have already seen, octagonal, after the manner of those found in the private *thermae* in the houses of very rich men. It lies inside three rows of steps leading concentrically downwards. These steps are in part decorated with mosaics, as is also the floor of the pool, which in its decorations shows the Maeander, and those little stylized fishes which, amongst others, also remind Augustine of those who are born anew of water by their faith, "of us little fishes who like our great *Ichthys*, Jesus Christ, were born in water".[103] Now the basin is filled by "living", that is to say, by streaming, water. It murmurs and rushes, it eddies and foams, for the water streams from above out of the mouths of gaping lions' heads which are fixed on the superstructure above the pillars. The water that is thus poured in makes the pool a living thing and gurgles as it flows away:

> Lo, not a cloud's to be seen up above, yet it rains in the house here;
>   Clear is the sky, and yet limpid the showers that descend.
> Ever the water flows from the holy mouth of the marble,
>   Still unceasing the gleam of the dew that's begotten of stone.
> Barren the baldaquin—strange, but it teems with glistening fountains;
>   Rushing, they strike from above those undergoing below
> Holy rebirth. From etherial sluice comes the life-giving water . . .

Even the vomiting lions inspire this poetaster:

> See how kindly the lion, forgetting his natural wildness
>   (Changed is his turbulent heart), spews forth the water that saves.
> Water flows from his mouth, and his lips hold precious refreshment;
>   Stripped of the traits of his kind, a beast assuages our thirst.
> Out of the formerly bloodthirsty throat comes streaming the crystal-clear water—
> Thus is the savage heart made clean through the health-bringing flood.[104]

Living, that is to say moving, water was essential. Standing water, a natural seat of corruption, could never have been the symbol of the new life which was not subject to corruption, nor could it ever have represented the soul's new potentiality for life.

And now there comes into the bishop's mind every image which this element of water is capable of calling into life. The pool is now for him the fountain of living water, the water that overflows into eternal life, the water which, once drunk, quenches thirst for ever. He thinks of the mysterious connection between water, life and spirit. Possibly the fact that fire plays a part in all this (for, owing to the coldness of the night, the water is heated as in an ordinary *calidarium*) may well have turned his thoughts to the subject of fire and so to the glow of the divine spirit. Certainly, as Augustine must have known very well, there were other spiritual guides whose thoughts on this occasion turned to that fire of the spirit with which Christ said he would baptize; indeed, there was an Italian bishop, a spiritual kinsman of Augustine's own Ambrose, who grew quite eloquent on this subject. In a carefully prepared and somewhat rhetorical address to baptismal candidates, entitled *Invitation to the Baptismal Pool,* this man used the following words: "See how the living water, which both the spirit and a warming fire have made bearable, invites you with its pleasant murmurs. The master of the baths awaits you with girded loins, holding in his hand the *denarius* on which is stamped the image of triune God." Possibly this last was a reference to the baptismal coin which it was sometimes the practice to throw into the pool.[105]

Yet a mere playing with words on such an occasion would have been alien to Augustine's nature, for the moment was one of intense solemnity. Silence would fall, as, surrounded by the packed throng, a priest—it may have been Augustine himself, we are not certain on the point—consecrated the water, making over it the sign of the cross and saying a prayer to God and to Christ, that he might condescend to cleanse the element of water of all evil, sanctify it and endow it with divine power;[106] for this element of water receives its cleansing power only through the sufferings of Christ and through his blood. That is why it was once foreshadowed by the Red Sea.[107] Many see in this prayer, which seems to have been the established form for consecrating the water, a kind of counterpart of the solemn *prex* over the altar gifts at the Eucharist. We happen also to know that priests occasionally failed to recite it correctly or even to understand it—we have already seen that even in the towns their educational standards sometimes left something to be desired; what was even worse, phrases of an unorthodox character were sometimes allowed to slip in.[108] Augustine, however, never doubted that the soundness of the celebrant's intention would outweigh such defects. And he was confident that the validity of the baptisms would not be endangered by a mere piece of *gaucherie*, all the more so since the sacrament was only really completed by the baptismal formula with the names of the three persons of the Trinity. For this baptismal formula is the "word of faith" which in the Church of God has such power that so long as this Church continues to believe, to sacrifice, to bless and to baptize, it can even cleanse a little child, and this despite the fact that such a child cannot believe with its heart "unto its own justification" nor "testify with its mouth to its own salvation".[109] We may, however, rest assured that Augustine took the necessary steps to ensure that his own priests were adequately educated for their task.

But to return to our picture. The candidates now remove all their clothing, probably in the niches of the ambulatory surrounding the pool (Plate 17), or in the adjoining rooms. They loose their hair and remove their girdles. Not a hairpin must remain on the head, not an earring on the ear nor a ring on the finger nor an amulet about the neck. They enter the mystical womb of their mother the Church as they have come out of that of their earthly mother. There is no embarrassment, for they have all been accustomed from childhood on to the freedom practised in the baths, and at home they invariably sleep naked under the bedclothes. The men stand on one side, the women on the other, the latter being assisted by the deaconesses and older women.[110] Under the light of the lamps one after the other passes through the curtains, which have been slightly withdrawn, and descends the steps down into the streaming water, the subdeacons and godfathers lending them a hand. First come the children, then the men. The women come last of all.

The person being baptized must, as Augustine points out, "step downwards, for participation in the sufferings of the Lord demands humility".[111] The water in the pool is not deep. It reaches up to the breast of a boy standing on the mosaic floor, while an adult is scarcely immersed up to the navel (Plates 16, 18).[112] When the candidate has entered the pool the ancient questions are put:

Dost thou believe in the Father?
Dost thou believe in the Son?
Dost thou believe in the Holy Ghost?
Dost thou believe in the Holy Church, the remission of sins, the resurrection of the body?

and there follows the answer, spoken with great earnestness: "I believe." Three times the candidate is baptized in the water, the first time in the name of the Father, then in the name of the Son, and finally in the name of the Holy Ghost. We do not know how this threefold "baptism, dipping and immersion", proceeded—it was also sometimes known by the word *tinguere*, to wet;[113] possibly the person concerned was taken by the shoulders by the deacon and held "with bowed neck" under the stream of the inflowing water, or again he may have squatted down and then have had his head or his shoulders pushed down into the full *piscina* or he may have been considered to have been baptized if the inflowing stream had thoroughly poured over his head and breast, while he himself stood up to his knees or his hips in the consecrated water. We only know that the actual act of baptism was performed three times, each time accompanied by the naming of one of the persons of the Trinity.[114] There is some reason to believe that the bishop himself did the actual baptizing, but it is widely assumed that in the case of mass baptisms it was usually done by one of the deacons, who baptized considerable numbers simultaneously. If this is so the *piscina* must have been very large indeed, or we must assume that some were baptized on the steps while others underwent baptism in the pool, or alternately that there were several pools;[115] but none of this is borne out either by the remains of baptisteries that have been excavated, or by the relevant texts. On the whole, the evidence seems to point to Augustine's performing this office himself, for he several times reminds his children that though it is he who performs the actual bodily task, it is Christ who lends him the support of his divinity. "A man need not hesitate to approach a very subordinate servant, if this servant serves an exalted master."[116]

And now there begins the new life of those who have been born anew in the name of the Blessed Trinity, and with it the mystical indwelling in them of the divine Persons, whose sojourn, though those Persons are themselves everlasting, may, alas, sometimes only be temporary.[117] Immediately he has left the baptismal pool the man who has thus been reborn appears before his bishop, where, in a rite "as solemn as baptism itself", he is confirmed, sealed and strengthened by the Holy Ghost. We do not know the exact nature of this rite, or, for that matter, where it took place, but this may well have been in the great room next to the baptistery, which is plainly recognizable in all excavations.[118] Now, born anew by water and the Spirit, the newly-baptized are anointed and nourished by the same Spirit of Christ. This too takes place under an eloquent and threefold sacramental sign.[119]

This last-named sign consists, first of all, of an anointing of the head "with the oil of joy and of the kindling of love", the external anointing being the symbol of that which takes place within. Augustine compares it to the spiritual anointing of Christ after his baptism in Jordan, of which Peter speaks in the Acts of the Apostles.[120] Augustine says concerning this: "Christ anoints us with oil in order to make us wrestlers with the devil", and "as all are called Christians because of the mystical chrism they have received, so men are called priests because they are the members of a Priest", for they are the priests of God and Christ and "they will reign with him for a thousand years".[121] The bishop had consecrated the oil as a chrism.[122] Concerning the sign as such, he says that oil always tends to rise, like love.[123]

The second of the signs is the laying of hands upon the head. While this is being done a prayer was said, invoking the sevenfold gift of the Spirit spoken of by Isaiah. Only the truly converted and those actuated by love are capable of receiving this, and those alone are capable of communicating it who live in the unity of the Spirit, that is to say, within the confines of the Catholic

Church. For this reason the laying-on of hands must be repeated in the case of returning schismatics, who, needless to say, must be animated by sincere repentance.[124]

The third sign was the sealing or *consignatio*, which perhaps was merely another aspect of the anointing with oil. As a sheep is branded with the initials of its owner, as a soldier receives the badge of his regiment, so is the name and image of Christ impressed upon the soul. In this spirit it is written in the psalm, "the light of thy countenance, O Lord, is signed upon us."[125] This mark, the sign of the Lord, *character dominicus*, indelibly stamps the soul, while the visible signing of the forehead can be extinguished. With this his owner's mark or *titulus* upon him the newly-sealed Christian goes forth into the world. He is branded as a sheep of the Good Shepherd and recognizable by his insignia as a soldier of Christ, for "our King, nay, our Emperor, is Christ".[126]

This form of confirmation was but one step, and that not the most conspicuous, in the general process of initiation. The three different rites in question were probably not distinguished one from the other, at least, not so far as the ordinary simple faithful were concerned; and these normally used the comprehensive term "unction" to denote them. For all that, Augustine often singled out for special note the sevenfold gifts of the Holy Ghost, which were indispensible for the victory of the spirit over the flesh, and, what is more, often did this on days when there were no baptisms. Through this gift the fleshly man is turned to a spiritual man, and in it that spirit is received which triumphs over the dead letter.[127] In treating of the separate gifts, he does not, like Ambrose, lay special stress on those of fear and counsel, but rather stresses that of wisdom, like Origen and the Greeks. He also links up the seven gifts with the Ten Commandments, thus bringing law and grace into harmony, and so he exalts the figure seventeen as the mark of the Spirit, which fulfils the letter of the law, and which is therefore the key figure for the relation between the old dispensation and the new.[128]

From now on the baptized are known as *neophytes*, or newly-born, or, for short, as *infantes*, that is to say, "children". They are the newly-born children of that virginal but fruitful mother, the Church—an idea that is perpetually occurring in Augustine's works and sermons.[129] Every one of them now receives a white garment of linen. Even the linen is here symbolic, for since the days of the Pythagoreans linen, the cool vegetable product, has signified ritual purity, and is thus contrasted with the animal product, wool. In the present instance the linen garment is the antitype of the animals' skins which those who are now reborn had, as *competentes*, trodden underfoot. It is the symbol of their own inward purity and of the stainless life to which they are now committed. Augustine further recalls that "best garment" which the servants brought to the Prodigal Son upon his return, the original garment of grace of our first parent Adam, which is now returned to the baptized, who are his sons.[130] It is a white dress, white being the colour of purity and of joy, and since ancient times the dress of those who have been set free—the dress of priests; and, so the story went, of the angels when they appeared. No tanned animal hide must now touch their feet. They probably put on felt sandals, and during their octave were most careful not to touch the earth with the sole of the foot. We have already noted one of Augustine's more sarcastic remarks, contained in a letter to Januarius, that his people found it a more reprehensible thing to touch the earth with their bare feet than to celebrate the festive occasion by getting drunk.[131] It is strange that Augustine, who has an explanation for everything, only has one passage explaining this custom. In this he makes an indirect allusion to Ephesians vi.15, ". . . and your feet shod with the preparation of the gospel of peace". "The foot, therefore," he says, "does not hide the Gospel nor does it seek any earthly ground for its support",[132] from which we infer that a light sandal was customary on these occasions.

And so without a single fibre of animal substance upon their bodies, without a bracelet or even a hairpin, in new clothes and with their hair loose, reborn, anointed, sealed and with the gifts of the Spirit upon them, the newly-illuminated come into the festive basilica to take part, in the midst of the congregation, of the sacrament of the faithful. They do not yet fully know its nature. For the first time they remain standing within the church after the catechumens have been dismissed and the doors closed. They stand right up at the front and close to the altar. They have often heard allusions to what they are now about to receive and are vaguely aware that here is the very heart of the Christian mysteries. But what manner of thing will it be when they come to see it with their own eyes?

Augustine appears by this time to have been usually so exhausted as to give the newly initiated no further explanation, but allow them to partake of the feast without a full understanding of its nature.[133] They thus witness what is done without fully knowing its meaning. They listen attentively and hear the bishop pray; they hear him repeat Christ's own words over the bread and the wine, and then they hear the loud "Amen" of the congregation. For the first time they hear the singing over this table with bread and wine upon it of the psalm "Come ye and taste how sweet is the Lord", and in this manner on this first occasion they receive that of which they cannot as yet have a true understanding. At this moment a festive drink is handed to them, a little milk and honey, the ancient ritual food of the newly-born.[134] These gifts, too, have been standing ready at the altar, and have had a special blessing spoken over them.[135] It is only rarely that Augustine speaks of the spiritual meaning of these elements, but they are intended to convey that the new life is indeed the Promised Land, a spiritual Canaan, flowing with milk and honey.[136] Milk, that typically pure gift which is given by the mother freely and without reward, is the symbol of that grace which we drink in from the breast of our mother, the Church. It is, further, that light form of nourishment which one should give those who, in the words of the Apostle, are not yet able to receive heavier foods.[137] The honey stands for that sweetness which one experiences when, thanks to the wisdom imparted by the Holy Ghost, one is able to penetrate to the inner meaning of the *sacramenta* and the various symbols and when, in a word, one is able to understand the word of God. This is the sucking of honey from the rock, for the rock is Christ.[138] And so this nocturnal initiation comes to an end, and now each one of those concerned can say, *Accepi* [*sci., gratiam*]—"I have received it", or as we should say, turning the phrase about, "I have been received."

The bishop has still to explain the mystery of the sacrament of the altar. He probably does this on this same Easter day at the Mass which is celebrated during the morning. Some authorities believe, however, that the addresses in which we find the explanations of the Eucharist were given at the time of the sacrifice on Easter Monday. At best the neophytes would have heard the explanation of this mystery at the second of the celebrations attended by them.[139]

The bishop only begins to speak when the actual sermon is over and the *missa* has already taken place; the doors are now closed and the faithful are all to themselves, while the sacrificial gifts stand ready upon the altar. He speaks immediately before the *Dominus vobiscum* of the Preface. We have seven such addresses preserved for us. In most of them he speaks very soberly. In only a few places does he throw away all restraint, and some doubt has arisen as to the genuineness of these excessively detailed expositions, which are held by some to be interpolations.[140] The actual form varies from year to year, and the theme in what are undoubtedly the genuine parts of the sermons is always the same: that in which you are now about to take part is your becoming one in the body of Christ; you will become one with him and with one another. Through the eating of this body you will yourselves become the body of Christ, which is the Church. This is what bread and wine signify and bring about.

Here are some of his words:

> Today, here at the altar of God, we owe a sermon to the *infantes* dealing with this altar's sacrament. We have preached to them concerning the sacrament of the *symbolum*, telling them what they must believe. We have preached concerning the sacrament of the Lord's Prayer, telling them how they must pray. We have further preached concerning the sacrament of the

pool [the consecration of the water] and that of baptism. You have had all these things explained to you and you have solemnly accepted the explanation given you. Nevertheless, you have as yet heard nothing concerning the sacrament of the holy altar.[141]

Then he develops his favourite theme, that of the faithful becoming one in the body of Christ. Then he considers the preparation of the bread, in which again he sees an allegorical relation to the rites of initiation, for in the passion of the bread the Lord enjoins us to become that which we have now ourselves become through the passion of our initiation, namely, his mystical body, "one and yet many". Thus he speaks, standing at the altar, which is laden with the gifts:

What you see standing here upon the altar, beloved, is bread and wine. Yet this bread and this wine become, by reason of the word which is added to them, the body and blood of the Word. Because it was for ourselves that the Word underwent his passion, he has left behind for us in this sacrament his body and blood, for we too have become his body and through his mercy we are ourselves that of which we partake.

And reflect for a moment what manner of thing this created substance was ere it grew great upon the field; how it was born of the earth, nourished by the rain and grew up to be an ear of corn. Then it was brought by labouring men to the threshing floor, was threshed, passed through a sieve, stored away and brought forth again, then it was milled, sprinkled with water and baked. Thus, finally it became bread. Consider this and then think upon yourselves. You also at one time did not exist and then were created, brought to the threshing floor of the Lord and were threshed by heavily labouring oxen, namely by the preachers of the Gospel. When, as catechumens, you had to undergo a waiting period, you also were as the corn that is stored in the barn. Thereupon you had yourselves inscribed, and by means of exorcisms and fasting the milling of you began. Then you were brought to the water and you were sprinkled and leavened and made into a dough, and finally, through the glow of the Holy Ghost, you were baked and made into the bread of the Lord.[142]

On another occasion he says:

In the night that is passed you saw what stands here upon the altar, but what manner of thing it is, what it signifies, and the great mystery that it shows forth, these things you do not yet know. Well then, what you see is bread and a chalice. Your own eyes tell you that, but the Faith that you have yet to learn is this: that the bread is Christ's body and the chalice is his blood. It is briefly said and that must be sufficient for your faith. Yet to your faith there must be added instruction, though the prophet says, "If you do not believe, you will not understand." You may therefore say to me at this moment, "Since you have ordered us to believe, you must now explain the matter to us, so that we may understand it." In each of us the thought may now arise that our Lord Jesus obtained his flesh, as we know, from the Virgin Mary. As a child he was given suck and so nourished and grew great. He became a young man, was killed upon the wood, was taken down from the wood, and buried. On the third day, which was the day of his choosing, he rose again and ascended into heaven. To heaven he raised his body, and from thence he will come again to judge both the living and the dead, and there he sits on the right hand of the Father. How is it possible that this bread is his body, and the chalice, or what the chalice contains, is his blood? These things, my brethren, are called sacraments because we are to understand something other concerning them than that which we see. Hear, therefore, what the Apostle says: "Ye are the members and body of Christ." If, then, you are Christ's body and members, then it is your own mystery that lies here upon the table of the Lord, and it is your own mystery that you receive. It is to what you are yourselves that you reply "Amen", for you hear the words "body of Christ", and you reply "Amen". Be therefore truly a member of Christ's body, that your "Amen" may be sincere. It is this to which you subscribe with your answer.

And why does this thing happen just with bread? Again, we shall say nothing in our own name, but rather let the Apostle speak. He speaks of this sacrament when he says, "For we, being many, partake of one bread, one body." Understand it and rejoice, for it means unity, truth, piety, love. "One bread"! Who is this one bread? "Many one body"! Remember that bread is made not from a single grain of wheat but from many. When the exorcism was spoken over you, you were milled; when you were baptized you were wetted into a dough, and when you received the fire of the Holy Ghost you were baked. Be, therefore, what you are, and receive what you are. It is this that the Apostle says concerning bread. What we have to understand concerning the chalice he says plainly enough, even if he does not say it in so many words, for what is true of the coming into being of the visible form of bread is also true of the wine. Remember, brethren, how wine comes into being. Many grapes hang together in one bunch, but the juice of the berries flows together into a unity. In this manner our Lord Christ has indicated his will that we should belong to him, for he has consecrated the mystery of our peace and our unity upon his table.[143]

With this reference to the symbolism of "Church–Unity", Augustine has expressed his principal thought. Apart from this, however, he comes now and then to speak of the unique reality that these sacramental symbols conceal. There is reason to believe that he always did so. We cannot establish this, since the copyists were bound by the discipline of secrecy,[144] but in the utterances in which the reference is plain he is bold enough to compare the hidden transformation that takes place in the baptized person with that which takes place in the bread and wine upon the altar:

> You who are reborn to a new life, above all you who see this thing for the first time, hear the explanation which we have promised you—and you too of the faithful who are used to the sight, hear me, for it is good to be reminded, lest you fall into forgetfulness. What you behold upon the table of the Lord is that which, so far as its outward appearance is concerned, you see upon your own tables; yet only the appearance is the same, not the power. Similarly, you yourselves have remained what you were; you did not return to us with new faces when you returned from the baptismal pool. Yet you have been made anew; your fleshly form is the old one, but you are new through the grace of holiness. In exactly this way this is something new; for what you see, what stands here, is bread and wine, but once the consecration has taken place, the bread becomes the body of Christ and the wine his blood. The name of Christ brings this about, the mercy of Christ brings this about, namely, that though one sees what one saw before, it no longer counts for what it counted for before.[145]

There has been preserved yet another address of Augustine, in which Augustine makes plain the meaning of the unspeakable mystery through a very clear explanation of the eucharistic feast. So forthright is this passage that many, despite the unmistakable Augustinian style, have doubted the genuineness of this sermon, for its whole character is different from the more or less uniform group of sermons which deal symbolically with the Eucharist.

> Very shortly now you will hear a second time what you heard yesterday, but today there will be explained to you what you heard, and possibly answered, yesterday, and what, if you yourselves were silent, was answered by others. In any case, you heard yesterday what you have to answer today.
> After the well-known greeting, "The Lord be with you", you heard the command, "Lift up your hearts." The whole life of the true Christian is a perpetual lifting up of the heart. That indeed is the way of any Christian who is not a Christian in name alone but is a Christian in fact. Now, what is meant by this lifting up of the heart? It means trusting in God and not in oneself. You yourselves are here below and God is above. If you rely upon yourselves, then your heart is here below and not up above. When you hear the priest say, "Lift up your hearts", you reply, "We have, to the Lord";

see to it that your answer be true, for God himself takes cognizance of it. Let it be as you say it is. Let not your tongue speak what your conscience denies. And because it is God who gives you the power to lift your heart up (for the strength to do so does not come from yourself) the priest, after you have said that your heart is with God, continues with the words, "Let us give thanks unto the Lord our God." For what do we thank him? Why, we thank him because we ourselves have lifted up our heart, for if he had not drawn our heart towards him, we should still be lying here on the ground with it.

And that which takes place by means of the holy prayers which you then hear is that these elements, these gifts, become, as soon as the word is added to them, the body and blood of Christ. Without the word they are bread and wine; once the word is added they are something else. And what is this something else? The body of Christ and the blood of Christ! Take away the word and it is bread and wine. Add the word and it is a sacrament. And to this you answer "Amen". To say "Amen" is to add, as it were, your signature. "Amen" signifies "Indeed" or "Verily".

Then the Lord's Prayer is prayed, which you have received and repeated to us. Why is it said just before we receive the body and blood of Christ? Hear, then, the answer to this question. If, as is the way of human weakness, something that is not fitting has come into our minds, if some word has escaped us that was not altogether proper, if the eye has glanced in an improper manner upon something, or if the ear has listened to something with immoderate delight, if anything of this kind has occurred by reason of the weakness of this our earthly nature and the temptations of the world, it is extinguished by the Lord's Prayer, for in that prayer we say, "Forgive us our trespasses", and thus we may approach the altar with a quiet mind and need not fear that we partake of that which we eat and drink to our damnation.

Immediately after this the words "Peace be with you" are said; a great sacrament, is this kiss of peace. Let your kiss be an expression of a true love. Do not be a Judas! Judas kissed Christ with his mouth, while in his heart he was already plotting against him. If any man has feelings of enmity towards you and you cannot win him over, you must bear with him. See that in your hearts you do not return evil for evil. If he has hatred towards you, you must love him; then you may kiss him with a quiet conscience.

You have heard only a small number of things, but those things are great things. Do not, therefore, treat them lightly because they are few. Rather, have them in great regard because they are weighty. Nor is there any reason why you should learn all things at once. Now it will be easy for you to remember the few things I have told you.[146]

We see that Augustine not only restricted the diet of his children to the milk of St. Paul, but fed that milk with a liturgical spoon. Even if the passage about the transformation of the elements were a later interpolation (though it follows the authentic Augustinian formula "a word is added to the element and it becomes a sacrament"), it would still remain a masterpiece of clarity and simplicity. The preacher concentrates on what is truly essential—the solemn prayers with their age-old introduction—something that is relatively easy to understand, once it is explained. He then draws attention to the *dimitte nobis*, to the acts of love and perfect contrition, and to the need for that disposition of the soul that can make even the kiss of peace into a sacrament. In connection with the *gratias agamus* he works in a refutation of Pelagianism, though without actually mentioning the name. Yet he says not a word about the sacrifice as such, and if indeed this sermon has been handed down in its entirety, it is the only one in which the main theme which he treats every year is not mentioned, namely, that of the Eucharist as a symbol of unity.

Here, finally, is the text of a somewhat remarkable sermon which Morin treats as genuine, while others regard it as a work of the sixth century, but which, whatever its authorship, is generally recognized as a masterpiece of its kind. It is a short address in which the newly-baptized are, during the Easter Mass, prepared for their first Communion:

> The duty of preaching and the solicitude with which we were long in labour for you, in order at least to see Christ born within you, enjoins us to make certain matters clear, for you are children who have just been reborn out of water and the spirit, and you now see in a new light the food and drink which you behold standing on the table of the Lord; and of this food and drink you will shortly be partaking with a new piety. It is therefore necessary that I should explain to you the nature of this great and divine mystery. I must tell you of this most holy physic, this pure oblation which it is so easy to bring, of this sacrifice which is offered not alone in the earthly Jerusalem, not in the tabernacle of Moses, nor in the temple of Solomon—for these indeed were not foreshadowings of things to come—but "from the rising of the sun unto the going down thereof",[147] as the Prophets foretold; this sacrifice which, in the husbandry of salvation of the New Testament, is offered as a sacrifice of praise to God.
>
> Here is no necessity for a bloody sacrifice out of a herd of cattle, here no sheep or goat is led to the altar of God; the victim in our day is the flesh and blood of the priest himself. Of him it was said long ago in the Psalms, "Thou art a priest for ever according to the order of Melchizedech",[148] and we have read in the Book of Genesis and have taken note how Melchizedech,

as priest of the highest God, brought bread and wine, when he blessed our father Abraham.

Now Christ, our Lord, who in his passion offered up for us that which he had received from us at his birth, and so became for ever the supreme priest, has given to us the form of sacrifice which you will here behold, namely, the offering of his body and his blood; for his body, being pierced with a lance, gave forth that water and blood whereby he took away your sins. Therefore should you who, mindful of his mercy, "wish to effect your own salvation",[149] approach the communion of this altar in fear and trembling, for it is God who will work within you. Recognize, therefore, in the bread that which hung upon the cross, in the chalice that which flowed from his side.

The old sacrifices of the Chosen People were in their various ways nothing but a foreshadowing of this one sacrifice. Christ is both the sheep, because of the innocence of his sinless character, and the goat, because he assumed our sinful human flesh. Thus also everything else which was foreshadowed in the various sacrifices of the Old Testament refers to this one sacrifice which was revealed under the new dispensation.

Take therefore and eat the body of Christ, you who in the body of Christ have become members of Christ; take and drink the blood of Christ. Eat the bond which binds you to him, that you may not be loosed from him again; drink your own ransom, so that you may not again consider yourselves worthless. Even as this is transformed into a part of yourselves, when you eat and drink of it, so also you are turned into the body of Christ, so long as you live in obedience and in the fear of God, for as the Pasch approached and he celebrated it with his disciples, he ate of the bread, blessed it and said, "This is my body, which shall be delivered for you." In like manner he gave the cup and said, "This is my blood of the New Testament which is shed for many unto the forgiveness of sins."[150]

You have read or heard this in the Gospels, but you did not yet know that this Eucharist was the Son himself. Now, however, "having your hearts sprinkled from an evil conscience and your bodies washed with clean water,[151] come ye to him and be enlightened, and your faces shall not be confounded."[152] For if you worthily receive this thing, this pledge of the new covenant, on the strength of which you may hope for your everlasting inheritance, and if you keep the commandment to love one another, then you have the Life within you, for you have taken unto yourselves that flesh, of which the Life himself said, "The bread which I shall give you is my flesh, for the life of the world" and "Except you eat of my flesh and drink my blood you shall not have life in you."[153]

If it is in him that you have your life, you will also be one flesh with him, for this sacrament does not give you the body of Christ in such a manner that you are separated from him. The Apostle has reminded us of the prophecy in Holy Scripture, "And they shall be two in one flesh.... This is a great sacrament but I speak in Christ and the Church"[154]—and in another passage he says concerning this same Eucharist, "We, being many, are one bread, one body."[155] You will, therefore, from this day forth, receive what you will be yourselves, assuming of course that you receive it worthily and do not eat and drink judgement to yourselves. For the Apostle also says the following: "Whosoever shall eat this bread or drink the chalice of the Lord unworthily, shall be guilty of the body and blood of the Lord. Then let a man prove himself, and so let him eat of that bread and drink of that chalice. For he that eateth and drinketh unworthily eateth and drinketh judgement to himself."[156]

Worthily do you receive if you guard against the leaven of false doctrine, and feast on the unleavened bread of sincerity and truth[157] or, better still, if you keep within yourselves that leaven of love, which the woman mixed with three measures of flour until the whole was leavened (for this woman is the wisdom of God, which, through the Virgin, became Man and put on our mortal flesh). She it is who spreads the Gospel, as among the three measures of flour; she spreads it over the whole earth, which she restored after the Flood through the three sons of Noah, and she spreads it until the whole is leavened. In this whole, which the Greeks call *holon*, you too will be included, while you preserve the bond of peace; that is to say, you will be *kath'holon*, in accord with the whole, the whole from which the *Catholic* Church takes her name.[158]

This address is in many respects different from the others, and primarily so through the strong emphasis it places on the sacrificial character of the Eucharist. It draws attention to the more important foreshadowings of that Eucharist such as the prophecy of Malachy, the priesthood of Christ according to the order of Melchizedech, and it explains the fulfilment of the sacrifices of the Old Testament in the one sacrifice of the new dispensation. There are in the address yet other remarkable ideas, such as the origin of this sacrament in the wound in our Lord's side, that is to say, in his death, and the identity of cross and altar. Also noteworthy are the references to the passages from John vi and 1 Cor. xi, and the account of the words of consecration. This last, by the way, is a precious treasure of Church history, in so far as it contains the African formula of the words of consecration, which differs somewhat from the Roman, and corresponds to the West Gothic and Mozarabic one. Further, there is the reference to the verse *Accedite et illuminamini*; there is the description of the fruits of the good Communion and of the disastrous consequences of the unworthy one. Finally, there is the essentially Augustinian theme that the Eucharist makes manifest the unity of the Church, and in this the preacher bases himself on the passage from Ephesians concerning the two in one flesh. At the end he repeats this theme, weaving into it the allegory of the woman with the leaven, who is the divine *logos*, and mingles the glad tidings with three measures of flour, these in their turn being the world, with its three continents, which will ultimately rise together in a common leavening and become that "whole" from which the Catholic Church takes her name. If Augustine is indeed the author, one can only say that this is indeed a remarkable collection of unique passages.

However that may be, these seven sermons in which we see how Augustine initiates the newly-baptized into the most delicate of the mysteries are a good illustration of his ability to represent a complicated sacramental reality, and one which, because of its multiple aspects, it is difficult to present as a whole, to men and women of great simplicity of mind. Augustine, as we have seen, concentrates on the symbolic aspect of the sacrament, interpreting it by the words of Scripture. Beyond that he does not go. He is still influenced by the traditional reserve of the early Church. It does not occur to him, on this occasion, to bring out the suggestive character of this divinely instituted symbol, a character which it most certainly possesses, nor does he endeavour to surround it with any kind of human tenderness. He confines himself to its original significance, and if in this instance we find his expositions somewhat barren, we must admit that he says nothing that can in any way belittle the majesty of this mystery, and nothing that in any way narrows the width of the sacramental horizon.

The Octave of Easter

During Easter Week the neophytes showed great zeal in celebrating the "sacrament of the holy octave". They continued to wear their linen garments and their felt sandals, practised continence, denied themselves elaborate meals and, of course, all visits to the theatre, and stood every day in their white garments within the choir close to the altar. The sermons of this week were largely given for their benefit.[159] On these occasions Augustine spoke briefly but warm-heartedly on the resurrection of the body, a theme most full of comfort, though it was one which was a special stumbling-block to the pagan. He also spoke of the happy life in the world to come, of the eternal Eastertide, of the last Sabbath and of the final octave of all octaves;[160] it was the theme he had treated in his lovely dialogue on "The Happy Life", and one which, shortly afterwards, formed the subject of that unforgettable conversation which, before her death, he had with his mother at the window of the inn at Ostia.

During this season he kept to the pericopes which it had long been customary to read on these occasions; namely, those dealing with the appearances of our Lord during the forty days of his glorified life which are described in the final chapters of the four Gospels. On Sunday there were readings from Matthew, on Monday from Mark, on Tuesday and Wednesday from Luke, and on Thursday, Friday, Saturday and Sunday from John.[161] Small wonder that Augustine's lively spirit fairly overflowed with mystical explanations when these visions of future glory thus flashed before his eyes. When, on the Thursday after Easter, we hear the Lord say "Touch me not", this signifies that the Lord can be more effectively reached and touched by faith than by a fleshly finger. This brings Augustine to meditate on the great distance between ourselves and our Lord—"a distance so great that we cannot even estimate it"; yet if we believe we do touch him, and that is sufficient. There are some who seek after his flesh and take him for a man and to whom his divinity is not sufficiently present by faith; but it was not for such as these that he ascended to his Father. It is along these lines that he explains the apparently insoluble question, why our Lord "would not allow himself to be touched by women, but only by men. He permits Thomas to touch him but not Mary Magdalene, and in this he gave as an explicit reason that he had not yet ascended to his Father."[162]

On Friday there was read the wonderful story of his appearance at Lake Tiberias, and of the mysterious meal at the coal fire with the seven disciples and of the catch of the 153 fishes. Augustine was thoroughly in his element here. He spoke of the significance of the number 153, and in this case gave a different explanation to that which he had previously given to Januarius. In the present instance his explanation is as follows. 153 is the sum of all the numbers from one to seventeen, seventeen being, of course, the key numeral for the relation between law and grace, since it is made up of ten and seven, ten being for the Ten Commandments, and seven for the gifts of the Holy Ghost. At the same time, 153 is three times the number of fullness (which is fifty, fifty being made up of seven times seven plus one) plus three, so that 153 signifies the fullness which has been taken up into the triune God. And so at length Augustine cries out, "Let us who are in the seventeen fear nought! For if we are in the seventeen, we shall attain to the 153, and if we are in the 153, we shall stand at the right hand, and if we stand at the right hand, then we shall attain the Kingdom of Heaven"—a conclusion which no doubt called forth the wildest applause and satisfied everybody.[163]

But after these games, which he carried on in the most incredible earnest, he spoke in even greater earnest on another matter. The great mass of Christians here on earth, he said sadly, were all too like the unsorted fishes in an overfull net. It was a theme on which he dwelt every year. This net, he said, which never actually reaches the point of tearing, signifies the Church, which also cannot be torn, but is nevertheless much too full, and is crowded with bad fish which do not belong there at all. And then he warned the newly-caught *pisciculi* that they would find good and bad and above all mediocre fish within the net of the Church; that they would find there more stumbling-blocks than edification, more bad examples than good; that they should neither be offended by these bad examples nor be induced by them to swim with the sinful majority. Rather should they wait until the net was turned out to the right and the catch was thoroughly sorted upon the shore; in other words, until the Last Judgement.

Special addresses for the newly-baptized, and ones intended primarily for these, seem to have been given during this period, probably in the afternoon. On these occasions the other faithful were freely permitted to attend, and everyone was allowed to ask questions, while the bishop sat in his usual place in the centre. During one such period of Christian instruction, the discussion turned to the wonderful knowledge of certain pagans, and someone raised the question whether it had indeed been possible for the demons to prophecy the carrying off of Serapion—a thing which actually took place quite suddenly in 391 under Bishop Theophilus. Augustine's reply excited so much interest that he was asked to put his views into writing, and this he actually did.[164] In Easter week of the year 413[165] he began that series of carefully prepared addresses (which he committed to writing in advance) on the First Epistle of St. John; these contain a positive treasury of ideas on a variety of subjects. Here he discusses the love and mercy of God, the Christian conception of the *caritas* which comes from above, the *sacramentum dominicum*, which is the Lord's Prayer, the spiritual unction of Christ, and above all, the Eucharist and the external unity of the Church.

On Low Sunday the *infantes* were solemnly released from the *cancelli*, and even before they had changed their white garments, allowed for the first time "to mingle with the people".[166] This, too, provided a welcome occasion for Augustine the preacher, for then he regularly reminded his congregation of the significance of the eighth day, the ultimate and eternal (for eight is the superfluity of the perfection of seven); he also enjoins them to be watchful, lest in putting off their baptismal garments they should permit that slower process to start which is the putting off of the Christ-like man, whom they have just put on. Tomorrow, he then says, the legal holiday comes to an end and the courts will again be in session, but is that any reason for starting to litigate again, and for tearing each other to pieces?[167] Then he reminds his hearers for the last time that the great mass of Christians no longer form an elect. The new Christians had to decide themselves to which party they wished to belong.

Choose the narrow way, he cries, choose in this octave of Easter—*pro octavo*, as the superscription says in certain psalms; that is to say, choose the final and enduring thing. Avoid those who move about in a circle, *in circulo ambulantes*,[168] those who move in that great vicious circle of vanities because they do not see the ultimate goal. They bark at you from all sides, but do you say *pro octavo* on this octave day. Upwards towards that which endures! In the midst of those who are a stumbling-block to you continue to pray, even as it says in the psalm: "Save me O Lord, for there is now no saint. Truths are decayed from among the children of men. They speak lies one to another."[169] Choose your examples from the side of the good. Do not say, Surely that man is supposed to be one of the faithful, yet he drinks too much; though married, he keeps a concubine, and every day he forswears himself for the sake of gain. He is a usurer and he consults fortune-tellers when he has a headache, and when he is afraid of dying he binds magic strips about his neck. Yes; such things, and such Christians, attract attention; but the good does not attract attention and there are so many good. But only the good know that.[170]

After that the "lambs" were lost to sight. They laid aside their eight-day-old skins in the *secretarium* and disappeared into the crowd in that curious sheepfold in which sheep, goats and wolves are all indistinguishable from one another.

Penance after Baptism

Although, in accordance with ancient usage, Christians were still called saints, yet these saints were already falling row by row from their pedestals; *deficit sanctus*, and nobody any longer seemed to be particularly put out by this. So long as things were not too raw, people were willing to close an eye —even in a Christian city. Public opinion would not tolerate much laxity among the clergy, and even less from the ascetics, while from nuns and widows[171] the very strictest propriety was expected; but with layfolk it was prepared to tolerate pretty well everything. In the case of people of rank it was expected that, as Christians, they should at least avoid causing grave scandal, and that if they misbehaved they should use a reasonable discretion about it, for even a catechumen was not supposed to behave like a pagan. A more severe standard, however, was applied to those who had actually been baptized. If a baptized person publicly misconducted himself, he would, if he was prudent, keep away from the church, and would certainly avoid showing himself in the sanctuary to receive the body of the Lord, for Augustine knew well enough how to maintain the discipline of his Church: "Those who know that I know of their sins [in this case, adultery] should keep away from Communion, so that I need not forbid them entry to the *cancelli*."[172]

In cases of public scandal, such as an adulterous relationship which was known to the whole town, or a compromise with heretics, blasphemy or lapses from the Faith, or in cases of murder, of the infliction of grievous bodily harm, and of similar crimes, where these had escaped retribution from the civil law, Augustine put the individuals concerned under the ban of the Church and so secured their exclusion. This the dignity of the Church demanded. The community of the saints would thus occasionally extrude the all-too-unsaintly from among their midst. The corrupt member was cut off, and in accordance with the Lord's command was accounted by the rest as a publican and a sinner.

Round about the year 400 excommunication was looked upon in Africa as a great disgrace and was an insuperable bar to social intercourse. The person who incurred this penalty had little ground for joking about it. Only once, however, do we hear from Augustine of a bishop who misused his powers, and even this was in the rather special case of a young hothead;[173] it may be safely said that the African bishops never thought of using the power of the ban for party purposes or to satisfy some personal grievance—a course of action that would seriously have weakened its effectiveness. On the contrary, the bishops seem only to have used it when public opinion and the good name of their congregations made its use unavoidable. In the main also, when serious public scandal had been caused, the offenders themselves did not wait until an outcry had arisen, but more often than not went to the bishop of their own accord, made their confession and requested the imposition of the great ecclesiastical penance, which a man might always perform at least once in his life.

For long men had known that those who had entered the communion of the saints by the door of baptism, but had had to leave that communion through their own fault, still had open to them the way of return. It was considered a sad thing that men should have to resort to such an expedient but, such as it was, it was in the nature of a second baptism. Despite their fury, the rigorists had not succeeded, even in Africa (though it was here that Tertullian's sarcasms had attained their shillest pitch), in completely closing this last door of the desperate (though one of Augustine's female correspondents could still encounter a follower of Novatian).[174] In 400 men believed more firmly than ever that even after baptism the true Church could still forgive even the gravest of sins and that she did forgive them at least once. Thanks to the power of the keys which gave the right to open and to shut, the true Church, and she alone, could open this portal of need. She could publicly reawaken to life the stinking Lazarus, "this corrupt and stinking carcase", however loathsome were the sins from which he had died.[175] "Whoever be the servant who lays upon the sinner the hands of reconciliation, it is the love of the Church which remits the sins of those who remain linked to her, and retains the sins of those who have broken the link."[176] It is therefore to be noted that the servant concerned acts in the name of the Catholic Church, and that a heretic or a schismatic has not the power of the keys.[177]

The "great public penance of repentance and lamentation", as it was called, was not something that should occur at all in the normal Christian life.[178] It is not known for certain how often such a penance was witnessed in the average Christian community, nor can we say whether it was performed under moral pressure or at the penitent's own request, but this public penance was certainly considered imperative when a sin was of such a nature that grave public scandal had been caused, and this either because there had been a complaint to the police or because the matter was one of Church discipline—as, say, in the case of an astrologer (who would naturally be accounted as a helper of the demons and a public cheat), or of a Christian who had gone over to the Donatists and had undergone a second baptism, or of a man who lived in flagrant adultery. Of course there were many who could avoid publicity in their evildoing and who quietly went on communicating, and thus were a cause of great offence to such of their fellow Christians as their secret sins happened to be known to; for the cynical conduct of such persons tended to bring the very sacrament itself into contempt.[179] In cases where the sin had been public, the bishop was in the habit of publicly imposing the penance in the form of an ecclesiastical judgement. It was left to him to decide whether the penance was to be performed "in the presence of many" or in the presence of the whole congregation. In either case, however, the consent of the person concerned was always obtained.[180] Also, the *reconciliatio* took place in such cases in the church and in the presence of the congregation, the thing being done from the steps of the apse. Again it was the bishop himself who performed the laying-on of hands; an ordinary priest could only do this when he had special powers, or during the bishop's absence.[181] This reconciliation was considered a true remission of the guilt of sin.[182] In cases of mortal sins that had remained partly or wholly secret, one could go to the bishop in private. The latter would then personally but again privately pronounce the ban, would give the penitent a homily, and would later (again privately) relax the ban. Any person punished in this way was accounted as a penitent and was expected to keep away from the *cancelli* on his own initiative.[183] Only the bishop could decide whether the penance was to take place wholly or partly in public, and Augustine confessed that he was often very uncertain what the decision in such a case should be. Nor do we know whether his conduct in such matters was characterized by marked mildness, or was strict. He certainly said in his sermons that not only the three sins of idolatry, murder and impurity, but that all grave sins against the Ten Commandments fell under the power of the keys—all sins, in fact, of which St. Paul says that whoever commits them can have no part in the kingdom of God.[184] He took the view, however, that sins which had remained secret did not require public penance: "The evil must die where it has taken place"—namely, in secret, even when it was a question of murder,[185] but he deplored the fact that on such occasions he could draw nobody into consultation, for, he says, "it is often the case that when I impose a public penance, a man will go to his ruin because of his obstinacy, while if I impose no penance, another will go to his ruin through fury at the other. I gladly confess that I fail daily to solve these problems." Nevertheless, even where the penance was shirked, he guarded his penitents' secrets. It was his desire to heal and not to accuse. Always he was silent, sometimes in order to avoid getting a man arrested, for a man who was presumed to have committed a criminal act was arrested on the strength of the merest rumour and was in all circumstances charged. The bishop could urge such a man to expiate his crime, but his duty of silence forbade him to accuse him. Often he saw the criminal escape both the penance and the law, to his great chagrin, and also to the annoyance of the officials concerned, who had strong suspicions of what was afoot and were not exactly pleased that such rascals should be able to stop the bishop's mouth, while escaping not only the ecclesiastical but the civil penalty as well.[186] We do not know to what extent a public confession of the sin in question was demanded, nor in what form it took place, but we have preserved for us a most moving address to penitents. "There are", he says, "only three syllables in *peccavi*, but the sacrificial flame of the heart arises out of them."[187] We do not, however, know whether he is referring to an internal confession to oneself, a confession made in private or to a public confession.

Every baptized person has the right to ask for a penance to be imposed.[188] It was always understood, however, that this was the first and would be the last time it was performed. A cleric, in such circumstances, was deprived of his priestly office and of his jurisdiction, while a layman was compelled to practise continence; all were expected to fast and to pray and were excluded from the Lord's table. If after this reconciliation a man fell again into sin, the Church could not help him. The man who fell a second time might indeed hope for forgiveness from God, but he could no longer obtain it from the Church,[189] and here was possibly the reason why those who had incurred the ban often hesitated to ask for reconciliation, and why those who had grave sins on their conscience tended to postpone their request for a penance till they lay dying. Penance on the deathbed counted as the equivalent of the "great public penance", exactly as though it had been performed in the presence of the whole congregation.[190] Since this possibility always continued to exist, many were reluctant even to start the lengthy mortifications of the penance while they still had their health, while others did not complete them, for once they had effected their reconciliation, they would in this life have had nothing further to hope for from the Church. So some stretched out the time of their penance while others continued in a state of mortal sin until there was perhaps an earthquake or a pestilence. Then every man who was already "bound", as the saying went, begged desperately for absolution, while whole crowds came to ask for the great penance to be imposed on them.[191] Yet even then the bishops had to turn away those "who had fallen a second time", and could only enjoin them to lay strict penances on themselves privately, to give alms, pray in secret and practise continence. They could still hope for forgiveness from God, though not from the earthly community of saints, which they had desecrated a second time.

The sincere and spontaneous penance of great sinners could in those days still make a profound impression, as is shown by the case of Fabiola. Fabiola was a Roman lady of high degree who had been married to a corrupt libertine and had then married another during this first husband's lifetime. After the death of her second husband she suddenly appeared in the crowded church of the Lateran in rags, barefooted, without a veil and with her hair loose, and went silently to the place of penance. At this sight all those present began loudly to weep. After her reconciliation she built a hospital, and gave the remainder of her fortune to the poor and afterwards lived a life of the strictest mortification.[192] Augustine too knew of penitents who "raged against themselves", beat their breasts, tore out their hair and for long periods wore a hair shirt next to their skin.[193] However, some of his utterances lead us to believe that much of this had already become a matter of mere habit and was of little spiritual significance. There were too many people standing among the *poenitentes* who had sins on their conscience which they were careful to keep concealed, and which in all probability they continued to commit. People who had already lost their reputation made a point of standing among the penitents at least once in their lives. By doing so they put their humility on display and made a great show of their piety. As against this, it was not considered in any way a disgrace to stand in the sinners' corner. It simply meant that you were a non-communicant. Moreover, penances which were carried out over a number of years came to be a matter of routine. There was also the circumstance that a custom had grown up, according to which any of the faithful seem on certain occasions to have been able to secure for themselves the laying-on of hands by simply asking for it. It counted as a kind of general absolution but was, admittedly, distinguishable from the sacramental *absolutio*. When the time came, there were always crowds of applicants for this benefit—"as though", Augustine said bitterly, "the laying-on of hands could be of any benefit to anybody where there was no change in the manner of life."[194]

For ordinary people who led decent lives and gave offence to nobody there was nothing in the nature of confession, except that which they made to God in their prayers. They expiated their daily sins and sins of weakness by beating their breasts at the "Forgive us our trespasses", by giving alms and by other works of charity, which, as we know, covers a multitude of sins.[195] Time and again they would be told by their stern bishop that God forgives sins of this kind, when there is prayer, fasting and almsgiving.[196] They also heard him say that all baptized laymen fall into sins of this kind, and this through the possession and administration of worldly goods, and also through the "more intimate bonds of marriage". By reason of such worthless things, even the lives of the good are covered, "if not with filth, then at least with dust", and a scabrous state may well develop, unless the physic of daily penance is applied.[197]

Yet even honest folk were at times disturbed in their minds, and then they seem to have come to the bishop to pour their heart out. If on such occasions Augustine saw no reason for believing that mortal sin had been committed and no necessity for the imposition of the ban or of a penance, they would return comforted to their homes, and were made whole through the secret physic of brotherly exhortation which Augustine had administered in his consulting-room. God, Augustine would say on these occasions, would forgive them their sins because of their humble acceptance of his rebuke.[198] And perhaps many did what was done by Augustine himself when he lay dying: repeated the penitential psalms for days on end with a humble and contrite heart.

13

A SUNDAY IN HIPPO

IT is a cool Sunday morning; a continuous muffled noise echoes through the white capital city, for except for the ascetics and for those who are both free and well-to-do, there is little in the nature of Sunday rest from servile tasks. Slaves trot through the back streets, the shops are open and the market gardeners and muleteers watch the faithful go up to the great church. The faces of these dark-eyed people seem strangely pale in the sunlight and contrast with their light and usually colourful clothing. People of rank, with their clients about them, bring up the tail of the procession and often come too late. Around the fountain under the parched plane-trees there squat the everlasting idlers of this country, who in those days sat near the church as today they sit near the mosque, while high above, on the top of the coping of the basilica, there gleams the golden emblem of the Lord Jesus Christ.

The blazing white façade reflects the light, the bronze doors have been opened inwards, and the people who pass through them and push on under the drawn curtain exchange the harsh sunlight with an almost startling suddenness for the cool semidarkness of the nave. There is a hum of muffled voices, and in the lattices of the windows the veined alabaster makes a splesh of bright orange. The little oil lamps in the great lampholders flicker over the altar, towards which the crowd continually pushes forward.

Bishop Aurelius Augustinus, with his flaming dark eyes and shaven head, is at this moment sitting in the *secretarium*[1] surrounded by his clergy, and is just concluding his short morning audience, which he is in the habit of giving before Mass. He hears few compliments on this occasion, but mostly complaints, petitions, mixed, it is feared, with a great deal of talebearing; the atmosphere is very much that of a kind of pious business office, as it still is today in many a Mediterranean presbytery—"l'un des deux cloaques de la poésie", as Balzac expressed it. The audience continues until the moment when the celebrant gives the signal for the solemn entrance to the church. Then Augustine follows a long row of assistants—*pompa ministerii*—passes under the updrawn curtain between two pillars and ascends the apse. The packed multitude awaits him, the men standing on one side, the women on the other.[2]

The doors still stand wide open and still the people stream in, but now there is a sudden silence, and from the steps of the apse Augustine greets his people.[3]

The Lord be with you.
And with thy spirit.

The Instructional Service

Immediately after this greeting the reader begins in his clear boy's voice to read "the Apostle". He reads on a high note with few inflections of the voice.[4]

> Lesson from the Epistle from the holy Apostle Paul to Titus: For this cause I left thee in Crete: that thou shouldst set in order the things that are wanting and shouldst ordain presbyters in every city ... A bishop must be without crime as the steward of God: not proud, not subject to anger, not given to wine, no striker, not greedy of filthy lucre: but given to hospitality, gentle, sober, just, holy, continent: embracing that faithful word which is according to doctrine, that he may be able to exhort in sound doctrine and to convince the gainsayers ...[5]

There, then, stands the people of Hippo, fishermen, sailors, business folk and strangers who are passing through, and even as it was in the days of St. Paul, so it is now: there were "not many wise according to the flesh, not many mighty, not many noble".[6] Right in front are the children, who stare upward into the apse, their eyes being lower than the top of the balustrade; at a place set apart are the dedicated virgins and the widows in their dark veils, the penitents and catechumens being similarly cut off from the rest; the last-named will, of course, have to leave the church in some one and a half hours. The *curiales* of the city have taken a place right in front, as have the commandant of the coastal guard and the other notables. These people's children are in the care of slaves, waiting-women looking after the girls, while the boys are in the charge of wretched-looking "paedagogues".

All is now attention. Even the well-to-do ladies, who a moment ago were smiling with their dark eyes at their acquaintances from under their veils, now observe a decorous silence; their earrings and bracelets sparkle in the light and they know well how to be attractive, even while they make the sign of the cross with a polished fingernail. Behind the great and wealthy in their silken cloaks and their neatly-braided tunics, which, in remarkable contrast to the ancient Roman dress, reach down to the ankles and have long wide sleeves,[7] there stand the artisans in their colourless *birri* and shabby capes,[8] their dusty feet in light sandals.

Last, there is the great crowd of semiromanized Berbers, mixed with the scum of a Mediterranean port, the whole having that rather sinister and forbidding aspect that seems to cling even to this day to the ordinary people of the ports on this strip of coast. They are an evil-smelling lot, though picturesquely decked out. Many have inflamed, red-rimmed eyes, and the men's faces often have a blueish tinge, where their shaving has been imperfect; the women's eyes are bold and penetrating, their tightly-closed lips impart an air of obstinacy, and they are remarkable for their raven-black hair. Possibly one would have seen brighter eyes and more brown skins among them than today, for the prematurely aged faces, the long clothing of the men, together with the habit of the women of screening themselves as much as possible from the light of day and of keeping their heads covered both outdoors and in, are part of a refined culture that tends to shun the daylight, and only date back to the days of the Arab conquest, when the African Church had been destroyed.

On the higher part of the apse sit the company of priests, with the bishop in the middle, and the latter sits listening on his richly draped *cathedra*, while the deacons stand to the left and to the right; it is an ascetic-looking shaven-pated group, for all are monks. The white ecclesiastical senate has turned into a monastic choir.

"Peace be with thee", says Augustine to the boy who has just read from the Apostle;[9] then he turns to an acolyte and says, "Psalm Twenty-Nine." The acolyte turns aside and passes this on to the precentor and also to one of the lectors,[10] who now steps to the reading desk and starts the bizarre *melope* of the psalm[11] in that nasal voice which the Berbers will, one feels, always retain:

> I will extol thee, O Lord, for thou hast upheld me
> And hast not made my enemies to rejoice over me.[12]

And immediately the whole people repeat the verse, draggingly and unevenly, as a refrain, for they follow the ancient custom of antiphonal chanting. Then the soloist sings the following verses, which are always answered by the refrain sung by the congregation:

> O Lord, my God, I have cried to thee:
> And thou hast healed me.
> Thou hast brought forth, O Lord, my soul from hell:
> Thou hast saved me from them that go down into the pit.
> Sing to the Lord, O ye his saints:
> And give praise to the memory of his holiness.
> Thou hast turned for me my mourning into joy:
> Thou hast cut my sackcloth and hast compassed me with gladness.
> To the end that my glory may sing to thee and I may not regret:
> O Lord my God, I will give praise to thee for ever.

After this the thirteenth verse the response sounds again through the great nave:

> I will extol thee, O Lord, for thou hast upheld me
> And hast not made my enemies to rejoice over me.

The singing of the psalm is over.

The day is one of those in which he has the freedom to choose the lessons, and Augustine has done so, including the third, which is the Gospel.[13] While everyone listens "with rapt attention, as though the Lord himself were in their midst",[14] a deacon reads the seventh chapter of the Gospel according to St. John from the fourteenth to the twenty-fourth verse. He recites the passage melodiously and with deep conviction.

> Now, about the midst of the feast, Jesus went up into the temple and taught. And the Jews wondered, saying: How doth this man know letters, having never learned? Jesus answered them and said: My doctrine is not mine, but his that sent me. If any man shall do the will of him, he shall know of the doctrine, whether it be of God, or whether I speak of myself.

And he closes with the words

Judge not according to the appearance, but judge just judgement.

Then the bishop seats himself again on the *cathedra*.[15] As the crowd presses ever more closely against the steps of the apse he looks, as he has so often looked before, at all those faces, known and unknown, that gaze up towards him; then he starts to preach:

> The letter of the holy Apostle concerning the setting-up of bishops, most dearly beloved, must without any doubt personally remind us that we must keep watch upon ourselves, but you also are reminded in it that you should not judge us, and that lesson is reinforced by the last sentence of the passage from the Gospel which you have just heard: "Judge not according to the appearance, but judge just judgement." He who does not judge justly of himself will certainly not judge justly of others. The holy Apostle says in another place: "I so fight not as one beating the air. But I chastise my body and bring it into subjection, lest perhaps when I have preached to others, I myself become a castaway."[16] By this fear concerning himself he frightens us all, for what is a lamb to do when the ram begins to tremble with fear?[17]

Then he broaches his real theme, and he does so with some apprehension, since his argument can be turned against himself, for that theme is that he may "embrace the faithful word of sound doctrine and convince the gainsayers". What a task is this! he cries. What a burden! And how steep is this way! The poet of the Psalms says somewhere: "Deliver me from the snare of the hunter and from the sharp word",[18] and nothing deters the steward of God more from the refutation of his gainsayers than the fear that they may reply with evil words. He goes on:

> But first I must explain to you what is meant by this phrase about "refuting the gainsayers". Let no man believe that we are here concerned with a verbal argument. Hardly anyone gainsays us with words, but many do so by their deeds, when they live evil lives. When does a Christian dare to tell me to my face that it is good to steal the property of others? He will not even dare to assert that it is a good thing to cling too tenaciously to one's own possessions. Reflect for a moment on that man who wanted to build great barns. Did he seek the property of others? No, he wanted only to look after his own property which he had honestly earned without doing injury to any man—and now listen to what this man was given to hear from the mouth of God: "Thou fool, this very night shall thy soul be demanded of thee."[19] This man who went so thoughtfully to work was called a fool by God. It is almost as though God had said to him, "Now that you have guarded it, you shall lose it. Had you given it away, it would have been preserved for you." This thrifty person was called a fool, yet if one who husbands his own goods is called a fool, what name shall be given to the man who steals the property of others? If the impulse of the thrifty man is sordid, then the thief is a boil full of poison—not like the man whose sores were licked by the dogs, for that man was full of pus upon his body, whereas the thief has the foulness in his heart.
>
> But perhaps somebody will say, "The man whom God called a fool was not really punished so heavily after all." But God does not speak here like a man. Such a word of God concerning a man is in the nature of a judgement. Does God give eternal life to fools? And yet what is there left to those who do not receive it but the pains of hell? Perhaps you think that is only a supposition on our part? But let us look carefully into the matter. Even the rich man who lived for his pleasures while the poor man lay covered with sores before his door—even that rich man was no thief. We are told that he was rich. We are not told that he was a slanderer, or that he was an oppressor of the poor, or a thief, or a receiver of stolen goods, or a publican, nor is it written that he robbed widows and orphans. There is nothing of any of this. All that we know is that he was rich. Is that anything very remarkable? He was rich, rich, because of his own possessions. From whom had he stolen? Or would the Lord perhaps have kept silent about this, or allowed his judgement to be influenced by respect for a person? Let us therefore not endeavour to find any evil deeds in this man.

17 Ambulatory of the baptistery at Cuicul

18 Font at Timgad

Let us seek no more than what is given us to hear as the truth. He was rich, clothed in purple and fine linen and had splendid banquets every day. What was his crime? That he left this man with the sores lying before his door and did not help him—that he was inhuman, that he had no heart and no crumb left over for this poor devil; and that was why he ended in torture from whence he lifted up his eyes and saw the poor in Abraham's bosom. But why should I say more? He who refused the crumbs was left to pant for a drop of water. If such be the punishment of those who have overmuch love of good living, what must a thief expect?

But such a man, who has stolen the property of others, may now say to me, "I am not as this rich man. I help the poor, I send food to those in prison, clothe the naked and show hospitality to travellers." So you think you are a generous man! Stop your thieving—then you would be generous indeed. The man to whom you have given something is happy, but he from whom you have stolen sits there and weeps. Which of the two of you will God hear? And even so you keep almost everything for yourself and only give away a trifle. "Thou fool," says God to such a man, "I have commanded thee to give but have I commanded thee to give alms out of the goods of others?" On the last day Christ will say to you, "What thou hast done to the least of these my brethren thou hast done unto me." Recognize, O fool, you who give alms out of stolen goods, that when you feed a Christian you feed Christ, and that if you strip a Christian, it is Christ that is stripped by you, and if a man to whom Christ says, "I was naked and you clothed me not", comes into the fire of hell, what place in those same fires of hell will that man be given to whom Christ will say, "I was clothed and you stripped me naked?"

And now, perhaps, you have begun to fear such a judgement, and you make up your mind not to strip Christians but only the heathen; but even then Christ will one day say to you—nay, any one of his servants will say it to you—"Do not harm me thus, for if you strip a heathen, you deter him from becoming a Christian." And if you then come along with the excuse that you do not do this out of hatred but out of love, so that a healthy chastisement will bring him to a different frame of mind—why, when I hear that kind of talk, I might be ready to believe you, if you restored to him when he was a Christian what you had taken from him as a heathen.

Now we have spoken concerning this one sin whereby human affairs are continually being turned upside down, the sin of theft—and nobody has contradicted us, for who dares to contradict such a palpable truth with words? Therefore we are not doing that which the Apostle enjoins us to do; we are not refuting our gainsayers. We speak to people who offer no objections, we instruct people who applaud. No, we refute no gainsayers. Yet if they do not gainsay us with words, they do so with their lives. I utter these warnings, yet a man steals. I instruct, yet he still steals. I command, I accuse, but the stealing goes on, and therefore I can only say that which I feel I must go on saying: My brethren, my children, put aside this habit of stealing. Put it right away from you, and you whom the hands of the thieves cause continually to sigh, see that the desire to steal does not enter your minds. One man has the chance of stealing and does so, another sighs under the depredations of thieves, but only refrains from stealing because he lacks the opportunity. When you have the opportunity to steal and then curb your greed, then I will praise you. Holy Scripture praises as happy the man "who does not hunt after money, who is able to transgress the law but does not do so",[20] but if you can say to yourself, "Never have I refused to restore the goods of others", then it is as good as certain that nobody has ever lent you anything, or that the loan was made before witnesses. Tell me honestly, whether you would have restored it if only you yourself and the lender had been present at the transaction and God had been the only witness? If you make restoration in such circumstances as these, if after the death of the lender you make restoration to his son, who knows nothing of the matter, then indeed I will praise you, because you did not hunt after money, and were able to transgress the law but did not do so— I will praise you, for instance, if you find another man's purse lying in the road when nobody sees you, and yet restore it to the owner forthwith. Come, my brethren, examine yourselves, look into your hearts, cross-question yourselves and give yourselves honest answers; judge yourselves without respect of persons and give honest judgement. See, you are Christians, you go regularly to church and hear the word of God and you feel moved by joy when you hear God's word explained to you——

At this point the congregation starts to cheer the preacher, for indeed they love to hear him explain the word of God; but Augustine interrupts the cheering and hastily calls out:

You praise him who preaches the word of God, I ask that your actions be in accord with it.

And because his words are lost in the applause, he repeats:

I say that you praise him who preaches the word of God; I seek the man who does it. What I wish to say to you is that you prove yourselves in this matter. Let this thing occupy your minds. Mount the judgement throne of the spirit, render an account to yourselves, and then do you yourselves pass judgement, and if the judgement goes against you, then mend your ways. What I am seeking to impress on you is that you have a plain duty to restore to the owners goods that you happen to find. Thus, if a man finds a purse containing money, he must give it back to the person to whom it belongs. And what if you do not know the owner, you say? Let me tell you that nobody pleads that kind of ignorance who is not actuated by greed.

Beloved, I should like to tell you a story, for by God's mercy there are among his people those who do not hear his word in vain. I will tell you the story of a man, a pitifully poor man and what he did while we were living in Milan . . .

Immediately there is a deathly stillness, and even at the very back of the church people listen with open mouths. "A story!" they say, and the reverend gentlemen in the apse think to themselves, "Aha! A *narratio*!" Meanwhile, Augustine is already in full flow:

. . . So poor that he was house-porter to a schoolmaster, but a good Christian, although the schoolmaster himself was a pagan, so that the man who watched the curtain at the door was in this case indeed higher than he who sat on the cathedra. This man found a purse with, if I remember rightly, some two hundred *solidi* in it. Being mindful of the law, he had a notice put up, for he knew that he had to restore the money, but he did not know how to set about it. So he had the following paper publicly exhibited: "Let the man who has lost the *solidi* come to such and such a place and ask for such and such a man." The man who had lost the money and was running around, bewailing his lot, saw the notice, read it, and came to see the man concerned. The latter, being anxious to ensure that his caller should not appropriate what did not belong to him, asked him to describe the quality of the purse, the seal, the number of coins and so on, and when the other had described everything correctly, he gave him what he had found. The owner of the purse was so overjoyed that he wanted to do something in return, and offered the finder ten per cent, twenty *solidi*, as his reward. These were refused, whereupon he offered ten *solidi*, but the result was the same. When he had vainly besought his benefactor to accept at least five *solidi*, he flew into a rage and threw the purse away. "I have lost nothing!", he cried. "If you will accept nothing from me then I have lost nothing!" What noble emulation! What a strange battle! What an edifying conflict of souls! The world is indeed a stage and God the Audience. At last the finder gave in and took the money offered, but when he had done so, he immediately distributed it to the poor, keeping not a penny for himself.

And what then? If I have achieved something within your hearts, if the word of God has taken root within you, then, my brethren, you cannot think you are the losers if ever you act in the way this man acted, for it can only be a great gain if you do what I say.

Then he adjures his hearers, who have listened to him with such close attention, to translate their admiration for the word into deeds and always to return anything they find to the rightful owner. As for such people who would like nothing better than to pocket things that they happen to find, but do not do so through fear of the law of the land, these persons are no whit better than actual robbers. If a wolf hears the dogs barking and slinks away, does that make him any less of a wolf? True, he who came snarling goes away all a-tremble, but, trembling or snarling, he remains a wolf. He is like a man who keeps out of sin simply through fear of hell.

If you refrain from evil simply through fear of hell, you are still far from perfect. I will even venture to say that if you keep clear of evil for no other reason than the fear of hell, then you do indeed possess the Faith, for you do indeed believe that God's judgement will one day come, and I am glad that you should have that belief—yet I still remain uneasy because of your evil will. What do I mean by that? Why, that if your reason for doing no evil is nothing but the fear of hell, then the good that you may do is not done from a love of justice.

He then closes with a peroration on the pure love of God which banishes fear and which should be the only motive of Christian conduct:

This pure love must be within you, this love which causes you to desire not the beholding of heaven or earth or the flowing stretches of the sea, neither does it cause you to desire the glitter of precious stones or childish theatrical performances, but engenders the desire for one thing only: the sight of God and the continued loving of him. For it is written, "Dearly beloved, we are now the sons of God, and it hath not yet appeared what we shall be. We know that when he shall appear we shall be like to him: because we shall see him as he is."[21] Mark that it is for that highest beholding of God that we should do good and let evil be, for if you truly desire to behold God, if on this earthly pilgrimage you faint with love for him, then God puts you to the test. Then it is as though he were saying to you, "Come now, do what you please, satisfy your desires, let your malice wax great and your impurities mount, and treat all that you lust after as permissible. I will not punish you for it or cast you down into hell. All I will do is to withdraw my countenance." If then you tremble, then you truly love. If those words, "God will withdraw his countenance from you" cause your heart to quake, and if you look upon it as a heavy punishment not to see God, then and then alone you have true selfless love.

Ah, if, on hearing my words, you can only find in your heart one little spark of this selfless love, then give it nourishment. Spur yourselves on to stir it up by prayer, by heavy penance, by humility, by your true love of justice, by good works, by a blameless life and by true friendship. This spark of true love, O breathe upon it, give it that whereon it can feed within yourselves; for this little spark of true love, once it has grown great and shot up to be a blazing flame, consumes all the chaff of your fleshly desires."[22]

The sermon is over. An air of relaxation passes through the crowd, which has grown stiff from standing. During his long sermon the bishop has stood up several times, and the concluding words are spoken standing and almost hurled into the nave. Then he says, using the old fixed formula, "Let us now, turning to the Lord . . .",[23] and immediately all stretch out their hands upwards and outwards in the customary attitude of prayer (though we do not know whether or no they turned towards the door when it was the door and not the apse that lay towards the east). Augustine begins the prayer with a short exhortation: "Beg him for ourselves, and for all the people who are now assembled together in the courts of his house, that he may deign to guard and protect it: through Jesus Christ, his son, our Lord, who lives and reigns with him from eternity to eternity. Amen."

He has spoken for more than an hour; the worship lasts for nearly an hour and a half and the children are beginning to get restless. Indeed the people themselves are beginning to tire. However, there are no notices to read, and the time of listening is over.[24] Now the catechumens come forward and receive, one after the other, their piece of the bread of exorcism together with salt.[25] When the prayer of dismissal, which is named *missa*, is spoken over their bowed heads,[26] they leave the basilica, a lengthy train, and when all have gone —they have been let go "in peace", though they are not yet admitted to the mysteries—the heavy bronze doors are shut. There is a dull thud as the locks shut, and the metallic sound echoes long and almost plaintively through the church, which is now empty at the end. The bolts are shot home. Out the profane! For now "it is good to guard the secret of the King". The faithful are alone.

The Sacrifice of the Faithful

Now there begins the divine mystery of the sacrifice. The crowd turns away from the apse, from where the instructional service was conducted, and turns to the *cancelli,* which surround the low wooden altar in the nave. The basilica now has another centre (Plates 4 and 8). What has gone before could well have taken place elsewhere, and indeed, we hear of Augustine, on the feast of the Twenty Martyrs, having the lessons and the sermon in the *memoria* of the latter and then celebrating the mystery of the altar in his own church.[27] Within the railing stands the little altar; the pattern of the mosaic floor winds around it, alternating intertwined ribbons, ovals filled with crosses and rosettes, peacocks between branches of acanthus, and doves which sip from jugs with handles. Below the white altarcloths, which hang down on all sides, the inscription of the *memoria* gleams on the ground with the names of the martyrs that rest here. The altar, a delicate and attractive thing, stands on a field of blue-green and dead-white stones. The flowers and candles have been removed;[28] the altar is bare in expectation of what is to come.

Augustine rises in the midst of his priests and together they descend the steps of the apse and betake themselves to "the place of prayer".[29] The people throng around him but remain outside the *cancelli*. The clergy pass inside these, and group themselves around the altar grave. No-one kneels; it is the day of the Lord.[30] In a loud voice Augustine begins the great "common prayer of the faithful"; he speaks the introductory words and every petition is preceded by an introductory exhortation from a deacon.[31]

> The Lord be with you,
> And with thy spirit.
>
> Let us pray, beloved, for the Holy Church of God, that our Lord and God may deign to grant her peace, unity and protection everywhere on earth, may make princes and powers subject to her and grant us a quiet peaceful life, so that we may glorify God the almighty Father.

Here the deacon calls out, not as on weekdays, "Let us bend the knee", but, it being Sunday, "Let us pray."

After a short pause, while utter stillness reigns over the church and all pray in silence, the bishop continues:

> Almighty everlasting God, who didst reveal thy glory to all peoples, protect the works of thy mercy, so that thy Church, spread out over the whole earth, may continue steadfast in the Faith and in the confessing of thy name. Through Jesus Christ, our Lord.

And the "Amen" comes echoing from the people.

Then follows the second prayer, led by the bishop, with the people joining themselves to him in silence. That prayer of the bishop's which, as it were, gathers together the hearts of the faithful, was what we should today call a *collect*.

A third and a fourth prayer follow, a regular litany in fact, for all ranks and classes, for the Empire, for the needs and troubles of the Christian people, and also for their enemies. They pray for the Hierarchy, for the bishops, priests, deacons, subdeacons, acolytes, exorcists, lectors, porters, ascetics, virgins, widows, and for the whole people of God. Then with great emphasis, and with words that are very carefully chosen, they pray for the Christian and orthodox Emperor, for his Court and those of his palace, and for the success of his armies against the barbarians. They also pray for the Empire, which makes it possible for the Church to lead "a quiet and peaceful life";[32] they pray for the catechumens, that God may "give them the desire for the bath of rebirth, so that they may become part of the body of Christ"; they pray for their city, for their congregation, for their land and for the whole earth, that God may disperse all errors, take away all sickness, banish hunger, open the prisons and loose all bonds, vouchsafe to travellers a safe return, to the sick, recovery, and to seafarers, a safe haven. They pray for heretics and schismatics and for the unbelieving Jews and for the heathen. Although we no longer possess the rubrics of the African Churches, we can nevertheless reconstruct them with tolerable accuracy; for the "common prayer" was very like that which we still use on Good Friday. For though this last is actually somewhat older than the one in question and came from Rome, it seems to have been prayed very much in the same manner, as is plain from a number of *verbatim* allusions which we can find in Augustine himself. It was to these centuries-old prayers that Augustine appealed in his controversy with the Pelagians, who, he complained, "robbed them completely of their force and meaning".[33]

The last "Amen" dies away and the actual petitionary prayers (which Augustine calls *precationes*)[34] are over. The sacrifice begins. There is now considerable movement in the basilica; the deacons receive the sacrificial offerings which the faithful have brought,[35] though in many cases these have already been deposited in the *secretarium*, and sort out that part of the bread and wine that is intended for the altar. (For some time now nothing else had been allowed to stand there.) The wine is poured into a large golden mixing vessel with handles, and a little water is added.[36] The little oval loaves with their light brown crusts—they have been baked with a cruciform dent, so that they can be more easily broken—are laid on flat golden saucers, while during all this the singers drown the noise with a joyful psalm (this last is a Carthaginian innovation).[37] Then the cups and the little bread-saucers are placed upon the altar; they stand there quite alone upon the white altar cover, the pure gold shining bravely upon the linen.

Silence is complete. Innumerable flames tremble in the hanging lamps. Augustine steps up to the altar, possibly together with his priests—we do not know for certain—though he is certainly the only one who remains standing upright behind the balustrade.[38] He stretches out his arms before the little white-covered table and raises them upward, his sharp-featured face turned to the east:

The Lord be with you.

And with thy spirit.

Lift up your heart.[39]

We have, to the Lord.

Let us give thanks unto the Lord, our God.

It is worthy and right.

Truly it is worthy and right everywhere and at all times to give thee thanks, O Father . . .

The petitionary prayers are now followed by prayers of thanks and praise; they form a single whole, and are spoken by the bishop "while the bread upon the altar is blessed, consecrated and broken". In his letter to Paulinus of Nola, in which he endeavours to trace the forms of prayer from 1 Tim. ii.1 in the liturgies of the Greeks and Latins, Augustine calls these prayers *orationes* and *proseuchai*.[40] Of this whole part, which really comprises our Canon, he says elsewhere that in it we "give thanks to the Lord, our God", and that "this is the great sacrament in the sacrifice of the New Testament".[41] We no longer know the actual wording of these prayers, or how many parts they consisted of. It seems, however, that Augustine was in the habit of improvising the first part as a solemn *praefatio*,[42] and also that there was as yet no Sanctus, for it is nowhere mentioned. We are told that the real kernel, which he called the holy or mystical high prayer, was composed from "the words and mysteries of the Gospel".[43]

So Augustine thanks the Father in the fullness of his heart for his great deeds, and the congregation take in every word, for who is more fitted to utter a prayer on behalf of that congregation than Augustine? Within the framework of traditional forms, he will surely, on this occasion, have expressed all his favourite ideas. He will have thanked the heavenly Father for the miracle of creation and of the Redemption. He will have remembered the works of Christ and the Word that was fulfilled. Perhaps he may have made some mention of the six ages which God has planned and which lead like steps to perfection. He will have said something of that incomparable ground of faith, the Prophets, and praised their fulfilment in Jesus Christ, who, in the fullness of time, was born of the Virgin Mary and redeemed mankind, which had been damned, by the humility of his suffering; and who, through his resurrection and ascent into heaven, opened to us the Kingdom of the Blessed, where "the angels and the saints, in pure and glowing contemplation, continually draw in the triune God in holy silence."[44] When these prayers of thanks and praise are over, Augustine passes on to the mystical high prayer, whose words followed a fixed form,[45] though we no longer know what it actually was. It is now that he celebrates the memory of the death of Christ;

he makes the sign of the cross over the sacrificial offerings,[46] and the words of the Last Supper sound aloud through the basilica. And "this bread, which you see lying on the altar, is consecrated through the word of God, and this chalice, or rather what it contains, is consecrated through the word of God."[47]

And continuing, he recommends to the Father not only his own congregation but the whole Church that is spread out over the world. He prays for freedom and unity, he prays for the living, naming by name all those who have recommended themselves to him, and further, for those benefactors whom he wishes specially to remember, reading their names from little tablets which have been handed up to him.[48] He also prays for the dead;[49] first he recalls the martyrs who have shed their blood for the Church in Hippo and for the other Churches of Africa, Italy and Rome, those heroes of ancient times, whose names he reads from carefully prepared lists of the dead and "for whom there is no necessity to pray, but who should rather be besought to pray for us".[50] Then he prays for all his dead predecessors, for dedicated virgins, for those who have died recently, and for all those "whom Mother Church embraces without calling them by name".[51] And when "that which is offered up has been consecrated",[52] and "that which has been received from the fruits of the earth has been consecrated, and that which has been shaped by human hands into the form which our eyes behold has, by the unseen working of the Spirit of God, become so high a sacrament",[53] then this long prayer comes to an end, and the people confirms[54] all that has been said with a long, united "Amen."

The sacrifice has been offered; the altar becomes the table of our Lord. "We dare to say", Augustine slowly recites, and then follow the seven petitions of the *Our Father*: the people listen and join silently in the prayer.[55] At the words "Forgive us our trespasses", the church resounds with loud sighs and with the noise of people beating their breasts.[56] Then Augustine turns to his oldest priest, kisses him upon the cheek and says, "Peace be with thee", and the priest returns this salutation with the words "And with thy spirit."[57] Then the men exchange the kiss of peace with one another, as do also the women. The noblest of the matrons comes to the *cancelli* of the virgins to receive the kiss from their superior, who is Augustine's sister.[58]

Before the Lord's Prayer the bread upon the little saucers has already been broken.[59] The bishop hands it to the priests and to the other clerics, to the ascetics and the other virgins; then it is given to all the rest as they form long rows and present themselves at the *cancelli*, the children receiving it first, then the men, and the women last of all. Augustine watches carefully who is before him, for he does not lack the courage to send a public sinner away, should such a one be bold enough to present himself.[60] The bread is handed to the recipient with the words "Body of Christ", and everyone answers, "Amen." They receive it in the palms of their right hands and carry it to their mouths with their left hands supporting their right.[61] "Bent over and without stretching out their hands", they take a sip from the great mixing vessel, which a deacon hands them with the words "Blood of Christ", and again they answer "Amen."

While these words are being murmured,[62] and the communicants reverently come forward and retreat, the choir joyfully sings the refrain of the thirty-third psalm: "Come ye to him and be enlightened: and your faces shall not be confounded."

It is the psalm that has already for years accompanied the distribution of the altar gifts in the East, and which now has also been introduced in Africa:

> I will praise the Lord at all times;
> His praise shall be always in my mouth.
> In the Lord shall my soul be praised;
> Let the meek hear and rejoice.
> O magnify the Lord with me;
> And let us extol his name together.
>
> I sought the Lord and he heard me;
> And he delivered me from all my troubles.
> Come ye to him and be enlightened;
> And your faces shall not be confounded.
> This poor man cried and the Lord heard him;
> And saved him out of all his troubles.
>
> O, taste and see that the Lord is sweet;
> Blessed is the man that hopeth in him.
> Fear the Lord, O ye his saints;
> For there is no want to them that fear him.
> The rich have wanted and have suffered hunger;
> And they that seek the Lord shall not be deprived of any good.[63]

What is left over from the mysteries is carried into the *secretarium*. The singing has now ceased. The deacon calls for the final prayer,[64] which is spoken by the bishop. It passes over into a prayer for all classes of men and ends with a recommendation of all those present to the divine mercy. Then follows the solemn dismissal: "Go in peace."

And as the flame of the oil lamps slants sideways from the draught of the sudden opening of the doors, the faithful stream out of the warm basilica. Outside the forecourt awaits them, a chalk-white oven blazing under a blue sky. It is not yet midday and Christians can still take their morning meal at the accustomed hour.

PART 3
PREACHING

14

THE HANDBOOK FOR PREACHERS

The Fourth Book of *Christian Knowledge*

How did Augustine preach? The answer to that question is short and concise. His sermons all have their starting points either in passages in the liturgy, or in extracts chosen by himself from the Bible, and Augustine preached out of, with, and by means of, the Bible. It is no coincidence that the short homiletic guide which we possess from his hand concerning the general practice of edification by word of mouth should really form the fourth book which he subsequently added on to his earlier work on the correct understanding of Holy Scripture.[1] This work, begun in 397 and concluded in 417, bears the title *Christian Knowledge*, though in our time it would probably have had some such name as *Exegetical Handbook, with a Guide to the Biblical Instruction of Christians*. It is a book definitely intended for preachers and its assumption is that whoever ascends the pulpit must have a thorough knowledge of Holy Scripture. The first three books discuss the value of this most helpful of sciences and explain the rules for interpreting the various meanings of Scripture, particularly its mystical and allegorical meanings. Augustine does not think it necessary to prove or defend the pre-eminent importance of this last; people in those days were already far too convinced of the greater significance of the mystical and allegorical meaning of Scripture as compared with its literal meaning. The fourth book, which takes up less than thirty folio columns, really does little more than describe the manner in which those giving sermons or addresses should express and deliver what they have found in the Bible.

In many respects this last book is a disappointment. Yet apart from another book that is rather more detailed, namely, his *Instruction for Beginners*, it contains everything that Augustine wrote on the art of preaching and instruction. However, we do not find here any systematic treatise on spiritual eloquence or on the construction of the Christian homily, but only a number of pieces of very excellent advice, all delightfully expressed, combined with a number of examples designed to serve as models. Finally there is a sort of legacy of the old school, namely the division, following Cicero, of the art of speaking into three kinds. Here is a short summary of the contents.

The Bible and Rhetoric

Augustine begins by saying that he does not intend to restate the rules of rhetoric, though this might be what some readers might be expecting him to do. These rules are no doubt excellent, and most useful to the preacher. Sometimes they may well prove most serviceable weapons in a debate;[2] but, says Augustine, they are not indispensable—a very bold observation, even though Quintilian had been dead some three hundred years. Indeed, this is another of those occasions on which Augustine, without willing it, brings about a minor educational revolution. The rules belonged to the normal school curriculum, and, like Cicero, Augustine thought they should be studied in youth. After that there was little point in bothering about them, for the preacher has his Bible, and if he uses it well, the work is already half done. The right manner can automatically be acquired if one diligently reads the great authors of the Church—here he refers particularly to his favourites, Cyprian and Ambrose—and for a time one should also listen to good speakers. But Augustine places no value on the conscious study of the speaker's art. Nothing ever really comes of that, particularly when one is no longer young, for an older man speaks quite differently from a young one. In any case, it takes much too much time to learn all the tricks of the old technique of oratory. With these words the liveliest speaker of the old school impatiently throws overboard all the useless antique ballast that cluttered up this subject.[3]

Preaching sometimes means both teaching and explaining, but that is not really difficult, particularly when one has a public, as one has in the Church, that is ready to go along with one. To prove something is sometimes less easy, though it is the kind of thing that always holds people's attention. But to preach on a theme with which one's hearers are already acquainted—that means saying something that is already known, in such a manner that it goes to people's hearts. That is difficult, and is the real test of the artist. A blasé society is liable to be very demanding, and Augustine himself confesses that he pays more attention to style when in Carthage than when he is preaching in the provincial town of Hippo. In the *cathedra*, however, things are doubly difficult, for here it is better to speak in a relatively unemotional manner and to depend on the soundness of one's matter than to attempt to move people by empty words.[4]

After these general observations, Augustine deals with the choice of themes and discusses what is their main and largely their exclusive source, namely, Holy Scripture.

The Necessity of Interpretation

A preacher is nothing but "an interpreter and expounder of Holy Scripture",[5] and his primary aim must be to understand it, to know as much of it as possible by heart and to present it with a certain amount of eloquence.[6] Holy Scripture indeed already possesses an eloquence of its own—whatever the heathen may say—and how could it be otherwise, for eloquence always goes together with true wisdom. True eloquence has nothing to do with being puffed up, a state which the detractors of eloquence often confuse with the true power of the word; wisdom gives to speech an unmistakable exaltation of style which can be attained in no other way. Augustine somewhat weakens this moving observation by immediately seeking to substantiate it by a reference to Rom. v.3–6 ("knowing that tribulation worketh patience") and by a further reference to 2 Cor. xi.16–17, that passionate sequence with the words "That which I speak, I speak not according to God, but as it were in foolishness, in this matter of glorying." He claims that these passages constitute an incomparable *climax* and that they are superb examples of a *periodos*. It is perhaps unfortunate that he had no other terminology but the unduly formalized clichés of Antiquity. He also draws attention to the rich imagery of the Prophets, and analyses Amos vi.1–6 by way of example.[7]

This defence of Holy Scripture may today seem strange to us, but at that time it was supremely necessary that it should be undertaken. Much as today people of taste take exception to the mechanical droning out of prayers, and to the crude sentimentality of some of our images, so in Augustine's day cultured people were repelled by the translations of the Bible into a particularly barbarous kind of Latin.[8] Today the educated unbeliever looks upon the Bible largely as a mythological work but one of tremendous power. In Augustine's day it appeared to him as the possible repository of a certain amount of historic truth, but as something that, from a literary point of view, was not worth serious consideration. The very favour that it enjoyed among the masses may well have increased the educated man's disdain. There is a celebrated passage in the second book of *Christian Knowledge* in which Augustine tells us that people who had, so to speak, grown up with the Bible, often felt certain correct Latin usages which happened to be unscriptural to be more foreign than the expressions which they had grown used to from Scripture, but which were definitely out of keeping with the classical tradition.[9] Indeed, in Augustine's own case it is obvious from a number of passages that he really admired biblical Latin as a living language and considered it more moving and expressive than the pure but dead Latin of the schools.[10] Many a man of the ancient world must have rubbed his eyes to see whether he read aright as he read such words as these, as indeed must the five Jesuits who, some thousand years later, mutilated our hymns by direction of Pope Urban VIII. Augustine made a better defence of pure poesy than the première of *Hernani*.

After this he speaks of the obscurity of Holy Scripture. It is a thing that must be reverently accepted, but not imitated. God has himself spread this obscurity over it in order to exercise the human spirit and to veil his secrets. However, these obscure passages should only be read to the people when this is absolutely necessary. They are more suitable for study circles or private discussion.[11]

Quite naturally he comes to deal with the question of clarity in interpretation. One should always be as clear as possible, even at the expense of purity of style. What is the point of interpreting at all? Clearly, to make plain the meaning. People must understand us. Else it were better for us to be silent altogether. He reminds his readers of the great freedom which even Cicero had allowed when it was a matter of interpreting texts and tells them to use colloquial expressions whenever the necessity for this arises. If there are two words for the same subject, one correct, the other vulgar but clear, choose the vulgar one. It is even quite permissible, for instance, when speaking of the singular of *ossa* and seeking to distinguish it from that of *ora*, to speak of *ossum* instead of *os*,[12] for if a man is to be edified by anything the first necessity is for him to understand it. It is not always easy to make oneself understood. I often find it a sad thing, he says elsewhere, that my words do not suffice to express that which is in my heart.[13]

The need for clarity is even greater in a sermon than in discussion, for in church people cannot put questions. It is true that audiences often show by their reactions when they have clearly understood something, and if the signs of this are lacking then what has been said must be repeated, turned about and restated until the desired reaction is plain to see. Immediately after this, however, a fresh subject should be broached, though that is, of course, impossible for those who "are reciting a sermon that has been prepared word for word and learned by heart". It is no fault if well-known and greatly loved passages of Scripture are frequently brought into the discourse, for one keeps on hearing them read and whether one hears a thing read or spoken comes to much the same thing, assuming always that the codex has been correctly copied. (One must, of course, remember that in those days there were no punctuation marks and the words were written one running into the other: as against this, people always read aloud even when they were reading to themselves.) The object of all preaching is to unlock meanings, even if when doing so one sometimes has to make do with a wooden key. If the key is of gold, then all the better, but the only thing that matters is that it should fit.[14]

On the other hand clarity alone, if there are no other ingredients, can become as tiresome as a continual repetition of the same food, however nourishing, and so a certain charm, *suavitas*, is indispensable. Even the prestige of sheer rhetorical ability plays a certain part, and for this reason it is a good thing for a Christian speaker now and then to show people that he can do that sort of thing as well as the next man; and to illustrate his point he quotes a rather

19 Floor mosaic in the Basilica of Cresconius (Cuicul)

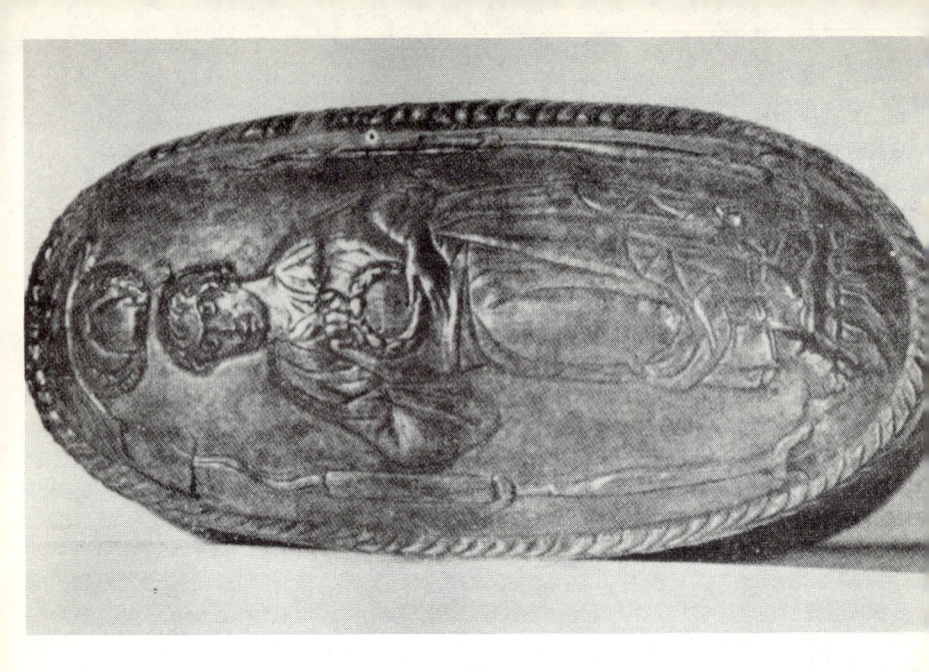

20 Reliquary from Aïn Zirara (Vatican)

pompous passage from Cyprian's letter to Donatus. While doing so, however, he remarks that the saint later abandoned this style. Finally, he says that before preaching one should pray that one's hearers may understand one. One should be a man of prayer first and an orator afterwards.[15]

THE THREE AIMS: EXPLANATION, EDIFICATION, CONVERSION

After thus explaining in a general way how the essential purpose of preaching is to be achieved, he goes on to discuss the technique of the different types of preaching, in this following "a certain orator Cicero". He distinguishes three kinds, the simple, the flowery and the pathetic, which are, respectively, designed to instruct, to hold the attention and to convince; or, to use the language of the Church, to explain, to edify and to convert.[16] To these three categories correspond three kinds of delivery, the quiet, the moderate and the grandiose—*submisse, temperate, granditer*—which in their turn again are the means of instructing, holding the attention and convincing.

Fundamentally, the material that is dealt with in the *cathedra* is always of the "grandiose" kind, for if God grants that we happen to speak well of the cup of cold water, does not a flame, a fire, shoot up out of that cold chalice which can inflame men to works of mercy? One can also say that many things which are discussed in a court of law are of little account, for they are mostly money matters, yet when the standard of Christian perfection is applied, then the least question concerning the fulfilment of duty becomes great. The matter of justice is like that of roundness; a large disk is just as round as a small coin,[17] but this does not say that every such matter must be treated *granditer*. That would be unendurable, for nothing wearies men so quickly as the grandiose manner.[18] It is best of all to mingle the three styles (though the *exordium* must always be kept subdued), for each one of them has its advantages and its defects. The interpretative passages should dispense with decorative elaboration, but should glow with clarity of argument. Exhortations, on the other hand, can really be made more effective by rhetorical elaboration, and here is the true field for verbal brilliance. When an exalted theme comes to be dealt with, then passion will produce its own suitable type of declamation; this will tend to move the hearers and to spur them to action. Applause usually follows a shrewd argument or the elaborated periods of an eloquent exhortation. It is when one speaks *granditer* that the tears begin to flow.[19]

These sayings are rather like flowers from a *herbarium*, yet they do not strike us as faded, for they have recovered in the fresh water of Augustine's own experience. Actually, Augustine gives an example of each of the three styles, taking them from Holy Scripture, from Cyprian and from Ambrose. For the *granditer* he chooses 2 Cor. vi.2–10, the series of antitheses which closes with the words "as having nothing and possessing all things". Then he chooses Rom. viii.28–39, "Who then shall separate us from the love of Christ?", and Gal. iv.10–20, "I am afraid of you lest perhaps I have laboured in vain among you", and from each of the Church Fathers he picks a very severe tirade against feminine adornment.[20] At the end he cites Gal. iv.1 and the passage that follows—"Now I say: As long as the heir is a child . . ."—as an example of an emotional passage and of a powerful cumulative effect, but he also uses this passage to show that St. Paul was not expert in the *numerus clausularum*, the harmonious cadences of the different parts of the sentences, and that he did not watch the rhythms of the concluding phrases—matters to which he himself, as he confesses, gave considerable attention.[21]

So he chats away with that easy informality which was the secret of much of the charm of ancient writing, and he tells us that on one occasion he, as it were, visualized all three styles, ranged one behind the other, together with the different effects that each produced. It was, according to his own account, some eight years previously—in 418, that is to say. He had gone, by direction of the Pope, to Caesarea in Mauretania, and had heard from the local bishop that the whole town at a certain time tended to be divided into two camps which did battle with one another in a most desperate fashion. This feud, which had by now become habitual, and was known as "the great row", cost in each year several lives. Augustine was now asked to preach on the matter. At first there was much applause, then the hearers showed close attention, then they were moved to tears, and Augustine was able to say, "Now I've got them where I want them." The feud was ended, and in the eight years which passed between the event and the account of it nothing more occurred.[22]

Among his other observations, he notes that the more entertaining style, by which he means the moderate or temperate (in which, of course, Augustine the virtuoso came into his own), should not become an end in itself, and that a truth which is all too temptingly presented is liable for that reason to fail to convince certain types of people, though if the matter is handled skilfully a certain gracefulness of presentation is particularly suitable for the work of Christian edification, for it assists internal consent.[23] The circumstance that quiet explanation so often provokes applause is explained by the fact that truth always delights, and when, on top of that, the thing is illuminated by a kind of natural harmony, which is enhanced by the rhythmical speech to which it inspires the speaker, why, then, there is so much applause that the matter can hardly be said to remain at the *submisse* stage.[24]

The Need for Living Example

At the end he utters a warning. He leaves all theory aside and becomes the old pastor pure and simple. His last word is this: People are more likely to accept what you preach, if you preach it by your own example. It is truth rather than the word that has a really salutary effect on men. "Christ sent me", says the Apostle, "not in wisdom of speech, lest the cross should be made void." If a man is not a good speaker, then this is no great matter; it is better for him to say wisely what he cannot say eloquently than to say eloquently what he cannot say wisely. If a man simply cannot speak at all, then let the eloquence be in his life. "Eloquent is the man whose life can speak." (*Sit ejus quasi copia dicendi' forma vivendi.*)[25]

There is also something that very much concerns his professional colleagues. If a man has a good delivery but lacks an inventive mind, he should not hesitate to appropriate other people's ideas, for there can be no stealing of the word of God, and though Jeremiah says, "I am against the prophets, saith the Lord, who steal my words, everyone from his neighbour",[26] the reference is here to hypocrites; but every man who ascends the pulpit should first pray, like Esther, "Give, O Lord, a sweet-sounding word into my mouth." He should pray for the people, for himself, for the man who takes the sermon down in shorthand, for all who may later read it, and last but not least, for the author of the book on preaching.[27]

15

THE SERVANT OF THE WORD

Augustine as Preacher

ALL the works of Augustine show signs of an unusual personality, and everywhere the tone is distinctly individual, but in his sermons he is particularly distinctive. He has, it is true, neither the satirical genius of Asterius, nor the suppleness and clarity of the realist with the Golden Mouth. He is far removed from the artificial solemnity of Ambrose and shows little of the grandeur of Leo, but through his genius for the right word he surpasses all the Church Fathers. Never once does he fail to make an idea unforgettable. Never once does he fail, when he desires to do so, to turn a simple statement into an aphorism. He never uses the sharpness of his mind to wound; on the contrary, every word he says carries its conviction by reason of an irresistible tenderness. Everyone who reads a number of his sermons will carry away the same impression as the men of his day, for no words from the pulpit have ever so fully come from the heart or combined that quality with such brilliance as did the words spoken by this one man in this remote corner of Africa.

No man has ever disputed his gifts. His opponent, Secundinus the Manichee, declares in one of his letters that he had never been able "to discern a Christian in him, but on all occasions a born orator, a veritable god of eloquence". "The *intarsia* of the palace of the Anicii," so he wrote, "despite all their polish and inlay work, do not have so powerful an effect, as do your writings by reason of the brilliance of their eloquence."[28] Yet it was not to his writings alone that he owed his fame. When Paulinus of Nola congratulated his African friend Romanianus on Augustine's consecration as a bishop, he wrote: I congratulate you on this new acquisition, not on the mere fact of his having become a bishop, but because the Churches of Africa can now hear him; for the trumpet of the Lord blows through Augustine's mouth.[29]

What is true of all good speakers is certainly true of Augustine, namely, that the bare text which has been reconstructed from the notes of stenographers does not even give an approximate idea of the reality. That stream of words that ceaselessly rushes on, sparkling and shimmering as it goes, has here been reduced to a shadow of its true self. One must have heard the man himself, writes Possidius, however well what he says looks on paper.[30] On the great feasts Augustine's audience hung with delight and astonishment on those lips, whose eloquence seemed so inexhaustible. Their rapt attention was so noticeable that Augustine himself occasionally was moved to praise it.[31] It so happens that the first sermon of his chosen successor, a sermon which he gave in the bishop's presence, has been preserved for us. Poor Eraclius! His sermon is charming, so far as its contents are concerned, and perfect in form, but it is one long excusing of himself, and confirms his own words—that he is a cricket chirping when the swan is silent.[32]

Augustine had a weak voice. "We beg you for silence", he once began in a crowded church in Carthage: "Then, after the strain which was put upon it yesterday, our voice may last out for at least a short while."[33] On occasion he could even complain: "Forgive me, you know how quickly I tire. I cannot speak so loud." "Yesterday", he begins another time, "the crowd stood packed together into the uttermost corners and people were not very quiet, which made it difficult for our voice, for that voice is not strong enough to be heard by everybody unless there is absolute silence." On this occasion he was not in flow and did not get round to the subject he really intended to talk about, and so had the same Gospel read on the following day, so that he could deal with the matter he had omitted to touch on that day.[34] When, on St. Laurence's day, he saw how few people were present, he said, "Hear then, you who are few, my words which are also few, for we also are not worth much today owing to our bodily exhaustion and to the heat" (it was the tenth of August). That sermon was indeed a short one.[35] He may, however, have thought on this day, Ambrose also soon gets hoarse.[36]

Whoever begins to read the *sermones* of the Bishop of Hippo knows after the first few pages that the theory in the last part of *Christian Knowledge* had been lived and experienced long before it was written down. The portrait that is there drawn, in a few rapid strokes, of the servant of the word might well be an involuntary self-portrait of Augustine himself, for all that is written there applies to him. Augustine follows his own precept. He preaches in truly popular fashion and is always clear, he is careful not to be solemn for too long or to sound perpetual notes of triumph, and like the Bishop of Meaux, he ignores all difficulties with a contemptuous eagle eye. With a facility that is quite inimitable he masters his three categories and mingles them one with another; improvises sudden transitions, or neglects to make any transition at all. When he is really in flow he speaks in all three styles at once, now in the strange staccato of an imaginary dialogue (admittedly difficult to understand upon the printed page, but clear enough in the spoken word); then, with a period taking up a whole paragraph, which flows on like a river with many winding turns. He can spread himself over everything, can let himself go, take hold of himself again, pick up seemingly forgotten threads and then, even after the wearisome repetitions which impromptu speaking is liable to bring with it (a feature which sometimes recalls the celebrated parentheses of Dickens) he suddenly catches the attention of his audience again by an apt comparison, a piece of verbal play, a spark struck from a bare half-dozen words, and conjures from the faces of the listeners a look of comprehension, and a sudden acclamation from their lips.

The Traditional Material

By far the greater number of the sermons were much more spontaneous than is usually realized; they were delivered first and written down afterwards. The bishop did not concern himself with the actual labour of writing—no writer of Antiquity ever did that. When he was at home he dictated, and walked up and down as he did so. Even his greater works came into being in this way, for the actual business of writing was too great a physical strain. Moreover, he could command the services of a whole staff of shorthand writers, the *notarii* (Plate 21), who scratched the *notae* and who were probably found from among the clerics of his own household.[37] Every ecclesiastical personage of any importance had one or more *notarii* available, and he also speaks of *librarii*, who gave him readable copies of what he had dictated, copies which then received from him their final correction. Augustine needed all of his staff; thus we find him writing to his brother bishop and friend, Evodius of Uzalis, that he would have to send over his own *notarius* if he wanted a copy of one of Augustine's works.[38] There was for the most part no question of a paper shortage, but parchment was accounted a luxury.[39] Augustine was definitely fond of dictating; he looked upon it as a relaxation and was ready to sacrifice his night's rest to do it.[40]

His sermons, however, were never actually dictated in the strict sense of the term. Indeed, his actual preparation consisted, for all practical purposes, in prayer or, occasionally, in a short meditation. What he really did was to improvise on the Bible texts that had just been read. Sometimes he had some special theme to discuss, such as the consecration of a bishop or a basilica, or it might be the anniversary of a saint which he had to commemorate in that saint's *memoria*.[41] Certain days were, however, free, and Augustine could exercise his own choice as to what texts were to be read and discussed.[42] On these occasions he would himself name the psalm that was to be sung and tell the precentor, who was usually a boy with an unbroken voice. On one occasion the precentor had misunderstood the number of the psalm and had sung Psalm cxxxviii, with its twenty-four verses, instead of the short one which Augustine had chosen; Augustine took up the theme of the psalm that had actually been sung. "I had prepared myself for one of the short psalms," he said on this occasion, "and had asked for it to be sung, but the lector seems to have been somewhat confused, and sang a different one. In these circumstances I prefer to conform to the error of the lector and the will of God rather than to follow my own."[43] Once, when no specific instructions had been given, the young lad started off in a determined fashion with Psalm 1, the *Miserere* (it being fast-time) and the people immediately answered, "Turn away thy face from my sins: and blot out all my iniquities." Augustine treated this as a cue to preach on the need for readiness to do penance: "We had prepared no sermon for you, beloved, we desired that you should do no more than chew the cud, for we had considered the meal of which you had partaken to be exceedingly nourishing; but you get hungry again every day, and now we have received the command of God to say something on the need for penance, for it was not we ourselves who instructed the lector to sing this psalm; he himself decided to do this, because his young heart felt you had need of it."[44] One day when he was a guest preacher in Carthage, it was his host, Aurelius, who selected and announced the psalm—to Augustine's considerable discomfiture, but in no wise to the detriment of the quality of the sermon.[45] On more than one occasion he professed to see divine guidance in such chance happenings, and in much the same way he looked upon the ideas that came to him during the readings of the Bible as a sort of divine pointer in the choice of his theme.[46]

Sometimes he chose the three readings in such a way that they all treated the same subject. Thus, on one occasion in the basilica of Celerina in Carthage, he preached on 1 Tim. i.15: "A faithful saying, and worthy of all acceptation: That Christ Jesus came into the world to save sinners", and in the same sermon spoke about the story of Zacchaeus. Needless to say, this developed into a sermon against the Pelagians.[47] On another occasion he had this same text read as the Epistle, and chose Psalm xciv, probably because the sixth verse of this was used as the refrain: "Come let us adore and fall down: and weep before the Lord that made us." Finally, for the Gospel he chose the story of the ten lepers. All this formed the basis of a sermon on gratitude, and of course again developed into an attack on the apostles of self-sufficiency, the ungrateful Pelagians.[48] When preaching he quoted the Bible from memory. Only when it was a case of longer extracts did he get the lector to hand up one of the codices onto the high apse where he sat when preaching. In one instance, however, we can see very well that he had consulted a whole row of selected texts beforehand, and had them ready prepared as a sort of armoury.[49]

That in spite of all this nearly a thousand sermons have been preserved,[50] we owe to the shorthand writers, those indispensable assistants:

> Every phrase of speech their scribbling rapidly follows
> And their briefest of notes capture each word that is said.[51]

True enough that sermons were not rattled off too quickly, for the speakers of Antiquity spoke more slowly than we; they savoured the hidden power of every word and did words a sort of honour. It was not the ecclesiastical shorthand writers alone, however, who played a part in this business, for there were those among Augustine's audience who "not only took in with their ears and their hearts what was spoken, but also put their pencils to use", which means that they made a short summary of the sermon or had it written down by paid shorthand writers of their own.[52] It seems probable enough that the bishop undertook some revision of sermons that had been transcribed in his own circle, such as those on the Psalms. Occasionally Augustine would work out his own summary after he had given a sermon, and this he would keep; in the fifteenth book on the Trinity he actually quotes such a summary and copies a whole passage, on the procession of the Holy Ghost,[53] out of it. Augustine did not by any means do this exclusively for his own benefit, for he took it as a matter of course that others should collect and use his sermons. All he asked was that they should pray for the author.[54]

When engaged in controversy Augustine would not speak unless minutes were taken, which he would afterwards work out in greater detail and have signed by witnesses. At ecclesiastical elections also he would only speak in the presence of the episcopal *notarii*.[55] Augustine was not the only one, however, whose sermons were thus copied down; shortly after Aurelius, following the example of Valerius in Hippo, had introduced the practice of permitting ordinary priests to preach, both Augustine, who was himself at that time still a priest, and his friend Alypius, began to receive from the capital the first sermons of Carthaginian priests, all carefully copied out, though whether the purpose of such despatches was for the information of the recipients or constituted an invitation to criticism we do not know.[56]

It so happens that we know something of the manner in which the largest collection of sermons, the so-called *Enarrationes in Psalmos*, came into being. It is a remarkable compilation, and its theme eminently suited to Augustine; a book in which there is an inexhaustible, an almost confusing, wealth of ideas. Its subject is the Psalter, and the author seems to share all the transports of David and to luxuriate in veritable orgies of allegory—so much so that Jerome once, in a fit of ill-temper, spoke of "those little commentaries, of which I have read a couple, and of which I would be compelled to say, were I called upon to discuss them, that they are at variance with the exegesis—I will not speak of my own, but of the old Greeks."[57]

This book of sermons became Augustine's greatest work. It is twice as large as the *City of God* and occupies an entire folio volume in the Maurist edition. He began it as a young bishop and completed it between 415 and 417.[58] It is a collection that had a natural growth. In part it consists of sermons improvised both in Hippo and Carthage; the rest is made up of material designed to complete the whole and dictated within Augustine's domestic circle.

Now, we happen to know that at one time several copies of this book were in circulation in which there was no mention of Psalm cxviii. It was at a considerably later date that he began his analysis of this the longest of the psalms, by saying that the brethren were particularly dissatisfied about this omission in his *opuscula*.[59]

The 124 sermons on the Gospel according to St. John, which are marked by such meticulous workmanship and full of such profound thought, were all first set down in writing, despite the fact that they were designed as homilies to accompany a *lectio continua* of the Gospel concerned. The first twelve were delivered in alternation with the *Enarrationes* to Psalms cxix–cxxxiii (*psalmi graduales*) between December 415 and Easter 416; the rest were dictated in 418, and then afterwards read out to the people. The ten sermons on the First Epistle of St. John were delivered in the great church of Hippo[60] in 413, in Easter week and at the time of the Ascension.[61] The more loosely constructed of the *sermones*, however, were improvised.

Augustine's sermons became known all over the world within his own lifetime. Cassiodorus quotes from one of them, but the fact that they have been preserved is probably chiefly due to his admirer Caesarius of Arles, who, a century after Augustine's death, had everything that he could lay his hands on collected and copied. The continual play with scriptural texts, many of which are not even well known, lend the sermons an air of subtlety which often makes it difficult to believe that many of them were improvised, but we must remember that, quite apart from the fact of Augustine's genius, the continual reading aloud of the Bible both in church and out resulted in a great many people knowing it virtually by heart.

The Popular Form

Undoubtedly many of Augustine's sermons were popular in form. He spoke not for the educated but for ordinary people. Moreover, he did not speak in order to make a name for himself. He was anything but a vain man in the pulpit. In his introduction to his edition of the sermons Erasmus has put the truth in a quite incomparable manner: "Christian love seeks rather to be of use to the people than to win the applause of an élite, for it thirsts more after the salvation of a brother than after fame."[62] All knew that, of course, nor were the great majority of bishops vain or boastful men, but who was proof against the peculiar seductions that always await the orator?

Augustine was one of the few educated people of his day who were really alive to the fact that Christianity is not something designed to make an exclusive appeal to aesthetes or people of taste. He knew that the practical Christian must never lose sight of this fact. Arnauld and others who, more than a thousand years later, wanted to banish oratory completely from the pulpit, are not wrong in appealing to Augustine's authority. What a contrast this man was to the great pulpit personalities of this time—to Aetius, to Severianus, to Antiochus of Ptolemais and Asterius of Amaseia, all men who, year in, year out, made so great a show in the *martyria* with their panegyrics and their diatribes!

All connoiseurs of the eloquence of Antiquity, and not least those who, in the seventeenth century, were conspicuous for their admiration of Augustine, have marvelled at the unpolished nature of his speech and the informality of his composition. Yet the true nature of this last must be correctly understood. A certain looseness and spontaneity in composition was wholly in the tradition of Antiquity. It was considered the mark of a good writer or a good speaker that he allowed a number of facts or ideas to pass pleasantly in procession before the mind and it was considered more important that he should please and entertain than that he should deeply move his audience. Above all, it was thought essential that what he presented should have a good beginning and a fine resonant end. A speech was like a garden with an entrance and a background; it was decorated here and there with neatly planted shrubs of digression and beds of narration which sometimes tended, in their luxuriance, to hide the very borders of the garden itself. Charm, in those days, seemed incompatible with any kind of visible articulation. Transition passages which were clearly recognizable as such, and clearly discernible *points d'appui*, were not in favour, nor was a clearly discernible framework. The prose of Antiquity was essentially a seamless garment. Nature herself, people felt, keeps her articulations covered. And people of sensibility who, in the other arts, liked to see an all-too-patent symmetry corrected by a slight deflection, and preferred to see a pillar taper upwards or lean inwards ever so slightly out of the true, knew well enough that in literature, too, an excessively rigid pattern is liable, where simple people are concerned, to destroy clarity rather than to enhance it, and that it tends to impair the charm of forms which might otherwise be seductive enough. We can hardly imagine how they would have stared at the great frame of a cathedral of the year 1200, but we may be certain that they would have stopped their ears at the mechanical twanging of the musical box of scholasticism. They did what all mature artists do; they veiled the framework and gave full freedom to the flowing line.

Yet the average sermon of Augustine makes such a disorderly impression that his unpretentious manner seems almost to suggest downright carelessness. One can almost say that he did two contradictory things at once; namely, that he made his sermons deliberately artless, and at the same time showed positive genius in his strict observance of all artistic rules. The planning that was inculcated by the schools is completely absent. He despised what others had thought indispensable—namely, the arrangement of his speech under certain heads—and a couple of lines usually suffice him for an exordium. Usually he plunges straight into his subject, his opening being always pleasant but sometimes on the banal side. Indeed, he seldom strikes a solemn note in his opening sentences and on occasions lets his good humour run away with him when there is a particularly large attendance.[63] In his exordium, which really cannot be called a proper exordium at all, he briefly indicates his theme, developing, as he does so, a train of thought that seems to stretch like a tendril of acanthus from one text to another. There is rarely any sign of a detailed *propositio* of his material, and never an express arrangement into parts. He is governed by the prevailing mood of his audience, and if attention lags he will pass on to a fresh subject. If his time is up, or his audience has grown restless, or if he himself has grown tired, he simply stops. The peroration comes in automatically, usually ending with a concluding sentence that has something like a Shakespearian force about it. The only comment that one can really make is that Augustine was a man who was never at a loss for an idea or for a word. That which was the essential distinguishing mark between the old orators and the new, Augustine possessed to an astonishing degree, namely a plenitude of words; *copia*, or amplitude, was in those days considered an essential mark of genius. It was not alone to the statues of Fortuna that people looked for the overflowing horn. *Prolixitas* was held in honour. Brevity was accounted as the sign of a poor and ill-furnished mind and was looked upon as a mark of weakness. A single idea must be made to sparkle in a hundred forms—and how well Augustine knew the art, not only of conjuring up new ideas, but of exhibiting new facets of those he had already used!

There is thus no sign in Augustine's sermons of a rigidly laid out plan being strictly adhered to. Whatever one may say about them, whether they strike one as brilliant, moving, wearisome or even confused, they were certainly no *oeuvres de raison* and were the complete opposite of those formalized and solemn exhibitions which could be heard many centuries later from the classical French pulpit. They were not speeches but talks like those which became common in the medieval pulpit, though they were woven according to the stylistic pattern of Antiquity and used Antiquity's vocabulary. Sometimes they were in the nature of spiritual addresses, sometimes they were really little more than conversations. Because he spoke *ex pectore*, that is, from the fullness of his heart, and because he was in living contact with his audience, Augustine disregarded any need for logical construction and observed only that order which was dictated by circumstances and by his own heart. Thus, as Pascal says,[64] in following the order of the heart he followed the order of love, and in doing so he did nothing other than what our Lord himself had done, as did also St. Paul; for these too despised all ordering and formalizing of the Spirit with principles and argumentations. It was Augustine's aim to follow the example of Holy Scripture and carry his point by the directness and by the positive character of his utterance. His was not to deduce or prove but to proclaim, to reveal; in a word, to preach, *intimare*. Yet though this was his feeling in the matter, this man who held the view that there was something in every sermon that could be treated *granditer*, was himself extremely reluctant to do anything like ride the high horse. He never declaimed; he spoke and explained until the subject, without his actually willing it, took hold of him and carried him along. That is what makes it easy for us to follow him and that is why, even today after fifteen hundred years, we are as much moved as he was himself, when we merely read his sermons. How encouraging this is for those who have something to say, but who rarely, if ever, have anything to declaim; and how humiliating this must be for those all-too-numerous people who mount the pulpit like so many wound-up alarm clocks, rattle off their piece *fortissimo*, and then descend, limp as the uncoiled clockspring, with nothing of what they have said echoing within them, a living example of the tinkling cymbal in the First Epistle to the Corinthians. If for a moment one could forget his polish (a legacy of the eighteenth century) and his psychological subtleties (an anticipation of the twentieth), then one could sometimes see a certain resemblance between Augustine and Newman. Neither thought for a moment about his manner of delivery, neither ever worked himself into an artificial frenzy, and both avoided demonstrative pathos; both tended to be enraptured by the supernatural perspectives that arose out of the flow of their own words,[65] the only difference being that the man of Antiquity really spoke, while the modern one read out his sermons. It is the difference between two whole worlds.

In the order of love the stones of rhetoric were worthless compared with the bread of the word. That was why Augustine preferred to adapt himself to the taste of his hearers; he broke the bread in the way they liked best. Not only did he forget literature; he also forgot his elevated episcopal throne. It was not in his nature to look upon himself as an omniscient man of learning, and on that score to feel superior to the common herd. In the pulpit he stood, as it were, in the company of his own people under the light of the word; he did not address them as "you", but invariably used the word "we". He would publicly recall his own faults, and if, as he sometimes did, he administered a quite sharp rebuke, he was ready to take this as applying, if necessary, to himself: "Why do I preach? Why do I sit here upon the *cathedra*? What do I live for? For this one thing alone, that we may one day live with Christ! This is my endeavour, my honour, my fame, this is my joy and my treasured possession! And if you have not heard me attentively, and I have for all that not remained silent, then I have at least saved my own soul, but I do not desire to attain everlasting salvation without you."[66]

Actually, Augustine's people would not accept this. That they themselves should beat their breasts at the words "Forgive us our trespasses" was quite in order; they were all sinners. " 'But not you, holy bishop! Yes, we are sinners, but you also? Oh no! Sir, do not wrong yourself!' I do myself no wrong, I speak the truth, we too owe a debt, and that not because of monetary difficulties, but because of sin. 'If we say that we are without sin, we deceive ourselves and the truth is not in us.' Although we are baptized, we are still debtors."[67] He does not seek to keep any kind of distance nor does he covet any theatrical dignity: "You all belong to one great family and we are only the administrators of this family, and we all stand under one Lord. Who knows how many such future administrators are standing here among the people? Once we ourselves stood there, where you now stand today, and once we ourselves, whom you see up above here handing out the bread to our fellow servants, stood down below to receive our share. I stand here and speak as a bishop before laymen, but for that very reason I know how many future bishops I am addressing."[68]

The apparent slipshodness of phrase which characterized his speech was deliberate, for he meant business with his theory about clarity. Too meticulous a choice of words would either cause his speech to be imperfectly understood or at least would rob it of much of its force when he addressed the masses; for this reason he preferred the colloquial language of the day to that of the schools. "What business is this of any schoolmaster?", he once remarked concerning the word *foeneratur*, which he had deliberately used instead of the more correct *foenerat*, simply because it was used in the Bible. "It is better", he said, "that we should use these barbarisms and be understood by you than be artists in speech and talk past you. I prefer that the schoolmasters should have a ground of complaint against us rather than that you should fail to understand what we are trying to say."[69] It need hardly be said, however, that he never made himself guilty of actual mistakes of grammar; he used few new formations, though those he did use were always excellent, and in reality only made use of a barbarism when it was part of the recognized Christian vocabulary and was to be found in those essentially popular documents, the translations of the Bible—all of which did not prevent him from apologizing on occasion for his own manner of speech and even for the Bible translations themselves. It was in this spirit that he once said that people were now in the habit of singing *floriet* instead of *florebit* and that there was really nothing that one could do about it.[70]

After some twenty years spent as a teacher of rhetoric in the great cities, he was naturally never at a loss for a synonym, but when it was a matter of a detailed analysis he tended naturally to choose words and phrases from popular speech. There were whole lists of vulgar or at any rate not particularly elevated expressions which were technically correct Latin and certainly did not belong to the dog-Latin of a later day, but which a well-trained speaker would have been ashamed to use on any important occasion, much as today there are expressions which a new member of the Académie française, making his maiden speech, would be careful to avoid. Now, it is true that Augustine did not make an actual point of using "words that are not said" (and indeed, the choice of one's vocabulary was looked upon as more important than style itself), but he certainly went further than any of his contemporaries, and although one would compare his age with that of Amyot and Rabelais rather than with that of Boileau, he nevertheless uses words from the pulpit which Jerome avoided even in his satires. He appropriated any felicitous popular phrase and loved those paradoxical juxtapositions which are known by the name of *oxymoron*, or indeed any combination of words that would enable him to end a passage with a bang. Nor did he have any difficulty in achieving rhythmic cadences of phrase. When he improvised these flowed from his lips without effort and without his being aware of the fact.[71]

Augustine's manner of exposition assumes at one and the same time in his audience a high degree of natural intelligence and an almost equal measure of naïveté. Often he has occasion to speak of the common popular misconceptions concerning God—and in this connection we should remember that as a young man he had himself thought of the infinite God who penetrates the cosmos as of water in a huge sponge, till the works of neo-Platonism opened his eyes.[72] When he speaks of the life of the saints after death and in this connection quotes the verse from the psalms, "Thou shalt hide them in the secrets of thy face", he asks, "Are we to understand this in a fleshly sense, which would mean that God has a very large face in which he keeps an actual physical storage place in which he stores the saints?" It must be admitted that his manner of correcting this particular misconception was not very simple, for his argument is that God alone knows "the barns and vessels", he alone knows the true dispositions of the souls of the saints, so that these are indeed hidden in his divine face, that is to say, in his divine knowledge.[73]

The same assumption of naïveté on the part of his audience marks his exposition of such matters as the nature and everlasting birth of the Word, the threefold reality in Christ (the divine, the human and the theandric) and the image of the Trinity in man.[74] He withholds nothing from his people of his profound, daring and grandiose thought, he gives the best he has; but he is at pains to say it all as simply as possible, and to explain it in the greatest possible detail. He does not weary of repeating his principal ideas over and over again, so that one can trace each one of them in three or four different sermons dressed every time in pretty much the same garb and illustrated by the same examples; a glance at the notes at the end of this book will fully confirm this. It is because this was Augustine's attitude that we find his boldest flights of thought so often followed by what seems to us a reasonable but somewhat pedestrian explanation, in which we suddenly detect the atmosphere of improvisation and the true note of the popular Church.

There is a sermon of Augustine's on the resurrection of the dead. It is a particularly carefully prepared piece of work and, incidentally, contains that picture of the cynical sympathizers at a funeral to which allusion has already been made. In this sermon he makes some remarks about the Pauline conception *in atomo* and goes into great detail in his explanation of the concept of divisibility; he illustrates this first by the example of a stone, which can be broken up into smaller stones, which can in their turn be broken up into gravel; this again can be made into rubble and rubble into dust. Then he takes the example of a month, which can be divided into days, these again into hours, hours into moments and these into atoms of time.[75] He loves to dwell on points of philology and to make things clear by etymological explanations which are sometimes excellent, often witty, but sometimes again distinctly forced. This was an old legacy of his teaching activity, for words and verbal analysis were the starting-point, in those days, of every textual exposition, and here, too, we find a wonderful mixture of the subtle and the ordinary. Yet one can say that if there is anything that makes Augustine's sermons difficult, it is not the choice of words or the structure of sentences, but rather, a tendency on Augustine's part to jump about in his explanations from one point to the other, combined with the packed fullness of the ideas that surge up in whole groups at a time, so that in the end the nature of the matter does get the better of the popular form.

Augustine has earned considerable fame—and it is well deserved—for the sureness of touch with which he will suddenly sketch a scene from everyday life, or, in a few inspired strokes, conjure up before us a particular psychological situation; concentrate the problem in question into a dialogue of a few short staccato sentences, or rapidly deal with and controvert any possible objections, and then invariably end up with a real punch in his concluding sentence—in which sentence the solution of the problem will be contained. The skill he displays in telling one of his charming little stories[76] is unique, and no man has ever been able to adduce more telling—or more simple—examples to illustrate a point, or any that have the same quality of making a problem suddenly crystal clear. Take him, for instance, on the problem of evil: "Just as evil men misuse the good creatures of God, so our good Creator makes good use of what is evil. God, who created the whole of the human race, knows well enough what he is to do with it. A painter knows well enough when to lay on black so as to put beauty into his picture; should God, then, not know where to put the sinner in order to achieve an ordered creation?" "Let us leave everything else on one side and ask what purpose that abominable Antiochus served. Through him God's people was chastised and proved and through him the holy youths [the Maccabaean brothers] gained the crown of martyrdom.[77] Everyone complains that the world is ill ordered, but are things evil in themselves, or are they made evil through bad use? Is the sun to blame for the fact that people are alway litigating with one another in such disgraceful fashion about the enjoyment of the sunlight, each man trying to get more sun into his home than the next, so that sometimes we see a rich man having the house of his poor neighbour pulled down, and, when the poor man tries to stand upon his rights, doing everything possible to have him driven out of the town—and sometimes out of the world?"[78] Again, here is what he says about habitual sins: "Every sin is made to appear lighter through habit. It soon reaches the point where a man no longer believes he is committing it at all. He has become hard and incapable of the feeling of contrition. What has become thoroughly decayed no longer causes pain, but when in this manner any part of one no longer causes pain, one must not look upon it as healthy but as already being dead."[79] On the avarice of the rich: "You believe that they are satisfied? Far from it! they no longer desire to drink from a beaker because they thirst after the whole river."[80] On being tied to earthly things: "What you love here upon earth is lime which prevents your spiritual wings, the virtues, from flying to God. You do not wish to be caught, but you still love your bird-lime."[81] On daily sins, he points out how some people commit them daily and no longer notice them. Would you take no notice, he asks these, if a ship were taking in water every day? If a ship has sprung a leak and nobody stops it or bails out the water, will it not sink sooner or later? If all your faults were tied together in a bundle, would the whole be light because it consists of a large number of things that are in themselves of little account? And what does it matter whether it is a piece of lead or a heap of sand that lies on you? The lead is solid, while sand can run through your fingers, but cannot a heap of sand that has grown to an avalanche bury you just because it consists of innumerable small grains? Cannot a river, which is made up of drops of rain, sweep away an entire farm? A lion can kill a man with a single bite, but throw him into a hole full of fleas—will he not, in the long run, perish in exactly the same way from the bites and stings of tens of thousands of these minute and feeble little creatures?[82]

If anyone doubts the essentially popular character of his delivery let him consider Augustine's perpetual play upon words.

Usually he contents himself with a few simple tricks, such as the antithesis of a couple of words that are roughly similar in sound, or (a favourite device of profane oratory) with the contrast of two verbs that have the same stem but different prefixes. Unfortunately, the actual point of this type of performance often has in fact very little point to it, or verges on mere clowning. Consider, for example, this from an opening sentence: "Tunc requiescit verbum dei in nobis, quando nos acquiescimus verbo dei."[83] Or consider him again, when he steers Catholic orthodoxy between the Scylla of Sabellianism and the Charybdis of Arianism—sure, of course, of the huge delight of his hearers.[84] "Not their *militia* but their *malitia* prevents soldiers from behaving decently", he says, in the middle of a most serious sermon on the occasion of the lynching affair that has been described earlier on.[85]

In the main, we must confess, some of these efforts of Augustine strike us today as far-fetched and not always in the best possible taste. What, for instance, is one to say to the following passage, which relates to some tightrope walkers who had just put up their tent before the theatre? "Look at this clown! By dint of a tremendous effort he has taught himself to walk upon the rope, and while he hangs in this fashion you hang upon him with your eyes. Rather let your mind be fixed upon somebody who performs even greater feats of skill! This man can walk upon a rope, but let a man try to walk upon the sea! Forget the theatre and consider Peter, who was not a tight-rope walker but might rather be called a sea-walker!"[86]

Many of Augustine's fireworks are, if the truth be told, simply unbearable for our modern ears. Perhaps the least offensive in this category are his remarks about St. Paul, who was "the small, the man of little account" (let people think of *post paulum, paulo post, paulo ante*, he adds), for Paul is the least of the Apostles.[87] Quadratus, however, he insists, was given this name as an anticipation of his steadfastness in martyrdom, for it denotes "the unshakeable and perfect"; the ideal *quadratus* or cube cannot fall over, "it always stands and never falls", and is therefore the perfect geometric figure.[88] He tells us in all seriousness that Adam (A.D.A.M.) had the whole world contained in his name, since it is made up of the four directions of the wind under their Greek names, *anatole, dysis, arkton, mesembria,* after which, however, follows the brilliant notion that the fallen Adam—mankind that is to say—was torn asunder into the four quarters of heaven after his fall, so that dissension reigns everywhere instead of unity.[89] Also, the man who composed the doggerel against the Donatists is not above delivering rhyming jingles from the pulpit. Thus on the feast of the Ascension he begins a sermon on the transfigured life with the following untranslatable piece of rhyming prose:

> Christus descendit, inferi patuerunt;
> Christus ascendit, superna claruerunt.

> Christus in ligno, insultent furentes,
> Christus in sepulchro, mentiantur custodientes.
> Christus in inferno, visitentur quiescentes;
> Christus in coelo, credant omnes gentes.*[90]

Many of his similes might be said to have come straight off the streets. Thus, he likens to full sacks those rich who have spiritually detached themselves from their wealth, while those who are proud and sufficient to themselves are likened to empty sacks that have been inflated. Both seem to have the same dimensions, but one is full while the other contains nothing at all: "If you look at them, you are misled, but if you weigh them, you soon find out the truth. The filled sacks can only be lifted with difficulty, the empty ones require no effort at all." A presumptuous rich man is like an empty sack: "In the flesh he cuts a great figure, but in his heart he is a beggar. He is not full but merely inflated."[91] Those who are everlastingly making promises to live like good Christians but never make a beginning of doing so are like the crows who cry *cras, cras* but continue to fly about outside.[92]

When he is dealing with his own congregation he does not seem to mind how familiar he becomes. He had no hesitation in speaking of a fellow citizen who was known to all present in a manner which made him appear in far from favourable light.[93] In a sermon on the subject of swearing, a habit which was ingrained in all classes, and one which involved calling upon God as a witness, he made the honest confession that he himself used at one time to indulge in this practice every day, but that at length the story of Herod thoroughly frightened him, for he saw what the consequences of this practice could be. Since then, he says, with God's help I have fought against the habit and have conquered it. "See, I live amongst you and who has ever heard me swear? Now, in my opinion nothing is easier than not to swear and by telling you this, beloved, I wish to exhort you and to prevent you from saying that it cannot be done. Ah, if men would only fear God and if the forswearers could really be made to tremble, then the tongue would find its wings, truth would never suffer, and all swearing would disappear from the world!"[94]

Even when he is speaking in the capital he usually begins with a few very free and easy words of introduction, for he feels at his ease even in such large congregations as these. "Our most saintly father, the bishop who is here present today, has unexpectedly proposed this psalm to me. At first I was rather frightened, but his prayer has given me courage, so now, my beloved,

---

* Christ descended, the gates were opened below;
Christ ascended, the heavens with light did glow.
Christ on the wood, let the wicked despise;
Christ in the grave, let the guards turn to lies.
Christ in hell, for the waiting reprieve;
Christ in heaven, let all men believe.

give me your attention."[95] When he was begged to continue with his interpretation of Psalm ciii, he delivered a charming exordium roughly along the following lines: We owe a sermon not only to God and to your father the bishop here, but also to the violence with which you demand it of us; and it is not only our duty but our love which calls us to deliver it; but the psalm is a very difficult one, for it is a veritable tissue of mystical symbols. I therefore ask you to be rather more quiet. It is going to be a short sermon, I fear, for, as you know, we have to go off to a funeral, and also we have no desire to repeat what was previously explained to you. If some of those present missed this last, they must blame themselves for not being present. Perhaps, however, it is actually a good thing if they hear nothing of what the others heard in a previous sermon, for then they will get out of the habit of staying away; so we will go rapidly through the psalm.[96] Here we have the tone of perfect understanding between speaker and audience.

It has been said that Augustine despises the more refined devices of oratory but is very fond of using such popular, primitive and natural aids as assonance, rhymes, alliteration, simple antitheses—the kind of thing, in fact, which we can at all times find in nursery rhymes, proverbs and popular songs;[97] nevertheless, in a work of distinction such as *The City of God* we find once more that polish of period and discrimination in the use of words that is lacking in the sermons.[98] The embellishments of the sermons belong to that category of spontaneous creation in which thought and sound form an indissoluble unity, though the pregnancy of the expression has a slighter effect than the actual audible charm of the sound. And in all this there is one thing of which we must in no circumstance lose sight: it is that what we now read is merely a dead transcript the living matter of which was once hurled down from the *exedra* with all the skill of the practised orator, accompanied by all the Southerner's liveliness of gesture, and delivered in such a manner that every member of his audience not only heard it but could take in the most delicate shades of expression.

Neither in Hippo nor in Carthage did Augustine have ground for complaining that his hearers were not receptive to their fingertips, and indeed in that day an orator who sought contact with his audience never failed to find it. Augustine certainly did so. Even the transcriptions of the *notarii*, from which much light and shade has naturally disappeared, show us that many sermons were punctuated by loud applause, sometimes, indeed, by complete dialogues between speaker and audience, all of which have been faithfully reproduced. Applause on these occasions was not so much a token of praise as of concurrence, or it was simply an indication that the listeners had followed the argument. Where a modern audience might do no more than slightly nod their heads or purse their lips, the people of Antiquity would use their voices to let the speaker know that they had understood him, that they had recognized a text or grasped a pun. This practice was so universal that Augustine actually reckoned with it, and even encouraged it, dividing his audience, on one occasion, into shouters and silent. "This lot of people indicated to me by their shouts that they had understood me, while the others indicated by their silence that they needed a more detailed explanation."[99] Sometimes the shouts were confined to those who had been baptized—as, for instance, when there was some reference to the eucharistic feast which the catechumens could not understand. Thus the bishop, who at the time was dealing with the story of Joseph in Egypt, when "he heard a speech he did not understand", once called out to the unbaptized: Be baptized, then you will understand a language which as yet has no meaning for you! Then you will learn where your heart should truly be. When, upon this, the faithful, who recognized the reference to the *sursum corda*, acclaimed him, he went on: When I say these things many understand me and call out to me, while others remain mute, because they have never heard the language which they now fail to understand.[100]

It is very apparent from all this that Augustine could always reckon on a lively interest, even when dealing with questions of pure dogma. When he began to quote a text that was popular or well known, they would interrupt him at the first words. They knew his favourite texts by heart, such texts as that from 1 Tim. i.5, for instance: "Now the end of the commandment is charity from a pure heart, and a good conscience, and an unfeigned faith."[101] When the great battle was on to bring the Donatists back into the Church, Augustine had only to quote from Psalm cxlvii, "Who hath placed peace in thy borders", to release the cheers and the acclamations for the great champion of peace.[102] It was truly remarkable how many such texts they knew by heart, and it was no idle remark that Augustine once made when he said to them, "As your learning and your love instruct you".[103] On one occasion he spoke about a man who, on his way to woo his bride, was attacked by a lion, and strangled it; immediately the church was filled with shouts of "Samson!"[104] And they knew, for instance, that Augustine saw a symbol of the Church in the woman of Proverbs, "who wove a twofold garment for her husband", the meaning being that she praised her Bridegroom both as God and Man.[105] Once, when he was preaching in the basilica of Restitutus in Carthage on the passion of our Lord, he closed a superb climax with the words, "And last of all, *domini exitus mortis*—'With the Lord are the issues of death'." Immediately came the cheers, for they had recognized three words from the Psalms. Yes, he agreed, it is in the Psalms.[106] On another occasion he was thundering against those who squandered their money on theatrical performers, simply because it made a splash, instead of giving it to the poor; he used the example of such people to show that certain sins tend to be accounted a sign of good taste. In this connection he quoted the Psalm text "The sinner is praised because of the lusts of his heart", and quite spontaneously the congregation interrupted him, for all remembered the second half of the verse, "and good things are said of him that doeth evil." Hereupon Augustine proceeded, "You have called out to me together, because you know the Scriptures that we quoted, but now those who do not know them shall hear the text again, for Holy Scripture says, or rather prophesies, that men are praised when they do evil."[107] They also recognized certain daring allegories which he frequently repeated. Once in Carthage he was endeavouring to explain that the twins of the Song of Solomon that are born "from the shorn sheep that come up white from the washing" denote the fruits that are given one if one observes the two greatest of the Commandments. They began immediately to shout. "Yes," he rejoined, "you still know what I am referring to; you have remembered it. You are well instructed and start shouting your applause when you realize I am going to speak of this matter. I have not actually told you which are the two Commandments in question, though I can guess from your spontaneous acclamations that you know which they are. Nevertheless, for the benefit of those who rarely come to church, I will name them."[108] Naturally it was his play on words, and not always the best examples of this, that won the most applause. After reading the *passio* of some martyrs Augustine pointed out in a sermon that Primus came first and Victoria Perpetua, the life without end, at the end. In these holy martyrdoms, he said, the will to live conquered the will to survive—and again the applause followed at once.[109] Sometimes the applause tended to be premature. On one occasion the congregation guessed that he was going to analyse the idea of *mundus* and give it its double meaning of "wicked world" and of the "pure world created by God". They showed plainly that they had divined his purpose and Augustine cried out, "What have I said? What is there to cheer about? We are still battling with the problem and you have already started to cheer!"[110]

Time and again it is plain that the applause brings him on to a new idea, and he almost invariably reacts to it in some positive way. On occasion he could parry and strike back. Once, when loud applause greeted one of his tirades against the "bird-lime" of worldly pleasures—and his audience knew well enough that this was a hit at the theatre, which they all too often frequented—he cried out angrily, "What I want is good conduct. Let your praise of wisdom be in the manner of your lives and express it not through noise but through harmony—with the law of God."[111] It often happened that he gave expression to his pleasure in being understood: "Your cries show me that you have understood, but I ask permission of those who have understood me to give a brief explanation of what has been said, for the benefit of those who have not."[112]

He did not find this everlasting repetition of applause in the least wearisome, despite the fact that, strictly speaking, he should have disapproved of it. He most certainly never ceased to react to it. When once they cheered at the words "for the joy of beholding my Lord", he immediately burst in upon them, exclaiming, "Why do you call out? Why are you carried away? Why do you so gladly hear this? Is it not because a little of this love [of God] is glowing within you?"[113] And yet he was quite capable of interrupting the applause when it took him away from a subject which he wanted to pursue, or was by way of being a pretext on the part of his audience to avoid having to hear some unpalatable truth. For how many there were who, as he said, loudly raised their voices to encourage him, but never to discourage their own sins. This was a perpetual worry to him and he continually felt constrained to speak about it: "It is so easy to listen to Christ and so convenient to praise the Gospels, it is so easy to acclaim the preacher, but to endure to the end—that really means hearkening to the voice of the Shepherd."[114] Finally, he also really did discern in this kind of thing a snare for himself, for he was in danger of being made vain. On the anniversary of his consecration as a bishop he once broached this subject. Certainly, he said, I like applause and it would be dishonest to say otherwise, but I do not want praise from men who lead an evil life; that I hate and abominate. It causes me pain instead of pleasure. But praise from decent folk—if I were to say that I do not wish for that, you would, I fear, think me a boaster rather than a righteous man. What, then, am I to say? I do not altogether wish to have it nor to do without it. I do not desire to have it, lest I be brought to fall through human praise; I do not desire to be without it, because I do not want to have an audience that is wholly unappreciative; but I think of the burden of my responsibility, for I must render an account even for your applause. Time and again I am praised, but I am anxious about the manner of life of those who thus praise me.[115] On another occasion he remarks, "How many people say, he preaches for applause and that that is the only reason for his preaching!"[116]

This Augustine, who pays so much attention to the reactions of his audience, might well remind some of his critics of the Archbishop of Granada and his homilies in the satire of Lesage, but Augustine, who always had his heart upon his tongue, was much too big a man to be compared to the aged fop in *Gil Blas*. It would never have occurred to Augustine to have his lackeys burn incense before him, but in those days applause was the only possible way of expressing thanks for the proclaiming of the word. It was in this light that he really saw the matter, and that is why he permitted it. He was grateful for a good reception and did not hesitate to say so. He was pleased as a child when he saw that his people, with all the *idiotae* that were amongst them, had understood him or could, here and there, recognize a word or a thought.[117]

He knew as well as Shaw that a preacher is always trying to put more into people's heads than can come out of them; he is so happy when anything comes spontaneously out of them at all.

He felt so much at home with his people that he could really do almost anything he liked with them. Once a sermon of his on the eight beatitudes had become rather long; he broke off suddenly while dealing with the last of them, and, when it became obvious that his people wanted him to continue, he waved their request aside, saying, "It is better that you should chew over what you have received and thoroughly reflect on it."[118] They were, it must be admitted, an easy audience to handle. They heard the word with pleasure; it always moved and fascinated them afresh and they "praised their preacher gladly".[119]

In those days the people of the towns loved a good speaker. In his explanation of Psalm ciii, Augustine opens with the following words: "You have reminded me, my dear people, of the fact that we still owe you the explanation of the remaining psalm, and I need no introduction in order to attract your attention, for I see that you hang eagerly on my lips to obtain an understanding of these words of prophecy [*prophetica sacramenta*]." [120] He could permit himself to put real questions instead of merely rhetorical ones, as is shown by the following example: "What would you rather lose, your eyes or your reason? Choose and tell me. What would you rather be? A man that is blind or an animal? Good, you have given me your answer, you have made your choice, but on what basis? Because you saw something? No, because you thought. You used your reason, and it is with your reason that you believe. So, even if nothing is visible to you, choose the Faith." [121] And what is one to say to the following close to a sermon: "Unhappy man that I am! Who will release me from this death-bringing body? Not always is the desire there within me to conquer [temptation], and there are times when I do want my rest. Hear me, my brethren, and keep to this rule. Serve the law of God with your spirit and the law of sin with your flesh, but only under necessity, not with consent, only because your desires torture you. Sometimes desires are so insistent with the saints that they attain while the latter are asleep what they cannot attain during their waking hours. [Here the whole church resounded with sighs.] Why have you called out? Is it because you understand what I mean? We are ashamed to dwell upon this matter, but that should not prevent us from crying out to God."[122] Is there a similar scene to be found anywhere in the records of Antiquity or one which throws a more striking light on the naïveté of these simple folk?

The sermon was not only a form of popular education[123] but also of popular entertainment. "You must not believe, brethren, that the Lord intended us to be entirely without theatrical spectacles of some kind. If there were none here would you have come together in this place?"—another remark that immediately provoked loud cheering.[124] These people listened with such childlike excitement that a burst of joy filled the church when their beloved bishop spoke the words "eternal life", or quoted some particularly moving text such as the verse of the psalm, "One thing I have asked of the Lord, this will I seek after: that I may dwell in the house of the Lord all the days of my life." We can find, not one, but numerous instances of this.[125]

He did not grudge his hearers their pleasure in the tricks with which he would imperceptibly combine his most profound thoughts—and also those games, which he took so seriously, with mystical numbers and allegorical meanings. As he wove his discourse he sometimes let the shuttle of his mind travel so rapidly to and fro that they could hardly follow it, while the friction between the thoughts that kept tumbling over one another produced a veritable cascade of sparks. Yet despite the whirl of word and trope and quick glitter of the sentences, Augustine always remained the man who spoke from heart to heart. Of all the inexhaustible treasures of his heart and spirit, he kept nothing for himself. He knew that if a man truly mastered a subject, he had only to say what was in his mind with honesty and conviction; then he would have no difficulty in remaining in the popular vein and in being at all times understood.

The Depth of Augustine's Thought

As to the actual content of his thought, no man surely will venture to map that ocean that washes the continents of the Bible. Even those priests who only read his shorter sermons and the often admirably selected samples in the Breviary know well enough that this sea is bottomless. There is always wealth in that thought; there are almost always surprises, and the average reader will almost always be overwhelmed by it. Nobody can fail to be astonished at what Augustine can get out of a single text. Whole generations of the devout have been delighted by the manner in which he can take three or four texts at once and strike a harmonious chord out of their juxtaposition. He is at times far-fetched, at times dumbfounding, rarely uncertain in aim or touch, and always honest—a characteristic which alone suffices to win us over. His real secret, which he shares with all orators who really succeed in fascinating us, is that he has such an enormous amount to say. He truly has something to give and does not have to go about wearily searching for it. So filled is he with the experiences of his own inner life that he can always speak of it without effort. This abundance that keeps welling up from the bottom of his heart causes the symphonic richness of his great works to be perceptible even in the shortest address, and we hear the full orchestral effects of the mightiest chapters of the *City of God* in the simple sentences of the sermons on the Gospel according to St. John, or in that on the anniversary of a martyr. When Augustine speaks the whole landscape seems to echo his words, and even some of the addresses designed only for his own circle of intimates never make one feel that there is less than the whole man within them.

This inner richness that is the mark of the Augustinian sermon forms a marvellous contrast to the simplicity of their form. It is as though a ray of sunshine were falling through the narrow windows of a village church. The contrast is as paradoxical as that of Augustine himself, for is there not a paradox in the fact that this great spirit was bound to the common people and suffered himself to be so bound? Indeed, one could briefly describe the essential character of the content of his sermons by saying that they contain the sum of his profoundest spiritual knowledge and experience adapted to the pattern of everyday practical life.

Augustine makes high demands upon himself, and it is this that is truly great in his sermons. The best was not good enough for him, and even when he was speaking to *rudes* and *idiotae* he kept nothing back. What he gave out amongst them was that by which he himself lived: "To give you all bread which you can touch and see, that is something which I cannot do," he once said at a distribution of alms on the anniversary of his consecration, "but this word is your portion. I give you the nourishment on which I myself subsist. I am your fellow-servant, not the father of your household."[126] It was wholly alien to Augustine to seek to achieve some higher *gnosis* for himself and to preach some kind of vulgarized religion to his people. He knew no ranks in the school of God, and if there was one thing that he really considered vulgar, it was not popular religion but the whole idea of *gnosis*.

As a young freethinker he had observed in people of simple faith like his mother a kind of unerring instinct in such matters, a *sensus catholicus*, and had regarded it with something like shy envy. Later this same thing touched him and filled him with joy, but it always kept him humble. Was it not to children that the truth had been revealed? That was what convinced him that what he himself had attained in so laboured and circuitous a fashion was in the last resort nothing more than the simple faith of quite ordinary folk. What he could at last touch, after years of hairsplitting, his people accepted—indeed, they fairly gulped it down—without bothering their heads about refined philosophical definitions, as though it was indeed the milk of Scripture's eloquence, and by the power given them by faith, hope and charity they understood. "He who makes these his true support and clings to them, has no longer any need of Scripture, save for the instruction of others. There are many who live wholly by these three, even in the desert and without books."[127] What right had he, as a steward of God according to the letter to Titus, to thin out the divine milk?

And so he gave no skim milk to his people; he preached what was essential. That which he had stated in his great works in packed and highly articulated form he gave bit by bit in his sermon, never giving too much at once, but giving what he did give without adulteration. That is why, in his sermons, we find all of his favourite themes. What filled his mind in his hours of study came forth from him in the pulpit. Whoever wants to re-experience Christianity as Augustine saw and experienced it need read neither the *City of God* nor the distinctly theological *Handbook for Laurentius*. It is sufficient for him to read the two model catechisms at the end of the *Catechism for Beginners,* or a number of the sermons on the great mysteries of the Faith.

The starting-point is always the same, as is the horizon that subsequently opens up. Earthly and heavenly love are in perpetual conflict with one another: the one builds the city of the flesh, the other the city of God.[128] Every evil has its origin in earthly love, in the selfishness that forgets God in the pursuit of its own ends. All good serves heavenly love, which forgets itself for the sake of God. He who has this love belongs to the holy city; he who lets himself be bound by the other belongs to the city of the devil; as yet, however, it is impossible fully to distinguish between the two cities, since they are intermingled. Time and again he will start out with the question which puzzles all philosophers, the question of the happy life—and ever again he ends with the rest in God.[129] Ever and again he repeats the same great thoughts, which are none other than those which dominate his great works; the primacy of love; the greatness and wretchedness of man; the image of God which is visible in our souls, and the possibility, which is granted us, thanks to the mighty operation of freely granted grace, of rising from the darkness of our sensuality to the light of God; the appearance of the Son of God in humility in the form of Jesus Christ (for that was how he formulated the Pauline "he emptied himself") was particularly dear to him, for it appeared to him to be the determining element in Christian doctrine and was what had torn him away from neo-Platonism.[130] Further, there was the indispensibility, holiness and unity of the Catholic Church, and finally the greatness of God, whom he praised as the highest truth, beauty and goodness.

Time and again he divides the history of human salvation into the same six ages and describes them in the same broad strokes with the same ten or twelve personalities—all of which was taken over and more or less faithfully repeated by the Middle Ages, both in the glosses of their books and in the statuary and stained glass of their cathedrals. He grouped them like a sort of forest of prophecy around the central figures, Christ and the Church. He sees history moving toward its appointed end like a sort of clockwork of mysterious numbers and time-relations, and marvels at it as a projection of the divine counsel into space and time.[131]

There are the same *lacunae* in the sermons, as in the great works. It is quite obvious that the humanity of Christ only moves him as the visible form of the divine Wisdom, and as the revelation of God "in the humility of suffering". He hangs with his whole heart on the Lord, whose image, he tells us, he could never banish from his mind in his youth, and from whom a light continued to fall on him even in his Manichean period, for even then he still "humbly held fast to the humble Lord Jesus".[132] But human tenderness for the humanity of Christ is alien to him. He does not see the scenes from the Gospel as an onlooker from the outside, he does not enact them before his mind, but transfigures them as though they were symbols; they are merely significant facts which point to things beyond themselves. Centuries separate him from the meditations of Bonaventure and the "composition of place" to be found in Bernard and Ignatius. Sometimes the reality of the Gospel is so compelling that the strictness of his attitude is shaken and a sound of human sympathy breaks from his lips. Then he speaks of the "head of the poor", then he describes in a pathetic climax the way of humility from the Crib to the Cross,[133] and shows us the Man of Sorrows in his silent patience.[134] Ordinarily, however, he seeks in Christ the inner teacher, and his spirit cleaves to the mystery of the Word made flesh. If, therefore, there is something lacking in his sermons, then it is only because he did not possess it himself, for everything that he possessed, even to the uttermost, he gave as a gift to men.

He has no hesitation in broaching problems which are solved indirectly or by implication in Scripture but are not explicitly stated or treated there. One recalls, for instance, the explanations in his sermons of how we draw near to God, not "in a spatial sense, moving, as it were from point to point, but by becoming like unto him",[135] or of how we can reach God with the sharp inner insight of the spirit and become happy in that contemplation,[136] or his remarks on the incorporeal and transcendant nature of God,[137] on the relations between the three divine persons,[138] on aspects of Christology, on the Holy Ghost as the soul of the Church,[139] or on the illumination which God grants to the soul so that she is enabled to gain knowledge.[140] He speaks of all this quite freely and in such simple terms that the unlearned can follow him. Concerning happiness in heaven, for instance, he says this: "Whatever enters into your mind, whatever you may think or imagine, it is not like that, because if it were like that it could not have entered the mind."[141] On another occasion, when a certain explanation had been oversubtle, he remarked, "I fear that those who are indolent will be unable to follow me—nevertheless I must bid those who can do so understand it."[142]

Many of his sermons on some verse of the Psalms seem to have a bearing on that neo-Platonist practice of inward contemplation that was peculiar to him: the tenor of Augustine's thought is that he who seeks to rise to a knowledge of God should make his own soul his starting-point, for this is a reflection and an image of God.[143] Time and again he stresses the transitoriness and unreliability of sense experience in order to tear the soul away from the deceptive impressions of earthly reality and make it more receptive for what God's illumination, the only *agens* of true knowledge, permits the "heart" of man to contemplate. And although upon the *cathedra* he does not explicitly mention either the light of knowledge or the world of intelligible ideas, and only speaks of the workings of divine grace, his representation of those workings remains unmistakably confined to the concepts of light, seeing and contemplation, and to that of the ascent from the lower to the higher, and so to the true reality behind all images.

It is not really surprising that he made concessions to the interest that prevailed at this time in intellectual problems (and also to a certain curiosity and love of sensation) by discussing the live questions of the day—and also the standard objections against the Faith. One of the difficulties thus raised was that of the possibility and manner of the resurrection of the flesh, a theme over which Christians, Jews and pagans could all become heated; Augustine never passed over this subject lightly. Indeed, he dealt with it at some length, though with a certain reserve, in addresses which have become famous.[144] As against this he had as little as possible to do with all profane learning. He hated the forced display of erudition that was cultivated by professional orators. It is true that his refutations from the pulpit concerned themselves not only with well-known heresies but also with the somewhat confused ideas of Plato and Porphyry on the origin of creation, and with such notions as that of the world-soul and the transmigration of souls.[145] When exceptionally, or through inadvertence, he quoted one of his favourite poets, generally without naming him, he did so because the quotation made some point particularly clear.[146] He thought it a bad thing that most of his audience should only know the poets from the theatre, but the fact that they were unacquainted with them from actual reading[147] did not greatly disturb him. And yet what delight he derived from his own acquaintance with them! "Those who promised an everlasting duration to an earthly empire", he once said, "were not guided by truth, but allowed their flattery to lead them into lies. Thus one of the poets allows Jupiter to appear and say to the Romans, 'These I give no measure of time or bound to their empire; theirs an eternal dominion . . .'" As against this, however, the remark escaped him shortly afterwards that Vergil had indeed "sold his words to the Romans as a form of flattery" but had nevertheless put the lie into the mouth of the god of lies, and had in another passage declared the Empire to be transient.[148] Yet who is not moved by the fact that these proud verses once resounded through the basilica of Hippo from the mouth of such a man as this?

He gave the best that was in him but he did not give it all at once. Like the servants at the marriage of Cana, he wanted to serve no water, since Christ had provided the wine; but he poured the wine into little cups, "and kept the good wine till last". To him who could not yet take the wine of contemplation he gave the milk of exhortation.

It is impossible to reproduce the leading ethical ideas in his sermons in a few sentences. The attempt has already been made by a much more competent authority and does not belong in the framework of this book. Everyone knows that his doctrine of heavenly and earthly love is the key even to this side door of the great cathedral of his thought. And any reader can see that he mastered his three categories not only in regard to their form but also in regard to their content; a lengthy piece of exposition is usually concluded with a short but powerful exhortation. Thus, in one of his improvised sermons on a number of passages, all of different kinds, the textual explanations continually alternate with moral applications of their meaning, the way the different elements are distributed being altogether excellent and always producing a stimulating effect. Always his more profound observations make occasion for little moral exhortations; this is the other and less valuable feature of this tremendous corpus of sermons. There is little in the way of casuistry here, but a whole treasury of practical Christian wisdom; a number of decisions which do undoubtedly belong to the realm of serious moral theology, and a great deal of inculcation of small moral duties. He speaks at considerable length of the different kinds of daily sin, of their dangers, and of how such sins can be wiped out.[149] He speaks of the correct attitude in prayer and of distractions—"Is it not true that when we pray our thoughts are almost always on other things?"[150] With a kind of sparkling simplicity he explains a method whereby one can get rid of the habit of swearing in three days.[151] He goes into some detail about the proper conduct for a workman and shows himself strict in this respect. He complains of the cobbler who keeps on promising "that he will have the shoes ready today" and then gives a late customer precedence over one that has come earlier.[152] It will be seen from the above that Augustine knew the way to hold up before each section of society both its peculiar duties and its peculiar failings; his voice, with its unceasing exhortations, was often that of one crying in the wilderness, a wilderness of bad habit and theatre-mania, but for all that it never lost the sound of charity. All these exhortations, both the exalted and the simple, were really only variations on a single theme: See that you have charity and then do what you will!

> For it is only charity that distinguishes the children of God from those of the devil. Though they all sign themselves with the sign of the cross, though they answer "Amen" and sing "Alleluia", and though they come to

church and build up the walls of the basilicas, it is charity that distinguishes the children of God from those of the devil. He who has charity is born of God, he who has it not is not born of God. That is how one knows the one from the other; that is the great distinguishing mark.[153]

Three Casts of Thought

Anybody who is acquainted with the oratory of Antiquity must immediately be struck, on reading Augustine's sermons, by the unusual variety of his thought forms, a variety which imparts to even the shortest of his addresses a colourful character that is quite alien to the classical spirit. There is, in particular, the contrast between the biblical parallelism and the antitheses that swing from sentence to sentence. Unceasingly the typically Jewish meditative utterance is transformed into some pointed aphorism. The solemn pronouncement is turned into an epigram of which an antithesis is necessarily the foundation; eventually the concepts all flow into one another and are lost in the twinkle and glitter, as the eternally selfsame images cast their reflections this way and that in the endless hall of mirrors of typological symbolism. Is this a world of genuine concepts or of biblical facts volatilized into symbols? We do not know; we can only hesitate and think: it is both. In a sense both propositions are true. This Christian prose, with its many peculiarities of speech and its new atmosphere so charged with piety and the fear of God, affects us as strangely, with its mixture of real and unreal, as the Christian art of the basilicas, that art that seems at one and the same time so remote and yet so familiar. The texts from Proverbs and the Psalms run parallel like little rows of stones, the Prophets intertwine with the Epistles of St. Paul, there are the hieratic ovals of the four Gospels, and all this combines with the criss-crossing of the rhetorical antitheses—in a word, all seems to combine to produce an effect very similar to the delicately-inlaid expressionist mosaics of early Christianity, those mosaics which we see in the baptistery at Naples and in the mausoleum of Augustine's unfortunate empress, Galla Placidia, in Ravenna. In one way it all seems curiously modern, though there hangs over it all a certain melancholy, a melancholy engendered by the memories stirred up by certain noble forms of the past, which have about them an air as of faded flowers, as they are re-employed in this new and more spiritual atmosphere. Actually, this new rhetorical style is not a uniform thing; in this loosely planned yet neatly kept ancient park there have been planted a multitude of biblical and Christian shrubs, and yet the paths of the logic are sometimes overgrown with weeds.

Of the three forms of thought which dominate the whole only one can be considered to belong truly to the ancient world. We have, first of all, the proclaiming of biblical truth; next, allegorical exegesis; and finally, the clear reasoning of Antiquity, a thing which can never die. Certainly these elements are to some extent in conflict with one another, and readers of Houston Stewart Chamberlain and Nietzsche might well find in this fact a confirmation of the chaotic and hybrid character of early Christianity and of the whole culture of that time. Yet others will reply that the biblical and classical forms of thought harmonize with each other just as successfully as do the survivals of classical draughtsmanship with the hieratical forms of composition in the great mosaics of the churches. However that may be, the fact remains that both the sermons and the mosaics are unique and wholly without precedent and that whoever has read them or seen them can never forget the experience. The figures which look down upon us from the shell-like niches of the naves are very like the voice that we hear in the sermons, friendly and yet compelling; but they are things which undoubtedly repel certain types of people. Some are alienated because the world to which these things belong is so very far away, others simply because of things like a predilection for the nude or other aesthetic preconceptions; yet others, because this world that they now behold is so deadly serious and so lacking in the quality of humour. Finally, there are those who simply take offence at the circumstance that the world of Augustine accepts the mystical and miraculous as a fact.

Now, after its own fashion each of these dominant forms of thought strikes us as strange, and indeed each in its turn carries the peculiar imprint of that time. The proclamation of biblical truth is probably more comprehensible to us than the other aspects of Augustine's thought I have mentioned. The determining element in this respect was, as it is today, the fact that the Church believed in the divine character of the sacred books, and also—and this to a far greater extent than today—in the all-embracing importance of Holy Scripture, an importance which the system of allegorical interpretation naturally made paramount. Further, this reverence for the word of God was to some extent reinforced by the traditional reverence of Antiquity for the word as such. It is not too much to say that the Bible simply replaced Homer and Vergil, though at a much higher level.

Nevertheless, the manner in which Augustine gets the Bible across tends to have the effect on our minds of something fragmentary and inconsequential. It is very much as though a short-sighted man were reading a letter without his spectacles and reading it line by line. He never gives a comprehensive view over a whole book of the Bible, nor does he even treat a single reading as a whole or lay bare its connecting thread. True, there is sometimes an inspired synthesis, but the whole planning of his sermons, and even of his learned commentaries, concerns itself with a single verse and sometimes with a single word. People have long drawn the conclusion that the explanation is to be found in the method of instruction prevailing in the secular schools.[154] The preachers followed in their homilies the method pursued by the authors of the Bible glossaries, and the latter followed that to which they had grown accustomed in the schools. This was, of course, the method adopted by the professors when they lectured on Vergil along the lines of the handbooks of Servius and Donatus; the professors naturally cared for little beside the treadmill of grammatical word-analysis. The lectures consisted of a number of specious comments, in which attention was continually drawn to the better-known commonplaces. They gave neither an introduction nor a general survey, but confined themselves to what was really an etymological and often a somewhat argumentative moralizing explanation of every sentence, part of a sentence and expression. Bit by bit and word by word, the celebrated texts would slide by under the microscope of pedantic erudition. This had been the manner in which the *grammaticus* had for centuries dealt with Homer and Vergil in the routine of the schools, and for centuries more this was the way the learned bishops were unconsciously to follow the example in the expounding of their pericopes and their exegesis of the biblical books. The texts had changed; the method remained the same.

Augustine was no exception to this rule. When dealing with a psalm or one of the speeches of Christ in the Gospel according to St. John, he too hardly ever entertained the idea of naming the nature of his theme. When he does so it is quite incidentally, and he immediately hurries on to the first verse in order to make a start on what is obviously his real subject, which is the explanation of individual words and verses. It is only when he encounters some difficulty that he traces the connection between one word, or one verse, and another. Never does he base the vision he begins to see once he starts preaching on one or two complete chapters of St. John or of the Acts. Those entrancing structures of thought which tower to heights that positively make one dizzy, real castles in the air, are usually built on a single sentence; indeed, on half a sentence. In fact, upon a single word of the Psalms he can construct a fugue in which he pulls out all the biblical stops so that it is as thunder in our ears—and that really is the other side of Augustine's preaching, for it is in this way that he makes people feel the sheer power of the Bible. Here he is once again the tempest of God that goes roaring through the wood, and one tends to forget his abstruse explanations of this word and that in the rush of his grandiose intuition.

The quotations that have already been given in this book will give the reader some idea of the essentially biblical character of Augustine's preaching. As soon as he touches a text it seems to open up like a flower. And when the text in its turn touches Augustine, it becomes indeed a "fountain flowing over into life everlasting"—a stream of living water from the hidden places of Holy Scripture; for he lives so much in Holy Scripture that a single associational link suffices to call some unfamiliar word into life and bring out the sweetness of its meaning. Needless to say, he lives by every word in the New Testament, but it is for all that usually some text from the Psalms that causes that all-pervading *suavitas* to master him which, he feels, should break out somewhere in every sermon. It is the Psalms, that great book of songs, the *carmina scripturarum*, which touch him like some living thing. He loves his Psalter above everything, and it is for him, as it was for Bossuet, "a Gospel of Jesus Christ transformed into song, into emotion, into the giving of thanks and into pious desires. The first psalm shows the happiness of that man who follows God's law, and in the second one sees Jesus Christ appear with all the powers of the world gathered together against him; God mocks them from high heaven, and, himself directing his words to Jesus Christ, he recognizes him as his Son begotten before all worlds. That is from the beginning the theme of all psalms."[155] This reproduces exactly what Augustine, with his thousands of quotations and allusions, is trying to say. In every psalm and in every verse of every psalm he thinks of Christ, and the Maurists were right in setting a vignette of David with his harp at the foot of a glorified cross over their edition of the *Enarrationes,* and putting over it the Lord's own words, "All things must be fulfilled which are written in the Psalms concerning me."[156]

What Augustine can get out of a single verse of a psalm often approaches the incredible and sometimes the ludicrous, and then again it sometimes happens that everything suddenly begins to partake of the crystal clarity which marks certain passages in the dialogues of Plato. Then there begins to become apparent something of that certainty and simplicity to which a Christian of this decadent period of Antiquity could attain through the reading of the Bible.

As an example of this, there is set forth below a passage based on the psalm text "Where is thy God?"[157] It is a small part of an address in which he expounds the first page of the Bible which, even at that time, was read out as the first lesson on the Vigil of Easter; and in it Augustine speaks of the invisibility of God and the possibility of attaining to a knowledge of him from introspection.

> One who truly loves the invisible God says, as he sighs for the love of him, "My tears have been my bread day and night, whilst it is said to me daily: Where is thy God?" And why should the tears and sighs of one who thus loves not become his bread, why should they not be food to him and satisfy his hunger, why should he not gladly weep until such time as he actually sees that which he loves, and while he still hears daily said to him "Where is thy God?" If I ask a heathen, "Where is thy God?" then he

shows me his statues. If I break his statues to pieces, then he shows me a mountain, a tree, an ordinary stone from a riverbed; for that which he picks up from among a number of stones, sets in a place of honour and then bows down low and worships—that is his god. If then I laugh at his stone and take it and break it or contemptuously throw it away, he points with his finger to the sun or the moon, he shows me this star or that, calling one Saturn, another Mercury, another Jupiter and yet another Venus. Of everything that happens to come into his mind, of everything that he can point to with his finger, he says to me, "That is my god", and since I see the sun before me and cannot break it in pieces, and since I cannot fetch down the stars, he thinks he has very much got the better of me, for he can indicate things which are visible and point with his finger at all kinds of things and say, "This is my god", and then he turns to me and says, "Where is *thy* God?"

When I hear this, when I hear him say, "Where is *thy* God?", then I have nothing which I can show to the eye and I find only blind spirits who raise their voices against me; to his actual eyes, which are the only things that such a man can see with, I have nothing to show. I should indeed like to weep over this and eat my bread in tears, for my God is invisible, and he who speaks with me demands something visible when he asks, "Where is thy God?" But in order to force my way through to my God I have, as the psalm says, "remembered these things and poured out my soul in me".[158] For my God stands not beneath but over my soul. You say, "Show me your God." I say, "Show me your soul!" Why can you not do this? Because it is invisible. For all that, it is the best thing within you. Now you say that you know your soul from your works, and you say this rightly. Well, in exactly the same way, I know my God, for he who has created all that you can admire when it is within yourself—he is my God.[159]

Here quiet exposition rises to the more lively manner of *granditer*, and despite the weakness of his voice, emotional speaking, *granditer* in fact, was Augustine's special province—but only on that higher level, where it passes into silence of its own accord. And what can be more suitable than that for a servant of the word?

As to the allegorical interpretation of Scripture, this was, in the natural order of things, the best method of freeing the classical manner of exposition from the slavery of the letter and of assisting it to rise to greater heights than the pedestrian analysis of a sequence of words. Actually, Augustine himself first conceived a certain reverence for Holy Scripture when he heard Ambrose expound it in just this allegorical fashion.[160] He suddenly saw these barbaric myths filled by a higher and spiritual meaning. This was definitely a decisive moment in his life (a fact of which we become conscious in almost every one of his sermons), for he remained to his death a convinced believer in the existence of this spiritual meaning. It was rather in the nature of a well-grounded belief than of an actual certainty established by proof. Augustine could appeal to the circumstance that both the Lord himself and the Apostles Peter and Paul were in the habit of quoting texts from the Old Testament to substantiate the New, and of interpreting them in the sense of the New Testament, but without reading back into a previous age[161] the new salvation which had come to man. He might also have appealed to a tradition, which was by now centuries old, which continually harked back to the Old Testament in the liturgy, the catechism and in theology.

Definite proof for the allegorist claim was never really forthcoming. Those who made it averred that it was a direct inference from the undoubted existence of a spiritual sense. Today typology, as it is called, is looked upon as an affectation, particularly outside the Church, yet in those days anybody who concerned himself with the bare texts of Scripture and went no further was considered a trifler. The conviction that Holy Scripture without such spiritual interpretation must of necessity appear "of the flesh", and the feeling that even on the face of it, its mere words, even if taken literally, were mysterious and full of a peculiar suggestiveness, dates back to Clement of Alexandria and his times.[162] The analogy between the Old Testament and the New, which had, as we have seen, already been confirmed by the utterances of the Apostles, had been tersely and brilliantly expressed by Origen in the words "Before Jesus Christ the Old Testament was water, now it is wine." If God was indeed the Author of this book, then everything that was in it must be worthy of God—otherwise it could have no sense at all. It had again been Origen who had compared the critics of the hidden spiritual sense of Holy Scripture with the wicked servants who stopped up Abraham's wells—"but these are being cleaned out again by those possessed of knowledge, and the water now streams forth again into eternal life."[163]

Tyconius, the learned Donatist (a man of moderation), called the Bible an immeasurable forest of prophecy.[164] Augustine, who had a high opinion of Tyconius and whose rules "for the finding of paths in this forest" he took over into his *Christian Knowledge*, believed that this forest rustled with one single truth and that every leaf whispered a prophecy for him who knew how to listen. In all its treetops, he said, there rustled but the single word—the Word. It was in accord with his theory of illumination that he believed that everything that was discovered in Holy Scripture by readers who were believers, had been foreseen by the Spirit of God and was intended to be discovered, and that it had been kernelled by the word of God inside the words of this all-comprehending book. This is the remarkable theory of the several senses of

Scripture "under the same letter"; however different those senses might be, and by whomsoever they were discovered, so long as they agreed with truths already established, then they were intended by the Spirit of God and were unassailable for that reason. Apart from the literal historical sense Augustine professes to see an etiological, an "analogous" and an allegorical sense, and Scripture's power of proof is no less strong when derived from the last-named of these senses than from the first.[165] It is small wonder that St. Thomas could not share this view. Although he admitted that the divine Author might have intended there to be more senses than one in the same phrase, St. Thomas insisted that there must be a connection between the etiological and analogous senses on the one hand and the literal-historical one on the other; and expressly declares that any explanation or argument must be based on the literal sense and not on an allegorical explanation. This does not in any way imply a belittling of Holy Scripture, since all truths necessary for the Faith are, after all, contained in it somewhere or other in the literal sense, and that very plainly.[166]

Augustine saw in the fact that the Bible was full of riddles the will of the divine Educator. Its very obscurity, according to him, is intended to be a spur to our lethargy and also to train our spirit.[167] This training of the spirit is the purpose of all the various auxiliary sciences which help to an understanding of Holy Scripture. At the same time, despite its obscurities, Scripture is very simple, and accessible to all. What is written in the difficult parts is, after all, the same as that contained in those that are easy to understand, so that the result of the sublime allegories really coincides with the straightforward passages.[168] This veiling of divine truth is very much like what happens in a throne room. There the hidden and withdrawn character of the Emperor exercises a mysterious attraction; the more the curtains that hide him, the more he is feared as a wielder of power, and the greater a prince he appears to be. No doubt, when he spoke like this Augustine was thinking of the stories his brother bishops brought back of the imperial court ceremonial, that ceremonial which Diocletian had introduced into the most un-Roman palace at Salona, and which was now in full flower in the dark Byzantine *palatium* of Ravenna, the city of lagoons.

That which can be true, freely approached, becomes commonplace. It is an unending and an incomparable joy to gain a partial perception of truth and at the same time to be less perfectly aware of it under the lovely veil of the symbol.[169] For instance, one can say quite simply, "The children of the Church are born of the bath of baptism, and it is expected of them that they shall keep the two greatest of the Commandments, those which enjoin the love of God and the love of their neighbour", but it is surely more delightful to express this thought by addressing the Church in the words of the Song of

Solomon: "Thy teeth are as flocks of sheep that are shorn, which come up white from the washing, all with twins: and there is none barren among them."[170]

An allegorical explanation seemed natural enough to everybody, even in interpretations of Homer and Vergil. Had not all myths, even the most objectionable, been made acceptable by this? There was also a tendency for anybody who thought about the meaning of things to live in a neo-Platonist world of imperishable ideas, and thus to float high above the world of mere historical reality, with the law of cause and effect reduced to the relation between image and symbol, the material world to numbers and history to the play of shadows. Augustine himself only fought free of this world with difficulty; he could never quite forget it. Holy Scripture caused his mind to become less rigidly fixed on timeless things and induced him to concern himself with actual happenings in time, since even revelation rested on historical fact, and the Bible was itself one great history. Yet it is no mere coincidence that his antagonism to Holy Scripture had only disappeared when he heard Ambrose say from his *cathedra* that it could be allegorically as well as literally interpreted. It is typical of his outlook that somewhat later he allowed it to appear between the lines that poets sometimes see deeper into things (as indeed they have always done) than the propagators of some allegedly scientific philosophy of nature.[171]

When we examine it more closely the mystical explanation is less forced than the theory might lead us to suppose. Many of the allegorical interpretations were really established clichés which had been hallowed by liturgical use and by the consensus of many of the Fathers. This is true of a great part of biblical typology, of which Augustine gives us a fine summary in the demonstration at the end of his *Instruction for Beginners*, and which has been preserved in that elucidatory guide to medieval mysticism and iconography, the concordance between the two Testaments. It is particularly true of Augustine himself, for his own explanations, which constantly recur, are for the most part rooted in tradition. Most of them go back to Origen, but Augustine was able to discover them more immediately in Ambrose and other contemporaries, though the latter, it is true, often avoided making any mention of that ancient but somewhat suspect, though incomparable, master. Time and again the figure of the woman with an issue of blood is used to represent the Church in the pagan world, the issue of blood being vice, the mantle of Christ representing the Apostles, and the hem which she touches the Apostle Paul—not, as one might perhaps suppose, because he went to the "edges" of the earth, but because he was the "edge" of the cloth, that is to say, the least of the Apostles.[172] Regularly John the Baptist is the voice, while Christ is the word, John is the lantern while Christ is the daylight.[173] Jacob, who, with deceitful intent, covers his hands with hairy goatskin, is Christ, who clothes himself with sinful human nature and with the misdeeds of others, so that the disguise is not a lie, but a *mysterium* which forecasts the future.[174] Moses is the epitome of the Law, Elijah of the Prophets; thus, when they do homage to Christ on Mount Tabor, they represent the Old Testament, which here in its totality acknowledges the New, and when all three of them fast for forty days, this means that all three are pointing to the same mystery.[175]

A great *sacramentum* is the opening of the eyes of the man born blind, in "the pool of Siloam, which means 'envoy' ". "For what is it that the Lord does? He spits upon the earth and makes a dough of his spittle, and in this he makes us aware of a great mystery, for the Word has been made flesh, the spittle from the head of the Father having been mingled with the clay of our human nature. When his eyes have been smeared, the blind man cannot yet see; he is still a catechumen. A catechumen has been anointed, but he has not yet been washed; first he must be baptized in the 'envoy', that is to say, in Christ." "For you know who this envoy is. If Christ had not been sent, none of us would be absolved from his sins."[176] Sometimes his thought makes amazing leaps. The five pebbles which David took from the brook in order to slay Goliath are the five books of Moses—that is to say, the Law; and the fact that they came from the streaming brook and were put into the pouch of the first good shepherd denotes that the law of God (which is the only firm thing in the temporal or "flowing" life of one who lives according to the Law) at length passed over into grace.[177] The commandment of Exodus, "Thou shalt not bathe a lamb in the milk of its mother", is understood by him as referring to the Lamb of God, and he sees this commandment fulfilled in the massacre of the innocents at Bethlehem, for the Lamb was the only infant that escaped.[178]

Every year we read in the Second Nocturn of the Ninth Sunday after Pentecost the well-known passage from the sermon on Elijah. There Elijah, who has been cast out, is the symbol of Christ, who has not been recognized by his people; and for that reason the raven who daily comforts him with a piece of bread in his loneliness is the Church, for the Church, in the heathen world, is black as a raven, having been conceived amidst injustice. Therefore can she sing, in the Song of Solomon, "I am black but beautiful, O ye daughters of Jerusalem." This will again serve as typical of the Augustinian manner, though as a matter of fact this sermon is not authentic, and is ascribed to Caesarius of Arles; in the eighteenth century it was removed from many French breviaries.[179]

Often his similes carry ingenuity to excess. When in the story of the Prodigal Son he comes to the words "he fell about his neck", Augustine, playing on the words *incubuit super*, says: "The arm which the Father puts about the neck of degraded man is the Son. This arm is a light yoke about his neck and a sweet burden; it is so light that rather than press down, it raises up. He who pushes this arm away from him does not feel relief, but, rather, feels a weight upon himself. That this is not untrue can be illustrated from examples in nature, though these are strange and even incredible. A bird falls down if it brushes its wings. Now, the burden of the arms of Christ is just as light as the feathers which a bird carries and which also carry the bird. It is a burden light as a feather. It was for this burden that the man yearned who said, 'O for the wings of a dove, that I may fly away and rest.' It was therefore an arm which honoured while it raised and one that formed no burden at all [*honoravit, non oneravit*]; and how can it be made possible for a man to carry the weight of God unless it is God himself who carries him?"[180]

There are plenty of other examples. In a sermon about Lazarus, who was dead and was recalled to life, a sermon that is very definitely penitential in character, he compares the desire for adultery with death in bed, the adulterer's state after the sin with the corruption and stink of the corpse, the sinful habit with the stone before the grave, and the priests of the Church to the servants to whom Christ said, "Unbind him and let him go."[181] When speaking on one occasion in Carthage on the famous deeds of the martyrs, he made a point of throwing particular light on certain moving details which might have escaped the listener's attention when he merely heard a reading of the story. There was, for instance, the condemned bishop who, when he saw that the faithful in their thousands had made up their minds to spend the last night with him, immediately begged his people to take great care of the young girls, failing which he would prefer them not to come. When he comes to that part of the story where the bishop is lifted into the cart between two court officials, he thinks immediately of Christ between the two thieves.[182]

Strangely enough, to our way of thinking, the sermons that most captured his hearers and called forth their delighted applause were just those that contained the most far-fetched allegories, the mystical antitheses and the correspondences of numbers. When the web of gossamer really held together and they could see it, applause would always follow. They loved nothing better, either in Hippo or Carthage, than to listen to Augustine displaying his conjuror's art in the *Commentaries on the Psalms*—unless perhaps it was hearing his profound variations on the theme of the Gospel according to St. John. Nobody thought of the lyrical qualities of the Psalms themselves when Augustine began experimenting on them with his allegory. Allegories were known to them from the theatre. Augustine knew this and once made an ironical remark about it: "If I speak of allegory and you think that I am referring to the theatre, then you might just as well believe that Christ had the amphitheatre in view when he spoke the Parables. This is the kind of thing that happens when a city is positively crawling with theatres. In the country I run no risk when I mention this subject. There the people, if they have heard of allegories at all, think they are something to do with Holy Scripture." In this same sermon he refers to Gal. iv.24, in which St. Paul uses the word "allegory" to denote the deeper meaning of the story of the two wives of Abraham, and in doing so Augustine tells us what it means and also, in no uncertain terms, what it does not mean: "Christ is called a lamb but does this mean that he is one of the cattle? He is called a rock, but does this mean that he is hard? He is called a mountain, but does this mean that he is a piece of high earth? So you see that many words have a different meaning from what their sound might lead us to suppose. It is this that is called allegory."[183]

Augustine never lost an opportunity of reminding his people that Holy Scripture must first and foremost be taken in the literal and historical sense. He did this to keep his feet upon the ground. Actually, he sometimes began even his mystical expositions with some such words as these: "We have heard the facts, now let us examine the mystery."[184]

Finally, let us never forget that he endeavoured to correct his own allegorical exegesis by giving a literal interpretation of the extremely difficult opening passages of Genesis which he had once interpreted mystically. He revised this work at a later date but was never really satisfied with it.[185]

It is strange that Augustine, who saw hidden meanings in everything, would not permit the pagans to rescue their own myths through a similar reinterpretation—by allowing the Mother of the Gods, for instance, to stand for Mother Earth, from which come all things, or Saturn, who devours his own children, to be a symbol for time, which also devours whatever it begets.[186]

As to the third aspect of Augustine's thought in his sermons—the way, that is to say, in which the reasoning actually unfolds—the dual nature of the spirituality of the time is here seen at its clearest. The truths of faith are reverently proclaimed, but immediately the rationality of Antiquity insinuates itself and explains them without a shadow of hesitation, and with unfailing acumen. Side by side with the intuitions of Holy Scripture and the quiet certitude which they seem to exhale we become aware of a ceaseless Hellenistic chatter, posing questions, analysing, engaging in endless arguments and making endless deductions. The sacred texts remain the starting-points, but the processes of thought which arrange the argument, build the sentences and weave the connecting thread of the whole presentation—these processes are those of classical intellectualism. That is why the sermons, despite their glow and their forthright speech, have, of necessity, to possess a certain ingenuity, one might almost say, a certain perverse ingenuity, and an intellectualist air.

The mystical allegorical method which underlies Augustine's interpretation of most texts is based on the effect of the impact of the text on his intuition; and that is why his mind is always breaking through the confines of logical reality. Despite this, however, this method is pursued by means of the weapons of the ancient logic. It is not, and is not looked upon as, a form of play. The image, though it may delight us in itself and work upon our minds by the power of suggestion, is not, in the last resort, intended to work upon our feelings, but, in theory at least, to appeal to our reason. The whole method of allegorical interpretation is essentially a form of intellectual reasoning on a non-intellectual basis. We hear deduction after deduction—but the intervening sentences are based on that far-reaching belief in the correspondence of the two Testaments and the neo-Platonist assumption that all things are symbols or shadows of a higher reality. And the modern man finds some difficulty in agreeing with these assumptions—indeed he often finds it impossible to do so. Nevertheless, these allegorical interpretations are expounded with the greatest exactitude, though they are sometimes, as in the case of Ambrose, furnished with a question mark or with a *fortasse*; if there are several meanings they are kept distinct from one another. Sometimes the syllogistic method of proof is used, and then there are quite precious and formal deductions. The superficial reader will sometimes be tempted to look upon the bolder allegories as pure poetry. Yet the kind of visions that symbolists like Valéry, Thompson and Claudel make us see in a magical and transient flash are, in these sermons, made the subjects of laboured proof. The poets show us a fleeting gleam; we catch it and are convinced, even if the thing itself is incredible, and we have the feeling that we understand everything forthwith; with Augustine, our experience seems at first not altogether dissimilar. When he begins, there is a kind of illumination about his words and we are immediately prepared to greet the harmony which we only half understand, but then, quite suddenly, the ancient classical thinking machine starts its wheezy revolutions, and once again we feel that we are witnessing the last phases of a dying culture; a culture that has, it is true, been baptized, but still continues endlessly and patiently to reason about things that cannot be grasped by logic at all. We are still only standing in the outer court of the great cathedral of the West.

Results

What were Augustine's views about the general effect of his words and his sermons? We can only answer that they were extremely modest. He knew well enough that it was not the preachers who moulded men's hearts as though they were wax. Commenting once on the words in the First Epistle of St. John, "You have no need that any man instruct you, for his unction has instructed you in all things", he once says in one of his sermons, "Now I ask myself—nay, I ask none other than the Apostle, and may he graciously hear his little questioner—I ask the Apostle St. John, 'Did those to whom you preached have unction? For you say that unction instructs above all things. Why, then, did you write this letter? Why did you instruct, enlighten and edify them?' Behold, therefore, my brethren, a great mystery, for the sound of my voice reaches your ear, but the real teacher is within you. Do not believe that anything can be learned from a mere man. We can exhort you by the sound of our voice, but unless there is one within you who teaches you this sound achieves nothing. Come, brethren, will you have the truth? Do you not all hear this sermon? Yet how many depart from this place without having been instructed by it? As to myself, I have spoken to you all, but those who have not this inner unction, those whose hearts have not been instructed by the Holy Ghost, go uninstructed away. The external instruction is a help and a spur, but he who instructs your heart has his pulpit in heaven. Therefore, this teacher himself says in the Gospel, 'Be ye not called teacher here on earth, for one is your teacher, Christ.' "[187] It was also a purely philosophical preconception that made Augustine take a very modest view of the effectiveness of his words. His theory of knowledge made it impossible for him to believe that one man could really instruct another, for nothing really passes from one spirit to another. Whatever is known by a man is known by reason of the divine light which shines from above, and does not come from without at all. The word that comes from without does not knock at the door of the soul; the latter is quite unreceptive to any such intrusion, nor is the higher set in motion by the lower. Moreover, the very hearing of God's word involves an active function of the soul, which has a determining effect on the lower and sensual function of the actual ear. What, then, can a preacher do? He can open up a possibility to those who hear him, and encourage them to enter upon the way of faith; for faith comes by hearing. He can show them what their attitude should be, if they wish to recognize the divine light of truth; but no man can see this light on behalf of another, or see it to another's profit. No man can infuse true wisdom into others; he can only pray for others and teach them to ask for this wisdom themselves; he can point towards true knowledge, but he cannot bestow it. This inner joy, *delectatio liberatrix*, by which the will is truly freed from the fetters of sense, so that the mist of the senses is dissipated and the spirit begins to behold things in the light of faith, is pure grace, and effected by God. The real teacher is within us, namely Christ the only light of true knowledge. This was the neo-Platonist point of view from which Augustine saw the ancient truth of Revelation. Its essence was that it is not the preacher who opens a door, but that a door *is opened for him*; it is the preacher who plants and Apollo who waters, but God alone can make the plant flourish. Thus it was that, as the years went by, Augustine confined himself more and more to what was simple and essential, and placed continually increasing emphasis on the importance of the will. Although he still clung to his habit of giving elaborate explanations of words and of arguing, he no longer attempted to give proofs. He proclaimed, urged and exhorted (as Holy Scripture itself does) in those interminable disquisitions which conflict all too often with the order of straightforward logical development, because they are dictated by the order of love. He began to set less and less store by grandiose demonstrations. The older he became, the shorter, more powerful and the better became his sermons. No man knew better than he that "we preach but God instructs. Not he who is instructed by man can be called blessed, but only he whom thou, O Lord, dost instruct."[188] "We work like the peasants on the land—from the outside. If none were working from within, then the seed corn would remain in the ground and send up no shoots; no stem would develop into a firm stalk. No twig would then bear fruit, nor would any leaf burst forth, for though the earth is worked, it is the heavens that send down moisture, for they send down such moisture from the face of God",[189] and only God "can clear out the corrupt dregs from the heart of man".[190]

Often he could himself see the spiritual fruits of his words. The story which has already been told of the "Great Row" in Caesarea shows what overwhelming results he could sometimes achieve at one stroke.[191] At home it was the same, and here he did not hesitate to point to the growth that God had granted. I have to inform you, he could then say on one occasion, that the labour which was cost me by yesterday's sermon was not in vain. One of the heretical Eunomians, a doctor from Theuita, has abjured Arius and Eunomius and has become a Catholic. Yesterday I said to you, "Beware of him." Today I say to you, "Take him in with good will and pray for the three others."[192] One day he asked his brother priests at table in the refectory whether they had not noticed that the beginning of his sermon had not completely harmonized with the end? Quite suddenly, he said, the notion came to me of working in an excursus on Manicheism, and I did so. I presume that this was the doing of God, in whose hands are both we ourselves and our sermons. A few days later, the merchant Firmus came into the monastery, deeply moved, and threw himself weeping at the feet of Augustine, who was seated in the midst of his clerics. He confessed to Augustine that he had been trapped in error, for he had lent money to some of the Manichean *electi*; but Augustine's unexpected explanation had struck him like lightning. The *coup de grâce* was final. The man underwent a complete change and later became a priest in Italy.[193]

These and other examples argue a deep faith that God directly concerned himself with making Augustine's words bear fruit, and we also have to note a strong belief in the effectiveness of the examples themselves. In his sermons the edifying account of the miraculous is his strongest argument; for nothing moves the masses so much as the faithful recounting of an actual miracle. In telling such a story Augustine is a true master. Then he forgets his more sophisticated thought and elaboration of expression; he forgets the allegories and does not even trouble to argue; then the oldest and most fascinating of all forms of literature is sufficient for him. He becomes simply a pastor who has something to tell his people. Augustine knows well enough how strong is his influence over his people, as the following example clearly shows:

> I want to tell you a little story, my beloved ones, and one that I have never yet told, though it concerns an incident that took place in this community. There used to live here a certain simple, harmless good Christian, and many of you Hipponesians—nay, all of you—will have known him. His name was Tutuslymeni. Which of you in this town does not know of Tutuslymeni? Well, what I am about to tell you I heard from his own lips.
>
> A certain person who had borrowed something from our friend, or, anyway, owed him some money, declared that this money was his own, and went surety for his assertion. Our friend grew very angry and summoned the other to make this assertion under oath. This other did so, and so our friend lost his money; but whatever he had lost, the other had lost himself body and soul by his act. Now Tutuslymeni, who is a serious and trustworthy person, has told me that in that same night he was brought before a judge. Quite suddenly he was led away and there, terrified to death, he stood before the president of the court, a most distinguished-looking man, surrounded by equally worthy servants. This person told him to be calm and put the following question to him: "Why", he said, "Why did you force a man to swear on oath when you were certain that in doing so he would perjure himself?" The man replied, "He would not restore me my property." To this he received the reply, "Would it not have been better to have lost the property which you claim than to let a man destroy his soul by a false oath?" Thereafter he caused him to be chastised all over his body. He was beaten so unmercifully that the traces of the lashes were still visible on his shoulders when he awoke. After the chastisement he was told, "We are willing to set to your credit that you acted in good faith, but in future be careful and do not do this again."
>
> This man made himself guilty of a grave sin and was chastised for it; but he who after this sermon and after my warning and exhortation would dare to act in similar fashion would commit an even graver sin.[194]

Who would not envy the parishioners of Hippo and who could have any doubts concerning the fruit from such a tree?

16

INSTRUCTION FOR BEGINNERS

The Guide for Deogratias and Its Plan

THE Carthaginian deacon Deogratias was a man of pleasing address, and was for that reason continually being sent to the reception room[1] to impart the first catechism to new converts, for, having to work in the great city of Carthage, Bishop Aurelius found no time for such a task. In due course, however, Deogratias began to be concerned whether he was applying the right method. He also began to worry over the fact that this work in which he tended to be continuously occupied gave him so little satisfaction.

He laid his difficulties before Augustine in a letter and asked how should he, who was "treading this well-worn path", expound the substance of the Faith? With what should he begin and with what should he end? Should there be at the end a vigorous exhortation, or merely a review of the Ten Commandments and all that went with that? Finally, he said, my instruction appears to me to be so dry, and so lifeless whenever it has to be continued for any appreciable length of time.[2]

Augustine answered by writing a most delightful book, the *Instruction for Beginners*,[3] which he dedicated to Deogratias. In this book he deals with Deogratias' questions and difficulties, but only from the point of view of a pastor of souls. He develops a theory concerning the first catechism—that is to say, he does not write out a model catechism, but gives a kind of guiding thread for catechists (not, let it be said, for professors of theology). The little book comprises two parts.[4] In the first of these the author encourages Deogratias by telling him some of his own experiences. Then he gives his opinion of the best way of planning the two constituent parts that are essential in the introductory catechism, namely the *narratio* of the story of salvation, which must be directed to the understanding, and an exhortation, which must be directed to the will. After this he discusses the more delicate shades of difference in method which must be applied to suit the character of different types of catechumen. At the end he deals with the qualities that a good catechist should possess, and shows the way in which these can be acquired.[5] In the second part of the book he gives two examples of a complete catechism, the first one being long, the second being short, and both constructed on the principles that have been earlier laid down.[6] In order to bring out Augustine's way of looking at this problem as clearly as possible, his advice in regard both to pupil and instructor has been placed at the beginning of the subjoined summary. Then follows his theory about the *narratio* and the exhortation, and immediately after that the examples which illustrate this theory.

THE TYPES OF CATECHUMEN

The first question must be this: With what kind of a man or with what kind of men have I to deal? Are there many of them, so that I must give a kind of sermon? Or is there only a single one, in which case I must offer him a chair and start a conversation with him? Are they peasants or townsmen, gentlefolk or men and women of the people? Most important of all, are they uneducated *idiotae*? Or half-educated? Or are they intellectuals, "whose minds have already been trained by familiarity with the deeper problems"?[7]

As to the last-named—people, that is to say, who have been trained in the liberal arts—one can usually assume that they have already read a considerable amount about the Christian faith. Most of them will already be acquainted with Holy Scripture and with the principal doctrines, and they only come so that they can partake of the sacraments. With such people one should be brief and avoid all semblance of pretension; one should interrupt one's discourse with a confidential "Of course, you know this already." One should also ask them what made them come. Was it their reading of books? If so, was it through reading Holy Scripture, or the ecclesiastical writers? If they name certain books, a word of praise should be said about them, but one should not fail to remark that, compared with the more musical and polished style of profane writers, Holy Scripture, despite the fact that it is a divine work, strikes one as a simple and modest affair. Such people should also be enlightened if, without knowing it, they have absorbed error through the reading of heretical books. One should also remember that there are occasionally objectionable passages to be found among the works of writers who died Catholics.[8]

In the case of the half-educated a different technique is required. These puffed-up people, who have usually visited the ordinary schools of the *grammatici* and the rhetoricians, should be warned to be more careful in avoiding faulty morals and to be less concerned with faulty grammar. Such people should especially have their attention drawn to the dignified and essentially unpretentious character of Holy Scripture, and the peculiar value of allegorical interpretation should be pointed out to them. They must, indeed, be taught not to rest content with the fleshly meaning of Scripture, and that "the real significance of a passage is a greater matter than its literal sense, even as the soul is a greater matter than the body", and that truth is more important than beauty of form, even as an understanding friend is better than a good-looking one. "They should also be made to realize that no voice reaches the ear of God save that of the movement of the heart." Then they will no longer laugh at the mistakes of grammar of which a bishop or a servant of the Church may occasionally be guilty. In court the quality of a speech is judged by its sound, in the Church by the good intention of its utterer. Therefore a *bona dictio* may well be possible before a judge, but never a *benedictio*. In the matter of the "sacrament of salt", only slow-witted and dull people will need a detailed explanation.[9]

You must be particularly careful, says Augustine, to ascertain the true grounds of their coming, for there are people who become Catholics to win the favour of their superiors, or from fear of drawing their disfavour upon them. Such men are dissimulators, for the Faith is not a matter of outer conformity, but of inner conviction. However, such people often attain a better frame of mind during the actual catechism. It is, nevertheless, a good thing to make enquiries elsewhere about their motives. If this is impossible, they must be asked directly, and if they give a praiseworthy reason—the best is that they long for the peace of eternal life—they should be congratulated on the good disposition of their mind, for then, if they are hypocrites, you heap coals of fire upon their heads. You should say the same if they say they fear the judgement or have had a fright, or if they say that they have received a warning from God in a dream. In this latter case, however, they should immediately be told that they should hold to the reliable oracles of Holy Scripture, which are a smooth road, not for sleepwalkers but for the awake.[10]

The Catechist

Then the bishop turns to Deogratias personally and gives a word of encouragement. Do not think, he says, that what you tell people is commonplace or boring. Quite possibly the man you are talking to has a very different opinion. Why do they always ask for you to be called and not for another? Not that I do not understand your discouragement. No, I have exactly the same feeling myself. That which gives me joy in my own heart, is a much better thing than that which I am able to express in words. But what can one do? Language is a very inadequate medium of expression. It is not nearly so direct in its effect as the expression on one's face, and it is an unsatisfactory business to have to translate into halting syllables the intuition that suddenly illuminates us within like a flash of lightning. And yet even this is only possible because that flash of lightning leaves certain traces behind in our memory. How very different, still, is our rendering of what we have experienced! What was drunk in one draught by the spirit comes out of the mouth longwindedly, and because we are eager to express everything with the same vividness with which it is apparent to our minds, we become discouraged—the contrast between what we desire and what we can achieve is too great for it to be otherwise.

Yet, he says, I can see by watching my people that the thing is not as bad as it seems, and that they do not share my disappointment. And that is understandable, for they do not share the experiences that I have within myself. They listen attentively—I can see that—and the same is surely true of yourself, otherwise you would not be called upon so often to give this type of instruction. True, we can never dissipate the mist of our fleshliness. Even love cannot penetrate it, any more than it can penetrate the "mirrors" and riddles. Never shall we attain to supreme clarity about the nature of things with the words we are able to utter. What we desire is "to behold in a more than ordinary manner", and that is why we grow weary of "our ordinary speech".[11]

Nevertheless, nothing is more dangerous than this feeling of weariness; for what is the secret of the good catechist? His joyfulness! That quality is infectious and radiates like the sun. It is the sun that allows all things to flourish—except poison weeds. Remember also, he adds, what has been written: God loveth a cheerful giver.[12]

As for yourself, he goes on, you have been well prepared, and have no lack of words, but I will tell you the real causes of the repugnance you experience and will also name the means for getting rid of it.

First of all, there is the contrast between what you perceive in the stillness of your soul and what you actually say. Further, it is much more pleasant to hear or read something that is perfect in form than to take the risk upon yourself, and extemporize a suitable form for your thoughts on your own account. Finally, you are afraid you may be guilty of some slip of the tongue. But does one not really perform an act of self-denial every time one steps down into our petty reality? Think how great must have been the difference for our Lord between our fleshly nature and his own likeness to God. St. Paul most aptly describes our situation when he says, "For whether we be transported in mind it is to God: or whether we be sober, it is for you."[13] Is it not the love of Christ which urges us on—is it not the love of him who became weak with the weak in order to win the weak?[14] He came to us as a little Child and nourished us like a wet-nurse. Is it a pleasure, unless love drives us to it, to go on murmuring maimed and broken words? And yet all parents want children so that they may be able to do just that, and a mother finds it much sweeter to put little morsels which she has chewed up beforehand into her infant's mouth than to eat large mouthfuls herself. Think also of the text about the hen and her chicks. And if our spirit finds its greatest delight within our own selves, "where everything lies plain to see", our love, after its self-denying downward descent, hurries all the more speedily to its resting place within us, and its homeward journey is assisted by a clear conscience.[15]

On the matter of slips of the tongue Augustine has the following to say: If it should so happen that we express ourselves less felicitously than we would have wished, then the hearer can learn from this that content is the main thing, and not form. If you really make a mistake, then it is God's wish to try you by this means. He wants to see whether you will quietly correct it, should this really be necessary. If nobody has noticed the mistake, then you need do nothing about it; you must not repeat it, but you must accept it as a salutary lesson for the future. When a suitable opportunity occurs you can then put the matter right. If on the other hand it has been noticed and you see that it has excited malicious pleasure, then you must practise patience. If you notice that a truth has caused some kind of offence among your audience, then you must substantiate it by reasoning and by the relevant texts from Scripture, and you must certainly do this if there are audible objections from your audience. If they remain quiet and you have no positive grounds for believing that you have upset them, God will himself soon heal the wound.[16]

A further cause of our reluctance to speak, he continues, is the fact that we ourselves have known the subject of our discourse for so long. Lads that have almost attained manhood dislike frequenting infants' schools. Yet does not your own city seem clean and new to you when you have to show it to a good friend? So a sermon which seems cold to us, because it contains that with which usage has made us familiar, may grow warm through the keen attention of the audience.[17]

A third reason, he says, is lack of receptivity on the part of the person listening to us. We become sad because the word of God seems to have so little success. But what do we know about the truth of the matter? Perhaps he is shy by nature, or perhaps he is shy in religious matters, and this makes him reserved. Perhaps he has not understood. Or again, he may really be indifferent. In all such cases it is best to try and loosen up the person concerned and get him to assume a more easy attitude. One can, for instance, ask him whether he has heard any of the things we are telling him before. One can arrest his attention by explaining one of the mystical passages in Holy Scripture. If he is really sluggish of spirit and unreceptive, then it will be sufficient very briefly to go through the most necessary truths of the Faith: the unity of the Catholic Church, the danger of temptations and the necessity for the leading of a moral life and the certainty of a terrible judgement. With such people it is better "to speak much about them to God than much about God to them". Sometimes it happens that a man involuntarily gives in to an impulse to yawn. At first he listened attentively, but now he is tired of standing up, and would really like to get away. In that case, tell an amusing story or recount something strange, or even something sad; then his interest will be reawakened. But don't let him guess that you are aware of how he feels. That might be embarrassing. On one occasion it happened to me, he says, that a peasant in the last row of a group suddenly felt compelled to yawn, and slipped unobtrusively away. It was the first time he had come and he did not come again. Perhaps he had to leave the room for a moment and did not dare to say so. Such happenings are, in my opinion, unfortunate, though it does not matter if one who has already been initiated goes away. The best thing is to offer your visitor a chair and immediately to ask him to sit down along with us. This is the practice in certain Churches abroad and I am in favour of it, especially when there are two or three people. If we only have a single person before us, it is in my opinion actually dangerous not to offer him a chair. Are we bishops too exalted for that? Did not Christ permit Mary—a woman, that is to say—to sit at his feet? [18]

A final cause of your ill-humour, concludes Augustine, is that you have your head too full of other matters and are not in the mood for the task. We are suddenly given this assignment and are torn away from some other business which seems to us much more pressing. But can we really be so certain which of the two tasks in question is the more useful? By no means. Our arrangement of our day may well be upset, so long as God's will is done and we fulfil our duty. Let us rather reflect that an alms can quench like water the fire that smoulders in our hay, and let us rejoice that we can give such an alms; for we are not so foolish as to believe that bread is a better alms than the word of God. If, however, it is not so much that our own work happens to be making demands upon us, but, rather, that we have suffered some disappointment or discouragement by reason of some lapse or some failure, then it is the work of catechising that will certainly help in raising us up. A convert must of necessity be a source of comfort to us, for he represents a new possibility and therefore a spur to us to start all over again.[19]

The Story of Redemption as the Essence of Instruction

Now comes the question of what one is to tell him and in what sequence. Augustine answers: Tell him little, but tell him everything that is important, and that in the form of a story, *narratio*, of which the principal theme should be the love of God. Here, then, are three points:

First of all, only a few things are to be dealt with, which means that the presentation should cover everything but that it should do it briefly. This is possible if one concentrates on the telling of the *mirabiliora*, those points of the story that are out of the ordinary and excite wonder, the events which excite joy and satisfaction in the hearer, and at the same time "make up the skeleton of the whole". The reference is, of course, to the decisive climaxes and turning-points in the Gospel story. These decisive moments must be highlighted and must be dwelt on like a scroll, which must be opened up at the relevant passages. It is no good just showing the opened *volumen* and then putting it back into its container.

Further, he says, you must tell a story, for what has been revealed to us is a story and not a theory of salvation. The truth of this story is something which Augustine assumes without actually endeavouring to prove it. About the year 400 his thinking was biblical enough to be undisturbed in this respect by his earlier neo-Platonist and anti-historic point of view. The catechist must bring the glad tidings, even as Philip brought them in the chariot of the chamberlain of Queen Candace, for when Philip proclaimed to the latter "the glad tidings of Jesus", he interpreted the prophecies to him and explained how they had been fulfilled. This is how, in Augustine's view, the good tidings should be brought. It is and should be a *narratio*, this last being a technical term, taken from the handbook of Quintilian, for the rhetorical telling of a story. But this *narratio*, this story, is no haphazard sequence of events; it is inspired by the Holy Ghost, and is therefore informed by the spirit of prophecy. Everything contained in Holy Scripture, from Genesis to the Revelation of St. John, is either a foreshadowing of what is to come or a fulfilment of prophecy. Everything points to Christ and the Church and has its fulfilment in these. This applies to the Old Testament as much as to the New, for this, too, contains nothing but mysteries that bear on Christ, who thus stretches out his hand to hold the heel of those born before him, even as his foreshadowing figure, Jacob, held Esau's heel in his hand in the womb of Rebecca. The whole story, therefore, must have Christ as its central point; it must begin with the Creation and must end with an account of the present position of the Church.[20]

Finally, the story should contain an emotional element, and the whole tremendous narrative should be attuned to that. This element can be summed up in the words "God so loved the world." The story must be the story of God's love. Nothing is more calculated to cause a man's love to blaze forth than the story of the great deeds that God's love has wrought. The love of God is not a love that comes from one below to one above, it is not a love "arising from necessity", but one that is moved by compassion and moves from above downwards. That is why, among other things, it teaches us that which is the beginning of all virtues—namely, humility. This humble love, however, must also be built up on fear, for a certain fear will always be present, even in a hypocrite. We must act as though it were genuine and purify it both by the threat of the Judgement, and by telling of God's deeds of love.[21]

It is clear that Augustine does not wish the substance of the Faith to be systematically explained in the initial stages of instruction. A true system is latently present, but the story is the main thing, its desired effect being to arouse the love of God. What matters is that the story should have radiance; the *epos*, says Augstine, should "shine". If a good teacher can draw wise lessons even from the fables of the gods, should we not be able to cause the gleam of truth to shine forth when we can obtain it from Holy Scripture, instead of from tales that are merely curious and full of vain sweetness? The "several jewels of our narrative must shine in the bright gold setting" of divine love. In contrast to Cyril of Jerusalem (and also to the Roman and Heidelberg catechisms), Augustine begins neither with the mysteries within the Divinity nor with our own sense of sin and our conversion in the Faith. The mystery of the Trinity is hardly touched on by him; he only names the names of Father, Son and Holy Ghost. Nor is his starting-point the question, "What is thy only comfort in this life?" What he does is to tell the great deeds of God in the historical sequence of Revelation, as do the Apostles in the Acts, and as did also the oldest liturgies in the great prayer of thanksgiving at the altar. It has therefore been correctly said that Augustine's catechism treats of the same themes as the oldest of the "eucharists" that have been preserved for us. The fact that he did not adopt the same sequence as the profession of faith is explained by the circumstance that, as we have already seen, the text of the *symbolum* was only entrusted to the *competentes* verbally a few weeks before their baptism, and was nowhere set down in writing nor recited on any occasion save in the baptismal liturgy. It was by liturgical tradition a kind of *arcanum*.[22]

Augustine defends his method partly by an appeal to Holy Scripture, and partly by pointing to its psychological effectiveness and to the power of conviction inherent in the "proofs of prophecy". Thus he writes elsewhere that pagans seem to be thunderstruck by the fact of the confirmation of the prophecies, when they become acquainted with it, by the "trustworthy prophetic word", of which Peter speaks. They are much more impressed by this than by miracles.[23] This is the principal ground put forward by him for accepting the Faith, the *motivum credibilitatis*, and he formulates his view as follows: See how everything up to the present day has been fulfilled in Christ and his Church! You can be assured from this that the terrible Last Judgement and the life everlasting will also be found to be realities.[24] This mode of proof is related to yet another which Augustine is also fond of adducing, namely the spectacle of the tremendous moral revolution that had taken place in the ageing world of Antiquity. It was the argument of his youth; if Plato and Socrates had seen what we have seen, they, too, would have believed![25]

Exhortation

In addition to the *narratio*, which should cause love to flame forth, there is need of a moral spur to the will. This cannot be provided better than by the doctrine of the Last Things, above all by that of eternal punishment. Further, it is essential to pay great attention to the doctrine of the resurrection of the body, not only because of the hope it arouses, but to refute objections (which, at that time, were very common). The catechumen must also be armed against the various scandals that he is bound to encounter. Point out to him, says Augustine, that all this was predicted, and that scandals must come, from Jews, pagans, schismatics and heretics, but above all from bad Christians. Teach him not to put his faith in man, but to be long-suffering of evil, as is God himself, and to pay attention to the good, of whom there are many. At least, he who himself is a true Christian and is prepared to see good where it exists will find it so. Actually, however, he does not develop these ideas till he comes to the second part of his book, which contains the two model catechisms.

Example of a Two-Hour Catechism

Both of the examples given, says Augustine, are designed for the average level of education prevailing in Deogratias' city and for the kind of people whom Deogratias would, for the most part, be bound to have before him.[26] The first is fairly detailed, with a large number of digressions. Incidentally, certain exhortatory passages are worked into the narrative. Augustine assumes that the catechumen has given a satisfactory answer to the first question, "Whether he has come in the hope of worldly gain or from an honest desire for the peace of the next world", and begins forthwith with his catechism.

"*Deo gratias*, brother! With all my heart I wish you happiness, and rejoice that among the many dangerous storms of this world you have thought of the one true and sure refuge"—for many pursue vanities, riches and office and find no rest: "All flesh is as the grass; the grass withereth and the flower is fallen, but the word of the Lord endureth for ever."[27] Others seek their satisfaction in the pleasures of the palate, in the titillations of the baths, in the delights of vice and in the free entertainment of the theatres in the great cities, but without noticing what is happening to them they slip into evil doing and into debt; they become housebreakers and end up in prison. Or again, they sit in the theatre and, together with others, act like devils and incite men to murder and homicide. But a slight fever can sweep all their pleasures away. Others, again, get baptized but do so with a bad intention. Let them have no illusions. Today they are in the Church but tomorrow they will be in the fire. And if they have become Catholics because they think this will bring them luck in their life in this world, they will soon feel cheated and will surely soon fall away. He, however, who comes to obtain everlasting peace and out of the fear of hell, can become a true Christian. With God's help he will progress. He will reach a point where he loves God more than he fears hell. Yes, if God were then to say to him, "Enjoy yourself according to the flesh and sin as much as you like, nothing will happen to you save only that you will no longer be with me", he would shudder at such a thought.[28]

Now, the seventh day on which God rested from creation is a prefiguration of our eternal rest—this thought serves Augustine as a transition to the *narratio* proper. There follows the story of salvation set forth in a few hurriedly sketched but nevertheless incomparable pictures. The six days of creation represent the six ages of the history of the world. He now treats these one after the other, laying emphasis on their various turning-points; the time up to Noah, Abraham, King David, the Babylonian Captivity, Christ and the end of the world. Then, in the seventh period, God rests in his saints, having in the previous or sixth period shown his power in their good works.

Creation was accomplished through Christ, the Word of God, "while the angels and all the purest spirits in heaven rested wordless in holy silence". Man, however, lost this rest in God through sin, but when the Word became Man, man received it back. The saints of earlier days foresaw our own time and believed in its coming, for since the beginning of the world this mystery of God becoming Man has been ceaselessly indicated and proclaimed in symbols.[29]

Then he tells of the creation of man, who, "because of his reason", is lord over all other creatures, and was created immortal and without sexual lust in the garden of Eden. Further, he speaks in detail of the problem of evil. Although the Lord knew that sin would occur, he permitted it for the sake of the freedom of man's will, for even a sinner, who is free, is better than a beast, which is not. Whatever man may do, God in his own deeds will always be worthy of praise, for if a man does good, God is just in his reward of him; and if he does evil he is just in his punishment; and if a man penitently confesses his wrongdoing and returns to him he is just in his merciful forgiveness. And did not the Lord know in advance those saints of his who came forth from this brood of death? The fallen angels did not harm their Creator, but only themselves. And "God knows well how to make use in his plan of those souls [later corrected to "spirits"[30]] who have fallen away from him, and to adorn the lowest parts of his creation (where is the habitation of the demons) with the misery which they deserve, this being according to the most fitting and appropriate laws of a most marvellous providence."

Among men also and even in the Church there are many who are evil, but the "huge heap of chaff" must not mislead us, for the few who follow God are more powerful than the many who despise him. Even a peasant knows very well what he will do with the heap of chaff. The two cities, of God and of the devil, are still intermingled, and the wheat is intermingled with the chaff; they lie all together upon the threshing floor, and God has patience; for a hundred years before the Flood he permitted Noah to preach to the mockers in order that we too might learn patience, for we do not know whether those to whom we preach will be converted like the inhabitants of Nineveh or whether they will remain stubborn like the contemporaries of Noah.[31]

So he comes to "the sacrament of the Flood". The wooden Ark is an image of the Church that was to come, in which Christ the King, by the wood of the cross, saves the saints from drowning in the sea of the world. Let it be noted, he says, that there were bad men in the Ark, as there are in the Church, and that the worship of idols began again at once. But between the faithless lives of the citizens of the holy city of God, and the first man, stands Abraham, to whom was promised the sacrament of God's Son, and who, by the example of his faith, has deserved to become the father of all the faithful. He was the original parent of that people which alone served the true God, and in which the Church is much more clearly prefigured; for here, too, a fleshly multitude performed the external rites and only a few thought of their future rest. Only to these few was the coming humiliation of God in Jesus Christ revealed; they belong to their head, Christ, as Jacob's hand, which had already left his mother's body, belonged to his body, which was as yet unborn. Their whole lives, their words, their marriages and progeny—all these are a picture of the Church which is to come.[32] The passage of the Red Sea is an indication of baptism. Here, as in the Flood, the element of water consumes the wicked, for the Egyptians are our sins, and here, too, redemption came through a piece of wood, namely through the staff of Moses. The Easter lamb is the image of the sufferings of Christ, and the blood-marks on the doorposts are the sign of the cross upon our foreheads. God's finger writing upon the tables means that the Spirit which distributes the various gifts loaded the stony hearts of the people of old with many sacraments, which, however, in their turn, were signs of future freedom. These gifts of God were like fingers of a hand; they were separate, that is to say, but were united in the palm of one hand, which was the love of God. The earthly kingdom of the City of Jerusalem, which means "Vision of Peace", is an image of the heavenly kingdom, while David is an image of the heavenly king, Christ. The things that happened in the Promised Land are prefigurations of many things which have happened within the Church, but "that is a matter of which you can only gradually obtain knowledge through the reading of Holy Scripture."[33]

We should note, says Augustine, that a part of the city is compelled to live in exile, namely, in "Babylon", which means "Confusion"; and this too we see fulfilled in the Church, for she also was compelled to live under worldly princes who for a long time were hostile to her; but even as some of the princes of Babylon recognized God, so the Roman emperors were also ultimately converted. And even as the Jews prayed for the princes of Babylon, so must we, too, pray for our Christian emperors, and that before all others; this is clearly shown in St. Paul's letter to Timothy, where they are placed at the beginning of the list.[34] We must obey them and pay taxes and understand why it is that they carry the sword; slaves, too, must obey their masters. For us the "seventy years", the predestined time of trial, are passed, "for through the Christian kings the Church received the gift of peace, and even if this only lasts for a time, we are at least permitted during that time spiritually to build our houses and to plant our houses and gardens without hindrance. For you yourselves", he continues, "have been planted and built by us in this moment through our sermon, and by reason of the peace ensured us by the Christian emperors this is now occurring all over the world, so that the words of the Apostles are confirmed, when he says, 'You are God's acre, you are God's building.' "[35] These beautiful words were dedicated by Augustine to the Christian State and to the civic duties of Christians.[36]

Yet the Prophets show that the rebuilding of the Temple was only to be a temporal thing, and the ruin of the fleshly Israel has made place for the spiritual Israel, in which Christ is at work. Five of the great periods had passed,[37] and it was only the sixth that was to bring the life of the Spirit for all people. It was on the sixth day that man was created in the image of God, and on this sixth day the human spirit will be "restored to God".[38] For this reason "Christ, the Lord, when he became Man, despised all worldly goods in order to show that they were contemptible, and for this reason he bore all earthly suffering and enjoined us to bear it, so that we may not tend to see our happiness in the former nor our misfortune in the latter." Then this Father of the Church writes his most moving Life of Jesus:

> For he was born of a mother who conceived though she was untouched by man, and who remained untouched for all time, conceiving as a virgin, bearing as a virgin and dying a virgin, though she was betrothed to an artisan. Thus he destroyed all pride in the nobility of the flesh. Moreover, he was born in the town of Bethlehem, which was of so little account among the princely cities of Judah that today it is reckoned as no more than a country estate. He did not wish that at some future time any man should be able to boast of the greatness of his city. He became a poor man, he to whom all belonged and through whom all was created, so that no man who believes in him should venture to boast of his worldly riches. He would not be a king among men, because he wished to show the way of humility to

those unhappy souls who were separated from him by pride; and yet the whole of creation testifies to his kingship.

He suffered hunger, he who nourishes all; he suffered thirst, he who gave all men to drink and who is himself the spiritual bread of the hungry and the fountain of the thirsty. He grew weary from his earthly wanderings, he who made himself the road to heaven for us all. Deaf and dumb did he become towards those who blasphemed against him, he who gave speech to the dumb and who gave the deaf their hearing. He was fettered, he who loosed the fetters of sickness. He was whipped, he who drives the whips of pain from the body of man. He was crucified, he who made an end of all our crosses, and he died, he who raised the dead to life. But he rose once more never to die again, so that none might learn from him so to despise death that he could dispense with life for ever.[39]

After the Lord had ascended to heaven, he sent on the fiftieth day the finger of God, which had once written the Law but now gave the power to fulfil this Law, which consists, as it were, of the ten fingers of the Ten Commandments and which ultimately rests, as on two hands, on the Two Commandments of love. Its power was shown in the miracle of the speaking with tongues, in the conversion of the three thousand Jews and the disappearance of all worldly greed among the first Christians, "who had all things in common". It had to be so. This kernel community, which had almost a monastic character, was persecuted and remained isolated. Thus its members might be likened to soldiers, whose pay was found by the heathen, amongst whom Paul was sent, and who in their turn may be likened to provincials. And indeed it is in keeping with this idea that St. Paul should have instituted a collection among them for the Church in Jerusalem—here the founder of the first African monasteries brings in a short *oratio pro domo*—yet both of these are united in the cornerstone, Christ.[40]

The vine of the Church has been made to grow by the blood of the martyrs and by the pruning-knife of the persecutors; the first barren shoots that are the heretics and schismatics have begun to fall away. They will end as was foretold of them, for all that was foretold of them is coming to pass.[41] Have faith, therefore, says Augustine, that all else that has been foretold will also come to pass. One day the citizens of both cities will be resurrected in the body. Remain firm in this faith and continue to believe in the Resurrection: "You can also come to this conclusion from your own reason, for since you, who once were not, now are here, you will also exist in the future after you have ceased to be." For where, he asks, was the substance of which your body was made, some time ago? God can in an instant cover the sky with banks of cloud: and no man knows how; is this same God not able to recall the bodies which he called into being and then sent away? Fly from the pains of hell, and desire heaven, where you will be even as the angels of God, where there will be no heavy toil and rest will not be wearisome, where you will neither have the desire to provide for your own maintenance nor be at pains to work for others, where one day, if such be our deserts, we shall no longer testify with the words of faith and with mere spoken words to the equality of Father, Son and Holy Ghost, and to the unity of these three Persons, in which all three are God, but in the silence of heaven drink in the reality in pure glowing contemplation.[42]

Do not, he goes on, be misled by Jews, heathens and bad Christians, and above all, not by the last, for you will soon observe that it is the same people who fill the churches on Sundays and the theatres on the festival days. If, then, you come to think after a time, "I can permit myself that, too", you will be in grave error, for your Christian name will then do you no service: "Not everyone that saith unto me Lord, Lord, shall enter into the kingdom of heaven." Many will come on the last day and say, "Lord, in thy name have I eaten and drunk", but their end will be the judgement of damnation. Keep close to the good, for there are sufficient of them. If the friends of a popular charioteer tend to feel united in the circus, the friends of God will surely come together and help one another, nor will God permit that you should be tempted beyond your strength.[43]

Finally, there are a few words about the salt—i.e., the spiritual sense—of Scripture.[44]

Example of a Half-Hour Catechism

The shorter catechism is very similar to the longer one, save only that certain of the more subtle transition passages are replaced by simpler ones and the more discursive expositions are omitted. It begins, not with the theme of the "eternal rest of the seventh day", but with that of the imperishable. All things pass away here below, but God's only Son releases us from this universal corruption. As all men died in the first Adam, so all will live for ever in the second Adam.[45] Then follows the story of salvation with the dominant theme roughly along these lines: All that you see in the Church has been predicted—in the Flood, in Abraham's people and in all the other prefigurations of Christ. The life of Christ and the oecumenical Church and even the schisms have been prophesied. Till now, all prophecies have been fulfilled; therefore, all else will come to pass as foretold. The resurrection of the body means that we shall be incorrupt as the angels are incorrupt. The catechism ends with the same exhortations and, as it so happens, with the same words as the other.[46]

Taken together, the two catechisms form what is probably the most impressive summary of the ancient popular catechism that we possess. They represent the best thought of a great spirit in its simplest form. At the same time they reproduce in a most lifelike way the general atmosphere of the popular churches of that time, as well as the most common themes of its iconography and the well-known subjects of these pericopes that were perpetually repeated on feast days in their classical typological connection. They bring alive again the background of the liturgy of the early Church and early Christian art. They also prove the somewhat self-contradictory fact that the preaching of God's word demands that a man must personally experience what he speaks about, and must put his whole personality into the task, and that nevertheless, despite the fact that it thus absorbs the whole person, it can never be bound or limited by any mere person whatever, for the word of God "can never be bound in fetters".

PART 4
POPULAR PIETY

17

THE CULT OF THE MARTYRS

WHAT were Augustine's views on the subject of popular devotion? Everyone knows what was the essential nature of the popular devotion of that age, and that it consisted of manifold variations on the single theme of the honouring of the martyrs, a practice which was carried to the very furthest extremes. The cult found expression in a number of ways—in the foundation of churches and memorial chapels—*memoriae*—over the graves (which meant that these buildings were usually situated in the cemetery outside the town); in the invocation of martyrs with regard to all manner of spiritual and temporal needs, either by a simple prayer or by pilgrimages to the *memoriae*, or even by the purchase of a grave near the sacred vault. Although the actual justification of the veneration thus paid lay in the idea of the communion of saints, it should really be regarded more in the light of a general manifestation of popular piety.

Augustine and the Cult of the Martyrs

Fundamentally Augustine had a profound veneration for all those who had given the testimony of blood, and he might well have read in a letter of Cyprian's, dating back some hundred and fifty years, how, at a time when the prisons were full of the faithful, people were concerned to preserve their memory after their death and how they compiled lists of names which could then have the date of death inscribed upon them (for it was felt that the Christian community must forget neither the name nor the date of death).[1] The community of the saints had always venerated the saints, and the saints were those who had testified to Jesus not with ink but with blood. These were the real witnesses, the *martyres*. It was the martyrs' and not the teachers' memory that was held in honour.

In this veneration of the martyrs Augustine recognizes a justifiable ecclesiastical tradition, though one that is relatively young, and a tradition that has been confirmed by public oecumenical practice. It has nothing whatever to do with the ancient cult of heroes. The statement that Christians replaced the gods and heroes by martyrs is wholly slanderous,[2] though it would be incorrect to say as much of all the pious customs that accompanied this form of veneration. Often such customs were confined to one locality and were pointless outside it. They were often of an extravagant nature and rightly suspect. Some were quite undoubtedly of pagan origin, and even the best of them were inessential, which meant that as far as Augustine was concerned they were *ipso facto* superfluous;[3] for in the second book of his *Christian Knowledge*, in which he examines the value of all the various human activities and forms of life, he summarily says, "What has been instituted by man is sometimes superstition and sometimes not." But everything is superstition which involves the giving of divine honours to a creature or to some part of a creature, or the making of some pact with demons, even if this is done unconsciously and out of foolish loyalty to one of a thousand nonsensical customs. Whatever belongs to superstition must be rooted out. Human institutions which do not partake of superstition may be divided into those which are useful and even necessary, and those which are superfluous;[4] and within the Church Augustine looks upon all that is superfluous as inadmissible. He is particularly anxious to cut off without hesitation "all those customs the meaning of which has been completely lost and which differ from one place to another"; but because this is not always possible, they are for the present permitted to endure, "for the Church is tolerant of much".[5] But because a thing cannot actually be called a superstition, it does not, for that reason, immediately appear of value in Augustine's eyes; for in such matters Augustine is a man of common sense and most certainly practical. He was less a zealot than an educator who condemned abuses. He felt as all sensible people must feel in a time of lively popular devotion: that in such a time it is a bishop's function, as a true overseer, to restrain rather than to incite.

While there are certain biblical personages, such as the Blessed Virgin and the Apostle Peter, whom he continually exalts as though they were a kind of symbol of the Catholic Church, he does not see in the martyrs a personification of Christian witness; rather does he see in them so many highly individual witnesses who interest him as individual human beings. In words that are simple and yet profoundly moving he can recall the details of each one's death, the manner of his previous life, his last words and his name. Time and again his rhetorical genius takes fire from these essentially simple heroes, who did not, like so many demi-gods, carry off an easy victory over hydras and dragons, but nevertheless overcame the world and themselves; who preached no philosophic system by words and personal eccentricity, but sealed divine truth with their blood. Indeed, Augustine loves to compare these popular heroes, who are wholly creatures of divine grace and, in their love of God, utterly forget themselves and so reach the supreme heights, with the old, lewd gods. How can Venus compare with the young maid Agnes? "How poor a thing is Juno when set against some simple old woman who has the Faith! How contemptible is even Hercules when set against any Christian, though that Christian be already trembling all over his body with age. Hercules overcame Cacus, Hercules overcame the lion, Hercules conquered the hell-hound Cerberus, but Fructuosus overcame the whole world and the maid Agnes overcame the devil."[6] He could never marvel enough over the women martyrs who put the stronger sex to shame. Once when he was speaking on the feast of Maxima, Secunda and Donatilla, the martyrs of Thurburbo, and quoted the words, "Come and follow me", he suddenly interrupted his discourse and cried, "But you say, 'Who does this?' Blush, O you strong man, blush for shame! Women did it, the women whose memory we celebrate today. By taking the narrow way himself and going ahead of us, the Lord has transformed this narrow way into a broad avenue, a royal military road that is protected on all sides, a road along which women have walked with ardour in their hearts. And you hesitate? You say you cannot do it, but boys and maidens, tender, delicately-nurtured children, have had the strength to do it."[7]

He recognizes their high place in the intermediate condition of the next world. They are the *coronati*, those who have already won the crown—a description that is in harmony with the manner in which they were represented in the arts of that time, for these show them receiving a wreath in their veiled hands, or being crowned with a crown of laurel from the hand of God which reaches out of an opening of the heavens. (Plate 20.)[8] "Where are they now, do you think, these saints? There where all things are well with them. What more do you ask? You do not know the place, but think of their deserts. Wherever they are, they are with God. They sit upon the seats of the holy [*sedes sanctorum*], they sit at the heavenly feast where the Lord feasts them upon his divinity. There is a great *mensa*, where the Lord of the feast is himself the repast. No man feasts his guests upon himself, but Christ the Lord does this thing; he himself is both host and also food and drink to his guests. O happy souls, your suffering is over and your glory is come!"[9] The others have indeed been sorted out, and are in God's hands, but their fate after death is not yet finalized and is in any case unknown to us. The wicked are chastised without respite, together with the wealthy glutton.[10] Those that are unclean are "purified by a chastising fire" in hidden places, and this cleansing is worse than any earthly pain.[11] In other places which are also hidden, and are called "paradise" or "Abraham's bosom", the just take their rest. Here they receive refreshment from the heavenly meal which does not yet give absolute illumination to their souls, but brings them both rest and a certain satisfaction of their hunger.[12] All this, however, cannot be compared with the sure and glorious *refrigerium* of the martyrs. Elsewhere Augustine sometimes speaks of the condition of the ordinary pious dead in terms that he usually reserves for that preliminary blessedness enjoyed by the martyrs. In the heavenly city of Jerusalem there dwell all the righteous and holy; they enjoy the word of God without reading it and without letters, for that which we must read in books they see through the contemplation of the face of God.[13] He had once written of his dead friend Nebridius, "Now he lives in Abraham's bosom. What this may be and what Abraham's bosom may mean we do not know, but Nebridius no longer puts his ear to my mouth, but puts his spiritual mouth to thy fountain, and from thence he drinks all the wisdom that he can drink, drinking it with that greed that was peculiar to him—and his happiness is great beyond all measure."[14] But in his sermons he says that all such glory is only a dream of the Lord's return. It is a shadow, a solace for the delay, a small part of the promise that will one day be fulfilled.[15] Departed souls, "although they have escaped from the shadow-world of the flesh, cannot behold the unchanging substance [of God] in the manner in which the angels can behold it. The life everlasting with the angels begins only after the Last Judgement, and in the time between death and the Judgement the natural desire of souls to serve the body has a restraining effect on their upward progress, and prevents them from rising to the highest heaven of fire in the Empyreum."[16] Yet despite this he seems, in the *Retractations*, unwilling to deny that such souls may possibly enjoy something that might be described as a contemplation of the face of God, and truly see him face to face with the inward eye.[17] The secret revelation only speaks of the martyrs of blood as reigning with Christ, but others also, in a certain sense, reign with Christ. Both the living and the dead do so in his kingdom of the Church, but it is only the martyrs that reign with him in the true sense of the word; the others only later reach that condition.[18] Although the names of the martyrs are read out at the altar in the intercessionary prayers at the end of the *prex mystica*, we do not pray for them as we pray for the ordinary dead whose names are handed in and placed on the diptychs so that they may be read out and recalled to the minds of the community and recommended to their prayers.[19] The martyrs are the jewels; they are the teeth of the Church. In commenting on the psalm verse "Blessed be the Lord, who hath not given us to their teeth", he says that the Church, too, has flashing white teeth, for of her it is said, "Thy teeth are as flocks of sheep that are shorn which come up from the washing." These are the martyrs, the flower of the baptized, shorn clean of their worldly wool; these are they who "bite men out of their errors", grind them small and absorb them in the body of the Church.[20] He loves to compare the time of the martyrs with his own. When he sees the great crowds before him on feast days, he thinks of that other multitude which in its rage and at that very place demanded the death of these men. Then the Church was great in a few; at the time of speaking she consisted of many and was far more widely spread; but what great courage was needed for her to grow great from such small beginnings! And it is still a question, which kind of greatness carries off the victory.[21]

General and Local Devotion to the Saints

It goes without saying that Augustine was more concerned with the great historical figures than with unknown local saints. The majority of the sermons which were given *in natali martyrum* speak of that not-overlarge group of saints whose names were known to everybody and among whom the African Church had numerous representatives.

Around the year 400 this group included among biblical personages the names of John the Baptist,[22] the Princes of the Apostles, Peter and Paul,[23] the Holy Innocents,[24] the Maccabaean brothers[25] and above all the protomartyr, Stephen.

The relics of St. Stephen, "little pieces of the saint's bones and a small heap of dust which is all that remains of his corrupted body", were found at Gaza in the year 415 as a result of a vision seen in a dream, together with the relics of Nicodemus, Gamaliel, and his son Habib. A small quantity of the relics of St. Stephen, in themselves of small importance and only indirectly connected with the saint, were brought to the West by Paulus Orosius and excited much attention in Africa. Augustine said of him, "Stephen made that other place famous by his suffering, but now, after his death, he has visited our country."[26] A number of inscriptions which have been found mention his name.[27] A small vessel containing his blood, its authenticity being established by yet another vision seen in a dream, came into the hands of Bishop Evodius of Uzalis. The matter happened as follows. A nun who, when the matter was mentioned in a sermon, had cast doubts on the new acquisition from the East, saw in a dream how an unknown priest placed a vessel to the mouth of her brother, who was a monk, and spoke the words, "Do you wish to know how to recognize the genuineness of martyr's relics?" and immediately fire came forth from his eyes and ears. Evodius thereupon organized a great procession with the relics. Sitting in a chariot, and surrounded by a crowd that stretched out further than the eye could see, and carried burning torches and sang psalms, he brought them with great solemnity into the town. He also kept a miracle book in which were recorded the answering of prayers. It is clear that the whole town literally dreamed of St. Stephen in broad daylight. One day a panic broke out in the market-place because a fiery dragon had appeared in a sky which had become pitch dark. All fled and rushed to the churches and the *memoriae*, and there hurled themselves to the ground. When the monster disappeared among the hurrying clouds it was said with one voice that St. Stephen had driven it away. On the next day a shrewd business man (perhaps an angel, says Evodius) offered an Italian curtain for sale to one of the subdeacons of Uzalis, having first taken the precaution of finding out where he came from; this curtain showed a beardless "Christ the Dragon-Killer", with a cruciform staff over his shoulder, a motif taken from Psalm xc and well known to us from a number of monuments. When this curtain was hung up before the *memoria*, everyone immediately recognized St. Stephen with the dragon—and a miracle in the purchase of the curtain.[28] It was much the same in Calama under Possidius, in Aquae Tibilitanae, in the fort at Siniti, near Hippo. In these places and in some country estates, shrines were erected over the relics of St. Stephen, which soon attracted many pilgrims.[29] At length, in the year 424, Eraclius erected a chapel near the cathedral of Hippo over what was no more than a handful of dust, which was in this case all that there was of the relics of St. Stephen; but "even this handful of dust brings great crowds together, and though the dust is hidden from view, the help and healing are there for all to see."[30]

Apart from the biblical martyrs, the most famous ones, both in the West and in the East, were the Romans Laurence and Agnes,[31] the Spaniards Vincent of Saragossa[32] and Fructuosus of Tarragona, with his two deacons, Augurius and Eulogius.[33] There was also Eulalia of Merida,[34] and Gervase and Protase[35] (who were discovered by Ambrose at Milan), and finally there was the African Cyprian,[36] while Perpetua and Felicity also came from Africa.[37] We possess a certain number of mosaic inscriptions from the covers of reliquaries—in those days the latter were usually kept beneath the floor—and on these mosaic covers there are often whole lists of all the relics concerned, many of which seem only indirectly related to the saints in question; the interesting thing, however, is that these saints come from every quarter of the globe. Besides those already mentioned we find, among Roman saints Hippolytus and Sebastian, and from Milan and Bologna, Nabor and Felix, Liberalis and Pastor; somewhat later we even find the simple confessor Martin of Tours, while from the East we have Menas, the patron saint of camel-drivers, who practised his sanctity in the desert west of Alexandria. Further, we have Romanus of Antioch, Euphemia of Chalcedon, Pantaleon and Anastasia, though some of the last-named may well date from the time of the Byzantine restoration. We even encounter relics of the three youths who passed through the fiery furnace in Babylon, and as early as the fourth century we have in inscriptions references to earth from the Holy Land, and to fragments of the Holy Cross.[38]

The first-named saints in the above list are mentioned by name by Augustine in his sermons, and at one time or another he preached in honour of most of them. Among the famous saints of the East he makes one mention of Thecla, the virgin of Seleucia and the legendary companion of St. Paul; also of Phocas of Sinope, the patron saint of sailors and fishermen, who can hardly have been unknown in any harbour town.[39] For many saints who were universally venerated the people of Africa showed little interest. Even for Peter and Paul they had only the most moderate enthusiasm. Relics of the latter are, it is true, mentioned on African inscriptions, but they are only indirect relics, *brandea*, as they are called—pieces of cloth which were let down through the grilles of the *confessio* into the vault for a moment—for, unlike the Greeks, the Romans refused to desecrate a grave.[40] On the feast of St. Laurence the church in Carthage was almost empty, though in Rome, as Augustine almost regretfully remarks, the crowd is so enormous that it is impossible to reach the vault.[41] But if the enthusiasm for the world's better-known saints was slight, ardour for the local ones, of whom there were considerable numbers, was all the greater.

In Carthage people venerated Agileus, Mappalicus, also Castus and Aemilius, who had once been *lapsi*, and the deacon Catholinus, who rested with a number of his companions in the basilica of Faustus.[42] Most important of all, however, were Perpetua and Felicity, whose feast was on the 7th of March, and the hero of the 18th day before the Calends of October (September 12th)—Bishop Cyprian, whose *passio* had been formally recorded in the *acta proconsularia* and had only recently been sung by the Spaniard Prudentius.[43] Cyprian's congregation had built three churches in his honour. One was on the spot where he had shed his blood, which since then had been called *ad mensam Cypriani*, a second was over his grave, *in Mappalibus*, which also lay outside the walls, while a third was near the harbour.[44] His feast was so popular and so much was made of it, that the Greek-speaking sailors applied the word *ta kupriana* both to the feast days and to the September storms, and everyone knew what they were referring to.[45] Theveste boasted of a certain Crispina,[46] and Utica boasted of Bishop Quadratus[47] and of his parishioners, the three hundred martyrs on the estate of Massa Candida, "that great white company, that splendid wall *in opus signinum*, in which all these souls have joined themselves together as living stones."[48] Lambaesis venerated the lector Marinus and the deacon Jacobus,[49] Thurburbo had its three martyred women,[50] while Scilli had those celebrated martyrs whose profoundly moving *acta* we still possess[51]—they are the oldest in Africa. The memory of all these saints was duly celebrated by Augustine; in the case of the Carthaginian ones among them, the celebration often took place on the very spot with which their names were associated.

But Hippo too had its saints. There was first of all Bishop Theogenes (a contemporary of Cyprian's), whose name occurs in the list of bishops at the council of 256, and who had a *memoria* dedicated to him[52] in the town. Further, there were "the Eight", in whose honour Augustine had a basilica built through his priest Leporius.[53] Then there were "the Twenty", among whom was Bishop Fidentius, and the women Valeriana and Victoria, names that provided Augustine with the occasion for some word-play on the subject of faith (*fides*) and victory (*victoria*); these too rested in a basilica.[54] Finally, there was the miracle-working handful of dust from the grave of St. Stephen. Felix, whose name, needless to say, was made use of by the bishop for further verbal conceits, was at home in the neighbouring Tunisia,[55] while at the Villa Victoriana, thirty miles from the town, stood the *memoria* of Gervase and Protase.[56]

And so it was everywhere. Excavations have confirmed in a most convincing manner what Augustine says in one of his letters, namely that "all Africa is full of holy bodies".[57] The whole peaceful country between the desert and the sea was strewn with structures that called the saints and martyrs to mind; there were great basilicas, little chapels, modest *cellae* and simple tables of stone under the open sky, designed for the feasts for the dead. These *mensae* were shaped in the form of a *sigma*. They were all objects of reverence, and were regarded as true *memoriae*. On these *mensae*, when they stood by themselves, the names of those saints whose graves or relics they covered were usually inscribed, just as they were inscribed on the mosaic floors of the churches.

Excavations have brought many such inscriptions to light. Some are carried out in mosaic and form part of the floor underneath or next to the altar, others were situated in a special apse on the west side of the church. Many are decorated with intertwining bands and with a cross, with a few lambs, with drinking doves and with peacocks or with the initials of Christ. Most of them contain no more than a list of names, though a few have something more; the so-called "catalogue" of Uppenna in Byzacena is a case in point—

> These are the names of the martyrs: Peter,
> Paul, Saturninus the priest.
> Also Saturninus, Bindemius, Saturnin
> us, Donatus, Saturninus, Gududa
> Paula, Clara, Lucilla, Fortun[atus]
> Jader, Cecilius, Emilius. They suffered on . . .
> of the Nones of August. Buried on 6, before the Ides
> of November. Gloria in esce
> lsis deo et in terra pacs ominibus.

Under the mosaic was found a small box with a few pieces of brocade and some parchment dust. Still further down were the foundations of an earlier apse also equipped with an altar; deeper still lay a similar inscription, and underneath this, again, a small pitcher with parchment dust in it.[58] One is particularly moved by the few inscriptions that give precise details of the

Diocletian persecution, and which undoubtedly cover the graves of genuine martyrs. The following one from the grave at Milevis is a good example.

> On the third day before the Ides of June burial of the blood of the holy martyrs who suffered under Praeses Florus in the city of Milevis in the time of the offering of incense; among others there rests here in peace Inno[centius].[59]

There is also the famous mosaic inscription found twenty years ago in the floor of a basilica in Haidra, an inscription which is rather difficult to translate:

> To the glorious and blessed martyrs who suffered for the divine laws under the persecution of Diocletian and Maximianus. Their bodies are buried here. They live everlastingly with God. He in whom God's compassion inspired this thought has bestowed their names [relics] and their most honourable bodies here, and that together with a decoration of little [mosaic] stones and also [altar?] pillars and a *mensa*, in return for all of which he, together with all his house, hopes for the divine favour. The most noble Marcellus, who wished to honour the *memoria* of these martyrs, has thus thankfully fulfilled his oath. May he who reads this attentively always live happily, but happier still will be he who fully believes in almighty God through his Christ.[60]

Actual graves have only rarely been found. Some time ago there was discovered in Carthage the remains of the Basilica Majorum, or Restituta, in which Perpetua and Felicity were buried;[61] in Tipasa there was also recently discovered the basilica of the virgin Salsa.[62] However, a great many small shrines have been discovered, built of marble or sandstone, which once contained a few bones or indirect relics, and which probably, as a general rule, stood under the altar. Such a small reliquary shrine was discovered in Bellezma in Numidia recently; it had upon it the following charming inscription:

> Behold here the place where you can seek the Lord with your whole heart. Yes, Christ, so be it. In this holy vessel the members of Christ will be gathered.[63]

There is also a square stone *theca* which has become famous. It was discovered in distant Ain Zirara by the Numidian lakes. In the middle of the nave of a ruined church a flagstone was found on which was inscribed the following:

> Here is the house of God . . . here prayers are heard, here the *memoria* of Peter, Paul, Laurence . . . Hippolitus . . . The consecration of the holy church . . .

and in a corner close to the apse lay the *theca*, shaped like a stone cube. It contained a small silver box, no larger than a man's hand. On the lid of this there was enchased the figure of a young martyr. He stands between two burning candelabra on the Hill of Paradise with its four streams, and holds his crown of victory in his hand while the hand of God holds a second crown over his head. On the sides are stags drinking from the streams of a mountain on which are the initials of Christ, while lambs run out of the two cities of Jerusalem and Bethlehem (which are symbols of circumcised Jewry and the uncircumcised world of the Gentiles) to the Lamb of God that stands upon the mountain. The cube itself was covered with a stone *mensa*-slab with a bowl fixed upon it, in which was placed the food at the feasts of the dead. The reliquary, the most beautiful that the whole of Antiquity has to show, is from the very period of Augustine.[64]

This discovery confirms that even in this little spot in the interior of Numidia direct relics of the four most famous Roman saints were venerated. Probably these relics had been placed in the central nave directly under the altar, and they probably had some kind of connection with the altar. In Calama, where Possidius was bishop, an inscription has been found that suggests that relics from the East, and even a memento of Tours, were venerated here, and that these lay under the altar-cloth, that is to say, under the floor onto which the altar-cloth hung down:

> † Under this holy altar-cloth lie the *memoriae* of the saints of Massa Candida, the sainted Heliodorus, the three holy youths, the sainted Martin, the sainted Romanus.[65]

Sometimes, however, such collections of relics were hidden under a *mensa* of stone that stood apart, as is clear from the rough table for the feasting of the dead that was found in Ain Tixter, a village of Mauretania Sitifensis. This table dates from the year 359. The inscription enumerates sacred objects which come from Carthage, Rome and Palestine:

> Victorinus Miggin Septimus
> . . . on the ides of September
> P.X.
> Sainted memory
> and Dabula and of the wood of the Cross
> from the Holy Land where Christ was born
> of the Apostles Peter and Paul; the names
> [=relics] of the martyrs Datianus, Dona-
> tianus, Ciprianus, Nemesanus,
> Citinus and Victor
> ia. provincial year
> three hundred and twenty
> Erected by Venenatus and Pecuaria[66]

These inscriptions and a hundred other similar ones confirm what we are already led to infer from the story of the carrying in procession of the relics of St. Stephen—namely, that in Africa as elsewhere people were no longer content to venerate the graves of local saints, but, whether they had such local saints or no, were anxious to have the *memoriae* of foreign saints as well. The possibility of satisfying this desire arose when the practice came into force in the East of dividing up the bodies of saints and making gifts of relics. In the West, above all in Rome, people were for centuries unwilling to have a hand in what they considered to be a desecration of the resting-place of the dead; but both in the West and in the East the custom had grown up since the fourth century, in the more important holy places, of giving pilgrims all kinds of mementos, or of selling them to visitors or sending them to far-off Churches which requested this to be done. They were mementos and nothing more—dust from a gravestone, oil from a votive lamp, flowers from the altar, *brandea*, pieces of cloth which had touched the relics, or engraved vessels with healing water from a nearby spring.[67] Soon, however, all these objects began to count as true relics with miraculous powers. With each of them it was customary to preserve a strip of parchment with the name of the holy place and of the cemetery or church concerned, and also of the saints who lay buried there; and both the parchment strip which carried this information and the object itself were hidden at home in the ground or under the altar of one's own chapel or basilica, which in this way was raised to the status of a *memoria*. Indeed, it became a memorial church of the saint concerned. A man with good connections like Paulinus of Nola received precious relics from all kinds of people. So the shrine under that altar of his in Nola, "which was always surrounded by a blaze of lights", received first of all a piece of the Holy Cross, a gift from the elder Melania in Jerusalem; further, it contained the body of the town's saint, Felix, also relics of the Princes of the Apostles—these came from Rome. There were, further, relics of Andrew that came from Patras in Argos, of Thomas and Luke, of Euphemia—this from Chalcedon—while from Bologna came relics of Vitalis, Agricola and Proculus; finally there came from Milan those of Nazarius, Gervase and Protase, these being a gift from Ambrose.[68]

This custom multiplied the *memoriae* to such an extent that the boundary between the grave proper of many a saint and his votive grave began to disappear. People were not satisfied till every little church on a country estate, every little monastery in the mountains, and every chapel in the town, had a stone bearing a number of famous names. The result of this was that the various foreign saints who ran about the world under the guise of unverifiable relics thrust the native saints into the background and that Africa's wealth in saints became well-nigh unlimited.

Africa was in this particular already richer than any other country.[69] Augustine tells us that for every day in the year there were already several saints in the calendar, but that they did not make a feast-day for every one of them, since a perpetual succession of feast-days would, as Augustine rightly saw, be wearisome, whereas the making of a break between such occasions tended to foster piety.[70] However, though the number of actual feast-days continued to be limited, there was no limit to the number of graves. Even if we ignore the names that come from overseas, more than half of the names that we can decipher from the inscriptions occur only in Africa and occur nowhere else, not even in the *Martyriologium Hieronymianum,* that compilation of the sixth century, in which Africa is so impressively represented, even though hundreds of names are entered without indication of their precise place of origin and only under the general designation "from Africa". We must, in this connection, remember that the Donatists also venerated countless martyrs, so that it is impossible to say, when we dig up an inscription with names that are unknown to us, whether we are dealing with heretics or with the orthodox, with genuine or with self-made saints—though we do sometimes get indications of a negative kind, as when we get such a characteristic expression as *Deo Laudes* or some other typically Donatist turn of phrase.[71] Failing evidence of that kind, we are completely in the dark even in the case of inscriptions that are in themselves profoundly moving—such, for instance, as the following one which was dedicated by their parents in the year 329 to the four youthful martyrs from Renault in Mauretania:

> Memoria of the most blessed martyrs, namely Rogatus, Majentus, Nasseus, Maxima, which has been dedicated to them by their parents Primosus and Cambus. They suffered on the twelfth of the Calends of November in [the year] 290 of the province.[72]

Who knows whether their posterity of the Byzantine age, when Donatism had long been overcome, did not read all these inscriptions in good faith and treat them as their own heritage? Many things were forgotten in the unhappy days of the Vandals, when so many churches were laid in ruins and so many inscriptions destroyed. In the curious calendar which we possess from sixth-century Carthage and which embraces the whole year save for the fasting period, we already miss many well-known names.[73]

Apparently Africa around the year 400 was not only crowded with ancient *memoriae,* but was continually being enriched by new ones. The isolated stone tables in particular, the *mensae,* shot up everywhere out of the ground like mushrooms. Many a credulous African of the people had similar experiences to that of the priest Lucius of Caphargamala in the matter of the relics of St. Stephen. People would have a dream in which some unknown martyr would complain that his bones were neglected, and indicate the place where they lay. A search would be organized, and if any such remains were found they would be elevated to the status of martyrs' relics and placed under a stone slab. If any discovery of human remains happened to be made, there was always somebody who would immediately cry, "Martyrs!" One can well understand why the fierce old Abbot Shenoute once asked his Egyptian monks, "Are martyrs the *only* people that have ever been buried?" The abuse became so widespread that a canon of the Carthaginian synod of the year 401, which was repeated word for word in 438, enjoined the bishops, in the following words, to put an end to it: "The altars which have been erected everywhere in fields and by the wayside, and of which it cannot be proved that they contain a body or a relic, are to be destroyed by whatever bishop exercises ecclesiastical authority over the place concerned. If this cannot be carried out without arousing a popular tumult, bishops should warn the faithful not to visit these places, so that men of good will may no longer be superstitiously attached to them, and not a single *memoria* should be regarded as being even probably genuine, unless a body or relics of unquestionable authenticity are to be found at such a place, or unless there is at least a tradition that is worthy of belief concerning their resting place, ownership and passion. Above all, the bishops should put a stop to the practice that now obtains, of erecting altars on the strength of dreams, and alleged revelations vouchsafed to all kinds of simple people."[74] Despite these injunctions the large number of isolated *memoriae* which excavation has revealed proves very clearly that they most certainly did not all disappear at once. In most cases, however, there are no means of ascertaining whether the *mensae* that have been found actually served as altars, nor, unless there is an actual inscription, have we any means of knowing whether they were used in connection with the veneration of martyrs or merely in the customary family cult. In Tipasa the entire cemetery around the church of St. Salsa, which was a centre of pilgrimage, is literally filled with *mensae*. One of them stands on the left-side nave of a second-cemetery basilica lying towards the west, that of the *justi priores*. Quite close to the entrance of the first-named church there have been found the remains of an open apse, also a passageway and a fairly large burial vault with numerous sarcophagi; the vault, to judge from the masonry, dates back to the fourth century and there is here a fountain with a drain—probably for the use of those who took part in the feasting of the dead. The implication seems to be that in this case what we have before us are ordinary family feasting-tables that have been set up around the grave of a martyr.[75] Elsewhere the nature of the finds is more difficult to establish. *Mensae* equipped with a hollow space for the holding of relics, however, can definitely be regarded as altars, and the number of these is certainly large enough.

Every community had the somewhat disedifying habit of boasting of its martyrs, while the collecting of relics became a veritable mania. Some forty years before, Julian the Apostate had pointed out to the Christians of the East that it was not in accordance with their own tradition to run riot over graves, or to spend their money on monuments and fill the whole place with graves and charnel-houses.[76] What would he have said about the things that were happening in Africa in Augustine's day? Even the oaths which the people used when they wished to make a declaration before a priest or, for that matter, to emphasize an ordinary statement, were taken, so says Augustine, from the vocabulary of the martyr-cult. Much as in Italy today people say *per bacco*, so in Numidia it was customary to underline a statement by the words *Si vincas* ("If thou wilt conquer"), while the expression *Per coronam tuam* ("By thy crown") was current in Byzacena, African Proconsularis and Tripolitana.[77] Strange examples indeed of purely local oaths! But one suspects that, with all due respect to Augustine, their origin is probably to be found in the circus rather than in the cult of martyrs; and yet the enthusiasm of a southern people for the heroes of its faith may not have been so very far removed from the kind of feelings they had for the champions of sport.

The Mother of our Lord

One cannot but be struck by the fact that Mary, the virgin Mother of God, was not among the most famous and universally venerated of the saints. This is no coincidence and is true of other places besides Africa. However many martyrs' feasts were celebrated, nobody observed the day of the Mother of God. People thought about her and knew about her and listened greedily to legends about her youth and the last years of her life, while every year her praises were sung on the feast of Christmas. For all that, she was not venerated. There were stories current about the grave of St. John the Apostle,[78] but no man spoke in the West of Mary's grave in Jerusalem. Everyone prayed to St. Stephen, but no-one turned to Mary. Although she was named in the Creed and in some places in the East in the prayers for intercession at the altar, and although the apocryphal stories which people in Syria and Egypt had woven around her life were known in the West, Mary remained in the background of the Gospel and had no place in popular devotion. As long as bishops still disputed about the human nature of Christ, she from whom he had taken flesh remained in the shadows. It was only when men's attention began to be fixed on the oneness of the person of Christ that they began to take more account of Mary and to see her in a different, a more exalted light.

But even if learned speculation concerned itself but little with her, the virginal figure of Mary still filled all ascetics with reverence. Ambrose drew the attention of his dedicated sister to her—"A clear mirror for you virgins and most worthy of honour."[79] And in whose spirit was she more alive than in that of Augustine, who wrote so many lovely things about his own mother that all that the sons of Antiquity have ever written about their mothers pales before it?

He recognizes what had by then become the classical antithesis between Mary and Eve as a great sacrament.[80] He knows of Mary's privileges and of her virginity before, during and after the birth of Christ;[81] he knows of her sinlessness. Though he recognizes the righteousness of Joseph, yet he counts both Joseph and all the other righteous men of the past among the sinners, but where Mary is concerned he will "for the honour of the Lord, not hear of such a thing as sin".[82] One of the expressions in his later work is so strong[83] that some have drawn an erroneous conclusion from it, and have held that Augustine had already surmised the secret of her special release from sin.

Yet the glory in Mary is, he realizes, pure grace: "How did all this become your portion? I ask the Virgin. It sounds irreverent, it is indeed unfitting that my voice should touch these shy ears. But see, the Virgin almost timidly gives me an answer, and says to me, 'You ask whence this became my portion. I hesitate to give you an answer myself concerning this my good. Hearken rather to the salutation of the angel, and then recognize that in me is also your own salvation. Believe on him on whom I also believe. Why do you ask me? The angel shall answer you.' 'Tell me, angel, whence did all this become Mary's portion?' 'I said it already in my greeting: *Blessed art thou, full of grace.*'"[84]

Above all, in his Christmas sermons he praised her as being most wonderfully both mother and virgin.[85] Like his teacher Ambrose, he looked upon Mary as the mirror of virgins;[86] but most of all he extols her as incomparable in her faith,[87] for as a virgin mother "she is very like the Church". He who "'was more comely in form than the sons of men' allowed his bride, the Church, to resemble his mother, for he has made her a mother to us all and has yet kept her as a virgin for himself."[88]

Her faith makes her the perfect picture of the Church, that is, the distributor of graces. It was her faith which made her great; indeed, she was greater through her faith than through her wonderful motherhood, and it was this that caused her to be honoured by her Son when he answered the praise of the woman from the multitude with the words, "Yea, blessed are they that hear the word and keep it"; the Spirit also moved Elizabeth to say, "Blessed art thou who hast believed." Who was ever a more steadfast daughter in the faith of that Abraham, "who believed and it was accounted to him for righteousness" and with whom the words of the *Magnificat* show that she felt herself to be bound up (for she too believed in God's promise)? Through the faith of this virgin the flesh of Christ entered the world. Therefore, too, it was not the "flesh of sin". He merely came to us in the form of our sinful flesh.[89] How very differently from the pious Zacharias she received the message![90]

Indeed, Augustine lays a wonderful intellectual offering at her feet. He sees in Mary the earthly foundation of Christ. She herself is earth, therefore the human nature of Christ, which was taken out of her, is also earth, and so it may be said of this the most precious of all our earth, which is itself the footstool of God's feet: "Fall down before the footstool of God's feet."[91] On the words "Truth is sprung out of the earth" he says: The truth is Christ. Who, then, is the earth out of which he is sprung? Mary! For she belonged to "our mass" (a favourite expression of Augustine's: it is the Pauline $\phi\acute{u}\rho\alpha\mu\alpha$), she is a daughter of that mass which is formed out of the earth.[92] When he speaks on the pericope from the Gospel concerning the kinsmen of our Lord who sought him, and of our Lord's sharp answer, he says, "This is a knotty problem. How could he leave his mother (and what a mother!) thus on one side without doing violence to his filial affection? Yet he did leave her on one side, because he did not wish her motherly love to interfere with and hinder his work. What, then, was he doing? He was speaking to the people, tearing the old man down and building up the new, and at such a moment they came to him with a message of human affection. You have heard what he answered and I will not repeat it to you. What could his mother avail him in the work on which he was engaged? Let mothers take note of this! Then they will no longer let their fleshly cares hinder their sons in their good works. In no way did he condemn the love of his mother, but in himself he showed by a moving example that a man must even despise his mother for the sake of God's work."[93] Yet a moment later, says Augustine, he praises her because in a quite especial way she had kept the word of God. "If ever anybody did so, it was Mary who fulfilled the word of the Father. Therefore it is more to Mary's honour to have been a disciple of Christ than to have been his mother. For this reason is Mary blessed. It is because before she gave birth she carried her own Teacher in her womb." For what was it the Lord said immediately after this? "Blessed are they who hear the word and keep it." But then Mary is also among the blessed, for she heard the word of God and kept it. It was even better to have had God's truth in her heart than his flesh in her body.[94]

Through her twofold dignity as virgin and mother, Mary is "that holy and most excellent member of the Church who towers over all others", the pride, the honour and the hope of all women. Augustine is the first chivalrous champion of our Lady among the Church Fathers, the first to sound the theme *Notre Dame, honneur des dames*. Thus he says, "Christ wished to bear the male sex in his person and he deigned to honour the female sex in his mother. Had Christ come as a Man without at the same time doing anything to recommend the female sex to us, then women would have lost heart, particularly since it was through their sex that man first fell. Now he has honoured them both, recommended both of them to us, and taken both of them to himself: he was born of a woman. Be of good cheer then, you men, for Christ condescended to be a Man. Be of good cheer, you women, for Christ condescended to be born of a woman. Together must both sexes strive towards the salvation of Christ. Let both man come and woman; in the Faith there is neither woman nor man."[95]

All this was, of course, partly drawn from the resources of his own mind, partly from learned tradition, but it was not yet part of the living substance of popular devotion. The day was, however, to come when this sowing was to put forth shoots and bear blossoms of a beauty that none had dreamed of.

Augustine's Criticism of Erroneous Views

It is nowhere written that Augustine made any attempt to abolish the *mensae*. What he abolished were not the tables but the carousals that were connected with them. In his old age he was firmly convinced that martyrs indicated by means of dreams the places where their relics were to be found. He was particularly sure of this in the case of St. Gervase, St. Protase and St. Stephen. For instance, in the year 424 he said in a sermon, "In this way, if it pleases God the bodies of the saints come to light."[96] In his youth he was not so credulous, and seems to have had a very keen eye for the more questionable side of this wild enthusiasm, and for the growing exaggerations of this cult. Despite his natural ardour Augustine did not, as a young priest and bishop, do anything to stoke this particular fire. In his book *The Work of Monks*, he utters a warning against monks who go peddling false relics.[97] One is struck by the fact that though in his sermons on feast days in honour of the martyrs he concentrates on certain aspects of the record that has just been read, he avoids dwelling on the unusual or extraordinary. The names he mentions are well known and have plenty of historical evidence behind them, or are collective names which indicate all the martyrs in a particular locality; the Massiliani, the Carthaerienses and "martyres Bolitani"[98] are cases in point. It sometimes happens that the superscriptions over the sermons mention the saint of the day or the one after whom the basilica was named in which the sermon was given, while the sermon itself omits all direct reference to the individual concerned. Thus we have three sermons in honour of the Scillitani, the martyrs of the town of Scilli who suffered in 180 (we still possess the moving record of their martyrdom); there is no indication in the actual sermon that it is supposed to be on the martyrs at all, the only reference to this being the superscription, in which their name is twice mentioned, and which also contains the noble answer of Donata, "Honour the Emperor as Emperor, but fear God."[99] There are a number of sermons which have been grouped together under the general title *In Natali Sanctorum Martyrum*,[100] which are also variations on this theme, a sort of *commune martyrum* for the pulpit. This reticence tends markedly to diminish in later years, especially after the relics of St. Stephen had come to Hippo and after a votive chapel had been erected next to the Cathedral in 424. In the last years of Augustine's life both his sermons and his writings are full of anecdotes and of the stories of miracles.

In the matter of the theory concerning the veneration of saints, however, Augustine does not change. In this connection his pastoral work is confined to moderating, pruning and forbidding. No sermon on the martyrs is without a warning against erroneous conceptions, and some begin with a piece of very thorough instruction. He expresses what may be called the classical conception of that time: the cult of the martyrs is lawful and useful, but it should consist of veneration, not of adoration. There should be no *colere* about it; this word *colere* still had the old overtone of giving something that belongs to God alone. This shade of meaning was, it is true, lost in the Church Latin of a later day, and even in some parts of Augustine's work it is evident that he was familiar with the sense of this word that was now beginning to be accepted, for in the eighth and tenth books of the *City of God* he uses this word for the veneration of the saints.[101]

The only purpose of the cult of the martyrs is to honour them as protagonists, to encourage the imitation of their example and to ask their intercession: "The Christian people celebrates the *memoriae* of the martyrs with such solemn piety because it looks upon them as examples to be followed, as advocates, and so that it may share in their merits and be fortified by their prayers; but there is always this reservation: our altars are not erected to any martyr but to the God of the martyrs—even though they lie within the martyrs' *memoriae*."[102]

They themselves are in need of no prayers. "At the *mensa* [he means here the altar] we do not think of them as we do of those others who rest in peace. We do not pray for them, but rather beg that they may pray for ourselves, so that we may follow in their footsteps; for they have that fullness of love of which the Lord has said that there cannot be a greater."[103] "To pray for a martyr is an insult; rather do we ourselves wish to be recommended by their prayers,[104] for they are not our clients but our defenders. We can do nothing for them except increase their joy by following their virtues; for to venerate them without following them is dishonest flattery. This [i.e., the following of their example] is the only ground we can give them for aiding us in our temporal needs."[105] In his book on dedicated virgins he writes: They do not desire to

21 Grave mosaic from Tabraca (Musée du Bardo, Tunis)

22 The Four Seasons, on a country estate (Musée du Bardo, Tunis)

be linked to us in any other way save through the example of faith, and the same is also true, first and foremost, of the Virgin Mary.[106]

To both heathens and Christians he continually repeats that the martyrs are no gods, nor are they deified human beings, like so many figures in the ancient Pantheon.[107] They can do many things but not everything. "God remains God without them, but what are they without God?"[108] The decisive thing is this: we do not dedicate any temples to them, or any altars, or any priesthood. Above all, we bring them no sacrifices, for the essence of *latria* is sacrifice. To his own imperfectly-instructed flock he says, "The martyrs have an honoured place. Reflect that when their names are read at the altar [during the prayers for intercession] they are named first [before all the other dead]. But they are not adored in place of Christ. When have you ever heard me or another bishop or any priest say at the altar in the *memoria* of Theogenes, 'This I offer to thee, St. Theogenes', or 'To thee I sacrifice, O Peter', or, 'I sacrifice to thee, Paul'? You have never heard this and there is no such practice nor may there be."[109] He says the same thing, though rather more emphatically, in the *City of God*. Which of the faithful, even though he stands at an altar which has been erected over the holy remains of a martyr for the purposes of the worship of God, ever says in the Great Prayer [*in precibus*], "I bring this sacrifice to thee, Peter"—or "Paul" or "Cyprian"?[110] "And even if that famous place by the sea, on the Field of Sextus before the walls of Carthage, that place where the great Cyprian was beheaded, is called *mensa Cypriani*, it is not because Cyprian receives sacrifices there or that his shadow is fed there or provides food for others." "As all of you that live in Carthage know, a *mensa* was there erected to God, and if it is now called *mensa Cypriani*, it is not because Cyprian has ever eaten there, but because he was torn to pieces like a sacrificial victim. Thus, through the sacrifice of himself, he prepared this table, a table on which he neither receives food nor provides it for others, but on which a sacrifice is brought to our God, to whom he once offered the sacrifice of himself."[111] In this sense, he argues, it is true to say that Cyprian himself prepared this *mensa*; for at that other time the many that hated him came together at this place to shed his blood, while now the multitude of those who do him honour come together here in order to drink the blood of Christ at his table and to drink it with all the more delight because it was in Christ's name that Cyprian's blood was shed.[112]

The saints desire from us *honorari* but not *coli*: "If somebody asks you, 'Do you give divine honours [*colis*] to Peter?' then give the answer that was given by the deacon Eulogius [the *martyrium* of Eulogius of Tarragona had just been read out], the answer he gave to the judge: 'I do not give divine honours to Peter, but to God, to whom Peter himself renders such honours.' If you do this Peter will look down on you with pleasure; but if you would have Peter instead of God, then you would strike yourself against a *petra*—and take heed that you do not break your bones on this *petra*."[113] When Eraclius had completed the votive chapel near the Cathedral, the chapel that was for the relics of St. Stephen, Augustine had four lines of verse of his own composition put up in it, which gave a sort of general direction about the nature of the legitimate veneration that might be given a saint, and the manner in which it might proceed; in a sermon given on a feast day or possibly at the consecration ceremony he said, "Do but read the four verses which we have put up in this chapel. Read them, let them sink into your minds and keep them in your hearts. We have put them up there so that everyone may read them and do so whenever they will. All should remember these verses; that is why I have made them few. All should read them; that is why they have been publicly exhibited. Here you need not seek a codex; this little enclosure of mosaic can be your codex."[114] In the last chapter of the eighth book of the *City of God* he once more finally declares for the benefit both of Christians and heathen that though the basilicas were indeed the successors of the temples, the saints were in no way the successors of the gods. The saints have neither priests nor altars of their own, no sacrifice is offered to them, not even by the simple people that hold a feast for the dead upon their graves. The cult of the saints is really directed to him who has made them what they are. Moreover, it does not consist in the dramatizing of immoral stories or in shameful popular representations in their honour, or in the jugglery and illusions of the demons. Rather does their example spur us on to the new and Christian form of heroism: to virtue. If one accepts the fact of a life of blessedness after death, then clearly these spirits may be honoured. Even a person of very modest understanding would not doubt this;[115] and in another passage he says that the graves of saints only confer a secondary honour on a basilica. The basilica remains exclusively dedicated to God.[116]

Nevertheless it is obvious that he has a genuine interest in the sequence of yearly feasts, and he adheres to them with the greatest strictness. On the anniversary, or *natale*, on which the death and crowning of a martyr was celebrated, he would go, together with his own congregation, or with that of the church to which he had been invited, to the *memoria*, which was usually in a cemetery outside the town. Here High Mass would be celebrated in the cemetery basilica, which would be decorated with garlands, sprays of laurel and hangings, and would be ablaze with light from clusters of lamps hanging down from the ceiling and candelabra that stood upon the floor carrying wax candles. Here, at the altar over the famous grave, Augustine would celebrate the Eucharist. Then the relevant pericopes from Scripture would be read, and also the *passio* of the hero, if one was available.[117] Sometimes this last would consist of an illuminating account out of the records of the trial, as was the case with the account of the *passio* of Fructuosus, or Crispina, or the "Twenty" of Hippo, or the Scillitani. In the case of Cyprian's execution the *acta proconsularia* also served this purpose.[118]

The masterpiece of this type of writing is of course the *passio* of Perpetua, Felicity and their companions, though Augustine is at pains to warn his audience here that these are not canonical writings;[119] it probably did not enter his mind that the established version went back to Tertullian, and that the visions represented a defence of the Montanist Pneumatics. But he knew very well that very few, if any, of the accounts of the *passiones* of martyrs are authentic. In the matter of local saints he remarks that in most cases there are not even *gesta* available.[120] His judgement coincides in a remarkable way with that of Gregory the Great, who, a hundred years later, replied to the request of the Patriarch Eulogius of Alexandria for information about Roman martyrs with the following words: "I could only find a single codex among my archives and this contained no details of the *passiones*, but only gave names, dates and place of martyrdom, the dates of many martyrs often falling on the same day."[121] There is a document dating from about the year 500 which tells us why no martyrs' records were allowed to be read out in the church at Rome; the reason was that the authors of such accounts were unknown, and the accounts themselves did not appear to be reliable, and indeed often seemed to be pure invention.[122] This corresponds entirely with the views of Gregory of Tours, who, in his book *The Glory of the Martyrs*, had shortly before this remarked concerning Rome that many martyrs lay buried there, but that the accounts which had survived of their *passiones* were incomplete.[123] The judgement of Duchesne and Delehaye is very similar. The fact is, however, that it is just this gigantic gap that explains the astonishing improbability of the legends with which popular imagination filled it up and, with it, filled the Second Nocturns of the Breviary which is still in use.

Finally Augustine was bold enough to unmask the self-made martyr. Once when in Carthage, on St. Cyprian's day, the incomparable *acta* had been read out and it fell to Augustine to preach, he made a point of comparing the *deo gratias* with which the saint heard the judgement read out which condemned him to death, with the *deo laudes* of the schismatic Donatist suicides, the cry with which these unhappy men hurled themselves into the abyss. He told how the celebrated Donatus himself had taken his life after this fashion, while Marculus had leapt into a pool. It was an impertinence to blame the Government for these deaths and a sacrilege to refer to these men as martyrs.[124] Even in his own camp, however, he refused to award the martyr's crown to people who had nothing but their folly to recommend them for it—such, for instance, as the sixty iconoclasts of Colonia Sufetana, whose reputation he dealt with in four masterly lines. These persons, he claimed, had found a place in the martyrology by some mischance, and he refused to recognize them as martyrs at all.[125] Even those to whose avocation it happened to belong to remove the statues of the gods in 399 could only claim a mere shadow of martyrdom if they lost their lives during this work.[126]

As against this he championed the cause of one who had been maligned, namely, Deacon Nabor, whom his community had refused to honour because, before his martyrdom, he had been a Donatist. In this case Augustine himself composed the epitaph, which expresses his opinion in no uncertain terms.

Thus in the chorus of eulogists who sing the praises of the martyrs, Augustine has an unmistakable voice of his own. He cannot compete with the pious fireworks let off by Asterius nor with the polished panegyrics with which Gregory of Nazianzus entrances the faithful. He has nothing to show like the *engkomia*, the praises or the apostrophes which were at one time the rage, or the ponderous biographies, stylized to the point of unintelligibility, with which the *pannychis* of the East were carried through. He was, as always, brief, gave little thought to anything in the nature of an *ekphrasis*, but invariably at a certain point plunged right into the business of instruction or exhortation. It never entered his mind to retell with flourishes and embellishments the *passio* that had just been read. He was only concerned for the honour of his heroes and set out to make sure that their dignity and the faith of his listeners received full measure. That their anniversaries had become regular feasts was a matter that could only give him joy, and he loved to compare the vast number of their venerators with the much smaller number of the persecutors who once had demanded their death. Yet the mere fact of changed times did not blind him to realities, nor did it escape him that the same sort of people who now cried "Hosanna!" had once cried, "Crucify him!" Hosannas do not mean the conversion of Jerusalem. Once he said, on the feast of a saint, "Naturally you, too, celebrate the feasts of the martyrs. 'Today is a saint's day', you say, 'I'll go to church and perhaps I'll wear my best tunic.' It were better you saw to it what kind of conscience you brought to church. Take to heart that which you now are engaged on, imitate that which you celebrate, and follow that which you praise."[127]

Burial *Ad Sanctos*

On one of the most common of the pious practices of his time Augustine's judgement was extremely cool. This was the purchasing of a grave of one's own close to the vault of a martyr. People liked to have their graves as near to such a vault as possible, to lie side by side with the saint, *ad sanctos* or *retro sanctos*. Many inscriptions from all parts of the Empire testify to this[128] and everyone who has visited the ancient Christian cemeteries of the period after

313 knows that the saints are almost without exception wedged in between a heap of other graves. It was this practice that, after the religious settlement, caused three-quarters of the catacombs to be burrowed out into a labyrinth of corridors which worked their way around the famous graves of an earlier necropolis. The nearer one comes to the grave of a saint, the thicker becomes the swarm of the dead; indeed, one is made aware that one is approaching the steps of the sacred spot by the narrowing of the passages and by the increasing number of the graves. Above ground the thing was even worse— particularly in the great basilicas which were built after the settlement in the cemeteries, and in which the holy graves found a place that shut them off and protected them. Every foot of ground before and behind the *confessio* and all around it was filled up with the dead. Sometimes whole layers of them extended over the entire length of the floor-space. The excavations carried out between 1915 and 1931 showed that the entire floor of the basilica of the Princes of the Apostles on the Via Appia, which is now called San Sebastiano, was covered with graves piled one on top of the other over the whole breadth of the central and lateral naves; the dead there lie in troughs, in coffins, in walled-in chambers and even in jars. This church is today still surrounded by a dense circle of mausolea in a cemetery that is packed completely full and is itself connected on one side with a catacomb.[129] To the left of the old church of St. Peter there lay in Augustine's day the imperial mausolea and behind the apse those of the patricians. The popes, in the third century, had been buried in humble chambers in the catacombs—in the episcopal vault, for instance, in the general cemetery which bears the name of Calixtus; but after the peace of 313 all of them wished to be buried in the basilica which they themselves had erected over the grave of one of their most beloved martyrs, or had at any rate spent great pains in beautifying. Or they desired burial in the cemetery of Priscilla, Calepodius, Laurence or Balbina, or, failing this, on one of the other cemeteries made famous by one of the martyrs, cemeteries which were usually underground, and surrounded the city like a garland. Alternately— and this later became the rule—they would be buried in St. Peter's. In his description of the new complex of buildings around the grave of St. Felix in Nola, Paulinus mentions four chapels which were attached to the basilica and were designed for purposes of prayer and meditation, but which were also intended for the burial of his housemates *ad sanctum Felicem*.[130]

The same picture meets us everywhere. The old heathen mausolea on the military roads towered enormous into the sky, the new Christian ones crowded around the graves of holy proletarians. The Christian graves clung to the cemetery basilicas as barnacles cling to the side of a vessel after a long voyage. If the saint lay in a cemetery, then from the religious settlement onward the dead crowded around him like a swarm of bees around their queen. Where there was no cemetery, or at least no Christian cemetery (as, for instance, on the Vatican, where Peter lay buried in a heathen necropolis, or on the Via Ostiensis, where Paul lay alone amidst forgotten freedmen), there they invariably called one into being in or near a church. The older catacombs were torn down, partly because the new basilica had actually to touch the sacred spot, partly to make room for an expensive new necropolis *retro sanctos*; we see a good example of this at the graves of St. Agnes and St. Laurence. Yet it was not long before demand outstripped supply; there was a crowd of applicants, and people haggled for every foot of ground. Although a man's own grave was legally regarded as *locus sacer*, and although the purchasers of graves had the most fearful curses inscribed upon them in case any attempt should be made at violation, nevertheless the lesser clerics and the gravediggers who administered the graveyards, and the basilicas connected with them, from the titular churches in the Eternal City,[131] were apparently not always incorruptible. Here and there a gravestone comes to light with its inscription partly obliterated or with a new one on the back of it, and about the year 400 people already knew about these things. A deacon of St. Laurence-outside-the-Walls in Rome had the following lines inscribed upon his tombstone:

> Bootless it is, yea, a burden, to cleave to the graves of the holy;
> Nearer one comes to these by an immaculate life.[132]

And an unknown man tells us in his epitaph, from the year 382, that "many desire this thing but only a few fortunate ones attain it."[133] Even the mighty ones of the earth had no dearer wish than to rest near the saints—in the best and most expensive places. High and low alike, everyone wanted to be buried close to a martyr, and in a certain sense this was a stronger wish than that of an ordinary modern man to be buried in consecrated ground. Ambrose buried his favourite brother Satyrus close to the grave of St. Victor.[134] In Sitifi an inscription was discovered dating from the year 324 which informs us, in the current African idiom, that a virgin "while she had life and health, had a holy *mensa* set up" which here can only mean that she had purchased a grave, together with a *mensa*, near a martyr's grave.[135]

The new saints, too, the ascetics, wished to rest near the old ones. The pious, distinguished and cultured ascetic Paulinus of Nola buried his only child near the martyrs of Complutum (Alcala de Henares). The rest of his life was dedicated to the grave of St. Felix, an unknown martyr of Nola; he sang of it in his *carmina* and built a shrine over it, in which he hoped one day to rest together with Therasia. We do not know whether he guessed that Augustine's attitude towards this pious practice was marked by a certain reserve; we find, however, that he wrote on the subject to Augustine. The mother of a certain young man who had died asked for him to be buried close to the grave of St. Felix, and Paulinus now asked Augustine to give him his views as an exegete and theologian on the value of this pious custom.[136] Augustine answered him in 421 in a lovely little book, which he entrusted to the priest Candidianus.

In this book, which deals with a number of questions, Augustine gives a laconic reply to Paulinus' principal enquiry. The *memoria* of a martyr helps to freshen the *memoria* of those who visit it; it is therefore possible that they will pray better at such a spot than in some other place. If a mother has her son buried in a basilica and really believes that the merits of the titular saint can help her child, then this belief is in itself a form of silent prayer and every visit to the place will make it more eloquent, while the bending of the knee, the stretching out of hands and the sighs, may well come from a genuine motion of the spirit and so serve to make the prayer more sincere.[137] The effectiveness of the prayer, nevertheless, is not dependent on its being made in this place, and it can be just as well made at home and may be just as good a prayer if so made. Yes—and here follow words that might well have caused the whole of Antiquity and many even of Augustine's own contemporaries to leap up in fury—no harm is done to the soul even if the body has no resting-place in the grave at all; the body might even be given to the dogs to eat, or burnt and its ashes scattered to the winds; or again (as Augustine had read in Rufinus' translation of the *Ecclesiastical History* of Eusebius,[138] concerning the martyrs of Lyons under Septimius Severus) it might be thrown into a river. He speaks with admiration of the indifference shown by Monica in the matter of her own burial, an indifference that astonished both Alypius and himself. In dying she had had no thought of the distant grave of her husband, where she had once ardently desired to find her last resting-place, but had only asked one thing— that she should be remembered at the altar of the Lord.[139] Augustine had by now learned to think of this matter as his mother thought of it; for him the place of burial was of no consequence, all that mattered was prayer.

There are, however, two passages in his correspondence with Paulinus which treat the matter of our duty to the dead from a slightly different point of view, one of them being a copy of an actual passage in the *City of God*. Our duty to honour the dead, he says, is part of that *pietas* which even our ancestors, who had not the Christian faith, held in high esteem.[140] Elsewhere he says that even a Christian may give expression to his grief and shed tears, but his sorrow "should not last too long".[141] The honouring of the dead should follow the custom of the country, and Christ himself has shown this by his example, for he praised Mary because she prepared his burial and he suffered himself to be buried with all the ceremonies of his country, "according to the custom of the Jews".[142] Even if the finest and most edifying funeral is more a comfort to the surviving than a help to the dead, it would still not be right to dispense with these solemnities or to be negligent in them, for our *pietas* would take offence at this, and rightly so. If we surround our mortal shell with reverence, then this derives from the universal feeling of mankind which prevents men from hating their own flesh.[143] It is true enough that Augustine did not look upon the concern for worthy funerals and graves as a spiritual work of mercy, but rather as a strict duty of *pietas*. It is also true that he may, on occasion, have grumbled about the ostentatious mausolea of the rich; for all that, however, his little book breathes a genuine reverence for the dead human body as the withered shell of the soul and the vessel of the Resurrection. He gives all the examples he can find in Holy Scripture of this duty of reverence toward the dead, pointing out how Tobias buried the dead at night under difficulties, and also referring to the anointing of the Lord by Mary, and his being laid in the grave by the two counsellors on the evening of Good Friday.[144]

To the main question, however, he merely replied by saying that visitors to a *memoria* might possibly pray better. That was all. On the last page he says, a little more cautiously, "It seems to me that . . .", but his main thesis remains unchanged.[145] Some years later he repeats it in exactly the same words in reply to a similar question from Count Dulcitius.[146]

When we survey Augustine's remarks on the martyr-cult as a whole our impression is that he recognized the element of value that it undoubtedly possessed but also laid bare its dangerous aspects and fought against its abuses. Its theoretical justification, which is quite plain to the Christian who lives in and by the Communion of the Saints, has been explained by him in words which none that have read them can ever forget. As to the abuses of the cult which flourished at that time, it may well have been impossible even for the sharpest eye to see what is obvious to a quite ordinary intelligence which surveys the problem from a distance of fifteen hundred years—namely, that in addition to the official public worship it was above all the activities which centred in and around the *memoriae* that thrust the ancient cults out of the minds of the great mass of people and taught even the ignorant to seek refuge with "those of Christ". Two generations previously, people had lain down in the temple of Aesculapius to receive the healing temple sleep; now people went in crowds to the famous basilicas to eat, to sleep and to pray. If there was a cure, the afflicted person would return to put up an *ex voto* or make a votive gift.[147] He who had previously consulted an oracle, now went to the martyr's grave, put his head under the altar-cover and his mouth close to the *confessio*, and prayed to hear the voice of God. The martyrs, who owed a great deal of the respect they enjoyed to such beliefs, finally triumphed over the heroes of mythology. Saints thus took the place of the old gods, with all their obscenities; legends concerning the saints replaced the ancient myths, stories of the passions of saints, which, childish and fantastic as they often were, had nevertheless about them a supernatural purity of sentiment, gradually filled men's minds and hearts and conquered one bishopric after another. Soon all the lands of Christendom were full of them, and of the unseen Christian race of which they spoke. These were men and women who were at home everywhere and nowhere, men and women surrounded by the golden gleam of legend, who were nevertheless made real and even tangible by the fact that their names were inscribed for ever in the lists of the ecclesiastical calendar. Legendary and yet publicly known, they live on in our baptismal name up to the present day.

Augustine could not yet visualize this process of the cleansing of a people's phantasy that was silently proceeding under his eyes, for he could not see what the end of it was to be, and the great changeover had only partly been completed within his own lifetime; yet he saw what was happening rather more clearly than anybody else, and had a certain dim idea of its importance. And it is to his honour that instead of meandering off into panegyrics he should have preserved towards this, the first important manifestation of popular Christian devotion, an attitude that was sober and even critical. Nobody showed greater deliberation or greater objectivity than Augustine when he performed the double function of both curbing and stimulating the veneration of the saints. Unfortunately there was one thing connected with this cult that was to him a source of endless annoyance. This was the feasting of the dead.

18

THE FEASTS OF THE DEAD

THERE was a very good reason why the covers of the graves of the saints should be called *mensae*. They had the shape of a dining-table, being straight on one side and rounded on the other in the form of a C. Whether a sigma-shaped couch was made to fit to the *mensa* or whether people squatted down or sat on loose cushions, they most certainly had meals at this table, for since men could remember a periodical feast in honour of the dead had always taken place at every grave. Nobody any longer knew what the custom really signified, but, as with many other customs of a similar kind, it seemed perfectly natural that it should continue. A certain irreducible minimum of *pietas* that was in everybody, a sentiment that had very little to do with religion, would not allow it to be otherwise. Thus the feast in honour of the dead was not something by any means peculiar to the cult of the martyrs, but was proper to every burial-place. It went back to the general cult of the dead and was after its fashion a family feast.

THE FAMILY FEAST

The men of old could forget many things but not their dead. Their piety consisted very largely in the honourable burial of their family and friends, in the celebration of their commemorative feasts and in the conscientious care of their graves. To have no grave was the greatest of evils[1] and no failure of duty was more heinous than the neglect of a tomb containing the remains of one's near relations. Not only the old tales but all the fancy of late Antiquity was filled with plaintive shadows that wandered about and appeared to people, and often took their revenge on friends and relations who proved themselves deficient in *pietas*; and whatever might have changed in the old ideas, most of the old usages were still alive at the end of the fourth century. The dead were still washed and arrayed in their festive garments; sometimes those who could afford this subjected their dead to a rapid embalming which converted them into sweet-smelling bandaged bundles not unlike the little figure of Lazarus which we see in contemporary representations, awakened to life by Christ and his miracle-working staff. The dead were carried to the grave accompanied by torches and usually in the evening, in memory of the ancient and noble times when burials only took place by torchlight. The cemetery, or the private and more elaborate grave, lay outside the town. Burial within the town walls was everywhere forbidden. The dead were either buried in cheap coffins of terra cotta or in expensive sarcophagi which were often decorated with reliefs. The coffins were laid in the ground, the sarcophagi were usually placed in niches in a wall or protected with a roof. Sometimes they were placed in the central niche of a kind of veranda built of brick, or given a chapel of their own. In other cases they would be put on the first storey of a tower-like mausoleum. Both the open apses and the closed chapels were called *cellae*, while all the larger tombs and mausolea were referred to as *memoriae*. The remains of such ostentatious tombs, built right around the grave of a saint and dating from Augustine's day, or possibly to a slightly earlier time, can still be seen and admired today at San Sebastiano on the Via Appia,[2] or, better still, in the two cemeteries of Manastirine and Marusinac before the walls of Salona in Dalmatia. In this last practically all the Western types of burial can be seen, and it is possible to reconstruct an open burial church (an apse to which are joined three galleries surrounding an open courtyard) as well as a two-storey martyr's grave, the resting-place of St. Anastasius.[3] A few objects were given to the dead that were suitable to their position in life; a child would be given a doll or some knuckle-bones, an official his spurs and shoulder-strap, while an ordinary mother would receive a little glass, a ring or a bracelet. On the third day the relations would come to the grave to mourn and to partake of a meal, and this would be repeated on the ninth day, for the *novemdialia* had, since ancient times, been the customary period of mourning. The nine days did not, however, end the solemnities whereby the dead were commemorated. In some cases the thirtieth day was the occasion of further honour to them and invariably the dead man's *anniversarium* (which meant not the anniversary of his death, for that was a day of ill fortune, but of his birth, his true *genesia*) was remembered. Then not only his relations but his clients, his old friends, his heirs and his servants would appear. A man who in his life had never gone abroad unless accompanied by a crowd of hangers-on would, it was thought, have liked to order his followers around him in the grave at least once a year. Sometimes the heirs were ordered in the will not only to care for the garden round the grave but to pay regular visits to it and to refresh it with a drink-offering and some talk. This last happened quite frequently. In many cases it was to some grave that citizens would take their evening walk, for these were as fond of sitting in the garden of a grave as the Turks were of sitting in the cemetery of Eyub some fifty years ago.

There was yet another occasion on which the dead would be especially recalled to memory, and that was during February, the month of the dead, the ancient world's All Souls' month. From 13 to 22 February the *parentalia* were held, the annual commemoration of all the dead of one's family, on the last day of which the *caristia* or *cara cognatio* was celebrated, and when all relations met together for a meal in honour of the dead, at which all departed members of the family were remembered.

Of all these things the meal long remained the most important. It is possible to see from all the richer graves, even when these are in poor repair, that they were equipped for the holding of a meal. Even the more modest graves are designed to provide for a drink-offering, and some kind of trifling refreshment. The older pagan graves were equipped with couches and tables, sometimes of an obviously provisional kind, though on occasion a quite elaborate set-up was actually built in with a kitchen, water-supply, drainage and ovens. In the rich mausolea people lay in comfort on sofas in a cool *cella*, and sometimes not before the grave at all, but in a small room situated above it, so that when drinking people could let the libations flow down through holes in the floor. Sometimes, also, the mosaic floors of such vaults have pipes in them which lead down right into the grave.[4] It would be difficult to say to what extent people were actually aware of the original significance of these feasts in honour of the dead. At one time those who forgathered at them as donors really brought drink and refreshment to the dead. They put the dishes as an offering to the latter upon the table, for they believed the shades of the dead to be actually present; indeed, they gave the dead man a place of honour—in a *cathedra*, an empty chair.[5] In the evening, the hour of mystery—for the meal was always in the evening—they called the dead man's name and invited him to partake of the offering, and to join them in eating and sacrifice.[6] The meal had at one time been called "round-the-table", or περίδειπνον; later, and even still in Christian times, it became known as the refreshment or *refrigerium*,[7] for it was not only the fear of the power of a ghost that drew the company together, but also care for the pale wandering shade, the little εἴδωλον that longed for men who would think of it, cherish its memory and give it back a faint semblance of life.

Those who could not pay for a mausoleum had their meal in the open or under some kind of a shelter, not too distant, or they would squat on the ledge of a wall, or sit in a circle on the ground, or bring folding chairs along,[8] and have a sort of picnic. Those who could not even pay for a meal would at least hang a garland of flowers on the grave, kiss the stone, and speak a few words of reverence or affection. Then they would take a bowl of porridge and a cold chicken out of a basket, place it in the centre of the stone, eat some of it and pour a little wine on to the grave before emptying their glasses.

As darkness began to fall, they would sit together and talk of the departed, always in terms of praise, offer incense and oil through the small holes in the gravestone, and make themselves comfortable. The meal tended, under a colouring of religion, to be a sort of family gathering, particularly when the person concerned had been dead for some time. The intimate atmosphere that tended to prevail in these affairs is well illustrated by an inscription found in Sitifi, not far from Hippo, from the year 399. In it some women of an unknown family tell how they have dedicated a memorial stone on the grave of their aged mother.

> To the memory of Aelia Secundula
> We have already spent much on Mother Secundula's tomb
> Now we have decided to put up at the place where she rests
> A stone table, where we will together remember
> All the things that she did.
> Then when the food has been brought and the cups have been filled and the cushions
> Have been laid around, then in order to heal the painful wound
> Till late in the evening we shall discuss gladly and with praises
> Our honourable mother—and the old lady will sleep.
> Now she who nourished us lies here in eternal sobriety.
> She lived 72 years. Provincial year 260. Erected by Statulenia Julia.[9]

There was not always so perfect an idyll. Synesius of Cyrene, who was almost a contemporary of Augustine, shows, in a little thumbnail sketch, a very different picture—that of an overdressed young niece who sits at her uncle's grave on a folding chair with silver feet on it and complains that he should elect to have his "third day" just when, as it so happens, she has an appointment with a friend. She has missed the funeral, wears jewellery and a golden hair-net and does not bother about the period of mourning at all, for would not her young man look upon it as a bad sign if he were to notice anything of that kind? On the seventh day the relations see her, not at the feast in honour of the dead, but driving across the market square in a mule cart and chatting away most cheerfully.[10]

The average Christian of the fourth century was far from being willing to abandon these immemorial customs, which belonged to the very stuff of civic life and among which the feasting in honour of the dead played an important part; and so far, indeed, had abandoned very little of them. Some time earlier the carrying of torches in daylight at funerals had been forbidden, though the prohibition was afterwards withdrawn. There was also a prohibition against putting a wreath of flowers on a dead man's head, though the strewing of flowers and the weaving of garlands was permitted; despite the book written by Tertullian during his Montanist period, the reason for these things remain hidden from us.[11] There was a very strong feeling against the cremation of the dead and from Hadrian's time onwards the practice had fallen largely into disuse;[12] it had ceased even among the pagans by 320. In the period of persecution the Christians were known for the simplicity of their funerals. We do it quietly, says Minucius Felix in the third century, even as we live quietly. They had their own cemeteries and had some affection for them.[13] Yet though men were struck by the retiring character of their lives, little attention was paid to their customs. Like other cemeteries the Christian ones were surrounded by a wall; in Africa, however, with few exceptions,[14] they lay on a flat piece of ground and were easily accessible. As *loci sacri* they were under the special protection of the law and inviolable, and on only one or two occasions during a space of nearly two hundred years were Christians forbidden to forgather in them, which means that, like others, they were permitted to hold their *parentalia*. Once only was entry forbidden them altogether and there was also a confiscation of the *areae*.[15]

Now, it is perfectly true that even in the earliest times Christianity had created an entirely new atmosphere around the grave; it is a matter on which we need not dwell at any length, since the fact is too obvious from the inscriptions. These simple inscriptions are really the first public testimony to a belief in eternal life. All are inspired by a clear certitude and are filled by a sense of the glory of the resurrected (who is never named by name) and by a profound sense of peace amid the general despair. As to the feasts in honour of the dead, as far back as the second century the Church had really caused the Eucharist to displace the deliberate or implicit offering of a sacrifice to the supposed shade of the departed. She had, however, never actually forbidden the traditional feast on the third day or on the birthday of the dead, the two things that had always been connected.[16] Moreover, in much the same manner, the giving of food to the shades was replaced by a distribution of food among the poor —at least for those who were anxious to mark the occasion in some suitable way and could afford the outlay. The sacrificial meal, as such, was thus displaced, while the family feast remained. In apostolic times the Eucharist had here and there been connected with an *agape*, and thus in the cemeteries and the μνῆμαι and *memoriae* there developed a connection between the feast of the dead and the Eucharist. Here probably lie the origins of our own Mass for the Dead, and also of the offerings *in natura* which still obtain in many countries. Exactly how this Eucharist was celebrated we do not know, but it was certainly offered up for the departed, probably after a comparatively short rite. It is possible that many of the curiously archaic-sounding passages of our own office for the dead are a reverent harking back to the prayers spoken on this occasion. Small wonder that the burials of Christians excited attention only by reason of their unpretentiousness.

All this was changed when, after 313, the great masses of this somewhat rough-and-ready people came streaming into the Church. The pious quiet that had once marked the Christian way towards the dead disappeared. It was replaced by the easy-going and somewhat noisy routine to which, from time immemorial, a people that was not conspicuously religious had been accustomed; the new half-Christians were still bogged down in pagan traditions. It was not long before most cemeteries were Christian in name, but in fact they had very much less to do with the Faith than in the days of the persecution; sometimes through sheer force of habit the letters D.M.S.—*dis manibus sacrum*—appeared over the initials of Christ.[17] Both in Rome and in Africa traces have been found of the old cult of the dead which seems to have been carried on pretty well in its entirety. There are still to be seen such things by the graves as the built-in chair for the dead man to sit at his feast in; there are the holes in the graves for the wine to flow down and even in the graves of the poor pipes for the dried balsam; there are the family *cubiculum*, kitchens and arrangements for water supply, and, above all, perfectly clear representations of the feast itself. In Augustine's own day the third and seventh days were still the customary ones for a visit to the grave, and sometimes still the thirtieth and the fortieth[18] day and the anniversary were still held in honour; and so, one must regretfully note, was 22 February.

Augustine himself would have nothing to do with the ninth day because both the *novemdialia* and the *parentalia* were of nine days' duration and the figure nine tended thus to be given a heathenish flavour. He recommended the seventh day, which was the one observed by good Christians, and naturally he particularly recommended the third. The seventh day was, "by reason of the sacrament of the Sabbath", a symbol of rest. Moreover, Holy Scripture said, "The mourning for a dead man is seven days", but for a fool all the days of his life.[19] Ambrose makes a passing remark that many keep the third and thirtieth days, and others, such as the Christians of Milan, the seventh and fortieth; elsewhere he says that the practice is to return to the grave on the seventh day, because this is the symbol of future rest.[20] Actually only the third, the seventh and the thirtieth days have been preserved in our liturgy for the dead. For the anniversary the Christians invariably chose the date of death, for Christians did not fear death nor did the day of death appear to them to be one of misfortune. Thus the idea of the *dies natalis* obtained a new meaning[21] and almost every inscription contained the date of death:

depositus die N.N.
obiit die N.N.

The Christian atmosphere in pious circles was a pure one. After a death Christians would read or sing hymns and psalms in alternation, exactly as happened in old Russia. While doing so they would sit in the cemetery "like the pelican of the wilderness", for the burial usually followed on the day after death.[22]

The Eucharist was celebrated on the third day, at that time probably in the cemetery chapel, for every cemetery had by that time a sanctuary of some kind, great or small. In Italy, apparently, the burial and the Mass for the Dead formed a single unity, for Augustine tells us that at Monica's funeral "the sacrifice of our redemption was offered up while the body lay on its bier next to the grave".[23] We do not know whether these most earnest people were also in the habit of partaking of a meal in honour of the dead—probably they did not, though there may have been an alms distribution carried out by the deacons; even this, however, is doubtful. Yet if people like those of Augustine's family had already broken with the old traditions, the ordinary folk clung all the more tenaciously, even after they had become Christian, to the familiar feast for the dead. They heard in church that it was unlawful to drink to the dead or to make them an offering, but the tables had not themselves been forbidden and were to be found in as great profusion on the Christian cemeteries as anywhere else. Was the thing behind this nothing more than a desire for social intercourse or the pleasure of convivial drinking? It is difficult to reach any other conclusion than that the persistence of the equivocal custom was connected with an unconscious or half-conscious religious conviction, and that men tended the graves of the departed as carefully as they did because they believed the fate of the soul to be dependent on the care they showed in this matter, and in general on the *pietas* of the relations.

All this scarcely improved the general tone in the cemeteries. A number of things, it is true, are merely the evidences of the ancient *pietas* and need give the Christian no particular ground for offence. At the cemetery at Manastirine near Salona, for instance, one can see glazed clay plates on the sarcophagi, which stand there in the open and which served for the feast in honour of the dead held by Christian families.[24] Similarly, there are shallow saucers in the catacombs of Malta, while in the chambers of the catacombs at Rome there are supports for benches and seats hewn out of the limestone; there are also niches for lamps and small sockets into which to fit the plates[25]—all this, let us repeat, is evidence of a custom with nothing more essentially pagan behind it than the ancient *pietas*, and we may say much the same about the various *mensae* which have been found in the cemetery at Tarragona[26] and at Tipasa in Mauretania.

Somewhat less edifying are the frescoes in certain of the catacombs, particularly those of Peter and Marcellinus, of which it is impossible to say whether they are intended to be a sort of snapshot of an actual meal or a transposition of such a meal into the next world, for the pictures are so uninhibited that they might just as well be held to represent an earthly family feast as the heavenly one. Both were referred to as *refrigerium*, and the one may possibly be looked upon as a foretaste or symbol of the other.

23 Mosaic of Theodoulos (Museum of Sousse)

24 Market-place, Timgad

In a number of subterranean burial chambers a certain dauber has repeatedly represented this feast. The impression created is of a cosy drinking party in which a number of men are reclining on the customary sigma-shaped couches with a little three-legged table with bread and fish upon it before them. Above the heads of the serving girls, who are hastening to supply the guests, stand the words: "Agape, mix my wine! Eirene, give me some warm water!"—phrases which certainly do not elevate the ladies Love and Peace to the status of heavenly allegories; incidentally these ladies make their appearance no less than four times—the painter was obviously repeating a stereotype.[27]

In another small chamber one sees a young lady labelled BINKENTIA lying relaxed upon her couch. She is raising a *rhyton* of some earthly or heavenly *refrigerium*-drink, while a number of youths are coming towards her with napkins over their arms like waiters, carrying jug and cups.[28] In yet another chamber there is to be seen an elderly man dressed like a workman in a knee-length tunic with circular insertions; he sits behind a bowl of food that has been stuck on top of a post. He points to the meal and opposite him there is depicted one of the scenes with Agape and Eirene. The learned have dubbed this man the Tricliniarch, but he suggests a porter rather than a *maître d'hôtel*. Probably it was merely the painter's intention to show how during the feast for the dead the purchaser of the grave thinks of the souls of his wife or his child at the heavenly feast.[29] Not only the old eulogistic phrases concerning the dead lived on, but also the old invocation of the shades. Sometimes in deep earnest, sometimes almost jovially, the old cry, *Refrigera bene!*, was still to be heard: "Take good refreshment, eat and drink!" and occasionally εἰς ἀγάπην—"To the heavenly feast!" Above all one still heard, *In pace!*[30]

In the catacomb of Domitilla is the gravestone of the sculptor Eutropos. It shows us the artist at work on a sarcophagus with a drill; next to him stands his son, who drinks to his dead father with the words "Holy God-fearing Eutropos, in peace."[31] In the same catacomb is the gravestone of little four-year-old Criste. On it the father drinks to his daughter with his left hand while pouring out wine for himself with his right.[32]

To drink to the dead was a pleasure which everyone could afford, even the poorest, and it was not an unpleasant duty. This seems clear from a *graffito* of the catacomb of Priscilla in which certain members of the Church inform us in their curious gutter Latin that

> In peace
> on the Ides of February
> under the third Consulate of Gratian and that of Equitius,
> We have, to the health of Florentinus Fortunatus and
> [Fel]ix, emptied our little glass[33]

Such things as these—all of them date back to the fourth century—show us that, at any rate in Rome, there was a tone about the cemeteries very different from that of previous ages. How very different is the atmosphere of the loose-mannered scenes of feasters from the catacomb of Peter and Marcellinus from that of the earnest representations of *refrigeria* in the third century, such as those, for instance, on the *attika* of the grave of Clodius Hermes and on the walls of the "sacrament chamber" of the catacomb of Callistus; and that of the famous "Breaking of Bread" in what is wrongly called the Greek Chapel of the funerary banqueting-chamber of Priscilla.[34] Here there is hardly ever lacking some allusion to the Bread of Life or to the physic of immortality; we also continually come across the seven baskets and the seven feasters, both of them subjects which have a bearing on the mystical banquets in the Gospels.

What is believed to be the oldest representation of a Christian feast in honour of the dead (that from the catacomb of Callistus) shows us the standing figure of a man who stretches out his hand to a small three-legged table with bread and fish. Opposite him stands the soul in a gesture of prayer, begging for her redemption in the next world.[35] The whole is marked by so earnest a spirit that when the thing was first discovered, it was thought to be a representation of the Eucharist. Even on one or two quite intimate scenes depicting a meal of bread and wine, which are on the lids of certain older sarcophagi and date back to before Constantine, there is always some reference to the Eucharist, and also some secondary theme of an eschatological character, such as the saving of Jonah and his repose beneath the gourd. The people who chiselled these mystical allusions did their work in the midst of pagans and in the midst of persecution;[36] but that reverent atmosphere is now definitely a thing of the past. The food upon the tables, once a thing so full of meaning, has achieved vestigial survival, but those at the table now have manners more suited to a pothouse, while the crude decorations represent nothing more than the husks of an ancient symbolism which now garnish the wine jugs of an ordinary, and distinctly convivial, wake.

The Commemorative Celebrations of the Church

What the family did on behalf of its departed was done for those bishops who had gone to their repose, and particularly for the martyrs, by the Christian congregation. The congregation of Smyrna did it for Bishop Polycarp as far back as 156. A hundred years later Cyprian was enjoining his clerics to make exact records of the dates of the deaths of martyrs, including those that had perished in prison.[37] The original ceremonial practised on these occasions was exceedingly simple. On the anniversaries the bishop would offer the sacrifice for them in the midst of the faithful, and later, in their honour. He did this at the grave in the cemetery, where the *passio* of the martyr concerned would also be read. In this way their place of burial, which was often marked by an almost excessive simplicity (for people accounted themselves fortunate if they were able quietly to hide away the holy remains), was prevented from being wholly forgotten.

Often the heathen went so far as actually to forbid the burial—indeed they would on occasion burn the corpse and scatter the ashes to the winds. Usually, however, the law was observed, and relatives were permitted to fetch the body; and it is hardly to be wondered at that, since burial was legally permitted, it should, in the age of persecution and in cases where the congregation was large and the martyrdom had been spectacular, have developed into something resembling a Christian triumph. After Cyprian's execution the Christians of Carthage waited till the crowd had dispersed, then they accompanied their famous bishop at night by torchlight from the Ager Sexti as far as the burial plot of the Procurator Macrobius Candidus on the Via Mappalia by the ponds. Neither spot was ever forgotten.[38]

We do not know whether in the earliest times there was, in addition to the Eucharist, a distribution of alms, or an *agape*, or privately-instituted feast in honour of the dead. In 1915, however, a monument was discovered in Rome which makes it quite clear that the Roman Christians of that time honoured the resting-places of the Princes of the Apostles by just such a feast. It is a roomy verandah with stone benches built into the wall and a small open terrace. This was in a necropolis, since buried, near to a little gorge on the Via Appia at the place called *ad catacumbas* ("on the slope"). It is to be presumed that around the year 258 the relics of Peter and Paul were transferred here provisionally and as a precautionary measure; however that may be, there was here a *memoria* of the two Apostles.[39] This building was obviously designed as a place for eating meals in, for a gutter has been found close to the benches and the drain leading off from it contained fragments of glass, chicken and fish bones, ashes and sand. (At the bottom of the gorge is a spring.) The monument was called a *triclia* or dining-room, and on the red-lead-painted rear wall one can still read the naïve invocations in Greek and Latin which pilgrims scratched there between the years 260 and 350.[40] The *triclia* disappeared in the year 350 in order to make room for the great basilica of San Sebastiano. Some of the invocations are as follows

> Paul and Peter pray
> for Victor

> For Peter and Paul
> Have I Tomius Coelius
> had the *refrigerium*

> On the fourteenth of the Calends of April
> have I held the *refrigerium*
>
> Parthenius in God and in God we all
>
> Paul and Peter
> pray for Nativus
> to all eternity
>
> Paul and Peter
> in your memory
> keep Sozomenus
> you who read this do likewise
>
> Peter and Paul
> pray for my parents
>
> Paul Peter
> pray for
> Eratus
>
> Dalmatius
> has made a vow
> to provide a *refrigerium*

This is the oldest and simplest of all the monuments that have to do with the popular cult of feasts in honour of the martyrs, though we have no means of knowing whether the *graffiti* date from before or after the religious settlement. In any case people did not forget to invoke the saints, and looked upon the provision of such a feast as a work that was pleasing to God—which does not, of course, mean that the Roman clergy actually asked for these feasts to be instituted.

As far back as the end of the third century the clergy in Rome seem to have replaced the feasts of 22 February by an ecclesiastical commemoration service for all departed bishops. Honour was now done to the spiritual predecessor instead of the fleshly ancestor, to the *cathedra* of Peter instead of to the dead upon their shadowy *cathedra*, to the dignity of the spiritual office rather than to bond of blood relationship. At the same time, this day was also used to celebrate the installation of the bishop of the day, and so the *natale episcoporum* became a kind of family feast for the congregation, not centring round a throne of shades, but around the throne of office, which in this case was the Chair of Peter. In the popular speech of Greece, 22 February had for a long time been known as the *kathedra*; from now on this day was known in Rome as *cathedra Petri*.[41]

Even so, this new spiritual feast could not altogether drive the old feasts at the grave out of existence. Even if the congregation as such did not think of communal feasts, and even though the clergy refused to organize anything but distributions of alms, the ordinary folk refused to abandon the ancient custom, and drank in swarms upon the graves of the new heroes. The quiet tribute was thus turned into a thoroughly noisy coming and going. Since the edict of toleration of 313, it was no longer a matter of determined believers going to a martyr's grave on his anniversary; visits were now made by hordes of pilgrims and holiday-makers from far and near.

The mood at such feasts was one of unqualified popular rejoicing; it was the mood of a crowd that thinks of a fallen leader after a successful revolt, and even the stern preacher of Hippo felt called upon to use the language of honest enthusiasm.[42] The grave of the martyr no longer lay in a carefully secluded private graveyard behind a wall of tiles; it lay covered with flowers in a recess in the floor of a brand-new marble basilica and over the grave stood the *mensa* of an altar.[43] Magnificent churches suddenly arose on the shabby cemeteries of the people; in Carthage there were three of them for Cyprian alone, one by the harbour, one over his grave, and another at the spot where he was beheaded in the midst of the Christians who held out cloths to catch his blood. In each of these three churches Augustine preached.

At the most impossible site of all—behind the walls of Rome, in the hollow of the Vatican Hill, where all the subterranean springs came to the surface—Constantine had the greatest of all Christian churches built at the State's expense, for here St. Peter lay buried. In order to make this possible the course of the water was diverted, half the hill was carried away, a new approach avenue was constructed from Nero's bridge over the Tiber and—an incredible undertaking—a complete heathen necropolis was destroyed. In the marshes by the reeds of the Tiber there arose on the road to Ostia, first a smaller, then a great, basilica over the grave of St. Paul, and what capital cities did in the grand manner was carried out in provincial cities on a more modest scale. Everywhere in the cemeteries basilicas began to arise in honour of the martyrs. Often they occupied the largest sites that a city had to offer—and they never remained empty.

The spectacle that was to be seen on days of pilgrimage is, as it happens, known to us from a Good Friday address, to a gathering of bishops, that has been put into the mouth of the Emperor Constantine and was obviously composed by one of his officials. The speech has a certain engaging courtesy about it, and contains the following passage: "Then hymns, psalms and songs of praise are sung in honour of him who sees all things, and in memory of these people there is celebrated the Sacrifice from which all blood and violence have been banished. Here is to be sought neither perfume or incense nor a funeral pyre, but only pure light to illuminate those who pray here; and often there is connected with this a modest meal for the benefit of the poor and unfortunate."[44]

We can hardly doubt that in reality this feast was a rather less distinguished affair than these words might lead one to suppose. The truly popular always tends to have about it the smell of the mob.

THE *REFRIGERIA* AFTER THE MASS CONVERSIONS

It is in particular the preachers of the East who provide us with our descriptions of these feasts, though such descriptions are usually quite incidental. The picture is always the same: a swarming crowd, open churches illuminated by day and night, a stream of people moving unceasingly in and out, people camping under the open sky, overcrowded *xenodochia*, a festival preacher whom no-one can understand—in fact, the usual picture of a pilgrimage centre working at high pressure.[45]

As is always the case in the East, the speakers tended to indulge in wild exaggeration. In one of his *encomia* Asterius of Amaesia in Pontus declares: "But for the martyrs our life would be without comfort or feasts. What can be compared to these *panegyreis*? What is more glorious or more beautiful than the spectacle of an entire city leaving its walls and going on to the sacred spot, where piety and truth perform the purest mysteries?"[46] And yet there were so many feasts that the calendar has not a single free day to show.[47] After Asterius has shown in some detail that this kind of veneration in no way diminishes the sovereignty of God, but rather that this is honoured in the person of the martyr, he declares that the Eunomians, those "stormers of sanctuaries", hate these practices, for they detest these antechambers of the grave more than they do the temples of the old gods—as do the demons themselves.[48]

Here too the business of eating plays an important part. Sinope was a famous place of pilgrimage, the saint being the holy gardener Phocas, who, according to Asterius, "gave shelter to his own executioners and waited on them because the duty of hospitality enjoined this". Phocas belonged to Sinope but was venerated by all seafaring men of both East and West, "and was known wherever there were Christians".[49] This same Asterius describes the pilgrimage to St. Phocas in the following terms:

> This [Phocas] now draws all men in great crowds to his resting-place and the military roads are full of people who come from every part of the world to this place of prayer on pilgrimage. This splendid temple, which now has the honour of sheltering the holy body of this witness, then becomes the place where the sorrowful once more have ease, it becomes the house of the physician [$ἰατρεῖον$] where the sick are healed—let people think of Epidaurus

—and the table of the hungry. Greater is the hospitality of Phocas after his death than that of Joseph of Egypt during his lifetime, for Joseph exchanged wheat for gold, while Phocas gives without return to those in need. Whole crowds of beggars and tramps hurry to the Isthmus of Sinope as to a common storehouse of provisions. That is what happens here; and if the martyr has here and there founded a small colony of his native city by means of his relics, then such places are also worthy of our admiration and are justly the object of longing to all Christians. These too will become the resting-place of the guests of the feast, as is this our own city. For precious in the eyes of the Lord is the death of his saints, and although his relics are scattered over many places, they nevertheless all sustain the fame of the thrice-blessed one without impairment. Yea, even in the Imperial City, the capital of Italy and the empress of the world, the martyr has a following and a cult which embraces the whole people.[50]

Although this last sentence may be called exaggerated (and a statement by the same author that Rome had purchased the head of the saint is also open to criticism), nevertheless this description of the *pannychis* on the Pontic isthmus is the clearest of its kind that we possess dating from this time. Phocas was certainly famous enough. The seafaring folk east and west, so Asterius tells us, turned their rowing songs into hymns of praise in his honour. The saint seems, moreover, to have had a habit of appearing at sea, where he would hoist the sails and draw the dozing helmsman's attention to his steering-oar. It was also the rule among sailors that one ration daily went to Phocas; this ration was then bought back and the proceeds were given to the poor when the ship reached shore,[51] for the holy shade did not keep offerings for himself, and the dead man's feast had everywhere been turned into a means of helping the poor.

In the matter of the business and bustle of the pilgrimages, the West was in no way behind the East. It is just that no one happens to have written about it, and the relatively late verses which Paulinus and Prudentius have dedicated to this pious activity are lost among a thousand other bombinations of religious prosody. Moreover, all these effusions are dedicated to shrines that have long since disappeared and are consequently unknown to us. Three graceless but simple pieces of doggerel have been found in the floor mosaic of the cemetery church of Justi Priores at Tipasa (an exact replica was later discovered at Djemila) which give us a description of African pilgrims:

> Christian folk both the young and the old come hither together
> Touching the holy threshold with joy and joyfully singing
> Hymns of praise while their hands stretch out for the sacrament holy.*[52]

> * Undique visendi studio Christiana aetas circumfusa venit
> liminaque sancta pedibus contingere laeta
> omnis sacra canens sacramento manus porrigere gaudens.

From Paulinus we have an account of the celebration of a feast in the basilica of Felix at Nola—snow-white curtains between the pillars, lamp-holders packed with lamps over the altar, the church blazing with light night and day, crowds of churchgoers so that little Nola was like Rome on 29 June. Despite the uncomfortable journey Paulinus went every year to this Roman feast, though as a monk he politely declined the invitation to the Pope's birthday.[53]

A strophe from one of Ambrose's hymns in honour of Peter and Paul gives us a momentary glimpse of this Rome as it was on the feast of the Apostles. We see the whole city on pilgrimage by different roads to the two graves, those going to the Vatican passing along the Via Cornelia and those going to the Church of St. Paul by the Via Ostiensis, while pilgrims making for the mysterious *memoria apostolorum* over which the *triclia* had since been replaced by a great basilica would be taking the Via Appia:

> Around the mighty city now
> The columns dense are stretched out
> Three separate roads the folk do fill
> As to the martyrs' feast they go.*[54]

It so happens that we know of this same Rome that feasts in honour of the dead took place in the Vatican basilica *ad sanctum Petrum* not only on 29 June but all the year through. In Augustine's eyes this was a thoroughly bad custom, from the guilt of which he would gladly have absolved the Roman clergy in the eyes of his flock at Hippo.[55] In the year 399 the pious aristocrat Pammachius instituted a feast in honour of the dead on the occasion of the death of his wife Paula (who, incidentally, was a pupil of Jerome). The feast was given in the galleries of the *atrium* round about the fir-cone fountain and in the great central nave. Although the feast was held in honour of the dead woman, it was nevertheless intended to be an *agape* for the poor, a fact which caused Paulinus of Nola to praise the donor in one of his letters. In this he contrasts the action of Pammachius with the senseless games which other senators were in the habit of providing for the people.[56] Incidentally, both Paulinus and Prudentius observed, without a shadow of displeasure, the little private feasts which ordinary folk held in honour of the dead, and have sung of them in their poems, the one picturesquely, the other in a more exalted tone. Neither shows the least disdain for these affairs. Poets can, of course, take delight in the pious jollifications of the people, for no poet was ever really a Jansenist or a Puritan—not even the Puritan Milton. Paulinus smiles good-

---

* Tantae per urbis ambitum
stipata tendunt agmina
trinis celebratur viis
festum sanctorum martyrum.

naturedly over the peasants from Campania on pilgrimage to St. Felix with their fatted pigs, of which they will have little more than the entrails to spare for the poor, and over their tales of stolen oxen and diseased chickens. All he has to say about these abuses is that such people come from far and near, braving the heat and cold, and then make merry the whole night through by the pine logs according to ancient custom. How sad that they do not say any salutary prayers, and that they carry their tippling right up to the sacred threshold! Naturally enough the "sober company" which sings psalms in my house, he says, has a better standard of conduct. But—oh, well, we must pardon these little folk their jollifications. Their action is wrong but they don't really think about what they are doing:

> Even piety brings the simple-minded to stumble.
> Saints, they believe, in the grave relish the scent of the wine-cup.*[57]

It is true that he thunders here against the devil, who thus carries on his work, sometimes screaming through the mouths of the possessed, sometimes singing via the tipplers—

> Fiend, avaunt from the sacred spot—O serpent, no games here!

Yet he leaves his own parishioners in peace. All that he does is to paint the walls of the *atrium* with a remarkable assortment of pictures—the creation of Adam, the crossing of the Jordan with the Ark, Orpha and Ruth, Abraham passing out of the land of Ur of the Chaldees, Isaac carrying the wood for the sacrifice, the youths in the fiery furnace, Lot's hospitality and his flight, the pillar of salt, Amalek destroying the wells, Jacob flying before Esau, Joseph's flight before Potiphar's wife and his imprisonment, scenes from the Book of Exodus, and many others. It was his intention, as he explains in a letter to his friend Bishop Nicetas of Remesiana (to whom he described the whole project with many pious allegories), that this pious spectacle should dissuade pilgrims from drinking.[58] Even the unapproachable grandee Prudentius delights in the hot kisses on the cool silver, in the violets and roses on the *confessio*, and in the sweet-scented water which pilgrims pour through the railings onto the grave of the saint:

> We shall grace the covered bones
> With violets sweet and many leaves,
> Sprinkling the grave and these cold stones
> With sweetly smelling water-sprays.†[59]

---

* Simplicitas pietate cadit, male credula sanctos perfusis, halante mero, gaudere sepulcris.

† Nos tecta fovebimus ossa
violis et fronde frequenti
titulumque et frigida saxa
liquido spargemus odore.

> Early at morn they come to bring greeting and all the great concourse
> Comes and goes and returns to the very last hour of the daylight.
> See how they fix their lips with a kiss on the glittering silver
> Pouring the balsam down—tears running down from their eyes.*[60]

And was it really so terrible if a pious soul supposed that the saint could actually smell the balsam? Does not Holy Scripture tell us that God smells the scent of incense and of prayer?

A much more serious matter was that the drinking grew steadily worse. The open verandahs had been replaced by churches and on some days these were turned into pot-houses. In certain smaller places there developed a combination of saint's day and festive gathering, a combination of the Mass with a hospitable spread, all ending up with a jolly excursion—very much as today a religious procession may be part of a general festival in which a fair and a shooting competition all have a place.

In the great churches the pious offering of wine gradually degenerated into a carousal which no-one could definitely forbid because it took place under the pretext of pious observance and in obedience to an ancient tradition, and was therefore in a certain sense protected. Drinking became the essential element on these occasions. The half-symbolic, half-realistic feasts from the catacomb of Pietro Marcellino may be quite safely accepted as snapshots of a popular feast on the anniversary of a martyr, although in reality they are connected with nothing more than old family customs. Moreover, it is by no means certain that the gentlemen who came together in the catacomb of Priscilla to "empty their little glass" did not empty their glasses to all the saints that lay buried there.

Apparently things were nowhere quite as bad as they were in Africa. On the great feasts the early morning worship usually went off in a reasonably dignified way, but the evening before the feast,[61] the vigil, and above all the afternoon worship of the feast day, with its wine parties and all the rest of the celebrations, often degenerated into a regular fair, and that in the church itself, where the *mensa* stood. In Carthage St. Cyprian's day, which fell on 16 September, was, in the year 360, celebrated very much after the fashion of 14 July in Paris—*le jour de boire est arrivé*. On the night of the feast people even sang rather loose songs to the accompaniment of the zither in the great memorial church on the Area Macrobii (after 400, older people could still remember this), and there was also some gay dancing.

"The Lord said in the Gospel," Augustine once said in a sermon given in

---

* Mane salutatum concurritur; omnis adorat
  pubis eunt, redeunt solis adusque occasum
  oscula perspicuo figunt impressa metallo
  balsama defendunt, fletibus ora rigant.

this church, " 'We have sung for you and you have not danced.' How could I say this if it were not written? The frivolous laugh, but one who has authority helps me out here. Yet had I not told you beforehand who it was that uttered these words, could any of you have borne hearing me say this? Is it proper that here where psalms are sung there should be dancing—and yet not so very long ago the frowardness of the dancers had penetrated even to this very place [etiam istum locum invaserat petulantia saltatorum]."[62] On another occasion he says: "Was it perhaps not necessary to introduce into this place a true vigil watched through in the name of Christ in order to drive the zither-players from this church?"[63] Shortly before Augustine uttered these words Bishop Aurelius, a man of some energy, had at Augustine's request taken the bull by the horns and driven the mob out of the church and celebrated the vigil of the feast by a carefully-ordered act of worship. It had not been easy to carry this prohibition into effect, for when he forbade people to make music when they entered the church, there was something of an uproar —a matter over which Augustine often displayed some heat when it fell to him to preach in the capital.[64]

As to the pleasures of the table, it is sufficient to note that a certain church which in point of fact we cannot identify was actually called the *basilica tricliarum*.

The First Protests

As far as we know it was Ambrose who first forbade the holding of feasts in honour of the dead actually inside a church.

When Monica, who went daily to church, first came to Milan, she followed African custom and, desiring to carry out her pious practices on the graves of the saints, entered the church with a small basket containing porridge, bread and undiluted wine. She was stopped by the porter at the door with the words: "Good lady, this is not allowed here. It has been forbidden by the bishop."

On this occasion the lady from the provinces obeyed without a word of protest—a most praiseworthy act for a woman, her son thought, all the more so since Monica was the last person to perform this rite in anything but a spirit of the greatest piety. At home she had always used the same little glass on every visit to a grave, had put in much more water than wine and had herself only taken the very smallest sip from it. There was certainly no question of indulgence here. Thus to obey the porter's order, Augustine states, was not an easy decision for her to make, and his belief is that she only acted as she did out of her love for Ambrose.[65] In telling us all this Augustine also relates what were the grounds of Ambrose's action. These were that such feasts in honour of the dead merely provided people with an excuse for getting drunk and that also since they were really a sort of *parentalia*, they had too close a resemblance to heathen superstition. Nor did Ambrose have any great liking for the traditional family feasts. He knew that in many cases they were kept within very modest bounds, but his advice was that such people should rather give alms directly to the poor and that instead of bringing a little basket with fruit it would be better to bring a heart full of prayers and good resolutions into church, and to take part in the communion of the body of the Lord, which was celebrated in that very place.[66] Although these family feasts were no longer consciously connected with the old cult of the dead and had for a long time been no more than a convention of ordinary people's lives, nevertheless they were based on the idea of a sacred community of sacrifice with the dead, and every good Christian should have known that among Christians the only possible community of sacrifice was that centring around their own unique sacrifice of the Eucharist.

Ambrose gave a lead to Northern Italy, for both Zeno of Verona and Gaudentius of Brescia followed his example and forbade the feasts, while in Africa it was in this case again Augustine who followed his master, as he had done in so many other matters. Even as a young priest he took the initiative in issuing a prohibition. It was a ticklish business, for nowhere was this custom more deeply rooted than in Africa;[67] it was no question of the correct direction of the spiritual exercises of a few pious ladies, but of an extremely popular ecclesiastical custom, though of course it was only the ordinary folk who were concerned here: the elite in Africa,[68] as elsewhere, had little part in these affairs. It was a dangerous thing to touch this honouring of the dead, but the spectacle of riotous conduct and drunkenness in a holy place was decisive, for on saints' days the whole church at Hippo was full of Christians who were distinctly merry.[69]

He had been a priest only a year when he thought he saw his opportunity. Shortly before, his friend Aurelius had mounted the *cathedra* in Carthage. He knew him as a champion of reform in these matters, for even as a deacon, Aurelius had been opposed to these abuses and had sought to resist them; also, he was a born ruler. Augustine therefore wrote him his celebrated Letter 22, which deals with the highly involved series of problems connected with the honouring of the dead.

In this letter he distinguishes between the traditional *pietas* and the various degenerations of that sentiment that had recently manifested themselves. Ambrose was for doing away with the whole business and abolishing all forms of feast in honour of the dead. Augustine, however, suggests that the placing of food and drink on graves should be permitted, providing some moderation is observed and that the thing is looked upon as a form of alms, for the poor who will go to such places of their own accord or can be invited to do so. In a word, he approves what was really the practice of his mother, and probably has a form of such a feast in mind which was to be found occasionally in his own country and also in Syria.[70]

It is true that he points to the dangerous possibility that the faithful might be induced to believe that they were actually giving a *suffragium* to the dead, for, he says, "fleshly and ignorant folk really believe that their drinking and guzzling in the cemeteries [istae in coemeteriis ebrietates et luxuriosa convivia] not only honours the martyrs but at the same time refreshes the departed."[71] Yet because he recognizes the possibility that the dead may indeed be helped by a *suffragium* that has been earned in advance, he is against abolishing outright the feasts that take this form.

For there are three ways in which a soul that has earned such assistance while still on earth can be helped after death; first, through the offering up of our redemption—that is to say, by the Eucharist; then, through prayer, above all the intercessionary prayers of the Church; and finally, through the giving of alms.[72] Why, then, could these last not be given in the form of a distribution to the poor at the grave, in certain circumstances at the grave of a saint and in his honour? And now he gives certain indications how these *agapes* can be ennobled, which is quite possible when they are confined to a small circle around a normal family grave. "The offerings for the souls of the dead which are placed on the *memoriae*, should not, if they are really to be of use, be of too extravagant a kind. They should be handed as a gift to all that ask for them, and this readily and without condescension; they should in no circumstances be sold. If anybody wishes to give money for a pious purpose this should be given to the poor there and then."[73] It is strange that the diaconate is not even mentioned in this connection.

But for the carousals which took place in the churches not only on feast days but daily,[74] and which were nominally in honour of the martyrs, he has not a good word to say. The time for concessions is over. He speaks again of the delusions which are nourished by the abuses, but the fact that people gorge themselves within the church walls is in itself quite sufficient to determine his judgement, for what has become of these feasts in honour of the dead is gluttony and drunkenness. When quoting the passage from St. Paul's Epistle to the Romans in which the various vices are named, he remarks that of the three kinds of sin which the Apostle enumerated, chambering and impurities are everywhere looked upon as the most grave while gluttony and drunkenness are not regarded as grave at all, and drinking is even looked upon as a way of honouring the martyrs. And these abominations are not only practised on feast days, but can be seen every day. It is "one of the fleshly foulnesses and sicknesses [carnales foeditates et aegritudines] under which the African Church suffers in many but over which she groans in few, and from which she can only be saved by the intervention of a council or of Aurelius himself".[75] But he continues, let us for the moment disregard the extravagance that is practised in private circles and let us receive the body of Christ together with such men (with whom, strictly speaking, we are forbidden to break bread); but let us at least keep this disgraceful thing far from the graves of our saints, from the place of sacraments, from the house of prayer. For who would dare to forbid something that takes place in the intimacy of the family circle when it is permitted in a holy place and there is treated as an honouring of the martyrs?"[76] "If Africa were to be the first to seek to abolish these things, her example would deserve to be imitated. Actually, however, these practices have disappeared completely in Italy and in almost all other overseas Churches, either because they never existed there at all or because they were utterly extirpated by the care and diligence of holy bishops who held to true doctrine concerning the future life. With so excellent an example before us, should we hesitate to extinguish such a blot upon our manners [morum labem]—all the more so since we have a bishop from that part of the world amongst us?" (Aurelius was an Italian.) "Yet this pestilence is so evil that in my opinion it can only be cured by a council. Yet if any one Church is to start the application of the physic, it should be that of Carthage, for it would be as impertinent to persist in an abuse which the Church of Carthage has corrected as it would be presumptuous to seek to change what Carthage has preserved. And what bishop would one rather choose than the man who, already as a deacon, was full of detestation for this thing?"[77] Let him therefore abolish what he at that time complained of, not harshly of course, for it is written, 'with love and in the spirit of gentleness'.[78] The unmistakable signs of honest affection which I find in your letter give me confidence to speak my mind to you as I should speak it to myself. So far as I can judge we should not seek to abolish these things with harshness or in an imperious manner, but by persuasion rather than by command, by advice rather than by threats [magis docendo quam jubendo, magis monendo quam minando]. When we are dealing with the multitude, we must proceed cautiously; a strict attitude is only suited for dealing with individual sinners. If, however, we really have to threaten, we must do so with a heavy heart and basing ourselves on the judgement of Holy Scripture, so that men may not fear us because of our personal power, but rather because they fear God by reason of our words. In this way an impression is first made on the spiritually-minded and on those that are closely bound to them, and through the influence of these and our own kindly but ceaseless and pressing exhortations the resistance of the people as a whole is ultimately broken down."

After this excursion into pastoral theology, he continues: "We shall be able to deal with more success with these abominable things if we quote passages from Holy Scripture showing that these prove them to be unlawful, and make a point of saying that the offerings for those that have fallen asleep should not be of a sumptuous kind, and should be given freely and without demur to all that ask. Then there will be no question of our seeking to persuade them to leave untended the graves of those who are near to them, and that which takes place in the church can proceed in a worthy and lawful fashion."[79]

The rest of the letter deals with the subject of disunity, and Augustine does not omit to excuse himself for his boldness, which he covers by the Pauline words "Let none think contemptuously of thy youth" and "Bear one another's burdens." One remark about clerical jealousy in his own circle is made the more pointed by the observation that there are many things which he would rather not confide to paper, and he adds that, "between my heart and yours there should be no communication other than that between my mouth and your ear."[80]

The letter, however, was not without its effect, for Aurelius was Augustine's intimate friend and immediately acted on his proposals. As chairman of the plenary council which met in Hippo in the following year of 393 he raised this very matter, which was ultimately settled along the lines suggested by Augustine. By Canon 29 bishops and clergy were forbidden to arrange meals in the church, save only when they were under the pressing necessity of entertaining guests, and they were to "dissuade the people as much as possible from instituting such meals".[81] The resolution was published in 394 and no-one in Hippo was in any doubt as to the identity of the driving force behind this matter.

For the views which he had formulated in a letter were fully expressed by Augustine from the steps of the apse.[82] When the Manicheans reproached the Catholics with drunkenness at the side of the grave and with believing "that they could put the Shades in a good temper by offerings of food and wine", Augustine answered them by saying that he certainly did not wish to excuse people who got publicly drunk, but that it was better that a man should return to his home the worse for drink than that he should, like certain other people, offer the martyrs sacrifices.[83] Nevertheless, the whole business filled him with shame, and he could find no way of making the thing that was actually going on appear less unlovely than it was. Indeed, in 388 he had openly conceded in a book against the Manichees that "you must not judge by the great mass of insufficiently-instructed people who have either remained superstitious even while in the true faith, or are so enslaved by the pleasures of sense that they forget what they have promised to God. I know well enough that there are those who adore painted figures and worship tombs and who drink with the utmost self-indulgence over the dead and set food before them. In doing so they bury themselves at such graves, and then attribute their gluttony and drunkenness to religion [novi multos qui ... super sepultos se ipsos sepeliant et voracitates ebrietatesque suas deputent religioni]."[84]

It was the same in his sermons. "The martyrs hate your wine-jugs and cooking-pots and your gluttony."[85] These unhappy people "whom one sees running off to the *memoriae* and who supposedly consecrate their cups thereon and then come home drunk, since they can no longer persecute the *coronati* with stones ... pursue them with wine-cups."[86] This sounds like a passage from Zeno of Verona: "God is displeased by those who run along to the gravesides, offer their lunch to stinking corpses and then and in their desire to eat and drink suddenly, with pot and glass, conjure up martyrs at the most unfitting places."[87]

But even drinking at family graves is a clear piece of folly. It gives not a jot of help to the poor souls concerned. "There they bring bread and wine to the grave and call the dead by name. How often after his death they must have called out the name of the wealthy glutton when they got drunk in his mausoleum, and yet not a drop fell on his parched tongue."[88] The Donatist bands knew no restraint whatever; they not only got drunk on the graves of their suicides, but committed every kind of sin there at once. Here were "those gangs of vagabonds who bury their own selves upon their graves in loathsome promiscuity, seducing one another into all manner of vice".[89] This last was an accusation which Augustine never made against his own people. For all that, the scandal was considerable and it was natural enough that Augustine should have been concerned to rid the Church of it. He succeeded. How he did so he described in a detailed and delightful letter to Alypius, with whom he discussed the whole matter, and who prayed with him for its success.[90] This letter shows something of the arts of the "hellfire" preacher and in it is preserved a sort of *tour de force*, in that direction, on the part of Augustine.

The Prohibition in Hippo

Round about the time of the Feast of the Ascension in 395 and shortly before the feast day of a particularly popular saint, the rumour spread in Hippo that Augustine was about to forbid the *laetitia*, as the feasts in honour of the dead were called.[91] On the day before the Ascension it happened, "through a secret dispensation of God", that he should have to treat of the Gospel text "Ye shall not give that which is holy to the dogs, nor shall ye cast your pearls before swine." The letter to Alypius has the following to say about this: "The reference, then, was to dogs and pigs, and it was made in such a manner that those who obstinately barked against God's commandments and those who were given up to the sordid lusts of the flesh, must needs be ashamed. In the end I showed how abominable it was to do certain things inside the church under the cover of piety, while we forbid those who do such things at home to have access to the holy things and to the pearls of the Church."[92] Those who heard him received his words well and were visibly impressed, though unfortunately only a few had come to church. Nevertheless the news ran through the town like wildfire, and "there were many protests".

On the feast of the Ascension he delivered his rhetorical masterpiece. He was in excellent form, and opinion changed in a flash. Augustine had gathered together all that Holy Scripture had to say on this theme, and a pile of codices lay ready to hand for him on the pulpit, a whole arsenal of texts which he could hurl into the faces of his packed congregation in a brilliant climax. He began with the reading of the account of the cleansing of the Temple, and on this occasion the bishop himself read the pericope over after it had already been once read by the deacon. Then he said: "If Christ himself would not suffer a trade which was at that time permitted in the Temple for the offering of the sacrifices of that day, what would he do in the matter of these drunkards today? I ask you: What more closely resembles a den of thieves—men who sell an article of common use and necessity, or men who get drunk? In that temple where the body and blood of the Lord was not offered up at all, there was no dining even of the most modest kind, and there was only one occasion when the fleshly folk of Israel got drunk in the name of religion, namely at the adoration of the Golden Calf." Here he took up the Pentateuch which lay before him and read the twenty-second chapter of Exodus. Then he cried out— "as sorrowfully as he could", so he tells us—"Moses could at least break the stone tables of the Law, but the Apostle says that the law of the New Testament was no more written on stone tables than his own letter, but is engraved upon the hearts of Christians. Hearts, however, are not things that can thus be broken in pieces."[93]

With this he put the Pentateuch aside and he reached, *exaggerans*, for the heavy guns of the codex of St. Paul. "Hear in the company of what sins St. Paul names drunkenness: 'If any man that is named a brother be a fornicator or covetous or a server of idols or a railer or a drunkard or an extortioner: with such a one not so much as eat'—and shortly afterwards: 'Do not err: Neither fornicators nor idolators nor adulterers, nor the effeminate nor drunkards shall possess the Kingdom of God. And such some of you were. But you are washed.' How can you hear it said, 'You are washed', when you still suffer to remain in your hearts the filth which shut you out from the Kingdom of Heaven? Again, it is written: 'When you come together it is not now to eat the Lord's supper. For every one taketh before his own supper to eat. And one indeed is hungry and another is drunk. What, have you not houses to eat and to drink? Or despise ye the Church of God?' Does the Apostle ask whether you have houses to get drunk in? He says 'to drink in' and this drinking he permits only in the house and not in the church, while we in our day would be almost content to watch the decay of our manners if drunkenness could only be confined to the house."[94]

Then he harked back to the Gospel of the previous day, "By their fruits ye shall know them." Among which fruits has drunkenness its place? The answer is in the letter to the Galatians: "Now the works of the flesh are manifest, which are fornication, uncleanness, immodesty, luxury, idolatry, witchcraft, enmities, drunkenness, revellings and such-like. Of the which I foretell you, as I have foretold to you, that they who do such things shall not obtain the kingdom of God." What, are Christians now to be recognized by the fruit of drunkenness? How can it be that we should not only have our own enjoyment of the works of the flesh but should cause them to redound to the honour of the Church? Nay, some would even have us fill the whole space of this great basilica with drunken and feasting men and women.[95]

Thereupon he gave the reader back the book and began the prayer. Then as best he could "and with such power as God lent me on this occasion" he sought to set before them the dangers and the scandal of their conduct and their responsibility to one another. He recalled to their minds their supreme shepherd, and sought to bring before their eyes his humiliation, how he was despised and spat upon, and the buffets he received; his crowning with thorns, his crucifixion and the shedding of his blood. He adjured them by the grey hairs of his bishop, who was also the bishop of them all, and who had so often said that the coming of his priest meant that his most ardent prayer had been heard. He adjured them to have pity on themselves, on him and on Valerius. The old man must not have lived thus long only to learn that he had rejoiced over their common ruin. At the end came the warning. He was convinced and trusted God in this matter, God could not lie, and had, in anticipation of our Lord Jesus Christ, declared through the mouth of his prophets that "if they despise the readings and the preaching and forsake his law and walk not in his judgements, if they profane his justices, he will visit their iniquities with a rod and their sins with stripes." But his mercy he would not take away, and he would not permit them to be judged with this world.[96]

The congregation could no longer contain itself and burst into tears. The speaker had to stop, and, so he writes, it was not he that caused them to weep, rather was it they who set him weeping. And when for a time they had thus wept with one another, he made an end to his sermon in the firm hope that they would mend their ways.

When the next day broke, the day for which they were in the habit of "holding their belly and their gullet in readiness", Augustine waited tensely in the episcopal residence—and indeed he was later to declare from the pulpit that the situation had been very tense indeed and the general mood a distinctly dangerous one.[97] During the morning he was informed that there was some murmuring in the streets, in which even those who had heard his sermon were joining. People were asking why the prohibition should be made at this late stage. Were the people who had previously refrained from forbidding the practice not Christians too? Hereat he really did not know where to bring up "heavier guns"[98] from, but he took note, for all eventualities, of a passage in Ezekiel: "The watchman hath delivered his soul if he tell the wicked man that he may be converted from his ways, even if he be not converted."[99] And he resolved that if the business should turn out badly, he would shake the dust of the place from his feet and go away.

Yet before he mounted the apse, the very same people who, as he had heard, were in opposition to him, came to visit him. He received them in friendly fashion and succeeded in persuading them with comparatively few words—so much so that in his sermon he decided to omit the passage from Ezekiel and dealt quite summarily with the most pertinent of his critics' questions by simply saying, "The best and quickest way of answering the question 'Why only now?' is simply to say, 'Well, now's the time!'"[100]

In order not to place his predecessors in the wrong, however, in so far as these had not felt equal to the decision which Valerius now allowed him to make, he again, in masterly fashion, explained his own point of view, and in doing so contrived to create the impression that he was defending the tradition of the Church. He explained to his audience how these abuses had come into being and why they had been tolerated for so long. "For when after such long and violent persecutions a period of peace set in, the heathen came in shoals asking to take the name of Christian, but the chief thing that held them back was that they had been accustomed to celebrate the feasts of their idols with heavy eating and drinking, and they felt that they could not deny themselves this indulgence. For this reason our predecessors considered it right for a time to make allowances for this weakness and to permit them to celebrate feasts in honour of the martyrs in place of those they were giving up, and these feasts, though not marked by actual sacrilege, nevertheless had a certain similarity with the pagan festivals by reason of the riotous conduct which accompanied them."[101]

That so much had to be conceded was looked upon as a necessary evil. It had been felt necessary to make some allowance to a people that had streamed into the Church but was unwilling to give up all its reprehensible habits at once. But things could not be allowed to go on indefinitely in this fashion, and in any case such happenings had not taken place overseas at all; or at any rate the practices, if they had ever obtained, had now ceased there. As to Rome, he knew, of course, as well as anybody else, that drinking parties were a daily occurrence in St. Peter's. But he had heard that such practices had been frequently forbidden there. Unfortunately the church concerned[102] was very far from the episcopal residence (the Lateran lay on the other side of the town, still within the Aurelian wall) and was full of newcomers who had been attracted by the great city. Such newcomers would hardly be likely to take orders from anybody; it was impossible to exercise any control over such people and the Roman clergy was virtually powerless, though the thing was of course a scandal. Meanwhile, he said, when we wish to honour Peter we can prove our piety much better by carefully examining his letter, in which his intention is clearly expressed, than by looking about in his basilica, where he is nowhere to be seen—and, taking the codex in his hand, he read the words from the great Epistle: "For the time past is sufficient to have fulfilled the will of the Gentiles for them that have walked in riotousness, lust, excess of wine, revellings, banquetings and unlawful worshipping of idols."[103]

He concluded by advising his hearers to consider the matter and come to the church that afternoon, where they could sing psalms and hear the word of God in common. Then it would be possible to see from the number of those who came who was serving his reason and who his belly. In the afternoon the church was even more full than it had been in the morning. When Augustine entered it together with Valerius, the reading and singing of psalms had been going on for some time. After two more psalms had been sung the old bishop asked his priest to say a few short words. "I had little inclination to do so," the latter wrote, "and only wished to have this dangerous day behind me." Nevertheless he began a short sermon, in which he gave thanks to God. Yet this short concluding address became a masterpiece, for he suddenly heard that the Donatists were celebrating the saint of the day in the accustomed fashion. This meant that within the same block of buildings the feast was in full blast in the schismatic church; actually the noise could be heard right where he was. He commented that white is even brighter when contrasted with black, and the day even more beautiful when contrasted with night. Then he stressed the difference between the worthy and spiritual celebration, which they were themselves conducting, and the "carnal gorging"—*carnalis ingurgitatio*—next door of those whose god was their belly.

He added an eloquent conclusion, quoting the text from Psalm xxxiii: "Come and taste ye, how sweet is the Lord", and the apostolic "Food is for the belly and the belly for food, but God will destroy both." Then came an exhortation to seek only that which is imperishable, and the sermon was thus protracted till the hour of Vespers. These were then sung, and when he was going away with Valerius while his brethren still sang songs of praise, a considerable number of Christians remained in the church and sang psalms until darkness fell.[104]

The perilous day had passed. Later, when he was already a bishop, he admitted that he had been rather nervous.[105] But the abuses were thus finished with.

The Acceptance of the Family Feasts

As to the *agapes*, the private feasts at the family mausolea,[106] there is no indication that as a bishop Augustine took any exception to an institution concerning which as a priest he had expressed himself with such moderation in his letter to Aurelius. In an address on the resurrection of the flesh he spoke of the mockers who continually say, "Dead is dead, so what use is it to put food on a dead man's grave?" In this manner he brought up for discussion the question of the feasts in honour of the dead. He states that he knows of indifferent people who assert that even Holy Scripture pokes fun at the practice, for of people who do not know the good things of life it is written that it is as though man were to put food on the grave of the dead. But the biblical writer is clearly thinking of heathen customs. It is a fanciful expression for the sick, who keep their mouths closed when dainties are put before them. The Patriarchs kept no *parentalia*. This was the usage of the heathen. The Patriarchs only arranged a funeral, and the Jews who came later ascribed no particular power or effectiveness to such a burial. They only held onto a solemn and ancient custom.[107] Augustine also dealt with the text from Tobias which was often quoted in the East, though he employs a curious variant from the original: "Lay out thy bread and pour out wine upon the burial of a just man, but give it not to the wicked."[108] This has little to do with the subject we are discussing, he says, but my hearers can well understand its meaning. It is known to you that the faithful are permitted to do something of this kind at the *memoriae* of their relatives, providing that they do it with pious intention, "for the just man lives by faith". Neither of these two texts says that no help can be rendered to the dead. Let no man, therefore, make a wound out of this physic, nor turn the Holy Scriptures into a cord, out of which he can make a noose to throw around his soul: "Nemo ergo quaeret de medicina vulnus, et de scripturis conetur torquere vinculum ut laqueum mortis injiciat animae suae." It is quite clear how these passages of Scripture should be interpreted, and the Christian ceremony is transparent and salutary.[109] Augustine thus tacitly assumes that this ceremony can be allowed to continue without hurt or impropriety, and is only concerned with the one object of proving to those that deny the resurrection of the body that help for the dead is possible; in other words, that they live on and that their condition is not yet definitively established.

When in his old age, in the *City of God*, he again had occasion to speak of feasts in honour of the dead, he was no longer concerned to criticize the lack of moderation with which these affairs were conducted, but merely to prove that Christians did not sacrifice to the dead and to confute those who expressed this opinion. In doing so he has especially in mind the little gifts which people put not only on the graves of relatives but, like Monica, privately, on those of the martyrs; and also, of course, the bread and wine of the Eucharist, which were ordered and paid for. Those who do this, he says, do not sacrifice to the dead, and at the Eucharist the sacrificial prayers are directed to God, to whom we give thanks upon the graves of our heroes for their victories, palms and crowns. Such celebrations are "a gracing of the *memoria*; they are not a sacrifice offered to the dead as though they were gods", and "as far as those are concerned who carry their food to such places, good Christians do not do this, and in most countries the custom is unknown, but all those Christians who engage in this practice put the food on the grave, say prayers and then take the food away and either eat it or give it to the poor. Their intention in acting thus is as follows. This food is to be sanctified by the merits of the martyrs in the name of the Lord of Martyrs. There can be no question here of sacrifices which are offered to the martyrs, and that is a fact known to everybody who has been instructed concerning the one unique sacrifice of Christ, for this very sacrifice is offered up at these very graves."[110]

Here speaks the apologist who is under compulsion of making out a case for something which in point of fact he does not permit among his own congregation. The feasts in honour of the dead did not disappear at one fell swoop, either in the case of family gatherings at the graves or in that of the graves of the saints, and it was in connection with the latter that the persistence of the custom was most obstinate. In a number of sermons given by men who came after Augustine we still hear the complaint that people were putting offerings on graves on the traditional 22 February. It would be better for such people to pray for their *cari*, says one of these preachers, with an allusion to the *caristia*.[111] One of these sermons is still read by us in our breviaries.[112] It is clear from a prohibition of the Second Council of Tours that in Gaul in 567 Christians were still, in some cases, in the habit of eating food that had been placed on the graves of the dead, though they did this secretly and not openly.[113] Incidentally, old people in Serbian villages still do this today, and what is more, they do it openly in the cemeteries in the presence of an Orthodox priest.

19

BELIEF IN MIRACLES

Primitive Popular Beliefs

THE drinking-parties on the graves of the saints represent something more than a coarse popular custom. There was a good bit of pagan superstition in them, and this pagan superstition threatened to turn into a Christian superstition. There were many such remains of paganism and Augustine forbade them one after the other. "The old superstition cannot be submerged deep enough, the new faith cannot be sufficiently perfected."[1] That was his dominant theme when he was called upon to pronounce judgement on this kind of thing. He did not want the faithful to light bonfires on the eve of 24 June, for "if they do not do this in actual honour of the demons, it is nevertheless done in the same fashion as it would be were such honour being rendered"—this though the honour was nominally being done to John the Baptist. "Yesterday evening the whole town glowed red with these stinking fires. If you care little for the scandal of religion, then at least think of the damage that is caused. We know of course that the whole thing was the work of young scalliwags, and these most certainly did not bother their heads about the summer solstice, but their elders should put a stop to it."[2]

On the actual feast many went to the sea in order there to baptize themselves—a practice which Augustine once used particularly stern words to forbid, although his people assured him that they did not take this self-baptism seriously, and merely did it to honour John the Baptist and the baptism of Christ. Yet because there was some murmuring in the town, because his priests had put some people who had been guilty of the practice under the ban of the Church, he took the precaution of warning his congregation some six months in advance.[3] He had to concede, however, that the pagan survivals had been given a certain modest Christian covering and that with every year they tended to become less noticeable.

A much more serious consideration was that there were still so many erroneous ideas on the meaning and use of the sacraments, so that a real Christian superstition was taking the place of the pagan one. And how could it be otherwise? The very real and strong faith of these simple people had expressed itself, as it was bound to do, in very primitive conceptions. In the world of late Antiquity, replete as it was with spiritual forces, with its heavens full of spirits, with the air between earth and moon crowded with demons and the stars guided by more spirits, and its whole cosmos like a huge many-souled animal—in such a world the boundary between matter and spirit was of necessity shadowy. When a fashionable theory tends to make light of the material world, material things tend inevitably to be regarded as mere shells and ultimately as the vessels and carriers of the spirit. In this way the purest idealism, if it is brought among the multitude in coarsened form, may quite easily turn into its opposite and lead to a kind of unconscious animism which is wholly in the service of man's lowest needs.

If the material *sacramenta* are channels for divine grace, so these primitive people argued, then they can never do any harm, but can be used for every purpose. It was the very faith in the effectiveness of the many *sacramenta*, which most Christians could hardly really tell apart from each other, that caused many people to regard these signs of spiritual grace as means for the securing of temporal ends. People saw in them "good" *remedia* which were entirely lawful to the Christian; they saw in them instruments of protection, and even looked upon them as a form of medicine which could be directly applied. In much the same way men were ready to ascribe spectacular improvements in the condition of the sick and similar happenings, which we might in our day quite possibly ascribe to the hearing of prayer, to the direct effect of a *sacramentum*; to the intervention of a saint, to the taking of advice miraculously given in a dream, or to the touching of a relic. Simple souls always like to translate highly spiritual realities into the concrete, and tend when so doing to think more about *sacramenta* and saints than about the distant majesty of God.

Augustine never made any mistake about the real merits of this simple faith, but he set himself against the very earthly frame of mind and the materialism that were here behind it—and that in the most determined fashion. He did not, of course, attack the wonderworking nature of the sacraments, but rather the brazenness of those who hoped for temporal advantages from them. This was avarice and carnality. It did not lie in the man to deny that the finger of God might manifest itself even in some trifling change of circumstance, but he could not sanction the conduct of people who tried to use the Gospels as a means of fortune-telling. That meant interpreting the divine oracles, which bear wholly on eternal things, in terms of temporal trivialities; although of course it was a much graver matter to make use of magic books for such a purpose.[4] Yet even Augustine was unwilling to forbid people to lay the Gospels on their heads if they had a headache, for it was at least something gained if they used the Gospels rather than the magic strips known as *ligaturae*. "But if they put it on their heads to heal their headaches they should also put it on their heart to heal it of its sins."[5] Augustine's Christians also had the habit of using the holy names from the Bible for this purpose, a practice of which he could as little approve as that of extracting oracles from the New Testament with the jab of a pin,[6] "because it is written that he who calls on the name of the Lord will be saved you must not think that this means that he will immediately be cured of fever, gout, pestilence and other bodily pains".[7]

We do not know whether the practice existed in Africa of using strips of papyrus with the conjuration "By the holy blood" as a means of blessing the house,[8] as was done in Egypt, or whether the Syrian custom obtained of using the initials $X.M.\Gamma.$ ("Christus, Michael, Gabriel") or alternately texts from the Bible, to fix up over the door as a protection. There are few apotropaic inscriptions to be found among the ruins of Africa.

Most definitely, however, he set himself against the misuse of the great *sacramenta* for unspiritual purposes. He knew of mothers who brought their children to the baptismal pool because they had ideas about some mysterious water-cure that would immunize them against disease and death, and not about the grace of their spiritual rebirth.[9] Many looked upon the baptismal pool as a vessel of miraculous water, not unlike the spring near the sanctuary of St. Menas which was close by, and not unlike Lourdes of today. The water from the baptismal pool played a particular part in popular imagination; they swore by this pool as they did by the mysteries of the altar, and strange as it may sound, Augustine himself in his old age seems to have believed in some of the stories of sudden miraculous cures in the baptismal pool which current reports sometimes held to have taken place[10]—this despite his frequent protests to baptismal candidates against their all-too-worldly expectations of the results that baptism might bring. However, Augustine continued to preach at great length against all who requested baptism because they looked upon it as a form of physical medicine or as a leap into a sort of lucky fountain or even as a means of winning a bet.

It seems, moreover, not unlikely that he took part in the councils of Hippo in 393 and of Carthage in 397, when prohibitions were issued against putting a piece of eucharistic bread into a dead man's mouth, "for thus the Fathers justified their command—The Lord said, 'Take ye and eat', and the dead can neither take nor eat."[11] It is clear that the simple folk among the faithful wished to give their beloved dead the most sacred pledge that they had, to take along upon the long journey into the next world. Thus the body of Christ took the place of the coin that had once been given for paying Charon the Ferryman. Although it is uncertain whether the old house Communion still existed, people could still take away some of the altar-bread without exciting comment, and carry it home with them, and then use it as a thing that communicated the divine blessing. It was thus used in much the same manner as the Agnus Dei was used in the last century. It was carried on journeys as a protection against mishaps and as a form of viaticum against all eventualities. This was particularly true of people taking a voyage by sea, for the sea in those days was always perilous and shipwreck a very real possibility. Sometimes people sewed the Eucharist into their clothes; Satyrus, the favourite and as yet uninitiated brother of Ambrose, received it from some of his baptized fellow-travellers on the occasion of just such a shipwreck, "so that he should not depart this life without the Mystery". He had asked for it "not out of an inquisitive desire to see that which was kept secret but in order to assure the fortification of his faith. For this reason he had it bound in a kerchief which he tied about his neck, and having done this, he plunged into the sea. He did not even look around for a plank that might be floating past; all he had asked for were the weapons of the Faith."[12]

There are a number of such stories—such, for instance, as that of the Arian ship's captain who in an hour of extreme peril during a tornado renounced his errors and received the holy mysteries from the hands of a bishop who was carrying them with him, and who was his passenger.[13] Augustine himself tells of a pious mother and her five-year-old son Acacius who, as the son himself was later to tell, was born with good eyes but with the eyelids grown together. The mother did not want a doctor to operate on the child, but made a sort of dough of the holy bread and stuck it on the diseased eyelids like a plaster. The child was healed, and Augustine certainly has no criticism to make, though he leaves in some doubt whether the mother acted out of genuine piety, out of fear of the lancet, or from a desire to save the doctor's bill.[14] It is also possible that the woman's action is to be explained by the custom then prevailing of touching one's eyes with the holy gift before receiving the Eucharist. It is clear from some catechetical writings of Cyril that the faithful in Jerusalem would sanctify their eyes "by touching them with the holy body with a firm hand", taking great care, while doing so, not to drop a single crumb upon the ground. We also learn that after they had partaken of the chalice, which they did bending down as though in adoration, they afterwards touched their damp lips with their fingers and "sanctified" their eyes, forehead and other parts, with the fingers that had thus been moistened, which probably means that as they touched them they made the sign of the cross upon them. St. Gregory Nazianzen speaks of the mystically sealed eyelids of his mother Nonna.[15] Augustine never mentions this matter but since he shows no signs of taking exception to the manner in which the Eucharist was received, we must presume that he had no ground for objecting to it.

Visions

The people not only honoured the holy powers of the *sacramenta*, but clung unshakably to the belief in the intervention of ghosts and all manner of spirits. Holy objects had the power of radiating their influence unseen, but supernatural personalities intervened actively in human affairs and appeared visibly to certain people. The evil spirits came to destroy and to torture, the good angels and the martyrs came to help and to warn;[16] the souls of the dead could come for either purpose. They usually came to men in dreams. It had always been the belief of Antiquity that both gods and ghosts preferred to have their dealings with men in the twilit seclusion of dreamland. It is true that certain irrational insights were supposed to be granted to men when in a state of Dionysiac exaltation, and that raving oracular priestesses would proclaim mysterious and equivocal decisions at critical junctures of people's lives; usually, however, counsel from above came to men in their sleep, and there was a celebrated temple at which people would lie down to sleep, for the god to speak to them. An interpreter of dreams was always at hand in order to explain whatever dream might have been granted to them, and so men tended to return to their homes after such an experience with a new certainty in their hearts; the sick man knew what he had to do to get well, the doubter received direction as to the way he was to take. And precisely in this manner the dead spoke at their graves. The temples of Aesculapius had been closed or pulled down, the oracles were silent and the demons had been exposed as cheats, but the faith in the meaning of certain dreams remained, as had the habit of indulging in the "temple sleep" in certain holy places, and of waiting for a word or a vision from the saint concerned. It is no mere coincidence that Bishop Evodius should have asked Augustine's advice concerning a number of curious visions that had been seen in dreams by persons within his own house, dreams which were all ultimately fulfilled;[17] nor is it in any way remarkable that Monica's dreams should have been carefully recorded in the *Confessions*. Monica knew from a certain vision that she would live to see her son's conversion. On this she built as on a rock, and it was by reference to a dream that she comforted the rough seafaring folk during a storm. "We shall not be lost," she said, "for I know this from God." But she also showed plainly that she could distinguish between a trick of the imagination and a true inspiration from above, or a certain and definite premonition.[18]

The written recording and the interpretation of dreams was no easy matter for those who practised this branch of literature or for those who studied it. Centuries before Calderon, Christians were convinced that dreams are sometimes revelations from God and from his servants. Did not Holy Scripture frequently tell how just such messages from God were given in dreams, and did not the angels of God appear as often in dreams as they did in broad daylight? That there was sometimes intercourse between spirits and men was a fact that nobody who heard Holy Scripture read could possibly doubt; it was not without good reason that the good spirits were called *angeloi* or "messengers". The proclamation of the glad tidings had now for all time replaced the lying messages of Mercury and other demonic heralds.

The most noteworthy of these dream visions were, in the year 400, connected with the martyr-cult. It was in the basilicas of the martyrs that the sick lay down to sleep, and upon the graves of the saints that the saints themselves appeared to pilgrims to warn or bless them; and if their bones chanced to be neglected, it was in a dream that they would appear to some pious person and ask that a *mensa* should be erected to them and their name made famous. The two most famous discoveries of relics in Augustine's day both derived from visions; the first of these was the finding of the bodies of Gervase and Protase in the year 386 under the floor of a church in Milan, close to the graves of Nabor and Felix. Ambrose, who actually ordered the digging to be begun at this place and was the one who found the relics (which he then had transferred to the Ambrosiana), spoke of nothing more than a premonition which had guided him in the matter, but the people immediately spoke of a vision in which Ambrose had received instructions to begin the excavations, and the bishop said nothing either to confirm or deny this.[19]

The second such incident was the discovery of the relics of St. Stephen and his companions in the year 415. This resulted from a vision of Gamaliel, who twice appeared to the priest Lucius of Caphergamala.[20] In both instances Augustine unhesitatingly believed that the visions in question were genuine. He is continually referring to them and makes them the theme of one of his sermons. There are also edifying accounts woven into his writings and sermons of various other manifestations that took place at night.[21]

In such accounts we hear the voice of the practical pastor of souls. We happen, however, to know exactly what, in the year 421, were his views of such occurrences, whether these took the form of dreams or of visions by daylight. In this year of 421 he gave to Paulinus of Nola, at the latter's request, a detailed account of his views on the possibility and nature of such visions and their different forms. He did this in the little book to which allusion has already been made and which bears the title *Our Duty to Care for the Dead*.[22] He was at that time sixty-seven years of age and the way he puts the matter makes it worth citing the passage in its entirety, especially in view of the examples he gives.

He begins by distinguishing, as is his habit, between what happens in the natural order and what happens in miraculous fashion, "although God is present in nature in that he permits it to continue to exist and, contrariwise, does not eliminate nature by his miracles".[23]

He divides the natural manifestations into three groups. The first comprises visions seen in dreams; it would indeed be presumptuous to deny that the dead have occasionally appeared to the living—in order to show where their unburied bones were to be found and either pitifully to request burial or imperiously to demand it. This does not, however, mean that they are really concerned about the matter, let alone tortured by it, or even that they are aware of their own appearances to men. Even the living can appear to others in dreams without being aware of the fact.[24] How is this possible? I should like to assume, he says, that it is through the power of such angels as have charge of these matters. For we are here concerned with something that is essentially good—either with the comforting of relatives or with the inculcation of the duty of *pietas*. Alternatively, dreams and visions can be sent to mislead us, as in the case of Aeneas, who, "in the poetical language of lies, professed to have seen the nether regions", and who was thus confirmed in his delusion that the soul can find no rest as long as the body is unburied.[25] Now, human power of perception is so weak that when people see one of the dead in a dream they immediately think that they have seen his soul, while if they should dream of some acquaintance who is still among the living such a thought would never occur to them. In this latter case they think it is simply the "phantom", the image, of the person concerned. The strange thing is that this illusory image sometimes reveals things that really come true. Once when a certain Milanese had received a legacy and was suddenly dunned for one of the testator's alleged debts, his father appeared to him in a dream and said: "Do not pay it! I have already settled the matter. The receipt is in such and such a place." And indeed that receipt was found at the place indicated. While I still lived in Milan myself, he continues, I appeared in a dream to my sometime pupil Eulogius the Orator in Carthage. He, after preparing one of his lectures, was for a long time unable to sleep because there was an obscure passage in Cicero which he could not understand. In that dream I resolved his difficulty. What the explanation of the thing can be, I do not know—but why should it be different from that of any other dream?[26]

The second group of manifestations, he continues, are those by which the insane are afflicted, for these are continually speaking in broad daylight with persons or things which, they imagine, are actually present.[27] A third kind is to be found in that mysterious state of unconsciousness that is deeper than sleep. I once experienced this, he says, in the neighbourhood of Hippo. A peasant named Curma who was on the local council of the *municipium Tulliense* and also a catechumen, lay unconscious for days and gave no other sign of life save that he breathed very feebly. When he came to himself he said somebody should go at once to Curma the Smith, for this man was dying, now that he had himself returned to life. He had heard it himself "over yonder". Over yonder they had said: "Not Curma the Councillor, but Curma the Smith", and indeed the smith had just died. The living Curma had, however, in his state of unconsciousness, seen many of the living and of the dead in the world beyond, and also a country estate where a priest had said to him: "Go to Hippo, for the bishop there is just baptizing"—and then he had seen Hippo, and also myself and the basilica and the baptismal church, and had, in the spirit, experienced his own baptism. Finally, he had been in paradise, and when he left that place he had been told: "Go and be baptized if thou wouldst come to this place of the blessed. Be baptized by Augustine!" and when he replied: "But I am baptized already" he received the reply: "No, thou didst only see this in a vision. Now go and be truly baptized." And so, when he had come to himself, Curma went unnoticed into the town. Easter was not far off and he was enrolled among the *competentes*, though he was silent on this matter and did not attract any particular attention. After Low Sunday he returned again to his village. It so happens, Augustine goes on, that I did not hear about this matter till some years later, though my informant was somebody who knew the man well. Then I had him come to me and personally went into the matter.[28] As to the explanation of the rest of it, any man can of course believe what he pleases, but my own view is that it is not the dead but the angels who are behind these manifestations, whether these be sent to exhort or to warn us, or to comfort us or help us; for if it were truly the dead who were here concerned, then they would be mixing themselves up in our affairs everywhere. They would simply be unable to leave us alone and would be continually seeking to speak with us. "Then my own dear mother, to say nothing of others, would never have left me alone for a single night, for she travelled by water and by land to be near me. It is, after all, unthinkable that her happier present state has made her hard-hearted"—so that she would no longer wish to comfort her son, whom, while she lived, she could never bear to see unhappy. No, he says; here the words of Psalm xxvi apply: "For my father and my mother have left me but thou, Lord, hast taken me up."[29] Neither our parents nor any others among the dead have any more care for us than the Patriarchs had care for their people. It is as Isaiah said: "Abraham knows us no more."[30] They see the misery of those that belonged to them as little as did King Josiah.[31] The dead are in a place where they neither know nor care what we do and where also they neither see their own graves nor know what has become of their mortal remains. Even the rich glutton, who was so full of care for his brethren, knew not what they did, and Abraham, who, according to the Prophets, no longer knew his own, had to be instructed by the beggar Lazarus. No, they care for us as did this rich man for his brethren, knowing nothing, yet passionately begging.[32] How, then, do the dead hear of what is happening to us? Perhaps, he says, they hear something of it from the dead that have newly arrived; but above all they must learn of it from the angels who minister to them, in so far as God wills this, for these angels go betwixt the living and the dead, and it was these same angels who carried Lazarus away from the dogs and placed him in Abraham's bosom. As Paul was removed into paradise, so also the dead can be removed into the company of the living. Even Holy Scripture testifies to something of this kind in the case of Samuel, who, as Jesus Son of Sirach tells us, continued to prophesy after his death, though there are some who do not recognize this book of the Bible, and believe that it was a demon who appeared in the cave of the Witch of Endor under the guise of a man of God.[33] Nevertheless, there are other passages which prove this point, such as the appearance of Moses on Mount Tabor.[34] So much for the natural manifestations. There are, however, says Augustine, others. Martyrs have also appeared to men. Your own Felix of Nola appeared at the siege of Nola by the Vandals—a fact confirmed by reliable witnesses. Such manifestations come from God and quite otherwise than through the natural order.[35] Yet how the martyrs help those that honour them, or whether they appear in several places at once or only at their *memoriae*, whether they merely intercede for us in a general way or know us, who pray to them, individually, and are actually cognizant of our personal problems—these are questions, says Augustine, to which I do not know the answer. Through the service of his angels God can hear the prayers that we make together, and can hear them how, when and where he pleases. But he is particularly well able to do this through the *memoriae* of his saints, for he knows how these build up the faith in Christ (a special tribute, this, to the great builder Paulinus). But this is too deep a question, he adds, and I am not competent to deal with it—indeed, it is too abstract to be dealt with at all. Therefore I will not commit myself as to whether prayers are heard through the personal presence of saints, through the mediation of angels or through both things together.[36] Does then nobody know the truth about this matter? I should hesitate to say this, but, continues Augustine, we should ask somebody who has the gift of the discernment of spirits. I know such a person at least from hearsay. It is the monk John, who prophesied the end of the civil war to Theodosius, and who also promised a woman whom, as a monk, he could not receive, that he would appear to her that very night, and actually did appear as he had promised. I have heard this from a highly-placed personality whose word in such a matter must be taken seriously. I would like to put this whole question to this same John, who, so they say, is always ready to allow himself to be questioned in detail. Further, he has the gift of prophecy, and if he really appeared to this woman and it was not merely a phantom of himself, then he is also a worker of miracles. Finally, I would ask him whether it is not perhaps the angels who harry the demons at the *memoriae*, for this really happens. In

Milan the demons have called both the living and the dead by name, Ambrose being among them, though he was not present and knew nothing of the matter. I assume that the angels brought this about, for the martyrs in their exalted rest must be occupied by quite another spectacle.[37]

He concludes that these manifestations, therefore, all appear in dreams—that is to say, in the imagination of the person concerned. From other passages it is clear that Augustine assumes the possibility of visions occurring in a waking state or in one of ecstasy. If these come from good spirits they are true revelations and can be compared with the messages of angels in the stories of the saints. For the angels appear in three different ways, as we can see: bodily—*solida corpulentia*—in the case, for instance, of the one who wrestled with Jacob at the stream Jabbok; or by means of an inner voice; or in dreams. On how this comes about Augustine refuses to express an opinion, "for there would be no point in trying to determine by enquiry what one can pass over without incurring the imputation of presumption".[38] Finally he takes into account visions of a purely spiritual kind—that is to say, conditions of great internal concentration, a "contemplation with the sharp edge of the soul" which can be heightened till it attains to the actual contemplation of God himself, though here on earth such experience has only been granted to Moses and possibly to St. Paul.

Ordinary visions in dreams, however, were at that time so numerous that they were accounted as no more than a fairly common form of edifying experience. Many of those concerned were persons in his own circle of acquaintance. His friend Bishop Evodius tells him, in a particularly beautiful letter, of his secretary, a refined and quiet young man who had formerly been a stenographer in the office of the proconsul but had later gone over to the bishop's residence and become wholly absorbed in Holy Scripture. He was in the habit of reading to his bishop till late into the night and of putting questions to him while so doing. He had now died at the age of twenty-two. His last words were cries of joy from the Psalms, and his last gesture was to try and raise his hand to his mouth in order to make the sign of the cross, though his strength was insufficient to do so. After his death, a pious widow saw a silver palace which a crowd of widows and virgins were preparing for him under the direction of a certain deacon who was also dead. She also heard an old man tell two persons who were dressed in white to carry the body to heaven; and suddenly, when he had been taken up, roses blossomed on his grave.[39] His death had been foretold to this young man in a dream by a former comrade and fellow-stenographer who had died some eight months before. After his own death this young man appeared to yet another of his colleagues and told him that he would soon fetch his own father, who was a priest and had sought comfort in a monastery after the burial of his son. And again the prediction proved true, for the priest died a few days later. Then men remembered that on his deathbed this young man had kissed his father three times and had said, "Let us go together! God be praised!"

In this same letter Evodius tells that a priest had seen whole crowds of the dead coming out of the baptismal chapel in the night in the form of shining figures, and gliding into the main body of the church to pray there. Everywhere where the dead lay buried, but particularly in the basilicas, there was rustling and murmuring at night and one could hear loud praying. How was this possible? Did it really happen that one saw the dead outside of dreams, and did their souls on occasion truly assume a visible form made up of air or aether?[40] It is clear from the stories told that Augustine, like his friend, could derive edification from such incidents. He had no hesitation in preaching about the behaviour of demons at the *memoriae* of the saints, and assured his hearers that they avoided the sanctuaries as though these were plague-spots, and that they flew out of the mouths of possessed persons with the cry: "I am on fire!"[41] On the graves of Gervase and Protase in Milan they cried out to Ambrose to spare them, though the latter was not present.[42] Augustine clearly looked upon the holy graves as a place where the good angels wrestled with the demons, and the demons were nothing other than the satellites of the old gods; indeed, they were the gods themselves.

To this extent, indeed, Augustine was ready to concede that the *memoriae*, as places of supernatural influence and supernatural encounters, had filled the gap left by the temples of the demons. At one time the demons had spat gall and poison against the Christians and through the persons of their idolatrous priests the mob had shed the blood of the martyrs in torrents. Now they whimpered helplessly around the graves of their victims. Once they had enmeshed the whole world in the deceitful net of dreams, signs and visions; now the net was torn and see!—in their place the martyrs appeared, and in their dreams people learned the truth. When the heathen insult us (so wrote Augustine in the *City of God*) because we have allegedly replaced the cult of the gods with the adoration of dead human beings, they forget that many of their own gods are dead and deified human beings. When Hermes Trismegistus had mournfully prophesied that the day would come when in holy Egypt, the land crowded with temples, people would only honour corpses, then it was a demon that inspired him to say this, for the demons knew very well that the martyrs would carry off the victory over them. Their oracles were silent while the saints, though also silent, nevertheless spoke in that silence. They hated the *memoriae* where the martyrs forced confessions from them through the mouths of the possessed, exactly as happened in the Gospel, and where they tortured them and ultimately drove them out.[43]

We must not forget that in the year 400 Christians still lived wholly within the picture of the ancient world, though the spell which that world had once inspired had been completely broken. No demons, no powers, no spirits, not even death itself, could any longer separate men from the love of Christ, and men's fate lay in the hands of the Father of our Lord Jesus Christ. The devils still pursued their crafty ways on earth, but were impotent against the cross. For all that, the cosmos was still full of sinister powers, and the demons remained "embittered stirrers-up of unrest". The older it grew, the less the world resembled the cruel machine of Lucretius; but also, the older it grew, the more it seemed like a thing in which spirits served and which was filled with personal being. When it became dark and the hour of sleep approached and some vision of terror rose up before men in their dreams, or if somebody was inexplicably afflicted by God with some infirmity, or if nature was disturbed by a violation of her own laws, then people did not think of the subconscious, or of mental sickness, or of the blind forces of nature, but of highly personal powers which might be either friendly or hostile and which in either case were in no way to be underestimated. Even Augustine, who was so constantly and continuously filled with God and whose thoughts were so much occupied with him, could not entirely withdraw from the power of this conception of a world that seemed always to be something halfway between matter and spirit. When he thought of the reality which he knew in all its innumerable manifestations, with its ceaseless alternation from life to death and from death to life, with its precarious equilibrium in virtue and what were often its enormous excesses in evil, then he could not feel other than that the world, though redeemed, was still the theatre of a violent war between the angels and the hordes of demons. The traces of heathenism which were still persistently visible, despite the abolition of the temple cults, were for Augustine the manifest signs of the continuance of an unseen struggle between the two cities, the City of God and that of the demons. True, he believed that the advantage was with the angels; his world has more similarity with that of Newman than with that of Antiquity. For him the spiritual reality was the decisive thing, yet at the same time he looked upon the material world entirely as a vessel, stage and instrument of spiritual powers. The divine ordering of things permitted both angels and demons to make use of this material apparatus. For this reason both could appear in dreams and reveal themselves in visible signs. It was in this way, too, that he understood the appearances of those sent by God in the Bible. It was thus he construed St. Paul's words about spiritual powers and principalities and the evil spirits of the air. For spirits were clearly localized, for Augustine as for the rest of Antiquity; that was the general view, and no one doubted it. Even the artists knew that the angels who appeared as envoys from God had their home in the fiery immaterial void of heaven, above the crystal sphere of the fixed stars, the place of ethereal light known as the *empyreum*. The mosaic workers who in 431, the year after Augustine's death, were asked to depict the story of our Lord's childhood years on the triumphal arch of the Esquiline basilica in Rome, actually portrayed the angels who appear to Mary and Joseph and the Magi, and provide a guard of honour for the divine Child, as appearing out of the upper fire of heaven; their hair and faces are still bathed in the red glow of the aether, which they have brought with them on their flight through the heavenly spheres from the empyrean. And at the same time their colleagues in Rome and Naples were portraying our Lord with a cruciform cloud of aether round his head (Vergil's *nubes divina*), and the blue-glass sphere of heaven, with its concentric globes, small and twinkling at his feet—like the footstool mentioned in the Psalms (Plate 12).[44]

MIRACLES

The great mass of the people honoured the *memoriae* as, above all, places where bodily miracles took place. The famous sanctuaries soared up on their horizon like so many minor heavens. These were the places where mighty powers came down from heaven to earth—tiny, still vaults lit by lamps and hidden away under flowers and curtains and offerings, where the sighs and entreaties of the pilgrims rose unceasingly, or vast churches resounding with the murmur of prayers and echoing with the halting steps of people who would finally throw themselves down on to the marble floor, beat their foreheads on the ground and cover the grille of the *transenna* over the grave with kisses. These basilicas were centres for spiritual powers, strongholds against devils, places for prayer, meeting-places, festival-places, but above all places where miracles took place, for the chief thing that everyone came to them for was bodily and spiritual healing. The ancient world was peppered with such places, where people came to pray for help whenever they were in any kind of need —not only really pious people, like those who today would go on a pilgrimage to Lourdes or Fatima, but the sort of people who today would go and see a specialist or go to some special place for treatment. The letters and sermons of the outstanding intellectuals of the day—Chrysostom, Jerome, Paulinus of Nola—vie with each other in their uninhibited descriptions of the remarkable scenes that took place at the burial-places of the saints. Devils could be heard through the mouths of human beings—howling like wolves, barking like dogs, roaring like bulls and lions, hissing like snakes. People possessed could be seen spinning round like dervishes and bending over backwards until their heads touched the ground, women would stand on their hands with their legs in the air without their skirts falling down... All this would be repeated and written down here, there and everywhere until no-one really knew who had seen what, where "tamen spectata profabor" as Paulinus said. But who had actually seen it?[45]

For a long time Augustine paid no attention to what went on amongst these hordes of "enthusiastic", or stolidly submissive, or—for the most part—merely curious pilgrims. In his early days he had been convinced that miracles no longer happened. Not long after he had been baptized, he observed that now that the Church had spread over the whole earth, "the miracles of earlier times are by divine disposition no longer permitted. This is to prevent the spirit from going on seeking after visible things. If miracles were to become an everyday occurrence they would cease to affect human beings, whereas in the early days they inspired them by their novelty."[46]

Again, about thirteen years later, he said in a sermon on the healing of the blind man in Jericho: "Today the dead do not rise again; instead, souls that lay dead in living corpses are restored to life." Today, he says, eyes that have lost their sight and ears that have lost their hearing are no longer opened, and no dead are restored to life; but in countless cases inner eyes and ears are being opened to the real truth, and innumerable are the people who are being resurrected to a new kind of life. Therefore it is not right to rate those earlier days higher than the present, for spiritual healing is more valuable than any healing of the body.[47] These words are said in praise of the *apertio aurium*, inner "enlightenment" and rebirth through initiation into Christianity. They have their roots in words used in the liturgy, and we also meet the idea in the iconography of sarcophagi of a slightly earlier date; but their chief interest is that they show how Augustine cannot really imagine any actual miracle occurring in his own day.

By the time he was forty-five he was talking quite differently. Then, when two of his household were accusing each other of having committed a certain serious misdemeanour, and neither was able to prove the other guilty, he sent them both to the grave of St. Felix of Nola to be judged by God, for according to him everyone knew that there, as at the graves of Gervase and Protase in Italy, thieves and liars as well as devils were "forced to confess" as a result of "terrible judgements from God"—and moreover, Paulinus was there to exert the necessary control.[48] And it is quite clear, especially after 415, that Augustine had no hesitation in regarding the answers given to prayers at the recognized *memoriae* as genuine miracles. The long succession of miracles that accompanied the entry of the relics of St. Stephen into Italy seems to have settled the matter for him more than anything else. He, the people's bishop, at last began to realize what the people themselves had known all along: that God still remained wonderful in his saints. In his later years he apologized for his earlier scepticism. He described how, when Ambrose was taking the relics of Gervase and Protase into Italy, he himself saw a blind man touch the shrine with his handkerchief and at once be healed, as though for a sign against the Arians, who at that very time were lying in wait for Ambrose. In those days, he says, he had still not been baptized, and passed by such prodigious happenings regardless. Now, he would like to make up for his laxity.[49] In the *Retractations* he expressly repudiates his earlier assertion that miracles had ceased after apostolic times.[50]

At about the same time he was describing in detail, in the last book of the *City of God*, miracles he had come across in his own circle, or knew of by hearsay from people he regarded as trustworthy; and it is worth considering the context into which he introduces these signs, and the use he makes of them.

The last book of the *City of God* is a genuine finale. With it, the whole work, like clothing settling into broad folds as someone sits down, ends in the calm and peace of the unending Sabbath. This city, after one final judgement, has ultimately been separated from the devil's city and now harbours all the company of the saints, at peace, body and soul, in their Lord. But even here the dream of the visionary has to give way to polemic, and here this is concerned not so much with the Transfiguration itself as with the problem exercising all the thinkers of the day, as to how earthly bodies could be taken up into the highest heaven. How could an earthly husk dare to pollute the *empyreum*? What could a heap of dust, the dross of the cosmos, be doing in that fiery heaven, on those purest heights? How could such dregs be transfigured, and a prison shutting out the light become a home of light? This made a mockery of the teachings of whole generations of wise men, and contradicted the established order of the old world-picture. For by its mere weight any earthly element was bound to fall down, down through air and water, and come to rest at the lowest place it could find.[51]

Augustine shows that these objections are quite arbitrary and abstract. Earthly elements can undergo a metamorphosis and change into one another. It is just as possible for an earthly body, changed in this way, to exist in the fiery heaven as it is for fire to exist upon the earth. Do not volcanoes spit fire from the bowels of the earth, and cannot fire be struck from stone? As the fire of the highest heaven neither smokes nor scorches nor destroys, so even an earthly body can put off its mortal nature up there, and still remain a body.

After this theoretical refutation of the opposing arguments he passes on to his real proof, the only really satisfactory one: the fact of the resurrection of our Lord's body and its ascension into heaven. This is a real miracle, the greatest of all miracles. It both transcends and buttresses all the other miracles that help to support revelation. And anyone who is not prepared to believe in this miracle has to try to explain another one, the fact that the whole world does in fact believe it; for anyone who is not prepared to believe what the whole world believes is himself something of a miracle. And this second miracle becomes all the greater by reason of a third miracle, the fact that our Lord's ascension into heaven was announced at a time when the general level of culture was high, when people had a sharp eye for the incredible—and, furthermore, was announced by very simple people. And these people were only believed because they could back up what they said by signs. Here Augustine refers to the way the Apostles spoke "with tongues", to the healing of the sick with a single word, or with such things as a kerchief, or Peter's shadow. Now, this fourfold interlinked chain of miracles binds the whole world to the fact that our own flesh has been assumed into heaven, so that we ourselves have already in principle been resurrected. And so the world believes, not because it has been convinced by human argumentation, but because, faced with the power of the divine signs, it has had to own up to being defeated —which means, in fact, that it believes on the basis of the authority of God himself.[52]

But, people ask, why do these miraculous signs no longer occur? Augustine answers: "I might perhaps say that their aim was to bring the world to belief, and the world does now believe, and the unbeliever has become an unbelievable exception and is himself something of a miracle. But I will not say this, because unbelievers do not in fact accept the miracles related in the Bible. Yet why don't they? It may indeed appear incredible, and incapable of proof, that our Lord should have ascended into heaven and now sits at God's right hand, but this has in fact become credible through other incredible but at the same time solidly attested visible facts, and is, moreover, believed throughout the world. These other miracles are all set down in Holy Scripture—the most authentic book in the world—with full details as to the why and the wherefore. The great mass of the people have not only heard about them, but have accepted them." "At first they were made widely known so as to awaken people's faith, but now they are becoming even more widely known because of the faith they have in fact awakened. They are read out to the people as testifying to the Faith, but they would not get read out if they were not already believed. And today miracles still go on happening in our Lord's name, through the sacraments he instituted and through the prayers and *memoriae* of his saints."[53]

In the last two sentences one link in the chain of reasoning is missing. Augustine seems to be arguing as follows. Contemporary miracles take place in the name of the heavenly, risen Christ, and if Christ had not risen and ascended into heaven they would not be possible. Further, they take place through the medium of his sacraments, that is to say, through ceremonies like baptism and Holy Communion, which symbolize his resurrection and transfigured humanity, and transform them into present realities. Finally, they take place through the medium of martyrs—that is to say, people who by their death testified to the Resurrection and the transfigured life.

To the question, how the current miracles actually come about, Augustine gives no answer. He will not discuss whether God does them directly or through his ministering angels. And as to the question whether, in this latter case, only the angels are involved, or whether the souls of the martyrs are involved too, and whether the saints can only pray, or whether they play a more active part—all this, he says, he cannot decide upon, as it is by no means apparent from what actually happens. It is something beyond the grasp of mortal beings. But however that may be, the current miracles provide eloquent testimony to the Faith that preaches the resurrection of the body.[54]

Augusine is also of the opinion that the miracles related by the old writers in connection with their gods and temples—miracles he never doubted for a moment—though not to be compared with the ones that take place at the *memoriae*, may, nevertheless, have a deceptive similarity to them; for instance, the miracle of the staff performed by the Egyptian magician, which was similar to the one performed by Moses.[55] But just as Moses put the Egyptians to shame, so the saints surpass the devils. One only has to compare the results in the two cases, to see which is sham and which reality; in the one case empty boasting, fake sacrifices, priests serving indecent gods, self-divinization; in the other, witness to the truth, praise of the power of God, and the establishment of the true faith in the one God, who was also Christ. Whatever redounds to God's honour is good, whatever works against it or has no connection with it —like empty curiosity, for example—is either a sham or demonic deceit. The devils do their miracles so as to be regarded as gods, the martyrs to honour God. This is an excellent criterion for distinguishing between spirits; it had been used as early as the second century by the Fathers of the Church.[56]

The current miracles are naturally not as well known as the ones in the Bible, for they have not been made known to the general public. Usually even the neighbours of anyone thus favoured do not come to hear of it, especially in a big city, and if a miracle does get talked about it has no authoritative power, even amongst Christians.[57]

Augustine frankly regrets this; the fact that indifference and ingratitude were as great amongst the favoured ones as amongst their fellow-citizens was to him incomprehensible and unforgivable. It was for this reason that he took such great care that everything that took place within his own district was properly recorded and made generally known. What the priests of Serapis had done in the dim and distant past with their oracles and cures at the Canopus sanctuary near Alexandria, and the priests of Aesculapius with the miracles at Epidaurus, he now did in Hippo: the facts should be saved from oblivion and no distortion allowed by mere rumour. In this the old critical intellectual appears again for a moment. In 424, when the *cella* that was being erected in honour of St. Stephen near the cathedral was completed, he began to keep a record of the miracles that took place there, and in fact he took down statements, or *libelli*. The *libellus* was written down by a *notarius* or, if he could write, by the person who had been cured. It was signed in the presence of the bishop, provided, in certain circumstances, with the testimony of witnesses, and read out in church at the appointed time.[58] Augustine publicized this scheme successfully among the local bishops, and within two years he had collected no less than sixty such statements in Hippo alone. In Calama, Possidius had even more; there was a *memoria* to Stephen there, too.[59] In Uzalis, which contained the oldest sanctuary to St. Stephen in Africa, no such records were collected at first; so, with Evodius' agreement, Augustine once asked a woman of Carthage who had been the subject of a miracle there to write a report on it herself, which she willingly did.[60] Later, a list of records seems to have been made here too, for we still have a copy of a book of miracles connected with the church in Uzalis, written by Evodius.[61]

The Miracle Record

Most of the twenty-five miracles which Augustine described in the twenty-second book of the *City of God*[62] take place in and around Hippo and in Uzalis, and are probably taken from the list of miracles. Persons and places are clearly specified. Augustine himself was directly acquainted with some of these miracles, but all, without exception, he seems to find uncommonly edifying—as, more than a thousand years later, did Peter Canisius and Bellarmine.

In some cases no more is involved than answers to prayers of the usual kind. One story, of the healing of a lawyer, Innocentius, with whom he was staying in Carthage in 388, he describes, not without humour, as an eye-witness. Innocentius had had a lot of trouble with a number of anal fistulas, which had had to be cut out. When it was discovered that the doctors had overlooked one, and that this, as his own doctor immediately pointed out to him, would have to come out too, he was so enraged that he first of all sent the surgeons packing, and then summoned a specialist from Alexandria. When this gentleman arrived and agreed with Innocentius' own doctor, but refused to go on with the operation without the help of the local surgeons, for whose earlier work he expressed great admiration, Innocentius cursed the whole pack of them, but did not care to send the gentleman from Alexandria away. Beside himself with anxiety, he suddenly decided that this time he would be bound to die under the scalpel. On the night before the operation the house was like a morgue, and Alypius and Augustine were hard put to it to calm the sobbing servants. Around the anxious victim sat the usual visitors—Bishop Saturninus of Uzalis, a priest, a handful of deacons from Carthage, including the future prelate Aurelius—all of whom did their best to talk to the patient and promised to be present at the operation the following morning. A general prayer was said, but the man collapsed so utterly and sobbed so heartbrokenly that Augustine himself was unable to join in—I don't know whether the others were similarly put off, he says—and instead, thought to himself: "Lord, if you will not hear this prayer, what prayer will you ever hear?" The bishop gave his blessing, and everyone went off to bed.

Then comes the remarkable scene that took place the following morning. All the clergy are gathered round the bed; the man lies there on his stomach, shivering, and the dread instruments—*tremenda ferramenta*—glitter in the surgeons' hands. The bandage is taken off, the specialist takes a look, puts out his hand—can feel nothing: the fistula has closed up and is covered by a scab. The tears of joy and shouts of praise were well-nigh indescribable, says our reporter. All this is not presented as any kind of satire on the usual comfort handed out to the sick, or on the medical profession, but as a proof of faith.[63]

Other answers to prayer Augustine described more solemnly. I know a bishop, he writes, who once prayed for a young man he had never seen who was possessed by a devil, and the devil at once left him. Perhaps Augustine himself was the bishop? In Hippo he also knew a nun who was freed from a devil by rubbing herself with an ointment that a priest had wetted with his tears while he was praying.[64] One day a very distinguished gentleman sent a request to the priests of Hippo, asking them to get rid of devils who were doing a great deal of harm to the slaves and livestock on his country estate. Augustine himself happened to be away, so a priest went off to the villa, offered up a Mass there, and prayed as hard as he could; and the trouble ceased. By way of self-protection, the master of the house had hung a little bag of Jerusalem earth up in his bedroom, but now that the trouble was over he was too awestruck to keep it, and some time later, when Augustine visited the area with his colleague, Bishop Maximinus, the former Donatist, the gentleman asked them to come and see him, and offered to bury the precious keepsake on the premises and build a chapel over it. The two bishops had no objection, the chapel was built, and soon afterwards a crippled young peasant boy was healed there.[65] Soil from the Holy Land was much sought after in Africa, as is clear from the inscriptions on a number of *mensae*. Is it not paradoxical, says the bishop in a letter, that the Donatists, who detest the whole of the East, including the Holy Land, and would like to confine the Church to Africa, nevertheless deeply honour any soil from Palestine?[66]

The waters of baptism also worked many miracles. Cripples recovered their power of movement from it. A former revue artiste from Curubis was cured not only of his lameness but of a swelling in the scrotum; Augustine, not satisfied with the reports of eyewitnesses, asked him to come and see him personally in Hippo.[67] We are told, again, of a distinguished lady of Carthage who suffered from cancer of the breast. Her doctor had decided upon the second of Hippocrates' two methods of treatment—which were, amputation, and letting the complaint run its course—so that the lady herself was simply praying to get better. She was told in a dream to go to the baptistery at Easter, and install herself amongst the serving matrons on the women's side of the church, and ask the first woman who emerged from the baptismal water to make the sign of the cross over the affected part. This she did, and was immediately cured, to the boundless amazement of her doctor.[68] Then there is the story of the doctor suffering from gout who, shortly before he was baptized, dreamed that frizzy-haired young negroes—devils, of course—were trying to get him not to let himself be baptized that year, at the same time stamping on his feet and causing him unbearable pain. Nevertheless, he did get baptized; as a reward for which, when he was in the basin he was relieved, not only of his more recent pains, but also of his gout.[69]

All this, in Augustine's view, reveals the power of prayer and the sacraments; but the lion's share of the miracles is due to martyrs' relics. One such miracle took place in the solitary little chapel dedicated to SS. Gervase and Protase that stood on the Victorian estate about twenty miles out of Hippo. A boy had been attacked by epilepsy—"had caught a devil"—while grooming his horse, and had been carried unconscious into the cool interior of the chapel and left there. Towards evening the lady of the house went along to the chapel with her two maidservants and a few nuns, to sing Vespers as usual. All at once the boy recovered, put his arms round the altar and began to emit strange hollow noises; whereupon the devil began to yell for mercy. He confessed, screaming, how and where he had fastened upon him, and said that he must now let him go free, and would remove himself from him limb by limb. He struggled out of him and vanished. The noise brought people running up from all sides and they found the boy calmly standing up, the only thing wrong with him being that one of his eyes had jumped out of its socket and "seemed to be hanging down on his cheek by a slender little vein as though it was growing on a root, and the pupil instead of being black had turned quite white." They were talking about sending for a doctor when one of the boy's friends thought: "If God can drive the devil away by the prayers of the saints, then he can give this boy his eye back too." Whereupon he pressed the eye back into place, bound it up with his handkerchief, left it like that for a week —and then found the eye was quite healed. And many other sick people got well at the same place.[70]

The sanctuaries in Hippo come into the picture too. An old tailor, Florentius, who was a poor but religious man, had lost his only overcoat (*casula*), and he went to the *memoria* to the Twenty Martyrs and prayed very audibly for a new one. Nor did he forget to mention the price, with the result that a number of urchins who had been watching him heard this and went running after him shouting, "He's praying for five hundred *folles*." But on the very same day—and with the aid of his tormenting spirits—he caught a tremendous fish that had been thrown up on to the beach by the tide, and sold it to the cook Catosus for three hundred *folles*. Not only that, but Catosus brought him a ring that he had found in the fish's belly, which was worth more than the remaining two hundred *folles*, and he handed it to the good little tailor with the words: "Just look how the Twenty have set you up in clothes!"[71]

Nearly all the other miracles centre round St. Stephen. In Aquae Tibilitanae a blind woman was led to the bishop whilst he was taking the relics to the *memoria*. She laid a wreath on the casket containing the relics, picked it up again, passed it over her eyes, and could see.[72] In Siniti, near Hippo, Bishop Lucillus had disappear a tumour that was due to be cut out by the doctor, during a procession with his new relic.[73] (The accounts of both these miracles can still be read today in the Nocturns for 3 August.) In Calama a resident Spanish priest was cured of the stone. Later, he had a serious illness and seemed to have died; his thumbs had already been bound up when someone laid his shirt on the *memoria*, and then back on his body, whereupon he woke to life again. Two men suffering from gout were also cured, one of them having previously been told in a dream what he had to do.[74] The same place witnessed a moving little episode concerning an old heathen aristocrat for whom the Church was like a red rag to a bull, and who was in danger of dying unbaptized. His son-in-law, after being gruffly dismissed from the bedside of the dying man, turned as a last refuge to the *memoria*, and there "with tears and in unfeigned love of God" implored him at this last hour to change his father-in-law's mind. As he was leaving he noticed flowers on the altar, and took a few of them away with him and pushed them surreptitiously under the dying man's pillow while he was asleep. As soon as the invalid woke up he shouted, "Fetch the bishop!" When the bishop failed to turn up (he happened to have come to see me, says Augustine), a priest went along instead and the man died baptized, sighing: "Lord Jesus, receive my spirit!"—thus wonderfully repeating the words of his intercessor Stephen, whom he had never even known about.[75] On the Audurus estate, a little boy was playing by the *memoria* when he was run over by an ox-wagon. He first went into convulsions and then seemed to have died, but his mother took him into the chapel, and there he recovered consciousness and was perfectly all right.[76] On another piece of property, known as Caspaliana, a nun was lying on her deathbed. Her tunic was taken into the chapel, and she passed away; but when her parents laid the garment on the *memoria* and came back to her and covered her over with it, life returned to her body.[77] The same thing happened in Hippo itself in connection with the young daughter of Bassus the Syrian. While he was on his knees in the cathedral, praying with his daughter's dress in his hands, his slaves came along, intending to tell him that she was already dead. They were restrained from doing so just in time by friends of the household; but when he was on his way back to the house he heard the wail of the mourning from afar. But the dress made the child arise again, like a second *"Talitha kumi"*.[78] In Hippo, too, the following event occurred. His neighbours went along to pay their last respects to a cashier's son who was lying on his bier, and someone suggested that the child should be rubbed for one last time with oil from the lamp at the *memoria*—whereupon he came back to life.[79] The *vir tribunitius* Eleusinus (whom we have already come across as the founder of a monastery) laid his little boy, who had lost all signs of life, on the *memoria* to St. Stephen in his own country house, wept and prayed—and when he lifted him up again, he was alive.[80] Anything connected with the valued relics at the chapel of Eraclius, Augustine took very seriously. So, for instance, we learn from a letter of introduction he wrote for the widow Galla and her daughter Simpliciola to their bishop, that he had also given her a little relic of St. Stephen, either as a gift for his fellow-bishop or to protect her on her journey.[81]

He has an amazing story to tell about a distinguished lady from Carthage called Petronia. He suggested that she should herself write a *libellus* about the way she had been cured in Uzalis, and she in fact describes not merely the miracle itself, but also a sign she was given while she was on her way to Uzalis. She had once been sold the stone from the kidney of an ox by a Jew, who told her to put it under the stone in one of her rings and wear it as a lucky charm in a hair belt next to her skin, like a kind of *ligatura*. She had been wearing it in this way for quite a long time, but when she was on her pilgrimage and was just about to cross a river, the ring suddenly fell out and rolled at her feet. She felt under her clothes for the belt; it was still fastened round her waist but the ring was no longer there. Then she realized that the saint wanted to give her a sign, hurled belt and ring into the water and, thus freed from all black magic, hastened in great relief to the *memoria* at Uzalis to be cured. So may those people—ends the storyteller—who do not believe that our Lord came *clauso utero* from a virgin, and appeared through closed doors, take note of this miracle, which this high-class lady, living in a big city and well known there, can vouch for.[82]

Of all these miracles, which are lumped together indiscriminately, as though the fall of a lucky charm and a successful cure of haemorrhoids exist on the same level as a case of resurrection from the dead, Augustine says expressly that though they caused a stir where they actually occurred, they were not known outside a very limited circle. Even when *libelli* are read out in church, he says, they are only heard by the people who happen to be there at the time, and these people only hear them once, and soon forget about them, and hardly ever repeat them to the people who were not there. In this connection, Augustine makes a notable statement about the woman cured of cancer of the breast. Her doctor insisted on her telling him what method she had used, and when she told him what had really happened, he looked disgusted and said, "I thought you were going to tell me something really interesting." When she looked astonished at such cynicism he went on, "What is there special about Christ's healing a case of cancer when he brought a man back to life after he had been dead four days?" This he said, according to Augustine, out of respect and veneration for our Lord; but it seems doubtful whether his readers will agree with him about this. He himself complained to the woman that no-one seemed to know anything about the miracle. Had she kept quiet about it? No, she said. "Did you know about it, then?" Augustine immediately asked the group of friends who happened to be visiting the lady at the time. No, no-one knew anything about it. "Just look", he mocked her, "how quiet you have in fact kept about it!" And then the spell was broken and the whole story came out, to the accompaniment of ah's and oh's from the ladies, who were in ecstasies about the whole thing and praised God for it.[83] This was in the year 400, but one cannot help being reminded a little of what was to take place after the miracle of the Holy Thorn in the anteroom at Port-Royal.

Nevertheless, at least one miracle had taken place in Hippo itself that everyone had heard about, many people had seen, and no-one was ever to forget. It was, indeed, a most unusual occurrence and left a very powerful impression behind, and it is described for us in full detail in a *libellus*, four sermons, and the last book of the *City of God*.[84] As it appears in these three different sources, it gives not only the atmosphere of the extraordinary event itself, and of a particular group of people, but the flavour of the whole period. Faith, autosuggestion, dream, atavistic longings for healing by pilgrimage and sleeping in temples—all these things are to be found lumped together in this story, and yet at the same time faith stands out above them all, in both the favoured few and the great mass of the people, and in the prime witness, Augustine himself.

The Tale of the Ten Accursed Children of Cappadocia

The story goes as follows. A widow living in Caesarea in Cappadocia had been insulted and beaten by her eldest son, and none of her nine other children had done anything to protect her. In her rage she had rushed off to the church where they had all been baptized to call down a curse upon her child at the font—again this devotion to the mystical source of life! On her way she met her brother, who asked her where she was going, and when she had told him the whole story he said, "Curse all ten of them!"—for it was actually a devil who had taken the shape of her brother. Whereupon the wretched woman, with bared bosom and hair all awry, hurled herself down in front of the font and cursed her ten children. She implored God to let the curse take visible effect and make them all stray far from their native town, as a terrible example to the whole of mankind. And behold, her request was granted. All the children, from the oldest to the youngest, seven boys and three girls, were immediately afflicted by an incurable nervous twitch and became a laughing-stock to the whole town. As they were not without means, they resolved, one by one, to go off on pilgrimage. Their mother, only now beginning to realize what she had done, fell into despair and hanged herself.[85] But the children wandered hither and thither over the whole world, from one holy place to another, doing penance and praying to the martyrs. The eldest finally arrived at the *memoria* to St. Laurence in Ravenna, where, not many years later, this saint was to be portrayed in brilliant mosaic with his fire, gridiron and books (Plate 7), on the rear wall of the *memoria* to Galla Placidia. The sixth and seventh children, Paulus and Palladia, travelled round together visiting the most famous *memoriae* to St. Stephen, who was just beginning to be known in Ancona, in Rome, and, when they reached Africa, in Uzalis too. But it was all to no avail. Then, in a dream, Palladia saw a grey-haired old man, who assured her that they would be cured within three months, in Africa, and when they happened to come across Augustine in another town they recognized him as the grey-haired old man they had seen in the dream. Shortly afterwards he also appeared to her brother in a dream. From this time onwards the other brothers and sisters kept arriving in Hippo and they all prayed daily in the *memoria* near the cathedral for a fortnight, while the whole town went in terror at the sight of their mysterious complaint.

Early on Easter Sunday morning, when a vast congregation had already gathered in the body of the church and Augustine was waiting in the sacristy for his solemn entry, a loud scream suddenly rang out from behind the grating in St. Stephen's chapel. Paulus, who, still twitching, had been clutching the *cancelli*, fell to the ground unconscious, lay there motionless, and stopped trembling, "as though he was asleep, for then, too, he always stopped trembling". A great uproar arose and no-one knew what to do. Should they carry him out? No, that would be too dangerous. Let him go on lying there, then, and wait and see what happened—for those marked by God still spread paralysing fear abroad. But the man suddenly came back to his senses, stood up, and now he was no longer trembling; no, he stood there cured, "looking at those who looked at him". Only then did the people realize what had happened, and the whole church echoed to the sound of their hymns of praise. One after another they streamed to the sacristy in a long chain to announce the news, and finally the cured man himself appeared, to a deafening chorus of jubilation: "Praise be to God, thanks be to Christ!" Augustine took him in his arms and kissed him before the whole people. The jubilation showed no signs of abating, and broke out again when the bishop made his entrance and greeted the congregation from the apse.[86] When finally silence reigned and the readings from the Bible were over, Augustine began to speak. "You are accustomed to hearing accounts of the miracles that take place through St. Stephen's intercession", he said. "Well, in this case the account of what happened is before your very eyes. Instead of hearing a report, you can see with your own eyes what has happened; instead of a document, you have been presented with a play. What formerly caused you pain when you looked at him who stands before you, you can now read with joy, to the greater honour and glory of God, and also to impress upon your minds what will also be written down in words. But now forgive me if I speak no longer; you know how tired I am. I have also to thank St. Stephen for the fact that I was able to endure so much so calmly yesterday without succumbing, and can still speak to you today. Let us now, turning to God . . ." and so he went on to say the brief prayer that brought the sermon to an end.[87]

Then he had something to eat with the cured man and asked him to prepare a *libellus*. The man readily promised to do so, but at the same time asked for urgent prayers to be said for his poor sister. On the following day, Easter Monday, Augustine said to his congregation: "Yesterday, as you know, I said that your report must this time be what you had witnessed yourself, but Paulus has told me further details that for the sake of God's honour you must know. So tomorrow you will hear a report."[88] On Easter Tuesday, after the sermon, he led the cured man up on to the steps of the apse along with his sister, so that the people could judge the greatness of the miracle by comparing the two cases. Then he had the account read out. The whole thing has come down to us, and although it begins with the words: "I beg you, most blessed Father Augustine, to let this my report, which I have drawn up at your command, be read out to the holy people", its faultless Latin is undoubtedly that of a *notarius*, for Paulus was a Greek. In any case, he kept nothing back, and the people learned the full story of the dreadful things that had happened earlier.[89]

Then the bishop delivered a sermon that in its brevity was if anything more affecting than the document. "Let us hope", he began, "that all these brothers and sisters will still, through the mercy of God, be cured. And may children learn from this to be respectful to their parents, and parents to refrain from anger. For that which was written has been fulfilled: 'The curse of the mother rooteth out the foundations.'[90] In so far as the unfortunate mother is concerned—was she not more dreadfully punished, the more promptly her request was answered? Learn, then, to desire from God only those things which can bring you no harm when you are given them." Then he asked for prayers to be said for the girl, and went on to describe the vision she had had. "Who am I, to have appeared to them without knowing it? I am only a man like other men, not one of the great, yet they were sent to our town, and were not healed in Ancona or Uzalis, even though both these towns can pride themselves on more famous pilgrimages." Then followed a dissertation on Ancona, wherein he answered the question how it came about that a *memoria* had existed there before 415. The relic that was there, he said, was not in fact a piece of a limb, but a stone that had struck St. Philip's elbow (*angkoon*) when he was stoned. It had been picked up by a religious man and taken to Italy; somehow they had found out about it in the town of Ancona—the name being wonderfully apt, of course . . . And then he went on to talk about the miracles in Uzalis, and began to describe a few of them, including the one about the mother who saw her son die at her breast and cried out: "My son is dead and is only a catechumen!"[91]

At this moment loud cries came from the *cella* to St. Stephen. "God be praised! Thanks be to God!" All the people near the apse turned round, and hurried through the nave to the chapel, but immediately came back, for behold, the girl was there, thoroughly cured, at the centre of the wildly excited crowd. After the first surge of excitement was over and had changed into the sound of loud sobbing, Augustine spoke—as calmly as he could and with a ready pun on his lips: "It says in the Psalms, 'I will confess my transgressions unto the Lord; and thou forgavest the iniquity of my sin.'[92] I say, I will indeed acknowledge it: even before I had finished speaking you had dismissed me [i.e., made my words unnecessary]. I commended this poor girl—this girl who *was* a poor girl—to your prayers. We were about to pray for her, but we had already been heard. Our joy shall be our thanksgiving. Our Mother the Church found her prayers answered with blessings more rapidly than the other mother was answered with ruin!"[93]

Only on the following day, the Wednesday of Easter Week, did he end his story of the mother of Uzalis; this woman, "who mourned her child, not as a mother, but as a believer", went to the *memoria* and cried to the martyr, "You know why I am weeping! Give me back my child so that he may appear before the face of God who has crowned you with glory!" And she prayed so passionately "that her tears seemed to be a demand rather than a plea". The child came back to life and the mother took it to the priests, who baptized it, blessed it and anointed it. Also they laid their hands upon it; and when all the sacraments had been administered, it passed away. The mother accompanied it to the grave, looking as though she was laying it not in a grave but in St. Stephen's lap. "Now judge the matter yourselves: if God performed such a miracle in Uzalis through his martyr, why couldn't he have healed these people there too? And yet he sent them to us."[94] With these words he rose up from the *cathedra* to say the prayer of thanksgiving that brought this unforgettable episode to an end.

Augustine's Critical Sense and His Credulity

Whoever reads these uncompromising stories can see how Augustine regards his people's belief in miracles. The pious activity at the great miracle centres is played out against a background of preternatural dimensions in a landscape filled with dreams, devils and spirits. And strangely enough, Augustine fits into this landscape. He appears as the typical Southerner controlling the behaviour of the massed crowds with a practised hand, sometimes as the incomparable rhetorician always ready with his answer, but at the same time the upright Christian fully believing in miracles. He is a typical child of his age, even in matters where we should not expect him to be so.

Not that he does not have his moments of criticism. The common sense that appears in the council resolution of the year 401—against the erecting of *mensae* solely on the basis of dreams—led him to write the passage about faces that appear in dreams in the little book to Paulinus. But this common sense does not come into it when it is a case of checking a matter of fact in eyewitnesses' accounts. When he is arguing about theory his critical sense is as acute as it could possibly be, but things that he can distinguish over quite clearly in theory, he accepts in practice without criticism. There is nothing wrong with his theories, but the factual material, as he presents it, reveals a credulity which to us today seems incredible.

The only weak point in his theory is the fact that he does not start from any sharply defined concept as to what a miracle is. He never gives any criterion for distinguishing between a genuine miracle and something that is merely unusual or remarkable. What, in Augustine's view, was a miracle? An occurrence that caused astonishment and apparently broke the laws of nature. It supplied its own evidence, for it was, by its nature, "unbelievable". Thus, all explained *mirabilia* in nature also fall under the heading of miracles as long as they remain unexplained. Augustine calls things miracles—*miracula, portenta, prodigia, signa*—that everyone else called miracles, that is to say, an undifferentiated sequence of astonishment-arousing things of a natural or preternatural kind.

Some of these do not belong to sacred history, without, for all that, being always the work of devils. Varro, for example, relates how a vestal virgin, having been wrongfully accused, proved her innocence by carrying water in a sieve from the Tiber to the town hall. Augustine believes this story implicitly;

he is not ready to say whether the miracle was effected by good angels or devils, but he prefers the former, and uses the fact itself as a weapon against people who deny the Resurrection. For if a "god" or an angel can keep water up in the air, is there any reason why the living, almighty God should not be able to deal with human weight in such a way that a body can be brought back to life and live in the bright upper air where the life-giving Spirit chooses to dwell?[95]

A miracle can, therefore, take place either through the agency of angels or through the agency of devils. In the latter case it belongs to secular history. The number of miracles described by heathen historians he reckons to be absolutely unlimited. He believes what the old writers say; believes that when the processional coach for the Mother of the Gods wouldn't budge, the chaste Claudia Quinta was able to pull it along with her own two hands; that the Trojan Penates ran before Aeneas, and that Tarquin cut the grindstone with a razor. All these things were the work of devils; but what significance have such signs when compared with the miracles of sacred history?[96] And yet, on the other hand, he says that many of these things were not really against nature—which is Varro's definition of a miracle—but only against nature in so far as we understand her. He emphasizes this again a little later on, when he remarks that miracles of this kind help us to remember that the Maker of the laws of nature can also make exceptions to them—which again raises the question, wherein exactly the difference is to be found between unusual natural phenomena and supernatural intervention by God.[97]

In practice Augustine is inclined to accept a natural explanation when he is faced with signs that are morally dubious, and to believe in miracles when he is told something edifying. Of a lamp burning unceasingly at the sanctuary to Venus, he says that it may have been able to go on burning like that as the result of some clever mechanical device—for example, by using a stone called asbestos. But he is not prepared to dismiss the possibility of black magic entirely.[98] He was fond of marvels, he had read widely in the collections of stories about natural phenomena which formed the only physics textbooks of the time,[99] and he loved to bring in references to this side of the old education. All who read the *City of God* must be amazed at the really astonishing things that Augustine can produce to prove some knotty point. For instance, he mentions his neighbour, the priest Restitutus of Calama, who could lie senseless, as though he were dead, just like a fakir, whenever he felt inclined; and people who could move their hair, or their ears, and even each ear separately, or fill their stomach up several times and then "empty it like a bag", or "sing" shamelessly through a certain part of their body—like the devil in Dante's hell. All these things are supposed to prove that it is possible to make sexual excitement entirely dependent upon the will, as in his opinion must have been the case in the ideal reproductive conditions of the Garden of Eden.[100] The possibility of burning indestructibly in hell he illustrates by three examples—the salamander, that lives in fire, Mount Etna, which burns without being consumed, and the flesh of peacocks, which does not decay; all things out of the old world of fable—though he can tell us from his own experience that a peacock's intestines, which he kept by way of experiment after eating the cooked meat, had still not gone rotten after being kept for weeks, and even after a year were a bit shrivelled up but otherwise quite unaffected.[101]

Religious tales that were generally believed in he himself accepted more or less without question. With regard to the more-than-remarkable things which everyone said were going on at the grave of John the Apostle in Ephesus, he does not in fact accept the current explanation, because this seems to contradict Holy Scripture. But he has no doubt about the miracle itself. What people were saying was that the earth that was being scraped up and taken away from the grave by pilgrims was self-renewing and that a fine dust was always being blown up against the open upper edge of the grave, as though by a wind. The saint himself was believed to be blowing this up from below with his own breath, as a sign that he was still really alive, as the Lord had prophesied: "So I will have him to remain till I come." John, therefore, was asleep in his grave, but alive.[102] In his sermon on the last chapter of St. John's Gospel Augustine comes to these words, and immediately the miracle at Ephesus comes into his mind. And commenting on the words "And Jesus did not say to him: He should not die, but: So I will have him to remain till I come, what is it to thee?", he repeats the legend that John had been buried alive. He reminds his hearers that even in the apocryphal story—according to which, at the age of a hundred, and still sound in wind and limb, John had a grave prepared for himself and lay down in it as though it was a bed—he was still described as giving up the ghost. So he did in fact die. But Augustine has no doubt about the authenticity of the miracle itself. God may have given this wonderful sign so that John, who was not to earn his fame as a martyr, should still be glorious in the manner of his death. There may have been other reasons too. The Apostle is not merely asleep, since Holy Scripture refers to his death, but the miracle itself Augustine is not prepared to deny. "People who know that place can decide whether the earth there does what it is said to do or not. For my own part, I have not heard the story from gullible people."[103]

It always comes down to the same thing. His final argument is the reliability of the witnesses, but all too often their statements are situated far away in place and time. Without a trace of incredulity he believes everything he hears at third or fourth hand from anyone who says it is so, or anything he reads in the work of any serious author. In those days an almost boundless awe of the written word still reigned, and there was no thought of any sort of historical criticism. In Augustine, as in the textbooks on casuistry, the proper estimation of any argument is unwittingly replaced by the heaping up of "authorities", the only difference being that the handbooks are concerned, not with highly picturesque accounts of miracles, but with ticklish questions of conscience, in which literary grace and irony would be strictly out of place. No doubt, even in the *City of God*, Augustine distinguishes between what he knows from his own experience or from the testimony of reliable witnesses, and what he has got from books; he does this particularly when *mirabilia* are involved. Some things—for instance, the properties of asbestos, chalk, oil, magnets, peacocks' flesh—he has been able to test for himself; others, like the Apple of Sodom and the torch-lighting brook near Grenoble, he only knows from hearsay. As regards the rest—things depending on written evidence—he is not prepared to vouch for these unreservedly, but he is quite prepared to use them in the course of an argument when the people he is arguing against have no doubts about their veracity.[104] But even though he may hesitate in theory and in fields which do not lie near to his heart, in practice he almost always plumps for belief, especially in what is for him the most fundamental field of all—namely, where he can find something edifying for himself and his readers. When for instance he describes in the pulpit how the pelican feeds its young with blood taken from its own breast, he says by way of qualification, "Perhaps this is true, perhaps it isn't", but he nevertheless regards it as a striking image of Christ, and portrays it most vividly for the benefit of his hearers.[105] No one was ever less superstitious than Augustine, but he was just as credulous as the rest of the people of his day. But however susceptible he may be to rumour, he uses everything that fills him with wonder as an opportunity to praise God in all his works. These events that were regarded as miracles helped to make the ancient world, brutal and chance-ridden as it was, a place of light in which one could feel at home, and to turn it bit by bit into a secure universe in which God's providence was the be-all and the end-all of existence, where no grain of dust on any grave, and not even the slightest mishap, could fall outside the range of the heavenly Father's loving care. For all these strange things brought peace of mind rather than terror, more love than fear. Miracles gave this world its first glimmer of the world to come. In their own way they helped to create virtue and faith—as Augustine explains at the end of his chapter on miracles in the *City of God*. "Thus it is in the Lord that we praise the souls of the martyrs. So let us believe them, as witnesses who brought us the truth and did wonders. As bringers of the truth they suffered, so that later they might work miracles. And the most important of their truths is this, that Christ rose from the dead, and in the flesh has shown us immortality, which he has firmly promised to us too, if only when the new world dawns and this present one comes to an end."[106]

Certainly the great mass of the people were not only credulous but absolutely athirst for miracles. Augustine, in his care of souls, took care to ensure that this longing for miracles did not become a form of selfishness. He always condemned speculations slanted toward worldly advantage as fleshliness. But he allowed the "golden legend" to persist. And in his last years he shared it to the full.

Credulity can lead to superstition, but on the other hand it is usually found where there is a living faith, and thus can frequently be regarded as an almost inevitable overflow of faith. De Maistre says in his *Soirées de Saint-Pétersbourg* that superstition is essentially the result of an excess of religion and to that extent a precursor of religiosity. Now, if such an excess is admirable in love, friendship, truth and honour, why should it not be so in religion? "As far as I am concerned," De Maistre says, "I am inclined to believe that the outcry against excrescences in this field comes from the enemies of the thing. It is certainly not believers who ever get annoyed about the manifestations of an over-simple faith."

Many of the phenomena described by Augustine may have been pious imaginations and many of the miracles exaggerated accounts of answers to prayers. But does prayer lose its value thereby? All too often Augustine seems to have turned the rational world-picture of Antiquity into one single, great, impenetrable divine mystery.[107] But is the truth in other philosophies so especially transparent, and do we really know what actually took place before Augustine's eyes? With regard to precisely these stories of miracles in the *City of God* Montaigne remarked, in words too admirable to be translated: "C'est une hardiesse dangereuse et de consequence, oultre l'absurde temerité qu'elle traisne quand et soy, de mespriser ce que nous ne concevons pas: car aprez que, selon vostre bel entendement, vous avez estably les limites de la verité et de la mensonge, et qu'il se treuve que vous avez necessairement à croire des choses où il y a encores plus d'estrangeté qu'en ce que vous niez, vous vous estes desia obligé de les abandonner."[108] In this observation lies more truth and less malice than people have supposed. Augustine, the great believer, had no need of signs, but he read the universe as a book full of signs —and what is more, he knew how to read it. He was familiar with a symbolic alphabet, perhaps the best that has ever been discovered. Whatever Augustine's vision lacked, it was certainly not anything to do with God's honour and the salvation of souls. This tree too is to be known by its fruits. It was really not such a bad thing that historical criticism should have been kept back for a thousand years, if Christ was to continue to be preached and God's name to be magnified in all things.

EPILOGUE

20

AUGUSTINE AND OUR OWN DAY

WHAT total picture emerges of this great master of the spiritual life? What is the essential characteristic of his concern for souls, and wherein lies the importance of this for us today?

The very various and often charmingly picturesque individual details that have been gathered together in this book, will, it seems to me, suggest that we must proceed cautiously. Before we can come to any final judgement about Augustine's position as a master of the spiritual life, we need to make careful distinctions.

The Stamp of the Age

The fact that we must frequently find Augustine disappointing cannot be denied; but this is because of the age he lived in. For even he was, and remains, a child of his age. Even he was hemmed in by all the fateful limitations inseparably connected with a period of transition, when old things have still not been thrown away for good and the new things have still not properly emerged—when the dissolution is evident, but the renewal still lies hidden. Like all his contemporaries, he, too, was filled with a naïve belief in miracles, and like most of his contemporaries with a taste for philosophy, he found it easier to give his unqualified assent to the value of invisible truth than to that of the visible world by which he was surrounded. This extreme idealism was in the air in those days and Augustine shared it with such very different thinkers as the neo-Platonist mystics, the Manichees, and those who still clung to the myth of Rome. Augustine, too, had been brought up on an educational system received at third hand, and he had no more sense of historical veracity or the historical point of view than anyone else, even though, especially towards the end of his life, he showed the greatest liking for historical facts to help him to prove his points. He could argue in perfect good faith over the curiosities in Pliny's natural history and Strabo's geography. With the Greek Fathers already beginning to doubt them, he still believed in the prophetic powers of the Sybils and the Messianism of Vergil's "prophetic" *Eclogue*—to the great benefit, incidentally, from both the religious and the literary point of view, of medieval poetry.[1] As a philosopher he had depended on collections made in second-class textbooks, on Cicero, on translations like the one by Marius Victorinus of Plotinus's *Enneads*, and, ultimately, on himself. Thus a sober scholar like Marrou, despite his tremendous admiration for Augustine, is not afraid to call him, incomparable though he is, a typical rhetor, a philosophical dilettante, by modern standards a very wise but still a relatively uneducated person. Fundamentally, what he knew was his own language and his Bible; Varro, Cicero, Ambrose and Cyprian at first hand; the rest, like almost all the people of his day, from collections. The general framework which his great mind burst, but without completely escaping from it, seems to us today, after some fifteen hundred years, to have been remarkably narrow and one-sided in a literary sort of way. But he did indeed burst it. He kept his treatment of curiosities almost entirely to where they belonged —that is to say, the study, for the initiated; in the pulpit, enchanting medieval "examples" came out of them. Working entirely on his own, he beat a way right through ancient history's half-mystical, half-epic, yet strikingly human world of magic—a way that has made him an acceptable figure to many different races. Indeed, one may go further: ancient history developed a deeper meaning as he treated it because he saw it as being from beginning to end the expression of a supra-temporal struggle between good and evil, and fundamentally a reflection of the divine decree. Working entirely on his own, he built up a universe of new ideas, simply on the basis of facts gained from a handful of books, including at most three or four masterpieces but also—and decisively—God's own book, the Bible. In point of fact even his interpretation of the Bible was not all gain. The penetrating but artificial arc-lamp of Origen's genius sheds a sharp but unreal light over the landscape of his Bible. Again and again he staggers us with arbitrary allegorical explanations, which were precisely the things that enchanted his hearers and readers. With regard to his attitude towards bodily goods, and in particular the physical side of marriage, this is to be seen as a result of his age's reaction against the widespred putrefaction of heathen life, rather than as a Christian, or, if you like, philosophical denigration of the physical, deriving from neo-Platonism. In these matters he was not so much a strict rigorist as a child of the fifth century; that is to say, someone who had to fight against a well-nigh unavoidable danger of infection.

Despite his belief in the miraculous, and even though he remains a stranger to any really critical attitude, he is nevertheless at times quite reasonable, and rounds sharply upon fantasticalities. He prefers, of course, sweeping away the cobwebs of the immoral old Graeco-Roman myths to getting rid of the comparatively recent dust of the legendary Christian tales. He unmasks "fate" and all the trash about the gods, but a great many uncanny things, on earth and in heaven, can still go on haunting his world-picture under harmless names. The stars, it is true, are no longer dangerous, but they are still like beings with souls; the demons and the old gods are now called devils and fill the air. But none of these phantom figures comes sufficiently into the foreground for his world-picture to seem at all stifling; they sit in hiding in nooks and corners, waiting for their secret worshippers and dark practices—and thus, banished, and yet still preserving themselves in existence, they were to penetrate into the imaginative world of the Middle Ages and come once again to the fore, cut in stone around the bases of Romanesque fonts in Sweden and Artois, huddled together in miniatures, and with the grinning, gaping mouths of gargoyles on cathedrals.

It may be said that in his judgements on critical questions Augustine is usually master of the situation, really explains difficulties (at least those that come within the scope of revelation), and is, generally speaking, far in advance of his time. He was the inheritor of a civilization that was, in spite of everything, essentially intellectualist, and in his early days he even dreamed of a new kind of teaching which would drop the ballast of the old fables and shift the emphasis to grammar, logic, mathematics and history. Thus lightened, it would become a rapid and effective method for the study of wisdom. Later he came to see the futility of any such attempt and discovered a more suitable starting-point in faith. But despite his theologian's hood, and his idealistic, Bible-drenched and sometimes visionary philosophical attitude, he remained in a certain sense a rationalist throughout his life. In his teaching about the Beatific Vision he remained to the end a philosopher of the old intellectualist stamp. This vision is in perfect line with his general theory of knowledge, even though it is only possible in the other world, and is essentially the luminous transparency of evidences of higher things. It remains all intellectual insight, and therefore a work of reason. It is the topmost rung of a whole ladder of knowledge that already exists within us, and which, with the help of grace, and enlightened by the teacher within us, Christ, we can ascend without any fear of the mists of the physical world. So we proceed from believing to seeing, from seeing to contemplating, without coming across any gaps between nature and supernature.

As a teacher Augustine is not only one of the greatest fathers of the medieval allegory, which turned the cosmos into an open-air theatre of symbols, and the cathedrals, again, into symbols of the cosmos; he is also the precursor of medieval intellectualism, which built up its whole system of ethics on the basis of the four major virtues of Antiquity, supported its biblical quotations with logical arguments, and in practice managed to prune the overgrowths of popular religion again and again.

No doubt his world-picture appears, from the cosmological point of view, to derive entirely from that of Antiquity, and, from the metaphysical point of view, too, to be to a great extent the inheritor of the old civilization. But it was Augustine, above all others, who first christianized this world-picture and so passed it on, in a state of comparative perfection, to the Christian Middle Ages.

Augustine's universe is an intricate system of concentric spheres that reach their culmination high up above in an *empyreum* of flaming aether. It is the same picture as we find almost unchanged nearly a thousand years later in Dante. The whole cosmos is imbued with powerful spiritual forces, and gives the impression of being a kind of enormous animal. Although at the end of his life Augustine was not certain whether he could call the world an animal or not, he still believed that as a whole and in all its parts it was subject to spiritual forces—he prefers to say, kept in motion by holy angels.[2] Contrariwise, he seems to accept the fact that angels (or some of them at least) possess ethereal bodies and demons airy ones.

Metaphysically speaking, at the basis of his universe lies the idea of a highly differentiated participation in the divine nature. But towards the end of his life he christianized this idea—one of the fundamental concepts of the old Platonism—by tracing the differences—that is to say, the different degrees of being—back to the transcendental relationships between the divine Persons. God as the Creator is the source of the being of everything: as the Word, he is the light of the intellect and the origin of all truth; as the dispenser of grace —the Holy Ghost—he is the source of all goodness and blessedness.[3] The Creation thus consists of an inexhaustible supply of images and symbols which owe their unity, beauty and truth to the divine prototype and highest symbol, the ideal image of the Father, the eternal Word, "in whom all things are made". To use a simple parallel, one might say that the universe is like a building made of crystal, which gets all its light from a point in the centre of a dome which itself can never be seen—a Hagia Sophia on the cosmic scale, with the heavenly spheres representing the shells of the dome, constructed on the plan of imperishable Ideas rising one above the other and reaching their summit in the divine zenith. It is a Platonic-Christian structure, rising up steeply like a late Byzantine church, climbing up transparently from the depths of our souls and vanishing away above in forms and symbols of increasing purity and unbearable brightness arranged in stages, on the pattern of the old Pythagorean theory of numbers, in a sort of ladder that finally opens out into the all-encompassing round dome of the last *kentron*, God. And this wonderful temple is then projected into the little chapel of our own minds by the divine light, for here too all light of knowledge comes from above. Not a single ray of knowledge comes in through any of the organs of sense or any other mind; our minds can only grasp the intelligible temple of ideas in the immaterial light that is poured into them, which enables us to know without itself being known. Signs of God are indeed to be found on every hand in this cosmic temple, but they are not all equally clear. To poor wretches like us, standing on the ground, the feeblest and most humble signs, forming the physically perceptible substructure, seem the clearest, though they are in fact the furthest removed from the centre of knowable truth, the world of the *intelligibilia et aeterna*. For the cosmos comes from God like a reflected halo, and what seems to us to be the floor is in fact the outmost ridge of the roof and the beginning of nothingness. It was this rigid world of ideas which came involuntarily into the young Augustine's mind when in the Gospel he read our Lord's words, "My kingdom is not of this world." Then he said to himself, But that is exactly what Plato says! As an old man he partly renounced this idea in the *Retractations*, for the Lord, he had come to see, had, rather, meant the new earth and the new heaven of the coming Kingdom—"though Plato in no way erred when he maintained that there is an intelligible world, that is to say, an eternal and unchanging ground of being through which God created the world."[4]

But this world with its shining essence of eternal ideas, clouded round by the material cosmos as though by an immense halo spiritualized into its furthermost corners, which manifests not mere causality, but the eternal meaning of things, and which at heart remains unchangingly itself, and only seems to move at the outermost edge of its field of illumination; this world where there is no time and no history, and where the immortal soul of the individual dissolves and vanishes like a beam in the sunlight: this motionless, outspread, abstract domed space, resting in perfect harmony upon itself, never disappeared from his view even after his years and years of reading the Holy Scriptures as priest and bishop. That must be admitted. Yet he saw it gradually pale and change. It was suddenly no longer empty to him, but taken unawares, stormed and occupied by the hosts of the Bible. He heard it being filled with sounds divine and human, first softly, then echoing and re-echoing ever more strongly until finally the sound of God's own mighty voice began to be heard.

The temple of ancient wisdom, once so remote, became a people's church, where everyone could hear the divine Word, Christ. The old proud mirror of ideas became the mirror of medieval history. In Augustine's eyes eternity was crossed by time, and the vertical philosopher's world cut through the horizontal one of revelation, which was a story of holy deeds in time and in souls. To Augustine's inward gaze the old world-picture moved gradually in the direction of God, and was peopled with all the uncountable elect whom God willed to attract towards him in his love; it was, as it were, wrenched open by his free choice. And so it has lost its strangeness for us too, and to many of us even becomes friendly again.

Augustine's Originality

It is certainly important not to forget that Augustine was a child of his time, but it is far more important to remember that he was in himself a person of tremendous stature and of powerful emotions.

He did not create any absolutely new, self-enclosed system of thought, with its own clearly defined, consistent terminology. Nor had he the ability to work patiently to arrange all the little details of such a system in their separate compartments. He absorbed them all rapidly, almost unwittingly, into a visionary synthesis, embracing God, human beings and things; this was his constant inspiration and he was always seeking new modes of expression for it, so that his words and even his definitions were continually changing, like variations on one inexhaustible theme. He gave the full chord, the harmony; he was never master of the manifold detail of reality. Thus he never produced any real moral or pastoral theology. It was not Augustine but Mausbach and Roland-Gosselin who created—as far as it can be created—Augustinian ethics. This man who opened up so many new ways for our thinking, our praying and our action, who can frequently say more in a few pages than whole schools put later into their completed systems, actually provided us with little that is really new in the field of the ordinary and extraordinary care of souls, especially from the theoretical point of view. He wrote no *De Officiis*; rather he tried continually to transcend the natural ethics of Antiquity by means of the heavenly virtues of faith, hope and charity, and even this he achieved more by way of glowing asides than in any work specially designed for the purpose. Anyone who approaches the Augustinian ethos finds himself faced, not by a system, but by the panoramic view of the *City of God*, a landscape as vast as this world's history and only slightly smaller than the Apocalypse. Here is enacted the life-and-death struggle between the love that forgets itself for God and the other kind that forgets God in favour of itself; and here no-one asks for ethics, but high above the din of the battle between the two *civitates*, both sprung from the same father, Adam,[5] can be seen fluttering already the two standards of the Ignatian *Exercises*, and the King of Eternity on his white steed in the skies.

Time and time again this great, often wilful thinker has been admiringly analysed, at first, and for several centuries, with undivided admiration, and then with mixed feelings of admiration and estrangement. The artist has occasionally been forgotten for a moment for the word-juggling rhetorician, with his endless repetitions, his far-fetched turns of phrase and everlasting literary parallels. But everyone has sensed behind all this the man of giant integrity, to whom it was given to express so inimitably all that is holiest and most inexpressible in the human heart. It is not surprising that Pascal and those who followed him were so fond of him. He was an *homme de cœur*, blessed with the *esprit de finesse*. He is the father of Western piety, and, despite his intellectualism, the teacher of all who are unable to live by argument alone. In this connection one can only repeat, once again, that passage from the *Pensées*: "Jesus Christ and St. Paul exist in the order of love, not in the intellectual order, for they aimed to bring fire, not to teach. Likewise St. Augustine. The main point about this order is that every detail of it refers to the ultimate object and is always returning to it."[6] Although his "heart" is to be understood not as a symbol of the will but as the seat of knowledge, and his "contemplation" is to be taken in the intellectualist sense, nevertheless, no-one can doubt for a moment that he did not simply approach divine truth with the surface of the personality, with the cold intellect, as a concept, but also experienced it as a profound reality in the furthest depths of his soul. When one studies his arguments one is impressed not so much by his powers of reasoning as by the personal passion that lies behind the arguments. One can always sense the man who dared to say of God, It was your beauty that drew me to you. Heaven and earth were shouting to me from all sides that I must love you. "I question them, and they answer, We are not your God, look beyond us. And to all the things standing at the door of my flesh I say: Tell me, O tell me something about him! And they all answer, in a loud voice, he created us"—*Ipse fecit nos!*—words that still echo unforgettably for us today in the melody of the Gregorian chant.[7] Instead of asking questions, he looked around him, and beauty gave him the answer. Few saints illustrate so overwhelmingly the thesis that in the existential order of things *prière et poésie* stand next to each other, the one being perhaps simply the continuation of the other. Augustine is the greatest poet of Christian Antiquity, without ever having written any poetry worth mentioning. His ecstasies, his lightning-like appraisal, sometimes, of the whole graded system of the universe, moved and lit by the sun of the divine love, he expresses endlessly with a candour and enthusiasm that make him irresistible. He possesses the fifth talent, the most valuable of all, the gift of endless wonderment; remaining in this like the little children to whom the Kingdom of Heaven was promised. And who ever made this talent yield more fruit? Most of all he admired God's bounty as one experiences it in one's own soul and as it has been revealed in the outside world in the person of our Lord. Thus his teaching becomes a personal testimony to the reality of salvation, a Bible as seen in the light of a soul. It is hardly surprising that he should have had such a profound understanding of souls.

In the practical care of souls, he was thus a man who followed his own intuition. And he cannot be considered to have displayed an outstandingly practical bent. As a matter of fact, in the view of many people, the early Church as a whole had little practical technique in this matter. Missionary activity, whether directed within or without, was foreign to her: the care of souls was very much conducted as from above. Augustine, with his championing of the ascetic communities (like so many others of his day), is separated by a millennium and a half from our modern forms of pastoral apostolate. It has been pointed out that neither he nor the African Church as a whole succeeded in educating the indigenous masses. Even his immediate preoccupation was the towns and the upper classes—and two hundred years later the whole province proved helpless in the face of the onslaught of Islam; indeed, the tribes beyond the *limes* were not even baptized.

But such criticisms concern his time more than Augustine himself. He and his associates had no time to educate the poor Berbers into being independent Christians. They led them into the proper pastures and revealed the true springs of the sacraments to them. But when, after their death, the great framework of the Roman Church was shattered into fragments, the barbarous Vandals driving out the bishops, murdering the clergy, burning down the little country chapels, seizing their property, closing or occupying the town churches for decades on end, and turning the Latin-speaking middle classes into Arians —then nothing really was left for the natives to cling to. They were quite prepared to receive the sacraments they felt so helplessly dependent on in some heretical church, or else to cease receiving them altogether. During the Byzantime restoration, which went on for a good hundred years and yet still remained such a shadowy affair, they sought to atone in tens of thousands, and returned in penitence to the true Church; even amongst the Berbers, who had crossed the *limes* and fallen upon the land, great numbers accepted the Roman faith. Then, two hundred and fifty years after Augustine's death, came Islam. The first of the enchanting mosques of Kairouan was founded by Sidi Okba, who came in the name of God but brought with him no mysteries, no ritual, and not many commandments either, tolerant towards superstition, lax in his morality, intolerant only of any other faith. For a time we go on hearing of a few bishops, the heroic Berber Queen Kahina, a Jewish woman who opposed Islam, and the Christian hero Koceila, who twice rebelled. But then darkness falls upon this old land of the Church. African Christianity, with all its five hundred and sixty dioceses, disappears so completely from the face of the earth that when we come to count the masses of ruins that are still being revealed we can hardly believe our eyes. The puzzle of this decline has still not been solved, but whoever may have been to blame it was certainly not the indefatigable Bishop of Hippo, who in the remotest corners of his own diocese installed priests and bishops who, though educated in Latin, were Punic-speaking too. The African Church produced an incomparable elite, but no Christian people. The barbarisms and the schism gave it no time to do so, But if it is still remembered today, this is chiefly due to Augustine.

He was no more of an organizer on the practical level than he was strictly systematic in matters of theory. He had more fondness for the spontaneous act performed out of conviction than for the minute patient diplomacy whereby the precision experts prepare their great deeds. For this reason, too, he never became a casuist, despite his talent for giving acute answers to concrete questions. His solutions tend, rather, to depend on direct insight. They always reveal a great mind and a warm heart, just as the dreadfully schoolmasterish theoretical treatises of his early years nevertheless affect the reader like shot silk which still goes on shining whichever way it is folded. But the great insights with which he was inspired he had partly earned the hard practical way, and then made more precise to himself under the pressure of circumstance. He described these again and again most effectively, with all the tricks of a winning and at the same time unbeatable dialectic, and he translated them into practical terms. It was thus that people found them so striking. And as a result of the successes he gained, his less far-seeing colleagues regarded him forthwith as a kind of oracle in the matter of pastoral questions.

We even know something about one or two of the novelties he introduced. He had only just become a priest when he opened up new lines in the instruction of *competentes* by basing their catechism on the Creed, and laying the emphasis on being able to explain passages instead of learning them by heart—the explanation itself not being limited to any dogmatic interpretation, but being broadened in scope by his emphasis, here too, on the will. He taught Deogratias—and the whole of the Middle Ages—to teach the mysteries of Faith in the light of the whole concrete plan of sacred history. He introduced communal singing and collaborated in revising the Latin translations of the Bible. He got rid of abuses and waged war against all forms of red tape. His hand can be traced in many passages of the *Codex Canonum Ecclesiae Africanae*. And everything he wrote and did was shot through with the same great leading ideas, and always revolved round the same themes—the longing for the life of bliss, with abstinence as the way to it; purification of the inward eye as a means to seeing God; and finally faith, hope and charity as the ways leading to God. With regard to the community, the holiness and unity of the Church, the contrast between the heavenly city to come and the earthly Church, and yet again the incomparable unity and objective holiness of the latter; finally, the conflict between the heavenly love and the earthly love on which the two different cities are, respectively, founded—all these things he not only described in unforgettable language but, beyond anyone else, transposed into the actual life of the Church; and for almost a millennium western Christianity kept his innumerable suggestions, counsels and rules before its eyes, almost as though they were instructions and final decisions.

His Model: Ambrose

It may be said that in all practical matters Augustine had a quite definite model before his eyes—his father in Christ, Ambrose. His relation to Ambrose during his Italian years is a much discussed problem, on which opinions conflict.[8] Many people are of the opinion that Ambrose intentionally adopted a reserved attitude towards him in order not to give the impression that he had sided with his mother, who often went to see him, against him; others believe that it was, rather, Augustine who tended to avoid Ambrose because fundamentally he felt no great attraction towards him. He himself says that the man of God gave him a fatherly welcome and loved him, restlessly seeking as he was after truth, as a bishop should.[9] It is clear from the *Confessions* that he could not bring himself to open his heart to Ambrose, even though in the rare interludes between audiences he "often" tried to do so. Every time, however, after a long wait, he would creep out of the antechamber so as not to disturb the bishop reading in his sitting-room, which does not make it quite clear whether or not, either out of modesty or embarrassment, he was glad to have had an excuse to put the conversation off.[10] It is, indeed, quite clear that the courtly bishop was a figure of uncommon interest to the sceptical professor, now no longer greatly concerned about his own career. He had listened with a critical ear to his sermons in the great Portian Basilica. And what an orator he was! Not so ingratiating in his manner, to be sure, as the Manichean spellbinder Faustus, but undoubtedly more learned,[11] and, what was more to the point, with something to say. As he explained them, the crudely written books of the Bible had, it seemed to Augustine, a definite meaning. Everyone went to these sermons, Sunday after Sunday: the number of the congregation went into thousands. Compared with this, what was the value of all the verbiage that he himself was producing for the benefit of a handful of rich young men, only three or four of whom were really prepared to work? Later on in life he put down in words what he had thought of this man, the spiritual leader of his age, at the time. He had regarded him as a fortunate and successful person, in the worldly sense of the words, but thought that celibacy was too high a price to pay for it.[12] He admired his independent attitude towards the all-powerful Court, and began to understand how someone could exchange the toga of a *consularis Liguriae et Aemiliae* for an archbishop's homely pallium. This was one of the chief impressions that remained with him from those days of inward crisis. Human beings, especially his father and his teachers, had previously had little influence on him. He avoided his mother, and amongst his friends he had always been the one who gave. He had lived in books and in his own thoughts. Ambrose gave him a polite welcome, and soon afterwards got to know, and esteem, his simple middle-class mother. He had many conversations with her and congratulated Augustine on having her. But the cool patrician did not take overmuch notice of her gifted problem child, who, to make matters worse, was still under the influence of the avowed freethinker, Symmachus—which only increased his prestige in Augustine's eyes. For Augustine saw how two strong-minded Christian characters like Monica and Ambrose immediately understood each other. This was his first contact with the fellowship of the saints. In the *Confessions* he says Ambrose had no time, but in the *Soliloquies* a lament is sounded: How much, he says, I regret that I was unable to show my affection for him.[13] When he gave up teaching he wrote to Ambrose asking him which book of the Bible he should begin by studying. The answer came back: Isaiah. But this was not, apparently, the right answer, for he was unable to understand the first chapter, and put off reading any more until later. So this exchange of letters, too, failed to lead to any closer contact.[14] From a letter to Casulanus it appears that when he was a catechumen he again went for an audience with Ambrose, to ask him a question from his mother about Saturday fasting—only on his mother's behalf, of course, for she was a very religious woman and had scruples about such things and, when it came to the point, he was prepared to go through fire for her. But he was not the slightest bit interested in the matter himself and it was dealt with in a couple of words.[15] Thereafter he is silent about the bishop who meant so much to him and who in fact baptized him—incidentally, it was the priest Simplicianus, Ambrose's own catechist and later his successor as bishop, who prepared Augustine for his baptism.[16] But the great impression remained, and he seems later to have turned it, with pleasure and slight stylization, into a spiritual father-son relationship. It was he, too, who later, when the Italian deacon Paulinus was staying with him for a while, prevailed upon him to write Ambrose's life. In questions concerning the authority of the Church and local tradition he referred again and again, like the good African he was, to the ideal bishop martyr of the past, Cyprian; but of his contemporaries he put no-one above Ambrose. It was Ambrose who showed him in person what potentialities existed in the union between *romanitas* and the Church. He, too, it was who brought him into contact with the two special treasures of the Christian East, Origen's biblical alchemy and the ideal of virginity. Ambrose showed him, unwittingly, first through his sermons and then in his exegetical and ascetical writings, the two roads along which he was to travel for the rest of his life. He rightly called Ambrose his "planter and waterer".[17] Ambrose's decision about the preservation of the local liturgy he had, as he wrote to Januarius, always before his eyes, and regarded it "as the word of a heavenly oracle".[18] He quoted sayings from his works as unsurpassed models of a Christian style;[19] in matters regarding the interpretation of dogma and the Bible he considered him an authority, and defended his orthodoxy against Pelagius and Julian.[20] But, about all, in really practical matters he followed Ambrose in detail,[21] if with all the warmth of his own heart and all the variability of a sensitive nature utterly foreign to that of his exemplar. He did not adopt everything he had seen in Italy. He respected his own country's form of ritual; we hear of no washing of the feet after baptism, or of any opening of the ears in the case of catechumens, or of any alterations in the celebration of Holy Communion—with the exception of the introduction of a few hymns to fill in the time. It was not Italy that was his model, but Ambrose. This silent adherence to the first of the Latin Fathers is one of the most striking and informative features in the total picture of Augustine the spiritual genius.

Was Augustine a Rigorist?

The fact that Augustine is a really unforgettable character is not due to what he had in common with his age, or to his strongly emotional personality, or his inner bond with Ambrose, but to his Christian fundamentalism. This brings us to the old question: Was Augustine, the spiritual minister, a rigorist? And to the other no less famous question: Did he reject civilization in the name of religion? And if not, what did he renounce, and why?

To the first question the answer is that his practice fortunately contradicts the strictness of his own theory. Like so many other spiritual giants, he was what ordinary people were later so rightly to describe as "lions in the pulpit and lambs in the confessional". He has no wish to offend his flock, not even with the truth, and even in his severest anti-Pelagian sermons he never fails to redeem the shock he has given with his iron logic by the happy inconsequentiality of his heart. In matters of practical asceticism he dwells longer and more lovingly on God's activity upon the fine point of the soul, and the stage-by-stage "ascent in the heart" of which the Psalmist speaks,[22] than on the sorrowful spectacle of our depravity.

That from the purely dogmatic point of view he was a rigorist cannot be denied. Since the time of the Council of Trent, which emphasized grace without doing any damage to nature, all Catholic Christians know that on the questions of grace and freedom he was just as fallible as his opponents. His own experience and his whole system of thought tended to make him ascribe as much as possible to God and as little as possible to man, God's masterpiece. As a philosopher he grants creation neither knowledge, on its own account, nor any fundamental reality. The latter is supplied by the *rationales seminales*, the former by the light of divine knowledge. In his struggle against the Pelagian overestimation of self his faith was not indeed too great—such a thing is impossible—but his logic was too severe. This man who believed that a catechumen who died before baptism was a lost soul, who before the end of his life even advanced the opinion that the good thief must undoubtedly have been baptized (because he was determined not to diminish in any way the need for the first sacrament),[23] undoubtedly went too far; we know that now, the Church has said so. There were many people in Carthage who silently protested, anyway, against what he said about the fate of unbaptized children, centuries before the majority of the theologians rose up against him.[24] He forgot that he had earlier consigned these children to a painless limbo—"halfway between reward and punishment"—for he never retracted this passage in the *Retractations*.[25]

It is one of the ironies of the intellectual history of mankind that this man who was so human, and wanted to remain so no matter what the circumstances, allowed himself to be led astray into expressions of a terrifying rigorism through a remarkable combination of logical necessity and passionate attachment to a personal conviction (not through the Bible), imagining all the time that he was following the teachings of Holy Scripture. It is still more ironical that this fundamentalist, but at the same time lovable and even at times quite charming Christian, should first have had such a decisive influence on the manly but pitiless father of Calvinism, and then, later, brought into being the earnest but testy spirit of Port-Royal. His obstinate attachment to certain inhuman consequences quite foreign to the spirit of the Gospels is an example of the quirks that can affect even the greatest minds, "ut sciant gentes, quoniam homines sunt". With his own now famous aphorism, "Better the ignorance of the believer than the knowledge of the upstart",[26] he did, in fact, condemn himself. But on the other hand he unwittingly showed again and again that he was trying to make his pitiless theories ineffective through the charity of his practice. In the matter of strict ethics he held theoretically, no doubt, to his pessimistic conception of the life of the will; where there is no grace there must be sin, everything in this world is a matter of the lust of the eyes, the lust of the flesh and the pride of life (these words, which Bossuet was to take as the text for a *Traité de la Concupiscence*, were one of Augustine's favourite passages), and there is no moral value whatsoever apart from the love of God. Conscience is faith; the whole of heathen virtue was conscienceless and flaunting depravity. All he can see is *caritas* and mere appetite, with nothing in between. He does not seem to have any place for the natural virtues. He is hardly prepared to recognize the joys of family life; marriage must quietly fade away, he says at one point, then the number of the elect will be reached sooner and the end will come more quickly. But this is all theory. In practice he is no stricter than his contemporaries over most questions, and only over a few is he any stricter than we are.

It is true that he is not prepared to admit the need for a white lie under any circumstances; he also considers it unlawful to kill an unjust attacker in self-defence. Sexual intercourse is only permissible for the sake of procreation. Nor is he prepared to tolerate empty talk, though he was not, for all that, a hermit who refused to allow himself any relaxation. He loved companionship and a good talk. If he bars the Vanity Fair of literature to his followers, we must remember that in those days the stalls there really were too accommodating in the market of the mind; if he utters warnings against processions, old customs and popular amusements, we must remember that all these things still reeked of the filth of heathen ways of life. This incurable infection, still coming from the active germs of the heathen past, also explains his horror of the theatre—a thing which the author of the *Maximes contre le théâtre*, writing a thousand years later, overlooked when he weighed in with the same arguments against a theatre infinitely more squeamish, which could quite sufficiently have been described as a mere vanity of vanities. Augustine was a man who had liberated himself from all things earthly; he was determined to renounce the world, not quietly, but with a public gesture, and he renounced it with the whole of his passionate nature. But he was no life-denier. He did not condemn riches, or good literature, or friendship. He did not retreat in horror from the sensual imagery of the "Song of Songs", and saw nothing to be afraid of in the delights of affective prayer. And above all, he did not look down on the natural religious feeling of ordinary human beings.

There is no trace in him of any mistrust of living worship, of the spheres laid down for the different sacraments, the visible symbols of overflowing grace. He speaks unaffectedly of honouring the martyrs and calling upon them for intercession; of merit and insufficiency, reward and punishment. Though he wrote that God, in rewarding our merits, is only bringing his own gifts to completion, he never tried to denigrate the dignity of the saints. He has no doubt that there is only one true way to sanctity, and that is the way of voluntary renunciation. But he makes a clear distinction between the counsels of perfection and the ordinary social duties.[27] All in all, his judgements on most everyday things show not the slightest sign of that mean-hearted and narrow-minded spiritualism that was later to produce the muscular type of Puritan Christian. Augustine was much concerned about keeping the Faith unspotted, and forthright in his condemnations of the old heathen customs, but he was no opponent of the good works of the simple-minded, nor was he cut off from popular piety. When Vigilantius attacked candles and relics, "unseemly" all-night vigils and monkish life-negation—whereupon Jerome hurled back even more angry abuse against Vigilantius, "or rather Dormitantius, who has opened his stinking trap against martyrs' relics once again" (but had also, unfortunately, dared to allude to Jerome's erstwhile sympathy for Origen)[28]—Augustine calmly let all the candles go on burning, let any rich people who wanted to go on founding monasteries do so, and any religious people who felt like living in them do so too; let his successor build chapels to house new relics, and only kept an eye on the all-night vigils. He recognized no barriers between the liturgy and personal piety, any more than the Jesuits do today. He did not pull a face when he saw hordes of pilgrims; on the contrary he mixed with them and delivered a sermon for the occasion. No indulgent smiles at the stupidity of ordinary people; he had no higher form of piety which he kept to himself. On the contrary, he says repeatedly that simple souls can get along quite satisfactorily with faith, hope and charity— once, even, that they can get along without Holy Scripture. The proper study of wisdom, which cannot be gainsaid, has no other foundation; and it gives at its best a foretaste of divine contemplation. The illusions he had had about this in his early days rapidly disappeared; he saw that they were the result of overweening folly, a hangover from the neo-Platonic system of thought, lacking humility. He had realized what heights of knowledge and wisdom the simple believer could achieve; he had only to think of his own mother. One thing became clearer and clearer to him, and was expressed ever more clearly in his sermons as time went on: What is left of a man when he cuts himself off from society? What is a Christian without the Church? Nothing in the Church of his day was alien to him.

Even his lack of interest in church decoration and his dislike of any sort of dramatic representation of the mysteries of the Faith was quite in line with the tradition of the African Church. His indifference to these things, which stands out so strikingly when compared with his friend Paulinus of Nola's enthusiasm, is characteristic of the whole period. It was Paulinus and Prudentius who were the exceptions, not Augustine. In the West images were not regarded as ugly or evil, but they were considered unimportant, and people were inclined to catch "uneducated" painters out on slight mistakes, with the theological pedantry that we later find in John Molanus. Thus, when Calvin, in the powerful introduction to his *Institutiones*, quotes passages from Augustine on the subject of worship and popular religion, we must remember, firstly, that they were carefully chosen, secondly, that they refer to conditions in the fifth century, and thirdly, that in Augustine's name he plays off these earlier stages against the current ones, towards which in fact the former, and many other ecclesiastical institutions, had been developing within the intervening thousand years.

Augustine's pessimistic teaching on inherited sin is closely bound up with his opinion of secular civilization. This brings us to the second question. Did Augustine really condemn civilization, and is he therefore a typical Christian fundamentalist?

Many people would answer this question in the affirmative, and try to convince others that it is so. In the eyes of such people, anyone who does not share their views is an incorrigible humanist trying to emasculate the splendidly independent fundamentalism of a Father of the Church. This changes the historical problem to one of principle, and Augustine's name becomes a rallying-cry for all who believe that an uncompromising decision for Christianity on the one hand or civilization on the other is absolutely essential.

This cry is a very old one. A whole line of great and serious-minded people have appealed to—after Holy Scripture—Augustine, in this matter of severity, including Peter Damian and Bernard of Clairvaux, Waldo and Calvin, De Rancé and the great Arnauld, and—believe it or not—both Pascal and Bossuet. On closer inspection we find others in this group—Tertullian, who did not know Augustine, Gregory the Great, who had a great veneration for him, and many modern Calvinists who neither quite dismiss him nor quite endorse his views. These people have ultimately only one thing in common: a more or less harshly rigoristic and pessimistic renunciation of some or all of the good things of civilization for the sake of "the one thing necessary", which may or may not be bound up with a pessimistic conception of fallen nature and a Barthian theory of God's transcendence. Bossuet needed his version of Augustine in his fight against the theatre and a vain dilettantism of the intellect, De Rancé against scientific work in monasteries, Calvin against cultural self-satisfaction and the forms taken by popular piety in the Church of Rome, many modern Calvinists against the general tendency to compromise the things of God with merely creaturely achievements. From this point of view, the Cluniacs, Mabillon, the Tridentine theologians and most Catholic scholars undoubtedly belong to the other side, but many of them claim to be just as good Augustinians as their adversaries. They say that the libraries at Cluny and Saint-Germain-des-Prés represent a direct continuation of the well-stocked episcopal shelves in Hippo; that Augustine would not have put either the imposing abbey church of St. Hugo with its nine towers and three hundred glass windows, or the works of the Maurists, or even Fénelon's *Maximes*, on the same level as the literary trifles of the fifth century; and finally, that not all scientific investigation, not all intellectual attempts to penetrate the mysteries of the Faith, not all of politics and the whole relative order and unity in the sphere of the State, are necessarily part of the devil's domain—which does not mean to say that they may not in fact sometimes belong to it.

Augustine was not by nature an obscurantist. It has been said that in his attitude to beauty and his theory of knowledge he remained in a way an optimistic humanist of the old stamp. He had fortunate endowments which prevented him in practice from denying human things. Had he not said, on his entry into the *episcopium*, Although I am a monk, my doors must remain open here; I must always be ready to receive visitors, for a bishop may not give the impression that he is "inhuman"?[29] Think too of those other unforgettable words: "May nothing that is horrible happen, nothing that is inhuman."[30] Anyone who studies Augustine's life and work finds in fact two Augustines and two kinds of Augustinianism. At one time he is the rapt inward-looking artist brought up on neo-Platonism, rising above the appearances of things and even the sacramental signs until he reaches the divine flash-point where black and white dissolve in purest light. Then, at others, he is the man who contemplates, now his own life, now the whole history of mankind, seeing all human souls as one vast mass doomed to perdition and falling into nothingness, falling further and further down, in the terrifying mystery of God's permissive will, until God himself takes a hand with the incarnation of his Son and reveals that he will grant his grace to the few who from that time onwards, led by his providential hand, keep to the strait and narrow way. The two views are radically opposed to each other; the first may be called the classic-optimistic attitude, the second the eschatological, orientated towards history, i.e., the facts in the Bible. For many people the gulf between the two is unbridgeable, like the gulf between the foolish wisdom of the heathen and biblical revelation. But since the time of the Council of Trent it must be clear to the children of the true Church that one must go beyond the two views before one can read Holy Scripture, not in this or that particular light, but in its own light. The first view has eternity as its horizon, the second time. Now, as we are born in time and held therein by sin, "we cannot pass over into eternity, unless the Eternal comes to us through birth [in time]"; this took place in Jesus Christ.[31] For Christ sees the eternal God being introduced into time through the incarnation of the Word, and so the Incarnation, the turning-point of history, becomes the point at which time and eternity meet, and the riddle of the conflict between them is solved. "The purified mind sees eternity; during the purification it believes in the temporal." One day we shall see the one true God; now we believe in him whom he has sent, Jesus Christ.[32]

As far as Augustine personally is concerned, the optimistic convert of the year 388 was thus soon transformed by his study of the Epistle to the Romans into a man broodingly contemplating the spectacle of sin and grace. And the spectacle presented to him year after year by the average run of parish life and the frightful disunity of African Christianity, and finally the far worse spectacle of the bumptious asceticism around Pelagius, left him with little of his earlier naïve optimism save a few bits of jargon. Nevertheless, he did not wholly give it up, any more than he gave up the philosophy which was its basis, but rather sublimated it, still silently holding on to it even in the sinister sheet-lightning flickering against the sombre background of the Bible. If it is wrong to regard sacred history as a tragedy, it is equally wrong to think of it as a transfiguring idyll; it is in fact the story of Paradise Lost and Paradise Regained. The optimistic view is always conscious of the fact that light will ultimately triumph, and therefore, from the supratemporal point of view, has already triumphed: *Christos voskres!* Christ has risen, no dead remain in their graves! The pessimistic view lives in the world of time, the vale of tears, crushed under the burden of sin and evil. It can see good only in the future. The first view can already see, like Stephen, the transfigured Christ as a present reality, and heaven wide open; the second looks forward to his second coming. Augustine united the two views (with a certain tendency towards the second), but at the same time he brought man's higher intellectual powers suspiciously near to the life of God, continually stressing the fact of their being in direct line with the divine, and cutting off all connection with the lower powers—unlike Thomas Aquinas, who both regards the mind as being so closely bound up with sense impressions, and also says that it would be nonsensical to regard human nature as a thing good in itself and at the same time utterly corrupt. There cannot be an absolutely corrupt nature; it would be an insult to the Creator to imagine such a thing as a possibility. The Church, though she tells us that the world beyond sense is an absolute mystery, has regarded it as her duty to make it clear that in this matter too there is no point in turning a mystery that lies beyond sense into nonsense.

Everything comes from grace; but we who are favoured with grace do not remain unfruitful. "Yea, the Lord shall give that which is good; and our land shall yield her increase."[33] Augustine, in brilliantly simply language, commenting on the words of the Psalm, "Yea, the darkness hideth not from thee", says, "Do not make your darkness even darker! For God does not make it dark, but brings light into it!" and in another place: "Go on, spring forward, to meet the light!" (the "divine flash-point" we spoke of earlier on). And these words can also be applied to the person who said them.[34] Every Christmas we hear, "The grace of God our Saviour hath appeared to all men", and shortly afterwards, "The goodness and kindness of God our Saviour appeared."[35] Despite himself, this strict Father of the Church found himself obliged again and again to speak with the comforting accents of Holy Scripture—and it is hard to think of anyone who excelled him in this. When one studies his finest sayings one always finds more light than darkness in them.

But it is not these more refined aspects of Augustine's intransigence that are really characteristic of his attitude towards secular civilization, but the intransigence itself. All true Christians are intransigent. Civilization, for them, is essentially a civilization of exile, for the City of God is not at home in this world; it is only *en route* for a world to come. This world is therefore a sort of thoroughfare, and civilization only supplies a sort of preliminary apprenticeship. As soon as Augustine became a priest he really treated the things that had become useless by the year 400 as though they were useless. He even put forward the idea of another "lust", the *libido sciendi*,[36] and dared to say so out loud—as he had a perfect right to do, being no world-forsaking ascetic but an educated man of letters, a man sated with education. He measured everything by one standard—the extent to which it served God, and whether there was any charity in it; and when that has been done there is not much left over, obviously, of most of the things considered important, certainly not in the fields of art and literature or the political struggle for power. And it was not philosophy—as was the case with the imprisoned Boethius—that drove the nine Muses out of his camp. It was concern for souls, his own and others!

After his consecration he wasted no more time on trifles. He did not want to seem for a second longer to be the aesthete which in fact he really was. Even in the power of beauty, he maintained, lurked demonry. No remark in secular literature can have touched him more deeply than the old words of Plato's about the poets, whom a properly ordered republic must send into exile; this, now that he saw it in the light of Scripture, became for him one of those bitter truths which one can only come to believe when one has to fight for them against one's earlier convictions, and persuades oneself to act according to them. He was never able to forget Vergil's poetry; but in his study and in the depths of his conscience he was engrossed in the problems of grace and freedom, sin and justification. He was a convert, a "turned-round" man, a man seized upon by God. The easy conception, held by the Cappadocian Fathers, of a cosmos already, in principle, divinized, would have remained alien to him, if he had been familiar with it, despite its Platonic background. He has left us no hymns about Christ,[37] no sensitive descriptions of splendid churches, or carefully polished collections of poems. He showed no enthusiasm for Hellenism, like the Christian humanists of the East. The white-haired Bishop of Hippo may have remembered with a shake of the head the highly-strung young scholar who, as soon as he had been baptized, could think of nothing better to do than to write a series of handbooks designed to provide a blue-print for a Platonic-Christian philosophy. How far behind him lay the dilettantism of Cassiciacum, when he had the psalms of atonement nailed up on the wall as he lay on his death-bed!

He died alone and penitent, concerned for the fate of the Empire, so far from perfect Christianity and yet so memorable an achievement, but infinitely more concerned about the future of the Church and the salvation of souls. This was not only the fruit of heroic self-mastery and lifelong mortification; it was the insight of genius. That sensitive nose had smelt the decay of a whole civilization. When he heard that Aquileia, Bononia, even Rome, were in flames, he cannot but have reflected that it was inevitable, that the whole thing had become senseless—"Ut quid locum occupat?" He was attached with his whole soul to the old Roman Empire, but in the *City of God* he finally settled his account with the Hegelians of the day, the circle centring round

Claudianus, Macrobius and Symmachus, who had created the myth of Rome and its syncretistically expounded folk-lore, the forerunners of the apostles of bourgeois virtue of 1791 and a certain Charles Maurras. He sensed how worthless, ultimately, all that old wisdom was which he had had handed down to him (in poor third-hand selections—a thing he did not know) from the ancients; all those collections of profound ideas, deep sayings, astonishing facts about nature and history and the artificial exercise of the will. Though he never did anything but praise Plato in his writings,[38] he nevertheless said in the pulpit that what the philosophers had discovered through their lust for knowledge—and that was a great deal—they had ruined with their pride. (There was nothing he would draw back from saying in his sermons!) Speaking on the words from the Psalms, "Their judges are overthrown in stony places", he explains that the rock is Christ, and the judges who fade away into nothingness, the philosophers. "Take Aristotle, put him near to the Rock, and he fades away into nothingness. Who is Aristotle? When he hears the words, 'Christ said', then he shakes in hell. 'Pythagoras said this', 'Plato said that'—put them near to the Rock and compare these arrogant people with him who was crucified!"[39]

If he spoke thus of the great, what must he have thought of the small ones of this world? He no longer paid any attention to their refinements. He had come to see that there was no point in going on polishing away at literature like Ausonius and Symmachus, or amassing knowledge like Macrobius and Martianus Capella, in an attempt to preserve the dead past. Marrou, who has published the most recent study of the general state of civilization at this time, says that Augustine was aware that he was living in a world of false values, and consciously avoided it. He sought something better, something lasting and eternal at the centre of all these crumbling buildings, collapsing boundaries, tottering authorities, dissolving relationships, this moribund scholarship. Augustine was one of the first to leave the house that was falling in ruins, taking with him only the things he would need to build something new—the old tools of the mind and the "study of wisdom", both only means to an end. In his three books on "Christian Knowledge" he puts it unequivocally: first faith, then a course of philosophy for the intellectuals, but for all people a knowledge of the Bible. In the second book, in which he inquires into the essential value of all human activities and institutions, he divides the institutions not infected by anything devilish into two groups, the useful ones and the unnecessary ones. To the first group belong many necessary forms of life and government and social relationships, and things like writing, money, weights and measurements; in the second he includes, besides literature and the plastic arts, anything that smacks of empty curiosity in, for instance, the fields of philosophy, philology and history, and cannot help in any way towards a better understanding of Holy Scripture. The study of chronology, on the other hand, he regards as useful, because it can be ancillary to exegesis. Furthermore, history acquaints us with many things that are not solely human in origin, but go back to forgotten traditions instituted by God himself. A certain knowledge of logic and rhetoric—*disputationis disciplina*—can also be useful on the understanding that any tendency towards sophistry is excluded. Further, it is permissible to extract the truth contained in the best philosophers, especially the Platonists, and it is also useful to learn the biblical languages.[40] But what is all this learning, compared with the knowledge of the one thing necessary? The contemplative life is higher than the active life. Rachel is greater than Leah, and Mary is more advanced than Martha.[41] If "anyone has an unshakable foundation of faith, hope and charity, he does not even need Holy Scripture, unless he has to teach others. Many people live entirely on these three things, without books, in the wilderness; in them is fulfilled what is written, 'Whether prophecies shall be made void, or tongues shall cease, or knowledge shall be destroyed... And now there remain faith, hope, charity, these three.'"[42] For intellectuals the contemplative life is synonymous with philosophy, but its basis is and always will be unshakable faith in Holy Scripture. The "study of wisdom" begins with submission to the supernatural influences coming from God, which liberate the will from fleshliness through grace, and the mind from scepticism through faith. Anyone who wants to go beyond hearing and believing must pray, study diligently, and live well; only then will he be able to develop an insight into what he believes—but even here the emphasis lies on the first thing, prayer.[43] Thus philosophy has its origin in piety—*pietas est sapientia*;[44] it is the human mind's activity around the things of faith, which, because of our condition as pilgrims in the world of time, are also historical facts, concrete, temporal, changeable and preliminary, for we come to them through the biblical facts of salvation, Holy Scripture and the tradition of the Church. By giving the human mind this transcendental aim and providing it with a new kind of teaching, decisively throwing out the old ballast at the same time, the Bishop of Hippo performed a greater service than Symmachus or even Boethius.

Exit Antiquitas

Augustine is the author of the most deeply personal, the most striking, but at the same time the most forcible book of the whole of Antiquity. No-one has ever caused more shock, aroused more religious feeling and more ardent enthusiasm for God's honour and the salvation of souls, through his books and sermons, than Augustine. In this he is a true representative of Christianity, in so far as this implies a spiritual revolution.

For never in the history of the human spirit has there been such a sudden change, arousing such a tremendous spiritual dynamism, as Christianity, in the tired old world of those days. It was as though mankind, the human personality, even the very soul itself, were given a new dimension, which found expression in the utterly new language of the Bible, in new types of character, new passions, new, unlimited aims and objects, and finally, after 313, even a new kind of art—an architectural art which suddenly produced the massive basilica, all focused upon a tiny altar erected for the reception of mystical gifts and the edification of the people, and a representational art devoted to portraying the all-important act of salvation and pictures of the saints. *Sophrosyne, gravitas, moderatio*—what remained of these ideals, still officially prized? They were masks, explained the new wise men.

There were still unbending thinkers who gave all their allegiance to the old wisdom (even today this has been so: did not Gilbert Murray ascribe our modern *pathos* to late Antiquity's "failure of nerve"?).[45] But what happened in the case of people generally, and the leading minds? Instead of a variety of different opinions, there was a single faith. Instead of manly resignation in the face of star-decreed fate, and the struggle for self-redemption by way of the intellect, there was a firm faith in a Redeemer of all men, who had been raised up above all the elements of the world. Above all, though, there was a demand for a genuine conversion of the heart, an *epistrophe*, instead of religious tricks of the trade and external observances. A powerful seriousness, a new kind of excitement, filled all the best minds of the day. The old ideas still held sway in certain restricted circles. The old gods, even those who figured at the heart of the mystery religions or had been sublimated into symbols in systems of philosophy, were not very demanding; you could take your choice amongst them, and ultimately they were no more than the puppets of fate. And then, all of a sudden, God was there, quite close, and his word was like a two-edged sword, penetrating to the very marrow of the bones and the depths of the heart. Sermons were being preached here, there and everywhere, not for the devotees of any single school, but for the people as a whole. No-one had any thought any longer for imposing temples, or for the "balanced" men with their harmonious words—no-one wanted them. The mighty cosmos, so delicately poised, with its contraries cancelling each other out in beauty—that comforting but heartless world-picture faded away. Now each individual fate was a drama of sin and grace, more important than the whole cosmos. Each separate soul hung with its own particular helplessness and its own particular responsibility between God and the devil, heaven and hell; with, over it and before it, no equivocal mythical figures of cosmocratic starry spirits, but Jesus, hanging upon the cross and calling out to it; no *polis*, not even a world empire any more, only fallen, redeemed, but still incomplete mankind. No-one was alone any more, and no-one had any right any longer to aristocratic isolation; the fate of the individual was inseparably bound up with that of the whole community of saints, and based on the demand for absolute humility. The proud cosmos had come to seem what it really was, a transitory world of appearances tortured by lust, sin and judgement, and of less importance than the least in the Kingdom of Heaven. The divine love drew everyone through this cosmos, between angels and demons, until he came face to face with the God of Justice.

All this utterly unexpected broadening out and uprooting of human feeling had been brought about by Revelation, through one book, the Bible, and one society, the Christian Church. Christianity took the earlier balanced and rationally conceived world picture, which was everywhere falling to pieces, and suddenly raised it into a fourth dimension, filling it with a new kind of emotion that overflowed all previous boundaries. In the first few centuries it had been the unshaken serenity of the martyr, the life in the world but not of it. This had perhaps included here and there a certain truculent element, of the sort characterizing small-minded people with one idea in their heads—or so it had seemed to the Emperor Marcus Aurelius—but fundamentally it had given a peace as pure as that experienced by Socrates, and one more firmly rooted, because it came straight from God. This had taken concrete form in innumerable simple people. Now in the fourth and fifth centuries the rich were renouncing their wealth and thousands were renouncing the joys of marriage and social life in the towns, because "poverty of spirit" was the only way to God and material poverty was a means to this; because the sexual impulse had the shadow of original sin over it and continence purified the eye for contemplation, because solitude was preferable to the distractions of civilization, and, finally, witness was a thing to be given not by words in the fashion of the talkers, the philosophers, but by self-discipline, patience and the fruits of the Spirit—since it could no longer be given by blood. Thus the hundreds who had witnessed with their blood were now followed by tens of thousands who testified through renunciation.

But even the more ordinary form of Christianity must have seemed strange, a sort of barbarous excess, to the heathens, who had suddenly become so out-of-date. They regarded it as a universal philosophy based on a series of puzzling misconceptions about the scandalously magnetic figure of Christ—as, incidentally, our modern heathens do too. Let us imagine that someone in Sulla's time had prophesied that within four hundred years there would be a big building in every town where on every seventh day a speech was made to the entire population, always about the same thing and the same Person, and in connection with a book, partly ancient-Jewish in origin, inspired with the spirit of God, surrounded by new symbols and mysteries and within the general framework of a rational sacramental sacrificial feast; that the impressive old sacrifices would be forbidden, and the open-air butchery, the smell of fat, the blazing altar fire, the thick smoke, the sound of the flute, the dressed-up priests, would all have disappeared. That instead of all this, thousands would be listening in silence to the news of the topsy-turvying appearance of God amongst us; that then everyone would stand up and say simple prayers together round a table covered with a white cloth and lit by the gentle radiance of innumerable lamps, with mixing jugs and a dish of bread, in the half-light of a pillared hall, amid deep stillness. And not just a few solemn faces and the officiating priest present, but the ordinary people, the average man of the day, and even cynics and aristocrats. And in spite of routine and habit, always the same incomparable sense of *pathos*; an outlook transcending the visible universe, the equality of all before God, the true voice of God being heard endlessly, and everything filled with the figure of Christ.

It was this contrast with the whole of the past that Augustine pondered over more than any of his contemporaries. He was the first human being in history to trace the historical contrast between the ancient world and the Christian Church back to the supratemporal contrast between fallen nature and divine intervention. He realized more clearly than anyone else that now that the fullness of time was come everything had changed; everything in the ancient world had only had a relative value, but now things had an absolute value. Compared with Christianity, what significance was there in things, admittedly good in themselves, like the order, unity and authority of the Roman Empire? What was he to think of the romanticism of *romanitas* as it existed in heathen circles in Rome—for is it not romanticism to see things classical as always existing in the past, and even today, for instance, to speak of the Ages of Faith as things dead and done with? Were even the old ethical insights worthy to serve as a basis for the scientific investigation of revelation? "All mortal things are only symbols"; they can therefore lead, on the one hand, to error, on the other, to fruitless resignation at the prospect of the unbridgeable gulf that is to be found equally in all fields of the spirit. In the year 400 all earthly things were recognized as relative, even the immortal Empire and the supposedly final wisdom of the ancients.

It was this fundamentally Christian realization that enabled Augustine, despite his refinement, not to love civilization for its own sake alone. Even religious activity did not seem to him to have an absolute value. Everything done here on earth, even caring for souls, belonged in his view to the sphere of the rhythmically revolving, perishable and largely illusory world, which, with its appearance and its truth, its good and evil, goes sweeping by, alternately light and dark like the revolving beams of a lighthouse. All earthly things belong to the rotation of opposites, whereby the cosmos "is perfect on the left side too",[46] because the opposites lead to a final harmony; but the movement only comes to rest when it is redeemed from all evil and can ultimately come to a stop in the final new creation, and God's Sabbath peace is manifested even in things. Till then "our days vanish into God's today", and all values, no matter how great they may be, remain relative.

Augustine the Man of the Early Church: Augustine the Genius: Augustine the Unconditional Christian

The significance of Augustine's spiritual travail for our own day lies, it seems to me, in the unconditioned character of its Christianity—not in the highly emotional character of his activity, and certainly not in the peculiar characteristics of the Church of his day. This last point needs especial emphasis, for there are still a great number of people about who are not prepared to give up their romantic view of the early Church at any price. But the early Church had its darker side too.

These admirers of the past have no lack of material, and they love to use it to put the modern Church to shame. How natural and self-confident the Church was in the year 400, they say. How independent, faced with the tremendous prestige of the old civilization! What joy it must have been, to have shared in the rise of Christianity and realized for the first time its great potentialities! How unexpectedly large looms Christian freedom, how small the attachment to law and precept! How direct and adaptable the form of worship was, how simple and open to everyone, how comprehensible and lucid! Even simple people were nourished by the fat and marrow of Holy Scripture. They knew their Psalms, used to sing them in their own language, and—very strange, this—obviously listened to the Sunday sermon with rapt attention. Who knows the Scriptures today? Who still sings psalms, except in a few monasteries? Isn't the Psalter in danger of becoming the exclusive property of dissidents, Benedictines and the well-bred people who arrange sung Vespers? How rarely sermons are drawn from Scripture, and how often from the world of action rather than that of contemplation. What remains of the old liturgy? It has become a kind of treasure-chest, containing the precious remnants of forms of piety long since dead and done with, which have been incorporated into modern ritual—two elements which, whether expressly or not, find themselves together to their constant surprise. The old plain chant has been filled out with neo-Gregorian offices, rather as the old cathedrals in Clermont-Ferrand and Moulins were enriched with neo-Gothic, *trompe-l'oeil* additions. The liturgy today is an incomparable, inexhaustible, but mongrel whole, alternately repelling and inspiring the initiated, either leaving ordinary people cold or occasionally delighting them, and filling the dilettantes with dainty aesthetic feelings. There is nothing on earth that reminds one of heaven as much as a High Mass in an old, well-filled cathedral, on one of the Sundays after Pentecost, with a good choir and congregational singing. But who enjoys this paradise, or can enjoy it, without the libretto called a missal? What remains of Christian freedom? How many ordinances make this sweet yoke a burden? Do we not all suffer, in both our churches and our moral theology, our ritual and our religious life, from this overloading which we have suddenly become aware of, and which is the reverse side of each new acquisition? And the pessimists end their complaints with a lament that the Church is so old.

But there is no lack of optimists either. Early, primitive things have their own incomparable charm, they say, but they can never be mature. One can appreciate the bud without losing one's pleasure in the full blossom. Should the liturgy have become fossilized, then, round about the year—well, when, as a matter of fact? After Leo the Great, or before Cluny? And as far as this torrent of new feasts is concerned, what precisely *is* a new feast? In A.D. 100 Easter was as new as a new pin, as Christmas was in 325, and in a few hundred years' time perhaps—who knows?—China will be celebrating the age-old feast of Christ the King with texts adapted from the forgotten liturgy for the Epiphany. And can anyone deny that today millions of Christians sing a *Kyrie* that was once sung only in some lonely Carolingian abbey, and later on only by paid choristers? And then, again, how difficult it is to estimate Christians' standard of life in the year 400. They really only went to Church because Christ was master of the world, and mightier than the demons. Are we to envy people who went in need of bread and were given the stone of allegory; who would sew a bit of the eucharistic bread into their clothes when they were going on a journey, believed the first story about miracles they came across, and were on the look-out for demons at the first suggestion of anything untoward? What has all this to do with having a proper estimation of our Lord's human nature, not to speak of a profound reverence for his holy humanity? How far people then were from giving any consideration to the God-Man's inner life, how far from the idea of our Lord as the bridegroom of the soul, and of the Sacred Heart of Jesus! The ardent heart and mind in Hippo went almost abstractly from the Son to the Father. In Augustine's eyes Christ was above all else an interior teacher. He speaks just as coolly from the Christological point of view as the anonymous creators of the sober Roman liturgy (who may to some extent at least have been contemporary with him); and much less mystagogically. Word and sacrament are today, from the external point of view, not as closely connected as they were once; but how much more evident has the difference become between what is essential and what is inessential. Spiritual direction is much more thoroughly differentiated; there is a much deeper awareness that everything in the Christian life is a pure gift of grace; daily meditation is practised to a far greater extent. The experience of sacrifice is lived far more vividly, the eucharistic life is much more interiorized, as is awareness of Christ's real presence in the Eucharist. The real meaning of Scripture is no longer hidden under allegorical fantasies; on the contrary, a recent biblical encyclopaedia has felt obliged to redirect our attention to the vast treasures of meaning that lie hidden within the spiritual meaning. How much centuries-old nonsense has disappeared, how much apparently consecrated confusion has been cleared away by criticism increasingly perceptive, if not always correct or even justifiable! How much freer from all sorts of slavery to the written word, and to that extent how much more spiritual, the general picture of sacred history has become: less archaic, but not less splendid. When we compare our parishes with those of ancient Africa we have to admit that there is a great deal of routine and ignorance amongst us, but hardly any exaggerated belief in miracles and practically no superstition. How simple the question of authority has become; how orderly the government of the Church! What a privilege to be able to be a member of the Church on earth today, now that she is two thousand years old!

In a certain sense both views are correct, but in another sense they are also mistaken, for in 400 the life of the Church was clearly as complicated as it is today, but in another way. The really wonderful thing about the ever-changing life of the Church lies in the fact that it is continually being differentiated and refined without disintegrating, or necessitating violent reactions, or over-drastic reforms. Fundamentally, the life of the Church never changes. In the early days the bishops consulted more with each other (and also, unfortunately, with the Emperor); today they consult more with the first bishop. In 400 masses of people went on pilgrimages to the *martyria*, today they go to the shrines of the Mother of God—if they go anywhere at all. In the early days the body and blood of the Lord were eaten and drunk as a mystery of faith, without much personal feeling; today, for most Christians, Holy Communion means a mysterious personal meeting rich with grace, carefully prepared for, and followed by an even more conscientious thanksgiving, which a hundred years ago used to last for several days. But the belief in the visible hierarchy, the invisible communion of the saints, the mystery of the altar, and the real experience of all these realities, have remained fundamentally the same. A Christian of the year 400 set down in a modern church would feel quite at home as soon as the first strangeness had had time to wear off, and would go on to experience the same mysteries, with different feelings no doubt, but in the same depths of the heart.

The early Church is a relatively small landscape, reflected in the upper stretches of a narrow river; our present-day Church is a broad plain on the lower stretches of the same river. The landscape is different, and the old one has become almost legendary, but the stream is the same and the continuity of the banks unbroken. There was not an early Church which suddenly came to an end somewhere—became medieval and thereby changed. To the end of time the Church will always remain equally appropriate to the times she lives in, because she brings each new epoch into contact with the whole of what lies ahead. It is not the early Church that can provide the light for our feet to walk by, but the glad tidings of Jesus Christ, which sound as clearly today as they did in those other days long ago.

Seen in this way, it is not, in the first place, Augustine the man, living in the year 400, who is of significance for us, but rather the Christian and the bishop as manifested in a man of his make-up. The man who was contemporary with the Anicii Probi and the sons of Theodosius remains a stranger to us, but we can understand the bishop perfectly, just as well as the people of Hippo did when he was alive. For there is an Augustine beyond all Augustinianism—the man who had one passion only, the love of God, and one devotion only, to the Church. If only we could learn to be like him! In his care of souls this man is in every respect typical of the Church. In his writings he may at times be a sort of theological El Greco, bringing forth the divine form like a flame and covering the human background with leaden white-edged clouds, but this man in the grasp of God, with his Latin that at times "sets one's teeth on edge",[47] is always, when he is in the pulpit, an announcer of the divine light. The essence of all his preaching and spiritual care is the announcement of the glad tidings.

What he announces is simple and always the same. God the Creator of all things is a just and loving Father, indeed, love itself. There is no such thing as fate, but election. Our love of God is purged by a chaste fear, quite different from the fear felt by the adulterer and the slave;[48] it has nothing in common with the pride of Pelagius or the anguish of a Kierkegaard. Man is neither good nor hopelessly lost, but affected with an hereditary taint and guilty and therefore susceptible to damnation; but in Christ he is redeemed from sin, death and hell.

Christ: the only-begotten Son of God, his word and image, and our redeemer. He is the way, the truth and the life. When he became man he became our only way; there is no other:

> Walk in the footsteps of this man and you will come to God. Look for no other way to come to God except this one. For if he had not himself become a way, we should always go astray. I do not say to you, look for

the way! This way comes to you itself; rise up and go. Go along this way by the way you behave, not with your feet. Many go along well with their feet, but badly in the way they behave. And of those who go well many go astray, for they meet people who live well but are not Christians. They can see well, but not along the way. The further they go, the further they go astray, for they are off the right way. But if such people get on to the right way and keep to it, how safe they are then! Then they not only go along well; they never go astray again! But if they fail to keep to the way, how sad it is for them, however well they may run! It is better to go stumbling along the right way than to go astray with steps as light as a feather.[49]

Mankind is one single family, in sin, in grace and in the Church, and no amount of patriotism or empire can obscure this truth, especially as empires are commonly the fruit of robbery. Only the soul is immortal, and it is in the soul that Christ can become a fountain of life and water overflowing to everlasting life. Christian perfection consists in humble love (which is why there is nothing greater than martyrdom),[50] and in the specially gifted (we are still in Antiquity) this love can become contemplative *sapientia*. He who has created us demands us wholly: "Hear what he asks of you through the mouth of Wisdom: My son, give me your heart!"[51] In eternity he himself will be the measure of his measureless love, but on earth too "the presence of his majesty will change us, when it finds the wide space of love in us."[52] Lastly, the world is no mere natural cycle, endlessly returning upon itself, but a history, ending in the triumph of grace over sin. Until then we live in exile, and "our conversation is in heaven".[53]

So if civilization is to have a meaning it must serve love as a whole, not Eros, who comes from below, but Agape, Christ, who comes from above. "The first man was of the earth, earthly, the second man from heaven, heavenly." In the same part of Holy Scripture it is written, "Knowledge puffeth up, but charity edifieth", and "Every plant which my heavenly Father hath not planted shall be rooted up."[54]

This is what Augustine of Hippo never stopped saying, and he never stopped translating it into reality. It is also his last word on the relationship between Christianity and earthly civilization. What he says is also valid for us, for it is but an echo of the divine voice that spoke the words of eternal love.

NOTES

INTRODUCTION

1. *CF*, 3, 1, 1.
2. *CF*, 6, 13, 23 and 15, 25.
3. *SE*, 356, 13.
4. *SE*, 302, 17 (date 10 August *circa* 400).
5. "Catholici te conditorem antiquae rursus fidei venerantur atque suscipiunt." (Jerome, *Ep.*, 141 (*CSEL*, 56, 2, ed. Hilberg=*Ep.*, 195, *inter ep. Aug.*).)
6. *VA*, 2.
7. Possidius, *Vita Augustini* (vol. 11, 285, in the Maurist edition of the *Works*); also in *AS*, 6, Aug., 215–28 and ed. Weiskotten, Princeton, 1919 and Vega, Escorial, 1934. Cf. Harnack in *PAWP*, 177, Berlin, 1930.
8. Sébastien Lenain de Tillemont, *Mémoires pour servir à l'histoire ecclésiastique des six premiers siècles*, Paris, 1702, vol. 13; cf. also the *Vita* in vol. 11, 1–492, of the Maurist edition (Paris, 1700) and that published by the Bollandists in *AS*, 6, Aug., 213–460.
9. I agree with the view of M. Gilson in his *Introduction à l'étude de S. Augustin*, Paris, 1929, and particularly with that of E. Hendrikx, *Augustins Verhältnis zur Mystik*, Würzburg, 1936. The divergence from the conceptions of Boyer and Cayré is chiefly to be explained by a difference in the definition of mysticism involved.
10. *EP*, 118, 17; cf. *CF*, 7, 20.
11. *WS*, 11, 6=*SE*, 142, 6.
12. *VA*, 29.
13. *VA*, 31 and Matt. v. 19.
14. *S. Aurelii Hipponensis Episcopi Operum, Opera et Studio Monachorum O.S.B. e Congregatione S. Mauri*, Parisiis, 1679–1700, 11 vols.; "S. Augustini Sermones post Maurinos Reperti", ed. Germanus Morin, in *MA*, 1, Rome, 1930; also the letters in *CSEL*, 34, 44, 57 and 58, ed. Goldbacher, Vienna, 1895–1923.
15. I do not know of any comprehensive study of the pastoral practice of St. Augustine. The numerous monographs on various points of detail are predominantly concerned with his educational theory, his catechetical practice and his ideas on moral theology. The essay of B. Altaner, "Augustinus als Seelsorger", in *Sacramentum Ordinis*, ed. E. Puzik and O. Kuss, Breslau, 1942, 29 pp.; H. Pope, O.P., *St. Augustine of Hippo*, London, 1937 (at the time of writing, out of print); J. Burnaby, *Amor Dei, A Study of the Religion of St. Augustine*, Hulsean Lectures, London, 1938 (at the time of writing, out of print)—these, unfortunately, I could not use. Vernon J. Bourke, *Augustine's Quest of Wisdom*, Milwaukee, Wis., 1945, and M. Pontet, *L'Exégèse de S. Augustin prédicateur*, Paris, 1946, were accessible to me too late to be consulted.

As to the liturgy, almost all the relevant texts can be found in Roetzer's *Des hl. Augustins Schriften als liturgiegeschichtliche Quelle*, Munich, 1930. The researches of Dom Busch concerning the *initiatio christiana* under Augustine in *EL*, 52 (1938), are rather in the nature of a critical reconstruction; both, however, concentrate more on the liturgy of that day than on Augustine's own practice. Pope's chapter on this subject was not accessible to me.

Certain details are to be found in the little essay of J. Zellinger, *Augustinus und die Volksfrömmigkeit*, Munich, 1933, and above all in F. X. Eggersdorfer, *Der hl. Augustinus als Pädagoge*, Freiburg, 1907. Other works and essays of which repeated use has been made are alluded to in subsequent notes.

PART 1

THE CHURCH OF HIPPO REGIUS

1. A Prisoner in the Lord

1. Cf. Morin, *RB* (1928), 366–7.
2. *VA*, 3. ("Agens in rebus" means a member of the imperial corps of couriers or orderlies: *Quaestiones de Notitia Dignitatem*, Or. II, Oc. 9, ed. Seeck, 1876) and *SE*, 355, 2 (*amicum*).
3. *CF*, 9, 6.
4. Ibid.
5. *VA*, 4, and *SE*, 355, 2.
6. *SE*, 355, 2 (*hortum*) and *VA*, 5 ("monasterium intra ecclesiam").
7. Eph. iv.1.
8. *EP*, 10, 2.
9. Jerome, *Ep.*, 52, 7 (*CSEL*, 54, 428, ed. Hilberg (with reference to 1 Cor. xiv.30–3)).
10. *VA*, 5 and *Pereg. Aether.*, 25, 1; vol. 3, p. 31 in the edition of Heraeus, Heidelberg, 1929. (Date, A.D. 395–400; according to Lambot, in *Revue Mabillon*, 49–69 (1938), A.D. 411–16; as against this see Loefstedt, *Philol. Kommentar*, Uppsala, 1936, 2 (after 550) and K. Meister, in *RMU*, 64, 327 f. (about 533–40)).
11. Paulinus of Nola in *Ep.*, 32, 2 (*inter epp. Aug.*), with references to the subsequent consecration of Augustine as bishop.
12. *VA*, 5; cf. *EP*, 41. Aurelius permits priests to preach in Carthage.
13. *EP*, 21.
14. *SE*, 216, 1, 2 ("rudimenta ministerii mei", "contirones mei") and *SE*, 20, 5.
15. *VA*, 7.
16. *DFS*, *RE*, 1, 17.
17. *VA*, 8.
18. *CCR*, 3, 80 and 4, 64. Date of consecration, 395; according to Morin, *RB*, 366–7 (1928), in the first half of January, according to Zarb, *AGM*, 261–85 (1933), in June or July.
19. *EP*, 38 (*Ad Profuturum*), 2.
20. *FSA*, 2, 4=*SE*, 339, 4.
21. *DSI*, 17, 8.
22. Leo the Great, *Ep.*, 12, 10 (*PL*, 54, 654–5; *BLO*, 667; cf. canon 6 of the Council of Sardica, *MC*, vol. 3, 10; cf. F. D. Moorrees, *De organisatie van de Chr. Kerk van Noord-Africa in het licht van de brieven van Augustinus*, Groningen and The Hague, 1926; G. Lapeyre, *L'Ancienne Église de Carthage*, Paris, 1932.
23. *BH*, 25 and canon 26 of the Third Council of Carthage; cf. *CCEA*, 39, *MC*, 3, 923, 884 and 734.
24. *EP*, 97, 2.
25. Batiffol, *Le Catholicisme de S. Augustin*, Paris, 1920, vol. 2, pp. 438, *n*, 445 and 446.
26. Batiffol, *Catholicisme*, p. 448; the council was adjourned a month later.
27. *CJ*, 1, 85.
28. *DEP*, 1, 1, 12.
29. Cf. the celebrated text in *EP*, 43, 7.
30. Batiffol, *Catholicisme*, pp. 455, 460–72; for greater detail see Trevor G. Jalland, *The Church and the Papacy*, London, 1946, pp. 287 onward; cf. the same author on the matter of Apiarius, p. 290.
31. *EP*, 122, 1.
32. *EP*, 10, 1–2.
33. *EP*, 216, 6; *EP*, 185, 18.
34. *IP*, 144, 1; *SE*, 306 (Utica), *DSI*, 17 (Bulla Regia); *IP*, 34 (at a synod).
35. *SE*, 94.
36. *RE*, 1, prologue.

37. *DDC*, 4, 24.
38. *DT*, 9, 10.
39. Lapeyre in *MA*, 2, 91–148 (St. Augustine and Carthage); De Bruyne, ibid., 321–5 (twenty-five *enarrationes in psalmos*=in all, thirty-four sermons given in Carthage).
40. *SE*, 312, 6; 311, 5; *DSI*, 14, 15, 22 (on the feast); *FSA*, 5 (on 8 September); *GUE*, 26.
41. *SE*, 258 (Easter, 410?), 261 (Ascension 410), 29 (Vergil of Pentecost).
42. *EP*, 34, 5.
43. *FSA*, 5, 6.
44. *EP*, 22, 9.
45. *EP*, 122, 1 (probably 410, cf. *SE*, 118, 34).
46. Gerontius, *Vita Melaniae Junioris*, 21 and 22; see Ch. 21 of the Greek *Life* in *AB*, 22, 21 (1903).
47. *EP*, 124, 1 and 2 (winter 410–11, after the conference with the Donatists).
48. *EP*, 124, 1.
49. *FSA*, 2, 1–4; *EP*, 86.
50. *DOM*, 29, 37; *VA*, 19 and 24; *EP*, 48, 1.
51. *FSA*, 2, 4.
52. *EP*, 110, 5; cf. *EP*, 139, 3.
53. *SE*, 8, 1, *De Jejun. Decimi Mensis*; *BLO*, 1, 59.
54. Sulpicius Severus, *Ep.*, 3, 10 and 11 (*CSEL*, 1, 148 (ed. Halm)).

2. THE TOWN AND COUNTRY

1. *Municipium* since Augustus, *colonia* since the time of Trajan; *GI*, no. 109 (*municipium*), *DCD*, 22, 8, 11 and 20 (*colonia*); *EP*, 35, 3 (*romana civitas*). Concerning Hippo see *DACL*, 6, 2483–531 and the bibliography there; further, De Labriolle in *DHGE*, 5, 440–73 and Homes van Mater Denis, *Hippo Regius from Earliest Times until the Vandal Invasion*, Princeton Dissertation, 1925. There is a map in *GA*, plate P, and pp. 5–11. See also *CIL*, 8, 5226–64. Cf. note 8 *infra*.
2. *VA*, 28 and 29; *VHP*, 1, 3, 11 (*CSEL*, 7, 6, ed. Petschenig); Procopius of Caesarea, *De Bello Vandal.*, 2, 4 (p. 438 in Haury's edition, Leipzig, 1936); George of Cyprus, *Descriptio Orbis Romani*, ed. Gelzer, 34 (*PG*, 152).
3. The church was designed in the Byzantino-Arabic style by the Abbé Pouget, who also built the Cathedral of Carthage, consecrated in 1890.
4. *CIL*, 8, 5276.
5. For twenty or so Christian inscriptions see *DACL*, 6, 2499–503; *CIL*, 8, 2562–4, 1744–5, 1741–4; W. Seston in *REA*, 38, 340 and 350 (1936); Gagé, *RHPR*, 1929 and in the *Bulletin de l'académie d'Hippone*, 1935.
6. *DACL*, 4, fig. 3582; *RBA*, 1894, p. 56; Strzygowski, *OC*, 1, 83–7 (1911).
7. *Bulletin de l'académie d'Hippone*, 35, 1925.
8. The results of the latest excavations are summed up in E. Marec, *Hippone la royale, antique Hippo Regius*, Algiers, 1954; id., *Augustinus Magister*, Paris, 1954, pp. 1–18; Leschi, *Revue Africaine*, 97, 258 f. (1953).
9. *EP*, 126, 4 (*aeris morbidi*); *EP*, 118, 34.
10. For the ruined towns of North Africa see *GMA*; J. Toutain, *Les Cités romaines de la Tunisie*, Paris, 1895; Cagnat, Boesillwald and Ballu, *Timgad*, Paris, 1905; R. Cagnat, *Carthage, Timgad, Tébesse et les villes antiques de l'Afrique du nord*, Paris, 1912; id., *En pays romain*, Paris, 1927, pp. 210–54 (on Dougga, Djemila and Khamissa); M. Douel, *L'Algérie romaine, forums et basiliques*, Paris, 1930; Berthier, Logeart and Martin, *Vestiges du christianisme antique dans la Numidie centrale*, Algiers, 1942 (contains data on Donatism); R. Batoccini, *Le antichità della Tripolitana*, Milan, 1926; S. Aurigemma, *Tripoli*, Milan, 1927; Ward Perkins and Goodchild, "The Christian Antiquities of Tripolitania", *Archeologia*, 1–84 (1953) (gives some archaic ground plans typical of the pre-Byzantine period); S. Gsell and Joly, *Khamissa*, Paris, 1914; id., *Announa*, 1918; id., *Mdaourouch*, 1922; S. Gsell, *Promenades archéologiques aux environs d'Alger*, 1926 (for Cherchel and Tipasa); for the floor mosaics see the list of Gauckler, *Basiliques chrétiennes de Tunisie*, Paris, 1913, vol. 2, pts. 1 and 2, 913 and 914 (Tunis), and De

Pachtère, *Inventaire des mosaïques de la Gaule et de l'Afrique*, 1911-25, vol. 3 (Algeria). For the earlier economic history see Rostovtseff, *The Social and Economic History of the Roman Empire*, Oxford, 1926, pp. 274-93. There is a detailed bibliography in C. A. Julien, *Histoire de l'Afrique du nord*, Paris, 1931.

11. *IP*, 53, 1; 55, 1; 58, 1, 1.

12. They depict the triumph of Amphitrite; a hunting scene; fishermen in the bay of Hippo, and a view of the monuments of the town (figs. 20, 55 and 50 respectively in Marec, *Hippone la royale, antique Hippo Regius*). The two mosaic floors on the east side of the adjacent *basilica major* (grapes and cupids, and the Muses) belonged to the villa which had been acquired by the Church. Marec ("Lybica", *Archéologie*, 1, 95 ff. (1953) takes it to be the villa of Julian mentioned in *EP*, 99 and *SE*, 355.

13. *CIL*, 7, 5276.

14. *SE*, 9, 13; *IP*, 53, 10; *SE*, 241, 5 (where there is an assumption of its being a general habit to visit the theatre).

15. *FM*, 1, superscription.

16. Geographically and ecclesiastically Hippo belonged to Numidia, though from the administrative aspect it had belonged since Diocletian's day to Africa Zeugitana, that is to say to the old Africa Proconsularis. In legal matters Augustine had to apply to the Proconsul in Carthage, *EP*, 133, 3 (to Marcellinus) and *EP*, 134 (to the latter's brother, Apringius, the Proconsul).

17. Cf. Busch in *EL*, 52, 402 (1938).

18. *CIL*, 8, 5351 ("curator frumenti comparandi in annonam urbis").

19. *SE*, 180, 5.

20. *RE*, 1, 17.

21. *EP*, 105.

22. *VA*, 28.

23. *SE*, 260 (Low Sunday); 262 (Ascension); cf. the old superscriptions (cf. *EP*, 29).

24. *SE*, 273, 7 ("memoria s. Theogenis"); *DCD*, 22, 8 and 9 ("memoria ad viginti martyres"); *SE*, 356, 10 ("basilica ad octo martyres"). See below.

25. *SE*, 356, 10 and *VA*, 31.

26. Timgad: *GMA*, 2, 309-12 and P. Monceaux, *Timgad chrétien*, Paris, 1911; Tigzirt: ibid., 2, 294-306 and the monograph of Gavault (1897). On the African basilicas see generally *GMA* and Gauckler, *Basiliques chrétiennes*; most of the monographs are referred to in J. Sauer, "Der Kirchenbau Nordafricas in den Tagen des hl. Augustinus", *Aurelius Augustinus, Festschrift Görresgesellschaft*, 1930, pp. 234-300; in regard to the Christian inscriptions see *MEC* (first published under the title "Enquête sur l'épigraphie chrétienne d'Afrique" in *RA*, 1903-6, then continued in *Mémoires Ac. IBL*, 12, pp. 161-339, 1908); P. Delattre, *L'Épigraphie funéraire chrétienne à Carthage*, Tunis, 1926; many details in *ILVC*, 1-3; the latest excavations are dealt with in the *Proceedings of the Third and Fourth Congresses of Christian Archeology*, Rome, 1934, pp. 387-427 and 1940, pp. 145-244 (dealing with the years 1920-38). The report for the years 1939-54 (that of the Congress held at Arles) has not yet been published. For Tripolitania see the monograph by Ward Perkins and Goodchild, referred to above in *n*. 10. The most imposing block of ecclesiastical building is that of Cuicul-Djemila. Concerning Cuicul-Djemila, see Albertini in *Atti del III Congr. Arch. Christ.*, Rome, 1934, pp. 411-18; Y. Allais, *Ruines de Djemila*, Paris, 1938; earlier finds in *GMA*, vol. 2, pp. 194-7, Monceaux in *CAIB*, 1922, pp. 290 ff., 380-407, and the proceedings of the Pontifical Academy, 3rd series, memor. 1, 1 (*Miscell. De Rossi*, Rome, 1923, 1, 106). The five-naved main basilica was built after the reunion with the Donatists in 411 by Bishop Crescon ius, a contemporary of Augustine.

27. "Basilica major seu pacis", *SE* 325, 2 (*major*) 258, ditto or *majorum*, i.e., in Carthage; *EP*, 213, 1 (*ecclesia pacis*).

28. For the word *baptisterium* see, for instance, *DCM*, 15.

29. *DCD*, 22, 8, 22; *SE*, 319, 7; 323, 4; 356, 7.

30. *SE*, 355, 2 and *VA*, 5; for the *secretarium* as a court of justice, see *SE*, 47, 4; as sacristy, *DCD*, 22, 8, 22; for the verses of Paulinus, *Ep.*, 22 (*CSEL*, 16, 29, 291 and 292): "Hic locus est veneranda penus qua conditur et qua promitur alma sacri pompa ministeril."

Weyman (*BGCP*, p. 99) thinks that *pompa* and *penus* mean the same thing. The sense would then be:

> "This is in truth the place where the sacred vessels are guarded
> Hence the glory sets out, bound for the worship of God."

31. *EP*, 29, 11.
32. *QIH*, qu. 177, 5; *SE*, 15, 1 (in Carthage, a gilt tabernacle-cover).
33. *DCR*, 13, 39.
34. *DCD*, 2, 28.
35. *DACL*, 2, 2, fig. 1159; *CIL*, 8, 17810; *ILVC*, vol. 1, 1856, p. 356; cf. Pseudo-Ambrose, *De Lapsu Virg.*, 6, 24 (*PL*, 16, 374 (363)).
36. *CCR*, 3, 47. In many ruins the sockets of the altar-feet have been found, but no stone remains. Baldachins were not yet known around 400; a certain number of baptismal pools, as, for instance, that in Cuicul, are surrounded by pillars which probably held the curtains, and were partly roofed over (plate 16).
37. *Cancelli*: *SE*, 392, 5, 322.
38. *DCD*, 22, 8, 22; for a pulpit for the lector in Cyprian, see *Ep.*, 38, 2 (*CSEL*, 3, 1, 581, ed. Hartel).
39. *EP*, 23, 3.
40. *EP*, 29, 8; *DCD*, 22, 8, 22 (*exedra*).
41. *EP*, 23, 3; cf. the mosaics of the dome of the baptistery of Neon in Ravenna, as also the strange anecdote in *Pontii Vita Cypriana*, 16 (*CSEL*, 3, 3, 108 ("linteum super sedile")).
42. *SE*, 91, 5 and *GUE*, 32, 4.
43. *IP*, 126, 3.
44. *CL*, 2, 6, 5 ("De superiore loco stamus vel sedemus"); *GUE*, 32, 9; *DSI*, 17, 2 (*superior locus*=*exedra*); 23, 1 ("altiore loco stamus"; Augustine was at the time already a bishop—20 Jan., about 410).
45. *EP*, 29, 6.
46. *SE*, 51, 5.
47. *SCA*, vol. 5, pl. 121, 1 and 3.
48. *IP*, 113, 2, 6; cf. *CCR*, 3, 29 ff. and *GZ* (*CSEL*, 26, 18, ed. Ziwsa: a record of the confiscation of the Church of Cirta, dated 14 May 303, with a full account of the case).
49. *SE*, 338, 2, 2 ("quando candelabra dedicantur"; they were also called *cereofala*).
50. *EP*, 190, 19; *SE*, 359, 9.
51. *DACL*, 4, 2, 2230–3; the mosaic is to be found behind the choir of the fourth-century basilica and dates approximately from the year 400. The inscription is: "ECCLESIA MATER VALENTIA IN PACE." The Orléansville lamp in the form of a church gives no details of the interior; cf. *DACL*, 2, 582, fig. 1143.
52. Cf. the vignette which serves as a headpiece to the Maurist edition of the sermons (Paris, 1683), fol. 2 (vol. 5 of the *Complete Works*).
53. *VHP*, 2, 17 (*CSEL*, 7, 30, ed. Petschenig).
54. *EP*, 86; 88 (superscription and 12); also 111, 1.
55. *GI*, nos. 134, 109; *GA*, pl. 9, no. 86.
56. *EP*, 139, 1 ("ecclesias in diocesi constitutas"); 209, 2 ("ad Parochiam Hipponensis ecclesiae pertinebat"); 103, 3 ("ad Hipponensium Regiorum diocesim").
57. *DCM*, 12, 15.
58. *EP*, 209, 2 (*milibus quadraginta*=approximately 36 miles).
59. *SE*, 125, 5.
60. *SE*, 70, 2.
61. *GI*, nos. 89, 93, 131, 285; *EP*, 66, 1 (imperial); *EP*, 58, 1 and 46 (senatorial).
62. *EP*, 21, 5 (*villa ecclesiae*); *EP*, 126, 7 (*praediorum ecclesiae*).
63. *EP*, 139, 2 (*procurator*).
64. *EP*, 35, 4 and 46, 2; 105, 1 (*conductor*); *EP*, 247, 1, 3 (*actor, Ponticanus*).
65. *IP*, 32, 3, 18 and *SE*, 345, 1.
66. *EP*, 66, 1; 58, 1; 105, 4.
67. *EP*, 47, 3.
68. *IP*, 70, 17.
69. *EP*, 58, 1.

70. *EP*, 66, 1 (the *Mappalienses* under Crispinus).
71. *EP*, 84, 2; 66, 12; 209, 3 (at Fussala); *SE*, 167, 4 (in the town not all understand Punic; Augustine is translating a proverb); cf. *GI*, 14 (Berber inscription with added Latin translation).
72. In the bishopric of Hippo alone we hear of *ecclesiae* in Subsana (*EP*, 63, 4; 62, 1), Verbalis (63, 4), Malliana (236, 1 and 3), Fussala (209), Mutugenna (23, 2), at the Villa Victoriana (*DCD*, 22, 8), in Asna (*EP*, 29, 12), *Germaniciana* (251), on the Fundus Gippi (65; *ecclesia Gippitana*), Spanianum (35, 2 and 4), and an *ecclesia Strabonianense* (65, 1); special rural bishops resided later in Thiava (*EP*, 83, 1), Siniti (*EP*, 92, 3; 105, 4; *CC*, 1, 202 (*MC*, 4, 153), Turris (*EP*, 34, 6; 63, 4) and in the Municipium Tulliense (*DCM*, 12, 15; cf. Fifth Council of Carthage, 525 (*MC*, 8, 647)).
73. *ILVC*, vol. 1, 1828, p. 360 or *DACL*, 6, 2, 250:

> que primitie nos
> tre virtutis sunt ex le
> ctione et aspectu pro
> bantur nam novum edi
> ficium quod cernis nos
> tro labore hoc incept
> um atque perfectum
> est

74. Gsell in *Mélanges d'archéologie et de l'histoire de l'École française de Rome*, 1894, 24.
75. *EP*, 63. The priest of Subsana also came with his lector Timotheus to Turris, Cizau and Verbalis; this lector was consecrated as a subdeacon in Subsana without Augustine's knowledge, but Augustine summoned him back.
76. *GA*, pl. 9 and p. 62; for the epitaph, *CIL*, 8, 17445: "Cu †stos subdiaconus bixxit in pacci annos XCIII."
77. *SE*, 46, 39; *IP*, 148, 10 (*nuda Getulia*).
78. *IP*, 90, 2, 6.
79. *IP*, 125, 13.
80. *SE*, 252, 5.
81. *IP*, 80, 1.
82. *IP*, 101, 2, 10.
83. *SE*, 277, 5.
84. *DME*, 2, 16, 42.
85. *MO*, 12, 1.
86. *EP*, 185, 44.
87. *IP*, 47, 9.
88. *IP*, 128, 13.
89. *IP*, 99, 4: "Maxime jubilant qui in agris."

3. THE PAGANS

1. *SE*, 302, 19, 21; *EP*, 199, 38 (a list of callings. He mentions incidentally "those who plough, drive, buy, educate children, sit in an office").
2. *IP*, 54, 13; cf. *EP*, 136, 3.
3. *EP*, 189, 4–8; 151, 14; 158, 5.
4. Council of Elvira, canons 2–4 (*MC*, 2, 6: (*flamines*)); cf. *Codex Theodosianus*, 12, 1, 112 (16 June 386), *CTM*, 690 (prohibition against bestowing the office of Pontifex Maximus on a Christian); Duchesne, in *Mélanges Rénier*, 24.
5. *SE*, 51, 4: "Intus est jam pene tota nobilitas."
6. *IP*, 90, 2, 4.
7. *Contra Symmachum*, 574–7 (*CSEL*, 61, 240). He is speaking of the aristocracy, particularly the Roman Senate; shortly afterwards he says the same thing of the common people.

> Vix pauca invenies gentilibus obsita nugis
> ingenia, obtritos aegre retinentia cultus
> et quibus exactas placeat servare tenebras
> splendentemque die medio non cernere diem.

8. *IP*, 46, 5 and 48, 2, 1 (concerning apparent conversions).
9. *EP*, 227.
10. *IP*, 83, 7; 25, 2, 2; *SE*, 141, 4.
11. *SE*, 24, 2 (delivered in Carthage).
12. *MO*, 1, 2 and 3 (23 June 401).
13. *DDD*, 10, 14; cf. *IP*, 90, 1, 4.
14. *DSI*, 17, 7 (refers to Bulla Regia); cf. *SE*, 61, 11.
15. *FSA*, 8, 5 and *IP*, 137, 14.
16. *EP*, 138, 20.
17. *SE*, 15, 6; 5, 8; cf. *IP*, 25, 2, 14.
18. *SE*, 47, 28.
19. *SE*, 352, 9; *IP*, 101, 1, 10 (concerning penance).
20. *EP*, 227.
21. *EP*, 16, 2. On the martyrs mentioned see Baxter in *JTS*, 26, 21–38.
22. *EP*, 16, 4.
23. *EP*, 17.
24. *SE*, 273, 3 and *DCD*, 8, 26.
25. The same theme is more broadly developed in *DCD*, 4, 8.
26. *EP*, 16, 1 ff.
27. *EP*, 234, 1, 3.
28. *EP*, 233.
29. *EP*, 135, 1 and 2.
30. *EP*, 234, 1.
31. Cf. *EP*, 232, 1 and 2.
32. *EP*, 232, 3–7.
33. *EP*, 91, 3.
34. *EP*, 138, 18 and 19.
35. *DCD*, 8, 12.
36. Cf. *DCR*, 8.
37. *EP*, 102.
38. Jerome, *Ep.*, 107, 1 (*Ad Laetam*) (*CSEL*, 55, 291, ed. Hilberg).
39. *EP*, 132.
40. *EP*, 135.
41. *EP*, 136.
42. *EP*, 137.
43. Cf. St. Leo the Great, *Ep.*, 165 (quotes *Ep.*, 137, 9); *BLO*, 1, 1391.
44. *EP*, 138.
45. *IP*, 80, 17.
46. *IP*, 68, 1, 12; 34, 2, 8; 93, 15; cf. 40, 1.
47. *IP*, 136, 9.
48. *Cod. Theod.*, 16, 10, 8 and 10 and 12 (*CTM*, 899 and 900): laws of 30 Nov. 382, 24 Feb. and 16 June 391 and 8 Nov. 392.
49. *Cod. Theod.*, 16, 10, 13 and 15–20 (*CTM*, 901–3): laws of 7 Aug. 395 (confirmation of the Theodosian prohibition of sacrifice): 29 Jan. 399 (sacrifices forbidden but damaging of public buildings not permitted): 10 July 399 (the temples in the territory in the East to be unobtrusively demolished): 20 Aug. 399 (directive to Appolodorus, Proconsul of Africa, to forbid sacrifice but retain popular festivals): 20 Aug. 399 (directive to the abovementioned: empty temples are not to be torn down but put to better use): 15 Nov. 407 and 408 (all sacrifices and festivals forbidden; the appropriation abolished; statues to be removed from temples). Cf. Sirmond. 12: *CTM*, 916: laws of 25 Nov. and 30 Aug. 415 (law of 408 concerning personnel and temple property again confirmed).
50. *DCD*, 7, 26 and 2, 4.
51. *DCD*, 18, 54.
52. *SE*, 22, 4, *DSI*, 24, 7, *CL*, 2, 19, 2, *MO*, 266, *CAS*, 2, 114, 2, *MO*, 416.
53. *DCE*, 1, 27, 42.
54. *EP*, 91, 8; 103, 1; 97, 2.
55. *EP*, 185, 19.
56. *Liber in S. Babylam*, 14 and 16 (*PG*, 50, 554 and 557); Sozomen, *Historia Ecclesiastica*, 5, 9; Ps. cxiii.8.

57. *SE*, 24, 6; for the date see Morin in *MA*, 1, 593, *n*. 15.
58. *EP*, 232, 3.
59. *IP*, 103, 4, 4; cf. *DCD*, 18, 54.
60. *DCD*, 5, 25 and 26.
61. *SE*, 62, 18.
62. *EP*, 50.
63. *EP*, 91, 8: "contra recentissimas leges", namely, the law of 17 a.d. kal. Dec. 407, which came into force in Carthage in June 408 and by which it was forbidden "to organize a festival in honour of a sacrilegious rite". (*Cod. Theod.*, 16, 10, 19; *CTM*, 903 and 917.)
64. *EP*, 91, 8 and 104, 5.
65. *EP*, 90; cf. 91, 10.
66. *EP*, 91.
67. *EP*, 97, 1–4.
68. *Cod. Theod.*, 16, 5, 46 and Sirmond., 14 (15 Jan. 409), *CTM*, 870 and 918.
69. *EP*, 103.
70. *EP*, 104.
71. *SE*, 105, 12.
72. *SE*, 62, 18.
73. *EP*, 185, 12; *SE*, 62, 17; *CEP*, 1, 10, 16.
74. *EP*, 185, 12; cf. the Council of Elvira (314), c. 60 (*MC*, 2, 15).
75. *SE*, 62, 17 and 18.
76. *EP*, 47, 3; *CG*, 1, 38, 51.
77. *CG*, 1, 38, 51; *SE*, 163, 1 and 2.
78. *IP*, 80, 1 ("Deus non pluit, duc ad christianos"); cf. *DCD*, 2, 3 ("Pluvia defit causa christiani").
79. *SE*, 296, 6; 105, 10; 81, 9.
80. *DCD*, 6, 8.
81. *IP*, 137, 14.
82. *IP*, 40, 1; *DCD*, 18, 54; cf. 53, 2 and 22, 25.
83. *RE*, 2, 43: "quos usitato nomine paganos vocamus"; the expression is already customary by 17 Feb. 370 (*Cod. Theod.*, 16, 2, 18: *CTM*, 841); cf. Sirmond. 14, *CTM*, 919: "gentiles quos vulgo paganos appellant"; see Zeiller, "Paganus", in *Collect. Friburg.*, 1917, 1, 17.
84. *EP*, 199, 12, 46: "In Africa barbarae innumerabiles gentes"; cf. G. Metzger, *Kirche und Mission in den Briefen Augustinus*, Gütersloh, 1936.

4. The Legacy of Paganism

1. *EP*, 232, 1 and *IP*, 98, 2.
2. *SE*, 359, 8.
3. *SE*, 248–251, *WS*, 13; *TJ*, 122.
4. *IP*, 39, 10 (*super numerum*).
5. Isa. ix.3.
6. *DCR*, 7, 11.
   Venari lavari ludere ridere occ est vivere.
7. Cagnat, *Carthage, Timgad, Tébesse*, Paris, 1912, p. 70.
8. *DCR*, 25, 48; cf. *SE*, 250, 3; 252, 4; *IP*, 30, 2.
9. De Labriolle in *Arch. Lat. Med. Aevi*, 2, pp. 177 ff. (1925), and Rahner in *ZKT*, 55, pp. 272 ff. (1931).
10. *EP*, 138, 14.
11. *CF*, 3, 2.
12. e.g., *DSI*, 14, 3; cf. *IP*, 50, 1; 80, 23 (a few words following the sermon).
13. *SE*, 290, 2.
14. *DSI*, 15, 2; Quodvultdeus, *De Symb. ad. Catech.*, 2, 5 (vol. 6, p. 558, in the Maurist Complete Works); Ps. lxxiii.19.
15. Cf. G. Boissier, *La Fin du paganisme*, Paris, 1891, vol. 2, pp. 171 ff. (the letters of Symmachus); further, Ambrose, *De Offic.*, 2, 21, 109 (*PL*, 16, 140 and 141). There is a description of a *venatio* in *SGD*, 6, 2 9–13 (*CSEL*, 8, 126 and 127).

16. *SE*, 32, 20.
17. *IP*, 147, 7 and 12; cf. *SE*, 21, 10; *IP*, 149, 10.
18. *SE*, 51, 2.
19. *CA*, 1, 2.
20. *IP*, 147, 7.
21. *CF*, 6, 8.
22. *SE*, 20, 3; *IP*, 101, 10; see also *IP*, 25, 9 (a servant of God waits in the amphitheatre for a gladiator whom he wishes to buy out); in regard to the official prohibition cf. *Cod. Theod.*, 15, 12, 1; Prudentius, *Contra Symmach.*, 2, 1414–29; Kirsch in *RQ*, 26, 210 (1910) and Delehaye in *AB*, p. 421 (1914); cf. Theodoret, *Historia Ecclesiastica*, 5, 26.
23. *IP*, 80, 23.
24. *IP*, 50, 1; *SE*, 19, 6.
25. *IP*, 147, 7.
26. *IP*, 50, 2.
27. *IP*, 39, 7.
28. *IP*, 39, 10.
29. *IP*, 39, 9.
30. *IP*, 80, 11 and 2.
31. *IP*, 39, 6.
32. *IP*, 53, 10; 39, 8–18; *SE*, 198, 3.
33. *IP*, 149, 10; 33, 6; *SE*, 332, 1.
34. *IP*, 72, 34.
35. *IP*, 39, 8.
36. *SGD*, 6, 3, 14–19 (*CSEL*, 8, 127–9, ed. Pauly); cf. Ovid, *Ars Amatoria*, 1, 99 and 100 ("Ille locus casti damna pudoris habet"); Tertullian, *De Spectac.*, 10 and 17 (*CSEL*, 20, 11–13 ("proprie sacrarium Veneris est")), also 18 and 19; Cyprian, *Ad Donat.*, 8, 1 (*CSEL*, 3, 1, 9 and 10, ed. Hartel); Pseudo-Cyprian, *De Spectac.*, 6 (*CSEL*, 3, 3, 8 and 9; Lactantius, *Divinarum Institutionum*, 6, 20 (*CSEL*, 19, 555–62, ed. Brandt)).
37. *EP*, 91, 5; *DCD*, 7, 26; 2, 8; 1, 32.
38. *DDC*, 2, 25, 38.
39. *CF*, 1, 13, 20–22; *SE*, 241, 5.
40. *CF*, 4, 2, 3 and 3, 5.
41. *IP*, 96, 10 (*choraulum*).
42. *EP*, 91, 5; cf. 138, 14.
43. *IP*, 39, 9; *EP*, 9, 3; 120, 5 (*histriones, funambuli*).
44. *SE*, 241, 5.
45. *CL*, 2, 19, 7; *MO*, 270; *SE*, 198, 3 ("the devils rejoice").
46. *DSI*, 14, 3.
47. *IP*, 147, 8.
48. *SE*, 9, 13.
49. *IP*, 103, 1, 13 ("ubi abundant spectacula").
50. *IP*, 50, 11.
51. *CIL*, 8, 5276.
52. *DSI*, 17, 7 ("Si non tanta erit solitudo, ut sibi erubescat turpitudo").
53. Ibid., 17, 8 and 9 ("onerant, non honorant").
54. *Cod. Theod.*, 16, 10, 3 and 17 and 19 (*CTM*, 898, 902, 903): laws of 342, 399 and 407; cf. Sirm. 12, *CTM*, 917.
55. *SE*, 198, 1; cf. *SE*, 196, 4 and 197; on the persistence of the New Year jollifications in Gaul see R. Boese, *Superstitiones Arelatenses e Caesario Collectae*, Marburg, 1909.
56. *SE*, 196, 4.
57. *TJ*, 7, 6 (27 March 418); cf. *DCD*, 2, 4; 6, 1–3; 7, 24–6.
58. Ibid., 7, 24.
59. *IP*, 26, 2, 19.
60. *IP*, 98, 14; *SGD*, 8, 2, 9–13 (*CSEL*, 8, 194–6, ed. Pauly); *EHC*, 507.
61. *IP*, 62, 7.
62. *IP*, 26, 2, 19; 43, 1, 7; cf. *RE*, 2, 43; *EP*, 169, 1 and *DSI*, 21, 6.
63. *IP*, 40, 3.
64. *IP*, 73, 25 ("Frater ipse catholicus torquet os") and *SE*, 361, 6.

65. *SE*, 62, 7 and 10 ("recumbere in idolio").
66. *Pythonissae, alligatores, praecantatores*: *TJ*, 6, 17; *IP*, 33, 2, 8, 18; 34, 1, 6; 35, 7; 59, 11; 90, 1, 4; 93, 20; 140, 18; *SE*, 9, 3; 56, 12; 88, 25; *DCR*, 7, 11; 25, 48; 27, 55; *MPB*, 25, 3; cf. M. E. Keenan, *The Terminology of Witchcraft in the Works of St. Augustine*, Chicago, 1940, pp. 274 ff.
67. *IP*, 26, 2, 19; 96, 12; cf. 35, 7; 66, 2.
68. *IP*, 91, 7; cf. 133, 2.
69. *IP*, 133, 2.
70. *IP*, 91, 7.
71. *MO*, 8, 3; DSI, 21, 4; on headaches: *SE*, 4, 36; *IP*, 70, 1, 17; *TJ*, 7, 7.
72. *GUE*, 18, 2; *MO*, 8, 2.
73. *DDC*, 2, 20, 30.
74. *SE*, 286, 7.
75. *SE*, 4, 36.
76. *MPB*, 25, 3; concerning *arrepticios*, see *SSA*, 167.
77. *MO*, 8, 3.
78. *TJ*, 7, 6.
79. *DSI*, 7, 3 (*flagellum-saccellum*) and 21, 4; *IP*, 127, 11.
80. *DCR*, 7, 11; 25, 48; 27, 55.
81. *EP*, 98, 1-4; cf. Cyprian, *De Lapsis*, 25 and 26 (*CSEL*, 3, 1, 255, ed. Hartel).
82. *EP*, 245, 1 and 2; cf. *DDC*, 2, 20, 30; *QIH*, 1, 111 (concerning Gen. xxxv.2—*idolorum phylacteria*).
83. *DDC*, 2, 20, 30.
84. *DDC*, 2, 20, 31.
85. *DDC*, 2, 21, 32; cf. *IEJ*, 3, 9; *SE*, 9, 3, 3; *IP*, 59, 11; the name itself is already in Tacitus, *Annals*, 2, 32 and Suetonius, *Tiberius*, 36. Concerning the astrology of that day, see F. Boll, *Sternglaube und Sterndeutung*, Leipzig-Berlin, 1926, 3; Bouché-Leclercq, *L'Astrologie grecque*, Paris, 1899; L. de Vreese, *Augustinus en de Astrologie*, Maastricht, 1933; P. Duhem, *Le Système du monde*, Paris, 1913-14, vol. 2, pp. 410, 430.
86. *CF*, 4, 3, 4-6.
87. *CF*, 5, 7, 12; 7, 6.
88. *CF*, 7, 6, 9.
89. *DDQO*, qu. 45.
90. *DDC*, 2, 21, 32.
91. *DCD*, 5, 2-6.
92. *DGL*, 2, 17, 35-7; cf. *DDQS*, qu. 2, 1 and 3 and Rom. ix.10; *DDC*, 2, 22, 33-5.

Quantaque quam parvi faciant discrimina motus.

93. Manilius, *Astronomica*, 2, 808.
94. *DDQO*, qu. 45.
95. *DCD*, 5, 3.
96. *DCD*, 5, 5-7.
97. *DCD*, 5, 9.
98. *DCD*, 5, 1.
99. 1 Cor. x.20.
100. Ps. cxl.4; cf. *IP*, 140, 6 and 31, 2, 16.
101. *IP*, 140, 9; cf. *EP*, 246, 1-3; *IP*, 31, 2, 16; 128, 9; 61, 23.
102. *IP*, 91, 3; cf. *MPB*, 17, 2; *IP*, 58, 1, 14.
103. *DCD*, 5, 1.
104. *SE*, 199, 3.
105. *IP*, 140, 6.
106. *IP*, 58, 1, 14.
107. *SE*, 199, 3 ("Servos tuos in domo peccantes verberare—deos suos in coelo radiantes blasphemare").
108. *IP*, 140, 9; cf. *EP*, 246.
109. *TJ*, 8, 11.
110. *IP*, 61, 23; cf. Acts xix.19 and Ps. iv.3.
111. *Ephemerides*, *IP*, 40, 3; *EEG*, 34 and 35.
112. *EP*, 55, 7, 13; *DCD*, 5, 7; cf. *SE*, 190, 1.

113. *EEG*, 35.
114. *ENC*, 21, 79 and 80: cf. Gal. iv.11.
115. *SE*, 9, 11, 18.
116. *SE*, 9, 3, 3.
117. *TJ*, 8, 8.
118. *EP*, 55, 7, 12.
119. Gen. i.14; cf. *DGL*, 2, 14, 29; *EP*, 55, 7, 13; *TJ*, 2, 4; 7, 30; 8, 20; 17, 1; also 31, 6 and 104, 2 and the remarks which follow.
120. *TJ*, 8, 8.
121. *CFA*, 2, 5.
122. John x.18; *TJ*, 8, 10–12; 27, 9.
123. 2 Cor. vi.2 and Isa. xlix.8.
124. *SE*, 199, 3.
125. *CFA*, 2, 5.
126. *SE*, 200, 1; 201, 1.
127. Gregory the Great, *Hom.*, 10, 4 (*In Evang.*) (*PG*, 76, 112).
128. *EEG*, 34 and 35 and Gal. iv.10 ff.
129. *DCD*, 5, 7; Juvenal, *Sat.*, 6, 553–91 (on superstition about the stars among women).
130. *IP*, 133, 2.
131. *TJ*, 10, 5.
132. *IP*, 10, 3 and 4 (*sol et luna=Christus et ecclesia*); *IP*, 93, 4 (*sol=Christus*); *EP*, 55, 5, 8 (*sol=sapiens, luna=stultus*); *IP*, 88, 2, 5 (*luna=caro*); cf. *EP*, 55, 6, 10 (*luna= caro et ecclesia*); ibid., 5, 8 (=*caro in Adam*; see also the detailed allegories in *IP*, 103); cf. Ps. lxxxviii.38 and lxxi.7.
133. *IP*, 93, 5 and Phil. ii.15.
134. *IP*, 93, 4; cf. Ps. cxiii.4.
135. *EP*, 55, 7, 12 and Matt. x.16.
136. *DCD*, 5, 8.
137. *EP*, 228, 12 (with reference to Prov. xviii.18).
138. *CA*, 1, 7, 20 ("huius aëris animalibus quibusdam vilissimis quos daemones vocant"); *DCD*, 10, 11, where he commends Porphyry's opinion that the demons are "non in aethere, sed in aëre sub luna".
139. Cf. Col. i.13 and 16; Eph. ii.2 and vi.12.
140. *DCD*, 8, 14 and 16.
141. Ps. xcv.5; cf. *DCD*, 2, 10 and 23 and 24; 4, 27; 7, 27 and 28, 33 and 35 and, above all, 8, 14–24; 10, 11; 18, 18; *IP*, 26, 2, 19; 96, 12.
142. *DDD*; cf. Courcelle (ibid., 591) 166 (Porphyry).
143. *EHC*, 2, 646; concerning the date see R. Herzog in *Pisciculi*, 117 ff. (1939); for Porphyry Serapis was the head of the evil demons.
144. *DCD*, 8, 14 and 15; 9, 2 and 3 and 18–22.
145. *DDD*, 3, 7; 4, 8; cf. (in shorter form), *DGL*, 2, 17, 37; *CA*, 1, 7, 20; with reference to works of art, *DT*, 3, 7, 12; 4, 11, 14.
146. *DDD*, 6, 10 and *DCD*, 9, 22.
147. *DDD*, 5, 9 and *RE*, 2, 30.
148. *DDD*, 7, 11–19, 13.
149. *DGL*, 11, 28, 35.
150. *DCD*, 5, 7; *DDC*, 2, 23, 35; *DGL*, 2, 17, 37; cf. *IP*, 96, 12 (on the presence of the demons behind the temple cults).
151. *DDC*, 2, 20, 30 ff.
152. *DDC*, 2, 24, 37.
153. *DDC*, 2, 23, 35 and *DCD*, 5, 7.
154. Ibid., cf. Deut. xiii and Acts xvi.16 ff.
155. *DGL*, 2, 17, 37 and *DCD*, 5, 7.
156. *DDQO*, 83, qu. 79, 1 (concerning the demonic sacraments of the Magi).
157. *DCD*, 9, 18 and 20.
158. *DT*, 13, 12–16 to 14, 19.
159. *SE*, 263, 1; 134, 5 and 6; cf. *GUE*, 21, 2; *MO*, 17, 5 (here also the image of the fish biting the hook).

160. *DCD*, 10, 22.

161. *DCD*, 5, 25. The idea that possession is due to the desire of the demons for carnal intercourse is found very early. (Pseudo-Clement, *Hom.*, 9, 10 (*PL*, 2, 247). There is no indication, however, that Augustine shared this view.

162. *DCD*, 10, 22 and 8, 26, conclusion.

163. *DDQO*, qu. 79, 1; cf. *IP*, 145, 5 ("sit licet corpus angelicum").

164. Martianus Capella, 6, 584 (p. 290 in Dick's edition, Leipzig, 1925).

> Tellus quae rapidum consistens suscipit orbem
> Puncti instar medio haeserat ima loco.

Cf. Boethius, *De Consol. Phil.*, 2, prose 7, 3 (p. 52 in Smith's edition, London, 1925): "Omnem terrae ambitum ad coeli spatium puncti constat obtinere rationem, id est ut, si ad coelestis globi magnitudinem conferatur, nihil spatii prorsus habere judicetur." (And see elsewhere in the same work.)

165. *DT*, 13, 12, 16; *DCD*, 10, 22.

166. *OPO*, 11, 14; cf. the reservation in *DGL*, 2, 18, 38 and *DCE*, 1, 23, 35 and *RE*, 1, 11, 4 (concerning the world-soul) as against the daring remark in *DDQO*, 83, qu. 79, 1.

167. *ENC*, 15, 58.

168. *DCD*, 5, 1.

169. *IP*, 93, 5.

170. *EP*, 55, 7, 12; *DGL*, 13, 38.

171. *DDC*, 2, 29, 46.

172. *DDQO*, qu. 45, 1; *SE*, 68, 2 and 3.

173. *IP*, 45, 1; *SE*, 68, 2 and 3.

174. *IP*, 41, 7.

175. *SE*, 241, 2; *SE*, 29, 1.

176. *SE*, 68, 2 and Wisd. xiii.9.

177. *IP*, 10, 3; cf. *EP*, 55, 6, 10.

178. *IP*, 18, 1, 1 and 2, 2.

179. *IP*, 93, 2; for the feria cf. *QE*, 1, 7.

180. Ibid.

181. *DCE*, 1, 23, 32 (refers to the case of Caesar for the month of July and also to Virgil's *Ninth Eclogue*, 1, 47).

182. *IP*, 95, 5; cf. *IP*, 131, 11 (he knows two readings of Ps. cxxxi.6—*saltuum* and *silvae*); cf. *IP*, 96, 12 (demons and the temple cults).

183. *IP*, 95, 5.

184. *EP*, 47; cf. below.

185. *EP*, 46.

186. Dan. vii.13–14.

5. THE JEWS

1. *SE*, 196, 4; cf. P. Bérard, *S. Augustin et les Juifs*, Besançon, 1913; P. de Labriolle, *La Réaction païenne*, Paris, 1938, pp. 457–60; B. Blumenkranz, *Die Judenpredigt Augustins*, Basle, 1946, which relies extensively on the work of Augustine's old age, *Tractatus Adversus Judaeos*.

2. *GUE*, 5, 4.

3. *IP*, 50, 1.

4. *SE*, 9, 3; cf. *DSI*, 17, 9.

5. *SE*, 62, 18.

6. *GUE*, 10, 3.

7. *DSI*, 24, 14; 12, 3; *GUE*, 2, 2; *IP*, 45, 12.

8. *TAJ*, 5, 6.

9. *DSI*, 5, 2.

10. *DCD*, 12, 23; Eusebius of Caesarea, *Praeparatio Evangelica*, 9, 10 (ed. Vigerus, Paris, 1628, pp. 412–13; ed. Gifford, Oxford, 1903, 412–13, 9, 3 (Vigerus, 404–7) deals with the Essenes). Origen, *Contra Celsum*, 5, 25 (*GCS*, 2, 26, ed. Koetschau).

11. *GUE*, 2, 1.

12. *SE*, 5, 5; *IP*, 136, 18.

13. *TAJ*, 1, 1 and 10, 15; cf. Rom. xi.18–22.
14. *CL*, 2, 8–11; *MO*, 260–62.
15. *CL*, 2, 8, conclusion.
16. *MPB*, 26, 2; *DSI*, 24, 2.

6. The Pars Donati and the Heretics

1. *EP*, 29, 11. On Donatism see L. Duchesne, "Le Dossier du Donatisme", in *MAH*, 10, pp. 589–650 (1890), and in *EHC*, 2, 79–97; 3, 76–103; P. Monceaux in *HL*, vols. 4–7; id., "L'Épigraphie donatiste", in *RP*, 33, 112–21 (1909); cf. *HL*, 4, 437–84; P. Batiffol, *Le Catholicisme de S. Augustin*, Paris, 1929, 4, 77–191, 201–348; H. von Soden, *Urkunden zur Entstehungsgeschichte des Donatismus*, Bonn, 1913, *Kleine Texte*, 122; on the Circumcellions: Martroye in *RQH*, 355–464 (1904), and in *Mém. Soc. nat. d'antiqu. de France*, 73, 23–140 (1914); Vannier in *Mélanges Martroye*, Paris, 1941, 101–6 (heresies in Africa); id., in *RHI*, 535–41 (1934) (Arianism in Africa).
2. *SE*, 46, 18.
3. *EP*, 129, 6: Optatus on Lucilla, 1, 16 (*CSEL*, 26, 18, ed. Ziwsa).
4. *IP*, 21, 2, 2 and 95, 5; cf. *SE*, 46, 41 (against the appeal to the "African" Simon of Cyrene, "as though there had been Donatists in the Pentapolis").
5. *OPD*, 1, 22 and 3, 3 (*CSEL*, 26, 25 and 73, ed. Ziwsa); *LP*, 2, 92, 205.
6. Cf. *EP*, 87, 4 and 5.
7. *LP*, 2, 30, 68.
8. At Ksarel-Kelb in Central Numidia a covering plate was found in the ruins of a Donatist basilica with the inscription "Memoria Domni Marchuli", together with a facing-stone with "Deo Laudes Hic Omnes Dicamus"; the church dates approximately from the year 347; see Cayré in *MAH*, 51, pp. 114–142 (1934); Courcelle in the same, 53 (1936); and *AB*, 53, 81–9 (1935); concerning the *Deo laudes* cf. *HL*, 4, 439–42 and Leclercq, *DACL*, 3, 651.
9. *LP*, 2, 1 and 2; *CC*, 1, 14 (*MC*, 4, 60) ("sincerae christianitatis episcopi et catholicae veritatis"); 3, 258 (*MC*, 4, 235 ("episcopi veritatis catholicae").
10. *OPD*, 2, 14 (*CSEL*, 26, 48, ed. Ziwsa).
11. *EP*, 87, 1.
12. *OPD*, 2, 4 (*CSEL*, 26, 37–9, ed. Ziwsa); *EP*, 53, 2.
13. *OPD*, 51, 26, 121.
14. Cf. the Angels of the Seven Churches in Apoc. i. and the Angel of the Pool of Bethesda.
15. *OPD*, 2, 6–9 and 1, 11 (*CSEL*, 26, 42–5 and 14, ed. Ziwsa).
16. *OPD*, 2, 2 and 3 (*CSEL*, 26, 36 and 37).
17. *IP*, 132, 3 and *CG*, 1, 32 (for the name); *EP*, 185, 13–16; (the people's word was *circelliones*).
18. *EP*, 111, 1; *EP*, 88, 12; *VA*, 10; *CCR*, 3, 42, 46.
19. *EP*, 185, 15.
20. *Epistula x Constantini de Basilica Catholicis Erepta* (in app. Optat. *CSEL*, 26, 215); for the laws cf. *CEP*, 1, 8, 13 and *LP*, 2, 205 and 97, 224.
21. *OPD*, 3, 4 (*CSEL*, 26, 81, ed. Ziwsa); *IP*, 132, 6.
22. *EP*, 108, 14 and 18 (on the robbery of churches).
23. *PCPD*, v. 154; (*fustes Israelis*).
24. *EP*, 111, 1.
25. Ps. xiii.3; during the liquidation this was applied by the Donatists to the Catholics; *EP*, 108, 14.
26. *IP*, 132, 6; *LP*, 2, 65, 146.
27. *GUE*, 28, 6.
28. Ibid. 28, 4; cf. *CG*, 1, 37, 49; cf. *TJ*, 11, 15, where he refers to their principal saints, Donatus and Marculus, as suicides.
29. *VA*, 10 ("velut sub professione continentium ambulantes").
30. "Caede traditorium vexata meruit dignitatem martyrii" (*ILVC*, 1, 2052, p. 405); concerning their cult of martyrs, see *CEP*, 3, 6, 29.
31. *CC*, 1, 133 (*MC*, 4, 110).

32. *OPD*, 2, 15 (*CSEL*, 26, 50; for the Donatist martyrs Marculus and Donatus see ibid., 3, 8; cf. 3, 1 (*CSEL*, 26, 90 and 91, and 68); *TJ*, 11, 15.
33. *OPD*, 2, 16 (*CSEL*, 26, 152–8 (on the purification of churches)); cf. 2, 29; 2, 21 (*CSEL*, 26, 55–6, 57 and 58).
34. *EP*, 87, 8.
35. *Cod. Theod.*, 16, 5, 21 (16 June 392) (CTM, 862) and *CEP*, 1, 12, 19; *EP*, 185, 25.
36. *CCR*, 3, 47, 51.
37. *VA*, 7.
38. *CCR*, 4 and *passim*; cf. *IP*, 36, 2, 20.
39. This argument is found again in the sermons—e.g., *SE*, 57, 15. The two synods are those of Cabarsussi in the year 393 (Maximianists) and Bagai, 394 (the adherents of Primianus mostly came from Numidia).
40. *EP*, 108, 2, 4 and 5.
41. *SE*, 57, 15 and *IP*, 21, 31.
42. *CEP*, 3, 29; *EP*, 108, 16.
43. *EP*, 93, 20.
44. *BH*, 37 (*MC*, 3, 924) and Council of Carthage, Sept. 401 (*MC*, 3, 771 E, 774 AB).
45. *DPC*, 1, 31, 53; *BC*, 3, 4.
46. *CCR*, 3, 44 and 45, 49 and 50; *hesternus tyro; doctissima annositas* (the references are to Mach. ii.62, Prov. xxiii.9, Job xxxiv.27).
47. *VA*, 12; *ENC*, 5, 17.
48. *CCR*, 3, 46, 50; *VA*, 12; *EP*, 105, 4.
49. *EP*, 185, 27; *CCR*, 3, 43, 47.
50. *EP*, 93, 16 and 17; 185, 25; cf. *CCEA*, 93 (*MC*, 3, 794–8).
51. *EP*, 185, 27; *CCR*, 3, 43, 47.
52. *EP*, 185, 26; cf. the laws of *Cod. Theod.*, 16, 5, 38 and 6, 4 (12 Feb. 405) (*CTM*, 867 and 881) and 16, 11, 2 (promulgation, March 405) (*CTM*, 905).
53. *EP*, 98, 1, 77; *CC*, 1, 135 and 129 (*MC*, 4, 119 and 107).
54. *EP*, 88, 10.
55. *BC*, 11, 23; *EP*, 86, 88, 12; *CC*, 1, 133, 139, 189 (*MC*, 4, 117, 123, 142) (on the events in Bagai, Cirta and Sitifi).
56. *EP*, 97, 2 and 3 (Nov. 408).
57. 286 Catholics out of 470; 279 Donatists out of about an equal number.
58. *EP*, 128, 2 and 3 (letter of the Catholic bishops to the *cognitor*); *BC*, 1, 5.
59. *EP*, 88, 10 (A.D. 406).
60. *CC, sententia cognitoris* (*MC*, 4, 264, middle).
61. *SE*, 358, 2; cf. Ps. lxxi.8 and cxviii.96; also 1 Tim. i.51.
62. *SE*, 357, 3 and 4 (*de laude pacis*).
63. *SE*, 358, 6.
64. *CC*, 1, 219 (*MC*, 4, 166) (for the reference to the eleven hours); concerning the arguments referred to cf. 1, 139, 134 and 126 (*MC*, 4, 123, 118, 110).
65. *CC*, 3, 258 (*MC*, 4, 235 (for the document, 235–41)).
66. *CC*, 3, 261 81 (*MC*, 4, 241–6); further in *BC*, 3, 9–25, 15–43 (this also in *MC*, 4, 245–63).
67. *CC, sententia cognitoris* (*MC*, 4, 263–5; *Cod. Theod.*, 16, 5, 52 (30 Jan. 412) (*CTM*, 872 and 873)); later laws, ibid., 873, 878.
68. *CCEA*, cc. 123 and 124 (*MC*, 3, 822).
69. *VA*, 13; *EP*, 204, 2; *CG*, 1, 24, 27.
70. *EP*, 185, 36 (about 417).
71. *SE*, 359, 8; cf. *EP*, 93, 2 (A.D. 407–10?).
72. *EP*, 133, 1 (A.D. 411); 185, 13 and 30 (A.D. 417).
73. *CG*, 1, 24, 27; *EP*, 185, 13 and 30.
74. *VA*, 14 (concerning Emeritus of Caesarea (A.D. 418)); *CG*, 1, 17, 19 (concerning Gaudentius of Thamugadi).
75. *SE*, 358, 4; 359, 5; *EP*, 128, 3.
76. *CG*, 1, 37, 47 and 48.
77. *EP*, 23, 6 and 7 and *PCPD*.
78. *EF*, 2.
79. *SE*, 302, 18, 16.

80. *VA*, 12; *CCR*, 3, 47, 50; cf. *EP*, 66, 1; 88, 7.
81. Ps. lvii.7; cf. *IP*, 57, 15.
82. *EP*, 185, 7.
83. See above all *EP*, 185 (*Ad Bonifatium*), a complete dissertation (dated 417) especially 10f. and 23f. Cf. further *EP*, 86 (A.D. 405), 87 and 88 (406), 89 and 93 (408), 97 and the important *EP*, 100 (*Ad Donatum*) (409); 105, 133 and 134 (411 and 412), 143 (416), 204 (420); 191, 2; cf. Richard in *REA*, *Mélanges Radet*, 498–507 (Lactantius', Themistius' and Augustine's conceptions of toleration).
84. *EP*, 134, 4.
85. *EP*, 139, 2.
86. *EP*, 100, 2 (A.D. 409).
87. *EP*, 185 (*Ad Bonifatium*, 417) and 133, 2 (*Ad Marcellium*, 411–12).
88. *EP*, 133, 2 and 134, 2; cf. 185, 21.
89. *IP*, 54, 16; cf. for the year 405, *EP*, 83, 1 and 85, 29.
90. Luke xiv.23; cf. *EP*, 185, 6, 24.
91. *DUJ*, 9, 11 and 12 (cf. Jer. xvi.16. Refers to the heathen; date, before 400).
92. *SE*, 359, 7 and 8.
93. *EP*, 89, 2 (A.D. 406).
94. *EP*, 185, 5, 19; *DCD*, 5, 26 (in praise of Theodosius).
95. *EP*, 185, 21.
96. *EP*, 43, 1.
97. See above.
98. *EP*, 69, 2.
99. *SE*, 360.
100. *DACL*, 6, 2, 2500 with bibliography; text in *ICR*, vol. 2, pt. 1, p. 481, and *RBA*, 1887, pp. 150 and 151; Monceaux, *MEQ*, p. 473, n. 191; *pia laude* is a deliberate contrast to *Deo laudes*:

VERSUS SANCTI AUGUSTINI EPISCOPI

D onatistarum crudeli caede peremptum
I nfossum hic corpus pia est cum laude nabori[s]
A nte aliquot tempus cum donatista fuisset
C onversus pacem pro qua moreretur amavit.
O ptima purpureo vestitus sanguine causa.
N on errore perit non se ipse furor peremit.
V erum martyrium vera est pietate probatum.
S uscipe litterulas primas; ibi nomen honoris.

Cf. Weyman in *BGCP*, p. 110 (the epitaph shows some similarity to that of Damasus for Hippolytus, ibid., 37).
101. *EP*, 144, 1 and 2.
102. *EP*, 141.
103. *GE*, 4.
104. *DPC*, 34, 57–35, 58.
105. Ps. cxix.6.
106. *RE*, 2, 59; *CG*, 1, 1.
107. *EP*, 204, 3.
108. *CG*, 1, 20, 22.
109. *CG*, 2, 37, 47.
110. *GE*, 1, 3 and 12; *VA*, 14; *RE*, 2, 51; cf. Prov. xix.21.
111. Pseudo-Aug., *Sermo de cataclysmo*, 5 (vol. 6, 605 in the Maurist edition).
112. *EP*, 23, 105, 4; 83, 1, 57, 1 and 2.
113. About 373–5? *LP*, 2, 83, 184.
114. *EP*, 78, 8 (A.D. 404?).
115. *SE*, 252, 5.
116. *EP*, 34, 2–4.
117. *EP*, 35, 2.
118. *SE*, 46, 13, 31
119. *EP*, 35, 4.

120. *EP*, 33, 5; 23, 5; cf. *EP*, 20, 3, 6 (to the partners of a mixed marriage).
121. *VA*, 7: "Ipsi haeretici concurrentes cum catholicis ingenti ardore audiebant."
122. *IP*, 57, 9 (A.D. 396?) cf. Ps. lvii.6.
123. *VA*, 6; *FM*, 1 and *RE*, 1, 16.
124. *EP*, 23.
125. A.D. 407; *EP*, 105, 4.
126. *PCPD*, complete text given by Lambot in *RB*, pp. 312-30 (1935); cf. the edition in *CSEL*, 51, 3-15 by Petschenig, and above all Vroom, *Le Psaume abécédaire de S. Aug. et la poésie latine rythmique*, Nijmegen, 1933; cf. C. Daux, *Le Chant abécédaire de S. Aug.*, Arras, 1905; Engelbrecht in *ZOG*, 59, 580f. (1908); Ermini in *MA*, 2, 341-52; *HL*, 4, p. 494 and 7, pp. 80f.; Batiffol, *Catholicisme de S. Augustin*, pp. 131-5; Rose in *JTS*, 28, 383-92 (1926-7).
127. *RE*, 1, 20; cf. *EP*, 55, 34.
128. E. Tréhorel in *Revue des études latines*, 17, 2, 309-29 (1939) (in the refrain, *vos* instead of *omnes*).
129. *PCPD*, 5, 1-20 (Lambot, *RB*, 318 (1935), with the *prooemium* 1-26):

> Vos qui gaudetis de pace   modo verum judicate
>
> Foeda res est causam audire   et personas accipere
> omnes injusti non possunt   regnum dei possidere.
> vestem alienam conscindas   nemo potest tolerare:
> quanto magis pacem Christi   qui conscidit dignus est morte.
> et quis est ista qui fecit   quaeramus hoc sine errore.
> Vos qui gaudetis de pace   modo verum judicate.

A

> Abundantia peccatorum   solet fratres conturbare.
> propter hoc dominus noster   voluit nos praemonere
> Comparans regnum caelorum   reticulo miso in mare
> congreganti multos pisces   omne genus hinc et inde.
> quos cum traxissent ad litus   tunc coeperunt separare,
> bonos in vasa miserunt   reliquos malos in mare.
> quisquis novit evangelium   recognoscat cum timore.
> videt reticulum ecclesiam   videt hoc saeculum mare;
> genus autem mixtum piscis   iustus est cum peccatore;
> saeculi finis est litus: tunc est tempus separare;
> qui modo retia ruperunt   multum dilexerunt mare;
> vasa sunt sedes sanctorum   quo non possunt pervenire.
> Vos qui gaudetis de pace   modo verum judicate.

B

> Bonus auditor fortasse   quaerit, qui ruperint rete.
> homines multum superbi   qui justos se dicunt esse.
> sic fecerunt conscissuram   et altare contra altare.
> diabolo se tradiderunt,   cum pugnant de traditione
> et crimen quod commiserunt   in alios volunt transferre.
> ipsi tradiderunt libros   et nos audent accusare...

130. *PCPD*, 137, 157 and 158 (Lambot, *RB*, 165 and 166 (1935)):

> si crudeles erant illi   et nobis displicent valde;
> si autem falsa de illis dicunt   deus potest iudicare.

131. *PCPD*, 137, 146-55 (Lambot, *RB*, 141-62 (1935)).
132. *PCPD*, 226-8 (Lambot, *RB*, 235-8 (1935)):

> sed quid illi prodest forma,   si non vivit in radice?
> venite, fratres, si vultus   ut inseramini in vite.
> dolor est cum vos videmus   praecisos ita jacere.

133. *PCPD*, 229–31 (Lambot, *RB*, 238–41 (1935)):
   numerate sacerdotes   vel ab ipsa Petri sede
   et in ordine illo petrum   quis cui successit videte:
   ipsa est petra quam non vincunt   superbae inferorum partae.
134. *PCPD*, 233–44 (Lambot, *RB*, 242–53 (1935)).
135. *PCPD*, 246–57 (Lambot, *RB*, 252–66 (1935)).
136. *PCPD*, 261–88 (Lambot, *RB*, 270–97 (1935)):
   quid si ipsa mater ecclesia   vos alloquatur cum pace
   et dicat: "O filii mei   quid queremini de matre?
   quare me deseruistis   iam volo a vobis audire.
   accusatis fratres vestros   et ego laceror valde.
   quando me premebant gentes   multa tuli eum dolore.
   multi me deseruerunt   sed fecerunt in timore;
   vos vero nullus coegit   sic contra me rebellare.
   dicitis mecum vos esse   sed falsum videtis esse
   ego catholica dicor   et vos de Donati parte
   iussit me apostolus Paulus   pro regibus mundi orare;
   vos invidetis, quod reges   iam sunt in christiana fide.
   si filii estis, quid invidetis   quia auditae sunt preces meae?
   quando enim dona miserunt   noluistis acceptare.
   et obliti estis prophetas   qui illud praedicerunt ante,
   quod gentium reges magni   missuri essent dona ecclesiae.
   quae dona cum respuistis   ostendistis vos non esse
   et Macarium coegistis   suum dolerem vindicare.
   sed ego quid vobis feci   vestra mater in toto orbe?
   expello malos quos possum   quos non possum cogor ferre;
   fero illos, donec sanentur   aut separentur in fine.
   vos me quare dimisistis   et crucior de vestra morte?
   si multum malos odistis   quales habetis videte.
   si et vos toleratis malos   quare non in unitate,
   ubi nemo rebaptizat   nec altare est contra altare?
   malos tantos toleratis   sed nulla bona mercede,
   quia quod debetis pro Christo   pro Donato vultis ferre."
   cantavimus vobis, fratres   pacem, si vultis audire.
   venturus est iudex noster: nos damus, exigit ille.
137. *EP*, 33.
138. *EP*, 34, 6 and 2–4.
139. *EP*, 35; cf. 34, 4.
140. *EP*, 43, 1–27.
141. *EP*, 44 particularly 1–7 and 12.
142. *EP*, 49.
143. *EP*, 51.
144. *EP*, 66; cf. *LP*, 2, 83, 184; 99, 228.
145. *EP*, 52 (*Ad Severinum*).
146. *EP*, 53; cf. 56, 57 (*Ad Celerem*).
147. *DB*, 2, 5 and 6, 6–9.
148. *LP*, 2, 51–5, 117–25.
149. *LP*, 3, 16 and 17, 19 and 20.
150. *GUE*, 32, 11.
151. *IP*, 36, 2, 16–23.
152. *IP*, 36, 3, 19 and 20; cf. *IP*, 128, 4.
153. *EP*, 76, 1 and 4, conclusion.
154. *EP*, 83, 1.
155. *TJ*, 6, 25.
156. *RE*, 2, 27.
157. *EP*, 150, 1, 3 and 4; *CCR*, 3, 46, 50 and 48, 53 ("amictu iunceo dehonestatus").
158. *EP*, 108, 14.
159. *EP*, 133, 1; 134, 4 (A.D. 411).

160. *EP*, 139, 2.
161. *SE*, 359, 8.
162. *EP*, 139, 1 and 2.
163. *EP*, 111, 1–2.
164. *EP*, 58, 1–3.
165. *EP*, 112, 3.
166. *EP*, 89, 8.
167. *EP*, 57.
168. *EP*, 173.
169. *EP*, 209, 2–10 and below.
170. *EP*, 124, 2.
171. Rom. x.2.
172. *CAS*, 1, 133, 14; *MO*, 411; short extract, *SE*, 296, 12.
173. Ibid., 15; cf. *SE*, 296, 12.
174. *VA*, 6; *FM*, 1 and 2, pref.; *RE*, 1, 16.
175. *AFM*, 2, 21, conclusion; *RE*, 2, 8 and *VA*, 16.
176. *DAA*; *EF*; *DNB*; *SM*; and especially *CFA*.
177. *RE*, 1, 22; *IP*, 140, 10 (where Augustine refers to the Manichean *electi*).
178. *ALP*, 1, 1 and *RE*, 2, 58 (A.D. 420).
179. *SA* (A.D. 418); *RE*, 2, 52.
180. See *TJ*, 98, 8; *EP*, 158, 6; *DCE*, 1, 10, 15 and 16 and *EP*, 237, 2–9.
181. *DH*, 87.
182. *DH*, 86.
183. e.g., *SE*, 139.
184. *EP*, 44, 6.
185. *EP*, 242, 1.
186. *EP*, 170, 1 and 10; *EP*, 171; the man is probably the doctor in *GUE*, 17, 4.
187. *EP*, 238–41 and *VA*, 17.
188. *EP*, 238, 1 and 2 and 4b.
189. *EP*, 238, 4a, 3, 4c–6.
190. *EP*, 238, 7.
191. *EP*, 238, 8.
192. *EP*, 238, 10–26.
193. *EP*, 238, 27 and 29.
194. *EP*, 239.
195. *EP*, 240.
196. *EP*, 241, 1.
197. *SE*, 140, 4 and superscription; *CM*, 2, 22.
198. *VA*, 17; *CCM*; *CM*; cf. 140, 4, 4.
199. *EHC*, 3, 122; according to statements from the chronicle of Hydatius for the year 440.
200. *DNG*, 6, 6: "fortissima et celerrima ingenia".
201. *EP*, 188, 13.
202. *SE*, 131, 6 (Sept. 416).
203. *CF*, 10, 31, 45; cf. *EP*, 157, 9 and 10; *DNG*, 43, 50; *SL*, 13, 22.
204. *EP*, 157.
205. *EP*, 194.
206. *EP*, 216, 1.
207. *EP*, 225 and 226.
208. *SE*, 46, 39; for the main arguments see, for instance, *EP*, 173, 5 and 6 (*Ad Donatum Presbyterum Partis Donati*).
209. *SE*, 51, 11.
210. *SE*, 46, 28 (*perdix*, from Jer. xvii.11, is equivalent to *diabolus*); *DCD*, 20, 19 (*multos antichristos*); *SE*, 71, 19, 32 and 33 (*sine spiritu*).
211. *EP*, 93, 17.
212. Ps. cxlvii.14: "qui posuit fines tuos pacem"; *IP*, 147, 15 (vol. 9, 622 in the Maurist edition).
213. *Sermo ad Caesar. ecclesiae plebem*, 6 (vol. 9, 605 in the Maurist edition).
214. *MPB*, 92; *MO*, 333; cf. *IP*, 88, 2, 14; *LP*, 3, 9, 10 and 216, 8.

7. Day-to Day Pastoral Work

1. *EP*, 191, 1; cf. 194, 1 (if this Leo is indeed the man who was later Pope, which is always possible; the latest biography looks upon this as very probable. See Trevor Jalland, *The Life and Times of St. Leo the Great*, London, 1941, p. 34).
2. *FSA*, 8, 5.
3. *SGD*, 7, 15, 63 (*CSEL*, 8, 176, ed. Pauly); "Nam sicut in sentinam profundae navis conluviones omnium sordium, sic in mores eorum quasi de omni mundo vitia fluxerunt." Cf. ibid., 7, 13, 56 and 57; 8, 173.
4. As against this Salvianus, in *SGD*, 7, 15, 63–4 (*CSEL*, 18, 176), speaks of unreliability and immorality as the chief vices of the Africans. Concerning the Christians in Africa see J. Vérin, *S. Augustini Auditores*, St. Blois, 1869; A. Degert, *Quid ad Mores Ingeniaque Afrorum Cognoscenda Conferant S. Augustini Sermones*, Paris, 1894; M. Getty, *The Life of the North Africans as Revealed in the Sermons of St. Augustine*, Washington, 1931; M. E. Keenan, *The Life and Times of St. Augustine as Revealed in his Letters*, Washington, 1935; G. Metzger, *Die Afrikanische Kirche*, Tübingen, 1934.
5. *EP*, 189, 7.
6. *EP*, 93, 48 and 49.
7. *SE*, 252, 4; and see below.
8. *SE*, 225, 4; *TEJ*, 4, 4 (on feast days and drinking days: "se inebriare quasi sollemniter").
9. *EP*, 36, 12, concluding paragraph.
10. *IP*, 18, 2, 1; *DOM*, 17, 20; *IP*, 84, 15 (*adulterina carmina*); *SE*, 153, 10 (*turpissima cantilena*).
11. Jerome, *Ep.*, 130, 5 (*CSEL*, 56, 180, ed. Hilberg).
12. Ambrose, *Exp. in Ev. Luc.* (*CSEL*, 32, 4, 168, ed. Schenkl).
13. *EP*, 213, 6.
14. *EP*, 230, 4.
15. *EP*, 169, 13.
16. *EP*, 211, 13.
17. Paulinus, *Ep.*, 32, 16 (*CSEL*, 29, 291, ed. Hartel);

> Si quem sancta tenet meditandi in lege voluntas
> hic poterit residens sacris intendere libris.

18. *IP*, 36, 1, 2. Concerning private reading of the Scriptures in Augustine's day, cf. Chrysostom, *Hom.*, 11, 1 and 32, 3 (*In Jo.*) (ed. Montfaucon, 8, 62 and 8, 188; 9, 1); *In Col.*, ibid., 11, 391; Ambrose, *In Ps. cxviii. Expos.*, 12, 28, 22, 19; *CF*, 8, 6, 14; and A. Harnack, *Bible Reading in the Early Church*, London, 1912, pp. 53f.
19. *TJ*, 1, 9, 14; cf. *SE*, 70, 2; *TJ*, 7, 12 and *EP*, 55, 37.
20. *CF*, 1, 9, 14; cf. *SE*, 70, 2.
21. *CF*, 2, 3, 8; cf. 3, 3, 6; 5, 12, 22 (on student life).
22. *DDQO*, 83, q. 78; cf. *DDC*, 2, 25, 39.
23. *EP*, 135, 1 and 2 for instance (at a men's club); cf. *EP*, 187, 7, 22–25, cf. below.
24. *EP*, 118, 2, 9.
25. *DH*, 87.
26. *IP*, 51, 14, middle.
27. *SE*, 170, 4.
28. Eph. vi.5 and 1 Tim. vi.1–2.
29. *DCD*, 19, 21; cf. 19, 16; *TJ*, 6, 25; *IP*, 124, 7.
30. *DCD*, 19, 15.
31. *IP*, 36, 1, 12; 124, 7.
32. *SE*, 356, 6 and 7.
33. *IP*, 96, 12; 73, 16.
34. *SE*, 161, 9.
35. *IP*, 122, 6 (v. 2).
36. *SE*, 21, 6; cf. *CCEA*, 64, 4n, 82 (*MC*, 3, 770 and 782) and *EP*, 185, 15 (*tabulas frangere*); *SE*, 159, 4, 5; *IP*, 25, 9 (the strange story of the cleric who waits in the amphitheatre for the liberation of a gladiator).
37. *SE*, 159, 4, 5.

38. *DOM*, 22, 25 and 26; Eph. vi.9.
39. Seneca, *Ep.*, 47.
40. Jerome, *Ep.*, 108, 5 (*Epitaphium Sanctae Paulae*) (*CSEL*, 55, 310, ed. Hilberg): concerning works of mercy in general, cf. *SE*, 37, 30; 50, 7; 311, 9.
41. *SE*, 211, 5, 4.
42. *SDM*, 1, 19, 59.
43. *TJ*, 41, 4.
44. *SE*, 36, 8.
45. *CF*, 6, 6, 9.
46. *IP*, 99, 4; 132, 2; 32, 2, 8.
47. *IP*, 103, 3, 16; cf. 40, 2 and 103, 16–17.
48. *SE*, 178, 4.
49. *SE*, 178, 8; the complete text below.
50. *SE*, 32, 21.
51. *SE*, 345, 1; *IP*, 32, 3, 12.
52. *IP*, 51, 14.
53. *SE*, 345, 1; *IP*, 32, 2, 12; 48, 1, 3.
54. *SE*, 38, 7, 9; 18, 4, 4; 60, 8, 8; *FSA*, 9, 4; *MO*, 2, 6; 12, 4.
55. *IP*, 36, 3, 6.
56. *SE*, 32, 23.
57. *SE*, 61, 13.
58. *SE*, 51, 5; *IP*, 41, 9.
59. *IP*, 48, 1, 13; *DCM*, 2, 4 (*marmoreum tumulum*).
60. *Vita Pauli*, 17; cf. 12 (*PL*, 23, 29–30 and 26).
61. *SE*, 289, 6; Ps. lxxii.13.
62. *SE*, 36, 10.
63. *SE*, 61, 2.
64. *IP*, 51, 14.
65. *IP*, 127, 16.
66. *SE*, 21, 10; *IP*, 149, 10.
67. *IP*, 72, 12; cf. 7.
68. *SE*, 64, 5.
69. Ibid.; cf. *IP*, 128, 4; *SE*, 331, 5, 38, 70, 2.
70. *SE*, 344, 7; cf. *SE*, 259, 3.
71. *EP*, 124, 1–2; 22, 9.
72. *SE*, 46, 10, 21.
73. *EP*, 124, 2; cf. 122, 1 (Winter 410/11).
74. *EP*, 9, 4.
75. *SE*, 259, 3; *EP*, 34, 3; *CF*, 9, 9.
76. *SE*, 49, 7 and 9.
77. *SE*, 302, 19 and 20.
78. *SE*, 302, 17, 19 and 16.
79. *EP*, 126; cf. C. Daux., "Un Incident à la basilique d'Hippone en 411", in *RQH*, 41, 36, 31–73 (1906); Rampolla, *S. Melania Giuniore, Senatrice Romana*, Rome, 1905, 205–10.
80. *EP*, 124.
81. *EP*, 126, 1f.
82. *EP*, 126, 1–5.
83. *EP*, 125, 1–5.
84. *EP*, 126, 1 and 6, 7–14.
85. *Mémoires pour servir à l'histoire ecclésiastique des six premiers siècles*, Paris, 1701–12, vol. 13, 514 and 515.
86. Palladius, *Hist. Laus.*, 119 and 121 (*PG*, 34, 1227–28 and 1233).
87. *RE*, 2, 50; *DGC*, 1, 1.
88. *EP*, 202, 2.
89. Paulinus, *Ep.*, 29, 12 (*CSEL*, 29, 259 and 260, ed. Hartel).
90. *EP*, 228, 8.
91. *SE*, 196.
92. *SE*, 19, 6 (probably *circa* 419, cf. vol. 5, p. 105, *n*.a in the Maurist edition).

93. *UE*, 6, 7 (vol. 6, 627 in the Maurist edition); *SE*, 19, 6; *EP*, 228, 8, A.D. 398, shortly before the evil consulate of the eunuch Eutropius; cf. O. Seeck, *Gesch. d. Untergangs der antiken Welt*, Berlin, 1895, 5, 305, appendix 563, which connects the panic with Claud., *In Eutrop.*, 1, 4.
94. *CF*, 2, 3 and 3, 4.
95. *IP*, 90, 2, 6.
96. *DSI*, 20, 6.
97. *FSA*, 2, 7 and 8; see Ecclus. v.8–9.
98. *SE*, 27, 6.
99. *FSA*, 2, 8b–9.
100. *SE*, 132, 1 and 2.
101. *EP*, 151, 14, cf. 4.
102. Cf. *EP*, 138, 9.
103. *EP*, 258, 1–5.
104. *SE*, 232, 8 and *SE*, 393, exordium.
105. *The Possessed*.
106. *SE*, 91, 3; cf. Ps. xxxiii.17.
107. *SE*, 361, 5 and 6.
108. *DFO*, 26, 48; *ENC*, 67; *DCD*, 21, 17–27, above all 21, 22, 25.
109. *EP*, 164, 14; cf., however, ibid., 15f. (1 Pet. iii.18–21, understood as an allegory).
110. *ENC*, 112; cf., however, *DCD*, 21, 17 and *EP*, 102, 22–27.
111. *SE*, 302, 18.
112. *EP*, 46; cf. 94, 2–3 (*Paulin. ad Aug.*, about 408); this Publicola is almost certainly identical with that of *EP*, 46; cf. *EHC*, 3, 134; concerning the frontier regions in the fourth century cf. J. Guey, "Notes sur le *limes* romain de Numidie", in *Mélanges d'archéologie et d'histoire de l'École française de Rome*, 56, 178–248 (1939).
113. *EP*, 46, 1–5.
114. *EP*, 46, 6–10.
115. *EP*, 46, 11.
116. *EP*, 46, 12 and 13; cf. Matt. v.39.
117. *EP*, 46, 14–18.
118. *EP*, 46, 18; cf. Deut. vii.26.
119. *EP*, 47.
120. Cf. *CFA*, 32, 13; *DDC*, 2, 23, 36 and 24, 37.
121. Ps. xxiii.1; 1 Cor. x.26 and 1 Tim. iv.4.
122. *EP*, 47, 2–6.
123. "Quod praesens est, acrem habet sensum" (*SE*, 25, 3; cf. *SE*, 311, 8; *IP*, 33, 2, 17; *CL*, 2, 19, 7 and 8; *MO*, 270; *CL*, 2, 92, 1; *MO*, 272).
124. *DSI*, 24, 13; cf. *CL*, 2, 19, 8.
125. Jerome, *Ep.*, 127, 13 and 14 (*CSEL*, 56, 155 and 156, ed. Hilberg).
126. *DCD*, 1, 32 and 33; *SGD*, 6, 12, 69 and 70 (*CSEL*, 8, 144, ed. Pauly) (on Cirta and Carthage); 6, 17, 76 and 77; 6, 19, 83 and 20, 84–22, 100; above all, 22, 94 (ibid., 180, 182, 183–188 and 186).
127. *UE*, 3 (vol. 6, 624 in the Maurist edition); *SE*, 105, 12 and 13; cf. Jerome, *Ep.*, 127, 11–14 (*CSEL*, 56, 153–6, ed. Hilberg); cf. (for about A.D. 428) *VA*, 28f.
128. *EP*, 111.
129. *EP*, 99, 1 and 2.
130. *EP*, 122, 2.
131. *SE*, 105, 12 and 13; *CAS*, 1, 133, 9; *SE*, 81, 7 and 9; 296, 7.
132. *SE*, 296, 6; *CAS*, 1, 133, 6.
133. *SE*, 105, 13; cf. *DCD*, 5, 23.
134. *UE*, 2.
135. Ibid., 2–9.
136. *SE*, 81, 8 and 9; 105, 12 and 13; 296, 6–10; cf. *CAS*, 1, 133, 9–12; *IP*, 138, *FSA*, 3, 7 and *UE*, 2–9.
137. This theme of *oleum* and *amurca* is also frequently met with elsewhere, e.g., *DSI*, 24, 11; *SE*, 15, 9; *IP*, 80, 1, 136, 9 and 10 (where the hearers recognize it and cheer).
138. 2 Cor. iv.17–18.
139. *CAS*, 1, 133, 6–7, 10 and 12; cf. *SE*, 296, 6.

140. *CAS*, 9; *SE*, 296, 7 and *SE*, 81, 9.
141. Ibid., 11 and *SE*, 296, 9.
142. *FSA*, 3, 7.
143. *SE*, 105, 12.
144. *DCD*, 20, 19, 3; *SE*, 15, 10; cf. also *DCD*, 4, 7.
145. Ausonius, *Epitaphia*, 32, 9 and 10 (ed. Peiper, Leipzig, 1886, 84):

> Miremur periisse homines monumenta fatiscunt
> mors etiam saxis nominibusque venit?

146. *IP*, 124, 7.
147. *DCD*, 5, 17, 1 and 2, 19.
148. *DCD*, 19, 17; cf. Rom. xiii.1–7 and Matt. xxii.21; *DCR*, 21, 37.
149. *EP*, 151, 14; 155, 10; 220, 7f.
150. See above.
151. *SE*, 302, 13 and 19–21.
152. *DCD*, 5, 24–26.
153. Cf. *DCD*, 4, 4; 5, 17; 15, 4 and also, for example, *DCR*, 21, 37.
154. *EP*, 151, 3f.
155. *EP*, 220, 8f.
156. *EP*, 220, 7–9.
157. *MO*, 8, 2.
158. *MO*, 8, 3.
159. *MO*, 8, 3 and *WS*, 12, 3.
160. *WS*, 12, 5.
161. *MO*, 8, 2; Ps. xciii.14–15.
162. *MO*, 8, 5; 1 Pet. ii.21.
163. *SE*, 250, 2; *IP*, 25, 2, 4.
164. *IP*, 91, 8; cf. *DCR*, 18 and 19, 31.
165. *IP*, 53, 10; cf. Ps. liii.8.
166. *TJ*, 34, 3; cf. 4 and Ps. xxxv.7.
167. *EP*, 130.
168. *SCA*, 1, pl. 35, 1.
169. Ps. xxvi.4; cf. *TJ*, 3, 20 and 21.
170. *EP*, 130, 4, 9–8, 15.
171. Luke xviii.1–8 and 1 Tim. v.5.
172. *EP*, 130, 1, 1; 2, 3–6 and 3, 7–9.
173. *EP*, 130, 8, 17 and 2 Cor. vi.13–14.
174. *EP*, 130, 9, 18.
175. Phil. iv.6.
176. *EP*, 130, 10, 18.
177. *EP*, 130, 10, 19 and 20; cf. *SDM*, 3, 12 and 13 (around 391–4).
178. *SE*, 130, 11, 21–12, 23; cf. *SDM*, 2, 4, 15–11, 39.
179. Ps. lxxvi.3; *EP*, 130, 13, 24.
180. *EP*, 130, 14, 25–27.
181. *EP*, 130, 15, 28: "quaedam docta ignorantia".
182. *EP*, 16, 29–31.
183. *SE*, 311, 13: "quotidie surgis, et oras".
184. e.g., *SE*, 311, 13.
185. *SE*, 57, 3.
186. *IP*, 118, 29, 3 and 4.
187. *DCD*, 22, 8, 9.
188. *DCD*, 22, 8, 13.
189. *TJ*, 3, 21: "genua trita in orationibus".
190. *DCM*, 5, 7 (prostration and the spreading out of the arms in the form of a cross); *SE*, 311, 13; 90, 9 (the touching of the floor with the forehead); *SE*, 324.
191. *IP*, 140, 18; cf. 141, 18 and 19; 137, 2; *SE*, 19, 2; 332, 4; *SE*, 135, 7 and 351, 6 (the priests on the altar).
192. Cf. *DCM*, 5, 7; *SE*, 311, 13; Gerontius, *Vita Melaniae Junioris*, 5.
193. *IP*, 31, 2, 11.

194. *SE*, 332, 4: *peccata pavimentare*.
195. *IP*, 140, 18; cf. *SE*, 56, 8, 12.
196. *SE*, 361, 4; cf. 51, 1 (Christmas morning).
197. *MPB*, 126, 1; *MO*, 356.
198. *TJ*, 8, 13.
199. *MPB*, 126, 1; *SE*, 51, 1 (continues the sermon of Christmas morning).
200. Cf. *EP*, 140, 5, 13 and *IP*, 72, 34 (but in the year 411?).
201. *IP*, 72, 34; cf. *IP*, 103, 1 and 147, 21.
202. *SE*, 264.
203. *IP*, 21, 2, 24a; 148, 1.
204. *SE*, 252, 4; cf. *SE*, 210, 8, 10.
205. *TEJ*, 4, 4: "se inebriare quasi sollemniter".
206. *SE*, 225, 4 and 252, 9 ("tu tractasti...").
207. *FSA*, 3, 6: "procedam, inquis, cum meliore tunica".
208. *SE*, 252, 4 (probably refers to Carthage, cf. below).
209. *CF*, 3, 3.
210. *IP*, 39, 8.
211. *In XII Psalmos Praefatio*, no. 5, 6, 7.
212. *SE*, 128, 4, 6: "matutina coepimus, hora prandii non urget" (early-morning worship); *MPB*, 125, 1.
213. *SE*, 259, 6 and *EP*, 34, 2.
214. *IP*, 88, 1, 2; *DSI*, 22, 1, *FSA*, 8, 1; *MPB*, 125, 1 (Saturday).
215. *EP*, 29, 3: "ad horam tractationis".
216. *DSI*, 11, 7: "tempus agimus lucernarium"; *EP*, 29, 11: "acta sunt vespertina quae cotidie solent".
217. Cf. *DH*, 57; *EP*, 130, 9–18; Cassian, *Conlationes*, 21, 26 (*CSEL*, 13, 2, 602, ed. Petschenig: many lay-folk do not pray in church till the morning); *IP*, 33, 2, 14: "quotidie ad basilicam surgo" (to the Eucharist with Lauds?).
218. *EP*, 54, 2, 2; *SE*, 58, 12 (the Eucharist); *EP*, 29, 11 (Vespers); on daily visits to church see *TJ*, 3, 21; *IP*, 33, 2, 14; 49, 23; 66, 3; *MO*, 8, 3; *CF*, 5, 9, 17.
219. *DCD*, 22, 8, 17.
220. *IP*, 49, 23; cf. 14.
221. *IP*, 66, 3.
222. *DSI*, 18, 6; *barbatus*=adult; cf. *IP*, 132, 7.
223. *IP*, 93, 21; 90, 1, 4.
224. *IP*, 90, 1, 4.
225. *SE*, 19, 2.
226. *IP*, 93, 21.
227. *SE*, 355, 1.
228. *SE*, 298, 1 and 2.
229. *SE*, 51, 1 and 2.
230. *SE*, 303, 1.
231. *DSI*, 13, 1.
232. Cf. *SE*, 176, 1; 165, 1; a lesson from the Prophets in *SE*, 45, 1; 48, 1, 2 and 289, 3; for the psalm cf. *IP*, 119, 1 and 2, 176, 1 (antiphon *Venite adoremus*, Ps. xciv.6).
233. Third Council of Carthage (397) canon 36 (*MC*, 3, 924); *SE*, 280, 1; 274, conclusion; 275, 1; *DSI*, 16, 7.
234. *SE*, 274, conclusion.
235. Cf. *DCR*, 13, 19.
236. Cf. *SE*, 355, 2; *IP*, 90, 1, 12 (broken off and postponed); *IP*, 32, 2, 12 (the same).
237. *IP*, 58, 2, 3; 147, 21; *SE*, 269, 1.
238. *IP*, 72, 34; *IP*, 147, 21.
239. *IP*, 93, 30.
240. *IP*, 147, 21.
241. *TJ*, 3, 1.
242. *TJ*, 6, 1; 7, 1; 12, 1.
243. *TJ*, 17–23; cf. *SE*, 58, 12.
244. *MPB*, 125, 1; *MO*, 353.
245. *SE*, 128, 4, 6 and *MPB*, 125, 1 are nevertheless early sermons.

246. *EP*, 54, 3, 4; cf. *EP*, **228**, 6.

247. *EP*, 54, 2, 2 and 7, 9; and again in *TJ*, 26, 15: "alicubi quotidie alicubi certis intervallis dierum"; concerning the East, *SDM*, 2, 7, 25 and 26.

248. *DCD*, 10, 20; cf. *SE*, 58, 12 (in Lent); *CF*, 5, 9, 17 (Monica's daily attendance at Mass); cf. *TJ*, 17–23; for daily visits to the church, see above *nn*. 216 and 218; also *SE*, 57, 7.

249. *SE*, 392, 5; cf. *EP*, 54, 3, 4.

250. *EP*, 54, 6, 8; cf. Tertullian, *Ad Uxor.*, 2, 5 (*PL*, 1, 1408).

251. Tertullian, *De Oratione*, 19 (*CSEL*, 20, 192); *Ad Uxor.*, 2, 5 (*PL*, 1, 1408); Cyprian, *De Lapsis*, 26 (*CSEL*, 3, 1, 256, on the unworthy man struck dead by the Ark).

252. Concerning the daily Eucharist see Cyprian, *Ep.*, 57, 3 (*CSEL*, 2, 2, 652) and *Ep.*, 63, 16 (ibid., 714) (*mane*); *Ep.* 58, 1 (ibid., 657); *De Dom Orat.*, 18 (*CSEL*, 3, 1, 280 and 281); concerning the care not to drop a particle cf. Origen, *Hom. in Exod.*, 13, 3 (*GCS*, 6, 274, ed. Baehrens); Hippolytus, *Trad. Apost.*, 32 (ed. Dix, London, 1937, 58–9); Hauler, *Didascaliae Apostolorum Fragmenta Veronensia Latina*, Leipzig, 1900, 117; according to Freestone ("The Sacrament Reserved", *Alcuin Club Collections*, 21, pp. 35–50, London, 1917). Communion in the home fell into disuse at the end of the fourth century.

253. Basil, *Ep.*, 93 (*PG*, 32, 484 and 485) (in Caesarea four times a week, i.e., Sunday, Wednesday, Friday and Saturday, also on the feasts of martyrs; in Alexandria people communicate at home as often as they wish); Jerome, *Ep.*, 48, 15 (*CSEL*, 54, 377, ed. Hilberg) ("alius in publico, alius domi"; Jerome will permit neither the one nor the other *post coitum*).

254. *CJ*, 3, 162; Ambrose, *De Obitu Funebris, Fratris Laudatio Satyri*, 1, 43 and 44 (*FP*, 15, 37 and 38; *PL*, 16, 1360 and 1361).

255. *EP*, 54, 3, 4; see below.

256. *EP*, 54, 4, 5 and 7, 10 (baths); *SE*, 209, 3 (flesh); concerning the usual diet, *DME*, 2, 13, 29. On the *hora nona*, *EP*, 54, 7, 9 and *DME*, loc. cit.; for a criticism of laxity in fasting see *SE*, 210, 10, 12.

257. *SE*, 209, 2; 210, 9, 11 and 10, 12.

258. *SE*, 205, 2; cf. 206, 3; 207, 2; 208, 1; 209, 3; 210, 7, 9.

259. *DME*, 33, 70: "semel sub noctem reficiendo corpus, quod est usquequaque usitatissimum"; *CFA*, 30, 5: "per quadragesimam fere omnes".

260. In Carthage, for instance, before St. Cyprian's day, *FSA*, 5, 6; there was also a *jejunium quinquagesimale*, i.e., before Whitsun, cf. *SE*, 7 and 28; also the *Indiculus* of Possidius, 109 and 110 (Lambot, in *RB*, 114–24 (1935)).

261. *SE*, 198, 2–3 and 196, 4 (on the Calends of January).

262. Holy Saturday, *EP*, 36, 13, 31; *SE*, 210, 1, 2 (fasting together with the baptismal candidates).

263. *EP*, 36, 13, 30f.

264. *EP*, 36, 13 and 14, 31 and 32.

265. *DME*, 1, 33, 70; *CFA*, 5, 9; 30, 5; *EP*, 26, 12, 27; *EP*, 54, 4, 5.

266. *SE*, 205–10 and *DUJ* (vol. 6, 613–22 in the Maurist edition).

267. *SE*, 209, 3.

268. *SE*, 205–10, *passim*; *EP*, 55, 15, 28.

269. *DUJ*, 7.

270. *SE*, 205–10, *passim*.

271. *SE*, 210, 8–11.

272. *DME*, 2, 13, 29 and 30 (where there is an enumeration of vegetable and fruit dishes of that time).

273. *SE*, 208, 1; 210, 8, 10; cf. *CFA*, 30, 5; *DUJ*, 4; cf. *DME*, 1, 71.

274. *Ritus: SE*, 332, 4 (the bishop signs the marriage contract); *EP*, 23, 5 (in praise of faithfulness: "plerumque per Christum"); *SE*, 51, 13, 22 (witness to the betrothal); *VA*, 27 (the bishop's blessing); cf. Tertullian, *Ad. Uxor.*, 2, 9 (*PL*, 1, 1415) (eucharistic blessing); Augustine compares marriage with the sacraments of baptism and holy orders in *DNC*, 1, 10, 11; *DBC*, 29, 32; and of course, with the oneness between Christ and his Church, the contract between whom is the Gospel: *SE*, 238, 1, 268, 4; cf. J. Peters, *Die Ehe nach der Lehre des hl. Augustin*, Paderborn, 1918, as also the monographs of Serrier (Paris, 1928) and Pereira (Paris, 1930); A. Reuter, *S. Dur. Aug. Doctrina de Bonis Matrimonii*, Rome, 1942.

275. *SGD*, 7, 16, 65 (*CSEL*, 8, 176, ed. Pauly); *SE*, 9, 11 and 12.
276. *SE*, 9, 3-4, 9-11; 82, 8, 11; 162, 1 and 2; 343 (concerning Susannah and Joseph).
277. *SE*, 392, 4; cf. above all *SE*, 9, 10, 14.
278. *SE*, 9, 3 and 4.
279. The expression is from Jerome.
280. *EP*, 259, 1 and 3.
281. *SE*, 9, 4, 4; cf. Jerome, *Ep.*, 128, 3 (*CSEL*, 56, 159, ed. Hilberg).
282. *SE*, 82, 8, 11; 224, 2.
283. *SE*, 224, 3; cf. *SE*, 392, 2 and 132, 4.
284. *SE*, 392, 2; cf. Jerome, *Ep.*, 77, 3 (*CSEL*, 55, 38-9 (Fabiola's first husband)).
285. *DSI*, 20, 6.
286. *DFO*, 19, 35; cf. 6, 8; 15, 25; cf. *SE*, 392, 2; *DCR*, 7, 11.
287. *IP*, 149, 14 and 15; cf. *SDM*, 1, 14, 39.
288. *SE*, 392, 3.
289. *SE*, 392, 4 and 5; cf. *SE*, 332, 4.
290. *SE*, 82, 8, 11.
291. *SE*, 9, 3, 3.
292. *SE*, 343, 7.
293. *SE*, 9, 12.
294. *EP*, 259, 3.
295. Tertullian, *De Cult. Fem.*, 1, 9 and 2, 5-7 (*PL*, 1, 1427 and 1435-9); Jerome, *Ep.*, 38, 3 and 130, 18 (*CSEL*, 56, 199, ed. Hilberg); Paulinus, *Carmina*, 25f., 43, 90f., 125 (*CSEL*, 30, 239-41, 242, ed. Hartel).
296. *EP*, 245, 1.
297. *SE*, 32, 25; cf. *IP*, 143, 12.
298. *SE*, 161, 10 (the terms are *lacerna* and *byrrhus*).
299. *IP*, 32, 2, 7 and *SE*, 297, 5, 8.
300. *IP*, 149, 15.
301. *DBC*, 10, 10; *DCA*, 2, 12, 12.
302. *SE*, 51, 13, 22; 278, 9, 9; 11, 18; *IP*, 80, 21; *DNC*, 1, 4, 5.
303. 1 Cor. vii.6; *SE*, 51, 13, 22; *DNC*, 1, 14 and 15, 16 and 17; *DBC*, 6, 6 and 7.
304. *DBC*, 22, 27; 26, 34; *SE*, 51, 13, 22-15, 25.
305. *RE*, 2, 22.
306. *SE*, 51, 15, 25 conclusion; concerning lust; *DNC*, 1, 5, 6-8, 9; *DGL*, 9, 10, 16f.
307. *DBC*, 10, 10; 1 Tim. i.5 and 1 Cor. vii.7.
308. *SE*, 132, 3; so also *SE*, 354, 9.
309. *DBC*, 21, 25 and 26; 19, 22; 23, 29 and 30.
310. *DMO*, 19, 40.
311. *SEL*, 392, 6.
312. *QIH*, i, qu. 153; *DBC*, 6, 6; *DCA*, 2, 8, 7f.; *SE*, 332, 4.
313. *CF*, 9, 9.
314. *EP*, 262, 1-11.
315. *DH*, 86; *DBV*, 4, 6-5, 7; cf. ibid., 9, 12, 12-15.
316. Cf. also passages such as *EP*, 54, 4 (*Ad Furiam*) (*CSEL*, 54, 468f., ed. Hilberg).
317. *RE*, 2, 22; *DBC*, 26, 34; *DNC*, 2, 23; *DH*, 82.
318. *DBC*, and *DSV*, *passim*; on humility see *DSV*, 30-54; *SE*, 354, 8 and 9; *IP*, 83, 4.
319. *SE*, 354, 8 and 4.
320. *GUE*, 18, 12; *MO*, 501; *EP*, 20, 3; cf. 35, 5; 23, 5 (on mixed marriage); cf. *EP*, 15, 2 (*domesticum gaudium*); *IP*, 144, 22 (on a rich wife).
321. *SE*, 51, 21.
322. *SE*, 9, 4 and 45, 2; cf. again also *IP*, 93, 17 (sending a child away through despair); cf. *SE*, 349, 2 (the love of parents is natural; even a lion puts aside his savage nature when he approaches his young).
323. *IP*, 55, 17.
324. *SE*, 13, 9; *IP*, 50, 24; *TJ*, 51, 13; *CF*, 2, 3, 5-8.
325. *SE*, 57, 2.
326. *IP*, 137, 8; cf. *EP*, 98, 6 (on foundlings taken up by virgins) and 194, 32 ("infans de sacrilego stupro exponitur"); similarly, *DNC*, 1, 15.

327. *DNC*, 1, 13 and 15; cf. Dölger, *AC*, 455, 59 and 60f.; concerning *orbitas* in general cf. Ambrose, *De Virginitate*, 7, 36 (*PL*, 16, 289); in Egypt and Africa more virgins take the veil than there are children born in Milan; cf. however, *De Virginibus*, 1, 10, 57 (*PL*, 16, 216).

328. *DME*, 2, 18, 65: "Nonne vos estis, qui nos solebatis monere, ut quantum fieri posset, observaremus tempus, quo ad conceptum mulier post genitalium viscerum purgationem apta esset, eoque tempore a concubitu temperamus, ne carni anima implicatur."

329. *SE*, 302, 21, 19.

330. *SE*, 73, 4: "Putatis quia ista zizania non ascendunt apsidas?" cf. *SE*, 90, 4.

331. *GUE*, 18, 2.

332. *IP*, 32, 2, 4: "Ipsa lingua popularis plerumque est doctrina salutaris"; cf. Ps. xxxii.i.

333. *DME*, 1, 33, 70–4.

334. *SE*, 354.

335. *DME*, 1, 34, 75.

336. *EP*, 159, 3 and 4.

337. *IP*, 39, 8.

338. *CF*, 8, 6.

339. Orosius, *Hist. Adv. Pag.*, 7, 42, 17 (*CSEL*, 5, 558 and 559, ed. Zangemeister): "incertum zelo stimulatus an auro corruptus"; Jerome, *Dial. Adv. Pelag.*, 3, 19 (*PL*, 23, 616); Augustine, *Ep.*, 151.

340. *EP*, 151, 9 and 8, opening.

341. *EP*, 151, 8.

342. *EP*, 220, 2–5, 7–12.

343. Prov. ix.8; cf. *SE*, 114, delivered "ad mensam Cypriani praesente comite Bonifatio".

344. Gregory of Nazianzus, *Orat.*, 18, 9 and 10 (*PG*, 35, 996 and 997).

345. *CF*, 9, 11, 28; on and in praise of the life of Monica, ibid., 9, 8–11.

346. *CF*, 5, 9, 16.

347. *SE*, 392, 6; cf. *IP*, 140, 18 (... "however far you advance" ...).

348. *IP*, 99, 12.

349. *SE*, 15, 9.

350. *DUC*, 17, 35.

351. Lactantius, *Div. Inst.*, 6, 12 (*CSEL*, 19, 524–32, ed. Brandt) (particularly the conclusion).

352. *DME*, 1, 35, 80 and 2 Cor. iv.16.

353. *DME*, 1, 30, 63.

8. The Clergy and the Ascetics

1. Ambrose, *Ep.*, 63, 66 and 71 (*PL*, 16, 1258 and 1260); *Ser.*, 56, 4 (*PL*, 17, 744) (Eusebius of Vercelli); Paulinus, *Ep.*, 5, 15–19; 23, 8, 18, 4 and 5 (*CSEL*, 29, 34–38, 166, 131 and 132, ed. Hartel) (Victricius of Rouen); *VA*, 3, 5, 11; and *SE*, 355, 35 (Augustine); Sulpicius Severus, *Vita S. Martini*, 10 (*CSEL*, 1, 119 and 120, ed. Halm) (Martin of Tours); concerning the bishopric of Hippo and the life there cf. Leclercq in *DACL*, 3, 224–35; Monceaux in *Mélanges Div. Thomas*, 529–37 (1930); Moricca in *MA*, 2, 934–75 (self-defence); M. Mellet in *La Vie spirituelle*, 40, 196–202 (July-Aug. 1934), and *L'Itinéraire et l'idéal monastiques de S. Augustin*, Paris, 1934; Lambot in *Rev. litt. et. monast.*, 15, 292–304 (1930); P. Merlin, *S. Augustin et la vie monastique*, Albi, 1933; Vermeersch in *GM*, 11, 1930; J. Wirges, *Die Anfänge der Chorherrenstifte*, Betzdorf, 1928, 61f.; E. A. Foran, *The Augustinians*, London, 1938 (about seventy orders and congregations follow the Rule of St. Augustine); Lambot in *RB*, 41–58 (1941) (concerning the Rule).

2. *SE*, 355, 2.

3. Cf. the canons on celibacy of the Council of Rome of the year 386. Pope Siricius sent them, with a letter, to the bishops of Africa (*MC*, 3, 670).

4. Cf. *BH*, 37 (*MC*, 3, 924: "Tanta inopia clericorum ... ut quaedam loca omnino deserta").

5. Third Council of Carthage, canons 11–12 and 14 (*MC*, 3, 882 and 883); *BH*, 11 and 12 (*MC*, 3, 921); *CCEA*, 15 and 21 (*MC*, 3, 718 and 722).
6. *SE*, 355, 6.
7. *VA*, 21.
8. *SE*, 355 and 356, about 425.
9. *SE*, 355, 1f.
10. *SE*, 355, 2, 3.
11. *SE*, 355, 3, 4–4, 6.
12. *SE*, 355, 4, and 6 and 7.
13. *SE*, 356, 1 and 2 (opening).
14. *SE*, 356, 3.
15. *SE*, 356, 3–10.
16. *SE*, 356, 15 and 11.
17. *SE*, 356, 12 and 13; 15 (conclusion).
18. *SE*, 356, 14.
19. J. M. Vidal, *Dans l'entourage du Caulet*, Castillon-en-Couserans, 1939 (from the *Bulletin historique du diocèse de Pamiers*) and *Lexikon für theologie und kirche*, 2, 796.
20. *CF*, 6, 14, 24.
21. *CF*, 8, 6, 13–15 and 8, 19.
22. *CF*, 8, 6, 15; *DME*, 1, 33, 70.
23. *DME*, 1, 31, 65 and 66.
24. *DME*, 1, 31, 67 and 68.
25. *VA*, 3; *EP*, 216, 6 ("congregatio propositi non voti"), and *SE*, 355, 2; 356, 3; Acts iv.32–5.
26. *EP*, 10, 2: "in otio deificari".
27. *SE*, 355, 1, 2.
28. *EHC*, 3, iii, 36; cf. Jerome, *Ep.*, 39, 5 and 45, 4; cf. 127, 5 (*CSEL*, 56, 149, ed. Hilberg).
29. Cf. *EP*, 22, 2, 7 (concerning jealousy among the clergy); in regard to a somewhat later time see the superb passage in *SGD*, 8, 4, 19–22 (*CSEL*, 8, 197–9, ed. Pauly).
30. Cf. *Cod. Theod.*, 16, 2, 32 (*CTM*, 846).
31. *EP*, 60, 1.
32. Council of Carthage, 401, canon 13 (*MC*, 3, 971); *CCEA*, 80 (*MC*, 3, 779).
33. *LP*, 3, 40, 48.
34. *EP*, 78, 9.
35. *DOM*, 28, 36.
36. *DOM*, 31, 39; 32, 40; 33, 41; cf. Jerome, *Ep.*, 22, 28 (*CSEL*, 54, 185, ed. Hilberg).
37. *SDM*, 2, 12, 41.
38. *DOM*, cf. *RE*, 2, 21; cf. also the curious commentary of Jean-Pierre Camus, Bishop of Belley, *S. Augustin, De l'ouvrage des moines*, Rouen, 1633, and Alvarez, *Religión y Cultura*, 11, 224–38 (1930) and 12, 10f. (1937).
39. *DOM*, 13, 14; cf. 3–20, 4–24 (section about St. Paul).
40. *Celeuma* (*DOM*, 17, 20).
41. *DOM*, 21, 25; 25, 33; cf. *EP*, 211, 6 and 9.
42. *DOM*, 22, 26.
43. *DOM*, 23, 27–24, 31.
44. *DME*, 1, 31, 65–8; cf. *IP*, 99, 12; *SE*, 161, 12; *CFA*, 5, 9.
45. *EP*, 48, 2 and 3.
46. Gerontius, *Vita Melaniae Junioris*, 20 (*AB*, 22, 21 (the Greek *Life*)); Rampolla, *S. Melan. Giun.*, Rome, 1905, p. 55.
47. *EP*, 262, 1–11.
48. *EP*, 130, 4; cf. 1 Tim. v.5.
49. *EP*, 130, 1–8, above all 7; 1 Cor. xv.54; Ps. lxi.11 and 1 Tim. v.6.
50. *DSI*, 20, 12; cf. Ps. xxxviii.5.
51. *SE*, 161, 12 and Ps. xliv.3.
52. *EP*, 10, 2: "in otio deificari".
53. *EP*, 211, 16.
54. *SO*, 1, 10.

55. *VA*, 26; cf. Jerome's advice to Nepotianus: "Dilige aut ignora omnes aequaliter", *Ep.*, 52, 5 (*CSEL*, 54, 423 and 424, ed. Hilberg); clerics were permitted to live with their mothers, aunts and nieces: Third Council of Carthage, canon 17 (*MC*, 3, 883; *BH*, 16 (*MC*, 3, 921)); for visits to a women's cloister, the bishop's permission was required, as was the presence of witnesses (Third Council of Carthage, canon 25 (*MC*, 3, 884); *BH*, 24 (*MC*, 3, 922)).

56. *DCD*, 5, 18.
57. *EP*, 130, 7 and 8.
58. *CF*, 6, 16, 26.
59. *IP*, 132, 2.
60. *IP*, 132, 3 and 6; cf. *EP*, 211, 5.
61. *IP*, 99, 10 and 11; cf. 12 and *SE*, 355, 3 (*pueri*).
62. *IP*, 99, 14; cf. ibid., 13; cf. the portrait of the unspiritual and the true monk in Paulinus' letter to Sulpicius Severus, *Ep.*, 22, 1 and 2 (*CSEL*, 29, 154–6, ed. Hartel).
63. *CFA*, 5, 9; cf. *DCR*, 23, 43; concerning the African monasteries, cf. Monceaux in *MA*, 2, 61–89 ("Augustin et S. Antoine"); Dom Besse, *Les Moines de l'Afrique romaine*, Paris, 1903.
64. *DME*, 31, 68; *EP*, 211, 12 and 13 and 98, 6.
65. *IP*, 99, 12.
66. Pseudo-Ambrose (Nicetas of Remesiana?), *De Lapsu Virg.*, 6, 24 (*PL*, 16, 390).
67. *EP*, 23, 3.
68. Ambrose, *Hymn.*, 18, 3; *AVK*, p. 140:

> Quocumque tendis, virgines
> sequuntur atque laudibus
> post te canentes cursitant
> hymnosque dulces personant.

69. Ambrose, *Hymn.*, 18, 4:

> Nescire prorsus omnia
> corruptionis vulnera.

70. *EP*, 150, conclusion.
71. Jerome, *Ep.*, 130 (*Ad Demetriadem*) (*CSEL*, 56, 175f.).
72. *EP*, 188; *EHC*, 200; the letter of Pelagius, *PL*, 30, 15.
73. Jerome, *Ep.*, 130, 5 and 6 (*CSEL*, 56, 180 and 182).
74. Ambrose, *De Virginibus*, 3, 1–3 (*PL*, 16, 231–6).
75. *VA*, 26.
76. *EP*, 211, 4 and 1.
77. *EP*, 210, 1 and 2.
78. *EP*, 211; concerning the Rule cf. Besse in *DTC*, 1, 2472–83 and Baxter in *JTS*, 188–99 (1922); Vega, *La Regla de San Agustín*, Escorial, 1933.
79. Cf. Gal. v.7–9 and 1 Cor. v.6; *EP*, 211, 1–3.
80. *EP*, 211, 4.
81. *EP*, 211, 5–15.
82. *EP*, 211, 15.
83. Col. i.10.
84. *EP*, 211, 12 and 13.
85. *EP*, 211, 8 and 9.
86. *EP*, 211, 10.
87. Jerome, *Ep.*, 22, 27 (*CSEL*, 54, 184, ed. Hilberg): "imitantur noctuas et bubones".
88. *EP*, 211, 6 and 9; cf. *DOM*, 21, 25; 25, 23.
89. *EP*, 7.
90. *EP*, 8.
91. Caesarius of Arles, *Ep.*, 1, 5 (*Ad Sanctimoniales*), in *Regula ad Virg.*, ed Morin; *FP*, Bonn, 1933, 34, 37; cf. ibid., 14 (*statuta* xxxvi.): "Uno vel duobus lectoribus quos aetas et vita commendat, qui aliquotiens missas facere debeant"; the reference is thus not to a reader in the monastic community.
92. *EP*, 211, 12–13 and above all *DME*, 31, 68.
93. *EP*, 211, 10, 13.

94. *EP*, 211, 14.
95. *EP*, 211, 11 and 14; cf. Sulpicius Severus, *Dial. I*, 9 (*CSEL*, 7, 159–61 and 173–4, ed. Halm); also ibid., 8 and 21 (on eating a lot and allowing oneself to be spoilt by widows and nuns); cf. Aug., *SE*, 99, 12.
96. *EP*, 211, 10; cf. Prov. xxvii.20 (according to the Septuagint).
97. *EP*, 211, 16.
98. Third Council of Carthage, canon 25 (*MC*, 3, 884); *CCEA*, 35 (*MC*, 3, 734).
99. Isa. xxvi.1 (the well-known Vespers antiphon of the second Sunday in Advent).
100. Cf. Morin in *RB*, 43, 145–52 (1931); cf. Lambot in *Mélanges Mt. Cassin.*, 40–50, 51–7 (1929) (arguing that there is similarity but no actual borrowing; this is also true of the anonymous *Regula Secunda*, which dates from the fifth century) and De Bruyne, *RB*, 42, 316–42 (1930) (who sees a connection between this *Regula* and the Rule of St. Benedict, as against which view see Morin).
101. *CCEA*, 49 (*MC*, 3, 739); *VHP*, 3, 9, 34 (*CSEL*, 7, 89, ed. Petschenig).
102. *SE*, 356, 3–11 and 15; *EP*, 213, 1.
103. Third Council of Carthage, canon 4 (*MC*, 3, 880); *BH*, 1 (*MC*, 3, 919); *CCEA*, 16 (*MC*, 3, 718); *DCE*, 1, 10, 15: "pueri qui adhuc pueriliter in gradu lectorum christianas litteras norunt"; *SE*, 352, 1.
104. Jerome, *Adv. Jovinian.*, 1, 34 (*PL*, 23, 269 and 270).
105. Cf. also *EP*, 78, 9.
106. *EP*, 22, 7.
107. *EP*, 21, 1; cf. *SE*, 355, 6: "scio ... quanti ament clericatum".
108. *DCR*, 9, 13.
109. *DB*, 6, 25, 47.
110. Third Council of Carthage, canon 23 (*MC*, 3, 884; *BH*, 21 (*MC*, 3, 922)); First Council of Milevis (402) (*MC*, 4, 330; for the nomenclature and style of the prayers, cf. *EP*, 149, 16, and below).
111. *EP*, 221, 2.
112. *EP*, 34, 6; cf. the views of Aurelius: "diaconum vel inliteratum", *CCEA*, 56 (*MC*, 3, 763).
113. *EP*, 222; 239; cf 83 ("Ordinatus ad ecclesiam N."), 35, 2 (*subdiaconus* with two *concolonae*); cf. *Cod. Theod.*, 16, 2, 23 (*CTM*, 846).
114. Cf. Third Council of Carthage, canon 21 (*MC*, 3, 883 and 884) (no cleric from elsewhere may be ordained without the consent of his bishop).
115. Cf. Council of Carthage, 421, canons 4 and 9 (*MC*, 4, 449 and 450).
116. Council of Carthage, 421, canon 10 (*MC*, 4, 450; cf. Council of Hippo (date uncertain), canons 5 and 9 (*MC*, 4, 441, 442)).
117. *EP*, 64, 3.
118. *EP*, 62, 1–2 and 63, 1–4; Council of Milevis, 402 (*MC*, 3, 787c).
119. Third Council of Carthage, canon 45 (*MC*, 3, 889 and 890; *CCEA*, 55 (*MC*, 3, 756)).
120. *CCEA*, 53 (*MC*, 3, 742 and 743; Third Council of Carthage, canons 42 and 43 (*MC*, 3, 887 and 888)).
121. *EP*, 22, 3, 7: "rustica et minus instructa clericorum turba".
122. *EP*, 35, 2.
123. *EP*, 108, 19 and 106; cf. Pseudo-Aug., *Sermo de Rusticiano Subdiacono*, 4, vol. 9, 679 in the Maurist edition (according to the Maurists, a somewhat unreliable account which confuses two different stories).
124. *EP*, 65, 1 and 2.
125. *EP*, 64, 3.
126. *EP*, 219, 1.
127. *EP*, 78, 2–5 and 9; Apoc. xxii.11.
128. *EP*, 85 and 96, 2 and 3.
129. *DGL*, 12, 17 (an excellent description of a case of hysteria).
130. *EP*, 209, 2–7, 9–10.
131. Sixth Council of Carthage, 426; *Ep. Synod ad Coelestium* ("optaremus") (*MC*, 4, 515 and 516; cf. Batiffol, *Catholicisme de S. Augustine*, Paris, 1929, 443f., 449, 464–6 (Apiarius); 456f. (Antonius); *EHC*, 3, 256 and 257).
132. Jerome, *Ep.*, 52, 5–6, 9 and 11 (*CSEL*, 54, 424–6, 430–5 and *Ep.*, 22, 28 (*CSEL*, 54, 185 and 186, ed. Hilberg)).

133. *EP*, 208, 2 and 3.
134. Cyprian, *Ep.*, 4, 1–5 (*CSEL*, 3, 2, 472–8).
135. *IP*, 99, 12; cf. Tertullian, *De Exhort. Castit.*, 12 (*PL*, 2, 976 and 977).
136. Jerome, *Ep.*, 52, 6 (*CSEL*, 54, 425, ed. Hilberg); *Cod. Theod.*, 16, 2, 20 (30 July 370). *CTM*, 841, cf. 16, 2, 27 (21 June 390) (*CTM*, 843 and 844).
137. *EP*, 78, 6; cf. Ps. lxviii.13.
138. *EP*, 251.
139. *SE*, 351, 4, 11.
140. Jerome, *Ep.*, 22, 13 (on nuns) and 22, 16 (on priests) (*CSEL*, 54, 160 and 164, ed. Hilberg).
141. *DME*, 32, 69.
142. *SE*, 355, 6.
143. *EP*, 21, 1.
144. *VA*, 29.

9. The Bishop

1. Wilpert, *Die römischen Mosaiken und Malereien*, Freiburg, 1916, pls. 83 and 84; F. Reggiori, *La Basilica Ambrosiana*, Milan, 1941, pp. 216–37, 256–8 (the author considers the mosaic to be practically undamaged, but the portion between the two hands has certainly suffered damage and the small cross dates from the nineteenth century; like the figure of Maternus that stands beside him, Ambrose holds a codex between his left hand, which is covered, and his right, which is not—the attitude that is typical of the art of the time. Mgr. Ratti (who later became Pius XI), Wilpert and Dartein date the mosaic from the beginning of the fifth century, Toesca from the end of it; see Plate 10.

2. *DCD*, 22, 8, 9 (mentions the *casula* of a workman); *SE*, 356, 13 (the *birrus*); in *SE*, 161, 10 Augustine distinguishes between the *lacerna* (summer garment) and *birrus* (winter garment), but this refers to layfolk; Paulinus, *Ep.*, 22, 2 (*CSEL*, 29, 155, ed. Hartel), speaks of a *sagulum*; Sulpicius Severus, *Dial. I*, 21 (*CSEL*, 1, 174, ed. Halm) distinguishes between the *byrrum rigidum* and the *fluentem lacernam* for clerics. Paulinus girded his underclothing with a string rather than with a girdle; there is also evidence that he kept his hair short; the true ascetics, he says, are "nec inproba adtonsi capitis fronte criniti sed casta informitate capillum ad cutem caesi et inaequaliter sermitonsi et destituta fronte praerasi" (*Ep.*, 22, 2 (*CSEL*, 29, 155)); cf. also *DACL*, 2, 1, 907–10, under "Birrus", and also ibid., 1, 2, 2128–34, under "Capuchon".

3. *EP*, 218, 4 and 48, 4 (a pun on "Capraria").

4. Wilpert, *MKR*, pl. 140, 2 (cf. ibid., 297); circa 600; the inscription is:

+diversi diversa paeres sed hic omnia dixit
romano eloquio mystica sensa tonans

Cf. Wilpert in *MA*, 2, 1–3; see Plate 11.

5. Cf. B. Legewie, *Augustinus, eine Psychographie*, Bonn-Berlin, 1925, and in *MA*, 2, 5–21; F. Dinkler, "Die Anthropologie Augustins", in *Forsch. z. Kirchengesch. und Geistesgesch.*, 4, Stuttgart, 1934.

6. *EP*, 10, 1.
7. *EP*, 122, 1; 124, 1 (410 and 411).
8. *EP*, 151, 13.
9. *VA*, 7, 12 and 14; cf. *EP*, 269.
10. *CF*, 5, 9, 16 and 17 (the sickness of 383 at Rome); 9, 5, 13 (Milan, 386; his asthma and consequent retirement); *CA*, 1, 3; 3, 15; *DVB*, 4; *DO*, 1, 5, 26, 33; *SO*, 1, 1, 16 and 12, 21 (complaints about his stomach, chest and voice; Cassiciacum, 386).
11. *EP*, 38 (A.D. 397: "rhagadis vel exochadis dolore et tumore"); *EP*, 118, 34; 122, 1 (A.D. 410); *VA*, 28 and 29.
12. *SE*, 277, 8.
13. *VA*, 24.
14. *EP*, 224, 2; cf. Ambrose, *Ep.*, 47, 1 (*PL*, 16, 1199 and Augustine, *Ep.*, 139, 3 (night work in the years 311 and 412)); concerning his working power cf. Sizoo in *Stemmen des Tijds*, 1934, pp. 503–34.
15. *EP*, 126, 7.

16. Mosaic inscription over the inner door (De Rossi, *Musaici delle chiese di Roma anteriori al secolo xv*, Rome, 1872, nos. 3 and 4):

> Pauperibus locuples, pauper sibi; qui bona vitae
> praesentis fugiens meruit sperare futuram.

17. *FSA*, 2, 4; *SE*, 14, 1, 2; 339, 3, 3; *VA*, 23; *EP*, 185, 9, 35; cf. *SSA*, 221.
18. *FSA*, 2, 4 (for the basis of the idea of the feast for the poor see Luke xiv.12–13).
19. *EP*, 263, 1.
20. *EP*, 218, 4 (*cilica*); cf. *EP*, 48, 4; cf. *SE*, 356, 13.
21. *VA*, 22.
22. *SE*, 356, 13.
23. *VA*, 25; on swearing cf. *SE*, 180, 5 and 6 and *CL*, 2, 6, 6; *MO*, 255; *EP*, 33, 5 (by the "wreath" of the bishop); *TJ*, 35, 3 ("per lumina mea").
24. *VA*, 22:

> Quisquis amat dictis absentium rodere vitam
> hanc mensam indignam noverit esse sibi

Variant:

> hac mensa indignam noverit esse suam.

(thus in the Weiskotten edition of 1919); the translation would then read:

> He who loves in his talk to carp at the lives of the absent
> May be assured that his own way of life is unworthy of this table.

Cf. Weyman in *BGCP*, pp. 11–13.

25. *EP*, 38, 2.
26. *VA*, 24.
27. *EP*, 126, 9.
28. *VA*, 24; cf. Ambrose, who made his brother Satyrus administrator of his bishopric, *De Excess. Fratr. Sui Satyri*, 1, 20 (*FP*, 15, 25 (*PL*, 16, 1353)).
29. *VA*, 24.
30. *DSI*, 21, 18.
31. *IP*, 80, 4 (for the place cf. ibid., 24).
32. *IP*, 103, 3, 12; cf. 146, 17.
33. *VA*, 24; cf. Ambrose, *De Offic.*, 2, 28, 136 (*PL*, 16, 148).
34. *EP*, 258, 1 and 2; concerning his social life see Lesaar in *MA*, 233f. and Cazzulani in *SC*, 292–9 (1931).
35. *VA*, 27, towards the end.
36. *CC*, 1, 207 and 208 (*MC*, 4, 157 and 158); on Alypius, cf. Lesaar in *MA*, 220f.
37. *EP*, 31, 9; 24, 6; 32, 3 (Paulinus sends five of these to laymen).
38. *EP*, 269, 110 and 84, 1; cf. 261.
39. *EP*, 33, 1 and 5.
40. *EP*, 63, 1.
41. *EP*, 96, 2 and 3.
42. *EP*, 59, 1 and 2.
43. *EP*, 84, 1 and 2.
44. *EP*, 200, 1; 220, 1 (Firmus and Paulus); 191, 1; 193, 1 (Albinus and Leo).
45. *EP*, 221, 2.
46. See above; *LP*, 3, 16–17, 19–20 and *GUE*, 32, 11.
47. *CJ*, 1, 68 and 3, 35; cf. 1, 6 and 7, 42; 3, 199 and *CF*, 9, 8.
48. *EP*, 200, 2 and 3.
49. *EP*, 96, 1 and 97, 1.
50. *EP*, 100 and 112, 2 (Donatus) and 134 (Apringius).
51. *EP*, 153, 1f. and 155 (about 413 and 414); Macedonius to Augustine, *EP*, 152, 154.
52. *EP*, 204 (*circa* 420, see below); cf. *RE*, 2, 59 and *DDPQ*, preface.
53. *EP*, 185, 185a, 189 (about 417) and 220 (427–8).
54. *EP*, 86 and 151 (413).
55. *EP*, 128 and 129 (official letters); 133; 138; 139 and 143 (personal); Marcellinus to Augustine, *EP*, 136.
56. *EP*, 151, 8.

57. *RE*, 1, 2 and *DBVA*, 1.
58. *EP*, 147, ed. Schmaus, in *FP*, 23 (Bonn, 1930).
59. *EP*, 200.
60. *DDPQ*, preface.
61. *DCD*, 1, 1 and *EP*, 136, 3; 138, 20; cf. 193, 3 (*De Bapt. Parvulorum*) and 143, 4 (*DGL* and *DT*).
62. *EP*, 72, 1, 1 and above all *EP*, 75, 7, 22 ("qui iuvenis es et in pontificali culmine constitutus").
63. *EP*, 72, 1, 2.
64. *EP*, 28 and 40; Jerome's angry letters are *inter Aug. epp.*, *EP*, 68 and 72.
65. *EP*, 149, 2.
66. *EP*, 202a, 1, 1.
67. *EP*, 200, 1.
68. *EP*, 59, 2.
69. Cf. *EP*, 192 and 209 (Celestine); 191 and 194 (Sixtus); the papal letters, *EP*, 181-4, are merely office jobs.
70. *Aug. Opera*, ed. Froben, Basle, 1528-9, preface to the reader; cf. C. Favez in *Mus. Helveticum*, 65-8 (1944) (*EP*, 92, 259, 263 are essentially letters of consolation in the old style; only the pagan clichés are missing).
71. *EP*, 110, 5; cf. 139 and *FSA*, 2, 4.
72. *EP*, 224, 2; cf. *RE*, prolog., and *VA*, 18.
73. *EP*, 27 and 31; also 42; 45; 80; 95 and 149; Paulinus to Augustine: *EP*, 25, 30; 94 and 121.
74. *EP*, 28; 40; 67; 71; 73; 166; 167; Jerome to Augustine: 39, 68; 72; 81; 123; 172; 195.
75. *EP*, 82, 2, 22.
76. *EP*, 74.
77. *EP*, 131.
78. *EP*, 130, cf. above.
79. *EP*, 150.
80. *EP*, 127, to Armentarius and Paulina; similarly to Paulina, *EP*, 147, *liber de Videndo Deo*.
81. *EP*, 229, 1 and 2; cf. 230, 4.
82. *EP*, 230, 1-6.
83. *EP*, 231, 1-7; cf. Persius, 1, 47 and Plutarch, *Themist.*, 2.
84. *EP*, 154, 1 and 2.
85. *EP*, 155.
86. *EP*, 137 and 138; cf. above.
87. *EP*, 263, 1-4 and Col. iii.1.
88. *EP*, 200, 1-3.
89. *EP*, 117.
90. *EP*, 118, above all 1, 2, 9 and 11; J. Koopmans, *Aug. briefwisseling met Dioscorus*, Amsterdam, 1949.
91. *EP*, 187, 7, 22; the questioner, Dardanus, was a layman of rank.
92. *DDPQ*.
93. *EP*, 143, 1; Exod. vii.20-22; cf. viii.22; ix.4; vi.26; x.23; xi.7.
94. *EP*, 135, 2 (around 412).
95. *EP*, 260 and 261, 4.
96. *EP*, 164; cf. 1 Pet. iii.18-21; *EP*, 147 and 120.
97. *EP*, 111.
98. *EP*, 175, 5 and 179, 4.
99. *EP*, 23, 3.
100. Cf. *SE*, 101, 4.
101. *IP*, 126, 3, also 1 and 2; *SE*, 23, 1; cf. *SE*, 17, 2.
102. e.g., *SE*, 340 and 339; concerning such celebrations cf. *SE*, 111, towards the end (Aurelius), and *LP*, 2, 23 and *EP*, 108, 2, 5 (Optatus of Thamugadi, known also as Gildonianus).
103. *GUE*, 32, 1.
104. *GUE*, 32, 4.

105. *GUE*, 32, 6, 9 and 8.
106. *DAC*; *RE*, 2, 3; D'Alès in *GM*, 131–45 (1930); cf. on the simple style of his prose writings J. Finaert in *Rev. des études lat.*, 16 (1938).
107. *VA*, 28; cf. Cassiodorus, *Institutiones Divinarum et Saecularium Litterarum*, 16 (p. 54 in Mynors' edition, Oxford, 1937) (citing *SP* and *DAC*; *DDQO*; *DVR* and *DCD*).
108. *Werke*, Leipzig, 1903, 13, 302, 334; cf. the letter to Overbeck of 31 March 1885 and De Lagarde, *Schriften für das deutsche volk*, ed. Fischer, Munich, 1934, p. 267.
109. *EP*, 19, 2 (*PL*, 16, 1024).
110. Cf. below.
111. Luke xii.13–14.
112. *VA*, 19; cf. *SE*, 47, 4 (the *secretarium* as a court of law).
113. *SE*, 161, 4.
114. *VA*, 19; cf. 1 Tim. v.20.
115. *SE*, 83, 8, 11; cf. *EP*, 95, 3 and below in the chapter on penance.
116. *EP*, 133, 2; cf. 185, 21.
117. *IP*, 46, 5; *EP*, 90 and 91, 7; cf. above.
118. *EP*, 139, 3.
119. *IP*, 25, 13 and *SE*, 47, 4.
120. *SE*, 137, 14.
121. *VA*, 27 and 24; Ambrose, *Ep.*, 82, 1–3 (*PL*, 16, 1331–2).
122. *EP*, 154, 1.
123. *EP*, 152, 2.
124. *EP*, 153, 1–26, cf. 10.
125. Cf. *Cod. Theod.*, 4, 3, 2; Sirmond., 13 (21 Dec. 419) (*CTM*, 917).
126. *EP*, 116, final paragraph.
127. *EP*, 247, 1–4.
128. *IP*, 128, 4; cf. *SE*, 9, 3–5.
129. *SE*, 82, 2.
130. *SE*, 46, 8.
131. *SE*, 137, 14.
132. *EP*, 113–15; 151, 3, 11; 268; cf. *Cod. Theod.*, 9, 45, 1–3 (*CTM*, 519) and 9, 45, 4 (limitations in regard to *publici debitores* and Jews) (*CTM*, 520).
133. *EP*, 151, 3 and 11.
134. *GUE*, 25 (after *SE*, 302); *MO*, 528.
135. *EP*, 268, 1–3.
136. *EP*, 250 and 250a.
137. *EP*, 133, 2; cf. above.
138. *EP*, 114; 115 and 113; concerning Generosus cf. *EP*, 53; cf. *Cod. Theod.*, 9, 2, 6 (January 409).
139. *EP*, 151, 5.
140. *SE*, 302, 17.
141. *CF*, 6, 3, 3.
142. *EP*, 253–5.
143. *EP*, 266, 1.
144. *EP*, 261, 1; 110, 5.
145. *EP*, 224, 2.
146. *EP*, 139, 3.
147. *DOM*, 29, 37.
148. *FP*, 48, 1; Matt. v.41 and Ps. lxxviii.11.
149. *SE*, 340, 1.
150. *SE*, 339, 4.
151. *EP*, 228; cf. *VA*, 30; cf. 2 Cor. xi.29.
152. Ps. lxxii.23.
153. Ps. xxxv.7.
154. Hahn, "Tyconiusstudien", in *Stud. z. Gesch. d. Theol. und d. Kirche*, 6 (1901); cf. *EP*, 208, 2.
155. *History of Dogma*.
156. *Acta ecclesiastica*, *EP*, 213, 1–7.
157. *EP*, 213, 7.

158. *VA*, 29–31 (Augustine d. 28 August 430, aged 76). Cf. *VHP*, 1, 3, 11 (*CSEL*, 7, 6, ed. Petschenig).
159. *VA*, 27.
160. *VA*, 29.

THE CULTUS

10. The Theoretical Aspect

1. *EP*, 54 and 55 (*Ad Inquisitiones Januarii*, bks. 1 and 2); *RE*, 2, 20; *EP*, 55, 39.
2. *DCD*, 10, 1; concerning λατρεια cf. *DCD*, 5, 15; 6, praef., 7, 32; 10, 1–3; 19, 17; *EP*, 170, 2 and 3 (*latria*).
3. *DCD*, 10, 3.
4. *CFA*, 20, 21.
5. *EP*, 54, 1, 1; cf. 55, 2f.; also, in *IP*, 103, 1, 9, he says "munus sacramentorum in baptismo, in eucharistia, in ceteris sacramentis".
6. *CFA*, 19, 13; "praenuntiativa erant Christi venturi"; cf. *DDC*, 3, 6, 10.
7. *DCD*, 2, 26; "cuncta obscoenitatis officia".
8. *DDC*, 3, 6, 8, 10–12.
9. *DDC*, 3, 9, 13.
10. *EP*, 55, 19, 35: "Religionem quam paucissimis et manifestissimis celebrationum sacramentis misericordia dei liberam esse voluit"; *EP*, 55, 7–13; *DSI*, 3, 1: "tam mundum et facile sacramentum"; cf. Newman, *Parochial and Plain Sermons*, 3, 277 and 278, and 5, 139.
11. *SE*, 227, *passim*; *SE*, 228, 3 (see text below).
12. *DDC*, 3, 10, 14; "sacramentorum velata mysteria": *SP*, preface.
13. *EP*, 55, 7, 13.
14. *CFA*, 19, 11; *Summa Theologica*, 3, qu. 61, ad. 1, *sed contra*; in the *Summa contra Gentiles*, 4, 56 ("De Necessitate Sacramentorum"), St. Thomas names three grounds for the sacraments' character of visible signs; the natural means of recognition possessed by men, the necessary correspondence of the instrument with the First Cause (in this case the Word of God made visible), and the showing-forth of the natural goodness of visible created things, provided they are used in accordance with right order. The argument from community is missing here.
15. *IP*, 103, 1, 9; *DB*, 3, 16, 21; cf. Ps. ciii. and 1 Cor. xii.31.
16. *DB*, 3, 17, 22.
17. *DB*, 1, 10, 14; cf. *EP*, 98, 5.
18. *TJ*, 26, 13 and 15, also 1 Cor. x.17.
19. *SE*, 57, 7, 227; 229; *TJ*, 26, 13; *EP*, 185, 50; *DSI*, 3, 3 (authenticity dubious) 6, 1–2; *GUE*, 7, 1.
20. *SE*, 272 shortly after the middle; cf. *GUE*, 7, 1 and 2.
21. *DCD*, 10, 6; *TJ*, 26, 13; 1 Cor. x.17.
22. *SE*, 227, beginning; 229; 272; *DSI*, 6, 1; *GUE*, 7, 2.
23. *GUE*, 7, 1.
24. Paul Valéry, *Existence du Symbolisme*, Maestricht, 1939, 33; cf. *CF*, 10, 33, 49 and 50.
25. *EP*, 54, 1; cf. 55, 19, 35 (text below).
26. Cf. the objections in *EP*, 36, 9, 21 and 22 (*Ad Casulanum*) concerning fasting on Saturdays.
27. *DB*, 2, 7, 12.
28. *DB*, 2, 9, 14.
29. *EP*, 54, 1 and 55, 15, 27 and 16, 29.
30. *EP*, 54, 2, 3; *EP*, 36, 13, 31–14, 32.
31. *EP*, 55, 13, 23.
32. Cumont in *RHR*, 103, 70f. (1931); the same thought is to be found in the model catechisms of *DCR*, 17f. and 27f.
33. *EP*, 55, 9, 16–13, 23.

34. Bücheler, *Carmina Latina Epigraphica*, Leipzig, 1897, 2, 420, no. 908, 1–4; likewise *ICR*, vol. 2, 161, 2:

> Octochorum s[an]c[t]os templum surrexit in usus
> Octagonus fons est munere dignus eo
> hoc numero decuit sacri baptismatis aulam
> surgere quo populis vera salus rediit.

Cf. Riva in *Ambrosius*, 12, 5–13 (1936) (baptisteries in Milan); Dölger in *AC*, 4, 153–187 (1934); Mercati in *BZ*, 36, 514 (1936). Octagonal baptisteries have been preserved in Rome, Vega del Mar, Albenga, Ventimiglia, Fréjus, and in Ravenna (two), all dating from the fourth and fifth centuries; there are octagonal *piscinae*, with concentrically descending steps, for instance in Africa at Timgad, Siagu and Tabraca.

35. *EP*, 55, 24; cf. 1 John iii.14 (Augustine reads "transivimus de morte ad vitam") and 2 Cor. iv.16; cf. *IP*, 140, 25 and *DSI*, 7, 1 (spurious?) concerning the Hebrew word.
36. *EP*, 55, 1 and 2 and 3, 5.
37. See above.
38. *EP*, 55, 15, 27.
39. *EP*, 55, 4, 6–8; cf. H. Rahner, *Griechische Mythen in christlicher Deutung*, Zürich, 1945, p. 215.
40. *EP*, 55, 5, 8–6, 10; cf. Ecclus. xxvii.12; Rom. v.12 and Ps. lxxxviii.38; cf. *IP*, 10, 3.
41. *EP*, 55, 3, 5 and 8, 14.
42. *EP*, 55, 16, 30.
43. *EP*, 55, 15, 28; concerning the numbers 40, 50 and 153 cf. also *SE*, 252, 7–12.
44. *EP*, 55, 16, 29–17, 31; cf. *SE*, 252, 7–12. For another and later explanation of the figure 153 see below.
45. *EP*, 54, 14, 24; cf. Eph. iii.18 and Phil. i.23; Ps. cxviii.120; cf. *TJ*, 118, 5: "quod signum nisi adhibeatur, nihil ... rite perificitur".
46. See below.
47. *SE*, 261–5, *MO*, 9, 1; cf. *EP*, 54, 1, 1.
48. *EP*, 55, 16, 29 and 30; *DCR*, 23 and 20; *MPB*, 158, 4–7.
49. *EP*, 55, 17, 32.
50. *SE*, 190, 1; on the date cf. *DT*, 4, 5, 9 and *SE*, 203, 1, 1; up to the time of Aurelian the *natale solis invicti* was only celebrated in Rome, cf. Noiville in *REA*, 38, pp. 145–76 (1939).
51. *SE*, 287, 4; cf. 292, 1 and *FSA*, 8, 5.
52. *SE*, 202, 2; B. Botte, *Les Origines de la Noël et de l'Épiphanie*, Louvain, 1932.
53. *EP*, 55, 2, 2.
54. *EP*, 54, 2, 2.
55. *EP*, 54, 2, 3.
56. *EP*, 36, 1, 2–14, 32.
57. *EP*, 54, 3, 4.
58. *EP*, 54, 4, 5–7, 10.
59. *EP*, 55, 18, 33.
60. *TJ*, 56, 4.
61. *EP*, 54, 2, 2 and *EP*, 36, 1, 2.
62. *EP*, 54, 5, 6.
63. *EP*, 54, 6, 8; cf. 1 Cor. xi.33–4.
64. *EP*, 55, 19, 35; cf. *EP*, 54, 5, 6.
65. Third Council of Carthage, 397, canon 23 (*MC*, 3, 884); *BH*, 393, canon 21 (*MC*, 3, 922); Council of Milevis, 402 (*MC*, 4, 330; cf. above).
66. *EP*, 36, 9, 22; cf. Ps. xliv.14–15.
67. *EP*, 138; cf. *DCD*, 10, 5 (the same thought and the same quotation from Ps. xv.2); for the Augustinian conception of the *sacramentum* see also J. Hymmen, *Die Sakramentslehre Augustins*, Bonn, 1905; M. Pontet, *L'Exégèse de S. Augustin, prédicateur*, Paris, 1946, p. 257; J. Huhn, *Die Bedeutung des wortes Sacramentum bei Ambrosius*, Fulda, 1928; Spallanzoni in *SC*, 1927, 175–88, 256–68; cf. also De Ghellinck and others, *Pour l'histoire du mot "sacramentum"*, Louvain-Paris, 1924, vol. 1, pp. 16 and 307–12 (the word's prehistory); Casel in *JFL*, 8, 225–32 (1928); Dölger in *AC*, 2, pp. 268–80

(1930) on the *sacramentum militiae*; R. Kuypers, *Der Zeichen- und Wortbegriff im Deneken Augustins*, Amsterdam, 1934; Lekkerkerker in *Vox Theologica*, 15, 516 ("Augustinus en Calvijn"; cf. Dankbaar, *De Sakramentsleer van Calvijn*, Amsterdam, 1941; R. Russell, "The Concept of a Sacrament in St. Augustine", *Eastern Churches Quarterly*, 1, pp. 73–9, 121–31 (1936); H. M. Féret, "Sacramentum et res dans la langue de Saint Augustin", *Rev. de Sc. phil. et rel.*, 218–43 (1940). Augustine is the first who uses *sacramentum* as equivalent to *signum*; the distinction *res-signum* is the key to medieval sacramental theology.

68. *TJ*, 80, 3; cf. *CFA*, 19, 16: "quasi visibilia, sacrosancta quidem, verumtamen mutabilia et temporalia"; cf. also Calvin, *Institutes*, 4, 14, 6.
69. Cf. *DT*, 13, 1, 4; cf. 9, 10, 10, 1 and *CFA*, 19, 16.
70. *EP*, 55, 6, 11.
71. *DCR*, 26, 50.
72. *DDC*, 3, 30, 42.
73. *MPB*, 130, 1; *MO*, 377 and 378.
74. Gen. i.14 and above; *IP*, 10, 3 and 4, 93, 4 and 5.
75. *EP*, 55, 7, 13, concluding words.
76. *EP*, 55, 11, 21.
77. *DCR*, 9, 13; cf. the beautiful example in *DDC*, 2, 6, below.
78. *EP*, 137, 5, 18.
79. Cf. *DM* and *IEJ*, 3, 13.
80. Dionysius, *De Eccl. Hierarch.*, 2, 3, 2: τα μέναισδημῶς ἱερα τῶν νοητῶν απεικονισματα και ’επ ἀυτα χειραμωμα και ὁδος: Richard Hooker, *Treatise of the Laws of Ecclesiastical Polity*, 4, 1, 3 and 4: "Ceremonies are resemblances framed according to things spiritually understood, whereunto they serve as a hand to lead, and a way to direct" (quoted by F. Paget, *An Introduction to the Fifth Book of Hooker's Treatise*, Oxford, 1907, p. 54); Baudelaire, *Fusées*, ed. Schiffrin, Paris, 1930, p. 136.
81. *All Things Considered*, London, 1908, p. 281.
82. *DCD*, 10, 3.
83. *EP*, 167, 3, 11; *EP*, 140, 18, 45; Ps. lxxii.28.
84. *IP*, 103, 1, 9.
85. *EP*, 55, 1, 2–3, 4.
86. *CFA*, 19, 13, 16 (*annuntiant, personant*).
87. *CFA*, 19, 13, 16, further on; cf. *CCR*, 4, 16, 19: "propria sanctitate atque veritate".
88. *CEP*, 2, 13, 28 and 29 (*character*).
89. Rom. vi.4.
90. *EP*, 98, 9 and 10; in the last sentence *christiano=Christi*.
91. *TJ*, 80, 3.
92. *DSI*, 6, 3 (spurious?).
93. *DB*, 3, 17, 22–3 and 1, 10, 14 (the Church); *CEP*, 2, 11, 24 (on the Spirit considered as an alternative to the Church).
94. *DB*, 4, 23, 30 and 24, 31.
95. *DB*, 4, 23, 30.
96. *DB*, 1, 10, 14 and *EP*, 98, 5; on infant baptism cf. *CJ*, 2, 101 and *DPMR*, 1, 34, 62.
97. Cf. P. Ellerbeck, "Schets van een anthropologie der sacramenten", *Bijdragen Phil. Theol. Facult. der Ned Jezuieten*, 1943, 6, 1.
98. *Adorare*: e.g., *IP*, 21, 1, 30; *EP*, 140, 27, 66.
99. *CAM*, 12, 3; cf., e.g., *IP*, 3, 1: "Convivium in quo corporis et sanguinis sui figuram discipulis commendavit et tradidit"; cf., for the beginning of the third century, Hippolytus, *Trad. Apost.*, 23, Dix, *The Shape of the Liturgy*, p. 40 (*antitypum*); for the fourth century, *Euchologion Serapionis*, 13, 12 (*FP*, 7, 61) (ὁμοίωμα); Ambrose, *De Sacr.*, 4, 5, 21 (*FP*, 7, 160) (*figura*). For the Augustinian doctrine on the Eucharist see K. Adam, *Die Eucharistielehre des hl. Augustins*, Paderborn, 1908, and *TQ*, 112, 490–536 (1931); G. Lecordier, *La Doctrine de l'Eucharistie chez S. Augustin*, Paris, 1930; A. Pons, *Le Banquet du Seigneur ou la communion d'après les docteurs et la practique de l' ancienne Église d'Afrique*, Tunis, 1930 (though I was not able to make use of this myself); J. Geiselmann, *Die Abendmahlslehre an der Wende der christlichen Spätantike zum Frühmittelalter*, Munich, 1933; P. Bertocci, *Il simbolismo ecclesiologico dell' Eucarestia*, Bergamo,

1937; E. Hendrikx, "Augustinus en de transsubstantiatie", in *Theol. Opstell. opg. aan Mgr. v. Noort*, Utrecht, 1944, pp. 106–17; Camelot, "Réalisme et symbolisme dans la doctrine eucharistique de Saint Augustin", *Rev. des. sc. phil et theol.*, 31 (1947); H. Lang, S. Aug. *Textus Eucharistici Selecti*, Bonn, 1933, *FP*, 35; cf. also Batiffol, *Études d'hist. et de théol. positive*, Paris, 1930, 2nd series.

100. *CAM*, 12, 3; cf. Deut. xii.23.
101. *GUE*, 7, 1 (see text below); cf. Ambrose, *De Mysteriis*, 8 and 9 (*FP*, 7, 131–7); *De Sacr.*, 4, 4, 14 and 15, 5 and 6 (*FP*, 158, 160), and 4, 4–6 (*FP*, 158–62): on Ambrose as the author of *De Sacr.*, cf. Faller in *ZKT*, 53, 41–65 (1929); Dölger, *AC*, 1, 35, n. 144a (1929); Morin, *JFL*, 8, 86–106 (1928); Casel, *JFL*, 11, 6 (1931); Faller in *ZKT*, 64, 1–14 and 81–101 (1940); Frank in *TQ*, 121, 67–82 (1940) (for); Baumstark in *Miss. Rom.*, Nijmegen, 11 (1929); Atchley in *JTS*, 30, 281–6 (1929) (against).
102. *EP*, 140, 19, 48 and *DT*, 3, 10, 21.
103. On the discipline of the *arcanum* cf. *IP*, 103, 1, 14; *SE*, 307, 3; 131, 1; 132, 1 and below.
104. *EP*, 54, 3, 4.
105. *IP*, 98, 9; Ambrose, *De Spir. S.*, 3, 11, 79 and 80 (*PL*, 16, 828 and 829; cf. Ps. xcviii.9).
106. *IP*, 33, 1, 10; cf. 1 Kings xxi.13 and *IP*, 33, 1, 6.
107. *EP*, 140, 27, 66 and *IP*, 21, 1, 30 and Ps. xxi.30 and 27.
108. *CFA*, 20, 13.
109. *IP*, 98, 9, conclusion.
110. *DDC*, 3, 16, 24.
111. Cf. *TJ*, 26, 12 and *IP*, 98, 9.
112. *CFA*, 12, 10.
113. *CF*, 9, 12, 32 and 13; 36; cf. Col. ii.14.
114. *CFA*, 20, 18.
115. *QE*, 2, 33, 5.
116. *DCD*, 17, 20, 2; for the unworthy cf. *SE*, 71, 17; *DB*, 5, 8.
117. *CFA*, 20, 21.
118. *DPMR*, 1, 24, 34.

11. Augustine's Liturgical Practice

1. Minutes of 14 May 303, quoted in the *Gesta apud Zenophilum*, A.D. 320 (*CSEL*, 26, 187, ed. Ziwsa) (*in app. Optat.*); cf. *IP*, 113, 2, 6 and *CCR*, 3, 29; the inventory comprised two golden and six silver chalices, six silver jars (*urceola*), a silver vessel (*cuccumellum*), seven silver lamps, two silver candelabra (*cereofala*), eleven bronze hanging lamps with chains. We may compare with two other later non-African and non-Augustinian documents. The first is the inventory of a village church near Tivoli, which is referred to in the deed of gift of the year 471 (*Charta Cornutiana*; Bruzza, *Regesto della chiesa di Tivoli*, 15–17); one silver paten, one large chalice and two smaller ones, one small sacrificial jug, one sieve, one incense container (for burning, not for censing), one lamp with chains and eighteen holders, four hanging lamps with chains, a pair of standing candelabra, two doors with keys for the *confessio* (the grave with the relics under the altar), in all, 54 lb. 7 oz. of silver, weighed in the municipal weighing-office; further, two copper chandeliers each with eight holders, six saucers of copper for the standing candelabra and twelve smaller saucers and two copper lilies, two standing candelabra of copper; a number of curtains of embroidered silk and linen. Books: four Gospels, one "Apostle", one psalter and 1 *comes*, in which the lessons were recorded.

The second document is the *Liber Pontificalis*, in which, above all for the fifth and sixth centuries, the following articles are enumerated: large plates for the bread (*patenae*), chalices for the consecrated wine (*scyphi*), smaller chalices for the distribution (*calices ministeriales*, which were filled from the *scyphi*), large tubs (for all that was sacrificed?—*amae*, containing up to 3 *medimnae*, which is about 4½ bushels capacity); further, pans for the incense (*thymiamateria*), pitchers (*aquamanilia*), large vessels (*metretae*, for oil or wine?) and finally a curtain between every pair of pillars (*vela*); cf. Duchesne in the edition of 1886, 1, introd., 145.

2. *VA*, 24, cf. above.

3. *SE*, 356, 12.
4. See above.
5. *DCE*, 1, 10, 16: the representation of the theme "Dominus legem dat" is found, for instance, in the mosaic of the baptistery at Naples (*MM*, plate 32), on the little ivory box from Samagher in Pola, on a golden glass from Porta (Garrucci, *Vetri Ornati di figure in oro trovati nei cemiteri dei Christiani primitivi di Roma*, Rome, 1858, 10, 8 and 9; Boll. 186, 38) and further on a number of sarcophagi from Milan, Rome and Arles, of the time of Theodosius (*SCA*, 188, 1: from Milan, 150, 1 and 2. Aix and Verona, 14, 3; Ancona, 12, 5 and 39, 1; Vatican, 12, 4; Arles, 17, 1; S. Paulo fuori le mure, 121, 4; the Lateran, 174, 31, 2; S. Sebastiano, 17, 2; Marseilles, cf. 141, 6; Ravenna. See also Kraus, *Geschichte d. chr. Kunst*, i, 58–65 and Nicodemi in *Pubbl. Commem. Milano*, 1931, 500–8).
6. *DT*, 8, 4, 7 and 5, 7.
7. *DFS*, 7, 14.
8. *DH*, 7; Lampridius, *Vita Alex. Sev.*, 29, 2.
9. *JP*, 5, 2–6.
10. *IP*, 113, 2, 4–6; cf. Calvin, *Institutes*, 1, 11, 10.
11. *RE*, 1, 1, 3; cf. *CA*, 2, 3: "Philocalia et Philosophia".
12. *DDC*, 2, 25, 39.
13. *EP*, 91, 5.
14. Calvin, *Institutes*, 1, 11, 5; cf. 11 *passim*.
15. *DDQO*, 83, qu. 78.
16. *DCD*, 11, 23; cf. the expositions of Alois Riegl in *Spätrömische Kunstindustrie*, Vienna, 1927, 2, 399.
17. *EP*, 18, 2: "Omnis porro pulchritudinis forma unitas."
18. *DO*, 2, 15, 42; ibid., 18, 48 on the unity of the individual; *numerus*=rhythm (ibid., 14, 40); cf. the conversation with an architect in *DVR*, 32, 59f.
19. *DDC*, 3, 13, 18.
20. Gregory Nazianzen, *Carm.*, 2, 12, 739–45 (*PG*, 37, 1219); cf. *Asterii Hom. in S. Euphemiam*, ed. Combefis, Paris, 1648, 208 (Euphranor).
21. *SE*, 243, 6; cf. 2, 24, 4.
22. *CF*, 10, 6, 8.
23. De Fontanes.
24. Cf. the Greek names φωισμός and φωτιστηριον for "baptism" and "baptismal Church" and Ambrose's hymn *Splendor Paternae Gloriae*; also *TJ*, 44, 2.
25. Ps. cxxxviii.12; Eph. v.8 (in *SE*, 222); Isa. lx.1; 2 Cor. iv.6 (Augustine reads: *qui dixit clarescere—claruit, WS*, 4, 5); Ps. cxxxviii.11 (*GUE*, 5); Ps. xii.4 (*WS*, add. M. 717); Ps. lxxv.5 (*WS*, add. M. 716); cf. below, the lesson on Easter Eve.
26. Ps. xvii.29, in *GUE*, 5, 1; cf. *WS*, 4, 2.
27. *SE*, 219, conclusion.
28. *GUE*, 5, 1 and 2.
29. *SE*, 316, 5.
30. *CFA*, 22, 73; cf. Gregory of Nyssa, *Sermo de Deitate Filii et Spir. S.* (*PG*, 46, 572); for the iconography of Abraham's sacrifice cf. Wilpert in *RQ*, 1887, 126f. and in *MKR*, 1903, § 99; Alison Moore Smith in *AJA*, 2, 159f. (1922).
31. *IP*, 103, 1, 7.
32. *EP*, 55, 18, 34 conclusion and 19, 35; on popular singing, J. Quasten, *Musik und Gesang in den Kulten de heidnischen Antike und der christliche Frühzeit*, Münster, 1930; Gennrich, *Der Gemeindegesang in der altchristliche und mittelalterl. Kirche*, Leipzig-Hamburg, 1936; Dohmes in *Lit. Leben*, 128–51 (1938) (the singing of psalms was the first real participation in worship); Glibotic in *EL*, 50, 99–153 (1936) (on the Allelulia); cf. also T. Gerold, *Les Pères de l'Eglise et la musique*, Paris, 1931.
33. *EP*, 55, 18, 34; cf. *RE*, 1, 20.
34. All these are vouched for for Africa; *DSI*, 6, 3; *GUE*, 7, 3; *SE*, 227 (dialogue before the *praefatio*); *IP*, 31, 21; 148, 5; *SE*, 25, 7; 53, 13, 14; 68, 4, 5; 237, 3; 343, 4 (*sursum cor*); *DSI*, 6, 3 ("Amen" after the Canon); *DDC*, 2, 11, 16 and *TJ*, 41, 3 (*Amen*); *DCD*, 22, 8, 22 and *EP*, 213, 2–7 ("Deo gratias", "Christo laudes", "Exaudi, Christe", "Fiat, fiat").
35. *SE*, 119, 1: "Psalmus quem modo nobis cantatum audivimus, et cantando respondimus."

36. *CF*, 9, 7–15 and 6, 14; Ambrose, *In Ps. XII praef.*, 5, 6, 7.
37. *Liber Pontificalis*, 1, 230 and 231, under Celestine I, 422–32, who was Augustine's contemporary.
38. *IP*, 18, 2, 1; 32, 2, 4; 43, 13.
39. *IP*, 138, 1; cf. *SE*, 352, 1.
40. *IP*, 119, 1 (antiphonal); 44, 1 (community singing, in Carthage); Ps. xc.40, 1 and 7 (Verse 6 as refrain); 29, 2, 1; 25, 5 (Verse 9 as refrain); *SE*, 176, 1 (singing in unison of Ps. xciv, at any rate of verses 2 and 6), *DSI*, 9, 1 ("Alleluia" as the refrain, Ps. xciv).
41. *RE*, 2, 11.
42. Caesarius of Arles, *SE*, 286, 1 and 285, 1, *in app. op. Aug.*, vol. 5, 475–6 and 474 in the Maurist edition.
43. *IP*, 132, 1.
44. *DOM*, 17, 20; cf. Jerome, *Ep.*, 46, 12 (*CSEL*, 54, 342–4, ed. Hilberg); *Vita Malchi*, 5 (*PL*, 23, 58); *DGL*, 12, 17 (the *chorus piorum psallentium* seen in a vision during a nerve crisis).
45. *DO*, 1, 8, 22; Ps. lxxix.8.
46. *CF*, 9, 6, 14.
47. Synod of the year 430 ("Talis partus decet deum" quoted in support of the *theotokos*), (*MC*, 4, 550); cf. Faustus of Riez, *Ep.*, 6 (*MG*, *Auct. Ant.*, 8, 286; *PL*, 58, 854 (quotes from the same hymn, "Procedat e thalamo suo geminae gigas substantiae")): for the Ambrosian hymns see *AVK*; A. Steier, *Untersuchungen über die Echtheit der Hymnen des Ambrosius*, Leipzig, 1903; Ermoni in *DACL*, 1, 1348f.; Walpole in *JTS*, 428–36 (1908).
48. *CF*, 9, 7, 15 and Ambrose, *C. Auxentium*, 34 (*Ep.*, 20) (*PL*, 16, 1060).
49. R. C. Trench in *Sacred Latin Poetry*, London, 1874, 87f. (*AVK*, p. 3); cf. Deut. xxvii.5 and 6 and Exod. xx.25.
50. C. Mohrmann, "Gebondenheid en vrijheid in de oudchrist. lat. Poëzie", *Annalen VWKN*, 31, 2, 1–31 (1939).
51. "Aeterne Rerum Conditor" (*ad gallicantum*); "Splendor Paternae Gloriae" (genuine? *in aurora*); "Iam Surgit Hora Tertia"; "Nunc Sancte Nobis Spiritus" (genuine? *ad horam tertiam*); "Rector Potens Verax Deus" (genuine? *ad horam sextam*); "Rerum Deus Tenax Vigor" (genuine? *ad horam nonam*); "Deus Creator Omnium" (*ad horam incensi= lucernarii*), *AVK*, 129–33, *AH*, 50, nos. 1–7.
52. "Hic Est Dies Verus Dei" (*in die Paschae*); "Intende Qui Regis Israel" (*in natali domini*); "In luminans Altissimis" (*in epiphaniis domini*); "Agnes, Beatae Virginis"; "Victor, Nabor, Felix, pii" (genuine?); "Grates Tibi, Jesu, Novas" (*Gervasii et Protasii*); texts in *AVK*, 133–38, and *AH*, 51, nos. 8–14; the five hymns "Apostolorum Passio" (*Petri et Pauli*), "Apostolorum Supparem" (*Laurentii*), "Amore Christi Nobilis" (*Johannis Evang.*); "Aeterna Christi Munera" (*in natali martyrum*); "Jesus Corona Virginum" (texts, *AVK*, 138–40) are not by Ambrose.
53. *Veredicos versus*: *CF*, 9, 12, 32.
54. "Fove, Precantes, Trinitas": *DVB*, 35 (Oct. 386).
55. *CF*, 9, 12, 32; *AH*, 7, p. 132:

> Deus, creator omnium
> polique rector, vestiens
> diem decoro lumine,
> noctem soporis gratia.
>
> artus solutos ut quies
> reddat laboris usui
> mentesque fessas allevet
> luctusque solvet anxios.

56. *CF*, 9, 12, 32 ("Deus Creator Omnium"); *RE*, 1, 21, 1 ("Aeterne Rerum Conditor"); *DNG*, 63, 74 ("Iam Surgit Hora Tertia"); *SE*, 372, 3 ("Intende Qui Regis Israel").
57. *SE*, 372, 3; *AH*, 8, 1, 2, 5 and 6, p. 133 (Augustine quotes only the fifth and sixth strophes):

> Intende, qui regis Israel,
> super Cherubim qui sedes,
> appare Ephrem coram, excita
> potentiam tuam et veni.

> veni, redemptor gentium,
> ostende ppartum virginis,
> miretur omne saeculum:
> talis partus decet deum.
>
> procedat e thalamo suo
> pudoris aula regia
> geminae gigas substantiae
> alacris ut currat viam.
>
> egressus eius a patre,
> regressus eius ad patrem.
> excursus usque ad inferos
> recursus ad sedem dei.

Cf. Ps. lxxix.2 and 3 and Ps. xviii.6 and 7; a line from the fourth stophe ("alvus tumescit virginis") is quoted in the Pseudo-Augustine, *Sermo de Symb. ad Catech.*, 4, 4 (vol. 6, 578 in the Maurist edition).

58. "Ante saecula qui manens"; cf. C. Blume, *Unsere liturg. Lieder*, Regensburg, 1932, pp. 41 f.
59. *DCR*, 25, 47.
60. *DCD*, 17, 14.
61. *CF*, 10, 33, 49 and 50 (according to the rendering of Alfred Hollman in *Biblioth. der Kirchenväter*; cf. *IP*, 18, 2, 1; *JP*, 4, 66.
62. *IP*, 44, 3.
63. *IP*, 32, 2, 5; 42, 5; 56, 16; 70, 2, 11; 80, 5; *DDC*, 16, 26 and 18, 28 (the usefulness of a knowledge of technical terms).
64. *IP*, 87, 1 (*praecentor* and *succentor*).
65. *TJ*, 41, 3 and *DSI*, 6, 3.
66. *GUE*, 8, 2; *MPB*, 92.
67. *IP*, 32, 2, 8; 46, 7; 94, 3; 97, 4; 102, 8.
68. *IP*, 32, 2, 8.
69. *CF*, 8, 12, 29.
70. *IP*, 66, 6; 137, 10; *DOM*, 17, 20.
71. *MPB*, 15, 1; *MO*, 297; Ps. lxx.4.
72. *SE*, 159, 2.
73. *DCD*, 22, 24, 3.
74. *EP*, 166, 5, 13; cf. below.
75. *IP*, 41, 9.
76. *DCR*, 26, 50.
77. *IP*, 18, 21, 1 and Ps. xviii.13.
78. *IP*, 93, 3.
79. *TJ*, 3, 21.
80. *IP*, 137, 2; 141, 19; *SE*, 19, 2; 135, 7; 351, 6; 332, 4 (beating one's breast); *IP*, 140, 18; *SE*, 90, 9; 311, 13; *DCM*, 5, 7 (touching the floor with one's forehead); cf. below.
81. *SDM*, 2, 5, 18; on the *gallicinium* see G. van der Leeuw in *Meded. Kon. Akad.*, new series, 4, no. 19.
82. For this whole line of thought and the relevant texts see F. Dölger, *Sol Salutis*, Münster, 1925.
83. *IP*, 118, 29, 4.
84. *SE*, 362, 1; 342, 1; *IP*, 62, 13; 133, 3; 62, 5; cf. Justin, *Apologia I*, 55, 4 (p. 47 in Krüger's ed.); Tertullian, *De Orat.*, 17 (*CSEL*, 20, 190: "Ne ipsis quidem manibus sublimius elatis, sed temperate ac probe elatis, ne vultu quidem in audacio erecto"); *Adv. Nat.*, 1, 12 (*CSEL*, 20, 82); *Adv. Marc.*, 3, 18 (*CSEL*, 47, 407 (on previous significations of the symbol)); Minucius Felix, 29 (*CSEL*, 2, 43, ed. Halm): the cross-pattern in the masts and yards of ships, in prayers and on banners).
85. *DCM*, 5, 7.
86. *DSI*, 9 (Mohrmann considers spurious *DSI*, 7, with its wonderful exposition in accordance with which the word "Alleluia" should be taken as synonymous with "Laudemus eum qui est"); *SE*, 252, 9; 254, 8; 255, 1; 256, 1 and 3; *IP*, 117, 2; *DDC*, 2, 11, 16.

87. *GUE*, 7, 3 (*Dominus vobiscum*); *DSI*, 6, 3; *GUE*, 7, 3; *SE*, 227 (the dialogue); *SE*, 25, 7; 53, 13 and 14; 68, 4, 5; 237, 3; 343, 4; *IP*, 31, 21; 148, 5 (*Sursum cor*).

88. *IP*, 140, 18; *SE*, 351, 3, 6; *EP*, 265, 8, *FSA*, 9, 5 (*Dimitte nobis*); *SE*, 137, 14 (*propitius esto*); for the *confiteor*, see below.

89. *SE*, 332, 4.

90. *MPB*, 13, 3.

91. *SE*, 67, 1; Matt. xi.25.

92. *MPB*, 126, 2; *MO*, 356; *SE*, 29, 2; *IP*, 117, 1; 137, 2; 144, 13; 141, 19; cf. *QIM*, 9; *DSI*, 9.

93. *IP*, 50, 1; *SE*, 32, 13.

94. *RE*, 2, 11.

95. *EP*, 71, 3, 5 and *EP*, 75, 6, 21 and 7, 22; cf. *EP*, 82, 5, 35 (Augustine prefers the Latin translation *cucurbita*, for *edera* is incorrect and *ciceion* unknown); the word in dispute is *kikajoon* (=*ciceion*, the *ricinus* of John. iv.6); the Septuagint has *kitton* (=*efeu*, *edera*). Augustine writes that the Jews of Oea had assured him that the Hebrew word had the same meaning as *kitton* and *cucurbita*. Jerome replied (*Ep.*, 22, 75 *inter epp. Aug.*) that the Jews of this little African town either knew no Hebrew or were simply making fun of the "pumpkin-growers"; cf. Jerome, *In Jonam*, 4 and 6 (*PL*, 25, 1147–9).

96. See, for example, *SCA*, pls. 53, 3 and 54, 3.

97. *SE*, 232; cf. *SE*, 218 (*In Parasceve*) (a collection of texts from Matthew).

98. Dom Busch has refuted the theories of Krawutzky, Rentschka and Eggersdorfer on this subject; see *EL*, 52, 443–4, 446–71 (1938); see Kunzelmann in *MA*, 2, 461, *n.* 2.

99. *CF*, 5, 9, 17.

100. *SE*, 90, 9 and *SE*, 219.

101. *DDC*, 2, 15, 22 (Italian version); De Bruyne in *MA*, 2, 521–606 ("St. Augustin reviseur de la Bible").

102. *DDC*, 2, 15, 22; cf. *DCD*, 18, 42.

103. *EP*, 82, 5, 34 and 35; *DCD*, 18, 43 (where the Hebrew and Greek texts are used to supplement one another); *IP*, 87, 10; *Ad Hier. Ep.*, 28, 2; cf. 71, 2, 4–4, 6; 75, 5, 19–7, 22 (Jerome); 82, 5, 34 and 35.

104. *IP*, 93, 29.

105. Cf. *TJ*, 8–10, 19–23, 34–6, read on successive days; there is an attempt at reconstructing the *lectionarium* by Roetzer (104–8).

106. *TEJ*, prologue; *SE*, 232, 1 and 239, 1; cf. *SE*, 231–63 (all *exordia*); according to *TJ*, 12, 1, the *lectio continua* took precedence on Sundays.

107. *SE*, 315, 1; cf. *SE*, 227; *TJ*, 6, 18.

108. *SE*, 302, 1.

109. *TJ*, 50, 6.

110. *CEP*, 2, 15–34.

111. *DPMR*, 1, 24, 34.

112. *SE*, 269, 2.

113. *TEJ*, 3, 13.

12. Becoming a Christian

1. *DCR*, 8, 12; there is a thorough analysis of initiation in Dom B. Busch's "*De Modo quo S. Augustinus Descripserit Initiationem Christianam*" and "*De Initiatione Secundum S. Augustinum*", in *EL*, 52, 385–483 and 158–78 (1938).

2. For Christianity as ἐπιστροφή see A. D. Nock's fine book *Conversion*, Oxford, 1933.

3. *EP*, 54, 1, 1 and *supra*.

4. *DCM*, 12, 15.

5. *TJ*, 50, 22.

6. *CF*, 9, 6; cf. Ambrose, *De Myster.*, 1, 2 (*FP*, 7, 3, Bonn, 1936, 114): "Sacramentorum rationem... quam ante baptismum si putassemus insinuandum nondum initiatis, prodidisse potius quam edidisse aestimaremur; deinde, quod in opinantifus melius se ipsa lux mysteriorum infuderit, quam si eam sermo aliquis praecucurisset."

7. *EP*, 217, 6, 19 (A.D. 427); *EP*, 149, 2, 22; *SE*, 324; *DGL*, 10, 11, 19 and 14, 25; *TJ*, 38, 6; cf. *IP*, 64, 15: "Parvulis et infirmis stillantur quaedam de sacramentis." There is a short description of infant baptism in *DPMR*, 1, 34, 62.

8. *EP*, 98, 6.
9. *DDP*, 13, 31; *EP*, 217, 6, 19.
10. *DCD*, 13, 4.
11. *CF*, 1, 11, 17 and 18.
12. *DGL*, 10, 23, 39; on the apostolic origin of infant baptism cf. *DB*, 4, 23, 30 and 24, 31; see above.
13. *SE*, 293, 10.
14. *SE*, 115, 4.
15. *DPMR*, 1, 19, 25; those who make the responses for the children are often called the *fidedictores* (see for instance *EP*, 98, 7).
16. *CEP*, 2, 13, 29 and 30; also *DB*, 7, 53, 101–54, esp. 103.
17. *CF*, 4, 4, 8 and 9.
18. *DFO*, 6, 8 and 9; see Dölger in *AC*, 2, 258–67 (1930).
19. *DB*, 1, 13, 21.
20. *SE*, 393, opening.
21. *DCA*, 1, 26, 33 and 28, 35.
22. *EP*, 168, 1 (*PL*, 54, 1209 and 1210; A.D. 459); for baptism at the Epiphany and during the octave cf. Gregory Nazianzen, *Orat.*, 39, 1 and 40, 1 (*PG*, 36, 336 f. and 360 f. For Asia Minor in the fourth century see *VHP*, 2, 17, 47 (*CSEL*, 7, 42–3 (Petschenig)); also Africa in the sixth century, that is, during the Byzantine restoration.
23. *SE*, 210, 1, 2.
23a. *DCR*, 13, 19 and 5, 9, 5.
24. *DCR*, 5, 9; 6, 10; 8, 12; cf. *SE*, 47, 10, 18.
25. *DCR*, 5, 9.
26. *SE*, 47, 10, 17 (the reference here is to a convert from Donatism).
27. *DCR*, 26, 50.
28. *Exsufflatio* (in the case of the Donatists, at least: *CCR*, 2, 5, 7); we hear nothing about any in-breathing (*inhalatio*), nor do we learn whether the laying-on of hands was accompanied by any anointing with oil on the head or the breast, as was already customary in Rome *circa* A.D. 200. This anointing, like that on the seats of pain in the sick, had an anti-daimonic character; sickness and the daimons were regarded as related.
29. *CF*, 1, 11; *DPMR*, 2, 26, 42; *DCR*, 26, 50; all bread was unleavened.
30. *MPB*, 94, 1; cf. Quodvultdeus, *De Symb. ad Catech.*, 1, 1 and 4, 1 (vol. 6, 555 and 575 in the Maurist edition).
31. *TJ*, 11, 4.
32. *IP*, 103, 1, 14.
33. Cf. *DT*, 15, 27, 48 (the concluding sentence, "*fidelibus, non infidelibus, loquens*".
34. *IP*, 109, 17; cf. *IP*, 102, 19 ("quod omnes audire possunt dico"); on the discipline of the *arcana*, which was already fully developed by just after A.D. 400, cf. *EP*, 140, 19, 48; *SE*, 307, 3; 131, 1; 132, 1; on the previous history and general scope of the subject see Othmar Perler in *Reallexikon f. Antike u. Christentum*, Leipzig, 1943, 1, 5, 667–76.
35. *SE*, 49, 8; Fourth Council of Carthage, 436, canon 84 (*MC*, 3, 958).
36. *SE*, 46, 31.
37. *TJ*, 50, 2 and 36, 4; cf. Dölger in *AC*, 1929, 1, 88 f. and 202 f., concerning tattooing; see Morin, *MA*, 1, 89, *n*.
38. *SE*, 302, 3.
39. *IP*, 36, 2, 4.
40. *TJ*, 3, 2.
41. *GUE*, 2, 1 and *TJ*, 118, 5.
42. *GUE*, 3, 4.
43. *IP*, 141, 9.
44. *DSI*, 17, 8; *IP*, 85, 14 and *IP*, 50, 1.
45. *SDM*, 1, 6, 16.
46. *IP*, 64, 9 and 11.
47. *QE*, 2, 43; cf. Origen, *Hom. in Gen.*, 5, 2 (*GCS*, 6, 59, ed. Baehrens); Augustine, *DFO*, 25, 47; *DCD*, 10, 8 and 16, 30; *SE*, 105, 7; *IP*, 75, 16.
48. *DCR*, 26, 50.
49. Third Council of Carthage, 397, canon 5 (*MC*, 3, 880 and 881); cf. *DPMR*, 2, 26, 42.

50. *DB*, 7, 53, 101 is concerned with those who have undergone the baptismal instruction out of mere curiosity.
51. Fourth Council of Carthage, 436, canon 84 (*MC*, 3, 958).
52. *SE*, 132, 1; cf. *SSA*, 90; the word *catechumenus* is first to be found in Tertullian, *De Praescr. Haeret.*, 41 (*PL*, 2, 68); *De Cor.*, 2 (*PL*, 2, 97); *Adv. Marcion.*, 5, 7 (*PL*, 2, 518); cf. *De Bapt.*, 20 (*CSEL*, 20, 217–18), where the mortifications of the candidates for baptism are enumerated.
53. *TJ*, 11, 3.
54. *TJ*, 44, 2; cf. *SE*, 136, 3 and also the *Sermo ad Catechumenos* published in *RB*, 50, 186–93 (1938).
55. "De... simul petendo atque unum aliquid appetendo" (*SE*, 216, 1 (*Ad Competentes*, 391)).
56. i.e., he was a *tiro*; *IP*, 26, 1, 1; *SE*, 216, (*contirones*).
57. *DFO*, 6, 8 and *SE*, 351, 2, 2; cf. 252, 1, 2; *IP*, 80, 10; on the fasting and abstinence see the Fourth Council of Carthage, 436, canon 85 (*MC*, 3, 958); cf. Ecclus. xxxiv.31; Matt. xvii.20).
58. *DFO*, 18, 33, 6, 9–7, 11 and 27, 49.
59. The catechist of *SE*, 216 was Augustine, but as priest, not as bishop.
60. According to *SE*, 392, 2, the *competentes* were present at the usual sermons.
61. *EP*, 194, 46; *SE*, 216, 11 contains, perhaps, a reference to the bodily examination (with an eye on diabolical possession?); on the ethical character of the *scrutinium* see Dondeyne in *RHE*, 28, 14–18 (1932); on the *exsufflatio* see Dölger, *Der Exorzismus im altchr. Taufritual*, Paderborn, 1909, 60 and 118; cf. also. Quodvultdeus, *De Symbol. ad Catech.*, 2, 1 (vol. 6, 555 in the Maurist edition) on the bodily examination; L'Allevi in *SC*, 1942, 428–40.
62. *CJ*, 4, 7, 2, 181, 3, 199 (against the Pelagians); *GUE*, 2, 3 and *EP*, 23, 4 (against the Donatists).
63. For *despuere* and *exsufflare* cf. Dölger in *AC*, 3, 192–203 (1932); Tert., *De Idol.*, 11 (*CSEL*, 20, 42): "Quo ore [christianus] fumantes aras despuet et exsufflabit quibus ipse prospexit?"
64. *OPD*, 4, 6 (*CSEL*, 26, 110, ed. Ziwsa) (where we also find "maledicte exi foras").
65. *SE*, 216, 6.
66. *SE*, 216, 10 and 11; *DCD*, 15, 20, 4; Quodvultdeus, *De Symb. ad Cat.*, 2, 1 (vol. 6, 555 in the Maurist edition); *Con. Mendacium*, 10, 24 (where goatskins=sins); the theme of Adam and Eve's animal-skins as the symbol of sinfulness and consciousness of guilt is still preserved in the old *Ordo Expulsandi Publice Poenitentium* of the *Pontificale Romanum*; cf. Quasten in *HTR*, 35, 3 (1942) (Theodore of Mopsuestia on the *cilicium*).
67. *CF*, 7, 18.
68. *CF*, 9, 6.
69. Thus Probst, Kattenbusch and Kunzelmann; P. de Puniet, Wiegand, Dondeyne, Zarb and Roetzer argue for the Saturday before Laetare (see Busch, *EL*, 52, 445–6 (1938) and *RHE*, 28, 14 (1932)).
70. On the text see Badcock in *RB*, 45, 3–9 (1933); for the most part Augustine uses the Romano-Milanese formula (cf. *SE*, 213, 214; *DSC*, 1; *ENC*, 15; but in *SE*, 212 and 215 it has been thought that traces of an African formula have been found—for example, the etymology of the word *symbolum* in *SE*, 213).
71. *SE*, 214, 1.
72. *SE*, 212, 2 and Jer. xxxi.33.
73. *SE*, 212, 213 (part of which=*GUE*, 1), 214; *DSC*, 1; on the question of authenticity see Sizoo in *Geref. Theol. Tijds.*, August, 1940 (against Kattenbusch); *SE*, 215 is clearly spurious.
74. *GUE*, 1, 11.
75. *SE*, 58, 1 and 13; and also *DSC*, 1, 1, where we also find the theme of the *symbolum* as a means of protection: "... vestro symbolo vos munite".
76. Thus Probst, Kattenbusch, Kunzelmann and Busch; others, for example Huyben, De Puniet, Eggersdörfer, Zarb, Dondeyne and Roetzer, think otherwise—*traditio* on the day before Judica Sunday, *redditio* on Palm Sunday; in Rome we find the *traditio* on the Wednesday after Laetare Sunday instead (cf. *Sacr. Gelas.*, ed. Wilson, Oxford, 1894, 57–9).
77. *SE*, 57, 1; cf. Rom. x.14–15.

78. *SE*, 56-9.
79. *EP*, 21, 7, 2; for the letter to Proba, *EP*, 130, 11, 21-12, 23, see above.
80. *GUE*, 1, 9.
81. *SE*, 58, 1 and 12.
82. *De Excessu Fr. Sui Satyri*, 1, 43 (*FP*, 15, Bonn, 1921, 37).
83. *EP*, 54, 7, 10.
84. *EP*, 55, 18, 33.
85. *EP*, 54, 5, 6-7 and 7, 9.
86. *SE*, 210, 1; *EP*, 36, 13, 31.
87. Good Friday sermons: see *SE*, 218, *GUE*, 2 and 3; *IP*, 21, 2; cf. *SE*, 231, 1, 1 (the Passion according to Matthew); *TJ*, 13, 14 (Ps. xxi.).
88. *GUE*, 5, 4; *SE*, 221; cf. *WS*, add. M.719.
89. *DSI*, 2, 1. Readings: *DSI*, 2 (Gen. i.); *WS*, 5, 2; *MO*, 687 (*cantic. Moysis*); *LP*, 2, 211 (*hist. et cant. trium puerorum*); *EP*, 105, 2, 7 (*amen post eandem lectionem*).
90. Comeau in *RSR*, 23, 264 f. (1933), reckons up over eighty for the whole octave, that is, *SE*, 219-58, and about fifty in Morin; for the Easter Vigil four in the Maurist edition (five probably belong rather to Whit Sunday) and twelve in Morin; for the morning of Easter Sunday five and eight respectively.
91. Eph. v.8.
92. *WS, frag. add. M.*, 716 and 717.
93. *GUE*, 7, 1 and Rom. vi.4.
94. *SE*, 58, 11.
95. *NOA*, 3, 9, 12 (on the story of Perpetua's little brother Dinocrates).
96. *EP*, 227.
97. *CF*, 8, 2, 5 and 6; cf. 4, 9 (*circa* 355).
98. Rom. xiii.13-14.
99. *SE*, 294, 11 and 12; 215, 1; 216, 1 and 2; cf. Jerome, *Ep.*, 130, 7 (*CSEL*, 56, 196, ed. Hilberg); cf. the αποταγὴ and συνταγὴ of *Const. Ap.*, 7, 40; for the *pompa diaboli* see Rahner in *ZKT*, 55, 272 f. (1931) and De Labriolle in *Arch. Lat. Med. Aevi*, 2, 177 f. (1925); Wassink in *Vig. Chr.*, 13-41 (1947); see also Quodvultdeus, *De Symb. ad Cat.*, 2, 3-5, 3, 1-4, 1 (vol. 6, 556-8, 569 and 576 respectively in the Maurist edition).
100. *IP*, 67, 5 and 76, 4; cf. *IP*, 67, 5 ("qui ascendit super occasum"); *EP*, 98, 7 and *DPMR*, 1, 34, 63 ("conversio ad deum").
101. *IP*, 41, 1.
102. The most beautiful and best preserved baptistery in Djemila-Cuicul.
103. Tertullian, *De Bapt.*, 11 (p. 15 in Borleff's edition, Leiden, 1931); cf. Augustine, *EP*, 30, 8, 16.
104. In the verses of Calbulus a hart appears as a water conduit; the reference is to a baptistery in Africa Proconsularis at the end of the fifth century (*ICR*, 2, 240, no. 4); Ennodius (*Carm.*, 2, 149 (*CSEL*, 6, 607), ed. Hartel) describes water flowing from an upper cornice in the baptistery of Eustorgius in Milan:

> En sine nube pluit sub tectis imbre sereno
> et coeli facies pura ministrat aquas.
> proflua marmoribus decurrunt flumina sacris
> atque iterum rorem parturit ecce lapis.
> arida in liquidos effundit pergula fontes,
> et rursus natus unda superna venit.
> sancta per aetherios emanat limpha recessus,
> Eustorgi vatis ducta ministerio.

Ennodius also mentions water flowing out of a lion's mouth (*Carm.*, 2, 19 (*CSEL*, 5, 564 and 565)):

> De leone marmoreo qui aquam mittit in domo
> aspice deposita blandum feritate leonem:
> ore vomit limphas pectoris obsequio.
> unda fluit rostro, dens mortis pocula mandit,
> naturam perdens belua nos satiat.
> effera dum vitreos effundunt guttura fontes
> dira salutiferis corda lavantur acquis.

Zeno of Verona, too (*Tr.*, 2, 35 (*PL*, 11, 480)) speaks of "superfluentis amni undae subjecti"; cf. T. Klauser in *Pisciculi*, Münster, 1939, pp. 157 f. (on "living water") and J. Zellinger, *Bad und Bäder in der altchr. Kirche*, Munich, 1928.

105. Zeno of Verona, *Tr.*, 2, 35 (*PL*, 11, 480); for the baptismal coin see *Tr.*, 1, 14 (*unus denarius*) and 2, 42 (*unum stipendium*) (*PL*, 11, 359 and 492) and also Dölger in *AC*, 1–24 (1932).

106. *SE*, 352, 3; *TJ*, 118, 5 (the sign of the cross); cf. *DB*, 3, 10, 15 and 5, 20, 27 and 28; also Cyprian, *Ep.*, 70, 1 (*CSEL*, 3, 2, 767) (cleansing and healing: "Oportet vero mundari et sanctificari aquam prius a sacerdote").

107. *IP*, 105, 10; 106, 3; 80, 8; *SE*, 213, 8; *GUE*, 1, 9; about A.D. 200 the consecration, at Rome, was carried out at dawn. Hippolytus, *Trad. Apost.*, 21; Dix, *The Shape of the Liturgy*, London, 1945, p. 33.

108. *DB*, 6, 25, 47; cf. *DCR*, 9, 13; on the water consecration see Neunheuser in *EL*, 44 (1930), 194 f., 258 f., 369 f. and especially 393 f. (on Augustine), and 455; also Karl Adam, *TQ*, 112, 518 (1931), as against *Geiselmann, Die Abendmahlslehre an der Wende der chr. Spätantike, zum Frühmittelalter*, Munich, 1933, 203. On the prayer of consecration itself see H. Scheidla, *Die Taufwasser-Weihegebete*, Münster, 1935.

109. *TJ*, 80, 3; cf. Eph. v.26 (*verbum fidei*); concerning this *verbum fidei* see Adam, *TQ*, 112, 518 (1931), and Hocedez in *RSR*, 9, 20 (1919) and Busch, *EL*, 52, 456 and 457 (1938).

110. *DCD*, 22, 8, 3; the women's side.

111. *SE*, 125, 6.

112. The African type of font was from 2 ft. 8 in. to 4 ft. 3 in. deep and had a diameter of from 3 ft. to 11 ft.

113. *TJ*, 80, 3, 15, 3; *SE*, 213, 8; cf. Kirsch, *RQ*, 31, 98 (1923).

114. The *triplex immersio* is to be found as early as in Tertullian, *Adv. Prax.*, 26 (*CSEL*, 47, 3: "... nec semel sed ter, ad singula nomina in personas singulos tinguimur." The term *submersio* is in Augustine, *TJ*, 81, 2; *submergere*=the Donatist repetition of baptism; cf. *LP*, 2, 83, 184; for *cervicem flectere* see e.g., *DB*, 5, 9, 11, and for the trinitarian formula see, e.g., *LP*, 2, 80, 178; 3, 8, 9; and *EP*, 23, 4.

115. Thus Leclercq in *DACL*, 2, 398, article "Baptistère".

116. *TJ*, 15, 3.

117. *TJ*, 76, 4.

118. Rightly or wrongly called the *consignatorium*.

119. Galtier, in *RSR*, 4, 350–82 (1911) and *RHE*, 13, 257–301 (1912) and 467–76; against this view De Puniet, *RHE*, 13, 450–66 (1912); Coppens, *L'Imposition des mains et les rites connexes*, Paris, 1925; F. Hofmann, *Der Kirchenbegriff des hl. Augustinus*, Munich, 337 f. (1933); F. Dölger, *Sphragis*, Paderborn, 1911; Zähringer, *Das kirchliche Priestertum nach dem. hl. Augustinus*, Paderborn, 1931, 95; Busch in *EL*, 52, 461–5 (1938).

120. *LP*, 2, 103, 237 (anointing of the head); on the significance of this cf. *IP*, 108, 26, *SE*, 71, 12, 19; *DT*, 15, 26, 46; cf. Acts x.38.

121. *TJ*, 33, 3; *DCD*, 20, 10; Apoc. xx.6.

122. Third Council of Carthage, canon 36 (*MC*, 3, 885); Optatus, *De Bapt.*, 7, 4 (*CSEL*, 26, 175, ed. Ziwsa).

123. *TJ*, 6, 20.

124. *GUE*, 15, 2; *SE*, 249, 3; 250, 3; 251, 6; 269, 2; 270, 5; *DB*, 3, 16, 21; *TEJ*, 6, 10 (cf. Isa. xi.2; this passage was apparently read also—*GUE*, 15, 2 and *SE*, 249, 3).

125. *TJ*, 40, 9; cf. Ps. iv.7: "Signatum est super nos lumen vultus tui, domine."

126. *IP*, 21, 2, 31; *EP*, 173, 3 (*characterem dominicum*).

127. *FSA*, 1, 17; *SE*, 270, 2; *TJ*, 122, 8; cf. *IP*, 119, 2.

128. *SE*, 249, 3; 250, 3; 251, 6; *IP*, 150, 2.

129. *SE*, 223, 1 (*infantes*); *SE*, 228, 1.

130. Cf. the allusion to the *prima stola* of Luke xv.22 in *EP*, 55, 9, 17; Jerome, *EP.*, 64, 19, 3 (*CSEL*, 54, 610, ed. Hilberg) ("tunicas pellicias deponere").

131. *EP*, 55, 19, 35; see Dölger in *AC*, 5, 115–19 (1936).

132. *DCE*, 2, 30, 75; cf. Eph. vi.15 and Mark vi.9.

133. Cf. *SE*, 228, 1 and 3, conclusion.

134. P. Browe, in *Alg. Ned. Euch. Tijdschr.*, 10, 11-17 (1931); cf. Tertullian, *De Cor.*, 3 (*PL*, 2, 98) and Hippolytus, *Trad. Ap.*, 23 (Dix, *The Shape of the Liturgy*, 40, cf. Hauler, 112).

135. Third Council of Carthage, canon 24 (*MC*, 3, 884), *BH*, 24 (*MC*, 3, 922), *CCEA*, 37 (*MC*, 3, 734).

136. *IP*, 110, 8.

137. *IP*, 143, 2; *TJ*, 98, 5.

138. *IP*, 80, 22.

139. Cf. *SE*, 227 and *DSI*, 6, 9, also the beginning of *SE*, 272.

140. *SE*, 227, 228, 3, 229, 272, and also *GUE*, 7 and *DSI*, 6; *DSI*, 3 is considered by many to be spurious.

141. Adam and Geiselmann view *DSI*, 6 also as spurious (but the key section of *SE*, 229 as, on the contrary, genuine); according to Busch (*EL*, 52, 397, *n*. 46 (1938)), Morin also accepts the possibility of certain interpolations.

142. *DSI*, 6, 1.

143. *SE*, 272 (almost complete); the scriptural texts are from Isa. vii.2, 1 Cor. xii.27 and 1 Cor. x.17.

144. Cf. the sudden end of *SE*, 228; the promised threefold explanation is missing.

145. *GUE*, 7, 1.

146. *DSI*, 6, 3; for the explanation of the dialogue before the Preface, cf. *GUE*, 7, 3, and *SE*, 227.

147. Col. ii.17; Heb. x.1; Mal. ii.1.

148. Ps. cix.4.

149. Phil. ii.12-13.

150. 1 Cor. xi.24-5.

151. Heb. x.22.

152. Ps. xxxiii.6.

153. John vi.54.

154. Eph. v.31-2.

155. 1 Cor. x.17.

156. 1 Cor. xi.27-9.

157. 1 Cor. v.8.

158. *DSI*, 3, 1-4.

159. *SE*, 223, 1; 146, 2; *EP*, 34, 2 (*MPB*, 94, 7) (within the *cancelli*); *SE*, 260, 1 ("sacramentum octavarum vestrarum"); *EP*, 55, 19, 35 ("per octavas suas"); on the question of abstinence cf. the Fourth Council of Carthage, 436, canon 86 (*MC*, 3, 958): "aliquemdiu abstineant".

160. See especially *MPB*, 94, 2-5.

161. *SE*, 232, 1 and *RB*, 31, 134, *n*. 1 (1919) (originally Luke came before Mark, cf. *SE*, 232, 235, but later this was changed); *SE*, 237, 1; 242, 2; 246, 1; 284, 4; 253, 1; 259, 1.

162. *GUE*, 16, 1 and 2; cf. *SE*, 243, 1 and 2; 244, 2 and 3; 245, 2-4; 246, 3-5.

163. *WS*, 13, conclusion; cf. *SE*, 248-51 *passim*; *TJ*, 122, 7-9.

164. *DDD*, 1, 1 and *supra*.

165. Zarb, in *AGM*, 10 (1933), 60 f. and table 103 (Augustine would have begun the series on 1 John in the Easter octave of the year 413 and continued it around Ascensiontide of the same year).

166. *SE*, 260, 1: "qui hodie miscendi sunt populo"; cf. *GUE*, 18, 2; sermons on Whit Sunday: *DSI*, 8 (spurious?), *MPB*, 89 and 94, *GUE*, 18 and 19; *SE*, 223 (the title notwithstanding), 259, 260.

167. *SE*, 259, 6: *dies feriales; Cod. Theod.*, 2, 8, 19 (*CTM*, 87 and 88 (A.D. 389: seven days before Easter and seven after)); cf. *Cod. Theod.*, 2, 8, 21 (*CTM*, 88) ("diebus quindecim paschalibus") and 2, 8, 24 (*CTM*, 89) (A.D. 405: "septem diebus quadragesimae, septem paschalibus"); cf. *EP*, 34, 2: "Severitas legum sceleratissimos parcit."

168. Ps. xi.9; *MPB*, 94, 4, conclusion.

169. Ps. xi.2; *MPB*, 94, 3.

170. *GUE*, 18, 2.

171. Cf. *EP*, 78, 6.

172. *SE*, 392, 5.

173. *EP*, 250; cf. *SE*, 351, 4, 10.
174. *EP*, 265, 1 f.
175. *SE*, 352, 3, 8; cf. *SE*, 98, 6; on the power of the keys cf. *SE*, 278, 12; 351, 4, 9 and 5, 12; cf. also *DSC*, 7, 14 and *SE*, 98, 6.
176. *TJ*, 121, 4.
177. *SE*, 71, 17, 28; 18, 30; 20, 33 and 23, 37; cf. *ENC*, 17, 65.
178. "Poenitentia major, insignis, luctuosa et lamentabilis"; the most important texts are in *SE*, 351; 352, 3, 8; *DSC*, 7, 14 and 8, 15; also *EP*, 265, 7 and 8 (cf. *SE*, 71). See also Karl Adam, *Die kirchliche Sündenvergebung nach dem hl. Augustinus*, Tübingen, 1917; id., in *TQ*, 1–66 (1929); id., *Die geheime Kirchenbusze beim hl. Augustinus*, Kempten, 1921 (where he ascribes to Augustine the introduction of private auricular confession); for the opposite view see Poschmann in *ZKT*, 208–28 (1921) and *Kirchenbusse und "correptio secreta" bei Augustinus*, Bonn, 1923; id., *Textus Selecti de Paenitentia* (*FP*, 38, Bonn, 1934); on the early penance in general see J. Jungmann, *Die lateinischen Bussriten in ihrer geschichtlichen Entwicklung*, Innsbruck, 1932; P. Galtier, *L'Église et la rémission des péchés aux premiers siècles*, Paris, 1932; for a different view see C. Mortimer, *The Origins of Private Penance*, Oxford, 1939, and a reply in *GM*, 21, 183 (1940); Poschmann (*Poenitentia Secunda*, Bonn, 1940) only deals with the period up to Cyprian.
179. *SE*, 351, 4, 10; *DFO*, 26, 48; *DSC*, 7, 15; cf. *IP*, 61, 23 (the case of an astrologer); *SE*, 296, 11, 18 (a scene with a reconciled Donatist); cf. *DB*, 3, 16, 21 and 5, 23, 33.
180. *SE*, 351, 4, 9.
181. *BH*, canon 30 (*MC*, 3, 1923 (*ante absidem*)); Third Council of Carthage, canon 32 (*MC*, 3, 885); *CCEA*, 43 (*MC*, 3, 735).
182. *SE*, 98, 6 (the bonds of Lazarus "sunt vincula ipsius reatus"); *TJ*, 121, 4.
183. *SE*, 82, 7, 10; 351, 4, 9; there is an exhortation to personal readiness for penance in *DCG*, 5, 7.
184. *SP*, 19; *SE*, 351, 4, 7; 278, 12.
185. *SE*, 82, 8, 11; cf. 351, 4, 9.
186. *SE*, 82, 8, 11; *SE*, 351, 4, 10; cf. also *EP*, 153, 3, 7; 6, 18 and 20 and 22 (referring to the episcopal intervention *ad Macedonium*).
187. *SE*, 393, 39.
188. *IP*, 61, 23.
189. *EP*, 153, 3, 7; cf. the decree of Pope Siricius in the year 385 (Jaffé, 255).
190. *EP*, 151, 9; cf. *SE*, 393.
191. *EP*, 228, 8.
192. Jerome, *Ep.*, 77, 4–6 (*CSEL*, 55, 40–3).
193. *CL*, 2, 11, 5; *MO*, 258; cf. Ambrose, *De Poenit.*, 1, 16, 90.
194. *SE*, 232, 7, 8; but cf. the texts on the reconciliation by the laying-on of hands of those who had returned from schism, in *DB*, 3, 16, 21; 5, 23, 33. The *oratio super populum* at the conclusion of the eucharistic celebration is probably a simple prayer of dismissal (thus Callewaert, in *EL*, 51, 310–18 (1937) and Eisenhöfer, *EL*, 52, 258–311 (1938)) and not a blessing for penitents (Jungmann, *Die lateinischen Bussriten*, Innsbruck, 1932, 5–44, 295–316 and in *EL*, 52, 77–96, esp. 95, n. 47 (1938)).
195. *EP*, 153, 5, 15.
196. *SE*, 9, 11, 17 and 18; 17, 5; 131, 7; *ENC*, 19, 71 (daily prayer); on forgiveness through the *dimitte nobis*, see *SE*, 17, 5; 131, 7; 351, 6 (*FSA*, 9, 5); *IP*, 140, 18; *ENC*, 19, 71; *DFO*, 26, 48.
197. *SE*, 351, 3, 5; cf. *ENC*, 21, 78.
198. On *correptio* see *DFO*, 26, 48; *DDQO*, 83, 1 and 26.

13. A Sunday in Hippo

1. *DCD*, 22, 8, 22; for the African liturgy of the period in general see F. Probst in *Der Katholik*, 61, 449–70, 561–81 (1881) and in his *Liturgie des 4 Jahrhunderts und dessen Reform*, Münster, 1893, 272–303; F. Cabrol in *DACL*, 1, 591–657 (620–57 are on the post-Nicene liturgy); W. C. Bishop in *JTS*, 13, 250–79 (1912) (on the relation with Spain). I was not able to make use of Roetzer, *Des hl. Augustins Schriften als liturgiegeschichtliche Quelle* (Munich, 1930) and Pope, *St. Augustine of Hippo* (London, 1937).

2. *DCD*, 2, 28.
3. *GUE*, 7, 3; cf. *MO*, 7, 3 and *DCD*, 22, 8, 22.
4. *SE*, 165, 1; 176, 1 (*apostolus*); for the previous reading of the title (e.g., "To the Romans", "To the Ephesians"), at least, among the Donatists, cf. *EP*, 53, 3; for the Gospel, see *SE*, 253, 1 (*secundum Joannem*).
5. Tit. i.5–9.
6. 1 Cor. i.26.
7. *DDC*, 3, 12, 20.
8. *Casula*; cf. *DCD*, 22, 8, 9.
9. *EP*, 53, 3.
10. Cf. *IP*, 138, 1.
11. *IP*, 119, 1; *SE*, 176, 1 (refrain *Venite Adoremus*); *IP*, 44, 1 (congregational singing), 40, 1 and 7; 29, 2, 1; 25, 5 (refrain).
12. Ps. xxix.2; for the text cf. *IP*, 29:

> Exaltabo te, domine, quoniam suscepisti me
> nec jocundasti inimicos meos super me.

and further on, Ps. xxix.3–5 and 12–13:

> Domine deus meus, clamavi ad te
> et sanasti me
> domine, reduxisti ab inferis animam meam;
> salvum fecisti me a descendentibus in lacum.
> psallite domino, sancti ejus:
> et confitemini memoriae sanctitatis ejus.
> Convertisti planctum meum in gaudium mihi;
> conscidisti saccum meum, et accinxisti me laetitia:
> ut cantet tibi gloria mea, et non compungar,
> domine deus meus, in aeternum confitebor tibi.

13. Cf. *SE*, 362, 1; also *SE*, 178, 1.
14. *SE*, 302, 1 ("Evangelicam lectionem intentissime accepimus") and *TJ*, 30, 1.
15. *SE*, 355, 2; *DCR*, 13, 19.
16. 1 Cor. ix.26–7.
17. *SE*, 178, exordium.
18. Ps. xc.3.
19. Luke xii.20.
20. Ecclus. xxxi.8 and 10.
21. 1 John iii.2.
22. *SE*, 178, abbreviated.
23. "Conversi ad dominum": three such concluding prayers have been preserved to us: *DSI*, 2, 5; *SE*, 362, 31 and *SE*, 67, 10; cf. Dölger, *Sol Salutis*, Münster, 1925, 331–3.
24. For notices and announcements see *EP*, 23, 3.
25. See above: Third Council of Carthage, canon 5 (*MC*, 3, 880); *DPMR*, 2, 26, 42.
26. *SE*, 49, 8.
27. *SE*, 325, conclusion.
28. Cf. the Tabraca mosaic and *DCD*, 22, 8, 13.
29. *SE*, 49, 8.
30. *EP*, 55, 17, 32; there are references to not kneeling on Sunday and at paschaltide as early as Hippolytus and Tertullian, *De Cor.*, 3 (PL, 2, 80).
31. *EP*, 55, 18, 34: "Communis oratio voce diaconi indicitur."
32. "Quietam et tranquillam vitam"; cf. *EP*, 149, 17 and 1 Tim. ii.1 and 2.
33. See especially *EP*, 217, 1, 2; 2, 6 and 7; 7, 26; *EP*, 149, 17; *DH*, 88; *DDP*, 7, 15; 23, 63.
34. *EP*, 149, 16.
35. Cf. Monica's daily offering for the sacrifice (*CF*, 5, 9, 17; cf. *EP*, 111, 8; *IP*, 129, 7).
36. *BH*, canon 23 (bread and wine with water only; no other *primitiae* (such as grapes and wheat)) (*MC*, 3, 992); so also Third Council of Carthage, canon 24 (*MC*, 3, 884) and *CCEA*, 37 (*MC*, 3, 734).
37. *RE*, 2, 11.

38. Cf. *CEP*, 2, 14: "Nam cum episcopo solus [the reading is uncertain here, and some would read *episcopus sanus*] intus est, populus et orat cum illo, et quasi subscribens ad ejus verba respondet Amen."
39. *Cor* throughout, instead of *corda*; see *SE*, 25, 7; 53, 13, 14; 68, 4, 5; 237, 3; 345, 4; *IP*, 31, 21; 148, 5; there are explanations of the dialogue in *DSI*, 6, 3 and *GUE*, 7, 3 and in *SE*, 227.
40. *EP*, 149, 16.
41. *EP*, 140, 48.
42. Cyprian, *De Dom. Orat.*, 31 (*CSEL*, 3, 1, 289) calls the *sursum corda* the *praefatio*; a Council of Milevis (canon 12, *MC*, 4, 330) speaks of *praefationes*, which had been approved by the council and explained as obligatory; there are also in question variable *praefationes*, which, according to Jungmann (*Gewordene Liturgie*, Innsbrück, 1941) are to be taken as *vere-dignum* texts, like our variable prefaces; on pp. 69 and 70 there is also an explanation of the passage quoted above from *EP*, 149, 16.
43. *Preces sanctae* (*DSI*, 6, 3); "prex mystica" (*DT*, 3, 4, 10); "Prex sacerdotis verbis et mysteriis evangelicis conformata" (*LP*, 2, 30, 68).
44. *DCR*, 25, 47.
45. "Carmen . . . memoriam teneat" (*LP*, 2, 30, 68).
46. *TJ*, 118, 5.
47. *SE*, 227; cf. *DSI*, 6, 3.
48. *EP*, 78, 4 (on the erasure of names); *CEP*, 3, 6, 29; cf. Cyprian, *Ep.*, 62, 5 (*CSEL*, 3, 2, 700 and 701, ed. Hartel) (on benefactors).
49. *DCD*, 20, 9, 2; *DCM*, 1, 1, 3; *SE*, 172, 2.
50. *SE*, 159, 1; *TJ*, 84, 1; cf. *SE*, 297, 2, 3.
51. *DSV*, 45, 46 (*sanctimoniales*); *DCM*, 4, 6 ("generalis commemoratio pro omnibus").
52. *SE*, 227.
53. *DT*, 3, 4, 10; perhaps an allusion to an *epiklesis*. See S. Salaville, "L'Epiclèse africaine de saint Augustin", in *Ech. d'Or.*, 1941 and 1942, 268 (the centre of the Canon; references to texts in Fulgentius. There are only hints in Cyprian, Optatus and Augustine).
54. *DSI*, 6, 3; cf. *SE*, 227 (a reference to the "Amen" at the Communion).
55. *EP*, 149, 16; *SE*, 58, 10, 12 (prayed by the priest alone, after the *fractio panis*); cf. Herzog in the *Rev. internationale de théologie*, 641–58 (1906) and Roetzer, *Des hl. Augustins Schriften als liturgiegeschichtliche Quelle*, pp. 128–30; cf. also *SE*, 110, 5, 5 (*audemus dicere*).
56. *SE*, 351, 3, 6; *EP*, 265, 8; *IP*, 140, 18.
57. *DSI*, 6, 3; *SE*, 227; *IP*, 124, 10.
58. Cf. the Pseudo-Ambrose, *De Lapsu Virg.*, 6, 24 (*PL*, 16, 374).
59. *EP*, 149, 16; 36, 12, 28; *SE*, 234, 2.
60. *SE*, 392, 5.
61. *CEP*, 2, 7–13 ("conjunctis manibus"); *LP*, 2, 23, 53 (". . . in cujus [sc. episcopi] manibus eucharistiam ponebatis, cui vicissim danti manus porrigebatis"); for the East, see Cyril of Jerusalem, *Cat. Myst.*, 5, 21 (*FP*, 7, 2, 108–9), Theodore of Mopsuestia, *S. Catech.*, 6 (p. 36 in the editions of Mingana (Cambridge, 1933)) and Rükker (Münster, 1933); John Damascene, *De Fide Orthodox.*, 4, 13 (*PG*, 94, 1149).
62. *SE*, 272; *DSI*, 6, 3; *CFA*, 12, 10; *SE*, 181, 5, 7 and *IP*, 32, 2, 4 ("quo subscribatis amen").
63. Ps. xxxiii.2–11 (for the text, see *IP*, 33, 2):

> Benedicam dominum in omni tempore
> semper laus ejus in ore meo.
> in domino laudabitur anima mea;
> audiant mansueti et laetentur.
> magnificate dominum mecum
> et exsaltemus nomen ejus in idipsum.
> inquisivi dominum et exaudivit me
> et ex omnibus tribulationibus meis eruit me.
> accedite ad eum, et illuminamini
> et vultus vestri non erubescent,

gustate et videte quoniam sauvis est dominus.
beatus vir qui sperat in eum.
timete dominum omnes sancti ejus
quia nihil deest timentibus eum.
divites eguerunt et esurierunt
inquirentes autem dominum non minuentur omni bono.

Cf. *RE*, 2, 11; *SE*, 225, 4 (quoting Ps. xxxiii.6); *IP*, 33, 12 and *DSI*, 3, 3.

64. *EP*, 149, 16. *Interpellationes*, in Italy called *postulationes*, were connected with the *gratiarum actio*; perhaps they were identical with the *missae* of the Council of Milevis (402), canon 1, and with the *orationes super populum*; cf. *EP*, 175, 5 and 179, 4, where there are perhaps quotations from similar prayers of blessing over the people.

PART 3

PREACHING

14. THE HANDBOOK FOR PREACHERS

1. *DDC*, 4, 1, 1 and 1, 1, 1, and *RE*, 2, 4, 30; on the fourth book see J. Pschmadt, in *TG*, 83–41 (1916). See also the edition of Sullivan (Washington, 1930) and that of Vogels (with the three other books) in *FP*, 24 (Bonn, 1930).

2. On the uses of rhetoric see *CCR*, 1, 1, where is to be found the definition "Eloquentia vero facultas dicendi est, congruenter explicans quae sentimus"; cf. *DCR*, 2, 3.

3. *DDC*, 4, 1, 2 and 3, 5.

4. *DDC*, 4, 4, 6–5, 7.

5. *DDC*, 4, 6: "scripturarum tractator et doctor".

6. *DDC*, 5, 8; cf. 2, 9, 14.

7. *DDC*, 6, 9–7, 20.

8. Cf. for example, *DDC*, 2, 13, 19; 4, 7, 14 and 10, 24; *CF*, 3, 5; Jerome, *Ep.*, 53, 10 (*CSEL*, 54, 463 and 464).

9. *DDC*, 2, 14, 21.

10. e.g., *DCR*, 8, 12, 3; 9, 13; cf. *EP*, 132, 1 (*Ad Volusianum*), where reference is made to the directness of the style of the Scriptures. Cf. also Sizoo in *Geref. Theol. Tijds.*, Sept., 1935, and again in *Eloquentia Divina*, Amsterdam, 1939; he makes the point that Augustine discovered a new criterion for the stylistic beauty of the Bible, the uniting of *veritas*, *puritas* and *soliditas*.

11. *DDC*, 4, 8, 22–9, 23.

12. Cf. *IP*, 138, 20.

13. *DDC*, 4, 10, 24; cf. *DCR*, 2, 3 and 10, 15.

14. *DDC*, 10, 25–11, 26.

15. *DDC*, 13, 29–15, 32.

16. *DDC*, 12, 27 f. and 26, 56.

17. *DDC*, 18, 35.

18. *DDC*, 18, 37–19, 38; cf. 22, 51.

19. *DDC*, 23, 52–26, 56.

20. On the subject of *granditer* see *DDC*, 4, 20, 42–44 and 49, 50 (2 Cor. vi.2–10; Rom. viii.28–39 and Gal. iv.10–20; Cyprian, *De Hab. Virg.*, 15 f.; Ambrose, *De Virg.*, 1, 6, 28); on *submisse*, *DDC*, 4, 20, 39 and 21, 45 and 46 (Gal. iv.21–6; iii.15–22; Cyprian, *Ep.*, 63, 2 and 3; Ambrose, *De Spir. S.*, 1, prol., 2 f.); on *temperate*, *DDC*, 4, 20, 40 and 21, 47 and 48 (Rom. xii.6–16; xiii.12–14; Cyprian, *De Hab. Virg.*, 3, 23; Ambrose, *De Virg.*, 2, 1, 7 and 8).

21. *DDC*, 4, 20, 41 and 44; according to Marrou (*S. Augustin et la fin de la culture antique*, Paris, 1938, p. 81), these *clausulae* are rhythmic; metrical *clausulae* appear only in the *De Civitate Dei*.

22. *DDC*, 24, 53 (*caterva*).

23. *CF*, 5, 5.

24. *DDC*, 4, 26, 56.
25. *DDC*, 27, 59–28, 61 and 1 Cor. i.17.
26. Jer. xxiii.30; *DDC*, 4, 29, 62.
27. *DDC*, 4, 30, 63.

15. THE SERVANT OF THE WORD

28. *Secundini Manichaei, Ep. III* (vol. 8, 369–71 in the Maurist edition).
29. *Inter Aug. epp.*, 32, 2 and 3.
30. *VA*, 31.
31. *IP*, 103, 1, 1; 147, 21; *IP*, 72, 34; 93, 30, cf. above.
32. *Sermo Presb. Eraclii*, 2 and 3, conclusion (vol. 5, 1523 in the Maurist edition).
33. *IP*, 50, 1.
34. *MPB*, 126, 1.
35. *SE*, 303, 1.
36. *CF*, 6, 3, 3.
37. *EP*, 213, 2 (*notarii ecclesiae*); 158, 1 (the *notarius* of Evodius); 41, 2 (sermons recorded in Carthage); *IP*, 44, 6 (*notarii veloces*); *DDC*, 2, 26, 40 (*Notarii: a notis*); *VA*, 6, 16 and 17; *EP*, 33, 4; 141, 2 (at disputations); *SE*, 24, 6 (the recording of the cry *dii Romani*); *EP*, 172, 2 (the lack of people who understand Latin in Bethlehem).
38. *EP*, 169, 4, 13.
39. *EP*, 15, 1; 118, 34 (*charta et membranae*).
40. *VA*, 24 and *EP*, 139, 3; 224, 2.
41. *SE*, 302, 1 (St. Laurence's day); on his preparation for his sermons see Deferrari in *AJP*, 43, 97–123, 193–219 (1922), and Mohrmann, *SSA*, 22–6.
42. e.g., *SE*, 362, 1 (the Gospel and Epistle for a sermon on the Resurrection).
43. *IP*, 138, 1.
44. *SE*, 352, 1.
45. *IP*, 86, 1.
46. *SE*, 180, 4 (on cursing); *SE*, 71, 8 (on blasphemy); *SE*, 52, 1.
47. *SE*, 174; 1 Tim. i.15 and Luke xix.2 ff.
48. *SE*, 176; 1 Tim. i.15 and Ps. xciv.6 and Luke xvii.12–19.
49. *EP*, 29, 4, cf. *infra*.
50. 205 *enarrationes in cl. psalmos*; 124 *tract. in Jo.*; 10 *tract. in ep. 1 Jo.*; 363 *sermones* (130 *post Maurinos reperti*, ed. Morin, 1930); cf. also one or two more in *RB*, 47 (1935), 49 (1937), and 50 (1938). On the chronology of the preaching see Cavallera in *BLE*, 21–30 (1930); De Bruyne in *RB*, 43, 185–93 (1931); Morin in *RB*, 75 f. (1932); De Bruyne in *RB*, 299–302 (1932); Kunzelmann in *MA*, 2, 417–520; Lambot in *RB*, 114–24 (1925); and also the list by Possidius published by Wilmart in *MA*, 2, 161–208.
51. Prudentius, *Peristephanon*, 9, 23 and 24 (*In Honorem S. Cassiani Forocorneliensis*, i.e., of Imola) (*CSEL*, 61, 367):

> Verba notis brevibus comprendere cuncta peritus
> raptimque punctis dicta praepetibus sequi.

52. *IP*, 51, 1 and *VA*, 18; also the Indiculus of Possidius.
53. *DT*, 15, 27, 48; the sermon is *TJ*, 99; according to *RE*, 2, 93, 2, Augustine did not get as far as a revision of the collected sermons as a whole.
54. *DDC*, 4, 29, 62–30, 63.
55. *EP*, 213, 2.
56. *EP*, 41, 2.
57. *EP*, 72, 3, 5 (Jerome, *Ep.*, 105).
58. Or was it begun before 403–4? Cf. *EP*, 72, 3, 5. For the date 415–17 cf. *EP*, 169, 1. See also Wilmart's final conclusion in *MA*, 2, 300, according to which 86 were dictated and 119 actually delivered, and also his list (ibid., 321–5) of the *Enarrationes*, which were probably delivered in Carthage.
59. *EP*, 169, 1 (the request to complete the missing portion); *IP*, 118, 1, 1.
60. Thus La Landais in *RSR*, 35, 226–50 (1948). A different view is taken by Zarb in *AGM*, 10, 50–110 (1933); cf. De Bruyne in *RB*, 246, 247–347 f. (1931); another view again

is taken by Huyben in *MA*, Nijmegen, 1930, 256–74 (for the date 418–19); see also M. Comeau, *La Rhétorique de S. Augustin d'après les tr. in Jo.*, Paris, 1930, and *S. Augustin exégète du 4e évangile*, Paris, 1930.

61. Cassiodorus, *De Incarnat.*, 7 (=*TJ*, 2; cf. *RSR*, 273 (1922), and also in *MA*, 2, 257–315.
62. The preface in Froben's Basle edition of 1529.
63. e.g., *TJ*, 6, 1 ("in spite of the cold") and 7, 1; for the more solemn note see 3, 1 and 1, 1.
64. *Pensées* (p. 283 in Brunschvicq's edition).
65. Cf. *DDC*, 4, 20, 42.
66. *SE*, 17, 2; cf. *SE*, 340, 1.
67. *SE*, 56, 11.
68. *SE*, 101, 4.
69. *IP*, 36, 3, 6; cf. *IP*, 138, 20 (the use of *ossum* instead of *os*); 123, 8 (*forsitan* for *putas*); 50, 19 (*sanguinibus* instead of *sanguine*); *TJ*, 2, 14 (the same).
70. *DDC*, 2, 13, 20.
71. Over 4,000 such cases have been counted in the sermons alone; according to Marrou (*S. Augustin et la fin de la culture antique*, p. 81), he does not use any metrical *clausulae* in his sermons.
72. *CF*, 5, 10, 20 and particularly 7, 1, 1–2 and 8, 13 f.; also 10, 16 f.
73. *SE*, 362, 3 and Ps. xxx.21.
74. *SE*, 52, 19 (the image of the Trinity); 117, 1–17 (the Word) and *SE*, 341, 1–12 (the threefold discourse on Christ).
75. *SE*, 362, 20.
76. e.g., *SE*, 178, 7, 8 (cf. above) and 308, 5 (cf. below).
77. *SE*, 301, 5, 4.
78. *SE*, 50, 7.
79. *SE*, 17, 2.
80. *SE*, 50, 6.
81. *SE*, 311, 4.
82. *SE*, 56, 12 and *SE*, 9, 11, 17; cf. *IP*, 148, 10, where he speaks of the minute organs with which fleas and midges suck blood.
83. *CAS*, 1, 133, 1.
84. *GUE*, 11, 4.
85. *SE*, 302, 15; see *supra*.
86. *IP*, 39, 9.
87. *CL*, 2, 11, 8; *MO*, 260; *GUE*, 23, 5; *SE*, 279, 5.
88. *MO*, 15, 2; *DSI*, 18, 3; cf. *IP*, 86, 3 (on the *quadratus* in itself).
89. *IP*, 95, 15; *TJ*, 9, 14.
90. Liverani, 8, 1; *MO*, 391: see also the collection of Augustine's sermon verse in Lietzmann's *Kleine Texte*.
91. *SE*, 36, 2.
92. *SE*, 82, 14; *SE*, 224, 4.
93. *SE*, 308, 5.
94. *SE*, 307, 5.
95. *IP*, 86, 1.
96. *IP*, 103, 2, 1.
97. De Capua in *MA*, 2, 607–764; on the sermons see 750–64; see also Sizoo in *Geref. Theol. Tijds.*, Sept., 1935.
98. Mohrmann in *MYE*, 3, 33–61 (1935–6).
99. *SE*, 101, 9; cf. 319, 8 and *DSI*, 15, 3; cf. J. Zellinger, "Der Beifall in der altchr. Predigt", in *Festgabe Knöpfler*, 1917, 403–15.
100. *IP*, 80, 8.
101. *SE*, 358, 4.
102. *IP*, 147, 15: "qui posuit fines tuos pacem" (finis=a boundary or zone). Cf. Ps. cxlvii.14.
103. *IP*, 149, 13.
104. *IP*, 88, 1, 10.

105. *SE*, 37, 12, 17.
106. *SE*, 19, 4; cf. Ps. lxvii.21.
107. *FSA*, 5, 5; Ps. ix.2–3.
108. *DSI*, 15, 3; cf. *IP*, 136, 9 and 10 (the reader will recognize again the image of the oil and grounds in the olive-press).
109. *FSA*, 6, 1 and 2; De Capua in *MA*, 2, 763, reads Telica (=*finalis*, hence the word-play on Perpetua, i.e., *sine fine*) instead of Primus, and cites the *Passio Martyrum Abitinensium*; cf. *RB*, 43, 9–14 (1931).
110. *SE*, 96, 4.
111. *SE*, 311, 4.
112. *FSA*, 6, 2.
113. *TJ*, 3, 21.
114. *TJ*, 45, 13; cf. *SE*, 137, 14; 178, 7; 180, 14; *MO*, 15, 4.
115. *FSA*, 2, 1.
116. *IP*, 141, 8.
117. *IP*, 53, 7 ("exclamatis ad verbum"); 88, 1, 10; *TJ*, 18, 8; *SE*, 37, 12, 17; 131, 5 (acclamations at "Exultate cum tremore"); 151, 8.
118. *MO*, 11, 14.
119. *SE*, 187, 7 and *IP*, 103, 1, 1 (at Carthage).
120. *IP*, 103, 3, 1.
121. *GUE*, 20, 2.
122. *SE*, 151, 8, conclusion.
123. On the church as a popular educational centre see *EP*, 91, 3.
124. *TJ*, 7, 6.
125. *TEJ*, 3, 11 and *IP*, 26, 2, 8; cf. *TJ*, 3, 20 and 21 ("ut inhabitam in domo domini" (Ps. xxvi.4)).
126. *FSA*, 2, 4 (and partly in *SE*, 339, 4).
127. *DDC*, 1, 39, 43; cf. 4, 6, 9 and 10.
128. *SE*, 344, 1, e.g., the *exordium*; *DCD*, 14, 28 and 14, 1.
129. e.g., *SE*, 150, 3, 4 and *DCD*, 10, 3.
130. *EP*, 118, 17; cf. *CF*, 7, 18 f.
131. Cf. below the comparison of *DCR*, 16, 24–25, 49.
132. *CF*, 7, 18, 24.
133. *SE*, 14, 9 (see also 14, 10): the inward cry "Domine Jesu, pupillum quaero; cito responde ut inveniam"; *DCR*, 22, 40.
134. *SE*, 49, 9 (against anger).
135. *IP*, 99, 5.
136. *SE*, 117, 3, 5 (*aspectus mentis*).
137. *SE*, 4, 4, 5–7.
138. *SE*, 341.
139. *SE*, 267, 4.
140. *IP*, 118, 18, 4, on the *illuminatio mentis*; not delivered as a sermon; cf. *SE*, 52, 18 and 19 and *IP*, 42, 6 (on the soul).
141. *IP*, 26, 2, 8.
142. *IP*, 44, 5.
143. See below *DSI*, 2, 4; *IP*, 41, 7; on the likeness of God in man, *SE*, 9, 8, 9; *SE*, 52, 7, 18 and 19 (the image of the Trinity).
144. *SE*, 361 and 362; 240, 241, 242; cf. *IP*, 88, 5 (this dogma under the heaviest of attack); cf. *ENC*, 23, 84–92; *SE*, 176 on the properties of the resurrected body.
145. e.g., *SE*, 241, 5–8.
146. About twenty allusions to this have been counted; cf. *SE*, 81, 9; 241, 5; 105, 10.
147. *SE*, 241, 5.
148. *SE*, 105, 10; Vergil, *Aeneid*, 1, 278.

> His ego nec metas rerum nec tempora pono:
> imperium sine fine dedi,

and the same passage quoted in *DCD*, 2, 29; cf. however the *peritura regna* of *Georgics*, 2, 498.

149. e.g., *SE*, 56, 8, 12 and 13; cf. *supra*.
150. Cf. *SE*, 56, 8, 12 and *IP*, 140, 18.
151. *SE*, 180, 14.
152. *IP*, 70, 17.
153. *TEJ*, 5, 7.
154. Cf. Marrou's exposition.
155. *Élévations sur les mystères*, 10th week, 3rd elevation; Cf. Urs von Balthasar, *Aurel. Aug. über die Psalmen*, Leipzig, 1936.
156. Luke xxiv.44.
157. Ps. xli.4.
158. Ps. xli.5.
159. *DSI*, 2, 4; cf. *IP*, 41, 7.
160. *CF*, 6, 4, 6.
161. M. Pontet, *L'Exégèse de Saint Augustin prédicateur*, Paris, 1946; L. Goppelt, *Typos, Die typologische Deutung des alten Testaments in Neuen*, Gutersloh, 1939.
162. e.g., *Strom.*, 7, 18 (*CGS*, 3, 76–9, ed. Stählin).
163. *Hom. in Gen.*, 13, 1–4 (*GCS*, 6, 113–121, ed. Baehrens).
164. *DDC*, 3, 30, 43.
165. *DDC*, 3, 27, 38 and *CF*, 12, 30, 41–31, 42; on the fourfold sense of Scripture cf. *DUC*, 3.
166. *S. Th.*, 1, qu. 1, a. 10; here he is distinguishing a historical or literal sense from a threefold spiritual or mystical sense, that is, allegorical, moral and anagogical.
167. *EP*, 137, 5, 18; *DDC*, 2, 6, 7.
168. Cf. *DDC*, 2, 5, 6.
169. *DCR*, 9, 13 and *DDC*, 2, 6, 7 and 8; cf. *EP*, 137, 5, 18.
170. *DDC*, 2, 6, 7; there is the same image in *DSI*, 15, 3; cf. Cant. iv.2 and vi.5.
171. *CF*, 3, 6 (the myths are better than the Manichean gnosis, because we know that they are made up).
172. *MPB*, 25, 2 and 3; cf. *SE*, 77, 8 (*MO*, 7, 2 and 3; *GUE*, 23, 5; 24, 5); *SE*, 22, 2 (*DSI*, 11, 1).
173. *FSA*, 7, 5; *MPB*, 101, 1.
174. *SE*, 4, 12–22; cf. *C. Mendac.*, 10, 24; *SE*, 288.
175. *SE*, 205, 1; 210, 9; 125, 9.
176. *TJ*, 44, 2 (*Saliva=quasi verbum*); at the end there is the word-play on *missus-dimissus*); cf. *SE*, 135, 1.
177. *SE*, 32, 7.
178. *QIH*, 2, 90; cf. Exod. xxiii.19.
179. Previously *SE*, 201, *De Temp.* (thus also in the Breviary); App., *SE*, 40, 1 in the Maurist edition; (Caesarius of Arles, *Ser.*, 20).
180. *CL*, 2, 6 and Ps. liv.7.
181. *MPB*, 125, 2.
182. *SE*, 309, 4 and 3.
183. *IP*, 103, 1, 13.
184. *TJ*, 50, 6.
185. *DGM* (A.D. 389); *De Gen. ad Litt., Op. Imp.* (392); *DGL* (about 412); cf. *DGL*, 8, 1 and 2.
186. *DCD*, 6, 8.
187. *TEJ*, 3, 13.
188. *SE*, 153, 1.
189. *SE*, 152, 1; cf. *IP*, 67, 10 (*coeli distillaverunt*); cf. Ps. lxvii.9.
190. *CF*, 9, 1: "a fundo cordis mei exhauriens abyssum corruptionis".
191. *DDC*, 4, 24, 53.
192. *GUE*, 17, 4 (cf. *EP*, 170, *circa* A.D. 410).
193. *VA*, 15.
194. *SE*, 308, 5.

16. Instruction for Beginners

1. *DCR*, 2, 4; 1, 1.
2. *DCR*, 1, 1.
3. *DCR*, ed Krüger, Tübingen, 1934. See also J. Christopher's commentary (Washington, 1926); Eggersdörfer, *Der hl. Augustinus als Pädagoge*, Freiburg, 1907, 174–99; Wundt in *ZNW*, 22, 135 (1923); Robbers in *MA*, 151 f.; Souter in *MA*, 2, 253–5 (text) (*rudis*=novices); cf. Cyprian, *Ep.*, 70, 2 (*CSEL*, 3, 2, 769); Jerome, *Ep.*, 107, 1 (*CSEL*, 55, 290, ed. Hilberg); Ambrose, *In Ps. cxviii*, Ser., 18, 26 (*PL*, 15, 1537) ("rudis adhuc in fide"); *DCR*, 1, 1; 2, 4; 8, 12; 10, 14; 11, 16; 15, 23—the non-intellectuals, or people of average education; 9, 13, the illiterate, *idiota*, cf. 8, 12; 16, 24.
4. *DCR*, 2–15 and 16–27.
5. *DCR*, 1–2 (introduction), 3–4 (*narratio*), 5–7 (questioning and admonition; 8–9 and 15, the various types of catechumens; 10–14 the *hilaritas* of the catechist).
6. *DCR*, 16–25 and 26, 51–27; cf. also *CFA*, 13, 7.
7. *DCR*, 15, 23.
8. *DCR*, 8, 12.
9. *DCR*, 9, 13.
10. *DCR*, 5, 9 and 6, 10. The testing of motives is already to be found in Origen, *C. Cels.*, 3, 51 (*GCS*, 1, 247, ed. Koetschau).
11. *DCR*, 2, 3–4 and 10, 15.
12. 2 Cor. ix.7.
13. 2 Cor. v.13.
14. 2 Cor. v.14; cf. 1 Cor. ix.22.
15. *DCR*, 10, 14 and 15.
16. *DCR*, 11, 16.
17. *DCR*, 12, 17.
18. *DCR*, 13, 19.
19. *DCR*, 14, 20.
20. *DCR*, 3, 5 and 6.
21. *DCR*, 4, 7 and 8.
22. See *supra*.
23. 2 Pet. i.19; cf. *CFA*, 13, 7 and *SE*, 43, 4, 5 (ibid., 3, 4: "Crede ut intelligas").
24. *DCR*, 24, 45 and 27, 53; there is the same theme in sermons—*MO*, 8, 1 (spurious?), 13, 4.
25. *DCR*, 7, 11; on the "milk diet" of exhortation see Origen *In Jud.*, 5, 6 (*GCS*, 7, 496, ed. Baehrens) and *C. Cels.*, 3, 52 (*GCS*, 1, 248, ed. Koetschau).
26. *DCR*, 16, 24.
27. 1 Pet. i.24–5 and Isa. xl.6–8.
28. *DCR*, 16, 24 and 25; 17, 26–7.
29. *DCR*, 17, 28.
30. *RE*, 2, 14.
31. *DCR*, 18, 29 and 30; 19, 31.
32. *DCR*, 19, 32 and 33.
33. *DCR*, 20, 34–6.
34. 1 Tim. ii.1 and 2; cf. Rom. xiii.7.
35. 1 Cor. iii.9.
36. *DCR*, 21, 37.
37. *DCR*, 21, 38.
38. *DCR*, 22, 39.
39. *DCR*, 22, 40: "numquam moriturus ... quasi numquam victurus".
40. *DCR*, 23, 41–3.
41. *DCR*, 24, 44.
42. *DCR*, 25, 46–7.
43. *DCR*, 25, 48–9.
44. *DCR*, 26, 50.
45. *DCR*, 26, 51–2.
46. *DCR*, 27, 53–5.

PART 4

POPULAR PIETY

17. The Cult of the Martyrs

1. Cyprian, *Ep.*, 12, 2 (*CSEL*, 3, 2, 503, ed. Hartel); cf. *Ep.*, 39, 3 (*CSEL*, 3, 2, 583). On this chapter see *OCM*; on Augustine's standpoint see Reul in *TG*, 22, 438 (1930). See also B. Kötting's book *Peregrinatio Religiosa*, Münster, 1950.
2. See in particular *DCD*, 8, 27; *CFA*, 20, 21; *SE*, 273, 7; also 318, 1; 310, 2; 319, 1.
3. *EP*, 55, 19, 35.
4. *DDC*, 2, 19, 29 and 20, 30; cf. 25, 38.
5. *EP*, 55, 19, 35; cf. above.
6. *SE*, 273, 6.
7. *FSA*, 3, 6.
8. On the *coronatio* see Borella in *Ambrosius*, 15, 149–55 (1939).
9. *SE*, 329, 1 and 2; cf. 298, 3 ("Finierunt dolores et acceperunt honores").
10. *QE*, 2, q. 38, 1–3 and 280, 5.
11. *IP*, 37, 3; *DCD*, 21, 13, 16; *ENC*, 29, 109 and 110.
12. *SE*, 109, 4 (Abraham's bosom); *TJ*, 49, 10 (*circa* 415); *ENC*, 29, 109 (*circa* 428); *DPS*, 12, 24 (*circa* 428).
13. *IP*, 119, 6.
14. *CF*, 9, 3, 6.
15. *SE*, 280, 5 and 328, 6 (for the martyrs).
16. *DGL*, 12, 35, 38.
17. *RE*, 1, 14, 2.
18. *DCD*, 20, 9, 2; *TJ*, 49, 10.
19. *SE*, 159, 1; 284, 5; 285, 5; 297, 2, 3; *TJ*, 84, 1.
20. *DSI*, 15, 1–3; Ps. cxxiii.6 and Cant. iv.2 and vi.5; cf. *DDC*, 2, 6, 7.
21. *DSI*, 15, 1; *MO*, 15, 1.
22. *SE*, 287–93; *FSA*, 7 and 8; *MPB*, 101; *GUE*, 22; *SE*, 307 and 308 (*decollatio*).
23. *SE*, 295–9; *MPB*, 19; *CAS*, 1, 133; *GUE*, 23 and 24.
24. Cf. Augustine, *IP*, 47, 5; *SE*, 199, 2; 373, 3 refers to them as martyrs; cf. *DLA*, 3, 23, 68.
25. *SE*, 300 and 301; *DSI*, 17, 7; they had been honoured as early as the fourth century, with a basilica in Antioch, and at Rome also from A.D. 432, on 1 August. See Ferrua in *Civ. Catt.*, 3, 234–97 and 318–37 (1938).
26. *SE*, 317, 1; cf. *SE*, 314–19 and 320–4; *Ep. Luciani, inter op. August.*, vol. 7, app. 3–11 in the Maurist edition, *PL*, 41, 808–15; cf. *OCM*, 80.
27. *MEQ*, 4, nos. 228, 245, 303, 306; *OCM*, 401.
28. *De Miraculis S. Stephani*, 1, 1, 2 and 2, 4 (*inter op. August.*, vol. 7 in the Maurist edition, app. 26 and 27, also 39 and 40; *PL*, 41, 834 and 850 f.).
29. *DCD*, 22, 8, 10–16, 20 and 21.
30. *SE*, 317 (the chapel); *DCD*, 22, 8, 22, 17–20; *SE*, 356, 7; 319, 7; 322; 323, 4.
31. *DSI*, 13 (in Carthage); *GUE*, 25 (after *SE*, 302); *SE*, 302–5 (Laurence); *SE*, 273, 6 (the feast of St. Agnes); *SE*, 354, 5 (on the name of St. Agnes).
32. *SE*, 274–7; *CL*, 1, 47; *MO*, 243.
33. *SE*, 273, 2.
34. *MO*, 2, 3 (Spain).
35. *DCD*, 22, 8, 7 and *SE*, 286, 5.
36. Cyprian; *DSI*, 11 (the vigil), 14, 15 and 22; *GUE*, 26–8; *SE*, 309–13.
37. *SE*, 280–2.
38. Cf. *OCM*, 400–1; on earth from Palestine see Augustine, *EP*, 52, 2 and *DCD*, 22, 8, 6; also *MEQ*, iv, 300 and Burel in *La Vie et les arts liturgiques*, 11, 5, 20 (1924).
39. *DSV*, 44 (Thecla) and *DSI*, 5, 6 (Phocas); on St. Phocas see especially *AB*, 30, 252–95 (1911).

40. *SE*, 298, 1 and 2; concerning the *brandea* see *Reg. Greg.*, 4, 30 (ed. Ewald and Hartmann, 1, 264–5); also Gregory of Tours, *De Glor. Martyr.*, 28 (*PL*, 71, 728–9) (the *brandea* which have been let down on to the *confessio* of St. Peter weigh heavier in the scales afterwards).
41. *DSI*, 13, 1 and *SE*, 303, 1.
42. *SE*, 285; cf. Cyprian, *De Lapsis*, 13 (*CSEL*, 3, 1, 246) (Castus and Aemilius); also the *Indiculus* of Possidius (Agileus and Catholinus); on Mappalicus see *OCM*, 280; for the Basilica Fausti, *SE*, 23 and 261.
43. Prudentius, *Peristephanon*, 13 (*CSEL*, 61, 423–7).
44. *VHP*, 1, 5, 16 (*CSEL*, 7, 8, ed. Petschenig) and *CF*, 5, 8, 15; *DSI*, 14 and 15; *SE*, 114, 131, 154, 169 (*in mensa*); cf. *IP*, 80, 4, 23.
45. Procopius, *De Bello Vandal.*, 1, 20 and 21, ed. Haury, Leipzig, 1936, 398 and 403.
46. *MO*, 2, 3; cf. *IP*, 120, 15 and 137, 3; he mentions her in *SE*, 286, 2; 354, 5, and *DSV*, 44.
47. *DSI*, 18; *MO*, 15; *DSI*, 24 (the Basilica of Quadratus in Hippo Zarytus); Lambot in *RB*, 6, 16–20 (1938).
48. *MO*, 14 and 15; cf. *IP*, 49, 9, and *SE*, 306; 311, 10; *IP*, 144, 1, 17 (the basilica in Utica); Prudentius, *Peristephanon*, 13, 76–87 (the *passio*) and 83 (the number 300) (*CSEL*, 61, 426).
49. *SE*, 284.
50. *FSA*, 3, 6.
51. *DSI*, 16; sermons: *GUE*, 30, 2; *SE*, 37, 16, 23; two in the *Indiculus*; *SE*, 155 (the basilica in Carthage).
52. *SE*, 273, 7; *MPB*, 158, 2; *DB*, 6, 21, 36; Leontius, who also had a basilica dedicated to him in the town (*SE*, 262, cf. *EP*, 29 (the old address) (*CSEL*, 34, 114 (Goldbacher))), is considered by Delehaye to have been one of the town's bishops, not a martyr; cf. *Origines*, 396.
53. *SE*, 356, 10; *MO*, 2, 3.
54. *DCD*, 22, 8, 9; *SE*, 148, 325, apparently also 326; *MO*, 2, 3.
55. *IP*, 127, 6.
56. *DCD*, 22, 8, 7; cf. *SE*, 286, 5.
57. *EP*, 78, 3.
58. *ILVC*, 2096, p. 411; *MEQ*, 238; for the inscription underneath, ibid., 334, 238. Gauckler, *Inventaire des mosaïques de la Tunisie*, Paris, 1909, nos. 259 and 260, pp. 89–103; Id., *Basiliques chrétiennes de Tunisie*, Paris, 1913, 23 and 24.
59. *ILVC*, 1, 2100; *MEQ*, 263.
60. *GMA*, 2, 323 and 333; Grandidier in *Atti II Congresso Arch. Crist.*, Rome, 1902, 51–77; L. Poinssot in *Bull. arch. du comité des trav. hist., procès-verbaux de la commiss. de l'Afrique du Nord*, 20 Feb. 1934, 11 f.; Delehaye in *AB*, 54, 312–14 (1936).
61. On the *basilica majorum* see *VHP*, 1, 3, 9 (*CSEL*, 7, 5, ed. Petschenig); for the grave inscription see *ILVC*, 1, 2040, 403; Delattre in *CAIB*, 118 f., 193 f., 515 f.; 1908, 59 f. (1907) and 566–83 (1911) and in *BSAF*, 198 f. (1908).
62. Gagé in *AEHG*, 1, 181–230 (1937); Grégoire in *Byzantion*, 12, 213–24 (1937) (where he groundlessly holds the saint as having been invented); Delehaye, *OCM*, 393.
63. Cf. *AB*, 54, 303 f. (1936) on the surroundings of Sitifis.
64. De Rossi, *La Capsella Argentea Africana*, Rome, 1889 (the original, 16 × 8 × 10 cm., is in the Museo Cristiano in the Vatican), fig. 20; Arnason in *Art. Bull.*, 20, 216 f. (1928).
65. *ILVC*, 1, 2070, 407.
66. *ILVC*, 1, 2068, 407; Gsell, *MAH*, 10, 1890, 441, and plates in *DACL*, 1, 1, 828 (130 cm. square; now in the Louvre).
67. Menas *ampullae* from Egypt were widely distributed (including in Hippo). There is a collection of oil *ampullae* with *pittacia* in the Cathedral Museum of Monza (16 metal ones from Palestine, 28 glass ones from the Roman shrines); cf. A. Colombo, *I Dittici Eburnei e le ampolle metalliche della basilica reale di Monza*, Monza, 1934.
68. *EP*, 32, 11 and 17 (*CSEL*, 29, 287 and 292–3) (Nola and Fundi; in Fundi, "sub accensis altaribus"); cf. *Carm.*, 27, 503–39 and 280–1.
69. *OCM*, 371–6; details in 376–401.
70. *DSI*, 13, 1.

71. Like the words "Caede traditorum vexata" in an inscription of the year 434 in Ala Miliaria (Benian) in Mauretania Caesariensis (*ILVC*, 1, 2052, p. 405); or again, "Deo laudes hic omnes dicamus", and "Memoria domni Marchuli" on a stone from a church at Ksarel-Kelb (Vegesela) in Numidia, dating from the fourth century (cf. *AB*, 53, 81–9 (1935) and Cayrol in *MAH*, 51, 114–42 (1934); 53, 166–77 (1936); cf. *TJ*, 11, 15.
72. *ILVC*, 1, 2071, 408; *OCM*, 393.
73. The gap in the fasting period runs from 17 Feb. to 19 April; see the edition of Lietzmann, *Kleine Texte*, Bonn, 1911, 2, 4–6.
74. Council of Carthage, 438, canon 14 (*MC*, 3, 971); *CCEA* (*MC*, 3, 782); cf. *De Miraculis S. Stephani*, 1, 2, *inter op. Aug.*, vol. 7, app. 27 in the Maurist edition (on dreams); the quotation from Abbot Shenoute is in *OCM*, 89.
75. On Tipasa see Gsell in *MAH*, 11, 179 (1891); 14, 358 f. (1894); id. in his monograph on Tipasa (1892); Hirogani in *MAH*, 1930; on the saints, see above.
76. Cyril of Alexandria, *C. Julian.*, 10 (*PG*, 76, 1016).
77. *CL*, 2, 6, 6; *MO*, 25, 5; cf. *EP*, 33, 5.
78. *TJ*, 124, 2 and 3.
79. Ambrose, *De Virg.*, 2, 2 (*PL*, 16, 219–23).
80. *DAC*, 22, 24; cf. Friedrich, *Die Mariologie des hl. Augustins*, 1907; Neveu in *Divus Thomas*, 522–30 (1931); H. Pope, O.P., "The Teaching of St. Augustine on Our Blessed Lady", in *The Clergy Review*, 16, 23–41 (1939).
81. *EP*, 137, 5, 8; 162, 6; 186, 1; 188, 4; 191, 2; 215, 3; *DSI*, 25, 3.
82. *DNG*, 36, 42.
83. *CJ*, 4, 122.
84. *SE*, 291, 6, conclusion.
85. *SE*, 186, 1 (the Mother of God); *SE*, 291, 6; 290, 4; 289.
86. *SE*, 191, 4; 192, 2.
87. *SE*, 215, 4 and particularly *SE*, 290, 4–6 and *DSI*, 25, 7.
88. *SE*, 195, 2; *DSI*, 2, 5, 8; *GUE*, 1, 8; *SE*, 188, 4; 191, 3; 192, 2, conclusion; *DSV*, 2.
89. *MPB*, 95, 7.
90. *SE*, 290, 4–6.
91. *IP*, 98, 9 and Ps. xcviii.5.
92. *FSA*, 4, 2 and Ps. lxxxiv.12; *DSI*, 5, 5 ("de massa nostra").
93. *DSI*, 25, 3 and Matt. xii.46–50.
94. *DSI*, 25, 7; *DSV*, 3.
95. *DSI*, 25, 4; thus also *DAC*, 22, 24 and *SE*, 190, 3.
96. *SE*, 318, 1 and following.
97. *DOM*, 28, 36.
98. *SE*, 283 (Massilitani); the *Indiculus* of Possidius (Carthaerienses); *SE*, 156 (Bolitani).
99. *GUE*, 30, 2; cf. *SE*, 37, 16, 23 and *DSI*, 16; cf. Lambot in *RB*, 7, 20–4 (1938); *SE*, 155 was delivered in the basilica of the Scillitan martyrs in Carthage; cf. *VHP*, 73, 9 (*CSEL*, 7, 5, ed. Petschenig).
100. *SE*, 327–35.
101. *CFA*, 20, 21; *DCD*, 8, 27 and 10, 1.
102. *CFA*, 20, 21.
103. *TJ*, 84, 1.
104. *SE*, 159, 1.
105. *SE*, 325, 1 and 317, 1.
106. *DSV*, 3 and 5.
107. Particularly *DCD*, 8, 27; *CFA*, 20, 21; *SE*, 273, 7; 318, 1; 310, 2; 319, 1.
108. *SE*, 319, 8 and 128, 3.
109. *SE*, 273, 7; cf. *SE*, 297, 3, 3; 159, 1.
110. *DCD*, 8, 27.
111. *SE*, 310, 2; we may note the word-play on *epulatus-immolatus*. On the *mensa Cypriani* cf. *IP*, 80, 4, 23; *SE*, 13, 114, 131, 154, 169; *DSI*, 14 and 15.
112. *SE*, 310, 2.
113. *SE*, 273, 3, 7.
114. Cf. *SE*, 356, 7.
115. *DCD*, 8, 27.
116. *SE*, 336, 6.

117. Third Council of Carthage, canon 36 (*MC*, 3, 924; cf. *SE*, 302, 1 (readings for St. Laurence's day); *SE*, 362, 1 (*congruas lectiones*).

118. *DSI*, 14, 3; *GUE*, 27, 2 and 4; 28, 6; *SE*, 309, 1–6 (the *acta proconsularia* of Cyprian); *DSI*, 16, 7 (the Scillitans); *IP*, 120, 13; 137, 3 (Crispina); *SE*, 273, 2 and 3 (Fructuosus); *SE*, 325, 1; 362, 2 (the Twenty of Hippo).

119. *NOA*, 1, 10, 12; cf. *SE*, 280, 1 and 2.

120. *SE*, 315, 1.

121. *Reg. Greg., Ep.*, 8, 29 (*PL*, 77, 930–1).

122. Thiel, *Epist. Rom. Pontif.*, 454.

123. *De Glor. Mart.*, 40 (*PL*, 71, 741).

124. *TJ*, 11, 15.

125. *EP*, 50.

126. *EP*, 185, 3, 12.

127. *FSA*, 3, 6.

128. There are examples in *OCM*, 132–4.

129. *RM*, 2, pl. 3c, 10, 12; cf. pl. 1 (a reconstruction of the whole complex); there is a ground-plan by Fornari in *RAC*, 9, 201 (1932) and *Atti III Congr. A.C.*, Rome, 1934.

130. Paulinus, *Ep.*, 32, 12 (*CSEL*, 29, 287, ed. Hartel); cf. *Carm.*, 19, 478.

131. De Rossi in *RRS*, 3, 478–533 (1876) and G. P. Kirsch, *Die römische Titelkirchen im Altertum*, Paderborn, 1918.

132. "Epitaphium Sabini diaconi in pronae S. Laurentii in Agro Verano", *ILVC*, 1, 2126, 416 and 417; cf. Bücheler, *Carmina Latina Epigraphica*, Leipzig, 1897, 2, 677, no. 1423, 5–6; cf. *RBA*, 1864, 33:

> [N]il juvat immo gravat tumulis haerere piorum
> sanctorum meritis optima vita prope est.

133. *ICR*, 1, no. 319, 142.

134. *ILVC*, 1, 2165, 424; cf. also Ambrose, *De Excess. Frat. Sui Satyri*, 1, 18 (*PL*, 16, 1352: *FP*, 15, 24).

135. *MEC*, no. 301, cf. nos. 243, 330 and 332.

136. *DCM*, 1, 1; cf. Paulinus, *Carm.*, 31, 608 f. (*CSEL*, 30, 329, ed. Hartel) (his child's grave in Complutum).

137. *DCM*, 4, 6; 5, 7.

138. *DCM*, 2, 4 (he is quoting *DCD*, 1, 12) and 6, 8.

139. *CF*, 9, 11, 27.

140. *DCM*, 2, 3; 3, 5 (he is quoting *DCD*, 1, 13), 7, 9 and 9, 11; on *pietas* cf. SE, 172 and 173.

141. *EP*, 263, 3 (*Ad Sapidam*); cf. *SE*, 172 and 173; *CF*, 9, 12, 33.

142. *TJ*, 120, 4 and John xix.40.

143. *DCM*, 7, 9.

144. *DCM*, 3, 5.

145. *DCM*, 18, 22.

146. *DDQP*, 2, 2 and 3.

147. Cf. the text from Theodoret of Cyrrthus's *Graecarum Affectionum Curatio*, 8, 49 and 63 (*circa* 437) cited in *OCM*, 114 and 115.

18. The Feasts of the Dead

1. Cf. *DCD*, 1, 12 and *DCM*, 2, 3 and 4.

2. F. Fornari, *San Sebastiano Extra Moenia*, Rome, 1934; id. in *Atti III Congr. A.C.*, Rome, 1934, 315–24; A. Prandi, *La Memoria Apostolorum in Catacumbas*, 1, Vatican City, 1936; illustrations in *RM*, 2, pls. 1–12.

3. *Forschungen in Salona*, 2, Vienna, 1926 (Egger-Bulic on Manastirine) and 3 (1939) (Dyggve-Egger on Marusinac); particularly 6 f. and pls. 5 and 23 (the remains); 80–106 and pls. 107–27 (reconstruction); cf. Dyggve in *ZKG*, 59, 103–13 (1940) and on the contrary viewpoint Klauser in *Kriegsvorträge*, Bonn, 1942, no. 62; on the one-storey mausolea see Dyggve, Poulsen and Rhomaios, *Das Heroon von Kalydon*, Copenhagen, 1934; for the fourth-century mausoleum in Pécs (Fünfkirchen=Sopianae), Dyggve in *Pannonia*, 3, Pécs, 1935; cf. the later grave of Theodoric in Ravenna.

4. On the graves of the first and second centuries in the Vatican necropolis and those located directly under S. Sebastian, see *RM*, pl. 37b and *RK*, pls. 53 (the Vatican libation tubes); on the holes in the *mensa* slab see Orsi in *Notizie degli Scavi*, 1893, 292.

5. T. Klauser, *Die Cathedra im Totenkult der heidn. und christ, Antike*, Münster, 1927.

6. Cf. Ambrose, *De Helia et Jejun.*, 17, 62 (*CSEL*, 32, 2, 448, ed. Schenkl) ("in vesperam bibunt"); cf. the texts in Dölger, *Ichthys*, Rome, 1910, 2, 13.

7. On the *refrigerium* see P. Paolucci, *Refrigerium*, Camerino, 1923; A. M. Schneider, Freiburg, 1928; Klauser in *TG*, 599–608 (1928); Delehaye in *Sanctus*, Brussels, 136–54 (1927); Buonaiuti in *Ricerche Relig.*, 5, 60–7 (1929); G. van der Leeuw in *MYE*, 3, 125–49 (1936); A. Parrot, *Le Refrigerium dans l'au-delà*, Paris, 1937; Grossi-Gondi, *Diss. Pont. Acc.*, 1920, 269 ff.; J. Quasten, in *HTR*, 253 (1940); Cumont, *Le Symbolisme funéraire chez les Romains*, Paris, 1942, 352, 387.

8. Synesius of Cyrene, *Ep.*, 3 (*PG*, 66, 1324).

9.   Memoriae Aeliae Secundulae

               Funeri mu[l]ta quid[e]m condigna iam misimus omneS
               Insuper ar[ea] equ[e] depost[a]e Secundulae matrI
               Lapideam placuit nobis atponere mensaM
               In qua magna eius memorantes plurima factA
               Dum cibi ponuntur calicesq[ue] e[t] copertaE
               Vulnus ut sanetur nos rod[ens] pectore saevuM
               Libenter fabul[as] dum sera red[d]imus horA
               Castae matri bonae laudesq[ue] vetula dormiT
               Ipsa q[uae] nitr[i]t iaces et sobria sempeR
               V[ixit] a[nnis] LXXV. A[nno] pr[ovinciali] CCLX.
               Statulenia Julia fecit.

CIL, 8, 20277; *ILVC*, 1, 1570, 301; in the second line I should read "ar[ea] equ[e]" instead of "ar[a]equ[e]". It will be noted that the opening and closing letters give "Fili dulci simae matr". (Gsell, *MAH*, 15, 49 (1895).)

10. Synesius of Cyrene, *Ep.*, 3 (*PG*, 66, 1324), circa 404–8; cf. Dölger, *Ichthys*, 2, 588.

11. Cf. Minucius Felix, 38, 3 (Waltzing, 67) with *Acta Cypriani*, 5 (*CSEL*, 3, 3, app. 113) (the reference to torches; "cum cereis et stolacibus"); cf. the Council of Elvira, canon 34: there are to be no garlands in the graveyards, "so that the spirits of the saints may not be disturbed" and this is a matter of the ban of the Church (canon 37); there are to be no lamps lighted by day (*MC*, 11 and 12); see again Minucius Felix, as cited above, and Tertullian, *De Corona*, 10, 1, 439, ed. Oehler (*PL*, 2, 109) (on garlands); on burial customs in general see *RRS*, 3, 495–505 and R. Ruland, *Gesch. der kirchl. Leichenfeier*, Regensburg, 1901; A. Frantz, *Das Gebet für die Todten nach den Schriften des hl. Augustinus*, Nordhausen, 1857.

12. P. Styger in *Pisciculi*, Münster, 1939, 266 f.

13. Cf. Tertullian, *Ad Scapulam*, 3 (*PL*, 1, 779); Cyprian, *Ep.*, 12, 2; 39, 3 (*CSEL*, 3, 3, 503, 583, ed. Hartel).

14. On the four Catacombs of Hadrumetum in Byzacena cf. A. Leynaud, *Les Catacombes africaines, Sousse, Hadrumète*, Algiers, 1937.

15. The edict of Valerian says: "Ne cimeteria ingrediantur, conciliabula ne fiant." It was withdrawn by Gallienus in 260. From 303 to 311, under Diocletian, there was the confiscation, with restorations in 311 and 314; see the *Acta Cypriani* and Eusebius, *Historia Ecclesiastica*, 7, 11, 18 (*GCS*, 2, 656 and 657, ed. Schwartz).

16. *Acta Johannis*, 85 and 86 (Bonnet's edition); *Acta Apostol. Apocr.*, 2, 1, 1898, 93 (on the Eucharist), also 109 and 110 (*op. cit.*, 207 and 208 (on the Third Day); cf. *Canon. Hippol.*, 33, canon 169 f., and Achelis in *TU*, 6, 4, 106 (Leipzig, 1891) (*anamnesis* for the dead, with celebration of the Eucharist, and the bread of exorcism, before the beginning of the feast in honour of the dead); Lietzmann, *Messe und Herrenmahl*, Bonn, 1926, 199 and 240.

17. *ILVC*, 3, pp. 426–7.

18. For Africa see *EP*, 158, 2 (the third day); for Syria around 370, *Const. Ap.*, 8, 42 (Funk, 1, 552): in this case the third day (in memory of the Resurrection) and also the ninth and the fortieth (mourning for Moses) and the anniversary; cf. Freistedt, *Altchr. Totengedächtnistage*, **Münster, 1928.**

19. *QIH*, 1, 172 on Gen. l.10 and Ecclus. xxii.13.
20. Ambrose, *De Obitu Theodosii*, 3 (*PL*, 16, 1448); *De Excessu Fratr. Sui Satyri*, 2, 2 (*PL*, 16, 1372 and 1373); *De Fide Resurrect.*, 1 (*PL*, 16, 1315); Augustine, *QIH*, 1, 172.
21. Ambrose, *De Excess. Frat. Sui Satyr.*, 2, 5 (*PL*, 16, 1374); Cf. Tertullian, *De Cor.*, 3, 1, 422 (ed. Oehler, *PL*, 2, 98); *De Monog.*, 10, 1, 776 (ed. Oehler, *PL*, 2, 942) and *De Exhort. Cast.*, 11, 1, 1, 753 (ed. Oehler, *PL*, 2, 926).
22. *EP*, 158, 2; cf. Ps. ci.7.
23. *CF*, 9, 12, 32; cf. *SE*, 313, 5 (the altar).
24. E. Dyggve in *ZKG*, 59, 1940, 103-13.
25. Especially, in a dozen *cubicula* of the *coemeterium majus*; for Malta see Becker, *Malta Soterranea*, Strasburg, 1913, 112.
26. Serra Villaró in *Riv. di Arch. Crist.*, 14 (1937) 243-80 and in *memoria* 88 and 89 of the Junta Superior de Escavaciones y Antiguedades, 1927 and 1929.
27. *MKR*, 2 pls. 21, 2; 157, 1; 133, 2; 184; 157, 2; without the two women, 133, 3; 167, 1; 65, 3; 62, 2 (with the poor?); cf. 7, 4 (*in Domitilla*); Dölger in *AC*, 2 (1930), 81-99 and fig. 3 (offering to the dead on the slab of a grave in the catacomb of Petrus and Marcellinus; cf. pl. 6 (holes for the wine in the slab); *Germania*, 1934, 113 and *Bonner Jahrbuch*, 1932, 192 (feast of the dead in Xanten).
28. *MKR*, pl. 107, 3 and 1.
29. *MKR*, pl. 159, 2 (contrast with pl. 133, 2).
30. The epitaph of Theodoulos (*MKR*, text 415, fig. 41, p. 472; cf. also *CIL*, 6, 2357: "Hospes ad hunc tumulum ne meias ossa precantur tecta hominis sed si gravus homo es misce bibe da mi"; also Epiphanius, *Ancoratus*, 86, 5 (*GCS*, 1, 106 (Holl)).
31. See for example Kaufmann, *Handbuch d. altchr. Epigraphik*, Freiburg, 1927, pl. 15; the stone is now in Urbino.
32. Klauser, *Cathedra*, Münster, 1927, pl. 19, 2; cf. 22, 1 and 19, 3 (pagan).

33.
                    in pace
                    I idus febr.
           conss. gratiani iii et equiti
            florentinus fortunatus et
           [fel] ix ad calice benimus

ILVC, 1, 1568, p. 300; *RBA*, 1890, 72-80 and fig. 6; ibid., 1888, p. 103, figs. 6 and 7; Marucchi in *Nuovo Bullett.*, 1901, 100.
34. For dating see F. Wirth, *Römische Wandmalerei vom Untergang Pompejis bis zum Ende des 3 Jahr.*, Berlin, 1934; fig. 101 (Clodius Hermes, about 230); Wilpert, *MKR*, 27, 2 (=A2); 15, 2 (=A6); 41, 3 (=A3); 41, 4 (=A5) (the chapel of the Sacrament in the catacomb of Callistus, circa 220-50); ibid., 15, 1 (Greek chapel, circa 290).
35. *MKR*, pl. 21, 1 (chamber A3).
36. *SCA*, pl. 53, 3 (from Baebia Hertofile); 53, 1; 163, 1-3; 255, 4; 27, 1; 29, 1; cf. 2, 1 (the meal with the praying figure and philosophers); on the origin and development of these Christian feast scenes see F. Gerke, *Die christl. Sarkophage der Vorkonstant. Zeit.*, Berlin, 1940, 120 f. and 411-12 (index).
37. *Martyrium Polycarpi*, 18, 2; Cyprian, *Ep.*, 12, 2 (*CSEL*, 3, 2, 503 (Hartel)).
38. *Acta Cypriani*, 5 (*CSEL*, 3, 3 add. 113).
39. Lietzmann, *PAWP*, 1936, 29, 21 (*translatio*) and *LG*, 3, 330.
40. For illustrations of *triclia* and *graffiti* see *RM*, pl. 15, 16 (reconstruction), 17-25; *RK*, pl. 50 and 51, text on p. 339 f.; on the *refrigerium* see Delehaye in *AB*, 45, 297-310 and Grossi-Gondi in *RQ*, 29 (1915) 229 and on *Diss. Pont. Accad.*, 2, 14 (1926) 261-77; on the *memoria* see Styger in *Atti Pont. Accad.*, 2, 13 (1918) 1-114; also Von Gerkan in *LPE*, 167 f.; Lanciani in *Diss. Acc. Rom. di Arch.*, 2, 14 (1920) 59-111; Mancini in *Notizie degli Scavi*, 1923, 3-79; Fornari in *Atti III Congr. A.C.*, Rome, 1934, 315-29 (photographs); also A. Prandi, *La Mem. Apost. in Catacumbas*, 1, Vatican City, 1936; on the feast of 29 June see Kirsch, *JFL*, 3 (1923) 33-50.
41. *LPE*, 18-21 and *LG*, 3, 331.
42. Cf. for example *SE*, 273, 2 and 9; also 309, 1; 310, 4.
43. All the relevant texts are in F. Wieland, *"Mensa" und "Confessio"*, Münich, 1906, and *Altar und Altargrab der chr. Kirchen im vierten Jahrhundert*, Leipzig, 1912.

44. *Oratio ad Sanctorum Coetum*, 12 (*GCS*, Eus., 1, 171, 19–26 (Heikel)); there was a long controversy over its genuineness—see *Philol. Wochenschau*, 50 (1930) 366 f.
45. The texts from Chrysostom and the Cappadocians are quoted in *OCM*, 44–9.
46. Asterius, *Encomium in SS. Martyres*, ed. Combefis, Paris, 1648, 181.
47. *Encomium*, 189.
48. *Encomium*, 186–91.
49. *Encomium*, 176 and 172.
50. *In Phocam Martyrem* (ibid., 177).
51. *In Phocam Martyrem*, 180.
52. Cf. *Aeneid*, 2, 63 and 2, 239; *ILVC*, 1, 1825, 11–13, p. 359; Bücheler, *Carm. Lat. Epigr.*, Leipzig, 1897, 2, 833, no. 1808; *MAH*, 1894, 389–92; see the almost identical inscription of Cuicul-Djemila; Monceaux in *CAIB*, 1920, 290 f., 380–407, and in *Misc. De Rossi*, Rome, 1923, 1, 106; Gagé in *AEHG*, 1937, 1, 195–206.
53. Paulinus, *Carmina*, 14, 82 f., 98 f., 103 (*CSEL*, 30, 49 (Hartel)); *EP*, 20, 2 (*CSEL*, 29, 144–5).
54. *AH*, p. 138, *hymnus* 15, 7 (*PL*, 17, 1215); on the genuineness of this see *Jahrbuch für klass. Philologie*, supplementary vol. 28, 656; on the three routes see Marius in *Ambrosius*, 1938, 14, 137–43.
55. *EP*, 29, 10; cf. below.
56. Paulinus, *Ep.*, 13, 11–15 (*CSEL*, 29, 92–6 (Hartel)).
57. *Carm.*, 27, 566–7 (*CSEL*, 30, 287).
58. *Carm.*, 27, 545–67; 30, 286–7 (the pilgrimages); 568–79; 287 (the tirade against Satan); 511–45 and 580–635; 285–6 and 288–90 (the frescoes); cf. *Carm.*, 18, 219 f., 107 f. (the tales about the stolen oxen). Cf. also Boissier, *La Fin du paganisme*, Paris, 1891, 2, 94–9 and Pichon in *REA*, 9, 236.
59. Prudentius, *Cathem.*, 10, 169–72 (*CSEL*, 61, 63) (he is referring to the usual type of family mausoleum).
60. Prudentius, *Peristephanon*, 11, 189 and 190, 193 and 194 (*CSEL*, 61, 418) (he is referring to the grave of Hippolytus in Rome (or perhaps that of Laurence, having changed round the two sanctuaries?)).
61. Cumont thinks there may be a survival of Semitic religion here—see *Recherches sur le Symbolisme funéraire des Romains*, Paris, 1942, 353, n. 4; 380, n. 2; people began in the evening even in Italy—see Ambrose, *De Helia et Jeju.*, 17, 62 (*CSEL*, 32, 2, 448 (Schenkl)) (*PL*, 14, 754: "Illic in vesperam bibunt").
62. *SE*, 311, 5; on dancing in the church cf. Gougaud in *RHE*, 15, 5–22 (1914); also Spanke in *Neuphilol. Mitt.*, 31, 143–76 (1930).
63. *IP*, 32, 2, 5; following *IP*, 32, 3, 9 ("ad mensam Cypriani"); on music in secular festivals cf. *IP*, 41, 9 and *DGL*, 12, 22.
64. *DSI*, 13, 4; *SE*, 311, 5; 252, 4.
65. *CF*, 6, 2, 2.
66. *CF*, 6, 2, 2; Ambrose, *De Hel. et Jejun.*, 17, 62 (*CSEL*, 32, 448 (Schenkl)).
67. *Consuetudo*; *EP*, 22, 4; cf. *EP*, 29, 8–10.
68. *DCD*, 8, 27; *EP*, 29, 10.
69. *EP*, 29, 6.
70. *Const. Apost.*, 8, 42 (1, 522 in Funk's edition): "... and each shall give of his possessions to the poor".
71. *EP*, 22, 6.
72. *SE*, 172, 2; *ENC*, 29, 110 and *DCM*, 17, 22; cf. *CF*, 9, 12, 32.
73. *EP*, 22, 6.
74. *EP*, 22, 3.
75. *EP*, 22, 2.
76. *EP*, 22, 3; 1 Cor. v.11.
77. *EP*, 22, 3.
78. Gal. vi.1 and 1 Cor. iv.21.
79. *EP*, 22, 5, 6.
80. *EP*, 22, 7–9.
81. *BH*, 29 (*MC*, 3, 923); Third Council of Carthage, canon 30 (*MC*, 3, 885); *CCEA*, 42 (*MC*, 3, 735).
82. *IP*, 48, 1, 15; *SE*, 64, 4; 326, 1; *FSA*, 6, 3.

83. *CFA*, 20, 21.
84. *DME*, 1, 34, 75.
85. *SE*, 273, 8.
86. *DSI*, 13, 4 (Carthage); cf. *IP*, 59, 15 and 137, 14.
87. Zeno of Verona, 1, 6, 15 (*PL*, 11, 366).
88. *IP*, 48, 1, 15.
89. Pseudo-Augustine, *De Unit. Eccl.*, 19, 50 (vol. 9, 373 in the Maurist edition); on the question of authenticity see Bardenhewer, 4, 470; cf. *GUE*, 28, 5 and *EP*, 29, 11 (in the Donatist Church of Hippo).
90. *EP*, 29, 2.
91. *EP*, 29, 2.
92. *EP*, 29, 2.
93. *EP*, 29, 3 and 4.
94. *EP*, 29, 5 and 1 Cor. v.11; vi.9–11; xi.20-2.
95. *EP*, 29, 6; Matt. vii.16; Gal. v.19, 23.
96. *EP*, 29, 7 and Ps. lxxxviii.31-4.
97. *SE*, 252, 4: "quanto periculo nostro".
98. "Majores machinas".
99. Ezek. xxxiii.9.
100. *EP*, 29, 8.
101. "Vel non simili sacrilegio quamvis simili luxu". (*EP*, 29, 9.)
102. Grossi-Gondi, *RQ*, 29, 229 (1915), unjustifiably identifies it with the Basilica Apostolorum on the Via Appia.
103. *EP*, 29, 10 and 1 Pet. iv.1–3.
104. *EP*, 29, 11.
105. *SE*, 252, 4.
106. The word *agapes* occurs in *SE*, 259, 5 and 178, 4.
107. *SE*, 361, 6 and Ecclus. xxx.18.
108. Tob. iv.18.
109. *SE*, 361, 6.
110. *DCD*, 8, 27.
111. Pseudo-Augustine, *SE*, 191, 2 (vol. 5, app. 319 in the Maurist edition).
112. Pseudo-Augustine, *SE*, 191 (vol. 5, app. 318 and 319 in the Maurist edition); nocturns of 22 Feb., lect. 4–6.
113. Second Council of Tours, canon 22 (*MC*, 9, 803).

19. Belief in Miracles

1. *FSA*, 8, 5; for this chapter see J. Zellinger, *Augustinus und die Volksfrömmigkeit*, Munich, 1923.
2. *FSA*, 8, 5.
3. *SE*, 196, 4.
4. *EP*, 55, 37; cf. the "Tolle, lege" of *CF*, 8, 12, 29 and 4, 3, 5.
5. *TJ*, 7, 12.
6. On getting "oracles" out of the Scriptures by opening them at random see Zellinger, 44–5.
7. *SE*, 169, 11 and Joel ii.32.
8. Dölger in *AC*, 5, 248–54 (1936).
9. *EP*, 98, 5; cf. *DCD*, 13, 4.
10. See below.
11. 3rd Council of Carthage, canon 6 (*MC*, 3, 881); *BH*, 4 (*MC*, 3, 919); *CCEA*, 18 (*MC*, 3, 719).
12. Ambrose, *De Excessu Fratr. Sui Satyri*, 1, 43 and 44 (*FP*, 15, 37 and 38): Dölger in *AC*, 5, 232–47 (1936).
13. Marcus Diaconus, *Vita Porphyrii*, 8, 57 (*PG*, 65, 1237; 47 in the Grégoire-Kugener edition); cf. Gregory the Great, *Dial.*, 3, 36 (*PL*, 77, 304).
14. *CJ*, 3, 162.

15. Cyril of Jerusalem, *Cat. Myst.*, 5, 21 and 22 (*FP*, 7, 2 (Bonn, 1935), 109 and 110; *PG*, 33, 1125), repeated word for word by Chrysostom, *Hom.*, 47 (12, 771 in Montfaucon's edition); Gregory Nazianzen, *Orat.*, 18, 10 (*PG*, 35, 997; cf. the texts cited in *FP* from Theodoret of Cyrus and Theodore of Mopsuestia; σταυροειδῶς is to be found also in John Damascene, *De Fide Orthod.*, 4, 13 (*PG*, 94, 1149); *AC*, 3, 231–44 (1923).

16. e.g., Gregory of Nyssa, *Laud. in Sanctos xl Martyres* (*PG*, 46, 784).

17. *EP*, 158, 3 and 10.

18. Cf. Monica's dreams in *CF*, 3, 11, 19; 5, 9, 17; 6, 1 and 13, 23.

19. *CF*, 9, 7, 16 ("per visum aperuisti"); cf. Ambrose, *Ep.*, 22, 1 and 2 (*PL*, 16, 1062 and 1963); *DCD*, 22, 8, 7; *SE*, 318, 1; 286, 5, 4 (the case of the blind man restored to sight, who attached himself to the shrine where the healing occurred); *OCM*, 75–8.

20. *OCM*, 80–2.

21. e.g., *SE*, 308, 5; cf. above.

22. *DCM*, 10, 12–12, 15; 13, 16–16, 20, discusses the knowledge that the dead have of earthly things.

23. *DCM*, 16, 19.

24. Cf. *SE*, 322, 323, 2 (Palladia appears to Augustine himself).

25. *DCM*, 10, 12.

26. *DCM*, 11, 13.

27. *DCM*, 12, 14.

28. *DCM*, 12, 15; Reitzenstein in *Vorträge Bibl. Warburg*, Leipzig, 1924, 2, 62 (he considers the story to be made up); Jülicher in *Hermes*, 54, 94 (1919) (he considers it certainly true).

29. Ps. xxvi.10.

30. Isa. lxiii.16.

31. 4 Kings xxii.18.

32. *DCM*, 13, 16 and 14, 17.

33. Ecclus. xlvi.23; *RE*, 2, 4 and *DDC*, 2, 8, 13 (on the authenticity of Ecclesiasticus); also *DDQS*, 2, q. 4.

34. *DCM*, 15, 18.

35. *DCM*, 16, 19.

36. *DCM*, 16, 20.

37. *DCM*, 17, 21; cf. *EP*, 78, 3.

38. *ENC*, 15, 59 (the play on words "discrimine . . . sine crimine" is untranslatable).

39. *EP*, 158, 1–3.

40. *EP*, 158, 10 and 5–9.

41. *IP*, 65, 17.

42. *DCM*, 17, 21; cf. Ambrose, *Ep.*, 22, 16 (*PL*, 16, 1067).

43. *DCD*, 8, 23 and 26, conclusion.

44. The Baptistery at Naples (Alinari, no. 33748); details of the triumphal arch of S. Maria Maggiore are in *MM*; cf. also Plate 10, the *nubes divina* on the mosaic of Abraham's hospitality in the nave of the same church.

45. Jerome, *Ep.*, 108, 13 (*CSEL*, 55, 323) (Hilberg) (at the graves of John the Baptist, Eliseus and Abdias in Sebaste (which is Samaria)); also, in almost the same strain, Paulinus, *Carm.*, 23, 82–98 (*CSEL*, 30, 197) and *Carm.*, 14, 21–37 (*CSEL*, 30, 46 and 47, ed. Hartel).

46. *DVR*, 25, 47.

47. *SE*, 88, 2, 3.

48. *EP*, 78, 3; cf. *DCD*, 8, 26, 3; *DCM*, 17, 21 and *CF*, 9, 7, 16.

49. *CF*, 9, 7, 16.

50. *RE*, 1, 13, 7.

51. *DCD*, 22, 4, 5 and 11.

52. *DCD*, 22, 7 and 5.

53. *DCD*, 22, 8, 1.

54. *DCD*, 22, 9.

55. Cf. *DDQO*, q. 79, 1–5.

56. *DDQO*, 9, 1–5 and *DCD*, 22, 10; cf. Irenaeus, *Adv. Haer.*, 2, 31, 2 and 3 (*PG*, 7, 824–5).

57. *DCD*, 22, 8, 1, conclusion.

58. *DCD*, 22, 8, 20; cf. *SE*, 319, 6 and 7, 322, and 286, 7; the *libelli* have been compared with the ἰαματα in the temples of Aesculapius (of which a number have been published by Herzog in his *Die Wunderheilungen von Epidauros*, Leipzig, 1931); cf. Kötting, *Peregrinatio Religiosa*, Münster, 1950, 15, *n.* 5; see also Harnack, *PAWP*, 8, Berlin, 1910 (on the arguments); against his view see Delehaye, *AB*, 29, 427–34 (1910); 43, 74–85 (1925), and *OCM*, 124 f. and 130 f.; also *Forsch. und Fortschr.*, 7, 223–4 (1931).
59. *DCD*, 22, 8, 20.
60. *DCD*, 22, 8, 21.
61. *De Miraculis S. Stephani Protomartyris* (vol. 7, app. 25–42 in the Maurist edition, or *PL*, 41, 850 f.).
62. *DCD*, 22, 8, 2–22; cf. Stolz in *TG*, 18, 843–55 (1926).
63. *DCD*, 22, 8, 3.
64. *DCD*, 22, 8, 8.
65. *DCD*, 22, 8, 6.
66. *EP*, and see above; *MEC*, 4, 300.
67. *DCD*, 22, 8, 5.
68. *DCD*, 22, 8, 3.
69. *DCD*, 22, 8, 4.
70. *DCD*, 22, 8, 7.
71. *DCD*, 22, 8, 9.
72. *DCD*, 22, 8, 10.
73. *DCD*, 22, 8, 11.
74. *DCD*, 22, 8, 12 and 14.
75. *DCD*, 22, 8, 13.
76. *DCD*, 22, 8, 15.
77. *DCD*, 22, 8, 16.
78. *DCD*, 22, 8, 17.
79. *DCD*, 22, 8, 18.
80. *DCD*, 22, 8, 19; cf. *SE*, 356, 15.
81. *EP*, 212.
82. *DCD*, 22, 8, 21.
83. *DCD*, 22, 8, 3.
84. *SE*, 322 (the *libellus*), *SE*, 320–4 and *DCD*, 22, 8, 22.
85. *SE*, 322.
86. *DCD*, 22, 8, 22 and *SE*, 322.
87. *SE*, 320.
88. *SE*, 321.
89. *SE*, 322 (*libellus*).
90. Ecclus. iii.11.
91. *SE*, 323, 1–3.
92. Ps. xxxi.5.
93. *SE*, 323, conclusion.
94. *SE*, 324.
95. *DCD*, 22, 11, 3; cf. 10, 16.
96. *DCD*, 10, 16, 2.
97. Cf. *DCD*, 21, 8, 1–4.
98. *DCD*, 21, 6.
99. *DCD*, 21, 4–8.
100. *DCD*, 14, 24.
101. *DCD*, 21, 4, 1.
102. John xxi.22; cf. Hennecke, *Handbuch z. d. ntl. Apokryphen*, Tübingen, 1914, 543 and M. R. James, *The Apocryphal New Testament*, Oxford, 1926, 268–70.
103. *TJ*, 124, 2 and 3; John xxi.20–3.
104. *DCD*, 21, 7, 1 conclusion and 2.
105. *IP*, 101, 1, 8.
106. *DCD*, 22, 10.
107. *DCD*, 21, 3, 8, 21 and *EP*, 162, 9.
108. *Essais*, bk. i, ch. 26.

EPILOGUE

20. AUGUSTINE IN OUR OWN DAY

1. *DCD*, 10, 27; *EER*, 3; cf. *EP*, 258, 5; Prüm in *Scholastik*, 4, 54–7 (1929). On Augustine's place in the history of culture see Reitzenstein, "Augustinus als antiker und als mittelalterlicher Mensch", in *Vorträge Bibl. Warburg*, Leipzig, 2, 1922–3, 1934, 24–65; H. I. Marrou, *S. Augustin et la fin de la culture antique*, Paris, 1938; also the extremely interesting second edition of 1949 with the postscript *Retractatio*, in which Marrou gives less emphasis to the *fin de l'antique* in Augustine's performance in order to bring out more the creative beginning of the Middle Ages. See also P. Courcelle, *Les Lettres grecques en occident, de Macrobe à Cassiodore*, Paris, 1943, 137–209; E. K. Rand, *Founders of the Middle Ages*, Cambridge (Mass.), 1929, 251–84 (St. Augustine and Dante).

2. *RE*, 1, 11, 4 (the world-soul); cf. *DCD*, 23, 7 and 15, 23; *DDQO*, 83, q. 79, 1; *IP*, 145, 5 (*corpus angelicum*); *DGL*, 2, 28.

3. Étienne Gilson, *Introduction à l'étude de S. Augustin*, Paris, 1929, 274.

4. John xviii.13. Cf. *DO*, 1, 11, 32 and *RE*, 1, 3, 2.

5. *DCD*, 12, 27, 14, 28.

6. *Pensées* (p. 283 in the edition of Brunschvicq).

7. *CF*, 7, 17, 23; 10, 6, 9.

8. Tillemont (*Mémoires pour servir à l'histoire ecclésiastique des six premiers siècles*, vol. 13, 54) does not deal with the question; cf. Davids in *MA*, 242 f.; Romano Guardini, *Die Bekehrung des hl. Augustinus*, Leipzig, 1935, 174 f.

9. *CF*, 5, 13, 23.

10. *CF*, 6, 3, 3 and 4.

11. *CF*, 5, 13, 23.

12. *CF*, 6, 3, 3.

13. *CF*, 6, 11, 18 and *SO*, 2, 14, 26.

14. *CF*, 9, 5, 13.

15. *EP*, 36, 14–32; cf. *EP*, 54, 2, 3.

16. *CF*, 8, 2, 3, 5, 10.

17. *EP*, 147, 23, 25.

18. *EP*, 54, 2, 3.

19. *DDC*, 4; cf. above.

20. *DGC*, 43, 47 and 44, 48; *CJ*, 1, 3, 10; 2, 4–10 *passim*; *EP*, 147, 7, 19; 16, 39 and 23, 52; 75, 6, 20; 148, 3, 12 and 1, 6. There are quotations in his letters: *EP*, 82, 2, 21 and 3, 24; 31, 8; 147, 6, 17 and 18.

21. *VA*, 27.

22. Ps. lxxxiii.6 (in Ps. lxxxiii.16 he reads *ascensus*); cf. *CF*, 13, 9, 10; the seven degrees are in *DDC*, 2, 7, 9–11, and also in his youthful work *De Quant. Anim.*, 33, 70–6.

23. *RE*, 2, 18; 2, 55; *DA*, 3, 9, 12; elsewhere he accepts a *baptisma deputatum* or baptism of blood; cf. *DDQO*, q. 62; *DB*, 4, 22; *DA*, 1, 9, 11; *QIH*, 3, 84.

24. *SE*, 294, 1 and 5 f.

25. *DLA*, 3, 23, 66; on the other side see *EP*, 166, 23 (that is, *coarctor*), *DDP*, 12, 30; *SE*, 294; *CJ*, 3, 199; *ENC*, 93 (*mitissima poena*).

26. *SE*, 27, 4: "Melior est enim fidelis ignorantia quam temeraria scientia."

27. *DSV*, 14, 14; cf. *EP*, 157, 4, 36 and 37.

28. Jerome, *Ep. ad Riparium*, 109, 1 (*CSEL*, 55, 352), and above all *C. Vigilant.*; see *EHC*, 3, 152.

29. *SE*, 355, 1, 2.

30. "Nihil fiat immaniter, nihil inhumaniter."

31. *DT*, 4, 18, 24; cf. ibid., 4, 20, 28.

32. *DT*, 4, 18, 24 and John xvii.3.

33. Ps. lxxxiv.13.

34. *IP*, 138, 15 and Ps. cxxxviii.12; the word-play on *transiliens* (sc. *idithun*) refers to *IP*, 76, 1–3.

35. Tit. ii.11; iii.4.

36. *CF*, 10, 35, 54.

37. Cf. the few very abstract lines "in praise of a wax candle" (a Paschal candle?) in *DCD*, 15, 22.
38. *DCD*, 8, 5 and 8, conclusion; cf. 8, 1 and *RE*, 1, 3, 2.
39. *IP*, 140, 19; cf. Ps. cxl.6 (Augustine reads: "... absorpti sunt juxta petram iudices eorum").
40. *DDC*, 2, 25, 38–42, 63, conclusion.
41. *DCE*, 1, 5, 8 and *CFA*, 22, 52 (Rachel and Leah); *GUE*, 29; *SE*, 103, 104, 169, 14, 17; 179, 3–6; 255, 6 (Martha and Mary).
42. *DDC*, 1, 39, 43; cf. 1 Cor. xiii.8 and 13.
43. *DT*, 15, 27, 49.
44. *EP*, 167, 3, 11; *DCD*, 14, 28; *ENC*, 1, 1 and 2; *DT*, 14, 1, 1 ("pietas est sapientia"); Job. xxviii.28.
45. *Five Stages of Greek Religion*, Oxford, 1930, 2.
46. *SO*, 1, 1, 2; cf. *DCD*, 11, 18.
47. Henri Bremond.
48. *IP*, 118, 12, 3; 127, 8; 53, 10; 52, 8.
49. *SE*, 141, 4.
50. On martyrdom see *IP*, 67, 36; also *SE*, 159, 7, 8; *IP*, 130, 14; 31, 2, 5; 41, 12 (humility); cf. *EP*, 118, 17 and *CF*, 7, 18 f. (on the humility of Christ).
51. *SE*, 34, 4, 7 and Prov. xiii.26; cf. Ep. cix.2 (Severus).
52. *SE*, 163, 1: "Deambulat autem in nobis praesentia majestatis, si latitudinem invenerit caritatis."
53. Phil. iii.20.
54. 1 Cor. xv.47; viii.1; Matt. xv.13.

LIST OF ABBREVIATIONS FOR MAIN WORKS REFERRED TO

AB	Analecta Bollandiana
AC	Antiquité chrétienne
AEHG	Annales de l'École des hautes études de Gand
AFM	De Actis cum Felice Manichaeo
AGM	Angelicum
AH	Dreves, Analecta Hymnica
AJA	American Journal of Archaeology
AJP	American Journal of Philology
ALP	Contra Adversarium Legis et Prophetarum
AS	Acta Sanctorum
AVK	Dreves, Aurelius Augustinus, der Vater des Kirchengesanges, Freiburg, 1893
BC	Breviculus Collationis
BGCP	Weyman, Beiträge zur Geschichte der christlich-lateinischen Poesie, Munich, 1926
BH	Breviarium Hipponense
BLE	Bulletin de littérature ecclésiastique
BLO	Ballerini, Sancti Leonis Magni Opera
BSAF	Bulletin de la Société des antiquaires de France
BZ	Byzantinische Zeitschrift
CA	Contra Academicos
CAIB	Compte-rendu de l'Académie des inscriptions et de belles-lettres
CAM	Contra Adimantum Manichaei Discipulum Liber Unus
CAS	Bibliotheca Casinensis
CC	Collatio Carthaginensis
CCEA	Codex Canonum Ecclesiae Africanae
CCM	Collatio cum Maximino Arianorum Episcopo
CCR	Contra Cresconius
CEP	Contra Epistolam Parmeniani Libri Tres
CF	Confessiones
CFA	Contra Faustum Manichaeum Libri Triginta Tres
CG	Contra Gaudentium Donatistam Episcopum Libri Duo
CIL	Corpus Inscriptionum Latinarum
CJ	Contra Secundam Juliani Responsionem Imperfectum Opus
CL	Caileau and Saintyves, Sancti Aurelii Augustini Sermones Inediti
CM	Contra Maximinum Arianum Libri Duo
CSEL	Corpus Scriptorum Ecclesiasticorum Latinorum
CTM	Mommsen and Meyer, Codex Theodosianus
DA	De Anima et ejus Origine Libri Quatuor
DAA	De Duabus Animabus contra Adimantum
DAC	De Agone Christiano
DACL	Dictionnaire d'archéologie chrétienne et de liturgie
DB	De Baptismo
DBC	De Bono Conjugali Liber Unus
DBV	De Bono Viduitatis Liber seu Epistola ad Julianam Viduam
DBVA	De Beata Vita
DCA	De Conjugiis Adulterinis Libri Duo
DCD	De Civitate Dei
DCE	De Consensu Evangelistarum Libri Quatuor
DCG	De Correptione et Gratia, ad Valentinum et cum illo Monachos Hadrumeticos
DCM	De Cura Pro Mortuis Gerenda
DCR	De Catechizandis Rudibus
DDC	De Doctrina Christiana
DDD	De Divinatione Daemonum
DDP	De Dono Perseverantiae
DDPQ	De Octo Dulcitii Quaestionibus
DDQO	De Diversis Quaestionibus LXXXIII Liber Unus
DDQS	De Diversis Quaestionibus ad Simplicianum Libri Duo
DEP	De Duas Epistolas Pelagianorum
DFO	De Fide et Operibus Liber Unus
DFS	De Fide et Symbolo
DGC	De Gratia Christi et de Peccato Originali, contra Pelagianum et Coelestinum, Libri Duo

DGL	*De Genesi at Litteram Libri Duodecim*
DGM	*De Genesi contra Manichaeos Libri Duo*
DH	*De Haeresibus*
DHGE	*Dictionnaire d'histoire et de géographie ecclésiastique*
DLA	*De Libero Arbitrio*
DM	*De Magistro*
DME	*De Moribus Ecclesiae Catholicae et de Moribus Manichaeorum Libri Duo*
DMO	*De Mendacio*
DNB	*De Natura Boni*
DNC	*De Nuptiis et Concupiscentia ad Valerium Libri Duo*
DNG	*De Natura et Gratia, ad Timasium et Jacobum, contra Pelagium, Liber Unus*
DO	*De Ordine*
DOM	*De Opere Monachorum*
DPC	*Ad Donatistas Post Collationum*
DPMR	*De Peccatorum Meritis et Remissione et de Baptismo Parvulorum, ad Marcellinum, Libri Tres*
DPS	*De Praedestinatione Sanctorum Liber ad Prosperum et Hilarium Primus*
DSC	*De Symbolo ad Catechumenos*
DSD	*De Schismate Donatistarum*
DSI	Denis, *Sancti Aurelii Augustini Sermones Inediti*
DSV	*De Sancta Virginitate*
DT	*De Trinitate Libri Quindecim*
DTC	*Dictionnaire de théologie catholique*
DUC	*De Utilitate Credendi*
DUJ	*De Utilitate Jejunii*
DVB	*De Vita Beata*
DVR	*De Vera Religione*
EEG	*Expositio Epistolae ad Galatas*
EER	*Epistolae ad Romanos Inchoata Expositio*
EF	*Contra Epistolam Manichaei quam Vocant Fundamenti Liber Unus*
EHC	Duchesne, *The Early History of the Church*, London, 1931
EL	*Ephemerides Liturgicae*
ENC	*Enchiridion ad Laurentium sive De Fide, Spe et Caritate Liber Unus*
EP	*Epistolae*
FM	*Acta seu Disputatio contra Fortunatus Manichaeus, Liber Unus*
FP	*Florilegium Patristicum*
FSA	Frangipane, *Sancti Aurelii Augustini Hipponensis Episcopi Sermones X*
GA	Gsell, *Atlas archéologique de l'Algérie*, Paris, 1902–11
GCS	*Die griechischen christlichen Schriftsteller der ersten drei Jahrhunderten*
GE	*De Gestis cum Emerito*
GI	Gsell, *Inscriptions latines de l'Algérie*, Paris, 1922
GM	*Gregorianum*
GMA	Gsell, *Les Monuments antiques de l'Algérie*, Paris, 1901
GUE	*Codex Guelferbytanus 4096*
GZ	*Gesta apud Zenophilum*
HL	Monceaux, *Histoire littéraire de l'Afrique chrétienne*, Paris, 1912–13
HTR	*Harvard Theological Review*
ICR	De Rossi, *Inscriptiones Christianae Urbis Romae*
IEJ	*In Epistolam I Johannis Tractatus*
ILVC	Diehl, *Inscriptiones Latinae Christianae Veteres*
IP	*Enarrationes in Psalmos*
JFL	*Jahrbuch für Liturgiewissenschaft*
JP	*Contra Julianum Haeresis Pelagianae Defensorum Libri Sex*
JTS	*Journal of Theological Studies*
LG	Lietzmann, *Geschichte der alten Kirche*, Berlin, 1938
LP	*Contra Litteras Petiliani Donatistae Cirtensi Episcopi Libri Tres*
LPE	Lietzmann, *Petrus und Paulus in Rom*, Berlin-Leipzig, 1927
LTK	*Lexikon für Theologie und Kirche*
MA	*Miscellanea Agostiniana*
MAH	*Mélanges de l'archéologie et d'histoire*
MC	Mansi, *Sacrorum Conciliorum Nova et Amplissima Collectio*
MEC	Monceaux, *L'Épigraphie chrétienne de l'Afrique*, Paris, 1907
MEQ	Monceaux, "Enquête sur l'épigraphie chrétienne d'Afrique", *Revue archéologique*, 1903–6.

MKR	Wilpert, *Malereien der Katakomben Roms*, Freiburg, 1903
MM	Wilpert, *Die römischen Mosaiken und Malereien*, Freiburg, 1916
MO	Morin, *Sancti Augustini Sermones post Maurinos Reperti* (*Miscellanea Agostiniana*, 1)
MPB	Mai, *Novae Patrum Bibliothecae*
MYE	*Mnemosyne*
NOA	*De Anima et ejus Origine contra Vincentium Victorem Libri Quatuor*
OC	*Oriens Christianus*
OCM	Delehaye, *Les Origines du culte des martyres*, Brussels, 1933
OPD	Optatus of Milevis, *Contra Parmenianum Donatistam*
OPO	*Ad Orosium contra Priscillianistas et Origenistas Liber Unus*
PAWP	*Sitzungsberichte, Preussischen Akademie der Wissenschaften, Philologische-historische Klasse*
PCPD	*Psalmus contra Partem Donati*
PG	Migne, *Patrologia Graeca*
PL	Migne, *Patrologia Latina*
QE	*Quaestionum Evangeliorum Libri Duo*
QIH	*Quaestiones in Heptateuchum libri Duo*
QIM	*Quaestiones Septemdecim in Evangelium Secundum Mattheum*
RA	*Revue archéologique*
RAC	*Rivista di archeologia Cristiana*
RB	*Revue bénédictine*
RBA	De Rossi, *Bulletino di archeologia cristiana*
RE	*Retractationes*
REA	*Revue des études anciennes*
RHE	*Revue d'histoire ecclésiastique*
RHI	*Revue historique*
RHPR	*Revue d'histoire et de philosophie religeuses*
RHR	*Revue de l'histoire des religions*
RIT	*Revue internationale de théologie*
RK	Styger, *Römischer Katakomben*, Berlin, 1933
RM	Styger, *Römische Märtyrergrüfte*, Berlin, 1935
RMU	*Rheinisches Museum für Philologie*
RP	*Revue de philologie*
RQ	*Römische Quartalschrift*
RQH	*Revue des questions historiques*
RRS	De Rossi, *Roma Sotteranea*
RSPT	*Revue des sciences philosophiques et théologiques*
RSR	*Recherches de science religieuse*
SA	*Contra Sermonum Arianorum Liber Unus*
SC	*Scuola Cattolica*
SCA	Wilpert, *I Sarcofagi cristiani antichi*, Rome, 1930
SDM	*De Sermone Domini in Monte*
SE	*Sermones*
SGD	Salvianus, *De Gubernatione Dei*
SL	*De Spiritu et Littera Liber Unus*
SM	*Contra Secundinum Manichaeum Liber Unus*
SO	*Soliloquia*
SP	*Speculum*
SSA	Mohrmann, *Die altchristlichen Sondersprache in den Sermones des hl. Augustin*, Nijmegen, 1932
TAJ	*Tractatus Adversus Judaeos*
TEJ	*In Epistolam Joannis Tractatus Decem*
TG	*Theologie und Glaube*
TJ	*In Evangelium Joannis Tractatus Centum Viginti Quatuor*
TQ	*Theologische Quartalschrift*
TU	*Texte und Untersuchungen*
UE	*De Urbis Excidio*
VA	Possidius, *Vita Augustini*
VHP	Victor Vitensis, *Historia Persecutionis Africae Provinciae*
WS	*Sermones Wilmartianos*
ZKG	*Zeitschrift für Kirchengeschichte*
ZKT	*Zeitschrift für katholische Theologie*
ZNW	*Zeitschrift für die neutestamentliche Wissenschaft*
ZOG	*Zeitschrift für die österreichischen Gymnasien*

INDEX

ABELITES, 119, 134
Abgar of Edessa, 251
Abora, Bishop of, 84
abortion, 189-90
Abraham's sacrifice, picture of, 324
absolution, general, 152, 386
Abundantias, 229
Académie française, 422
acclamations (in church), 270, 271, 272, 325-6, 339, 414, 428, 429, 430. See also Augustine, Sermons of, congregation's reactions to
Adam and Eve, paintings of, 318-19
Adam, name of, 425
Addas Adimantus, 118, 312
Adeodatus (son of Augustine), 3, 208, 328
Admonition and Grace, see Augustine, writings of
adornment, feminine, Augustine on, 183
adultery, Augustine on, 180-3
Aesculapius, temples of, 496, 531, 543
aesthetics, 319, 320
Aetheria, 6
Aetius, 418
African Church, xvi, xvii, xviii, 10, 11, 12, 231, 242, 298, 390, 517, 568, 575
saints of, 482
Against Cresconius, Against Faustus the Manichee, Against the Letter of Parmenianus, Against the Letters of Petilianus, Against the Pars Donati, see Augustine, writings of
Agnes, St., 472, 473, 476, 494
Alaric, 148, 159, 161
Albina, 14, 143, 145, 146, 153, 245
Augustine's letter to, 146-7
Albinus (acolyte), 243
Albinus, Pontifex Maximus, 35
Alexander Severus, 318
Allais, Mlle, xxiii
allegory, 73, 301-2, 304, 346, 405, 416, 429, 432, 439, 447, 452, 563, 586. See also Bible, allegorical interpretation of
almsgiving, 65, 137, 148, 167, 179, 386, 387
alphabetical psalm (Augustine's, against Donatists), 104-9, 332, 425
Alypius, xvii, 11, 14, 49, 90, 101, 120, 143, 144, 145, 146, 194, 207, 208, 209, 219,

Alypius, *contd.*
242, 244, 249, 328, 359, 416, 495, 520, 544
Ambrose, St., xv, 4, 22, 32, 110, 120, 124, 131, 143, 183, 199, 207, 221, 235, 238, 241, 243, 258, 261, 266, 273, 287, 288, 300, 312, 313, 317, 326, 328, 329, 332, 349, 361, 366, 369, 406, 409, 412, 413, 442, 445, 449, 476, 481, 484-5, 494, 503, 515, 516, 530, 532, 536, 537, 540, 541, 562, 570-2
hymns of, 328-31
portrait of, 235
amphitheatre (at Hippo), 18, 53
amphitheatres, 48, 157
size of, 50
amulets, 58, 59
angels, 33, 71, 72, 534, 535-6, 536-8, 543, 554, 564, 583
animal-baiting, 48-9
Anthony of Egypt, St., xxi, 207, 212
Antiochus of Ptolemais, 418
Antonius, 230-1, 233
"apes of God", demons as, 55, 59
Apiarius, 231
Appollonius of Tyana, Augustine on, 34
Apringius, 96, 192, 245, 246
Apuleius, Augustine on, 29, 34-5
Aquinas, St. Thomas, 124, 282, 444, 578
architecture, 321, 582
Arianism, Arians, 110, 118, 119-23, 159, 194, 329, 330, 360, 425, 530, 541, 568
Augustine's debates with, 120-3
Aristotle, 580
Arnauld, 4, 418, 576
Arnauld, Angélique, 221
Arnobius, 130
art, Christian, 319, 322, 582
plastic, Augustine's view on, 318-20, 321. See also Church art and Pictures, religious, Augustine's views on
Ascension, Augustine's verse on, 425-6
asceticism, ascetics, 125, 178, 207, 208, 209, 213, 215, 217-19, 382, 494, 568
Asterius of Amaseia, 322, 492, 510, 511
astrologer (converted), 64
astrologers, astrology, 47, 56, 57, 60-7, 69, 70, 72, 73, 384

astrologers, astrology, *contd.*
  Augustine on, 57, 60–7. See also Horoscopes, Stars, influence of
asylum, right of, 136, 159, 263–5
Athanasius, St., 332, 333
Attis, 55
audientes, 357
Augustine, St., as arbitrator, 259–67
  as preacher, 12–13, 130, 412–52. See also Sermons of
  as rigorist, 572–81
  baptism of, 149, 349, 350, 571
  church-building by, 239–40
  consecrated bishop, 9, 272
  convent founded by, 221
  death of, 273–4
  diet of, 238–9
  dress of, 25, 235–6, 238, 317
  education of, 34, 133–4
  elected priest, 4, 6
  father of, see Patricius
  friendships of, 241–7
  health of, 14, 236–7
  imputations against, 9, 112
  journeyings of, 11, 12, 236, 241
  letters of, xix, 7–8, 33, 34, 35–6, 41, 86, 94, 96, 99, 104, 111, 115, 116, 118, 119–20, 122, 125, 129, 141, 146–7, 151, 155–6, 158, 163, 165–8, 177, 181, 194, 213, 214, 215, 221, 222, 226, 231–2, 236, 238, 242, 243, 247–55, 265–7, 341, 360, 516–19
  literary output of, 237–8
  literary style of, 237, 248–9, 255, 258
  monasteries founded by, 199 ff., 208, 210, 233, 234
  mother of, see Monica, St.
  personal appearance of, 25, 236
  poverty of, 238
  representation of, 236
  seminary founded by, 200, 234
  sermons of, xix, 6, 7, 8, 12, 13, 14, 28, 30, 38, 39, 48, 49, 52, 53–4, 55, 73, 77, 84, 94, 103–4, 112, 116–17, 119, 124, 129, 130, 133, 135–6, 138, 140–3, 149, 150, 152–3, 157, 159–61, 170, 172–5, 178, 185, 190–1, 201–3, 214, 232, 237, 240, 256–7, 260, 263, 264, 266, 284, 323, 340, 341, 344–5, 360, 362, 369, 371–3, 391–7, 405, 412–52, 476, 485, 487–8, 514–15, 521–3, 540, 551, 575, 580
    congregation's reactions to, 138, 140, 143, 270–2, 339–40, 414, 421, 427–432, 522
  sermons: style of, 28, 413, 414, 416, 417–33, 446–7; word-play in, 147, 424–6, 446, 478. See also Preacher, Augustine as
  sisters of, 20, 221, 401

Augustine, St., *contd.*
  son of, see Adeodatus
  working methods of, 238, 267, 414
  writings of: *Admonition and Grace*, 125
    Against Cresconius, 111
    Against Faustus the Manichean, 278, 282, 314, 315
    Against the Letter of Parmeianus, 111
    Against the Letters of Petilianus, 111
    Against the Pars Donati, 111
    Against the Two Letters of the Pelagians, 11
    Admonition and Grace, 125
    Alphabetical Psalm, 104–9, 332, 425
    Breviculus Collationis, 99
    Christian Knowledge, 59, 69, 344, 405–11, 413, 443, 472, 580
    Christian's Battle, The, 258
    City of God, The, 22, 43, 44, 68, 70, 75, 157, 162, 236, 246, 252, 261, 267, 277, 336, 416, 427, 432, 434, 488, 489, 490, 495, 525, 537, 541, 549, 554, 556, 557, 566, 579
    Commentary on Genesis Written Against the Manichees, 209
    Confessions, xv, 3, 112, 132, 244, 249, 251, 322, 326, 333, 343, 349, 531, 570, 571
    Contemplation of God, The, 246
    Customs of the Catholic Church and the Customs of the Manichees, 178, 208, 209, 233
    Demons' Art of Prophecy, The, 68
    Enarrationes in Psalmos, 416, 417, 441, 447
    Excellence of Widowhood, The, 187, 246
    Faith, Hope and Love (Handbook for Laurentius), 246, 251, 434
    Faith and Works, 181
    Faith in Things Unseen, 251
    Gift of Steadfastness, The, 125
    Good in Marriage, The, 187
    Grace and Free Will, 125
    Grace of Christ, The, 147
    Handbook for Laurentius (Faith, Hope and Love), 246, 251, 434
    Instruction for Beginners, 59, 244, 353, 405, 434, 445, 453–67
    Mirror, The, 258
    On Baptism, 111, 246, 286, 310, 349
    On the Happy Life, 246
    On Holy Virginity, 187
    On the Letter and the Spirit, 246
    On Marriage and Desire, 189, 246, 252
    On Music, 209, 320, 334
    On the Quantity of the Soul, 5
    On the Trinity, xvii, 119, 416
    On the True Religion, 209
    On the Uses of Faith, 6, 246
    On the Work of Monks, 211, 487

INDEX 663

Augustine, St., writings of, *contd.*
  Original Sin, 147
  Our Duty to Care for the Dead, 532
  Predestination of the Saints, The, 125
  Retractations, 13, 238, 277, 319, 474, 541, 565, 573
  Schism of the Donatists, The, 82
  Soliloquies, 5, 215, 216, 571
  Teacher, The, 3, 209
  To the Donatists after the Conference, 99
  True Faith, The, 7
  True Worship of God, The, 32
Aurelius, Bishop of Carthage, 8–11, 13, 14, 56, 85, 87, 119, 202, 209–10, 211, 219, 226, 229, 242, 252, 265, 415, 416, 453, 515, 518, 519, 525, 545
  Augustine's letter to (Letter 22), 516–19
Ausonius, 162, 218, 580
authors, classical, 75, 134, 319, 436, 561–2, 579–80
Auxentius, Bishop, 120
Auxilius of Nurco, Bishop, 265
avarice, 139, 140, 145, 146, 424
Avvakum, Archpriest, 83

BABYLAS, 38
Bagai, Bishop of, 88, 89
Balzac, 388
baptism, 21, 47, 280, 282, 283, 284, 285, 286, 295, 300, 307–11, 315, 316, 323, 345, 347–58, 361–73, 444, 463, 542
  ceremony of, 337, 349, 361–73
  deferring of, 29, 148–51, 166, 181, 182, 197, 348, 350, 356, 357. Augustine's sermons on, 149–51, 357; letters on, 151
  emergency, 350, 351, 352
  infant, 308–9, 310, 311, 350–1. Augustine's letter on, 308–9
  necessity of, for salvation, 350, 352, 572–3
baptisteries, 21, 288, 365, 368: octagonal, 288
baptistery at Hippo, 21
barbarians, 12, 153, 154, 157, 163, 194
Barnabas (priest), 205
Basil, St., 177
Bassus the Syrian, 548
baths, public, 17, 18, 51, 154–5, 177, 224, 321, 361, 367
Baudelaire, 75, 153, 303
beauty (Augustine's attitude to), 73, 319, 320, 321, 322, 567, 576, 579
Benedict, St., 210, 216, 220, 225
Berbers, 28, 45, 194, 241, 389–90, 568
Bernard of Clairvaux, St., xxi, 305, 435, 576
Bertrand, xv
Bible, 35, 44, 120, 285–7, 291–3, 297, 300–2, 304–5, 313, 314, 325, 330, 333, 341–6, 353, 356, 378, 379, 405–11, 414, 415, 420, 432, 433, 435, 439–41, 455, 457, 463, 525, 531–2, 536, 538, 542, 562,

Bible, *contd.*
  565, 569, 570, 573, 575, 576, 577, 578, 580, 581, 582, 583, 589
  allegorical interpretation of, 356, 442–3, 444, 445–9, 454, 459, 562, 587
  popular knowledge of, 133, 156, 341, 407, 417, 428, 429, 454, 580, 585
bishops, multiplicity of, 10–11
bishop, office of: Augustine on, 14–15, 255–8
birrus, 235
Blesilla, 209
"Blood Day", 55
Boethius, 579, 581
Bonaventure, St., 435
Bône, 16–17
Boniface, Bishop: Augustine's letter to, 308–9, 311
Boniface, Count, 19, 96, 122, 163, 194, 202, 243, 246, 251
Boniface, Pope, 11, 230, 231
Bossuet, xvii, xxi, 94, 128, 441, 573, 576
Bourdaloue, 180
Breviculus Collationis, see Augustine, writings of
Brom, Professor, xxii
Bulla Regia, sermon at, 53–4
burial *ad sanctos*, 492–7

CAECILIANUS, BISHOP OF CARTHAGE, 79, 86, 90, 93, 110
Caecilianus, Count, 151, 193, 246, 265
Caesaria, "great row" at, 410, 451
Caesarius of Arles, St., 224, 327, 417, 446
Calama, pagan riots, at, 40–2
Calvin, 124, 297, 319, 320, 573, 575, 576
Candidianus, 495
Cappodocia, "ten accursed children of", 549–53
Carpocratians, 318
Carthage, xv, xvi, 11, 12, 13, 19, 37, 38, 47, 48, 51–3, 56, 57, 76, 79, 85, 87–8, 99, 112, 117, 119, 124, 134, 157, 170, 171, 172, 178, 190, 191, 192, 193, 209, 212, 225, 227, 228, 229, 231, 240, 245, 262, 263, 279, 324, 327, 341, 361, 406, 413, 415, 417, 427, 429, 447, 477, 479, 482, 491, 507, 509, 514, 518, 544, 548, 573
  Conference of, 90–3, 99, 117, 170, 192, 242. Augustine on, 91–2
  Synod of, 90
  theatre at, 51–53
Cassian, 36
Cassiodorus, 216, 417
Castorius, 98
casuistry, 155, 437
casula, 235
Casulanus, Augustine's letter to, 294, 296, 298, 571
catacombs, 493, 494, 504, 505, 506, 514

catechism, xviii, 244, 453–67, 569. See also *Instruction for Beginners*, under Augustine, writings of
catechists, 455–8
catechumenate, catechumens, 59, 148–51, 280, 348, 350, 352–7, 365, 370, 382, 389, 397, 399, 428, 453–5. Augustine's sermon on, 357
Cato, 60
Celer, 115
Celestine, Pope St., 116, 231, 248, 328
Celsus, 77
cenobites, 208
Ceretius, Bishop: Augustine's letter to, 118–19
cervulum facere, 54–5
chariot-racing, 50
charity, Augustine on, 437–8, 579, 589
chastity, 185, 215
Chesterton, G. K., 303–4
Chiliasts, 288
childlessness, 188–9
children, exposure of, 189
children, unbaptized: fate of, 573
children, vocations of, 214–15
Christ as the "way", Augustine's sermon on, 588–9
Christ, divinity of, 121
Christian Knowledge, see Augustine, writings of
Christians, exemplary, 191–3
Christianity, effects of, 190–8, 583–4
opposition to, 31–4
Christians, nominal, 190–1, 382, 466
Christmas, 292, 293, 485
Chrysostom, St. John, 133, 539
church art, Augustine's views on, 317–20, 575
church, attendance at, 49, 50, 53–4, 55, 169–77
conduct in, 168–9, 171–2
Church, Augustine's apostrophe to the, 197–8
ban of, 294, 383, 384, 385, 387
benefactions to, 201–5
Church, unity of, xvii, 77, 82, 126–7, 162, 282–6, 293, 381, 569
church-building, Augustine on, 240
churches, appearance of, 24–5
rural, 27, 227
Cicero, 62, 134, 151, 166, 241, 248, 253, 405, 406, 408, 562
cilicia, 236
Cincinnatus, 216
Circumcellions, 12, 28, 42, 82–3, 88, 93, 94, 95, 102–3, 107, 126, 141
attacks by, 82–3, 88, 89, 114, 115. See also Donatists
circus, 50, 53, 466
Cirta, 19, 83, 98, 111, 112, 242, 265, 317
City of God, The. See Augustine, writings of

City of God, the, 163, 538, 578
civilization, secular, Augustine's views on, 575–6, 584, 589
clarity, 408, 409, 421
Classicianus, Count, 265
Claudel, Paul, 449
Clement of Alexandria, 443
clergy, 198–234
country, 227–9
criticism of, 232
educational standards of, 226–8, 366, 367
election of, 4, 143–7, 225
monastic, 210
renunciation of property among, 200–6
respect for, 226, 233
scandals among, 201, 226, 228–33
clerical office, Augustine on, 7–8, 233–4
Codex Canonum Ecclesiae Africanae, 569
coloni, 26, 111, 227, 262
Communion, daily, 177, 294, 295
house, 176, 177, 529
method of giving, 401–2, 572
community, life in, 199–203, 206, 208, 210
competentes, 8, 148, 181–2, 280, 284, 348, 356–61, 369, 460, 569
concubines, 181, 185, 382
confession, auricular, beginnings of, 260, 383–5, 387
Confessions, see Augustine, writings of
confirmation, 21, 354, 369
congregation, Augustine's, character of, 6, 29, 132
consecration (at Mass), form of, 378–9
Consentius, 255
consignatio, 368
Constantine, Emperor, 29, 39, 71, 83, 161, 509
Constantinople, vision at, 149
Constantius, Emperor, 81, 83, 84
continence (in marriage), 177–9, 180, 185, 186, 187, 189, 200, 216, 250, 253, 358
continentes, 6, 19–20, 143, 178, 179, 187, 191, 200, 216, 217, 220, 234
convents, see Nunneries
conversions, pagan, motives behind, 30–1
Council of Milevis, 226, 228
Council of Trent, 572, 577
councils, 8, 11, 13, 19, 242, 529
Cresconius, 111, 112
criniti, 211
Crispinus, 95, 110–11
Cross, the, 289–91
sign of the, 72, 280, 340, 354–5, 357
Cuicul, 20
cults, pagan, 37, 46, 69, 74, 75, 279, 538
culture, literary, 134
cultus, 277–402
Curma, 533–4
customs, local, Augustine on, 295–6, 297, 298, 337

INDEX

Customs of the Catholic Church and the Customs of the Manichees, The, see Augustine, writings of

Cyprian, St., 19, 49, 52, 59, 81, 111, 176, 183, 232, 240, 286, 307, 317, 351, 360, 406, 409, 471, 476, 477, 489, 491, 506, 507, 509, 514, 562, 571

Cyril of Jerusalem, St., 349, 460, 530

DANTE, 75, 554, 564

Darius, Count, Augustine's correspondence with, 251, 252

days of week, names of, 74

De Labriolle, 249

De Maistre, 557

De Rancé, 576

Dea Coelestis, 57, 279, 290

dead, honouring of, Augustine's views on, 495–7, 516, 517–20
 prayers for the, 401, 474
 feasts for, see Feasts for the dead

death, intermediate state after, 473–4
 penalty for heresy: Augustine on, 96, 100

Delehaye, 33, 491

Demetrias, 219, 220, 245

demons, devils, 39, 41, 55, 56, 59, 67–75, 95, 153, 288, 289, 362, 381, 384, 472, 535, 536, 537, 538, 540, 543, 545, 546, 550, 553, 554, 563, 564, 583, 586

demons, Augustine on, 68–9, 70–5

"Deo laudes" (of Donatists), 81, 83, 482

Deogratias, 35, 59, 244, 356, 453, 455, 461, 569
 Instruction for Beginners written for, 356, 453–67

devotion, popular, xix, 471, 472, 487, 497, 574, 575

Dickens, Charles, 414

Didache, 284–5

Diocletian, 80, 444, 479

Dioscuros, Augustine's letter to, 253

Dioscuros (physician), 363

discipline of secrecy, 35, 312, 349, 354, 359, 374, 460

disinheritance of family (in favour of Church), 201–2, 204–5

divorce, 181, 182, 184, 186, 352

"Dominus legem dat", representations of, 317–18

Donatists, xx, 4, 10, 13, 14, 20, 21, 27, 28, 41, 42, 43, 66, 79–117, 119, 122, 125–8, 131, 134, 140, 163, 192, 210, 228, 229, 230, 231, 239, 244, 255, 257, 258, 269, 282, 283, 311, 325, 332, 358, 360, 384, 425, 428, 482, 491, 492, 520, 524, 545
 Augustine's alphabetical psalm against, see Augustine, writings of
 Augustine's public debates with, 90–3, 99, 100–1, 110, 117, 170, 192, 242

Donatists, *contd.*
 forcible conversion of, 84–5, 89, 93–7, 100, 103, 113, 116, 141
 laws against, 84, 85, 86, 89, 93–4, 95, 111
 property, confiscation of, 85, 89, 93, 113
 rebaptism by, 5, 27, 80, 83, 85, 87, 89, 98, 104, 106–8, 109, 111, 115, 116, 229, 286, 307, 315, 384
 schism among, 85–6, 87, 95, 99, 100, 111. See also Maximianus
 suicides among, 42, 83–4, 98, 100, 134, 491, 520. See also Circumcellions

Donatus (Donatist priest of Mutugenna), 115–16

Donatus (founder of Donatist sect), 81, 90, 97, 491

dreams, 487, 531, 532–3, 536, 537, 538, 546, 547, 549, 550, 553
 Augustine's views on, 532–6. See also Visions

drunkenness (at graves of martyrs), 131, 171, 513, 514, 516, 517, 519, 520, 521–3, 527
 Augustine's letter on, 516–19
 sermons on, 514–15, 521–4

Duchesne, 209, 491

Dulcitius, 100, 192, 246, 254, 496

EARLY CHURCH, two views on, 585–7

Easter, 286, 288–93, 308, 309, 344, 361, 362, 371, 376
 date of, 65, 287, 288–90

Easter eve, baptismal rites on, 295, 322–3, 352, 361–79

Easter, octave of, 172, 280, 379–82

Ecdicia, 186, 213

Ecclesiastical History, 495

education, 133–4, 188, 440

Egypt, monks and hermits of, 167, 199, 207–8, 216, 483

eight, mystical significance of, 287–8, 291, 381. See also Numbers, mystical significance of

"Eight Martyrs", 19, 205, 477

Eleusinus, 205, 548

Elpidius (Arian), Augustine's letter to, 119

Emeritus, 93, 100–1

empyreum, 71, 539, 541, 564

entertainment, popular, sermons as, 431–2

Epiphany, 293

episcopium (in Hippo), monastic community at, 20, 199–209, 238–9

Eraclius, xvii, 123, 204, 240, 270–3, 323–4, 413, 476, 490
 elected Augustine's successor, 270–3

Erasmus, 236, 248, 267, 417

Escobar, 155

ethics, Augustinian, 566, 573

666 INDEX

Eucharist, 280, 282, 283, 284, 285, 286, 295, 300, 307–9, 311–16, 345, 348, 350, 354–5, 356, 361, 366, 370, 371–9, 381, 382, 401–2, 502, 504, 506, 507, 516, 517, 526, 530, 587
  as bond of unity, 282–5, 371–3, 376, 377–9
  Augustine's sermons on, 284, 371–8
  practices connected with, 529–30, 586
Eudoxia, Empress, 220
Eudoxius, Abbot of Capraria, 213, 268
Eulogius the Orator, 533
Eulogius, Patriarch of Alexandria, 491
Eunomians, 119, 120, 451, 510
eunuchs, 37
Eusebius, 495
Eustochium, 327
Evagrius, 223
evil, problem of, Augustine on, 423–4
  eye, the, 59
Evil One (expelled at baptism), 358–9
Evodius, Bishop of Uzalis, 132, 208, 242, 254, 414, 475, 476, 531, 536, 537, 544
examination, bodily, before baptism, see *Scrutinium*
excavations, discoveries made by, xxiii, 17, 20–2, 81, 84, 132, 368, 478, 479, 480, 483, 493, 507
excommunicati, 151–2
excommunication, 383
exorcism (at baptism), 354, 358–9, 372, 373, 397
exposition of texts (by Augustine), 338–9, 345–6, 440
exsufflatio (at baptism), 358, 359
extreme unction, 280, 315, 350, 355

FABIOLA, 386
Faltonia Proba, see Proba, Faltonia
family, disinheritance of, in favour of Church, see Disinheritance
Fascius, 264
fasting, 13, 167, 177–9, 191, 208, 216, 277, 287, 292, 294, 295, 298, 358, 361, 372, 387, 571
  before Communion, 296
fatum, 62, 65, 66, 67
Fauchet, Bishop, 206
Faustinus (banker), 30–1
Faustinus (ex-soldier), 204
Faustus (Manichee), 60, 314, 315, 570
Faventius, 265
feasts for the dead: drunkenness at, 131, 171, 513, 514, 516, 517, 519, 520–3, 527
  family, 57, 498–506, 512–13, 516, 520, 525–6
  in honour of martyrs, 131, 171, 478, 480, 483, 487, 490, 497, 506–23, 526
  on graves of St. Peter and St. Paul, 507–8, 523

feasts for the dead, *contd.*
  on graves of martyrs, 131, 171, 487, 509, 513–14, 516–19, 520–3, 527
  prohibition of, in churches, 515, 516, 517, 518, 519, 520–6
  representations of, 504–6, 514
feasts for the dead, Augustine's letters on, 516–20
  sermons on, 514–15, 519–25
Felicitas (superior of convent), 221–2
Felicia (converted Donatist), 231–2
Felicity, St., see Perpetua and Felicity, SS.
Felix of Aptunga, 79, 110
Felix (Manichee converted by Augustine), 118
Felix of Nola, St., 148, 493, 494–5, 512, 513, 535, 540
festivals, pagan, 46, 47, 54–5, 57, 74, 178
Festus (landowner), 115
Firmus, 81
Flaubert, 208
Flavianus, Vicarius Africae, 85
Flood, "sacrament" of the, 463
Florentina, Augustine's letter, 267
folk song, origin of, 332
forcible conversion of Donatists, Augustine's views on, 95–100, 113, 115–16
Fortunatus (Manichee), Augustine's debate with, 18, 118
Fortunatus of Sicca, 41
Fortunius (Donatist bishop), Augustine's debate with, 110
France, Anatole, 208
Francis of Sales, St., xxi, 98, 99, 128, 225
free will, 62, 63, 75, 125, 462, 572, 579
freedmen, 136. See also Slaves, freed, in monasteries
Fructuosus of Tarragona, 473, 476, 491
Fussala, 26, 102, 116, 230, 231, 232

GAISERIC, 10, 123
Galla Placidia, see Placidia, Galla
games, gladiatorial, 18, 49
  public, 32, 48–50, 54, 139, 157, 200, 219
  Augustine on, 49–50
Gaudentius of Brescia, 516
Gaudentius of Thamugadi (Donatist), 100
Gennadius, 192
Genesis, Augustine on, 5, 8
Generosus, 111
Generosus (*consularis*), Augustine's letter to, 265
Genseric, 157, 194, 234
Gervase and Protase, SS., 476, 478, 481, 487, 532, 540, 546
ghosts, 531, 537
Gil Blas, 430
Gildo, 81, 100, 163
Glory of the Martyrs, 491

God, invisibility of, Augustine's sermon on, 441-2
Goddess of Heaven, 37, 56
gods, 32-3, 38, 39, 44, 56, 57, 69, 74, 154, 158, 472-3, 490, 543, 562, 582
Goths, 14
grace, 124, 125, 308, 434, 436, 572, 577-9, 581, 582, 589
graffiti, 505, 507-8
Gratus of Carthage, Bishop, 11
Gregory the Great, Pope St., 66, 236, 320, 491, 576
Gregory Nazianzen, St., 194, 492, 530
Gregory of Nyssa, St., 324
Gregory of Tours, St., 491
Gsell, 17

HADRUMETUM, abbot of, 125
"happy life", ideal of, 166, 305-6, 379, 434
Harnack, xviii, 269
hell, 153, 462. See also Punishment, eternal
Heraclian, 81, 163
Hercules, destruction of statue of (in Byzacena), 39-40
heresies, Augustine on, 243-4
Hermes Trismegistus, 537
hexameron, 287, 330
  Ambrose's hymns on, 330
Hilarus (*vir tribunitius*), 327, 341
Hilarius, 125
Hilary of Poitiers, St., 332
Hippo, province of, 25-9
Hippo Regius, xvi, 3-5, 9-11, 16-20, 48, 53, 76, 79, 85, 88, 98, 99, 102, 103, 104, 110, 113, 116, 122, 129-30, 141, 144, 147, 148, 157, 178, 190, 191, 193, 194, 197, 237, 255, 268, 270, 326, 341, 348, 361, 406, 417, 427, 447, 452, 477, 488, 519, 543, 544, 546, 548, 549
  basilica major in, 20-5
  basilicas in, 19, 24-5
  congregation in, 129, 140-3, 147, 169 ff. See also People of
  council of, 19, 87, 519
  description of, 16-20
  Donatists in, 4, 79, 102-17
  education in, 132-4
  excavations at, 17, 20-1, 22
  monastery in, 200-6, 210, 217
  nunnery in, 215, 221-5
  people of, 130-43, 147, 148, 169, 190
  poverty in, 135, 137-40
  present-day, 16-17
  saints of, 477-8
  siege of, 16, 19, 194, 268
  Sunday in, 388-402
Hippolytus of Rome, St., 289
Holy Ghost, gifts of, 369
Holy Thorn, miracle of, 549

Homer, 439, 440, 445
homoousion, 120, 121
honey (given to *infantes* after baptism), 370-1
Honoratus (catechumen), 312
Honoratus (Donatist bishop), 110
Honoratus of Thiava, 268
Honorius, Emperor, 11, 37, 41, 54, 81, 89, 90, 94, 95, 210
Hooker, Richard, 303
Horace, 318
horoscopes, 60-1, 62, 64-5, 66, 70
house-chapels, 27
humility, Augustine's emphasis on, xxii, 187, 215, 268, 459
Huneric, 234

IAMBLICHUS, 35
Ideas, eternal, 5, 445, 564-5
idiotae, 341, 430, 433, 454
idols, destruction of, 38, 39, 42, 492
  trade in, 41, 42
Ignatius Loyola, St., 435, 566
illiteracy, 132
Incarnation, xxii, 36
indifferent, the, Augustine's views on, 152-3
infantes, 21, 131, 171, 196, 292, 312, 369, 371, 381-2
initiatio Christiana, 346-87
Innocent, Pope St., 11, 210
Innocentius (miraculous cure of), 544
Innocentius (victim of Donatists), 114, 115
inscriptions, 17, 18, 20, 22, 24, 27, 53, 84, 188, 478-82, 483, 492, 494, 501, 502, 503, 505, 507-8, 511, 529, 545
Institutiones (Calvin), 575
Instruction for Beginners, see Augustine, writings of
instruction, Augustine on, 458-60
instructional service, 388-402
intercourse (marital, before Communion), 177-8
Invitation to the Baptismal Pool, 366
Irenaeus, St., 289
Islam, 568
Italica, 158

JANSENISTS, 81, 298. See also Port-Royal
Januarius (layman), letters to, 67, 176, 177, 277, 278, 280, 286, 290, 291, 292, 293, 294, 302, 340, 370, 380, 571
Januarius (priest), 201, 232, 239
Jerome, St., 6, 11, 35, 129, 131, 139, 147, 177, 183, 187, 200, 209, 211, 219, 221, 223, 225, 231, 233, 247, 249, 250, 255, 336, 341, 343, 416, 422, 539, 574
  Augustine's letters to, 249, 255, 336, 341
Jesus, Augustine's "Life" of, 464-5
Jews, 53, 54, 55, 76-8, 79, 135, 149, 179, 297, 341-2, 354, 356, 466

John the Apostle, St., miracle at grave of, 555
John (monk), 535
John Chrysostom, St., 133, 412, 539
Jonah, sermon on, 341
Jovinian, 185, 187
Julian the Apostate, 38, 77, 81, 83, 84, 102, 162, 484
Julian of Eclanum, 189, 238, 244, 316, 318, 572
Juliana, 214, 219, 245, 246
Julianus, 202
Justin, St., 339
Justina, Empress, 329

KAHINA, QUEEN, 568
Khlysti, 134
Kierkegaard, 588
Koceila, 568

LANDOWNERS, 26, 27, 29, 102, 114, 115
latreia, 119, 277, 278, 306, 315, 489
Laurence, St., 174, 477, 494, 550
Laurentius, 246
law, civil (vested in bishops), 259-60
laymen, Augustine's friends among, 245-6, 253, 277
Lazarus (deacon), 203
Leo (acolyte), 243
Leo Africanus, 16
Leo the Great, Pope, St., 10, 15, 36, 129, 352, 412, 586
Leo X, Pope, 127
Leporius, 20, 205, 229, 477
Leschi, Professor, xxiii, 17
Letter 22 (on honouring the dead), 516-19
Letter 211 (rule for nuns), 222, 225
letters, Augustine's, 247-55: see also Augustine, letters of
  difficulties in sending, 247-8
Lettres provinciales, 101, 155
Libanius, 212
libelli, 544, 548, 549, 551
Liberius, Pope, 221
libido sciendi, 578-9, 580
libraries, 16, 132, 133, 223, 576
Licentius, 328
"life" (Eucharist known as), 316, 345
ligaturae, 58, 69, 382, 528-9, 548
light, Augustine's sermons on, 323, 362-3
liturgy, 277, 278-80, 285, 286, 287, 297, 317, 322, 338-40, 342-6, 571, 575, 585, 586
Longinianus (Augustine's letters to), 33-4
lots, drawing of, 67
love, earthly and heavenly, 434, 437, 566
  God's, 459, 463, 565, 567, 588, 589
Lucilla, 79-80
Lucillus, Bishop (miraculous cure of), 547
Lucillus (deacon), 243
Lucius of Caphergamala, 482, 532
Lucretius, 329, 538

Luther, 15, 112, 127
lynched officer, case of the, 142-3, 153, 190, 264

MACARIUS, 84, 89, 107, 108
Macedonius, 264
Macedonius (Vicarius Africae), 192, 246, 252, 261, 262
Macrobius, 580
Macrobius, Bishop, 83, 114, 115
Madaura, 29, 32, 34, 134
magic, 57, 58, 59, 60, 67, 69, 164, 382, 528, 548
Majorinus, 80, 106
Manichees, 5, 60, 104, 117, 118, 179, 180, 187, 190, 191, 208, 227, 246, 314, 351, 412, 435, 451, 519, 561, 570
  Augustine's debates with, 18, 104, 118, 412
Manlius Theodorus, 246
manumission (of slaves), 132, 135-6
Marcella, 157, 327
Marcellina (gnostic), 318
Marcellina (sister of Ambrose), 221
Marcellinus, Count, 36, 43, 90, 94, 96, 99, 151, 163, 192, 193, 246, 248, 252, 254, 260, 265, 267
  Augustine's letters to, 36
Marcianus, Emperor, 220
Marcianus (friend of Augustine's), 151
Marculus, 491
Marcus Aurelius, 583
Marec, Erwam, 17
Marinus, Count, 192, 193, 263, 265
Marius Victorinus, 364, 562
marriage, Augustine on, 181-7, 215, 216, 387, 562, 573-4
  mixed, 103
  second, 187
Marrou, H. I., 562, 580
Martin of Tours, St., 15, 199, 332, 476
martyrs, cult of, 6, 19, 32, 33, 55-6, 71, 174-5, 340, 397, 447, 471-97, 498, 506, 507, 508, 509, 510, 532, 537, 543, 550, 556, 574, 583
  Augustine's sermons on, 472-5, 487-9, 520
  graves of, 52, 71, 131, 483, 506-7, 509, 526.
    See also Feasts for the dead and *Memoriae*
  martyrs, warnings against erroneous views on, 487-92
Martyriologium Hieronymianum, 482
Mary, mother of Christ, 472, 484-7
  Augustine's sermons on, 485-7
Mass, daily, 176-7
  order of, 399-402
massa damnata, 196, 577
mathematici, see astrologers
Maurists, 441, 576
Maurras, Charles, 580

Mausbach, 566
Maximianists, 86, 87, 95, 99, 100, 111
Maximianus, 85-6
Maximinus (Arian bishop), 122-3
Maximinus, Donatist Bishop of Siniti, 104, 113, 114, 545
Maximus (pagan orator), Augustine's correspondence with, 32-3, 34
meditation, 168, 587
Megalius of Calama, 9
Melania (the elder), 148, 153, 481
Melania (the younger), 14, 27, 35, 136, 143, 145, 147, 153, 213, 245
memoriae, 13, 19, 27, 49, 169, 397, 398, 414, 471, 475, 476, 477, 478, 479, 480, 481, 482-3, 488, 489, 490, 495, 542, 543, 544, 547, 550, 552
of Apostles (in Rome), 158-61, 507-9
mensae, 240, 478, 479, 480, 482, 483, 487, 488, 489, 494, 498, 504, 509, 514, 532, 553
Middle Ages, 148, 162, 221, 290, 311, 313, 434, 562, 563-4, 569
Milan, singing in basilica of, 326, 328-31, 349
milk (given to *infantes*), 370-1
Minucius Felix, 75, 502
miracle record, 475, 544-8. See also *libelli*
miracles, 164, 253, 460, 476, 488, 535, 539-57, 561-2, 586, 587
  Augustine's credulity over, 553-7, 562
  pagan, 34, 543, 553-4
  worked by Augustine, 274
Mohrmann, Dr. Christine, xxii
Molanus, John, 575
monasteries, 14, 20, 191, 196, 199-217, 226, 233, 234
  founded by Augustine, 19-20, 22, 199-217, 233, 234, 465
  in Hippo, 199-206, 210
  in Tagaste, 208-9
Monica, St. (mother of Augustine), 3, 5, 133, 186, 195, 221, 244, 294, 328, 329, 330, 331, 343, 350, 379, 433, 495, 504, 515, 517, 531, 534, 570-1, 575
monks, 209-13, 216-17, 390
  idle, 212-13
  runaway, 210
  wandering, 210-11
  work of, 211, 212, 217. See also *On the Work of Monks* under Augustine, writings of
Montaigne, 557
Montanists, 491, 501. See also Pneumatics
moon, as symbol of Church, 66, 73, 287, 290
morality, sexual, Augustine on, 180-90
Morin, Dom, xxii, 376
mosaics, 16, 19, 23-4, 235, 365, 397-8, 478, 479, 511, 539
munera, 48-9, 219
"murmurers", 157-61

music, Augustine views on, 320, 333-7
musicians, 321
Mysteries, The, 312
Mystical Body, 283-4, 285, 343, 372, 373

NABOR, AUGUSTINE'S EPITAPH ON, 98, 492, 532
narratio, 452, 453, 459, 460, 461, 462
nature, Augustine's similes from, 28
Navigius (brother of St. Augustine), 221
Nebridius, 3, 5, 60, 209, 236, 248, 308, 474
Nectarius, 41
neophytes, 369, 379, 381. See also *infantes*
neo-Platonism, neo-Platonists, xxi, 5, 44, 186, 288, 289, 299, 303, 304, 319, 332, 364, 422, 434, 435, 445, 449, 450, 459, 561, 562, 575, 577
Nestorius, 328
Nero, 161
Newman, Cardinal, 19, 420, 538
Nicetas of Remesiana, Augustine's letter to, 513
Nietzsche, 258, 334, 439
notarii, 39, 121, 270, 414, 415-16, 427, 536, 544, 551
Nonna, Mother, 194-5, 530
Novatian, 187, 383
Novatus, Bishop of Sitifi, 243
numbers, mystical significance of, 287, 288, 290, 291, 293, 301, 316, 369, 380, 381, 432, 447, 503
numbers, Pythagorean theory of, 334, 564
nunneries, 212, 215, 217-25, 234
nunnery in Hippo, Augustine's letters to, 215, 221-2, 225
nuns, dress of, 223
  rule for, 215, 222-5

OLD BELIEVERS, 83, 134
omens, 59-60
On Baptism, On the Excellence of Widowhood, On the Happy Life, On Holy Virginity, On the Letter and the Spirit, On Marriage and Desire, On Music, On the Trinity, On the Quantity of the Soul, On the Uses of Faith, On the Work of Monks, see Augustine, writings of
Olympiodorus, 41, 90, 245
On the Virgins (Ambrose), 221
Optatus of Milevis, St., 82, 84, 95, 96, 107
Optatus of Thamugadi, Donatist bishop, 81, 83, 125
orbitas, see Childlessness
Origen, 15, 287, 300, 310, 343, 351, 369, 443, 445, 562, 571, 574
original sin, 185-7, 244, 311, 351, 358, 575, 583
Original Sin, see Augustine, writings of
Orosius, 248, 475

Ostia, 195, 330, 379
Our Duty to Care for our Dead, see Augustine, writings of
Our Father, Augustine on, 167, 284, 360-1

PACIANUS, BISHOP OF BARCELONA, 55
paganism, pagans, 29-75, 154-6, 157, 158, 209, 252, 279, 354, 356, 364, 381, 466, 583
paganism, Augustine on, 43-4
    ending of, 37-45
    laws against, 37-9, 41, 54. Augustine's views on, 38, 39, 40, 41
    legacy of, 46-75, 79, 164, 209, 472, 503, 527, 538, 574
pagans, riots caused by, 39-41. Augustine's letter on, 40
Palatinus, 238
Palestrina, 321
Palladia, 550
Pammachius, 115, 512
Parmenianus (Donatist, bishop of Carthage), 82, 90, 105, 325
parentalia, 499-500, 502, 503, 516, 525
Pascal, Blaise, 156, 420, 566-7, 576
Pascentius (Arian), Augustine's public debates with, 120-2
Pasch, 288-9
passiones (of martyrs), 491, 492
Patricius (Augustine's father), 149, 186, 570
Paul, St., 70, 135, 156, 164, 165, 167, 177, 181, 212, 236, 249-50, 283, 284, 289, 297, 318, 333, 339, 358, 376, 385, 389, 410, 420, 425, 445, 448, 456, 464, 465, 476, 521, 536, 538
    grave of, 158-61, 493-4, 507, 509, 512
    feast for the dead at, 507
Paula, 327, 512
Paulina, Augustina's letter to, 246, 254
Paulinus of Nola, 41, 143, 148, 199, 242, 247, 248, 249, 250, 255, 322, 400, 412, 481, 493, 494, 495, 511, 512, 532, 535, 539, 540, 553, 575
    Augustine's letters to, 247, 248, 249, 250, 255, 400
    Our Duty to Care for the Dead written for, 532, 553
Paulus (one of "ten accursed children"), 550, 551
Paulus, Bishop of Cataqua, 230, 233, 243
Péguy, 351
Pelagianism, Pelagians, 11, 12, 122, 124, 242, 246, 248, 311, 358, 376, 399, 415, 572
Pelagius, 147, 219, 246, 572, 577, 588
penance (after baptism), 382-7
penance, public, 151, 273, 384-6
pericopes, 344-5, 380, 440
Perpetua and Felicity, Saints, 476, 477, 479, 491

Peter, chair of, 12, 107, 111
Peter, St., grave of: see Paul, St., grave of
Petilianus of Cirta, 92, 112, 210
Petronia, 548
Phocas, St., 476, 510
Pico della Mirandola, 245
pictures, religious, Augustine on, 318-19, 323-4
pietas, 495, 496, 498, 504, 516
piety, mockery of, 174
pilgrimages, 510-13, 587
Pinianus, 14, 143-7, 245. Augustine's letters on, 146-7
Placidia, Empress Galla, 122, 163, 194, 220, 251, 438
Plato, 436, 441, 460, 565, 579, 580
Platonism, Platonists, 34-5, 207, 258, 320, 321, 564, 581
Plenary Council of Africa, 8-9
Pliny, 561
Plotinus, 35, 305, 562
Pneumatics, 491. See also Montanists
poenitentes, Augustine's sermons on, 151-2
Polycarp, St., Bishop of Smyrna, 506
pompa diaboli, 47-56, 364
Pontitianus, Count, 192, 207
Porphyry, 35, 332, 436
Port-Royal, xix, xxi, 4, 81, 101, 297, 549, 573
possession, cases of, 539
Possidius, xviii, xix, xxii, 16, 29, 40, 41, 59, 95, 132, 183, 225, 235, 239, 240, 241, 242, 247, 259, 274, 412, 476, 480, 544
poverty, Augustine's sermons on, 137-40
Praesidius, 250
prayer, at Mass, 398-40
    Augustine on, 164-9, 214, 250, 338-9, 360-1, 437, 581
    conduct during, 168-9, 338-9, 397, 398
    ejaculatory, 167
preaching, (Augustine on), 405-11
Predestination of the Saints, see Augustine, writings of
Priscillianists, 119
Primianus, Donatist Bishop of Carthage, 85-7
Principia, 157
Proba, Faltonia, 164-5, 166, 168, 214, 216, 219, 245, 250, 360
    Augustine's letter to (on prayer), 164-9, 214, 250, 360
probabilism (of Augustine), 153-6, 352
Probas, 166
Proculeianus (Donatist bishop), 109, 114, 243
Prodigal Son, sermon on, 77-8, 446-7
Profuturus, 242
property (of clergy, renunciation of), 200-6
prophecy, 460, 465, 466, 535
    demonic, 70, 537
Prosper, 125, 248

Prudentius, 30, 321, 322, 477, 511, 512, 513, 575
psalms, singing of, 6, 326–8, 333, 336, 341, 390–1, 402, 414–15, 585
 Augustine's sermons on, 13, 49, 127, 170, 334, 335–6, 337, 416. See also *Enarrationes in Psalmos*, under Augustine, writings of
Pseudo-Dionysius, 303
"pseudo-sacraments", Augustine on, 297
psychology, modern, 311
Publicola, Valerius, Augustine's letter to, 153–6
Pulcheria, Empress Aelia, 220
Punic (language), 26–8, 32, 81, 105, 111, 116, 131, 228, 230, 258, 345, 568
punishment, eternal, 35, 153, 461, 554–5
purification rites, 33
Puritans, 138, 298, 303

QUADRATUS, BISHOP, 425, 477
Quintilian, 406, 459
Quodvulteus, 48, 101, 227, 243

RAGE, AUGUSTINE'S SERMONS ON, 141–3
Raskolniki, 134
Ravenna, xvii, 11, 89, 90, 163, 219–220, 235, 243, 244, 245, 252, 263, 265, 438, 444
Real Presence, 312–13, 314, 372, 375, 377
reconciliato, 152, 384, 385, 386
Redemption, the, 289
refrigerium, 500, 504, 506, 508, 510–15
relics, 78, 475–8, 479, 480, 482, 483, 487, 511, 532, 546, 552, 574, 575
refectory, inscription in Augustine's, 239
remedia, 58, 69, 164, 528
Restitutus (murdered by Donatists), 96, 114, 115
resurrection (of the body), 35, 57, 187, 288, 379, 423, 436, 461, 465–6, 525, 541–3
Retractations, see Augustine, writings of
Rhadagasus, 158
rhetoric, 406–9, 422
rich, the, 135, 137–40, 148
riches, sermons on, 138–40
Riegl, Alois, 320
rites, local, 286
Robba, 84
Rogatists, 86, 131
Roland-Gosselin, 566
Roman Empire, Augustine's views on, 135, 162–4, 273, 579, 534
Romanianus, 48, 207, 412
Rome, fall of, 14, 43, 157–62, 579. Augustine's views on, 158–9, 160–4
 refugees from, 157, 158
Romulus, Augustine's letter to, 262
Rufinus, 495
rule for nuns (Augustine's), 215, 222–5

Rusticianus, 228–9
Rusticus, 221–2
Rutilius Numatianus, 211

SABELLIANISM, 425
"sacrament of salt", 337, 354, 355–6, 397, 455, 466
sacramenta, Christian, 280, 281
sacramenta, Old Testament, 279–80, 281, 299, 315, 348, 377, 378, 463
sacraments, 106, 278–86, 291, 298–316, 342, 344–6, 347, 354, 371–4, 376–9, 527, 568, 574. See also Baptism, confirmation, Eucharist, extreme unction
sacraments, as symbols, 298–316, 337, 379
 objective character of, 307, 310
 outside Church, 283, 307, 310
 validity of, 106, 283, 307, 310, 316, 351, 366
Sacraments, The, 312
sacrifices, pagan, 154–6, 584
saints, burial near: see Burial *ad sanctos*
 local, 475, 477, 481, 482, 491
 veneration of, Augustine on, 488–92
salvation, 300–1, 304, 306, 307, 308, 310, 453
"salvation" (baptism known as), 316, 345
Salvianus, 56, 130, 157, 180
Salvius of Membressa, 86
Samsucius, 109, 227
sanctimoniales, 218
Sapida, 238, 252
Sassen, Professor, xxii
Satan, 62, 70, 71
Saturninus, Bishop of Uzalis, 544–5
Satyrus (brother of Ambrose), 494, 530
Scilli, martyrs of, 477, 487, 491
scruples, 153–6, 178–9
scrutinium, 358
Second Coming, 363
Secundinus the Manichee, 412
Secundula, Aelia, epitaph on, 501
self-baptism, 55
self-glorification, Augustine's sermon on, 266
seminary (founded by Augustine), 200, 234
sensus catholicus, 433
Septuagint, 343–4
Serapion, carrying off of, 68, 381
serfs, 115, 227
Sermon on the Mount, Augustine on, 8
sermons (of Augustine): see Augustine, sermons of
Severianus, 418
Severus of Milevis, 41, 204, 208, 228, 242, 243, 248, 270, 271
Shaw, Bernard, 431
Shenoute, Abbot, 483
Sidi Okba, 568
Sigisvult, Count, 122
signs, 299–304, 308, 310, 312, 314, 345, 346, 347, 356, 368. See also Symbols

INDEX

Simon Magus, 283, 307
Simplicianus, Bishop of Milan, 243, 248, 261, 571
sin, habitual, Augustine on, 424
singing, congregational, 105, 168, 172, 173, 325–38, 341, 349, 370, 390–1, 399, 414–15, 524, 585. Augustine's views on, 332–8. See also Psalms, singing of
Sinnius (deacon), 247
Sixtus (archdeacon), Augustine's letter to, 125
skin, animal (trodden on at baptism), 359
Skoptsi, 134
slavery, slaves, 26, 27, 28, 49, 77, 135–6, 137, 181, 197, 204, 212, 217–18, 219, 260, 388, 389, 464
slaves, freed, in monasteries and convents, 135, 204, 212, 218, 219
manumission of, 132, 135–6
Socrates, 460, 583
Sol Invictus, feast of, 292
solitude, 216
Sozomen, 245
Spain, Communists in, 158
spiritualism, 69
stars, influence of, 61–2, 63, 64, 65, 66, 67, 70, 72
Augustine on, 62–6, 72–3, 300–301, 563
Stephen, St., 21, 22, 475, 476, 478, 484, 544, 547–8, 550, 551, 552–3, 578
miracles attributed to, 547–8, 550–3
relics of, 20, 475, 476, 478, 481, 482, 487, 488, 490, 532, 540, 547, 548
Stilicho, 40, 89, 114, 245
Stoics, 136
Strabo, 561
strena, 54–5
subjectivism, religious, 305–6
Suetonius, xviii, 18
suicides (among Donatists), see Donatists, suicides among
Sulla, 583
sun (representing Christ), 73
Sunday (as Lord's Day), 286–9
in Hippo, 388–402
superstition, 56–60, 69, 472, 527, 557, 587
Christian, 527–9, 530, 586
symbolism, symbols, 281, 282, 285, 287, 290, 291, 293, 298–316, 323, 337, 342–3, 346, 355, 356, 359, 364, 368–9, 371, 373, 374, 379, 427, 435, 438, 444, 445, 462, 557, 563, 564, 583
purpose of, Augustine on, 301–2
and realism, 299, 306–16
Symbolists, 303
symbolum, 280, 352, 353, 359, 360, 363, 364, 371, 460
"giving back" of, 280, 360, 363, 364
Symbolum for Catechumens (four sermons of Augustine's), 360

Symmachus, 32, 571, 580, 581
Synesius of Cyrene, 501

TAGASTE, 3, 14, 48, 89, 99, 116, **134**, **141**, 143, 145, 147, 208, 209, 217, 236, 242, 267
Augustine's monastery in, 3, 208–9
Tanit, 37, 290
tattooing (of cross on forehead), 355
Teacher, The, see Augustine, writings of
"temple sleep", 496, 531, 549
temples, pagan, closing or destruction of, 34, 37, 38–9, 43, 54, 56, 75, 156, 538
"ten accursed children", see Cappadocia, "ten accursed children" of
Tertullian, 10, 47, 51, 75, 176, 178, 183, 187, 298, 339, 383, 491, 501, 576
Tertullianists, 119
Testaments, correspondence between Old and New, 292, 443, 445, 446, 449, 459
theatre, 13, 17, 18, 31, 47, 48, 50, 51–4, 67, 76, 105, 131, 157, 161, 164, 171, 174, 175, 196, 200, 263, 327, 336, 355, 364, 379, 429, 436, 447, 461, 466, 574. Augustine on, 48, 50–4, 574
at Hippo, 17, 18, 48, 53
Thecla, baptistery of, 288
Thecla, St., 476
theft, Augustine's sermon on, 392–7
Themistocles, 251
Theodore of Mopsuestia, 36, 349
Theodosius, Emperor, 37, 39, 60, 85, 95, 163, 182, 220, 535
Theogenes, Bishop, 19, 477, 489
Theophilus, Bishop, 68, 381
Thérèse of Lisieux, St., xxii
thermae, see Baths, public
Thurburbo, martyrs of, 473, 477
Tillemont, Le Nain de, xviii, xix, 147
To the Donatists after the Conference, see Augustine, writings of
toleration, 42, 43, 97
torture, Augustine's views on, 41, 96, 265
tradition, 285–6, 296, 297, 340, 351, 445
local, 12, 340, 341
traditores, 80, 84, 87, 94
tramps, Augustine's views on, 138
transmigration, 436
Trent, Council of, 572, 577
triclia, 507, 512, 514
Trinity, the, xvii, 119, 120, 121, 291, 304, 330, 351, 354, 359, 360, 366, 367–8, 422, 435, 460, 466
True Faith, True Worship of God, see Augustine, writings of
Tutuslymeni, sermon on, 452
"Twenty Martyrs", 19, 397, 477, 491, 547
Tyconius (Donatist), 81, 269, 300, 443
typology, 443, 445

UNDERSTANDING (ON PART OF CONGREGATION), 337–42, 343, 371, 373, 405
universe, concepts of, 71–2, 445, 538–9, 563–5, 567, 582–3, 585

VALENS, 204
Valentinian II, 37
Valentinian III, 194
Valentinus, Abbot of Hadrumetum, 125
Valerii, 141, 143, 148, 245
Valerius, Bishop, 4, 5, 6, 7, 8, 9, 15, 104, 143, 209, 226, 272, 416, 522, 523, 524
  consecration of Augustine by, 9, 143, 272
  ordination of Augustine by, 4, 5, 6, 7, 8, 189
Valerius, Count, 189, 192, 243, 245, 248, 252
  Marriage and Desire written for, 189, 252
Valerius Publicola, see Publicola, Valerius
Valéry, Paul, 285, 449
Vandals, 16, 21, 25, 101, 122, 157, 158, 163, 225, 251, 268, 482, 535, 568
Varro, 553, 554, 562
vendettas, 142
Vespers, 172, 173, 524, 546
vessels, liturgical, 317
vestal virgin, "miracle" of, 553–4
Victor Vitensis, 25
Victorianus, 115, 158, 255
Victorinus, Bishop, 248
Victricius of Rouen, St., 199

Vigilius, Bishop of Trent, 258
Vincentius (Rogatist), Augustine's letter to, 86
Vindicianus, 60
Vigilantius, 574
visions, 531–9, 552. See also Dreams
  Augustine on, 532–6
Vergil, 52, 75, 329, 436, 439, 440, 445, 539, 561, 579
virginity, 185, 187, 214–16, 218
Virgin Birth, 254
Virgin's Hymn, 218
Voltaire, 233
Volusianus, Augustine's correspondence with, 35–6, 254

WASHING OF FEET (BY BISHOPS), 295, 572
water, baptismal: miracles attributed to, 350, 529, 545–6, 549
  symbolism of, 365–6
  verses on, 365
widowhood, 166, 168, 213, 214
wives, duties of, 182–3, 186, 213–14
women, Augustine's attitude to, 182–5, 215, 221

Zeno of Verona, St., 516, 520
Zosimus, Pope, 13, 236

INDEX TO NOTES

ABRAHAM'S SACRIFICE, ICONOGRAPHY OF, 630 n. 30
Adam, Karl, 628 n. 99; 637 nn. 108, 109; 638 n. 141; 639 n. 178
Aesculapius, temples of, 657 n. 58
Agnes, St., 648 n. 31
Albertini, 596 n. 26
Allais, Y., 596 n. 26
alphabetical psalm, 608 nn. 129, 130, 132; 609 nn. 133, 136
Altaner, B., 593 n. 15
Alvarez, 619 n. 38
Alypius, 623 n. 36
Ambrose, St., 600 n. 15; 611 nn. 12, 18; 616 n. 254; 618 nn. 327, 1; 620 nn. 68, 69, 74; 622 nn. 1, 14; 623 nn. 28, 33; 628 n. 99; 629 nn. 101, 105; 630 n. 24; 631 nn. 36, 47, 48, 52; 632 n. 57; 633 n. 6; 639 n. 193; 642 n. 20; 647 n. 3; 650 n. 79; 651 n. 134; 652 n. 6; 653 nn. 20, 21; 654 n. 61; 656 n. 19
Apiarius, 594 n. 30; 621 n. 131
Apringius, 596 n. 16; 623 n. 50
Arianism, 605 n. 1
Armentarius, 624 n. 80
Arnason, 649 n. 64
ascetics, 622 n. 2
Asterius, 654 n. 46
astrology, 602 n. 85
Atchley, 629 n. 101
Augustine, 593 n. 15; 607 n. 83; 622 n. 10; 631 nn. 37, 57; 633 n. 95; 634 n. 47; 635 n. 70; 637 n. 114; 638 n. 165; 639 n. 178; 641 n. 53; 642 n. 10; 643 n. 53; 648 nn. 1, 24, 38; 653 n. 20; 656 n. 24; 658 n. 1; 659 n. 39
Aurelian, 627 n. 50
Aurelius, 594 n. 12; 621 n. 112; 624 n. 102
Ausonius, 614 n. 145

BADCOCK, 635 n. 70
Baehrens, 646 n. 163
Bagai, Council of, 606 n. 39
Ballu (with Cagnat and Boesillwald), 595 n. 10
baptism, 616 n. 274; 634 n. 22
 infant, 633 n. 7; 634 nn. 12, 15
 of blood, 658 n. 23

baptisteries, 597 n. 41; 627 n. 34; 630 n. 5; 636 nn. 102, 104; 656 n. 44
Bardenhewer, 655 n. 89
Basil, St., 616 n. 253
Batiffol, 594 nn. 25, 26, 30; 605 n. 1; 608 n. 126; 621 n. 131; 629 n. 99
Batoccini, R., 595 n. 10
Baudelaire, 628 n. 80
Baumstark, 629 n. 101
Baxter, 620 n. 78
Becker, 653 n. 25
Benedict, St., 621 n. 100
Bérard, P., 604 n. 1
Berthier (with Logeart and Martin), 595 n. 10
Bertocci, P., 628 n. 99
Besse, Dom, 620 nn. 63 and 78
Bible, allegorical sense of, 646 n. 166
Bishop, W. C., 639 n. 1
Blume, C., 632 n. 58
Blumenkranz, B., 604 n. 1
Boese, R., 601 n. 55
Boesillwald (with Cagnat and Ballu), 595 n. 10
Boethius, 604 n. 164
Boissier, G., 600 n. 15; 654 n. 58
Boll, F., 602 n. 85
Bollandists, 593 n. 8
Bonnet, 652 n. 16
Borella, 648 n. 8
Botte, B., 627 n. 52
Bouché-Leclercq, 602 n. 85
Bourke, Vernon J., 593 n. 15
Boyer, 593 n. 9
Brandt, 618 n. 351
Bremond, Henri, 659 n. 47
Browe, P., 638 n. 134
Bücheler, 627 n. 34; 651 n. 132; 654 n. 52
Bulla Regia, 594 n. 34
Buonaiuti, 652 n. 7
Burel, 648 n. 38
Burnaby, J., 593 n. 15
Busch, Dom, 593 n. 15; 596 n. 17; 633 nn. 98, 1; 635 nn. 69, 76; 637 n. 109; 638 n. 141

CAESAR, 604 n. 181
Cabrol, F., 639 n. 1
Caesarius of Arles, 620 n. 91; 631 n. 42; 646 n. 179
Cagnat, R., 595 n. 10; 600 n. 7

Calbulus (verses on baptismal water), 636 n. 104
Callewaert, 639 n. 194
Calvin, 628 n. 68; 630 nn. 10, 14
Camelot, 629 n. 99
Camus, J. P., 619 n. 38
Carthage, Third Council of, 594 n. 23; 615 n. 233; 619 n. 5; 620 n. 55; 621 nn. 98, 103, 110, 114, 115, 116, 119, 120; 627 n. 65; 634 n. 49; 637 n. 122; 638 n. 135; 639 n. 181; 640 n. 25, 36; 651 n. 117; 654 n. 81; 655 n. 11
    Fourth Council of, 634 n. 35; 635 nn. 51, 57; 638 n. 159
    Fifth Council of, 598 n. 72
    Sixth Council of, 621 n. 131
Casel, 627 n. 67; 629 n. 101
Cassian, 615 n. 217
Cassiodorus, 625 n. 107; 644 n. 61
catechumens, 647 n. 5
Cavallera, 643 n. 50
Cayré, 593 n. 9; 605 n. 8
Cayrol, 650 n. 71
Cazzulani, 623 n. 34
Celestine I, 631 n. 37
childlessness, 618 n. 327
Circumcellions, 605 n. 1
Christmas, 615 nn. 196, 199
Chrysostom, St. John, 611 n. 18; 654 n. 45; 656 n. 15
Cirta, 597 n. 48; 613 n. 126
Colombo, A., 649 n. 67
Comeau, 636 n. 90; 644 n. 60
Communion, house, 616 n. 253
competentes, 635 n. 60
confession, auricular, 639 n. 178
Coppens, 637 n. 119
Courcelle, P., 603 n. 142; 605 n. 8; 658 n. 1
Cresconius, Bishop, 596 n. 26
cross, sign of the, 637 n. 106
Cuicul (Cuicul-Djemila), 596 n. 26; 597 n. 36; 636 n. 102; 654 n. 52
Cumont, 626 n. 32; 652 n. 7; 654 n. 61
Cyprian, 597 n. 38; 601 n. 36; 602 n. 81; 616 n. 252; 616 n. 260; 622 n. 134; 637 n. 106; 639 n. 178; 641 nn. 42, 48, 53; 642 n. 20; 647 n. 3; 648 n. 36; 649 n. 42; 651 n. 118; 652 n. 13
Cyril of Alexandria, St., 650 n. 76
Cyril of Jerusalem, St., 641 n. 61; 656 n. 15

Damasus, I, Pope St., 607 n. 100
Dankbaar, 628 n. 67
Dardanus, 624 n. 91
Dartein, 622 n. 1
D'Alès, 625 n. 106
Daux, C., 612 n. 79
Davids, 658 n. 8

De Bruyne, 621 n. 100; 633 n. 101; 643 nn. 50, 60
De Capua, 644 n. 97; 645 n. 109
Deferrari, 643 n. 41
De Fontanes, 630 n. 23
De Ghellinck, 627 n. 67
Degert, A., 611 n. 4
De Labriolle, 595 n. 1; 600 n. 9; 604 n. 1; 636 n. 99
De Lagarde, 625, n. 108
Delehaye, 601 n. 22; 648 n. 1; 649 nn. 52, 60, 62; 652 n. 7; 653 n. 40; 657 n. 58
Delattre, P., 596 n. 26; 649 n. 61
demons, 603 nn. 138, 143, 150, 156; 604 n. 161; 604 n. 182; 634 n. 28
Denis, H. van M., 595 n. 1
De Pachtère, 595-6 n. 10
De Puniet, 635 nn. 69, 76; 637 n. 119
De Rossi, 623 n. 16; 649 n. 64; 651 n. 131
De Vreese, L., 602 n. 85
Deo laudes, 605 n. 8; 607 n. 100
Diocletian, 596 n. 16; 652 n. 15
Dinkler, F., 622 n. 5
Dionysius, 628 n. 80
discipline of secrecy, 629 n. 103; 634 n. 34
Dix, 616 n. 252; 628 n. 99; 637 n. 107; 638 n. 134
Dohmes, 630 n. 32
Dölger, F., 618 n. 327; 627 n. 67; 629 n. 101; 632 n. 82; 634 nn. 18, 37; 635 nn. 61, 63; 637 nn. 105, 119, 131; 640 n. 23; 652 nn. 6, 10; 653 n. 27; 655 nn. 8, 12
"Dominus legem dat", 630 n. 5
Donatists, 596 n. 26; 605 nn. 1, 4, 8, 25, 28; 606 n. 57; 634 n. 28; 635 n. 62; 637 n. 114; 639 n. 179; 640 n. 4; 655 n. 89
Donatus, 605 n. 28; 606 n. 32
Dondeyne, 635 nn. 61, 76
Douel, M., 595 n. 10
Duchesne, 598 n. 4; 605 n. 1; 629 n. 1
Duhem, 602 n. 85
Dyggve, 651 n. 3; 653 n. 24

Egger-Bulic, 651 n. 3
Eggersdörfer, F. X., 593 n. 15; 633 n. 98; 635 n. 76; 647 n. 3
Eight Martyrs, 596 n. 24
Eisenhöfer, 639 n. 194
Ellerbeck, P., 628 n. 97
Elvira, Council of, 598 n. 4; 600 n. 74; 652 n. 11
Emeritus of Caesarea, 606 n. 74
Engelbrecht, 608 n. 126
Enarrationes, 643 nn. 50, 58
Ennodius, 636 n. 104
Ermini, 608 n. 126
Ermoni, 631 n. 47
Essenes, 604 n. 10

INDEX TO NOTES

Eucharist, 628 *n.* 99
Eusebius of Caesarea, 604 *n.* 10
Eusebius of Vercelli, 618 *n.* 1
Eustorgius, baptistery of, 636 *n.* 104
Eutropius, 613 *n.* 93
Evodius, 643 *n.* 37
Ewald, 649 *n.* 40
excavations, 595 *n.* 8; 596 *n.* 26
exsufflatio, 634 *n.* 28; 635 *n.* 61

FABIOLA, 617 *n.* 284
Faller, 629 *n.* 101
fasting, 616 *nn.* 256, 260, 262; 626 *n.* 26; 635 *n.* 57; 650 *n.* 73
Faustus of Riez, 631 *n.* 47
Favez, C., 624 *n.* 70
Féret, H., 628 *n.* 67
festivals, pagan, 599 *n.* 49; 600 *n.* 63
Firmus, 623 *n.* 44
Foran, E. A., 618 *n.* 1
Fornari, 651 *nn.* 129, 2
Frank, 629 *n.* 101
Frantz, 652 *n.* 11
Freestone, 616 *n.* 252
Freistedt, 652 *n.* 18
Friedrich, 650 *n.* 80
Froben, 624 *n.* 70; 644 *n.* 62
Fructuosus, St., 651 *n.* 118
Fulgentius, 641 *n.* 53
Funk, 654 *n.* 70
Fussala, 598 *n.* 72

GAGÉ, 595 *n.* 5; 649 *n.* 62; 654 *n.* 52
Gallienus, 652 *n.* 15
Galtier, P., 637 *n.* 119; 639 *n.* 178
Gauckler, 595 *n.* 10; 596 *n.* 26; 649 *n.* 58
Gaudentius of Thamugadi, 606 *n.* 74
Gavault, 596 *n.* 26
Geiselmann, J., 628 *n.* 99; 637 *n.* 108
Generosus, 625 *n.* 138
Gennrich, 630 *n.* 32
George of Cyprus, 595 *n.* 2
Gerke, F., 653 *n.* 36
Gerold, T., 630 *n.* 32
Gerontius, 595 *n.* 46; 614 *n.* 192; 619 *n.* 46
Getty, M., 611 *n.* 4
Gifford, 604 *n.* 10
Gilson, Etienne, 593 *n.* 9; 658 *n.* 3
Glibotic, 630 *n.* 32
Goldbacher, 649 *n.* 52
Goodchild (with Ward Perkins), 595 *n.* 10; 596 *n.* 26
Goppelt, L., 646 *n.* 161
Gougaud, 654 *n.* 62
graffiti, 653 *n.* 40
Grandidier, 649 *n.* 60
Grégoire, 649 *n.* 62
Grégoire-Kugener, 655 *n.* 13

Gregory the Great, Pope St., 603 *n.* 127; 655 *n.* 13
Gregory of Nazianzus St., 618 *n.* 344; 630 *n.* 20; 634 *n.* 22; 656 *n.* 15
Gregory of Nyssa, St., 630 *n.* 30; 656 *n.* 16
Gregory of Tours, St., 649 *n.* 40
Grossi-Gondi, 652 *n.* 7; 653 *n.* 40; 655 *n.* 102
Gsell, S., 595 *n.* 10; 598 *n.* 74; 652 *n.* 9
Guardini, Romano, 658 *n.* 8
Guey, J., 613 *n.* 112

HADRUMETUM, 652 *n.* 14
Hahn, 625 *n.* 154
Halm, 618 *n.* 1; 622 *n.* 2
Hartel, 612 *n.* 89; 617 *n.* 295; 620 *n.* 62; 622 *n.* 2; 636 *n.* 104; 641 *n.* 48; 648 *n.* 1; 651 *n.* 136; 652 *n.* 13; 653 *n.* 37; 654 *nn.* 53, 56
Hartmann, 649 *n.* 40
Harnack, A., 593 *n.* 7; 611 *n.* 18; 657 *n.* 58
Haury, 649 *n.* 45
Heikel, 654 *n.* 44
Hendrikx, 593 *n.* 9; 629 *n.* 99
Hennecke, 657 *n.* 102
Herzog, R., 603 *n.* 143; 641 *n.* 55; 657 *n.* 58
Hilberg, 613 *n.* 127; 616 *n.* 253; 617 *nn.* 281, 295; 620 *n.* 55; 621 *n.* 132; 622 *n.* 136; 631 *n.* 44; 636 *n.* 99; 637 *n.* 130; 647 *n.* 3; 656 *n.* 45
Hippolytus, 607 *n.* 100; 616 *n.* 252; 628 *n.* 99; 637 *n.* 107; 638 *n.* 134; 640 *n.* 30; 654 *n.* 60
Hippo, Council of, 621 *n.* 116
Hirogani, 650 *n.* 75
Hocedez, 637 *n.* 109
Hofmann, F., 637 *n.* 119
Hollman, A., 632 *n.* 61
Hooker, Richard, 628 *n.* 80
Huhn, J., 627 *n.* 67
humility, Augustine's emphasis on, 617 *n.* 318
Huyben, 635 *n.* 76; 644 *n.* 60
Hydatius, 610 *n.* 199
Hymmen, J., 627 *n.* 67
hymns (of Ambrose), 631 *nn.* 47, 51, 52, 55, 57

IDIOTAE, 647 *n.* 3
initiatio christiana, 593 *n.* 15; 633 *n.* 1
inscriptions, 595 *n.* 5; 596 *n.* 26; 597 *n.* 51; 598 *n.* 71; 598 *n.* 73 (on chapel in Hippo); 605 *n.* 8; 623 *n.* 16; 649 *n.* 58
Irenaeus, 656 *n.* 56

JAFFÉ, 639 *n.* 189
Jalland, Trevor G., 594 *n.* 30; 611 *n.* 1
James, M. R., 657 *n.* 102
Jerome, St., 593 *n.* 5; 594 *n.* 9; 611 *n.* 11; 612 *n.* 40; 613 *nn.* 125, 127; 616 *n.* 253; 617 *nn.* 279, 281, 284, 295; 618 *n.* 339; 619 *nn.* 28, 36; 620 *nn.* 55, 73, 87; 621 *nn.* 104, 132; 622 *nn.* 1 6, 140; 624

INDEX TO NOTES

Jerome, St., *contd.*
    nn. 64, 74; 631 *n.* 44; 636 *n.* 99; 637 *n.* 130; 639 *n.* 192; 642 *n.* 8; 647 *n.* 3; 656 *n.* 45; 658 *n.* 28
Jews, 625 *n.* 132; 633 *n.* 95
Joly, 595 *n.* 10
John Damascene, St., 641 *n.* 61; 656 *n.* 15
Jülicher, 656 *n.* 28
Julien, C. A., 596 *n.* 10
Jungmann, J., 639 *nn.* 178, 194; 641 *n.* 42
Justin, 632 *n.* 84
Juvenal, 603 *n.* 129

KATTENBUSCH, 635 *nn.* 69, 73, 76
Kaufmann, 653 *n.* 31
Keenan, M. E., 602 *n.* 66; 611 *n.* 4
Kirsch, 601 *n.* 22; 637 *n.* 113; 651 *n.* 131; 653 *n.* 40
Klauser, 637 *n.* 104; 651 *n.* 3; 652 *nn.* 5, 7; 653 *n.* 32
Koetschau, 647 *nn.* 10, 25
Koopmans, 624 *n.* 90
Kötting, 648 *n.* 1; 657 *n.* 58
Krawutzky, 633 *n.* 98
Krüger, 632 *n.* 84; 647 *n.* 3
Kunzelmann, 633 *n.* 98; 635 *nn.* 69, 76; 643 *n.* 50
Kuss, O., 593 *n.* 15
Kuypers, R., 628 *n.* 67

LA LANDAIS, 643 *n.* 60
Lactantius, 601 *n.* 36; 607 *n.* 83; 618 *n.* 351
L'Allevi, 635 *n.* 61
Lambot, 594 *n.* 9; 608 *nn.* 126, 130, 131, 132; 609 *nn.* 133, 134, 135, 136; 616 *n.* 260; 618 *n.* 1; 621 *n.* 100; 643 *n.* 50; 649 *n.* 47; 650 *n.* 99
Lampridius, 630 *n.* 8
Lanciani, 653 *n.* 40
Lang, H., 629 *n.* 99
Lapeyre, G., 594 *n.* 23; 595 *n.* 39
Leclercq, 618 *n.* 1
Lecordier, G., 628 *n.* 99
Legewie, B., 622 *n.* 5
Lekkerkerker, 628 *n.* 67
Leo the Great, Pope St., 594 *n.* 22; 599 *n.* 43; 611 *n.* 67
Lesaar, 623 *nn.* 34, 36
Leschi, 595 *n.* 8
Leynaud, A., 652 *n.* 14
libelli, 657 *nn.* 58, 84, 89
Lietzmann, 644 *n.* 90; 650 *n.* 73
Liverani, 644 *n.* 90
Loefstedt, 594 *n.* 10
Logeart (with Berthier and Martin), 595 *n.* 10

MACEDONIUS, 623 *n.* 51
Magi, the, 603 *n.* 156
Mancini, 653 *n.* 40
Manichees, 610 *n.* 177; 646 *n.* 171

Manilius, 602 *n.* 93
Marec, E., 595 *n.* 8; 596 *n.* 12
Marcellinus, 596 *n.* 16; 623 *n.* 55
Marculus, 605 *n.* 28; 606 *n.* 32
Marcus Diaconus, 655 *n.* 13
marriage, 616 *n.* 274
marriage, mixed, 608 *n.* 120; 617 *n.* 320
Marrou, H. I., 642 *n.* 21; 644 *n.* 71; 646 *n.* 154; 658 *n.* 1
Martianus Capella, 604 *n.* 164
Martin of Tours, St., 618 *n.* 1
Martroye, 605 *n.* 1
Marucchi, 653 *n.* 33
Mass, daily, 616 *n.* 248
Maurists, 593 *n.* 8; 597 *n.* 52; 610 *n.* 212; 612 *n.* 92; 613 *nn.* 93, 127; 616 *n.* 266; 621 *n.* 123; 631 *n.* 42; 632 *n.* 57; 635 *n.* 61; 636 *nn.* 90, 99; 643 *nn.* 28, 32; 646 *n.* 179; 648 *nn.* 26, 28; 650 *n.* 74; 655 *nn.* 89, 111, 112; 657 *n.* 61
Maximianists, 606 *n.* 39
Meister, K., 594 *n.* 10
Mellet, M., 618 *n.* 1
Mercati, 627 *n.* 34
Merlin, P., 618 *n.* 1
Metzger, G., 611 *n.* 4
Middle Ages, 658 *n.* 1
Mingana, 641 *n.* 61
Minucius Felix, 632 *n.* 84; 652 *n.* 11
Milevis, Council of, 621 *nn.* 110, 118; 627 *n.* 65; 641 *n.* 42; 642 *n.* 64
Mohrmann, C., 631 *n.* 50; 632 *n.* 86; 644 *n.* 98
moon (representing Church), 603 *n.* 132
Monceaux, P., 596 *n.* 26; 605 *n.* 1; 607 *n.* 100; 618 *n.* 1; 620 *n.* 63; 654 *n.* 52
Monica, St., 616 *n.* 248; 618 *n.* 345; 640 *n.* 35; 656 *n.* 18
Montfaucon, 611 *n.* 18; 656 *n.* 15
Moore Smith, A., 630 *n.* 30
Moricca, 618 *n.* 1
Morin, 593 *n.* 14; 594 *nn.* 1, 18; 600 *n.* 57; 621 *n.* 100; 629 *n.* 101; 634 *n.* 37; 636 *n.* 90
Mortimer, C., 639 *n.* 178
mosaics, 595 *n.* 10; 596 *n.* 12; 597 *n.* 51; 622 *n.* 1; 623 *n.* 16; 630 *n.* 5; 640 *n.* 28
Mynors, 625 *n.* 107

NABOR, AUGUSTINE'S EPITAPH ON, 607 *n.* 100
narratio, 647 *n.* 5
Nepotianus, 620 *n.* 55
Neunheuser, 637 *n.* 108
Neveu, 650 *n.* 80
New Year, festivities at, 601 *n.* 55
Newman, 626 *n.* 10
Nock, A. D., 633 *n.* 2
Noiville, 627 *n.* 50
notarii, 643 *n.* 37

OEHLER, 652 n. 11; 653 n. 21
Optatus of Milevis, St., 605 n. 3; 637 n. 122; 641 n. 53
Optatus of Thamugadi, 624 n. 102
Origen, 604 n. 10; 616 n. 252; 634 n. 47; 647 nn. 10, 25
Orosius, 618 n. 339
Ovid, 601 n. 36

PAGANS (APPARENT CONVERSION OF), 599 n. 8
Paget, F., 628 n. 80
Palladia, 656 n. 24
Palladius, 612 n. 86
Paolucci, P., 652 n. 7
Parrot, A., 652 n. 7
Paulina, 624 n. 80
Paulinus of Nola, 594 n. 11; 596 n. 30; 611 n. 17; 612 n. 89; 618 n. 1; 620 n. 62; 622 n. 2; 623 n. 37; 624 n. 73; 651 nn. 130, 136; 654 nn. 53, 56; 656 n. 45
Pauly, 601 nn. 36, 60; 611 n. 3; 617 n. 275; 619 n. 29
Pelagius, 620 n. 72; 635 n. 62
penance, 599 n. 19
major, 639 n. 178
Pensées, 658 n. 6
Perler, Othmar, 634 n. 34
Perpetua, 636 n. 95; 645 n. 109
Persius, 624 n. 83
Peters, J., 616 n. 274
Petschenig, 608 n. 126; 615 n. 217; 626 n. 158; 634 n. 22; 649 n. 44; 650 n. 99
Phocas, St., 648 n. 39
Pichon, 654 n. 58
pilgrimages, 654 n. 58
Plutarch, 624 n. 83
Poinssot, 649 n. 60
pompa diaboli, 636 n. 99
Pons, A., 628 n. 99
Pontet, M., 593 n. 15; 627 n. 67; 646 n. 161
Pope, H., O.P., 593 n. 15; 639 n. 1; 650 n. 80
Porphyry, 603 nn. 138, 142, 143
Poschmann, 639 n. 178
possession, 604 n. 161
Possidius, 593 n. 7; 616 n. 260; 643 n. 50, 52; 649 n. 42; 650 n. 98
Pouget, Abbé, 595 n. 3
Poulsen, 651 n. 3
Prandi, A., 651 n. 2
Primianus, 606 n. 39
Proba, 636 n. 79
Probst, 635 nn. 69, 76; 639 n. 1
Procopius of Caesaria, 595 n. 2; 649 n. 45
Prudentius, 598 n. 7; 601 n. 22; 643 n. 51; 649 nn. 43, 48; 654 nn. 59, 60
psalms, singing of, 630 n. 32
Pschmadt, J., 642 n. 1
Pseudo-Ambrose, 597 n. 35; 620 n. 66; 641 n. 58

Pseudo-Augustine, 607 n. 111; 632 n. 57; 655 nn. 89, 111, 112
Pseudo-Clement, 604 n. 161
Pseudo-Cyprian, 601 n. 36
Publicola, 613 n. 112
Punic (language), 598 n. 71
Puzik, E., 593 n. 15

QUASTEN, J., 630 n. 32; 635 n. 66; 652 n. 7
Quodvultdeus, 600 n. 14; 634 n. 30; 635 nn. 61, 66; 636 n. 99

RAHNER, 636 n. 99
Rampolla, 612 n. 79; 619 n. 46
Rand, E. K., 658 n. 1
Ratti, Mgr., 622 n. 1
refectory, inscription in Augustine's, 623 n. 24
refrigerium, 652 n. 7; 653 n. 40
Reggiori, F., 622 n. 1
Reitzenstein, 656 n. 28; 658 n. 1
Rentschka, 633 n. 98
resurrection (of body), 645 n. 144
Reul, 648 n. 1
Reuter, A., 616 n. 274
rhetoric, 642 n. 2
Rhomaios, 651 n. 3
Richard, 607 n. 83
Riegl, Alois, 630 n. 16
Riva, 627 n. 34
Robbers, 647 n. 3
Roetzer, 593 n. 15; 633 n. 105; 635 nn. 69, 76; 639 n. 1; 641 n. 55
Rome, Council of (386), 618 n. 3
Rose, 608 n. 126
Rostovtseff, 596 n. 10
Rükker, 641 n. 61
Ruland, R., 652 n. 11
Russell, 628 n. 67

SACRIFICE, PAGAN, FORBIDDEN, 599 n. 49
Salaville, S., 641 n. 53
Salvianus, 611 n. 4
Sardica, Council of, 594 n. 22
Satyrus, 623 n. 28
Scheidla, H., 637 n. 108
Schenkl, 611 n. 12; 652 n. 6; 654 n. 66
Schenoute, Abbot, 650 n. 74
Schmaus, 624 n. 58
Schneider, A. M., 652 n. 7
Scillitan martyrs, 650 n. 99; 651 n. 118
scrutinium, 635 n. 61
Secundula, Aelia, epitaph on, 652 n. 9
Seeck, O., 613 n. 93
Seneca, 612 n. 39
Serapis, 603 n. 143
Serrier, 616 n. 274
Seston, W., 595 n. 5
singing, congregational, 640 n. 11

INDEX TO NOTES

Siricius, Pope, 618 *n.* 3; 639 *n.* 189
Sirmond, 599, *n.* 49
Sizoo, 635 *n.* 73; 642 *n.* 10; 644 *n.* 97
skins, animal, at baptism, 635 *n.* 66
Sol Invictus, 627 *n.* 50
Souter, 647 *n.* 3
Spallanzoni, 627 *n.* 67
Spanke, 654 *n.* 62
Stählin, 646 *n.* 162
stars, 603 *n.* 129
Steier, A., 631 *n.* 47
Strzygowski, 595 *n.* 6
Styger, P., 652 *n.* 12
Subsana, priest of, 598 *n.* 75
Suetonius, 602 *n.* 85
Sullivan, 642 *n.* 1
Sulpicius Severus, 595 *n.* 54; 618 *n.* 1; 620 *n.* 62; 621 *n.* 95; 622 *n.* 2
sun (representing Christ), 603 *n.* 132
symbolum, 635 *nn.* 70, 75
Symmachus, 600 *n.* 15
Synesius of Cyrene, 652 *nn.* 8, 10

TACITUS, 602 *n.* 85
tattooing (of cross), 634 *n.* 37
temple cults, 603 *n.* 150; 604 *n.* 182
temples, demolition of, 599 *n.* 49
Tertullian, 601 *n.* 36; 616 *nn.* 250, 251, 274; 617 *n.* 295; 622 *n.* 135; 632 *n.* 84; 635 *n.* 52; 637 *n.* 114; 638 *n.* 134; 640 *n.* 30; 652 *nn.* 11, 13; 653 *n.* 21
theatre, 596 *n.* 14
Thecla, baptistery of, 627 *n.* 34
Themistius, 607 *n.* 83
Theodore of Mopsuestia, 635 *n.* 66; 641 *n.* 61; 656 *n.* 15
Theodoret, 601 *n.* 22
Theodoret of Cyrus, 656 *n.* 15
Theodoric, 651 *n.* 3
Theodosius, 599 *n.* 49
Theodoulos, epitaph on, 653 *n.* 30
Thiel, 651 *n.* 122
Tillemont, Lenain de, 593 *n.* 8; 658 *n.* 8
Timotheus, 598 *n.* 75
Toesca, 622 *n.* 1
toleration, 607 *n.* 83
Tours, Second Council of, 655 *n.* 113
Toutain, J., 595 *n.* 10
Tréhorel, E., 608 *n.* 128

Trench, R. C., 631 *n.* 49
triclia, 653 *n.* 40
Trinity, the, 645 *n.* 143
Twenty Martyrs, 596 *n.* 24; 651 *n.* 118

URS VON BALTHASAR, 646 *n.* 155

VALERIAN, EDICT OF, 652 *n.* 15
Valéry, Paul, 626 *n.* 24
Van der Leeuw, G., 652 *n.* 7
Vannier, 605 *n.* 1
Vega, 620 *n.* 78
Vérin, J., 611 *n.* 4
Vermeersch, 618 *n.* 1
vessels, liturgical, 629 *n.* 1
Victricius of Rouen, 618 *n.* 1
Vidal, J. M., 619 *n.* 19
Vigerus, 604 *n.* 10
Villarò, Serra, 653 *n.* 26
Virgil, 604 *n.* 181; 645 *n.* 148
Vogels, 642 *n.* 1
Von Gerkan, 653 *n.* 40
Von Soden, H., 605 *n.* 1
Vroom, 608 *n.* 126

WALPOLE, 631 *n.* 47
Ward Perkins (with Goodchild), 595 *n.* 10; 596 *n.* 26
Wassink, 636 *n.* 99
water, baptismal, verses on, 636 *n.* 104
Weiskotten, 623 *n.* 24
Weyman, 597 *n.* 30; 607 *n.* 100; 623 *n.* 24
Wiegand, 635 *n.* 69
Wieland, F., 653 *n.* 43
Wilmart, 643 *n.* 58
Wilpert, 622 *nn.* 1, 4; 630 *n.* 30; 653 *n.* 34
Wirth, F., 653 *n.* 34
word-play, 646 *n.* 176; 650 *n.* 111; 656 *n.* 38

ZÄHRINGER, 637 *n.* 119
Zangemeister, 618 *n.* 339
Zarb, 594 *n.* 18; 635 *nn.* 69, 76; 638 *n.* 165
Zeiller, 600 *n.* 83
Zellinger, J., 593 *n.* 15; 637 *n.* 104; 644 *n.* 99; 655 *nn.* 1, 6
Zeno of Verona, 637 *n.* 104; 655 *n.* 87
Ziwsa, 605 *nn.* 3, 5, 10, 12, 15, 21; 629 *n.* 1; 635 *n.* 64; 637 *n.* 122

Revised November, 1964

harper ☦ torchbooks

HUMANITIES AND SOCIAL SCIENCES

American Studies

JOHN R. ALDEN: The American Revolution, 1775-1783.† *Illus.* TB/3011
BERNARD BAILYN: The New England Merchants in the Seventeenth Century TB/1149
RAY STANNARD BAKER: Following the Color Line: American Negro Citizenship in the Progressive Era.‡ *Illus. Edited by Dewey W. Grantham, Jr.* TB/3053
RAY A. BILLINGTON: The Far Western Frontier, 1830-1860.† *Illus.* TB/3012
JOSEPH L. BLAU, Ed.: Cornerstones of Religious Freedom in America. *Selected Basic Documents, Court Decisions and Public Statements. Revised and Enlarged Edition* TB/118
RANDOLPH S. BOURNE: War and the Intellectuals: *Collected Essays, 1915-1919.‡ Edited by Carl Resek* TB/3043
A. RUSSELL BUCHANAN: The United States and World War II. † *Illus.* Vol. I TB/3044
Vol. II TB/3045
ABRAHAM CAHAN: The Rise of David Levinsky: *a novel. Introduction by John Higham* TB/1028
JOSEPH CHARLES: The Origins of the American Party System TB/1049
THOMAS C. COCHRAN: The Inner Revolution: *Essays on the Social Sciences in History* TB/1140
T. C. COCHRAN & WILLIAM MILLER: The Age of Enterprise: *A Social History of Industrial America* TB/1054
EDWARD S. CORWIN: American Constitutional History: *Essays edited by Alpheus T. Mason and Gerald Garvey* TB/1136
FOSTER RHEA DULLES: America's Rise to World Power, 1898-1954.† *Illus.* TB/3021
W. A. DUNNING: Reconstruction, Political and Economic, 1865-1877 TB/1073

A. HUNTER DUPREE: Science in the Federal Government: *A History of Policies and Activities to 1940* TB/573
CLEMENT EATON: The Freedom-of-Thought Struggle in the Old South. *Revised Edition. Illus.* TB/1150
CLEMENT EATON: The Growth of Southern Civilization, 1790-1860.† *Illus.* TB/3040
HAROLD U. FAULKNER: Politics, Reform and Expansion, 1890-1900.† *Illus.* TB/3020
LOUIS FILLER: The Crusade against Slavery, 1830-1860.† *Illus.* TB/3029
EDITORS OF FORTUNE: America in the Sixties: *the Economy and the Society. 72 two-color charts* TB/1015
DIXON RYAN FOX: The Decline of Aristocracy in the Politics of New York.‡ *Edited by Robert V. Remini* TB/3064
LAWRENCE HENRY GIPSON: The Coming of the Revolution, 1763-1775.† *Illus.* TB/3007
FRANCIS J. GRUND: Aristocracy in America: *Jacksonian Democracy* TB/1001
ALEXANDER HAMILTON: The Reports of Alexander Hamilton.‡ *Edited by Jacob E. Cooke* TB/3060
OSCAR HANDLIN, Editor: This Was America: *As Recorded by European Travelers to the Western Shore in the Eighteenth, Nineteenth, and Twentieth Centuries. Illus.* TB/1119
MARCUS LEE HANSEN: The Atlantic Migration: 1607-1860. *Edited by Arthur M. Schlesinger, Sr.; Introduction by Oscar Handlin* TB/1052
MARCUS LEE HANSEN: The Immigrant in American History. *Edited with a Foreword by Arthur M. Schlesinger, Sr.* TB/1120
JOHN D. HICKS: Republican Ascendancy, 1921-1933.† *Illus.* TB/3041
JOHN HIGHAM, Ed.: The Reconstruction of American History TB/1068

† The New American Nation Series, edited by Henry Steele Commager and Richard B. Morris.
‡ American Perspectives series, edited by Bernard Wishy and William E. Leuchtenburg.
* The Rise of Modern Europe series, edited by William L. Langer.
‖ Researches in the Social, Cultural, and Behavioral Sciences, edited by Benjamin Nelson.
§ The Library of Religion and Culture, edited by Benjamin Nelson.
Σ Harper Modern Science Series, edited by James R. Newman.
º Not for sale in Canada.

1

DANIEL H. HUNDLEY: Social Relations in our Southern States.‡ Edited by William R. Taylor TB/3058

HELEN HUNT JACKSON: A Century of Dishonor: The Early Crusade for Indian Reform.‡ Edited by Andrew F. Rolle TB/3063

ROBERT H. JACKSON: The Supreme Court in the American System of Government TB/1106

THOMAS JEFFERSON: Notes on the State of Virginia.‡ Edited by Thomas Perkins Abernethy TB/3052

JOHN F. KENNEDY: A Nation of Immigrants. Revised and Enlarged Edition. Illus. TB/1118

WILLIAM L. LANGER & S. EVERETT GLEASON: The Challenge to Isolation: The World Crisis of 1937-1940 and American Foreign Policy   Vol. I TB/3054
Vol. II TB/3055

WILLIAM E. LEUCHTENBURG: Franklin D. Roosevelt and the New Deal, 1932-1940.† Illus. TB/3025

LEONARD W. LEVY: Freedom of Speech and Press in Early American History: Legacy of Suppression TB/1109

ARTHUR S. LINK: Woodrow Wilson and the Progressive Era, 1910-1917.† Illus. TB/3023

ROBERT GREEN McCLOSKEY: American Conservatism in the Age of Enterprise, 1865-1910 TB/1137

BERNARD MAYO: Myths and Men: Patrick Henry, George Washington, Thomas Jefferson TB/1108

JOHN C. MILLER: Alexander Hamilton and the Growth of the New Nation TB/3057

JOHN C. MILLER: The Federalist Era, 1789-1801.† Illus. TB/3027

PERRY MILLER: Errand into the Wilderness TB/1139

PERRY MILLER & T. H. JOHNSON, Editors: The Puritans: A Sourcebook of Their Writings
Vol. I TB/1093
Vol. II TB/1094

GEORGE E. MOWRY: The Era of Theodore Roosevelt and the Birth of Modern America, 1900-1912.† Illus. TB/3022

WALLACE NOTESTEIN: The English People on the Eve of Colonization, 1603-1630.† Illus. TB/3006

RUSSEL BLAINE NYE: The Cultural Life of the New Nation, 1776-1801.† Illus. TB/3026

RALPH BARTON PERRY: Puritanism and Democracy TB/1138

RALPH BARTON PERRY: The Thought and Character of William James: Briefer Version TB/1156

GEORGE E. PROBST, Ed.: The Happy Republic: A Reader in Tocqueville's America TB/1060

WALTER RAUSCHENBUSCH: Christianity and the Social Crisis.‡ Edited by Robert D. Cross TB/3059

HEINRICH STRAUMANN: American Literature in the Twentieth Century. Revised Edition TB/1168

FRANK THISTLETHWAITE: America and the Atlantic Community: Anglo-American Aspects, 1790-1850 TB/1107

TWELVE SOUTHERNERS: I'll Take My Stand: The South and the Agrarian Tradition. Introduction by Louis D. Rubin, Jr.; Biographical Essays by Virginia Rock TB/1072

A. F. TYLER: Freedom's Ferment: Phases of American Social History from the Revolution to the Outbreak of the Civil War. Illus. TB/1074

GLYNDON G. VAN DEUSEN: The Jacksonian Era, 1828-1848.† Illus. TB/3028

WALTER E. WEYL: The New Democracy: An Essay on Certain Political and Economic Tendencies in the United States.‡ Edited by Charles Forcey TB/3042

LOUIS B. WRIGHT: The Cultural Life of the American Colonies, 1607-1763.† Illus. TB/3005

LOUIS B. WRIGHT: Culture on the Moving Frontier TB/1053

Anthropology & Sociology

BERNARD BERELSON, Ed.: The Behavioral Sciences Today TB/1127

JOSEPH B. CASAGRANDE, Ed.: In the Company of Man: 20 Portraits of Anthropological Informants. Illus. TB/3047

W. E. LE GROS CLARK: The Antecedents of Man: An Introduction to the Evolution of the Primates.° Illus. TB/559

THOMAS C. COCHRAN: The Inner Revolution: Essays on the Social Sciences in History TB/1140

ALLISON DAVIS & JOHN DOLLARD: Children of Bondage: The Personality Development of Negro Youth in the Urban South ‖ TB/3049

ST. CLAIR DRAKE & HORACE R. CAYTON: Black Metropolis: A Study of Negro Life in a Northern City   Vol. I TB/1086; Vol. II TB/1087

CORA DU BOIS: The People of Alor. New Preface by the author. Illus.   Vol. I TB/1042; Vol. II TB/1043

EMILE DURKHEIM et al.: Essays on Sociology and Philosophy: With Analyses of Durkheim's Life and Work. ‖ Edited by Kurt H. Wolff TB/1151

LEON FESTINGER, HENRY W. RIECKEN & STANLEY SCHACHTER: When Prophecy Fails: A Social and Psychological Account of a Modern Group that Predicted the Destruction of the World ‖ TB/1132

RAYMOND FIRTH, Ed.: Man and Culture: An Evaluation of the Work of Bronislaw Malinowski ‖ ° TB/1133

L. S. B. LEAKEY: Adam's Ancestors: The Evolution of Man and his Culture. Illus. TB/1019

KURT LEWIN: Field Theory in Social Science: Selected Theoretical Papers. ‖ Edited with a Foreword by Dorwin Cartwright TB/1135

ROBERT H. LOWIE: Primitive Society. Introduction by Fred Eggan TB/1056

R. M. MacIVER: Social Causation TB/1153

BENJAMIN NELSON: Religious Traditions and the Spirit of Capitalism: From the Church Fathers to Jeremy Bentham TB/1130

TALCOTT PARSONS & EDWARD A. SHILS, Editors: Toward a General Theory of Action: Theoretical Foundations for the Social Sciences TB/1083

JOHN H. ROHRER & MUNRO S. EDMONSON, Eds.: The Eighth Generation Grows Up: Cultures and Personalities of New Orleans Negroes ‖ TB/3050

ARNOLD ROSE: The Negro in America: The Condensed Version of Gunnar Myrdal's An American Dilemma TB/3048

HENRI DE SAINT-SIMON: Social Organization, The Science of Man, and Other Writings. ‖ Edited and translated by Felix Markham TB/1152

KURT SAMUELSSON: Religion and Economic Action: A Critique of Max Weber's The Protestant Ethic and the Spirit of Capitalism.‖ ° Trans. by E. G. French; Ed. with Intro. by D. C. Coleman TB/1131

PITIRIM SOROKIN: Contemporary Sociological Theories. *Through the First Quarter of the Twentieth Century* TB/3046

MAURICE R. STEIN: The Eclipse of Community: *An Interpretation of American Studies* TB/1128

SIR EDWARD TYLOR: The Origins of Culture. *Part I of "Primitive Culture."*§ *Introduction by Paul Radin* TB/33

SIR EDWARD TYLOR: Religion in Primitive Culture. *Part II of "Primitive Culture."*§ *Introduction by Paul Radin* TB/34

W. LLOYD WARNER & Associates: Democracy in Jonesville: *A Study in Quality and Inequality* TB/1129

W. LLOYD WARNER: A Black Civilization: *A Study of an Australian Tribe.* ∥ *Illus.* TB/3056

W. LLOYD WARNER: Social Class in America: *The Evaluation of Status* TB/1013

Art and Art History

WALTER LOWRIE: Art in the Early Church. *Illus. Revised Edition* TB/124

EMILE MÂLE: The Gothic Image: *Religious Art in France of the Thirteenth Century.*§ *190 illus.* TB/44

MILLARD MEISS: Painting in Florence and Siena after the Black Death: *The Arts, Religion and Society in the Mid-Fourteenth Century. 169 illus.* TB/1148

ERICH NEUMANN: The Archetypal World of Henry Moore. *107 illus.* TB/2020

ERWIN PANOFSKY: Studies in Iconology: *Humanistic Themes in the Art of the Renaissance. 180 illustrations* TB/1077

ALEXANDRE PIANKOFF: The Shrines of Tut-Ankh-Amon. *Edited by N. Rambova. 117 illus.* TB/2011

JEAN SEZNEC: The Survival of the Pagan Gods: *The Mythological Tradition and Its Place in Renaissance Humanism and Art. 108 illustrations* TB/2004

OTTO VON SIMSON: The Gothic Cathedral: *Origins of Gothic Architecture and the Medieval Concept of Order. 58 illus.* TB/2018

HEINRICH ZIMMER: Myths and Symbols in Indian Art and Civilization. *70 illustrations* TB/2005

Business, Economics & Economic History

REINHARD BENDIX: Work and Authority in Industry: *Ideologies of Management in the Course of Industrialization* TB/3035

THOMAS C. COCHRAN: The American Business System: *A Historical Perspective, 1900-1955* TB/1080

ROBERT DAHL & CHARLES E. LINDBLOM: Politics, Economics, and Welfare: *Planning and Politico-Economic Systems Resolved into Basic Social Processes* TB/3037

PETER F. DRUCKER: The New Society: *The Anatomy of Industrial Order* TB/1082

ROBERT L. HEILBRONER: The Great Ascent: *The Struggle for Economic Development in Our Time* TB/3030

ABBA P. LERNER: Everybody's Business: *Current Assumptions in Economics and Public Policy* TB/3051

ROBERT GREEN McCLOSKEY: American Conservatism in the Age of Enterprise, 1865-1910 TB/1137

PAUL MANTOUX: The Industrial Revolution in the Eighteenth Century: *The Beginnings of the Modern Factory System in England* ° TB/1079

WILLIAM MILLER, Ed.: Men in Business: *Essays on the Historical Role of the Entrepreneur* TB/1081

PERRIN STRYKER: The Character of the Executive: *Eleven Studies in Managerial Qualities* TB/1041

PIERRE URI: Partnership for Progress: *A Program for Transatlantic Action* TB/3036

Contemporary Culture

JACQUES BARZUN: The House of Intellect TB/1051

JOHN U. NEF: Cultural Foundations of Industrial Civilization TB/1024

NATHAN M. PUSEY: The Age of the Scholar: *Observations on Education in a Troubled Decade* TB/1157

PAUL VALÉRY: The Outlook for Intelligence TB/2016

History: General

L. CARRINGTON GOODRICH: A Short History of the Chinese People. *Illus.* TB/3015

BERNARD LEWIS: The Arabs in History TB/1029

SIR PERCY SYKES: A History of Exploration.° *Introduction by John K. Wright* TB/1046

History: Ancient and Medieval

A. ANDREWES: The Greek Tyrants TB/1103

P. BOISSONNADE: Life and Work in Medieval Europe: *The Evolution of the Medieval Economy, the Fifth to the Fifteenth Centuries.°* *Preface by Lynn White, Jr.* TB/1141

HELEN CAM: England before Elizabeth TB/1026

G. G. COULTON: Medieval Village, Manor, and Monastery TB/1022

HEINRICH FICHTENAU: The Carolingian Empire: *The Age of Charlemagne* TB/1142

F. L. GANSHOF: Feudalism TB/1058

J. M. HUSSEY: The Byzantine World TB/1057

SAMUEL NOAH KRAMER: Sumerian Mythology TB/1055

FERDINAND LOT: The End of the Ancient World and the Beginnings of the Middle Ages. *Introduction by Glanville Downey* TB/1044

CHARLES PETIT-DUTAILLIS: The Feudal Monarchy in France and England: *From the Tenth to the Thirteenth Century* ° TB/1165

STEVEN RUNCIMAN: A History of the Crusades. Volume I: *The First Crusade and the Foundation of the Kingdom of Jerusalem. Illus.* TB/1143

FERDINAND SCHEVILL: Siena: *The History of a Medieval Commune. Introduction by William M. Bowsky* TB/1164

HENRY OSBORN TAYLOR: The Classical Heritage of the Middle Ages. *Foreword and Biblio. by Kenneth M. Setton* [Formerly listed as TB/48 under the title *The Emergence of Christian Culture in the West*] TB/1117

J. M. WALLACE-HADRILL: The Barbarian West: *The Early Middle Ages, A.D. 400-1000* TB/1061

3

History: Renaissance & Reformation

R. R. BOLGAR: The Classical Heritage and Its Beneficiaries: *From the Carolingian Age to the End of the Renaissance* TB/1125

JACOB BURCKHARDT: The Civilization of the Renaissance in Italy. *Introduction by Benjamin Nelson and Charles Trinkaus. Illus.* Volume I TB/40
Volume II TB/41

ERNST CASSIRER: The Individual and the Cosmos in Renaissance Philosophy. *Translated with an Introduction by Mario Domandi* TB/1097

EDWARD P. CHEYNEY: The Dawn of a New Era, 1250-1453.* *Illus.* TB/3002

DESIDERIUS ERASMUS: Christian Humanism and the Reformation: *Selected Writings. Edited and translated by John C. Olin* TB/1166

WALLACE K. FERGUSON et al.: Facets of the Renaissance TB/1098

WALLACE K. FERGUSON et al.: The Renaissance: *Six Essays. Illus.* TB/1084

MYRON P. GILMORE: The World of Humanism, 1453-1517.* *Illus.* TB/3003

FRANCESCO GUICCIARDINI: Maxims and Reflections of a Renaissance Statesman: *Ricordi. Trans. by Mario Domandi. Intro. by Nicolai Rubinstein* TB/1160

JOHAN HUIZINGA: Erasmus and the Age of Reformation. *Illus.* TB/19

ULRICH VON HUTTEN et al.: On the Eve of the Reformation: *"Letters of Obscure Men." Introduction by Hajo Holborn* TB/1124

PAUL O. KRISTELLER: Renaissance Thought: *The Classic, Scholastic, and Humanist Strains* TB/1048

PAUL O. KRISTELLER: Renaissance Thought II: *Papers on Humanism and the Arts* TB/1163

NICCOLÒ MACHIAVELLI: History of Florence and of the Affairs of Italy: *from the earliest times to the death of Lorenzo the Magnificent. Introduction by Felix Gilbert* TB/1027

ALFRED VON MARTIN: Sociology of the Renaissance. *Introduction by Wallace K. Ferguson* TB/1099

GARRETT MATTINGLY et al.: Renaissance Profiles. *Edited by J. H. Plumb* TB/1162

MILLARD MEISS: Painting in Florence and Siena after the Black Death. *The Arts, Religion and Society in the Mid-Fourteenth Century. 169 illus.* TB/1148

J. E. NEALE: The Age of Catherine de Medici° TB/1085

ERWIN PANOFSKY: Studies in Iconology: *Humanistic Themes in the Art of the Renaissance. 180 illustrations* TB/1077

J. H. PARRY: The Establishment of the European Hegemony: 1415-1715 TB/1045

HENRI PIRENNE: Early Democracies in the Low Countries: *Urban Society and Political Conflict in the Middle Ages and the Renaissance. Introduction by John Mundy* TB/1110

J. H. PLUMB: The Italian Renaissance: *A Concise Survey of Its History and Culture* TB/1161

FERDINAND SCHEVILL: The Medici. *Illus.* TB/1010

FERDINAND SCHEVILL: Medieval and Renaissance Florence. *Illus.* Volume I: *Medieval Florence* TB/1090
Volume II: *The Coming of Humanism and the Age of the Medici* TB/1091

G. M. TREVELYAN: England in the Age of Wycliffe, 1368-1520° TB/1112

VESPASIANO: Renaissance Princes, Popes, and Prelates: *The Vespasiano Memoirs: Lives of Illustrious Men of the XVth Century. Introduction by Myron P. Gilmore* TB/1111

History: Modern European

FREDERICK B. ARTZ: Reaction and Revolution, 1815-1832.* *Illus.* TB/3034

MAX BELOFF: The Age of Absolutism, 1660-1815 TB/1062

ROBERT C. BINKLEY: Realism and Nationalism, 1852-1871.* *Illus.* TB/3038

CRANE BRINTON: A Decade of Revolution, 1789-1799.* *Illus.* TB/3018

J. BRONOWSKI & BRUCE MAZLISH: The Western Intellectual Tradition: *From Leonardo to Hegel* TB/3001

GEOFFREY BRUUN: Europe and the French Imperium, 1799-1814.* *Illus.* TB/3033

ALAN BULLOCK: Hitler, A Study in Tyranny.° *Illus.* TB/1123

E. H. CARR: The Twenty Years' Crisis, 1919-1939: *An Introduction to the Study of International Relations*° TB/1122

GORDON A. CRAIG: From Bismarck to Adenauer: *Aspects of German Statecraft. Revised Edition* TB/1171

WALTER L. DORN: Competition for Empire, 1740-1763.* *Illus.* TB/3032

CARL J. FRIEDRICH: The Age of the Baroque, 1610-1660.* *Illus.* TB/3004

LEO GERSHOY: From Despotism to Revolution, 1763-1789.* *Illus.* TB/3017

ALBERT GOODWIN: The French Revolution TB/1064

CARLTON J. H. HAYES: A Generation of Materialism, 1871-1900.* *Illus.* TB/3039

J. H. HEXTER: Reappraisals in History: *New Views on History and Society in Early Modern Europe* TB/1100

A. R. HUMPHREYS: The Augustan World: *Society, Thought, and Letters in Eighteenth Century England* TB/1105

HANS KOHN, Ed.: The Mind of Modern Russia: *Historical and Political Thought of Russia's Great Age* TB/1065

SIR LEWIS NAMIER: Vanished Supremacies: *Essays on European History, 1812-1918*° TB/1088

JOHN U. NEF: Western Civilization Since the Renaissance: *Peace, War, Industry, and the Arts* TB/1113

FREDERICK L. NUSSBAUM: The Triumph of Science and Reason, 1660-1685.* *Illus.* TB/3009

RAYMOND W. POSTGATE, Ed.: Revolution from 1789 to 1906: *Selected Documents* TB/1063

PENFIELD ROBERTS: The Quest for Security, 1715-1740.* *Illus.* TB/3016

PRISCILLA ROBERTSON: Revolutions of 1848: *A Social History* TB/1025

ALBERT SOREL: Europe Under the Old Regime. *Translated by Francis H. Herrick* TB/1121

4

N. N. SUKHANOV: The Russian Revolution, 1917: *Eyewitness Account*. Edited by Joel Carmichael
Vol. I TB/1066; Vol. II TB/1067

JOHN B. WOLF: The Emergence of the Great Powers, 1685-1715.* Illus. TB/3010

JOHN B. WOLF: France: 1814-1919: *The Rise of a Liberal-Democratic Society* TB/3019

Intellectual History

HERSCHEL BAKER: The Image of Man: *A Study of the Idea of Human Dignity in Classical Antiquity, the Middle Ages, and the Renaissance* TB/1047

J. BRONOWSKI & BRUCE MAZLISH: The Western Intellectual Tradition: *From Leonardo to Hegel* TB/3001

ERNST CASSIRER: The Individual and the Cosmos in Renaissance Philosophy. *Translated with an Introduction by Mario Domandi* TB/1097

NORMAN COHN: The Pursuit of the Millennium: *Revolutionary Messianism in medieval and Reformation Europe and its bearing on modern Leftist and Rightist totalitarian movements* TB/1037

ARTHUR O. LOVEJOY: The Great Chain of Being: *A Study of the History of an Idea* TB/1009

ROBERT PAYNE: Hubris: *A Study of Pride. Foreword by Sir Herbert Read* TB/1031

BRUNO SNELL: The Discovery of the Mind: *The Greek Origins of European Thought* TB/1018

ERNST LEE TUVESON: Millennium and Utopia: *A Study in the Background of the Idea of Progress. New Preface by the Author* TB/1134

Literature, Poetry, The Novel & Criticism

JAMES BAIRD: Ishmael: *The Art of Melville in the Contexts of International Primitivism* TB/1023

JACQUES BARZUN: The House of Intellect TB/1051

W. J. BATE: From Classic to Romantic: *Premises of Taste in Eighteenth Century England* TB/1036

RACHEL BESPALOFF: On the Iliad TB/2006

R. P. BLACKMUR et al.: Lectures in Criticism. *Introduction by Huntington Cairns* TB/2003

ABRAHAM CAHAN: The Rise of David Levinsky: *a novel. Introduction by John Higham* TB/1028

ERNST R. CURTIUS: European Literature and the Latin Middle Ages TB/2015

GEORGE ELIOT: Daniel Deronda: *a novel. Introduction by F. R. Leavis* TB/1039

ETIENNE GILSON: Dante and Philosophy TB/1089

ALFRED HARBAGE: As They Liked It: *A Study of Shakespeare's Moral Artistry* TB/1035

STANLEY R. HOPPER, Ed.: Spiritual Problems in Contemporary Literature§ TB/21

A. R. HUMPHREYS: The Augustan World: *Society, Thought, and Letters in Eighteenth Century England*º TB/1105

ALDOUS HUXLEY: Antic Hay & The Gioconda Smile.º *Introduction by Martin Green* TB/3503

HENRY JAMES: Roderick Hudson: *a novel. Introduction by Leon Edel* TB/1016

HENRY JAMES: The Tragic Muse: *a novel. Introduction by Leon Edel* TB/1017

ARNOLD KETTLE: An Introduction to the English Novel. Volume I: *Defoe to George Eliot* TB/1011
Volume II: *Henry James to the Present* TB/1012

ROGER SHERMAN LOOMIS: The Development of Arthurian Romance TB/1167

JOHN STUART MILL: On Bentham and Coleridge. *Introduction by F. R. Leavis* TB/1070

PERRY MILLER & T. H. JOHNSON, Editors: The Puritans: *A Sourcebook of Their Writings* Vol. I TB/1093
Vol. II TB/1094

KENNETH B. MURDOCK: Literature and Theology in Colonial New England TB/99

SAMUEL PEPYS: The Diary of Samuel Pepys.º *Edited by O. F. Morshead. Illus. by Ernest Shepard* TB/1007

ST.-JOHN PERSE: Seamarks TB/2002

O. E. RÖLVAAG: Giants in the Earth TB/3504

GEORGE SANTAYANA: Interpretations of Poetry and Religion§ TB/9

C. P. SNOW: Time of Hope: *a novel* TB/1040

HEINRICH STRAUMANN: American Literature in the Twentieth Century. *Revised Edition* TB/1168

DOROTHY VAN GHENT: The English Novel: *Form and Function* TB/1050

E. B. WHITE: One Man's Meat. *Introduction by Walter Blair* TB/3505

MORTON DAUWEN ZABEL, Editor: Literary Opinion in America. Vol. I TB/3013; Vol. II TB/3014

Myth, Symbol & Folklore

JOSEPH CAMPBELL, Editor: Pagan and Christian Mysteries. *Illus.* TB/2013

MIRCEA ELIADE: Cosmos and History: *The Myth of the Eternal Return*§ TB/2050

C. G. JUNG & C. KERÉNYI: Essays on a Science of Mythology: *The Myths of the Divine Child and the Divine Maiden* TB/2014

ERWIN PANOFSKY: Studies in Iconology: *Humanistic Themes in the Art of the Renaissance. 180 illustrations* TB/1077

JEAN SEZNEC: The Survival of the Pagan Gods: *The Mythological Tradition and its Place in Renaissance Humanism and Art. 108 illustrations* TB/2004

HELLMUT WILHELM: Change: *Eight Lectures on the I Ching* TB/2019

HEINRICH ZIMMER: Myths and Symbols in Indian Art and Civilization. *70 illustrations* TB/2005

Philosophy

HENRI BERGSON: Time and Free Will: *An Essay on the Immediate Data of Consciousness*º TB/1021

H. J. BLACKHAM: Six Existentialist Thinkers: *Kierkegaard, Nietzsche, Jaspers, Marcel, Heidegger, Sartre*º TB/1002

ERNST CASSIRER: The Individual and the Cosmos in Renaissance Philosophy. *Translated with an Introduction by Mario Domandi* TB/1097

ERNST CASSIRER: Rousseau, Kant and Goethe. *Introduction by Peter Gay* TB/1092

FREDERICK COPLESTON: Medieval Philosophyº TB/376

F. M. CORNFORD: From Religion to Philosophy: A Study in the Origins of Western Speculation§ TB/20
WILFRID DESAN: The Tragic Finale: An Essay on the Philosophy of Jean-Paul Sartre TB/1030
PAUL FRIEDLÄNDER: Plato: An Introduction TB/2017
ETIENNE GILSON: Dante and Philosophy TB/1089
WILLIAM CHASE GREENE: Moira: Fate, Good, and Evil in Greek Thought TB/1104
W. K. C. GUTHRIE: The Greek Philosophers: From Thales to Aristotle° TB/1008
F. H. HEINEMANN: Existentialism and the Modern Predicament TB/28
EDMUND HUSSERL: Phenomenology, and the Crisis of Philosophy. Translated with an Introduction by Quentin Lauer TB/1170
IMMANUEL KANT: The Doctrine of Virtue, being Part II of The Metaphysic of Morals. Translated with Notes and Introduction by Mary J. Gregor. Foreword by H. J. Paton TB/110
IMMANUEL KANT: Groundwork of the Metaphysic of Morals. Translated and analyzed by H. J. Paton TB/1159
IMMANUEL KANT: Lectures on Ethics.§ Introduction by Lewis W. Beck TB/105
QUENTIN LAUER: Phenomenology: Its Genesis and Prospect TB/1169
JOHN MACQUARRIE: An Existentialist Theology: A Comparison of Heidegger and Bultmann.° Preface by Rudolf Bultmann TB/125
MICHAEL POLANYI: Personal Knowledge: Towards a Post-Critical Philosophy TB/1158
WILLARD VAN ORMAN QUINE: From a Logical Point of View: Logico-Philosophical Essays TB/566
BERTRAND RUSSELL et al.: The Philosophy of Bertrand Russell. Edited by Paul Arthur Schilpp Vol. I TB/1095; Vol. II TB/1096
L. S. STEBBING: A Modern Introduction to Logic TB/538
ALFRED NORTH WHITEHEAD: Process and Reality: An Essay in Cosmology TB/1033
WILHELM WINDELBAND: A History of Philosophy Vol. I: Greek, Roman, Medieval TB/38
Vol. II: Renaissance, Enlightenment, Modern TB/39

Philosophy of History

NICOLAS BERDYAEV: The Beginning and the End§ TB/14
NICOLAS BERDYAEV: The Destiny of Man TB/61
WILHELM DILTHEY: Pattern and Meaning in History: Thoughts on History and Society.° Edited with an Introduction by H. P. Rickman TB/1075
RAYMOND KLIBANSKY & H. J. PATON, Eds.: Philosophy and History: The Ernst Cassirer Festschrift. Illus. TB/1115
JOSE ORTEGA Y GASSET: The Modern Theme. Introduction by Jose Ferrater Mora TB/1038
KARL R. POPPER: The Poverty of Historicism° TB/1126
W. H. WALSH: Philosophy of History: An Introduction TB/1020

Political Science & Government

JEREMY BENTHAM: The Handbook of Political Fallacies: Introduction by Crane Brinton TB/1069
KENNETH E. BOULDING: Conflict and Defense: A General Theory TB/3024
CRANE BRINTON: English Political Thought in the Nineteenth Century TB/1071
EDWARD S. CORWIN: American Constitutional History: Essays edited by Alpheus T. Mason and Gerald Garvey TB/1136
ROBERT DAHL & CHARLES E. LINDBLOM: Politics, Economics, and Welfare: Planning and Politico-Economic Systems Resolved into Basic Social Processes TB/3037
JOHN NEVILLE FIGGIS: Political Thought from Gerson to Grotius: 1414-1625: Seven Studies. Introduction by Garrett Mattingly TB/1032
F. L. GANSHOF: Feudalism TB/1058
G. P. GOOCH: English Democratic Ideas in the Seventeenth Century TB/1006
ROBERT H. JACKSON: The Supreme Court in the American System of Government TB/1106
DAN N. JACOBS, Ed.: The New Communist Manifesto and Related Documents TB/1078
DAN N. JACOBS & HANS BAERWALD, Eds.: Chinese Communism: Selected Documents TB/3031
KINGSLEY MARTIN: French Liberal Thought in the Eighteenth Century: Political Ideas from Bayle to Condorcet TB/1114
JOHN STUART MILL: On Bentham and Coleridge. Introduction by F. R. Leavis TB/1070
JOHN B. MORRALL: Political Thought in Medieval Times TB/1076
KARL R. POPPER: The Open Society and Its Enemies Vol. I: The Spell of Plato TB/1101
Vol. II: The High Tide of Prophecy: Hegel, Marx, and the Aftermath TB/1102
HENRI DE SAINT-SIMON: Social Organization, The Science of Man, and Other Writings. Edited and Translated by Felix Markham TB/1152
JOSEPH A. SCHUMPETER: Capitalism, Socialism and Democracy TB/3008

Psychology

ALFRED ADLER: Problems of Neurosis. Introduction by Heinz L. Ansbacher TB/1145
ALFRED ADLER: The Individual Psychology of Alfred Adler. Edited by Heinz L. and Rowena R. Ansbacher TB/1154
ANTON T. BOISEN: The Exploration of the Inner World: A Study of Mental Disorder and Religious Experience TB/87
LEON FESTINGER, HENRY W. RIECKEN, STANLEY SCHACHTER: When Prophecy Fails: A Social and Psychological Study of a Modern Group that Predicted the Destruction of the World TB/1132
SIGMUND FREUD: On Creativity and the Unconscious: Papers on the Psychology of Art, Literature, Love, Religion.§ Intro. by Benjamin Nelson TB/45
C. JUDSON HERRICK: The Evolution of Human Nature TB/545

ALDOUS HUXLEY: The Devils of Loudun: *A Study in the Psychology of Power Politics and Mystical Religion in the France of Cardinal Richelieu*§° TB/60

WILLIAM JAMES: Psychology: *The Briefer Course.* Edited with an Intro. by Gordon Allport TB/1034

C. G. JUNG: Psychological Reflections TB/2001

C. G. JUNG: Symbols of Transformation: *An Analysis of the Prelude to a Case of Schizophrenia.* Illus. Vol. I TB/2009; Vol. II TB/2010

C. G. JUNG & C. KERÉNYI: Essays on a Science of Mythology: *The Myths of the Divine Child and the Divine Maiden* TB/2014

SOREN KIERKEGAARD: Repetition: *An Essay in Experimental Psychology.* Translated with Introduction & Notes by Walter Lowrie TB/117

JOHN T. McNEILL: A History of the Cure of Souls TB/126

KARL MENNINGER: Theory of Psychoanalytic Technique TB/1144

ERICH NEUMANN: Amor and Psyche: *The Psychic Development of the Feminine* TB/2012

ERICH NEUMANN: The Archetypal World of Henry Moore. *107 illus.* TB/2020

ERICH NEUMANN: The Origins and History of Consciousness Vol. I Illus. TB/2007; Vol. II TB/2008

C. P. OBERNDORF: A History of Psychoanalysis in America TB/1147

RALPH BARTON PERRY: The Thought and Character of William James: *Briefer Version* TB/1156

JEAN PIAGET, BÄRBEL INHELDER, & ALINA SZEMINSKA: The Child's Conception of Geometry ° TB/1146

JOHN H. SCHAAR: Escape from Authority: *The Perspectives of Erich Fromm* TB/1155

RELIGION

Ancient & Classical

J. H. BREASTED: Development of Religion and Thought in Ancient Egypt. Introduction by John A. Wilson TB/57

HENRI FRANKFORT: Ancient Egyptian Religion: *An Interpretation* TB/77

WILLIAM CHASE GREENE: Moira: *Fate, Good and Evil in Greek Thought* TB/1104

G. RACHEL LEVY: Religious Conceptions of the Stone Age and their Influence upon European Thought. *Illus.* Introduction by Henri Frankfort TB/106

MARTIN P. NILSSON: Greek Folk Religion. Foreword by Arthur Darby Nock TB/78

ALEXANDRE PIANKOFF: The Shrines of Tut-Ankh-Amon. Edited by N. Rambova. *117 illus.* TB/2011

H. J. ROSE: Religion in Greece and Rome TB/55

Biblical Thought & Literature

W. F. ALBRIGHT: The Biblical Period from Abraham to Ezra TB/102

C. K. BARRETT, Ed.: The New Testament Background: *Selected Documents* TB/86

C. H. DODD: The Authority of the Bible TB/43

M. S. ENSLIN: Christian Beginnings TB/5

M. S. ENSLIN: The Literature of the Christian Movement TB/6

H. E. FOSDICK: A Guide to Understanding the Bible TB/2

H. H. ROWLEY: The Growth of the Old Testament TB/107

D. WINTON THOMAS, Ed.: Documents from Old Testament Times TB/85

Judaic Thought & Literature

MARTIN BUBER: Eclipse of God: *Studies in the Relation Between Religion and Philosophy* TB/12

MARTIN BUBER: Moses: *The Revelation and the Covenant* TB/27

MARTIN BUBER: Pointing the Way. Introduction by Maurice S. Friedman TB/103

MARTIN BUBER: The Prophetic Faith TB/73

MARTIN BUBER: Two Types of Faith: *the interpenetration of Judaism and Christianity*° TB/75

MAURICE S. FRIEDMAN: Martin Buber: *The Life of Dialogue* TB/64

FLAVIUS JOSEPHUS: The Great Roman-Jewish War, with The Life of Josephus. Introduction by William R. Farmer TB/74

T. J. MEEK: Hebrew Origins TB/69

Christianity: Origins & Early Development

AUGUSTINE: An Augustine Synthesis. Edited by Erich Przywara TB/335

ADOLF DEISSMANN: Paul: *A Study in Social and Religious History* TB/15

EDWARD GIBBON: The Triumph of Christendom in the Roman Empire *(Chaps. XV-XX of "Decline and Fall," J. B. Bury edition).*§ Illus. TB/46

MAURICE GOGUEL: Jesus and the Origins of Christianity.° Introduction by C. Leslie Mitton
Volume I: *Prolegomena to the Life of Jesus* TB/65
Volume II: *The Life of Jesus* TB/66

EDGAR J. GOODSPEED: A Life of Jesus TB/1

ADOLF HARNACK: The Mission and Expansion of Christianity in the First Three Centuries. Introduction by Jaroslav Pelikan TB/92

R. K. HARRISON: The Dead Sea Scrolls: *An Introduction*° TB/84

EDWIN HATCH: The Influence of Greek Ideas on Christianity.§ Introduction and Bibliography by Frederick C. Grant TB/18

WALTER LOWRIE: Art in the Early Church. *Illus.* Revised Edition TB/124

ARTHUR DARBY NOCK: Early Gentile Christianity and Its Hellenistic Background TB/111

ARTHUR DARBY NOCK: St. Paul° TB/104

F. VAN DER MEER: Augustine the Bishop: *Church and Society at the Dawn of the Middle Ages* TB/304

JOHANNES WEISS: Earliest Christianity: *A History of the Period A.D. 30-150.* Introduction and Bibliography by Frederick C. Grant Volume I TB/53
Volume II TB/54

Christianity: The Middle Ages and The Reformation

JOHANNES ECKHART: Meister Eckhart: *A Modern Translation* by R. B. Blakney TB/8

DESIDERIUS ERASMUS: Christian Humanism and the Reformation: *Selected Writings.* Edited and translated by John C. Olin TB/1166

G. P. FEDOTOV: The Russian Religious Mind: *Kievan Christianity, the tenth to the thirteenth centuries* TB/70

ÉTIENNE GILSON: Dante and Philosophy TB/1089

WILLIAM HALLER: The Rise of Puritanism TB/22

JOHAN HUIZINGA: Erasmus and the Age of Reformation. *Illus.* TB/19

DAVID KNOWLES: The English Mystical Tradition TB/302

JOHN T. McNEILL: Makers of the Christian Tradition: *From Alfred the Great to Schleiermacher* TB/121

A. C. McGIFFERT: Protestant Thought Before Kant. *Preface by Jaroslav Pelikan* TB/93

GORDON RUPP: Luther's Progress to the Diet of Worms° TB/120

Christianity: The Protestant Tradition

KARL BARTH: Church Dogmatics: *A Selection.* TB/95

KARL BARTH: Dogmatics in Outline TB/56

KARL BARTH: The Word of God and the Word of Man TB/13

WINTHROP HUDSON: The Great Tradition of the American Churches TB/98

SOREN KIERKEGAARD: Edifying Discourses. *Edited with an Introduction by Paul Holmer* TB/32

SOREN KIERKEGAARD: The Journals of Kierkegaard.° *Edited with an Introduction by Alexander Dru* TB/52

SOREN KIERKEGAARD: The Point of View for My Work as an Author: *A Report to History.§ Preface by Benjamin Nelson* TB/88

SOREN KIERKEGAARD: The Present Age.§ *Translated and edited by Alexander Dru. Introduction by Walter Kaufmann* TB/94

SOREN KIERKEGAARD: Purity of Heart TB/4

SOREN KIERKEGAARD: Repetition: *An Essay in Experimental Psychology. Translated with Introduction & Notes by Walter Lowrie* TB/117

SOREN KIERKEGAARD: Works of Love: *Some Christian Reflections in the Form of Discourses* TB/122

WALTER LOWRIE: Kierkegaard: *A Life* Vol. I TB/89
Vol. II TB/90

PERRY MILLER: Errand into the Wilderness TB/1139

PERRY MILLER & T. H. JOHNSON, Editors: The Puritans: *A Sourcebook of Their Writings*
Vol. I TB/1093
Vol. II TB/1094

KENNETH B. MURDOCK: Literature and Theology in Colonial New England TB/99

F. SCHLEIERMACHER: The Christian Faith. *Introduction by Richard R. Niebuhr* Volume I TB/108
Volume II TB/109

F. SCHLEIERMACHER: On Religion: *Speeches to Its Cultured Despisers. Intro. by Rudolf Otto* TB/36

PAUL TILLICH: Dynamics of Faith TB/42

EVELYN UNDERHILL: Worship TB/10

G. VAN DER LEEUW: Religion in Essence and Manifestation: *A Study in Phenomenology. Appendices by Hans H. Penner* Vol. I TB/100; Vol. II TB/101

Christianity: The Roman and Eastern Traditions

THOMAS CORBISHLEY, s. j.: Roman Catholicism TB/112

G. P. FEDOTOV: The Russian Religious Mind: *Kievan Christianity, the tenth to the thirteenth centuries* TB/70

G. P. FEDOTOV, Ed.: A Treasury of Russian Spirituality TB/303

DAVID KNOWLES: The English Mystical Tradition TB/302

GABRIEL MARCEL: Homo Viator: *Introduction to a Metaphysic of Hope* TB/397

GUSTAVE WEIGEL, s.j.: Catholic Theology in Dialogue TB/301

Oriental Religions: Far Eastern, Near Eastern

TOR ANDRAE: Mohammed: *The Man and His Faith* TB/62

EDWARD CONZE: Buddhism: *Its Essence and Development.° Foreword by Arthur Waley* TB/58

EDWARD CONZE et al., Editors: Buddhist Texts Through the Ages TB/113

ANANDA COOMARASWAMY: Buddha and the Gospel of Buddhism. *Illus.* TB/119

H. G. CREEL: Confucius and the Chinese Way TB/63

FRANKLIN EDGERTON, Trans. & Ed.: The Bhagavad Gita TB/115

SWAMI NIKHILANANDA, Trans. & Ed.: The Upanishads: *A One-Volume Abridgment* TB/114

HELLMUT WILHELM: Change: *Eight Lectures on the I Ching* TB/2019

Philosophy of Religion

RUDOLF BULTMANN: History and Eschatology: *The Presence of Eternity* TB/91

RUDOLF BULTMANN AND FIVE CRITICS: Kerygma and Myth: *A Theological Debate* TB/80

RUDOLF BULTMANN and KARL KUNDSIN: Form Criticism: *Two Essays on New Testament Research. Translated by Frederick C. Grant* TB/96

MIRCEA ELIADE: The Sacred and the Profane TB/81

LUDWIG FEUERBACH: The Essence of Christianity.§ *Introduction by Karl Barth. Foreword by H. Richard Niebuhr* TB/11

ADOLF HARNACK: What is Christianity?§ *Introduction by Rudolf Bultmann* TB/17

FRIEDRICH HEGEL: On Christianity: *Early Theological Writings. Edited by Richard Kroner and T. M. Knox* TB/79

KARL HEIM: Christian Faith and Natural Science TB/16

IMMANUEL KANT: Religion Within the Limits of Reason Alone.§ *Introduction by Theodore M. Greene and John Silber* TB/67

JOHN MACQUARRIE: An Existentialist Theology: *A Comparison of Heidegger and Bultmann.*° *Preface by Rudolf Bultmann* TB/125

PIERRE TEILHARD DE CHARDIN: The Phenomenon of Man° TB/83

Religion, Culture & Society

JOSEPH L. BLAU, Ed.: Cornerstones of Religious Freedom in America: *Selected Basic Documents, Court Decisions and Public Statements. Revised and Enlarged Edition* TB/118

CHRISTOPHER DAWSON: The Historic Reality of Christian Culture TB/305

C. C. GILLISPIE: Genesis and Geology: *The Decades before Darwin*§ TB/51

WALTER KAUFMANN, Ed.: Religion from Tolstoy to Camus: *Basic Writings on Religious Truth and Morals. Enlarged Edition* TB/123

JOHN T. McNEILL: A History of the Cure of Souls TB/126

BENJAMIN NELSON: Religious Traditions and the Spirit of Capitalism: *From the Church Fathers to Jeremy Bentham* TB/1130

H. RICHARD NIEBUHR: Christ and Culture TB/3

H. RICHARD NIEBUHR: The Kingdom of God in America TB/49

RALPH BARTON PERRY: Puritanism and Democracy TB/1138

PAUL PFUETZE: Self, Society, Existence: *Human Nature and Dialogue in the Thought of George Herbert Mead and Martin Buber* TB/1059

WALTER RAUSCHENBUSCH: Christianity and the Social Crisis.‡ *Edited by Robert D. Cross* TB/3059

KURT SAMUELSSON: Religion and Economic Action: *A Critique of Max Weber's The Protestant Ethic and the Spirit of Capitalism.* ‖° *Trans. by E. G. French; Ed. with Intro. by D. C. Coleman* TB/1131

ERNST TROELTSCH: The Social Teaching of the Christian Churches ° Vol. I TB/71; Vol. II TB/72

NATURAL SCIENCES AND MATHEMATICS

Biological Sciences

CHARLOTTE AUERBACH: The Science of Genetics∑ TB/568

A. BELLAIRS: Reptiles: *Life History, Evolution, and Structure. Illus.* TB/520

LUDWIG VON BERTALANFFY: Modern Theories of Development: *An Introduction to Theoretical Biology* TB/554

LUDWIG VON BERTALANFFY: Problems of Life: *An Evaluation of Modern Biological and Scientific Thought* TB/521

JOHN TYLER BONNER: The Ideas of Biology.∑ *Illus.* TB/570

HAROLD F. BLUM: Time's Arrow and Evolution TB/555

A. J. CAIN: Animal Species and their Evolution. *Illus.* TB/519

WALTER B. CANNON: Bodily Changes in Pain, Hunger, Fear and Rage. *Illus.* TB/562

W. E. LE GROS CLARK: The Antecedents of Man: *An Introduction to the Evolution of the Primates.*° *Illus.* TB/559

W. H. DOWDESWELL: Animal Ecology. *Illus.* TB/543

W. H. DOWDESWELL: The Mechanism of Evolution. *Illus.* TB/527

R. W. GERARD: Unresting Cells. *Illus.* TB/541

DAVID LACK: Darwin's Finches. *Illus.* TB/544

J. E. MORTON: Molluscs: *An Introduction to their Form and Functions. Illus.* TB/529

ADOLF PORTMANN: Animals as Social Beings.° *Illus.* TB/572

O. W. RICHARDS: The Social Insects. *Illus.* TB/542

P. M. SHEPPARD: Natural Selection and Heredity. *Illus.* TB/528

EDMUND W. SINNOTT: Cell and Psyche: *The Biology of Purpose* TB/546

C. H. WADDINGTON: How Animals Develop. *Illus.* TB/553

Chemistry

J. R. PARTINGTON: A Short History of Chemistry. *Illus.* TB/522

J. READ: A Direct Entry to Organic Chemistry. *Illus.* TB/523

J. READ: Through Alchemy to Chemistry. *Illus.* TB/561

Communication Theory

J. R. PIERCE: Symbols, Signals and Noise: *The Nature and Process of Communication* TB/574

Geography

R. E. COKER: This Great and Wide Sea: *An Introduction to Oceanography and Marine Biology. Illus.* TB/551

F. K. HARE: The Restless Atmosphere TB/560

History of Science

W. DAMPIER, Ed.: Readings in the Literature of Science. *Illus.* TB/512

A. HUNTER DUPREE: Science in the Federal Government: *A History of Policies and Activities to 1940* TB/573

ALEXANDRE KOYRÉ: From the Closed World to the Infinite Universe: *Copernicus, Kepler, Galileo, Newton, etc.* TB/31

A. G. VAN MELSEN: From Atomos to Atom: *A History of the Concept Atom* TB/517

O. NEUGEBAUER: The Exact Sciences in Antiquity TB/552

H. T. PLEDGE: Science Since 1500: *A Short History of Mathematics, Physics, Chemistry and Biology. Illus.* TB/506

GEORGE SARTON: Ancient Science and Modern Civilization TB/501

HANS THIRRING: Energy for Man: *From Windmills to Nuclear Power* TB/556

WILLIAM LAW WHYTE: Essay on Atomism: *From Democritus to 1960* TB/565

A. WOLF: A History of Science, Technology and Philosophy in the 16th and 17th Centuries.° *Illus.*
Vol. I TB/508; Vol. II TB/509

A. WOLF: A History of Science, Technology, and Philosophy in the Eighteenth Century.° *Illus.*
Vol. I TB/539; Vol. II TB/540

Mathematics

H. DAVENPORT: The Higher Arithmetic: *An Introduction to the Theory of Numbers* TB/526

H. G. FORDER: Geometry: *An Introduction* TB/548

GOTTLOB FREGE: The Foundations of Arithmetic: *A Logico-Mathematical Enquiry* TB/534

S. KÖRNER: The Philosophy of Mathematics: *An Introduction* TB/547

D. E. LITTLEWOOD: Skeleton Key of Mathematics: *A Simple Account of Complex Algebraic Problems* TB/525

GEORGE E. OWEN: Fundamentals of Scientific Mathematics TB/569

WILLARD VAN ORMAN QUINE: Mathematical Logic TB/558

O. G. SUTTON: Mathematics in Action.° *Foreword by James R. Newman. Illus.* TB/518

FREDERICK WAISMANN: Introduction to Mathematical Thinking. *Foreword by Karl Menger* TB/511

Philosophy of Science

R. B. BRAITHWAITE: Scientific Explanation TB/515

J. BRONOWSKI: Science and Human Values. *Illus.* TB/505

ALBERT EINSTEIN ET AL.: Albert Einstein: Philosopher-Scientist. *Edited by Paul A. Schilpp*
Volume I TB/502
Volume II TB/503

WERNER HEISENBERG: Physics and Philosophy: *The Revolution in Modern Science* TB/549

JOHN MAYNARD KEYNES: A Treatise on Probability.° *Introduction by N. R. Hanson* TB/557

STEPHEN TOULMIN: Foresight and Understanding: *An Enquiry into the Aims of Science. Foreword by Jacques Barzun* TB/564

STEPHEN TOULMIN: The Philosophy of Science: *An Introduction* TB/513

G. J. WHITROW: The Natural Philosophy of Time° TB/563

Physics and Cosmology

DAVID BOHM: Causality and Chance in Modern Physics. *Foreword by Louis de Broglie* TB/536

P. W. BRIDGMAN: The Nature of Thermodynamics TB/537

P. W. BRIDGMAN: A Sophisticate's Primer of Relativity TB/575

A. C. CROMBIE, Ed.: Turning Point in Physics TB/535

C. V. DURELL: Readable Relativity. *Foreword by Freeman J. Dyson* TB/530

ARTHUR EDDINGTON: Space, Time and Gravitation: *An outline of the General Relativity Theory* TB/510

GEORGE GAMOW: Biography of Physics∑ TB/567

MAX JAMMER: Concepts of Force: *A Study in the Foundation of Dynamics* TB/550

MAX JAMMER: Concepts of Mass *in Classical and Modern Physics* TB/571

MAX JAMMER: Concepts of Space: *The History of Theories of Space in Physics. Foreword by Albert Einstein* TB/533

EDMUND WHITTAKER: History of the Theories of Aether and Electricity
Volume I: *The Classical Theories* TB/531
Volume II: *The Modern Theories* TB/532

G. J. WHITROW: The Structure and Evolution of the Universe: *An Introduction to Cosmology. Illus.* TB/504

Code to Torchbook Libraries:

TB/1+	: The Cloister Library
TB/301+	: The Cathedral Library
TB/501+	: The Science Library
TB/1001+	: The Academy Library
TB/2001+	: The Bollingen Library
TB/3001+	: The University Library

A LETTER TO THE READER

Overseas, there is considerable belief that we are a country of extreme conservatism and that we cannot accommodate to social change.

Books about America in the hands of readers abroad can help change those ideas.

The U. S. Information Agency cannot, by itself, meet the vast need for books about the United States.

You can help.

Harper Torchbooks provides three packets of books on American history, economics, sociology, literature and politics to help meet the need.

To send a packet of Torchbooks [*] overseas, all you need do is send your check for $7 (which includes cost of shipping) to Harper & Row. The U. S. Information Agency will distribute the books to libraries, schools, and other centers all over the world.

I ask every American to support this program, part of a worldwide BOOKS USA campaign.

I ask you to share in the opportunity to help tell others about America.

EDWARD R. MURROW
Director,
U. S. Information Agency

[*retailing at $10.85 to $12.00]

PACKET I: *Twentieth Century America*
   Dulles/America's Rise to World Power, 1898-1954
   Cochran/The American Business System, 1900-1955
   Zabel, Editor/Literary Opinion in America (two volumes)
   Drucker/The New Society: *The Anatomy of Industrial Order*
   Fortune Editors/America in the Sixties: *The Economy and the Society*

PACKET II: *American History*
   Billington/The Far Western Frontier, 1830-1860
   Mowry/The Era of Theodore Roosevelt and the
      Birth of Modern America, 1900-1912
   Faulkner/Politics, Reform, and Expansion, 1890-1900
   Cochran & Miller/The Age of Enterprise: *A Social History of
      Industrial America*
   Tyler/Freedom's Ferment: *American Social History from the
      Revolution to the Civil War*

PACKET III: *American History*
   Hansen/The Atlantic Migration, 1607-1860
   Degler/Out of Our Past: *The Forces that Shaped Modern America*
   Probst, Editor/The Happy Republic: *A Reader in Tocqueville's America*
   Alden/The American Revolution, 1775-1783
   Wright/The Cultural Life of the American Colonies, 1607-1763

Your gift will be acknowledged directly to you by the overseas recipient. Simply fill out the coupon, detach and mail with your check or money order.

HARPER & ROW, PUBLISHERS · BOOKS USA DEPT.
49 East 33rd Street, New York 16, N. Y.

Packet I ☐   Packet II ☐   Packet III ☐

Please send the BOOKS USA library packet(s) indicated above, in my name, to the area checked below. Enclosed is my remittance in the amount of _____ for _____ packet(s) at $7.00 each.

_____ Africa   _____ Latin America

_____ Far East   _____ Near East

Name_____

Address_____

_____

NOTE: *This offer expires December 31, 1966.*